# THE
# RIGVEDA

# THE
# RIGVEDA

TRANSLATED BY RALPH T. H. GRIFFITH

pacps

Pacific Publishing Studio

Published in the United States by Pacific Publishing Studio.

www.PacPS.com

ISBN-13: 978-1456502942

ISBN-10: 1456502948

# BOOK ONE

### [01-001] HYMN I. Agni.

1 I Laud Agni, the chosen Priest, God, minister of sacrifice,
The hotar, lavishest of wealth.
2 Worthy is Agni to be praised by living as by ancient seers.
He shall bring hitherward the Gods.
3 Through Agni man obtaineth wealth, yea, plenty waxing day by day,
Most rich in heroes, glorious.
4 Agni, the perfect sacrifice which thou encompassest about
Verily goeth to the Gods.
5 May Agni, sapient-minded Priest, truthful, most gloriously great,
The God, come hither with the Gods.
6 Whatever blessing, Agni, thou wilt grant unto thy worshipper,
That, Angiras, is indeed thy truth.
7 To thee, dispeller of the night, O Agni, day by day with prayer
Bringing thee reverence, we come
8 Ruler of sacrifices, guard of Law eternal, radiant One,
Increasing in thine own abode.
9 Be to us easy of approach, even as a father to his son:
Agni, be with us for our weal.

### [01-002] HYMN II. Vayu.

1 BEAUTIFUL Vayu, come, for thee these Soma drops have been prepared:
Drink of them, hearken to our call.
2 Knowing the days, with Soma juice poured forth, the singers glorify
Thee, Vayu, with their hymns of praise.
3 Vayu, thy penetrating stream goes forth unto the worshipper,
Far-spreading for the Soma draught.
4 These, Indra-Vayu, have been shed; come for our offered dainties' sake:
The drops are yearning for you both.
5 Well do ye mark libations, ye Vayu and Indra, rich in spoil
So come ye swiftly hitherward.
6 Vayu and Indra, come to what the Soma. presser hath prepared:
Soon, Heroes, thus I make my prayer.
7 Mitra, of holy strength, I call, and foe-destroying Varuna,
Who make the oil-fed rite complete.
8 Mitra and Varuna, through Law, lovers and cherishers of Law,
Have ye obtained your might power
9 Our Sages, Mitra-Varuna, wide dominion, strong by birth,
Vouchsafe us strength that worketh well.

### [01-003] HYMN III. Asvins

1 YE Asvins, rich in treasure, Lords of splendour, having nimble hands,
Accept the sacrificial food.
2 Ye Asvins, rich in wondrous deeds, ye heroes worthy of our praise,
Accept our songs with mighty thought.
3 Nisatyas, wonder-workers, yours arc these libations with clipt grass:
Come ye whose paths are red with flame.
4 O Indra marvellously bright, come, these libations long for thee,
Thus by fine fingers purified.
5 Urged by the holy singer, sped by song, come, Indra, to the prayers,
Of the libation-pouring priest.
6 Approach, O Indra, hasting thee, Lord of Bay Horses, to the prayers.
In our libation take delight.
7 Ye Visvedevas, who protect, reward, and cherish men, approach
Your worshipper's drink-offering.
8 Ye Visvedevas, swift at work, come hither quickly to the draught,
As milch-kine hasten to their stalls.
9 The Visvedevas, changing shape like serpents, fearless, void of guile,
Bearers, accept the sacred draught
10 Wealthy in spoil, enriched with hymns, may bright Sarsavad desire,
With eager love, our sacrifice.
11 Inciter of all pleasant songs, inspirer o all gracious thought,
Sarasvati accept our rite
12 Sarasvati, the mighty flood,- she with be light illuminates,
She brightens every pious thought.

### [01-004] HYMN IV. Indri

1 As a good cow to him who milks, we call the doer of fair deeds,
To our assistance day by day.
2 Come thou to our libations, drink of Soma; Soma-drinker thou!
The rich One's rapture giveth kine.
3 So may we be acquainted with thine innermost benevolence:
Neglect us not, come hitherward.
4 Go to the wise unconquered One, ask thou of Indra, skilled in song,
Him who is better than thy friends.
5 Whether the men who mock us say, Depart unto another place,
Ye who serve Indra and none else;
6 Or whether, God of wondrous deeds, all our true people call us blest,
Still may we dwell in Indra's care.
7 Unto the swift One bring the swift, man-cheering, grace of sacrifice,
That to the Friend gives wings and joy.
8 Thou, Satakratu, drankest this and wast the Vrtras' slayer; thou
Helpest the warrior in the fray.
9 We strengthen, Satakratu, thee, yea, thee the powerful in fight,
That, Indra, we may win us wealth.
10 To him the mighty stream of wealth, prompt friend ot'him who pours the juice,
yea, to this Indra sing your song.

### [01-005] HYMN V. Indra.

1 O COME ye hither, sit ye down: to Indra sing ye forth, your song,
companions, bringing hymns of praise.
2 To him the richest of the rich, the Lord of treasures excellent,
Indra, wi th Soma juice outpoured.
3 May he stand by us in our need and in abundance for our wealth:
May he come nigh us with his strength.
4 Whose pair of tawny horses yoked in battles foemen challenge not:
To him, to Indra sing your song.
5 Nigh to the Soma-drinker come, for his enjoyment, these pure drops,
The Somas mingled with the curd.
6 Thou, grown at once to perfect strength, wast born to drink the Soma juice,
Strong Indra, for preeminence.
7 O Indra, lover of the song, may these quick Somas enter thee:
May they bring bliss to thee the Sage.
8 Our chants of praise have strengthened thee, O Satakratu, and our lauds
So strengthen thee the songs we sing.
9 Indra, whose succour never fails, accept these viands thousandfold,
Wherein all manly powers abide.

10 O Indra, thou who lovest song, let no man hurt our bodies, keep
Slaughter far from us, for thou canst.

## [01-006] HYMN VI. Indra.

1 They who stand round him as he moves harness the bright, the ruddy Steed
The lights are shining in the sky.
2 On both sides to the car they yoke the two bay coursers dear to him,
Bold, tawny, bearers of the Chief.
3 Thou, making light where no light was, and form, O men: where form was not,
Wast born together with the Dawns.
4 Thereafter they, as is their wont, threw off the state of babes unborn,
Assuming sacrificial names.
5 Thou, Indra, with the Tempest-Gods, the breakers down of what is firm '
Foundest the kine even in the cave.
6 Worshipping even as they list, singers laud him who findeth wealth,
The far-renowned, the mighty One.
7 Mayest thou verily be seen coming by fearless Indra's side:
Both joyous, equal in your sheen.
8 With Indra's well beloved hosts, the blameless, hastening to heaven,
The sacrificer cries aloud.
9 Come from this place, O Wanderer, or downward from the light of heaven:
Our songs of praise all yearn for this.
10 Indra we seek to give us help, from here, from heaven above the earth,
Or from the spacious firmament.

## [01-007] HYMN VII. Indra.

1 INDRA the singers with high praise, Indra reciters with their lauds,
Indra the choirs have glorified.
2 Indra hath ever close to him his two bay steeds and word-yoked car,
Indra the golden, thunder-armed.
3 Indra hath raised the Sun on high in heaven, that he may see afar:
He burst the mountain for the kine.
4 Help us, O Indra, in the frays, yea, frays, where thousand spoils are gained,
With awful aids, O awful One.
5 In mighty battle we invoke Indra, Indra in lesser fight,
The Friend who bends his bolt at fiends.
6 Unclose, our manly Hero, thou for ever bounteous, yonder cloud,
For us, thou irresistible.
7 Still higher, at each strain of mine, thunder-armed Indra's praises rise:
I find no laud worthy of him.
8 Even as the bull drives on the herds, he drives the people with his might,
The Ruler irresistible:
9 Indra who rules with single sway men, riches, and the fivefold race
Of those who dwell upon the earth.
10 For your sake from each side we call Indra away from other men:
Ours, and none others', may he be.

## [01-008] HYMN VIII. Indra.

1 INDRA, bring wealth that gives delight, the victor's ever-conquering wealth,
Most excellent, to be our aid;
2 By means of which we may repel our foes in battle hand to hand,
By thee assisted with the car.
3 Aided by thee, the thunder-armed, Indra, may we lift up the bolt,
And conquer all our foes in fight.
4 With thee, O India, for ally with missile-darting heroes, may
We conquer our embattled foes.
5 Mighty is Indra, yea supreme; greatness be his, the Thunderer:
Wide as the heaven extends his power
6 Which aideth those to win them sons, who come as heroes to the fight,
Or singers loving holy thoughts.
7 His belly, drinking deepest draughts of Soma, like an ocean swells,
Like wide streams from the cope of heaven.
8 So also is his excellence, great, vigorous, rich in cattle, like
A ripe branch to the worshipper.
9 For verily thy mighty powers, Indra, are saving helps at once
Unto a worshipper like me.
10 So are his lovely gifts; let lauds and praises be to Indra sung,
That he may drink the Soma juice.

## [01-009] HYMN IX. Indra.

1 COME, Indra, and delight thee with the juice at all the Soma feasts,
Protector, mighty in thy strength.
2 To Indra pour ye forth thejuice, the active gladdening juice to him
Ile gladdening, oinnific God.
3 O Lord of all men, fair of cheek, rejoice thee in the gladdening lauds,
Present at these drink-offerings.
4 Songs have outpoured themselves to thee, Indra, the strong, the guardian Lord,
And raised themselves unsatisfied.
5 Send to us bounty manifold, O Indra, worthy of' our wish,
For power supreme is only thine.
6 O Indra, stimulate thereto us emulously fain for wealth,
And glorious, O most splendid One.
7 Give, Indra, wide and lofty fame, wealthy in cattle and in strength,
Lasting our life-time, failing not.
8 Grant us high fame, O Indra, grant riches bestowing thousands, those
Fair fruits of earth borne home in wains.
9 Praising with songs the praise-worthy who cometh to our aid, we call
Indra, the Treasure-Lord of wealth.
10 To lofty Indra, dweller by each libation, the pious man
Sings forth aloud a strengthening hymn.

## [01-010] HYMN X. Indra.

1 THE chanters hymn thee, they who say the word of praise magnify thee.
The priests have raised thee up on high, O Satakratu, like a pole.
2 As up he clomb from ridge to ridge and looked upon the toilsome task,
Indra observes this wish of his, and the Rain hastens with his troop.
3 Harness thy pair of strong bay steeds, long-maned, whose bodies fill the girths,
And, Indra, Soma-drinker, come to listen to our songs of praise.

4 Come hither, answer thou the song, sing in approval, cry aloud.
Good Indra, make our prayer succeed, and prosper this our
sacrifice.
5 To Indra must a laud be said, to strengthen him who freely
gives,
That Sakra may take pleasure in our friendship and drink-
offerings.
6 Him, him we seek for friendship, him for riches and heroic
might.
For Indra, he is Sakra, he shall aid us while he gives us wealth.
7 Easy to turn and drive away, Indra, is spoil bestowed by thee.
Unclose the stable of the kine, and give us wealth O Thunder-
armed
8 The heaven and earth contain thee not, together, in thy
wrathful mood.
Win us the waters of the sky, and send us kine abundantly.
9 Hear, thou whose ear is quick, my call; take to thee readily my
songs
O Indra, let this laud of mine come nearer even than thy friend.
10 We know thee mightiest of all, in battles hearer of our cry.
Of thee most mighty we invoke the aid that giveth thousandfold.
11 O Indra, Son of Kusika, drink our libation with delight.
Prolong our life anew, and cause the seer to win a thousand gifts.
12 Lover of song, may these our songs on every side encompass
thee:
Strengthening thee of lengthened life, may they be dear delights
to thee.

### [01-011] HYMN XI. Indra.

1 ALL sacred songs have magnified Indra expansive as the sea,
The best of warriors borne on cars, the Lord, the very Lord of
strength.
2 Strong in thy friendship, Indra, Lord of power and might, we
have no fear.
We glorify with praises thee, the never-conquered conqueror.
3 The gifts of Indra from of old, his saving succours, never fail,
When to the praise-singers he gives the boon of substance rich in
kine.
4 Crusher of forts, the young, the wise, of strength unmeasured,
was he born
Sustainer of each sacred rite, Indra, the Thunderer, much-
extolled.
5 Lord of the thunder, thou didst burst the cave of Vala rich in
cows.
The Gods came pressing to thy side, and free from terror aided
thee,
6 I, Hero, through thy bounties am come to the flood addressing
thee.
Song-lover, here the singers stand and testify to thee thereof.
7 The wily Susna, Indra! thou o'er-threwest with thy wondrous
powers.
The wise beheld this deed of thine: now go beyond their eulogies.
8 Our songs of praise have glorified Indra who ruleth by his
might,
Whose precious gifts in thousands come, yea, even more
abundantly.

### [01-012] HYMN XII. Agni.

I WE choose Agni the messenger, the herald, master of all wealth,
Well skilled in this our sacrifice.
2 With callings ever they invoke Agni, Agni, Lord of the House,
Oblation-bearer, much beloved.
3 Bring the Gods hither, Agni, born for him who strews the sacred
grass:
Thou art our herald, meet for praise.
4 Wake up the willing Gods, since thou, Agni, performest
embassy:

Sit on the sacred grass with Gods.                    burn?
5 O Agni, radiant One, to whom the holy oil is poured, bum up
Our enemies whom fiends protect.
6 By Agni Agni is inflamed, Lord of the House, wise, young, who
bears
The gift: the ladle is his mouth.
7 Praise Agni in the sacrifice, the Sage whose ways are ever true,
The God who driveth grief away.
8 God, Agni, be his strong defence who lord of sacrificial gifts,
Worshippeth thee the messenger.
9 Whoso with sacred gift would fain call Agni to the feast of Gods,
O Purifier, favour him.
10 Such, Agni, Purifier, bright, bring hither to our sacrifice,
To our oblation bring the Gods.
11 So lauded by our newest song of praise bring opulence to us,
And food, with heroes for our sons.
12 O Agni, by effulgent flame, by all invokings of the Gods,
Show pleasure in this laud of ours.

### [01-013] HYMN XIII. Agni

1 AGNI, well-kindled, bring the Gods for him who offers holy
gifts.
Worship them, Purifier, Priest.
2 Son of Thyself, present, O Sage, our sacrifice to the Gods today.
Sweet to the taste, that they may feast.
3 Dear Narasamsa, sweet of tongue, the giver of oblations, I
Invoke to this our sacrifice.
4 Agni, on thy most easy car, glorified, hither bring the Gods:
Manu appointed thee as Priest.
5 Strew, O ye wise, the sacred grass that drips with oil, in order
due,
Where the Immortal is beheld.
6 Thrown open be the Doors Divine, unfailing, that assist the rite,
For sacrifice this day and now.
7 I call the lovely Night and Dawn to seat them on the holy grass
At this our solemn sacrifice.
8 The two Invokers I invite, the wise, divine and sweet of tongue,
To celebrate this our sacrifice.
9 Ila, Sarasvati, Mahi, three Goddesses who bring delight,
Be seated, peaceful, on the grass.
10 Tvastar I call, the earliest born, the wearer of all forms at will:
May he be ours and ours alone.
11 God, Sovran of the Wood, present this our oblation to the
Gods,
And let the giver be renowned.
12 With Svaha. pay the sacrifice to Indra in the offerer's house:
Thither I call the Deities.

### [01-014] HYMN XIV. Visvedevas.

1 To drink the Soma, Agni, come, to our service and our songs.
With all these Gods; and worship them.
2 The Kanvas have invoked thee; they, O Singer, sing thee songs
of praise
Agni, come hither with the Gods;
3 Indra, Vayu, Brhaspati, Mitra, Agni, Pusan, Bhaga,
Adityas, and the Marut host.
4 For you these juices are poured forth that gladden and
exhilarate,
The meath-drops resting in the cup.
5 The sons of Kanva fain for help adore thee, having strewn the
grass,
With offerings and all things prepared.
6 Let the swift steeds who carry thee, thought-yoked and
dropping holy oil,
Bring the Gods to the Soma draught.
7 Adored, the strengtheners of Law, unite them, Agni, with their
Dames:

3

Make them drink meath, O bright of tongue,
8 Let them, O Agni, who deserve worship and praise drink with
thy tongue
Tle meath in solemn sacrifice.
9 Away, from the Sun's realm of light, the wise invoking Priest
shall bring
All Gods awaking with the dawn.
10 With all the Gods, with Indra, with Vayu, and Mitra's
splendours, drink,
Agni, the pleasant Soma juice.
11 Ordained by Manu as our Priest, thou sittest, Agni, at each rite:
Hallow thou this our sacrifice.
12 Harness the Red Mares to thy car, the Bays, O God, the
flaming ones:
With those bring hitherward the Gods.

## [01-015] HYMN XV. RTU.

1 O INDRA drink the Soma juice with Rtu; let the cheering drops
Sink deep within, which settle there.
2 Drink from the Purifier's cup, Maruts, with Rtu; sanctify
The rite, for ye give precious gifts.
3 O Nestar, with thy Dame accept our sacrifice; with Rtu drink,
For thou art he who giveth wealth.
4 Bring the Gods, Agni; in the three appointed places set them
down:
Surround them, and with Rtu drink.
5 Drink Soma after the Rtus, from the Brahmana's bounty:
undissolved,
O Indra, is thy friendship's bond.
6 Mitra, Varuna, ye whose ways are firm - a Power that none
deceives-,
With Rtu ye have reached the rite.
7 The Soma-pressers, fain for wealth, praise the Wealth-giver in
the rite,
In sacrifices praise the God.
8 May the Wealth-giver grant to us riches that shall be far
renowned.
These things we gain, among the Gods.
9 He with the Rtu fain would drink, Wealth-giver, from the
Nestar's bowl.
Haste, give your offering, and depart.
10 As we this fourth time, Wealth-giver, honour thee with the
Rtus, be
A Giver bountiful to us.
11 Drink ye the meath, O Asvins bright with flames, whose acts
are pure. who with
Rtus accept the sacrifice.
12 With Rtu, through the house-fire, thou, kind Giver, guidest
sacrifice:
Worship the Gods for the pious man.

## [01-016] HYMN XVI. Indra.

1 LET thy Bay Steeds bring thee, the Strong, hither to drink the
Soma draught-
Those, Indra, who are bright as suns.
2 Here are the grains bedewed with oil: hither let the Bay
Coursers bring
Indra upon his easiest car.
3 Indra at early morn we call, Indra in course of sacrifice,
Indra to drink the Soma juice.
4 Come hither, with thy long-maned Steeds, O Indra, to- the
draught we pour
We call thee wher, the juice is shed.
5 Come thou to this our song of praise, to the libation poured for
thee
Drink of it like a stag athirst.

6 Here are the drops of Soma juice expressed on sacred grass:
thereof
Drink, Indra, to increase thy might.
7 Welcome to thee be this our hymn, reaching thy heart, most
excellent:
Then drink the Soma juice expressed.
8 To every draught of pressed-out juice Indra, the Vrtra-slayer,
comes,
To drink the Soma for delight.
9 Fulfil, O Satakratu, all our wish with horses and with kine:
With holy thoughts we sing thy praise.

## [01-017] HYMN XVII Indra-Varuna

1 I CRAVE help from the Imperial Lords, from Indra-Varuna;
may they
Both favour one of us like me.
2 Guardians of men, ye ever come with ready succour at the call
Of every singer such as I.
3 Sate you, according to your wish, O Indra-Varuna, with wealth:
Fain would we have you nearest us.
4 May we be sharers of the powers, sharers of the benevolence
Of you who give strength bounteously.
5 Indra and Varuna, among givers of thousands, meet for praise,
Are Powers who merit highest laud.
6 Through their protection may we gain great store of wealth, and
heap it up
Enough and still to spare, be ours.
7 O Indra-Varuna, on you for wealth in many a form I call:
Still keep ye us victorious.
8 O Indra-Varuna, - through our songs that seek to win you to
ourselves,
Give us at once your sheltering help.
9 O Indra-Varuna, to you may fair praise which I offer come,
joint eulogy which ye dignify.

## [01-018] HYMN XVIII. Brahmanaspati.

1 O BRAHMANAPSATI, make him who presses Soma glorious,
Even Kaksivan Ausija.
2 The rich, the healer of disease, who giveth wealth, increaseth
store,
The prompt,-may he be with us still.
3 Let not the foeman's curse, let not a mortal's onslaught fall on
us
Preserve us, Brahmanaspati.
4 Ne'er is the mortal hero harmed whom Indra, Brahmanaspati,
And Soma graciously inspire.
5 Do, thou, O Brahmanaspati, and Indra, Soma, Daksina,
Preserve that mortal from distress.
6 To the Assembly's wondrous Lord, to Indra's lovely Friend who
gives
Wisdom, have I drawn near in prayer.
7 He without whom no sacrifice, e'en of the wise man, prospers;
he
Stirs up the series of thoughts.
8 He makes the oblation prosper, he promotes the course of
sacrifice:
Our voice of praise goes to the Gods.
9 I have seen Narasamsa, him most resolute, most widely famed,
As 'twere the Household Priest of heaven.

## [01-019] HYMN XIX. Agni, Maruts.

1 To this fair sacrifice to drink the milky draught thou art
invoked:
O Agni, with the Maruts come.
2 No mortal man, no God exceeds thy mental power, O Mighty
one -
O Agni, with the Maruts come

3 All Gods devoid of guile, who know the mighty region of mid-air:
O Agni, with those Maruts come.
4 The terrible, who sing their song, not to be overcome by might:
O Agni, with those Maruts come.
5 Brilliant, and awful in their form, mighty, devourers of their foes':
O Agni, with those Maruts come.
6 Who sit as Deities in heaven, above the sky-vault's luminous sphere:
O Agni, with those Maruts come.
7 Who scatter clouds about the sky, away over the billowy sea:
O Agni, with those Maruts come.
8 Who with their bright beams spread them forth over the ocean in their might
O Agni, with those Maruts come.
9 For thee, to be thine early draught, I pour the Soma-mingled meath:
O Agni, with the Maruts come.

### [01-020] HYMN XX Rbhus.
1 FOR the Celestial Race this song of praise which gives wealth lavishly
Was made by singers with their lips.
2 They who for Indra, with their mind, formed horses harnessed by a word,
Attained by works to sacrifice.
3 They for the two Nasatyas wrought a light car moving every way:
They formed a nectar-yielding cow.
4 The Rbhus with effectual prayers, honest, with constant labour, made
Their Sire and Mother young again.
5 Together came your gladdening drops with Indra by the Maruts girt,
With the Adityas, with the Kings.
6 The sacrificial ladle, wrought newly by the God Tvastar's hand-
Four ladles have ye made thereof.
7 Vouchsafe us wealth, to him who pours thrice seven libations, yea, to each
Give wealth, pleased with our eulogies.
8 As ministering Priests they held, by pious acts they won themselves,
A share in sacrifice with Gods.

### [01-021] HYMN XXI. Indra-Agni.
1 INDRA and Agni I invoke fain are we for their song of praise
Chief Soma-drinkers are they both.
2 Praise ye, O men, and glorify Indra-Agni in the holy rites:
Sing praise to them in sacred songs.
3 Indra and Agni we invite, the Soma-drinkers, for the fame
Of Mitra, to the Soma-draught.
4 Strong Gods, we bid them come to this libation that stands ready here:
Indra and Agni, come to us.
5 Indra and Agni, mighty Lords of our assembly, crush the fiends:
Childless be the devouring ones.
6 Watch ye, through this your truthfulness, there in the place of spacious view
Indra and Agni, send us bliss.

### [01-022] HYMN XXII Asvins and Others
1 WAKEN the Asvin Pair who yoke their car at early morn: may they
Approach to drink this Soma juice.
2 We call the Asvins Twain, the Gods borne in a noble car, the best

Of charioteers, who reach the heavens.
3 Dropping with honey is your whip, Asvins, and full of pleasantness
Sprinkle therewith the sacrifice.
4 As ye go thither in your car, not far, O Asvins, is the home
Of him who offers Soma juice.
5 For my protection I invoke the golden-handed Savitar.
He knoweth, as a God, the place.
6 That he may send us succour, praise the Waters' Offspring Savitar:
Fain are we for his holy ways.
7 We call on him, distributer of wondrous bounty and of wealth,
On Savitar who looks on men.
8 Come hither, friends, and seat yourselves Savitar, to be praised by us,
Giving good gifts, is beautiful.
9 O Agni, hither bring to us the willing Spouses of the Gods,
And Tvastar, to the Soma draught.
10 Most youthful Agni, hither bring their Spouses, Hotra, Bharati, Varutri, Dhisana, for aid.
11 Spouses of Heroes, Goddesses, with whole wings may they come to us
With great protection and with aid.
12 Indrani, Varunani, and Agnayi hither I invite,
For weal, to drink the Soma juice.
13 May Heaven and Earth, the Mighty Pair, bedew for us our sacrifice,
And feed us full with nourishments.
14 Their water rich with fatness, there in the Gandharva's steadfast place,
The singers taste through sacred songs.
15 Thornless be thou, O Earth, spread wide before us for a dwelling-place:
Vouchsafe us shelter broad and sure.
16 The Gods be gracious unto us even from the place whence Visnu strode
Through the seven regions of the earth!
17 Through all this world strode Visnu; thrice his foot he planted, and the whole
Was gathered in his footstep's dust.
18 Visnu, the Guardian, he whom none deceiveth, made three steps; thenceforth
Establishing his high decrees.
19 Look ye on Visnu's works, whereby the Friend of Indra, close-allied,
Hath let his holy ways be seen.
20 The princes evermore behold that loftiest place where Visnu is,
Laid as it were an eye in heaven.
21 This, Vishnu's station most sublime, the singers, ever vigilant,
Lovers of holy song, light up.

### [01-023] HYMN XXIII. Vayu and Others.
1 STRONG are the Somas; come thou nigh; these juices have been mixt with milk:
Drink, Vayu, the presented draughts.
2 Both Deities who touch the heaven, Indra and Vayu we invoke
To drink of this our soma juice.
3 The singers' for their aid, invoke Indra and Vayu, swift as mind,
The thousand-eyed, the Lords of thought.
4 Mitra and Varupa, renowned as Gods of consecrated might,
We call to drink the Soma juice.
5 Those who by Law uphold the Law, Lords of the shining light of Law,
Mitra I call, and Varuna.
6 Let Varuna be our chief defence, let Mitra guard us with all aids
Both make us rich exceedingly.

7 Indra, by Maruts girt, we call to drink the Soma juice: may he
Sate him in union with his troop.
8 Gods, Marut hosts whom Indra leads, distributers of Pusan's gifts,
Hearken ye all unto my cry.
9 With conquering Indra for ally, strike Vrtra down, ye bounteous Gods
Let not the wicked master us.
10 We call the Universal Gods, and Maruts to the Soma draught,
For passing strong are Prsni's Sons.
11 Fierce comes the Maruts' thundering voice, like that of conquerors, when ye go
Forward to victory, O Men.
12 Born of the laughing lightning. may the Maruts guard us everywhere
May they be gracious unto Us.
13 Like some lost animal, drive to us, bright Pusan, him who bears up heaven,
Resting on many-coloured grass.
14 Pusan the Bright has found the King, concealed and bidden in a cave,
Who rests on grass of many hues.
15 And may he. duly bring to me the six bound closely, through these drops,
As one who ploughs with steers brings corn.
16 Along their paths the Mothers go, Sisters of priestly ministrants,
Mingling their sweetness with the milk.
17 May Waters gathered near the Sun, and those wherewith the Sun is joined,
Speed forth this sacrifice of ours.
18 I call the Waters, Goddesses, wherein our cattle quench their thirst;
Oblations to the Streams be given.
19 Amrit is in the Waters in the Waters there is healing balm
Be swift, ye Gods, to give them praise.
20 Within the Waters-Soma thus hath told me-dwell all balms that heal,
And Agni, he who blesseth all. The Waters hold all medicines.
21 O Waters, teem with medicine to keep my body safe from harm,
So that I long may see the Sun.
22 Whatever sin is found in me, whatever evil I have wrought.
If I have lied or falsely sworn, Waters, remove it far from me.
23 The Waters I this day have sought, and to their moisture have we come:
O Agni, rich in milk, come thou, and with thy splendour cover me.
24 Fill me with splendour, Agni; give offspring and length of days; the Gods
Shall know me even as I am, and Indra with the Rsis, know.

### [01-024] HYMN XXIV. Varuna and Others.
1 WHO now is he, what God among Immortals, of whose auspicious name we may bethink us?
Who shall to mighty Aditi restore us, that I may see my Father and my Mother?
2 Agni the God the first among the Immortals, - of his auspicious name let us bethink us.
He shall to mighty Aditi restore us, that I may see my Father and my Mother.
3 To thee, O Savitar, the Lord of precious things, who helpest us
Continually, for our share we come-
4 Wealth, highly lauded ere reproach hath fallen on it, which is laid,
Free from all hatred, in thy hands

5 Through thy protection may we come to even the height of affluence
Which Bhaga hath dealt out to us.
6 Ne'er have those birds that fly through air attained to thy high dominion or thy might or spirit;
Nor these the waters that flow on for ever, nor hills, abaters of the wind's wild fury.
7 Varuna, King, of hallowed might, sustaineth erect the Tree's stem in the baseless region.
Its rays, whose root is high above, stream downward. Deep may they sink within us, and be hidden.
8 King Varuna hath made a spacious pathway, a pathway for the Sun wherein to travel.
Where no way was he made him set his footstep, and warned afar whate'er afflicts the spirit.
9 A hundred balms are thine, O King, a thousand; deep and wide-reaching also be thy favours.
Far from us, far away drive thou Destruction. Put from us e'en the sin we have committed.
10 Whither by day depart the constellations that shine at night, set high in heaven above us?
Varuna's holy laws remain unweakened, and through the night the Moon moves on in splendor
11 I ask this of thee with my prayer adoring; thy worshipper craves this with his oblation.
Varuna, stay thou here and be not angry; steal not our life from us, O thou Wide-Ruler.
12 Nightly and daily this one thing they tell me, this too the thought of mine own heart repeateth.
May he to whom prayed fettered Sunahsepa, may he the Sovran Varuna release us.
13 Bound to three pillars captured Sunahsepa thus to the Aditya made his supplication.
Him may the Sovran Varuna deliver, wise, ne'er deccived, loosen the bonds that bind him.
14 With bending down, oblations, sacrifices, O Varuna, we deprecate thine anger:
Wise Asura, thou King of wide dominion, loosen the bonds of sins by us committed.
15 Loosen the bonds, O Varuna, that hold me, loosen the bonds above, between, and under.
So in thy holy law may we made sinless belong to Aditi, O thou Aditya.

### [01-025] HYMN XXV. Varuna.
I WHATEVER law of thine, O God, O Varurna, as we are men,
Day after day we violate.
2 give us not as a prey to death, to be destroyed by thee in wrath,
To thy fierce anger when displeased.
3 To gain thy mercy, Varuna, with hymns we bind thy heart, as binds
The charioteer his tethered horse.
4 They flee from me dispirited, bent only on obtaining wealths
As to their nests the birds of air.
5 When shall we bring, to be appeased, the Hero, Lord of warrior might,
Him, the far-seeing Varuna?
6 This, this with joy they both accept in common: never do they fail
The ever-faithful worshipper.
7 He knows the path of birds that fly through heaven, and, Sovran of the sea,
He knows the ships that are thereon.
8 True to his holy law, he knows the twelve moons with their progeny:
He knows the moon of later birth.

9 He knows the pathway of the wind, the spreading, high, and mighty wind
He knows the Gods who dwell above.
10 Varuna, true to holy law, sits down among his people; he,
Most wise, sits there to govern. all.
11 From thence percerving he beholds all wondrous things, both what hath been,
And what hereafter will be done.
12 May that Aditya, very -wise, make fair paths for us all our days:
May lie prolong our lives for us.
13 Varuna, wearing golden mail, hath clad him in a shining robe.
His spies are seated found about.
14 The God whom enemies threaten not, nor those who tyrannize o'er men,
Nor those whose minds are bent on wrong.
15 He who gives glory to mankind, not glory that is incomplete,
To our own bodies giving it.
16 Yearning for the wide-seeing One, my thoughts move onward unto him,
As kine unto their pastures move.
17 Once more together let us speak, because my meath is brought: priest-like
Thou eatest what is dear to thee.
18 Now saw I him whom all may see, I saw his car above the earth:
He hath accepted these my songs.
19 Varuna, hear this call of mine: be gracious unto us this day
Longing for help I cried to thee.
20 Thou, O wise God, art Lord of all, thou art the King of earth and heaven
Hear, as thou goest on thy way.
21 Release us from the upper bond, untie the bond between, and loose
The bonds below, that I may live.

## [01-026] HYMN XXVI. Agni.
1 O WORTHY of oblation, Lord of prospering powers, assume thy robes,
And offer this our sacrifice.
2 Sit ever to be chosen, as our Priest., most youthful, through our hymns,
O Agni, through our heavenly word.
3 For here a Father for his son, Kinsman for kinsman worshippeth,
And Friend, choice-worthy, for his friend.
4 Fiere let the foe-destroyers sit, Varuna, Mitra, Aryaman,
Like men, upon our sacred grass.
5 O ancient Herald, be thou glad in this our rite and fellowship:
Hearken thou well to these our songs.
6 Whate'er in this perpetual course we sacrifice to God and God,
That gift is offered up in thee
7 May he be our dear household Lord, Priest, pleasant and, choice-worthy may
We, with bright fires, be dear to him.
8 The Gods, adored with brilliant fires. have granted precious wealth to us
So, with bright fires, we pray to thee.
9 And, O Immortal One, so may the eulogies of mortal men
Belong to us and thee alike.
10 With all thy fires, O Agni, find pleasure in this our sacrifice,
And this our speech, O Son of Strength.

## [01-027] HYMN XXVII. Agni.
1 WITH worship will I glorify thee, Agni, like a long-tailed steed,
Imperial Lord of sacred rites.
2 May the far-striding Son of Strength, bringer of great felicity,
Who pours his gifts like rain, be ours.

3 Lord of all life, from near; from far, do thou, O Agni evermore
Protect us from the sinful man.
4 O Agni, graciously announce this our oblation to the Gods,
And this our newest song of praise.
5 Give us a share of strength most high, a share of strength that is below,
A share of strength that is between.
6 Thou dealest gifts, resplendent One; nigh, as with waves of Sindhu, thou
Swift streamest to the worshipper.
7 That man is lord of endless strength whom thou protectest in the fight,
Agni, or urgest to the fray.
8 Him, whosoever he may be, no man may vanquish, mighty One:
Nay, very glorious power is his.
9 May he who dwells with all mankind bear us with war-steeds through the fight,
And with the singers win the spoil.
10 Help, thou who knowest lauds, this work, this eulogy to Rudra, him
Adorable in every house.
11 May this our God, great, limitless, smoke-bannered excellently bright,
Urge us to strength and holy thought.
12 Like some rich Lord of men may he, Agni the banner of the Gods,
Refulgent, hear us through our lauds.
13 Glory to Gods, the mighty and the lesser glory to Gods the younger and the elder!
Let us, if we have power, pay the God worship: no better prayer than this, ye Gods, acknowledge.

## [01-028] HYMN XXVIII Indra, Etc.
1 THERE where the broad-based stone raised on high to press the juices out,
O Indra, drink with eager thirst the droppings which the mortar sheds.
2 Where, like broad hips, to hold the juice the platters of the press are laid,
O Indra, drink with eager thirst the droppings which the mortar sheds.
3 There where the woman marks and leans the pestle's constant rise and fall,
O Indra, drink with eager thirst the droppings which the mortar sheds.
4 Where, as with reins to guide a horse, they bind the churning-staff with cords,
O Indra, drink with eager thirst the droppings which the mortar sheds.
5 If of a truth in every house, O Mortar thou art set for work,
Here give thou forth thy clearest sound, loud as the drum of conquerors.
6 O Sovran of the Forest, as the wind blows soft in front of thee,
Mortar, for Indra press thou forth the Soma juice that he may drink.
7 Best strength-givers, ye stretch wide jaws, O Sacrificial Implements,
Like two bay horses champing herbs.
8 Ye Sovrans of the Forest, both swift, with swift pressers press to-day
Sweet Soma juice for Indra's drink.
9 Take up in beakers what remains: the Soma on the filter pour, and on the ox-hide set the dregs.

## [01-029] HYMN XXIX. Indra.
1 O SOMA DRINKER, ever true, utterly hopeless though we be,
Do thou, O Indra, give us hope of beauteous horses and of kine,

In thousands, O most wealthy One.

2 O Lord of Strength, whose jaws are strong, great deeds are thine, the powerful:
Do thou, O Indra, give us hope of beauteous horses and of kine,
In thousands, O most wealthy One.

3 Lull thou asleep, to wake no more, the pair who on each other look
Do thou, O Indra, give us, help of beauteous horses and of kine,
In thousands, O most wealthy One.

4 Hero, let hostile spirits sleep, and every gentler genius wake:
Do thou, O Indra,. give us hope of beauteous horses and of kine,
In thousands, O most wealthy One.

5 Destroy this ass, O Indra, who in tones discordant brays to thee:
Do thou, O Indra, give us hope of beauteous horses and of kine,
In thousands, O most wealthy One.

6 Far distant on the forest fall the tempest in a circling course!
Do thou, O Indra, give us hope of beauteous horses and of kine,
In thousands, O most wealthy One.

7 Slay each reviler, and destroy him who in secret injures us:
Do thou, O Indra, give us hope of beauteous horses and of kine
In thousands, O most wealthy One.

## [01-030] HYMN XXX. Indra.

1 WE seeking strength with Soma-drops fill full your Indra like a well,
Most liberal, Lord of Hundred Powers,

2 Who lets a hundred of the pure, a thousand of the milk-blent draughts
Flow, even as down a depth, to him;

3 When for the strong, the rapturous joy he in this manner hath made room
Within his belly, like the sea.

4 This is thine own. Thou drawest near, as turns a pigeon to his mate:
Thou carest too for this our prayer.

5 O Hero, Lord of Bounties, praised in hymns, may power and joyfulness
Be his who sings the laud to thee.

6 Lord of a Hundred Powers, stand up to lend us succour in this fight
In others too let us agree.

7 In every need, in every fray we call as friends to succour us
Indra the mightiest of all.

8 If he will hear us let him come with succour of a thousand kinds,
And all that strengthens, to our call.

9 I call him mighty to resist, the Hero of our ancient home,
Thee whom my sire invoked of old.

10 We pray to thee, O much-invoked, rich in all precious gifts, O Friend,
Kind God to those who sing thy praise.

11 O Soma-drinker, Thunder-armed, Friend of our lovely-featured dames
And of our Soma-drinking friends.

12 Thus, Soma-drinker, may it be; thus, Friend, who wieldest thunder, act
To aid each wish as we desire.

13 With Indra splendid feasts be ours, rich in all strengthening things wherewith,
Wealthy in food, we may rejoice.

14 Like thee, thyself, the singers' Friend, thou movest, as it were, besought,
Bold One, the axle of the car.

15 That, Satakratu, thou to grace and please thy praisers, as it were,
Stirrest the axle with thy strength.

16 With champing, neighing loudly-snorting horses Indra hath ever won himself great treasures
A car of gold hath he whose deeds are wondrous received from us, and let us too receive it.

17 Come, Asvins, with enduring strength wealthy in horses and in kine,
And gold, O ye of wondrous deeds.

18 Your chariot yoked for both alike, immortal, ye of mighty acts,
Travels, O Aivins, in the sea.

19 High on the forehead of the Bull one chariot wheel ye ever keep,
The other round the sky revolves.

20 What mortal, O immortal Dawn, enjoyeth thee? Where lovest thou?
To whom, O radiant, dost thou go?

21 For we have had thee in our thoughts whether anear or far away,
Red-hued and like a dappled mare.

22 Hither, O Daughter of the Sky, come thou with these thy strengthenings,
And send thou riches down to us.

## [01-031] HYMN XXXI. Agni.

1 Thou, Agni, wast the earliest Angiras, a Seer; thou wast, a God thyself, the Gods' auspicious
Friend.
After thy holy ordinance the Maruts, sage, active through wisdom, -with their glittering spears, were
born.

2 O Agni, thou, the best and earliest Angiras, fulfillest as a Sage the holy law of Gods.
Sprung from two mothers, wise, through all existence spread, resting in many a place for sake of
living man.

3 To Matarisvan first thou, Agni, wast disclosed, and to Vivasvan through thy noble inward power.
Heaven and Earth, Vasu! shook at the choosing of the Priest: the burthen thou didst bear, didst
worship mighty Gods.

4 Agni thou madest heaven to thunder for mankind; thou, yet more pious, for pious Pururavas.
When thou art rapidly freed from thy parents, first eastward they bear thee round, and, after, to the
west.

5 Thou, Agni, art a Bull who makes our store increase, to be invoked by him who lifts the ladle up.
Well knowing the oblation with the hallowing word, uniting all who live, thou lightenest first our folk

6 Agni, thou savest in the synod when pursued e'en him, farseeing One! who walks in evil ways.
Thou, when the heroes fight for spoil which men rush, round, slayest in war the many by the hands
of few.

7 For glory, Agni, day by day, thou liftest up the mortal man to highest immortality,
Even thou who yearning for both races givest them great bliss, and to the prince grantest abundant
food.

8 O Agni, highly lauded, make our singer famous that he may win us store of riches:
May we improve the rite with new performance. O Earth and Heaven, with all the Gods, protect us.

9 O blameless Agni lying in thy Parents' lap, a God among the Gods, be watchful for our good.
Former of bodies, be the singer's Providence: all good things hast thou sown for him, auspicious One!

10 Agni, thou art our Providence, our Father thou - we are thy brethren and thou art our spring of life.

in thee, rich in good heroes, guard of high decrees, meet hundred, thousand treasures, O infallible!

11 Thee, Agni, have the Gods made the first living One for living man, Lord of the house of Nahusa.

Ila they made the teacher of the sons of men, what time a Son was born to the father of my race.

12 Worthy to be revered, O Agni, God, preserve our wealthy patrons with thy succours, and ourselves.

Guard of our seed art thou, aiding our cows to bear, incessantly protecting in thy holy way.

13 Agni, thou art a guard close to the pious man; kindled art thou, four-eyed! for him who is unarmed.

With fond heart thou acceptest e'en the poor man's prayer, when he hath brought his gift to gain security.

14 Thou, Agni gainest for the loudly-praising priest the highest wealth, the object of a man's desire.

Thou art called Father, caring even for the weak, and wisest, to the simple one thou teachest lore.

15 Agni, the man who giveth guerdon to the priests, like well-sewn armour thou guardest on every side.

He who with grateful food shows kindness in his house, an offerer to the living, is the type of heaven.

16 Pardon, we pray, this sin of ours, O Agni, -- the path which we have trodden, widely straying,

Dear Friend and Father, caring for the pious, who speedest nigh and who inspirest mortals.

17 As erst to Manus, to Yayiti, Angiras, so Angiras! pure Agni! come thou to our hall

Bring hither the celestial host and seat them here upon the sacred grass, and offer what they love.

18 By this our prayer be thou, O Agni, strengthened, prayer made by us after our power and knowledge.

Lead thou us, therefore, to increasing riches; endow us with thy strength-bestowing favour.

## [01-032] HYMN XXXII. Indra.

1 I WILL declare the manly deeds of Indra, the first that he achieved, the Thunder-wielder.

He slew the Dragon, then disclosed the waters, and cleft the channels of the mountain torrents.

2 He slew the Dragon lying on the mountain: his heavenly bolt of thunder Tvastar fashioned.

Like lowing kine in rapid flow descending the waters glided downward to the ocean.

3 Impetuous as a bull, he chose the Soma and in three sacred beakers drank the juices.

Maghavan grasped the thunder for his weapon, and smote to death this firstborn of the dragons.

4 When, Indra, thou hadst slain the dragon's firstborn, and overcome the charms of the enchanters,

Then, giving life to Sun and Dawn and Heaven, thou foundest not one foe to stand against thee.

5 Indra with his own great and deadly thunder smote into pieces Vrtra, worst of Vrtras.

As trunks of trees, what time the axe hath felled them, low on the earth so lies the prostrate Dragon.

6 He, like a mad weak warrior, challenged Indra, the great impetuous many-slaying Hero.

He. brooking not the clashing of the weapons, crushed-Indra's foe-the shattered forts in falling.

7 Footless and handless still he challenged Indra, who smote him with his bolt between the shoulders.

Emasculate yet claiming manly vigour, thus Vrtra lay with scattered limbs dissevered.

8 There as he lies like a bank-bursting river, the waters taking courage flow above him.

The Dragon lies beneath the feet of torrents which Vrtra with his greatness had encompassed.

9 Then humbled was the strength of Vrtra's mother: Indra hath cast his deadly bolt against her.

The mother was above, the son was under and like a cow beside her calf lay Danu.

10 Rolled in the midst of never-ceasing currents flowing without a rest for ever onward.

The waters bear off Vrtra's nameless body: the foe of Indra sank to during darkness.

11 Guarded by Ahi stood the thralls of Dasas, the waters stayed like kine held by the robber.

But he, when he had smitten Vrtra, opened the cave wherein the floods had been imprisoned.

12 A horse's tail wast thou when he, O Indra, smote on thy bolt; thou, God without a second,

Thou hast won back the kine, hast won the Soma; thou hast let loose to flow the Seven Rivers.

13 Nothing availed him lightning, nothing thunder, hailstorm or mist which had spread around him:

When Indra and the Dragon strove in battle, Maghavan gained the victory for ever.

14 Whom sawest thou to avenge the Dragon, Indra, that fear possessed thy heart when thou hadst slain him;

That, like a hawk affrighted through the regions, thou crossedst nine-and-ninety flowing rivers?

15 Indra is King of all that moves and moves not, of creatures tame and horned, the Thunder-wielder.

Over all living men he rules as Sovran, containing all as spokes within the felly.

## [01-033] HYMN XXXIII. Indra.

1 Come, fain for booty let us seek to Indra: yet more shall he increase his care that guides us.

Will not the Indestructible endow us with perfect knowledge of this wealth, of cattle?

2 I fly to him invisible Wealth-giver as flies the falcon to his cherished eyrie,

With fairest hymns of praise adoring Indra, whom those who laud him must invoke in battle.

3 Mid all his host, he bindeth on the quiver he driveth cattle from what foe he pleaseth:

Gathering up great store of riches, Indra. be thou no trafficker with us, most mighty.

4 Thou slewest with thy bolt the wealthy Dasyu, alone, yet going with thy helpers, Indra!

Far from the floor of heaven in all directions, the ancient riteless ones fled to destruction.

5 Fighting with pious worshippers, the riteless turned and fled, Indra! with averted faces.

When thou, fierce Lord of the Bay Steeds, the Stayer, blewest from earth and heaven and sky the godless.

6 They met in fight the army of the blameless. then the Navagvas put forth all their power.

They, like emasculates with men contending, fled, conscious, by steep paths from Indra, scattered.

7 Whether they weep or laugh, thou hast o'erthrown them, O Indra, on the sky's extremest limit.

9

The Dasyu thou hast burned from heaven, and welcomed the prayer of him who pours the juice and
lauds thee.
8 Adorned with their array of gold and jewels, they o'er the earth a covering veil extended.
Although they hastened, they o'ercame not Indra: their spies he compassed with the Sun of morning.
9 As thou enjoyest heaven and earth, O Indra, on every side surrounded with thy greatness,
So thou with priests hast blown away the Dasyu, and those who worship not with those who
worship.
10 They who pervaded earth's extremest limit subdued not with their charms the Wealth-bestower:
Indra, the Bull, made his ally the thunder, and with its light milked cows from out the darkness.
11 The waters flowed according to their nature; he raid the navigable streams waxed mighty.
Then Indra, with his spirit concentrated, smote him for ever with his strongest weapon.
12 Indra broke through Ilibisa's strong castles, and Suspa with his horn he cut to pieces:
Thou, Maghavan, for all his might and swiftness, slewest thy fighting foeman with thy thunder
13 Fierce on his enemies fell Indra's weapon: with. his sharp bull he rent their forts in pieces.
He with his thunderbolt dealt blows on Vrtra; and conquered, executing all his purpose.
14 Indra, thou helpest Kutsa whom thou lovedst, and guardedst brave Dagadyu when he battled,
The dust of trampling horses rose to heaven, and Svitri's son stood up again for conquest.
15 Svitra's mild steer, O Maghavan thou helpest in combat for the land, mid Tugra's houses.
Long stood they there before the task was ended: thou wast the master of the foemen's treasure.

## [01-034] HYMN XXXIV. Asvins.

1 Ye who observe this day be with us even thrice: far-stretching is you bounty, Asvins and your
course.
To you, as to a cloak in winter, we cleave close: you are to be drawn nigh unto us by the wise.
2 Three are the fellies in your honey-bearing car, that travels after Soma's loved one, as all know.
Three are the pillars set upon it for support: thrice journey ye by night, O Asvins, thrice by day.
3 Thrice in the self-same day, ye Gods who banish want, sprinkle ye thrice to-day our sacrifice with
meath;
And thrice vouchsafe us store of food with plenteous strength, at evening, O ye Asvins, and at break
of day.
4 Thrice come ye to our home, thrice to the righteous folk, thrice triply aid the man who well deserves
your help.
Thrice, O ye Asvins, bring us what shall make us glad; thrice send us store of food as nevermore to
fail.
5 Thrice, O ye Asvins, bring to us abundant wealth: thrice in the Gods' assembly, thrice assist our
thoughts.
Thrice, grant ye us prosperity, thrice grant us fame; for the Sun's daughter hath mounted your threewheeled
car.
6 Thrice, Asvins, grant to us the heavenly medicines, thrice those of earth and thrice those that the

waters hold,
Favour and health and strength bestow upon my son; triple protection, Lords of Splendour, grant to
him.
7 Thrice are ye to be worshipped day by day by us: thrice, O ye Asvins, ye travel around the earth.
Car-borne from far away, O ye Nasatyas, come, like vital air to bodies, come ye to the three.
8 Thrice, O ye Asvins, with the Seven Mother Streams; three are the jars, the triple offering is
prepared.
Three are the worlds, and moving on above the sky ye guard the firm-set vault of heaven through
days and nights.
9 Where are the three wheels of your triple chariot, where are the three seats thereto firmly
fastened?
When will ye yoke the mighty ass that draws it, to bring you to our sacrifice. Nasatyas?
10 Nasatyas, come: the sacred gift is offered up; drink the sweet juice with lips that know the
sweetness well.
Savitar sends, before the dawn of day, your car, fraught with oil, various-coloured, to our sacrifice.
11 Come, O Nasatyas, with the thrice-eleven Gods; come, O ye Asvins, to the drinking of the meath.
Make long our days of life, and wipe out all our sins: ward off our enemies; be with us evermore.
12 Borne in your triple car, O Asvins, bring us present prosperity with noble offspring.
I cry to you who hear me for protection be ye our helpers where men win the booty.

## [01-035] HYMN XXXV. Savitar.

1 AGNI I first invoke for our prosperity; I call on Mitra, Varuna, to aid us here.
I call on Night who gives rest to all moving life; I call on Savitar the God to lend us help.
2 Throughout the dusky firmament advancing, laying to rest the immortal and the mortal,
Borne in his golden chariot he cometh, Savitar, God who looks on every creature.
3 The God moves by the upward path, the downward; with two bright Bays, adorable, he journeys.
Savitar comes, the God from the far distance, and chases from us all distress and sorrow.
4 His chariot decked with pearl, of various colours, lofty, with golden pole, the God hath mounted,
The many-rayed One, Savitar the holy, bound, bearing power and might, for darksome regions.
5 Drawing the gold-yoked car his Bays, white-footed, have manifested light to all the peoples.
Held in the lap of Savitar, divine One, all men, all beings have their place for ever.
6 Three heavens there are; two Savitar's, adjacent: in Yama's world is one, the home of heroes,
As on a linch-pin, firm, rest things immortal: he who hath known it let him here declare it.
7 He, strong of wing, hath lightened up the regions, deep-quivering Asura, the gentle Leader.
Where now is Surya, where is one to tell us to what celestial sphere his ray hath wandered?
8 The earth's eight points his brightness hath illumined, three desert regions and the Seven Rivers.
God Savitar the gold-eyed hath come hither, giving choice treasures unto him who worships.

9 The golden-handed Savitar, far-seeing, goes on his way between the earth and heaven,
Drives away sickness, bids the Sun approach us, and spreads the bright sky through the darksome
region.
10 May he, gold-handed Asura, kind Leader, come hither to us with his help and favour.
Driving off Raksasas and Yatudhanas, the God is present, praised in hymns at evening.
11 O Savitar, thine ancient dustless pathways are well established in the air's midregion:
O God, come by those paths so fair to travel, preserve thou us from harm this day, and bless us.

## [01-036] HYMN XXXVI. Agni.

1 WITH words sent forth in holy hymns, Agni we supplicate, the Lord
Of many families who duly serve the Gods, yea, him whom others also praise.
2 Men have won Agni, him who makes their strength abound: we, with oblations, worship thee.
Our gracious-minded Helper in our deeds of might, be thou, O Excellent, this day.
3 Thee for our messenger we choose, thee, the Omniscient, for our Priest.
The flames of thee the mighty are spread wide around: thy splendour reaches to the sky.
4 The Gods enkindle thee their ancient messenger, - Varuna, Mitra, Aryaman.
That mortal man, O Agni, gains through thee all wealth, who hath poured offerings unto thee.
5 Thou, Agni, art a cheering Priest, Lord of the House, men's messenger:
All constant high decrees established by the Gods, gathered together, meet in thee.
6 In thee, the auspicious One, O Agni, youthfullest, each sacred gift is offered up:
This day, and after, gracious, worship thou our Gods, that we may have heroic sons.
7 To him in his own splendour bright draw near in worship the devout.
Men kindle Agni with their sacrificial gifts, victorious o'er the enemies.
8 Vrtra they smote and slew, and made the earth and heaven and firmament a wide abode.
The glorious Bull, invoked, hath stood at Kanva's side: loud neighed the Steed in frays for kine.
9 Seat thee, for thou art mighty; shine, best entertainer of the Gods.
Worthy of sacred food, praised Agni! loose the smoke, ruddy and beautiful to see.
10 Bearer of offerings, whom, best sacrificing Priest, the Gods for Manu's sake ordained;
Whom Kanva, whom Medhyatithi made the source of wealth, and Vrsan and Upastuta.
11 Him, Agni, whom Medhyatithi, whom Kanva kindled for his rite,
Him these our songs of praise, him, Agni, we extol: his powers shine out preeminent.
12 Make our wealth perfect thou, O Agni, Lord divine: for thou hast kinship with the Gods.
Thou rulest as a King o'er widely-famous strength: be good to us, for thou art great.
13 Stand up erect to lend us aid, stand up like Savitar the God:
Erect as strength-bestower we call aloud, with unguents and with priests, on thee.

14 Erect, preserve us from sore trouble; with thy flame burn thou each ravening demon dead.
Raise thou us up that we may walk and live. so thou shalt find our worship mid the Gods.
15 Preserve us, Agni, from the fiend, preserve us from malicious wrong.
Save us from him who fain would injure us or slay, Most Youthful, thou with lofty light.
16 Smite down as with a club, thou who hast fire for teeth, smite thou the wicked, right and left.
Let not the man who plots against us in the night, nor any foe prevail o'er us.
17 Agni hath given heroic might to Kainva, and felicity:
Agni hath helped our friends, hath helped Medhyitithi, hath helped Upastuta to win.
18 We call on Ugradeva, Yadu, Turvasa, by means of Agni, from afar;
Agni, bring Navavastva and Brhadratba, Turviti, to subdue the foe.
19 Manu hath stablished thee a light, Agni, for all the race of men:
Sprung from the Law, oil-fed, for Kanva hast thou blazed, thou whom the people reverence.
20 The flames of Agni full of splendour and of might are fearful, not to be approached.
Consume for ever all demons and sorcerers, consume thou each devouring fiend.

## [01-037] HYMN XXXVII. Maruts.

1 SING forth, O Kanvas, to your band of Maruts unassailable,
Sporting, resplendent on their car
2 They who, self-luminous, were born together, with the spotted deer,
Spears, swords, and glittering ornaments.
3 One hears, as though 'twere close at hand, the cracking of the whips they hold
They gather glory on their way.
4 Now sing ye forth the God-given hymn to your exultant Marut host,
The fiercely-vigorous, the strong.
5 Praise ye the Bull among the cows; for 'tis the Maruts' sportive band:
It strengthened as it drank the rain.
6 Who is your mightiest, Heroes, when, O shakers of the earth and heaven,
Ye shake them like a garment's hem?
7 At your approach man holds him down before the fury of your wrath:
The rugged-jointed mountain yields.
8 They at whose racings forth the earth, like an age-weakened lord of men,
Trembles in terror on their ways.
9 Strong is their birth: vigour have they to issue from their Mother; strength,
Yea, even twice enough, is theirs.
10 And these, the Sons, the Singers, in their racings have enlarged the bounds,
So that the kine must walk knee-deep.
11 Before them, on the ways they go, they drop this offspring of the cloud,
Long, broad, and inexhaustible.
12 O Maruts, as your strength is great, so have ye cast men down on earth,
So have ye made the mountains fall.
13 The while the Maruts pass along, they talk together on the way:
Doth any hear them as they speak?

14 Come quick with swift steeds, for ye have worshippers among Kanva's sons
May you rejoice among them well.
15 All is prepared for your delight. We are their servants evermore,
To live as long as life may last.

## [01-038] HYMN XXXVIII. Maruts.

I WHAT now? When will ye take us by both hands, as a dear sire his son,
Gods, for whom sacred grass is clipped?
2 Now whither? To what goal of yours go ye in heaven, and not on earth?
Where do your cows disport themselves?
3 Where are your newest favours shown? Where, Maruts, your prosperity?
Where all your high felicities?
4 If, O ye Maruts, ye the Sons whom Prsni bore, were mortal, and Immortal he who sings your praise.
5 Then never were your praiser loathed like a wild beast in pasture-land,
Nor should he go on Yama's path.
6 Let not destructive plague on plague hard to be conquered, strike its down:
Let each, with drought, depart from us.
7 Truly, they the fierce and mighty Sons of Rudra send their windless
Rain e'en on the desert places.
8 Like a cow the lightning lows and follows, motherlike, her youngling,
When their rain-flood hath been loosened.
9 When they inundate the earth they spread forth darkness e'en in day time,
With the water-laden rain-cloud.
10 O Maruts, at your voice's sound this earthly habitation shakes,
And each man reels who dwells therein.
11 O Maruts, with your strong-hoofed steeds, unhindered in their courses, haste
Along the bright embanked streams.
12 Firm be the fellies of your wheels, steady your horses and your cars,
And may your reins be fashioned well.
13 Invite thou hither with this song, for praise, Agni the Lord of Prayer,
Him who is fair as Mitra is.
14 Form in thy mouth the hymn of praise expand thee like, a rainy cloud
Sing forth the measured eulogy.
15 Sing glory to the Marut host, praiseworthy, tuneful, vigorous:
Here let the Strong Ones dwell with us.

## [01-039] HYMN XXXIX Maruts.

1 WHEN thus, like flame, from far away, Maruts, ye cast your measure forth,
To whom go Ye, to whom, O shakers of the earth, moved by whose wisdom, whose design?
2 Strong let your weapons be to drive away your foes, firm for resistance let them be.
Yea, passing glorious must be your warrior might, not as a guileful mortal's strength.
3 When what is strong ye overthrow, and whirl about each ponderous thing,
Heroes, your course is through the forest trees of earth, and through the fissures of the rocks.
4 Consumers of your foes, no enemy of yours is found in heaven or on the earth:

Ye Rudras, may the strength, held in this bond, be yours, to bid defiance even now.
5 They make the mountains rock and reel, they rend the forest-kings apart.
onward, ye Maruts, drive, like creatures drunk with wine, ye, Gods with all your company.
6 Ye to your chariot have yoked the spotted deer: a red deer, as a leader, draws.
Even the Earth herself listened as ye came near, and men were sorely terrified.
7 O Rudras, quickly we desire your succour for this work of ours.
Come to us with your aid as in the days of old, so now for frightened Kanva's sake.
8 Should any monstrous foe, O Maruts, sent by you or sent by mortals threaten us,
Tear ye him from us with your power and with your might, and with the succours that are yours.
9 For ye, the worshipful and wise, have guarded Kanva perfectly.
O Maruts, come to us with full protecting help, as lightning flashes seek the rain.
10 Whole strength have ye, O Bounteous Ones; perfect, earth-shakers, is your might.
Maruts, against the poet's wrathful enemy send ye an enemy like a dart.

## [01-040] HYMN XL. Brahmanaspati

1 O BRAMANASPATI, stand up: God-serving men we pray to thee.
May they who give good gifts, the Maruts, come to us. Indra, most swift, be thou with them.
2 O Son of Strength, each mortal calls to thee for aid when spoil of battle waits for him.
O Maruts, may this man who loves you well obtain wealth of good steeds and hero might.
3 May Brahmanaspati draw nigh, may Sunrta the Goddess come,
And Gods bring to this rite which gives the five-fold gift the Hero, lover of mankind.
4 He who bestows a noble guerdon on the priest wins fame that never shall decay.
For him we offer sacred hero-giving food, peerless and conquering easily.
5 Now Brahmanaspati speaks forth aloud the solemn hymn of praise,
Wherein Indra and Varuna, Mitra, Aryaman, the Gods, have made their dwelling place.
6 May we in holy synods, Gods! recite that hymn, peerless, that brings felicity.
If you, O Heroes, graciously accept this word, may it obtain all bliss from you.
7 Who shall approach the pious? who the man whose sacred grass is trimmed?
The offerer with his folk advances more and more: he fills his house with precious things.
8 He amplifies his lordly might, with kings he slays: e'en mid alarms he dwells secure
In great or lesser fight none checks him, none subdues,-the wielder of the thunderbolt.

## [01-041] HYMN XLI. Varuna, Mitra, Aryaman.

1 NE'ER is he injured whom the Gods Varuna, Mitra, Aryaman,
The excellently wise, protect.
2 He prospers ever, free from scathe, whom they, as with full hands, enrich,
Whom they preserve from every foe.
3 The Kings drive far away from him his troubles and his enemies,
And lead him safely o'er distress.

4 Thornless, Adityas, is the path, easy for him who seeks the Law:
With him is naught to anger you.
5 What sacrifice, Adityas, ye Heroes guide by the path direct,-
May that come nigh unto your thought.
6 That mortal, ever unsubdued, gains wealth and every precious thing,
And children also of his own.
7 How, my friends, shall we prepare Aryaman's and Mitra's laud,
Glorious food of Varuna?
8 I point not out to you a man who strikes the pious, or reviles:
Only with hymns I call you nigh.
9 Let him not love to speak ill words: but fear the One who holds all four
Within his hand, until they fall.

## [01-042] HYMN XLII. Pusan.

I SHORTEN our ways, O Pusan, move aside obstruction in the path:
Go close before us, cloud-born God.
2 Drive, Pusan, from our road the wolf, the wicked inauspicious wolf,
Who lies in Wait to injure us.
3 Who lurks about the path we take, the robber with a guileful heart:
Far from the road chase him away.
4 Tread with thy foot and trample out the firebrand of the wicked one,
The double-tongued, whoe'er he be.
5 Wise Pusan, Wonder-Worker, we claim of thee now the aid wherewith
Thou furtheredst our sires of old.
6 So, Lord of all prosperity, best wielder of the golden sword,
Make riches easy to be won.
7 Past all pursuers lead us, make pleasant our path and fair to tread:
O Pusan, find thou power for this.
8 Lead us to meadows rich in grass: send on our way no early heat:
O Pusan, find thou power for this.
9 Be gracious to us, fill us full, give, feed us, and invigorate:
O Pusan, find thou power for this.
10 No blame have we for Pusan; him we magnify with songs of praise:
We seek the Mighty One for wealth.

## [01-043] HYMN XLIII. Rudra.

1 WHAT shall we sing to Rudra, strong, most bounteous, excellently wise,
That shall be dearest to his heart?
2 That Aditi may grant the grace of Rudra to our folk, our kine,
Our cattle and our progeny;
3 That Mitra and that Varuna, that Rudra may remember us,
Yea, all the Gods with one accord.
4 To Rudra Lord of sacrifice, of hymns and balmy medicines,
We pray for joy and health and strength.
5 He shines in splendour like the Sun, refulgent as bright gold is he,
The good, the best among the Gods.
6 May he grant health into our steeds, wellbeing to our rams and ewes,
To men, to women, and to kine.
7 O Soma, set thou upon us the glory of a hundred men,
The great renown of mighty chiefs.
8 Let not malignities, nor those who trouble Soma, hinder us.
Indu, give us a share of strength.

9 Soma! head, central point, love these; Soma! know these as serving thee,
Children of thee Immortal, at the highest place of holy law.

## [01-044] HYMN XLIV. Agni.

I IMMORTAL Jatavedas, thou many-hued fulgent gift of Dawn,
Agni, this day to him who pays oblations bring the Gods who waken with the morn.
2 For thou art offering-bearer and loved messenger, the charioteer of sacrifice:
Accordant with the Asvins and with Dawn grant us heroic strength and lofty fame.
3 As messenger we choose to-day Agni the good whom many love,
Smoke-bannered spreader of the light, at break of day glory of sacrificial rites.
4 Him noblest and most youthful, richly worshipped guest, dear to the men who offer gifts,
Him, Agni Jatavedas, I beseech at dawn that he may bring the Gods to us.
5 Thee, Agni, will I glorify, deathless nourisher of the world,
Immortal, offering-bearer, meet for sacred food, preserver, best at sacrifice.
6 Tell good things to thy praiser, O most youthful God, as richly worshipped, honey-tongued,
And, granting to Praskanva lengthened days of life, show honour to the Heavenly Host.
7 For the men, Agni, kindle thee as all possessor and as Priest;
So Agni, much-invoked, bring hither with all speed the Gods, the excellently wise,
8 At dawn of day, at night, Usas and Savitar, the Asvins, Bhaga, Agni's self:
Skilled in fair rites, with Soma poured, the Kanvas light thee, the oblation-wafting God.
9 For, Agni, Lord of sacrifice and messenger of men art thou:
Bring thou the Gods who wake at dawn who see the light, this day to drink the Soma juice.
10 Thou shonest forth, O Agni, after former dawns, all visible, O rich in light.
Thou art our help in battle-strife, the Friend of inan, the great high priest in sacrifice.
11 Like Manu, we will stablish thee, Agni, performer of the rite,
Invoker, ministering Priest, exceeding wise, the swift immortal messenger.
12 When as the Gods' High Priest, by many loved, thou dost their mission as their nearest Friend,
Then, like the far-resounding billows of the flood, thy flames, O Agni, roar aloud.
13 Heat-, Agni, who hast ears to hear, with all thy train of escort Gods;
Let Mitra, Aryaman,- seeking betimes our rite, seat them upon the sacred grass.
14 Let those who strengthen Law, who bountiUly give, the life-tongued Maruts, hear our praise.
May Law-supporting Varuna with the Asvins twain and Usas, drink the Soma juice.

## [01-045] HYMN XLV Agni.

I WORSHIP the Vasus, Agni! here, the Rudras, the Adityas, all
Who spring from Manu, those who know fair rites, who pour their blessings down.
2 Agni, the Gods who understand give ear unto the worshipper:
Lord of Red Steeds, who lovest song, bring thou those Three-and-Thirty Gods.
3 O Jatavedas, great in act, hearken thou to Praskanva's call,
As Priyamedha erst was heard, Atri, Virupa, Angiras.
4 The sons of Priyamedha skilled in lofty praise have called for help

On Agni who with fulgent flame is Ruler of all holy rites.

5 Hear thou, invoked withholy oil, bountiful giver of rewards,
These eulogies, whereby the sons of Kanva call thee to their aid.

6 O Agni, loved by many, thou of fame most wondrous, in their homes
Men call on thee whose hair is flame, to be the bearer of their gifts.

7 Thee, Agni, best to find out wealth, most widely famous, quick to hear,
Singers have stablished in their rites Herald and ministering Priest.

8 Singers with Soma pressed have made thee, Agni, hasten to the feast,
Great light to mortal worshipper, what time they bring the sacred gift.

9 Good, bounteous, Son of Strength, this day seat here on sacred grass the Gods
Who come at early morn, the host of heaven, to drink the Soma juice

10 Bring with joint invocations thou, O Agni, the celestial host:
Here stands the Soma, bounteous Gods drink this expressed ere yesterday.

## [01-046] HYMN XLVI. Asvins.

1 Now Morning with her earliest light shines forth, dear Daughter of the Sky:
High, Asvins, I extol your praise,

2 Sons of the Sea, mighty to save discoverers of riches, ye
Gods with deep thought who find out wealth.

3 Your giant coursers hasten on over the region all in flames, -
When your car flies with winged steeds.

4 He, liberal, lover of the flood, Lord of the House, the vigilant,
Chiefs! with oblations feeds you full.

5 Ye have regard unto our hymns, Nasatyas, thinking of our words:
Drink boldly of the Soma juice.

6 Vouchsafe to us, O Asvin Pair, such strength as, with attendant light,
May through the darkness carry us.

7 Come in the ship of these our hymns to bear you to the hither shore
O Asvins, harness ye the car.

8 The heaven's wide vessel is your own on the flood's shore your chariot waits
Drops, with the hymn, have been prepared.

9 Kanvas, the drops are in the heaven; the wealth is at the waters' place:
Where will ye manifest your form?

10 Light came to lighten up the branch, the Sun appeared as it were gold:
And with its-tongue shone forth the dark.

11 The path of sacrifice was made to travel to the farther goal:
The road of heaven was manifest.

12 The singer of their praise awaits whatever grace the Asvins give,
who save when Soma gladdens them.

13 Ye dwellers with Vivasvan come, auspicious, as to Manu erst;
come to the Soma and our praise.

14 O circumambient Asvins, Dawn follows the brightness of your way:
Approve with beams our solemn rites.

15 Drink ye of our libations, grant protection, O ye Asvins Twain,
With aids which none may interrupt.

## [01-047] HYMN XLVlI. Asvins.

1 ASVINS, for you who strengthen Law this sweetest Soma hath been shed.

Drink this expressed ere yesterday and give riches to him who offers it.

2 Come, O ye Asvins, mounted on your triple car three-seated, beautiful of form
To you at sacrifice the Kanvas send the prayer: graciously listen to their call.

3 O Asvins, ye who strengthen Law, drink ye this sweetest Soma juice.
Borne on your wealth-fraught car come ye this day to him who offers, ye of wondrous deeds.

4 Omniscient Asvins, on the thrice-heaped grass bedew with the sweet juice the sacrifice.
The sons of Kanva, striving heavenward, call on you with draughts of Soma juice out-poured.

5 O Asvins, with those aids wherewith ye guarded Kanva carefully,
Keep us, O hords of Splendour: drink the Soma juice, ye strengtheners of holy law.

6 O Mighty Ones, ye gave Sudas abundant food, brought on your treasure-laden car;
So now vouchsafe to us the wealth which many crave, either from heaven or from the sea.

7 Nasatyas, whether ye be far away or close to Turvasa,
Borne on your lightly-rolling chariot come to us, together with the sunbeams come.

8 So let your coursers, ornaments of sacrifice, bring you to our libations here.
Bestowing food on him who acts and gives aright, sit, Chiefs, upon the sacred grass.

9 Come, O Nasatyas, on your car decked with a sunbright canopy,
Whereon ye ever bring wealth to the worshipper, to drink the Soma's pleasant juice.

10 With lauds and songs of praise we call them down to us, that they, most rich, may succour us;
For ye have ever in the Kanvas' well-loved house, O Asvins, drunk the Soma juice.

## [01-048] HYMN XLVIII. Dawn.

1 DAWN on us with prosperity, O Usas, Daughter of the Sky,
Dawn with great glory, Goddess, Lady of the Light, dawn thou with riches, Bounteous One.

2 They, bringing steeds and kine, boon-givers of all wealth, have oft sped forth to lighten us.
O Usas, waken up for me the sounds of joy: send us the riches of the great.

3 Usas hath dawned, and now shall dawn, the Goddess, driver forth of cars
Which, as she cometh nigh, have fixed their thought on her, like glory-seekers on the flood.

4 Here Kanva, chief of Kanva's race, sings forth aloud the glories of the heroes' names,-
The. princes who, O Usas, as thou comest near, direct their thoughts to liberal gifts.

5 Like a good matron Usas comes carefully tending everything:
Rousing all life she stirs all creatures that have feet, and makes the birds of air fly up.

6 She sends the busy forth, each man to his pursuit: delay she knows not as she springs.
O rich in opulence, after thy dawning birds that have flown forth no longer rest.

7 This Dawn hath yoked her steeds afar, beyond the rising of the Sun:
Borne on a hundred chariots she, auspicious Dawn, advances on her way to Men.

8 To meet her glance all living creatures bend them down:
Excellent One, she makes the light.

Usas, the Daughter of the Sky, the opulent, shines foes and enmities away.

9 Shine on us with thy radiant light, O Usas, Daughter of the Sky,
Bringing to us great store of high felicity, and bearning on our solemn rites.

10 For in thee is each living creature's breath and life, when, Excellent! thou dawnest forth.
Borne on thy lofty car, O Lady of the Light, hear, thou of wondrous wealth, our call.

11 O Usas, win thyself the strength which among men is wonderful.
Bring thou thereby the pious unto holy rites, those who as priests sing praise to thee.

12 Bring from the firmament, O Usas, all the Gods, that they may drink our Soma juice,
And, being what thou art, vouchsafe us kine and steeds, strength meet for praist and hero might.

13 May Usas whose auspicious rays are seen resplendent round about,
Grant us great riches, fair in form, of all good things, wealth which light labour may attain.

14 Mighty One, whom the Rsis of old time invoked for their protection and their help,
O Usas, graciously answer our songs of praise with bounty and with brilliant
light.

15 Usas, as thou with light to day hast opened the twin doors of heaven,
So grant thou us a dwelling wide and free from foes. O Goddess, give us food with kine.

16 Bring us to wealth abundant, sent in every shape, to plentiful refreshing food,
To all-subduing splendour, Usas, Mighty One, to strength, thou rich in spoil and wealth.

## [01-049] HYMN XLIX. Dawn.

1 E'EN from above the sky's bright realm come, Usas, by auspicious ways:
Let red steeds bear thee to the house of him who pours the Soma, juice.

2 The chariot which thou mountest, fair of shape, O Usas light to move,-
Therewith, O Daughter of the Sky, aid men of noble fame today.

3 Bright Usas, when thy times return, all quadrupeds and bipeds stir,
And round about flock winged birds from all theboundaries of heaven.

4 Thou dawning with thy beams of light illumest all the radiant realm.
Thee, as thou art, the Kanvas, fain for wealth, have called with sacred songs.

## [01-050] HYMN L. Surya.

1 HIS bright rays bear him up aloft, the God who knoweth all that lives,
Surya, that all may look on him.

2 The constellations pass away, like thieves, together with their beams,
Before the all-beholding Sun'

3 His herald rays are seen afar refulgent o'er the world of men,
Like flames of fire that burn and blaze.

4 Swift and all beautiful art thou, O Surya, maker of the light,
Illuming all the radiant realm.

5 Thou goest to the hosts of Gods, thou comest hither to mankind,
Hither all light to be belield.

6 With that same eye of thine wherewith thou lookest brilliant Varuna,
Upon the busy race of men,

7 Traversing sky and wide mid-air, thou metest with thy beams our days,
Sun, seeing all things that have birth.

8 Seven Bay Steeds harnessed to thy car bear thee, O thou farseeing One,
God, Surya, with the radiant hair.

9 Surya hath yoked the pure bright Seven, the daughters of the car; with these,
His own dear team, he goeth forth.

10 Looking upon the loftier light above the darkness we have come
To Surya, God among the Gods, the light that is most excellent.

11 Rising this day, O rich in friends, ascending to the loftier heaven,
Surya remove my heart's disease, take from me this my yellow hue.

12 To parrots and to starlings let us give away my yellowness,
Or this my yellowness let us transfer to Haritala trees.

13 With all his conquering vigour this Aditya hath gone up on high,
Giving my foe into mine hand: let me not be my foeman's prey.

## [01-051] HYMN LI. Indra.

1 MAKE glad with songs that Ram whom many men invoke, worthy of songs of praise, Indra, the sea
of wealth;
Whose gracious deeds for men spread like the heavens abroad: sing praise to him the Sage, most
liberal for our good.

2 As aids the skilful Rbhus yearned to Indra strong to save, who fills mid-air, encompassed round
with might,
Rushing in rapture; and -o'er Satakratu came the gladdening shout that urged him on to victory.

3 Thou hast disclosed the kine's stall for the Angirases, and made a way for Atri by a hundred doors.
On Vimada thou hast bestowed both food and wealth, making thy bolt dance in the sacrificer's fight.

4 Thou hast unclosed the prisons of the waters; thou hast in the mountain seized the treasure rich in
gifts.
When thou hadst slain with might the dragon Vrtra, thou, Indra, didst raise the Sun in heaven for all
to see.

5 With wondrous might thou blewest enchanter fiends away, with powers celestial those who called
on thee in jest.
Thou, hero-hearted, hast broken down Pipru's forts, and helped Rjisvan when the Dasyus were struck
dead.

6 Thou savedst Kutsa when Susna was smitten down; to Atithigva gavest Sambara for a prey.
E'en mighty Arbuda thou troddest under foot: thou from of old wast born to strike the Dasyus dead.

7 All power and might is closely gathered up in thee; thy bounteous spirit joys in drinking Soma juice.
Known is the thunderbolt that lies within thine arms: rend off therewith all manly prowess of our foe.

8 Discern thou well Aryas and Dasyus; punishing the lawless give them up to him whose grass is
strewn.
Be thou the sacrificer's strong encourager all these thy deeds are my delight at festivals.

9 Indra gives up the lawless to the pious man, destroying by the Strong Ones those who have no
strength.
Vamra when glorified destroyed the gathered piles of the still waxing great one who would reach the
heaven.
10 The might which Usana hath formed for thee with might rends in its greatness and with strength
both worlds apart.
O Hero-souled, the steeds of Vata, yoked by thought, have carried thee to fame while thou art filled
with power.
11 When Indra hath rejoiced with Kavya Usana, he mounts his steeds who swerve wider and wider
yet.
The Strong hath loosed his bolt with the swift rush of rain, and he hath rent in pieces Susna's firmbuilt
forts.
12 Thou mountest on thy car amid strong Soma draughts: Saryata brought thee those in which thou
hast delight.
Indra, when thou art pleased with men whose Soma flows thou risest to unchallenged glory in the
sky.
13 To old Kaksivin, Soma-presser, skilled in song, O Indra, thou didst give the youthful Vrcaya.
Thou, very wise, wast Mena, Vrsanaiva's child: those deeds of thine must all be told at Soma feasts.
14 The good man's refuge in his need is Indra, firm as a doorpost, praised among the Pajras.
Indra alone is Lord of wealth, the Giver, lover of riches, chariots, kine, and horses.
15 To him the Mighty One, the self-resplendent, verily strong and great, this praise is uttered.
May we and all the heroes, with the princes, be, in this fray, O Indra, in thy keeping.

## [01-052] HYMN LII. Indra.

1 I GLORIFY that Ram who finds the light of heaven, whose hundred nobly-natured ones go forth
with him.
With hymns may I turn hither Indra to mine aid,-the Car which like a strong steed hasteth to the call.
2 Like as a mountain on firm basis, unremoved, he, thousandfold protector, waxed in mighty
strength,
When Indra, joying in the draughts of Soma juice, forced the clouds, slaying Vrtra stayer of their flow.
3 For he stays e'en the stayers, spread o'er laden cloud, rooted in light, strengthened in rapture by
the wise.
Indra with thought, with skilled activity, I call, most liberal giver, for he sates him with the juice.
4 Whom those that flow in heaven on sacred grass, his own assistants, nobly-natured, fill full like the
sea,-
Beside that Indra when he smote down Vrtra stood his helpers, straight in form, mighty, invincible.
5 To him, as in wild joy he fought with him who stayed the rain, his helpers sped like swift streams
down a slope,
When Indra, thunder-armed, made bold by Soma draughts, as Trta cleaveth Vala's fences, cleft him
through.
6 Splendour encompassed thee, forth shone thy warrior might: the rain-obstructer lay in mid-air's
lowest deep,

What time, O Indra, thou didst cast thy thunder down upon the jaws of Vritra hard to be restrained.
7 The hymns which magnify thee, Indra, reach to thee even as water-brooks flow down and fill the
lake.
Tvastar gave yet more force to thine appropriate strength, and forged thy thunderbolt of
overpowering might.
8 When, Indra, thou whose power is linked with thy Bay Steeds hadst smitten Vrtra, causing floods to
flow for man,
Thou heldst in thine arms the metal thunderbolt, and settest in the heaven the Sun for all to see.
9 In fear they raised the lofty self-resplendent hymn, praise giving and effectual, leading up to
heaven,
When Indra's helpers fighting for the good of men, the Maruts, faithful to mankind, joyed in the light.
10 Then Heaven himself, the mighty, at that Dragon's roar reeled back in terror when, Indra, thy
thunderbolt
In the wild joy of Soma had struck off with might the head of Vrtra, tyrant of the earth and heaven.
11 O Indra, were this earth extended forth tenfold, and men who dwell therein multiplied day by day,
Still here thy conquering might, Maghavan, would be famed: it hath waxed vast as heaven in majesty
and power.
12 Thou, bold of heart, in thine own native might, for help, upon the limit of this mid-air and of
heaven,
Hast made the earth to be the pattern of thy strength: embracing flood and light thou reachest to the
sky.
13 Thou art the counterpart of earth, the Master of lofty heaven with all its mighty Heroes:
Thou hast filled all the region with thy greatness: yea, of a truth there is none other like thee.
14 Whose amplitude the heaven and earth have not attained, whose bounds the waters of mid-air
have never reached,-
Not, when in joy he fights the stayer of the rain: thou, and none else, hast made all things in order
due.
15 The Maruts sang thy praise in this encounter, and in thee all the Deities delighted,
What time thou, Indra, with thy spiky weapon, thy deadly bolt, smotest the face of Vrtra.

## [01-053] HYMN LIII. Indra.

I WE will present fair praise unto the Mighty One, our hymns to Indra in Vivasvdn's dwelling-place;
For he hath ne'er found wealth in those who seem to sleep: those who give wealth to men accept no
paltry praise.
2 Giver of horses, Indra, giver, thou, of kine, giver of barley, thou art Lord and guard of wealth:
Man's helper from of old, not disappointing hope, Friend of our friends, to thee ,as such we sing this
praise.
3 Indra, most splendid, powerful, rich in mighty deeds, this treasure spread around is known to be
thine own.
Gather therefrom, O Conqueror, and bring to us: fail not the hope of him who loves and sings to thee.
4 Well pleased with these bright flames and with these Soma drops, take thou away our poverty with

seeds and kine.

With Indra scattering the Dasyu through these drops, freed from their hate may we obtain abundant
food.

5 Let us obtain, O Indra, plenteous wealth and food, with strength exceeding glorious, shining to the
sky:

May we obtain the Goddess Providence, the strength of heroes, special source of cattle, rich in
steeds.

6 These our libations strength-inspiring, Soma draughts, gladdened thee in the fight with Vrtra, Hero
Lord,

What time thou slewest for the singer with trimmed grass ten thousand Vrtras, thou resistless in thy
might.

7 Thou goest on from fight to fight intrepidly, destroying castle after castle here with strength.

Thou, Indra, with thy friend who makes the foe bow down, slewest from far away the guileful
Namuci.

8 Thou hast struck down in death Karanja, Parnaya, in Atithigva's very glorious going forth.

Unyielding, when Rjisvan compassed them with siege, thou hast destroyed the hundred forts of
Vangrida.

9 With all-outstripping chariot-wheel, O Indra, thou far-famed, hast overthrown the twice ten Kings of
men,

With sixty thousand nine-and-ninety followers, who came in arms to fight with friendless Susravas.

10 Thou hast protected Susravas with succour, and Turvayana with thine aid, O Indra.

Thou madest Kutsa, Atithigva, Ayu, subject unto this King, the young, the mighty.

11 May we protected by the Gods hereafter remain thy very prosperous friends, O Indra.

Thee we extol, enjoying through thy favour life long and joyful and with store of heroes.

## [01-054] HYMN LIV. Indra.

1 URGE us not, Maghavan, to this distressful fight, for none may comprehend the limit of thy
strength.

Thou with fierce shout hast made the woods and rivers roar: did not men run in crowds together in
their fear?

2 Sing hymns of praise to Sakra, Lord of power and might; laud thou and magnify Indra who hearcth
thee,

Who with his daring might, a Bull exceeding strong in strength, maketh him master of the heaven
and earth.

3 Sing forth to lofty Dyaus a strength-bestowing song, the Bold, whose resolute mind hath
independent sway.

High glory hath the Asura, compact of strength, drawn on by two Bay Steeds: a Bull, a Car is he.

4 The ridges of the lofty heaven thou madest shake; thou, daring, of thyself smotest through
Sambara,

When bold with gladdening juice, thou warredst with thy bolt, sharp and twoedged, against the
banded sorcerers.

5 When with a roar that fills the woods, thou forcest down on wind's head the stores which 8usga
kept confined,

Who shall have power to stay thee firm and eager-souled from doing still this day what thou of old
hast done?

6 Thou helpest Narya, Turvasa, and Yadu, and Vayya's son Turviti, Satakratu!

Thou helpest horse and car in final battle thou breakest down the nine-and-ninety castles.

7 A hero-lord is he, King of a mighty folk, who offers free oblations and promotes the Law,

Who with a bounteous guerdon welcomes hymns of praise: for him flows down the abundant stream
below the sky.

8 His power is matchless, matchless is his wisdom; chief, through their work, be some who drink the
Soma,

Those, Indra, who increase the lordly power, the firm heroic strength of thee the Giver.

9 Therefore for thee are these abundant beakers Indra's drink, stone-pressed juices held in ladles.

Quaff them and satisfy therewith thy longing; then fix thy mind upon bestowing treasure.

10 There darkness stood, the vault that stayed the waters' flow: in Vrtra's hollow side the rain-cloud
lay concealed.

But Indra smote the rivers which the obstructer stayed, flood following after flood, down steep
declivities.

11 So give us, Indra, bliss-increasing glory give us great sway and strength that conquers people.

Preserve our wealthy patrons, save our princes; vouchsafe us wealth and food with noble offspring.

## [01-055] HYMN LV. Indra.

1 THOUGH e'en this heaven's wide space and earth have spread them out, nor heaven nor earth may
be in greatness Indra's match.

Awful and very mighty, causing woe to men, he whets his thunderbolt for sharpness, as a bull.

2 Like as the watery ocean, so doth he receive the rivers spread on all sides in their ample width.

He bears him like a bull to drink of Soma juice, and will, as Warrior from of old, be praised for might.

3 Thou swayest, Indra, all kinds of great manly power, so as to bend, as't were, even that famed
mountain down. Foremost among the Gods is he through hero might, set in the van, the Strong One, for each arduous
deed.

4 He only in the wood is praised by worshippers, when he shows forth to men his own fair Indrapower.

A friendly Bull is he, a Bull to be desired when Maghavan auspiciously sends forth his voice.

5 Yet verily the Warrior in his vigorous strength stirreth up with his might great battles for mankind;

And men have faith in Indra, the resplendent One, what time he hurleth down his bolt, his dart of
death.

6 Though, fain for glory, and with strength increased on earth, he with great might destroys the
dwellings made with art,

He makes the lights of heaven shine forth secure, he bids, exceeding wise, the floods flow for his
worshipper.

7 Drinker of Soma, let thy heart incline to give; bring thy Bays hitherward, O thou who hearest praise.

Those charioteers of thine, best skilled to draw the rein, the rapid sunbeams, Indra, lead thee not
astray.

8 Thou bearest in both hands treasure that never fails; the famed One in his body holds
unvanquished might.
O Indra, in thy members many powers abide, like wells surrounded by the ministering priests.

## [01-056] HYMN LVI. Indra.

I FOR this man's full libations held in ladles, he hath roused him, eager, as a horse to meet the mare.
He stays his golden car, yoked with Bay Horses, swift, and drinks the Soma juice which strengthens
for great deeds.
2 To him the guidance-following songs of praise flow full, as those who seek gain go in company to
the flood.
To him the Lord of power, the holy synod's might, as to a hill, with speed, ascend the loving ones.
3 Victorious, great is he; in manly battle shines, unstained with dust, his might, as shines a mountain
peak;
Wherewith the iron one, fierce e'en against the strong, in rapture, fettered wily Sushna fast in bonds.
4 When Strength the Goddess, made more strong for help by thee, waits upon Indra as the Sun
attends the Dawn,
Then. he who with his might unflinching kills the gloom stirs up the dust aloft, with joy and
triumphing.
5 When thou with might, upon the framework of the heaven, didst fix, across, air's region firmly,
unremoved,
In the light-winning war, Indra, in rapturous joy, thou smotest Vrtra dead and broughtest floods of
rain.
6 Thou with thy might didst grasp,the holder-up of heaven, thou who art mighty also in the seats of
earth.
Thou, gladdened by the juice, hast set the waters free, and broken Vrtra's stony fences through and
through.

## [01-057] HYMN LVII. Indra.

I To him most liberal, lofty Lord of lofty wealth, verily powerful and strong, I bring my hymn,-
Whose checkless bounty, as of waters down a slope, is spread abroad for all that live, to give them
strength.
2 Now all this world, for worship, shall come after thee-the offerer's libations like floods to the depth,
When the well-loved one seems to rest upon the hill, the thunderbolt of Indra, shatterer wrought of
gold.
3 To him the terrible, most meet for lofty praise, like bright Dawn, now bring gifts with reverence in
this rite,
Whose being, for renown, yea, Indra-power and light, have been created, like bay steeds, to move
with speed.
4 Thine, Indra, praised by many, excellently rich! are we who trusting in thy help draw near to thee.
Lover of praise, none else but thou receives our laud: as earth loves all her creatures, love thou this
our hymn.
5 Great is thy power, O Indra, we are thine. Fulfil, O Maghavan, the wish of this thy worshipper.
After thee lofty heaven hath measured out its strength: to thee and to thy power this earth hath bowed itself.

6 Thou, who hast thunder for thy weapon, with thy bolt hast shattered into pieces this broad massive
cloud.
Thou hast sent down the obstructed floods that they may flow: thou hast, thine own for ever, all
victorious might.

## [01-058] HYMN LVIII., Agni.

I NE'ER waxeth faint the Immortal, Son of Strength, since he, the Herald, hath become Vivasvan's
messenger.
On paths most excellent he measured out mid-air: he with oblation calls to service of the Gods.
2 Never decaying, seizing his appropriate food, rapidly, eagerly through the dry wood he spreads.
His back, as he is sprinkled, glistens like a horse: loud hath he roared and shouted like the heights of
heaven?
3 Set high in place o'er all that Vasus, Rudras do, immortal, Lord of riches, seated as High Priest;
Hastening like a car to men, to those who live, the God without delay gives boons to be desired.
4 Urged by the wind be spreads through dry wood as he lists, armed with his tongues for sickles,
with a mighty roar.
Black is thy path, Agni, changeless, with glittering waves! when like a bull thou rushest eager to the
trees.
5 With teeth of flame, wind-driven, through the wood he speeds, triumphant like a bull among the
herd of cows,
With bright strength roaming to the everlasting air: things fixed, things moving quake before him as
he flies.
6 The Bhrgus established thee among mankind for men, like as a treasure, beauteous, easy to invoke;
Thee, Agni, as a herald and choice-worthy guest, as an auspicious Friend to the Celestial Race.
7 Agni, the seven tongues' deftest Sacrificer, him whom the priests elect at solemn worship,
The Herald, messenger of all the Vasus, I serve with dainty food, I ask for riches.
8 Grant, Son of Strength, thou rich in friends, a refuge without a flaw this day to us thy praisers.
O Agni, Son of Strength, with forts of iron preserve thou from distress the man who lauds thee.
9 Be thou a refuge, Bright One, to the singer, a shelter, Bounteous Lord, to those who worship.
Preserve the singer from distress, O Agni. May he, enriched with prayer, come soon and early.

## [01-059] HYMN LIX. Agni.

1 THE other fires are, verily, thy branches; the Immortals all rejoice in thee, O Agni.
Centre art thou, Vaigvdnara, of the people, sustaining men like a deep-founded pillar.
2 The forehead of the sky, earth's centre, Agni became the messenger of earth and heaven.
Vaisvanara, the Deities produced thee, a God, to be a light unto the Arya.
3 As in the Sun firm rays are set for ever, treasures are in Vaisvanara, in Agni.
Of all the riches in the hills, the waters, the herbs, among mankind, thou art the Sovran.
4 As the great World-halves, so are their Son's praises; skilled, as a man, to act, is he the Herald.

Vaisvanara, celestial, truly mighty, most manly One, hath many a youthful consort.

5 Even the lofty heaven, O Jatavedas Vaisvanara, hath not attained thy greatness.
Thou art the King of lands where men are settled, thou hast brought comfort to the Gods in battle.

6 Now will I tell the greatness of the Hero whom Prarti's sons follow as Vrtra's slayer:
Agni Vaisvanara struck down the Dasyu, cleave Sambara through and shattered down his fences.

7 Vaisvanara, dwelling by his might with all men, far-shining, holy mid the Bharadvajas,
Is lauded, excellent, with hundred praises by Purunitha, son of Satavani.

## [01-060] HYMN LX. Agni.

I As 'twere Some goodly treasure Matarisvan brought, as a gift, the glorious Priest to Bhrgu,
Banner of sacrifice, the good Protector, child of two births, the swiftly moving envoy.

2 Both Gods and men obey this Ruler's order, Gods who are worshipped, men who yearn and worship.
As Priest he takes his seat ere break of morning, House-Lord, adorable with men, Ordainer.

3 May our fair praise, heart-born, most recent, reach him whose tongue, e'en at his birth, is sweet as honey;
Whom mortal priests, men, with their strong endeavour, supplied with dainty viands, have created.

4 Good to mankind, the yearning Purifier hath among men been placed as Priest choice-worthy.
May Agni be our Friend, Lord of the Household, protector of the riches in the dwelling.

5 As such we Gotamas with hymns extol thee, O Agni, as the guardian Lord of riches,
Decking thee like a horse, the swift prizewinner. May he, enriched with prayer, come soon and early.

## [01-061] HYMN LXI Indra.

1 EVEN to him, swift, strong and high. exalted, I bring my song of praise as dainty viands,
My thought to him resistless, praise-deserving, prayers offered most especially to Indra.

2 Praise, like oblation, I present, and utter aloud my song, my fair hymn to the Victor.
For Indra, who is Lord of old, the singers have decked their lauds with heart and mind and spirit.

3 To him then with my lips mine adoration, winning heaven's light, most excellent, I offer,
To magnify with songs of invocation and with fair hymns the Lord, most bounteous Giver.

4 Even for him I frame a laud, as fashions the wright a chariot for the man who needs it,-
Praises to him who gladly hears our praises, a hymn well-formed, all-moving, to wise Indra.

5 So with my tongue I deck, to please that Indra, my hymn, as 'twere a horse, through love of glory,
To reverence the Hero, bounteous Giver, famed far and wide, destroyer of the castles.

6 Even for him hath Tvastar forged the thunder, most deftly wrought, celestial, for the battle,
Wherewith he reached the vital parts of Vrtra, striking-the vast, the mighty with the striker.

7 As soon as, at libations of his mother, great Visnu had drunk up the draught, he plundered.

The dainty cates, the cooked mess; but One stronger transfixed the wild boar, shooting through the mountain.

8 To him, to Indra, when he slew the Dragon, the Dames, too, Consorts of the Goda, wove praises.
The mighty heaven and earth hath he encompassed: thy greatness heaven and earth, combined, exceed not.

9 Yea, of a truth, his magnitude surpasseth the magnitude of earth, mid-air, and heaven.
Indra, approved by all men, self-resplendent, waxed in his home, loud-voiced and strong for battle.

10 Through his own strength Indra with bolt of thunder cut piece-meal Vrtra, drier up of waters.
He let the floods go free, like cows imprisoned, for glory, with a heart inclined to bounty.

11 The rivers played, through his impetuous splendour, since with his bolt he compassed them on all sides.
Using his might and favouring him who worshipped, he made a ford, victorious, for Turviti.

12 Vast, with thine ample power, with eager movement, against this Vrtra cast thy bolt of thunder.
Rend thou his joints, as of an ox, dissevered, with bolt oblique, that floods of rain may follow.

13 Sing with new lauds his exploits wrought aforetime, the deeds of him, yea, him who moveth swiftly,
When, hurling forth his weapons in the battle, he with impetuous wrath lays low the foemen.

14 When he, yea, he, comes forth the firm. Set mountains and the whole heaven and earth, tremble for terror.
May Nodhas, ever praising the protection of that dear Friend, gain quickly strength heroic.

15 Now unto him of these things hath been given what he who rules alone o'er much, electeth.
Indra hath helped Etasa, Soma-presser, contending in the race of steeds with Sarya.

16 Thus to thee, Indra, yoker of Bay Coursers, the Gotamas have brought their prayers to please thee.
Bestow upon them thought, decked with all beauty. May he, enriched with prayer, come soon and early.

## [01-062] HYMN LXII. Indra.

1. LIKE Angiras a gladdening laud we ponder to him who loveth song, exceeding mighty.
Let us sing glory to the far-famed Hero who must be praised with fair hymns by the singer.

2 Unto the great bring ye great adoration, a chant with praise to him exceeding mighty,
Through whom our sires, Angirases, singing praises and knowing well the places, found the cattle.

3 When Indra and the Angirases desired it, Sarama found provision for her offipring.
Brhaspati cleft the mountain, found the cattle: the heroes shouted with the kine in triumph.

4 Mid shout, loud shout, and roar, with the Navagvas, seven singers, hast thou, heavenly, rent the mountain;
Thou hast, with speeders, with Dasagvas, Indra, Sakra, with thunder rent obstructive Vala.

5 Praised by Angirases, thou, foe-destroyer, hast, with the Dawn, Sun, rays, dispelled the darkness.
Thou Indra, hast spread out the earths high ridges, and firmly fixed the region under heaven.

6 This is the deed most worthy of all honour, the fairest marvel of the Wonder-Worker,
That, nigh where heaven bends down, he made four rivers flow full with waves that carry down
sweet water.
7 Unwearied, won with lauding hymns, he parted of old the ancient Pair, united ever.
In highest sky like Bhaga, he the doer of marvels set both Dames and earth and heaven.
8 Still born afresh, young Dames, each in her manner, unlike in hue, the Pair in alternation
Round heaven and earth from ancient time have travelled, Night with her dark limbs, Dawn with
limbs of splendour.
9 Rich in good actions, skilled in operation, the Son with might maintains his perfect friendship.
Thou in the raw cows, black of hue or ruddy, storest the ripe milk glossy white in colour.
10 Their paths, of old connected, rest uninjured; they with great might preserve the immortal
statutes.
For many thousand holy works the Sisters wait on the haughty Lord like wives and matrons.
11 Thoughts ancient, seeking wealth, with adoration, with newest lauds have sped to thee, O
Mighty.
As yearning wives cleave to their yearning husband, so cleave our hymns to thee, O Lord most
potent.
12 Strong God, the riches which thy hands have holden from days of old have perished not nor
wasted.
Splendid art thou, O Indra, wise, unbending:strengthen us with might, O Lord of Power.
13 O mighty Indra, Gotama's son Nodhas hath fashioned this new prayer to thee Eternal,
Sure leader, yoker of the Tawny Coursers. May he, enriched with prayer, come soon and early.

## [01-063] HYMN LXIII. Indra.
1. THOU art the Mighty One; when born, O Indra, with power thou tcrrifiedst earth and heaven -
When, in their fear of thee, all firm-set mountains and monstrous creatures shook like dust before
thee.
2 When thy two wandering Bays thou drawest hither, thy praiser laid within thine arms the thunder,
Wherewith, O Much-invoked, in will resistless, thou smitest foemen down and many a castle.
3 Faithful art thou, these thou defiest, Indra; thou art the Rbhus' Lord, heroic, victor.
Thou, by his side, for young and glorious Kutsa, with steed and car in battle slewest Susna,
4 That, as a friend, thou furtheredst, O Indra, when, Thundcrer, - strong in act, thou crushedst Vrtra;
When, Hero, thou, great-souled, with easy conquest didst rend the Dasyus in their
distant dwelling.
5 This doest thou, and art not harmed, O Indra, e'en in the anger of the strongest mortal.
Lay thou the race-course open for our horses: as with a club, slay, Thunderarmed 1 our foemen.
6 Hence men invoke thee, Indra, in the tumult of battle, in the light-bestowing conflict.
This aid of thine, O Godlike One, was ever to be implored in deeds of might in combat.

7 Warring for Purukutsa thou, O Indra, Thunder-armed I breakest down the seven castles;
Easily, for Sudis, like grass didst rend them, and out of need, King, broughtest gain to Puru.
8 O Indra, God who movest round about us, feed us with varied food plenteous as water-
Food wherewithal, O Hero, thou bestowest vigour itself to flow to us for ever.
9 Prayers have been made by Gotamas, O Indra, addressed to thee, with laud for thy Bay Horses.
Bring us in noble shape abundant riches. May he, enriched with prayer, come soon and early.

## [01-064] HYMN LXIV. Maruts.
1. BRING for the manly host, wise and majestical, O Nodhas, for the Maruts bring thou a pure gift.
I deck my songs as one deft-handed, wise in mind prepares the water that hath power in solemn
rites.
2 They spring to birth, the lofty Ones, the Bulls of Heaven, divine, the youths of Rudra, free from spot
and stain;
The purifiers, shining brightly even as suns, awful of form like giants, scattering rain-drops down.
3 Young Rudras, demon-slayers, never growing old, they have waxed, even as mountains, irresistible.
They make all beings tremble with their mighty strength, even the very strongest, both of earth and
heaven.
4 With glittering ornaments they deck them forth for show; for beauty on their breasts they bind their
chains of gold.
The lances on their shoulders pound to pieces; they were born together, of themselves, the Men of
Heaven.
5 Loud roarers, giving strength, devourers of the foe, they make the winds, they make the lightnings
with their powers.
The restless shakers drain the udders of the sky, and ever wandering round fill the earth full with
milk.
6 The bounteous Maruts with the fatness dropping milk fill full the waters which avail in solenm
rites.
They lead, as 'twere, the Strong Horse forth, that it may rain: they milk the thundering, the neverfailing
spring.
7 Mighty, with wondrous power and marvellously bright, selfstrong like mountains, ye glide swiftly
on your way.
Like the wild elephants ye eat the forests up when ye assume your strength among the bright red
flames.
8 Exceeding wise they roar like lions mightily, they, all-possessing, are beauteous as antelopes;
Stirring the darkness with lances and spotted deer, combined as priests, with serpents' fury through
their might.
9 Heroes who march in companies, befriending man, with serpents' ire through strength, ye greet the
earth and heaven.
Upon the seats, O Maruts, of your chariots, upon the cars stands lightning visible as light.
10 Lords of all riches, dwelling in the home of wealth, endowed with mighty vigour, singers loud of
voice,

Heroes, of powers infinite, armed with strong men's rings, the archers, they have laid the arrow on
their arms.
11 They who with golden fellies make the rain increase drive forward the big clouds like wanderers
on the way.
Self-moving, brisk, unwearied, they o'erthrow the firm; the Maruts with bright lances make all things to reel.
12 The progeny of Rudra we invoke with prayer, the brisk, the bright, the worshipful, the active Ones
To the strong band of Maruts cleave for happiness, the chasers of the sky, impetuous, vigorous.
13 Maruts, the man whom ye have guarded with your help, he verily in strength surpasseth all
mankind.
Spoil with his steeds he gaineth, treasure with his men; he winneth honourable strength and
prospereth.
14 O Maruts, to the worshippers give glorious strength invincible in battle, brilliant, bringing wealth,
Praiseworthy, known to all men. May we foster well, during a hundred winters, son and progeny.
15 Will ye then, O ye Maruts, grant us riches, durable, rich in men, defying onslaught.
A hundred, thousandfold, ever increasing? May he, enriched with prayer, come soon and early.

### [01-065] HYMN LXV. Agni.
1 ONE-MINDED, wise, they tracked thee like a thief lurking in dark cave with a stolen cow:
Thee claiming worship, bearing it to Gods -. there nigh to thee sate all the Holy Ones.
2 The Gods approached the ways of holy Law; there was a gathering vast as heaven itself.
The waters feed with praise the growing Babe, born nobly in the womb, the seat of Law.
3 Like grateful food, like some wide dwelling place, like a fruit-bearing hill, a wholesome stream.
Like a steed urged to run in swift career, rushing like Sindhu, who may check his course?
4 Kin as a brother to his sister floods, he cats the woods as a King eats the rich.
When through the forest, urged by wind, he spreads, verily Agni shears the hair of earth.
5 Like a swan sitting in the floods he pants wisest in mind mid men he wakes at morn.
A Sage like Soma, sprung from Law, he grew like some young creature, mighty, shining far.

### [01-066] HYMN LXVI. Agni.
1. LIKE the Sun's glance, like wealth of varied sort, like breath which is the life, like one's own son,
Like a swift bird, a cow who yields her milk, pure and refulgent to the wood he speeds.
2 He offers safety like a pleasant home, like ripened corn, the Conqueror of men.
Like a Seer lauding, famed among the folk; like a steed friendly he vouchsafes us power.
3 With flame insatiate, like eternal might; caring for each one like a dame at home;
Bright when he shines forth, whitish mid the folk, like a car, gold-decked, thundering to the fight.
4 He strikes with terror like a dart shot forth, e'en like an archer's arrow tipped with flame;
Master of present and of future life, the maidens' lover and the matrons' Lord.

5 To him lead all your ways: may we attain the kindled God as cows their home at eve.
He drives the flames below as floods their swell: the rays rise up to the fair place of heaven.

### [01-067] HYMN LXVII. Agni.
1. VICTORIOUS in the wood, Friend among men, ever he claims obedience as a King.
Gracious like peace, blessing like mental power, Priest was he, offering-bearer, full of thought.
2 He, bearing in his hand all manly might, crouched in the cavern, struck the Gods with fear.
Men filled with understanding find him there, when they have sting prayers formed within their
heart.
3 He, like the Unborn, holds the broad earth up; and with effective utterance fixed the sky.
O Agni, guard the spots which cattle love: thou, life of all, hast gone from lair to lair.
4 Whoso hath known him dwelling in his lair, and hath approached the stream of holy Law,-
They who release him, paying sacred rites, -truly to such doth he announce great wealth.
5 He who grows mightily in herbs, within each fruitful mother and each babe she bears,
Wise, life of all men, in the waters' home,-for him have sages built as 'twere a seat.

### [01-068] HYMN LXVIII. Agni.
1. COMMINGLING, restless, he ascends the sky, unveiling nights and all that stands or moves,
As he the sole God is preeminent in great. ness among all these other Gods.
2 All men are joyful in thy power, O God, that living from the dry wood thou art born.
All truly share thy Godhead while they keep, in their accustomed ways, eternal Law.
3 Strong is the thought of Law, the Law's behest; all works have they performed; he quickens all.
Whoso will bring oblation, gifts to thee, to him, bethinking thee, vouchsafe thou wealth.
4 Seated as Priest with Manu's progeny, of all these treasures he alone is Lord.
Men yearn for children to prolong their line, and are not disappointed in their hope.
5 Eagerly they who hear his word fulfil his wish as sons obey their sire's behest.
He, rich in food, unbars his wealth like doors: he, the House-Friend, bath decked heaven's vault with
stars.

### [01-069] HYMN LXIX. Agni.
1. BRIGHT, splendid, like Dawn's lover, he bath filled the two joined worlds as with the light of
heaven.
When born, with might thou hast encompassed them: Father of Gods, and yet their Son wast thou.
2 Agni, the Sage, the humble, who discerns like the cow's udder, the sweet taste of food,
Like a bliss-giver to be drawn to men, sits gracious in the middle of the house.
3 Born in the dwelling like a lovely son, pleased, like a strong steed, he bears on the folk.
What time the men and I, with heroes, call, may Agni then gain all through Godlike power.
4 None breaks these holy laws of thine when thou hast granted audience to these chieftains here.

This is thy boast, thou smotest with thy peers, and joined with heroes dravest off disgrace.
5 Like the Dawn's lover, spreading light, well-known as hued like morn, may he remember me.
They, bearing of themselves, unbar the doors: they all ascend to the fair place of heaven.

## [01-070] HYMN LXX. Agni.

1. MAY we, the pious, win much food by prayer, may Agni with fair light pervade each act,-
He the observer of the heavenly laws of Gods, and of the race of mortal man.
2 He who is germ of waters, germ of woods, germ of all things that move not and that move,-
To him even in the rock and in the house: Immortal One, he cares for all mankind.
3 Agni is Lord of riches for the man who serves him readily with sacred songs.
Protect these beings thou with careful thought, knowing the races both of Gods and men.
4 Whom many dawns and nights, unlike, make strong, whom, born in Law, all things that move and stand,-
He bath been won, Herald who sits in light, making effectual all our holy works.
5 Thou settest value on our cows and woods: all shall bring tribute to us to the light.
men have served thee in many and sundry spots, parting, as 'twere, an aged father's wealth.
6 Like a brave archer, like one skilled and bold, a fierce avenger, so he shines in fight.

## [01-071] HYMN LXXI. Agni.

1. LOVING the loving One, as wives their husband, the sisters of one home have urged him forward,
Bright-coloured, even, as the cows love morning, dark, breaking forth to view, and redly beaming.
2 Our sires with lauds burst e'en the firmset fortress, yea, the Angirases, with roar, the mountain.
They made for us a way to reach high heaven, they found us day, light, day's sign, beams of morning.
3 They stablished order, made his service fruitful; then parting them among the longing faithful,
Not thirsting after aught, they come, most active, while with sweet food the race of Gods they strengthen.
4 Since Matarisvan, far-diffused, bath stirred him, and he in every house grown bright and noble,
He, Bhrgu-like I hath gone as his companion, as on commission to a greater Sovran.
5 When man poured juice to Heaven, the mighty Father, he knew and freed himself from close embracement.
The archer boldly shot at him his arrow, and the God threw his splendour on his Daughter.
6 Whoso, bath flames for thee within his dwelling, or brings the worship which thou lovest daily,
Do thou of double might increase his substance: may he whom thou incitest meet with riches.
7 All sacrificial viands wait on Agni as the Seven mighty Rivers seek the ocean.
Not by our brethren was our food discovered: find with the Gods care for us, thou who knowest.
8 When light bath filled the Lord of men for increase, straight from the heaven descends the limpid moisture.

Agni bath brought to light and filled with spirit the youthful host blameless and well providing.
9 He who like thought goes swiftly on his journey, the Sun, alone is ever Lord of riches.
The Kings with fair hands, Varuna and Mitra, protect the precious nectar in our cattle.
10 O Agni, break not our ancestral friendship, Sage as thou art, endowed with deepest knowledge.
Old age, like gathering cloud, impairs the body: before that evil be come nigh protect me.

## [01-072] HYMN LXXII. Agni.

1. THOUGH holding many gifts for men, he humbleth the higher powers of each wise ordainer.
Agni is now the treasure-lord of treasures, for ever granting all immortal bounties.
2 The Gods infallible all searching found not him, the dear Babe who still is round about us.
Worn weary, following his track, devoted, they reached the lovely highest home of Agni.
3 Because with holy oil the pure Ones, Agni, served thee the very pure three autumn seasons,
Therefore they won them holy names for worship, and nobly born they dignified their bodies.
4 Making them known to spacious earth and heaven, the holy Ones revealed the powers of Rudra.
The mortal band, discerning in the distance, found Agni standing in the loftiest station.
5 Nigh they approached, one-minded, with their spouses, kneeling to him adorable paid worship.
Friend finding in his own friend's eye protection, they made their own the bodies which they chastened.
6 Soon as the holy beings had discovered the thrice-seven mystic things contained within thee,
With these, one-minded., they preserve the Amrta: guard thou the life of all their plants and cattle.
7 Thou, Agni, knower of men's works, hast sent us good food in constant course for our subsistence:
Thou deeply skilled in paths of Gods becamest an envoy never wearied, offeringbearer.
8 Knowing the Law, the seven strong floods from heaven, full of good thought, discerned the doors of riches.
Sarama found the cattle's firm-built prison whereby the race of man is still supported.
9 They who approached all noble operations making a path that leads to life immortal,
To be the Bird's support, the spacious mother, Aditi, and her great Sons stood in power.
10 When Gods immortal made both eyes of heaven, they gave to him the gift of beauteous glory.
Now they flow forth like rivers set in motion: they knew the Red Steeds coming down, O Agni.

## [01-073] HYMN LXXIII. Agni.

I. HE who gives food, like patrimonial riches and guides aright like some wise man's instruction,
Loved like a guest who lies in pleasant lodging,-may he, as Priest, prosper his servant's dwelling.
2 He who like Savitar the God, true-minded protecteth with his power. all acts of vigour,
Truthful, like splendour, glorified by many, like breath joy-giving,-all must strive to win him.
3 He who on earth dwells like a king surrounded by faithful friends, like a God all-sustaining,

Like heroes who preside, who sit in safety: like as a blameless dame dear to her husband.

4 Thee, such, in settlements secure, O Agni, our men serve ever kindled in each dwelling.

On him have they laid splendour in abundance: dear to all men, bearer be he of riches.

5 May thy rich worshippers win food, O Agni, and princes gain long life who bring oblation.

May we get booty from jur foe in battle, presenting to the Gods their share for glory.

6 The cows of holy law, sent us by Heaven, have swelled with laden udders, loudly lowing;

Soliciting his favour, from a distance the rivers to the rock have flowed together.

7 Agni, with thee, soliciting thy favour, the holy Ones have gained glory in heaven.

They made the Night and Dawn of different colours, and set the black and purple hues together.

8 May we and those who worship be the mortals whom thou, O Agni, leadest on to riches.

Thou hast filled earth and heaven and air's mid-region, and followest the whole world like a shadow.

9 Aided by thee, O Agni, may we conquer steeds with steeds, men with men, heroes with heroes,

Lords of the wealth transmitted by our fathers: and may our princes live a hundred winters.

10 May these our hymns of praise, Agni, Ordainer, be pleasant to thee in thy heart and spirit.

May we have power to hold thy steeds of riches, laying on thee the God-sent gift of glory.

### [01-074] HYMN LXXIV. Agni.

1. As forth to sacrifice we go, a hymn to a hymn let us say, Who hears us even when afar;

2 Who, from of old, in carnage, when the people gathered, hath preserved

His household for the worshipper.

3 And let men say, Agni is born, e'en he who slayeth Vrtra, he Who winneth wealth in every fight.

4 Him in whose house an envoy thou lovest to taste his offered gifts,

And strengthenest his sacrifice,

5 Him, Angiras, thou Son of Strength, all men call happy in his God,

His offerings, and his sacred grass.

6 Hitherward shalt thou bring these Gods to our laudation and to taste.

These offered gifts, fair-shining One.

7 When, Agni, on thine embassage thou goest not a sound is heard of steed or straining of thy car.

8 Aided by thee uninjured, strong, one after other, goes he forth: Agni, the ofterer forward steps.

9 And splendid strength, heroic, high, Agni, thou grantest from the Gods,

Thou God, to him who offers gifts.

### [01-075] HYMN LXXV. Agni.

1. ACCEPT our loudest-sounding hymn, food most delightful to the Gods,

Pouring our offerings in thy mouth.

2 Now, Agni, will we say to thee, O wisest and best Afigiras,

Our precious, much-availing prayer.

3 Who, Agni, is thy kin, of men? who is thy worthy worshipper?

On whom dependent? who art thou?

4 The kinsman, Agni, of mankind, their well beloved Friend art thou,

A Friend whom friends may supplicate.

5 Bring to us Mitra, Varuna, bring the Gods to mighty sacrifice. Bring them, O Agni, to thine home.

### [01-076] HYMN LXXVI. Agni.

1. How may the mind draw nigh to please thee, Agni? What hymn of praise shall bring us greatest blessing?

Or who hath gained thy power by sacrifices? or with what mind shall we bring thee oblations?

2 Come hither, Agni; sit thee down as Hotar; be thou who never wast deceived our leader.

May Heaven and Earth, the all-pervading, love thee: worship the Gods to win for us their favour.

3 Burn thou up all the Riksasas, O Agni; ward thou off curses from our sacrifices.

Bring hither with his Bays the Lord of Soma: here is glad welcome for the Bounteous Giver.

4 Thou Priest with lip and voice that bring us children hast been invoked. Here with the Gods be seated.

Thine is the task of Cleanser and Presenter: waken us, Wealth-bestower and Producer.

5 As with oblations of the priestly Manus thou worshippedst the Gods, a Sage with sages,

So now, O truthfullest Invoker Agni, worship this day with joy-bestowing ladle.

### [01-077] HYMN LXXVII. Agni.

1. How shall we pay oblation unto Agni? What hymn, Godloved, is said to him refulgent?

Who, deathless, true to Law, mid men a herald, bringeth the Gods as best of sacrificers?

2 Bring him with reverence hither, most propitious in sacrifices, true to Law, the herald;

For Agni, when he seeks the Gods for mortals, knows them full well and worships them in spirit.

3 For he is mental power, a man, and perfect; he is the bringer, friend-,like, of the wondrous.

The pious Aryan tribes at sacrifices address them first to him who doeth marvels.

4 May Agni, foe-destroyer, manliest Hero, accept with love our hymns and our devotion.

So may the liberal lords whose strength is strongest, urged by their riches, stir our thoughts with vigour.

5 Thus Agni Jatavedas, true to Order, hath by the priestly Gotamas been lauded.

May he augment in them splendour and vigour: observant, as he lists, he gathers increase.

### [01-078] HYMN LXXVIII. Agni.

1. O JATAVEDAS, keen and swift, we Gotamas with sacred song exalt thee for thy glories' sake.

2 Thee, as thou art, desiring wealth Gotama worships with his song:

We laud thee for thy glories' sake.

3 As such, like Angiras we call on thee best winner of the spoil:

We laud thee for thy glories' sake.

4 Thee, best of Vrtra-slayers, thee who shakest off our Dasyu foes:

We laud thee for thy glories' sake.

5 A pleasant song to Agni we, sons of Rahugana, have sung:

We laud thee for thy glories' sake.

### [01-079] HYMN LXXIX. Agni.

1. HE in mid-air's expanse hath golden tresses; a raging serpent, like the rushing tempest:

Purely refulgent, knowing well the morn. ing; like honourable dames, true, active workers.

2 Thy well-winged flashes strengthen in their manner, when the black Bull hath bellowed round
about us.
With drops that bless and seem to smile he cometh: the waters fall, the clouds utter their thunder.

3 When he comes streaming with the milk of worship, conducting by directest paths of Order
Aryaman, Mitra, Varuna, Parijman fill the hide full where lies the nether press-stone.

4 O Agni, thou who art the lord of wealth in kine, thou Son of Strength,
Vouchsafe to us, O Jatavetlas, high renown.

5 He, Agni, kindled, good and wise, must be exalted in our song:
Shine, thou of many forms, shine radiantly on us.

6 O Agni, shining of thyself by night and when the morning breaks,
Burn, thou whose teeth are sharp, against the Raksasas.

7 Adorable in all our rites, favour us, Agni, with thine.aid,
When the great hymn is chanted forth.

8 Bring to us ever-conquering wealth, wealth, Agni, worthy of our choice,
In all our frays invincible.

9 Give us, O Agni, through thy grace wealth that supporteth all our life,
Thy favour so that we may live.

10 O Gotama, desiring bliss present thy songs composed with care
To Agni of the pointed flames.

11 May the man fall, O Agni, who near or afar assaileth us:
Do thou increase and prosper us.

12 Keen and swift Agni, thousand-eyed, chaseth the Raksasas afar:
He singeth, herald meet for lauds.

## [01-080] HYMN LXXX. Indra.

1. THUS in the Soma, in wild joy the Brahman hath exalted thee:
Thou, mightiest It thunder-armed, hast driven by force he Dragon from the earth, lauding thine own
imperial sway.

2 The mighty flowing Soma-draught, brought by the Hawk, hath gladdened thee,
That in thy strength, O Thunderer, thou hast struck down Vrtra from the floods, lauding thine own
imperial sway.

3 Go forward, meet the foe, be bold; thy bolt of thunder is not checked.
Manliness, Indra, is thy might: stay Vrtra, make the waters thine, lauding thine own imperial sway.

4 Thou smotest Vrtra from the earth, smotest him, Indra, from the sky.
Let these life-fostering waters flow attended by the Marut host, lauding thine own imperial sway.

5 The wrathful Indra with his bolt of thunder rushing on the foe,
Smote fierce on trembling Vrtra's back, and loosed the waters free to run, lauding his own imperial
sway.

6 With hundred-jointed thunderbolt Indra hath struck him on the back,
And, while rejoicing in the juice, seeketh prosperity for friends, lauding his own imperial sway.

7 Indra, unconquered might is thine, Thunderer, Caster of the Stone;
For thou with thy surpassing power smotest to death the guileful beast, lauding thine own imperial sway.

8 Far over ninety spacious floods thy thunderbolts were cast abroad:
Great, Indra, is thy hero might, and strength is seated in thine arms, lauding thine own imperial
sway.

9 Laud him a thousand all at once, shout twenty forth the hymn of praise.
Hundreds have sung aloud to him, to Indra hath the prayer been raised, lauding his own imperial
sway.

10 Indra hath smitten down the power of Vrtra,-might with stronger might.
This was his manly exploit, he slew Vrtra and let loose the floods, lauding his own imperial sway.

11 Yea, even this great Pair of Worlds trembled in terror at thy wrath,
When, Indra, Thunderer, Marut-girt, thou slewest Vrtra in thy strength, lauding thine own imperial
sway.

12 But Vrtra scared not Indra with his shaking or his thunder roar.
On him that iron thunderbolt fell fiercely with its thousand points, lauding his own imperial sway.

13 Whenwith the thunder thou didst make thy dart and Vrtra meet in war,
Thy might, O Indra, fain to slay the Dragon, was set firm in heaven, lauding thine own imperial sway.

14 When at thy shout, O Thunder-armed, each thing both fixed and moving shook,
E'en Tvastar trembled at thy wrath and quaked with fear because of thee, lauding thine own imperial
sway.

15 There is not, in our knowledge, one who passeth Indra in his strength:
In him the Deities have stored manliness, insight, power and might, lauding his own imperial sway.

16 Still as of old, whatever rite Atharvan, Manus sire of all,
Dadhyach performed, their prayer and praise united in that Indra meet, lauding his own imperial
sway.

## [01-081] HYMN LXXXI. Indra.

1. THE men have lifted Indra up, the Vrtra slayer, to joy and strength:
Him, verily, we invoke in battles whether great or small: be he our aid in deeds of might.

2 Thou, Hero, art a warrior, thou art giver of abundant spoil.
Strengthening e'en the feeble, thou aidest the sacrificer, thou givest the offerer ample wealth.

3 When war and battles are on foot, booty is laid before the bold.
Yoke thou thy wildly-rushing Bays. Whom wilt thou slay and whom enrich? Do thou, O Indra, make
us rich.

4 Mighty through wisdom, as he lists, terrible, he hath waxed in strength.
Lord of Bay Steeds, strong-jawed, sublime, he in joined hands for glory's sake hath grasped his iron
thunderbolt.

5 He filled the earthly atmosphere and pressed against the lights in heaven.
None like thee ever hath been born, none, Indra, will be born like thee. Thou hast waxed mighty over
all.

6 May he who to the offerer gives the foeman's man-sustaining food,
May Indra lend his aid to us. Deal forth -abundant is thy wealth-that in thy bounty 1 may share.

7 He, righteous-hearted, at each time of rapture gives us herds of kine.
Gather in both thy hands for us treasures of many hundred sorts. Sharpen thou us, and bring us
wealth.
8 Refresh thee, Hero, with the juice outpoured for bounty and for strength.
We know thee Lord of ample store, to thee have sent our hearts' desires: be therefore our Protector
thou.
9 These people, Indra, keep for thee all that is worthy of thy choice.
Discover thou, as Lord, the wealth of men who offer up no gifts: bring thou to us this wealth of theirs.

## [01-082] HYMN LXXXII. Indra.

1. GRACIOUSLY listen to our songs, Maghavan, be not negligent.
As thou hast made us full of joy and lettest us solicit thee, now, Indra, yoke thy two Bay Steeds.
2 Well have they eaten and rejoiced; the friends have risen and passed away.
The sages luminous in themselves have. praised thee with their latest hymn. Now, Indra, yoke thy
two Bay Steeds.
3 Maghavan, we will reverence thee who art so fair to look upon.
Thus praised, according to our wish come now with richly laden car. Now, Indra, yoke thy two Bay
Steeds.
4 He will in very truth ascend the powerful car that finds the kine,
Who thinks upon the well-filled bowl, the Tawny Coursers' harnesser. Now, Indra, yoke thy two Bay
Steeds.
5 Let, Lord of Hundred Powers, thy Steeds be harnessed on the right and left.
Therewith in rapture of the juice, draw near to thy beloved Spouse. Now, Indra, yoke thy two Bay
Steeds.
6 With holy prayer I yoke thy long-maned pair of Bays: come hitherward; thou holdest them in both
thy hands.
The stirring draughts of juice outpoured have made thee glad: thou, Thunderer, hast rejoiced with
Pusan and thy Spouse.

## [01-083] HYMN LXXXIII. Indra.

1. INDRA, the mortal man well guarded by thine aid goes foremost in the wealth of horses and of kine.
With amplest wealth thou fillest him, as round about the waters clearly seen afar fill Sindhu full.
2 The heavenly Waters come not nigh the priestly bowl: they but look down and see how far mid-air is spread:
The Deities conduct the pious man to them: like suitors they delight in him who loveth prayer.
3 Praiseworthy blessing hast thou laid upon the pair who with uplifted ladle serve thee, man and wife.
Unchecked he dwells and prospers in thy law: thy power brings blessing to the sacrificer pouring gifts.
4 First the Angirases won themselves vital power, whose fires were kindled through good deeds and sacrifice.
The men together found the Pani's hoarded wealth, the cattle, and the wealth in horses and in kine.
5 Atharvan first by sacrifices laid the paths then, guardian of the Law, sprang up the loving Sun.
Usana Kavya straightway hither drove the kine. Let us with offerings honour Yama's deathless birth.
6 When sacred grass is trimmed to aid the auspicious work, or the hymn makes its voice of praise

sound to the sky.
Where the stone rings as'twere a singer skilled in laud, --Indra in truth delights when these come near to him.

## [01-084] HYMN LXXXIV. Indra.

1. The Soma hath been pressed for thee, O Indra; mightiest, bold One, come.
May Indra-vigour fill thee full, as the Sun fills mid-air with rays.
2 His pair of Tawny Coursers bring Indra of unresisted might
Hither to Rsis' songs of praise and sacrifice performed by men.
3 Slayer of Vrtra, mount thy car; thy Bay Steeds have been yoked by prayer.
May, with its voice, the pressing-stone draw thine attention hitherward.
4 This poured libation, Indra, drink, immortal, gladdening, excellent.
Streams of the bright have flowed to thee here at the seat of holy Law.
5 Sing glory now to Indra, say to him your solemn eulogies.
The drops poured forth have made him glad: pay reverence to his might supreme.
6 When, Indra, thou dost yoke thy Steeds, there is no better charioteer:
None hath surpassed thee in thy might, none with good steeds o'ertaken thee.
7 He who alone bestoweth on mortal man who offereth gifts,
The ruler of resistless power, is Indra, sure.
8 When will he trample, like a weed, the man who hath no gift for him?
When, verily, will Indra hear our songs of praise?
9 He who with Soma juice prepared amid the many honours thee,-
Verily Indra gains thereby tremendous might.
10 The juice of Soma thus diffused, sweet to the taste, the bright cows drink,
Who for the sake of splendour close to mighty Indra's side rejoice, good in their own supremacy.
11 Craving his touch the dappled kine mingle the Soma with their milk.
The milch-kine dear to Indra send forth his death-dealing thunderbolt, good in their own supremacy.
12 With veneration, passing wise, honouring his victorious might,
They follow close his many laws to win them due preeminence, good in their
own supremacy.
13 With bones of Dadhyac for his arms, Indra, resistless in attack,
Struck nine-and-ninety Vrtras dead.
14 He, searching for the horse's head, removed among the mountains, found
At Suryanavan what he sought.
15 Then verily they recognized the essential form of Tvastar's Bull,
Here in the mansion of the Moon.
16 Who yokes to-day unto the pole of Order the strong and passionate steers of checkless spirit,
With shaft-armed mouths, heart-piercing, health-bestowing? Long shall he live who richly pays their service.
17 Who fleeth forth? who suffereth? who feareth? Who knoweth Indra present, Indra near us?
Who sendeth benediction on his offspring, his household, wealth and person, and the People?
18 Who with poured oil and offering honours Agni, with ladle worships at appointed seasons?
To whom to the Gods bring oblation quickly? What offerer, God-favoured, knows him thoroughly?
19 Thou as a God, O Mightiest, verily blessest mortal man.

O Maghavan, there is no comforter but thou: Indra, I speak my words to thee.
20 Let not thy bounteous gifts, let not thy saving help fail us, good Lord, at any time;
And measure out to us, thou lover of mankind, all riches hitherward from men.

## [01-085] HYMN LXXXV. Maruts.

1. THEY who are glancing forth, like women, on their way, doers of mighty deeds, swift racers, Rudra's Sons,
The Maruts have made heaven and earth increase and grow: in sacrifices they delight, the strong and wild.
2 Grown to their perfect strength greatness have they attained; the Rudras have established their
abode in heaven.
Singing their song of praise and generating might, they have put glory on, the Sons whom Prani bare.
3 When, Children of the Cow, they shine in bright attire, and on their fair limbs lay their golden ornaments,
They drive away each adversary from their path, and, following their traces, fatness floweth down,
4 When, mighty Warriors, ye who glitter with your spears, o'erthrowing with your strength e'en what is ne'er o'erthrown,
When, O ye Maruts, ye the host that send the rain, had harnessed to your cars the thought-fleet spotted deer.
5 When ye have harnessed to your cars the spotted deer, urging the thunderbolt, O Maruts, to the fray,
Forth rush the torrents of the dark red stormy cloud, and moisten, like a skin, the earth with waterfloods.
6 Let your swift-gliding coursers bear you hitherward with their fleet pinions. Come ye forward with your arms.
Sit on the grass; a wide scat hath been made for you: delight yourselves, O Maruts, in the pleasant food.
7 Strong in their native strength to greatness have they grown, stepped to the firmament and made their dwelling wide.
When Visnu saved the Soma bringing wild delight, the Maruts sate like birds on their dear holy grass.
8 In sooth like heroes fain for fight they rush about, like combatants fame-seeking have they striven in war.
Before the Maruts every creature is afraid: the men are like to Kings, terrible to behold.
9 When Tyastar deft of hand had turned the thunderbolt, golden, with thousand edges, fashioned more skilfully,
Indra received it to perform heroic deeds. Vrtra he slew, and forced the flood of water forth.
10 They with their vigorous strength pushed the well up on high, and clove the cloud in twain though it was passing strong.
The Maruts, bounteous Givers, sending forth their voice, in the wild joy of Soma wrought their glorious deeds.
11 They drave the cloud transverse directed hitherward, and poured the fountain forth for thirsting Gotama.
Shining with varied light they come to him with help: they with their might fulfilled the longing of the sage.
12 The shelters which ye have for him who lauds you, bestow them threefold on the man who offers.
Extend the same boons unto us, ye Maruts. Give us, O Heroes, wealth with noble offipring.

## [01-086] HYMN LXXXVI. Maruts.

1. THE best of guardians hath that man within whose dwelling place ye drink,
O Maruts, giants of the sky.
2 Honoured with sacrifice or with the worship of the sages' hymns,
O Maruts, listen to the call.
3 Yea, the strong man to whom ye have vouchsafed to give a sage, shall move

Into a stable rich in kine.
4 Upon this hero's sacred grass Soma is poured in daily rites: Praise and delight are sung aloud.
5 Let the strong Maruts hear him, him surpassing all men: strength be his
That reaches even to the Sun.
6 For, through the swift Gods' loving help, in many an autumn, Maruts, we
Have offered up our sacrifice.
7 Fortunate shall that mortal be, O Maruts most adorable, Whose offerings ye bear away.
8 O Heroes truly strong, ye know the toil of him who sings your praise,
The heart's desire of him who loves.
9 O ye of true strength, make this thing manifest by your greatness - strike
The demon with your thunderbolt.
10 Conceal the horrid darkness, drive far from us each devouring fiend.
Create the light for which we long.

## [01-087] HYMN LXXXVII Maruts.

1. LOUD Singers, never humbled, active, full of strength, immovable, impetuous, manliest, bestbeloved,
They have displayed themselves with glittering ornaments, a few in number only, like the heavens
with stars.
2 When, Maruts, on the steeps ye pile the moving cloud, ye are like birds on whatsoever path it be.
Clouds everywhere shed forth the rain upon your cars. Drop fatness, honey-hued, for him who sings
your praise.
3 Earth at their racings trembles as if weak and worn, when on their ways they yoke their cars for
victory.
They, sportive, loudly roaring, armed with glittering spears, shakers of all, themselves admire their mightiness.
4 Self-moving is that youthful band, with spotted steeds; thus it hath lordly sway, endued with power and might.
Truthful art thou, and blameless, searcher out of sin: so thou, Strong Host, wilt be protector of this prayer.
5 We speak by our descent from our primeval Sire; our tongue, when we behold the Soma, stirs itself.
When, shouting, they had joined Indra in toil of fight, then only they obtained their sacrificial names.
6 Splendours they gained for glory, they who wear bright rings; rays they obtained, and men to
celebrate their praise.
Armed with their swords, impetuous and fearing naught, they have possessed the Maruts' own
beloved home.

## [01-088] HYMN LXXXVIII. Maruts.

1. COME hither, Maruts, on your lightning laden cars, sounding with sweet songs, armed with
lances, winged with steeds.
Fly unto us with noblest food, like birds, O ye of mighty power.
2 With their red-hued or, haply, tawny coursers which speed their chariots on, they come for glory.
Brilliant like gold is he who holds the thunder. Earth have they smitten with the chariot's felly.
3 For beauty ye have swords upon your bodies. As they stir woods so may they stir our spirits.
For your sake, O ye Maruts very mighty and well-born, have they set the stone, in motion.
4 The days went round you and came back O yearners, back, to this prayer and to this solemn worship.

The Gotamas making their prayer with singing have pushed the well's lid up to drink the water.

5 No hymn way ever known like this aforetime which Gotama sang forth for you, O Maruts,
What time upon your golden wheels he saw you, wild boars rushing about with tusks of iron.

6 To you this freshening draught of Soma rusheth, O Maruts, like the voice of one who prayeth.
It rusheth freely from our hands as these. libations wont to flow.

## [01-089] HYMN LXXXIX. Visvedevas.

1. MAY powers auspicious come to us from every side, never deceived, unhindered, and victorious,
That the Gods ever may be with us for our gain, our guardians day by day unceasing in their care.

2 May the auspicious favour of the Gods be ours, on us descend the bounty of the righteous Gods.
The friendship of the Gods have we devoutly sought: so may the Gods extend our life that we may
live.

3 We call them hither with a hymn of olden time, Bhaga, the friendly Daksa, Mitra, Aditi,
Aryaman, Varuna, Soma, the Asvins. May Sarasvati, auspicious, grant felicity.

4 May the Wind waft to us that pleasant medicine, may Earth our Mother give it, and our Father
Heaven,
And the joy-giving stones that press the Soma's juice. Asvins, may ye, for whom our spirits long, hear this.

5 Him we invoke for aid who reigns supreme, the Lord of all that stands or moves, inspirer of the soul,
That Pusan may promote the increase of our wealth, our keeper and our guard infallible for our good.

6 Illustrious far and wide, may Indra prosper us: may Pusan prosper us, the Master of all wealth.
May Tarksya with uninjured fellies prosper us: Brhaspati vouchsafe to us prosperity.

7 The Maruts, Sons of Prani, borne by spotted steeds, moving in glory, oft visiting holy rites,
Sages whose tongue is Agni, brilliant as the Sun,-hither let all the Gods for our protection come.

8 Gods, may we with our ears listen to what is good, and with our eyes see what is good, ye Holy
Ones.
With limbs and bodies firm may we extolling you attain the term of life appointed by the Gods.

9 A hundred autumns stand before us, O ye Gods, within whose space ye bring our bodies to decay;
Within whose space our sons become fathers in turn. Break ye not in the midst our course of fleeting
life.

10 Aditi is the heaven, Aditi is mid-air, Aditi is the Mother and the Sire and Son.
Aditi is all Gods, Aditi five-classed men, Aditi all that hath been bom and shall be born.

## [01-090] HYMN XC. Visvedevas.

1. MAY Varuna with guidance straight, and Mitra lead us, he who knows,
And Aryaman in accord with Gods.

2 For they are dealers forth of wealth, and, not deluded, with their might
Guard evermore the holy laws.

3 Shelter may they vouchsafe to us, Immortal Gods to mortal men,
Chasing our enemies away.

4 May they mark out our paths to bliss, Indra, the Maruts, Pusan,

and Bhaga, the Gods to be adored.

5 Yea, Pusan, Visnu, ye who run your course, enrich our hymns with kine;
Bless us with all prosperity.

6 The winds waft sweets, the rivers pour sweets for the man who keeps the Law
So may the plants be sweet for us.

7 Sweet be the night and sweet the dawns, sweet the terrestrial atmosphere;
Sweet be our Father Heaven to us.

8 May the tall tree be full of sweets for us, and full of sweets the Sun:
May our milch-kine be sweet for us.

9 Be Mitra gracious unto us, and Varuna and Aryaman:
Indra, Brhaspati be kind, and Visnu of the mighty stride.

## [01-091] HYMN XCI Soma.

1. Thou, Soma, art preeminent for wisdom; along the straightest path thou art our leader.
Our wise forefathers by thy guidance, Indu, dealt out among the Gods their share of treasure.

2 Thou by thine insight art most wise, O Soma, strong by thine energies and all possessing,
Mighty art thou by all thy powers and greatness, by glories art thou glorious, guide of mortals.

3 Thine are King Varuna's eternal statutes, lofty and deep, O Soma, is thy glory.
All-pure art thou like Mitra the beloved, adorable, like Aryaman, O Soma.

4 With all thy glories on the earth, in heaven, on mountains, in the plants, and in the waters,-
With all of these, well-pleased and not in anger, accept, O royal Soma, our oblations.

5 Thou, Soma, art the Lord of heroes, King, yea, Vrtra-slayer thou:
Thou art auspicious energy.

6 And, Soma, let it be thy wish that we may
live and may not die:
Praise-loving Lord of plants art thou.

7 To him who keeps the law, both old and young, thou givest happiness,
And energy that he may live.

8 Guard us, King Soma, on all sides from him who threatens us: never let
The friend of one like thee be harmed.

9 With those delightful aids which thou hast, Soma, for the worshipper,-
Even with those protect thou us.

10 Accepting this our sacrifice and this our praise, O Soma, come,
And be thou nigh to prosper us.

11 Well-skilled in speech we magnify thee, Soma, with our sacred songs:
Come thou to us, most gracious One.

12 Enricher, healer of disease, wealth-finder, prospering our store,
Be, Soma, a good Friend to us.

13 Soma, be happy in our heart, as milch-kine in the grassy meads,
As a young man in his own house.

14 O Soma, God, the mortal man who in thy friendship hath delight,
Him doth the mighty Sage befriend.

15 Save us from slanderous reproach, keep us., O Soma, from distress:
Be unto us a gracious Friend.

16 Soma, wax great. From every side may vigorous powers unite in thee:

Be in the gathering-place of strength.

17 Wax, O most gladdening Soma, great through all thy rays of light, and be

A Friend of most illustrious fame t6 prosper us.

16 In thee be juicy nutriments united, and powers and mighty foe-subduing vigour,

Waxing to immortality, O Soma: win highest glories for thyself in heaven.

19 Such of thy glories as with poured oblations men honour, may they all invest our worship.

Wealth-giver, furtherer with troops of heroes, sparing the brave, come, Soma, to our houses.

20 To him who worships Soma gives the milchcow, a fleet steed and a man of active knowledge,

Skilled in home duties, meet for holy synod, for council meet, a glory to his father.

21 Invincible in fight, saver in battles, guard of our camp, winner of light and water,

Born amid hymns, well-housed, exceeding famous, victor, in thee will we rejoice, O Soma.

22 These herbs, these milch-kine, and these running waters, all these, O Soma, thou hast generated.

The spacious firmament bast thou expanded, and with the light thou hast dispelled the darkness.

23 Do thou, God Soma, with thy Godlike spirit, victorious, win for us a share of riches.

Let none prevent thee: thou art Lord of valour. Provide for both sides in the fray for booty.

### [01-092] HYMN XCII. Dawn.

1. THESE Dawns have raised their banner; in the eastern half of the mid-air they spread abroad their

shinine light.

Like heroes who prepare their weapons for the war, onward they come bright red in hue, the Mother

Cows.

2 Readily have the purple beams of light shot up; the Red Cows have they harnessed, easy to be

yoked.

The Dawns have brought distinct perception as before: red-hued, they have attained their fulgent

brilliancy.

3 They sing their song like women active in their tasks, along their common path hither from far

away,

Bringing refreshment to the liberal devotee, yea, all things to the worshipper who pours the juice.

4 She, like a dancer, puts her broidered garments on: as a cow yields her udder so she bares her

breast.

Creating light for all the world of life, the Dawn hath laid the darkness open as the cows their stall.

5 We have beheld the brightness of her shining; it spreads and drives away the darkiorne monster.

Like tints that deck the Post at sacrifices, Heaven's Daughter hath attained her wondrous splendour.

6 We have o'erpast the limit of this darkness; Dawn breaking forth again brings clear perception.

She like a flatterer smiles in light for glory, and fair of face hath wakened to rejoice

us.

7 The Gotamas have praised Heaven's radiant Daughter, the leader of the charm of pleasant voices.

Dawn, thou conferrest on us strength with offspring and men, conspicuous with kine and horses.

8 O thou who shinest forth in wondrous glory, urged onward by thy strength, auspicious Lady,

Dawn, may I gain that wealth, renowned and ample, in brave sons, troops of slaves, far-famed for horses.

9 Bending her looks on all the world, the Goddess shines, widely spreading with her bright eye westward.

Waking to motion every living creature, she understands the voice of each adorer.

10 Ancient of days, again again born newly, decking her beauty with the self-same raiment.

The Goddess wastes away the life of mortals, like a skilled hunter cutting birds in pieces.

11 She hath appeared discovering heaven's borders: to the far distance she drives off her Sister.

Diminishing the days of human creatures, the Lady shines with all her lover's splendour.

12 The bright, the blessed One shines forth extending her rays like kine, as a flood rolls his waters.

Never transgressing the divine commandments, she is beheld visible with the sunbeams.

13 O Dawn enriched with ample wealth, bestow on us the wondrous gift

Wherewith we may support children and children's sons.

14 Thou radiant mover of sweet sounds, with wealth of horses and of kine

Shine thou on us this day, O Dawn auspiciously.

15 O Dawn enriched with holy rites, yoke to thy car thy purple steeds,

And then bring thou unto us all felicities.

16 O Asvins wonderful in act, do ye unanimous direct

Your chariot to our home wealthy in kine and gold.

17 Ye who brought down the hymn from heaven, a light that giveth light to man,

Do ye, O Asvius, bring strength bither unto us.

18 Hither may they who wake at dawn bring, to drink Soma both the Gods

Health-givers Wonder-Workers, borne on paths of gold.

### [01-093] HYMN XCIII. Agni-Sona.

1 AGNI and Soma, mighty Pair, graciously hearken to my call,
Accept in friendly wise my hymn, and prosper him who offers gifts.

2 The man who honours you to-day, Agni and Soma, with this hymn,

Bestow on him heroic strength, increase of kine, and noble steeds.

3 The man who offers holy oil and burnt oblations unto you,
Agni and Soma, shall enjoy great strength, with offspring, all his life.

4 Agni and Soma, famed is that your. prowess wherewith ye stole the kine, his food, from Pani.

Ye caused the brood of Brsaya to perish; ye found the light, the single light for many.

5 Agni and Soma, joined in operation ye have set up the shining lights in heaven.

From curse and from reproach, Agni and Soma, ye freed the rivers that were bound in fetters.

6 One of you Mitarisvan brought from heaven, the Falcon rent the other from the mountain.

Strengthened by holy prayer Agni and Soma have made us ample room for sacrificing.

7 Taste, Agni, Soma, this prepared oblation; accept it, Mighty Ones, and let it please you.

Vouchsafe us good protection and kind favour: grant to the sacrificer health and riches.

8 Whoso with oil and poured oblation honours, with God-devoted heart, Agni and Soma,-

Protect his sacrifice, preserve him from distress, grant to the sacrificer great felicity.

9 Invoked together, mates in wealth, AgniSoma, accept our hymns:
Together be among the Gods.
10 Agni and Soma, unto him who worships you with holy oil
Shine forth an ample recompense.
11 Agni and Sonia, be ye pleased with these oblations brought to you,
And come, together, nigh to us.
12 Agni and Soma, cherish well our horses, and let our cows be fat who yield oblations.
Grant power to us and to our wealthy patrons, and cause our holy rites to be successful.

## [01-094] HYMN XCIV. Agni

1 FOR Jatavedas worthy of our praise will we frame with our mind this eulogy as 'twere a car.
For good, in his assembly, is this care of ours. Let us not, in thy friendship, Agni, suffer harm.
2 The man for whom thou sacrificest prospereth, dwelleth without a foe, gaineth heroic might.
He waxeth strong, distress never approacheth him. Let us riot, in thy friendship, Agni, suffer harm.
3 May we have power to kindle thee. Fulfil our thoughts. In thee the Gods eat the presented offering,
Bring hither the Adityas, for we long for them. Let us not in thy friendship, Agni, suffer harm.
4 We will bring fuel and prepare burnt offerings, reminding thee at each successive festival.
Fulfil our thought that so we may prolong our lives. Let us not in thy friendship, Agni, suffer harm.
5 His ministers move forth, the guardians of the folk, protecting quadruped and biped with their rays.
Mighty art thou, the wondrous herald of the Dawn. Let us not in thy friend. ship, Agni, suffer harm.
6 Thou art Presenter and the chief Invoker, thou Director, Purifier, great High Priest by birth.
Knowing all priestly work thou perfectest it, Sage. Let us not in thy friendship, Agni, suffer harm.
7 Lovely of form art thou, alike on every side; though far, thou shinest brightly
as if close at hand.
O God, thou seest through even the dark of night. Let us not in thy friendship, Agni, suffer harm.
8 Gods, foremost he his car who pours libations out, and let our hymn prevail o'er evil-hearted men.
Attend to this our speech and make it prosper well. Let us not in thy friendship, Agni, suffer harm.
9 Smite with thy weapons those of evil speech and thought, devouring demons, whether near or tar
away.
Then to the singer give free way for sacrifice. Let us not in thy friendship, Agni, suffer harm.
10 When to thy chariot thou hadst yoked two red steeds and two ruddy steeds, wind-sped, thy roar
was like a bull's.
Thou with smoke-bannered flame attackest forest trees. Let us not in thy friendship, Agni, suffer
harm.
11 Then at thy roar the very birds are terrified, when, eating-up the grass, thy sparks fly forth abroad.
Then is it easy for thee and thy car to pass. Let us not in thy friendship, Agni, suffer harm.
12 He hath the Power to soothe Mitra and Varuna: wonderful is the Maruts' wrath when they
descend.
Be gracious; let their hearts he turned to us again. Let us not in thy friendship, Agni, suffer harm.

13 Thou art a God, thou art the wondrous Friend of Gods, the Vasu of the Vasus, fair in sacrifice.
Under, thine own most wide protection may we dwell. Let us not in thy friendship, Agni, suffer harm.
14 This is thy grace that, kindled in thine own abode, invoked with Soma thou soundest forth most benign,
Thou givest wealth and treasure to the worshipper. Let us not in thy friendship, Agni, suffer harm.
15 To whom thou, Lord of goodly riches, grantest freedom from every sin with perfect wholeness,
Whom with good strength thou quikenest, with children and wealth-may we be they, Eternal Being.
16 Such, Agni, thou who knowest all good fortune, God, lengthen here the days of our existence.
This prayer of ours may Varuna grant, and Mitra, and Aditi and Sindhu, Earth and Heaven.

## [01-095] HYMN XCV. Agni

1. To fair goals travel Two unlike in semblance: each in succession nourishes an infant.
One bears a Godlike Babe of golden colour; bright and fair-shining, is he with the other.
2 Tvastar's ten daughters, vigilant and youthful, produced this Infant borne to sundry quarters.
They bear around him whose long flames are pointed, fulgent among mankind with native splendour.
3. Three several places of his birth they honour, in mid-air, in the heaven, and in the waters.
Governing in the cast of earthly regions, the seasons hath he stablished in their order.
4 Who of you knows this secret One? The Infant by his own nature hath brought forth his Mothers.
The germ of many, from the waters' bosom he goes forth, wise and great, of Godlike nature.
5 Visible, fair, he grows in native brightness uplifted in the lap of waving waters.
When he was born both Tvastar's worlds were frightened: they turn to him and reverence the Lion.
6 The Two auspicious Ones, like women, tend him: like lowing cows they seek him in their manner.
He is the Lord of Might among the mighty; him, on the right, they balm with their oblations.
7 Like Savitar his arms with might he stretches; awful, he strives grasping the world's two borders.
He forces out from all a brilliant vesture, yea, from his Mothers draws he forth new raiment.
8 He makes him a most noble form of splendour, decking him in his home with milk and waters.
The Sage adorns the depths of air with wisdom . this is the meeting where the Gods are worshipped.
9 Wide through the firmament spreads forth triumphant the far-resplendent strength of' thee the Mighty.
Kindled by us do thou preserve us, Agni, with all thy self-bright undiminished succours.
10 In dry spots he makes stream, and course, and torrent, and inundates the earth with floods that glisten.
All ancient things within his maw he gathers, and moves among the new fresh-sprouting grasses.
11 Fed with our fuel, purifying Agni, so blaze to us auspiciously for glory.
This prayer of ours may Varuna grant, and Mitra, and Aditi and Sindhu, Earth and Heaven.

## [01-096] HYMN XCVI. Agni.

1. HE in the ancient way by strength engendered, lo! straight hath taken to himself all wisdom.

The waters and the bowl have made him friendly. The Gods possessed the wealth bestowing Agni.

2 At Ayu's ancient call he by his wisdom gave all this progeny of men their being,
And, by refulgent light, heaven and the waters. The Gods possessed the wealth. bestowing Agni.

3 Praise him, ye Aryan folk, as chief performer of sacrifice adored and ever toiling,
Well-tended, Son of Strength, the Constant Giver. The Gods possessed the wealth bestowing Agni.

4 That Matarisvan rich in wealth and treasure, light-winner, finds a pathway for his offspring.
Guard of our folk, Father of earth and heaven. The Gods possessed the wealth bestowing Agni.

5 Night and Dawn, changing each the other's colour, meeting together suckle one same Infant:
Golden between the heaven and earth he shineth. The Gods possessed the wealth bestowing Agni.

6 Root of wealth, gathering-place of treasures, banner of sacrifice, who grants the suppliant's wishes:
Preserving him as their own life immortal, the Gods possessed the wealth-bestowing Agni.

7 Now and of old the home of wealth, the mansion of what is born and what was born aforetime,
Guard of what is and what will be hereafter,-the Gods possessed the wealth bestowing Agni.

8 May the Wealth-Giver grant us conquering riches; may the Wealth-Giver grant us wealth with heroes.
May the Wealth-Giver grant us food with offspring, and length of days may the Wealth-Giver send us.

9 Fed with our fuel, purifying Agni, so blaze to us auspiciously for glory.
This prayer of ours may Varuna grant, and Mitra, and Aditi and Sindhu, Earth and Heaven.

### [01-097] HYMN XCVII. Agni.

1. CHASING with light our sin away, O Agni, shine thou wealth on us.
May his light chase our sin away.

2 For goodly fields, for pleasant homes, for wealth we sacrifice to thee.
May his light chase our sin away.

3 Best praiser of all these be he; foremost, our chiefs who sacrifice.
May his light chase our sin away.

4 So that thy worshippers and we, thine, Agni, in our sons may live.
May his light chase our sin away.

5 As ever- conquering Agni's beams of splendour go to every side,
May his light chase our sin away.

6 To every side thy face is turned, thou art triumphant everywhere.
May his light chase our sin away.

7 O thou whose face looks every way, bear us past foes as in a ship.
May his light chase our sin away.

8 As in a ship, convey thou us for our advantage o'er the flood.
May his light chase our sin away.

### [01-098] HYMN XCVIII Agni.

1. STILL in Vaisvanara's grace may we continue: yea, he is King supreme o'er all things living.
Sprung hence to life upon this All he looketh. Vaisvanara hath rivalry with Surya.

2 Present in heaven, in earth, all-present Agni,-all plants that grow on ground hath he pervaded.

May Agni, may Vaisvanara with vigour, present, preserve us day and night from foemen.

3 Be this thy truth, Vaisvanara, to us-ward: let wealth in rich abundance gather round us.
This prayer of ours may Varuna grant, and Mitra, and Aditi and Sindhu, Earth and Heaven.

### [01-099] HYMN XCIX. Agni.

1. FOR Jatavedas let us press the Soma: may he consume the wealth of the malignant.
May Agni carry us through all our troubles, through grief as in a boat across the river.

### [01-100] HYMN C. Indra.

1. MAY he who hath his home with strength, the Mighty, the King supreme of earth and spacious heaven,
Lord of true power, to he invoked in battles,-may Indra, girt by Maruts, be our succour.

2 Whose way is unattainable like Surya's: he in each fight is the strong Vrtra-slayer,
Mightiest with his Friends in his own courses. May Indra, girt by Maruts, be our succour.

3 Whose paths go forth in their great might resistless, forthmilking, as it were, heaven's genial moisture.
With manly strength triumphant, foe-subduer,-may Indra, girt by Maruts, be our succour.

4 Among Angirases he was the chiefest, a Friend with friends, mighty amid the mighty.
Praiser mid praisers, honoured most of singers. May Indra, girt by Maruts, be our succour.

5 Strong with the Rudras as with his own children, in manly battle conquering his foemen '
With his close comrades doing deeds of glory,-may Indra, girt by Maruts, be our succour.

6 Humbler of pride, exciter of the conflict, the Lord of heroes, God invoked of many,
May he this day gain with our men the sunlight. May Indra, girt by Maruts, be oursuccour.

7 His help hath made him cheerer in the battle, the folk have made him guardian of their comfort.
Sole Lord is he of every holy service. May Indra, girt by Maruts, be our succour.

8 To him the Hero, on high days of prowess, heroes for help and booty shall betake them.
He hath found light even in the blinding darkness. May Indra, girt by Maruts, be our succour.

9 He with his left hand checketh even the mighty, and with his righthand gathereth up the booty.
Even with the humble he acquireth riches. May Indra, girt by Maruts, be our succour.

10 With hosts on foot and cars he winneth treasures: well is he known this day by all the people.
With manly might he conquereth those who hate him. May Indra, girt by Maruts, be our succour.

11 When in his ways with kinsmen or with strangers he speedeth to the fight, invoked of many,
For gain of waters, and of sons and grandsons, may Indra, girt by Maruts, be our succour.

12 Awful and fierce, fiend-slayer, thunder-wielder, with boundless knowledge, hymned by hundreds, mighty,
In strength like Soma, guard of the Five Peoples, may Indra, girt by Maruts, be our succour.

13 Winning the light, hitherward roars his thunder like the terrific mighty voice of Heaven.

Rich gifts and treasures evermore attend him. May Indra, girt by Maruts, be our succour.

14 Whose home eternal through his strength surrounds him on every side, his laud, the earth and
heaven,
May he, delighted with our service, save us. May Indra, girt by Maruts, be our succour.

15 The limit of whose power not Gods by Godhead, nor mortal men have reached, nor yet the Waters.
Both Earth and Heaven in vigour he surpasseth. May Indra, girt by Maruts, he our succour.

16 The red and tawny mare, blaze-marked, high standing, celestial who, to bring Rjrasva riches,
Drew at the pole the chariot yoked with stallions, joyous, among the hosts of men was noted.

17 The Varsagiras unto thee, O Indra, the Mighty One, sing forth this laud to please thee,
Rjrasva with his fellows, Ambarisa, Suradhas, Sahadeva, Bhayamana.

18 He, much invoked, hath slain Dasyus and Simyus, after his wont, and laid them low with arrows.
The mighty Thunderer with his fair-complexioned friends won the land, the sunlight, and the waters.

19 May Indra evermore be our protector, and unimperilled may we win the booty.
This prayer of ours may Varuna grant, and Mitra, and Aditi and Sindhu, Earth and Heaven.

## [01-101] HYMN CI. Indra.

1. SING, with oblation, praise to him who maketh glad, who with Rjisvan drove the dusky brood
away.
Fain for help, him the strong whose right hand wields the bolt, him girt by Maruts we invoke to be
our Friend.

2 Indra, who with triumphant wrath smote Vyamsa down, and Sambara, and Pipru the unrighteous
one;
Who extirpated Susna the insatiate, him girt by Maruts we invoke to be our Friend.

3 He whose great work of manly might is heaven and earth, and Varuna and Surya keep his holy law;
Indra, whose law the rivers follow as they flow,-him girt by Maruts we invoke to be our Friend.

4 He who is Lord and Master of the steeds and kine, honoured - the firm and sure- at every holy act;
Stayer even of the strong who pours no offering out, -him girt by Maruts we invoke to be our Friend.

5 He who is Lord of all the world that moves and breathes, who for the Brahman first before all found
the Cows;
Indra who cast the Dasyus down beneath his feet,-him girt by Maruts we invoke to be our Friend.

6 Whom cowards must invoke and valiant men of war, invoked by those who conquer and by those
who flee;
Indra, to whom all beings turn their constant thought,-him girt by Maruts we invoke to be our Friend.

7 Refulgent in the Rudras' region he proceeds, and with the Rudras through the wide space speeds
the Dame.
The hymn of praise extols Indra the far-renowned: him girt by Maruts we invoke to be our Friend.

8 O girt by Maruts, whether thou delight thee in loftiest gathering-place or lowly dwelling,
Come thence unto our rite, true boon-best-ower: through love of thee have we prepared oblations.

9 We, fain for thee, strong Indra, have pressed Soma, and, O thou sought with prayer, have made
oblations.
Now at this sacrifice, with all thy Maruts, on sacred grass, O team-borne God, rejoice thee.

10 Rejoice thee with thine own Bay Steeds, O Indra, unclose thy jaws and let thy lips be open.
Thou with the fair cheek, let thy Bay Steeds bring thee: gracious to us, he pleased with our oblation.

11 Guards of the camp whose praisers are the Maruts, may we through Indra, get ourselves the
booty.
This prayer of ours may Varuna grant, and Mitra, and Aditi and Sindhu, Earth and Heaven.

## [01-102] HYMN CII. Indra.

1. To thee the Mighty One I bring this mighty hymn, for thy desire hath been gratified by my laud.
In Indra, yea in him victorious through his strength, the Gods have joyed at feast and when the Soma
flowed.

2 The Seven Rivers bear his glory far and wide, and heaven and sky and earth display his comely
form.
The Sun and Moon in change alternate run their course, that we, O Indra, may behold and may have
faith.

3 Maghavan, grant us that same car to bring us spoil, thy conquering car in which we joy in shock of
fight.
Thou, Indra, whom our hearts praise highly in the war, grant shelter, Maghavan, to us who love thee
well.

4 Encourage thou our side in every fight: may we, with thee for our ally, conquer the foeman's host.
Indra, bestow on us joy and felicity break down, O Maghavan, the vigour of our foes.

5 For here in divers ways these men invoking thee, holder of treasures, sing hymns to win thine aid.
Ascend the car that thou mayest bring spoil to us, for, Indra, thy fixt winneth the victory.

6 His arms win kine, his power is boundless in each act best, with a hundred helps waker of battle's
din
Is Indra: none may rival him in mighty strength. Hence, eager for the spoil the people call on him.

7 Thy glory, Maghavan, exceeds a hundred yea, more than a hundred, than a thousand mid the folk,
The great bowl hath inspirited thee boundlessly: so mayst thou slay the Vrtras breaker-down of forts!

8 Of thy great might there is a three counterpart, the three earths, Lord men and the three realms of
light.
Above this whole world, Indra, thou hast waxen great: without a foe art thou, nature, from of old.

9 We invocate thee first among the Deities: thou hast become a mighty Conquer in fight.
May Indra fill with spirit this our singer's heart, and make our car impetuous, foremost in attack.

10 Thou hast prevailed, and hast not kept the booty back, in trifling battles in those of great account.
We make thee keen, the Mighty One, succour us: inspire us, Maghavan, when we defy the foe.

11 May Indra evermore be our Protector, and unimperilled may we win the booty.
This prayer of ours may Vartuna grant and Mitra, and Aditi and Sindhu, Earth and Heaven.

## [01-103] HYMN CIII. Indra.

1. THAT highest Indra-power of thine is distant: that which is here sages possessed aforetime.
This one is on the earth, in heaven the other, and both unite as flag with flag in battle.
2 He spread the wide earth out and firmly fixed it, smote with his thunderbolt and loosed the waters.
Maghavan with his puissance struck down Ahi, rent Rauhipa to death and slaughtered Vyarnsa.
3 Armed with his bolt and trusting in his prowess he wandered shattering the forts of Dasas.
Cast thy dart, knowing, Thunderer, at the Dasyu; increase the Arya's might and glory, Indra.
4 For him who thus hath taught these human races, Maghavan, bearing a fame-worthy title,
Thunderer, drawing nigh to slay the Dasyus, hath given himself the name of Son for glory.
5 See this abundant wealth that he possesses, and put your trust in Indra's hero vigour.
He found the cattle, and he found the horses, he found the plants, the forests and the waters.
6 To him the truly strong, whose deeds are many, to him the strong Bull let us pour the Soma.
The Hero, watching like a thief in ambush, goes parting the possessions of the godless.
7 Well didst thou do that hero deed, O Indra, in waking with thy bolt the slumbering Ahi.
in thee, delighted, Dames divine rejoiced them, the flying Maruts and all Gods were joyful.
8 As thou hast smitten Susna, Pipru, Vrtra and Kuyava, and Sambara's forts O Indra.
This prayer of ours may Varuna grant, and Mitra, and Aditi and Sindhu, Earth and Heaven.

## [01-104] HYMN CIV. Indra.

1. THE altar hath been made for thee to rest on: come like a panting courser and be seated.
Loosen thy flying Steeds, set free thy Horses who bear thee swiftly nigh at eve and morning.
2 These men have come to Indra for assistance: shall he not quickly come upon these pathways?
May the Gods quell the fury of the Dasa, and may they lead our folk to happy fortune.
3 He who hath only wish as his possession casts on himself, casts foam amid the waters.
Both wives of Kuyava in milk have bathed them: may they be drowned within the depth of Sipha.
4 This hath his kinship checked who lives beside us: with ancient streams forth speeds and rules the
Hero, Anjasi, Kulisi, and Virapatni, delighting him, bear milk upon their waters.
5 Soon as this Dasyu's traces were discovered, as she who knows her home, he sought the dwelling.
Now think thou of us, Maghavan, nor cast us away as doth a profligate his treasure.
6 Indra, as such, give us a share of sunlight, of waters, sinlessness, and reputation.
Do thou no harm to our yet unborn offspring: our trust is in thy mighty Indra-power.
7 Now we, I think, in thee as such have trusted: lead us on, Mighty One, to ample riches.
In no unready house give us, O Indra invoked of many, food and drink when hungry.
8 Slay us not, Indra; do not thou forsake us: steal not away the joys which we delight in.

Rend not our unborn brood, strong Lord of Bounty! our vessels with the life that is within them.
9 Come to us; they have called thee Soma-lover: here is the pressed juice. Drink thereof for rapture.
Widely-capacious, pour it down within thee, and, invocated, hear us like a Father.

## [01-105] HYMN CV. Visvedevas.

1. WITHIN the waters runs the Moon, he with the beauteous wings in heaven.
Ye lightnings with your golden wheels, men find not your abiding-place. Mark this my woe, ye Earth
and Heaven.
2 Surely men crave and gain their wish. Close to her husband clings the wife.
And, in embraces intertwined, both give and take the bliss of love. Mark this my woe, ye Earth and
Heaven.
3 O never may that light , ye Gods, fall from its station in the sky.
Ne'er fail us one like Soma sweet, the spring of our felicity. Mark this my woe ye Earth and Heaven.
4 I ask the last of sacrifice. As envoy he shall tell it forth.
Where is the ancient law divine? Who is its new diffuser now? Mark this my woe, ye Earth and
Heaven.
5 Ye Gods who yonder have your home in the three lucid realms of heaven,
What count ye truth and what untruth? Where is mine ancient call on you? Mark this my woe, ye
Earth and Heaven.
6 What is your firm support of Law? What Varuna's observant eye?
How may we pass the wicked on the path of mighty Aryaman? Mark this my woe, ye Earth and
Heaven.
7 I am the man who sang of old full many a laud when Soma flowed.
Yet torturing cares consume me as the wolf assails the thirsty deer. Mark this my woe, ye Earth and
Heaven.
8 Like rival wives on every side enclosing ribs oppress me sore.
O Satakratu, biting cares devour me, singer of thy praise, as rats devour the weaver's threads. Mark
this my woe, ye Earth and Heaven.
9 Where those seven rays are shining, thence my home and family extend.
This Trta Aptya knoweth well, and speaketh out for brotherhood. Mark this my woe, ye Earth and
Heaven.
10 May those five Bulls which stand on high full in the midst of mighty heaven,
Having together swiftly borne my praises to the Gods, return. Mark this my woe, ye Earth and
Heaven.
11 High in the mid ascent of heaven those Birds of beauteous pinion sit.
Back from his path they drive the wolf as he would cross the restless floods. Mark this my woe, ye
Earth and Heaven.
12 Firm is this new-wrought hymn of praise, and meet to be told forth, O Gods.
The flowing of the floods is Law, Truth is the Sun's extended light. Mark this my woe, ye Earth and
Heaven.
13 Worthy of laud, O Agni, is that kinship which thou hast with Gods.

Here seat thee like a man: most wise, bring thou the Gods for sacrifice. Mark this my woe, ye Earth
and Heaven.
14 Here seated, man-like as a priest shall wisest Agni to the Gods
Speed onward our oblations, God among the Gods, intelligent.
Mark this my woe, ye Earth and
Heaven.
15 Varuna makes the holy prayer. To him who finds the path we pray.
He in the heart reveals his thought. Let sacred worship rise anew.
Mark this my woe, ye Earth and
Heaven.
16 That pathway of the Sun in heaven, made to be highly glorified,
Is not to be transgressed, O Gods. O mortals, ye behold it not.
Mark this my woe, ye Earth and
Heaven.
17 Trta, when buried in the well, calls on the Gods to succour him.
That call of his Brhaspati heard and released him from distress.
Mark this my woe, ye Earth and
Heaven.
18 A ruddy wolf beheld me once, as I was faring on my path.
He, like a carpenter whose back is aching crouched and slunk away. Mark this my woe, ye Earth and
Heaven.
19 Through this our song may we, allied with Indra, with all our heroes conquer in the battle.
This prayer of ours may Varuna grant, and Mitra, and Aditi and Sindhu, Earth and Heaven.

## [01-106] HYMN CVI. Visvedevas.

1. CALL we for aid on Indra, Mitra, Varuna and Agni and the Marut host and Aditi.
Even as a chariot from a difficult ravine, bountiful Vasus, rescue us from all distress.
2 Come ye Adityas for our full prosperity, in conquests of the foe, ye Gods, bring joy to us.
Even as a chariot from a difficult ravine, bountiful Vasus, rescue us from all distress.
3 May the most glorious Fathers aid us, and the two Goddesses, Mothers of the Gods, who
strengthen Law.
Even as a chariot from a difficult ravine, bountiful Vasus, rescue us from all distress.
4 To mighty Narasamsa, strengthening his might, to Pusan, ruler over men, we pray with hymns.
Even as a chariot from a difficult ravine, bountiful Vasus, rescue us from all distress.
5 Brhaspati, make us evermore an easy path: we crave what boon thou hast for men in rest and stir.
Like as a chariot from a difficult ravine, bountiful Vasus, rescue us from all distress.
6 Sunk in the pit the Rsi Kutsa called, to aid, Indra the Vrtra-slayer, Lord of power and might.
Even as a chariot from a difficult ravine, bountiful Vasus, rescue us from all distress.
7 May Aditi the Goddess guard us with the Gods: may the protecting God keep us with ceaseless
care.
This prayer of ours may Varuna grant, and Mitra, and Aditi and Sindhu, Earth and Heaven.

## [01-107] HYMN CVII. Visvedevas.

1. THE sacrifice obtains the Gods' acceptance: be graciously inclined to us, Adityas.
Hitherward let your favour be directed, and be our best deliverer from trouble.

2 By praise-songs of Angirases exalted, may!he Gods come to us with their protection.
May Indra with his powers, Maruts with Maruts, Aditi with Adityas grant us shelter.
3 This laud of ours may Varuna and Indra, Aryaman Agni, Savitar find pleasant.
This prayer' of ours may Varuna grant, and Mitra, and Aditi and Sindhu, Earth and Heaven.

## [01-108] HYMN CVIII. Indra-Agni.

1. ON that most wondrous car of yours, O Indra and Agni, which looks round on all things living,
Take ye your stand and come to us together, and drink libations of the flowing Soma.
2 As vast as all this world is in its compass, deep as it is, with its far-stretching surface,
So let this Soma be, Indra and Agni, made for your drinking till your soul be sated.
3 For ye have won a blessed name together: yea, with one aim ye strove, O Vrtra-slayers.
So Indra-Agni, seated here together, pour in, ye Mighty Ones, the mighty Soma.
4 Both stand adorned, when fires are duly kindled, spreading the sacred grass, with lifted ladles.
Drawn by strong Soma juice poured forth around us, come, Indra-Agni, and display your favour.
5 The brave deeds ye have done, Indra and Agni, the forms ye have displayed and mighty exploits,
The ancient and auspicious bonds of friendship,-for sake of these drink of the flowing Soma.
6 As first I said when choosing you, in battle we must contend with Asuras for this Soma.
So came ye unto this my true conviction, and drank libations of the flowing Soma.
7 If in your dwelling, or with prince or Brahman, ye, Indra-Agni, Holy Ones, rejoice you,
Even frorn thence, ye mighty Lords, come hither, and drink libation of the flowing Soma.
8 If with, the Yadus, Turvasas, ye sojourn, with Druhyus, Anus, Purus, Indra-Agni!
Even from thence, ye mighty Lords, come hither, and drink libations of the flowing Soma.
9 Whether, O Indra-Agni, ye be dwelling in lowest earth, in central, or in highest.
Even from thence, ye mighty Lords, come hither, and drink libations of the flowing Soma.
10 Whether, O Indra-Agni, ye be dwelling in highest earth, in central, or in lowest,
Even from thence, ye mighty Lords, come hither, and drink libations of the flowing Soma.
11 Whether ye be in heaven, O Indra-Agni, on earth, on mountains, in the herbs, or waters,
Even from thence, ye mighty Lords, come hither, and drink libations of the flowing Soma.
12 If, when the Sun to the mid-heaven hath mounted, ye take delight in food, O Indra-Agni,
Even from thence, ye mighty Lords, come hither, and drink libations of the flowing Soma.
13 Thus having drunk your fill of our libation, win us all kinds of wealth, Indra and Agni.
This prayer of ours may Varuna grant, and Mitra, and Aditi and Sindhu, Earth and Heaven.

## [01-109] HYMN CIX. Indra-Agni.

1. LONGING for weal I looked around, in spirit, for kinsmen, Indra-Agni, or for brothers.

No providence but yours alone is with me so have I wrought for you this hymn for succour.
2 For I have heard that ye give wealth more freely than worthless son-in-law or spouse's brother.
So offering to you this draught of Soma, I make you this new hymn, Indra and Agni,
3 Let us not break the cords: with this petition we strive to gain the powers of our forefathers.
For Indra-Agni the strong drops are joyful-, for here in the bowl's lap are both the press-stones.
4 For you the bowl divine, Indra and Agni, presses the Soma gladly to delight you.
With hands auspicious and fair arms, ye Asvins, haste, sprinkle it with sweetness in the waters.
5 You, I have heard, were mightiest, Indra-Agni, when Vrtra fell and when the spoil was parted.
Sit at this sacrifice, ye ever active, on the strewn grass, and with the juice delight you.
6 Surpassing all men where they shout for battle, ye Twain exceed the earth and heaven in greatness.
Greater are ye than rivers and than mountains, O Indra-Agni, and all things beside them.
7 Bring wealth and give it, ye whose arms wield thunder: Indra and Agni, with your powers protect us.
Now of a truth these be the very sunbeams wherewith our fathers were of old united.
8 Give, ye who shatter forts, whose hands wield thunder: Indra and Agni, save us in our battles.
This prayer of ours may Varuna grant, and Mitra, and Aditi and Sindhu, Earth and Heaven.

## [01-110] HYMN CX. Rbhus.

1. THE holy work I wrought before is wrought again: my sweetest hymn is sung to celebrate your praise.
Here, O ye Rbhus, is this sea for all the Gods: sate you with Soma offered with the hallowing word.
2 When, seeking your enjoyment onward from afar, ye, certain of my kinsmen, wandered on your way,
Sons of Sudhanvan, after your long journeying, ye came unto the home of liberal Savitar.
3 Savitar therefore gave you immortality, because ye came proclaiming him whom naught can hide;
And this the drinking-chalice of the Asura, which till that time was one, ye made to be fourfold.
4 When they had served with zeal at sacrifice as priests, they, mortal as they were, gained immortality.
The Rbhus, children of Sudhanvan, bright as suns, were in a year's course made associate with prayers.
5 The Rbhus, with a rod measured, as 'twere a field, the single sacrificial chalice. wide of mouth,
Lauded of all who saw, praying for what is best, desiring glorious fame among Immortal Gods.
6 As oil in ladles, we through knowledge will present unto the Heroes of the firmament our hymn,-
The Rbhus who came near with this great Father's speed, and rose to heaven's high sphere to cat the strengthening food.
7 Rbhu to us is Indra freshest in his might, Rbhu with powers and wealth is giver of rich gifts.
Gods, through your favour may we on the happy day quell the attacks of those who pour no offerings forth.

8 Out of a skin, O Rbhus, once ye formed a cow, and brought the mother close unto her calf again.
Sons of Sudhanvan, Heroes, with surpassing skill ye made your aged Parents youthful as before.
9 Help us with strength where spoil is won, O Indra: joined with the gbhus give us varied bounty.
This prayer of ours may Varuna grant, and Mitra, and Aditi and Sindhu, Earth and Heaven.

## [01-111] HYMN CXI. Rbhus.

1. WORKING with skill they wrought the lightly rolling car: they wrought the Bays who bear Indra and bring great gifts.
The Rbhus for their Parents made life young again; and fashioned for the calf a mother by its side.
2 For sacrifice make for us active vital power for skill and wisdom food with noble progeny.
Grant to our company this power most excellent, that with a family all-heroic we may dwell.
3 Do ye, O Rbhus, make prosperity for us, prosperity for car, ye Heroes, and for steed.
Grant us prosperity victorious evermore, conquering foes in battle, strangers or akin.
4 Indra, the Rbhus' Lord, I invocate for aid, the Rbhus, Vajas, Maruts to the Soma draught.
Varuna, Mitra, both, yea, and the Asvins Twain: let them speed us to wealth, wisdom, and victory.
5 May Rbhu send prosperity for battle, may Vaja conquering in the fight protect us.
This prayer of ours may Varuna grant, and Mitra, and Aditi and Sindhu, Earth and Heaven.

## [01-112] HYMN CXII. Asvins.

1 To give first thought to them, I worship Heaven and Earth, and Agni, fair bright glow, to hasten their approach.
Come hither unto us, O Asvins, with those aids wherewith in fight ye speed the war-cry to the spoil.
2 Ample, unfailing, they have mounted as it were an eloquent car that ye may think of us and give.
Come hither unto us, O Asvins, with those aids wherewith ye help our thoughts to further holy acts.
3 Ye by the might which heavenly nectar giveth you are in supreme dominion Lords of all these folk.
Come hither unto us, O Asvins, with those aids wherewith ye, Heroes, made the barren cow give milk.
4 The aids wherewith the Wanderer through his offipring's might, or the Two-Mothered Son shows swiftest mid the swift;
Wherewith the sapient one acquired his triple lore,-Come hither unto us, O Asvins, with those aids.
5 Wherewith ye raised from waters, prisoned and fast bound, Rebha, and Vandana to look upon the light;
Wherewith ye succoured Kapva as he strove to win,-Come hither unto us, O Asvins, with those aids.
6 Wherewith ye rescued Antaka when languishing deep in the pit, and Bhujyu with unfailing help.
And comforted Karkandhu, Vayya, in their woe,-Come hither unto us, O Asvins, with those aids.
7 Wherewith ye gave gucanti wealth and happy home, and made the fiery pit friendly for Atri's sake;
Wherewith ye guarded Purukutsa, Prsnigu, -Come hither unto us, O Agvin;, with those aids.

8 Mighty Ones, with what powers ye gave Paravrj aid what time ye made the blind and lame to see
and walk;
Wherewith ye set at liberty the swallowed quail,-Come hither unto us, O Asvins, with those aids.
9 Wherewith ye quickened the most sweet exhaustless flood, and comforted Vasistha, ye who ne'er
decay;
And to Srutarya, Kutsa, Narya gave your help,-Come hither unto us, O Asvins, with those aids.
10 Wherewith ye helped, in battle of a thousand spoils, Vispala seeking booty, powerless to move.
Wherewith ye guarded friendly Vaga, Asva's son,-Come hither unto us, O Asvins, with those aids.
11 Whereby the cloud, ye Bounteous Givers, shed sweet rain for Dirghasravas, for the merchant
Ausija,
Wherewith ye helped Kaksivan, singer of your praise,-Come hither unto us, O Asvins, with those aids.
12 Wherewith ye made Rasa swell full with water-floods, and urged to victory the car without a
horse;
Wherewith Trisoka drove forth his recovered cows,-Come hither unto us, O Asvins, with those aids.
13 Wherewith ye, compass round the Sun when far away, strengthened Manddatar in his tasks as
lord of lands,
And to sage Bharadvija gave protecting help,-Come hither unto us, O Asvins, with those aids.
14 Wherewith, when Sambara was slain, ye guarded well great Atithigva, Divodisa, Kasoju,
And Trasadasyu when the forts were shattered down,-Come hither unto us, O Asvins, with those
aids.
15 Wherewith ye honoured the great drinker Vamra, and Upastuta and Kali when he gained his wife,
And lent to Vyasva. and to Prthi favouring help,-Come hither unto us, O Asvins, with those aids.
16 Wherewith, O Heroes, ye vouchsafed deliverance to Sayu, Atri, and to Manu long ago;
Wherewith ye shot your shafts in Syumarasmi's cause.-Come hither unto us, O Asvins, with those
aids.
17 Wherewith Patharva, in his majesty of form, shone in his course like to a gathered kindled fire;
Wherewith ye helped Suryata in the mighty fray,-Come hither unto us, O Asvins, with those aids.
18 Wherewith, Angirases! ye triumphed in your heart, and onward went to liberate the flood of milk;
Wherewith ye helped the hero Manu with new strength,-Come hither unto us, O Asvins, with those
aids.
19 Wherewith ye brought awife for Vimada to wed, wherewith ye freely gave the ruddy cows away;
Wherewith ye brought the host of kind Gods to Sudas-Come hither unto us, O Asvins, with those
aids.
20 Wherewith ye bring great bliss to him who offers gifts, wherewith ye have protected Bhujyu,
Adhrigu,
And good and gracious Subhara and Rtastup,-Come hither unto us, O Asvins, with those aids.
21 Wherewith ye served Krsanu where the shafts were shot, and helped the young man's horse to
swiftness in the race;
Wherewith ye bring delicious honey to the bees,-Come hither unto us, O Asvins, with those aids.

22 Wherewith ye speed the hero as he fights for kine in hero battle, in the strife for land and sons,
Wherewith ye safely guard his horses and his car,-Come hither unto us, O Asvins with those aids.
23 Wherewith ye, Lords of Hundred Powers, helped Kutsa, son of Aduni, gave Turviti and Dabhiti
strength,
Favoured Dhvasanti and lent Purusanti help,-Come hither unto us, O Asvins, with those aids.
24 Make ye our speech effectual, O ye Asvins, and this our hymn, ye mighty Wonder-Workers.
In luckless game I call on you for succour . strengthen us also on the field of battle.
25 With, undiminished blessings, O ye Asvins, for evermore both night and day protect us.
This prayer of ours may Varuna grant, and Mitra, and Aditi and Sindhu, Earth and Heaven.

**[01-113] HYMN CXIII. Dawn.**
1. This light is come, amid all lights the fairest; born is the brilliant, far-extending brightness.
Night, sent away for Savitar's uprising, hath yielded up a birth-place for the Morning.
2 The Fair, the Bright is come with her white offspring; to her the Dark One hath resigned her
dwelling.
Akin, immortal, following each other, changing their colours both the heavens move onward.
3 Common, unending is the Sisters' pathway; taught by the Gods, alternately they travel.
Fair-formed, of different hues and yet one-minded, Night and Dawn clash not, neither do they travel.
4 Bright leader of glad sounds, our eyes behold her; splendid in hue she hath unclosed the portals.
She, stirring up the world, hath shown us riches: Dawn hath awakened every living creature.
5 Rich Dawn, she sets afoot the coiled-up sleeper, one for enjoyment, one for wealth or worship,
Those who saw little for extended vision. All living creatures hath the Dawn awakened.
6 One to high sway, one to exalted glory, one to pursue his gain, and one his labour:
All to regard their different vocations, all moving creatures hath the Dawn awakened.
7 We see her there, the Child of Heaven apparent, the young Maid, flushing in her shining raiment.
Thou soyran Lady of all earthly treasure, flush on us here, auspicious Dawn, this morning.
8 She first of endless morns to come hereafter, follows the path of morns that have departed.
Dawn, at her rising, urges forth the living him who is dead she wakes not from his slumber.
9 As thou, Dawn, hast caused Agni to be kindled, and with the Sun's eye hast revealed creation.
And hast awakened men to offer worship, thou hast performed, for Gods, a noble service.
10 How long a time, and they shall be together,-Dawns that have shone and Dawns to shine
hereafter?
She yearns for former Dawns with eager longing, and goes forth gladly shining with the others.
11 Gone are the men who in the days before us looked on the rising of the earlier Morning.
We, we the living, now behold her brightness and they come nigh who shall hereafter see her.
12 Foe-chaser, born of Law, the Law's protectress, joy-giver waker of all pleasant voices,

Auspicious, bringing food for Gods' enjoyment, shine on us here, most bright, O Dawn, this morning.

13 From days eternal hath Dawn shone, the Goddess, and shows this light to-day, endowed with
riches.
So will she shine on days to come immortal she moves on in her own strength, undecaying.

14 In the sky's borders hath she shone in splendour: the Goddess hath thrown off the veil of
darkness.
Awakening the world with purple horses, on her well-harnessed chariot Dawn approaches.

15 Bringing all life-sustaining blessings with her, showing herself she sends forth brilliant lustre.
Last of the countless mornings that have vanished, first of bright morns to come hath Dawn arisen.

16 Arise! the breath, the life, again hath reached us: darkness hath passed away and light
approacheth.
She for the Sun hath left a path to travel we have arrived where men prolong existence.

17 Singing the praises of refulgent Mornings with his hymn's web the priest, the poet rises.
Shine then to-day, rich Maid, on him who lauds thee, shine down on us the gift of life and offpring.

18 Dawns giving sons all heroes, kine and horses, shining upon the man who brings oblations,-
These let the Soma-presser gain when ending his glad songs louder than the voice of Vayu.

19 Mother of Gods, Aditi's forui of glory, ensign of sacrifice, shine forth exalted.
Rise up, bestowing praise on our devotion all-bounteous, niake us chief among the people.

20 Whatever splendid wealth the Dawns bring with them to bless the man who offers praise and
worship,
Even that may Mitra, Varuna vouchsafe us, and Aditi and Sindhu, Earth and Heaven.

## [01-114] HYMN CXIV. Rudra.

1. To the strong Rudra bring we these our songs of praise, to him the Lord of Heros with the braided
hair,
That it be well with all our cattle and our men, that in this village all he healthy and well-fed.

2 Be gracious unto us, O Rudra, bring us joy: thee, Lord of Heroes, thee with reverence will we serve.
Whatever health and strength our father Manu won by sacrifice may we, under thy guidance, gain.

3 By worship of the Gods may we, O Bounteous One, O Rudra, gain thy grace, Ruler of valiant men.
Come to our families, bringing them bliss: may we, whose heroes are uninjured, bring thee sacred
gifts,

4 Hither we call for aid the wise, the wanderer, impetuous Rudra, perfecter of sacri fice.
May he repel from us the anger of the Gods: verily we desire his favourable grace.

5 Him with the braided hair we call with reverence down, the wild-boar of the sky, the red, the
dazzling shape.
May he, his hand filled full of sovran medicines, grant us protection, shelter, and a home secure.

6 To him the Maruts' Father is this hymn addressed, to strengthen Rudra's might, a song more sweet
than sweet.

Grant us, Immortal One, the food which mortals eat: be gracious unto me, my seed, my progeny.

7 O Rudra, harm not either great or small of us, harm not the growing boy, harm not the full-grown
man.
Slay not a sire among us, slay no mother here, and to our own dear bodies, Rudra, do not harm.

8 Harm us not, Rudra, in our seed and progeny, harm us not in the living, nor in cows or steeds,
Slay not our heroes in the fury of thy wrath. Bringing oblations evermore we call to thee.

9 Even as a herdsman I have brought thee hymns of praise: O Father of the Maruts, give us
happiness,
Blessed is thy most favouring benevolence, so, verily, do we desire thy saving help.

10 Far be thy dart that killeth men or cattle: thy bliss be with us, O thou Lord of Heroes.
Be gracious unto us, O God, and bless us, and then vouchsafe us doubly-strong protection.

11 We, seeking help, have spoken and adored him: may Rudra, girt by Maruts, hear our calling.
This prayer of ours may Varuna grant, and Mitra, and Aditi and Sindhu, Earth and Heaven.

## [01-115] HYMN CXV. Surya.

1. THE brilliant presence of the Gods hath risen, the eye of Mitra, Varuna and Agni.
The soul of all that moveth not or moveth, the Sun hath filled the air and earth and heaven.

2 Like as a young man followeth a maiden, so doth the Sun the Dawn, refulgent Goddess:
Where pious men extend their generations, before the Auspicious One for happy fortune.

3 Auspicious are the Sun's Bay-coloured Horses, bright, changing hues, meet for our shouts of
triumph.
Bearing our prayers, die sky's ridge have they mounted, and in a moment speed round earth and
heaven.

4 This is the Godhead, this might of Surya: he hath withdrawn what spread o'er work unfinished.
When he hath loosed his Horses from their station, straight over all Night spreadeth out her garment.

5 In the sky's lap the Sun this form assumeth that Varuna and Mitra may behold it.
His Bay Steeds well maintain his power eternal, at one time bright and darksome at another.

6 This day, O Gods, while Surya is ascending, deliver us from trouble and dishonour.
This prayer of ours may Varuna grant, and Mitra, and Aditi and Sindhu, Earth and Heaven.

## [01-116] HYMN CXVI. Asvins.

1. I TRIM like grass my song for the Nasatyas and send their lauds forth as the wind drives rainclouds,
Who, in a chariot rapid as an arrow, brought to the youthful Vimada a consort.

2 Borne on by rapid steeds of mighty pinion, or proudly trusting in the Gods' incitements.
That stallion ass of yours won, O Nasatyas, that thousand in the race, in Yama's contest.

3 Yea, Asvins, as a dead man leaves his riches, Tugra left Bhujyu in the cloud of waters.
Ye brought him back in animated vessels, traversing air, unwetted by the billows.

4 Bhujyu ye bore with winged things, Nasatyas, which for three nights, three days full swiftly
travelled,
To the sea's farther shore, the strand of ocean, in three cars, hundred-footed, with six horses.
5 Ye wrought that hero exploit in the ocean which giveth no support, or hold or station,
What time ye carried Bhujyu to his dwelling, borne in a ship with hundred oars, O Asvins.
6 The white horse which of old ye gave Aghasva, Asvins, a gift to be his wealth for ever,-
Still to be praised is that your glorious present, still to be famed is the braye horse of Pedu.
7 O Heroes, ye gave wisdom to Kaksivan who sprang from Pajra's line, who sang your praises.
Ye poured forth from the hoof of your strong charger a hundred jars of wine as from a strainer.
8 Ye warded off with cold the fire's fierce burning; food very rich in nouripliment ye furnished.
Atri, cast downward in the cavern, Asvins ye brought, with all his people, forth to comfort.
9 Ye lifted up the well, O ye Nasatyas, and set the base on high to open downward.
Streams flowed for folk of Gotama who thirsted, like rain to bring forth thousandfold abundance.
10 Ye from the old Cyavana, O Nasatyas, stripped, as 'twere mail, the skin upon
his body,
Lengthened his life when all had left him helpless, Dasras! and made him lord of youthful maidens.
11 Worthy of praise and worth the winning, Heroes, is that your favouring succour O Nasatyas,
What time ye, knowing well his case, delivered Vandana trom the pit like hidden treasure.
12 That mighty deed of yours, for gain, O Heroes, as thunder heraldeth the rain, I publish,
When, by the horse's head, Atharvan's offspring Dadhyac made known to you the Soma's sweetness.
13 In the great rite the wise dame called, Nasatyas, you, Lords of many treasures, to assist her.
Ye heard the weakling's wife, as 'twere an order, and gave to her a son Hiranyahasta.
14 Ye from the wolf's jaws, as ye stood together, set free the quail, O Heroes, O Nasatyas.
Ye, Lords of many treasures, gave the poet his perfect vision as he mourned his trouble.
15 When in the time of night, in Khela's battle, a leg was severed like a wild bird's pinion,
Straight ye gave Vispali a leg of iron that she might move what time the conflict opened.
16 His father robbed Rjrasva of his eyesight who for the she-wolf slew a hundred wethers.
Ye gave him eyes, Nasatyas, Wonder-Workers, Physicians, that he saw with sight uninjured.
17 The Daughter of the Sun your car ascended, first reaching as it were the goal with coursers.
All Deities within their hearts assented, and ye, Nasatyas, are close linked with glory.
18 When to his house ye came, to Divodasa, hasting to Bharadvaja, O ye Asvins,
The car that came with you brought splendid riches: a porpoise and a bull were yoked together.
19 Ye, bringing wealth with rule, and life with offspring, life rich in noble heroes; O Nasatyas,
Accordant came with strength to Jahnu's children who offered you thrice every day your portion.

20 Ye bore away at night by easy pathways Jahusa compassed round on every quarter,
And, with your car that cleaves the toe asunder, Nasatyas never decaying! rent the mountains.
21 One morn ye strengthened Vaga for the battle, to gather spoils that might be told in thousands.
With Indra joined ye drove away misfortunes, yea foes of Prthusravas, O ye mighty.
22 From the deep well ye raised on high the water, so that Rcatka's son, Sara, should drink it;
And with your might, to help the weary Sayu, ye made the barren cow yield milk, Nasatyas.
23 To Visvaka, Nasatyas! son of Krsna, the righteous man who sought your aid and praised you,
Ye with your powers restored, like some lost creature, his son Visnapu for his eyes to look on.
24 Asvins, ye raised, like Soma in a ladle Rebha, who for ten days and ten nights, fettered.
Had lain in cruel bonds, immersed and wounded, suffering sore affliction, in the waters.
25 1 have declared your wondrous deeds, O Asvins: may this be mine, and many kine and heroes.
May I, enjoying lengthened life, still seeing, enter old age as 'twere the house I live in.

## [01-117] HYMN CXVII. Asvins.

1. ASVINS, your ancient priest invites you hither to gladden you with draughts of meath of Soma.
Our gift is on the grass, our song apportioned: with food and strength come hither, O Nasatyas.
2 That car of yours, swifter than thought, O Asvins, which drawn by brave steeds cometh to the
people,
Whereon ye seek the dwelling of the pious,-come ye thereon to our abode, O Heroes.
3 Ye freed sage Atri, whom the Five Tribes honoured, from the strait pit, ye Heroes with his people,
Baffling the guiles of the malignant Dasyu, repelling them, ye Mighty in succession.
4 Rebha the sage, ye mighty Heroes, Asvins! whom, like a horse, vile men had sunk in water,-
Him, wounded, with your wondrous power ye rescued: your exploits of old time endure for ever.
5 Ye brought forth Vandana, ye Wonder-Workers, for triumph, like fair gold that hath been buried,
Like one who slumbered in destruction's bosom, or like the Sun when dwelling in the darkness.
6 Kaksivan, Pajra's son, must laud that exploit of yours, Nasatyas, Heroes, ye who wander!
When from the hoof of your strong horse ye showered a hundred jars of honey for the people.
7 To Krsna's son, to Visvaka who praised you, O Heroes, ye restored his son Visnapu.
To Ghosa, living in her father's dwelling, stricken in years, ye gave a husband, Asvins.
8 Rusati, of the mighty people, Asvins, ye gave to Syava of the line of Kanva.
This deed of yours, ye Strong Ones should be published, that ye gave glory to the son of Nrsad.
9 O Asvins, wearing many forms at pleasure, on Pedu ye bestowed a fleet-foot courser,
Strong, winner of a thousand spoils, resistless the serpent slayer, glorious, triumphant.
10 These glorious things are yours, ye Bounteous Givers; prayer, praise in both worlds are your
habitation.

O Asvins, when the sons of Paira call you, send strength with nourishment to him who knoweth.
11 Hymned with the reverence of a son, O Asvins ye Swift Ones giving booty to the singer,
Glorified by Agastya with devotion, established Vispala again, Nasatyas.
12 Ye Sons of Heaven, ye Mighty, whither went ye, sought ye, for his fair praise the home of Kdvya.
When, like a pitcher full of gold, O Asvins, on the tenth day ye lifted up the buried?
13 Ye with the aid of your great powers, O Asvins, restored to youth the ancient man Cyavana.
The Daughter of the Sun with all her glory, O ye Nasatyas, chose your car to bear her.
14 Ye, ever-youthful Ones, again remembered Tugra, according to your ancient manner:
With horses brown of hue that flew with swift wings ye brought back Bhujyu from the sea of billows.
15 The son of Tugra had invoked you, Asvins; borne on he went uninjured through the ocean.
Ye with your chariot swift as thought, well-harnessed, carried him off, O Mighty Ones, to safety.
16 The quail had invocated you, O Asvins, when from the wolf's devouring jaws ye freed her.
With conquering car ye cleft the mountain's ridges: the offspring of Visvac ye killed with poison.
17 He whom for furnishing a hundred wethers to the she-wolf, his wicked father blinded,
To him, Rjrasva, gave ye eyes, O Asvins; light to the blind ye sent for perfect vision.
18 To bring the blind man joy thus cried the she-wolf: O Asvins, O ye Mighty Ones, O Heroes,
For me Rjrasva, like a youthful lover, hath. cut piecemeal one and a hundred wethers.
19 Great and weal-giving is your aid, O Asvins, ye, objects of all thought, made whole the cripple.
Purandhi also for this cause invoked you, and ye, O mighty, came to her with succours.
20 Ye, Wonder-Workers, filled with milk for Sayu the milkless cow, emaciated, barren;
And by your powers the child of Purumitra ye brought to Vimada to be his consort.
21 Ploughing and sowing barley, O ye Asvins, milking out food for men, ye Wonder-Workers,
Blasting away the Dasyu with your trumpet, ye gave far-spreading light unto the Arya.
22 Ye brought the horse's head, Asvins, and gave it unto Dadhyac the offspring of Atharvan.
True, he revealed to you, O WonderWorkers, sweet Soma, Tvastar's secret, as your girdle.
23 O Sages, evermore I crave your favour: be gracious unto all my prayers, O Asvins.
Grant me, Nasatyas, riches in abundance, wealth famous and accompanied with children.
24 With liberal bounty to the weakling's consorts ye, Heroes, gave a son Hiranyahasta;
And Syava, cut into three several pieces, ye brought to life again, O bounteous Asvins.
25 These your heroic exploits, O ye Asvins, done in the days. of old, have men related.
May we, addressing prayer to you, ye Mighty, speak with brave sons about us to. the synod.

## [01-118] HYMN CXVIII. Asvins.
1. FLYING, with falcons, may your chariot, Asvins, most gracious, bringing friendly
help, come hither,-

Your chariot, swifter than the mind of mortal, fleet as the wind, three-seated O ye Mighty.
2 Come to us with your chariot triple seated, three-wheeled, of triple form, that rolleth lightly.
Fill full our cows, give mettle to our horses, and make each hero son grow strong, O Asvins.
3 With your well-rolling car, descending swiftly, hear this the press-stone's song, ye Wonder-
Workers.
How then have ancient sages said, O Asvins, that ye most swiftly come to stay affliction?
4 O Asvins, let your falcons bear you hither, yoked to your chariot, swift, with flying pinions,
Which, ever active, like the airy eagles, carry you, O Nasatyas, to the banquet.
5 The youthful Daughter of the Sun, delighting in you, ascended there your chariot, Heroes.
Borne on their swift wings let your beauteous horses, your birds of ruddy hue, convey you near us.
6 Ye raised up Vandana, strong WonderWorkers! with great might, and with power ye rescued
Rebha.
From out the sea ye saved the son of Tugra, and gave his youth again unto Cyavana.
7 To Atri, cast down to the fire that scorched him, ye gave, O Asvins, strengthening tbod and favour.
Accepting his fair praises with approval, ye gave his eyes again to blinded Kanva.
8 For ancient Sayti in his sore affliction ye caused his cow to swell with milk, O Asvins.
The quail from her great misery ye delivered, and a new leg for Vispala provided.
9 A white horse, Asvins, ye bestowed on Pedu, a serpent-slaying steed sent down by Indra,
Loud-neighing, conquering the foe, highmettled, firm-limbed and vigorous, winning thousand
treasures.
10 Such as ye are, O nobly horn, O Heroes, we in our trouble call on you for succour.
Accepting these our songs, for our wellbeing come to us on your chariot treasure-laden.
11 Come unto us combined in love, Nasatyas come with the fresh swift vigour of the falcon.
Bearing oblations I invoke you, Asvins, at the first break of everlasting morning.

## [01-119] HYMN CXIX. Asvins.
1. HITHER, that I may live, I call unto the feast your wondrous car, thought-swift, borne on by rapid
steeds.
With thousand banners, hundred treasures, pouring gifts, promptly obedient, bestowing ample room.
2 Even as it moveth near my hymn is lifted up, and all the regions come together to sing praise.
I sweeten the oblations; now the helpers come. Urjani hath, O Asvins, mounted on your car.
3 When striving man with man for glory they have met, brisk, measurcless, eager for victory in fight,
Then verily your car is seen upon the slope when ye, O Asvins, bring some choice boon to the prince.
4 Ye came to Bhujyu while he struggled in the flood, with flying birds, self-yoked, ye bore him to his
sires.
Ye went to the far-distant home, O Mighty Ones; and famed is your great aid to Divodisa given.
5 Asvins, the car which you had yoked for glorious show your own two voices urged directed to its goal.

Then she who came for friendship, Maid of noble birth, elected you as Husbands, you to be her Lords.
6 Rebha ye saved from tyranny; for Atri's sake ye quenched with cold the fiery pit that compassed him.
Ye made the cow of Sayu stream refreshing milk, and Vandana was holpen to extended life.
7 Doers of marvels, skilful workers, ye restored Vandana, like a car, worn out with length of days.
From earth ye brought the sage to life in wondrous mode; be your great deeds done here for him who honours you.
8 Ye went to him who mourned in a far distant place, him who was left forlorn by treachery of his
sire.
Rich with the light ofheaven was then the help ye gave, and marvellous your succour when ye stood
by him.
9 To you in praise of sweetness sang the honey-bee: Ausija calleth you in Soma's rapturous joy.
Ye drew unto yourselves the spirit of Dadhyac, and then the horse's head uttered his words to you.
10 A horse did ye provide for Pedu, excellent, white, O ye Asvins, conqueror of combatants,
Invincible in war by arrows, seeking heaven worthy of fame, like Indra, vanquisher of men.

## [01-120] HYMN CXX. Asvins.

1. ASVINS, what praise may win your grace? Who may be pleasing to you both?
How shall the ignorant worship you?
2 Here let the ignorant ask the means of you who know-for none beside you knoweth aught -
Not of a spiritless mortal man.
3 Such as ye: are, all-wise, we call you. Ye wise, declare to us this day accepted prayer.
Loving you well your servant lauds you.
4 Simply, ye Mighty Ones, I ask the Gods of that wondrous oblation hallowed by the mystic word.
Save us from what is stronger, fiercer than ourselves.
5 Forth go the hymn that shone in Ghosa Bhrgu's like, the song wherewith the son of Pajra worships you,
Like some wise minister.
6 Hear ye the song of him who hastens speedily. O Asvins, I am he who sang your praise.
Hither, ye Lords of Splendour, hither turn your eyes.
7 For ye were ever nigh to deal forth ample wealth, to give the wealth that ye had gathered up.
As such, ye Vasus, guard us well, and keep us safely from the wicked wolf.
8 Give us not up to any man who hateth us, nor let our milch-cows stray, whose udders give us food,
Far from our homes without their calves.
9 May they who love you gain you for their Friends. Prepare ye us for opulence with strengthening
food,
Prepare us for the food that floweth from our cows
10 1 have obtained the horseless car of Asvins rich in sacrifice, And I am well content therewith.
11 May it convey me evermore: may the light chariot pass from men
To men unto the Soma draught.
12 It holdeth slumber in contempt. and the rich who enjoyeth not:
Both vanish quickly and are lost.

## [01-121] HYMN CXXI, Indra.

1. WHEN Will men's guardians hasting hear with favour the song of Angiras's pious childern?

When to the people of the home he cometh he strideth to the sacrifice, the Holy.
2 He stablished heaven; he poured forth, skilful worker, the wealth of kine, for strength, that nurtures heroes.
The Mighty One his self-born host regarded, the horse's mate, the mother of the heifer.
3 Lord of red dawns, he came victorious, daily to the Angirases' former invocation.
His bolt and team hath he prepared, and stablished the heaven for quadrupeds and men two-footed.
4 In joy of this thou didst restore, for worship, the lowing company of hidden cattle.
When the three-pointed one descends with onslaught he opens wide the doors that cause man trouble.
5 Thine is that milk which thy swift-moving Parents brought down, a strengthening genial gift for
conquest;
When the pure treasure unto thee they offered, the milk shed from the cow who streameth nectar.
6 There is he born. May the Swift give us rapture, and like the Sun shine forth from yonder dawning,
Indu, even us who drank, whose toils are offerings, poured from the spoon, with praise, upon the altar.
7 When the wood-pile, made of good logs, is ready, at the Sun's worship to bind fast the Bullock,
Then when thou shinest forth through days of action for the Car-borne, the Swift, tile Cattle-seeker.
8 Eight steeds thou broughtest down from mighty heaven, when fighting for the well that giveth splendour,
That men might press with stones the gladdening yellow, strengthened with milk, fermenting, to exalt thee.
9 Thou hurledst forth from heaven the iron missile, brought by the Skilful, from the sling of leather,
When thou, O Much-invoked, assisting Kutsa with endless deadly darts didst compass Susna.
10 Bolt-armed, ere darkness overtook the sunlight, thou castest at the veiling cloud thy weapon,
Thou rentest, out of heaven, though firmly knotted, the might of Susna that was thrown around him.
11 The mighty Heaven and Earth, those bright expanses that have no wheels, joyed, Indra, at thine exploit.
Vrtra, the boar who lay amid the waters, to sleep thou sentest with thy mighty thunder.
12 Mount Indra, lover of the men thou guardest, the well-yoked horses of the wind, best bearers.
The bolt which Kavya Usana erst gave thee, strong, gladdening, Vrtra-slaying, hath he fashioned *
13 The strong Bay Horses of the Sun thou stayedst: this Etasa drew not the wheel, O Indra.
Casting them forth beyond the ninety rivers thou dravest down into the pit the godless.
14 Indra, preserve thou us from this affliction Thunder-armed, save us from the misery near us.
Vouchsafe us affluence in chariots, founded on horses, for our food and fame and gladness.
15 Never may this thy loving-kindness fail us; mighty in strength, may plenteous food surround us.
Maghavan, make us share the foeman's cattle: may we be thy most liberal feast companions.

## [01-122] HYMN CXXII Visvadevas.

1. SAY, bringing sacrifice to bounteous Rudra, This juice for drink to you whose wrath is fleeting!
With Dyaus the Asura's Heroes I have lauded the Maruts as with prayer to Earth and Heaven.
2 Strong to exalt the early invocation are Night and Dawn who show with varied aspect.

The Barren clothes her in wide-woven raiment, and fair Morn shines with Surya's golden splendour.

3 Cheer us the Roamer round, who strikes at morning, the Wind delight us, pourer forth of waters!

Sharpen our wits, O Parvata and Indra. May all the Gods vouchsafe to us this favour.

4 And Ausija shall call for me that famous Pair who enjoy and drink, who come to brighten.

Set ye the Offspring of the Floods before you; both Mothers of the Living One who beameth.

5 For you shall Ausija call him who thunders, as, to win Arjuna's assent, cried Ghosa.

I will invoke, that Pusan may be bounteous to you, the rich munificence of Agni.

6 Hear, Mitra-Varuna, these mine invocations, hear them from all men in the hall of worship.

Giver of famous gifts, kind hearer, Sindhu who gives fair fields, listen with all his waters 1

7 Praised, Mitra, Varuna! is your gift, a hundred cows to the Prksayamas and the Pajra.

Presented by car-famous Priyaratha, supplying nourishment, they came directly.

8 Praised is the gift of him the very wealthy: may we enjoy it, men with hero children:

His who hath many gifts to give the Pajras, a chief who makes me rich in cars and horses.

9 The folk, O Mitra-Varuna, who hate you, who sinfully hating pour you no libations,

Lay in their hearts, themselves, a wasting sickness, whereas the righteous gaineth all by worship.

10 That man, most puissant, wondrously urged onward, famed among heroes, liberal in giving,

Moveth a warrior, evermore undaunted in all encounters even with the mighty.

11 Come to the man's, the sacrificer's calling: hear, Kings of Immortality, joy-givers!

While ye who speed through clouds decree your bounty largely, for fame, to him the chariot rider.

12 Vigour will we bestow on that adorer whose tenfold draught we come to taste, so spake they.

May all in whom rest splendour and great riches obtain refreshment in these sacrifices.

13 We will rejoice to drink the tenfold present when the twicefive come bearing sacred viands.

What can he do whose steeds and reins are choicest? These, the all-potent, urge brave men to conquest.

14 The sea and all the Deities shall give us him with the golden car and neck bejewelled.

Dawns, hasting to the praises otthe pious, be pleased with us. both offerers and singers.

15 Four youthful sons of Masarsara vex me, three, of the king, the conquering Ayavasa.

Now like the Sun, O Varuna and Mitra, your car hath shone, long-shaped and reined with splendour.

## [01-123] HYMN CXXIII. Dawn.

1. THE Daksina's broad chariot hath been harnessed: this car the Gods Immortal have ascended.

Fain to bring light to homes of men the noble and active Goddess hath emerged from darkness.

2 She before all the living world hath wakened, the Lofty One who wins and gathers treasure.

Revived and ever young on high she glances. Dawn hath come first unto our morning worship.

3 If, Dawn, thou Goddess nobly born, thou dealest fortune this day to all the race of mortals,

May Savitar the God, Friend of the homestead, declare before the Sun that we are sinless.

4 Showing her wonted form each day that passeth, spreading the light she visiteth each dwelling.

Eager for conquest, with bright sheen she cometh. Her portion is the best of goodly treasures.

5 Sister of Varuna, sister of Bhaga, first among all sing forth, O joyous Morning.

Weak be the strength of him who worketh evil - may we subdue him with our car the guerdon.

6 Let our glad hymns and holy thoughts rise upward, for the flames brightly burning have ascended.

The far-refulgent Mornings make apparent the lovely treasures which the darkness covered.

7 The one departeth and the other cometh: unlike in hue day's, halves march on successive.

One hides the gloom of the surrounding Parents. Dawn on her shining chariot is resplendent.

8 The same in form to-day, the same tomorrow, they still keep Varuna's eternal statute.

Blameless, in turn they traverse thirty regions, and dart across the spirit in a moment.

9 She who hath knowledge Of the first day's nature is born refulgent white from out the darkness.

The Maiden breaketh not the law of Order, day by day coming to the place appointed.

10 In pride of beauty like a maid thou goest, O Goddess, to the God who longs to win thee,

And smiling youthful, as thou shinest brightly, before him thou discoverest thy bosom.

11 Fair as a bride embellished by her mother thou showest forth thy form that all may see it.

Blessed art thou O Dawn. Shine yet more widely. No other Dawns have reached what thou attainest.

12 Rich in kine, horses, and all goodly treasures, in constant operation with the sunbeams,

The Dawns depart and come again again assuming their wonted forms that promise happy fortune.

13 Obedient to the rein of Law Eternal give us each thought that more and more shall bless us.

Shine thou on us to-day, Dawn, swift to listen. With us be riches and with chiefs who worship.

## [01-124] HYMN CXXIV. Dawn.

1. THE Dawn refulgent when the fire is kindled, and the Sun rising, far diffuse their brightness.

Savitar, God, hath sentus forth to labour, each quadruped, each biped, to be active.

2 Not interrupting heavenly ordinances, although she minisheth human generations.

The last of endless morns that have departed, the first of those that come, Dawn brightly shineth.

3 There in the eastern region she, Heaven's Daughter, arrayed in garments all of light, appeareth.

Truly she fo1loweth the path of Order, nor faileth, knowing well, the heavenly quarters.

4 Near is she seen, as 'twere the Bright One's bosom: she showeth sweet things like a new songsinger.

She cometh like a fly awaking sleepers, of all. returning dames most true and constant.

5 There in the east half of the watery region the Mother of the Cows hath shown her ensign.

Wider and wider still she spreadeth onward, and filleth full the laps of both heir Parents.

6 She, verily, exceeding vast to look on debarreth from her light nor kin nor stranger.

Proud of her spotless form she, brightly shiming, turneth not from the high nor froom the humble.

7 She seeketh men, as she who hath no brother, mounting her car, as 'twere to gather riches.

Dawn, like a loving matron for her husband, smiling and well attired, unmasks her beauty.

8 The Sister quitteth, for the elder Sister, her place, and having looked on her departeth.

She decks her beauty, shining forth with sunbeams, like women trooping to the festal meeting.

9 To all these Sisters who ere now have vanished a later one each day in course succeedeth.

So, like the past, with days of happy fortune, may the new Dawns shine forth on us with riches.

10 Rouse up, O Wealthy One, the liberal givers; let niggard traffickers sleep on unwakened:

Shine richly, Wealthy One, on those who worship, richly, glad. Dawn while wasting, on the singer.

11 This young Maid from the east hath shone upon us; she harnesseth her team of bright red oxen.

She will beam forth, the light will hasten hither, and Agni will be present in each dwelling.

12 As the birds fly forth from their resting places, so men with store of food rise at thy dawning.

Yea, to the liberal mortal who remaineth at home, O Goddess Dawn, much good thou bringest.

13 Praised through my prayer be ye who should be lauded. Ye have increased our wealth, ye Dawns who love us.

Goddesses, may we win by your good favour wealth to be told by hundreds and by thousands.

## [01-125] HYMN CXXV. Svanaya.

1. COMING at early morn he gives his treasure; the prudent one receives and entertains him.

Thereby increasing still his life and offspring, he comes with brave sons to abundant riches.

2 Rich shall he be in gold and kine and horses. Indra bestows on him great vital power,

Who stays thee, as thou comest, with his treasure, like game caught in the net, O early comer.

3 Longing, I came this morning to the pious, the son of sacrifice, with car wealth. laden.

Give him to drink juice of the stalk that gladdens; prosper with pleasant hymns the Lord of Heroes.

4 Health-bringing streams, as milch-cows, flow to profit him who hath worshipped, him who now will worship.

To him who freely gives and fills on all sides full streams of fatness flow and make him famous.

5 On the high ridge of heaven he stands exalted, yea, to the Gods he goes, the liberal giver.

The streams, the waters flow for him with fatness: to him this guerdon ever yields abundance.

6 For those who give rich meeds are all these splendours, for those who give rich meeds suns shine in heaven.

The givers of rich meeds are made immortal; the givers of rich fees prolong their lifetime.

7 Let not the liberal sink to sin and sorrow, never decay the pious -chiefs who worship!

Let every man besides be their protection, and let affliction fall upon the niggard.

## [01-126] HYMN CXXVI. Bhavayavya.

1. WITH wisdom I present these lively praises of Bhavya dweller on the bank of Sindhu;

For he, unconquered King, desiring glory, hath furnished me a thousand sacrifices.

2 A hundred necklets from the King, beseeching, a hundred gift-steeds I at once accepted;

Of the lord's cows a thousand, I Kaksivan. His deathless glory hath he spread to heaven.

3 Horses of dusky colour stood beside me, ten chariots, Svanaya's gift, with mares to draw them.

Kine numbering sixty thousand followed after. Kaksivan gained them when the days were closing.

4 Forty bay horses of the ten cars' master before a thousand lead the long procession.

Reeling in joy Kaksivan's sons and Pajra's have grounded the coursers decked with pearly trappings.

5 An earlier gift for you have I accepted eight cows, good milkers, and tree harnessed horses,

Pajras, who with your wains with your great kinsman, like troops of subjects, have been fain for
glory.

6

## [01-127] HYMN CXXVII Agni.

1. AGNI I hold as herald, the munificent, the gracious, Son of Strength, who knoweth all that live, as
holy Singer, knowing all,

Lord of fair rites, a God with form erected turning to the Gods, He, when the flame hath sprung forth from the holy oil, the offered fatness, longeth for it with his
glow.

2 We, sacrificing, call on thee best worshipper, the eldest of Angirases, Singer, with hymns, thee,
brilliant One! with singers' hymns;

Thee, wandering round as 't were the sky, who art the invoking Priest of men,

Whom, Bull with hair of flame the people must observe, the people that he speed them on.

3 He with his shining glory blazing far and wide, he verily it is who slayeth demon foes, slayeth the
demons like an axe:

At whose close touch things solid shake, and what is stable yields like trees.

Subduing all, he keeps his ground and flinches not, from the skilled archer flinches not.

4 To him, as one who knows, even things solid yield: unrough fire-sticks heated hot he gives his gifts
to aid. Men offer Agni gifts for aid.

He deeply piercing many a thing hews it like wood with fervent glow.

Even hard and solid food he crunches with his might, yea, hard and solid food with might.

5 Here near we place the sacrificial food for him who shines forth fairer in the night than in the day,
with life then stronger than by day.

His life gives sure and firm defence as that one giveth to a son.

The during fires enjoy things given and things not given, the during fires enjoy as food.

6 He, roaring very loudly like the Maruts' host, in fertile cultivated fields adorable, in desert spots
adorable,

Accepts and eats our offered gifts, ensign of sacrifice by desert;

So let all, joying, love his path when he is glad, as men pursue a path for bliss.

7 Even as they who sarig forth hymns, addressed to heaven, the Blirgus with their prayer and praise
invited him, the Bhrgus rubbing, offering gifts.

For radiant Agni, Lord of all these treasures, is exceeding strong.

May he, the wise, accept the grateful coverings, the wise accept the coverings.

8 Thee we invoke, the Lord of all our settled homes, common to all, the household's guardian, to

enjoy, bearer of true hymns, to enjoy.

Thee we invoke, the guest of men, by whose mouth, even as a sire's,

All these Immortals come to gain their food of life, oblations come to Gods as food.

9 Thou, Agni, most victorious with thy conquering strength, most Mighty One, art born for service of

the Gods, like wealth for service of the Gods.

Most mighty is thine ecstasy, most splendid is thy mental power. Therefore men wait upon thee, undecaying One, like vassals, undecaying One.

10 To him the mighty, conquering with victorious strength, to Agni walking with the dawn, who

sendeth kine, be sung your laud, to Agni sung;

As he who with oblation comes calls him aloud in every place. Before the brands of fire he shouteth singerlike, the herald, kindler of the brands.

11 Agni, beheld by us in nearest neighbourhood, accordant with the Gods, bring us, with gracious

love, great riches with thy gracious love.

Give us O Mightiest, what is great, to see and to enjoy the earth. As one of awful power, stir up heroic might for those who praise thee, Bounteous Lord!

## [01-128] HYMN CXXVIII. Agni.

1. By Manu's law was born this Agni, Priest most skilled, born for the holy work of those who yearn

therefore, yea, born for his own holy work.

All ear to him who seeks his love and wealth to him who strives for fame,

Priest ne'er deceived, he sits in Ila's holy place, girt round in Ila's holy place.

2 We call that perfecter of worship by the path or sacrifice; with reverence rich in offerings, with

worship rich in offerings.

Through presentation of our food he grows not old in this his from;

The God whom Matarisvan brought from far away, for Manu brought from far away.

3 In ordered course forthwith he traverses the earth, swift-swallowing, bellowing Steer, bearing the

genial seed, bearing the seed and bellowing.

Observant with a hundred eyes the God is conqueror in the wood: Agni, who hath his seat in broad plains here below, and in the high lands far away.

4 That Agni, wise High-Priest, in every house takes thought for sacrifice and holy service, yea, takes

thought, with mental power, for sacrifice.

Disposer, he with mental power shows all things unto him who strives;

Whence he was born a guest enriched with holy oil, born as Ordainer and as Priest.

5 When through his power and in his strong prevailing flames the Maruts' gladdening boons mingle

with Agni's roar, boons gladdening for the active One,

Then he accelerates the gift, and by the greatness of his wealth,

Shall rescue us from overwhelming misery, from curse and overwhelming woe.

6 Vast, universal, good he was made messenger; the speeder with his right hand hath not loosed his

hold, through love of fame not loosed his hold.

He bears oblations to the Gods for whosoever supplicates.

Agni bestows a blessing on each pious man, and opens wide the doors for him.

7 That Agni hath been set most kind in camp of men, in sacrifice like a Lord victorious, like a dear

Lord in sacred rites.

His are the oblations of mankind when offered up at Ili's place. He shall preserve us from Varuna's chastisement, yea, from the great God's chastisement.

8 Agni the Priest they supplicate to grant them wealth: him, dear, most thoughtful, have they made

their messenger, him, offering-bearer have they made,

Beloved of all, who knoweth all, the Priest, the Holy one, the Sage-

Him, Friend, for help, the Gods when they are fain for wealth, him, Friend, with hymns, when fain for

wealth.

## [01-129] HYMN CXXIX Indra.

1. THE car which Indra, thou, for service of the Gods though it be far away, O swift One, bringest

near, which, Blameless One, thou bringest near,

Place swiftly nigh us for our help: be it thy will that it be strong. Blameless and active, hear this speech of orderers, this speech of us like orderers.

2 Hear, Indra, thou whom men in every fight must call to show thy strength, for cry of battle with the

men, with men of war for victory.

He who with heroes wins the light, who with the singers gains the prize,

Him the rich seek to gain even as a swift strong steed, even as a courser fleet and strong.

3 Thou, Mighty, pourest forth the hide that holds the rain, thou keepest far away, Hero, the wicked

man, thou shuttest out the wicked man.

Indra, to thee I sing, to Dyaus, to Rudra glorious in himself, To Mitra, Varuna I sing a far-famed hymn to the kind God a far-famed hymn.

4 We. wish our Indra here that he may further you, the Friend, beloved of all, the very strong ally, in

wars the very strong ally

In all encounters strengthen thou our prayer to be a help to us. No enemy-whom thou smitest downsubdueth thee, no enemy, whom thou smitest down.

5 Bow down the overweening pride of every foe with succour like to kindling-wood in fiercest flame,

with mighty succour, Mighty One.

Guide us, thou Hero, as of old, so art thou counted blameless still. Thou drivest, as a Priest, all sins of man away, as Priest, in person, seeking us.

6 This may I utter to the present Soma-drop, which, meet to be invoked, with power, awakes the

prayer, awakes the demon-slaying prayer.

May he himself with darts of death drive far from us the scorner's hate.

Far let him flee away who speaketh wickedness and vanish like a mote of dust.

7 By thoughtful invocation this may we obtain, obtain great wealth, O Wealthy One, with Hero sons,

wealth that is sweet with hero sons.

Him who is wroth we pacify with sacred food and eulogies, Indra the Holy with our calls inspired and true, the Holy One with calls inspired.

8 On, for your good and ours, come Indra with the aid of his own lordliness to drive the wicked hence,

to rend the evilhearted ones!

The weapon which devouring fiends cast at us shall destroy themselves.

Struck down, it shall not reach the mark; hurled forth, the fire-brand shall not strike.

9 With riches in abundance, Indra, come to us, come by an unobstructed path, come by a path from
demons free.
Be with us when we stray afar, be with us when our home is nigh.
Protect us with thy help both near and far away: protect us ever with thy help.

10 Thou art our own, O Indra, with victorious wealth: let might accompany thee, the Strong, to give
us aid, like Mitra, to give mighty aid.
O strongest saviour, helper thou, Immortal! of each warrior's car.
Hurt thou another and not us, O Thunderarmed, one who would hurt, O Thunder-armed!

11 Save us from injury, thou who art well extolled: ever the warder-off art thou of wicked ones, even
as a God, of wicked ones;
Thou slayer of the evil fiend, saviour of singer such as I.
Good Lord, the Father made thee slayer of the fiends, made thee, good Lord, to slay the fiends.

## [01-130] HYMN CXXX. Indra.

1. Come to us, Indra, from afar, conducting us even as a lord of heroes to the gatherings, home, like a
King, his heroes' lord.
We come with gifts of pleasant food, with juice poured forth, invoking thee,
As sons invite a sire, that thou mayst get thee strength thee, bounteousest, to get thee strength.

2 O Indra, drink the Soma juice pressed out with stones. poured from the reservoir, as an ox drinks
the spring, a very thirsty bull the spring.
For the sweet draught that gladdens thee, for mightiest freshening of thy strength.
Let thy Bay Horses bring thee hither as the Sun, as every day they bring the Sun.

3 He found the treasure brought from heaven that lay concealed, close-hidden, like the nestling of a
bird, in rock, enclosed in never-enffing rock.
Best Angiras, bolt-armed, he strove to win, as 'twere, the stall of kine;
So Indra hath disclosed the food concealed, disclosed the doors, the food that lay concealed.

4 Grasping his thunderbolt with both hands, Indra made its edge most keen, for hurling, like a
carving-knife for Ahi's slaughter made it keen.
Endued with majesty and strength, O Indra, and with lordly might,
Thou crashest down the trees, as when a craftsman fells, crashest them down as with an axe.

5 Thou, Indra, without effort hast let loose the floods to run their free course down,
like chariots, to the sea, like chariots showing forth their strength.
They, reaching hence away, have joined their strength for one eternal end,
Even as the cows who poured forth every thing for man, Yea, poured forth all thing- for mankind.

6 Eager for riches, men have formed for thee this song, like as a skilful craftsman fashioneth a car, so
have they wrought thee to their bliss;
Adorning thee, O Singer, like a generous steed for deeds of might,
Yea, like a steed to show his strength and win the prize, that he may bear each prize away.

7 For Puru thou hast shattered, Indra ninety forts, for Divodasa thy boon servant with thy bolt, O
Dancer, for thy worshipper.

For Atithigva he, the Strong, brought Sambara. from the mountain down,
Distributing the mighty treasures with his strength, parting all treasures with his strength.

8 Indra in battles help his Aryan worshipper, he who hath hundred helps at hand in every fray, in
frays that win the light of heaven.
Plaguing the lawless he gave up to Manu's seed the dusky skin;
Blazing, 'twere, he burns each covetous man away, he burns, the tyrannous away.

9 Waxed strong in might at dawn he tore the Sun's wheel off. Bright red, he steals away their speech,
the Lord of Power, their speech he steals away from them,
As thou with eager speed, O Sage, hast come from far away to hel
As winning for thine own all happiness of men, winning all happiness each day.

10 Lauded with our new hymns, O vigorous in deed, save us with strengthening help, thou Shatterer
of the Forts!
Thou, Indra, praised by Divodasa's clansmen, as heaven grows great with days, shalt wax in glory.

## [01-131] HYMN CXXXI. Indra.

1. To Indra Dyaus the Asura hath bowed him down, to Indra mighty Earth with wide-extending
tracts, to win the light, with wide-spread tracts.
All Gods of one accord have set Indra in front preeminent.
For Indra all libations must be set apart, all man's libations set apart.

2 In all libations men with hero spirit urge the Universal One, each seeking several light, each fain to
win the light apart.
Thee, furthering like a ship, will we set to the chariot-pole of strength,
As men who win with sacrifices Indra's thought, men who win Indra with their lauds.

3 Couples desirous of thine aid are storming thee, pouring their presents forth to win a stall of kine,
pouring gifts, Indra, seeking thee.
When two men seeking spoil or heaven thou bringest face to face in war,
Thou showest, Indra, -then the bolt thy constant friend, the Bull that ever waits on thee.

4 This thine heroic power men of old time have known, wherewith thou breakest down, Indra,
autumnal forts, breakest them down with conquering might.
Thou hast chastised, O Indra, Lord of Strength, the man who worships not,
And made thine own this great earth and these water-floods; with joyous heart these waterfloods.

5 And they have bruited far this hero-might when thou, O Strong One, in thy joy helpest thy
suppliants, who sought to win thee for their Friend.
Their battle-cry thou madest sound victorious in the shocks of war.
One stream after another have they gained from thee, eager for glory have they gained.

6. Also this morn may he be well inclined to us, mark at our call our offerings and our song of praise,
our call that we may win the light.
As thou, O Indra Thunder-armed, wilt, as the Strong One, slay the foe,
Listen thou to the prayer of me a later sage, hear thou a later sage's prayer.

7 O Indra, waxen strong and well-inclined to us, thou very mighty, slay the man that is our foe, slay the man, Hero! with thy bolt.

Slay thou the man who injures us: hear thou, as readiest, to hear.
Far be malignity, like mischief on the march, afar be all malignity.

## [01-132] HYMN CXXXII. Indra.

1. HELPED, Indra Maghavan, by thee in war of old, may we subdue in fight the men who strive with
us, conquer the men who war with us.
This day that now is close at hand bless him who pours the Soma juice.
In this our sacrifice may we divide the spoil, showing our strength, the spoil of war.
2 In war which wins the light, at the freegiver's call, at due oblation of the early-rising one, oblation
of the active one,
Indra slew, even as we know-whom each bowed head must reverence.
May all thy bounteous gifts be gathered up for us, yea, the good gifts of thee the Good.
3 This food glows for thee as of old at sacrifice, wherein they made thee chooser of the place , for
thou choosest the place of sacrifice.
Speak thou and make it known to us they see within with beams of light.
Indra, indeed, is found a seeker after spoil, spoil-seeker for his own allies.
4 So now must thy great deed be lauded as of old, when for the Angirases thou openedst the stall,
openedst, giving aid, the stall.
In the same manner for us here fight thou and be victorious:
To him who pours the juice give up the lawless man, the lawless who is wroth with us.
5 When with wise plan the Hero leads the people forth, they conquer in the ordered battle, seeking
fame, press, eager, onward seeking fame.
To him in time of need they sing for life with offspring and with strength.
Their hymns with Indra find a welcome place of rest: the hynins go forward to the Gods.
6 Indra and Parvata, our champions in the fight, di ive ye away each man who fain would war with
us, drive him far from us with the bolt.
Welcome to him concealed afar shall he the lair that he hath found.
So may the Render rend our foes on every side, rend them, O Hero, everywhere.

## [01-133] HYMN CXXXIII. Indra.

1. WITH sacrifice I purge both earth and heaven: I burn up great she-fiends who serve not Indra,
Where throttled by thy hand the foes were slaughtered, and in the pit of death lay pierced and
mangled.
2 O thou who castest forth the stones crushing the sorceresses' heads,
Break them with thy wide-spreading foot, with thy wide-spreading mighty foot.
3 Do thou, O Maghavan, beat off these sorceresses' daring strength.
Cast them within the narrow pit. within the deep and narrow pit.
4 Of whom thou hast ere now destroyed thrice-fifty with thy fierce attacks.
That deed they count a glorious deed, though small to thee, a glorious deed.
5 O Indra, crush and bray to bits the fearful fiery-weaponed fiend:
Strike every demon to the ground.

6 Tear down the mighty ones. O Indra, hear thou us. For heaven hath glowed like earth in fear, O
nunder-armed, as dreading fierce heat, Thunder-armed!
Most Mighty mid the Mighty Ones thou speedest with strong bolts of death,
Not slaying men, unconquered Hero with the brave, O Hero, with the thrice-seven brave.
7 The pourer of libations gains the home of wealth, pouring his gift conciliates hostilities, yea, the
hostilities of Gods.
Pouring, he strives, unchecked and strong, to win him riches thousandfold.
Indra gives lasting wealth to him who pours forth gifts, yea, wealth he gives that long shall last.

## [01-134] HYMN CXXXIV. Vayu.

1. Vayu, let fleet-foot coursers bring thee speedily to this our feast, to drink first of the juice we pour,
to the first draught of Soma juice.
May our glad hymn, discerning well, uplifted, gratify thy mind.
Come with thy team-drawn car, O Vayu, to the gift, come to the sacrificer's gift.
2 May the joy-giving drops, O Vayu gladden thee, effectual, well prepared, directed to the heavens,
strong, blent with milk and seeking heaven;
That aids, effectual to fulfil, may wait upon our skilful power.
Associate teams come hitherward to grant our prayers . they shall address the hymns we sing.
3 Two red steeds Vayu yokes, Vayu two purple steeds, swift-footed, to the chariot, to the pole to
draw, most able, at the pole, to draw.
Wake up intelligence, as when a lover wakes his sleeping love.
Illumine heaven and earth, make thou the Dawns to shine, for glory make the Dawns to shine.
4 For thee the radiant Dawns in the fardistant sky broaden their lovely gannents forth in wondrous
beams, bright-coloured in their new-born beams.
For thee the nectar-yielding Cow pours all rich treasures forth as milk.
The Marut host hast thou engendered from the womb, the Maruts from the womb of heaven.
5 For thee the pure bright quickly-flowing Soma-drops, strong in their heightening power, hasten to
mixthemselves, hasten to the water to be mixed.
To thee the weary coward prays for luck that he may speed away.
Thou by thy law protectest us from every world, yea, from the world of highest Gods.
6 Thou, Vayu, who hast none before thee, first of all hast right to drink these offerings of Soma juice,
hast right to drink the juice out-poured,
Yea, poured by all invoking tribes who free themselves from taint of sin,
For thee all cows are milked to yield the Soma-milk, to yield the butter and the milk.

## [01-135] HYMN CXXXV. Vayu, Indra-Vayu.

1. STREWN is the sacred grass; come Vayu, to our feast, with team of thousands, come, Lord of the
harnessed team, with hundreds, Lord of harnessed steeds!
The drops divine are lifted up for thee, the God, to drink them first.
The juices rich in sweets have raised thern for thy joy, have raised themselves to give thee strength.
2 Purified by the stones the Soma flows for thee, clothed with its lovely splendours, to the reservoir,
flows clad in its refulgent light.

For thee the Soma is poured forth, thy portioned share mid. Gods and men.
Drive thou thy horses, Vayu, come to us with love, come well-inclined and loving us.
3 Come thou with hundreds, come with thousands in thy team to this our solemn rite, to taste the
sacred food, Vayu, to taste the offerings.
This is thy seasonable share, that comes co-radiant with the Sun.
Brought by attendant priests pure juice is offered up, Vayu, pure juice is offered up.
4 The chariot with its team of horses bring you both, to guard us and to taste the well-appointed
food, Vayu, to taste the offerings!
Drink of the pleasant -flavoured juice the first draught is assigned to you.
O Vayu, with your splendid bounty come ye both, Indra, with bounty come ye both.
5 May our songs bring you hither to our solemn rites: these drops of mighty vigour have they beauti
fied, like a swift veed of mighty strength.
Drink of them well-inclined to us, come hitherward to be our help.
Drink, Indra-Vayu, of these Juices pressed with stones, Strength-givers! till they gladden you.
6 These Soma juices pressed for you in waters here, borne by attendant priests, are ofcredup to you:
bright, Vayu, are they offered up.
Swift through the strainer have they flowed, and here are shed for both ofyou,
Soma-drops, fain for you, over the wether's fleece, Somas over the wether's fleece.
7 O Vayu, pass thou over all the,slumberers, and where the press-stone rings enter ye both that
house, yea, Indra, go ye both within.
The joyous Maiden is beheld, the butter flows. With richly laden team come to our solemn rite, yea,
Indra, come ye to the rite.
8 Ride hither to the offering of the pleasant juice, the holy Fig-tree which victorious priests surround:
victorious be they still for us.
At once the cows yield milk, the barleymeal is dressed. For thee, O Vayu, never shall the cows grow thin, never for thee shall they be dry.
9 These Bulls of thine, O Vayu with the arm of strength, who swiftly fly within the current of thy
stream, the Bulls increasing in their might,
Horseless, yet even through the waste swift-moving, whom no shout can stay,
Hard to be checked are they, like sunbeams, in their course. hard to be checked by both the hands.

## [01-136] HYMN CXXXVI. Mitra-Varuna.

1. BRING adoration ample and most excellent, hymn, offierings, to the watchful Twain, the bountiful,
your sweetest to the bounteous Ones.
Sovrans adored with streams of oil and praised at every sacrifice.
Their high imperial might may nowhere be assailed, ne'er may their Godhead be assailed.
2 For the broad Sun was seen a path more widely laid, the path of holy law hath been maintained
with rays, the eye with Bhaga's rays of light.
Firm-set in heaven is Mitra's home, and Aryaman's and Varuna's.
Thence they give forth great vital strength which merits praise, high power of life that men shall
praise.
3 With Aditi the luminous, the celestial, upholder of the people,
come ye day by day, ye who watch

sleepless, day by day.
Resplendent might have ye obtained, Adityas, Lords of liberal gifts.
Movers of men, mild both, are Mitra, Varuna, mover of men is Aryaman.
4 This Soma be most sweet to Mitra, Varuna: he in the drinking-feasts, shall have a share thereof,
sharing, a God, among the Gods.
May all the Gods of one accord accept it joyfully to-day.
Therefore do ye, O Kings, accomplish what we ask, ye Righteous Ones, whate'er we ask.
5 Whoso, with worship serves Mitra and VaruiIa, him guard ye carefully, uninjured, from distress,
guard from distress the liberal man.
Aryaman guards him well who acts uprightly following his law,
Who beautifies their service with his lauds, who makes it beautiful with songs of praise.
6 Worship will I proress to lofty Dyaus, to Heaven and Earth, to Mitra and to bounteous Varuna, the
Bounteous, the Compassionate.
Praise Indra, praise thou Agni, praise Bhaga and heavenly Aryaman.
Long may we live and have attendant progeny, have progeny with Soma's help.
7 With the Gods' help, with Indra still beside us, may we be held self-splendid with the Maruts.
May Agni, Mitra, Varuna give us shelter this may we gain, we and our wealthy princes.

## [01-137] HYMN CXXXVII. Mitra-Varuna.

1. WITH stones have we pressed out: O come; these gladdening drops are blent with milk, these
Soma-drops which gladden you.
Come to us, Kings who reach to heaven, approach us, coming hitherward.
These milky drops are yours, Mitra and Varuna, bright Soma juices blent with milk.
2 Here are the droppings; come ye nigh the Soma-droppings blent with curd, juices expressed and
blent with curd.
Now for the wakening of your Dawn together with the Sun-God's rays,
juice waits for Mitra and for Varuna to drink, fair juice for drink, for sacrihce.
3 As 'twere a radiant-coloured cow, they milk with stones the stalk for you, with stones they milk the
Soma-plant.
May ye come nigh us, may ye turn hither to drink the Soma juice.
The men pressed out this juice, Mitra and Varuna, pressed out this Soma for your drink.

## [01-138] HYMN CXXXVIII. Pusan.

1. STRONG Pusan's majesty is lauded evermore, the glory of his lordly might is never faint, his song
of praise is never faint.
Seeking felicity I laud him nigh to help, the source, of bliss,
Who, Vigorous one, hath drawn to him the hearts of all, drawn them, the Vigorous One, the God.
2 Thee, then, O Pusan, like a swift one on his way, I urge with lauds that thou mayst make the
foemen flee, drive, camel-like, our foes afar.
As I, a man, call thee, a God, giver of bliss, to be my Friend,
So make our loudly-chanted praises glorious, in battles make them glorious.
3 Thou, Pusan, in whose friendship they who sing forth praise enjoy advantage, even in wisdom,
through thy grace, in wisdom even they are advanced.

45

So, after this most recent course, we come to thee with prayers for wealth.

Not stirred to anger, O Wide-Ruler, come to us, come thou to us in every fight.

4 Not stirred to anger, come, Free-giver, nigh to us, to take this gift of ours, thou who hast goats for steeds, Goat-borne! their gift who long for fame.

So, Wonder-Worker! may we turn thee hither with effectual lauds.

I slight thee not, O Pusan, thou Resplendent One: thy friendship may not be despised.

## [01-139] HYMN CXXXIX. Visvedevas.

1. HEARD be our prayer! In thought I honour Agni first: now straightway we elect this heavenly company, Indra and Vayu we elect.

For when our latest thought is raised and on Vivasvan centred well,

Then may our holy songs go forward on their way, our songs as 'twere unto the Gods.

2 As there ye, Mitra, Varuna, above the true have taken to yourselves the untrue with your mind, with wisdom's mental energy,

So in the seats wherein ye dwell have we beheld the Golden One, Not with our thoughts or spirit, but with these our eyes, yea, with the eyes that Soma gives.

3 Asvins, the pious call you with their hymns of praise, sounding their loud song forth to you, these living men, to their oblations, living men.

All glories and all nourishment, Lords of all wealth! depend on you.

The fellies of your golden chariot scatter drops, Mighty Ones! of your golden car.

4 Well is it known, O Mighty Ones: ye open heaven; for you the chariotsteeds are yoked for morning rites, unswerving steeds for morning rites,

We set you on the chariot-seat, ye Mighty, on the golden car. Ye seek mid-air as by a path that leads aright, as by a path that leads direct.

5 O Rich in Strength, through your great power vouchsafe us blessings day and night.

The offerings which we bring to you shall never fail, gifts brought by us shall never fail.

6 These Soma-drops, strong Indra! drink for heroes, poured, pressed out by pressing-stones, are welling forth for thee, for thee the drops are welling forth.

They shall make glad thy heart to give, to give wealth great and wonderful.

Thou who acceptest praise come glorified by hymns, come thou to us benevolent.

7 Quickly, O Agni, hear us: magnified by us thou shalt speck for us to the Gods adorable yea, to the Kings adorable:

When, O ye Deities, ye gave that Milch-cow to the Angirases, They milked her: Aryaman, joined with them, did the work: he knoweth her as well as I.

8 Ne'er may these manly deeds of yours for us grow old, never may your bright glories fall into decay, never before our time decay.

What deed of yours, new every age, wondrous, surpassing man, rings forth,

Whatever, Maruts! may be difficult to gain, grant us, whate'er is hard to gain.

9 Dadhyac of old, Anigiras, Priyamedha these, and Kanva, Atri, Manu knew my birth, yea, tbose of ancient days and Manu knew.

Their long line stretcheth to the Gods, our birth-connexions are with them.

To these, for their high station, 1 bow down with song, to Indra, Agni, bow with song.

10 Let the Invoker bless: let offerers bring choice gifts; Brhaspati the Friend doth sacrifice with Steers, Steers that have many an excellence.

Now with our ears we catch the sound of the press-stone that rings afar.

The very Strong hath gained the waters by himself, the strong gained many a resting-place.

11 O ye Eleven Gods whose home is heaven, O ye Eleven who make earth your dwelling,

Ye who with might, Eleven, live in waters, accept this sacrifice, O Gods, with pleasure.

## [01-140] HYMN CXL. Agni.

1 To splendid Agni seated by the altar, loving well his home, I bring the food as 'twere his place of birth.

I clothe the bright One with my hymn as with a robe, him with the car of light, bright-hued, dispelling gloom.

2 Child of a double birth he grasps at triple food; in the year's course what he hath swallowed grows anew.

He, by another's mouth and tongue a noble Bull, with other, as an elephant, consumes the trees.

3 The pair who dwell together, moving in the dark bestir themselves: both parents hasten to the babe,

Impetuous-tongued, destroying, springing swiftly forth, one to be watched and cherished, strengthener of his sire.

4 For man, thou Friend of men, these steeds of thine are yoked, impatient, lightly running, ploughing blackened lines,

Discordant-minded, fleet, gliding with easy speed, urged onward by the wind and rapid in their course.

5 Dispelling on their way the horror of black gloom , making a glorious show these flames Of his fly forth,

When o'er the spacious tract he spreads himself abroad, and rushes panting on with thunder and with roar.

6 Amid brown plants he stoops as if adorning them, and rushes bellowing like a bull upon his wives.

Proving his might, he decks the glory of his form, and shakes his horns like one terrific, bard to stay.

7 Now covered, now displayed he grasps as one who knows his resting-place in those who know him well.

A second time they wax and gather Godlike power, and blending both together change their Parents' form.

8 The maidens with long, tresses hold him in embrace; dead, they rise up again to meet the Living One.

Releasing them from age with a loud roar he comes, filling them with new spirit, living, unsubdued.

9 Licking the mantle of the Mother, far and wide he wanders over fields with beasts that flee apace.

Strengthening all that walk, licking up all around, a blackened path, forsooth, he leaves where'er he goes.

10 O Agni, shine resplendent with our wealthy chiefs, like a loud-snorting bull, accustomed to the house.

Thou casting off thine infant wrappings blazest forth as though thou hadst put on a coat of mail for war.

11 May this our perfect prayer be dearer unto thee than an imperfect prayer although it please thee well.

With the pure brilliancy that radiates from thy form, mayest thou grant to us abundant store of wealth.

12 Grant to our chariot, to our house, O Agni, a boat with moving feet and constant oarage,
One that may further well our wealthy princes and all the folk, and be our certain refuge.

13 Welcome our laud with thine approval, Agni. May earth and heaven and freely flowing rivers
Yield us long life and food and corn and cattle, and may the red Dawns choose for us their choicest.

### [01-141] HYMN CXLI. Agni.

1. YEA, verily, the fair effulgence of the God for glory was established, since he sprang from strength.
When he inclines thereto successful is the hymn: the songs of sacrifice have brought him as they flow

2 Wonderful, rich in nourishment, he dwells in food; next, in the seven auspicious Mothers is his
home.
Thirdly, that they might drain the treasures of the Bull, the maidens brought forth him for whom the
ten provide.

3 What time from out the deep, from the Steer's wondrous form, the Chiefs who had the power
produced him with their strength;
When Matarisvan rubbed forth him who lay concealed, for mixture of the sweet drink, in the days of
old.

4 When from the Highest Father he is brought to us, amid the plants he rises hungry, wondrously.
As both together join to expedite his birth, most youthful he is born resplendent in his light.

5 Then also entered he the Mothers, and in them pure and uninjured he increased in magnitude.
As to the first he rose, the vigorous from of old, so now he runs among the younger lowest ones.

6 Therefore they choose him Herald at the morning rites, pressing to him as unto Bhaga, pouring
gifts,
When, much-praised, by the power and will of Gods, he goes at all times to his mortal worshipper to
drink.

7 What time the Holy One, wind-urged, hath risen up, serpent-like winding through the dry grass
unrestrained,
Dust lies upon the way of him who burneth all, black-winged and pure of birth who follows sundry
paths.

8 Like a swift chariot made by men who know their art, he with his red limbs lifts himself aloft to
heaven.
Thy worshippers become by burning black of hue: their strength flies as before a hero's violence.

9 By thee, O Agni, Varuna who guards the Law, Mitra and Aryaman, the Bounteous, are made strong;
For, as the felly holds the spokes, thou with thy might pervading hast been born encompassing them round.

10 Agni, to him who toils and pours libations, thou, Most Youthful! sendest wealth and all the host of Gods.
Thee, therefore, even as Bhaga, will we set anew, young Child of Strength, most wealthy! in our battle-song.

11 Vouchsafe us riches turned to worthy ends, good luck abiding in the house, and strong capacity,
Wealth that directs both worlds as they were guiding-reins, and, very Wise, the Gods' assent in sacrifice.

12 May he, the Priest resplendent, joyful, hear us, he with the radiant car and rapid horses.

May Agni, ever wise, with best directions to bliss and highest happiness conduct us.

13 With hymns of might hath Agni now been lauded, advanced to height of universal kingship.
Now may these wealthy chiefs and we together spread forth as spreads the Sun above the rainclouds.

### [01-142] HYMN CXLII Apris.

1. KINDLED, bring, Agni, Gods to-day for him who lifts the ladle up.
Spin out the ancient thread for him who sheds, with gifts, the Soma juice.

2 Thou dealest forth, Tanunapat, sweet sacrifice enriched with oil,
Brought by a singer such as I who offers gifts and toils for thee.

3 He wondrous, sanctifying, bright, sprinkles the sacrifice with mead,
Thrice, Narasamsa from the heavens, a God mid Gods adorable.

4 Agni, besought, bring hitherward Indra the Friend, the Wonderful,
For this my hymn of praise, O sweet of tongue, is chanted forth to thee.

5 The ladle-holders strew trimmed grass at this well-ordered sacrifice;
A home for Indra is adorned, wide, fittest to receive the Gods.

6 Thrown open be the Doors Divine, unfailing, that assist the rite,
High, purifying, much-desired, so that the Gods may enter in.

7 May Night and Morning, hymned with lauds, united, fair to look upon,
Strong Mothers of the sacrifice, seat them together on the grass.

8 May the two Priests Divine, the sage, the sweet-voiced lovers of the hymn,
Complete this sacrifice of ours, effectual, reaching heaven to-day.

9 Let Hotri pure, set amang Gods, amid the Maruts Bhirati, Ila, Sarasvati, Mahi, rest on the grass,
adorable.

10 May Tvastar send us genial dew abundant, wondrous, rich in gifts,
For increase and for growth of wealth, Tvastar our kinsman and our Friend.

11 Vanaspati, give forth, thyself, and call the Gods to sacrifice.
May Agni, God intelligent, speed our oblation to the Gods.

12 To Vayu joined with Pusan, with the Maruts, and the host of Gods,
To Indra who inspires the hymn cry Glory! and present the gift.

13 Come hither to enjoy the gifts prepared with cry of Glory! Come,
O Indra, hear their calling; they invite thee to the sacrifice.

### [01-143] HYMN CXLIII. Agni.

1. To Agni I present a newer mightier hymn, I bring my words and song unto the Son of Strength,
Who, Offspring of the Waters, bearing precious things sits on the earth, in season, dear InvokingPriest.

2 Soon as he sprang to birth that Agni was shown forth to Matarisvan in the highest firmament.
When he was kindled, through his power and majesty his fiery splendour made the heavens and
earth to shine.

3 His flames that wax not old, beams fair to look upon of him whose face is lovely, shine with
beauteous sheen.
The rays of Agni, him whose active force is light, through the nights glimmer sleepless, ageless, like
the floods.

4 Send thou with hymns that Agni to his own abode, who rules, one Sovran Lord of wealth, like Varuna,

Him, All-possessor, whom the Bhrgus with their might brought to earth's central point, the centre of the world.

5 He whom no force can stay, even as the Maruts' roar, like to a dart sent forth, even as the bolt from heaven,

Agni with sharpened jaws chews up and cats the trees, and conquers them as when the warrior smites his foes.

6 And will not Agni find enjoyment in our praise, will not the Vasu grant our wish with gifts of wealth?

Will not the Inspirer speed our prayers to gain their end? Him with the radiant glance 1 laud with this my song.

7 The kindler of the flame wins Agni as a Friend, promoter of the Law, whose face is bright with oil.

Inflamed and keen, refulgent in our gatherings, he lifts our hymn on high clad in his radiant hues.

8 Keep us incessantly with guards that cease not, Agni, with guards auspicious, very mighty.

With guards that never slumber, never heedless, never beguiled. O Helper, keep our children.

## [01-144] HYMN CXLIV. Agni.

1. THE Priest goes forth to sacrifice, with wondrous power sending aloft the hymn of glorious
brilliancy.

He moves to meet the ladles turning to the right, which are the first to kiss the place where he
abides.

2 To him sang forth the flowing streams of Holy Law, encompassed in the home and birth-place of
the God.

He, when he dwelt extended in the waters' lap, absorbed those Godlike powers for which he is
adored.

3 Seeking in course altern to reach the selfsame end the two copartners strive to win this beauteous
form.

Like Bhaga must he be duly invoked by us, as he who drives the car holds fast the horse's reins.

4 He whom the two copartners with observance tend, the pair who dwell together in the same
abode,

By night as in the day the grey one was born young, passing untouched by eld through many an age
of man.

5 Him the ten fingers, the devotions. animate: we mortals call on him a God to give us help.

He speeds over the sloping surface of the land: new deeds hath he performed with those who gird
him round.

6 For, Agni, like a herdsman, thou by thine own might rulest o'er all that is in heaven and on the earth;

And these two Mighty Ones, bright, golden closely joined, rolling them round are come unto thy
sacred grass.

7 Agni, accept with joy, be glad in this our prayer, joy-giver, self-sustained, strong, born of Holy Law!

For fair to see art thou turning to every side, pleasant to look on as a dwelling filled with food.

## [01-145] HYMN CXLV. Agni.

1. Ask ye of him for he is come, he knoweth it; he, full of wisdom, is implored, is now implored.

With him are admonitions and with him commands: he is the Lord of Strength, the Lord of Power and
Might.

2 They ask of him: not all learn by their questioning what he, the Sage, hath grasped, as 'twere, with
his own mind.

Forgetting not the former nor the later word, he goeth on, not careless, in his mental power.

3 To him these ladles go, to him these racing mares: he only will give ear to all the words I speak.

All-speeding, victor, perfecter of sacrifice, the Babe with flawless help hath mustered vigorous might.

4 Whate'er he meets he grasps and then runs farther on, and straightway, newly born,creeps forward with his kin.

He stirs the wearied man to pleasure and great joy what time the longing gifts approach him as he comes.

5 He is a wild thing of the flood and forest: he hath been laid upon the highest surface.

He hath declared the lore of works to mortals, Agni the Wise, for he knows Law, the Truthful.

## [01-146] HYMN CXLVI. Agni.

1. I LAUD the seven-rayed, the triple-headed, Agni all-perfect in his Parents' bosom,

Sunk in the lap of all that moves and moves not, him who hath filled all luminous realms of heaven.

2 As a great Steer he grew to these his Parents; sublime lie stands, untouched by eld, far-reaching.

He plants his footsteps on the lofty ridges of the broad earth: his red flames lick the udder.

3 Coming together to their common youngling both Cows, fairshaped, spread forth in all directions,

Measuring out the paths that must be travelled, entrusting all desires to him the Mighty.

4 The prudent sages lead him to his dwelling, guarding with varied skill the Ever-Youthful.

Longing, they turned their eyes unto the River: to these the Sun of men was manifested.

5 Born noble in the regions, aim of all mens' eyes to be implored for life by great and small alike,

Far as the Wealthy One hath spread himself abroad, he is the Sire all-visible of this progeny.

## [01-147] HYMN CXLVII. Agni.

1. How, Agni, have the radiant ones, aspiring, endued thee with the vigour of the living,

So that on both sides fostering seed and offspring, the Gods may joy in Holy Law's fulfilment?

2 Mark this my speech, Divine One, thou, Most Youthful! offered to thee by him who gives most
freely.

One hates thee, and another sings thy praises: I thine adorer laud thy form, O Agni.

3 Thy guardian rays, O Agni, when they saw him, preserved blind Mamateya from affliction.

Lord of all riches, he preserved the pious the foes who fain would harm them did no mischief.

4 The sinful man who worships not, O Agni, who, offering not, harms us with double-dealing,-

Be this in turn to him a heavy sentence may he distress himself by his revilings.

5 Yea, when a mortal knowingly, O Victor, injures with double tongue a fellow-mortal,

From him, praised Agni! save thou him that lauds thee: bring us not into trouble and affliction.

## [01-148] HYMN CXLVIII. Agni.

1. WHAT Matarisvan, piercing, formed by friction, Herald of all the Gods. in varied figure,

Is he whom they have set mid human houses, gay-hued as light and shining forth for beauty.

2 They shall not harm the man who brings thee praises: such as I am, Agni my help approves me.

All acts of mine shall they accept with pleasure, laudation from the singer who presents it.
3 Him in his constant seat men skilled in worship have taken and with praises have established.
As, harnessed to a chariot fleet-foot horses, at his command let bearers lead him forward.
4 Wondrous, full many a thing he chews and crunches: he shines amid the wood with spreading brightness.
Upon his glowing flames the wind blows daily, driving them like the keen shaft of an archer.
5 Him, whom while yet in embryo the hostile, both skilled and fain to harm, may never injure,
Men blind and sightless through his splendour hurt not: his never-failing lovers have preserved him.

## [01-149] HYMN CXLIX. Agni.

1. HITHER he hastens to give, Lord of great riches, King of the mighty, to the place of treasure.
lie pressing-stones shall serve him speeding near us.
2 As Steer of men so Steer of earth and heaven by glory, he whose streams all life hath drunken,
Who hasting forward rests upon the altar.
3 He who hath lighted up the joyous castle, wise Courser like the Steed of cloudy heaven,
Bright like the Sun, with hundredfold existence.
4 He, doubly born, hath spread in his effulgence through the three luminous realms, through all the
regions,
Best sacrificing Priest where waters gather.
5 Priest doubly born, he through his love of glory hath in his keeping all things worth the choosing,
The man who brings him gifts hath noble offspring.

## [01-150] HYMN CL. Agni.

1. AGNI, thy faithful servant I call upon thee with many a gift,
As in the keeping of the great inciting God;
2 Thou who ne'er movest thee to aid the indolent, the godless man,
Him who though wealthy never brings an offering.
3 Splendid, O Singer, is that man, mightiest of the great in heaven.
Agni, may we be foremost, we thy worshippers.

## [01-151] HYMN CLI. Mitra and Varuna

1. HEAVEN and earth trembled at the might and voice of him, whom, loved and Holy One, helper of
all mankind,
The wise who longed for spoil in fight for kine brought forth with power, a Friend, mid waters, at the
sacrifice.
2 As these, like friends, have done this work for you, these prompt servants of Purumilha Somaofferer,
Give mental power to him who sings the sacred song, and hearken, Strong Ones, to the master ofthe
house.
3 The folk have glorified your birth from Earth and Heaven, to be extolled, ye Strong Ones, for your
mighty power.
Ye, when ye bring to singer and the rite, enjoy the sacrifice periormed with holy praise and strength.
4 The people prospers, Asuras! whom ye dearly love: ye, Righteous Ones, proclaim aloud the Holy
Law.
That efficacious power that comes from lofty heaven, ye bind unto the work, as to the pole an ox.
5 On this great earth ye send your treasure down with might: unstained by dust, the crowding kine are in the stalls.

Here in the neighbourhood they cry unto the Sun at morning and at evening, like swift birds of prey.
6 The flames with curling tresses serve your sacrifice, whereto ye sing the song, Mitra and Varuna.
Send down of your free will, prosper our holy songs: ye are sole Masters of the singer's hymn of praise.
7 Whoso with sacrifices toiling brings you gifts, and worships, sage and priest, fulfilling your desire,-
To him do ye draw nigh and taste his sacrifice. Come well-inclined to us unto our songs and prayer.
8 With sacrifices and with milk they deck you first, ye Righteous Ones, as if through stirrings of the mind.
To you they bring their hymns with their collected thought, while ye with earnest soul come to us gloriously.
9 Rich strength of life is yours: ye, Heroes, have obtained through your surpassing powers rich farextending might.
Not the past days conjoined with nights, not rivers, not the Papis have attained your Godhead and your wealth.

## [01-152] HYMN CLII. Mitra-Varuna.

1. THE robes which ye put on abound with fatness: uninterrupted courses are your counsels.
All falsehood, Mitra-Varuna! ye conquer, and closely cleave unto the Law Eternal.
2 This might of theirs hath no one comprehended. True is the crushing word the sage hath uttered,
The fearful four-edged bolt smites down the three-edged, and those who hate the Gods first fall and
perish.
3 The Footless Maid precedeth footed creatures. Who marketh, Mitra-Varuna, this your doing?
The Babe Unborn supporteth this world's burthen, fulfilleth Law and overcometh falsehood.
4 We look on him the darling of the Maidens, always advancing, never falling downward,
Wearing inseparable, wide-spread raiment, Mitra's and Varuna's delightful glory.
5 Unbridled Courser, horn but not of horses, neighing he flieth on with back uplifted.
The youthful love mystery thought-surpassing, praising in Mitra-Varuna, its glory.
6 May the milch-kine who favour Mamateya prosper in this world him who loves devotion.
May he, well skilled in rites, be food, and calling Aditi with his lips give us assistance.
7 Gods, Mitra-Varuna, with love and worship, let me make you delight in this oblation.
May our prayer be victorious in battles, may we have rain from heaven to make us prosper.

## [01-153] HYMN CLIII. Mitra-Varuna.

1. WE worship with our reverence and oblations you, Mitra Varuna, accordant, mighty,
So that with us, ye Twain whose backs are sprinkled with oil, the priests with oil and hymns support
you.
2 Your praise is like a mighty power, an impulse: to you, Twain Gods, a well-formed hymn is offered,
As the priest decks yon, Strong Ones, in assemblies, and the prince fain to worship you for blessings.
3 O Mitra-Varuna, Aditi the Milch-cow streams for the rite, for folk who bring oblation,
When in the assembly he who worships moves you, like to a human priest, with gifts presented.
4 So may the kine and heavenly Waters pour you sweet drink in families that make you joyful.
Of this may he, the ancient House-Lord, give us. Enjoy, drink of the milk the cow provideth.

## [01-154] HYMN CLIV. Visnu

1. I WILL declare the mighty deeds of Visnu, of him who measured out the earthly regions,
Who propped the highest place of congregation, thrice setting down his footstep, widely striding.
2 For this his mighty deed is Visnu lauded, like some wild beast, dread, prowling, mountain-roaming;
He within whose three wide-extended paces all living creatures have their habitation.
3 Let the hymn lift itself as strength to Visnu, the Bull far-striding, dwelling on the mountains,
Him who alone with triple step hath measured this common dwelling-place, long, far extended.
4 Him whose three places that are filled with sweetness, imperishable, joy as it may list them,
Who verily alone upholds the threefold, the earth, the heaven, and all living creatures.
5 May I attain to that his well-loved mansion where men devoted to the Gods are happy.
For there springs, close akin to the Wide-Strider, the well of meath in Visnu's highest footstep.
6 Fain would we go unto your dwelling-places where there are many-horned and nimble oxen,
For mightily, there, shineth down upon us the widely-striding Bull's sublimest mansion.

## [01-155] HYMN CLV. Visnu-Indra.

1. To the great Hero, him who sets his mind thereon, and Visnu, praise aloud in song your draught of juice,-
Gods ne'er beguiled, who borne as 'twere by noble steed, have stood upon the lofty ridges of the hills.
2 Your Soma-drinker keeps afar your furious rush, Indra and Visnu, when ye come with all your might.
That which hath been directed well at mortal man, bow-armed Krsanu's arrow, ye turn far aside.
3 These offerings increase his mighty manly strength: he brings both Parents down to share the genial flow.
He lowers, though a son, the Father's highest name; the third is that which is high in the light of heaven.
4 We laud this manly power of him the Mighty One, preserver, inoffensive, bounteous and benign;
His who strode, widely pacing, with three steppings forth over the realms of earth for freedom and for life.
5 A mortal man, when he beholds two steps of him who looks upon the light, is restless with amaze.
But his third step doth no one venture to approach, no, nor the feathered birds of air who fly with wings.
6 He, like a rounded wheel, hath in swift motion set his ninety racing steeds together with the four.
Developed, vast in form, with those who sing forth praise, a youth, no more a child, he cometh to our call.

## [01-156] HYMN CLVI. Visnu

1. FAR-SHINING, widely famed, going thy wonted way, fed with the oil, be helpful. Mitra-like, to us.
So, Visnu, e'en the wise must swell thy song of praise, and he who hath oblations pay thee solemn rites.
2 He who brings gifts to him the Ancient and the Last, to Visnu who ordains, together with his Spouse,

Who tells the lofty birth of him the Lofty One, shall verily surpass in glory e'en his peer.
3 Him have ye satisfied, singers, as well as ye know, primeval germ of Order even from his birth.
Ye, knowing e'en his name, have told it forth: may we, Visnu, enjoy the grace of thee the Mighty One.
4 The Sovran Varuna and both the Asvins wait on this the will of him who guides the Marut host.
Visnu hath power supreme and might iliat finds the day, and with his Friend unbars the stable of the kine.
5 Even he the Heavenly One who came for fellowship, Visnu to Indra, godly to the godlier,
Who Maker, throned in three worlds, helps the Aryan man, and gives the worshipper his share of Holy Law.

## [01-157] HYMN CLVII. Asvins.

1. AGNI is wakened: Surya riseth from the earth. Mighty, refulgent Dawn hath shone with all her light.
The Asvins have equipped their chariot for the course. God Savitar hath moved the folk in sundry ways.
2 When, Asvins, ye equip your very mighty car, bedew, ye Twain, our power with honey and with oil.
To our devotion give victorious strength in war: may we win riches in the heroes' strife for spoil.
3 Nigh to us come the Asvins' lauded three-wheeled car, the car laden with meath and drawn by fleet-foot steeds,
Three-seated, opulent, bestowing all delight. may it bring weal to us, to cattle and to men.
4 Bring hither nourishment for us, ye Asvins Twain; sprinkle us with your whip that drops with honey-dew.
Prolong our days of life, wipe out our trespasses; destroy our foes, be our companions and our Friends.
5 Ye store the germ of life in female creatures, ye lay it up within all living beings.
Ye have sent forth, O Asvins passing mighty, the fire, the sovrans of the wood, the waters,
6 Leeches are ye with medicines to heal us, and charioteers are ye with skill in driving.
Ye Strong, give sway to him who brings oblation and with his heart pours out his gift before you.

## [01-158] HYMN CLVIII. Asvins.

1. YE Vasus Twain, ye Rudras full of counsel, grant us, Strong Strengtheners, when ye stand beside us,
What wealth Aucathya craves of you, great Helpers when ye come forward with no niggard succour.
2 Who may give you aught, Vasus, for your favour, for what, at the Cow's place, ye grant through worship?
Wake for us understanding full of riches, come with a heart that will fulfil our longing.
3 As erst for Tugra's son your car, sea-crossing, strong, was equipped and set amid the waters,
So may I gain your shelter and protection as with winged course a hero seeks his army.
4 May this my praise preserve Ucathya's offspring: let not these Twain who fly with wings exhaust me.
Let not the wood ten times up-piled consume me, when fixed for you it bites the ground it stands on.
5 The most maternal streams, wherein the Dilsas cast me securely bound, have not devoured me.

When Traitana would cleave my head asunder, the Dasa wounded his own breast and shoulders.

6 Dirghatamas the son of Mamati hath come to length of days in the tenth age of human kind.

He is the Brahman of the waters as they strive to reach their end and aim: their charioteer is he.

### [01-159] HYMN CLIX. Heaven and Earth.

1. I PRAISE with sacrifices mighty Heaven and Earth at festivals, the wise, the Strengtheners of Law.

Who, having Gods for progeny, conjoined with Gods, through wonder-working wisdom bring forth

choicest boons.

2 With invocations, on the gracious Father's mind, and on the Mother's great inherent power I muse.

Prolific Parents, they have made the world of life, and for their brood all round wide immortality.

3 These Sons of yours well skilled in work, of wondrous power, brought forth to life the two great

Mothers first of all.

To keep the truth of all that stands and all that moves, ye guard the station of your Son who knows

no guile.

4 They with surpassing skill, most wise, have measured out the Twins united in their birth and in their home.

They, the refulgent Sages, weave within the sky, yea, in the depths of sea, a web for ever new.

5 This is to-day the goodliest gift of Savitar: this thought we have when now the God is furthering us.

On us with loving-kindness Heaven and Earth bestow riches and various wealth and treasure

hundredfold!

### [01-160] HYMN CLX. Heaven and Earth.

1. THESE, Heaven and Earth, bestow prosperity on all, sustainers of the region, Holy Ones and wise,

Two Bowls of noble kind: between these Goddesses the God, the fulgent Sun, travels by fixed decree.

2 Widely-capacious Pair, mighty, that never fail, the Father and the Mother keep all creatures safe:

The two world-halves, the spirited, the beautiful, because the Father hath clothed them in goodly

forms.

3 Son of these Parents, he the Priest with power to cleanse, Sage, sanctifies the worlds with his

surpassing power.

Thereto for his bright milk he milked through all the days the party-coloured Cow and the prolific

Bull.

4 Among the skilful Gods most skilled is he, who made the two world-halves which bring prosperity

to all;

Who with great wisdom measured both the regions out, and stablished them with pillars that shall

ne'er decay.

5 Extolled in song, O Heaven and Earth, bestow on us, ye mighty Pair, great glory and high lordly

sway,

Whereby we may extend ourselves ever over the folk; and send us strength that shall deserve the

praise of men.

### [01-161] HYMN CLXI. Rbhus.

1 WHY hath the Best, why hath the Youngest come to us? Upon what embassy comes he? What have we said?

We have not blamed the chalice of illustrious birth. We, Brother Agni, praised the goodness of the wood.

2 The chalice that is single make ye into four: thus have the Gods commanded; therefore am I come.

If, O Sudhanvan's Children, ye will do this thing ye shall participate in sacrifice with Gods.

3 What to the envoy Agni in reply ye spake, A courser must be made, a chariot fashioned here,

A cow must be created, and the Twain made young. When we have done these things, Brother, we

turn to you.

4 When thus, O Rbhus, ye had done ye questioned thus, Whither went he who came to us a

messenger?

Then Tvastar, when he viewed the four wrought chalices, concealed himself among the Consorts of

the Gods.

5 As Tvastar thus had spoken, Let us slay these men who have reviled the chalice, drinking-cup of

Gods,

They gave themselves new names when Soma juice was shed, and under these new names the

Maiden welcomed them.

6 Indra hath yoked his Bays, the Asvins' car is horsed, Brhaspati hath brought the Cow of every hue.

Ye went as Rbhus, Vibhvan, Vaja to the Gods, and skilled in war, obtained your share in sacrifice.

7 Ye by your wisdom brought a cow from out a hide; unto that ancient Pair ye gave again their youth.

Out of a horse, Sudhanvan's Sons, ye formed a horse: a chariot ye equipped, and went unto the Gods.

8 Drink ye this water, were the words ye spake to them; or drink ye this, the rinsing of the Munjagrass.

If ye approve not even this, Sudhanvan's Sons, then at the third libation gladden ye yourselves.

9 Most excellent are waters, thus said one of you; most excellent is Agni, thus another said.

Another praised to many a one the lightning cloud. Then did ye shape the cups, speaking the words

of truth.

10 One downward to the water drives the crippled cow, another trims the flesh brought on the

carving-board.

One carries off the refuse at the set of sun. How did the Parents aid their children in their task!

11 On the high places ye have made the grass for man, and water in the valleys, by your skill, O Men.

Rbhus, ye iterate not to-day that act of yours, your sleeping in the house of him whom naught can

hide.

12 As, compassing them round, ye glided through the worlds, where had the venerable Parents their

abode?

Ye laid a curse on him who raised his arm at you: to him who spake aloud to you ye spake again.

13 When ye had slept your fill, ye Rbhus, thus ye asked, O thou whom naught may hide, who now

hath wakened us?

The goat declared the hound to be your wakener. That day, in a full year, ye first unclosed our eyes.

14 The Maruts move in heaven, on earth this Agni; through the mid-firmament the Wind approaches.

Varuna comes in the sea's gathered waters, O Sons of Strength, desirous of your presence.

### [01-162] HYMN CLXII. The Horse.

1. SLIGHT us not Varuna, Aryaman, or Mitra, Rbhuksan, Indra, Ayu, or the Maruts,

51

When we declare amid the congregation the virtues of the strong Steed, God-descended.

2 What time they bear before the Courser, covered with trappings and with wealth, the grasped oblation,
The dappled goat goeth straightforward, bleating, to the place dear to Indra and to Pusan.

3 Dear. to all Gods, this goat, the share of Pusan, is first led forward with the vigorous Courser,
While Tvastar sends him forward with the Charger, acceptable for sacrifice, to glory.

4 When thrice the men lead round the Steed, in order, who goeth to the Gods as meet oblation,
The goat precedeth him, the share of Pusan, and to the Gods the sacrifice announceth.

5 Invoker, ministering priest, atoner, fire-kindler Soma-presser, sage, reciter,
With this well ordered sacrifice, well finished, do ye fill full the channels of the rivers.

6 The hewers of the post and those who carry it, and those who carve the knob to deck the Horse's stake;
Those who prepare the cooking-vessels for the Steed,-may the approving help of these promote our work.

7 Forth, for the regions of the Gods, the Charger with his smooth back is come my prayer attends him.
In him rejoice the singers and the sages. A good friend have we won for the Gods' banquet.

8 May the fleet Courser's halter and his heel-ropes, the head-stall and the girths and cords about him.
And the grass put within his mouth to bait him,-among the Gods, too, let all these be with thee.

9 What part of the Steed's flesh the fly hath eaten, or is left sticking to the post or hatchet,
Or to the slayer's hands and nails adhereth,-among the Gods, too, may all this be with thee.

10 Food undigested steaming from his belly, and any odour of raw flesh remaining,
This let the immolators set in order and dress the sacrifice with perfect cooking.

11 What from thy body which with fire is roasted, when thou art set upon the spit, distilleth,
Let not that lie on earth or grass neglected, but to the longing Gods let all be offered.

12 They who observing that the Horse is ready call out and say, the smell is good; remove it;
And, craving meat, await the distribution, -may their approving help promote labour.

13 The trial-fork of the flesh-cooking caldron, the vessels out of which the broth is sprinkled,
The warming-pots, the covers of the dishes, hooks, carving-boards,-all these attend the Charger.

14 The starting-place, his place of rest and rolling, the ropes wherewith the Charger's feet were fastened,
The water that he drank, the food he tasted, -among the Gods, too, may all these attend thee.

15 Let not the fire, smoke-scented, make thee crackle, nor glowing caldron smell and break to pieces.
Offered, beloved, approved, and consecrated,-such Charger do the Gods accept with favour.

16 The robe they spread upon the Horse to clothe him, the upper covering and the golden trappings,
The halters which restrain the Steed, the heel-ropes,-all these, as grateful to the Gods, they offer.

17 If one, when seated, with excessive urging hath with his heel or with his whip distressed thee,
All these thy woes, as with the oblations' ladle at sacrifices, with my prayer I banish.

18 The four-and-thirty ribs of the. Swift Charger, kin to the Gods, the slayer's hatchet pierces.
Cut ye with skill, so that the parts be flawless, and piece by piece declaring them dissect them.

19 Of Tvastar's Charger there is one dissector,-this is the custom-two there are who guide him.
Such of his limbs as I divide in order, these, amid the balls, in fire I offer.

20 Let not thy dear soul burn thee as thou comest, let not the hatchet linger in thy body.
Let not a greedy clumsy immolator, missing the joints, mangle thy limbs unduly.

21 No, here thou diest not, thou art not injured: by easy paths unto the Gods thou goest.
Both Bays, both spotted mares are now thy fellows, and to the ass's pole is yoked the Charger.

22 May this Steed bring us all-sustaining riches, wealth in good kine, good horses, manly offspring.
Freedom from sin may Aditi vouchsafe us: the Steed with our oblations gain us lordship!

## [01-163] HYMN CLXIII. The Horse.

1. WHAT time, first springing into life, thou neighedst, proceeding from the sea or upper waters,
Limbs of the deer hadst thou, and eagle pinions. O Steed, thy birth is nigh and must be lauded.

2 This Steed which Yama gave hath Trita harnessed, and him, the first of all, hath Indra mounted.
His bridle the Gandharva grasped. O Vasus, from out the Sun ye fashioned forth the Courser.

3 Yama art thou, O Horse; thou art Aditya; Trita art thou by secret operation.
Thou art divided thoroughly from Soma. They say thou hast three bonds in heaven that hold thee.

4 Three bonds, they say, thou hast in heaven that bind thee, three in the waters,
three within the ocean.
To me thou seernest Varuna , O Courser, there where they say is thy sublimest birth-place.

5 Here-, Courser, are the places where they groomed thee, here are the traces of thy hoofs as winner.
Here have I seen the auspicious reins that guide thee, which those who guard the holy Law keep safely.

6 Thyself from far I recognized in spirit,-a Bird that from below flew through the heaven.
I saw thy head still soaring, striving upward by paths unsoiled by dust, pleasant to travel.

7 Here I beheld thy form, matchless in glory, eager to win thee food at the Cow's station.
Whene'er a man brings thee to thine enjoyment, thou swallowest the plants most greedy eater.

8 After thee, Courser, come the car, the bridegroom, the kine come after, and the charm of maidens.
Full companies have followed for thy friendship: the pattern of thy vigour Gods have copied.

9 Horns made of gold hath he: his feet are iron: less fleet than he, though swift as thought, is Indra.
The Gods have come that they may taste the oblation of him who mounted, first of all, the Courser.

10 Symmetrical in flank, with rounded haunches, mettled like heroes, the Celestial Coursers

Put forth their strength, like swans in lengthened order, when they, the Steeds, have reached the
heavenly causeway.
11 A body formed for flight hast thou, O Charger; swift as the wind in motion is thy spirit.
Thy horns are spread abroad in all directions: they move with restless beat in wildernesses.
12 The strong Steed hath come forward to the slaughter, pondering with a mind directed God-ward.
The goat who is his kin is led before him the sages and the singers follow after.
13 The Steed is come unto the noblest mansion, is come unto his Father and his Mother.
This day shall he approach the Gods, most welcome: then he declares good gifts to him who offers.

## [01-164] HYMN CLXIV. Visvedevas.

1. OF this benignant Priest, with eld grey-coloured, the brother midmost of the three is lightning.
The third is he whose back with oil is sprinkled. Here I behold the Chief with seven male children.
2 Seven to the one-wheeled chariot yoke the Courser; bearing seven names the single Courser draws
it.
Three-naved the wheel is, sound and undecaying, whereon are resting all these worlds of being.
3 The seven who on the seven-wheeled car are mounted have horses, seven in tale, who draw them
onward.
Seven Sisters utter songs of praise together, in whom the names of the seven Cows are treasured.
4 Who hath beheld him as he sprang to being, seen how the boneless One supports the bony?
Where is the blood of earth, the life, the spirit? Who may approach the man who knows, to ask it?
5 Unripe in mind, in spirit undiscerning, I ask of these the Gods' established places; For up above the
yearling Calf the sages, to form a web, their own seven threads have woven.
6 I ask, unknowing, those who know, the sages, as one all ignorant for sake of knowledge,
What was that ONE who in the Unborn's image hath stablished and fixed firm these worlds' six
regions.
7 Let him who knoweth presently declare it , this lovely Bird's securely founded station.
Forth from his head the Cows draw milk, and, wearing his vesture, with their foot have drunk the
water.
8 The Mother gave the Sire his share of Order: with thought, at first, she wedded him in spirit.
She, the coy Dame, was filled with dew prolific: with adoration men approached to praise her.
9 Yoked was the Mother to the boon Cow's car-pole: in the dank rows of cloud the Infant rested.
Then the Calf lowed, and looked upon the Mother, the Cow who wears all shapes in three directions.
10 Bearing three Mothers and three Fathers, single he stood erect: they never make him weary.
There on the pitch of heaven they speak together in speech all-knowing but not all-impelling.
11 Formed with twelve spokes, by length of time, unweakened, rolls round the heaven this wheel of
during Order.
Herein established, joined in pairs together, seven hundred Sons and twenty stand, O Agni.

12 They call him in the farther half of heaven the Sire five-footed, of twelve forms, wealthy in watery
store.
These others say that he, God with far-seeing eyes, is mounted on the lower seven-wheeled, sixspoked
car.
13 Upon this five-spoked wheel revolving ever all living creatures rest and are dependent.
Its axle, heavy-laden, is not heated: the nave from ancient time remains unbroken.
14 The wheel revolves, unwasting, with its felly: ten draw it, yoked to the far-stretching car-pole.
The Sun's eye moves encompassed by the region: on him dependent rest all living creatures.
15 Of the co-born they call the seventh single-born; the six twin pairs are called Rsis, Children of
Gods.
Their good gifts sought of men are ranged in order due, and various in their form move for the Lord
who guides.
16 They told me these were males, though truly females: he who hath eyes sees this, the blind
discerns not.
The son who is a sage hath comprehended: who knows this rightly is his father's father.
17 Beneath the upper realm, above this lower, bearing her calf at foot the Cow hath risen.
Witherward, to what place hath she departed? Where calves she? Not amid this herd of cattle.
18 Who, that the father of this Calf discerneth beneath the upper realm, above the lower,
Showing himself a sage, may here declare it? Whence hath the Godlike spirit had its rising?
19 Those that come hitherward they call departing, those that depart they call directed hither.
And what so ye have made, Indra and Soma, steeds bear as 'twere yoked to the region's car-pole.
20 Two Birds with fair wings, knit with bonds of friendship, in the same sheltering tree have found a
refuge.
One of the twain eats the sweet Fig-tree's fruitage; the other eating not regardeth only.
21 Where those fine Birds hymn ceaselessly their portion of life eternal, and the sacred synods,
There is the Universe's mighty Keeper, who, wise, hath entered into me the simple.
22 The, tree whereon the fine Birds eat the sweetness, where they all rest and procreate their
offspring,-
Upon its top they say the fig is luscious none gaineth it who knoweth not the Father.
23 How on the Gayatri. the Gayatri was based, how from the Tristup they fashioned the Tristup forth,
How on the Jagati was based the Jagati,- they who know this have won themselves immortal life.
24 With Gayatri he measures out the praise-song, Sama with praise-song, triplet with the Tristup.
The triplet witli the two or four-foot measure, and with the syllable they form seven metres.
25 With Jagati the flood in heaven he stablished, and saw the Sun in the Rathantara Saman.
Gavatri hath, they say, three brands for kindling: hence it excels in majesty and vigour.
26 I invocate the milch-cow good for milking so that the milker, deft of hand, may drain her.
May Savitar give goodliest stimulation. The caldron is made hot; I will proclaim it.

27 She, lady of all treasure, is come hither yearning in spirit for her calf and lowing.
May this cow yield her milk for both the Asvins, and may she prosper to our high advantage.
28 The cow hath lowed after her blinking youngling; she licks his forehead, as she lows, to form it.
His mouth she fondly calls to her warm udder, and suckles him with milk while gently lowing.
29 He also snorts, by whom encompassed round the Cow laws as she clings unto the shedder of the
rain.
She with her shrilling cries hath humbled mortal man, and, turned to lightning, hath stripped off her
covering robe.
30 That which hath breath and speed and life and motion lies firmly stablished in the midst of
houses.
Living, by offerings to the Dead he moveth Immortal One, the brother of the mortal.
31 I saw the Herdsman, him who never stumbles, approaching by his pathways and departing.
He, clothed with gathered and diffusive splendour, within the worlds continually travels.
32 He who hath made him cloth not comprehend him: from him who saw him surely is he hidden.
He, yet enveloped in his Mother's bosom, source of much life, hath sunk into destruction.
33 Dyaus is my Father, my begetter: kinship is here. This great earth is my kin and Mother.
Between the wide-spread world-halves is the birthb-place: the Father laid the Daughter's germ
within it.
34 1ask thee of the earth's extremest limit, where is the centre of the world, I ask
thee.
1ask thee of the Stallion's seed prolific, I ask of highest heaven where Speech abideth.
35 This altar is the earth's extremest limit; this sacrifice of ours is the world's centre.
The Stallion's seed prolific is the Soma; this Brahman highest heaven where Speech abideth.
36 Seven germs unripened yet are heaven's prolific, seed: their functions they maintain by Visnu's
ordinance.
Endued with wisdom through intelligence and thought, they compass us about present on every
side.
37 What thing I truly am I know not clearly: mysterious, fettered in my mind I wander.
When the first-born of holy Law approached me, then of this speech I first obtain a portion.
38 Back, forward goes he, grasped by strength inherent, the Immortal born the brother of the mortal
Ceaseless they movelnopposite directions: men mark the one, and fail to mark the other.
39 Upon what syllable of holy praise-song, as twere their highest heaven, the Gods repose them,-
Who knows not this, what will he do with praise-song? But they who know it well sit here
assembled.
40 Forunate mayst thou be with goodly pasture, and may we also be exceeding wealthy.
Feed on the grass, O Cow, at every season, and coming hitherward drink limpid water.
41 Forming the water-floods, the buffalo hath lowed, one-footed or two-footed or fourfooted, she,

Who hath become eight-footed or hath got nine feet, the thou sand-syllabled in the sublimest heaven.
42 From her descend in streams the seas of water; thereby the world's four regions have their being,
Thence flows the imperishable flood and thence the universe hath life.
43 I saw from far away the smoke of fuel with spires that rose on high o'er that beneath it.
The Mighty Men have dressed the spotted bullock. These were the customs in the days aforetime,
44 Three with long tresses show in ordered season. One of them sheareth when the year is ended.
One with his powers the universe regardeth: Of one, the sweep is seen, but his figure.
45 Speech hath been measured out in four divisions, the Brahmans who have understanding know
them.
Three kept in close concealment cause no motion; of speech, men speak only the fourth division.
46 They call him Indra, Mitra, Varuna, Agni, and he is heavenly nobly-winged Garutman.
To what is One, sages give many a title they call it Agni, Yama, Matarisvan.
47 Dark the descent: the birds are golden-coloured; up to the heaven they fly robed in the waters.
Again descend they from the seat of Order, and all the earth is moistened with their fatness.
48 Twelve are the fellies, and the wheel is single; three are the naves. What man hath understood it?
Therein are set together spokes three hundred and sixty, which in nowise can be loosened.
49 That breast of thine exhaustless, spring of pleasure, wherewith thou feedest all things that are
choicest,
Wealth-giver, treasure. finder, free bestower,-bring that, Sarasvati, that we may drain it.
50 By means of sacrifice the Gods accomplished their sacrifice: these were the earliest ordinances.
These Mighty Ones attained the height of heaven, there where the Sadhyas, Gods of old, are
dwelling.
51 Uniform, with the passing days, this water mounts and fails again.
The tempest-clouds give life to earth, and fires re-animate the heaven.
52 The Bird Celestial, vast with noble pinion, the lovely germ of plants, the germ of waters,
Him who delighteth us with rain in season, Sarasvan I invoke that he may help us.

## [01-165] HYMN CLXV. Indra. Maruts.

1. WITH what bright beauty are the Maruts jointly invested, peers in age, who dwell together?
From what place have they come? With what intention? Sing they their strength through love of
wealth, these Heroes?
2 Whose prayers have they, the Youthful Ones, accepted? Who to his sacrifice hath turned the
Maruts?
We will delay them on their journey sweeping-with what high spirit!-through the air like eagles.
3 Whence comest thou alone, thou who art mighty, Indra, Lord of the Brave? What is thy purpose?
Thou greetest us when meeting us the Bright Ones. Lord of Bay Steeds, say what thou hast against us.
4 Mine are devotions, hymns; sweet are libations. Strength stirs, and hurled forth is my bolt of thunder.

They call for me, their lauds are longing for me. These my Bay Steeds bear me to these oblations.

5 Therefore together with our strong companions, having adorned our bodies, now we harness,
Our spotted deer with might, for thou, O Indra, hast learnt and understood our Godlike nature.
6 Where was that nature then of yours, O Maruts, that ye charged me alone to slay the Dragon?
For I in truth am fierce and strong and mighty. I bent away from every foeman's weapons.
7 Yea, much hast thou achieved with us for comrades, with manly valour like thine own, thou Hero.
Much may we too achieve, O mightiest Indra, with our great power, we Maruts, when we will it.
8 Vrtra I slew by mine own strength, O Maruts, having waxed mighty in mine indignation.
I with the thunder in my hand created for man these lucid softly flowing waters.
9 Nothing, O Maghavan, stands firm before thee; among the Gods not one is found
thine equal.
None born or springing into life comes nigh thee. Do what thou hast to do, exceeding mighty?
10 Mine only be transcendent power, whatever I, daring in my spirit, may accomplish.
For I am known as terrible, O Maruts I, Indra, am the Lord of what I ruined.
11 Now, O ye Maruts, hath your praise rejoiced me, the glorious hymn which ye have made me,
Heroes!
For me, for Indra, champion strong in battle, for me, yourselves, as lovers for a lover.
12 Here, truly, they send forth their sheen to meet me, wearing their blameless glory and their vigour.
When I have seen you, Matuts, in gay splendour, ye have delighted me, so now delight me.
13 Who here hath magnified you, O ye Maruts? speed forward, O ye lovers, to your lovers.
Ye Radiant Ones, assisting their devotions, of these my holy rites he ye regardful.
14 To this hath Minya's wisdom brought us, so as to aid, as aids the poet him who worships.
Bring hither quick! On to the sage, ye Maruts! These prayers for you the singer hath recited.
15 May this your praise, may this your song, O Maruts, sung by the poet, Mana's son, Mandarya,
Bring offspring for ourselves with food to feed us. May we find strengthening food in full abundance!

### [01-166] HYMN CLXVI. Maruts.
1. Now let us publish, for the vigorous company the herald of the Strong One, their primeval might.
With fire upon your way, O Maruts loud of voice, with battle, Mighty Ones, achieve your deeds of
strength.
2 Bringing the pleasant mcath as 'twere their own dear son, they sport in sportive wise gay at their
gatherings.
The Rudras come with succour to the worshipper; self-strong they fail not him who offers sacrifice.
3 To whomsoever, bringer of oblations, they immortal guardians, have given plenteous wealth,
For him, like loving friends, the Maruts bringing bliss bedew the regions round with milk abundantly.
4 Ye who with mighty powers have stirred the regions up, your coursers have sped forth directed by themselves.

All creatures of the earth, all dwellings are afraid, for brilliant is your coming with your spears
advanced.
5 When they in dazzling rush have made the mountains roar, and shaken heaven's high back in their
heroic strength,
Each sovran of the forest fears as ye drive near, aid the shrubs fly before you swift as whirling
wheels.
6 Terrible Maruts, ye with ne'er-diminished host, with grcat benevolence fulfil our heart's desire.
Where'er your lightning bites armed with its gory teeth it crunches up the cattle like a well-aimed
dart.
7 Givers of during gifts whose bounties never fail, free from ill-will, at sacrifices glorified,
They sing their song aloud that they may drink sweet juice: well do they know the Hero's first heroic
deeds.
8 With castles hundredfold, O Maruts, guard ye well the man whom ye have loved from ruin and from
sin,-
The man whom ye the fierce, the Mighty ones who roar, preserve from calumny by cherishing his
seed.
9 O Maruts, in your cars are all things that are good: great powers are set as 'twere in rivalry therein.
Rings are upon your shoulders when ye journey forth: your axle turns together both the chariot
wheels.
10 Held in your manly arms are many goodly things, gold chains are on your chests, and glistering
ornaments,
Deer-skins are on their shoulders, on their fellies knives: they spread their glory out as birds spread
out their wings.
11 Mighty in mightiness, pervading, passing strong, visible from afar as 'twere with stars of heaven,
Lovely with pleasant tongues, sweet singers with their mouths, the Maruts, joined with Indra, shout
forth all around.
12 This is your majesty, ye Maruts nobly born, far as the sway of Adid your bounty spreads.
Even Indra by desertion never disannuls the boon bestowed by you upon the pious man.
13 This is your kinship, Maruts, that, Immortals, ye were oft in olden time regardful of our call,
Having vouchsafed to man a hearing through this prayer, by wondrous deeds the Heroes have
displayed their might.
14 That, O ye Maruts, we may long time flourish through your abundant riches, O swift movers,
And that our men may spread in the encampment, let me complete the rite with these oblations.
15 May this your laud, may this your song, O Maruts, sung by the poet, Mana's son, Mandarya,
Bring offspring for ourselves with food to feed us. May we find strengthening food in full abundance.

### [01-167] HYMN CLXVII. Indra. Maruts.
1. A THOUSAND are thy helps for us, O Indra: a thousand, Lord of Bays, thy choice refreshments.
Wealth of a thousand sorts hast thou to cheer us: may precious goods come nigh to us in thousands.
2 May the most sapient Maruts, with protection, with best boons brought from lofty heaven,
approach us,

Now when their team of the most noble horses speeds even on the sea's extremest limit.

3 Close to them clings one moving in seclusion, like a man's wife, like a spear carried rearward,
Well grasped, bright, decked with gold there is Vak also, like to a courtly, eloquent dame, among them.

4 Far off the brilliant, never-weary Maruts cling to the young Maid as a joint possession.
The fierce Gods drave not Rodasi before them, but wished for her to grow their friend and fellow.

5 When chose immortal Rodasi to follow- she with loose tresses and heroic spirit-
She climbed her servant's chariot, she like Surya with cloud-like motion and refulgent aspect.

6 Upon their car the young men set the Maiden wedded to glory, mighty in assemblies,
When your song, Maruts, rose, and, with oblation, the Soma-pourer sang his hymn in worship.

7 I will declare the greatness of these Maruts, their real greatness, worthy to be lauded,
How, with them, she though firm, strong-minded, haughty, travels to women happy in their fortune.

8 Mitra and Varuna they guard from censure: Aryaman too, discovers worthless sinners Firm things
are overthrown that ne'er were shaken: he prospers, Maruts, who gives choice oblations.

9 None of us, Maruts, near or at a distance, hath ever reached the limit of your vigour.
They in courageous might still waxing boldly have compassed round their foemen like an ocean.

10 May we this day be dearest friends of Indra, and let us call on him in fight to-morrow.
So were we erst. New might attend us daily! So be with us! Rbhuksan of the Heroes!

11 May this your laud, may this your song, O Maruts, sung by the poet, Mana's
son, Mandarya,
Bring offspring for ourselves with. food to feed us. May we find strengthening food in full abundance.

## [01-168] HYMN CLXVIII. Maruts.

1. SWIFT gain is his who hath you near at every rite: ye welcome every song of himwho serves the Gods.
So may I turn you hither with fair hymns of praise to give great succour for the weal of both the worlds.

2 Surrounding, as it were, self-born, self-powerful, they spring to life the shakers-down of food and light;
Like as the countess undulations of the floods, worthy of praise when near, like bullocks and like kine.

3 They who, like Somas with their well-grown stalks pressed out, imbibed within the heart, dwell
there in friendly wise.
Upon their shoulders rests as 'twere a warrior's spear and in their hand they hold a dagger and a ring.

4 Self-yoked they have descended lightly from the sky. With your own lash, Immortals, urge
yourselve's to speed.
Unstained by dust the Maruts, mighty in their strength, have cast down e'en firm things, armed with
their shining spears.

5 Who among you, O Maruts armed with lightning-spears, moveth you by himself, as with the tongue
his jaws?
Ye rush from heaven's floor as though ye sought for food, on many errands like the Sun's diurnal Steed.

6 Say where, then, is this mighty region's farthest bound, where, Maruts, is the lowest depth that ye
have reached,
When ye cast down like chaff the firmly stablished pile, and from the mountain send the glittering water-flood?

7 Your winning is with strength, dazzling, with heavenly light, with fruit mature, O Maruts, fall of plenteousness.
Auspicious is your gift like a free giver's meed, victorious, spreading far, as of immortal Gods.

8 The rivers roar before your chariot fellies when they are uttering the voice of rain-clouds.
The lightnings laugh upon the earth beneath them, what time the Maruts scatter forth their fatness.

9 Prani brought forth, to fight the mighty battle, the glittering army of the restless Maruts.
Nurtured together they begat the monster, and then looked round them for the food that strengthens.

10 May this your laud, may this your song O Maruts, sung by the poet Mana's son,
Mandarya,
Bring offspring for ourselves with food to feed us. May we find strengthening food in full abundance.

## [01-169] HYMN CLXIX. Indra.

1. As, Indra, from great treason thou protectest, yea, from great treachery these who approach us,
So, marking well, Controller of the Maruts grant us their blessings, for they are thy dearest.

2 The various doings of all mortal people by thee are ordered, in thy wisdom, Indra.
The host of Marutg goeth forth exulting to win the light-bestowing spoil of battle.

3 That spear of thine sat firm for us, O Indra: the Maruts set their whole dread power in motion.
E'en Agni shines resplendent in the brush-wood: the viands hold him as floods hold an island.

4 Vouchsafe us now that opulence, O Indra, as guerdon won by mightiest donation.
May hymns that please thee cause the breast of Vayu to swell as with the mead's refreshing sweetness.

5 With thee, O Indra, are most bounteous riches that further every one who lives uprightly.
Now may these Maruts show us loving-kindness, Gods who of old were ever prompt to help us.

6 Bring forth the Men who rain down boons, O Indra: exert thee in the great terrestrial region;
For their broad-chested speckled deer are standing like a King's armies on the field of battle.

7 Heard is the roar of the advancing Maruts, terrific, glittering, and swiftly moving,
Who with their rush o'erthrow as 'twere a sinner the mortal who would fight with those who love him

8 Give to the Manas, Indra with Maruts, gifts universal, gifts of cattle foremost.
Thou, God, art praised with Gods who must be lauded. May we find strengthening food in full abundance.

**[01-170] HYMN CLXX. Indra. Maruts.**

1. NAUGHT is to-day, to-morrow naught. Who comprehends the mystery?
We must address ourselves unto another's thought, and lost is then the hope we formed.
2 The Maruts are thy brothers. Why, O Indra, wouldst thou take our lives?
Agree with them in friendly wise, and do not slay us in the fight.
3 Agastya, brother, why dost thou neglect us, thou who art our friend?
We know the nature of thy mind. Verity thou wilt give us naught.
4 Let them prepare the altar, let them kindle fire in front: we two
Here will spread sacrifice for thee, that the Immortal may observe.
5 Thou, Lord of Wealth, art Master of all treasures, thou, Lord of friends, art thy
friends' best supporter.
O Indra, speak thou kindly with the Maruts, and taste oblations in their proper season.

**[01-171] HYMN CLXXI. Maruts.**

1. To you I come with this mine adoration, and with a hymn I crave the Strong Ones' favour
A hymn that truly makes you joyful, Maruts. Suppress your anger and unyoke your horses.
2 Maruts, to you this laud with prayer and worship, formed in the mind and heart, ye Gods, is offered.
Come ye to us, rejoicing in your spirit, for ye are they who make our prayer effective.
3 The Maruts, praised by us, shall show us favour; Maghavan, lauded, shall be most propitious.
Maruts,, may all our days that are to follow be very pleasant, lovely and triumphant.
4 I fled in terrror from this mighty Indra, my body trembling in alarm, O Maruts.
Oblations meant for you had been made ready; these have we set aside: for this forgive us.
5 By whom the Manas recognize the day-springs, by whose strength at the dawn of endless
mornings,
Give us, thou Mighty, glory with Maruts. fierce with the fierce, the Strong who givest triumph.
6 Do thou, O Indra, guard the conquering Heroes, and rid thee of thy wrath against the Maruts,
With them, the wise, victorious and bestowing. May we find strengthening food in full abundance.

**[01-172] HYMN CLXXII. Maruts.**

1. WONDERFUL let your coming be, wondrous with help, ye Bounteous Ones,
Maruts, who gleam as serpents gleam.
2 Far be from us, O Maruts, ye free givers, your impetuous shaft;
Far from us be the stone ye hurl.
3 O Bounteous Givers, touch ye not, O Maruts, Trnskanda's folk;
Lift ye us up that we may live.

**[01-173] HYMN CLXXIII. Indra.**

1. THE praise-song let him sing forth bursting bird-like: sing we that hymn which like heaven's light
expandeth,
That the milk-giving cows may, unimpeded call to the sacred grass the Gods' assembly.
2 Let the Bull sing with Bulls whose toil is worship, with a loud roar like some wild beast that
hungers.
Praised God! the glad priest brings his heart's devotion; the holy youth presents twofold oblation.

3 May the Priest come circling the measured stations, and with him bring the earth's autumnal
fruitage.
Let the Horse neigh led near, let the Steer bellow: let the Voice go between both worlds as herald,
4 To him we offer welcomest oblations, the pious bring their strength-inspiring praises.
May Indra, wondrous in his might, accept them, car-borne and swift to move like the Nasatyas.
5 Praise thou that Indra who is truly mighty, the car-borne Warrior, Maghavan the Hero;
Stronger in war than those who fight against him, borne by strong steeds, who kills enclosing
darkness;
6 Him who surpasses heroes in his greatness: the earth and heavens suffice not for his girdles.
Indra endues the earth to be his garment, and, God-like, wears the heaven as 'twere a frontlet,
7 Thee, Hero, guardian of the brave in battles, who roamest in the van,-to draw thee hither,
Indra, the hosts agree beside the Soma, and joy, for his great actions, in the Chieftain.
8 Libations in the sea to thee are pleasant, when thy divine Floods come to cheer these people.
To thee the Cow is sum of all things grateful when with the wish thou seekest men and princes.
9 So may we in this One be well befriended, well aided as it were through praise of chieftains,
That Indra still may linger at our worship, as one led swift to work, to hear our praises.
10 Like men in rivalry extolling princes, our Friend be Indra, wielder of the thunder.
Like true friends of some city's lord within them held in good rule with sacrifice they help him.
11 For every sacrifice makes Indra stronger, yea, when he goes around angry in spirit;
As pleasure at the ford invites the thirsty, as the long way brings him who gains his object.
12 Let us not here contend with Gods, O Indra, for here, O Mighty One, is thine own portion,
The Great, whose Friends the bounteous Maruts honour, as with a stream, his song who pours
oblations.
13 Addressed to thee is this our praise, O Indra: Lord of Bay Steeds, find us hereby advancement.
So mayst thou lead us on, O God, to comfort. May we find strengthening food in full abundance.

**[01-174] HYMN CLXXIV. Indra.**

1. THOU art the King of all the Gods, O Indra: protect the men, O Asura, preserve us.
Thou Lord of Heroes, Maghavan, our saver, art faithful, very rich, the victory-giver.
2 Indra, thou humbledst tribes that spake with insult by breaking down seven autumn forts, their
refuge.
Thou stirredst, Blameless! billowy floods, and gavest his foe a prey to youthful Purukutsa.
3 With whom thou drivest troops whose lords are heroes, and bringest daylight now, much
worshipped Indra,
With them guard lion-like wasting active Agni to dwell in our tilled fields and in our homestead.
4 They through the greatness of thy spear, O Indra, shall, to thy praise, rest in this earthly station.
To loose the floods, to seek, for kine, the battle, his Bays he mounted boldly seized the booty.

5 Indra, bear Kutsa, him in whom thou joyest: the dark-red horses of the Wind are docile.
Let the Sun roll his chariot wheel anear us, and let the Thunderer go to meet the foemen.
6 Thou Indra, Lord of Bays, made strong by impulse, hast slain the vexers of thy friends, who give not.
They who beheld the Friend beside the living were cast aside by thee as they rode onward.
7 Indra, the bard sang forth in inspiration: thou madest earth a covering for the Dasa.
Maghavan made the three that gleam with moisture, and to his home brought Kuyavac to slay him.
8 These thine old deeds new bards have sung, O Indra. Thou conqueredst, boundest many tribes for ever.
Like castles thou hast crushed the godless races, and bowed the godless scorner's deadly weapon.
9 A Stormer thou hast made the stormy waters flow down, O Indra, like the running rivers.
When o'er the flood thou broughtest them, O Hero, thou keptest Turvaga and Yadu safely.
10 Indra, mayst thou be ours in all occasions, protector of the men, most gentle-hearted,
Giving us victory over all our rivals. May we find strengthening food in full abundance.

### [01-175] HYMN CLXXV. Indra.

1. GLAD thee: thy glory hath been quaffed, Lord of Bay Steeds, as 'twere the bowl's enlivening mead.
For thee the Strong there is strong drink, mighty, omnipotent to win.
2 Let our strong drink, most excellent, exhilarating, come to thee, Victorious, Indra1 bringing gain, immortal conquering in fight,
3 Thou, Hero, winner of the spoil, urgest to speed the car of man.
Burn, like a vessel with the flame, the lawless Dasyu, Conqueror!
4 Empowered by thine own might, O Sage, thou stolest Sarya's chariot wheel.
Thou barest Kutsa with the steeds of Wind to Susna as his death.
5 Most mighty is thy rapturous joy, most splendid is thine active power,
Wherewith, foe-slaying, sending bliss, thou art supreme in gaining steeds.
6 As thou, O Indra, to the ancient singers wast ever joy, as water to the thirsty,
So unto thee I sing this invocation. May we find strengthening food in full abundance.

### [01-176] HYMN CLXXVI. Indra.

1. CHEER thee with draughts to win us bliss: Soma, pierce Indra in thy strength.
Thou stormest trembling in thy rage, and findest not a foeman nigh.
2 Make our songs penetrate to him who is the Only One of men;
For whom the sacred food is spread, as the steer ploughs the barley in.
3 Within whose hands deposited all the Five Peoples' treasures rest.
Mark thou the man who injures us and kill him like the heavenly bolt.
4 Slay everyone who pours no gift, who, hard to reach, delights thee not.
Bestow on us what wealth he hath: this even the worshipper awaits.
5 Thou helpest him the doubly strong whose hymns were sung unceasingly.
When Indra fought, O Soma, thou helpest the mighty in the fray.

6 As thou, O Indra, to the ancient singers wast ever joy, like water to the thirsty,
So unto thee I sing this invocation. May we find strengthenifig food in full abundance.

### [01-177] HYMN CLXXVII. Indra.

1. THE Bull of men, who cherishes all people, King of the Races, Indra, called of many,
Fame-loving, praised, hither to me with succour turn having yoked both vigorous Bay Horses!
2 Thy mighty Stallions, yoked by prayer, O Indra, thy. Coursers to thy mighty chariot harnessed,-
Ascend thou these, and borne by them come hither: with Soma juice out. poured, Indra, we call thee.
3 Ascend thy mighty car: the mighty Soma is poured for thee and sweets are sprinkled round us.
Come down to us-ward, Bull of human races,come, having harnessed them, with strong Bay Horses.
4 Here is God-reaching sacrifice, here the victim; here, Indra,are the prayers, here is the Soma.
Strewn is thesacred grass: come hither, Sakra; seatthee and drink: unyoke thy two Bay Coursers.
5 Come to us, Indra, come thou highly lauded to the devotions of the singer Mana.
Singing, may we find early through thy succour, may we find strengthening food in full abundance.

### [01-178] HYMN CLXXVIII. Indra.

1. IF, Indra, thou hast given that gracious hearing where with thou helpest those who sang thy praises.
Blast not the wish that would exalt us may I gain all from thee, and pay all man's devotions.
2 Let not the Sovran Indra disappoint us in what shall bring both Sisters to our dwelling.
To him have run the quickly flowing waters.May Indra come to us with life and friendship.
3 Victorious with the men, Hero in battles, Indra, who hearsthe singer's supplication,
Will bring his car nigh to the man who offers, if he himself upholds the songs that praise him.
4 Yea,Indra, with the men, through love of gloryconsumes the sacred food which friends have offered.
The ever-strengthening song of him who worships is sung in fight amid the clash of voices.
5Aided by thee, O Maghavan, O Indra, may we subdue our foes who count them mighty.
Be our protector, strengthen and increase us.May we find strengthening food in full abundance.

### [01-179] HYMN CLXXIX. Rati.

1 'Through many autumns have I toiled and laboured, at night and morn, through age-inducing dawnings.
Old age impairs the beauty of our bodies. Let husbands still come near unto their spouses.
2 For even the men aforetime, law-fulfillers, who with the Gods declared eternal statutes,--
They have decided, but have not accomplished: so now let wives come near unto their husbands.
3 Non inutilis est labor cui Dii favent: nos omnes aemulos et aemulas vincamus.
Superemus in hac centum artium pugna in qua duas partes convenientes utrinque commovemus.
4 Cupido me cepit illius tauri (viri) qui me despicit, utrum hinc utrum illinc ab aliqua parte nata sit.

Lopamudra taurum (maritum suum) ad se detrahit: insipiens illa
sapientem anhelantem absorbet.
5 This Soma I address that is most near us, that which hath been
imbibed within the spirit,
To pardon any sins we have committed. Verily mortal man is full
of longings.
6 Agastya thus, toiling with strong endeavour, wishing for
children, progeny and power,
Cherished - a sage of mighty strength - both classes, and with the
Gods obtained his prayer's
fulfilment.
5 Membrum suum virile, quod vrotentum fuerat, mas ille retraxit.
Rursus illud quod in juvenem filiam
sublatum fuerat, non aggressurus, ad se retrahit.
6 Quum jam in medio connessu, semiperfecto opere, amorem in
puellam pater impleverat, ambo
discedentes seminis paulum in terrae superficiem sacrorum sede
effusum emiserunt.
7 Quum pater suam nilam adiverat, cum ea congressus suum
semen supra wrrarn effudit. Tum Dii
benigni precem (brahma) progenuerunt, et Vastoshpatim, legum
sacrarum custodem, formaverunt.
8 Ille tauro similis spumam in certamine jactavit, tunc discedens
pusillaximis huc profectus est. Quasi
dextro pede claudus processit, "inutiles fuerunt illi mei
complexus," ita locutus.
9 'The fire, burning the people, does not approach quickly (by
day): the naked (Rakasas approach) not
Agni by night; the giver of fuel, and the giver of food, he, the
upholder (of the rite), is born,
overcoming enemies by his might.'

## [01-180] HYMN CLXXX. Asvins.

1. LIGHTLY your coursers travel through the regions when round
thesea of air your car is flying.
Your golden fellies scatter drops of moisture: drinking the
sweetness ye atend the Mornings.
2 Ye as ye travel overtake the Courser who flies apart, the Friend
of man, most holy.
The prayer is that the Sister may convey you, all praised, meath-
drinkers! to support and strengthen.
3 Ye have deposited, matured within her, in the raw cow the first
milk of the milch-cow,
Which the bright offerer, shining like a serpent mid trees,
presents to you whose form is perfect.
4 Ye made the fierce heat to be full of sweetness for Atri at his
wish, like streaming water.
Fire-offering thence is yours, O Asvins, Heroes: your car-wheels
speed to us like springs of honey.
5 Like Tugra's ancient son may I, ye Mighty, bring you to give
your gifts with milk-oblations.
Your greatness compasseth Earth, Heaven, and Waters: decayed
for you is sorrow's net, ye Holy.
6 When, Bounteous Ones, ye drive your yoked team downward,
ye send, by your own natures,
understanding.
Swift as the wind let the prince please and feast you: he, like a
pious man, gains strength for
increase.
7 For verily we truthful singers praise you the niggard trafficker is
here excluded.
Now, even now do ye O blameless Advins, ye Mighty, guard the
man whose God is near him.
8 You of a truth day after day, O Asvins, that he might win the
very plenteous torrent,
Agastya, famous among mortal heroes, roused with a thousand
lauds like sounds of music.

9 When with the glory of your car ye travel, when we go speeding
like the priest of mortals,
And give good horses to sacrificers, may we, Nasatyas! gain our
share of riches.
10 With songs of praise we call to-day, O Asvins, that your new
chariot, for our own well-being,
That circles heaven with never-injured fellies. May we find
strengthening food in full abundance.

## [01-181] HYMN CLXXXI. Asvins

1. WHAT, dearest Pair, is this in strength and riches that ye as
Priests are bring from the waters?
This sacrifice is your glorification, ye who protect mankind and
give them treasures.
2 May your pure steeds, rain-drinkers, bring you hither, swift as
the tempest, your celestial coursers,
Rapid as thought, with fair backs, full of vigour, resplendent in
their native light, O Asvins.
3 Your car is like a torrent rushing downward: may it come nigh,
broad-seated, for our welfare,-
Car holy, strong, that ever would be foremost, thought-swift,
which ye, for whom we long, have
mounted.
4 Here sprung to life, they both have sung together, with bodies
free from stain, with signs that mark
them;
One of you Prince of Sacrifice, the Victor, the other counts as
Heaven's auspicious offspring.
5 May your car-seat, down-gliding, golden-coloured, according to
your wish approach our dwellings.
Men shall feed full the bay steeds of the other, and, Asvins they
with roars shall stir the regions.
6 Forth comes your strong Bull like a cloud of autumn, sending
abundant food of liquid sweetness.
Let them feed with the other's ways and vigour: the upper
streams have come and do us service.
7 Your constant song hath been sent forth, Disposers! that flows
threefold in mighty strength, O
Asvins.
Thus lauded, give the suppliant protection moving or resting hear
mine invocation.
8 This song of bright contents for you is swelling in the men's hall
where three-fold grass is.ready.
Your strong rain-cloud, ye Mighty Ones, hath swollen, honouring
men as 'twere with milk's
outpouring.
9 The prudent worshipper, like Pusan, Asvins! praises you as he
praises Dawn and Agni,
When, singing with devotion, he invokes you. May we find
strengthening food in full abundance.

## [01-182] HYMN CLXXXII. Asvins.

1. THIS was the task. Appear promptly, ye prudent Ones. Here is
the chariot drawn by strong steeds:
be ye glad.
Heart-stirring, longed for, succourers of Vispala, here are
Heaven's Sons whose sway blesses the
pious man.
2 Longed for, most Indra-like, mighty, most Marut-like, most
w6nderful in deed, car-borne, best
charioteers,
Bring your full chariot hither heaped with liquid sweet: thereon,
ye Mvins, come to him who offers
gifts.
3 What make ye there, ye Mighty? Wherefore linger ye with folk
who, offering not, are held in high
esteem?

Pass over them; make ye the niggard's life decay: give light unto the singer eloquent in praise.

4 Crunch up on. every side the dogs who bark at us: slay ye our foes, O Asvins this ye understand.
Make wealthy every word of him who praises you: accept with favour, both Nasatyas, this my laud.

5 Ye made for Tugra's son amid the water-floods that animated ship with wings to fly withal,
Whereon with God-devoted mind ye brought him forth, and fled with easy flight from out the mighty
surge.

6 Four ships most welcome in the midst of ocean, urged by the Asvins, save the son of Tugra,
Him who was cast down headlong in the waters, plunged in the thick inevitable darkness.

7 What tree was that which stood fixed in surrounding sea to which the son of Tugra supplicating
clung?
Like twigs, of which some winged creature may take hold, ye, Asvins, bore him off safely to your
renown.

8 Welcome to you be this the hymn of praises uttered by Manas, O Nasatyas, Heroes,
From this our gathering where we offer Soma. May we find strengthening food in full abundance.

### [01-183] HYMN CLXXXIII. Asvins.

1. MAKE ready that which passes thought in swiftness, that hath three wheels and triple seat, ye
Mighty,
Whereon ye seek the dwelling of the pious, whereon, threefold, ye fly like birds with pinions.

2 Light rolls your easy chariot faring earthward, what time, for food, ye, full of wisdom, mount it.
May this song, wondrous fair, attend your glory: ye, as ye travel, wait on Dawn Heaven's Daughter.

3 Ascend your lightly rolling car, approaching the worshipper who turns him to his duties,-
Whereon ye come unto the house to quicken man and his offspring, O Nasatyas, Heroes.

4 Let not the wolf, let not the she-wolf harm you. Forsake me not, nor pass me by or others.
Here stands your share, here is your hymn, ye Mighty: yours are these vessels, full of pleasant juices.

5 Gotama, Purumilha, Atri bringing oblations all invoke you for protection.
Like one who goes strai ht to the point directed, ye Nasatyas, to mine invocation.

6 We have passed o'er the limit of this darkness: our praise hath been bestowed on you, O Asvins.
Come hitherward by paths which Gods have travelled. May we find strengthening food in full
abundance.

### [01-184] HYMN CLXXXIV Asvins.

1. LET us invoke you both this day and after the priest is here with lauds when morn is breaking:
Nasatyas, wheresoe'er ye be, Heaven's Children, for him who is more liberal than the godless.

2 With us, ye Mighty, let yourselves be joyful, glad in our stream of Soma slay the niggards.
Graciously hear my hymns and invitations, marking, O Heroes, with your cars my longing.

3 Nasatyas, Pusans, ye as Gods for glory arranged and set in order Surya's bridal.
Your giant steeds move on, sprung from the waters, like ancient times of Varuna the Mighty.

4 Your grace be with us, ye who love sweet juices: further the hymn sung by the poet Mana,
When men are joyful in your glorious actions, to win heroic strength, ye Bounteous Givers.

5 This praise was made, O liberal Lords, O Asvins, for you with fair adornment by the Manas.
Come to our house for us and for our children, rejoicing, O Nasatyas, in Agastya.

6 We have passed o'er the limit of this darkness: our praise hath been'bestowed on you, O Asvins.
Come hitherward by paths which Gods have travelled. may we find strengthening food in full
abundance.

### [01-185] HYMN CLXXXV. Heaven and Earth.

1. WHETHER of these is elder, whether later? How were they born? Who knoweth it, ye sages?
These of themselves support all things existing: as on a car the Day and Night roll onward.

2 The Twain uphold, though motionless and footless, a widespread offspring having feet and moving.
Like your own fon upon his parents' bosom, protect us, Heaven and earth, from fearful danger.

3 I call for Aditi's unrivalled bounty, perfect, celestial, deathless, meet for worship.
Produce this, ye Twain Worlds, for him who lauds you. Protect us, Heaven and Earth, from fearful
danger.

4 May we be close to both the Worlds who suffer no pain, Parents of Gods, who aid with favour,
Both mid the Gods, with Day and Night alternate. Protect us, Heaven and Earth, from fearful danger.

5 Faring together, young, with meeting limits, Twin Sisters lying in their Parents' bosom,
Kissing the centre of the world together. Protect us, Heaven and Earth, from fearful danger.

6 Duly I call the two wide seats, the mighty, the general Parents, with the God's protection.
Who, beautiful to look on, make the nectar. Protect us, Heaven and Earth, from fearful danger.

7 Wide, vast, and manifold, whose bounds are distant,-these, reverent, I address at this our worship,
The blessed Pair, victorious, all-sustaining. Protect us, Heaven and Earth, from fearful danger.

8 What sin we have at any time committed against the Gods, our friend, our house's chieftain,
Thereof may this our hymn be expiation. Protect us, Heaven and Earth, from fearful danger.

9 May both these Friends of man, who bless, preserve me, may they attend me with their help and
favour.
Enrich the man more liberal than the godless. May we, ye Gods, be strong with food rejoicing.

10 Endowed with understanding, I have uttered this truth, for all to hear, to Earth and Heaven.
Be near us, keep us from reproach and trouble. Father and Mother, with your help preserve us.

11 Be this my prayer fulfilled, O Earth and Heaven, wherewith, Father and Mother, I address you.
Nearest of Gods be ye with your protection. May we find strengthening food in full abundance.

### [01-186] HYMN CLXXXVI. Visvedevas.

1. LOVED of all men, may Savitar, through praises offered as sacred food, come to our synod,
That you too, through-our hymn, ye ever-youthful, may gladden, at your visit, all our people.

2 To us may all the Gods come trooped together, Aryaman, Mitra, Varuna concordant,
That all may be promoters of our welfare, and with great might preserve our strength from slackness.
3 Agni I sing, the guest you love most dearly: the Conqueror through our lauds is friendly-minded.
That he may be our Varuna rich in glory and send food like a prince praised by the godly.
4 To you I seek with reverence, Night and Morning, like a cow good to milk, with hope to conquer,
Preparing on a common day the praise. song with milk of various hues within this udder.
5 May the great Dragon of the Deep rejoice us: as one who nourishes her young comes Sindhu,

With whom we will incite the Child of Waters whom vigorous course swift as thought bring hither.
6 Moreover Tvastar also shall approach us, one-minded with the princes at his visit.
Hither shall come the Vrtra-slayer Indra, Ruler of men, as strongest of the Heroes.
7 Him too our hymns delight, that yoke swift horses, like mother cows who lick their tender
youngling.
To him our songs shall yield themselves like spouses, to him the most delightful of the Heroes.
8 So may the Maruts, armed with mighty weapons, rest here on heaven and earth with hearts in
concord,
As Gods whose cars have dappled steeds like torrents, destroyers of the foe allies of Mitra.
9 They hasten on to happy termination their orders when they are made known by
glory.
As on a fair bright day the arrow flieth o'er all the barren soil their missiles sparkle.
10 Incline the Asvins to show grace, and Pusan, for power and might have they, their own
possession.
Friendly are Visnu, Vata, and Rbhuksan so may I bring the Gods to make us happy.
11 This is my reverent thought of you, ye Holy; may it inspire you, make you dwell among us,-
Thought, toiling for the Gods and seeking treasure. May we find strengthening food in full
abundance.

## [01-187] HYMN CLXXXVII. Praise of Food.
1. Now will I glorify Food that upholds great strength,
By whose invigorating power Trita rent Vrtra limb frorn limb.
2 O pleasant Food, O Food of meath, thee have we chosen for our own,
So be our kind protector thou.
3 Come hitherward to us, O Food, auspicious with auspicious help,
Health-bringing, not unkind, a dear and guileless friend.
4 These juices which, O Food, are thine throughout the regions are diffused.
like winds they have their place in heaven.
5 These gifts of thine, O Food, O Food most sweet to taste,
These savours of thy juices work like creatures that have mighty necks.
6 In thee, O Food, is set the spirit of great Gods.
Under thy flag brave deeds were done he slew the Dragon with thy help.
7 If thou be gone unto the splendour of the clouds,

Even from thence, O Food of meath, prepared for our enjoyment, come.
8 Whatever morsel we consume from waters or from plants of earth, O Soma, wax thou fat thereby.
9 What Soma, we enjoy from thee in milky food or barley-brew, Vatapi, grow thou fat thereby.
10 O Vegetable, Cake of meal, he wholesome, firm, and strengthening: Vatapi, grow thou fat thereby.
11 O Food, from thee as such have we drawn forth with lauds, like cows, our sacrificial gifts,
From thee who banquetest with Gods, from thee who banquetest with us.

## [01-188] HYMN CLXXXVIII. April
1. WINNER of thousands, kindled, thou shinest a God with Gods to-day.
Bear out oblations, envoy, Sage.
2 Child of Thyself the sacrifice is for the righteous blent with meath,
Presenting viands thousandfold.
3 Invoked and worthy of our praise bring Gods whose due is sacrifice:
Thou, Agni, givest countless gifts.
4 To seat a thousand Heroes they eastward have strewn the grass with might,
Whereon, Adityas, ye shine forth.
5 The sovran all-imperial Doors, wide, good, many and manifold,
Have poured their streams of holy oil.

6 With gay adornment, fair to see, in glorious beauty shine they forth:
Let Night and Morning rest them here.
7 Let these two Sages first of all, heralds divine and eloquent,
Perform for us this sacrifice.
8 You I address, Sarasvati, and Bharati, and Ila, all:
Urge ye us on to glorious fame.
9 Tvastar the Lord hath made all forms and all the cattle of the field
Cause them to multiply for us.
10 Send to the Gods, Vanaspati, thyself, the sacrificial draught:
Let Agni make the oblations sweet.
11 Agni, preceder of the Gods, is honoured with the sacred song:
He glows at offerings blest with Hail!

## [01-189] HYMN CLXXXIX. Agni.
1. BY goodly paths lead us to riches, Agni, God who knowest every sacred duty.
Remove the sin that makes us stray and wander. most ample adoration will we bring thee.
2 Lead us anew to happiness, O Agni; lead us beyond all danger and affliction.
Be unto us a wide broad ample castle bless, prosper on their way our sons and offspring.
3 Far from us, Agni, put thou all diseases let them strike lauds that have no saving Agni.
God, make our home again to be a bless ing, with all the Immortal Deities, O Holy.
4 Preserve us, Agni, with perpetual succour, refulgent in the dwelling which thou lovest.
O Conqueror, most youthful, let no danger touch him who praises thee to-day or after.
5 Give not us up a prey to sin, O Agni, the greedy enemy that brings us trouble;
Not to the fanged that bites, not to the toothless: give not us up, thou Conqueror, to the spoiler.
6 Such as thou art, born after Law, O Agni when lauded give protection to our bodies,

From whosoever would reproach or injure: for thou, God, rcscuest from all oppression.

7 Thou, well discerning both these classes, comest to men at early morn, O holy Agni.

Be thou obedient unto man at evening, to be adorned, as keen, by eager suitors.

8 To him have we addressed our pious speeches, I, Mana's son, to him victorious Agni.

May we gain countless riches with the sages. May we find strengthening food in full abundance.

## [01-190] HYMN CXC. Brhaspati.

1.GLORIFY thou Brhaspati, the scatheless, who must be praised with hymns, sweet-tongued and mighty,

To whom as leader of the song, resplendent, worthy of lauds, both Gods and mortals listen.

2 On him wait songs according to the season even as a stream of pious men set moving.

Brhaspati-for helaid out the expanses- was, at the sacrifice, vast Matarisvan.

3 The praise, the verse that offers adoration, may he bring forth, as the Sun sends his arms out,

He who gives daily light through this God's wisdom, strong as a dread wild beast, and inoffensive.

4 His song of praise pervades the earth and heaven - let the wise worshipper draw it, like a courser.

These of Brhaspati, like hunters' arrows, go to the skies that change their hue like serpents.

5 Those, God, who count thee as a worthless bullock, and, wealthy sinners, live on thee the Bounteous,-

On fools like these no blessing thou bestowest: Brhaspati, thou punishest the spiteful.

6 Like a fair path is he, where grass is pleasant, though hard to win, a Friend beloved most early.

Those who unharmed by enemies behold us, while: they would make them bare, stood closely compassed.

7 He to whom songs of praise go forth like torrents, as rivers eddying under banks flow sea-ward-

Brhaspati the wise, the eager, closely looks upon both, the waters and the vessel.

8 So hath Brhaspati, great, strong and mighty, the God exceeding powerful, been brought hither.

May he thus lauded give us kine and horses. May we find strengthening food in full abundance.

## [01-191] HYMN CXCI Water. Grass. Sun.

1. VENOMOUS, slightly venomous, or venomous aquatic worm,-
Both creatures, stinging, unobserved, with poison have infected me.

2 Coming, it kills the unobserved; it kills them as it goes away,
It kills them as it drives them off, and bruising bruises them to death.

3 Sara grass, Darbha, Kusara, and Sairya, Munja, Virana,
Where all these creatures dwell unseen, with poison have infected me.

4 The cows had settled in their stalls, the beasts of prey had sought their lairs,
Extinguished were the lights of men, when things unseen infected me.

5 Or these, thesereptiles, are observed, like lurking thieves at evening time.
Seers of all, themselves unseen: be therefore very vigilant.

6 Heaven is your Sire, your Mother Earth, Soma your Brother, Aditi
Your Sister: seeing all, unseen, keep still and dwell ye happily.

7 Biters of shoulder or of limb, with needle-stings, most venomous,
Unseen, whatever ye may be, vanish together and be gone.

8 Slayer of things unseen, the Sun, beheld of all, mounts, eastward, up,
Consuming all that are not seen, and evil spirits of the night.

9 There hath the Sun-God mounted up, who scorches much and everything.
Even the Aditya from the hills, all-seen, destroying things unseen.

10 I hang the poison in the Sun, a wine-skin in a vintner's house,
He will not die, nor shall we die: his path is far: he whom Bay Horses bear hath turned thee to sweet meath.

11 This little bird, so very small, hath swallowed all thy poison up.
She will not die, nor shall we die: his path is far: he whom Bay Horses bear hath turned thee to sweet meath.

12 The three-times-seven bright sparks of fire have swallowed up the poison's strength.
They will not die, nor shall we die: his path is far: he whom Bay Horses bear hath turned thee to sweet meath.

13 Of ninety rivers and of nine with power to stay the venom's course,-
The names of all I have secured: his path is far: he whom Bay Horses bear hath turned thee to sweet meath.

14 So have the peahens three-times-seven, so have the maiden Sisters Seven
Carried thy venom far away, as girls bear water in their jars.

15 The poison-insect is so small; I crush the creature with a stone.
I turn the poison hence away, departed unto distant lands.

16 Forth issuing from the mountain's side the poison-insect spake and said:
The scorpion's venom hath no strength Scorpion, thy venom is but weak.

# BOOK TWO

## [02-001] HYMN I. Agni.

1. THOU, Agni, shining in thy glory through the days, art brought to life from out the waters, from the stone:
From out the forest trees and herbs that grow on ground, thou, Sovran Lord of men art generatad (sic) pure.

2 Thine is the Herald's task and Cleanser's duly timed; Leader art thou, and Kindler for the pious man.
Thou art Director, thou the ministering Priest: thou art the Brahman, Lord and Master in our home.

3 Hero of Heroes, Agni! Thou art Indra, thou art Visnu of the Mighty Stride, adorable:
Thou, Brahmanaspati, the Brahman finding wealth: thou, O Sustainer, with thy wisdom tendest us.

4 Agni, thou art King Varuna whose laws stand fast; as Mitra, Wonder-Worker, thou must be implored.
Aryaman, heroes' Lord, art thou, enrich ing all, and liberal Amsa in the synod, O thou God.

5 Thou givest strength, as Tvastar, to the worshipper: thou wielding Mitra's power hast kinship with the Dames.

Thou, urging thy fleet coursers, givest noble steeds: a host of heroes art thou with great store of
wealth.
6 Rudra art thou, the Asura of mighty heaven: thou art the Maruts' host, thou art the Lord of food,
Thou goest with red winds: bliss hast thou in thine home. As Pusan thou thyself protectest
worshippers.
7 Giver of wealth art thou to him who honours thee; thou art God Savitar, granter of precious things.
As Bhaga, Lord of men! thou rulest over wealth, and guardest in his house him who hath served thee
well.
8 To thee, the people's Lord within the house, the folk press forward to their King most graciously
inclined.
Lord of the lovely look, all things belong to thee: ten, hundred, yea, a thousand are outweighed by
thee.
9 Agni, men seek thee as a Father with their prayers, win thee, bright-formed, to brotherhood with
holy act.
Thou art a Son to him who duly worships thee, and as a trusty Friend thou guardest from attack.
10 A Rbhu art thou, Agni, near to be adored thou art the Sovran Lord of foodful spoil and wealth.
Thou shinest brightly forth, thou burnest to bestow: pervading sacrifice, thou lendest us thine help.
11 Thou, God, art Aditi to him who offers gifts: thou, Hotri, Bharati, art strengthened by the song.
Thou art the hundred-wintered Ila to give strength, Lord of Wealth! Vrtra-slayer and Sarasvati.
12 Thou, Agni, cherished well, art highest vital power; in thy delightful hue are glories visible.
Thou art the lofty might that furthers each design: thou art wealth manifold, diffused on every side.
13 Thee, Agni, have the Adityas taken as their mouth; the Bright Ones have made thee, O Sage, to be
their tongue.
They who love offerings cling to thee at solemn rites: by thee the Gods devour the duly offered food.
14 By thee, O Agni, all the Immortal guileless Gods cat with thy mouth the oblation that is offered
them.
By thee do mortal men give sweetness to their drink. Bright art thou born, the embryo of the plants of
earth.
15 With these thou art united, Agni; yea thou, God of noble birth, surpassest them in majesty,
Which, through the power of good, here spreads abroad from thee, diffused through both the worlds,
throughout the earth and heaven.
16 The princely worshippers who send to those who sing thy praise, O Agni, guerdon graced with
kine and steeds,-
Lead thou both these and us forward to higher bliss. With brave men in the assembly may we speak
aloud.

## [02-002] HYMN II. Agni.

1. WITH sacrifice exalt Agni who knows all life; worship him 'with oblation and the song of praise,
Well kindled, nobly fed; heaven's Lord, Celestial Priest, who labours at the pole where deeds of might are done.
2 At night and morning, Agni, have they called to thee, like milch-kine in their stalls lowing to meet their young.

As messenger of heaven thou lightest all night long the families of men. Thou Lord of precious boons.
3 Him have the Gods established at the region's base, doer of wondrous deeds, Herald of heaven and
earth;
Like a most famous car, Agni the purely bright, like Mitra. to be glorified among the folk.
4 Him have they set in his own dwelling, in the vault, like the Moon waxing, fulgent, in the realm of
air.
Bird of the firmament, observant with his eyes, guard of the place as 'twere, looking to Gods and
men.
5 May he as Priest encompass all the sacrifice. men throng to him with offerings and with hymns of
praise.
Raging with jaws of gold among the growing plants, like heaven with all the stars, he quickens earth
and sky.
6 Such as thou art, brilliantly kindled for our weal, a liberal giver, send us riches in thy shine,
For our advantage, Agni, God, bring Heaven and Earth hither that they may taste oblation brought by
man.
7 Agni, give us great wealth, give riches thousandfold. unclose to us, like doors, strength that shall
bring renown.
Make Heaven and Earth propitious through the power of prayer, and like the sky's bright sheen let
mornings beam on us.
8 Enkindled night by night at every morning's dawn, may he shine forth with red flame like the realm
of light,-
Agni adored in beauteous rites with lauds of men, fair guest of living man and King of all our folk.
9 Song chanted by us men, O Agni, Ancient One, has swelled unto the deathless Gods in lofty
heaven-
A milch-cow yielding to the singer in the rites wealth manifold, in hundreds, even as he wills.
10 Agni, may we show forth our valour with the steed or with the power of prayer beyond all other
men;
And over the Five Races let our glory shine high like the realm of light and unsurpassable.
11 Such, Conqueror! be to us, be worthy of our praise, thou for whom princes nobly born exert
themselves;
Whose sacrifice the strong seek, Agni, when it shines for never-failing offspring in thine own abode.
12 Knower of all that lives, O Agni may we both, singers of praise and chiefs, be in thy keeping still.
Help us to wealth exceeding good and glorious, abundant, rich in children and their progeny.
13 The princely worshippers who send to those who sing thy praise, O Agni, guerdon, graced with kine and steeds,-
Lead thou both these and us forward to higher bliss. With brave men in the assembly may we speak aloud.

## [02-003] HYMN III. Apris.

1. AGNI is set upon the earth well kindled; he standeth in the presence of all beings.
Wise, ancient, God, the Priest and Purifier, let Agni serve the Gods for he is worthy.
2 May Narasamsa lighting up the chambers, bright in his majesty through threefold heaven,

Steeping the gift with oil diffusing purpose, bedew the Gods at chiefest time of worship.

3 Adored in heart, as is thy right, O Agni, serve the Gods first to-day before the mortal.

Bring thou the Marut host. Ye men do worship to Indra seated on the grass, eternal.

4 O Grass divine, increasing, rich in heroes, strewn for wealth' sake, well laid upon this altar,-

On this bedewed with oil sit ye, O Vasus, sit all ye Gods, ye Holy, ye Adityas.

5 Wide be the Doors, the Goddesses, thrown open, easy to pass, invoked, through adorations,

Let them unfold, expansive, everlasting, that sanctify the class famed, rich in heroes.

6 Good work for us, the glorious Night and Morning, like female weavers, waxen from aforetime,

Yielders of rich milk, interweave in concert the long-extended thread, the web of worship.

7 Let the two heavenly Heralds, first, most wise, most fair, present oblation duly with the sacred verse,

Worshipping God at ordered seasons decking them at three high places at the centre of the earth.

8 Sarasvati who perfects our devotion, Ila divine, Bharati all surpassing,-

Three Goddesses, with power inherent, seated, protect this holy Grass, our flawless refuge!

9 Born is the pious hero swift of hearing, like gold in hue, well formed, and full of vigour.

May Tvastar lengthen our line and kindred, and may they reach the place which Gods inhabit.

10 Vanaspati shall stand anear and start us, and Agni with his arts prepare oblation.

Let the skilled heavenly Immolator forward unto the Gods the offering thrice anointed.

11 Oil has been mixt: oil is his habitation. In oil he rests: oil is his proper province.

Come as thy wont is: O thou Steer, rejoice thee; bear off the oblation duly consecrated.

## [02-004] HYMN IV Agni.

1. FOR you I call theglorious refulgent Agni, the guest of men, rich in oblations

Whom all must strive to win even as a lover, God among godly people, Jatavedas.

2 Bhrgus who served him in the home of waters set him of old in houses of the living.

Over all worlds let Agni be the Sovran, the messenger of Gods with rapid coursers.

3 Among the tribes of men the Gods placed Agni as a dear Friend when they would dwell among them.

Against the longing nights may he shine brightly, and show the offerer in the house his vigour.

4 Sweet is his growth as of one's own possessions; his look when rushing fain to burn is lovely.

He darts his tongue forth, like a harnessed courser who shakes his flowing tail, among the bushes.

5 Since they who honour me have praised my greatness,-he gave, as 'twere, his hue to those who love him.

Known is he by his bright delightful splendour, and waxing old renews his youth for ever.

6 Like one athirst, he lighteth up the forests; like water down the chariot ways he roareth.

On his black path he shines in burning beauty, marked as it were the heaven that smiles through vapour.

7 Around, consuming the broad earth, he wanders, free roaming like an ox without a herdsman,-

Agni refulgent, burning up the bushes, with blackened lines, as though the earth he seasoned.

8 I, in remembrance of thine ancient favour have sung my hymn in this our third assembly.

O Agni, give us wealth with store of heroes and mighty strength in food and noble offspring.

9 May the Grtsamadas, serving in secret, through thee, O Agni, overcome their neighbours,

Rich in good heroes and subduing foemen. That vital power give thou to chiefs and singers.

## [02-005] HYMN V. Agni.

1. HERALD and teacher was he born, a guardian for our patrons' help,

Earner by rites of noble wealth. That Strong One may we grasp and guide;

2 In whom, Leader of sacrifice, the seven reins, far extended, meet;

Who furthers, man-like, eighth in place, as Cleanser, all the work divine.

3 When swift he follows this behest, bird-like he chants the holy prayers.

He holds all knowledge in his grasp even as the felly rounds the wheel.

4 Together with pure mental power, pure, as Director, was he born.

Skilled in his own unchanging laws he waxes like the growing boughs.

5 Clothing thern in his hues, the kine of him the Leader wait on him.

Is he not better than the Three, the Sisters who have come to us?

6 When, laden with the holy oil, the Sitster (sic) by the Mother stands,

The Priest delights in their approach, as corn at coming of the rain.

7 For his support let him perform as ministrant his priestly task;

Yea, song of praise and sacrifice: we have bestowed, let us obtain.

8 That so this man well skilled, may pay worship to all the Holy Ones.

And, Agni, this our sacrifice which wehave here prepared, to thee.

## [02-006] HYMN VI. Agni.

1. AGNI, accept this flaming brand, this waiting with my prayer on thee:

Hear graciously these songs of praise.

2 With this hymn let us honour thee, seeker of horses, Son of Strength,

With this fair hymn, thou nobly born.

3 As such, lover of song, with songs, wealth-lover, giver of our wealth!

With reverence let us worship thee.

4 Be thou for us a liberal Prince, giver and Lord of precious things.

Drive those who hate us far away.

5 Such as thou art, give rain from heaven, give strength which no man may resist:

Give food exceeding plentiful.

6 To him who lauds thee, craving help, most youthful envoy! through our song,

Most holy Herald! come thou nigh.

7 Between both races, Agni, Sage, well skilled thou passest to and fro,

As envoy friendly to mankind.

8 Befriend us thou as knowing all. Sage, duly worship thou the Gods,

And seat thee on this sacred grass.

## [02-007] HYMN VII. Agni.

1. VASU, thou most youthful God, Bharata, Agni, bring us wealth,
Excellent, splendid, much-desired.
2 Let no malignity prevail against us, either God's or man's.
Save us from this and enmity.
3 So through thy favour may we force through all our enemies a way,
As 'twere through streaming water-floods.
4 Thou, Purifier Agni, high shinest forth, bright, adorable,
When worshipped with the sacred oil.
5 Ours art thou, Agni, Bharata, honoured by us with barren cows,
With bullocks and with kine in calf
6 Wood-fed, bedewed with sacred oil, ancient, Invoker, excellent,
The Son of Strength, the Wonderful.

## [02-008] HYMN VIII.Agni.

1. Now praise, as one who strives for strength, the harnessing of Agni's car,
The liberal, the most splendid One;
2 Who, guiding worshippers aright, withers, untouched by age, the foe:
When worshipped fair to look upon;
3 Who for his glory is extolled at eve and morning in our homes,
Whose statute is inviolate;
4 Who shines refulgent like the Sun, with brilliance and with fiery flame,
Decked with imperishable sheen.
5 Him Atri, Agni, have our songs Strengthened according to his sway:
All glories hath he made his own.

6 May we with Agni's, Indra's help, with Soma's, yea, of all the Gods,
Uninjured dwell together still, and conquer those who fight with us.

## [02-009] HYMN IX. Agni.

1. ACCUSTOMED to the Herald's place, the Herald hath seated him, bright, splendid, passing mighty,
Whose foresight keeps the Law from violation, excellent, pure-tongued, bringing thousands, Agni.
2 Envoy art thou, protector from the foeman, strong God, thou leadest us to higher blessings.
Refulgent, be an ever-heedful keeper, Agni, for us and for our seed offspring.
3 May we adore thee in thy loftiest birthplace, and, with our praises, in thy lower station.
The place whence thou issued forth I worship: to thee well kindled have they paid oblations.
4 Agni, best Priest, pay worship with oblation; quickly commend the gift to be presented;
For thou art Lord of gathered wealth and treasure. of the bright song of praise thou art inventor.
5 The twofold opulence, O Wonder-Worker, of thee new-born each day never decreases.
Enrich with food the man who lauds thee, Agni: make him the lord of wealth with noble offspring.
6 May he, benevolent with this fair aspect, best sacrificer, bring the Gods to bless us.
Sure guardian, our protector from the foemen, shine, Agni, with thine affluence and splendour.

## [02-010] HYMN X. Agni.

1.AGNI, first, loudly calling, like a Father, kindled by man upon the seat of worship.
Clothed in his glory, deathless, keen of insight, must be adorned by all, the Strong, the Famous.

2 May Agni the resplendent hear my calling through all my songs,
Immortal, keen of insight.
Dark steeds or ruddy draw his car, or carried in sundry ways he makes them red of colour.
3 On wood supine they got the well-formed Infant: a germ in various-fashioned plants was Agni;
And in the night, not compassed round by darkness, he dwells exceeding wise, with rays of splendour.
4 With oil and sacred gifts I sprinkle Agni who makes his home in front of all things living,
Broad, vast, through vital power o'er all expanded, conspicuous, strong with all the food that feeds him.
5 I pour to him who looks in all directions: may he accept it with a friendly spirit.
Agni with bridegroom's grace and lovely colour may not be touched when all his form is fury.
6 By choice victorious, recognize thy portion: with thee for envoy may we speak like Manu.
Obtaining wealth, I call on perfect Agni who with an eloquent tongue dispenses sweetness.

## [02-011] HYMN XI. Indra.

1. HEAR thou my call, O Indra; be not heedless: thine may we be for thee to give us treasures;
For these presented viands, seeking riches, increase thy strength like streams of water flowing.
2 Floods great and many, compassed by the Dragon, thou badest swell and settest free, O Hero.
Strengthened by songs of praise thou rentest piecemeal the Dasa, him who deemed himself immortal.
3 For, Hero, in the lauds wherein thou joyedst, in hymns of praise, O Indra, songs of Rudras,
These streams in which is thy delight approach thee, even as the brilliant ones draw near to Vayu.
4 We who add strength to thine own splendid vigour, laying within thine arms the splendid thunder-
With us mayst thou, O Indra, waxen splendid, with Surya overcome the Dasa races.
5 Hero, thou slewest in thy valour Ahi concealed in depths, mysterious, great enchanter,
Dwelling enveloped deep within the waters, him who checked heaven and stayed the floods from flowing.
6 Indra, we laud thy great deeds wrought aforetime, we laud thine exploits later of achievement;
We laud the bolt that in thine arms lies eager; we laud thy two Bay Steeds, heralds of Surya.
7 Indra, thy Bay Steeds showing forth their vigour have sent a loud cry out that droppeth fatness.
The earth hath spread herself in all her fulness: the cloud that was about to move hath rested.
8 Down, never ceasing, hath the rain-cloud settled: bellowing, it hath wandered with the Mothers.
Swelling the roar in the far distant limits, they have spread wide the blast sent forth by Indra.
9 Indra hath hurled down the magician Vrtra who lay beleaguering the mighty river.
Then both the heaven and earth trembled in terror at the strong Hero's thunder when he bellowed.
10 Loud roared the mighty Hero's bolt of thunder, when he, the Friend of man, burnt up the monster,
And, having drunk his fill of flowing Soma, baffled the guileful Danava's devices.
11 Drink thou, O Hero Indra, drink the Soma; let the joy-giving juices make thee joyful.

They, filling both thy flanks, shall swell thy vigour. The juice that satisfies hath helped Indra.

12 Singers have we become with thee, O Indra: may we serve duly and prepare devotion.

Seeking thy help we meditate thy praises: may we at once enjoy thy gift of riches.

13 May we be thine, such by thy help, O Indra, as swell thy vigour while they seek thy favour.

Give us, thou God, the riches that we long for, most powerful, with stare of noble children.

14 Give us a friend, give us an habitation; Indra, give us the company of Maruts,

And those whose minds accord with theirs, the Vayus, who drink the first libation of the Soma.

15 Let those enjoy in whom thou art delighted. Indra, drink Soma for thy strength and gladness.

Thou hast exalted us to heaven, Preserver, in battles, through the lofty hymns that praise thee.

16 Great, verily, are they, O thou Protector, who by their songs of praise have won the blessing.

They who strew sacred grass to be thy dwelling, helped by thee have got them strength, O Indra.

17 Upon the great Trikadruka days, Hero, rejoicing thee, O Indra, drink the Soma.

Come with Bay Steeds to drink of libation, shaking the drops from out thy beard, contented.

18 Hero, assume the might wherewith thou clavest Vrtra piecemeal, the Danava Aurnavabha.

Thou hast disclosed the light to light the Arya: on thy left hand, O Indra, sank the Dasyu.

19 May we gain wealth, subduing with thy succour and with the Arya, all our foes, the Dasyus.

Our gain was that to Trta of our party thou gavest up Tvastar's son Visvarupa.

20 He cast down Arbuda what time his vigour was strengthened by libations poured by Trta.

Indra sent forth his whirling wheel like Surya, and aided by the Angirases rent Vala.

21 Now let that wealthy Cow of thine, O Indra, yield in return a boon to him who lauds thee.

Give to thy praisers: let not fortune fail us. Loud may we speak, with brave men, in the assembly.

## [02-012] HYMN XII. Indra.

1. HE who, just born, chief God of lofty spirit by power and might became the Gods' protector,

Before whose breath through greatness of his valour the two worlds trembled, He, O men, is Indra.

2 He who fixed fast and firm the earth that staggered, and set at rest the agitated mountains,

Who measured out the air's wide middle region and gave the heaven support, He, men, is Indra.

3 Who slew the Dragon, freed the Seven Rivers, and drove the kine forth from the cave of Vala,

Begat the fire between two stones, the spoiler in warriors' battle, He, O men, is Indra.

4 By whom this universe was made to tremble, who chased away the humbled brood of demons,

Who, like a gambler gathering his winnings seized the foe's riches, He, O men, is Indra.

5 Of whom, the Terrible, they ask, Where is He? or verily they say of him, He is not.

He sweeps away, like birds, the foe's possessions. Have faith in him, for He, O men, is Indra.

6 Stirrer to action of the poor and lowly, of priest, of suppliant who sings his praises;

Who, fair-faced, favours him who presses Soma with stones made ready, He, O men, is Indra.

7 He under whose supreme control are horses, all chariots, and the villages, and cattle;

He who gave being to the Sun and Morning, who leads the waters, He, O men, is Indra.

8 To whom two armies cry in close encounter, both enemies, the stronger and the weaker;

Whom two invoke upon one chariot mounted, each for himself, He, O ye men, is Indra.

9 Without whose help our people never conquer; whom, battling, they invoke to give them succour;

He of whom all this world is but the copy, who shakes things moveless, He, O men, is Indra.

10 He who hath smitten, ere they knew their danger, with his hurled weapon many grievous sinners;

Who pardons not his boldness who provokes him, who slays the Dasyti, He, O men, is Indra.

11 He who discovered in the fortieth autumn Sambara as he dwelt among the mountains;

Who slew the Dragon putting forth his vigour, the demon lying there, He, men, is Indra.

12 Who with seven guiding reins, the Bull, the Mighty, set free the Seven great Floods to flow at
pleasure;

Who, thunder-armed, rent Rauhina in pieces when scaling heaven, He, O ye men, is Indra.

13 Even the Heaven and Earth bow down before him, before his very breath the mountains tremble.

Known as the Soma-drinker, armed with thunder, who wields the bolt, He, O ye men, is Indra.

14 Who aids with favour him who pours the Soma and him who brews it, sacrificer, singer.

Whom prayer exalts, and pouring forth of Soma, and this our gift, He, O ye men, Is Indra.

15 Thou verily art fierce and true who sendest strength to the man who brews and pours libation.

So may we evermore, thy friends, O Indra, speak loudly to the synod with our heroes.

## [02-013] HYMN XIII. Indra.

1. THE Season was the parent, and when born therefrom it entered rapidly the floods wherein it
grows.

Thence was it full of sap, streaming with milky juice: the milk of the plant's stalk is chief and meet for
lauds.

2 They come trooping together bearing milk to him, and bring him sustenance who gives support to
all.

The way is common for the downward streams to flow. Thou who didst these things first art worthy
of our lauds.

3 One priest announces what the institutor gives: one, altering the forms, zealously plies his task,

The third corrects the imperfections left by each. Thou who didst these things first art worthy of our
lauds.

4 Dealing out food unto their people there they sit, like wealth to him who comes, more than the back
can bear.

Greedily with his teeth he eats the master's food. Thou who didst these things first art worthy of our
lauds.

5 Thou hast created earth to look upon the sky: thou, slaying Ahi, settest free the river's paths.

Thee, such, a God, the Gods have quickened with their lauds, even as a steed with waters: meet for
praise art thou.
6 Thou givest increase, thou dealest to us our food: thou milkest from the moist the dry, the rich in
sweets.
Thou by the worshipper layest thy precious store: thou art sole Lord of all. Meet for our praise art
thou.
7 Thou who hast spread abroad the streams by stablished law, and in the field the plants that
blossom and bear seed;
Thou who hast made the matchless lightnings of the sky,-vast, compassing vast realms, meet for our
praise art thou.
8 Who broughtest Narmara with all his wealth, for sake of food, to slay him that the fiends might be
destroyed,
Broughtest the face unclouded of the strengthening one, performing much even now, worthy art thou
of praise.
9 Thou boundest up the Dasa's hundred friends and ten, when, at one's hearing, thou belpest thy
worshipper.
Thou for Dabhiti boundest Dasyus not with cords; Thou wast a mighty help. Worthy of lauds art thou.
10 All banks of rivers yielded to his manly might; to him they gave, to him, the Strong, gave up their
wealth.
The six directions hast thou fixed, a five-fold view: thy victories reached afar. Worthy of lauds art
thou.
11 Meet for high praise, O Hero, is thy power, that with thy single wisdom thou obtainest wealth,
The life-support of conquering Jatusthira. Indra, for all thy deeds, worthy of lauds art thou.
12 Thou for Turviti heldest still the flowing floods, the river-stream for Vayya easily to pass
Didst raise the outcast from the depths, and gavest fame unto the halt and blind. Worthy of lauds art
thou.
13 Prepare thyself to grant us that great bounty, O Vasu, for abundant is thy treasure.

Snatch up the wonderful, O Indra, daily. Loud may we speak, with heroes, in assembly.

## [02-014] HYMN XIV. Indra.

1. MINISTERS, bring the Soma juice for Indra, pour forth the gladdening liquor with the
beakers.logeth ever
To drink of this the Hero offer it to the Bull, for this he willeth.
2 Ye ministers, to him who with the lightning smote, like a tree, the rain-withholding Vrtra-
Bring it to him, him who is fain to taste it, a draught of this which Indra here deserveth.
3 Ye ministers, to him who smote Drhhikas who drove the kine forth, and discovered Vala,
Offer this draught, like Vita in the region: clothe him with Soma even as steeds with trappings.
4 Him who did Urana to death, Adhvaryus! though showing arms ninety-and-nine in number;
Who cast down headlong Arbuda and slew him,-speed ye that Indra to our offered Soma.
5 Ye ministers, to him who struck down Svasna, and did to death Vyamsa and greedy Susna,

And Rudhikras and Namuci and Pipru,- to him, to Indra, pour ye forth libation.
6 Ye ministers, to him who as with thunder demolished Sambara's hundred ancient castles;
Who cast down Varcin's sons, a hundred thousand,-to him, to Indra, offer ye the Soma.
7 Ye ministers, to him who slew a hundred thousand, and cast them down upon earth's bosom;
Who quelled the valiant men of Atithigva, Kutsa, and Ayu,-bring to him the Soma.
8 Ministers, men, whatever thing ye long for obtain ye quickly bringing gifts to Indra.
Bring to the Glorious One what bands have cleansed; to Indra bring, ye pious ones, the Soma.
9 Do ye, O ministers, obey his order: that purified in wood, in wood uplift ye.
Well pleased he longs for what your hands have tended: offer the gladdening Soma juice to Indra.
10 As the cow's udder teems with milk, Adhvaryus, so fill with Soma Indra, liberal giver.
I know him: I am sure of this, the Holy knows that I fain would give to him more largely.
11 Him, ministers, the Lord of heavenly treasure and all terrestrial wealth that earth possesses,
Him, Indra, fill with Soma as a garner is filled with barley full: be this your labour.
12 Prepare thyself to grant us that great booty, O Vasu, for abundant is thy treasure.
Gather up wondrous wealth, O Indra, daily. Loud may we speak, with heroes, in assembly.

## [02-015] HYMN XV. Indra

1. Now, verily, will I declare the exploits, mighty and true, of him the True and Mighty.
In the Trikadrukas he drank the Soma then in its rapture Indra slew the Dragon.
2 High heaven unsupported in space he stablished: he filled the two worlds and the air's mid-region.
Earth he upheld, and gave it wide expansion. These things did Indra in the Soma's rapture.
3 From front, as 'twere a house, he ruled and measured; pierced with his bolt the fountains of the
rivers,
And made them flow at ease by paths far-reaching, These things did Indra in the Soma's rapture.
4 Compassing those who bore away Dabhiti, in kindled fire he burnt up all their weapons.
And made him rich with kine and cars and horses. These things did Indra in the Soma's rapture.
5 The mighty roaring flood he stayed from flowing, and carried those who swam not safely over.
They having crossed the stream attained to riches. These things did Indra in the Soma's rapture.
6 With mighty power he made the stream flow upward, crushed with his thunderbolt the car of Usas,
Rending her slow steeds with his rapid coursers. These things did Indra in the Soma's rapture.
7 Knowing the place wherein the maids were hiding, the outcast showed himself and stood before
them.
The cripple stood erect, the blind beheld them. These things did Indra in the Soma's rapture.
8 Praised by the Angirases he slaughtered Vala, and burst apart the bulwarks of the mountain.
He tore away their deftly-built defences. These things did Indra in the Soma's rapture.

9 Thou, with sleep whelming Cumuri and Dhuni, slewest the Dasyu, keptest safe Dabhiti.

There the staff-bearer found the golden treasure. These things did Indra in the Soma's rapture.

10 Now let that wealthy Cow of thine, O Indra , yield in return a boon to him who lauds thee.

Give to thy praisers: let not fortune fail us. Loud may we speak, with brave men, in assembly.

## [02-016] HYMN XVI. Indra.

1. To him, your own, the best among the good, I bring eulogy, like oblation in the kindled fire.

We invocate for help Indra untouched by eld, who maketh all decay, strengthened, for ever young.

2 Without whom naught exists, Indra the Lofty One; in whom alone all powers heroic are combined.

The Soma is within him, in his frame vast strength, the thunder in his hand and wisdom in his head.

3 Not by both worlds is thine own power to be surpassed, nor may thy car be stayed by mountains or by seas.

None cometh near, O Indra, to thy thunderbolt, when with swift steeds thou fliest over many a league.

4 For all men bring their will to him the Resolute, to him the Holy One, to him the Strong they cleave.

Pay worship with oblation, strong and passing wise. Drink thou the Soma, Indra, through the mighty blaze.

5 The vessel of the strong flows forth, the flood of meath, unto the Strong who feeds upon the strong, for drink,

Strong are the two Adhvaryus, strong are both the stones. They press the Soma that is strong for him the Strong.

6 Strong is thy thunderbolt, yea, and thy car is strong; strong are thy Bay Steeds and thy weapons powerful.

Thou, Indra, Bull, art Lord of the strong gladdening drink. with the strong Soma, Indra, satisfy thyself.

7 I, bold by prayer, come near thee in thy sacred rites, thee like a saving ship, thee shouting in the war.

Verily he will hear and mark this word of ours: we will pour Indra forth as 'twere a spring of wealth.

8 Turn thee unto us ere calamity come nigh, as a cow full of pasture turns her to her calf.

Lord of a Hundred Powers, may we once firmly cling to thy fair favours even as husbands to their wives.

9 Now let that wealthy Cow of thine, O Indra, yield in return a boon to him who lauds thee.

Give to thy praisers: let not fortune fail us. Loud may we speak, with heroes, in assembly.

## [02-017] HYMN XVII. Indra.

1. LIKE the Angirases, sing this new song forth to him, for, as in ancient days, his mighty powers are shown,

When in the rapture of the Soma he unclosed with strength the solid firm-shut stables of the kine.

2 Let him be even that God who, for the earliest draught measuring out his power, increased his majesty;

Hero who fortified his body in the wars, and through his greatness set the heaven upon his head.

3 Thou didst perform thy first great deed of hero might what time thou showedst power, through prayer, before this folk.

Hurled down by thee the car-borne Lord of Tawny Steeds, the congregated swift ones fled in sundry ways.

4 He made himself by might Lord of all living things, and strong in vital power waxed great above them all.

He, borne on high, o'erspread with light the heaven and earth, and, sewing up the turbid darkness, closed it in.

5 He with his might made firm the forward-bending hills, the downward rushing of the waters he ordained.

Fast he upheld the earth that nourisheth all life, and stayed the heaven from falling by his wondrous skill.

6 Fit for the grasping of his arms is what the Sire hath fabricated from all kind of precious wealth.

The thunderbolt, wherewith, loud-roaring, he smote down, and striking him to death laid Krivi on the earth.

7 As she who in her parents' house is growing old, I pray to thee as Bhaga from the seat of all.

Grant knowledge, mete it out and bring it to us here: give us the share wherewith thou makest people glad.

8 May we invoke thee as a liberal giver thou givest us, O Indra, strength and labours.

Help us with manifold assistance, Indra: Migthy One, Indra, make us yet more wealthy.

9 Now may that weaithy Cow of thine, O Indra, give in return a boon to him who lauds thee.

Give to thy praisers: let not fortune fail us. Loud may we speak, with heroes, in assembly.

## [02-018] HYMN XVIII. Indra

1. THE rich new car hath been equipped at morning; four yokes it hath, three whips, seven reins to guide it:

Ten-sided, friendly to mankind, light-winner, that must be urged to speed with prayers and wishes.

2 This is prepared for him the first, the second, and the third time: he is man's Priest and Herald.

Others get offspring of another parent he goeth, as a noble Bull, with others.

3 To Indra's car the Bay Steeds have I harnessed, that new well-spoken words may bring him hither.

Here let not other worshippers detain thee, for among us are many holy singers.

4 Indra, come hitherward with two Bay Coursers, come thou with four, with six when invoked.

Come thou with eight, with ten, to drink the Soma. Here is the juice, brave Warrior: do not scorn it.

5 O Indra, come thou hither having harnessed thy car with twenty, thirty, forty horses.

Come thou with fifty well trained coursers, Indra, sixty or seventy, to drink the Soma.

6 Come to us hitherward, O Indra, carried by eighty, ninety, or an hundred horses.

This Soma juice among the Sunahotras hath been poured out, in love, to glad thee, Indra.

7 To this my prayer, O Indra, come thou hither: bind to thy car's pole all thy two Bay Coursers.

Thou art to be invoked in many places Hero, rejoice thyself in this libation.
8 Ne'er be my love from Indra disunited still may his liberal Milch-cow yield us treasure.
So may we under his supreme protection, safe in his arms, succeed in each forth-going.
9 Now may that wealthy Cow Of thine, O Indra, give in return a boon to him who lauds thee.
Give to thy praisers: let not fortune fail us. Loud may we speak, with heroes, in assembly.

### [02-019] HYMN XIX. Indra.
1. DRAUGHTS of this sweet juice have been drunk for rapture, of the wise Soma-presser's offered
dainty,
Wherein, grown mighty in the days aforetime, Indra hath found delight, and men who worship.
2 Cheered by this meath Indra, whose hand wields thunder, rent piecemeal Ahi who barred up the
waters,
So that the quickening currents of the rivers flowed forth like birds unto their resting-places.
3 Indra, this Mighty One, the Dragon's slayer, sent forth the flood of waters to the ocean.
He gave the Sun his life, he found the cattle, and with the night the works of days completed.
4 To him who worshippeth hath Indra given many and matchless gifts. He slayeth Vrtra.
Straight was he to be sought with supplications by men who struggled to obtain the sunlight.
5 To him who poured him gifts he gave up Surya,-Indra, the God, the Mighty, to the mortal;
For Etasa with worship brought him riches that keep distress afar, as 'twere his portion.
6 Once to the driver of his chariot, Kutsa, he gave up greedy Surya, plague of harvest;
And Indra, for the sake of Divodasa demolished Sambara's nine-and-ninety castles.
7 So have we brought our hymn to thee, O Indra, strengthening thee and fain ourselves for glory.
May we with best endeavours gain this friendship, and mayst thou bend the godless scorner's
weapons.
8 Thus the Grtsamadas for thee, O Hero, have wrought their hymn and task as seeking favour.
May they who worship thee afresh, O Indra, gain food and strength, bliss, and a happy dwelling.
9 Now may that wealthy Cow of thine, O Indra, give in return a boon to him who lauds thee,
Give to thy praisers: let not fortune fail us. Loud may we speak, with heroes, in assembly.

### [02-020] HYMN XX. Indra.
1. As one brings forth his car when fain for combat, so bring we power to thee- regard us, Indra-
Well skilled in song, thoughtful in spirit, seeking great bliss from one like thee amid the Heroes.
2 Indra, thou art our own with thy protection, a guardian near to men who love thee truly,
Active art thou, the liberal man's defender, his who draws near to thee with right devotion.
3 May Indra, called with solemn invocations. the young, the Friend, be men's auspicious keeper,
One who will further with his aid the singer, the toiler, praiser, dresser of oblations.

4 With laud and song let me extol that Indra in whom of old men prospered and were mighty.
May he, implored, fulfil the prayer for plenty of him who worships, of the living mortal.
5 He, Indra whom the Angirases' praise delighted, strengthened their prayer and made their goings
prosper.
Stealing away the mornings with the sunlight, he, lauded, crushed even Asna's ancient powers.
6 He verily, the God, the glorious Indra, hath raised him up for man, best Wonder-Worker.
He, self-reliant, mighty and triumphant, brought low the dear head of the wicked Dasa.
7 Indra theVrtra-slayer, Fort-destroyer, scattered the Dasa hosts who dwelt in darkness.
For men hath he created earth and waters, and ever helped the prayer of him who worships.
8 To him in might the Gods have ever yielded, to Indra in the tumult of thebattle.
When in his arms they laid the bolt, he slaughtered the Dasyus and cast down their forts of iron.
9 Now may that wealthy Cow of thine, O Indra, give in return a boon to him who lauds thee.
Give to thy praisers: let not fortune fail us. Loud may we speak, with heroes, in assembly.

### [02-021] HYMN XXI.
1. To him the Lord of all, the Lord of wealth, of light; him who is Lord for ever, Lord of men and tilth,
Him who is Lord of horses, Lord of kine,of floods, to Indra, to the Holy bring sweet Soma juice.
2 To him the potent One, who conquers and breaks down, the Victor never vanquished who disposes
all,
The migbty-voiced, the rider, unassailable, to Indra everconquering speak your reverent prayer.
3 Still Victor, loved by mortals, ruler over men, o'erthrower, warrior, he hath waxen as he would;
Host-gatherer, triumphant, honoured mid the folk. Indra's heroic deeds will I tell forth to all.
4 The strong who never yields, who slew the furious fiend, the deep, the vast, of wisdom
unattainable;
Who speeds the good, the breaker-down, the firm, the vast,-Indra whose rites bring joy hath made
the light of Dawn.
5 By sacrifice the yearning sages sending forth their songs found furtherance from him who speeds
the flood.
In Indra seeking help with worship and with hymn, they drew him to themselves and won them kine
and wealth.
6 Indra, bestow on us the best of treasures, the spirit of ability and fortune;
Increase of riches, safety of our bodies, charm of sweet speech, and days of pleasant weather.

### [02-022] HYMN XXII. Indra.
I. At the Trikadrukas the Great and Strong hath drunk drink blent with meal. With Visnu hath he
quaffed the poured out Soma juice, all that he would.
That hath so heightened him the Great, the Wide, to do his mighty work.
So may the God attain the God, true Indu Indra who is true.
2 So he resplendent in the battle overcame Krivi by might. He with his majesty hath filled the earth
and heaven, and waxen strong.

One share of the libation hath he swallowed down: one share he left.
So may the God attend the God, true Indu Indra who is true.
3 Brought forth together with wisdom and mighty power thou grewest great; with hero deeds
subduing the malevolent, most swift in act;

Giving prosperity, and lovely wealth to him who praiseth thee. So may the God attend the God, true
Indu Indra who is true.
4 This, Indra, was thy hero deed, Dancer, thy first and ancient work, worthy to be told forth in
heaven,
What time thou sentest down life with a God's own power, freeing the floods.
All that is godless may he conquer with his might, and, Lord of Hundred Powers, find for us strength
and food.

## [02-023] HYMN XXIII. Brahmanaspati.

1. WE call thee, Lord and Leader of the heavenly hosts, the wise among the wise, the famousest of
all,
The King supreme of prayers, O Brahmanaspati: hear us with help; sit down in place of sacrifice.
2 Brhaspati, God immortal! verily the Gods have gained from thee, the wise, a share in holy rites.
As with great light the Sun brings forth the rays of morn, so thou alone art Father of all sacred prayer.
3 When thou hast chased away revilers and the gloom, thou mountest the refulgent car of sacrifice;
The awful car, Brhaspati, that quells the foe, slays demons, cleaves the stall of kine, and finds the
light.
4 Thou leadest with good guidance and preservest men; distress o'ertakes not him who offers gifts to
thee.
Him who hates prayer thou punishest, Brhaspati, quelling his wrath: herein is thy great mightiness.
5 No sorrow, no distress from any side, no foes, no creatures double-tongued have overcome the
man,-
Thou drivest all seductive fiends away from him whom, careful guard, thou keepest Brahmanaspati.
6 Thou art our keeper, wise, preparer of our paths: we, for thy service, sing to thee with hymns of
praise.
Brhaspati, whoever lays a snare for us, him may his evil fate, precipitate, destroy.
7 Him, too, who threatens us without offence of ours, the evilminded, arrogant, rapacious man,-
Him turn thou from our path away, Brhaspati: give us fair access to this banquet of the Gods.
8 Thee as protector of our bodies we invoke, thee, saviour, as the comforter who loveth us.
Strike, O Brhaspati, the Gods' revilers down, and let not the unrighteous come to highest bliss.
9 Through thee, kind -prosperer, O Brahmanaspati, may we obtain the wealth of Men which all
desire:
And all our enemies, who near or far away prevail against us, crush, and leave them destitute.
10 With thee as our own rich and liberal ally may we, Brhaspati, gain highest power of life.
Let not the guileful wicked man be lord of us:-still may we prosper, singing goodly hymns of praise.

11 Strong, never yielding, hastening to the battle-cry, consumer of the foe, victorious in the strife,
Thou art sin's true avenger, Brahmanaspati, who tamest e'en the fierce, the wildly passionate.
12 Whoso with mind ungodly seeks to do us harm, who, deeming him a man of might mid lords,
would slay,-
Let not his deadly blow reach us, Brhaspati; may we humiliate the strong ill-doer's wrath.
13 The mover mid the spoil, the winner of all wealth, to be invoked in fight and reverently adored,
Brhaspati hath overthrown like cars of war all wicked enemies who fain would injure us.
14 Burn up the demons with thy fiercest flaming brand, those who have scorned thee in thy
manifested might.
Show forth that power that shall deserve the hymn of praise: destroy the evil speakers, O Brhaspati.
15 Brhaspati, that which the foe deserves not which shines among the folk effectual, splendid,
That, Son of Law I which is with might refulgent-that treasure wonderful bestow thou on us.
16 Give us not up to those who, foes in ambuscade, are greedy for the wealth of him who sits at ease,
Who cherish in their heart abandonment of Gods. Brhaspati, no further rest shall they obtain.
17 For Tvastar, he who knows each sacred song, brought thee to life, preeminent o'er all the things
that be.
Guilt-scourger, guilt-avenger is Brhaspati, who slays the spoiler and upholds the mighty Law.
18 The mountain, for thy glory, cleft itself apart when, Angiras! thou openedst the stall of kine.

Thoul O Brhaspati, with Indra for ally didst hurl down water-floods which gloom had compa-sed
round.
19 O Brahmanaspati, be thou controller of this our hymn and prosper thou our children.
All that the Gods regard with love is blessed. Loud may we speak, with heroes, in assembly.

## [02-024] HYMN XXIV. Brahmanaspati.

1. BE pleased with this our offering, thou who art the Lord; we will adore thee with this new and
mighty song.
As this thy friend, our liberal patron, praises thee, do thou, Brhaspati, fulfil our hearts' desire.
2 He who with might bowed down the things that should be bowed, and in his fury rent the holds of
Sambara:
Who overthrew what shook not, Brahmapaspati,-he made his way within the mountain stored with
wealth.
3 That was a great deed for the Godliest of the Gods: strong things were loosened and the firmly
fixed gave way.
He drave the kine forth and cleft Vala through by prayer, dispelled the darkness and displayed the
light of heaven.
4 The well with mouth of stone that poured a flood of meath, which Brahmapaspati hath opened with
his might-
All they who see the light have drunk their fill thereat: together they have made the watery fount
flow forth.

5 Ancient will be those creatures, whatsoe'er they be; with moons, with autumns, doors unclose
themselves to you.
Effortless they pass on to perfect this and that, appointed works which Brahmanaspati ordained.
6 They who with much endeavour searching round obtained the Panis' noblest treasure hidden in the
cave,-
Those sages, having marked the falsehoods, turned them back whence they had come, and sought
again to enter in.
7 The pious ones when they had seen the falsehoods turned them back, the sages stood again upon
the lofty ways.
Cast down with both their arms upon the rock they left the kindled fire, and said, No enemy is he.
8 With his swift bow, strung truly, Brahmanaspati reaches the mark whate'er it be that he desires.
Excellent are the arrows wherewithal he shoots, keen-eyed to look on men and springing from his
ear.
9 He brings together and he parts, the great High Priest; extolled is he, in battle Brahmapaspati.
When, gracious, for the hymn he brings forth food and wealth, the glowing Sun untroubled sends
forth fervent heat.
10 First and preeminent, excelling all besides are the kind gifts of liberal Brhaspati.
These are the boons of him the Strong who should be loved, whereby both classes and the people
have delight.
11 Thou who in every way supreme in earthly power, rejoicing, by thy mighty strength hast waxen
great,-
He is the God spread forth in breadth against the Gods: he, Brahmanaspati, encompasseth this All.
12 From you, twain Maghavans, all truth proceedeth: even the waters break not your commandment.
Come to us, Brahmanaspati and Indra, to our oblation Iiie yoked steeds to fodder.
13 The sacrificial flames most swiftly hear the call: the priest of the assembly gaineth wealth for
hymns.
Hating the stern, remitting at his will the debt, strong in the shock of fight is Brahmanaspati.
14 The wrath of Brahmanaspati according to his will had full effect when he would do a mighty deed.
The kine he drave forth and distributed to heaven, even as a copious flood with strength flows
sundry ways.
15 O Brahmanaspati, may we be evermore masters of wealth well-guided, full of vital strength.
Heroes on heroes send abundantly to us, when thou omnipotent through prayer seekest my call.
16 O Brahmanaspati, be thou controller of this our hymn, and prosper thou our children.

All that the Gods regard with love is blessed. Loud may we speak, with heroes, in assembly.

## [02-025] HYMN XXV. Brahmanaspati.
1. HE lighting up the flame shall conquer enemies: strong shall he be who offers prayer and brings his
gift.
He with his seed spreads forth beyond another's seed, whomever Brahmanaspati takes for his friend.

2 With heroes he shall overcome his hero foes, and spread his wealth by kine wise by himself is be.
His children and his children's children
grow in strength, whomever Brahmanaspati takes for his friend.
3 He, mighty like a raving river's billowy flood, as a bull conquers oxen, overcomes with strength.
Like Agni's blazing rush he may not be restrained, whomever Brahmanaspati takes for his friend.
4 For him the floods of heaven flow never failing down: first with the heroes he goes forth to war for
kine.
He slays in unabated vigour with great might, whomever Brahmanaspati takes for his friend.
5 All roaring rivers pour their waters down for him, and many a flawless shelter hath been granted
him.
Blest with the happiness of Gods he prospers well, whomever Brahmanaspati takes for his friend.

## [02-026] HYMN XXVI. Brahmanaspati.
1. THE righteous singer shall o'ercome his enemies, and he who serves the Gods subdue the godless
man.
The zealous man shall vanquish the invincible, the worshipper share the food of him who worships
not.
2 Worship, thou hero, chase the arrogant afar: put on auspicious courage for the fight with foes.
Prepare oblation so that thou mayst have success. we crave the favouring help of Brahmanaspati.
3 He with his folk, his house, his family, his sons, gains booty for himself, and, with the heroes,
wealth,believing
Who with oblation and a true heart serves Brahmanaspati the Father of the Gods.
4 Whoso hath honoured him with offerings rich in oil, him Brahmanaspati leads forward on his way,
Saves him from sorrow, frees him from his enemy, and is his wonderful deliverer from woe.

## [02-027] HYMN XXVII. Adityas.
1. THESE hymns that drop down fatness, with the ladle I ever offer tothe Kings Adityas.
May Mitra, Aryanian, and Bhaga hear us, the mighty Varuna Daksa, and Amsa.
2 With one accord may Aryaman and Mitra and Varuna this day accept this praise-song-
Adityas bright and pure as streams of water, free from all guile and falsehood, blameless, perfect.
3 These Gods, Adityas, vast, profound, and faithful, with many eyes, fain to deceive the wicked,
Looking within behold the good and evil near to the Kings is even the thing most distant.
4 Upholding that which moves and that which moves not,
Adityas, Gods, protectors of all being,
Provident, guarding well the world of spirits, true to eternal Law, the debt-exactors.
5 May I, Adityas, share m this your favour which, Aryaman, brings profit e'en in danger.
Under your guidance, Varuna and Mitra, round troubles may I pass, like rugged places.
6 Smooth is your path, O Aryaman and Mitra; excellent is it, Varuna, and thornless.
Thereon, Adityas, send us down your blessing: grant us a shelter hard to be demolished.
7 Mother of Kings, may Aditi transport us, by fair paths Aryaman, beyond all hatred.

May we uninjured, girt by many heroes, win Varuna's and Mitra's high protection.
8 With their support they stay three earths, three heavens; three are their functions in the Gods' assembly.
Mighty through Law, Adityas, is your greatness; fair is it, Aryaman, Varuna, and Mitra.
9 Golden and splendid, pure like streams of water, they hold aloft the three bright heavenly regions.
Ne'er do they slumber, never close their eyelids, faithful, far-ruling for the righteous mortal.
10 Thou over all, O Varuna, art Sovran, be they Gods, Asura! or be they mortals.

Grant unto us to see a hundred autumns ours be the blest long lives of our forefathers.
11 Neither the right nor left do I distinguish, neither the cast nor yet the west, Adityas.
Simple and guided by your wisdom, Vasus! may I attain the light that brings no danger.
12 He who bears gifts unto the Kings, true Leaders, he whom their everlasting blessings prosper,
Moves with his chariot first in rank and wealthy, munificent and lauded in assemblies.
13 Pure, faithful, very strong, with heroes round him, he dwells beside the waters rich with pasture.
None slays, from near at hand or from a distance, him who is under the Adityas' guidance.
14 Aditi, Mitra, Varuna, forgive us however we have erred and sinned against you.
May I obtain the broad light free from peril: O Indra, let not during darkness seize us.
15 For him the Twain united pour their fulness, the rain from heaven: he thrives most highly favoured.
He goes to war mastering both the mansions: to him both portions of the world are gracious.
16 Your guiles, ye Holy Ones, to quell oppressors, your snares spread out against the foe, Adityas,
May I car-borne pass like a skilful horseman: uninjured may we dwell in spacious shelter.
17 May1 not live, O Varuna, to witness my wealthy, liberal, dear friend's destitution.
King, may1 never lack well-ordered riches. Lond may we speak, with heroes, in assembly.

## [02-028] HYMN XXVIII. Varuna

1. THIS laud of the self-radiant wise Aditya shall be supreme o'er all that is in greatness.
1 beg renown of Varuna the Mighty, the God exceeding kind to him who worships.
2, Having extolled thee. Varuna, with thoughtful care may we have high fortune in thy service,
Sinffing thy praises like the fires at coming, day after day, of mornings rich in cattle.
3 May we be in thy keeping, O thou Leader wide-ruling Varuna, Lord of many heroes.
O sons of Aditi, for ever faithful, pardon us, Gods, admit us to your friendship.
4 He made them flow, the Aditya, the Sustainer: the rivers run by Varuna's commandment.
These feel no weariness, nor cease from flowing: swift have they flown like birds in air around us.
5 Loose me from sin as from a bond that binds me: may we swell, Varuna, thy spring of Order.
Let not my thread, while I weave song, be severed, nor my work's sum, before the time, be shattered.

6 Far from me, Varuna, remove all danger accept me graciously, thou Holy Sovran.
Cast off, like cords that hold a calf, my troubles: I am not even mine eyelid's lord without thee.
7 Strike us not, Varuna, with those dread weapons which, Asura, at thy bidding wound the sinner.
Let us not pass away from light to exile. Scatter, that we may live, the men who hate us.
8 O mighty Varuna, now and hereafter, even as of old, will we speak forth our worship.
For in thyself, invincible God, thy statutes ne'er to be moved are fixed as on a mountain.
9 Move far from me what sins I have committed: let me not suffer, King, for guilt of others.
Full many a morn remains to dawn upon us: in these, O Varuna, while we live direct us.
10 O King, whoever, be he friend or kinsman, hath threatened me affrighted in my slumber-
If any wolf or robber fain would harm us, therefrom, O Varuna, give thou us protection.
11May I not live O Varuna, to witness my wealthy, liberal dear friend's destitution.
King, may I never lack well-ordered riches. Loud may we speak, with heroes, in assembly.

## [02-029] HYMN XXIX. Visvedevas.

I. UPHOLDERS of the Law, ye strong Adityas, remove my sin like her who bears in secret.
You, Varuna, Mitra and all Gods who listen, I call to help me, I who know your goodness.
2 Ye, Gods, are providence and ye are power: remove ye utterly all those who hate us.
As givers of good things deal with us kindly: this day be gracious to us and hereafter.
3 What service may we do you with our future, what service, Vasus, with our ancient friendship?
O Aditi, and VaruVa and Mitra, Indra and Maruts, make us well and happy.
4 Ye, O ye Gods, are verily our kinsmen as such be kind to me who now implore you.
Let not your car come slowly to our worship: of kinsmen such as you ne'er let us weary.
5 I singly have sinned many a sin against you, and ye chastised me as a sire the gambler.
Far be your nets, far, Gods, be mine offences: seize me not like a bird upon her offspring.
6 Turn yourselves hitherward this day, ye Holy, that fearing in my heart I may approach you.
Protect us, God; let not the wolf destroy us. Save us, ye Holy, from the pit and falling.
7 May I not live, O Varuna, to witness my wealthy, liberal, dear friend's destitution.
King, may I never lack well-ordered riches. Loud may we speak, with heroes, in assembly.

## [02-030] HYMN XXX. Indra and Others.

1. THE streams unceasing flow to Indra, slayer of Ahi, Savitar, God, Law's fulfiller,
Day after day goes on the sheen of waters. What time hath past since they were first set flowing?
2 His Mother-for she knew-spake and proclaimed him who was about to cast his bolt at Vrtra.
Cutting their paths according to his pleasure day after day flow to their goal the rivers.
3 Aloft he stood above the airy region, and against Vrtra shot his deadly missile.

Enveloped in a cloud he rushed upon him. Indra subdued the foe with sharpened weapons.

4 As with a bolt, Brhaspati, fiercely flaming, pierce thou Vrkadvaras', the Asura's, heroes.

Even as in time of old with might thou slewest, so slay even now our enemy, O Indra.

5 Cast down from heaven on high thy bolt of thunder wherewith in joy thou smitest dead the foeman.

For gain of children make us thine, O Indra, of many children's children and of cattle.

6 Whomso ye love, his power ye aid and strengthen; ye Twain are the rich worshipper's advancers.

Graciously favour us, Indra and Soma; give us firm standing in this time of danger.

7 Let it not vex me, tire me, make me slothful, and never let us say, Press not the Soma;

For him who cares for me, gives gifts, supports me, who comes with kine to me who pour libations.

8 Sarasvati, protect us: with the Maruts allied thou boldly conquerest our foemen,

While Indra does to death the daring chieftain of Sandikas exulting in his prowess.

9 Him who waylays, yea, him who would destroy us,-aim at him, pierce him with thy sharpened

weapon.

Brhaspati, with arms thou slayest foemen O King, give up the spoiler to destruction.

10 Perform, O Hero, with our valiant heroes the deeds heroic which thou hast to finish.

Long have they been inflated with presumption: slay them, and bring us hither their possessions.

11 I craving joy address with hymn and homage your heavenly host, the company of Maruts,

That we may gain wealth with full store of heroes, each day more famous, and with troops of

children.

## [02-031] HYMN XXXI. Visvedevas.

1. HELP, Varuna and Mitra, O ye Twain allied with Vasus, Rudras, and Adityas, help our car,

That, as the wild birds of the forest from their home, our horses may fly forth, glad, eager for renown.

2 Yea, now ye Gods of one accord speed on our car what time among the folk it seeks an act of might;

When, hasting through the region with the stamp of hoofs, our swift steeds trample on the ridges of

the earth.

3 Or may our Indra here, the Friend of all mankind, coming from heaven, most.wise, girt by the Marut

host,

Accompany, with aid untroubled by a foe, our car to mighty gain, to win the meed of strength.

4 Or may this Tvastar, God who rules the world with power, one-minded with the Goddesses speed

forth our car;

Ila and Bhaga the celestial, Earth and Heaven, Pusan, Purandhi, and the Asvins, ruling Lords.

5 Or, seen alternate, those two blessed Goddesses, Morning and Night who stir all living things to

act:

While with my newest song I praise you both, O Earth, that from what moves not ye may spread

forth threefold food.

6 Your blessing as a boon for suppliants we desire: the Dragon of the Deep, and Aja-Ekapad,

Trita, Rbhuksan, Savitar shall joy in us, and ihe Floods' swift Child in our worship and our prayer.

7 These earnest prayers I pray to you, ye Holy: to pay you honour, living men have formed them,

Men fain to win the prize and glory. May they win, as a car-horse might the goal, your notice.

## [02-032] HYMN XXXII. Various Deities.

1. GRACIOUSLY further, O ye Heaven and Earth, this speech striving to win reward, of me your

worshipper.

First rank I give to you, Immortal, high extolled! I, fain to win me wealth, to you the migbty Pair.

2 Let not man's guile annoy us, secret or by day: give not us up a prey to these calamities.

Sever not thou our friendship: think thereon for us. This, with a heart that longs for bliss, we seek

from thee.

3 Bring hither with benignant mind the willing Cow teeming with plenteous milk, full, inexhaustible.

O thou invoked by many, day by day I urge thee with my word, a charger rapid in his tread.

4 With eulogy I call on Raka swift to hear may she, auspicious, hear us, and herself observe.

With never-breaking needle may she sew her work, and give a hero son most wealthy, meet for

praise.

5 All thy kind thoughts, O Raka, lovely in their form, wherewith thou grantest wealth to him who

offers gifts-

With these come thou to us this day benevolent, O Blessed One, bestowing food of thousand sorts.

6 O broad-tressed Sinivali, thou who art the Sister of the Gods, Accept the offered sacrifice, and, Goddess, grant us progeny.

7 With lovely fingers, lovely arms, prolific Mother of many sons-Present the sacred gifts to her, to Sinlivali Queen of men.

8 Her, Sinivali, her, Gungu, her, Raka, her, Sarasvati, Indrani to mine aid I call, and Vartunani for my

weal.

## [02-033] HYMN XXXIII. Rudra.

1. FATHER of Maruts, let thy bliss approach us: exclude us not from looking on the sunlight.

Gracious to our fleet courser be the Hero may we transplant us, Rudra, in our children.

2 With the most saving medicines which thou givest, Rudra, may I attain a hundred winters.

Far from us banish enmity and hatred, and to all quarters maladies and trouble.

3 Chief of all born art thou in glory, Rudra, armed with the thunder, mightiest of the mighty.

Transport us over trouble to well-being repel thou from us all assaults of mis. chief.

4 Let us not anger thee with worship, Rudra, ill praise, Strong God! or mingled invocation.

Do thou with strengthening balms incite our heroes: I hear thee famed as best of all physicians.

5 May I with praise-songs win that Rudra's favour who is adored with gifts and invocations.

Ne'er may the tawny God, fair-checked, and gracious, swifthearing, yield us to this evil purpose.

6 The Strong, begirt by Maruts, hath refreshed me, with most invigorating food, imploring.

As he who finds a shade in fervent sunlight may I, uninjured, win the bliss of Rudra.

7 Where is that gracious hand of thine, O Rudra, the hand that giveth health and bringeth comfort,

Remover of the woe that Gods have sent us? O Strong One, look thou on me with compassion.

8 To him the strong, great, tawny, fair-complexioned, I utter forth a mighty hymn of praises.
We serve the brilliant God with adorations, we glorify, the splendid name of Rudra.
9 With firm limbs, multiform, the strong, the tawny adorns himself with bright gold decorations:
The strength of Godhead ne'er departs from Rudra, him who is Sovran of this world, the mighty.
10 Worthy, thou carriest thy bow and arrows, worthy, thy manyhued and honoured necklace.
Worthy, thou cuttest here each fiend to pieces: a mightier than thou there is not, Rudra.
11 Praise him the chariot-borne, the young, the famous, fierce, slaying like a dread beast of the forest.
O Rudra, praised, be gracious to the singer. let thy hosts spare us and smite down another.
12 I bend to thee as thou approachest, Rudra, even as a boy before the sire who greets him.
I praise thee Bounteous Giver, Lord of heroes: give medicines to us as thou art lauded.
13 Of your pure medicines, O potent Martits, those that are wholesomest and healthbestowing,

Those which our father Manu hath selected, I crave from. Rudra for our gain and welfare.
14 May Rudra's missile turn aside and spare us, the great wrath of the impetuous One avoid us.
Turn, Bounteous God, thy strong bow from our princes, and be thou gracious to our seed and offspring.
15 O tawny Bull, thus showing forth thy nature, as neither to be wroth, O God, nor slay us.
Here, Rudra, listen to our invocation. Loud may we speak, with heroes, in assembly.

## [02-034] HYMN XXXIV. Maruts

1. THE Maruts of resistless might who love the rain, resplendent, terrible like wild beasts in their
strength,
Glowing like flames of fire, impetuous in career, blowing the wandering raincloud, have disclosed the
kine.
2 They gleam with armlets as the heavens are decked with stars, like cloud-born lightnings shine the
torrents of their rain.
Since the strong Rudra, O Maruts with brilliant chests, sprang into life for you in Prsni's radiant lap.
3 They drip like horses in the racings of swift steeds; with the stream's rapid cars they hasten on
their way.
Maruts with helms of gold, ye who make all things shake, con e with your spotted deer, one-minded,
to our food.
4 They have bestowed of Mitra all that live, to feed, they who for evermore cause their swift drops to
flow;
Whose steeds are spotted deer, whose riches never fail, like horses in full speed, bound to the pole in
work.
5 With brightly-flarning kine whose udders swell with milk, idth glittering lances on your
unobstructed paths,
O Maruts, of one mind, like swans who seek their nests, come to the rapturous enjoyment of the
meath.
6 To these our prayers, O Maruts, come unanimous, come ye to our libations like the praise of men.

Make it swell like a mare, in udder like a cow, and for the singer grace the song with plenteous
strength.
7 Give us a steed, O Maruts migbty in the car; prevailing prayer that brings remembrance day by day;
Food to your praisers, to your bard in deeds of might give winning wisdom, power uninjured,
unsurpassed.
8 When the bright-chested Maruts, lavish of their gifts, bind at the time bliss their horses to the cars,
Then, as the milch-cow feeds her calf within the stalls, they pour forth food for all oblation-bringing
men.
9 Save us, O Maruts, Vasus, from the injurer, the mortal foe who makes us looked upon as wolves.
With chariot all aflame compass him round about: O Rudras, cast away the foeman's deadly bolt.
10 Well-known, ye Maruts, is that wondrous course of yours, when they milked Prsni's udder, close
akin to her.
Or when to shame the bard who lauded, Rudra's Sons, ye O infallible brought Trita to decay.
11 We call youi such, great Maruts, following wonted ways, to the oblation paid to Visnu Speeder-on.
With ladles lifted up, with prayer, we seek of them preeminent, golden-hued, the wealth which all
extol.
12 They, the Dasagvas, first of all brought sacrifice: they at the break of mornings shall inspirit us.
Dawn with her purple beams uncovereth the nights, with great light glowing like a billowy sea of
milk.
13 The Rudras have rejoiced thern in the gathered bands at seats of worship as in purple ornaments.
They with impetuous vigour sending down the rain have taken to themselves a bright and lovely hue.
14 Soliciting their high protection for our help, with this our adoration we sing praise to them,
Whom, for assistance, like the five terrestrial priests. Trita hath brought to aid us hither on his car.
15 So may your favouring help be turned to us-ward, your kindness like a Iowing cow approach us,
Wherewith ye bear your servant over trouble, and free your worshipper from scoff and scorning.

## [02-035] HYMN XXXV. Son of Waters.

1. EAGER for spoil my flow of speech I utter: may the Floods' Child accept my songs with favour.
Will not the rapid Son of Waters make them lovely, for he it is who shall enjoy them?
2 To him let us address the song well-fashioned, forth from the heart. Shall he not understand it'
The friendly Son of Waters by the greatness of Godhead hath produced all things existing.
3 Some floods unite themselves and others join them: die sounding rivers fill one common storehouse.
On every side the bright Floods have encompassed the bright resplendent Offspring of the Waters.
4 The never-sullen waters, youthful Maidens, carefully decking, wait on him the youthful.
He with bright rays shines forth in splendid beauty, unfed with wood. in waters, oil-enveloped.
5 To him three Dames are oftering food to feed him, Goddesses to the God whom none may injure.
Within the waters hath he pressed, as hollows, and drinks their milk who now are first made mothers.

6 Here was the horse's birth; his was the sunlight. Save thou our princes from the oppressor's
onslaught.
Him, indestructible, dwelling at a distance in forts unwrought lies and ill spirits reach not.
7 He, in whose mansion is the teeming Milch-cow, swells the Gods' nectar and cats noble viands.
lle Son of Waters, gathering strength in waters, shines for his worshipper to give him treasures.
8 He who in waters with his own pure Godhead shines widely, law-abiding, everlasting-
The other worlds are verily his branches, and plants are born of him with all their offspring.
9 The Waters' Son hath risen, and clothed in lightning ascended up unto the curled cloud's bosom;
And bearing with them his supremest glory the Youthful Ones, gold-coloured, move around him.
10 Golden in form is he, like gold to look on, his colour is like gold, the Son of Waters.
When he is seated fresh from golden birthplace those who present their gold give food to feed him.
11 This the fair name and this the lovely aspect of him the Waters' Son increase in secret.
Whom here the youthful Maids together kindle, his food is sacred oil of golden colour.
12 Him, nearest Friend of many, will we worship with sacrifice. and reverence and oblation.
I make his back to shine, with chips provide him; t offer food and with my songs exalt him.
13 The Bull hath laid his own life-germ Within them. He sucks them as an infant, and they kiss him.
He, Son of Waters, of unfading colour, hadi entered here as in another's body.
14 While here he dwelleth in sublimest station, resplendent with the rays that never perish,
The Waters, bearing oil to feed their ofispring, flow, Youthful Ones, in wanderings about him.
15 Agni, I gave good shelter to the people, and to the princes goodly preparation.
Blessed is all that Gods regard with favour. Loud may we speak, with heroes, in assembly.

## [02-036] HYMN XXXVI Various Gods.
1. WATER and milk hath he endued, sent forth to thee: the men have drained him with the filters and
the stones.
Drink, Indra, from the Hotar's bowlfirst right is thine-Soma hallowed and poured with Vasat and
Svaha.
2 Busied with sacrifice, with spotted deer and spears, gleaming upon your way with ornaments, yea,
our Friends,
Sitting on sacred grass, ye Sons of Bharata, drink Soma from the Potar's bowl, O Men of heaven.
3 Come unto us, ye swift to listen: as at home upon the sacred grass sit and enjoy yourselves.
And, Tvastar, well-content be joyful in the juice with Gods and Goddesses in gladsome company.
4 Bring the Gods hither, Sage, and offer sacrifice: at the three altars seat thee willingly, O Priest.
Accept for thy delight the proffered Soma meath: drink from the Kindler's bowl and fill thee with thy
share.
5 This is the strengthener of thy body's manly might: strength, victory for all time are placed within
thine arms.

Pressed for thee, Maghavan, it is offered unto thee: drink from the chalice of this Brahman, drink thy
fill.
6 Accept the sacrifice; mark both of you, my call: the Priest hath seated him after the ancient texts.
My prayer that bids them come goes forth to both the Kings: drink ye the Soma meath from the
Director's bowl.

## [02-037] HYMN XXXVII. Various Gods.
1. Enjoy thy fill of meath out of the Hotar's cup: Adhvaryus he desires a full draught poured for him.
Bring it him: seeking this he gives. Granter of Wealth, drink Sorna with the Rtus from the Hotar's cup.
2 He whom of old I called on, him I call on now. He is to be invoked; his name is He who Gives,
Here brought by priests is Soma meath. Granter of Wealth, drink Soma with the Rtus from the Potar's
cup.
3 Fat may the horses be wherewith thou specdest on: Lord of the Wood, unharming, strengthen thou
thyself.
Drawing and seizing, Bold One, thou who grantest wealth, drink Soma with the Rtus from the
Nestar's cup.
4 From Hotar's cup and Potar's he hath drunk and joyed: the proffered food hath pleased him from
the Nestar's bowl.
The fourth cup undisturbed, immortal, let him drink who giveth wealth, the cup of the wealth-giving
God.
5 Yoke, O ye Twain, to-day your hero-bearing car, swift-moving hitherward: your loosing-place is
here.
Mix the oblations, then come hither with the meath, and drink the Soma, ye rich in abundant
strength.
6 Agni, accept the fuel and our offered gift: accept the prayer of man, accept our eulogy,
Do thou with all, with Rtu, O thou Excellent, fain, make the great Gods all fain taste the gift we bring.

## [02-038] HYMN XXXVIII. Savitar.
1. UPRISEN is Savitar, this God, to quicken, Priest who neglects not this most constant duty.
To the Gods, verily, he gives rich treasure, and blesses him who calls them to the banquet.
2 Having gone up on high, the God broadhanded spreads his arms widely forth that all may mark
him.
Even the waters bend them to his service: even this wind rests in the circling region.
3 Though borne by swift steeds he will yet unyoke them: e'en the fleet chariot hath he stayed from
going.
He hath checked e'en their haste who glide like serpents. Night closely followed Savitar's dominion.
4 What was spread out she weaves afresh, re-weaving: the skilful leaves his labour half-completed.
He hath arisen from rest, and parted seasons: Savitar hath approached, God, holy-minded.
5 Tlirough various dwellings, through entire existence, spreads, manifest, the household light of
Agni.
The Mother gives her Son the goodliest portion, and Savitar hath sped to meet his summons.

6 He comes again, unfolded, fain for conquest: at home was he, the love of all things moving.

Each man hath come leaving his evil doings, after the Godlike Savitar's commandment.

7 The wild beasts spread through desert places seeking their watery share which thou hast set in waters.

The woods are given to the birds. These statutes of the God Savitar none disobeyeth.

8 With utmost speed, in restless haste at sunset Varuna seeks his watery habitation.

Then seeks each bird his nest, each beast his lodging. In due place Savitar hath set each creature.

9 Him whose high law not Varuna nor Indra, not Mitra, Aryaman, nor Rudra breaketh,

Nor evil-hearted fiends, here for my welfare him I invoke, God Savitar, with worship.

10 May they who strengthen bliss, and thought and wisdom, and the Dames' Lord and Narasamsa

aid us.

That good may come to us and wealth be gathered, may we be Savitar the God's beloved.

11 So come to us our hearts' desire, the bounty bestowed by thee, from heaven and earth and waters,

That it be well with friends and those who praise thee, and, Savitar, with the loud-lauding singer.

## [02-039] HYMN XX Asvins.

1. SING like the two press-stones for this same purpose; come like two misers to the tree of treasure;

Like two laud-singing Brahmans in the assembly, like the folk's envoys called in many places.

2 Moving at morning like two chr-borne heroes, like to a pair of goats ye come electing;

Like two fair dames embellishing their bodies, like a wise married pair among the people.

3 Like to a pair of horns come first to usward, like to a pair of hoofs with rapid motion;

Come like two Cakavas in the grey of morning, come like two chariot wheels at dawn, ye Mighty.

4 Bear us across the rivers like two vessels, save us as ye were yokes, naves, spokes and fellies.

Be like two dogs that injure not our bodies; preserve us, like two crutches, that we fall not.

5 Like two winds ageing not, two confluent rivers, come with quick vision like two eyes before us.

Come like two hands most helpful to the body, and guide us like two feet to what is precious.

6 Even as two lips that with the mouth speak honey, even as two breasts that nourish our existence,

Like the two nostrils that protect our being, be to us as our ears that hear distinctly.

7 Like two hands give ye us increasing vigour; like heaven and earth constrain the airy regions.

Asvins, these hymns that struggle to approach you, sharpen ye like an axe upon a whetstone.

8 These prayers of ours exalting you, O Asvins, have the GrtSamadas, for a laud, made ready.

Welcome them, O ye Heroes, and come bither. Loud may we speak. with brave men, in assembly.

## [02-040] HYMN XL. Soma and Pusan.

1 SOMA and Pusan, Parents of all riches, Parents of earth and Parents of high heaven,

You Twain, brought forth as the whole world's protectors, the Gods have made centre of life eternal.

2 At birth of these two Gods all Gods are joyful: they have caused darkness, which we hate, to vanish.

With these, with Soma and with Pusan, India generates ripe warm milk in the raw milch-cows.

3 Soma and Pusan, urge your chariot hither, the seven-wheeIed car that measures out the region,

That stirs not all, that moves to every quarter, fivc-reined and harnessed by the thought, ye Mighty.

4 One in the heaven on high hath made his dwelling, on earth and in the firmament the other.

May they disclose to us great store of treasure, much-longed for, rich in food, source of enjoyment.

5 One of you Twain is Parent of all creatures, the otherjourneys onward all-beholding.

Soma and Pusan, aid my thought with favour: with you may we o'ercome in all encounters.

6 May Pusan stir our thought, the all-impelling, may Soma Lord of riches grant us riches.

May Aditi the perfect Goddess aid us. Loud may we speak, with heroes, in assembly.

## [02-041] HYMN XLI. Various Deities.

1. O VAYU, come to us with all the thousand chariots that are thine,

Team-borne, to drink the Soma juice.

2 Drawn by thy team, O Vayu, come; to thee is offered this, the pure.

Thou visitest the presser's house.

3 Indra and Vayu, drawn by teams, ye Heroes, come today and drink.

Of the bright juice when blent with milk.

4 This Soma hath been shed for you, Lawstrengtheners, Mitra-Varuna!

Listen ye here to this my call.

5 Both Kings who never injure aught seat them in their supremest home,

The thousand-pillared, firmly-based.

6 Fed with oblation, Sovran Kings, Adityas, Lords of liberal gifts.

They wait on him whose life is true.

7 With kine, Nasatyas, and with steeds, come, Asvins, Rudras, to the house

That will protect its heroes well;

8 Such, wealthy Gods! as none afar nor standing nigh to us may harm,

Yea, no malicious mortal foe.

9 As such, O longed-far Asvins, lead us on to wealth of varied sort,

Wealth that shall bring us room and rest.

10 Verily Indra, conquering all, driveth e'en mighty fear away,

For firm is he and swift to act.

11 Indra be gracious unto us: sin shall not reach us afterward,

And good shall be before us still.

12 From all the regions of the world let Indra send security,

The foe-subduer, swift to act.

13 O all ye Gods, come hitherward: hear this mine invocation, seat

Yourselves upon this sacred grass.

14 Among ihe gunahotras strong for you is this sweet gladdening draught.

Drink ye of this delightsome juice.

15 Ye Martus led by Indra, Gods with Pri§an for your bounteousest,

Hear all of you this call of mine.

16 Best Mother, best of Rivers, best of Goddesses, Sarasvati, We are, as 'twere, of no repute and dear

Mother, give thou us renown.

17 In thee, Sarasvati, divine, all generations have their stay.
Be, glad with Sunahotra's sons: O Goddess grant us progeny.

18 Enriched with sacrifice, accept Sarasvati, these prayers of ours,
Thoughts which GrtSamadas beloved of Gods bring, Holy One,to thee.

19 Ye who bless sacrifice, go forth, for verily we choose you both,
And Agni who conveys our gifts.

20 This our.effectual sacrifice, reaching the sky, shall Heaven and Earth
Present unto the Gods to-day.

21 In both your laps, ye guileless Ones, the Holy Gods shall sit them down
To-day to drink the Soma here.

### [02-042] HYMN XLII Kapinjala.

1. TELLING his race aloud with cries repeated, he sends his voice out as his boat a steersman.
O Bird, be ominous of happy fortune from no side may calamity befall thee.

2 Let not the falcon kill thee, nor the eagle let not the arrow-bearing archer reach thee.
Still crying in the region of the Fathers, speak here auspicious, bearing joyful tidings.

3 Bringing good tidings, Bird of happy omen, call thou out loudly southward of our dwellings,
So that no thief, no sinner may oppress us. Loud may we speak, with heroes, in assembly.

### [02-043] HYMN XLIII. Kapinjala.

1. HERE on the right sing forth chanters of hymns of praise, even the winged birds that in due season speak.
He, like: a Sama-chanter utters both the notes, skilled in the mode of Trstup and of Gayatri.

2 Thou like the chanter-priest chantest the Sama, Bird; thou singest at libations like a Brahman's son.
Even as a vigorous horse when he comes near the mare, announce to us good forturue, Bird, on every
side, proclaim in all directions happy luck, O Bird.

3 When singing here, O Bird. announce good luck to us, and when thou sittest still think on us with
kind thoughts.
When flying off thou singest thou art like a lute. With brave sons in assembly may we speak aloud.

# BOOK THREE

### [03-001] HYMN I. Agni.

1. THOU, Agni, who wilt have the strong, hast made me the Soma's priest, to worship in assembly.
Thou shinest to the Gods, I set the pressstones. I toil; be joyful in thyself, O Agni.

2 East have we turned the rite; may the hymn aid it. With wood and worship shall they honour Agni.
From heaven the synods of the wise have learnt it: c'en for the quick and strong they seek
advancement.

3 The Prudent, he whose will is pure, brought welfare, allied by birth to Heaven and Earth in kinship.
The Gods discovered in the midst of waters beautiful Agni with the Sisters' labour.

4 Him, Blessed One, the Seven strong Floods augmented, him white at birth and red when waxen
mighty.

As mother mares run to their new-born you ling, so at his birth the Gods wondered at Agni.

5 Spreading with radiant limbs throughout the region, purging his power with wise purifications,
Robing himself in light, the life of waters, lie spreads abroad his high and perfect glories.

6 He sought heaven's Mighty Ones, the unconsuming, the unimpaired, not clothed and yet not naked.
Then they, ancient and young, who dwell together, Seven sounding Rivers, as one germ received
him.

7 His piles, assuming every form, are scattered where flow sweet waters, at the spring of fatness;
There stood the milch-kine with full-laden udders, and both paired Mighty Mothers of the Wondrous.

8 Carefully cherished, Son of Strength, thou shonest assuming lasting and refulgent beauties.
Full streams of fatness and sweet juice descended, there where the Mighty One grew strong by
wisdom.

9 From birth he knew even his Father's bosom, he set his voices and his streams in motion;
Knew him who moved with blessed Friends in secret, with the young Dames of heaven. He stayed
not hidden.

10 He nursed the Infant of the Sire and Maker: alone the Babe sucked many a teeming bosom.
Guard, for the Bright and Strong, the fellow-spouses friendly to men and bound to him in kinship.

11 The Mighty One increased in space unbounded; full many a glorious flood gave strength to Agni.
Friend of the house, within the lap of Order lay Agni, in the Sister Rivers' service.

12 As keen supporter where great waters gather, light-shedder whom the brood rejoice to look on;
He who begat, and will beget, the dawnlights, most manly, Child of Floods, is youthful Agni.

13 Him, varied in his form, the lovely Infant of floods and plants the blessed wood hath gendered.
Gods even, moved in spirit, came around him, and served him at his birth, the Strong, the Wondrous.

14 Like brilliant lightnings, mighty luminaries accompany the light-diffusing Agni,
Waxen, as 'twere in secret, in his dwelling, while in the boundless stall they milk out Amrta.

15 I sacrificing serve thee with oblations and crave with longing thy good-will and friendship.
Grant, with the Gods, thy grace to him who lauds thee, protect us with thy rays that guard the
homestead.

16 May we, O Agni, thou who leadest wisely, thy followers and masters of all treasures,
Strong in the glory of our noble offspring, subdue the godless when they seek the battle.

17 Ensign of Gods hast thou become, O Agni, joy-giver, knower of all secret wisdom.
Friend of the homestead, thou hast lightened mortals: carborne thou goest to the Gods, fulfilling.

18 Within the house hath sate the King immortal of mortals, filling full their sacred synods.
Bedewed with holy oil he shineth widely, Agni, the knower of all secret wisdom.

19 Come unto us with thine auspicious friendship, come speeding, Mighty, with thy mighty succours.
Grant us abundant wealth that saves from danger, that brings a good repute, a glorious portion.

20 To thee who art of old these songs, O Agni, have I declared, the ancient and the later.

These great libations to the Strong are offered: in every birth is Jatavedas stablished.

21 Stablished in every birth is Jatavedas, kindled perpetual by the Visvamitras.

May we rest ever in the loving-kindness, in the auspicious grace of him the Holy.

22 This sacrifice of ours do thou, O Mighty, O truly Wise, bear to the Gods rejoicing.

Grant us abundant food, thou priestly Herald, vouchsafe to give us ample wealth, O Agni.

23 As holy food, Agni, to thine'invoker give wealth in cattle, lasting, rich in marvels.

To us he born a son, and spreading offspring. Agni, be this thy gracious will to us-ward.

## [03-002] HYMN II. Agni.

1. To him, Vaisvanara, who strengthens Holy Law, to Agni we present our praise like oil made pure.

With thoughtful insight human priests bring him anear, our Herald from of old, as an axe forms a car.

2 He made the heaven and earth resplendent by his birth: Child of two Mothers he was meet to be implored,

Agni, oblation-bearer, gracious, ever-young, infallible, rich in radiant light, the guest of men.

3 Within the range of their surpassinq power, by might, the Gods created Agni with inventive thought.

I, eager to win strength, address him, like a steed, resplendent with his brilliance, with his ample light.

4 Eager to gain, we crave from him the friendly God strength confident, choiceworthy meet to be extolled:

The Bhrgus' bounty, willing, strong with sages' lore, even Agni shining forth with light that comes from heaven.

5 For happiness, men, having trimmed the sacred grass, set Agni glorious for his strength before them here;

Yea, with raised ladles, him bright, dear to all the Gods, perfecting aims of works, Rudra of solemn rites.

6 Around thy dwelling-place, O brightly-shining Priest, are men at sacrifice, whose sacred grass is trimmed.

Wishing to do thee service, Agni, they are there, desirous of thy friendship grant them store of wealth.

7 He hath filled heaven and earth and the great realm of light, when at his birth the skilful held him in their hold.

He like a horse is led forth to the sacrifice Sage, graciously inclined, that he may win us strength.

8 Honour the oblation-bearer, him who knows fair rites, serve ye the Household Friend who knows all things that be.

He drives the chariot of the lofty ordinance: Agni most active, is the great High Priest of Gods.

9 They who are free from death, fain for him, purified three splendours of the mighty Agni, circling all.

To man, for his enjoyment, one of these they gave: the other two have passed into the sister sphere.

10 Man's sacrificial food hath sharpened like an axe, for brightness, him the Sage of men, the people's Lord,

Busied with sacred rites he mounts and he descends. He hath laid down his vital germ within these worlds.

11 He stirs with life in wombs dissimilar in kind, born as a Lion or a loudly-bellowing Bull:

Vaisvanara immortal with wide-reaching might, bestowing goods and wealth on him who offiers gifts.

12 Vaisvanara, as of old, mounted the cope of heaven, heaven's ridge, well greeted, by those skilled in noble songs.

He, as of old, producing riches for the folk, still watchful, traversesthe common way again.

13 For new prosperity we seek to Agni, him whose course is splendid, gold-haired, excellently bright,

Whom Matarisvan stablished, dweller in the heaven, meet for high praise and holy, sage and true to Law.

14 As pure and swift of course, beholder of the light, who stands in heaven's bright sphere a sign, who wakes at dawn,

Agni, the head of heaven, whom none may turn aside-to him the Powerful with mighty prayer we seek.

15 The cheerful Priest, the pure, in whom no guile is found, Friend of the House, praise-worthy, dear to all mankind,

Fair to behold for beauty like a splendid car,- Agni the Friend of men we ever seek for wealth.

## [03-003] HYMN III. Agni.

1. To him who shines afar, Vaisvanara, shall bards give precious things that he may go on certain paths:

For Agni the Immortal serves the Deities, and therefore never breaks their everlasting laws.

2 He, wondrous envoy, goes between the earth and heaven, firm seated as the Herald, great High Priest of men.

He compassethwith rays the lofty dwelling-place, Agni, sent forward by the Gods, enriched with piayer.

3 Sages shall glorify Agni with earnest thoughts, ensign of sacrifice, who fills the synod full:

In whom the singers have stored up their holy acts to him the worshipper looks for joy and happiness.

4 The Sire of sacrifice, great God of holy bards, Agni, the measure and the symbol of the priests,

Hath entered heaven and earth that show in varied form: the Sage whom many love rejoiceth in his might.

5 Bright Agni with the bright car, Lord of green domains, Vaisvanara dweller in the floods, who finds the light,

Pervading, swift and wild, encompassed round with powers, him very glorious have the Gods established here.

6 Agni, together with the Gods and Manu's folk by thought extending sacrifice in varied form,

Goes, car-borne, to and fro with those who crown each rite, the fleet, the Household Friend, who turns the curse aside.

7 Sing, Agni, for long life to us and noble sons: teem thou with plenty, shine upon us store of food.

Increase the great man's strength, thou ever-vigilant: thou, longing for the Gods, knowest their hymns full well.

8 The Mighty One, Lord of the people and their guest, the leader of their thoughts, devoted Friend of
priests,
Our solemn rites' announcer, Jatavedas, men with worship ever praise, with urgings for their weal.

9 Agni the God resplendent, giver of great joy, hath on his lovely car compassed the lands with, might.
Let us with pure laudations in his house approach the high laws of the nourisher of multitudes.

10 I celebrate thy glories, O Vaisvanara, wherewith thou, O farsighted God, has found the light.
Thou filledst at thy birth both worlds, the earth and heaven: all this, O Agni, hast thou compassed of thyself.

11 By his great skill the Sage alone hath brought to pass a great deed, mightier than Vaisvanara's wondrous acts.
Agni sprang into being, magnifying both his Parents, Heaven and Earth, rich in prolific seed.

## [03-004] HYMN IV Apris.

1. BE friendly with each kindled log of fuel, with every flash bestow the boon of riches.
Bring thou the Gods, O God, unto our worship: serve, well-inclined, as Friend thy friends, O Agni.

2 Agni whom daily Varuna and Mitra the Gods bring thrice a day to this our worship,
Tanunapat, enrich with meath our service that dwells with holy oil, that offers honour.

3 The thought that bringeth every boon proceedeth to worship first the Priest of the libation,
That we may greet the Strong One with our homage. Urged, may he bring the Gods, best Sacrificer.

4 On high your way to sacrifice was made ready; the radiant flames went upward to the regions.
Full in the midst of heaven the Priest is seated: sirew we the sacred grass where Gods may rest
them.

5 Claiming in mind the seven priests' burntoblations, inciting all, they came in settled order.
To this our sacrifice approach the many who show in hero beauty at assemblies.

6 Night and Dawn, lauded, hither come together, both smiling, different are their forms in colour,
That Varuna and Mitra may accept us, and Indra, girt by Maruts, with his glories.

7. I crave the grace of heaven's two chief Invokers: the seven swift steeds joy in their wonted
manner.
These speak of truth, praising the truth eternal, thinking on Order as the guards of Order.

8 May Bharati with all her Sisters, Ila accordant with the Gods, with mortalls Agni,
Sarasvati with all her kindred Rivers, come to this grass, Three Goddesses, and seat them.

9 Well pleased with us do thou O God, O Tvastar, give ready issue to our procreant vigour,
Whence springs the hero, powerful, skilled in action, lover of Gods, adjuster of the press-stones.

10 Send to the Gods the oblation, Lord of Forests; and let the Immolator, Agni, dress it.
He as the truer Priest shall offer worship, for the Gods' generations well he knoweth.

11 Come thou to us, O Agni, duly kindled, together with the potent Gods and Indra.
On this our grass sit Aditi, happy Mother, and let our Hail delight the Gods Immortal.

## [03-005] HYMN V. Agni.

1. AGNI who shines against the Dawns is wakened. The holy Singer who precedes the sages.
With far-spread lustre, kindled by the pious, the Priest hath thrown both gates of darkness open.

2 Agni hath waxen mighty by laudations, to be adored with hymns of those who praise him.
Loving the varied shows of holy Order at the first flush of dawn he shines as envoy.

3 Amid men's homes hath Agni been established, fulfilling with the Law, Friend, germ of waters.
Loved and adored, the height he hath ascended, the Singer, object of our invocations.

4 Agni is Mitra when enkindled duly, Mitra as Priest, Varuna, Jatavedas;
Mitra as active minister, and House-Friend, Mitra of flowing rivers and of mountains.

5 The Earth's, the Bird's dear lofty place he guardeth, he guardeth in his might the course of Surya,
Guardeth the Seven-headed in the centre, guardeth sublime the Deities enjoyment.

6 The skilful God who knows all forms of knowledge made for himself a fair form, meet for worship.
This Agni guards with care that never ceases the Sonia's skin, the Bird's place rich in fatness.

7 Agni hath entered longingly the longing shrine rich with fatness, giving easy access.
Resplendent, pure, sublime and purifying, again, again he renovates his Mothers.

8 Born suddenly, by plants he grew to greatness, when tender shoots with holy oil increased him,
Like waters lovely when they hasten downward may Agni in his Parents' lap protect us.

9 Extolled, the Strong shone forth with kindled fuel to the earth's centre, to the height of heaven.
May Agni, Friend, adorable Matarisvan, as envoy bring the Gods unto our worship.

10 Best of all luminaries lofty Agni supported with his flame the height of heaven,
When, far from Bhrgus, Matarisvan kindled the oblation-bearer where he lay in secret.

11 As holy food, Agni to thine invoker give wealth in cattle, lasting, rich in marvels.
To us be born a son and spreading offspring. Agni, be this thy gracious will to us-word.

## [03-006] HYMN VI. Agni.

1. URGED on by deep devotion, O ye singers, bring, pious ones, the God-approaching ladle.
Borne onward to the right it travels eastward, and, filled with oil, to Agni bears oblation.

2 Thou at thy birth didst fill both earth and heaven, yea, Most Adorable, thou didst exceed them.
Even through the heaven's and through the earth's expanses let thy swift seventongued flames roll
on, O Agni.

3 Both Heaven and Earth and Gods who should be worshipped establish thee as Priest for every
dwelling,
Whenever human families, God-devoted, bringing oblations; laud thy splendid lustre.

4 Firm in the Gods' home is the Mighty seated, between vast Heaven and Earth the well-beloved-
Those Cows who yield, unharmed, their nectar, Spouses of the Far-Strider, everyoung, united.

5 Great are the deeds of thee, the Great, O Agni: thou by thy power hast spread out earth and heaven.

As soon as thou wast born thou wast an envoy, thou, Mighty One, was Leader of the people.

6 Bind to the pole with cords of holy Order the long-maned ruddy steeds who sprinkle fatness.
Bring hithier, O thou God, all Gods together: provide them noble worship, Jatavedas.

7 Even from the sky thy brilliant lights shone hither: still hast thou beamed through many a radiant morning,
That the Gods praised their joyous Herald's labour eagerly burning, Agni, in the forests.

8 The Gods who take delight in air's wide region, or those the dwellers in heaven's realm of
brightness,
Or those, the Holy, prompt to hear, our helpers, who, carborne, turn their horses hither, Agni---

9 With these, borne on one ear, Agni, approach us, or borne on many, for thy steeds are able.
Bring, witb their Dames, the Gods, the Three and-Thirty, after thy Godlike nature, and be joyful.

10 He is the Priest at whose repeated worship even wide Heaven and Earth sing out for increase.
They fair and true and holy coming forward stand at his sacrifice who springs from Order.

11 As holy food, Agni, to thine invoker give wealth in cattle, lasting, rich in marvels.
To us be born a son and spreading offspring. Agni, be this thy gracious will to usward.

## [03-007] HYMN VII.

1. THE seven tones risen from the whitebacked viand have made their way between the pair of
Mothers.
Both circumjacent Parents come together to yield us length of days they hasten forward.

2 The Male who dwells in heaven hath Mares and Milchkine: he came to Goddesses who bring sweet treasure.
To thee safe resting in the seat of Order the Cow alone upon her way proceedeth.

3 Wise Master, wealthy finder-out of riches, he mounted those who may with case be guided.
He, dark-backed, manifold with varied aspect, hath made them burst forth from their food the brushwood.

4 Strength-giving streams bear hither him eternal, fain to support the mighty work. of Tvastar.
He, flashing in his home with all his members, hath entered both the worlds as they were single.

5 They know the red Bull's blessing, and are joyful under the flaming-coloured Lord's dominion:
They who give shine from heavenwith fair effulgence, whose lofty song like Ila must be honoured.

6 Yea, by tradition from the ancient sages they brought great strength from the two mighty Parents,
To where the singer's Bull, the night's dispeller, after his proper law hath waxen stronger.

7 Seven holy singers guard with five Adhvaryus the Bird's beloved firmly-settled station.
The willing Bulls, untouched by old, rejoice them: as Gods themselves the ways of Gods they follow.

8 I crave the grace of heaven's two chief Invokers: the seven swift steeds joy in their wonted manner.
These speak of truth, praising the Truth Eternal, thinking on Order as the guards of Order.

9 The many seek the great Steed as a stallion: the reins obey the Lord of varied colour.
O heavenly Priest, most pleasant, full of wisdom, bring the great Gods to us, and Earth and Heaven.

10 Rich Lord, the Mornings have gleamed forth in splendour, fair-rayed, fair-speaking, worshipped
with all viands,
Yea, with the glory of the earth, O Agni. Forgive us, for our weal, e'en sin cornmitted.

11 As holy food, Agni, to thine invoker, give wealth in cattle, lasting, rich in marvels.
To us be born a son, and spreading offspring Agni, be this thy gracious will to usward.

## [03-008] HYMN VIII Sacrificial Post.

1. GOD-SERVING men, O Sovran of the Forest, with heavenly meath at sacrifice anoint thee.
Grant wealth to us when thou art standing upright as when reposing on this Mother's bosom.

2 Set up to eastward of the fire enkindled, accepting prayer that wastes not, rich in hero.
Driving far from us poverty and famine, lift thyself up to bring us great good fortune.

3 Lord of the Forest, raise. thyself up on the loftiest spot of earth. Give splendour, fixt and measured well, to him who brings the sacrifice.

4 Well-robed, enveloped he is come, the youthful: springing to life his glory waxeth greater.
Contemplative in mind and God-adoring, sages of high intelligence upraise him.

5 Sprung up he rises in the days' fair weather, increasing in the men-frequented synod.
With song the wise and skilful consecrate him: his voice the God-adoring singer utters.

6, Ye whom religious men have firmly planted; thou Forest Sovran whom the axe hath fashioned,-
Let those the Stakes divine which here are standing be fain to grant us wealth with store of children.

7 O men who lift the ladles up, these hewn and planted in the ground,
Bringing a blessing to the field, shall bear our precious gift to Gods.

8 Adityas, Rudras, Vasus, careful leaders, Earth, Heaven, and Prthivi and Air's mid-region,
Accordant Deities shall bless our worship and make our sacrifice's ensign lofty.

9 Like swan's that flee in lengthened line, the Pillars have come to us arrayed in brilliant coIour.
They, lifted up on high, by sages, eastward, go forth as Gods to the God's dwelling-places.

10 Those Stakes upon the earth with rings that deck them seem to the eye like horns of horned creatures;
Or, as upraised by priests in invocation, let them assist us in the rush to battle.

11 Lord of the Wood, rise with a hundred branches. with thousand branches may we rise to greatness,
Tlou whom this hatchct, with an edge well whetted for great felicity, hath brought before us.

## [03-009] HYMN IX.

1. WE as thy friends have chosen thee, mortals a God, to be our help,
The Waters' Child, the blessed, the resplendent One, victorious and beyond compare.

2 Since thou delighting in the woods hast gone unto thy mother streams,
Not to be scorned, Agni, is that return of thine when from afar thou now art here.

3 O'er pungent smoke host thou prevailed, and thus art thou benevolent.

Some go before, and others round about thee sit, they in whose friendship thou hast place.

4 Him who had passed beyond his foes, beyond continual pursuits, Him the unerring Ones,
observant, found in floods, couched like a lion in his lair.

5 Him wandering at his own free will, Agni here hidden from our view,
Him Matarisvan brought to us from far away produced by friction, from the Gods.

6 O Bearer of Oblations, thus mortals received thee from the Gods,
Whilst thou, the Friend of man, guardest each sacrifice with thine own power, Most Youthful One.

7 Amid thy wonders this is good, yea, to the simple is it clear,
When gathered round about thee, Agni, lie the herds where thou art kindled in the morn.

8 Offer to him who knows fair rites, who burns with purifying glow,
Swift envoy, active, ancient, and adorable: serve ye the God attentively.

9 Three times a hundred Gods and thrice a thousand, and three times ten and nine have worshipped Agni,
For him spread sacred grass, with oil bedewed him, and stablished him as Priest and Sacrificer.

## [03-010] HYMN X. Agni.

1. THEE Agni, God, Imperial Lord of all mankind, do mortal men
With understanding kindle at thesacrifice.

2 They laud thee in their solemn rites, Agni, as Minister and Priest,
Shine forth in thine own home as guardian of the Law.

3 He, verily, who honours thee with fuel, Knower of all life,
He, Agni! wins heroic might, he prospers well.

4 Ensign of sacrifices, he, Agni, with Gods is come to us,
Decked by the seven priests, to him who bringeth gifts.

5 ToAgni, the Invoking Priest, offer your best, your lofty speech,
To him Ordainer-like who brings the light of songs.

6 Let these our hymns make Agni grow, whence, meet for laud, he springs to life,
To mighty strength and great possession, fair to see.

7 Best Sacrificer, bring the Gods, O Agni, to the pious man:
A joyful Priest, thy splendour drive our foes afar

8 As such, O Purifier, shine on us heroic glorious might:
Be nearest Friend to those who laud thee, for their weal.

9 So, wakeful, versed in sacred hymns, the holy singers kindly thee.
Oblation-bearer, deathless, cherisher of strength.

## [03-011] HYMN XI. Agni.

1. AGNI is Priest, the great High Priest of sacrifice, most swift in act:
He knows the rite in constant course.

2 Oblation-bearer, deathless, well inclined, an eager messenger,
Agni comes nigh us with the thought.

3 Ensign of sacrifice from of old, Agni well knoweth with his thought
To prosper this man's aim and hope.

4 Agni, illustrious from old time, the Son of Strength who knows all life,
The Gods have made to their Priest.

5 Infallible is Agni, he who goes before the tribes of men,
A chariot swift and ever new.

6 Strength of the Gods which none may harm, subduing all his enemies,
Agni is mightiest in fame.

7 By offering sacred food to him the mortal worshipper obtains.
A home from him whose light makes pure.

8 From Agni, by our hymns, may we gain all things that bring happiness,
Singers of him who knows all life.

9 O Agni, in our deeds of might may we obtain all precious things:
Tle Gods are centred all in thee.

## [03-012] HYMN XII. Indra-Agni.

1. MOVED, Indra-Agni, by our hymn, come to the juice, the precious dew:
Dr.ink ye thereof, impelled by song.

2 O Indra-Agni, with the man who lauds you comes the wakening rite:
So drink ye both this juice assured.

3 Through force of sacrifice I choose Indra-Agni who love the wise:
With Sorna let these sate them here.

4 Indra and Agni I invoke, joint-victors, bounteous, unsubdued,
Foe-slayers, best to win the spoil.

5 Indra and Agni, singers skilled in melody hymn you, bringing lauds:
I choose you for the sacred food.

6 Indra and Agni, ye cast down the ninety forts which DAsas held,
Together, with one mighty deed.

7 To Indra-Agni eeverent thoughts go forward from the holy task
Along the path of sacred Law.

8 O Indra-Agni, powers are yours, and dwellings and delightful food
Good is your readiness to act.

9 Indra and Agni, in your deeds of might ye deck heaven's lucid realms:
Famed is that hero strength of yours.

## [03-013] HYMN XIII. Agni.

1. To Agni, to this God of yours I sing aloud with utmost power.
May he come to us with the Gods, and sit, best Offerer, on the grass.

2 The Holy, whose are earth and heaven, and succour waits upon his strength;
Him men who bring oblations laud, and they who wish to gain, for grace.

3 He is the Sage who guides these men, Leader of sacred rites is he.
Him your own Agni, serve ye well, who winneth and bestoweth wealth.

4 So may the gracious Agni grant most goodly shelter for our use;
Whence in the heavens or in the floods he shall pour wealth upon our lands.

5 The singers kindle him, the Priest, Agni the Lord of tribes of men,
Resplendent and without a peer through his own excellent designs.

6 Help us, thou Brahman, best of all invokers of the Gods in song.
Beam, Friend of Maruts, bliss on us, O Agni, a most liberal God.

7 Yea, grant us treasure thousandfold with children and with nourishment,
And, Agni, splendid hero strength, exalted, wasting not away.

## [03-014] HYMN XIV. Agni.

1 THE pleasant Priest is come into the synod, true, skilled in sacrifice, most wise, Ordainer.
Agni, the Son of Strength, whose car is lightning, whose hair is flame, hath shown on earth his lustre.

2 To thee I offer reverent speech: accept it: to thee who markest it, victorious, faithful!

Bring, thou who knowest, those who know, and seat thee amid the sacred grass, for help, O Holy.
3 The Two who show their vigour, Night and Morning, by the wind's paths shall haste to thee O
Agni.
When men adorn the Ancient with oblations, these seek, as on two chariot-seats, the dwelling.
4 To thee, strong Agni! Varuna and Mitra and all the Maruts sang a song of triumph,
What time unto the people's lands thou camest, spreading them as the Sun of men, with lustre.
5 Approaching with raised hands and adoration, we have this day fulfilled for thee thy longing.
Worship the Gods with most devoted spirit, a Priest with no unfriendly thought, O Agni.
6 For, Son of Strength, from thee come many succours, and powers abundant that a God possesses.
Agni, to us with speech that hath no falsehood grant riches, real, to be told in thousands.
7 Whatever, God, in sacrifice we mortals have wrought is all for thee, strong, wise of purpose!
Be thou the Friend of each good chariot's master. All this enjoy thou here, immortal Agni.

## [03-015] HYMN XV. Agni.

1. RESPLENDENT with thy wide-extending lustre, dispel the terrors of the fiends who hate us
May lofty Agni be my guide and shelter, the easily-invoked, the good Protector.
2 Be thou To us, while now the morn is breaking, be thou a guardian when the Sun hath mounted..
Accept, as men accept a true-born infant, my laud, O Agni nobly born in body.
3 Bull, who beholdest men, through many mornings, among the dark ones shine forth red, O Agni.
Lead us, good Lord, and bear us over trouble: Help us who long, Most Youthful God, to riches.
4 Shine forth, a Bull invincible, O Agni, winning by conquest all the forts and treasures,
Thou Jatavedas who art skilled in guiding, the chief high saving sacrifice's Leader.
5 Lighting Gods hither, Agni, wisest Singer, bring thou to us many and flawless shelters.
Bring vigour, like a car that gathers booty: bring us, O Agni, beauteous.Rarth and Heaven.
6 Swell, O thou Bull and give those powers an impulse, e'en Earth and Heaven who yield their milk in
plenty,
Shining, O God, with Gods in clear effulgence. Let not a mortal's evil will obstruct us.
7 Agni, as holy food to thine invoker, give wealth in cattle, lasting, rich in marvels.
To us be born a son and spreading ofrspring. Agni, be this thy gracious will to us-ward.

## [03-016] HYMN XVI. Agni.

1. THIS Agni is the Lord of great felicity and hero Strength;

Lord of wealth in herds of kine; Lord of the battles with the foe.
2 Wait, Maruts, Heroes, upon him the Prosperer in whom is bliss-increasing wealth;
Who in fights ever conquer evil-hearted men, who overcome the enemy.
3 As such, O Agni, deal us wealth and hero might, O Bounteous One!
Most lofty, very glorious, rich in progeny, free from disease and full of power.

4 He who made all that lives, who passes all in might, who orders service to the Gods,
He works among the Gods, he works in hero strength, yea, also in the praise of men.
5 Give us not up to indigence, Agni, nor want of hero sons,
Nor, Son of Strength, to lack of cattle, nor to blame. Drive. thou our enemies away.
6 Help us to strength, blest Agni! rich in progeny, abundant, in our sacrifice.
Flood us with riches yet more plenteous, bringing weal, with high renown, most Glorious One!

## [03-017] HYMN XVII. Agni.

1. DULY enkindled after ancient customs, bringing all treasures, he is balmed with unguents,-
Flame-haired, oil-clad, the purifying Agni, skilled in fair rites, to bring the Gods for worship.
2 As thou, O Agni, skilful Jatavedas, hast sacrificed as Priest of Earth, of Heaven,
So with this offering bring the Gods, and prosper this sacrifice today as erst for Manu.
3 Three are thy times of life, O Jatavedas, and the three mornings are thy births, O Agni.
With these, well-knowing, grant the Gods' kind favour, and help in stir aiid stress the man who
worships.
4 Agni most bright and fair with song we honour, yea, the adorable, O Jatavedas.
Thee, envoy, messenger, oblation-bearer, the Gods have made centre of life eternal.
5 That Priest before thee, yet more skilled in worship, stablished of old, healthgiver by his nature,-
After his custom offer, thou who knowest, and lay our sacrifice where Gods may taste it.

## [03-018] HYMN XVIII. Agni.

1. AGNI, be kind to us when we approach thee good as a friend to friend, as sire and mother.
The races of mankind are great oppressors burn up malignity that strives against us.
2 Agni, burn up the unfriendly who are near us, burn thou the foeman's curse who pays no worship.
Burn, Vasu, thou who markest well, the foolish: let thine eternal nimble beams surround thee.
3 With fuel, Agni, and with oil, desirous, mine offering I present for strength and conquest,
With prayer, so far as I have power, adoring-this hymn divine to gain a hundred treasures.
4 Give with thy glow, thou Son of Strength, when lauded, great vital power to those who toil to serve
thee.
Give richly, Agni, to the Visvamitras in rest and stir. Oft have we decked thy body.
5 Give us, O liberal Lord, great gtore of riches, for, Agni, such art thou when duly kindled.
Thou in the happy singer's home bestowest, amply with arms extended, things of beauty.

## [03-019] HYMN XIX. Agni.

1. Aow, quick, sage, infallible, all-knowing, I choose to be our Priest at this oblation.
In our Gods' service he, best skilled, shall worship: may he obtain us boons for strength and riches.
2 Agni, to thee I lift the oil-fed ladle, bright, with an offering, bearing our oblation.
From the right hand, choosing the Gods' attendance, he with rich presents hath arranged the

worship.

3 Of keenest spirit is the man thou aidest give us good offspring, thou who givest freely.

In power of wealth most rich in men. O Agni, of thee, the Good, may we sing forth fair praises.

4 Men as they worship thee the God, O Agni, have set on thee full many a brilliant, aspect.

So bring Most Youthful One, the Gods' asserrigly, the Heavenly Host which thou to-day shalt honour.

5 When Gods anoint thee Priest at their oblation, and seat thee for thy task as Sacrificer,

O Agni, be thou here our kind defender, and to ourselves vouchsafe the gift of glory.

## [03-020] HYMN XX Agni.

1. WITH lauds at break of morn the priest invoketh Agni, Dawn, Dadhikras, and both the Asvins.

With one consent the Gods whose light is splendid, longing to taste our sacrifice, shall hear us.

2 Three are thy powers, O Agni, three thy stations, three are thy tongues, yea, many, Child of Order!

Three bodies hast thou which the Gods delight in: with these protect our hymns with care unceasing.

3 O Agni, many are the names thou bearest, immortal, God, Divine, and Jatavedas.

And many charms of charmers, All-Inspirer! have they laid in thee, Lord of true attendants!

4 Agni, like Bhaga, leads the godly people, he who is true to Law and guards the seasons.

Ancient, all-knowing, he the Vrtra-slayer shall bear the singer safe through every trouble.

5 I call on Savitar the God, on Morning, Brhaspati, and Dadhikras, and Agni,

On Varuna and Mitra, on the Asvins, Bhaga, the Vasus, Rudras and Adityas.

## [03-021] HYMN XXI. Agni.

1. SET this our sacrifice among the Immortals: be pleased with these our presents, Jatavedas.

O Priest, O Agni, sit thee down before us, and first enjoy the drops of oil and fatness.

2 For thee, O Purifier, flow the drops of fatness rich in oil.

After thy wont vouchsafe to us the choicest boon that Gods may feast.

3 Agni, Most Excellent! for thee the Sage are drops that drip with oil.

Thou art enkindled as the best of Seers. Help thou the sacrifice.

4 To thee, O Agni, mighty and resistless, to thee stream forth the drops of oil and fatness.

With great light art thou come, O praised by poets! Accept our offering, O thou Sage.

5 Fatness exceeding rich, extracted from the midst,-this as our gift we offer thee.

Excellent God, the drops run down upon thy skin. Deal them to each among the Gods.

## [03-022] HYMN XXII. Agni.

1 THIS is that Agni whence the longing Indra took the pressed Soma deep within his body.

Winner of spoils in thousands, like a courser, with praise art thou exalted, Jatavedas.

2 That light of thine in heaven and earth, O Agni, in plants, O Holy One, and in the waters,

Wherewith thou hast spread wide the air's mid-region-bright is that splendour, wavy, manbeholding.

3 O Agni, to the sea of heaven thou goest: thou hast called hither Gods beheld in spirit.

The waters, too, come hither, those up yonder in the Sun's realm of light, and those beneath it.

4 Let fires that dwell in mist, combined with those that have their home in floods,

Guileless accept our sacrifice, great viands free from all disease.

5 Agni, as holy food to thine invoker give wealth in cattle, lasting, rich in marvels.

To us be born a son and spreading offspring. Agni, be this thy gracious will to us-ward.

## [03-023] HYMN XXIII. Agni.

1. RUBBED into life, well stablished in the dwelling, Leader of sacrifice, the Sage, the youthful,

Here in the wasting fuel Jatavedas, eternal, hath assumed immortal being.

2 Both Bharatas, Devasravas, Devavata, have strongly rubbed to life effectual Agni.

O Agni, look thou forth with ample riches: be, every day, bearer of food to feed us.

3 Him nobly born of old the fingers ten produced, him whom his Mothers counted dear.

Praise Devavata's Agni, thou Devasravas, him who shall be the people's Lord.

4 He set thee in the earth's most lovely station, in Ila's place, in days of fair bright weather.

On man, on Apaya, Agni! on the rivers Drsadvati, Sarasvati, shine richly.

5 Agni, as holy food to thine invoker give wealth in cattle, lasting, rich in marvels.

To us be born a son and spreading offspring Agni, be this thy gracious will to us-ward

## [03-024] HYMN XXIV. Agni.

1. AGNI, subdue opposing bands, and drive our enemies away.

Invincible, slay godless foes: give splendour to the worshipper.

2 Lit with libation, Agni, thou, deathless, who callest Gods to feast,

Accept our sacrifice with joy.

3 With splendour, Agni, Son of Strength, thou who art worshipped, wakeful One.

Seat thee on this my sacred grass.

4 With all thy fires, with all the Gods, Agni, exalt the songs we sing.

And living men in holy rites.

5 Grant, Agni, to the worshipper wealth rich in heroes, plenteous store,

Make thou us rich with many sons.

## [03-025] HYMN XXV. Agni.

1. THOU art the sapient Son of Dyaus, O Agni, yes and the Child of Earth, who knowest all things.

Bring the Gods specially, thou Sage, for worship.

2. Agni the wise bestows the might of heroes grants strengthening food, preparing it for nectar.

Thou who art rich in food bring the Gods hither.

3 Agni, infallible, lights Earth and Heaven, immortal Goddesses gracious to all men,-

Lord through his strength, splendid through adorations.

4 Come to the sacrifice, Agni and Indra come to the offerer's house who hath the Soma.

Come, friendly-minded, Gods, to drink the Soma.

5 In the floods' home art thou enkindled, Agni, O Jatavedas, Son of Strength, eternal,

Exalting with thine help the gatheringplaces.

[03-026] HYMN XXVI. Agni.

1. REVERING in our heart Agni Vaisvanara, the finder of the light, whose promises are true,
The liberal, gladsome, car-borne God we Kusikas invoke him with oblation, seeking wealth with
songs.
2 That Agni, bright, Vaisvanara, we invoke for help, and Matarisvan worthy of the song of praise;
Brhaspati for man's observance of the Gods, the Singer prompt to hear, the swiftly-moving guest.
3 Age after age Vaisvanara, neighing like a horse, is kindled with the women by the Kusikas.
May Agni, he who wakes among Immortal Gods, grant us heroic strength and wealth in noble steeds.
4 Let them go forth, the strong, as flames of fire with might. Gathered for victory they have yoked
their spotted deer.
Pourers of floods, the Maruts, Masters of all wealth, they who can ne'er be conquered, make the
mountains shake.
5 The Maruts, Friends of men, are glorious as the fire: their mighty and resplendent succour we
implore.
Those storming Sons of Rudra clothed in robes of rain, boon-givers of good gifts, roar as the lions roar.
6 We, band on band and troop following troop, entreat with fair lauds Agni's splendour and the
Maruts' might,
With spotted deer for steeds, with wealth that never fails, they, wise Ones, come to sacrifice at our
gatherings.
7 Agni am I who know, by birth, all creatures. Mine eye is butter, in my mouth is nectar.
I am light threefold, measurer of the region exhaustless heat am I, named burnt-oblation.
8 Bearing in mind a thought with light accordant, he purified the Sun with three refinings;
By his own nature gained the highest treasure, and looked abroad over the earth and heaven.
9 The Spring that fails not with a hundred streamlets, Father inspired of' prayers that men should
utter,
The Sparkler, joyous in his Parents' bosorn, -him, the Truth-speaker, sate ye, Earth and Heaven.

[03-027] HYMN XXVII. Agni.

1. IN ladle dropping oil your food goes in oblation up to heaven,

Goes to the Gods in search of bliss.
2 Agni I laud, the Sage inspired, crowner of sacrifice through song,
Who listens and gives bounteous gifts.
3 O Agni, if we might obtain control of thee the potent God,
Then should we overcome our foes.
4 Kindled at sacrifices he is Agni, hallower, meet for praise,
With flame for hair: to him we seek.
5 Immortal Agni, shining far, enrobed with oil, well worshipped, bears
The gifts of sacrifice away.
6 The priests with ladles lifted up, worshipping here with holy thought,
Have brought this Agni for our aid.
7 Immortal, Sacrificer, God, with wondrous power he leads the way,
Urging the great assembly on.
8 Strong, he is set on deeds ofstrength. In sacrifices led in front,
As Singer he completes the rite.

9 Excellent, he was made by thought. The Germ of beings have I gained,
Yea, and die Sire of active strength.
10 Thee have I stablished, Excellent, O strengthened by the sage's prayer,
Thee, Agni, longing, nobly bright.
11 Agni, the swift and active One, singers, at time of sacrifice,
Eagerly kindle with their food.
12 Agni the Son of Strength who shines up to the heaven in solemn rites,
The wise of heart, I glorify.
13 Meet to be lauded and adored, showing in beauty through the dark,
Agni, the Strong, is kindled well.
14 Agni is kindled as a bull, like a horsebearer of the Gods:
Men with oblations worship him.
15 Thee will we kindle as a bull, we who are Bulls ourselves, O Bull.
Thee, Agni, shining mightily.

[03-028] HYMN XXVIII. Agni.

1. AGNI who knowest all, accept our offering and the cake of meal,
At dawn's libation, rich in prayer!
2 Agni, the sacrificial cake hath been prepared and dressed for thee:
Accept it, O Most Youthful God.
3 Agni, enjoy the cake of meal and our oblation three days old:
Thou, Son of Strength, art stablished at our sacrifice.
4 Here at the midday sacrifice enjoy thou the sacrificial cake, wise, Jatavedas!
Agni, the sages in assemblies never minish the portion due to thee the Mighty.
5 O Agni, at the third libation takewith joy the offered cake of sacrifice, thou, Son of Strength.
Through skill in song bear to the Gods our sacrifice, watchful and fraught with riches, to Immortal
God.
6 O waxing Agni, knower, thou, of all, accept our gifts, the cake,
And that prepared ere yesterday.

[03-029] HYMN XXIX. Agni.

1. HERE is the gear for friction, here tinder made ready for the spark.
Bring thou the Matron: we will rub Agni in ancient fashion forth.
2 1n the two fire-sticks Jatavedas lieth, even as the well-set germ in pregnant women,
Agni who day by day must be exalted by men who watch and worship with oblations.
3 Lay this with care on that which lies extended: straight hath she borne the Steerwhen made
prolific.
With his red pillar-radiant is his splendour -in our skilled task is born the Son of Ila.
4 In Ila's place we set thee down, upon the central point of earth,
That, Agni Jatavedas, thou mayst bear our offerings to the Gods.
5 Rub into life, ye men, the Sage, the guileless, Immortal, very wise and fair to look on.
O men, bring forth the most propitious Agni, first ensign of the sacrifice to eastward.
6 When with their arms they rub him straight he shineth forth like a strong courser, red in colour, in
the wood.
Bright, checkless, as it were upon the Atvins' path, lie passeth by the stones and burneth up the grass.
7 Agni shines forth when born, observant, mighty, the bountiful, the Singar praised by sages;

Whom, as adorable and knowing all things, Gods set at solemn rites as offeringbearer.

8 Set thee, O Priest, in, thine own place, observant: lay down the sacrifice in the home of worship.

Thou, dear to Gods, shalt serve them with oblation: Agni, give long life to the sacrificer.

9 Raise ye a mighty smoke, my fellow-workers! Ye shall attain to wealth without obstruction.

This Agni is the battle-winning Hero by whom the Gods have overcome the Dasyus.

10 This is thine ordered place of birth whence sprung to life thou shonest forth.

Knowing this, Agni, sit thee down, and prosper thou the songs we sing.

11 As Germ Celestial he is called Tanunapat, and Narasamsa born diffused in varied shape.

Formed in his Mother he is Matarisvan; he hath, in his course, become the rapid flight of wind.

12 With strong attrition rubbed to life, laid down with careful hand, a Sage,

Agni, make sacrifices good, and for the pious bring the Gods.

13 Mortals have brought to life the God Immortal, the Conqueror with mighty jaws, unfailing.

The sisters ten, unwedded and united, together grasp the Babe, the new-born Infant.

14 Served by the seven priests, he shone forth from ancient time, when in his Mother's bosom, in her lap, he glowed.

Giving delight each day he closeth not his eye, since from the Asura's body hewas brought to life.

15 Even as the Maruts, onslaughts who attack the foe, those born the first of all knew the full power of prayer.

The Kusikas have made the glorious hymn ascend, and, each one singly in his home, have kindled fire.

16 As we, O Priest observant, have elected thee this day, what time the solemn sacrifice began,

So surely hast thou worshipped, surely hast thou toiled: come thou unto the Soma, wise and knowing all.

## [03-030] HYMN XXX. Indra.

1. THE friends who offer Soma long to find thee: they pour forth Soma and present their viands.

They bear unmoved the cursing of the people, for all our wisdom comes from thee, O Indra.

2 Not far for thee are mid-air's loftiest regions: start hither, Lord of Bays, with thy Bay Horses.

Made for the Firm and Strong are these libations. The pressing-stones are set and fire is kindled.

3 Fair cheeks hath Indra, Maghavan, the Victor, Lord of a great host, Stormer, strong in action.

What once thou didst in might when mortals vexed thee,-where now, O Bull, are those thy hero exploits?

4 For, overthrowing what hath ne'er been shaken, thou goest forth alone destroying Vrtras.

For him who followeth thy Law the mountains and heaven and earth stand as if firmly stablished.

5 Yea, Much-invoked! in safety through thy glories alone thou speakest truth as Vrtra's slayer.

E'en these two boundless worlds to thee, O Indra, what time thou graspest them, are but a handful.

6 Forthwith thy Bay steeds down the steep, O Indra, forth, crushing foemen, go thy bolt of thunder!

Slay those who meet thee, those who flee, who follow: make all thy promise true; be all completed.

7 The man to whom thou givest as Provider enjoys domestic plenty undivided.

Blest, Indra, is thy favour dropping fatness: thy worship, Much-invoked! brings gifts in thousands.

8 Thou, Indra, Much-invoked! didst crush to pieces Kunaru handless fiend who dwelt with Danu.

Thou with might, Indra, smotest dead the scorner, the footless Vrtra as he waxed in vigour.

9 Thou hast established in her seat, O Indra, the level earth, vast, vigorous, unbounded.

The Bull hath propped the heaven and air's mid-region. By thee sent onward let the floods flow hither.

10 He who withheld the kine, in silence I yielded in fear before thy blow, O Indra.

He made paths easy to drive forth the cattle. Loud-breathing praises helped the Much-invoked One.

11 Indra alone filled full the earth and heaven, the Pair who meet together, rich in treasures.

Yea, bring thou near us from the air's mid-region strength, on thy car, and wholesome food, O Hero.

12 Surya transgresses not the ordered limits set daily by the Lord of Tawny Coursers.

When to the goal he comes, his journey ended, his Steeds he looses: this is Indra's doing.

13 Men gladly in the course of night would look on the broad bright front of the refulgent Morning;

And all acknowledge, when she comes in glory, the manifold and goodly works of Indra.

14 A mighty splendour rests upon her bosom: bearing ripe milk the Cow, unripe, advances.

All sweetness is collected in the Heifer, sweetness which Indra made for our enjoyment.

15 Barring the way they come. Be firm, O Indra; aid friends to sacrifice and him who singeth.

These must be slain by thee, malignant mortals, armed with ill arts, our quiverbearing foemen.

16 A cry is beard from enemies most near us: against them send thy fiercest-flaming weapon.

Rend them from under, crush them and subdue them. Slay, Maghavan, and make the fiends our booty.

17 Root up the race of Raksasas, O Indra rend it in front and crush it in the middle.

How long hast thou bebaved as one who wavers? Cast thy hot dart at him who hates devotion:

18 When borne by strong Steeds for our weal, O Leader, thou seatest thee at many noble viands.

May we be winners of abundant riches. May Indra be our wealth with store of children.

19 Bestow on us resplendent wealth. O Indra let us enjoy thine overflow of bounty.

Wide as a sea our longing hath expanded, fulfil it, O thou Treasure-Lord of treasures.

20 With kine and horses satisfy this longing with very splendid bounty skill extend it.

Seeking the light, with hymns to thee, O Indra, Kusikas have brought their gift, the singers.

21 Lord of the kine, burst the kine's stable open: cows shall be ours, and strength that wins the booty.

Hero, whose might is true, thy home is heaven: to us, O Maghavan, grant gifts of cattle.

22 Call we on Maghavan, auspicious Indra, best Hero in this fight where spoil is gathered,

The Strong who listens, who gives aid in battles, who slays the Vrtras, wins and gathers riches.

## [03-031] HYMN XXXI. Indra.

1. WISE, teaching, following the thought of Order, the sonless gained a grandson from his daughter.

Fain, as a sire, to see his child prolific, he sped to meet her with an eager spirit.

2 The Son left not his portion to the brother, he made a home to
hold him who should gain, it.
What time his Parents gave the Priest his being, of the good pair
one acted, one promoted.
3 Agni was born trembling with tongue that flickered, so that the
Red's great children should be
honoured.
Great is their germ, that born of them is mighty, great the Bays'
Lord's approach through sacrifices.
4 Conquering bands upon the Warrior waited: they recognized
great light from out the darkness.
The conscious Dawns went forth to meet his coming, and the sole
Master of the kine was Indra.
5 The sages freed them from their firmbuilt prison: the seven
priests drove them forward with their
spirit.
All holy Order's pathway they discovered he, full of knowledge,
shared these deeds through worship.
6 When Sarama had found the mountain's fissure, that vast and
ancient place she plundered
thoroughly.
In the floods' van she led them forth, light-footed: she who well
knew came first unto their lowing.
7 Longing for friendship came the noblest singer: the hill poured
forth its treasure for the pious.

The Hero with young followers fought and conquered, and
straightway Angiras was singing praises,
8 Peer of each noble thing, yea, all excelling, all creatures doth he
know, he slayeth Susna.
Our leader, fain for war, singing from heaven, as Friend he saved
his lovers from dishonour.
9 They sate them down with spirit fain for booty, making with
hymns a way to life eternal.
And this is still their place of frequent session, whereby they
sought to gain the months through
Order.
10 Drawing the milk of ancient seed prolific, they joyed as they
beheld their own possession.
Their shout of triumph heated earth and heaven. When the kine
showed, they bade the heroes rouse
them.
11 Indra drove forth the kine, that Vrtra-slayer, while hymns of
praise rose up and gifts were offered.
For him the Cow, noble and far-extending, poured pleasant
juices, bringing oil and sweetness.
12 They made a mansion for their Father, deftly provided him a
great and glorious dwelling;
With firm support parted and stayed the Parents, and, sitting,
fixed him there erected, mighty.
13 What time the ample chalice had impelled him, swift waxing,
vast, to pierce the earth and
heaven,-
Him in whom blameless songs are all united: all powers
invincible belong to Indra.
14 I crave thy powers, I crave thy mighty friendship: full many a
team goes to the Vrtra-slayer.
Great is the laud, we seek the Princes' favour. Be thou, O
Maghavan, our guard and keeper.
15 He, having found great, splendid, rich dominion, sent life and
motion to his friends and lovers.
Indra who shone together with the Heroes begot the song, the
fire, and Sun and Morning.
16 Vast, the House-Friend, he set the waters flowing, all-lucid,
widely spread, that move together.
By the wise cleansings of the meath made holy, through days, and
nights they speed the swift streams onward.

17 To thee proceed the dark, the treasure-holders, both of them
sanctified by Surya's bounty.
The while thy ovely storming Friends, O Indra, fail to attain the
measure of thy greatness.
18 Be Lord of joyous songs, O Vrtra-slayer, Bull dear to all, who
gives the power of living.
Come unto us with thine auspicious friendship, hastening,
Mighty One, with mighty succours.
19 Like Angiras I honour him with worship, and renovate old
song for him the Ancient.
Chase thou the many godless evil creatures, and give us,
Maghavan, heaven's light to help m.
20 Far forth are spread the purifying waters convey thou us
across them unto safety.
Save us, our Charioteer, from harm, O Indra, soon, very soon,
make us win spoil of cattle.
21 His kine their Lord hath shown, e'en Vrtra's slayer, through
the black hosts he passed with red
attendants.
Teaching us pleasant things by holy Order, to, us hath he thrown
open all his portals.
22 Call we on Maghavan, auspicious Indra, best Hero in this fight
where spoil is gathered.
The Strong who listens, who gives aid in battles, who slays the
Vrtras, wins and gathers riches.

## [03-032] HYMN XXXII. Indra
1. DRINK thou this Soma, Indra, Lord of Soma; drink thou the
draught of noonday which thou Iovest.
Puffing thy cheeks, impetuous, liberal Giver, here loose thy two
Bay Horses and rejoice thee.
2 Quaff it pure, meal-blent, mixt with milk, O Indra; we have
poured forth the Soma for thy rapture.
Knit with the prayer-fulfilling band of Maruts, yea, with the
Rudras, drink till thou art sated;
3 Those who gave increase to thy strength and vigour; the Maruts
singing forth thy might, O Indra.
Drink thou, O fair of cheek, whose hand wields thunder, with
Rudras banded, at our noon libation.
4 They, even the Maruts who were there, excited with song the
meath-created strength of Indra.
By them impelled to act he reached the vitals Of Vrtra, though he
deemed that none might wound
him.
5 Pleased, like a man, with our libation, Indra, drink, for
enduring hero might, the Soma.
Lord of Bays, moved by sacrifice come hither: thou with the Swift
Ones stirrest floods and waters.
6 When thou didst loose the streams to run like racers in the swift
contest, having smitten Vrtra
With flying weapon where he lay, O Indra, and, godless, kept the
Goddesses encompassed.
7 With reverence let us worship mighty Indra, great and sublime,
eternal, everyouthful,
Whose greatness the dear world-halves have not measured, no,
nor conceived the might of him the
Holy.
8 Many are Indra's nobly wrought achievements, and none of all
the Gods transgress his statutes.
He beareth up this earth and heaven, and, doer of marvels, he
begot the Sun and Morning.
9 Herein, O Guileless One, is thy true greatness, that soon as born
thou drankest up the Soma.
Days may not check the power of thee the Mighty, nor the nights,
Indra, nor the months, nor autumns.
10 As soon as thou wast born in highest heaven thou drankest
Soma to delight thee, Indra;

And when thou hadst pervaded earth and heaven thou wast the first supporter of the singer.

11 Thou, puissant God, more mighty, slewest. Ahi showing his strength when couched around the waters.

The heaven itself attained not to thy greatness when with one hip of thine the earth was shadowed.

12 Sacrifice, Indra, made thee wax so mighty, the dear oblation with the flowing Soma.

O Worshipful, with worship help our worship, for worship helped thy bolt when slaying Ahi.

13 With sacrifice and wish have I brought Indra; still for new blessings may I turn him hither,

Him magnified by ancient songs and praises, by lauds of later time and days yet recent.

14 I have brought forth a song when longing seized me: ere the decisive day will I laud Indra;

Then may lie safely bear us over trouble, as in a ship, when both sides invocate him.

15 Full is his chalice: Glory! Like a pourer I have filled up the vessel for his drinking.

Presented on the right, dear Soma juices have brought us Indra, to rejoice him, hither.

16 Not the deep-flowing flood, O Much-invoked One! not hills that compass thee about restrain thee,

Since here incited, for thy friends, O Indra, thou breakest e'en the firm built stall of cattle.

17 Call we on Maghavan, auspicious Indra, best Hero in this fight where spoil is gathered,

The Strong who listens, who gives aid in battles, who slays the Vrtras, wins and gathers riches.

## [03-033] HYMN XXXIII. Indra.

1. FORTH from the bosom of the mountains, eager as two swift mares with loosened rein contending,

Like two bright mother cows who lick their youngling, Vipas and Sutudri speed down their waters.

2 Impelled by Indra whom ye pray to urge you, ye move as 'twere on chariots to the ocean.

Flowing together, swelling with your billows, O lucid Streams, each of you seeks the other.

3 I have attained the most maternal River, we have approached Vipas, the broad, the blessed.

Licking as 'twere their calf the pair of Mothers flow onward to their common home together.

4 We two who rise and swell with billowy waters move forward to the home which Gods have made us.

Our flood may not be stayed when urged to motion. What would the singer, calling to the Rivers?

5 Linger a little at my friendly bidding rest, Holy Ones, a moment in your journey.

With hymn sublime soliciting your favour Kusika's son hath called unto the River.

6 Indra who wields the thunder dug our channels: he smote down Vrtra, him who stayed our currents.

Savitar, God, the lovely-handed, led us, and at his sending forth we flow expanded.

7 That hero deed of Indra must be lauded for ever that he rent Ahi in pieces.

He smote away the obstructors with his thunder, and eager for their course forth flowed the waters.

8 Never forget this word of thine, O singer, which future generations shall reecho.

In hymns, O bard, show us thy loving kindness. Humble us not mid men. To thee be honour!

9 List quickly, Sisters, to the bard who cometh to you from far away with car and wagon.

Bow lowly down; be easy to be traversed stay, Rivers, with your floods below our axles.

10 Yea, we will listen to thy words, O singer. With wain and car from far away thou comest.

Low, like a nursing mother, will I bend me, and yield me as a maiden to her lover.

11 Soon as the Bharatas have fared across thee, the warrior band, urged on and sped by Indra,

Then let your streams flow on in rapid motion. I crave your favour who deserve our worship.

12 The warrior host, the Bharatas, fared over the singer won the favour of the Rivers.

Swell with your billows, hasting, pouring riches. Fill full your channels, and roll swiftly onward.

13 So let your wave bear up the pins, and ye, O Waters, spare the thongs;

And never may the pair of Bulls, harmless and sinless, waste away.

## [03-034] HYMN XXXIV. Indra.

1. FORT-RENDER, Lord of Wealth, dispelling foemen, Indra with lightnings hath o'ercome the Dasa.

Impelled by prayer and waxen great in body, he hath filled earth and heaven, the Bounteous Giver.

2 I stimulate thy zeal, the Strong, the Hero decking my song of praise forth; Immortal.

O Indra, thou art equally the Leader of heavenly hosts and human generations.

3 Leading, his band Indra encompassed Vrtra; weak grew the wily leader of enchanters.

He who burns fierce in forests slaughtered Vyamsa, and made the Milch-kine of the nights apparent.

4 Indra, light-winner, days' Creator, conquered, victorious, hostile bands with those who loved him.

For man the days' bright ensign he illumined, and found the light for his joy and gladness.

5 Forward to fiercely falling blows pressed Indra, herolike doing many hero exploits.

These holy songs he taught the bard who gaised him, and widely spread these Dawns' resplendent colour.

6 They laud the mighty acts of him the Mighty, the many glorious deeds performed by Indra.

He in his strength, with all-surpassing prowess, through wondrous arts crushed the malignant Dasyus.

7 Lord of the brave, Indra who rules the people gave freedom to the Gods by might and battle.

Wise singers glorify with chanted praises these his achievements in Vivasvan's dwelling.

8 Excellent, Conqueror, the victory-giver, the winner of the light and Godlike Waters,

He who hath won this broad earth and this heaven, -in Indra they rejoice who love devotions.

9 He gained possession of the Sun and Horses, Indra obtained the Cow who feedeth many.

Treasure of gold he won; he smote the Dasyus, and gave protection to the Aryan colour.

10 He took the plants and days for his possession; he gained the forest trees and air's mid-region.

Vala he cleft, and chased away opponents: thus was he tamer of the overweening.

11 Call we on Maghavan, auspicious Indra, best Hero in the fight where spoil is gathered,

The Strong, who listens, who gives aid in battles, who slays the Vrtras, wins and gathers treasures.

## [03-035] HYMN XXXV Indra.

1. MOUNT the Bay Horses to thy chariot harnessed, and come to us like Vayu with his coursers.
Thou, hastening to us, shalt drink the Soma. Hail, Indra. We have poured it for thy rapture.
2 For him, the God who is invoked by many, the two swift Bay Steeds to the pole I harness,
That they in fleet course may bring Indra hither, e'en to this sacrifice arranged completely.
3 Bring the strong Steeds who drink the warm libation, and, Bull of Godlike nature, be thou gracious.
Let thy Steeds eat; set free thy Tawny Horses, and roasted grain like this consume thou daily.
4 Those who are yoked by prayer I harness, fleet friendly Bays who take their joy together.
Mounting thy firm and easy car, O Indra, wise and all-knowing come thou to the Soma.
5 No other worshippers must stay beside them thy Bays, thy vigorous and smooth-backed Coursers.
Pass by them all and hasten onward hither: with Soma pressed we will prepare to feast thee.
6 Thine is this Sorna: hasten to approach it. Drink thou thereof, benevolent, and cease not.
Sit on the sacred grass at this our worship, and take these drops into thy belly, Indra.
7 The grass is strewn for thee, pressed is the Soma; the grain is ready for thy Bays to feed on.
To thee who lovest them, the very mighty, strong, girt by Maruts, are these gifts presented.
8 This the sweet draught, with cows, the men, the mountains, the waters, Indra, have for thee made
ready.
Come, drink thereof, Sublime One, friendly-minded, foreseeing, knowing well the ways thou goest.
9 The Maruts, they with whom thou sharedst Soma, Indra, who made thee strong and were thine
army,-

With these accordant, eagerly desirous drink thou this Soma with the tongue of Agni.
10 Drink, Indra, of the juice by thine own nature, or by the tongue of Agni, O thou Holy.
Accept the sacrificial gift, O Sakra, from the Adhvaryu's hand or from the Hotar's.
11 Call we on Maghavan, auspicious Indra, best Hero in the fight where spoil is gathered,
The Strong, who listens, who.gives aid in battles, who slays the Vrtras, wins and gathers riches.

## [03-036] HYMN XXXVI. Indra.

1. WITH constant succours, fain thyself to share it, make this oblation which we bring effective.
Grown great through strengthening gifts at each libation, he hath become renowned by mighty
exploits.
2 For Indra were the Somas erst- discovered, whereby he grew strong-jointed, vast, and skilful.
Indra , take quickly these presented juices: drink of the strong, that which the strong have shaken.
3 Drink and wax great. Thine are the juices, Indra, both Somas of old time and these we bring thee.
Even as thou drankest, Indra, earlier Somas, so drink to-day, a new guest, meet for praises.

4 Great and impetuous, mighty-voiced in battle, surpassing power is his, and strength resistless.
Him the broad earth hath never comprehended when Somas cheered the Lord of Tawny Coursers.
5 Mighty and strong he waxed for hero exploit: the Bull was furnished a Sage's wisdom.
Indra is our kind Lord; his steers have vigour; his cows are many with abundant offspring.
6 As floods according to their stream flow onward, so to the sea, as borne on cars, the waters.
Vaster is Indra even than his dwelling, what time the stalk milked out, the Soma, fills him.
7 Eager to mingle with the sea, the rivers carry the well-pressed Soma juice to Indra.
They drain the stalk out with their arms, quick-banded, and cleanse it with a stream of mead and
filters.
8 Like lakes appear his flanks filled full with Soma: yea, he contains libations in abundance.
When Indra had consumed the first sweet viands, he, after slaying Vrtra, claimed the Soma.
9 Then bring thou hither, and let none prevent it: we know thee well, the Lord of wealth and
treasure.
That splendid gift which is thine own, O Indra, vouchsafe to us, Lord of the Tawny Coursers.
10 O Indra, Maghavan, impetuous mover, grant us abundant wealth that brings all blessings.
Give us a hundred autumns for our lifetime: give us, O fair-checked Indra, store of heroes.
11 Call we on Indra, Maghavan, auspicious, best Hero in the fight where spoil is gathered,
The Strong, who listens, who gives aid in battles, who slays the Vrtras, wins and gathers riches.

## [03-037] HYMN XXXVII. Indra.

1. O INDRA, for the strength that slays Vrtra and conquers in the fight,
We turn thee hitherward to us.
2 O Indra, Lord of Hundred Powers, may those who praise thee hitherward.
Direct thy spirit and thine eye.
3 O Indra, Lord of Hundred Powers, with all our songs we invocate
Thy names for triumph over foes.
4 We strive for glory through the powers immense of him whom many praise,
Of Indra who supports mankind.
5 For Vrtra's slaughter I address Indra whom many invocate,
To win us booty in the wars.
6 In battles be victorious. We seek thee, Lord of Hundred Powers,
Indra, that Vrtra may be slain.
7 In splendid combats of the hosts, in glories where the fight is won.
Indra, be victor over foes.
8 Drink thou the Soma for our help, bright, vigilant, exceeding strong,
O Indra, Lord of Hundred Powers.
9 O Satakratu, powers which thou mid the Five Races hast displayed
These, Indra, do I claim of thee.
10 Indra, great glory hast thou gained. Win splendid fame which none may mar
We make thy might perpetual.
11 Come to us either from anear, Or, Sakra, come from far away.
Indra, wherever be thy home, come to us thence, O Thunder-armed.

## [03-038] HYMN XXXVIII. Indra.

1. HASTING like some strong courser good at drawing, a thought have I imagined like a workman.
Pondering what is dearest and most noble, I long to see the sages full of wisdom.
2 Ask of the sages' mighty generations firm-minded and devout they framed the heaven.
These are thy heart-sought strengthening directions, and they have come to be sky's upholders.
3 Assuming in this world mysterious natures, they decked the heaven and earth for high dominion,
Measured with measures, fixed their broad expanses, set the great worlds apart held firm for safety.
4 Even as he mounted up they all adorned him: self-luminous he travels clothed in splendour.
That is the Bull's, the Asura's mighty figure: he, omniform, hath reached the eternal waters.
5 First the more ancient Bull engendered offspring; these are his many draughts that lent him vigour.
From days of old ye Kings, two Sons of Heaven, by hymns of sacrifice have won dominion.
6 Three seats ye Sovrans, in the Holy synod, many, yea, all, ye honour with your presence.
There saw I, going thither in the spirit, Gandharvas in their course with wind-blown tresses.
7 That same companionship of her, the Milch-cow, here with the strong Bull's divers forms they
stablished.
Enduing still some new celestial figure, the skilful workers shaped a form around him.
8 Let no one here debar me from enjoying the golden light which Savitar diffuses.
He covers both all-fostering worlds with praises even as a woman cherishes her children.
9 Fulfil, ye twain, his work, the Great, the Ancient: as heavenly blessing keep your guard around us.
All the wise Gods behold his varied actions who stands erect, whose voice is like a herdsman's.
10 Call we on Indra, Maghavan, auspicious, best Hero in the fight where spoil is gathered,
The Strong, who listens, who gives aid in battles, who slays the Vrtras, wins and gathers riches.

## [03-039] HYMN XXXIX. Indra.

1. To Indra from the heart the hymn proceedeth, to him the Lord, recited, built with praises;
The wakening song sung forth in holy synod: that which is born for thee, O Indra, notice.
2 Born from the heaven e'en in the days aforetime, wakening, sting aloud in holy synod,
Auspicious, clad in white and shining raiment, this is the ancient hymn of our forefathers.
3 The Mother of the Twins hath borne Twin Children: my tongue's tip raised itself and rested silent.
Killing the darkness at the light's foundation, the Couple newly born attain their beauty.
4 Not one is found among them, none of mortals, to blame our sires who fought to win the cattle.
Their strengthener was Indra the Majestic he spread their stalls of kine the Wonder-Worker.
5 Where as a Friend with friendly men, Navagvas, with heroes, on his knees he sought the cattle.
There, verily with ten Dasagvas Indra found the Sun lying hidden in the darkness.
6 Indra found meath collected in the milch-cow, by foot and hoof, in the cow's place of pasture.

That which lay secret, hidden in the waters, he held in his right hand, the rich rewarder.
7 He took the light, discerning it from darkness: may we be far removed from all misfortune.
These songs, O Soma-drinker, cheered by Soma, Indra, accept from thy most zealous poet.
8 Let there be light through both the worlds for worship: may we be far from most overwhelming evil.
Great woe comes even from the hostile mortal, piled up; but good at rescue are the Vasus.
9 Call we on Maghavan, auspicious Indra, best Hero in the fight where spoil is gathered,
The Strong, who listens, who gives aid in battles, who slays the Vrtras, wins and gathers riches.

## [03-040] HYMN XL. Indra.

1. THEE, Indra, we invoke, the Bull, what time the Soma is expressed.
So drink thou of the savoury juice.
2 Indra, whom many laud, accept the strength-conferring Soma juice:
Quaff, pour down drink that satisfies.
3 Indra, with all the Gods promote our wealth-bestowing sacrifice,
Thou highly-lauded Lord of men.
4 Lord of the brave, to thee proceed these drops of Soma juice expressed,
The bright drops to thy dwelling-place.
5 Within thy belly, Indra, take juice, Soma the most excellent:
Thine are the drops celestial.
6 Drink our libation, Lord of hymns: with streams of meath thou art bedewed
Our glory, Indra, is thy gift.
7 To Indra go the treasures of the worshipper, which never fail:
He drinks the Soma and is strong
8 From far away, from near at hand, O Vrtra-slayer, come to us:
Accept the songs we sing to thee.
9 When from the space between the near and far thou art invoked by us,
Thence, Indra. come thou hitherward.

## [03-041] HYMN XLI. Indra.

1. INVOKED to drink the Soma juice, come with thy Bay Steeds, Thunder-armed
Come, Indra, hitherward to me.
2 Our priest is seated, true to time; the grass is regularly strewn;
The pressing-stones were set at morn.
3 These prayers, O thou who hearest prayer are offered: seat thee on the grass.
Hero, enjoy the offered cake.
4 O Vrtra-slayer, be thou pleased with these libations, with these hymns,
Song-loving Indra, with our lauds.
5 Our hymns caress the Lord of Strength, vast, drinker of the Soma's juice,
Indra, as mother-cows their calf.
6 Delight thee with the juice we pour for thine own great munificence:
Yield not thy singer to reproach.
7 We, Indra, dearly loving thee, bearing oblation, sing thee hymns
Thou, Vasu, dearly lovest us.
8 O thou to whom thy Bays are dear, loose not thy Horses far from us:
Here glad thee, Indra, Lord divine.
9 May long-maned Coursers, dropping oil, bring thee on swift car hitherward,
Indra, to seat thee on the grass.

**[03-042] HYMN XLII. Indra.**

1. COME to the juice that we have pressed, to Sorna, Indra, bleat with milk:
Come, favouring us, thy Bay-drawn car!
2 Come, Indra, to this gladdening drink, placed on the grass, pressed out with stones:
Wilt thou not drink thy fill thereof?
3 To Indra have my songs of praise gone forth, thus rapidly sent hence,
To turn him to the Soma-draught.
4 Hither with songs of praise we call Indra to drink the Soma juice:
Will he not come to us by lauds?
5 Indra, these Somas are expressed. Take them within thy belly, Lord
Of Hundred Powers, thou Prince of Wealth.
6 We know thee winner of the spoil, and resolute in battles, Sage!
Therefore thy blessing we implore.
7 Borne hither by thy Stallions, drink, Indra, this juice which we have pressed,
Mingled with barley and with milk.
8 Indra, for thee, in thine own place, I urge the Soma for thy draught:
Deep in thy heart let it remain,
9 We call on thee, the Ancient One, Indra, to drink the Soma juice,
We Kusikas who seek thine aid.

**[03-043] HYMN XLIII. Indra.**

1. MOUNTED upon thy chariot-seat approach us: thine is the Sorna-draught from days aforetime.
Loose for the sacred grass thy dear companions. These men who bring oblation call thee hither.
2 Come our true Friend, passing by many people; come with thy two Bay Steeds to our devotions;
For these our hymns are calling thee, O Indra, hymns formed for praise, soliciting thy friendship.
3 Pleased, with thy Bay Steeds, Indra, God, come quickly to this our sacrifice that heightens worship;
For with my thoughts, presenting oil to feed thee, I call thee to the feast of sweet libations.
4 Yea, let thy two Bay Stallions bear thee hither, well limbed and good to draw, thy dear companions.
Pleased with the corn-blent offering which we bring thee, may Indra, Friend, hear his friend's
adoration.
5 Wilt thou not make me guardian of the people, make me, impetuous Maghavan, their ruler?
Make me a Rsi having drunk of Soma? Wilt thou not give me wealth that lasts for ever?
6 Yoked to thy chariot, led thy tall Bays, Indra, companions of thy banquet, bear thee hither,
Who from of old press to heaven's farthest limits, the Bull's impetuous and well-groomed Horses.
7 Drink of the strong pressed out by strong ones, Indra, that which the Falcon brought thee when thou longedst;
In whose wild joy thou stirrest up the people, in whose wild joy thou didst unbar the cow-stalls.
8 Call we on Indra, Makhavan, auspicious, best Hero in the fight where spoil is gathered;
The Strong, who listens, who gives aid in battles, who slays the Vrtras, wins and gathers riches.

**[03-044] HYMN XLIV. Indra.**

1. May this delightsome Soma be expressed for thee by tawny stones.

Joying thereat, O Indra, with thy Bay Steeds come:. ascend thy golden-coloured car.
2 In love thou madest Usas glow, in love thou madest Surya shine.
Thou, Indra, knowing, thinking, Lord of Tawny Steeds, above all glories waxest great.
3 The heaven with streams of golden hue, earth with her tints of green and gold-
The golden Pair yield Indra plenteous nourishment: between them moves the golden One.
4 When born to life the golden Bull illumines all the realm of light.
He takes his golden weapon, Lord of Tawny Steeds, the golden thunder in his arms.
5 The bright, the well-loved thunderbolt, girt with the bright, Indra disclosed,
Disclosed the Soma juice pressed out by tawny stones, with tawny steeds drave forth the kine.

**[03-045] HYMN XLV. Indra.**

1. COME hither, Indra, with Bay Steeds, joyous, with tails like peacocks' plumes.
Let no men cheek thy course as fowlers stay the bird: pass o'er them as o'er desert lands.
2 He who slew Vrtra, burst the cloud, brake the strongholds and drave the floods,
Indra who mounts his chariot at his Bay Steeds' cry, shatters e'en things that stand most firm.
3 Like pools of water deep and full, like kine thou cherishest thy might;
Like the milch-cows that go well-guarded to the mead, like water-brooks that reach the lake.
4 Bring thou us wealth with power to strike, our share, 'gainst him who calls it his.
Shake, Indra, as with hooks, the tree for ripened fruit, for wealth to satisfy our wish.
5 Indra, self-ruling Lord art thou, good Leader, of most glorious fame.
So, waxen in thy strength, O thou whom many praise, be thou most swift to hear our call.

**[03-046] HYMN XLVI. Indra.**

1. OF thee, the Bull, the Warrior, Sovran Ruler, joyous and fierce, ancient and ever youthful,
The undecaying One who wields the thunder, renowned and great, great are the exploits, Indra.
2 Great art thou, Mighty Lord, through manly vigour, O fierce One, gathering spoil, subduing others,
Thyself alone the universe's Sovran: so send forth men to combat and to rest them.
3 He hath surpassed all measure in his brightness, yea, and the Gods, for none may be his equal.
Impetuous Indra in his might cxccdcth wide vast mid-air and heaven and earth together.
4 To Indra, even as rivers to the ocean, flow forth from days of old the Soma juices;
To him wide deep and mighty from his birth-time, the well of holy thoughts, aIl-comprehending.
5 The Soma, Indra, which the earth and heaven bear for thee as a mother bears her infant,
This they send forth to thee, this, vigorous Hero! Adhvaryus purify for thee to drink of.

**[03-047] HYMN XLVII. Indra.**

1. DRINK, Indra, Marut-girt, as Bull, the Soma, for joy, for rapture even as thou listest.

Pour down the flood of meath within thy belly: thou from of old art King of Soma juices.

2 Indra, accordant, with the banded Maruts, drink Soma, Hero, as wise Vrtra-slayer.
Slay thou our foemen, drive away assailants and make us safe on every side from danger.

3 And, drinker at due seasons, drink in season, Indra, with friendly Gods, our pressed-out Soma.
The Maruts following, whom thou madest sharers, gave thee the victory, and thou slewest Vrtra.

4 Drink Soma, Indra, banded with the Maruts who, Maghavan, strengthened thee at Ahi's slaughter,
'Gainst Sambara, Lord of Bays! in winning cattle, and now rejoice in thee, the holy Singers.

5 The Bull whose strength hath waxed, whom Maruts follow, free-giving Indra, the celestial Ruler,
Mighty, all-conquering, the victory-giver, him let us call to grant us new protection.

## [03-048] HYMN XLVIII. Indra.

1. SOON as the young Bull sprang into existence he longed to taste the pressed-out Soma's liquor.
Drink thou thy fill, according to thy longing, first, of the goodly mixture blent with Soma.

2 That day when thou wast born thou, fain to taste it, drankest the plant's milk which the mountains
nourish.
That milk thy Mother first, the Dame who bare thee, poured for thee in thy mighty Father's dwelling.

3 Desiring food he came unto his Mother, and on her breast beheld the pungent Soma.
Wise, he moved on, keeping aloof the others, and wrought great exploits in his varied aspects.

4 Fierce, quickly conquering, of surpassing vigour, he framed his body even as he listed.
E'en from his birth-time Indra conquered Tvastar, bore off the Soma and in beakers drank it.

5 Call we on Maghavan, auspicious Indra, best Hero in the fight where spoil is gathered;
The Strong, who listens, who gives aid in battles, who slays the Vrtras, wins and gathers riches.

## [03-049] HYMN XLIX. Indra.

1. GREAT Indra will I laud, in whom all people who drink the Soma have attained their longing;
Whom, passing wise, Gods, Heaven and Earth, engendered, formed by a Master's hand, to crush the
Vrtras.

2 Whom, most heroic, borne by Tawny Coursers, verily none subdueth in the battle;
Who, reaching far, most vigorous, hath shortened the Dasyu's life with Warriors bold of spirit.

3 Victor in fight, swift mover like a warhorse, pervading both worlds, rainer down of blessings,
To he invoked in war like Bhaga, Father, as 'twere, of hymns, fair, prompt to hear, strength-giver.

4 Supporting heaven, the high back of the region, his car is Vayu with his team of Vasus.
Illumining the nights, the Sun's creator, like Dhisana he deals forth strength and riches.

5 Call we on Maghavan, auspicious Indra, best Hero in the fight where spoil is gathered;
The Strong, who listens, who gives aid in battles, who slays the Vrtras, wins and gathers treasure.

## [03-050] HYMN L. Indra.

1. LET Indra drink, All-hail! for his is Soma,-the mighty Bull come, girt by Maruts, hither.
Far-reaching, let him fill him with these viands, and let our offering sate his body's longing.

2 I yoke thy pair of trusty Steeds for swiftness, whose faithful service from of old thou lovest.
Here, fair of cheek! let thy Bay Coursers place thee: drink of this lovely welleffused libation.

3 With milk they made Indra their good Preserver, lauding for help and rule the bounteous rainer.
Impetuous God, when thou hast drunk the Soma, enraptured send us cattle in abundance.

4 With kine and horses satisfy this longing with very splendid bounty still extend it.
Seeking the light, with hymns to thee, O Indra, the Kusikas have brought their gift, the singers.

5 Call we on Maghavan, auspicious Indra, best Hero in the fight where spoil is gathered;
The Strong, who listens, who gives aid in battles, who slays the Vrtras, wins and gathers riches.

## [03-051] HYMN LI. Indra.

1. HIGH hymns have sounded forth the praise of Maghavan, supporter of mankind, of Indra meet for
lauds;
Him who hath waxen great, invoked with beauteous songs, Immortal One, whose praise each day is
sung aloud.

2 To Indra from all sides go forth my songs of praise, the Lord of Hundred Powers, strong, Hero, like
the sea,
Swift, winner of the booty, breaker-down of forts, faithful and ever-glorious, finder of the light.

3 Where battle's spoil is piled the singer winneth praise, for Indra taketh care of matchless
worshippers.
He in Vivasvan's dwelling findeth his delight: praise thou the ever-conquering slayer of the foe.

4 Thee, valorous, most heroic of the heroes, shall the priests glorify with songg and praises.
Full of all wondrous power he goes to conquest: worship is his, sole Lord from days aforetime.

5 Abundant are the gifts he gives to mortals: for him the earth bears a rich store of treasures.
The heavens, the growing plants, the living waters, the forest trees preserve their wealth for Indra.

6 To thee, O Indra, Lord of Bays, for ever are offered prayers and songs: accept them gladly.
As Kinsman think thou of some fresh assistance; good Friend, give strength and life to those who
praise thee.

7 Here, Indra, drink thou Soma with the Maruts, as thou didst drink the juice beside Saryata.
Under thy guidance, in thy keeping, Hero, the singers serve, skilled in fair sacrifices.

8 So eagerly desirous drink the Soma, our juice, O Indra, with thy friends the Maruts,
Since at thy birth all Deities adorned thee for the great fight, O thou invoked of many.

9 He was your comrade in your zeal, O Maruts: they, rich in noble gifts, rejoiced in Indra.
With them together let the Vrtra-slayer drink in his home the worshipper's libation.

10 So, Lord of affluent gifts, this juice hath been pressed for thee with strength
Drink of it, thou who lovest song.

11 Incline thy body to this juice which suits thy Godlike nature well:
May it cheer thee who lovest it.
12 Brave Indra, let it work through both thy flanks, and through thy head by prayer,
And through thine arms, to prosper us.

## [03-052] HYMN LII. Indra.

1. INDRA, accept at break of day our Soma mixt with roasted corn,
With groats with cake, with eulogies.
2 Accept, O Indra, and enjoy the well-dressed sacrificial cake:
Oblations are poured forth to thee.
3 Consume our sacrificial cake, accept the songs of praise we sing,
As he who woes accepts his bride.
4 Famed from of old, accept the cake at our libation poured at dawn,
Forgreat, O Indra, is thy power.
5 Let roasted corn of our midday libation, and sacrificial cake here please thee, Indra,
What time the lauding singer, keen of purpose and eager as a bull, with hymns implores thee.
6 At the third sacrifice, O thou whom many praise, give glory to the roasted corn and holy cake.
With offered viands and with songs may we assist thee, Sage, whom Vaja and the Rbhus wait upon.
7 The groats have we prepared for thee with Pusan, corn for thee, Lord of Bay Steeds, with thy
horses.
Eat thou the meal-cake, banded with the Maruts, wise Hero, Vrtra-slayer, drink the Soma.
8 Bring forth the roasted corn to meet him quickly, cake for the bravest Hero mid the heroes.
Indra, may hymns accordant with thee daily strengthen thee, Bold One, for the draught of Soma.

## [03-053] HYMN LIII. Indra, Parvata, Etc.

1. ON a high car, O Parvata and Indra, bring pleasant viands, with brave heroes, hither.
Enjoy the gifts, Gods, at our sacrifices wax strong by hymns, rejoice in our oblation.
2 Stay still, O Maghavan, advance no farther. a draught of well-pressed Soma will I give thee.
With sweetest song I grasp, O Mighty Indra, thy garment's hem as a child grasps his father's.
3 Adhvaryu, sing we both; sing thou in answer: make we a laud acceptable to Indra.
Upon this sacrificer's grass he seated: to Indra shall our eulogy be uttered.
4 A wife, O Maghavan is home and dwelling: so let thy Bay Steeds yoked convey thee hither.
Whenever we press out for thee the Soma, let Agni as our Herald speed to call thee.
5 Depart, O Maghavan;again come hither: both there and here thy goat is Indra, Brother,
Where thy tall chariot hath a place to rest in, and where thqu loosest thy loud-neighing Courser.
6 Thou hast drunk Soma, Indra, turn thee homeward; thy joy is in thy home, thy racious Consort;
Where thy tall chariot hath a place to rest in, and thy strong Courser is set free with guerdon.
7 Bounteous are these, Angirases, Virupas: the Asura's Heroes and the Sons of Heaven.
They, giving store of wealth to Visvamitra, prolong his life through countless Soma-pressings.
8 Maghavan weareth every shape at pleasure, effecting magic changes in his body,

Holy One, drinker out of season, coming thrice, in a moment, through fit prayers, from heaven.
9 The mighty sage, God-born and God-incited, who looks on men, restrained the billowy river.
When Visvamitra was Sudas's escort, then Indra through the Kusikas grew friendly.
10 Like swans, prepare a song of praise with pressing-stones, glad in your hymns with juice poured
forth in sacrifice.
Ye singers, with the Gods, sages who look on men, ye Kutikas drink up the Soma's savoury meath.
11 Come forward, Kusikas, and be attentive; let loose Sudas's horse to win him riches.
East, west, and north, let the King slay the foeman, then at earth's choicest place perform his worship.
12 Praises to Indra have I sung, sustainer of this earth and heaven. This prayer of Visvamitra keeps
secure the race of Bharatas.
13 The Visvamitras have sung forth this prayer to Indra Thunder-aimed:
So let him make us prosperous.
14 Among the Kikatas what do thy cattle? They pour no milky draught, they heat no caldron.
Bring thou to us the wealth of Pramaganda;give up to us, O Maghavan, the low-born.
15 Sasarpari, the gift of Jamadagnis, hath lowed with mighty voice dispelling famine.
The Daughter of the Sun hath spread our glory among the Gods, imperishable, deathless.
16 Sasarpari brought glory speedily to these, over the generations of the Fivefold Race;
Daughter of Paksa, she bestows new vital power, she whom the ancient Jamadagnis gave to me.
17 Strong be the pair of oxen, firm the axles, let not the pole slip nor the yoke be broken.
May Indra, keep the yoke-pins from decaying: attend us, thou whose fellies are uninjured.
18 O Indra, give our bodies strength, strength to the bulls who draw the wains,
Strength to our seed and progeny that they may live, for thou art he who giveth strength.
19 Enclose thee in the heart of Khayar timber, in the car wrought of Sinsapa put firmness.
Show thyself strong, O Axle, fixed and strengthened: throw us not from the car whereon we travel.

20 Let not this sovran of the wood leave us forlorn or injure us.
Safe may we be until we reach our homes and rest us and unyoke.
21 With various aids this day come to us, Indra, with best aids speed us, Maghavan, thou Hero.
Let him who hatcth us fall headlong downward: him whom we hate let vital breath abandon.
22 He heats his very axe, and then cuts a mere Semal blossom off.
O Indra, like a caldron cracked and seething, so he pours out foam.
23 Men notice not the arrow, O ye people; they bring the red beast deeming it a bullock.
A sluggish steed men run not with the courser, nor ever lead an ass before a charger.
24 These men, the sons of Bharata, O Indra, regard not severance or close connexion.
They urge their own steed as it were another's, and take him, swift as the bow's string, to battle.

## [03-054] HYMN LIV. Visvedevas.

1. To him adorable, mighty, meet for synods, this strengthening hymn, unceasing, have they offered.

May Agni hear us with his homely splendours, hear us, Eternal One, with heavenly lustre.

2 To mighty Heaven and Earth I sing forth loudly: my wish goes out desirous and well knowing

Both, at whose laud in synods, showing favour, the Gods rejoice them with the living mortal.

3 O Heaven and Earth, may your great law he faithful: he ye our leaders for our high advantage.

To Heaven and Earth I offer this my homage, with food, O Agni, as I pray for riches.

4 Yea, holy Heaven and Earth, the ancient sages whose word was ever true had power to find you;

And brave men in the fightwhere heroes conquer, O Earth, have known you well and paid you honour.

5 What pathway leadeth to the Gods? Who knoweth this of a truth, and who will now declare it?

Seen are their lowest dwelling-places only, but they are in remote and secret regions.

6 The Sage who looketh on mankind hath viewed them bedewed, rejoicing in the seat of Order.

They make a home as for a bird, though parted, with one same will finding themselves together.

7 Partners though parted, with far-distant limits, on one firm place both stand for ever watchful,

And, being young for evermore, as sisters, speak to each other names that are united.

8 All living things they part and keep asunder; though bearing up the mighty Gods they reel not.

One All is Lord of what is fixed and moving, that walks, that flies, this multiform creation.

9 Afar the Ancient from of old I ponder, our kinship with our mighty Sire and Father,-

Singing the praise whereof the Gods by custom stand on the spacious far-extended pathway.

10 This laud, O Heaven and Earth, to you I utter: let the kind-hearted hear, whose tongue is Agni,

Young, Sovran Rulers, Varuna and Mitra, the wise and very glorious Adityas.

11 The fair-tongued Savitar, the golden-handed, comes thrice from heaven as Lord in our assembly.

Bear to the Gods this song of praise, and send us, then, Savitar, complete and perfect safety.

12 Deft worker, skiful-handed, helpful, holy, may Tvastar, God, give us these things to aid us,

Take your delight, Ye Rbhus joined with Pusan: ye have prepared the rite with stones adjusted.

13 Borne on their flashing car, the spear-armed Maruts, the nimble Youths of Heaven, the Sons of Order,

The Holy, and Sarasvati, shall hear us: ye Mighty, give us wealth with noble offspring.

14 To Visnu rich in marvels, songs And praises shall go as singers on the road of Bhaga,-

The Chieftain of the Mighty Stride, whose Mothers, the many young Dames, never disregard him.

15 Indra, who rules through all his powers heroic, hath with his majesty filled earth and heaven.

Lord of brave hosts, Fort-crusher, Vrtra-slayer, gather thou up and bring us store of cattle.

16 My Sires are the Nasatyas, kind tokinsmen: the Asvins' kinship is a glorious title.

For ye are they who give us store of riches: ye guard your gift uncheated by the bounteous.

17 This is, ye Wise, your great and glorious title, that all ye Deities abide in Indra.

Friend, Much-invoked! art thou with thy dear Rbhus: fashion ye this our hymn for our advantage.

18 Aryaman, Aditi deserve our worship: the laws of Varuna remain unbroken.

The lot of childlessness remove ye from us, and let our course be rich in kine and offspring.

19 May the Gods' envoy, sent to many a quarter, proclaim us sinless for our perfect safety.

May Earth and Heaven, the Sun, the waters, hear us, and the wide firmament and constellations.

20 Hear us the mouatains which distil the rain-drops, and, resting firm, rejoice in freshening moisture.

May Aditi with the Adityas hear us, and Maruts grant us their auspicious shelter.

21 Soft be our path for ever, well-provisioned: with pleasant meath, O Gods, the herbs besprinkle.

Safe be my bliss, O Agni, in thy friendship: may I attain the seat of foodful. riches,

22 Enjoy the offering: beam thou strength upon us; combine thou for our good all kinds of glory.

Conquer in battle, Agni, all those foemen, and light us every day with loving kindness.

### [03-055] HYMN LV. Visvedevas.

1. AT the first shining of the earliest Mornings, in the Cow's home was born the Great Eternal.

Now shall the statutes of the Gods be valid. Great is the Gods' supreme and sole dominion -

2 Let not the Gods here injure us, O Agni, nor Fathers of old time who know the region,

Nor the sign set between two ancient dwellings. Great is the Gods' supreme and sole dominion.

3 My wishes fly abroad to many places: I glance back to the ancient sacrifices.

Let us declare the truth when fire is kindled. Great is the Gods' supreme and sole dominion.

4 King Universal, born to sundry quarters, extended through the wood be lies on couches.

One Mother rests: another feeds the Infant. Great is the Gods' supreme and sole dominion.

5 Lodged in old plants, he grows again in younger, swiftly within the newly-born and tender.

Though they are unimpregned, he makes them fruitful. Great is the Gods' supreme and sole dominion.

6 Now lying far away, Child of two Mothers, he wanders unrestrained, the single youngling.

These are the laws of Varuna and Mitra. Great is the Gods' supreme and sole dominion.

7 Child of two Mothers, Priest, sole Lord in synods, he still precedes while resting as foundation.

They who speak sweetly bring him sweet addresses. Great is the Gods' supreme and sole dominion.

8 As to a friendly warrior when he battles, each thing that comes anear is seen to meet him.

The hymn commingles with the cow's oblation. Great is the Gods' supreme and sole dominion.

9 Deep within these the hoary envoy pierceth; mighty, he goeth to the realm of splendour,

And looketh on us, clad in wondrous beauty. Great is the Gods' supreme and sole dominion.

10 Visnu, the guardian, keeps the loftiest station, upholding dear, immortal dwelling-places.

Agni knows well all these created beings. Great is the Gods' supreme and sole dominion.

11 Ye, variant Pair, have made yourselves twin beauties: one of the Twain is dark, bright shines the other;
And yet these two, the dark, the red, are Sisters. Great is the Gods' supreme and sole dominion.
12 Where the two Cows, the Mother and the Daughter, meet and give suck yielding their lordly nectar,
I praise them at the seat of law eternal. Great is the Gods' supreme and sole dominion.
13 Loud hath she lowed, licking the other's youngling. On what world hath the Milch-cow laid her udder?
This Ila streameth with the milk of Order. Great is the Gods' supreme and sole dominion.
14 Earth weareth beauties manifold: uplifted, licking her Calf of eighteen months, she standeth.
Well-skilled I seek the seat of law eternal. Great is the Gods' supreme and sole dominion.
15 Within a wondrous place the Twain are treasured: the one is manifest, the other hidden.
One common pathway leads in two directions. Great is the Gods' supreme and sole dominion.
16 Let the milch-kine that have no calves storm downward, yielding rich nectar, streaming, unexhausted,
These who are ever new and fresh and youthful. Great is the Gods' supreme and sole dominion.
17 What time the Bull bellows in other regions, another herd receives the genial moisture;
For he is Bhaga, King, the earth's Protector. Great is the Gods' supreme and sole dominion.
18 Let us declare the Hero's wealth in horses, O all ye folk: of this the Gods have knowledge.
Sixfold they bear him, or by fives are harnessed. Great is the Gods' supreme and sole dominion.
19 Tvastar the God, the omniform. Creator, begets and feeds mankind in various manner.

His, verily, arc all these living creatures. Great is the Gods' supreme dominion.
20 The two great meeting Bowls hath he united: each of the Pair is laden with histreasure.
The Hero is renowned for gathering riches. Great is the Gods' supreme and sole dominion.
21 Yea, and on this our earth the All-Sustainer dwells like a King with noble friends about him.
In his protection heroes rest in safety. Great is the Cods' supreme and sole dominion.
22 Rich in their gifts for thee are herbs and waters, and earth brings all her wealth for thee, O Indra.
May we as friends of thine share goodly treasures. Great is the Gods' supreme and sole dominion.

## [03-056] HYMN LVI. Visvedevas.
1. NOT men of magic skill, not men of wisdom impair the Gods' first steadfast ordinances.
Ne'er may the earth and heaven which know not malice, nor the fixed hills, be bowed by sage devices.
2 One, moving not away, supports six burthens: the Cows proceed to him the true, the Highest.
Near stand three Mighty Ones who travel swiftly: two are concealed from sight, one is apparent.
3 The Bull who wears all shapes, the triple-breasted, three-uddered, with a brood in many places,

Ruleth majestic with his triple aspect, the Bull, the Everlasting Ones' impregner.
4 When nigh them, as their tracer he observed them: he called aloud the dear name of Adityas.
The Goddesses, the Waters, stayed to meet him: they who were wandering separate enclosed him.
5 Streams! the wise Gods have thrice three habitations. Child of three Mothers, he is Lord in synods.
Three are the holy Ladies of the Waters, thrice here from heaven supreme in our assembly.
6 Do thou, O Savitar, from heaven thrice hither, three times a day, send down thy blessings daily.
Send us, O Bhaga, triple wealth and treasure; cause the two worlds to prosper us, Preserver!
7 Savitar thrice from heaven pours down abundance, and the fair-handed Kings Varuna, Mitra;
And spacious Heaven and Earth, yea, and the Waters, solicit wealth that Savitar may send us.
8 Three are the bright realms, best, beyond attainment, and three, the Asura's Heroes, rule as Sovrans,
Holy and vigorous, never to be injured. Thrice may the Gods from heaven attend our synod.

## [03-057] HYMN LVII. Visvedevas.
1. MY thought with fine discernment hath discovered the Cow who wanders free without a herdsman,
Her who hath straightway poured me food in plenty: Indra and Agni therefore are her praisers.
2 Indra and Pusan, deft of hand and mighty, well-pleased have drained the heaven's exhaustless udder.
As in this praise the Gods have all delighted, may I win blessing here from you, O Vasus.
3 Fain to lend vigour to the Bull, the siste.. with reverence recognize the germ within him.
The Cows come lowing hither to the Youngling, to him endued with great and wondrous beauties.
4 Fixing with thought, at sacrifice, the press-stones, I bid the well-formed Heaven and Earth come hither;
For these thy flames, which give men boons in plenty, rise up on high, the beautiful, the holy.
5 Agni, thy meath-sweet tongue that tastes fair viands, which among Gods is called the farextended,-
Therewith make all the Holy Odes be seated here for our help, and feed them with sweet juices.
6 Let thy stream give us drink, O God, O Agni, wonderful and exhaustless like the rain-clouds.
Thus care for us, O Vasu Jatavedas, show us thy loving-kindness, reaching all men.

## [03-058] HYMN LVIII. Asvins.
1. THE Ancient's Milch-cow yields the things we long for: the Son of Daksina travels between them.
She with the splendid chariot brings refulgence. The praise of Usas hath awoke the Asvins.
2 They bear you hither by well-orderd statute: our sacred offerings rise as if to parents.
Destroy in us the counsel of the niggard come hitherward, for we have shown you favour.

3 With lightly-rolling car and well-yoked horses hear this, the press-stone's song, ye Wonder-Workers.

Have not the sages of old time, ye Asvins, called you most prompt to come and stay misfortune?

4 Remember us, and come to us, for ever men, as their wont is, invocate the Asvins.
Friends as it were have offered you these juices, sweet, blent with milk at the first break of morning.

5 Even through many regions, O ye Asvins high praisc is yours among mankind, ye Mighty-
Come, helpers, on the paths which Gods have travelled: here your libations of sweet meath are ready.

6 Ancient your home, auspicious is your friendship: Heroes, your wealth is with the house of Jahnu.
Forming again with you auspicious friendship, let us rejoice with draughts of meath together.

7 O Asvins, Very Mighty ones, with Vayu and with his steeds, one-minded, ever-youthful,
Nasatyas, joying in the third day's Soma, drink it, not hostile, Very Bounteous Givers.

8 Asvins, to you are brought abundant viands in rivalry with sacred songs, unceasing.
Sprung from high Law your car, urged on by press-stones, goes round the earth and heaven in one brief moment.

9 Asvins, your Soma sheds delicious sweetness: drink ye thereof and come unto our dwelling.
Your car, assuming many a shape, most often goes to the Soma-presser's place of meeting.

### [03-059] HYMN LIX. Mitra.

1. MITRA, when speaking, stirreth men to labour: Mitra sustaineth both the earth and heaven.
Mitra beholdeth men with eyes that close not. To Mitra bring, with holy oil, oblation.

2 Foremost be he who brings thee food, O Mitra, who strives to keep thy sacred Law, Aditya.
He whom thou helpest ne'er is slain or conquered, on him, from near or far, falls no affliction.

3 joying in sacred food and free from sickness, with knees bent lowly on the earth's broad surface,
Following closely the Aditya's statute, may we remain in Mitra's gracious favour.

4 Auspicious and adorable, this Mitra was born with fair dominion, King, Disposer.
May we enjoy the grace of him the Holy, yea, rest in his propitious loving-kindness.

5 The great Aditya, to be served with wor. ship, who stirreth men, is gracious to the singer.
To Mitra, him most highly to be lauded, offer in fire oblation that he loveth.

6 The gainful grace of Mitra,. God, supporter of the race of man,
Gives splendour of most.glorious fame.

7 Mitra whose glory spreads afar, he who in might surpasses heaven,
Surpasses earth in his renown.

8 All the Five Races have repaired to Mitra, ever strong to aid,
For he sustaineth all the Gods.

9 Mitra to Gods, to living men, to him who strews the holy grass,
Gives food fulfilling sacred Law.

### [03-060] HYMN LX. Rbhus.

1. HERE is your ghostly kinship, here, O Men: they came desirous to these holy rites with store of wealth,
With wondrous arts, whereby, with schemes to meet each need, Ye gained, Sudhanvan's Sons! your share in sacrifice.

2 The mighty powers wherewith. ye formed the chalices, the thought by which ye drew the cow from out the hide,
The intellect wherewith ye wrought the two Bay Steeds,-through these, O Rbhus, ye attained divinity.

3 Friendship with Indra havc thc Rbhus, fully gaincd: grandsons of Manu, they skilfully urged the work.
Sudhanvan's Children won them everlasting life, serving with holy rites, pious with noble acts.

4:In company with Indra come ye to the juice, then gloriously shall your wishes be fulfilled.
Not to be paragoned, ye Priests, are your good deeds, nor your heroic acts, Rbhus, Sudhanvan's Sons.

5 O Indra, with the Rbhus, Mighty Ones, pour down the Soma juice effused, well-blent, from both thy hands.
Maghalan, urged by song, in the drink-offerer's house rejoice thee with the Heroes, with Sudhanvan's Sons.

6 With Rbhu near, and Vaja, Indra, here exult, with Saci, praised of many, in the juice we pour.
These homes wherein we dwell have turned themselves to thee, - devotions to the Gods, as laws of men ordain.

7 Come with the mighty Rbhus, Indra, come to us, strengthening with thy help the singer's holy praise;
At hundred eager calls come to the living man, with thousand arts attend the act of sacrifice.

### [03-061] HYMN LXI. Usas.

1. O Usas, strong with strength, endowed witli knowledge, accept the singer's praise, O wealthy Lady.
Thou, Goddess, ancient, young, and full of wisdom, movest, all-bounteous! as the Law ordaineth.

2 Shine forth, O Morning, thou auspicious Goddess, on thy bright car awaking pleasant voices.
Let docile horses of far-reaching splendour convey thee hitherward, the goldencoloured.

3 Thou, Morning, turning thee to every creature, standest on high as ensign of the Immortal,
To one same goal ever and ever wending now, like a wheel, O newly-born, roll hi ther.

4 Letting her reins drop downward, Morning cometh, the wealthy Dame, the Lady of the dwelling;
Bringing forth light, the Wonderful, the Blessed hath spread her from the bounds of earth and heaven.

5 Hither invoke the radiant Goddess Morning, and bring with reverence your hymn to praise her.
She, dropping sweets, hath set in heaven her brightness, and, fair to look on, hath beamed forth her splendour.

6 From heaven, with hymns, the Holy One was wakened: brightly to both worlds came the wealthy Lady.
To Morning, Agni, when she comes refulgent, thou goest forth soliciting fair riches.

7 On Law's firm base the speeder of the Mornings, the Bull, hath entered mighty earth and heaven.
Great is the power of Varuna and Mitra, which, bright, hath spread in every place its splendour.

**[03-062] HYMN LXII. Indra and Others.**

1. YOUR well-known prompt activities aforetime needed no impulse from your faithful servant.
Where, Indra-Varuna, is now that glory wherewith ye brought support to those who loved you?
2 This man, most diligent, seeking after riches, incessantly invokes you for your favour.
Accordant, Indra-Varuna, with Maruts, with Heaven and Earth, hear ye mine invocation.
3 O Indra-Varuna, ours be this treasure ours be wealth, Maruts, with full store of heroes.
.May the Varutris with their shelter aid us, and Bharati and Hotri with the Mornings.
4 Be pleased! with our oblations, thou loved of all Gods, Brhaspati:
Give wealth to him who brings thee gifts.
5 At sacrifices, with your hymns worship the pure Brhaspati-
I pray for power which none may bend-
6 The Bull of men, whom none deceive, the wearer of each shape at will,
Brhaspati Most Excellent.
7 Divine, resplendent Pusan, this our newest hymn of eulogy,
By us is chanted forth to thee.
8 Accept with favour this my song, be gracious to the earnest thought,
Even as a bridegroom to his bride.
9 May he who sees all living things, see, them together at a glancc,-
May lie, may Pusan be our help.
10 May we attain that excellent glory of Savitar the God:
So May he stimulate our prayers.

11 With understanding, earnestly, of Savitar the God we crave
Our portion of prosperity.
12 Men, singers worship Savitar the God with hymn and holy rites,
Urged by the impulse of their thoughts.
13 Soma who gives success goes forth, goes to the gathering place of Gods,
To seat him at the seat of Law.
14 To us and to our cattle may Soma give salutary food,
To biped and to quadruped.
15 May Soma, strengthening our power of life, and conquering our foes,
In our assembly take his seat.
16 May Mitra-Varuna, sapient Pair, bedew our pasturage with oil,
With meatb the regions of the air.
17 Far-ruling, joyful when adored, ye reign through majesty of might,
With pure laws everlastingly.
18 Lauded by Jamadagni's song, sit in the place of holy Law:
Drink Soma, ye who strengthen Law.

# BOOK FOUR

**[04-001] HYMN I. Agni.**

1, THEE Agni, have the Gods, ever of one accord, sent hither down, a God, appointed messenger,
yea, with their wisdom sent thee down.
The Immortal, O thou Holy One, mid mortal men, the God-devoted God, the wise, have they brought
forth, brought forth the omnipresent God-devoted Sage.
2 As such, O Agni, bring with favour to the Gods thy Brother Varuna who loveth sacrifice,

True to the Law, the Aditya who supporteth men, the King, supporter of mankind.
3 Do thou, O Friend, turn hither him who is our Friend, swift as a wheel, like two car-steeds in rapid
course, Wondrous! to us in rapid course.
O Agni, find thou grace for us with Varuna, with Maruts who illumine all.
Bless us, thou Radiant One, for seed and progeny, yea, bless us, O thou Wondrous God.
4 Do thou who knowest Varuna, O Agni, put far away from us the God's displeasure.
Best Sacrificer, brightest One, refulgent remove thou far from us all those who hate us.
5 Be thou, O Agni, nearest us with succour, our closest Friend while now this Morn is breaking.
Reconcile to us Varuna, be bounteous enjoy the gracious juice; be swift to hear us.
6 Excellent is the glance, of brightest splendour, which the auspicious God bestows on mortals-
The God's glance, longed-for even as the butter, pure, heated, of the cow, the milch-cow's bounty.
7 Three are those births, the true, the most exalted, eagerly longed-for, of the God, of Agni.
He came invested in the boundless region, pure, radiant, friendly, mightily resplendent.
8 This envoy joyeth in all seats of worship, borne on his golden car, sweet-tongued Invoker:
Lovely to look on, with red steeds, effulgent, like a feast rich in food, joyous for ever.
9 Allied by worship, let him give man knowledge: by an extended cord they lead him onward.
He stays, effectual in this mortal's dwelling, and the God wins a share in his possessions.
10 Let Agni -for he knows the way- conduct us to all that he enjoys of God-sent riches,
What all the Immortals have prepared with wisdom, Dyaus, Sire, Begetter, raining down true blessings.
11 In houses first he sprang into existence, at great heaven's base, and in this region's bosom;
Footless and headless, both his ends concealing, in his Bull's lair drawing himself together.
12 Wondrously first he rose aloft, defiant, in the Bull's lair, the homeof holy Order,
Longed-for, young, beautiful, and far-resplendent: and sevendear frieuds sprang up unto the Mighty.
13 Here did our human fathers take their places, fain to fulfil the sacred Law of worship.
Forth drave they, with loud call, Dawn's teeming Milch-kine bid in the mountainstable, in the cavern.
14 Splendid were they when they had rent the mountain: others, around, shall tell forth this their exploit.
They sang their song, prepared to free the cattle: they found the light; with holy hymns they worshipped.
15 Eager, with thought intent upon the booty, the men with their celestial speech threw open,
The solid mountain firm, compact, enclosing, confining Cows, the stable full of cattle.
16 The Milch-cow's earliest name they comprehended: they found the Mother's thrice-seven noblest titles.
This the bands knew, and sent forth acclamation:with the Bull's sheen the Red One was apparent.
17 The turbid darkness fled, the heaven was sp, endid! up rose the bright beam of celestial Morning.

Surya ascended to the wide expanses, beholding deeds of men both good and evil.

18 Then, afterwards they looked around, awakened, when first they held that Heaven allotted
treasure.

Now all the Gods abide in all their dwellings. Varuna, Mitra, be the prayer effective.

19 I will call hither brightly-beaming Agni, the Herald, all-supporting, best at worship.

He hath disclosed, like the milch cows' pure udder, the Sorria's juice when cleansed and poured from
beakers.

20 The freest God of all who should be worshipped, the guest who is received in all men's houses,

Agni who hath secured the Gods' high favour,-may he be gracious, to us Jatavedas.

## [04-002] HYMN II. Agni.

1. THE, Faithful One, Immortal among mortals, a God among the Gods, appointed envoy,

Priest, best at worship, must shine forth in glory . Agni shall be raised high with man's oblations.

2 Born for us here this day, O Son of Vigour, between both races of born beings, Agni,

Thou farest as an envoy, having harnessed, Sublime One! thy strong-muscled radiant stallions.

3 I laud the ruddy steeds who pour down blessing, dropping oil, flectest through the thoualit of
Order.

Yoking red horses to and fro thou goest between you Deities and mortal races.

4 Aryaman, Mitra, Varuna, and Indra with Visnu, of the Gods, Maruts and Asvins-

These, Agni, with good car and steeds, bring hither, most bountiful, to folk with fair oblations.

5 Agni, be this our sacrifice eternal, with brave friends, rich in kine and sheep and horses,

Rich, Asura! in sacred food and children, in full assembly, wealth broad-based and during.

6 The man who, sweating, brings for thee the fuel, and makes his head to ache, thy faithful servant,-

Agni, to him be a self-strong Protector guard him from all who seek to do him mischief.

7 Who brings thee food, though thou hast food in plenty, welcomes his cheerful guest and speeds
him onward,

Who kindles thee devoutly in his dwelling,to him be wealth secure and freely giving.

8 Whoso sings praise to thee at eve or morning, and, with oblation, doth the thing thou lovest,-

In his own home, even as a goId-girt courser, rescue him from distress, the bounteous giver.

9 Whoso brings gifts to thee Immortal, Agni, and doth thee service with uplifted ladle,-

Let him not, sorely toiling, lose his riches; let not the sinner's wickedness enclose him.

10 Whose well-wrought worship thou acceptest, Agni, thou God a mortal's gift, thou liberal Giver,-

Dear be his sacrifice to thee, Most Youthful! and may we strengthen him when he adores thee.

11 May he who knows distinguish sense and folly of men, like straight and crooked backs of horses.

Lead us, O God, to wealth and noble offspring: keep penury afar and grant us plenty.

12 This Sage the Sages, ne'er deceived, commanded, setting him down in dwellings of the living.

Hence mayst thou, friendly God, with rapid footsteps behold the Gods, wonderful, fair to look on.

13 Good guidance hast thou for the priest, O Agni, who, Youngest God! with outpoured Soma serves
thee.

Ruler of men, thou joyous God, bring treasure splendid and plentiful to aid the toiler.

14 Now all that we, thy faithful servants, Agni, have done with feet, with hands, and with our bodies,

The wise, with toil, the holy rite have guided, as those who frame a car with manual cunning.

15 May we, seven sages first in rank, engender, from Dawn the Mother, men to be ordainers.

May we, Angirases, be sons of Heaven, and, radiant, burst the wealth-containing mountain.

16 As in the days of old our ancient Fathers, speeding the work of holy worship, Agni,

Sought pure light and devotion, singing praises; they cleft the ground and made red Dawns apparent.

17 Gods, doing holy acts, devout, resplendent, smelting like ore their human generations.

Enkindling Agni and exalting Indra, they came encompassing the stall of cattle.

18 Strong One! he marked them-and the Gods before them-like herds of cattle in a foodful pasture.

There they moaned forth their strong desire for mortals, to aid the True, the nearest One, the Living.

19 We have worked for thee, we have laboured nobly-bright Dawns have shed their light upon our
worship-

Adding a beauty to the perfect Agni, and the God's beauteous eye that shines for ever.

20 Agni, Disposer, we have sung these praises to thee the Wise: do thou accept them gladly.

Blaze up on high and ever make us richer. Give us great wealth, O thou whose boons are many.

## [04-003] HYMN III. Agni.

1. WIN, to assist you, Rudra, Lord of worship, Priest of both worlds, effectual
Sacrificer,

Agni, invested with his golden colours, before the thunder strike and lay you senseless.

2 This shrine have we made ready for thy coming, as the fond dame attires her for her husband.

Performer of good work, sit down before us, invested while these flames incline to meet thee.

3 A hymn, O Priest, to him who hears, the gentle, to him who looks on men, exceeding gracious,

A song of praise sing to the God Immortal, whom the stone, presser of the sweet juice, worships.

4 Even as true knower of the Law, O Agni, to this our solemn rite he thou attentive.

When shall thy songs of festival be sung thee? When is thy friendship shown within our dwelling?

5 Why this complaint to Varuna, O Agni? And why to Heaven? for what is our transgression?

How wilt thou speak to Earth and bounteous Mitra? What wilt thou say to Aryaman and Bhaga?

6 What, when thou blazest on the lesser altars, what to the mighty Wind who comes tobless us,

True, circumambient? what to Earth, O Agni, what wilt thou say to man-destroying Rudra?

7 How to great Pusan who promotes our welfare,- to honoured Rudra what, who gives oblations?

What sin of ours to the far-striding Visnu, what, Agni, wilt thou tell the Lofty Arrow.

8 What wilt thou tell the truthful band of Maruts, how answer the great Sun when thou art
questioned?
Before the Free, before the Swift, defend us: fulfil heaven's work, all-knowing Jatavedas.
9 I crave the cow's true gift arranged by Order: though raw, she hath the sweet ripe juice, O Agni.
Though she is black of hue with milk she teemeth, nutritious, brightly shining, all-sustaining.
10 Agni the Bull, the manly, hath been sprinkled with oil upon his back, by Law eternal.
He who gives vital power goes on unswerving. Prsni the Bull hath milked the pure wiiite udder.
11 By Law the Angirases cleft the rock asunder, and sang their hymns together with the cattle.
Bringing great bliss the men encompassed Morning: light was apparent at the birth of Agni.
12 By Law the Immortal Goddesses the Waters, with meath-rich waves, O Agni, and uninjured,
Like a strong courser lauded in his running, sped to flow onward swiftly and for ever.
13 Go never to the feast of one who harms us, the treacherous neighbour or. unworthy kinsman.
Punish us not for a false brother's trespass. Let us riot feel the might of friend or foeman.
14 O Agni, keep us safe with thy protection, loving us, honoured God! and ever guarding.
Beat thou away, destory severe affliction slay e'en the demon when he waxes mighty.
15 Through these our songs of praise be gracious, Agni; moved by ourprayers, O Hero, touch our
viands.
Accept, O Angiras, these our devotions, and let the praise which Gods desire address thee.
16 To thee who knowest, Agni, thou Disposer, all these wise secret speeches have I uttered,
Sung to thee, Sage, the charming words of wisdom, to thee, O Singer, with. my thoughts and Praises.

## [04-004] HYMN IV. Agni.

1. PUT forth like a wide-spreading net thy vigour; go like a mighty King with his attendants.
Thou, following thy swift net, shootest arrows: transfix the fiends with darts that burn most fiercely.
2 Forth go in rapid flight thy whirling weapons: follow them closely, glowing in thy fury.
Spread with thy tongue the winged flames, O Agni; unfettered, cast thy firebrands all around thee.
3 Send thy spies forward, flectest in thy motion; be, ne'er deceived, the guardian of this people
From him who, near or far, is bent on evil, and let no trouble sent from thee o'ercome us.
4 Rise up, O Agni, spread thee out before us: burn down our foes, thou who hast sharpened arrows.
Him, blazing Agni! who hath worked us mischief, consume thou utterly like dried-up stubble.
5 Rise, Agni, drive off those who fight against us: make manifest thine own celestial vigour.
Slacken the strong bows of the demondriven: destroy our foemen whether kin or stranger.
6 Most Youthful God, he knoweth well thy favour who gave an impulse to this high devotion.
All fair days and magnificence of riches hast thou beamed forth upon the good man's portals.
7 Blest, Agni, be the man, the liberal giver, who with his lauds and regular oblation

Is fain to please thee for his life and dwelling. May all his days be bright: be this his longing.
8 I praise thy gracious favour: sing in answer. May this my song sing like a loved one with thee.
Lords of good steeds and cars may we adorn thee, and day by day vouchsafe thou us dominion.
9 Here of free choice let each one serve thee richly, resplendent day by day at eve and morning.
So may we honour thee, content and joyous, passing beyond the glories of the people.
10 Whoso with good steeds and fine gold, O Agni, comes nigh thee on a car laden with treasure,
His Friend art thou, yea, thou art his Protector whose joy it is to entertain thee duly.
11 Through words and kinship I destroy the miglity: this power I have from Gotama my father.
Mark thou this speech of ours, O thou Most Youthful, Friend of the House, exceeding wise, Invoker.
12 Knowing no slumber, speedy and propitious, alert and ever friendly, most unwearied,
May thy protecting powers, unerring Agni, taking their places here, combined, preserve us.
13 Thy guardian rays, O Agni, when they saw him, preserved blind Mamateya from affliction.
Lord of all riches, he preserved the pious: the fees who fain would harm them did no mischief
14 Aided by thee with thee may we be wealthy, may we gain strength with thee to guide us onward.
Fulfil the words of both, O Ever Truthful: straightway do this, thou God whom power emboldens.
15 O Agni, with this fuel will we serve thee; accept the laud we sing to thee with favour
Destroy the cursing Raksasas: preserve us, O rich in friends, from guile and scorn and slander.

## [04-005] HYMN V. Agni.

1. How shall we give with one accord oblation to Agni, to Vaisvanara the Bounteous?
Great light, with full high growth hath he uplifted, and, as a pillar bears the roof, sustains it.
2 Reproach not him who, God and selfreliant, vouchsafed this bounty unto me a mortal,-
Deathless, discerner, wise, to me the simple, Vaisvanara most manly, youthful Aini.
3 Sharp-pointed, powerful, strong, of boundless vigour, Agni who knows the lofty hymn, kept secret
As the lost milch-cow's track, the doubly Mighty,-he hath declared to me this hidden knowledge.
4 May he with sharpened teeth, the Bounteous Giver, Agni, consume with flame most fiercely
glowing.
Those who regard not Varuna's commandments and the dear stedfast laws of sapient Mitra.
5 Like youthful women without brothers, straying, like dames who hate their lords, of evil conduct,
They who are full of sin, untrue, unfaithful, they have engendered this abysmal station.
6 To me, weak, innocent, thou, luminous Agni, bast boldly given as 'twere a heavy burthen,
This Prstha hymn, profound and strong and mighty, of seven elements, and with offered dainties.
7 So may our song that purifies, through wisdom reach in a moment him the Universal,
Established on the height, on earth's best .station, above the beauteous grassy skin of Prsni.
8 Of this my speech what shall I utter further? They indicate the milk stored up in secret

When they have thrown as 'twere the cows' stalls open. The Bird protects earths' best and wellloved
station.
9 This is the Great Ones' mighty apparition which from of old the radiant Cow hath followed.
This, shining brightly in the place of Order, swift, hasting on in secret, she discovered.
10 He then who shone together with his Parents remembered Prsni's fair and secret treasure,
Which, in the Mother Cow's most lofty station, the Bull's tongue, of the flame bent forward, tasted.
11 With reverence I declare the Law, O Agni; what is, comes by thine order, Jatavedas.
Of this, whate'er it be, thou art the Sovran, yea, all the wealth that is in earth or
heaven.
12 What is our wealth therefrom, and what our treasure? Tell us O Jatavedas, for thou
knowest,
What is our best course in this secret passage: we, unreproached, have reached a t)lace far distant.
13 What is the limit, what the rules, the guerdon? Like fleet-foot coursers speed we to the contest.
When will the Goddesses, the Immortal's Spouses, the Dawns, spread over us the Sun-God's
splendour?
14 Unsatisfied, with speech devoid of vigour, scanty and frivolous and inconclusive,

Wherefore do they address thee here, O Agni? Let these who have no weapons suffer sorrow.
15 The majesty of him the Good, the Mighty, aflame, hath shone for glory in the dwelling.
He, clothed in light, hath shone most fair to look on, wealthy in boons, as a home shines with riches.

## [04-006] HYMN VI. Agni.
1. PRIEST of our rite, stand up erect, O Agni, in the Gods' service best of sacrificers,
For over evei y thought thou art the Ruler: thou furtherest e'en the wisdom of the pious.
2 He was set down mid men as Priest unerring, Agni, wise, welcome in our holy synods.
Like Savitar he hath lifted up his splendour, and like a builder raised his smoke to heaven.
3 The glowing ladle, filled with oil, is lifted; choosing Gods' service to the right he circles.
Eager he rises like the new-wrought pillar which, firmly set and fixed, anoints the victims.
4 When sacred grass is strewn and Agni kindled, the Adhvaryu rises to, his task rej o cing.
Agni the Priest, like one who tends the cattle, goes three times round, as from of old he wills it.
5 Agni himself, the Priest, with measured motion, goes round, with sweet speech, cheerful, true to
Order.
His fulgent flames run forth like vigorous horses; all creatures are affrighted when he blazes.
6 Beautiful and auspicious is thine aspect, O lovely Agni, terrible when spreading.
Thy splendours are not covered by the darkness: detraction leaves no stain upon thy body.
7 Naught hindered his production, Bounteous Giver: his Mother and his Sire were free to send him.
Then as Friend benevolent, refulgent, Agni shone forth in human habitations.

8 He, Agni, whom the twice-five sisters, dwelling together, in the homes of men engendered,
Bright like a spear's tooth, wakened in the morning, with powerful mouth and like an axe wellsharpened.
9 These thy Bay Coursers, Agni, dropping fatness, ruddy vigorous, speeding straightly forward,
And red steeds, wonderful, of mighty muscle, are to this service of the Gods invited:
10 These brightly-shining games of thine, O Agni, that move for ever restless, allsubduing,
Like falcons hasting eagerly to the quarry, roar loudly like the army of the Maruts.
11 To thee, O flaming God, hath prayer been offered. Let the priest laud thee: give to him who
worships.
Men have established Agni as Invoker, fain to adore the glory of the living.

## [04-007] HYMN VII. Agni.
1. HERE by ordainers was this God appointed first Invoker, best at worship, to be praised at rites:
Whom Apnavana, and the Bhrgus caused to shine bright-coloured in the wood, spreading from home
to home.
2 When shall thy glory as a God, Agni, be suddenly shown forth.
For mortal men have held thee fast, adorable in all their homes,
3 Seeing thee faithful to the Law, most sapient, like the starry heaven,
Illumining with cheerful ray each solemn rite in every house.
4 Vivasvan's envoy living men have taken as their ensign, swift,
The ruler over all mankind, moving like Bhrgu in each home.
5 Him the intelligent have they placed duly as Invoking Priest,
Welcome, with sanctifying flame, best worshipper, with sevenfold might;
6 In his Eternal Mothers, in the wood, concealed and unapproached,
Kept secret though his flames are bright seekingon all sides, quickly found.
7 That as food spreads forth in this earthly udder, Gods may rejoice them in the home of Order,
Great Agni, served with reverence and oblation, flies ever to the sacrifice, the Faithful.
8 Bird of each rite, skilled in an envoy's duties, knowing both worlds and that which lies between
them,
Thou goest from of old a willing Herald, knowing full well heaven's innermost recesses.
9 Bright God, thy path is black: light is before thee: thy moving splendour is the chief of wonders.

When she, yet unimpregnate, hath conceived thee, even when newly born thou art an envoy.
10 Yet newly born, his vigour is apparent when the wind blows upon his fiery splendour,
His sharpened tongue he layeth on the brushwood, and with his teeth e'en solid food consumeth.
11 When he hath borne off food with swift flame swiftly, strong Agni makes himself a speedy envoy,
Follows the rustling of the wind, consuming, and courser-like, speeds, drives the swift horse onward.

## [04-008] HYMN VIII. Agni.
1. YOUR envoy who possesses all, Immortal, bearer of your gifts,
Best worshipper, I woo with song.
2 He, Mighty, knows the gift of wealth, he knows the deep recess of heaven:
He shall bring hitherward the Gods.

3 He knows, a God himself, to guide Gods to the righteous in his home:
He gives e'en treasures that we love.
4 He is the Herald: well-informed, he doth his errand to and fro,
Knowing the deep recess of heaven.
5 May we be they who gratify Agni with sacrificial gifts,
Whocherish and enkindle him.
6 Illustrious for wealth are they, and hero deeds, victorious,
Who have served Agni reverently.
7 So unto us, day after day, may riches craved by many come,
And power and might spring up for us.
8 That holy Singer in his strength shoots forth his arrows swifter than
The swift shafts of the tribes of men.

## [04-009] HYMN IX. Agni.

1. AGNI, show favour: great art thou who to this pious man art come,
To seat thee on the sacred grass.
2 May he the Immortal, Helper, bard to be deceived among mankind,
Become the messenger of all.
3 Around the altar is he led, welcome Chief Priest at solemn rites,
Or as the Potar sits him down.
4 Agni in fire at sacrifice, and in the house as Lord thereof,
And as a Brahman takes his seat.
5 Thou comest as the guide of folk who celebrate a sacrifice,
And to oblations brought by men.
6 Thou servest as his messenger whose sacrifice thou lovest well,
To bear the mortal's gifts to heaven.
7 Accept our solemn rite; be pleased, Angiras, with our sacrifice:
Give ear and listen to our call.
8 May thine inviolable car, wherewith thou guardest those who give,
Come near to us from every side.

## [04-010] HYMN X. Agni.

I. This day with praises, Agni, we bring thee that which thou lovest.
Right judgment, like a horse, with our devotions.
2 For thou hast ever been the Car-driver, Agni, of noble
Strength, lofty sacrifice, and rightful judgment.
3 Through these our praises come thou to meet us, bright as the sunlight,
O Agni, well disposed, with all thine aspects.
4 Now may we serve thee singing these lauds this day to thee, Agni.

Loud as the voice of Heaven thy blasts are roaring.
5 just at this time of the day and the night thy look is the sweetest.
It shineth near us even as gold for glory.
6 Spotless thy body, brilliant as gold, like clarified butter:
This gleams like gold on thee, O Self. dependent.
7 All hate and mischief, yea, if committed, Agni, thou turnest,
Holy One, from the man who rightly worships.
8 Agni, with you Gods, prosperous be our friendships and kinships.
Be this our bond here by this place, thine al tar.

## [04-011] HYMN XI. Agni.

1. THY blessed majesty, victorious Agni, shines brightly in the neighbourhood of Surya.
Splendid to see, it shows even at nighttime, and food is fair to look on in thy beauty.
2 Agni, disclose his thought for him who singeth, the well, Strong God! while thou art praised with
fervour.

Vouchsafe to us that powerful hymn, O Mighty, which, Radiant One! with all the Gods thou lovest.
3 From thee, O Agni, springs poetic wisdom, from thee come thoughts and hymns of praise that
prosper;
From thee flows wealth, with heroes to adorn it, to the true-hearted man who gives oblation.
4 From thee the hero springs who wins the booty, bringer of help, mighty, of real courage.
From thee comes wealth, sent by the Gods, bliss-giving; Agni, from thee the fleet impetuous charger.
5 Immortal Agni, thee whose voice is pleasant, as first in rank, as God, religious mortals
Invite with hyrnns; thee who removest hatred, Friend of the Home, the household's Lord, unerring.
6 Far from us thou removest want and sorrow, far from us all ill-will when thou protectest.
Son of Strength, Agni, blest is he at evening, whom thou as God attendest for his welfare.

## [04-012] HYMN XII. Agni.

1. WHOSO enkindles thee, with lifted ladle, and thrice this day offiers thee food, O Agni,
May he excel, triumphant through thy splendours, wise through thy mental power, O Jatavedas.
2 Whoso with toil and trouble brings thee fuel, serving the majesty of mighty Agni,
He, kindling thee at evening and at morning, prospers, and comes to wealth, and slays his foemen.
3 Agni is Master of sublime dominion, Agni is Lord of strength and lofty riches.
Straightway the self-reliant God, Most Youthful, gives treasures to the mortal who adores him.
4 Most Youthful God, whatever sin, through folly, we here, as human beings, have committed,
In sight of Aditi make thou us sinless remit, entirely, Agni, our offences.
5 Even in the presence of great sin, O Agni, free us from prison of the Gods or mortals.
Never may we who are thy friends be injured: grant health and strength unto our seed and offspring.
6 Even as ye here, Gods Excellent and Holy, have loosed the cow that by the foot was tethered,
So also set us free from this affliction long let our life, O Agni, be extended.

## [04-013] HYMN XIII. Agni.

1. AGNI hath looked, benevolently-minded, on the wealth-giving spring of radiant Mornings.
Come, Asvins, to the dwelling of the pious: Surya the God is rising with his splendour.
2 Savitar, God, hath spread on high his lustre, waving his flag like a spoil-seeking hero.
Their stablished way go Varuna and Mitra, what time they make the Sun ascend the heaven.
3 Him whom they made to drive away the darkness, Lords of sure mansions, constant to their object,
Him who beholds the universe, the Sun-God, seven strong and youthful Coursers carry onward.
4 Spreading thy web with mightiest Steeds thou comest, rending apart, thou God, the black-hued
mantle.
The rays of Surya tremulously shining sink, like a hide, the darkness in the waters.
5 How is it that, unbound and not supported, he falleth not although directed downward?

By what self power moves he? Who liath seen it? He guards the vault of heaven, a close-set pillar.

## [04-014] HYMN XIV. Agni.

1. THE God hath looked, even Agni Jatavedas, to meet the Dawns refulgent in their glories.
Come on your chariot, ye who travel widely, come to this sacrifice of ours, Nasatyas.
2 Producing light for all the world of creatures, God Savitar hath raised aloft his banner.
Making his presence known by sunbeams, Surya hath filled the firmament and earth and heaven.
3 Red Dawn.is come, riding with brightness onward,
distinguished by her beams, gay-hued and
mighty.
Dawn on her nobly-harnessed car, the Goddess, awaking men to happiness, approacheth.
4 May those most powerful steeds and chariot bring you, O Asvins, hither at the break of morning.
Here for your draugllt of meath are Soma juices: at this our sacrifice rejoice, ye Mighty.
5 How is it that, unbound and unsupported, he falleth not although directed downward?
By what self-power moves he? Who hath seen it? He guards the vault of heaven, a close-set pillar?

## [04-015] HYMN XV. Agni.

1. AGNI the Herald, like a horse, is led forth at our solemn rite, God among Gods adorable.
2 Three times unto our solemn rite comes Agni like a charioteer, Bearing the viands to the Gods.
3 Round the oblations hath he paced, Agni the Wise, the Lord of Strength,
Giving the offerer precious boons.
4 He who is kindled eastward for Srnjaya, Devavata's son, Resplendent, tamer of the foe.
5 So mighty be the Agni whom the mortal hero shall command, With sharpened teeth and bountiful.
6 Day after day they dress him, as they clean a horse who wins the prize.
Dress the red Scion of the Sky.
7 When Sahadeva's princely son with two bay horses thought of me,
Summoned by him I drew not back.
8 And truly those two noble bays I straightway took when offered me,
From Sahadeva's princely son.
9 Long, O ye Asvins, may he live, your care, ye Gods, the princely son.
Of Sahadeva, Somaka.
10 Cause him the youthful prince, the son of Sahadeva, to enjoy Long life, O Asvins, O ye Gods.

## [04-016] HYMN XVI. Indra.

1. IMPETUOUS, true, let Maghavan come hither, and let his Tawny Coursers speed to reach us.
For him have we pressed juice exceeding potent: here, praised with song, let him effect his visit.
2 Unyoke, as at thy journey's end, O Hero, to gladden thee today at this libation.
Like Usana, the priest a laud shall utter, a hymn to thee, the Lord Divine, who markest.
3 When the Bull, quaffing, praises our Iibation, as a sage paying holy rites in secret,
Seven singers here from heaven hath he begotten, who e'en by day have wrought their works while
singing.

4 When heaven's fair light by hymns was made apparent (they made great splendour shine at break
of morning),
He with his succour, best of Heroes, scattered the blinding darkness so that men saw clearly.
5 Indra, Impetuous One, hath waxed immensely: he with his vastness hath filled earth and heaven.
E'en beyond this his majesty extendeth who hath exceeded all the worlds in greatness.
6 Sakra who knoweth well all human actions hath with his eager Friends let loose the waters.

They with their songs cleft e'en the mountain open and willingly disclosed the stall of cattle.
7 He smote away the floods' obstructer, Vrtra; Earth, conscious, lent her aid to speed thy thunder.
Thou sentest forth the waters of the ocean, as Lord through power and might, O daring Hero.
8 When, Much-invoked! the water's rock thou cleftest, Sarama showed herself and went before thee.
Hymned by Angirases, bursting the cowstalls, much strength thou foundest for us as our leader.
9 Come, Maghavan, Friend of Man, to aid the singer imploring thee in battle for the sunlight.
Speed him with help in his irypired invokings: down sink the sorcerer, the prayerless Dasyu.
10 Come to our home resolved to slay the Dasyu: Kutsa longed eagerly to win thy friendship.
Alike in form ye both sate in his dwelling the faithful Lady was in doubt between you.
11 Thou comest, fain to succour him, with Kutsa,-a goad that masters both the Wind-God's horses,
That, holding the brown steeds like spoil for capture, the sage may on the final day be present.
12 For Kutsa, with thy thousand, thou at day-break didst hurl down greedy Susna, foe of harvest.
Quickly with Kutsa's friend destroy the Dasyus, and roll the chariot-wheel of Sarya near us.
13 Thou to the son of Vidathin, Rjisvan, gavest up mighty Mrgaya and Pipru.
Thou smotest down the swarthy fifty thousand, and rentest forts as age consumes a garment.
14 What time thou settest near the Sun thy body, thy form, Immortal One, is seen expanding:
Thou a wild elephant with might invested. like a dread lion as thou wieldest weapons.
15 Wishes for wealth have gone to Indra, longing for him in war for light and at libation,
Eager for glory, labouring with praisesongs: he is like home, like sweet and fair nutrition.
16 Call we for you that Indra, prompt to listen, him who hath done so much for men's advantage;
Who, Lord of envied bounty, to a singer like me brings quickly booty worth the capture.
17 When the sharp-pointed arrow, O thou Hero, flieth mid any conflict of the people,
When, Faithful One, the dread encounter cometh, then be thou the Protector of my body.
18 Further the holy thoughts of Vamadeva be thou a guileless Friend in fight for booty.
We come to thee whose providence protects us: wide be thy sway for ever for thy singer.
19 O Indra, with these men who love thee truly, free givers, Maghavan, in every battle,
May we rejoice through many autumns, quelling our foes, as days subdue the nights with splendour.

20 Now, as the Bhrgus wrought a car, for Indra the Strong, the Mighty, we our prayer have fashioned,
That he may, ne'er withdraw from us his friendship, but be our bodies' guard and strong defender.
21 Now, Indra! lauded, glorified with praises, let power swell. high like rivers for the singer.
For thee a new hymn, Lord of Bays, is fashioned. May we, car-borne, through song be victors ever.

## [04-017] HYMN XVII. Indra.

1. GREAT art thou, Indra; yea, the earth, with gladness, and heaven confess to thee thine high dominion.
Thou in thy vigour having slaughtered Vrtra didst free the floods arrested by the Dragon.
2 Heaven trembled at the birth of thine effulgence; Earth trembled at the fear of thy displeasure.
The stedfast mountains shook in agitation . the waters flowed, and desert spots were flooded.
3 Hurling his bolt with might he cleft the mountain, while, putting forth his strength, he showed his vigour.
He slaughtered Vrtra with his bolt, exulting, and, their lord slain, forth flowed the waters swiftly.
4 Thy Father Dyaus esteemed himself a hero: most noble was the work of Indra's Maker,
His who begat the strong bolt's Lord who roareth, immovable like earth from her foundation.
5 He who alone o'erthrows the world of creatures, Indra the peoples' King, invoked of many-
Verily all rejoice in him, extolling the boons which Maghavan the God hath sent them.
6 All Soma juices are his own for ever, most gladdening draughts are ever his, the Mighty,
Thou ever wast the Treasure-Lord of treasures: Indra, thou lettest all folk share thy bounty.
7 Moreover, when thou first wast born, O Indra, thou struckest terror into all the people.
Thou, Maghavan, rentest with thy bolt the Dragon who lay against the waterfloods of heaven.
8 The ever-slaying, bold and furious Indra, the bright bolt's Lord, infinite, strong and mighty,
Who slayeth Vrtra and acquireth booty, giver of blessings, Maghavan the bounteous:
9 Alone renowned as Maghavan in battles, he frighteneth away assembled armies.
He bringeth us the booty that he winneth may we, well-loved, continue in his friendship.
10 Renowned is he when conquering and when slaying: 'tis he who winneth cattle in the combat.
When Indra hardeneth his indignation all that is fixed and all that moveth fear him.
11 Indra hath won all kine, all gold, all horses,-Maghavan, he who breaketh forts in pieces;
Most manly with these men of his who help him, dealing out wealth and gathering the treasure.
12 What is the care of Indra for his Mother, what cares he for the Father who begat him?
His care is that which speeds his might in conflicts, like wind borne onward by the clouds that thunder.
13 Maghavan makes the settled man unsettled: he scatters dust that he hath swept together,
Breaking in pieces like Heaven armed with lightning: Maghavan shall enrich the man who lauds h;m.
14 He urged the chariot-wheel of Surya forward: Etasa, speeding on his way, he rested.
Him the black undulating cloud bedeweth, in this mid-air's depth, at the base of darkness,

15 As in the night the sacrificing priest.
16 Eager for booty, craving strength and horses, we-singers stir Indra, the strong, for friendship,
Who gives the wives we seek, whose succour fails not, to hasten, like a pitcher to the fountain.
17 Be thou our guardian, show thyself our kinsman, watching and blessing those who pour the Soma;
As Friend, as Sire, most fatherly of fathers giving the suppliant vital strength and freedom.
18 Be helping Friend of those who seek thy friendship . give life, when lauded, Indra, to the singer.
For, Indra, we the priests have paid thee worship, exalting thee with these our sacrifices.
19 Alone, when Indra Maghavan is lauded, he slayeth many ne'er-resisted Vrtras.
Him in whose keeping is the well-loved singer never do Gods or mortals stay or hinder.
20 E'en so let Maghavan, the loud-voiced Indra, give us true blessings, foeless, men's upholder.
King of all creatures, give us glory amply, exalted glory due to him who lauds thee.
21 Now, Indra! lauded, glorified with praises, let power swell high like rivers for the singer.
For thee a new hymn, Lord of Bays! is fashioned. May we, car-borne, through song be victors ever.

## [04-018] HYMN XVIII. Indra and Others.

1. THIS is the ancient and accepted pathway by which all Gods have come into existence.
Hereby could one be born though waxen mighty. Let him not, otherwise, destroy his Mother.
2 Not this way go I forth: hard is the passage. Forth from the side obliquely will I issue.
Much that is yet undone must I accomplish; one must I combat and the other question.
3 He bent his eye upon the dying Mother: My word I now withdraw. That way I follow.
In Tvastar's dwelling India drank the Soma, a hundredworth of juice pressed from the mortar.
4 What strange act shall he do, he whom his Mother bore for a thousand months and many autumns?
No peer hath he among those born already, nor among those who shall be born hereafter.
5 Deeming him a reproach, his mother hid him, Indra, endowed with all heroic valour.
Then up he sprang himself, assumed his vesture, and filled, as soon as born, the earth and heaven.
6 With lively motion onward flow these waters, the Holy Ones, shouting, as 'twere, together.
Ask them to. tell thee what the floods are saying, what girdling rock the waters burst asunder.
7 Are they addressing him with words of welcome? Will the floods take on them the shame of Indra?
With his great thunderbolt my Son hath slaughtered Vrtra, and set these rivers free to wander.
8 I cast thee from me, mine,-thy youthful mother: thee, mine own offspring, Kusava hath swallowed.
To him, mine infant, were the waters gracious. Indra, my Son, rose up in conquering vigour.
9 Thou art mine own, O Maghavan, whom Vyamsa struck to the ground and smote thy jaws in pieces.
But, smitten through, the mastery thou wonnest, and with thy bolt the Dasa's head thou crushedst.
10 The Heifer hath brought forth the Strong, the Mighty, the unconquerable Bull, the furious Indra.
The Mother left her unlicked Calf to wander, seeking himself, the path that he would follow.

11 Then to her mighty Child the Mother turned her, saying, My son, these Deities forsake thee.
Then Indra said, about to slaughter Vrtra, O my friend Vrtra, stride full boldly forward.

12 Who was he then who made thy Mother widow? Who sought to stay thee lying still or moving?
What God, when by the foot thy Sire thou tookest and slewest, was at hand to give thee comfort?

13 In deep distress I cooked a dog's intestines. Among the Gods I found not one to comfort.
My consort I beheld in degradation. The Falcon then brought me the pleasant Soma.

## [04-019] HYMN XIX. Indra.

1. THEE, verily, O Thunder-wielding Indra, all the Gods here, the Helpers swift to listen,
And both the worlds elected, thee the Mighty, High, waxen strong, alone to slaughter Vrtra.

2 The Gods, as worn witheld, relaxed their efforts: thou, Indra, born of truth, wast Sovran Ruler.
Thou slewest Ahi who besieged the waters, and duggest out their all-supporting channels.

3 The insatiate one, extended, hard to waken, who slumbered in perpetual sleep, O Indra,-
The Dragon stretched against the seven prone rivers, where no joint was, thou rentest with thy thunder.

4 Indra with might shook earth and her foundation as the wind stirs the water with its fury.
Striving, with strength he burst the firm asunder, and tore away the summits of the mountains.

5 They ran to thee as mothers to their offspring: the clouds, like chariots, hastened forth together.
Thou didst refresh the streams and force the billows: thou, Indra, settest free obstructed rivers.

6 Thou for the sake of Vayya and Turviti didst stay the great stream, flowing, allsustaining:
Yea, at their prayer didst check the rushing river and make the floods easy to cross, O Indra.

7 He let the young Maids skilled in Law, unwedded, like fountains, bubbling, flow forth streaming onward.
He inundated thirsty plains and deserts, and milked the dry Cows of the mighty master.

8 Through many a morn and many a lovely autumn, having slain Vrtra, lie set free the rivers.
Indra hath set at liberty to wander on earth the streams encompassed pressed together.

9 Lord of Bay Steeds, thou broughtest from the ant-hill the unwedded damsel's son whom ants were eating.
The blind saw clearly, as he grasped the serpent, rose, brake the jar: hisjoints again united.

10 To the wise man, O Sage and Sovran Ruler, the man who knoweth all thine ancient exploits,
Hath told these deeds of might as thou hast wrought them, great acts, spontaneous, and to man's advantage.

11 Now, Indra! lauded, glorified with praises, let powers swell high, like rivers, for the singer.
For thee a new hymn, Lord of Bays! is fashioned. May we, car-borne, through song be victors ever.

## [04-020] HYMN XX. Indra.

1. FROM near or far away may mighty Indra giver of succour, come for our protection
Lord of men, armed with thunder, with the Strongest, slaying his foes in conflict, in the battles.

2 May Indra come to us with Tawny Coursers, inclined to us, to favour and enrich us.

May Maghavan, loud-voiced and wielding thunder, stand by us at this sacrifice, in combat.

3 Thou, honouring this our sacrifice, O Indra, shalt give us strength and fill us full of courage.
To win the booty, Thunder-armed! like hunters may we with thee subdue in fight our foemen.

4 Loving us well, benevolent, close beside us, drink, Godlike Indra, of the wellpressed Soma.
Drink of the meath we offer, and delight thee with food that cometh from the mountain ridges.

5 Him who is sung aloud by recent sages, like a ripe-fruited tree, a scythe-armed victor,-
I, like a bridegroom thinking of his consort, call hither Indra, him invoked of many;

6 Him who in native strength is like a mountain, the lofty Indra born or old for conquest,
Terrific wielder of the ancient thunder. filled full with splendour as a jar with water.

7 Whom from of old there is not one to hinder, none to curtail the riches of his bounty.
Pouring forth freely, O thou Strong and Mighty, vouchsafe us riches, God invoked of many!

8 Of wealth and homes of men thou art the ruler, and opener of the stable of the cattle.
Helper of men, winner of spoil in combats, thou leadest to an ample heap of riches.

9 By what great might is he renowned as strongest, wherewith the Lofty One stirs up wild battles?
Best soother of the worshipper's great sorrow, he gives possessions to the man who lauds him.

10 Slay us not; bring, bestow onus the ample gift which thou hast to give to him who offers.
At this new gift, with this laud sung before thee, extolling thee, we, Indra, will declare it.

11 Now, Indra! lauded, glorified with praises, let power swell high, like rivers, for the singer.
A new hymn, Lord of Bays! for thee is fashioned. May we, car-born, through song be victors ever.

## [04-021] HYMN XXI. Indra.

1. MAY Indra come to us for our protection; here be the Hero, praised, our feast-companion.
May he whose powers are many, waxen mighty, cherish, like Dyaus, his own supreme dominion.

2 Here magnify his great heroic exploits, most glorious One, enriching men with bounties,
Whose will is like a Sovran in assembly, who rules the people, Conqueror, all-surpassing.

3 Hither let Indra come from earth or heaven, hither with speech from firmament or ocean;
With Maruts, from the realm of light to aid us, or from a distance, from the seat of Order.

4 That Indra will we laud in our assemblies, him who is Lord of great and lasting riches,
Victor with Vayu where the herds are gathered, who leads with boldness on to higher fortune.

5 May the Priest, Lord of many blessings, striving,-who fixing reverence on reverence, giving
Vent to his voice, inciteth men to worshipwith lauds bring Indra hither to our dwellings.

6 When sitting pondering in deep devotion in Ausija's abode they ply the press-stone,
May he whose wrath is fierce, the mighty bearer, come as the house-lord's priest within our chambers.

7 Surely the power of Bharvara the mighty for ever helpeth to support the singer;

That which in Ausija's abode lies hidden, to come forth for delight and for devotion.

8 When he unbars the spaces of the mountains, and quickens with his floods the water-torrents,
He finds in lair the buffalo and wild-ox when the wise lead him on to vigorous exploit.

9 Auspicious are thy hands, thine arms wellfashioned which proffer bounty, Indra, to thy praiser.
What sloth is this? Why dost thou not rejoice thee? Why dost thou not delight thyself with giving?

10 So Indra is the truthful Lord of treasure. Freedom he gave to man by slaying Vrtra.
Much-lauded! help us with thy power to riches: may I be sharer of thy Godlike favour.

11 Now, Indra! lauded, glorified with praises, let power swell high, like rivers, for,the singer.
For thee a new hymn, Lord of Bays! is fashioned. May we, care-borne, through song be victqrs ever.

## [04-022] HYMN XXII. Indra.

1. THAT gift of ours which Indra loves and welcomes, even that he makes for us, the Great and Strong One.
He who comes wielding in his might the thunder, Maghavan, gives prayer, praise, and laud, and
Soma.

2 Bull, hurler of the four-edged rain-producer with both his arms, strong, mighty, most heroic;
Wearing as wool Parusni for adornment, whose joints for sake of friendship he hath covered.

3 God who of all the Gods was born divinest, endowed with ample strength and mighty powers,
And bearing in his arrns the yearning thunder, with violent rush caused heaven and earth to tremble.

4 Before the High God, at his birth, heaven trembled, earth, many floods and all the precipices.
The Strong One bringeth nigh the Bull's two Parents: loud sing the winds, like men, in air's midregion.

5 These are thy great deeds, Indra, thine, the Mighty, deeds to be told aloud at all libations,
That thou, O Hero, bold and boldly daring, didst with thy bolt, by strength, destroy the Dragon.

6 True are all these thy deeds, O Most Heroic. The Milch-kine issued from the streaming udder.
In fear of thee, O thou of manly spirit, the rivers swiftly set themselves in motion.

7 With joy, O Indra, Lord of Tawny Coursers, the Sisters then, these Goddesses, extolled thee,
When thou didst give the prisoned ones their freedom to wander at their will in long succession.

8 Pressed is the gladdening stalk as 'twere a river: so let the rite, the toiler's power, attract thee
To us-ward, of the Bright One, as thc courser strains his. exceedingly strong leather bridle.

9 Ever by us perform thy most heroic, thine highest, best victorious deeds, O Victor.
For us make Vrtras easy to be conquered: destroy the weapon of our mortal foeman.

10 Graciously listen to our prayer, O Indra, and strength of varied sort bestow thou on us.
Send to us all intelligence arid wisdom O Maghavan, be he who gives us cattle.

11 Now, Indra! lauded, glorified with praises, let wealth swell hiah like rivers to the singer.
For thee a new hymn, Lord of Bays, is fashioned. May we, care-borne, through song be victqrs ever.

## [04-023] HYMN XXIII. Indra.

1. How, what priest's sacrifice hath he made mighty, rejoicing in the Soma and its fountain?
Delighting in juice, eagerly drinking, the Lofty One hath waxed for splendid riches.

2 What hero hath been made his feast-companion? Who hath been partner in his loving-kindness?
What know we of his wondrous acts? How often comes he to aid and speed the pious toiler?

3 How heareth Indra offered invocation? How, hearing, marketh he the invoker's wishes?
What are his ancient acts of bounty? Wherefore call they him One who filleth full the singer?

4 How doth the priest who laboureth, ever longing, win for himself the wealth which he possesseth?
May he, the God, mark well my truthful praises, having received the homage which he loveth.

5 How, and what bond of friendship with a mortal hath the God chosen as this morn is breaking?
How, and what love hath he for those who love him, who have entwined in him their firm affection?

6 Is then thy friendship with thy friends most mighty? Thy brotherhood with us, -when may we tell it?
The streams of milk move, as most wondrous sunlight, the beauty of the Lovely One for glory.

7 About to stay the Indra-less destructive spirit he sharpens his keen arms to strike her.
Whereby the Strong, although our debts' exactor, drives in the distant mornings that we know not.

8 Eternal Law hath varied food that strengthens; thought of eternal Law, removes transgressions.
The praise-hymn of eternal Law, arousing, glowing, hath oped the deaf ears of the living.

9 Firm-seated are eternal Law's foundations in its fair form are many splendid beauties.
By holy Law long lasting food they bring us; by holy Law have cows come to our worship.

10 Fixing eternal Law he, too, upholds it swift moves the might of Law and wins the booty.
To Law belong the vast deep Earth and Heaven: Milch-kine supreme, to Law their milk they render.

11 Now, Indra! lauded,- glorified with praises, let power swell high like rivers to the singer.
For thee a new hymn, Lord of Bays, is fashioned. May we, car-borne, through song be victors ever.

## [04-024] HYMN XXIV. Indra.

1. WHAT worthy praise will bring before us Indra, the Son of Strength, that he may grant us riches;
For he the Hero, gives the singer treasures: he is the Lord who sends us gifts, ye people.

2 To be invoked and hymned in fight with Vrtra, that well-praised Indra gives us real bounties.
That Maghavan brings comfort in the foray to the religious man who pours libations.

3 Him, verily, the men invoke in combat; risking their lives they make him their protector,
When heroes, foe to foe, give up their bodies, fighting, each side, for children and their offspring.

4 Strong God! the folk at need put forth their vigour, striving together in the whirl of battle.
When warrior bands encounter one another some in the grapple quit themselves like Indra.

5 Hence many a one worships the might of Indra: hence let the brew succeed the meal-oblation.
Hence let the Soma banish those who pour not: even hence I joy to pay the Strong One worship.

6 Indra gives comfort to the man who truly presses, for him who longs fot it, the Soma,
Not disaffected, with devoted spirit this man he takes to be his friend in battles.

7 He who this day for Indra presses Soma, prepares the brew and fries the grains of barley-
Loving the hymns of that devoted servant, to him may Indra give heroic vigour.

8 When the impetuous chief hath sought the confliet, and the lord looked upon the long-drawn battle,
The matron calls to the Strong God whom pressers of Soma have encouraged int the dwelling.

9 He bid a small price for a thing of value: I was content, returning, still unpurchased.
He heightened not his insufficient offer. Simple and clever, both milk out the udder.

10 Who for ten milch-kine purchaseth from rne this Indra who is mine?
When he hath slain the Vrtras let the buyer give him back to me.

11 Now, Indra! lauded, glorified with praises, let wealth swell high like rivers for the singer.
For thee a new hymn, Lord of Bays, is fashioned. May we, car-borne, through song be victors ever.

## [04-025] HYMN XXV. Indra.

1. WHAT friend of man, God-loving, hath delighted, yearning therefor, this day in Indra's friendship?
Who with enkindled flame and flowing Soma laudeth him for his great protecting favour?

2 Who hath with prayer bowed to the Soma-lover? What pious man endues the beams of morning?
Who seeks bond, fritridship, brotherhood with Indra? Who hath recourse unto the Sage for succour?

3 Who claims to-day the Deities' protection, asks Aditi for light, or the Adityas?
Of whose pressed stalk of Soma drink the Asvins, Indra, and Agni, well-inclined in spirit?

4 To him shall Agni Bharata give shelter: long shall he look upon the Sun up-rising,
Who sayeth, Let us press the juice for Indra, man's Friend, the Hero manliest of heroes.

5 Him neither few men overcome, nor many to him shall Aditi give spacious shelter.
Dear is the pious, the devout, to Indra dear is the zealous, dear the Soma-bringer.

6 This Hero curbs the mighty for the zealous: the presser's brew Indra possesses solely:
No brother, kin, or friend to him who pours not, destroyer of the dumb who would resist him.

7 Not with the wealthy churl who pours no Soma doth Indra, Soma-drinker, bind alliance,
He draws away his wealth and slays him naked, own Friend to him who offers, for oblation.

8 Highest and lowest, men who stand between diem, going, returning, dwelling in contentment,
Those who show forth their strength when urged to battle-these are the men who call for aid on Indra.

## [04-026] HYMN XXVI. Indra.

1. I WAS aforetime Manu, I was Surya: I am the sage Kaksivan, holy singer.
Kutsa the son of Arjuni I master. I am the sapient Usana behold me.

2 I have bestowed the earth upon the Arya, and rain upon the man who brings oblation.

I guided forth the loudly-roaring waters, and the Gods moved according to my pleasure.

3 In the wild joy of Soma I demolished Sambara's forts, ninety-and-nine, together;
And, utterly, the hundredth habitation, when helping Divodasa Atithigva.

4 Before all birds be ranked this Bird, O Maruts; supreme of falcons be this fleet-winged Falcon,
Because, strong- pinioned, with no car to bear him, he brought to Manu the Godloved oblation.

5 When the Bird brought it, hence in rapid motion sent on the wide path fleet as thought he hurried.
Swift he returned with sweetness of the Soma, and hence the Falcon hath acquired his glory.

6 Bearing the stalk, the Falcon speeding onward, Bird bringing from afar the draught that gladdens,
Friend of the Gods, brought, grasping fast, the Soma which be bad taken from yon loftiest heaven.

7 The Falcon took and brought the Soma, bearing thousand libations with him, yea, ten thousand.
The Bold One left Malignities behind him, wise, in wild joy of Soma, left the foolish.

## [04-027] HYMN XXVII. The Falcon.

1. I, As I lay within the womb, considered all generations of these Gods in order.
A hundred iron fortresses confined me but forth I flew with rapid speed a Falcon.

2 Not at his own free pleasure did he bear me: he conquered with his strength and manly courage.
Straightway the Bold One left the fiends behind him and passed the winds as he grew yet more mighty.

3 When with loud cry from heaven down sped the Falcon, thence hasting like the wind he bore the Bold One.
Then, wildly raging in his mind, the archer Krsanu aimed and loosed the string to strike him.

4 The Falcon bore him from heaven's lofty summit as the swift car of Indra's Friend bore Bhujyu.
Then downward bither fell a flying feather of the Bird hasting forward in his journey.

5 And now let Maghavan accept the beaker, white, filled with milk, filled with the shining liquid;
The best of sweet meath which the priests have offered: that Indra to his joy may drink, the Hero,
that he may take and drink it to his rapture.

## [04-028] HYMN XXVIII. Indra-Soma.

1. ALLIED with thee, in this thy friendship, Soma, Indra for man made waters flow together,
Slew Ahi, and sent forth the Seven Rivers, and opened as it were obstructed fountains.

2 Indu, with thee for his confederate, Indra swiftly with might pressed down the wheel of Surya.
What rolled, all life's support, on heaven's high summit was separated from the great oppressor.

3 Indra smote down, Agni consumed, O Indu, the Dasyus ere the noontide in the conflict.
Of those who gladly sought a hard-won dwelling he cast down many a thousand with his arrow.

4 Lower than all besides hast thou, O Indra, cast down the Dasyus, abject tribes of Dasas.
Ye drave away, ye put to death the foemen, and took great vengeance with your murdering weapons.

5 So, of a truth, Indra and Soma, Heroes, ye burst the stable of the kine and horses,

The stable which the bar or stone obstructed; and piercing through set free the habitations.

## [04-029] HYMN XXIX. Indra.

1. COME, lauded, unto us with powers and succours, O Indra, with thy Tawny Steeds; exulting,
Past even the foeman's manifold libations, glorified with our hymns, true Wealth-bestower.
2 Man's Friend, to this our sacrifice he cometh marking how he is called by Soma-pressers.
Fearless, and conscious that his Steeds are noble, he joyeth with the Soma-pouring heroes.
3 Make his cars hear, that he may show his vigour and may be joyful in the way he loveth.
May mighty Indra pouring forth in bounty bestow on us good roads and perfect safety;
4 He who with succour comes to his implorer, the singer here who with his song invites him;
He who himself sets to the pole swift Coursers, he who hath hundreds, thousands, Thunder-wielder.
5 O Indra Maghavan, by thee protected may we be thine, princes and priests and singers,
Sharing the riches sent from lofty heaven which yields much food, and all desire its bounty.

## [04-030] HYMN XXX. Indra.

1. O INDRA, Vrtra-slayer, none is better, mightier than thou:
Verily there is none like thee.
2 Like chariot-wheels these people all together follow after thee:
Thou ever art renowned as Great.
3 Not even all the gathered Gods conquered thee, Indra, in the war,
When thou didst lengthen days by night.
4 When for the sake of those oppressed, and Kutsa as he battled,
Thou stolest away the Sun's car-wheel.
5 When, fighting singly, Indra. thou o'ercamest all the furious Gods, thou slewest those who strove
with thee.
6 When also for a mortal man, Indra, thou speddest forth the Sun,
And holpest Etasa with might.
7 What? Vrtra-slayer, art not thou, Maghavan, fiercest in thy wrath?
So hast thou quelled the demon too.
8 And this heroic deed of might thou, Indra, also hast achieved,
That thou didst smite to death the Dame, Heaven's Daughter, meditating ill.
9 Thou, Indra, Mighty One, didst crush Usas, though Daughter of the Sky.
When lifting up herself in pride.
10 Then from her chariot Usas fled, affrighted, from her ruined car.
When the strong God had shattered it.
11 So there this car of Usas lay, broken to pieces, in Vipas,
And she herself fled far away.
12 Thou, Indra, didst. with magic power resist the overflowing stream
Who spread her waters o'er the land.
13 Valiantly didst thou seize and take the store which Susna had amassed,
When thou didst crush his fortresses.
14 Thou, Indra, also smotest down Kulitara's son Sambara,
The Dasa, from the lofty hill.
15 Of Dasa Varcin's thou didst slay the hundred thousand and the five,
Crushed like the fellies, of a car.

16 So Indra, Lord of Heroes, Powers, caused the unwedded damsel's son,
The castaway, to share the lauds.
17 So sapient Indra, Lord of Might, brought Turvaga and Yadu, those
Who feared the flood, in safel o'er.
18 Arpa and Citraratha, both Aryas, thou, Indra, slewest swift,
On yonder side of Sarayu,
19 Thou, Vrtra-slayer, didst conduct those two forlorn, the blind, the lame.
None may attain this bliss of thine.
20 For Divodasa, him who brought oblationt, 1ndra overthrew
A hundred fortresses of stone.
21 The thirty thousand Disas he with magic power and weapons sent
To slumber, for Dabhiti's sake.
22 As such, O Vrtra-slayer, thou art general Lord of kine for all,
Thou Shaker of all things that be.
23 Indra, whatever deed of might thou hast this day to execute,
None be there now to hinder it.
24 O Watchful One, may Aryaman the God give thee all goodly things.
May Risan, Bhaga, and the God Karulati give all things fair.

## [04-031] HYMN XXXI. Indra.

1. WITH what help will he come to us, wonderful, ever-waxing Friend;
With what most mighty company?
2 What genuine and most liberal draught will spirit thee with juice to burst
Open e'en strongly-guarded wealth?
3 Do thou who art Protector of us thy friends who praise thee
With hundred aids approach us.
4 Like as a courser's circling wheel, so turn thee hitherward to us,
Attracted by the hymns of men.
5 Thou seekest as it were thine own stations with swift descent of powers:
I share thee even with the Sun.
6 What time thy courage and his wheels together, Indra, run their course
With thee and with the Sun alike,
7 So even, Lord of Power and Might, the people call thee Maghavan,
Giver, who pauses not to think.
8 And verily to him who toils and presses Soma juice for thee
Thou quickly givest ample wealth.
9 No, not a hundred hinderers can check thy gracious bounty's flow,
Nor thy great deeds when thou wilt act.
10 May thine assistance keep us safe, thy hundred and thy thousand aids:
May all thy favours strengthen us.
11 Do thou elect us this place for friendship and prosperity,
And great celestial opulence.
12 Favour us, Indra, evermore with overflowing store of wealth:
With all thy succours aid thou us.
13 With new protections, Indra, like an archer, open thou forus
The stables that are filled with kine.
14 Our chariot, Indra, boldly moves endued with splendour, ne'er repulsed,
Winning for us both kine andsteeds.
15 O Surya, make our fame to be most excellent among the Gods,
Most lofty as the heaven on high.

## [04-032] HYMN XXXII. Indra.

1. O THOU who slewest Vrtra, come, O Indra, hither to our side,
Mighty One with thy mighty aids.

2 Swift and impetuous art thou, wondrous amid the well-dressed folk:
Thou doest marvels for our help.
3 Even with the weak thou smitest down him
who is stronger, with thy strength
The mighty, with the Friends thou hast.
4 O Indra, we are close to thee; to thee we sing aloud our songs:
Help hnd defend us, even us.
5 As such, O Caster of the Stone, come with thy succours wonderful,
Blameless, and irresistible.
6 May we be friends of one like thee, O Indra, with the wealth of kine,
Comrades for lively energy.
7 For thou, O Indra, art alone the Lord of strength that comes from kine
So grant thou us abundant food.
8 They turn thee not another way, when, lauded, Lover of the Song,
Thou wilt give wealth to those who praise.
9 The Gotamas have sung their song of praise to thee that thou mayst give,
Indra, for lively energy.
10 We will declare thy hero deeds, what Disa forts thou brakest down,
Attacking them in rapturous joy.
11 The sages sing those manly deeds which, Indra, Lover of the Song,
Thou wrougbtest when the Soma flowed.
12 Indra, the Gotamas who bring thee praises have grown strong by thee.
Give them renown with hero sons.
13 For, Indra, verily thou art the general treasure even of all .
Thee, therefore, do we invocate.
14 Excellent Indra, turn to us: glad thee among us with the juice
Of Somas, Soma-drinker thou.
15 May praise from us who think Qn thee, O Indra, bring thee near to us.
Turn thy two Bay Steeds hitherward.
16 Eat of our sacrificial cake: rejoice thee in the songs we sing.
Even as a lover in his bride.
17 To India for a thousand steeds well-trained and fleet of foot we pray,
And hundred jars of Soma juice.
18 We make a hundred of thy kine, yea, and a thousand, hasten nigh:
So let thy bounty come to us.
19 We have obtained, a gift from thee, ten water-ewers wrought of gold:
Thou, Vrtra-slayer, givest much.
20 A bounteous Giver, give us much, bring much and not a trifling gift:
Much, Indra, wilt thou fain bestow.
21 O Vrtra-slayer, thou art famed in many a place as bountiful
Hero, thy bounty let us share.
22 I praise thy pair of Tawny Steeds, wise Son of him who giveth kine
Terrify not the cows with these.
23 Like two slight images of girls, unrobed, upon a new-wrought post,
So shine the Bay Steeds in their course.
24 For me the Bays are ready when I start, or start not, with the dawn, Innocuous in the ways they take.

## [04-033] HYMN XXXIII. Rbhus.

I. I SEND my voice as herald to the Rbhus; I crave the white cow for the overspreading.

Wind-sped, the Skillful Ones in rapid motion have in an instant compassed round the heaven.
2 What time the Rbus had with care and marvels done proper service to assist their Parents,
They won the friendship of the Gods; the Sages carried away the fruit of their devotion.
3 May they who made their Parents, who were lying like posts that moulder, young again for ever,-
May Vaja, Vibhvan, Rbhu, joined with Indra , protect our sacrifice, the Soma-lovers.
4 As for a year the Rbhus kept the Milch-cow, throughout a year fashioned and formed her body,
And through a year's space still sustained her brightness, through these their labours they were
made immortal.
5 Two beakers let us make,- thus said the eldest. Lct us make three,- this was the younger's
sentence.
Four beakers let us make,- thus spoke the youngest. Tvastar approved this rede of yours, O Rbhus.
6 The men spake truth and even so they acted: this Godlike way of theirs the Rbhus followed.
And Tvastar, when he looked on the four beakers resplendent as the day, was moved with envy.
7 When for twelve days the Rbhus joyed reposing as guests of him who never may be hidden,
lley made fair fertile fields, they brought the rivers. Plants spread o'er deserts, waters filled the
hollows.
8 May they who formed the swift car, bearing Heroes, and the Cow omniform and all-impelling,
Even may they form wealth for us,-the Rbhus, dexterous-handed, deft in work and gracious.
9 So in their work the Gods had satisfaction, pondering it with thought and mental insight.
The Gods' expert artificer was Vaja, Indra's Rbhuksan, Varuna's was Vibhvan.
10 They whol made glad with sacrifice and praises, wrought the two Bays, his docile Steeds, for
Indra,-
Rbhus, as those who wish a friend to prosper, bestow upon us gear and growth of riches.
11 This day have they set gladdening drink before you. Not without toil are Gods inclined to
friendship.
Therefore do ye who are so great, O Rbhus, vouchsafe us treasures at this third libation.

## [04-034] HYMN XXXIV. Rbhus.

1. To this our sacrifice come Rbhu, Vibhvan, Vaja, and Indra with the gift of riches,
Because this day hath Dhisana the Goddess set drink for you: the gladdening draughts have reached
you.
2 Knowing your birth and rich in gathered treasure, Rbhus, rejoice together with the Rtus.
The gladdening draughts and wisdom have approached you: send ye us riches with good store of
heroes.
3 For you was made this sacrifice, O Rbhus, which ye, like men, won for yourselves aforetime.
To you come all who find in you their pleasure: ye all were-even the two elder-Vajas.
4 Now for the mortal worshipper, O Heroes, for him who served you, was the gift of riches.
Drink, Vajas, Rbhus! unto you is offered, to gladden you, the third and great libation.

5 Come to us, Heroes, Vajas and Rbhuksans, glorified for the sake of mighty treasure.
These draughts approach you as the day is closing, as cows, whose calves are newly-born, their
stable.
6 Come to this sacrifice of ours, ye Children of Strength, invoked with humble adoration.
Drink of this meath, Wealth-givers, joined with Indra with whom ye are in full accord, ye Princes.
7 Close knit with Varuna drink the Soma, Indra; close-knit, ilymn-lover! with the Maruts drink it:
Close-knit with drinkers first, who drink in season; close-knit with heavenly Dames who give us
treasures.
8 Rejoice in full accord with the Adityas, in concord with the Parvatas, O Rbhus;
In full accord with Savitar, Divine One; in full accord with floods that pour forth riches.
9 Rbhus, who helped their Parents and the Asvins, who formed the Milch-cow and the pair of horses,
Made armour, set the heaven and earth asunder,-far- reaching Heroes, they have made good
offspring.
10 Ye who have wealth in cattle and in booty, in heroes, in rich sustenance and treasure,
Such, O ye Rbhus, first to drink, rejoicing, give unto us and those who laud our present.
11 Ye were not far: we have not left you thirsting, blameless in this our sacrifice, O Rbhus.
Rejoice you with the Maruts and with Indra, with the Kings, Gods! that ye may give us riches.

## [04-035] HYMN XXXV. Rbhus.

1. Come hither, O ye Sons of Strength, ye Rbhus; stay not afar, ye Children of Sudhanvan.
At this libation is your gift of treasure. Let gladdening draughts approach you after Indra's.
2 Hither is come the Rbhus' gift of riches; here was the drinking of the well-pressed Soma,
Since by dexterity and skill as craftsmen ye made the single chalice to be fourfold
3 Ye made fourfold the chalice that wag single: ye spake these words and said, O Friend, assist us;
Then, Vajas! gained the path of life eternal, deft-handed Rbhus, to the Gods' assembly.
4 Out of what substance was that chalice fashioned which ye made fourfold by your art and wisdom?
Now for the gladdening draught press out the liquor, and drink, O Rbhus, of die meath of Soma.
5 Ye with your cunning made your Parents youthful; the cup, for Gods to drink, ye formed with
cunning;
With cunning, Rbhus, rich in treasure, fashioned the two swift Tawny Steeds who carry Indra.
6 Whoso pours out for you, when days are closing, the sharp libation for your joy, O Vajas,
For him, O mighty Rbhus, ye, rejoicing, have fashioned wealth with plenteous store of heroes.
7 Lord of Bay Steeds, at dawn thejuice thou drankest: thine, only thine, is the noonday libation.
Now drink thou with the wealth-bestowing Rbhus, whom for their skill thou madest friends, O Indra.
8 Ye, whom your artist skill hath raised to Godhead have set you down above in heaven like falcons.
So give us riches, Children of Sudhanvan, O Sons of Strength; ye have become immortal.

9 The third libation, that bestoweth treasure, which ye have won by skill, ye dexterous-handed,-
This drink hath been effused for you, O Rbhus . drink it with high delight, with joy like Indra's.

## [04-036] HYMN XXXVI. Rbhus.

1. THia car that was not made for horses or for reins, three-wheeled, worthy of lauds, rolls round the
firmament.
That is the great announcement of your Deity, that, O ye Rbhus, ye sustain the earth and heaven.
2 Ye Sapient Ones who made the lightly-rolling car out of your mind, by thought, the car that never
errs,
You, being such, to drink of this drinkoffering, you, O ye Vajas, and ye Rbhus, we invoke.
3 O Vajas, Rbhus, reaching far, among the Gods this was your exaltation gloriously declared,
In that your aged Parents, worn with length of days, ye wrought again to youth so that they moved
at will.
4 The chalice that wag single ye have made fourfold, and by your wisdom brought the Cow forth from the hide.
So quickly, mid the Gods, ye gained immortal life. Vajas and Rbhus, your great work must be extolled.
5 Wealth from the Rbhus is most glorious in renown, that which the Heroes, famed for vigour, have
produced.
In synods must be sung the car which Vibhvan wrought: that which ye favour, Gods! is famed among mankind.
6 Strong is the steed, the man a sage in eloquence, the bowman is a hero hard to beat in fight,
Great store of wealth and manly power hath he obtained whom Vaja, Vibhvan, Rbhus have looked
kindly on.
7 To you hath been assigned the fairest ornament, the hymn of praise: Vajas and Rbhus, joy therein;
For ye have lore and wisdom and poetic skill: as such, with this our prayer we call on you to come.
8 According to the wishes of our hearts may ye, who have full knowledge of all the delights of men,
Fashion for us, O Rbhus, power and splendid wealth, rich in high courage, excellent, and vital
strength.
9 Bestowing on us here riches and offspring, here fashion fame for us befitting heroes.
Vouchsafe us wealth of splendid sort, O Rbhus, that we may make us more renowned than others.

## [04-037] HYMN XXXVII. Rbhus.

1. COME to our sacrifice, Vajas, Rbhuksans, Gods, by the paths which Gods are wont to travel,
As ye, gay Gods, accept in splendid weather the sacrifice among these folk of Manus.
2 May these rites please you in your heart and spirit; may the drops clothed in oil this day approach you.
May the abundant juices bear you onward to power and strength, and, when imbibed, delight you.
3 Your threefold going near is God-appointed, so praise is given you, Vajas and Rbhuksans.
So, Manus-like, mid younger folk I offer, to you who are aloft in heaven, the Soma.
4 Strong, with fair chains of gold and jaws of iron, ye have a splendid car and well-fed horses.
Ye Sons of Strength, ye progeny of Indra, to you the best is offered to delight you.

5 Rbhuksans! him, for handy wealth, the mightiest comrade in the fight,
Him, Indra's equal, we invoke, most bounteous ever, rich in steeds.
6 The mortal man whom, Rbhus, ye and Indra favour with your help,
Must be successful, by his thoughts, at sacrifice and with the steed.
7 O Vajas and Rbhuksans, free for us the paths to sacrifice,
Ye Princes, lauded, that we may press forward to each point of heaven.
8 O Vajas and Rbhuksans, ye Nasatyas, Indra, bless this wealth,
And, before other men's, the steed, that ample riches may be won.

## [04-038] HYMN XXXVIII. Dadhikris.

1. FROM you two came the gifts in days aforetime which Trasadasyu granted to the Purus.
Ye gave the winner of our fields and plough-lands, and the strong smiter who subdued the Dasytis.
2 And ye gave mighty Dadhikras, the giver of many gifts, who visiteth all people,
Impetuous hawk, swift and of varied colour, like a brave King whom each true man must honour.
3 Whom, as 'twere down a precipice, swift rushing, each Puru praises and his heart rejoices,-
Springing forth like a hero fain for battle, whirling the car and flying like the tempest.
4 Who gaineth precious booty in the combats and moveth, winning spoil, among the cattle;
Shown in bright colour, looking on the assemblies, beyond the churl, to worship of the living.
5 Loudly the folk cry after him in battles, as 'twere a thief who steals away a garment;
Speeding to glory, or a herd of cattle, even as a hungry falcon swooping downward.
6 And, fain to come forth first amid these armies, this way and that with rows of cars he rushes,
Gay like a bridesman, making him a garland, tossing the dust, champing the rein that holds him.
7 And that strong Steed, victorious and faithful, obedient with his body in the combat,
Speeding straight on amid the swiftly ressing, casts o'er his brows the dust he tosses upward.
8 And at his thunder, like the roar of heaven, those who attack tremble and are affrighted;
For when he fights against embattled thousands, dread is he in his striving; none may stay him.
9 The people praise the overpowering swiftness of this fleet Steed who giveth men abundance.
Of him they say when drawing back from battle. Dadhikras hath sped forward with his thousands.
10 Dadhikras hath o'erspread the Fivefold People with vigour, as the Sun lightens the waters.
May the strong Steed who winneth bundreds, thousands, requite with sweetness these my words
and praises.

## [04-039] HYMN XXXIX Dadhikras.

1. Now give we praise to Dadhikras the rapid, and mention in our laud the Earth and Heaven.
May the Dawns flushing move me to exertion, and bear me safely over every trouble.
2 I praise the mighty Steed who fills my spirit, the Stallion Dadhikravan rich in bounties,
Whom, swift of foot aind shining bright as Agni, ye, Varuna and Mitra, gave to Purus.

3 Him who hath honoured, when the flame is kindled at break of dawn, the Courser Dadhikrivan,
Him, of one mind with Varuna and Mitra may Aditi make free from all transgression.
4 When we remember mighty Dadhikravan our food and strength, then the blest name of Maruts,
Varuna, Mitra, we invoke for welfare, and Agni, and the thunder-wielding Indra.
5 Both sides invoke him as they call on Indra when they stir forth and turn to sacrificing.
To us have Varuna and Mitra granted the Courser Dadhikris, a guide for mortals.
6 So have I glorified with praise strong Dadhikravan, conquering Steed.
Sweet may he make our mouths; may he prolong the days we have to live.

## [04-040] HYMN XL. Dadhikravan.

1. LET us recite the praise of Dadhikravan: may all the Mornings move me to exertion;
Praise of the Lord of Waters, Dawn, and Agni, Brhaspati Son of Angiras, and Surya.
2 Brave, seeking war and booty, dwelling with the good and with the swift, may he hasten the food
of Dawn.
May he the true, the fleet, the lover of the course, the bird-like Dadhikravan, bring food, strength, and
light.
3 His pinion, rapid runner, fans him m his way, as of a bird that hastens onward to its aim,
And, as it were a falcon's gliding through the air, strikes Dadhikravan's side as he speeds on with
might.
4 Bound by the neck and by the flanks and by the mouth, the vigorous Courser lends new swiftness
to his speed.
Drawing himself together, as his strength allows, Dadhikras springs along the windings of the paths.
5 The Hamsa homed in light, the Vasu in mid-air, the priest beside the altar, in the house the guest,
Dweller in noblest place, mid men, in truth, in sky, born of flood, kine, truth, mountain, he is holy Law.

## [04-041] HYMN XLI. Indra-Varuna.

1. WHAT laud, O Indra-Varuna, with oblation, hath like the Immortal Priest obtained your favour?
Hath our effectual laud, addressed with homage, touched you, O Indra-Varuna, in spirit?
2 He who with dainty food hath won you, Indra and Varuna, Gods, as his allies to friendship,
Jayeth the Vrtras and his foes in battles, and through your mighty favours is made famous.
3 Indra and Varuna are most liberal givers of treasure to the men who toil to serve them,
When they, as Friends inclined to friendship, honoured with dainty food, delight in flowing Soma.
4 Indra and Varuna, ye hurl, O Mighty, on him your strongest flashing bolt of thunder
Who treats us ill, the robber and oppressor: measure on him your overwhelming vigour.
5 O Indra-Varuna, be ye the lovers of this my song, as steers who love the milch-Cow.
Milk may it yield us as, gone forth to pasture, the great Cow pouring out her thousand rivers.
6 For fertile fields, for worthy sons and grandsons, for the Sun's beauty and for steer-like vigour,

May Indra-Varuna with gracious favours work marvels for us in the stress of battle.

7 For you, as Princes, for your ancient kindness, good comrades of the man who seeks for booty,
We choose to us for the dear bond of friendship, most liberal Heroes bringing bliss like parents.

8 Showing their strength, these hymns for grace, Free-givers I have gone to you, devoted, as to battle.
For glory have they gone, as milk to Soma, to Indra-Varuna my thoughts and praises.

9 To Indra and to Varuna, desirous of gaining wealth have these my thoughts proceeded.
They have come nigh to you as treasurelovers, like mares, fleet-footed, eager for the glory.

10 May we ourselves be lords of during riches, of ample sustenance for car and hones.
So may the Twain who work with newest succours bring yoked teams hitherward to us and riches.

11 Come with your mighty succours, O ye Mighty; come, Indra-Varuna, to us in battle.
What time the flashing arrows play in combat, may we through you be winners in the contest.

## [04-042] HYMN XLIL Indra-Varuna.

1. I AM the royal Ruler, mine is empire, as mine who sway all life are all Immortals.
Varuna's will the Gods obey and follow. I am the King of men's most lofty cover.

2 I am King Varuna. To me were given these first existinghigh celestial powers.
Varuna's will the Gods obey and follow. I am the King of men's most lofty cover.

3 I Varuna am Indra: in their greatness, these the two wide deep fairly-fashioned regions,
These the two world-halves have I, even as Tvastar knowing all beings, joined and held together.

4 I made to flow the moisture-shedding waters, and set the heaven firm in the scat of Order.
By Law the Son of Aditi, Law Observer, hath spread abroad the world in threefold measure.

5 Heroes with noble horses, fain for battle, selected warriors, call on me in combat.
I Indra Maghavan, excite the conflict; I stir the dust, Lord of surpassing vigour.

6 All this I did. The Gods' own conquering power never impedeth me whom none opposeth.
When lauds and Soma juice have made me joyful, both the unbounded regions are affrighted.

7 All beings know these deeds of thine thou tellest this unto Varuna, thou great Disposer!
Thou art renowned as having slain the Vrtras. Thou madest flow the floods that were obstructed.

8 Our fathers then were these, the Seven his, what time the son of Durgaha was captive.
For her they gained by sacrifice Trasadasyu, a demi-god, like Indra, conquering foemen.

9 The spouse of Purukutsa gave oblations to you, O Indra-Varuna, with homage.
Then unto her ye gave King Trasadasyu, the demi-god, the slayer of the foeman.

10 May we, possessing much, delight in riches, Gods in oblations and the kine in pasture;
And that Milch-cow who ahrinks not from the milking, O Indra-Varuna, give to us daily.

## [04-043] HYMN XLIII. Asvins.

1. WHO will hear, who of those who merit worship, which of all Gods take pleasure in our homage?
On whose heart shall we lay this laud celestial, rich with fair offerings, dearest to Immortals?

2 Who will be gracious? Who will come most uickly of all the Gods? Who will
bring liss most largely?
What car do they call swift with rapid coursers? That which the Daughter of the Sun elected.

3 So many days do ye come swiftly hither, as Indra to give help in stress of battle.
Descended from the sky, divine, strong-pinioned, by which of all your powers are ye most mighty?

4 What is the prayer that we should bring you, Asvins, whereby ye come to us when invoked?
Whether of you confronts e'en great betrayal? Lovers of sweetness, Dasras, help and save us.

5 In the wide space your chariot reacheth heaven, what time it turneth hither from the ocean.
Sweets from your sweet shall drop, lovers of sweetness! These have they dressed for you as dainty viands.

6 Let Sindhu with his wave bedew your horses: in fiery glow have the red birds come hither.
Observed of all was that your rapid going, whereby ye were the Lords of Siirya's Daughter.

7 Whene'er I gratified you here together, your grace was given us, O ye rich in booty.
Protect, ye Twain, the singer of your praises: to you, Nasatyas, is my wish directed.

## [04-044] HYMN XLIV. Asvins.

1. WE will invoke this day your car, farspreading, O Asvins, even the gathering, of the sunlight,-
Car praised in hymns, most ample, rich in treasure, fitted with seats, the car that beareth Surya.

2 Asvins, ye gained that glory by your Godhead, ye Sons of Heaven, by your own might and power.
Food followeth close upon your bright appearing when stately horses in your chariot draw you.

3 Who bringeth you to-day for help with offered oblation, or with hymns to drink the juices?
Who, for the sacrifice's ancient lover, turneth you hither, Asvins, offering homage?

4 Borne on your golden car, ye omnipresent! come to this sacrifice of ours, Nasatyas.
Drink of the pleasant liquor of the Soma give riches to the people who adore you.

5 Come hitherward to us from earth, from heaven, borne on your golden chariot rolling lightly.
Suffer not other worshippers to stay you here are ye bound by earlier bonds of friendship.

6 Now for us both, mete out, O WonderWorkers, riches exceeding great with store of heroes,
Because the men have sent you praise, O Asvins, and Ajamilhas come to the laudation.

7 Whene'er I gratified you here together, your grace was given us, O ye rich in booty.
Protect, ye Twain, the singer of your praises: to you, Nasatyas, is my wish directed.

## [04-045] HYMN XLV. Asvins

1. YONDER goes up that light: your chariot is yoked that travels round upon the summit of this
heaven.

Within this car are stored three kindred shares of food, and a skin filled with meath is rustling as the
fourth.
2 Forth come your viands rich with store of pleasant meath, and cars and horses at the flushing of the
dawn,
Stripping the covering from the surrounded gloom, and spreading through mid-air bright radiance like
the Sun.
3 Drink of the meath with lips accustomed to the draught; harness for the meath's sake the chariot
that ye love.
Refresh the way ye go, refresh the paths with meath: hither, O Asvins, bring the skin that holds the
meath.
4 The swans ye have are friendly, rich in store of meath, gold-pinioned, strong to draw, awake at
early morn,
Swimming the flood, exultant, fain for draughts that cheer: ye come like flies to our libations of-the
meath.
5 Well knowing solemn rites and rich in meath, the fires sing to the morning Asvins at the break of
day,
When with pure hands the prudent energetic priest hath with the stones pressed out the Soma rich
in meath.
6 The rays advancing nigh, chasing with day the gloom, spread through the firmament bright
radiance like the Sun;
And the Sun harnessing his horses goeth forth: ye through your Godlike nature let his paths be
known.
7 Devout in thought I have declared, O Asvins, your chariot with good steeds, which lasts for ever,
Wherewith ye travel swiftly through the regions to the prompt worshipper who brings oblation.

## [04-046] HYMN XLVI. Vayu. Indra-Vayu

1. DRINK the best draught of Soma-juice, O Vayu, at our holy rites:
For thou art he who drinketh first.
2 Come, team-drawn, with thy hundred helps, with Indra, seated in the car,
Vaya, and drink your fill of juice.
3 May steeds a thousand bring you both, Indra. and Vayu, hitherward
To drink the Soma, to the feagt.
4 For ye, O Indra-Vayu, mount the goldenseated car that aids
The sacrifice, that reaches heaven.
5 On far-refulgent chariot come unto the man who offers gifts:
Come, Indra-Vayu, hitherward.
6 Here, Indra-Vayu, is the juice: drink it, accordant with the Gods,
Within the giver's dwelling-place.
7 Hither, O Indra-Vayu, be your journey here unyoke your steeds,
Here for your draught of Soma juice.

## [04-047] HYMN XLVIL. Vayu. Indra-Vayu.

1. Vayu, the bright is offered thee, best of the meath at holy rites.
Come thou to drink the Soma juice, God, longed-for, on thy team-drawn car.
2 O Vayu, thou and Indra are meet drinkers of these Soma-draughts,
For unto you the drops proceed as waters gather to the vale.
3 O Indra-Vayu, mighty Twain, speeding together, Lords of Strength,

Come to our succour with your team, that ye may drink the Soma juice.
4 The longed-for teams which ye possess, O Heroes, for the worshipper,
Turn to us, Indra-Vayu, ye to whom the sacrifice is paid.

## [04-048] HYMN XLVIII. Vayu.

1. TASTE offerings never tasted yet, as bards enjoy the foeman's wealth.
O Vayu, on refulgent car come to the drinking of the juice.
2 Removing curses, drawn by teams, with 1ndra, seated by thy side,
O Vayu, on refulgent car come to the drinking of the juice.
3 The two dark treasuries of wealth that wear all beauties wait on thee.
O Vayu, on refulgent car come to the drinking of the juice.
4 May nine-and-ninety harnessed steeds who yoke them at thy will bring thee.
O Vayu, on refulgent car come to the drinking of the juice.
5 Harness, O Vayu, to thy car a hundred well-fed tawny steeds,
Yea, or a thousand steeds, and let thy chariot come to us with might.

## [04-049] HYMN XLIX. Indra-Brhaspati.

1. DEAR is this offering in your mouth, O Indra and Brhaspati:
Famed is the laud, the gladdening draught.
2 This lovely Soma is effused, O Indra and Brhaspati,
For you, to drink it and rejoice.
3 As Soma-drinkers to our house come, Indra and Brhaspati-and Indra-to drink Soma juice.
4 Vouchsafe us riches hundredfold, O Indra, and Brhaspati,
With store of horses, thousandfold.
5 O Indra. and Brhaspati, we call you when the meath is shed,
With songs, to drink the Soma juice.
6 Drink, Indra and Brhaspati, the Soma in the giver's house:
Delight yourselves abiding there.

## [04-050] HYMN L. Brhaspati.

1. Him who with might hath propped earth's ends, who sitteth in threefold seat, Brhaspati, with
thunder,
Him of the pleasant tongue have ancient sages, deep-thinking, holy singers, set before them.
2 Wild in their course, in well-marked wise rejoicing were they, Brhaspati, who pressed around us.
Preserve Brhaspati, the stall uninjured, this company's raining, ever-moving birthplace.
3 Brhaspati, from thy remotest distance have they sat down who love the law eternal.

For thee were dug wells springing from the mountain, which murmuring round about pour streams of
sweetness.
4 Brhaspati, when first he had his being from mighty splendour in supremest heaven,
Strong, with his sevenfold mouth, with noise of thunder, with his seven rays, blew and dispersed the
darkness.
5 With the loud-shouting band who sang his praises, with thunder, he destroyed obstructive Vala.
Brhaspati thundering drave forth the cattle, the lowing cows who make oblations ready.
6 Serve we with sacrifices, gifts, and homage even thus the Steer of all the Gods, the Father.
Brhaspati, may we be lords of riches, with noble progeny and store of heroes.

7 Surely that King by power and might heroic hath made him lord of all his foes' posses-ions,
Who cherishes Brhaspati well-tended, adorns and worships him as foremost sharer.
8 In his own house he dwells in peace and comfort: to him for ever holy food flows richly.
To him the people with free will pay homage-the King with whom the Brahman hatb precedence.
9 He, unopposed, is master of the riches.of his own subjects and of hostile people.
The Gods uphold that King with their protection who helps the Brahman when he seeks his favour.
10 Indra, Brhaspati, rainers of treasure, rejoicing at this sacrifice drink the Soma.
Let the abundant drops sink deep within you: vouchsafe us riches with full store of heroes.
11 Brhaspati and Indra, make us prosper may this be your benevolence to usward.
Assist our holy thoughts, wake up our spirit: weaken the hatred of our foe and rivals.

## [04-051] HYMN LI. Dawn.

1. FORTH from the darkness in the region eastward this most abundant splendid light hatb mounted.
Now verily the far-refulgent Mornings, Daughters of Heaven, bring welfare to the people.
2 The richly-coloured Dawns have mounted eastward, like pillars planted at our sacrifices,
And, flushing far, splendid and purifying, unbarred the portals of the fold of darkness.
3 Dispelling gloom this day the wealthy Mornings urge liberal givers to present their treasures.
In the unlightened depth of darkness round them let niggard traffickers sleep unawakened.
4 O Goddesses, is this your car, I ask you, ancient this day, or is it new, ye Mornings,
Wherewith, rich Dawns, ye seek with wealth Navagva, Dasagva Angira, the seven-toned singer?
5 With horses harnessed by eternal Order, Goddesses, swiftly round the worlds ye travel,
Arousing from their rest, O Dawns, the sleeping, and all that lives, man, bird, and beast, to motion.
6 Which among these is eldest, and where is she through whom they fixed the Rbhus' regulations?
What time the splendid Dawns go forth for splendour, they are not known aparto alike, unwasting.
7 Blest were these Dawns of old, shining with succour, true with the truth that springs from holy
Order;
With whom the toiling worshipper, by praises, hymning and lauding, soon attained to riches.
8 Hither from eastward all at once they travel, from one place spreading in the selfsame manner.
Awaking, from the seat of holy Order the Godlike Dawns come nigh like troops of cattle.
9 Thus they go forth with undiminished colours, these Mornings similar, in self-same fashion,
Concealing the gigantic might of darkness with radiant bodies bright and pure and shining.
10 O Goddesses, O Heaven's refulgent Daughters, bestow upon us wealth with store of children.
As from our pleasant place of rest ye rouse us may we be masters of heroic vigour.
11 Well-skilled in lore of sacrifice, ye Daughters of Heaven, refulgent Dawns, I thus address you.
May we be glorious among the people. May Heaven vouchsafe us this, and Earth the Goddess,

## [04-052] HYMN LIL Dawm.

1. THIS Lady, giver of delight, after her Sister shining forth, Daughter of Heaven, hath shown herself.-
2 Unfailing, Mother of the Kine, in colour like a bright red mare, The Dawn became the Asvins' Friend.
3 Yea, and thou art the Asvins' Friend, the Mother of the Kine art thou:
O Dawn thou rulest over wealth.
4 Thinking of thee, O joyous One, as her who driveth hate away, We woke to meet thee with our lauds.
5 Our eyes behold thy blessed rays like troops of cattle loosed to feed.
Dawn hath filled full the wide expanse.
6 When thou hast filled it, Fulgent One! thou layest bare the gloom with light.
After thy nature aid us, Dawn.
7 Thou overspreadest heaven with rays, the dear wide region of mid-air.
With thy bright shining lustre, Dawn.

## [04-053] HYMN LIII. Savitar.

1. OF Savitar the God, the sapient Asura, we crave this great gift which is worthy of our choice,
Wherewith he freely grants his worshiper defence. This with his rays the Great God hath vouchsafed
to us.
2 Sustainer of the heaven, Lord of the whole world's life, the Sage, he putteth on his golden-coloured
mail.
Clear-sighted, spreading far, filling the spacious realm, Savitar hath brought forth bliss that deserveth
laud.
3 He hath filled full the regions of the heaven and earth: the God for his own strengthening waketh
up the hymn.
Savitar hath stretched out his arms to cherish life, producing with his rays and lulling all that moves.
4 Lighting all living creatures, neer to be deceived, Savitar, God, protects each holy ordinance.
He hath stretched out his arms to all the folk of earth, and, with his laws observed, rules his own
mighty course.
5 Savitar thrice surrounding with his mightiness mid-air, three regions, and the triple sphere of light,
Sets the three heavens in motion and the threefold earth, and willingly protects us with his triple law.
6 Most gracious God, who brings to life and lulls to rest, he who controls the world, what moves not
and what moves,
May he vouchsafe us shelter, -Savitar the God,- for tranquil life, with triple bar against distress.
7 With the year's seasons hath Savitar, God, come nigh: may he prosper our home, give food and
noble sons.
May he invigorate us through the days and nights, and may he send us opulence with progeny.

## [04-054] HYMN LIV. Savitar.

1. Now must we praise and honour Savitar the God: at this time of the day the men must call to him,
Him who distributes wealth to Manu's progeny, that he may grant us here riches most excellent.
2 For thou at first producest for the holy Gods the noblest of all portions, immor-tality:
Thereafter as a gift to men, O Savitar, thou openest existence, life succeeding life.

3 If we, men as we are, have sinned against the Gods through want of thought, in weakness, or
through insolence,
Absolve us from the guilt and make us free from sin, O Savitar, alike among both Gods and men.
4 None may impede that power of Savitar the God whereby he will maintain the universal world.
What the fair-fingered God brings forth on earth's expanse or in the heightof heaven, that work of his
stands sure.
5 To lofty hills thou sendest those whom Indra leads, and givest fixed abodes with houses unto
these.
However they may fly and draw themselves apart, still, Savitar, they stand obeying thy behest.
6 May the libations poured to thee thrice daily, day after day, O Savitar, bring us blessing.
May Indra, Heaven, Earth, Sindhu with the Waters, Aditi with Adityas, give us shelter.

## [04-055] HYMN LV. Visvedevas.
1. WHO of you, Vasus, saveth? who protecteth? O Heaven and Earth and Aditi, preserve us,
Varuna., Mitra, from the stronger mortal. Gods, which of you at sacrifice giveth comfort?

2 They who with laud extol the ancient statutes, when they shine forth infallible dividers,
Have ordered as perpetual Ordainers, and beamed as holy-thoughted WonderWorkers.
3 The Housewife Goddess, Aditi, and Sindhu, the Goddess Svasti I implore for friendship:
And may the unobstructed Night and Morning both, day and night, provide for our protection.
4 Aryaman, Varuna have disclosed the pathway, Agni as Lord of Strength the road to welfare.
Lauded in manly mode may Indra-Visnu grant us their powerful defence and shelter.
5 I have besought the favourof the Maruts, of Parvata, of Bhaga God who rescues.
From trouble caused by man the Lord preserve us; from woe sent by his friend let Mitra save us.
6 Agree, through these our watery oblations, Goddesses, Heaven and Earth, with Ahibudhnya.
As if to win the sea, the Gharma-heaters have opened, as they come anear, the rivers.
7 May Goddess Aditi with Gods defend us, save us the saviour God with care unceasing.
We dare not stint the sacred food of Mitra and Varuna upon the back of Agni.
8 Agni is Sovran Lord of wealth, Agni of great prosperity:
May he bestow these gifts on us.
9 Hither to us, rich pleasant Dawn, bring many things to be desired,
Thou who hast ample store of wealth.
10 So then may Bhaga, Savitar, Varuna, Mitra, Aryaman, Indra, with bounty come to us.

## [04-056] HYMN LVI. Heaven and Earth.
1. MAY mighty Heaven and Earth, most meet for honour, be present here with light and gleaming
splendours;
When, fixing them apart, vast, most extensive, the Steer roars loudly in far-reaching courses.
2 The Goddesses with Gods, holy with holy, the Two stand pouring out their rain, exhaustless:

Faithful and guileless, having Gods for children, leaders of sacrifice with shining splendours.
3 Sure in the worlds he was a skilful Craftsman, he who produced these Twain the Earth and Heaven.
Wise, with his power he brought both realms, together spacious and deep, wellfashioned,
unsupported.
4 O Heaven and Earth, with one accord promoting, with high protection as of Queens, our welfare,
Far-reaching, universal, holy, guard us. May we, car-borne, through song be victors ever.
5 To both of you, O Heaven and Earth, we bring our lofty song of praise,
Pure Ones! to glorify you both.
6 Ye sanctify each other's form, by your own proper might ye rule,
And from of old observe the Law.
7 Furthering and fulfilling, ye, O Mighty, perfect Mitra's Law.
Ye sit around our sacrifice.

## [04-057] HYMN LVII. Ksetrapati, Etc.
1. WE through the Master of the Field, even as through a friend, obtain
What nourisheth our kine and steeds. In such may he be good to us.
2 As the cow yieldeth milk, pour for us freely, Lord of the Field, the wave that beareth sweetness,
Distilling meath, well-purified like butter, and let the. Lords of holy Law be gracious.
3 Sweet be the plants for us. the heavens, the waters, and full of sweets for us be air's mid-region.
May the Field's Lord for us be full of sweetness, and may we follow after him uninjured.
4 Happily work our steers and men, may the plough furrow happily.
Happily be the traces bound; happily may he ply the goad.
5 Suna and Sira, welcome ye this laud, and with the milk which ye have made in heaven
Bedew ye both this earth of ours.
6 Auspicious Sita, come thou near: we venerate and worship thee
That thou mayst bless and prosper us and bring us fruits abundantly.
7 May Indra press the furrow down, may Pusan guide its course aright.
May she, as rich in milk, be drained for us through each succeeding year.

8 Happily let the shares turn up the ploughland, happily go the ploughers with the oxen.
With meath and milk Parjanya make us happy. Grant us prosperity, Suna and Sira.

## [04-058] HYMN LVIII. Ghrta.
1. FORTH from the ocean sprang the wave of sweetness: together with the stalk it turned to Amrta,
That which is holy oil's mysterious title: but the Gods' tongue is truly Amrta's centre.
2 Let us declare aloud the name of Ghrta, and at this sacrifice hold it up with homage.
So let the Brahman hear the praise we utter. This hath the four-horned Buffalo emitted.
3 Four are his horns, three are the feet that bear him; his heads are two, his hands are seven in
number.
Bound with a triple bond the Steer roars loudly: the mighty God hath entered in to mortals.
4 That oil in triple shape the Gods discovered laid down within the Cow, concealed by Panis.

113

Indra produced one shape, Surya another: by their own power they formed the third from Vena.

5 From inmost reservoir in countless channels flow down these rivers which the foe beholds not.

I look upon the streams of oil descending, and lo! the Golden Reed is there among them.

6 Like rivers our libations flow together, cleansing themselves in inmost heart and spirit.

The streams of holy oil pour swiftly downward like the wild beasts that fly before the bowman.

7 As rushing down the rapids of a river, flow swifter than the wind the vigorous currents,

The streams of oil in swelling fluctuation like a red courser bursting through the fences.

8.Like women at a gathering fair to look on and gently smiling, they incline to Agni.

The streams of holy oil attain the fuel, and Jatavedas joyfully receives them.

9 As maidens dock themselves with gay adornment to join the bridal feast, I now behold them.

Where Soma flows and sacrifice is ready, thither the streams of holy oil are running.

10 Send to our eulogy a herd of cattle bestow upon us excellent possessions.

Bear to the Gods the sacrifice we offer the streams of oil flow pure and full of sweetness.

11 The universe depends upon thy power and might within the sea, within the heart, within all life.

May we attain that sweetly-flavoured wave of thine, brought, at its gathering, o'er the surfaceof the

floods.

# BOOK FIVE

### [05-001] HYMN I. Agni

1. Agni is wakened by the people's fuel to meet the Dawn who cometh like a milch-cow.

Like young trees shooting up on high their branches, his flames are rising to the vault of heaven.

2 For worship of the Gods the Priest was wakened: at morning gracious Agni hath arisen.

Kindled, his radiant might is made apparent, and the great Deity set free from darkness.

3 When he hath stirred the line of his attendants, with the pure milk pure Agni is anointed.

The strength-bestowing gift is then made ready, which spread in front, with tongues, erect, he

drinketh.

4 The spirits of the pious turn together to Agni, as the eyes of all to Surya.

He, when both Dawns of different hues have borne him, springs up at daybreak as a strong white

charger.

5 The noble One was born at days' beginning, laid red in colour mid the well-laid fuel.

Yielding in every house his seven rich treasures, Agni is seated, Priest most skilled in worship.

6 Agni hath sat him down, a Priest most skilful, on a sweet-smelling place, his Mother's bosom.

Young, faithful, sage, preeminent o'er many, kindled among the folk whom he sustaineth.

7 This Singer excellent at sacrifices, Agni the Priest, they glorify with homage.

Him who spread out both worlds by Law Eternal they balm with oil, strong Steed who never faileth.

8. He, worshipful House-Friend, in his home is worshipped, our own auspicious guest, lauded by

sages.

That strength the Bull with thousand horns possesses. In might, O Agni, thou excellest others.

9 Thou quickly passest by all others, Agni, for him to whom thou hast appeared most lovely,

Wondrously fair, adorable, effulgent, the guest of men, the darling of the people.

10 To thee, Most Youthful God! to thee, O Agni from near and far the people bring their tribute.

Mark well the prayer of him who best extols thee. Great, high, auspicious, Agni, is thy shelter.

11 Ascend to-day thy splendid car, O Agni, in splendour, with the Holy Ones around it.

Knowing the paths by mid-air's spacious region bring hither Gods to feast on our oblation.

12 To him adorable, sage, strong and mighty we have sung forth our song of praise and homage.

Gavisthira hath raised with prayer to Agni this laud far-reaching, like gold light to heaven.

### [05-002] HYMN II. Agni.

1. THE youthful Mother keeps the Boy in secret pressed to her close, nor yields him to the Father.

But, when he lies upon the arm, the people see his unfading countenance before them.

2 What child is this thou carriest as handmaid, O Youthful One? The Consort-Queen hath bome him.

The Babe unborn increased through many autumns. I saw him born what time his Mother bare him.

3 I saw him from afar gold-toothed, bright-coloured, hurling his weapons from his habitation,

What time I gave him Amrta free from mixture. How can the Indraless, the hymnless harm me?

4 I saw him moving from the place he dwells in, even as with a herd, brilliantly shining.

These seized him not: he had been born already. They who were grey with age again grow youthful.

5 Who separate my young bull from the cattle, they whose protector was in truth no stranger?

Let those whose hands have seized upon them free them. May he, observant, drive the herd to usward.

6 Mid mortal men godless have secreted the King of all who live, home of the people.

So may the prayers of Atri give him freedom. Reproached in turn be those who now reproach him.

7 Thou from the stake didst loose e'en Sunahsepa bound for a thousand; for he prayed with fervour.

So, Agni, loose from us the bonds that bind us, when thou art seated here, O Priest who knowest.

8 Thou hast sped from me, Agni, in thine anger: this the protector of Gods' Laws hath told me.

Indra who knoweth bent his eye upon thee: by him instructed am I come, O Agni.

9 Agni shines far and wide with lofty splendour, and by his greatness makes all things apparent.

He conquers godless and malign enchantments, and sharpens both his horns to gore the Raksas.

10 Loud in the heaven above be Agni's roarings with keen-edged weapons to destroy the demons.

Forth burst his splendours in the Soma's rapture. The godless bands press round but cannot stayhim.

11 As a skilled craftsman makes a car, a singer I, Mighty One! this hymn for thee have fashioned.

If thou, O Agni, God, accept it gladly, may we obtain thereby the heavenly Waters.

12 May he, the strong-necked Steer, waxing in vigour, gather the foeman's wealth with none to check him.

Thus to this Agni have the Immortals spoken. To man who spreads the grass may he grant shelter, grant shelter to the man who brings oblation.

### [05-003] HYMN III. Agni.

1. THOU at thy birth art Varuna, O Agni; when thou art kindled thou becomest Mitra.

In thee, O Son of Strength, all Gods are centred. Indra art thou to man who brings oblation.

2 Aryaman art thou as regardeth maidens mysterious, is thy name, O Self-sustainer.

As a kind friend with streams of milk they balm thee what time thou makest wife and lord oneminded.

3 The Maruts deck their beauty for thy glory, yea, Rudra! for thy birth fair, brightly-coloured.

That which was fixed as Visnu's loftiest station-therewith the secret of the Cows thou guardest.

4 Gods through thy glory, God who art so lovely! granting abundant gifts gained life immortal.

As their own Priest have men established Agni; and serve him fain for praise from him who liveth.

5 There is no priest more skilled than thou in worship; none Self-sustainer pass thee in wisdom.

Ile man within whose house as guest thou dwellest, O God, by sacrifice shall conquer mortals.

6 Aided by thee, O Agni may we conquer through our oblation, fain for wealth, awakened:

May we in battle, in the days' assemblies,O Son of Strength, by riches conquer mortals.

7 He shall bring evil on the evil-plottcr whoever turns against us sin and outrage.

Destroy this calumny of him, O Agni, whoever injures us with double-dealing.

8 At this dawn's flushing, God! our ancient fathers served thee with offerings, making thee their envoy,

When, Agni, to the store of wealth thou goest, a God cnkindled with good things by mortals.

9 Save, thou who knowest, draw thy father near thee, who counts as thine own son, O Child of Power.

O sapient Agni, when wilt thou regard us? When, skilled in holy Law, wilt thou direct us?

10 Adoring thee he gives thee many a title, when thou, Good Lord! acceptest this as Father.

And doth not Agni, glad in strength of Godhead, gain splendid bliss when he hath waxen mighty?

11 Most Youthful Agni, verily thou bearest thy praiser safely over all his troubles.

Thieves have been seen by us and open foemen: unknown have been the plottings of the wicked.

12 To thee these eulogies have been directed: or to the Vasu hath this sin been spoken.

But this our Agni, flaming high, shall never yield us to calumny, to him who wrongs us.

### [05-004] HYMN IV. Agni.

1. O AGNI, King and Lord of wealth and treasures, in thee is my delight at sacrifices.

Through thee may we obtain the strength we long for, and overcome the fierce attacks of mortals.

2 Agni, Eternal Father, offering- bearer, fair to behold, far-reaching, far-refulgent,

From well-kept household fire beam food to feed us, and measure out to us abundant glory.

3 The Sage of men, the Lord of human races, pure, purifying Agni, balmed with butter,

Him the Omniscient as your Priest ye stablish: he wins among the Gods things worth the choosing.

4 Agni, enjoy, of one accord with Ila, striving in rivalry with beams of Sarya,

Enjoy, O Jatavedas, this our fuel, and bring the Gods to us to taste oblations.

5 As dear House-Friend, guest welcome in the dwelling, to this our sacrifice come thou who knowest.

And, Agni, having scattered all assailants, bring to us the possessions of our foemen.

6 Drive thou away the Dasyu with thy weapon. As, gaining vital power for thine own body,

O Son of Strength, the Gods thou satisfiest, so in fight save us, most heroic Agni.

7 May we, O Agni, with our lauds adore thee, and with our gifts, fair-beaming Purifier!

Send to us wealth containing all things precious: bestow upon us every sort of riches.

8 Son of Strength, Agni, dweller in three regions, accept our sacrifice and our oblation.

Among the Gods may we be counted pious: protect us with a triply-guarding shelter.

9 Over all woes and dangers, Jatavedas, bear us as in a boat across a river.

Praised with our homage even as Atri praised thee, O Agni, be the guardian of our bodies.

10 As I, remembering thee with grateful spirit, a mortal, call with might on thee Immortal,

Vouchsafe us high renown, O Jatavedas, and may I be immortal by my children.

11 The pious man, O Jatavedas Agni, to whom thou grantest ample room and pleasure,

Gaineth abundant wealth with sons and horses, with heroes and with kine for his well-being.

### [05-005] HYMN V. Apris.

1. To Agni, Jatavedas, to the flame, the well-enkindled God, Offer thick sacrificial oil.

2 He, Narasamsa, ne'er beguiled, inspiriteth this sacrifice: For sage is he, with sweets in hand.

3 Adored, O Agni, hither bring Indra the Wonderful, the Friend, On lightly-rolling car to aid.

4 Spread thyself out, thou soft as wool The holy hymns have sung to thee.

Bring gain to us, O beautiful!

5 Open yourselves, ye Doors Divine, easy of access for our aid: Fill, more and more, the sacrifice.

6 Fair strengtheners of vital power, young Mothers of eternal Law,

Morning and Night we supplicate.

7 On the wind's flight come, glorified, ye two celestial Priests of man

Come ye to this our sacrifice.

8 I! Sarasvati, Mahl, three Goddesses who tring us weal, Be seated harmless on the grass.

9 Rich in all plenty, Tvastar, come auspicious of thine own accord Help us in every sacrifice.

10 Vanaspati, wherever thou knowest the Gods' mysterious names,

Send our oblations thitherward.

11 To Agni and to Varuna, Indra, the Maruts, and the Gods, With Svaha be oblation brought.

## [05-006] HYMN VI. Agni.

1. I VALUE Agni that good Lord, the home to which the kine return:
Whom fleet-foot coursers seek as home, and strong enduring steeds as home. Bring food to those
who sing thy praise.
2 'Tis Agni whom we laud as good, to whom the milch-kine come in herds,
To whom the chargers swift of foot, to whom our well-born princes come. Bring food to those who
sing thy praise.
3 Agni the God of all mankind, gives, verily, a steed to man.
Agni gives precious gear for wealth, treasure he gives when he is pleased. Bring food to those who
sing thy praise.
4 God, Agni, we will kindle thee, rich in thy splendour, fading not,
So that this glorious fuel may send forth by day its light for thee.
Bring food to those who sing thy
praise.
5 To thee the splendid, Lord of flame, bright, wondrous, Prince of men, is brought.

Oblation with the holy verse, O Agni, bearer of our gifts.
Bring food to those who sing thy praise.
6 These Agnis in the seats of the fire nourish each thing most excellent.
They give delight, they spread abroad, they move themselves continually. Bring food to those who
sing thy praise.
7 Agni, these brilliant flames of thine wax like strong chargers mightily,
Who with the treadings of their hoofs go swiftly to the stalls of kine. Bring food to those who sing thy
praise.
8 To us who laud thee, Agni, bring fresh food and safe and happy homes.
May we who have sung hymns to thee have thee for envoy in each house. Bring food to those who
sing thy praise.
9 Thou, brilliant God, within thy mouth warmest both ladies of the oil.
So fill us also, in our hymns, abundantly, O Lord of Strength,Bring food to those who sing thy praise.
10 Thus Agni have we duly served with sacrifices and with hymns.
So may he give us what we crave, store of brave sons and fleet-foot steeds. Bring food to those who
sing thy praise.

## [05-007] HYMN VII. Agni.

1. OFFER to Agni, O my friends, your seemly food, your seemly praise;
To him supremest o'er the folk, the Son of Strength, the mighty Lord:
2 Him in whose presence, when they meet in full assembly, men rejoice;
Even him whom worthy ones inflame, and living creatures bring to life.
3 When we present to him the food and sacrificial gifts of men,
He by the might of splendour grasps the holy Ordinance's rein.
4 He gives a signal in the night even to him who is afar,
When he, the Bright, unchanged by eld, consumes the sovrans of the wood.
5 He in whose service on the ways they offer up their drops of sweat,
On him is their high kin have they mounted, as ridges on the earth.

6 Whom, sought of many, mortal man hath found to be the Stay of all;
He who gives flavour to our food, the home of every man that lives.
7 Even as a herd that crops the grass he shears the field and wilderness,
With flashing teeth and beard of gold, deft with his unabated might.
8 For him, to whom, bright as an axe he, as to Atri, hath flashed forth,
Hath the well-bearing Mother borne, producing when her time is come.
9 Agni to whom the oil is shed by him thou lovest to support,
Bestow upon these mortals fame and splendour and intelligence.
10 Such zeal hath he, resistless one: he gained the cattle given by thee.
Agni, may Atri overcome the Dasyus who bestow no gifts, subdue the men who give no food.

## [05-008] HYMN VIII. Agni.

1. O AGNI urged to strength, the men of old who loved the Law enkindled thee,
the Ancient, for their aid,
Thee very bright, and holy, nourisher of all, most excellent, the Friend and Master of the home.
2 Thee, Agni, men have stablished as their guest of old, as Master of the household, thee, with hair of
flame;
High-bannered, multiform, distributor of wealth, kind helper, good protector, drier of the floods.
3 The tribes of men praise thee, Agni, who knowest well burnt offerings, the Discerner, lavishest of
wealth,
Dwelling in secret, Blest One! visible to all, loud-roaring, skilled in worship, glorified with oil.
4 Ever to thee, O Agni, as exceeding strong have we drawn nigh with songs and reverence singing
hymns.
So be thou pleased with us, Angiras! as a God enkindled by the noble with man's goodly light.

5 Thou, Agni! multiform, God who art lauded much! givest in every house subsistence as of old.
Thou rulest by thy might o'er food of many a sort: that light of thine when blazing may not be
opposed.
6 The Gods, Most Youthful Agni, have made thee, inflamed, the bearer of oblations and the
messenger.
Thee, widely-reaching, homed in sacred oil, invoked, effulgent, have they made the Eye that stirs the
thought.
7 Men seeking joy have lit thee worshipped from of old, O Agni, with good fuel and with sacred oil.
So thou, bedewed and waxing mighty by the plants, spreadest thyself abroad over the realms of
earth.

## [05-009] HYMN IX. Agni.

1. BEARING; oblations mortal men, O Agni, worship thee the God.
I deem thee Jatavedas: bear our offerings, thou, unceasingly.
2 In the man's home who offers gifts, where grass is trimmed, Agni is Priest,
To whom all sacrifices come and strengthenings that win renown.
3 Whom, as an infant newly-born, the kindling-sticks have brought to life,

Sustainer of the tribes of men, skilled in well-ordered sacrifice.
4 Yea, very hard art thou to grasp, like offspring of the wriggling snakes,
When thou consumest many woods like an ox, Agni, in the mead.
5 Whose flames, when thou art sending forth the smoke, completely reach the mark,
When Trta in the height of heaven, like as a smelter fanneth thee,
e'en as a smelter sharpeneth thee.
6 O Agni, by thy succour and by Mitra's friendly furtherance,
May we, averting hate, subbue the wickedness of mortal men.
7 O Agni, to our heroes bring such riches, thou victorious God.
May he protect and nourish us, and help in aining strength: be thou near us in 6rht for our success.

## [05-010] HYMN X. Agni.

1. BRING us most mighty splendour thou, Agni, resistless on thy way.
With overflowing store of wealth mark out for us a path to strength.
2 Ours art thou, wondrous Agni, bywisdom and bounteousness of power.
The might of Asuras rests on thee, like Mitra worshipful in act.
3 Agni, increase our means of life, increase the house and home of these,
The men, the princes who have won great riches through our hymns of praise.
4 Bright Agni, they who deck their songs for thee have horses as their meed.
The men are mighty in their might, they whose high laud, as that of heaven, awakes thee of its own accord.
5 O Agni, those resplendent flames of thine go valorously forth,
Like lightnings flashing round us, like a rattling car that seeks the spoil.
6 Now, Agni, come to succour us; let priests draw nigh to offer gifts;
And let the patrons of our rites subdue all regions of the earth.
7 Bring to us, Agni, Angiras, lauded of old and lauded now,
Invoker! wealth to quell the strong, that singers may extol thee.
Be near us in fight for our success.

## [05-011] HYMN XI. Agni.

1. THE watchful Guardian of the people hath been born, Agni, the very strong, for fresh prosperity.
With oil upon his face, with high heaventouching flame, he shineth splendidly, pure, for the Bharatas.
2 Ensign of sacrifice, the earliest Household-Priest, the. men have kindled Agni in his threefold seat,
With Indra and the Gods together on the grass let the wise Priest sit to complete the sacrifice.
3 Pure , unadorned, from thy two Mothers art thou born: thou camest fromVivasvan as a charming
Sage.

With oil they strengthened thee, O Agni, worshipped God: thy banner was the smoke that mounted
to the sky.
4 May Agni graciously come to our sacrifice. The men bear Agni here and there in every house.
He hath become an envoy, bearer of our gifts: electing Agni, men choose one exceeding wise.
5 For thee, O Agni, is this sweetest prayer of mine: dear to thy spirit be this product of my thought.
As great streams fill the river so our song of praise fill thee, and make thee yet more mighty in thy
strength.

6 O Agni, the Angirases discovered thee what time thou layest hidden, fleeing back from wood to
wood.
Thou by attrition art produced as conquer.ing might, and men, O Angiras, call thee the Son of
Strength.

## [05-012] HYMN XII. Agni.

I. To Agni, lofty Asura, meet for worship, Steer of eternal Law, my prayer I offer;
I bring my song directed to the Mighty like pure oil for his mouth at sacrifices.
2 Mark the Law, thou who knowest, yea, observe it: send forth the full streams of eternal Order.
I use no sorcery with might or falsehood the sacred Law of the Red Steer I follow.
3 How hast thou, follower of the Law eternal, become the knower of a new song, Agni?
The God, the Guardian of the seasons, knows me: the Lord of him who won this wealth I know not.
4 Who, Agni, in alliance with thy foeman, what splendid helpers won for them their riches?
Agni, who guard the dwelling-place of falsehood? Who are protectors of the speech of liars?
5 Agni, those friends of thine have turned them from thee: gracious of old, they have become
ungracious.
They have deceived themselves by their own speeches, uttering wicked words against the righteous.
6 He who pays sacrifice to thee with homage, O Agni, keeps the Red Steer's Law eternal;
Wide is his dwelling. May the noble offipring of Nahusa who wandered forth come hither.

## [05-013] HYMN XIII. Agni.

1. WITH songs of praise we call on thee, we kindle thee with songs of praise,
Agni, -with songs of praise, for help.
2 Eager for wealth, we meditate Agni's effectual praise to-day,
Praise of the God who touches heaven.
3 May Agni, Priest among mankind, take pleasure in our songs of praise,
And worship the Celestial Folk.
4 Thou, Agni, art spread widely forth, Priest dear and excellent; through thee
Men make the sacrifice complete.
5 Singers exalt thee, Agni, well lauded, best giver of our strength:
So grant thou us heroic might.
6 Thou Agni, as the felly rings the spokes, encompassest the Gods.
1 yearn for bounty manifold.

## [05-014] HYMN XIV. Agni.

1. ENKINDLING the Immortal, wake Agni with song of praise: may he bear our oblations to the Gods.
2 At high solemnities mortal men glorify him the Immortal, best At sacrifice among mankind.
3 That he may bear their gifts to heaven, all glorify him Agni, God,
With ladle that distilleth oil.
4 Agni shone bright when born, with light killing the Dasyus and the dark:
He found the Kine, the Floods, the Sun.
5 Serve Agni, God adorable, the Sage whose back is balmed with oil:
Let him approach, and hear my call.

6 They have exalted Agni, God of all mankind, with oil and hymns
Of praise, devout and eloquent.

## [05-015] HYMN XV. Agni.

1. To him, the far-renowned, the wise Ordainer, ancient and glorious, a song I offer.
Enthroned in oil, the Asura, bliss-giver, is Agni, firm support of noble, riches.
2 By holy Law they kept supporting Order, by help of sacrifice, in loftiest heaven,-
They who attained with born men to the unborn, men seated on that stay, heaven's firm sustainer.
3 Averting woe, they labour hard to bring him, the ancient, plenteous food as power resistless.
May he, born newly, conquer his assailants: round him they stand as round an angry lion.
4 When, like a mother, spreading forth to nourish, to cherish and regard each man that liveth,-
Consuming all the strength that thou hast gotten, thou wanderest round, thyself,
in varied fashion.
5 May strength preserve the compass of thy vigour, God! that broad stream of thine that beareth
riches.
Thou, like a thief who keeps his refuge secret, hast holpen Atri to great wealth, by teaching.

## [05-016] HYMN XVI. Agni.

1. GREAT power is in the beam of light, sing praise to, Agni, to the God
Whom men have set in foremost place like Mitra with their eulogies.
2 He by the splendour of his arms is Priest of every able man.
Agni conveys oblation straight, and deals, as Bhaga deals, his boons.
3 All rests upon the laud and love of him the rich, high-flaming God,
On whom, loud-roaring, men have laid great strength as on a faithful friend.
4 So, Agni, be the Friend of these with liberal gift of hero strength.
Yea, Heaven and Earth have not surpassed this Youthful One in glorious fame.
5 O Agni, quickly come to us, and, glorified, bring precious wealth.
So we and these our princes will assemble for the good of all. Be near in fight to prosper us.

## [05-017] HYMN XVII. Agni.

1. GOD, may a mortal call the Strong hither, with solemn rites, to aid,
A man call Agni to protect when sacrifice is well prepared.
2 Near him thou seemest mightier still in native glory, set to hold
Apart yon flame-hued vault of heaven, lovely beyond the thought of man.
3 Yea, this is by the light of him whom powerful siong hath bound to act,
Whose bearns of splendour flash on high as though they sprang from heavenly seed.
4 Wealth loads the Wonder-Worker's car through his, the very wise One's power.
Then, meet to be invoked among all tribes, is Agni ghorified.
5 Now, too, the princes shall obtain excellent riches by our lips.
Protect us for our welfare: lend thy succour, O thou Son of Strength. Be near in fight to prosper us.

## [05-018] HYMN XVIII. Agni.

1. AT dawn let: Agni, much-beloved guest of the house, be glorified;
Immortal who delights in all oblations brought by mortal men.
2 For Dvita who receives through wealth of native strength maimed offerings,
Thy praiser even gains at once the Soma-drops, Immortal Gods!
3 Nobles, with song I call that car of yours that shines with lengthened life,
For, God who givest steeds! that car hither and thither goes unharmed.
4 They who have varied ways of thought, who guard, the lauds within their lips,
And strew the grass before the light, have decked themselves with high renown.

5 Immortal Agni, give the chiefs, heroes who institute the rite,
Heroes' illustrious, lofty fame, who at the synod met for praise presented me with fifty steeds.

## [05-019] HYMN XIX. Agni.

1. ONE state begets another state: husk is made visible from husk:
Within his Mother's side he speaks.
2 Discerning, have they offered gifts: they guard the strength that never wastes.
To a strong fort have they pressed in.
3 Svaitreya's people, all his men, have gloriously increased in might.
A gold chain Brhaduktha wears, as, through this Soma, seeking spoil.
4 I bring, as 'twere, the longed-for milk, the dear milk of the Sister-Pair.
Like to a caldron filled with food is he, unconquered, conquering all.
5 Beam of light, come to us in sportive fashion, finding thyself close to the wind that fans thee.
These flames of his are wasting flames, like arrows keen-pointed, sharpened, on his breast.

## [05-020] HYMN XX. Agni.

1. AGNI, best winner of the spoil, cause us to praise before the Gods
As our associate meet for lauds, wealth which thou verily deemest wealth.
2 Agni, the great who ward not off the anger of thy power and might
Stir up the wrath and hatred due to one who holds an alien creed.
3 Thee, Agni, would we choose as Priest, the perfecter of strength and skill;
We who bring sacred food invoke with song thee Chief at holy rites.
4 Here as is needful for thine aid we toil, O Conqueror, day by day,
For wealth, for Law. May we rejoice, Most Wise One! at the feast, with kine, rejoice, with heroes, at
the feast.

## [05-021] HYMN XXI. Agni.

1. WE stablish thee as Manus used, as Manus used we kindle thee.
Like Manus, for the pious man , Angiras, Agni, worship Gods.
2 For well, O Agni, art thou pleased when thou art kindled mid mankind.
Straight go the ladles unto thee, thou highborn God whose food is oil.
3 Thee have all Gods of one accord established as their messenger.

Serving at sacrifices men adore thee as a God, O Sage.
4 Let mortal man adore your God, Agni, with worship due to Gods.
Shine forth enkindled, Radiant One. Sit in the chamber of the Law, sit in the chamber of the food.

## [05-022] HYMN XXII. Agni.

1. LIKE Atri, Visvasaman! sing to him of purifying light,
Who must be praised in holy rites, the Priest most welcome in the house.
2 Set Jatavedas in his place, Agni the God and Minister.
Let sacrifice proceed to-day duly, comprising all the Gods.
3 All mortals come to thee for aid, the God of most observant mind.
Of thine excelling favour we bethink us as we long for it.
4 Mark with attention this our speech, O Agni, thou victorious One.
Thee, Strong-jawed! as the homestead's Lord, the Atris with their lauds exalt, the Atris beautify with songs.

## [05-023] HYMN XXIII. Agni.

1. By thy fair splendour's mighty power, O Agni, bring victorious wealth,
Wealth that o'ercometh all mankind, and, near us, conquereth in fight.
2 Victorious Agni, bring to us the wealth that vanquisheth in war;

For thou art wonderful and true, giver of strength in herds of kine.
3 For all the folk with one accord, whose sacred grass is trimmed and strewn,
Invite thee to their worship-halls, as a dear Priest, for choicest wealth.
4 For he, the God of all men, hath gotten him might that quelleth foes.
O Agni, in these homes shine forth, bright God! for our prosperity, shine, Purifier! splendidly.

## [05-024] HYMN XXIV. Agni.

1. O AGNI, be our nearest Friend, be thou a kind deliverer and a gracious Friend.
2 Excellent Agni, come thou nigh to us, and give us wealth most splendidly renowned.
3 So hear us, listen to this call of ours, and keep us far from every sinful man.
4 To thee then, O Most Bright, O Radiant God, we come with prayer for happiness for our friends.

## [05-025] HYMN XXV. Agni.

1. I WILL sing near, for grace, your God Agni, for he is good to us.
Son of the Brands, may he give gifts, and, righteous, save us from the foe.
2 For be is true, whpm men of old enkindled, and the Gods themselves,
The Priest with the delicious tongue, rich with the light of glorious beams.
3 With wisdom that surpasseth all, with gracious will most excellent,
O Agni, worthy of our choice, shine wealth on us through hymns of praise.
4 Agni is King, for he extends to mortals and to Gods alike.
Agni is bearer of our gifts. Worship ye Agni with your thoughts.
5 Agni gives to the worshipper a son, the best, of mightiest fame,
Of deep devotion, ne'er subdued, bringer of glory to his sire.
6 Agni bestows the hero-lord who conquers with the men in fight.
Agni bestows the fleet-foot steed, the victor never overcome.

7 The mightiest song is Agni's: shine on high, thou who art rich in light.
Like the Chief Consort of a King, riches and strength proceed - from thee.
8 Resplendent are thy rays of light: loud is thy voice like pressing-stones.
Yea, of itself thy thunder goes forth like the roaring of the heaven.
9 Thus, seeking riches, have we paid homage to Agni Conqueror.
May he, most wise, as with a ship, carry us over all our foes.

## [05-026] HYMN XXVI. Agni.

1. O AGNI, Holy and Divine, with splendour and thy pleasant tongue
Bring hither and adore the Gods.
2 We pray thee, thou who droppest oil, bright-rayed! who lookest on the Sun,
Bring the Gods hither to the feast.
3 We have enkindled thee, O Sage, bright caller of the Gods to feast.
O Agni, great in Sacrifice.
4 O Agni, come with all the Gods, come to our sacrificial gift:
We choose thee as Invoking Priest.
5 Bring, Agni, to the worshipper who pours the juice, heroic strength:
Sit with the Gods upon the grass.
6 Victor of thousands, Agni, thou, enkindled, cherishest the laws,
Laud-worthy, envoy of the Gods.
7 Set Agni Jatavedas down, the bearer of our sacred gifts,
MostYouthful, God and Minister.
8 Duly proceed our sacrifice, comprising all the Gods, to-day:
Strew holy grass to be their seat.
9 So may the Maruts sit thereon, the Asvins, Mitra, Varuna:

The Gods with all their company.

## [05-027] HYMN XXVII. Agni.

1. THE Godlike hero, famousest of nobles, hath granted me two oxen with a wagon.
Trvrsan's son Tryaruna hath distinguished himself, Vaisvanara Agni! with ten thousands.
2 Protect Tryaruna, as thou art waxing strong and art highly praised, Vaisvanara Agni!
Who granteth me a hundred kine and twenty, and two bay horses, good at draught, and harnessed.
3 So Trasadasyu served thee, God Most Youthful, craving thy favour for the ninth time, Agni;
Tryaruya who with attentive spirit accepteth many a song from me the mighty.
4 He who declares his wish to me, to Asvamedha, to the Prince,
Pays him who with his verse seeks gain, gives power to him who keeps the Law.
5 From whom a hundred oxen, all of speckled hue, delight my heart,
The gifts of Asvamedha, like thrice-mingled draughts of Soma juice.
6 To Asvamedha who bestows a hundred gifts grant hero power,
O Indra-Agni! lofty rule like the unwasting Sun in heaven.

## [05-028] HYMN XXVIII. Agni.

1. AGNI inflamed hath sent to heaven his lustre: he shines forth widely turning unto Morning.
Eastward the ladle goes that brings all blessing, praising the Godswith homage and oblation.
2 Enkindled, thou art King of the immortal world: him who brings offerings thou attendest for his weal.

He whom thou urgest on makes all possessions his: he sets before thee, Agni, gifts that guests may
claim.
3 Show thyself strong for mighty bliss, O Agni, most excellent be thine effulgent splendours.
Make easy to maintain our household lordship, and overcome the might of those who hate us.
4 Thy glory, Agni, I adore, kindled, exalted in thy strength.
A Steer of brilliant splendour, thou art lighted well at sacred rites.
5 Agni, invoked and kindled, serve the Gods, thou skilled in sacrifice:
For thou art bearer of our gifts.
6 Invoke and worship Agni while the sacrificial rite proceeds:
For offering-bearer choose ye him.

## [05-029] HYMN XXIX. Agni.

1. MAN'S worship of the Gods hath three great lustres, and three celestial lights have they
established
The Maruts gifted with pure strength adore thee, for thou, O Indra, art their sapient Rsi.
2 What time the Maruts sang their song to Indra, joyous when he had drunk of Soma juices,
He grasped his thunderbolt to slay the Dragon, and loosed, that they might flow, the youthful Waters.
3 And, O ye Brahmans, Maruts, so may Indra drink draughts of this my carefully pressed Sorna;
For this oblation found for man the cattle, and Indra, having quaffed it, slew the Dragon.
4 Then heaven and earth he sundered and supported: wrapped even in these he struck the Beast
with terror.
So Indra forced the Engulfer to disgorgement, and slew the Danava. panting against him.
5 Thus all the Gods, O Maghavan, delivered to thee of their free will the draught of Soma;
When thou for Etasa didst cause to tarry the flying mares of Surya racing forward.
6 When Maghavan with the thunderbolt demolished his nine-and-ninety castles all together,
The Maruts, where they met, glorified Indra: ye with the Trstup hymn obstructed heaven.
7 As friend to aid a friend, Agni dressed quickly three hundred buffaloes, even as he willed it.
And Indra, from man's gift, for Vrtra's slaughter, drank ofr at once three lakes of pressed-out Soma.
8 When thou three hundred buffaloes' flesh hadst eaten, and drunk, as Maghavan, three lakes of
Soma,

All the Gods raised as 'twere a shout of triumph to Indra praise because he slew the Dragon.
9 What time ye came with strong steeds swiftly speeding, O Usana and Indra, to the dwelling,
Thou camest thither -conquering together with Kutsa and the Gods: thou slewest Susna.
10 One car-wheel of the Sun thou rolledst forward, and one thou settest free to move for Kutsa.
Thou slewest noseless Dasyus with thy weapon, and in their home o'erthrewest hostile speakers.
11 The lauds of Gauriviti made thee mighty to Vidathin's son, as prey, thou gavest Pipru.
Rjisivan drew thee into friendship dressing the sacred food, and thou hast drunk his Soma.
12 Navagvas and Dasgvas with libations of Soma juice sing hymns of praise to Indra.

Labouring at their task the men laid open the stall of Kine though firmly closed and fastened.
13 How shall I serve thee, Maghavan, though knowing full well what hero deeds thou hast
accomplished?
And the fresh deeds which thou wilt do, Most Mighty! these, too, will we tell forth in sacred synods.
14 Resistless from of old through hero courage, thou hast done all these many acts, O Indra.
What thou wilt do in bravery, Thunder-wielder! none is there who may hinder this thy prowess.
15 Indra, accept the prayers which now are offered, accept the new prayers, Mightiest! which we
utter.
Like fair and well-made robes, I, seeking riches, as a deft craftsman makes a car, have wrought them.

## [05-030] HYMN XXX. Indra.

1. WHERE is that Hero? Who hath looked on Indra borne on light-rolling car by Tawny Coursers,
Who, Thunderer, seeks with wealth the Soma-presser, and to his house goes, much-invoked, to aid
him?
2 I have beheld his strong and secret dwelling, longing have sought the Founder's habitation.
I asked of others, and they said in answer, May we, awakened men, attain to Indra.
3 We will tell, Indra, when we pour libation, what mighty deeds thou hast performed to please us.
Let him who knows not learn, who knows them listen: hither rides Maghavan with all his army.
4 Indra, when born, thou madest firm thy spirit: alone thou seekest war to fight with many.
With might thou clavest e'en the rock asunder, and foundest out the stable of the Milch-kine.
5 When thou wast born supremest at a distance, bearing a name renowned in far-off regions,
Since then e'en Gods have been afraid of Indra: he conquered all the floods which served the Dasa.
6 These blissful Maruts sing their psalm to praise thee, and pour to thee libation of the Soma.
Indra with wondrous powers subdued the Dragon, the guileful lurker who beset the waters.
7 Thou, Maghavan, from the first didst scatter foemen, speeding, while joying in the milk, the Giver.
There, seeking man's prosperity, thou torest away the head of Namuci the Dasa.
8 Pounding the head of Namuci the Dasa, me, too thou madest thine associate, Indra!
Yea, and the rolling stone that is in heaven both worlds, as on a car, brought to the Maruts.
9 Women for weapons hath the Dasa taken, What injury can his feeble armies To me?
Well he distinguished his two different voices, and Indra then advanced to fight the Dasyu.
10 Divided from their calves the Cows went lowing around, on every side, hither and thither.
These Indra re-united with his helpers, what time the well-pressed Soma made him joyful.
11 What time the Somas mixed by Babhru cheered him, loud the Steer bellowed in his habitations.
So Indra drank thereof, the Fort-destroyer, and gave him guerdon, in return, of milch-kine.
12 This good deed have the Rusamas done, Agni! that they have granted me four thousand cattle.
We have received Rnancaya's wealth, of heroes the most heroic, which was freely offered.

13 The Rusamas, O Agni, sent me homeward with fair adornment and with kine in thousands.
The strong libations have made Indra joyful, when night, whose course was ending, changed to
morning.
14 Night, well-nigh ended, at Rnancaya's coming, King of the Rusamas, was changed to morning.
Like a strong courser, fleet of foot, urged onward, Babhru hath gained four thousand as his guerdon.
15 We have received four thousand head of cattle presented by the Rusamas, O Agni.
And we, the singers, have received the caldron of metal which was heated for Pravargya.

## [05-031] HYMN XXXI. Indra.

1. MAGHAVAN Indra turns his chariot downward, the strength-displaying car which he hath
mounted.
Even as a herdsman driveth forth his cattle, he goeth, first, uninjured, fain for treasure.
2. Haste to us, Lord of Bays; be not ungracious: visit us, lover of gold-hued oblation.
There is naught else better than thou art, Indra: e'en to the wifeless hast thou given spouses.
3 When out of strength arose the strength that conquers, Indra displayed all powers that he
possesses.
Forth from the cave he drove the milky mothers, and with the light laid bare investing darkness.
4. Anus have wrought a chariot for thy Courser, and Tvastar, Much-invoked! thy bolt that glitters.
The Brahmans with their songs exalting Indra increased his strength that he might slaughter Ahi.
5 When heroes sang their laud to thee the Hero, Indra! and stones and Aditi accordant,
Without or steed or chariot were the fellies which, sped by Indra, rolled upon the Dasytis.
6 I will declare thine exploits wrought aforetime, and, Maghavan, thy deeds of late achievement,
When, Lord of Might, thou sunderedst earth and heaven, winning for man the moistly-gleaming
waters.
7 This is thy deed, e'en this, Wonderful! Singer! that, slaying Ahi, here thy strength thou showedst,
Didst check and stay e'en gusna's wiles and magic, and, drawing nigh, didst chase away the Dasytis.
8 Thou, Indra, on the farther bank forYadu and Turvaga didst stay the gushing waters.
Ye both assailed the fierce: thou barest Kutsa: when Gods and Usana came to you together.
9 Let the steeds bring you both, Indra and Kutsa, borne on the chariot within hearing-distance.
Ye blew him from the waters, from his dwelling, and chased the darkness from the noble's spirit.
10 Even this sage hath come looking for succour even to Vata's docile harnessed horses.
Here are the Maruts, all, thy dear companions: prayers have increased thy power and might, O Indra.
11 When night was near its close he carried forward e'en the Sun's chariot backward in its running.
Etaga brought his wheel and firmly stays it: setting it eastward he shall give us courage.
12 This Indra, O ye men, hath come to see you, seeking a friend who hath expressed the Soma.
The creaking stone is laid upon the altar, and the Adhvaryus come to turn it quickly.

13 Let mortals who were happy still be happy; let them not come to sorrow, O Immortal.
Love thou the pious, and to these thy people-with whom may we be numbered-give thou vigour.

## [05-032] HYMN XXXII. Indra.

1. THE well thou clavest, settest free the fountains, and gavest rest to floods that were obstructed.
Thou, Indra, laying the great mountain open, slaying the Danava, didst loose the torrents.
2 The fountain-depths obstructed in their seasons, thou, Thunderer! madest flow, the mountain's
udder.
Strong Indra, thou by slaying e'en the Dragon that lay extended there hast shown thy vigour.
3 Indra with violence smote down the weapon, yea, even of that wild and mighty creature.
Although he deemed himself alone unequalled, another had been born e'en yet more potent.
4 Him, whom the heavenly food of these delighted, child of the mist, strong waxing, couched in
darkness,
Him the bolt-hurling Thunderer with his lightning smote down and slew, the Danava's wrath-fire,
Susna.
5 Though he might ne'er be wounded still his vitals felt that, the God's bolt, which his powers
supported,
When, after offered draughts, Strong Lord, thou laidest him, fain to battle, in the pit in darkness.
6 Him as he lay there huge in length extended, still waxing in the gloom which no sun lightened,
Him, after loud-voiced threats, the Hero Indra, rejoicing in the poured libation, slaughtered.
7 When 'gainst the mighty Danava his weapon Indra uplifted, power which none could combat,
When at the hurling of his bolt he smote him, he made him lower than all living creatures.

8 The fierce God seized that huge and restless coiler, insatiate, drinker of the sweets, recumbent,
And with his mighty weapon in his dwelling smote down the footless evil-speaking ogre.
9 Who may arrest his strength or cheek his vigour? Alone, resistless, he bears off all riches.
Even these Twain, these Goddesses, through terror of Indra's might, retire from his dominion.
10 E'en the Celestial Axe bows down before him, and the Earth, lover-like, gives way to Indra.
As he imparts all vigour to these people, straightway the folk bend them to him the Godlike.
11 I hear that thou wast born sole Lord of heroes of the Five Races, famed among the people.
As such my wishes have most lately grasped him, invoking Indra both at eve and morning.
12 So, too, I hear of thee as in due season urging to action and enriching singers.
What have thy friends received from thee, the Brahmans who, faithful, rest their hopes on thee, O
Indra?

## [05-033] HYMN XXXIII. Indra.

1. GREAT praise to Indra, great and strong mid heroes, I ponder thus, the feeble to the Mighty,
Who with his band shows favour to this people, when lauded, in the fight where spoil is gathered.

2 So made attentive by our hymns, Steer! Indra! thou fastenedst the girth of thy Bay Coursers,
Which, Maghavan, at thy will thou drivest hither. With these subdue for us the men who hate us.
3 They were not turned to us-wtrd, lofty Indra! while yet through lack of prayer they stood
unharnessed.
Ascend this chariot, thou whose hand wields thunder, and draw the rein, O Lord of noble horses.
4 Thou, because many lauds are thine, O Indra, wast active warring in the fields
for cattle.
For Surya in his own abode thou, Hero, formedst in fights even a Dasa's nature.
5 Thine are we, Indra; thine are all these people, conscious of might, whose cars are set in motion.
Some hero come to us, O Strong as Ahi beauteous in war, to be invoked like Bhaga.
6 Strength much to be desired is in thee, Indra: the Immortal dances forth his hero exploits.
Such, Lord of Treasure, give us splendid riches. I praise the Friend's gift, his whose wealth is mighty.
7 Thus favour us, O Indra, with ihy succour; Hero, protect the bards who sing thy praises.
Be friendly in the fray to those who offer the skin of beautiful and well-pressed Soma.
8 And these ten steeds which Trasadasyu gives me, the goldrich chief, the son of Purukutsa,
Resplendent in their brightness shall convey me. Gairiksita willed it and so came I hither.
9 And these, bestowed as sacrificial guerdon, the powerful tawny steeds of Marutasva;
And thousands which kind Cyavatana gave me, abundantly bestowed for my adornment.
10 And these commended horses, bright and active, by Dhvanya son of Laksmana presented,
Came unto me, as cows into the Rsi Samvarana's stall, with magnitude of riches.

## [05-034] HYMN XXXIV. Indra.

1. BOUNDLESS and wasting not, the heavenly food of Gods goes to the foeless One, doer of
wondrous deeds.
Press out, make ready, offer gifts with special zeal to him whom many laud, accepter of the prayer.
2 He who filled full his belly with the Soma's juice, Maghavan, was delighted with the meath's sweet
draught,
When Usana, that he might slay the monstrous beast, gave him the mighty weapon with a thousand
points.
3 Illustrious is the man whoever presseth out Soma for him in sunshine or in cloud and rain.
The mighty Maghavan who is the sage's Friend advanceth more and more his beauteous progeny.
4 The Strong God doth not flee away from him whose sire, whose mother or whose brother he hath
done to death.
He, the Avenger, seeketh this man's offered gifts: this God, the source of riches, doth not flee from
sin.
5 He seeks no enterprise with five or ten to aid, nor stays with him who pours no juice though
prospering well.

The Shaker conquers or slays in this way or that, and to the pious gives a stable full of kine.

6 Exceeding strong in war he stays the chariot wheel, and, hating him who pours not, prospers him
who pours.
Indra the terrible, tamer of every man, as Arya leads away the Dasa at his will.
7 He gathers up for plunder all the niggard's gear: excellent wealth he gives to him who offers gifts.
Not even in wide stronghold may all the folk stand firm who have provoked to anger his surpassing
might.
8 When Indra Maghavan hath marked two wealthy men fighting for beauteous cows with all their
followers,
He who stirs all things takes one as his close ally, and, Shaker, with his Heroes, sends the kine to
him.
9 Agni! I laud the liberal Agnivesi, Satri the type and standard of the pious.
May the collected waters yield him plenty, and his be powerful and bright dominion.

## [05-035] HYMN XXXV. Indra.

1. INDRA, for our assistance bring that most effectual power of thine,
Which conquers men for us, and wins the spoil, invincible in fight.
2 Indra, whatever aids be thine, four be they, or, O Hero, three,
Or those of the Five Tribes of men, bring quickly all that help to us.
3 The aid most excellent of thee the Mightiest hitherward we call,
For thou wast born with hero might, conquering, Indra, with the Strong.
4 Mighty to prosper us wast thou born, and mighty is the strength thou hast.
In native power thy soul is firm: thy valour, Indra, slays a host.
5 O Satakratu, Lord of Strength, O Indra, Caster of the Stone.
With all thy chariot's force assail the man who shows himself thy foe.
6 For, Mightiest Vrtra-slayer, thee, fierce, foremost among many, folk
Whose sacred grass is trimmed invite to battle where the spoil is won.
7 Indra, do thou protect our car that mingles foremost in the fights,
That bears its part in every fray, invincible and seeking spoil.
8 Come to us, Indra, and protect our car with thine intelligence.
May we, O Mightiest One, obtain excellent fame at break of day, and meditate our hymn at dawn.

## [05-036] HYMN XXXVI. Indra.

1. MAY Indra come to us, he who knows rightly to give forth treasures from his store of riches.
Even as a thirsty steer who roams the deserts may he drink eagerly the milked-out Soma.
2 Lord of Bay Horses, Hero, may the Soma rise to thy cheeks and jaws like mountain-ridges.
May we, O King, as he who driveth coursers, all joy in thee with hymns, invoked of many!
3 Invoked of many, Caster of the Stone my heart quakes like a rolling wheel for fear of penury.
Shall not Puruvasu the singer give thee praise, O ever-prospering Maghavan, mounted on thy car?
4 Like the press-stone is this thy praiser, Indra. Loudly he lifts his voice with strong endeavour.
With thy left hand, O Maghavan, give us riches: with thy right, Lord of Bays, be not reluctant.

5 May the strong Heaven make thee the Strong wax stronger:
Strong, thou art borne by thy two
strong Bay Horses.
So, fair of cheek, with mighty chariot, mighty, uphold us, strong-willed, thunderarmed, in battle.
6 Maruts, let all the people in obeisance bow down before this youthful Srutaratha,
Who, rich in steeds, gave me two dark red horses together with three hundred head of cattle.

## [05-037] HYMN XXXVII. Indra.

1. BEDEWED with holy oil and meetly worshipped, the Swift One vies with Surya's beam in
splendour.
For him may mornings dawn without cessation who saith, Let us press Soma out for Indra.

2 With kindled fire and strewn grass let him worship, and, Soma-presser, sing with stones adjusted:
And let the priest whose press-stones ring forth loudly, go down with his oblation to the river.
3 This wife is coming near who loves her husband who carries to his home a vigorous consort.
Here may his car seek fame, here loudly thunder, and his wheel make a thousand revolutions.
4 No troubles vex that King in whose home Indra drinks the sharp Soma juice with milk commingled.
With heroes he drives near, he slays the foeman: Blest, cherishing that name, he guards his people.
5 May he support in peace and win in battle: he masters both the hosts that meet together.
Dear shall he be to Surya, dear to Agni, who with pressed Soma offers gifts to India.

## [05-038] HYMN XXXVIII. Indra.

1. WIDE, Indra Satakratu, spreads the bounty of thine ample grace:
So, Lord of fair dominion, Friend of all men, give us splendid wealth.
2 The food which, Mightiest Indra, thou possessest worthy of renown
Is bruited as most widely famed, invincible, O Golden-hued!
3 O Darter of the Stone, the powers which readily obey thy will,-
Divinities, both thou and they, ye rule, to guard them, earth and heaven.
4 And from whatever power of thine, O Vrtra-slayer, it may be,
Bring thou to us heroic strength: thou hast a man's regard for us.
5 In thy protection, with these aids of thine, O Lord of Hundred Powers,
Indra, may we be guarded well, Hero, may we be guarded well.

## [05-039] HYMN XXXIX. Indra.

1. STONE-DARTING Indra. Wondrous One, what wealth is richly given from thee,
That bounty, Treasure-Finder! bring filling both thy hands, to us.
2 Bring what thou deemest worth the wish, O Indra, that which is in heaven.
So may we know thee as thou art, boundless in thy munificence.
3 Thy lofty spirit, far-renowned as fain to give and prompt to win,-
With this thou rendest e'en the firm, Stone-Darter! so to gain thee strength.
4 Singers with many songs have made Indra propitious to their fame,
Him who is King of human kind, most liberal of your wealthy ones.

5 To him, to Indra must be sung the poet's word, the hymn of praise.
To him, accepter of the prayer, the Atris raise their songs on high, the Atris beautify their songs.

## [05-040] HYMN XL. Indra. Surya. Atri.

1. COME thou to what the stones have pressed, drink Soma, O thou Soma's Lord,
Indra best Vrtra-slayer Strong One, with the Strong.
2 Strong is the stone, the draught is strong, strong is this Soma that is pressed,
Indra, best Vrtra-slayer, Strong One with the Strong.
3 As strong I call on thee the Strong, O Thunder-armed, with various aids,
Indra, best Vrtra-slayer, Strong One with the Strong.
4 Impetuous, Thunderer, Strong, quelling the mighty, King, potent, Vrtra-slayer, Soma-drinker,
May he come hither with his yoked Bay Horses; may Indra gladden him at the noon libation.
5 O Surya, when the Asura's descendant Svarbhanu, pierced thee through and through with
darkness,
All creatures looked like one who is bewildered, who knoweth not the place where he is standing.
6 What time thou smotest down Svarbhanu's magic that spread itself beneath the sky, O Indra,
By his fourth sacred prayer Atri disoovered Surya concealed in gloom that stayed his function.
7 Let not the oppressor with this dread, through anger swallow me up, for I am thine, O Atri.
Mitra art thou, the sender of true blessings: thou and King Varuna be both my helpers.
8 The Brahman Atri, as he set the press-stones, serving the Gods with praise and adoration,

Established in the heaven the eye of Surya, and caused Svarbhanu's magic arts to vanish.
9 The Atris found the Sun again, him whom Svarbhanu of the brood
Of Asuras had pierced with gloom. This none besides had power to do.

## [05-041] HYMN XLI. Visvedevas

1. WHO, Mitra-Varuna, is your pious servant to give you gifts from earth or mighty heaven?
Preserve us in the seat of holy Order, and give the offerer power that winneth cattle.
2 May Mitra, Varuna, Aryaman, and Ayu, Indra Rbhuksan, and the Maruts, love us,
And they who of one mind with bounteous Rudra accept the hymn and laud with adorations.
3 You will I call to feed the car-horse, Asvins, with the wind's flight swiftest of those who travel:
Or also to the Asura of heaven, Worshipful, bring a hymn as 'twere libation.
4 The heavenly Victor, he whose priest is Kanva, Trta with Dyaus accordant, Vata, Agni,
All-feeding Pusan, Bhaga sought the oblation, as they whose steeds are fleetest seek the contest.
5 Bring ye your riches forward borne on horses: let thought be framed for help and gain of treasure.
Blest he the priest of Ausija through courses, the courses which are yours the fleet, O Maruts.
6 Bring hither him who yokes the car, your Vayu, who praises with his songs, the God and Singer;
And, praying and devout, noble and prudent, may the Gods' Spouses in their thoughts retain us.

7 I speed to you with powers that should be honoured, with songs distinguishing Heaven's mighty
Daughters,
Morning and Night, the Two, as 'twere all-knowing: these bring the sacrifice unto the mortal.
8 You I extol, the nourishers of heroes bringing you gifts, Vastospati and Tvastar-
Rich Dhisana accords through our obeisance - andTrees and Plants, for the swift gain of riches.
9 Ours be the Parvatas, even they, for offspring, free-moving, who are Heroes like the Vasus.
May holy Aptya, Friend of man, exalted, strengthen our word for ever and be near us.
10 Trta praised him, germ of the earthly hero, with pure songs him the Offspring of the Waters.
Agn; with might neighs loudly like a charger: he of the flaming hair destroys the forests.
11 How shall we speak to the great might of Rudra? How speak to Bhaga who takes thought for
riches?
May Plants, the Waters, and the Sky preserve us, and Woods and Mountains with their trees for
tresses.
12 May the swift Wanderer, Lord of refreshments listen to our songs, who speeds throuih cloudy
heaven:
And may the Waters, bright like castles, hear us, as they flow onward from the cloven mountain.
13 We know your ways, ye Mighty Ones receiving choice meed, ye Wonderful, we will proclaim it.
Even strong birds descend not to the mortal who strives to reach them with swift blow and weapons.
14 Celestial and terrestrial generations, and Waters will I summon to the feasting.
May days with bright dawns cause my songs to prosper, and may the conquered streams increase
their waters.
15 Duly to each one hath my laud been offered. Strong be Varutri with her powers to succour.
May the great Mother Rasa here befriend us, straight-handed, with the princes, striving forward.
16 How may we serve the Liberal Ones with worship, the Maruts swift of course in invocation, the
Maruts far-renowned in invocation?
Let not the Dragon of the Deep annoy us, and gladly may he welcome our addresses.
17 Thus thinking, O ye Gods, the mortal wins you to give him increase of his herds of cattle: the
mortal wins him, O ye Gods, your favour.
Here he wins wholesome food to feed this body: as for mine old age, Nirrti consume it
18 O Gods, may we obtain from you this favour, strengthening food through the Cow's praise, ye
Vasus.
May she who gives good gifts, the gracious Goddes. s, come speeding nigh to us for our well-being.
19 May Ila, Mother of the herds of cattle, and Urvasi with all the streams accept us;
May Urvasi in lofty heaven accepting, as she partakes the oblation of the living,
20 Visit us while she shares Urjavya's food.

**[05-042] HYMN XLII. Visvedevas.**
1. Now may our sweetest song with deep devotion reach Varuna, Mitra, Aditi, and Bhaga.

May the Five Priests' Lord, dwelling in oblations, bliss-giving Asura, hear, whose paths are open.
2 May Aditi welcome, even as a mother her dear heart-gladdening son, my song that lauds her.
The prayer they love, bliss-giving, God-appointed, I offer unto Varuna and Mitra.
3 In spirit him, the Sagest of the Sages; with sacrificial oil and meath bedew him
So then let him, God Savitar, provide us excellent, ready, and resplendent treasures.
4 With willing mind, Indra, vouchsafe us cattle, prosperity, Lord of Bays! and pious patrons;
And, with the sacred prayer by Gods appointed, give us the holy Deities' lovingkindness.
5 God Bhaga, Savitar who deals forth riches, Indra, and they who conquer Vrtra's treasures,
And Vaja and Rbhuksan and Purandhi, the Mighty and Immortal Ones, protect us!
6 Let us declare his deeds, the undecaying unrivalled Victor whom the Maruts follow.
None of old times, O Maghavan, nor later, none of these days hath reached thy hero prowess.
7 Praise him the Chief who gives the boon of riches, Brhaspati distributor of treasures,
Who, blessing most the man who sings and praises, comes with abundant wealth to his invoker.
8 Tended, Brhaspati, with thy protections, the princes are unharmed and girt by heroes.
Wealth that brings bliss is found among the givers of horses and of cattle and of raiment.
9 Make their wealth flee who, through our hymns enjoying their riches, yield us not an ample
guerdon.
Far from the sun keep those who hate devotion, the godless, prospering in their vocation.
10 With wheelless chariots drive down him, O Maruts, who at the feasts of Gods regards the demons.
May he, though bathed in sweat, form empty wishes, who blames his sacred rite who toils to serve
you.
11 Praise him whose bow is strong and sure his arrow, him who is Lord of every balm that healeth.
Worship thou Rudra for his great good favour: adore the Asura, God, with salutations.
12 May the House-friends, the cunning-handed Artists, may the Steer's Wives, the streams carved
out by Vibhvan,
And may the fair Ones honour and befriend us, Sarasvati, Brhaddiva, and Raka.
13 My newest song, thought that now springs within me, I offer to the Great, the Sure Protector,
Who made for us this All, in fond love laying each varied form within his Daughter's bosom.
14 Now, even now, may thy fair praise, O Singer, attain Idaspati who roars and thunders,
Who, rich in clouds and waters with his lightning speeds forth bedewing both the earth and heaven.
15 May this my laud attain the troop of Maruts, those who are youths in act, the Sons of Rudra.
The wish calls me to riches and well-being: praise the unwearied Ones whose steeds are dappled.
16 May this my laud reach earth and air's mid-region, and forest trees and plants to win me riches.
May every Deity be swift to listen, and Mother Earth with no ill ` thought regard me.
17 Gods, may we dwell in free untroubled bliss.

18 May we obtain the Asvins' newest favour, and gain their health-bestowing happy guidance.
Bring riches hither unto us, and heroes, and all felicity and joy, Immortals!

## [05-043] HYMN XLIII. Visvedevas.

1. MAY the Milch-cows who hasten to their object come harmless unto us with liquid sweetness.
The Singer, lauding, calls, for ample riches, the Seven Mighty Ones who bring enjoyment.
2 With reverence and fair praise will I bring hither, for sake of strength, exhaustless Earth and
Heaven.
Father and Mother, sweetof speech, fairhanded, may they, far-famed, in every fight protect us.
3 Adhvaryus, make the sweet libations ready, and bring the beautiful bright juice to Vayu.
God, as our Priest, be thou the first to drink it: we give thee of the mead to make thee joyful.
4 Two arms-the Soma's dexterous immo. lators-and the ten fingers set and fix the press-stone.

The stalk hath poured, fair with its spreading branches, the mead's bright glittering juice that dwells
on mountains.
5 The Soma hath been pressed for thee, its lover, to give thee power and might and high enjoyment.
Invoked, turn hither in thy car, O Indra, at need, thy two well-trained and dear Bay Horses.
6 Bring by God-traversed paths, accordant, Agni, the great Aramati, Celestial Lady,
Exalted, worshipped with our gifts and homage, who knoweth holy Law, to drink sweet Soma.
7 As on his father's lap the son, the darling, so on the fire is set the sacred caldron,
Which holy singers deck, as if extending and heating that which holds the fatty membrane.
8 Hither, as herald to invite the Asvins, come the great lofty song, most sweet and pleasant!
Come in one car, joy-givers! to the banquet, like the bolt binding pole and nave, come hither.
9 I have declared this speech of adoration to mightiest Pusan and victorious Vayu,
Who by their bounty are the hymns' inspirers, and of themselves give power as a possession.
10 Invoked by us bring hither, jatavedas the Maruts all under their names and figures.
Come to the sacrifice with aid all Maruts, all to the songs and praises of the singer!
11 From high heaven may Sarasvati the Holy visit our sacrifice, and from the mountain.
Eager, propitious, may the balmy Goddess hear our effectual speech, our invocation.
12 Set in his seat the God whose back is dusky, Brhaspati the lofty, the Disposer.
Him let us worship, set within the dwelling, the red, the golden-hued, the allresplendent.
13 May the Sustainer, high in heaven, come hither, the Bounteous One, invoked, with all his favours,
Dweller with Dames divine, with plants, unwearied, the Steer with triple horn, the life-bestower.
14 The tuneful eloquent priests of him who liveth have sought the Mother's bright and loftiest
station.
As living men, with offered gifts and homage they deck the most auspicious Child to clothe him.

15 Agni, great vital power is thine, the mighty: pairs waxing old in their devotion seek thee.
May every Deity be swift to listen, and Mother Earth with no ill thought regard me.
16 Gods, may we dwell in free untroubled bliss.
17 May we obtain the Asvins' newest favour, and gain their health-bestowing happy guidance.
Bring riches hither unto us, and heroes, and all felicity and joy, Immortals!

## [05-044] HYMN XLIV. Visvedevas.

1. As in the first old times, as all were wont, as now, he draweth forth the power turned hitherward
with song,
The Princedom throned on holy grass, who findeth light, swift, conquering in the' plants wherein he
waxeth strong.
2 Shining to him who leaves heaven's regions undisturbed, which to his sheen who is beneath show
fair in light,
Good guardian art thou, not to be deceived, Most Wise! Far from deceits thy name dwelleth in holy
Law.
3 Truth waits upon oblation present and to come: naught checks him in his way, this vic torybringing
Priest:
The Mighty Child who glides along the sacred grass, the undecaying Youth set in the midst of plants.
4 These come, well-yoked, to you for furtherance in the rite: down come the twinborn strengtheners
of Law for him,
With reins easily guided and commanding all. In the deep fall the hide stealeth away their names.
5 Thou, moving beauteously in visibly pregnant ones, snatching with trees the branching plant that
grasps the juice,
Shinest, true Singer! mid the upholders of the voice. Increase thy Consorts thou, lively at sacrifice.
6 Like as he is beheld such is he said to be.
They with effectual splendour in the floods have made
Earth yield us room enough and amply wide extent, great might invincible, with store of hero sons.
7 Surya the Sage, as if unwedded, with a Spouse, in battle-loving spirit moveth o'er the foes.

May he, self-excellent, grant us a sheltering home, a house that wards the fierce heat off on every
side.
8 Thy name, sung forth by Rsis in these hymns of ours, goes to the loftier One with this swift mover's
light.
By skill he wins the boon whereon his heart is set: he who bestirs himself shall bring the thing to
pass.
9 The chief and best of these abideth in the sea, nor doth libation fail wherein it is prolonged.
The heart of him who praiseth trembleth not in fear there where the hymn is found connected with
the pure.
10 For it is he: with though to of Ksatra, Manasa, of Yajata, and Sadhri, and Evavada,
With Avatsara's sweet songs will we strive to win the mightiest strength which even he who knows
should gain.
11 The Hawk is their full source, girth-stretching rapturous drink of Visvavara, of Mayin, and Yajata.

They ever seek a fresh draught so that they may come, know when thy time to halt and drink thy fill
is near.
12 Sadaprna the holy, Tarya, Srutavit, and Bahuvrkta, joined with you, have slain the foes.
He gains his wish in both the worlds and brightly shines-when he adores the host with welladvancing
steeds.
13 The worshipper's defender is Sutambhara, producer and uplifter of all holy thoughts.
The milch-cow brought, sweet-flavoured milk was dealt around. Who speaks the bidding text knows
this, not he who sleeps.
11 The sacred hymns love him who wakes and watches: to him who watches come the Sama verses.
This Soma saith unto the man who watches, I rest and have my dwelling in thy friendship.
15 Agni is watchful, and the gcas love him; Agni is watchful, Sama verses seek him.
Agni is watchful, to him saith this Soma, I rest and have my dwelling in thy friendship.

## [05-045] HYMN XLV. Visvedevas.
1. BARDS of approaching Dawn who know the heavens are come with hymns to throw the mountain
open.
The Sun hath risen and oped the stable portals: the doors of men, too, hath the God thrown open.
2 Surya hath spread his light as splendour: hither came the Cows' Mother, conscious, from the stable,
To streams that flow with biting waves to deserts; and heaven is stablished like a firm-set pillar.
3 This laud hath won the burden of the mountain. To aid the ancient birth of mighty waters
The mountain parted, Heaven performed his office. The worshippers were worn with constant
serving.
4 With hymns and God-loved words will I invoke you, Indra and Agni, to obtain your favour,
For verily sages, skilled in sacrificing, worship the Maruts and with lauds invite them.
5 This day approach us: may our thoughts be holy, far from us let us cast away misfortune.
Let us keep those who hate us at a distance, and haste to meet the man who sacrifices.
6 Come, let us carry out, O friends, the purpose wherewith the Mother threw the Cow's stall open,
That wherewith Manu conquered Visisipra, wherewith the wandering merchant gained heaven's
water.
7 Here, urged by hands, loudly hath rung the press-stone wherewith Navagvas through ten months
sang praises.
Sarama went aright and found the cattle. Angiras gave effect to all their labours.
8 When at the dawning of this mighty Goddess, Angirases all sang forth with the cattle,-
Their spring is in the loftiest place of meeting,-Sarama found the kine by Order's pathway.
9 Borne by his Coursers Seven may Surya visit the field that spreadeth wide for his long journey.
Down on the Soma swooped the rapid Falcon. Bright was the young Sage moving mid his cattle.
10 Surya hath mounted to the shining ocean when he hath yoked his fair-backed Tawny Horses.
The wise have drawn him like a ship through water: the floods obedient have descended hither.

11 I lay upon the Floods your hymn, lightwinning, wherewith Navagvas their ten months completed.

Through this our hymn may we have Gods to guard us: through this our hymn pass safe beyond
affliction.

## [05-046] HYMN XLVI. Visvedevas.
1. WELL knowing I have bound me, horselike, to the pole: I carry that which bears as on and gives us
help.
I seek for no release, no turning back therefrom. May he who knows the way, the Leader, guide me
straight.
2 O Agni, Indra, Varuna, and Mitra, give, O ye Gods, and Marut host, and Visnu.
May both Nasatyas, Rudra, heavenly Matrons, Pusan, Sarasvati, Bhaga, accept us.
3 Indra and Agni, Mitra, Varuna, Aditi, the Waters, Mountains, Maruts, Sky, and Earth and Heaven,
Visnu I call, Pusan, and Brahmanaspati, and Bhaga, Samsa, Savitar that they may help.
4 May Visnu also and Vata who injures none, and Soma granter of possessions give us joy;
And may the Rbhus and the Asvins, Tvastar and Vibhvan remember us so that we may have wealth.
5 So may the band of Maruts dwelling in the sky, the holy, come to us to sit on sacred grass;
Brhaspati and Pusan grant us sure defence, Varuna, Mitra, Aryaman guard and shelter us.
6 And may the Mountains famed in noble eulogies, and the fair-gleaming Rivers keep us safe from
harm.
May Bhaga the Dispenser come with power and grace, and far-pervading Aditi listen to my call.
7 May the Gods' Spouses aid us of their own freewill, aid us to offspring and the winning of the spoil.
Grant us protection, O ye gracious Goddesses, ye who are on the earth or in the waters' realm.
8 May the Dames, wives of Gods, enjoy our presents, Rat, Asvini, Agnayi, and Indrani.
May Rodasi and Varunani hear us, and Goddesses come at the Matrons' season.

## [05-047] HYMN XLVII. Visvedevas.
1. URGING to toil and making proclamation, seeking Heaven's Daughter comes the Mighty Mother:
She comes, the youthful Hymn, unto the Fathers, inviting to her home and loudly calling.
2 Swift in their motion, hasting to their duty, reaching the central point of life immortal,
On every side about the earth and heaven go forth the spacious paths without a limit.
3 Steer, Sea, Red Bird with strong wings, he hath entered the dwelling-place of the Primeval Father.
A gay-hued Stone set in the midst of heaven, he hath gone forth and guards mid-air's two limits.
4 Four bear him up and give him rest and quiet, and ten invigorate the Babe for travel.
His kine most excellent, of threefold nature, pass swiftly round the boundaries of heaven.
5 Wondrous, O people, is the mystic knowledge that while the waters stand the streams are flowing:
That, separate from his Mother, Two support him, closely-united, twins, here made apparent.
6 For him they lenghten prayers and acts of worship: the Mothers weave garments for him their offspring.

Rejoicing, for the Steer's impregning contact, his Spouses move on paths or heaven to meet him.
7 Be this our praise, O Varuna and Mitra may this be health and force to us, O Agni.
May we obtain firm ground and room for resting: Glory to Heaven, the lofty habitation!

## [05-048] HYMN XLVIII. Visvedevas.

1. WHAT may we meditate for the beloved Power, mighty in native strength and glorious in itself,
Which as a magic energy seeking waters spreads even to theimmeasurable middle region's cloud?
2 O'er all the region with their uniform advance these have spread out the lore that giveth heroes strength.
Back, with their course reversed, the others pass away: the pious lengthens life with those that are before.
3 With pressing-stones and with the bright beams of the day he hurls his broadest bolt against the Guileful One.
Even he whose hundred wander in his own abode, driving the days afar and bringing them again.
4 I, to enjoy the beauty of his form, behold that rapid rush of his as 'twere an axe's edge,

What time he gives the man who calls on him in fight wealth like a dwelling-house filled full with store of food.
5 Four-faced and nobly clad, Varuna, urging on the pious to his task, stirs himself with the tongue.
Naught by our human nature do we know of him, him from whom Bhaga Savitar bestows the boon.

## [05-049] HYMN XLIX. Visvedevas.

1. THIS day I bring God Savitar to meet you, and Bhaga who allots the wealth of mortals.
You, Asvins, Heroes rich in treasures, daily seeking your friendship fain would I turn hither.
2 Knowing full well the Asura's time of coming, worship God Savitar with hymns and praises.
Let him who rightly knoweth speak with homage to him who dealeth out man's noblest treasure.
3 Not for reward doth Pusan send his blessings, Bhaga, or Aditi: his garb is splendour.
May Indra, Visniu, Varuna, Mitra, Agni produce auspicious days, the Wonder-Workers.
4 Sending the shelter which we ask, the foeless Savitar and the Rivers shall approach us.
When I, the sacrifice's priest, invite them, may we he lords of wealth and rich possessions.
5 They who devote such worship to the Vasus, singing their hymns to Varuna and Mitra,
Vouchsafe them ample room, far off be danger. Through grace of Heaven and Earth may we be happy.

## [05-050] HYMN L. Visvedevas.

1. LET every mortal man elect the friendship of the guiding God.
Each one solicits him for wealth and seeks renown to prosper him.
2 These, leading God, are thine, and these here ready to speak after us.
As such may we attain to wealth and wait with services on thee.
3 So further honour as our guests the Hero Gods and then the Dames.
May he remove and keep afar our foes and all who block our path.

4 Where fire is set, and swiftly runs the victim dwelling in the trough,
He wins, with heroes in his home, friendly to man, like constant streams.
5 May these thy riches, Leader God! that rule the car, be blest to us,
Yea, blest to us for wealth and weal. This will we ponder praising strength, this ponder as we praise the God.

## [05-051] HYMN LI. Visvedevas.

1. WITH all assistants, Agni, come hither to drink the Soma-juice;
With Gods unto our sacred gifts.
2 Come to the sacrifice, O ye whose ways are right, whose laws are true,
And drink the draught with Agni's tongue.
3 O Singer, with the singers, O Gracious, with those who move at dawn,
Come to the Soma-draught with Gods.
4 To Indra and to Vayu dear, this Soma, by the mortar pressed,
Is now poured forth to fill the jar.
5 Vayu, come hither to the feast, wellpleased unto our sacred gifts:
Drink of the Soma juice effused come to the food.
6 Ye, Indra, Vayu, well deserve to drink the juices pressed by us.
Gladly accept them, spotless Pair come to the food.
7 For Indra and for Vayu pressed are Soma juices blent with curd,
As rivers to the lowland flow: come to the food.
8 Associate with all the Gods, come, with the Asvins and with Dawn,
Agni, as erst with Atri, so enjoy the juice.
9 Associate with Varuna, with Mitra, Soma, Visnu, come,
Agni, as erstwith Atri, so enjoy the juice.
10 Associate with Vasus, with Adityas, Indra, Viyu, come, Agni as erst with Atri, so enjoy the juice.
11 May Bhaga and the Asvins grant us health and wealth, and Goddess Adid and he whom none resist.
The Asura Pusan grant us all prosperity, and Heaven and Earth most wise vouchsafe us happiness.
12 Let us solicit Vayu for prosperity, and Soma who is Lord of all the world for weal;
For weal Brhaspati with all his company. May the Adityas bring us health and happiness.
13 May all the Gods, may Agni the beneficent, God of all men, this day be with us for our weal.
Help us the Rbhus, the Divine Ones, for our good. May Rudra bless and keep us from calamity.
14 Prosper us, Mitra, Varuna. O wealthy Pathya, prosper us.
Indra and Agni, prosper us; prosper us thou, O Aditi.
15 Like Sun and Moon may we pursue in full prosperity our path,
And meet with one who gives again, -who knows us well and slays us not.

## [05-052] HYMN LII Maruts.

1. SING boldly forth, Syavasva, with the Maruts who are loud in song,
Who, holy, as their wont is, joy in glory that is free from guile.
2 For in their boldness they are friends of firm and sure heroic strength.
They in their course, bold-spirited, guard all men of their own accord.
3 Like steers in rapid motion they advance and overtake the nights;
And thus the Maruts' power in heaven and on the earth we celebrate.
4 With boldness to your Maruts let us offer laud and sacrifice:

Who all, through ages of mankind, guard mortal man from injury.
5 Praiseworthy, givers of good gifts, Heroes with full and perfect strength -
To Maruts, Holy Ones of heaven, will I extol the sacrifice.
6 The lofty Heroes cast their spears and weapons bright with gleaming gold.
After these Maruts followed close, like laughing lightning from the sky, a splendour of its own accord.
7 They who waxed mighty, of the earth, they who are in the wide mid-air,
Or in the rivers' compass, or in the abode of ample heaven.
8 Praise thou the Maruts' company, the valorous and truly strong,
The Heroes, hasting, by themselves have yoked their deer for victory.
9 Fair-gleaming, on Parusni they have clothed themselves in robes of wool,
And with their chariot tires they cleave the rock asunder in their might.
10 Whether as wanderers from the way or speeders on or to the path,
Under these names the spreading band tend well the sacrifice for me.
11 To this the Heroes well attend, well do their teams attend to this.
Visible are their varied forms. Behold, they are Paravatas.
12 Hymn-singing, seeking water, they, praising, have danced about the spring.
What are they unto me? No thieves, but helpers, splendid to behold.
13 Sublime, with lightnings for their spears, Sages and Orderers are they.
Rsi, adore that Marut host, and make them happy with thy song.
14 Rsi, invite the Marut band with offerings, as a maid her friend.
From heaven, too, Bold Ones, in your might haste hither glorified with songs.
15 Thinking of these now let him come, as with the escort of the Gods,
And with the splendid Princes, famed for rapid courses, to the gifts.
16 Princes, who, when I asked their kin, named Prsni as their Mother-cow,
And the impetuous Rudra they, the Mighty Ones, declared their Sire.
17 The mighty ones, the seven times seven, have singly given me hundred gifts.
I have obtained on Yamuna famed wealth in kine and wealth in steeds.

### [05-053] HYMN LIII. Maruts.

1. Who knows the birth of these, or who lived in the Maruts' favour in the days of old

What time their spotted deer were yoked?
2 Who, when they stood upon their cars, hath heard them tell the way they went?
Who was the bounteous man to whom their kindred rains flowed down with food of sacrifice?
3 To me they told it, and they came with winged steeds radiant to the draught,
Youths, Heroes free from spot or stain: Behold us here and praise thou us;
4 Who shine self-luminous with ornaments and swords, with breastplates, armlets, and with
wreaths,
Arrayed on chariots and with bows.
5 O swift to pour your bounties down, ye Maruts, with delight I look upon your cars,

Like splendours coming through the rain.
6 Munificent Heroes, they have cast heaven's treasury down for the worshipper's behoof:
They set the storm-cloud free tostream through both the worlds, and rainfloods flow o'er desert
spots.
7 The bursting streams m billowy flood have spread abroad, like milch-kine, o'er the firmament.
Like swift steeds hasting to their journey's resting-place, to every side run glittering brooks.
8 Hither, O Maruts, come from heaven, from mid-air, or from near at hand
Tarry not far away from us.
9 So let not Rasa, Krumu, or Anitabha, Kubha, or Sindhu hold you back.
Let not the watery Sarayti obstruct your way. With us be all the bliss ye give.
10 That brilliant gathering of your cars, the company of Maruts, of the Youthful Ones,
The rain-showers, speeding on, attend.
11 With eulogies and hymns may we follow your army, troop by troop, and band by band,
And company by company.
12 To what oblation-giver, sprung of noble ancestry, have sped The Maruts on this course to-day?
13 Vouchsafe to us the bounty, that which we implore, through which, for child and progeny,
Ye give the seed of corn that wasteth not away, and bliss that reacheth to all life.
14 May we in safety pass by those who slander us, leaving behind disgrace and hate.
Maruts, may we be there when ye, at dawn, in rest and toil, rain waters down and balm.
15 Favoured by Gods shall he the man, O Heroes, Marutr! and possessed of noble sons,
Whom ye protect. Such may we be.
16 Praise the Free-givers. At this liberal patron's rite they joy like cattle in the mead.
So call thou unto them who come as ancient Friends: hymn those who love thee with a song.

### [05-054] HYMN LIV. Maruts.

1. THIS hymn will I make for the Marut host who bright in native splendour cast the mountains down.
Sing the great strength of those illustrious in renown, who stay the heat, who sacrifice on heights of
heaven.
2 O Maruts, rich in water, strengtheners of life are your strong bands with harnessed steeds, that
wander far.
Trita roars out at him who aims the lightning-flash. The waters sweeping round are thundering on
their way.
3 They gleam with lightning, Heroes, Casters of the Stone, wind-rapid Maruts, overthrowers of the
bills,
Oft through desire to rain coming with storm of hail, roaring in onset, violent and exceeding strong.
4 When, mighty Rudras, through the nights and through the days, when through the sky and realms
of air, shakers of all,
When over the broad fields ye drive along like ships, e'en to strongholds ye come, Maruts, but are not
harmed.
5 Maruts, this hero strength and majesty of yours hath, like the Sun, extended o'er a lengthened way,

When in your course like deer with splendour unsubdued ye bowed the hill that gives imperishable rain.

6 Bright shone your host, ye Sages, Maruts, when ye smote the waving tree as when the worm
consumeth it.
Accordant, as the eye guides him who walks, have ye led our devotion onward by an easy path.

7 Never is he, O Maruts, slain or overcome, never doth he decay ne'er is distressed or harmed;
His treasures, his resources, never waste away, whom. whether he be prince or Rsi, ye direct.

8 With harnessed team like heroes overcoming troops, the friendly Maruts, laden with their watercasks,
Let the spring flow, and when impetuous' they roar they inundate the earth with floods of pleasant
meath.

9 Free for the Maruts is the earth with sloping ways, free for the rushing Ones is heaven with steep descents.
The paths of air's mid-region are precipitous, precipitous the mountains with their running streams.

10 When, as the Sun hath risen up, ye take delight, O bounteous radiant Maruts, Heroes of the sky,
Your coursers weary not when speeding on.their way, and rapidly ye reach the end of this your path.

11 Lances are on your shoulders, anklets on your feet, gold chains are on your breasts, gems, Maruts, on your car.
Lightnings aglow with flame are flashing in your hands, and visors wroughtof gold are laid upon your heads.

12 Maruts, in eager stir ye shake the vault of heaven, splendid beyond conception, for its shining
fruit.
They gathered when they let their deeds of might flash forth. The Pious Ones send forth a farresounding
shout.

13 Sage Maruts, may we be the drivers of the car of riches ful I of life that have been given by you.
O Maruts, let that wealth in thousands dwell with us which never vanishes like Tisya from the sky.

14 Maruts, ye further wealth with longedfor heroes, further the Rsi skilled in chanted verses.
Ye give the Bharata as his strength, a charger, and ye bestow a king who quickly listens.

15 Of you, most swift to succour! I solicit wealth wherewith we may spread forth mid men like as the
Sun.
Accept, O Maruts, graciously this hymn of mine that we may live a hundred winters through its
power.

## [05-055] HYMN LV. Maruts.

1. WITH gleaming lances, with their breasts adorned with gold, the Maruts, rushing onward, hold
high power of life.
They hasten with swift steeds easy to be controlled. Their cars moved onward as they went to victory.

2 Ye, as ye wist, have gained of your own selves your power: high, O ye Mighty Ones, and wide ye shine abroad.
They with their strength have even measured out the sky.
Their cars moved onward as they went to victory.

3 Strong, born together, they together have waxed great: the Heroes more and more have grown to majesty
Resplendent as the Sun's beams in their light are they. Their cars moved onward as they went to victory.

4 Maruts, your mightiness deserves to be adored, sight to be longed for like the shining of the Sun.
So lead us with your aid to immortality.
Their cars moved onward as they went to victory.

5 O Maruts, from the Ocean ye uplift the rain, and fraught with vaporous moisture pour the torrents down.
Never, ye Wonder-Workers, are your Milch-kine dry. Their cars moved onward as they went to victory.

6 When to your car-poles ye have yoked your spotted deer to be your steeds, and put your golden
mantles on,
O Maruts, ye disperse all enemies abroad. Their cars moved onward as they went to victory.

7 Neither the mountains nor the rivers keep you back: whither ye have resolved thither ye, Maruts, go.
Ye compass round about even the heaven and earth. Their cars moved onward as they went to
victory.

Whate'er is ancient, Maruts, what of recent time, whate'er is spoken, Vasus, what is chanted forth,
They who take cognizance of all of this are ye. Their cars moved onward as they went to victory.

9 Be gracious unto us, ye Maruts, slay us not extend ye unto us shelter of many a sort.
Pay due regard unto our friendship and our praise. Their cars moved onward as they went to victory.

10 O Maruts, lead us on to higher fortune deliver us, when lauded, from afflictions.
Accept, ye Holy Ones, the gifts we bring you. May we be masters of abundant riches.

## [05-056] HYMN LVI. Maruts.

1. AGNI, that valorous company adorned with ornaments of gold, The people of the Maruts, I call down to-day even from the luminous realm of heaven.

2 Even as thou thinkest in thy heart, thither my wishes also tend. Those who have come most near to thine invoking calls, strengthen them fearful to behold.

3 Earth, like a bounteous lady, liberal of her gifts, struck down and shaken, yet exultant, comes to us.
Impetuous as a bear, O Maruts, is youi rush terrible as a dreadful bull..

4 They who with mighty strength o'erthrow like oxen difficult to yoke,
Cause e'en the heavenly stone to shake ' yea, shake the rocky mountain as they race along.

5 Rise up! even now with lauds I call the very numerous company,
Unequalled, of these Maruts, like a herd of kine, grown up together in their strength.

6 Bind to your car the bright red mares, yoke the red coursers to your car.
Bind to the pole, to draw, the fleet-foot tawny steeds, the best at drawing, to the pole.

7 Yea, and this loudly-neighing bright red vigorous horse who hath been sutioned, fair to see,
Let him not cause delay, O Maruts,, in your course, urge ye him onward in your cars.

8 The Maruts' chariot, ever fain to gather glory, we invoke, Which Rodasi hath mounted, bringing pleasant gifts, with Maruts in her company.

9 I call that brilliant band of yours, adorable, rapid on the car Whereon the bounteous Dame, auspicious, nobly born, shows glorious with the Marut host.

## [05-057] HYMN LVII. Maruts.

1. OF one accord, with Indra, O ye Rudras, come borne on your golden car for our prosperity.
An offering from us, this hymn is brought to you, as, unto one who th irsts for water, heavenly springs.

2 Armed with your daggers, full of wisdom, armed with spears, armed with your quivers, armed with
arrows, with good bows,
Good horses and good cars have ye, O Prsni's Sons: ye, Maruts, with good weapons go to victory.
3 From hills and heaven ye shake wealth for the worshipper: in terror at your coming low the woods
bow down.
Ye make the earth to tremble, Sons of Prsni, when for victory ye have yoked, fierce Ones! your
spotted deer.
4 Bright with the blasts of wind, wrapped in their robes of rain, like twins of noble aspect and of
lovely form,
The Maruts, spotless, with steeds tawnyhued and red, strong in their mightiness and spreading wide
like heaven.
5 Rich in adornment, rich in drops, munificent, bright in their aspect, yielding bounties that endure,
Noble by birth, adorned with gold upon their breasts, the Singers of the sky have won immortal fame.
6 Borne on both shoulders, O ye Maruts, are your spears: within your arms is laid your energy and
3trength.
Bold thoughts are in your heads, your weapons in your cars, all glorious majesty is moulded on your
forms.
7 Vouchsafe to us, O Maruts, splendid bounty in cattle and in steeds, in cars and heroes.
Children of Rudra, give us high distinction: may I enjoy your Godlike help and favour.
8 Ho! Maruts, Heroes, skilled in Law, immortal, be gracious unto us, ye rich in treasures,
Ye hearers of the truth, ye sage and youthful, grown mighty, dwelling on the lofty mountains.

## [05-058] HYMN LVIII. Maruts.

1. Now do I glorify their mighty cohort, the company of these the youthful Maruts,
Who ride impetuous on with rapid horses, and radiant in themselves, are Lords of Amrta.
2 The mighty glittering band, arm-bound with bracelets, givers of bliss, unmeasured in their
greatness,
With magical powers, bountiful, ever-roaring,-these, liberal Heroes, venerate thou singer.
3 This day may all your water-bringers, Maruts, they who impel the falling rain, approach us.
This fire, O Maruts, hath been duly kindled; let it find favour with you, youthful Sages.
4 Ye raise up for the folk an active ruler whom, Holy Ones! a Master's hand hath fashioned.
Ye send the fighter hand to hand, armmighty, and the brave hero, Maruts with good horses.
5 They spring forth more and more, strong in their glories, like days, like spokes where none are last
in order.
Highest and mightiest are the Sons of Prsni. Firm to their own intention cling the Maruts.
6 When ye have hastened on with spotted coursers, O Maruts, on your cars with strong-wrought
fellies,
The waters are disturbed, the woods are shattered. Let Dyaus the Red Steer send his thunder
downward.
7 Even Earth hath spread herself wide at their coming, and they as husbands have with power impregned her.

They to the pole have yoked the winds for coursers: their sweat have they made rain, these Sons of
Rudra.
8 Ho! Maruts, Heroes, skilled in Law, immortal, be gracious unto us, ye rich in treasures,
Ye hearers of the truth, ye sage and youthful, grown mighty, dwelling on the lofty mountains.

## [05-059] HYMN LIX. Maruts.

1. YOUR spy hath called to you to give prosperity. I sing to Heaven and Earth and offer sacrifice.
They bathe their steeds and hasten through the firmament: they spread abroad their radiance
through the sea of cloud.
2 Earth shakes and reels in terror at their onward rush, like a full ship which, quivering, lets the
water in.
Marked on their ways are they, visible from afar: the Heroes press between in mighty armament.
3 As the exalted horn of bulls for splendid might, as the Sun's eye set in the firmament's expanse,
Like vigorous horses ye are beauteous to behold, and for your glory show like bridegrooms, O ye Men.
4 Who, O ye Maruts, may attain the mighty lore of you the mighty, who may reach your manly deeds?
Ye, verily, make earth tremble like a ray of light what time ye bring your boons to give prosperity,
5 Like steeds of ruddy colour, scions of one race, as foremost champions they have battled in the van.
The Heroes have waxed strong like we.1grown manly youths; with floods of rain they make the Sun's
eye fade away,
6 Having no eldest and no youngest in their band, no middlomost, preeminent they have waxed in might,
These Sons of Prsni, sprung of noble ancestry: come hitberward to us, ye bridegrooms of the sky.
7 Like birds of air they flew with might in lengthened lines from heaven's high ridges to the borders
of the sky.
The steeds who carry them, as Gods and mortals know, have caused the waters of the mounuains to
desGend.
8 May Dyaus, the Infinite, roar for our banquet: may Dawns toil for us, glittering with moisture.
Lauded by thee, these Maruts, Sons o Rudra, O Rsi, have sent down the heavenly treasure.

## [05-060] HYMN LX. Maruts.

1. I LAUD with reverence the gracious Agni: here may he sit and part our meed among us.
As with spoil-seeking cars I bring oblation: turned rightward I will swell the Marut's, praise-song.
2 The Maruts, yea, the Rudras, who have mounted their famous spotted deer and cars swift-moving,-
Before you, fierce Ones! woods bow down in terror: Earth, even the mountain, trembles at your coming.
3 Though vast and tall, the mountain is affrighted, the height of heaven is shaken at your roaring
When, armed with lances, ye are sporting, Maruts, and rush along together like the waters.
4 They, like young suitors, sons of wealthy houses, have with their golden natures decked their bodies.
Strong on their cars, the lordly Ones, for glory, have set their splendours on their forms for ever.
5 None being eldest, none among them youngest, as brothers they have grown to happy fortune.

May their Sire Rudra, young and deft, and Prsni pouring much milk, bring fair days to the Maruts.

6 Whether, O blessed Maruts, ye be dwelling in highest, midmost, or in lowest heaven,
Thence, O ye Rudras, and thou also, Agni, notice the sacrificial food we offer.

7 O Maruts, Lords of all, when Agni and when ye drive downward from sublimest heaven along the heights,
Shakers of all, rejoicing, slayers of the foe, give riches to the Soma-pressing worshipper.

8 O Agni, with the Maruts as they gleam and sing, gathered in troop, rejoicing drink the Soma juice;
With these the living ones who cleanse and further all, joined with thy banner, O Vaisvanara, from of old.

## [05-061] HYMN LXI. Maruts.

1. O HEROES lordliest of all, who are ye that have singly come
Forth from a region most remote?

2. Where are your horses, where the reins? How came ye? how had ye the power?
Rein was on nose and seat on back.

3 The whip is laid upon the flank. The heroes stretch their thighs apart,
Like women when the babe is born.

4 Go ye, O Heroes, far away, ye bridegrooms with a lovely Spouse
That ye may warm you at the fire.

5 May she gain cattle for her meed, hundreds of sheep and steeds and kine,
Who threw embracing arms around the hero whom gyavaiva praised.

6 Yea, many a woman is more firm and better than the man who turns
Away from Gods, andoffers not.

7 She who discerns the weak and worn, the man who thirsts and is in want
She sets her mind upon the Gods.

8 And yet full many a one, unpraised, mean niggard, is entitled man:
Only in weregild is he such.

9 And she, the young, the joyous-spirited, divulged the path to Syava, yea, to me.
Two red steeds carried me to Purumilha's side, that sage of far-extended fame,

10 Him who, like Vaidadasvi, like Taranta, hath bestowed on me
A hundred cows in liberal gift.

11 They who are borne by rapid steeds, drinking the meath that gives delight,
They have attained high glories here.

12 They by whose splendour both the worlds are over-spread they shine on cars
As the gold gleams above in heaven.

13 That Marut band is ever young, borne on bright cars, unblamable,
Moving to victory, checked by none.

14 Who knoweth, verily, of these where the All-shakers take delight,
Born, spotless, after sacred Law?

15 Guides are ye, lovers of the song to mortal man through holy hymn,
And hearers when he cries for help.

16 Do ye, destroyers of the foe, worshipful and exceeding bright,
Send down the treasures that we crave.

17 OUrmya, bear thou far away to Darbhya this my hymn of praise,
Songs, Goddess, as if chariot-borne.

18 From me to Rathaviti say, when he hath pressed the Soma juice,

The wish I had departeth not.

19 This wealthy Rathaviti dwells among the people rich in kine,
Among the mountains, far withdrawn.

## [05-062] HYMN LXII. Mitra-Varuna

1. BY your high Law firm order is established there where they loose for travel Surya's horses.
Ten hundred stood together: there I looked on this the most marvellous Deities' one chief glory.

2 This, Mitra-Varuna, is your special greatness: floods that stood there they with the days attracted.
Ye cause to flow all voices of the cowpen: your single chariotfelly hath rolled hither.

3 O Mitra-Varuna, ye by your greatness, both Kings, have firmly stablished earth and heaven,
Ye caused the cows to stream, the plants to flourish, and, scattering swift drops, sent down the rainflood.

4 Let your well-harnessed horses bear you hither: hitherward let them come with reins drawn tightly.
A covering cloud of sacred oil attends you, and your streams flow to us from days aforetime.

5 To make the lustre wider and more famous, guarding the sacred grass with veneration,
Ye, Mitra-Varuna, firm, strong, awe-inspiring, are seated on a throne amid oblations.

6 With hands that shed no blood, guarding the pious, whom, Varuni3, ye save amid oblations.
Ye Twain, together, Kings of willing spirit, uphold dominion based on thousand pillars.

7 Adorned with gold, its columns are of iron. in heaven it glitters like a whip for horses;
Or stablished on a field deep-spoiled and fruitful. So may we share the meath that loads your carseat.

8 Ye mount your car gold-hued at break of morning, and iron-pillared when the Sun is setting,
And from that place, O Varuna and Mitra, behold infinity and limit~tion.

9 Bountiful guardians of the world! the shelter that is impenetrable, strongest, flawless,
Aid us with that, O Varuna and Mitra, and when we long to win may we be victors.

## [05-063] HYMN LXIII. Mitra-Varuna.

1. GUARDIANS of Order, ye whose Laws are ever true, in the sublimest heaven your chariot ye ascend.
O Mitra-Varuna whomsoe'er ye: favour, here, to him the rain with sweetness streameth down from heaven.

2 This world's imperial Kings, O Mitra-Varuna, ye rule in holy synod, looking on the light.
We pray for rain, your boon, and immortality. Through heaven and over earth the thunderers take their way.

3 Imperial Kings, strong, Heroes, Lords of earth and heaven, Mitra and Varuna, ye ever active Ones,
Ye wait on thunder with the many-tinted clouds, and by the Asura's magic power cause Heaven to rain.

4 Your magic, Mitra-Varuna, resteth in the heaven. The Sun, the wondrous weapon, cometh forth as light.
Ye hide him in the sky with cloud and flood of rain, and water-drops, Parjanya! full of sweetness flow.

5 The Maruts yoke their easy car for victory, O Mitra-Varuna, as a hero in the wars.

The thunderers roam through regions varied in their hues.
Imperial Kings, bedew us with the milk of
heaven.
6 Refreshing is your voice, O Mitra-Varuna: Parjanya sendeth out
a wondrous mighty voice.
With magic power the Maruts clothe them with the clouds. Ye
Two cause Heaven to rain, the red, the
spotless One.
7 Wise, with your Law and through the Asura's magic power ye
guard the ordinances, Mitra-Varuna.
Ye by eternal Order govern all the world. Ye set the Sun in heaven
as a refulgent car.

## [05-064] HYMN LX1V. Mitra-Varuna

1. You, foeman-slaying Varuna and Mitra, we invoke with song,
Who, as with penfold of your arms, encompass round the realm
of light.
2 Stretch out your arms with favouring love unto this man who
singeth hymns,
For in all places is sung forth your evergracious friendliness.
3 That I may gain a refuge now, may my steps be on Mitra's path.
Men go protected in the charge of this dear Friend who harms us
not.
4 Mitra and Varuna, from you may I, by song, win noblest meed.
That shall stir envy in the homes of wealthy chiefs and those who
praise.
5 With your fair splendours, Varuna and Mitra, to our gathering
come,
That in their homes the wealthy chiefs and they who are your
friends may thrive.
6 With those, moreover, among whom ye hold your high
supremacy,
Vouchsafe us room that we may win strength for prosperity and
wealth.
7 When morning flushes, Holy Ones! in the Gods' realm where
white Cows shine,
Supporting Arcananas, speed, ye Heroes, with your active feet
hither to my pressed Soma juice.

## [05-065] HYMN LXV Mitra-Varuna.

1. FULL wise is he who hath discerned: let him speak to us of the
Gods,-
The man whose praise-songs Varuna the beautiful, or Mitra,
loves.
2 For they are Kings of noblest might, of glorious fame most
widely spread;
Lords of the brave, who strengthen Law, the Holy Ones with
every race.
3 Approaching you with prayer for aid, together I address you
first
We who have good steeds call on you, Most Sage, to give us
strength besides.
4 E'en out of misery Mitra gives a way to dwelling at our case,
For he who worships hath the grace of Mitra, fighter in the van. '
5 In Mitra's shelter that extends to utmost distance may we dwell,
Unmenaced, guarded by the care, ever as sons of Varuna.
6 Ye, Mitra, urge this people on, and to one end direct their ways.
Neglect not ye the wealthy chiefs, neglect not us the Rsis: be our
guardians when ye quaff the milk.

## [05-066] HYMN LXVI. Mitra-Varuna.

1. O SAPIENT man, call the Two Gods, the very wise, who slay the
foe.
For Varuna, whose form is Law, place offerings for his great
delight.
2 For they have won unbroken sway in full perfection, power
divine.

And, like high laws, the world of man hath been made beautiful
as light.
3 Therefore we praise you that your cars may travel far in front of
ours-
You who accept the eulogy of Ratahavya with his hymns.
4 And ye show wMom, Wondrous Gods with fulness of
intellIgence.
By men's discernment are Ve marked, O ye whose might is
purified.
5 This is the Law sublime, O Earth: to aid the Rsis' toil for fame
The Two, wide-spreading, are prepared. They come with ample
overflow.
6 Mitra, ye Gods with wandering eyes, would that the
worshippers and we
Might strive to reach the realm ye rule, most spacious and
protected well,

## [05-067] HYMN LXVII. Mitra-Varuna.

1. YE Gods, Adityas, Varuna, Aryaman, Mitra, verily
Have here obtained supremest sway, high, holy, set apart for you.
2 When, Varuna and Mitra, ye sit in your golden dwelling-place,
Ye Twain, supporters of mankind, foeslayers, give felicity.
3 All these, possessors of all wealth, Varuna, Mitra, Aryaman,
Follow their ways, as if with feet, and guard from injury mortal
man.
4 For they are true, they cleave to Law, held holy among every
race,
Good leaders, bounteous in their gifts, deliverers even from
distress.
5 Which of your persons, Varuna or Mitra, merits not our praise?
Therefore our thought is turned to you, the Atris' thought is
turned to you.

## [05-068] HYMN LXVIII. Mitra-Varuna.

1. SING forth unto your Varuna and Mitra with a song inspired.
They, Mighty Lords, are lofty Law
2 Full springs of fatness, Sovran Kings, Mitra. and Varuna, the
Twain,
Gods glorified among the Gods.
3 So help ye us to riches, great terrestrial and celestial wealth:
Vast is your sway among the Gods.
4 Carefully tending Law with Law they have attained their
vigorous might.
The two Gods wax devoid of guile.
5 With rainy skies and streaming floods, Lords of the strength
that bringeth gifts,
A lofty seat have they attained.

## [05-069] HYMN LXIX. Mitra-Varuna.

1. THREE spheres of light, O Varuna, three heavens, three
firmaments ye comprehend, O Mitra:
Waxed strong, ye keep the splendour of dominion, guarding the
Ordinance that lasts for ever.
2 Ye, Varuna, have kine who yield refreshment; Mitra, your floods
pour water full of sweetness.
There stand the Three Steers, splendid in their brightness, who
fill the three world-bowls with genial
moisture.
3 I call at dawn on Aditi the Goddess, I call at noon and when the
Sun is setting.
I pray, O Mitra-Varuna, for safety, for wealth and progeny, in rest
and trouble.
4 Ye who uphold the region, sphere of brightness, ye who support
earth's realm Divine Adityas,
The Immortal Gods, O Varuna and Mitra, never impair your
everlasting statutes.

## [05-070] HYMN LXX. Mitra-Varuna.

1. EVEN far and wide, O Varuna and Mitra, doth your grace extend.
May I obtain your kind good-will.
2 From you, benignant Gods, may we gain fully food for sustenance.
Such, O ye Rudras, my wc bc.
3 Guard us, O Rudras. with your guar4 save us, ye skilled to save, my we
Subdue the Dasyus, we ourselves,
4 Or ne'er may we, O Wondrous Strong, enjoy another's solemn feast,
Ourselves, our sons, or progeny.

## [05-071] HYMN LXXI. Mitra-Varuna.

1. O Varuna and Mitra, ye who slay the foemen, come with might
To this our goodly sacrifice.
2 For, Varuna and Mitra, ye Sages are Rulers over all. Fill full our songs, for this ye can.
3 Come to the juice that we have pressed. Varuna, Mitra, come to drink
This Soma of the worshipper.

## [05-072] HYMN LXXIL Mitra-Varuna.

1 To Varuna and Mitra we offerwith songs, as Atri did. Sit on the sacred grass to drink the Soma
juice.
2 By Ordinance and Law ye dwell in peace secure, bestirring men.
Sit on the sacred grass to drink the Soma juice.
3 May Varuna and Mitra, for our help, accept the sacrifice.
Sit on the sacred grass to drink the Soma juice.

## [05-073] HYMN LXXIII. Asvins.

1. WHETHER, O Asvins, ye this day be far remote or near at hand,
In many spots or in mid-air, come hither, Lords of ample wealth.
2 These here, who show o'er widest space, bringing full many a wondrous act,
Resistless, lovingly I seek, I call the Mightiest to enjoy.
3 Another beauteous wheel have ye fixed there to decorate your car.
With others through the realms ye roam in might unto the neighbouring tribes.
4 That deed of yours that is extolled, Visvas! hath all been done with this.
Born otherwise, and spotless, ye have entered kinship's bonds with us.
5 When Surya mounted on your car that rolls for ever rapidly,
Birds of red hue were round about and burning splendours compassed you.
6 Atri bethinks himself of you, O Heroes, with a friendly mind,
What time, Nasatyas, with his mouth he stirs the spotless flame for you.
7 Strong is your swiftly moving steed, famed his exertion in the course
When by your great deeds, Atyins, Chiefs, Atri is brought to us again.
8 Lovers of sweetness, Rudras, she who streams with sweetness waits on you.
When ye have travelled through the seas men bring you gifts of well-dressed food.
9 Asvins, with truth they call you Twain bestowers of felicity;
At sacrifice most prompt to hear, most gracious ye at sacrifice.
10 Most pleasing to the Asvins be these prayers which magnify their might,
Which we have fashioned, even as cars high reverence have we spoken forth.

## [05-074] HYMN LXXIV. Asvins.

1. WHERE in the heavens are ye to-day, Gods, Asvins, rich in constancy?
Hear this, ye excellent as Steers: Atri inviteth you to come.
2 Where are they now? Where are the Twain, the famed Nasatyas, Gods in heaven?
Who is the man ye strive to reach? Who of your suppliants is with you?
3 Whom do ye visit, whom approach? to whom direct your harnessed car?
With whose devotions are ye pleased? We long for you to further us.
4 Ye, Strengtheners, for Paura stir the filler swimming in the flood,
Advancing to be captured like a lion to the ambuscade.
5 Ye from cyavana worn with age removed his skin as 'twere a robe.
So, when ye made him young again, he stirred the longing of a dame.
6 Here is the man who lauds you both: to see your glory are we here.
Now bear me, come with saving help, ye who are rich in store of wealth.
7 Who among many mortal men this day hath won you to himself?
What bard, accepters of the bard? Who, rich in wealth! with sacrifice?
8 O Asvins, may your car approach, most excellent of cars for speed.
Through many regions may our praise pass onward among mortal men.
9 May our laudation of you Twain, lovers of meath! be sweet to you.
Fly hitherward, ye wise of heart, like falcons with your winged steeds.

10 O Asvins, when at any time ye listen to this call of mine,
For you is dainty food prepared: they mix refreshing food for you.

## [05-075] HYMN LXXV. Asvins.

1. To meet your treasure-bringing car, the mighty car most dear to us,
Asvins, the Rsi is prepared, your raiser, with his song of praise. Lovers of sweetness, hear my call.
2 Pass, O ye Asvins, pass away beyond all tribes of selfish men,
Wonderful, with your golden paths, most gracious, bringers of the flood. Lovers of sweetness, hear
my call.
3 Come to us, O ye Asvin Pair, bringing your precious treasures, come
Ye Rudras, on your paths of gold, rejoicing, rich in store of wealth. Lovers of sweetness, hear my call.
4 O strong and Good, the voice of him who lauds you well cleaves to your car.
And that great beast, your chariot-steed, fair, wonderful, makes dainty food. Lovers of sweetness,
hear my call.
5 Watchful in spirit, born on cars, impetuous, listing to his cry,
Asvins, with winged steeds ye speed down to cyavana void of guile. Lovers of sweetness, hear my
call.
6 Hither, O Heroes, let your steeds, of dappled hue, yoked at the thought,
Your flying steeds, O Asvins, bring you hitherward, with bliss, to drink. Lovers of sweetness, hear my
call.
7 O Asvins, hither come to us; Nasatyas, be not disinclined.

Through longing for the pious turn out of the way to reach our home. Lovers of sweetness, bear my
call.
8 Ye Lords of Splendour, free from guile, come, stand at this our sacrifice.
Beside the singer, Asvins, who longs for your grace and lauds you both. Lovers of sweetness, hear
my call.
9 Dawn with her white herd hath appeared, and in due time hath fire been placed.
Harnessed is your immortal car, O WonderWorkers, strong and kind. Lovers of sweetness, bear my
call.

### [05-076] HYMN LXXVI. Asvins

1. AGNI, the bright face of the Dawns, is shining; the singers' pious voices have ascended.
Borne on your chariot, Asvins, turn you hither and come unto our full and rich libation.
2 Most frequent guests, they scorn not what is ready: even now the lauded Asvins are beside us.
With promptest aid they come at morn and evening, the worshipper's most blessed guards from
trouble.
3 Yea, come at milking-time, at early morning, at noon of day and when the Sun is setting,
By day, by night, with favour most auspicious. Not only now the draught hath drawn the Asvins.
4 For this place, Asvins, was of old your dwelling, these were your houses, this your habitation.
Come to us from high heaven and from the mountain. Come from the waters bringing food and
vigour.
5 May we obtain the Asvins' newest favour, and gain their health-bestowing happy guidance.
Bring riches hither unto us, and heroes, and all felicity and joy, Immortals!

### [05-077] HYMN LXXVII. Asvins.

1. FIRST worship those who come at early morning: let the Twain drink before the giftless niggard.
The Asvins claim the sacrifice at daybreak: the sages yielding the first share extol them.
2 Worship at dawn and instigate the Asvins:nor is the worshipper at eve rejected.
Besides ourselves another craves and worships: each first in worship is most highly favoured.
3 Covered with gold, meath-tinted, dropping fatness, your chariot with its freight of food comes
hither,
Swift as thought, Asvins, rapid as the tempest, wherewith ye travel over all obstructions.

4 He who hath served most often the Nasatyas, and gives the sweetest food at distribution,
Furthers with his own holy works his offspring, and ever passes those whose flames ascend not.
5 May we obtain the Asvins' newest favour, and gain their health-bestowing happy ildance.
Bring riches hither unto us, and heroes, and all felicity and joy, Immortals!

### [05-078] HYMN LXXVIII. Asvins.

1. YE Asvins, hither come to us: Nasatyas, be not disinclined.
Fly hither like two swans unto the juice we shed.
2 O Asvins, like a pair of deer, like two wild cattle to the mead:
Fly hither like two swans unto the juice we shed.

3 O Asvins rich in gifts, accept our sacrifice to prosper it:
Fly hither like two swans unto the juice we shed.
4 As Atri when descending to the cavem called on you loudly like a wailing woman.
Ye came to him, O Asvins, with the freshest and most auspicious fleetness of a falcon.
5 Tree, part asunder like the side of her who bringeth forth a child.
Ye Asvins, listen to my call: loose Saptavadhri from his bonds.
6 For Saptavadhri, for the seer affrighted when he wept and wafled,
Ye, Asvins, with your magic powers rent up the tree and shattered it.
7 Like as the wind on every side ruffles a pool of lotuses,
So stir in thee the babe unborn, so may the ten-month babe descend.
8 Like as the wind, like as the wood, like as the sea is set astir,
So also, ten-month babe, descend together with the after-birth.
9 The child who hath for ten months' time been lying in his mother's side,-
May he come forth alive, unharmed, yea, livingfrorn the living dame.

### [05-079] HYMN LXXIX. Dawn.

1. O HEAVENLY Dawn, awaken us to ample opulence to-day
Even as thou hast wakened us with Satyasravas, Vayya's son, high-born! delightful with thy steeds!
2 Daughter of Heaven, thou dawnedst on Sunitha Sucadratha's son,
So dawn thou on one mightier still, on Satyasravas, Vayya's son, high-born! delightful with thy
steeds!
3 So, bringing treasure, dawn to-day on us thou Daughter of the Sky,
As thou, O mightier yet. didst shine for Satyatravas, Vayya's son, high-born! delightful with thy
steeds!
4 Here round about thee are the priests who laud thee, Bright One, with their hymns,
And men with gifts, O Bounteous Dame, splendid with wealth and offering much, high-born!
delightful with thy steeds!
5 Whatever these thy bands perform to please thee or to win them wealth,
E'en fain they gird us round and give rich gifts which ne'er are reft away, high-born! delightful with
thy steeds!
6 Give to these wealthy patrons fame, O affluent Dawn, with hero sons,
To these our princes who have brought rich gifts ne'er to be reft away, highborn! delightful with thy
steeds!
7 Bring lofty and resplendent fame, O thou munificent Dawn, to these
Our wealthy patrons who bestow rich gifts on us of steeds and kine, high-born! delightful with thy
steeds!
8 Bring us, O Daughter of the Sky, subsistence in our herds of kine,
Together with the sunbeams, with the shine of pure refulgent flames, highborn! delightful with thy
steeds!
9 O Daughter of the Sky, shine forth; delay not to perform thy task.
Let not the Sun with fervent heat consume thee like a robber foe, high-born! delightful with the
steeds!

10 So much, and more exceedingly, O Dawn, it suits thee to bestow,
Thou Radiant One who ceasest not to shine for those who sing thy praise, highborn! delightful with
thy steeds!

## [05-080] HYMN LXXX. Dawn.

1. THE singers welcome with their hymns and praises the Goddess Dawn who bringeth in the
sunlight,
Sublime, by Law true to eternal Order, bright on her path, red-tinted, far-refulgent.
2 She comes in front, fair, rousing up the people, making the pathways easy to be travelled.
High, on her lofty chariot, all-impelling, Dawn gives her splendour at the days' beginning.
3 She, harnessing her car with purple oxen. injuring none, hath brought perpetual riches.
Opening paths to happiness, the Goddess shines, praised by all, giver of every blessing.
4 With changing tints she gleams in double splendour while from the eastward she displays her
body.
She travels perfectly the path of Order, nor fails to reach, as one who knows, the quarters.
5 As conscious that her limbs are bright with bathing, she stands, as 'twere, erect that we may see
her.
Driving away malignity and darkness, Dawn, Child of Heaven, hath come to us with lustre.
6 The Daughter of the Sky, like some chaste woman, bends, opposite to men, her forehead
downward.
The Maid, disclosing boons to him who worships, hath brought again the daylight as aforetime.

## [05-081] HYMN LXXXI. Savitar.

1. THE priests of him the lofty Priest well-skilled in hymns harness their spirit, yea, harness their holy
thoughts.
He only knowing works assigns their priestly tasks. Yea, lofty is the praise of Savitar the God.
2 The Sapient One arrays himself in every form: for quadruped and biped he hath brought forth good.
Excellent Savitar hath looked on heaven's high vault, and shineth after the outgoing of the Dawn.
3 Even he, the God whose going-forth and majesty the other Deities have followed with their might,
He who hath measured the terrestrial regions out by his great power, he is the Courser Savitar.
4 To the three spheres of light thou goest, Savitar, and with the rays of Sidrya thou combinest thee.
Around, on both sides thou encompassest the night: yea, thou, O God, art Mitra through thy
righteous laws.
5 Over all generation thou art Lord alone: Pusan art thou, O God, in all thy goings-forth.
Yea, thou hast domination over all this world. Syavasva hath brought praise to thee, O Savitar,

## [05-082] HYMN LXXXII. Savitar.

1. WE crave of Savitar the God this treasure much to be enjoyed.
The best, all-yielding, conquering gift of Bhaga we would gladly win.
2 Savitar's own supremacy, most glorious and beloved of all,
No one diminisheth in aught.

3 For Savitar who is Bhaga shall send riches to his worshipper. That wondrous portion we implore.
4 Send us this day, God Savitar, prosperity with progeny. Drive thou the evil dream away.
5 Savitar, God, send far away all sorrows and calamities, And send us only what is good.
6 Sinless in sight of Aditi through the God Savitar's influence, May we obtain all lovely things.
7 We with our hymns this day elect the general God, Lord of the good,
Savitar whose decrees are true.
8 He who for ever vigilant precedes these Twain, the Day and Night,

Is Savitar the thoughtful God.
9 He who gives glory unto all these living creatures with the song, And brings them forth, is Savitar.

## [05-083] HYMN LXXXIII. Parjanya.

1. SING with these songs thy welcome to the Mighty, with adoration praise and call Parjanya.
The Bull, loud roaring, swift to send his bounty, lays in the plants the seed. for germination.
2 He smites the trees apart, he slays the demons: all life fears him who wields the mighty weapon.
From him exceeding strong fices e'en the guiltless, when thundering Parjanya smites the wicked.
3 Like a car-driver whipping on his horses, he makes the messengers of rain spring forward.
Far off resounds the roaring of the lion, what time Parjanya fills the sky with rain-cloud.
4 Forth burst the winds, down come the lightning-flashes: the plants shoot up, the realm of light is
streaming.
Food springs abundant for all living creatures, what time Parjanya quickens earth with moisture.
5 Thou at whose bidding earth bows low before thee, at whose command hoofed cattle fly in terror,
At whose behest the plants assume all colours, even thou Parjanya, yield us great protection.
6 Send down for us the rain of heaven, ye Maruts, and let the Stallion's flood descend in torrents.
Come hither with this thunder while thou pourest the waters down, our heavenly Lord and Father.
7 Thunder and roar: the germ of life deposit. Fly round us on thy chariot waterladen.
Thine opened water-skin draw with thee downward, and let the hollows and the heights be level.
8 Lift up the mighty vessel, pour down water, and let the liberated streams rush forward.
Saturate both the earth and heaven with fatness, and for the cows let there be drink abundant.
9 When thou, with thunder and with roar, Parjanya, smitest sinners down,
This universe exults thereat, yea, all that is upon the earth.
10 Thou hast poured down the rain-flood now withhold it. Thou hast made desert places fit for travel.
Thou hast made herbs to grow for our enjoyment: yea, thou hast won thee praise from living
creatures.

## [05-084] HYMN LXXXIV. Prthivi.

1. THOU, of a truth,O Prthivi, bearest the tool that rends the hills: Thou rich in torrents, who with might quickenest earth, O Mighty One.
2 To thee, O wanderer at will, ring out the lauds with beams of day,

Who drivest, like a neighing steed, the swelling cloud, O bright of hue.

3 Who graspest with thy might on earth. e'en the strong sovrans of the wood,

When from the lightning of thy cloud the rain-floods of the heaven descend.

### [05-085] HYMN LXXXV. Varuna.

1. SING forth a hymn sublime and solemn, grateful to glorious. Varuna, imperial Ruler,

Who hath struck out, like one who slays the victim, earth as a skin to spread in front of Surya.

2 In the tree-tops the air he hath extended, put milk in kine and vigorous speed in horses,

Set intellect in hearts, fire in the waters, Siurya in heaven and Soma on the mountain.

3 Varuna lets the big cask, opening downward, flow through the heaven and earth and air's midregion.

Therewith the universe's Sovran waters earth as the shower of rain bedews the barley.

4 When Varuna is fain for milk he moistens the sky, the land, and earth to her foundation.

Then straight the mountains clothe them in the rain-cloud: the Heroes, putting forth their vigour,

loose them.

5 I will declare this mighty deed of magic, of glorious Varuna the Lord Immortal,

Who standing in the firmament hath meted the earth out with the Sun as with a measure.

6 None, verily, hath ever let or hindered this the most wise God's mighty deed of magic,

Whereby with all their flood, the lucid rivers fill not one sea wherein they pour their waters.


7 If we have sinned against the man who loves us, have ever wronged a brother, friend, or comrade,

The neighbour ever with us, or a stranger, O Varuna, remove from us the trespass.

8 If we, as gamesters cheat at play, have cheated, done wrong unwittingly or sinned of purpose,

Cast all these sins away like loosened fetters, and, Varuna let us be thine own beloved.

### [05-086] HYMN LXXXVI. Indra-Agni.

1. THE mortal man whom ye, the Twain, Indra and Agni, help in fight,

Breaks through e'en strongly-guarded wealth as Trta burst his way through reeds.

2 The Twain invincible in war, worthy to be renowned in frays, Lords of the Fivefold. People, these, Indra and Agni, we invoke.

3 Impetuous is their strength, and keen the lightning of the mighty Pair,

Which from their arms speeds with the car to Vrtra's slayer for the kine.

4 Indra and Agni, we invoke you both, as such, to send your cars: Lords of quick-coming bounty, ye who know, chief lovers of the song.

5 These who give increase day by day, Gods without guile for mortal man,

Worthy themselves, I honour most, Two Gods as partners, for my horse.

6 The strength-bestowing offering thus to Indra-Agni hath been paid, as butter, purified by stones.

Deal to our princes high renown, deal wealth to those who sing your praise, deal food to those who

sing your praise.

### [05-087] HYMN LXXXVII. Maruts.

1. To Visnu, to the Mighty whom the Maruts follow let your hymns born in song go forth,

Evayamarut;

To the impetuous, strong band, adorned with bracelets, that rushes on in joy and ever roars for

vigour.

2 They who with might were manifest, and who willingly by their own knowledge told it forth,

Evayamarut.

Maruts, this strength of yours no wisdom comprehendeth: through their gifts' greatness they are

moveless as the mountains.

3 Who by the psalm they sing are heard, from lofty heaven, the strong, the brightly shining Ones,

Evayamarut;

In whose abode there is no mightier one to move them, whose lightnings are as fires, who urge the

roaring rivers.

4 He of the Mighty Stride forth strode, Evayamarut, out of the spacious dwelling-place, their home in

common.

When he, himself, hath yoked his emulous strong horses on heights, he cometh forth, joy-giving, with

the Heroes.

5 Like your tremendous roar, the rainer with light flashing, strong, speeding, hath made all tremble,

Evayamarut,

Wherewith victorious ye, self-luminous, press onward, with strong reins, decked with gold,

impetuous and well-weaponed.

6 Unbounded is your greatness, ye of mighty power: may your bright vigour be our aid, Evayamarut;

For ye are visible helpers in the time of trouble: like fires, aglow with light, save us from shame and

insult.

7 So may the Rudras, mighty warriors, Evayamarut, with splendid brilliancy, like fires, be our

protectors;

They whose terrestrial dwelling-place is wide-extended, whom none suspect of sin, whose bands

have lofty courage.

8 Come in a friendly spirit, come to us, O Maruts, and hear his call who praises you, Evayamarut.

Like car-borne men, one-minded with the mighty Visnu, keep enmity far from us with your deeds of

wonder.

9 Come to our sacrifice, ye Hnly Ones, to bless it, and, free from demons, hear our call, Evayamarut.

Most excellent, like mountains in the air's raid-region, be irresistible, ye, Wise, to this man'a hater.

# BOOK SIX

### [06-001] HYMN I. Agni.

1. THOU, first inventor of this prayer, O Agni, Worker of Marvels, hast become our Herald.

Thou, Bull, hast made us strength which none may conquer, strength that shall overcome all other

prowess.

2 As Priest thou sattest at the seat of worship, furthering us, best Offerer, meet for honour.

So first to thee have pious men resorted, turning thy mind to thoughts of ample riches.

3 In thee, still watching, they have followed riches, who goest with much wealth as with an army,
The radiant Agni, lofty, fair to look on, worshipped with marrow, evermore resplendent.
4 They who approached the God's abode with homage, eager for glory, won them perfect glory:
Yea, they gained even sacrificial titles, and found delight in thine auspicious aspect.
5 On earth the people magnify thee greatly, thee their celestial and terrestrial riches.
Thou, Helper, must be known as our Preserver, Father and Mother of mankind for ever.
6 Dear priest among mankind, adorable Agni hath seated him, joy-giver, skilled in worship.
Let us approach thee shining in thy dwelling, kneeling upon our knees, with adoration.
7 Longing for bliss, pure-minded, God-devoted, Agni, we seek thee, such, meet to be lauded.
Thou, Agni, leddest forth our men to battle, refulgent with the heaven's exalted splendour.
8 Sage of mankind, all peoples' Lord and Master, the Bull of men, the sender down of blessings,
Still pressing on, promoting, purifying, Agni the Holy One, the Lord of riches.
9 Agni, the mortal who hath toiled and worshipped, brought thee oblations with his kindled fuel,
And well knows sacrifice with adoration, gains every joy with thee to guard and help him.
10 Mightily let us worship thee the Mighty, with reverence, Agni! fuel and oblations,
With songs, O Son of Strength, with hymns, with altar: so may we strive for thine auspicious favour.
11 Thou who hast covered heaven and earth with splendour and with thy glories, glorious and
triumphant.
Continue thou to shine on us, O Agni, with strength abundant, rich, and long enduring.
12 Vouchsafe us ever, as man needs, O Vasu, abundant wealth of kine for son and offspring.
Food noble, plenteous, far from sin and evil, he with us, and fair fame to make us happy.
13 May I obtain much wealth in many places by love of thee and through thy grace, King Agni;
For in thee Bounteous One, in thee the Sovran, Agni, are many boons for him who serves thee.

## [06-002] HYMN II. Agni.

1. THOU, Agni, even as Mitra, hast a princely glory of thine own.
Thou, active Vasu, makest fame increase like full prosperity.
2 For, verily, men pray to thee with sacrifices and with songs.
To thee the Friendly Courser, seen of all, comes speeding through the air.
3 Of one accord men kindle thee Heaven's signal of the sacrifice,
When, craving bliss, this race of man invites thee to the solemn rite.
4 Let the man thrive who travails sore, in prayer, far thee the Bountiful.
He with the help of lofty Dyaus comes safe through straits of enmity.
5 The mortal who with fuel lights thy flame and offers unto thee,
Supports a house with many a branch, Agni, to live a hundred years.
6 Thy bright smoke lifts itself aloft, and far-extended shines in heaven.
For, Purifier! like the Sun thou beamest with thy radiant glow.
7 For in men's houses thou must be glorified as a well-loved guest,

Gay like an elder in a fort, claiming protection like a son.
8 Thou, Agni, like an able steed, art urged by wisdom in the wood.
Thou art like wind; food, home art thou, like a young horse that runs astray.

9 E'en things imperishable, thou, O Agni, like a gazing ox,
Eatest, when hosts, Eternal One! of thee the Mighty rend the woods.
10 Agni, thou enterest as Priest the home of men who sacrifice.
Lord of the people, prosper them. Accept the ofrering, Angiras!
11 O Agni, God with Mitra's might, call hither the favour of the Gods from earth and heaven.
Bring weal from heaven, that men may dwell securely. May we o'ercome the foe's malign
oppressions, may we o'ercome them, through thy help o'ercome them.

## [06-003] HYMN III. Agni.

1. TRUE, guardian of the Law, thy faithful servant wins ample light and dwells in peace, O Agni,
Whom thou, as Varuna in accord with Mitra, guardest, O God, by banishing his trouble.
2 He hath paid sacrifices, toiled in worship, and offered gifts to wealth-increasing Agni.
Him the displeasure of the famous moves not, outrage and scorn affect not such a mortal.
3 Bright God, whose look is free from stain like Surya's, thou, swift, what time thou earnestly
desirest,
Hast gear to give us. Come with joy at evening, where, Child of Wood, thou mayest also tarry.
4 Fierce is his gait and vast his wondrous body: he champeth like a horse with bit and bridle,
And, darting forth his tongue, as 'twere a hatchet, burning the woods, smelteth them like a smelter.
5 Archer-like, fain toshoot, he sets his arrow, and whets his splendour like the edge of iron:
The messenger of night with brilliant pathway, like a tree-roosting bird of rapid pinion.
6 In beams of morn he clothes him like the singer, and bright as Mitra with his splendour crackles.
Red in the night, by day the men's possession: red, he belongs to men by day, Immortal.
7 Like Heaven's when scattering beams his voice was uttered: among the plants the radiant Hero
shouted,
Who with his glow in rapid course came hither to fill both worlds, well-wedded Dames, with treasure.
8 Who, with supporting streams and rays that suit him, hath flashed like lightning with his native
vigour.
Like the deft Maker of the band of Maruts, the bright impetuous One hath shone refulgent.

## [06-004] HYMN IV Agni.

1. As at man's service of the Gods, Invoker, thou, Son of Strength, dost sacrifice and worship,
So bring for us to-day all Gods together, bring willingly the willing Gods, O Agni.
2 May Agni, radiant Herald of the morning, meet to be known, accept our praise with favour.
Dear to all life, mid mortal men Immortal, our guest, awake at dawn, is Jatavedas.
3 Whose might the very heavens regard with wonder: bright as the Sun he clothes himself with
lustre.

He who sends forth,, Eternal Purifier, hath shattered e'en the ancient works of Asna.

4 Thou art a Singer, Son! our feast-companion: Agni at birth prepared his food and pathway.
Therefore vouchsafe us strength, O Strength-bestower. Win like a King: foes trouble not thy dwelling.

5 Even he who cats his firm hard food with swiftness,and overtakes the nights as Vayu kingdoms.
May we o'ercome those who resist thine orders, like a steed casting down the flying foemen.

6 Like Surya with his fulgent rays, O Agni, thou overspreadest both the worlds with splendour.
Decked with bright colour he dispels the darkness, like Ausija, with clear flame swifily flying.

7 We have elected thee as most delightful for thy beams' glow: hear our great laud, O Agni.
The best men praise thee as the peer of Indra in strength, mid Gods, like Viyu in thy bounty.

8 Now, Agni, on the tranquil paths of riches come to us for our weal: save us from sorrow.
Grant chiefs and bard this boon. May we live happy, with hero children, through a hundred winters.

## [06-005] HYMN V. Agni.

1. I INVOKE your Son of Strength, the Youthful, with hymns, the Youngest God, whose speech is
guileless;
Sage who sends wealth comprising every treasure, bringer of many boons, devoid of malice.

2 At eve and morn thy pious servants bring thee their precious gifts, O Priest of many aspects,
On whom, the Purifier, all things living as on firm. ground their happiness have stablished.

3 Thou from of old hast dwelt among these people, by mental power the charioteer of blessings.
Hence sendest thou, O sapient Jatavedas, to him who serves thee treasures in succession.

4 Agni, whoever secretly attacks us, the neighbour, thou with Mitra's might! who harms us,
Burn him with thine own Steers for ever youthful, burning with burning heat, thou fiercest burner.

5 He who serves thee with sacrifice and fuel, with hymn, O Son of Strength, and chanted praises,
Shines out, Immortal! in the midst of mortals, a sage, with wealth, with splendour and with glory.

6 Do this, O Agni, when we urge thee, quickly, triumphant in thy might subdue our foemen.
When thou art praised with words and decked with brightness, accept this chanted hymn, the
singer's worship.

7 Help us, that we may gain this wish, O Agni, gain riches, Wealthy One! with store of heroes.
Desiring strength from thee may we be strengthened, and win, Eternal! thine eternal glory.

## [06-006] HYMN VI. Agni.

1. HE who seeks furtherance and grace to help him goes to the Son of Strength with newest worship,
Calling the heavenly Priest to share the banquet, who rends the wood, bright, with his blackened
pathway.

2 White-hued and thundering he dwells in splendour, Most Youthful, with the loudvoiced and
eternal-
Agni, most variform, the Purifier, who follows crunching many ample forests.

3 Incited by the wind thy flames, O Agni, move onward, Pure One! pure, in all directions.
Thy most destructive heavenly Navagvas break the woods down and devastate them boldly.

4 Thy pure white horses from their bonds are loosened: O Radiant One, they shear the ground
beneath them,
And far and wide shines out thy flame, and flickers rapidly moving over earth's high ridges.

5 Forth darts the Bull's tongue like the sharp stone weapon discharged by him who fights to win the
cattle.
Agni's fierce flame is like a hero's onset: dread and resistless he destroys the forests.

6 Thou with the sunlight of the great Impeller hast boldly over-spread the earth's expanses.
So drive away with conquering might all perils. fighting out foemen burn up those who harm us.

7 Wondrous! of wondrous power! give to the singer wealth wondrous, marked, most wonderful, lifegiving.
Wealth bright, O Bright One, vast, with many heroes, give with thy bright flames to the man who
lauds thee.

## [06-007] HYMN VII. Agni.

1. Him, messenger of earth and head of heaven, Agni Vaisvanara, born in holy Order,
The Sage, the King, the guest of men, a vessel fit for their mouths, the Gods have generated.

2 Him have they praised, mid-point of sacrifices, great cistern of libations, seat of riches.
Vaisvanara, conveyer of oblations, ensign of worship, have the Gods engendered.

3 From thee, O Agni, springs the mighty singer, from thee come heroes who subdue the foeman.
O King, Vaisvanara, bestow thou on us excellent treasures worthy to belonged fo r.

4 To thee, Immortal! when to life thou springest, all the Gods sing for joy as to their infant.
They by thy mental powers were made immortal, Vaisvanara, when thou shonest from thy Parents.

5 Agni Vaisvanara, no one hath ever resisted these thy mighty ordinances,
When thou, arising from thy Parents' bosom, foundest the light for days' appointed courses.

6 The summits of the heaven are traversed through and through by the Immortal's light, Vaisvanara's
brilliancy.
All creatures in existence rest upon his head. The Seven swift-flowing Streams have grown like
branches forth,

7 Vaisvanara, who measured out the realms of air, Sage very wise who made the lucid spheres of
heaven,
The Undeceivable who spread out all the worlds, keeper is he and guard of immortality.

## [06-008] HYMN VIII. Agni.

1. AT Jatavedas' holy gathering I will tell aloud the conquering might of the swift red-hued Steer.
A pure and fresher hymn flows to Vaisvanara, even as for Agni lovely Soma is made pure.

2 That Agni, when in loftiest heaven he sprang to life, Guardian of Holy Laws, kept and observed
them well.

Exceeding wise, he measured out the firmament. Vaisvanara attained to heaven by mightiness.

3 Wonderful Mitra propped the heaven and earth apart, and covered and concealed
the darkness with his light.
He made the two bowls part asunder like two skins. Vaisvanara put forth all his creative power.

4 The Migbty seized him in the bosom of the floods: the people waited on the King who should be
praised.
As envoy of Vivasvan MatariSvan brought Agni Vaisvanara hither from far away.

5 In every age bestow upon the singers wealth, worthy of holy synods, glorious, ever new.
King, undecaying, as it were with sharpened bolt, smite down the sinner like a tree with lightningflash.

6 Do thou bestow, O Agni, on our wealthy chiefs, rule, with good heroes, undecaying, bending not.
So may we win for us strength. O Vaisvanara, hundredfold, thousandfold, O Agni, by thy help.

7 O thou who dwellest in three places, Helper, keep with effective guards our princely patrons.
Keep our band, Agni, who have brought thee presents. Lengthen their lives, Vaisvanara, when
lauded.

## [06-009] HYMN IX. Agni.

1. ONE half of day is dark, and bright the other: both atmospheres move on by sage devices.
Agni Vaisvanara, when born as Sovran, hath with his lustre overcome the darkness.

2 I know not either warp or woof, I know not the web they weave when moving to the contest.
Whose son shall here speak words that must be spoken without assistance from the Father near him?

3 For both the warp and woof he understandeth, and in due time shall speak what should be spoken,
Who knoweth as the immortal world's Protector, descending, seeing with no aid from other.

4 He is the Priest, the first of all: behold him. Mid mortal men he is the light immortal.
Here was he born, firm-seated in his station Immortal, ever waxing in his body.

5 A firm light hath been set for men to look on: among all things that fly the mind is swiftest.
All Gods of one accord, with one intention, move unobstructed to a single purpose.

6 Mine ears unclose to hear, mine eye to see him; the light that harbours in my spirit broadens.
Far roams my mind whose thoughts are in the distance. What shall I speak, what shall I now
imagine?

7 All the Gods bowed them down in fear before thee, Agni, when thou wast dwelling in the darkness.
Vaisvanara be gracious to assist us, may the Immortal favour us and help us.

## [06-010] HYMN X. Agni.

1. INSTALL at sacrifice, while the rite advances, your pleasant, heavenly Agni, meet for praises.
With hymns-for he illumines us-install him. He, Jatavedas, makes our rites successful.

2 Hear this laud, Radiant Priest of many aspects, O Agni with the fires of man enkindled,
Laud which bards send forth pure as sacred butter, strength to this man, as 'twere for selfadvantage.

3 Mid mortal men that singer thrives in glory who offers gifts with hymns of praise to Agni,
And the God, wondrous bright, with wondrous succours helps him to win a stable filled with cattle.

4 He, at his birth, whose path is black behind him, filled heaven and earth with far-apparent
splendour:
And he himself hath been. through night's thick darkness, made manifest by light, the Purifier.

5 With thy most mighty aid, confer, O Agni, wonderful wealth on us and on our princes,
Who stand preeminent, surpassing others in liberal gifts, in fame, and hero virtues.

6 Agni, accept this sacrifice with gladness, which, seated here, the worshipper presenteth.
Fair hymns hadst thou among the Bharadvajas, and holpest them to gain abundant vigour.

7 Scatter our foes, increase our store. May we he glad a hundred winters with brave sons.

## [06-011] HYMN XI. Agni.

1. EAGERLY Sacrifice thou, most skilful, Agni! Priest, pressing on as if the Maruts sent thee.
To our oblation bring the two Nasatyas, Mitra and Varuna and Earth and Heaven.

2 Thou art our guileless, most delightful Herald, the God, among mankind, of holy synods.
A Priest with purifying tongue, O Agni, sacrifice with thy mouth to thine own body.

3 For even the blessed longing that is in thee would bring the Gods down to the singer's worship,
When the Angirases' sagest Sage, the Poet, sings the sweet measure at the solemn service.

4 Bright hath he beamed, the wise, the far-refulgent. Worship the two widespreading Worlds, O
Agni,
Whom as the Living One rich in oblations the Five Tribes, bringing gifts, adorn with homage.

5 When I with reverence clip the grass for Agni, when the trimmed ladle, fullof oil, is lifted,
Firm on the seat of earth is based the altar: eye-like, the sacrifice is directed Sun-ward.

6 Enrich us, O thou Priest of many aspects, with the Gods, Agni, with thy fires, enkindled.
O Son of Strength, clad in the robe of riches, may we escape from woe as from
a prison.

## [06-012] HYMN XII. Agni.

1. KING of trimmed grass, Herald within the dwelling, may Agni worship the Impeller's World-halves.
He, Son of Strength, the Holy, from a distance hath spread himself abroad with light like Surya.

2 In thee, most wise, shall Dyaus, for full perfection, King! Holy One! pronounce the call to worship.
Found in three places, like the Speeder's footstep, come to present men's riches as oblations!

3 Whose blaze most splendid, sovran in the forest, shines waxing on his way like the - Impeller.
He knows himself, like as a guileless smelter, not to be stayed among the plants, Immortal.

4 Our friends extol him like a steed for vigour even Agni in the dwelling, jatave~as.
Trce-fed, he fights with power as doth a champion, like Dawn's Sire to be praised with sacrifices.

5 Men wonder at his shining glows when, paring the woods with case, o'er the broad earth he goeth,

And, like a rushing flood, loosed quickly, burneth, swift as a guilty thief, o'er desert places.
6 So mighty thou protectest us from slander, O Champion, Agni! with all fires enkindled.
Bring opulence and drive away affliction. May brave sons gladden us through a hundred winters.

## [06-013] HYMN XIII. Agni.

1. FROM thee, as branches from a tree, O Agni, from thee, Auspicious God! spring all our blessings-
Wealth swiftly, strength in battle with our foemen, the rain besought of heaven, the flow of waters.
2 Thou art our Bhaga to send wealth thou dwellest, like circumambient air, with wondrous splendour.
Friend art thou of the lofty Law, like Mitra, Controller, Agni! God! of many a blessing.
3 Agni! the hero slays with might his foeman; the singer bears away the Pani's booty-
Even he whom thou, Sage, born in Law, incitest by wealth, accordant with the Child of Waters.
4 The man who, Son of Strength 1 with sacrifices, hymns, lauds, attracts thy fervour to the altar,
Enjoys each precious thing, O God, O Agni, gains wealth of corn and is the lord of treasures.
5 Grant, Son of Strength, to men for their subsistence such things as bring high fame and hero children.
For thou with might givest much food in cattle even to the wicked wolf when he is hungry.
6 Eloquent, Son of Strength, Most Mighty, Agni, vouchsafe us seed and offspring, full of vigour.
May I by all my songs obtain abundance. May brave sons gladden us through a hundred winters.

## [06-014] HYMN XIV. Agni.

1. WHOSO to Agni hath endeared his thought and service by his hymns,
That mortal cats before the rest, and finds sufficiency of food.
2 Agni, in truth, is passing wise, most skilled in ordering, a Seer.
At sacrifices Manus' sons glorify Agni as their Priest.
3 The foeman's wealth in many a place, Agni, is emulous to help.
Men fight the fiend, and seek by rites to overcome the riteless foe.
4 Agni bestows the hero chief, winner of waters, firm in fray.
Soon as they look upon his might his enemies tremble in alarm.
5 For with his wisdom Agni, God, protects the mortal from reproach,
Whose conquering wealth is never checked, is never checked in deeds of might.
6 O Agni, God with Mitra's might call hither the favour of the Gods from earth and heaven.
Bring weal from heaven that men may dwell securely. May we o'ercome the foe's malign oppressions,
may we o'ercome them, through thy help o'ercome them.

## [06-015] HYMN XV. Agni.

1. WITH this my song I strive to reach this guest of yours, who wakes at early morn, the Lord of all the tribes.
Each time he comes from heaven, the Pure One from of old: from ancient days the Child cats everlasting food.
2 Whom, well-dis sed, the Blirgus stablished as a rriend, whom men must glorify, high-flaming in the wood.
As such, most friendly, thou art every day extolled in lauds by Vitahavya, O thou wondrous God.

3 Be thou the foeless helper of the skilful man, subduer of the enemy near or far away.
Bestow a wealthy home on men, O Son of Strength. Give Vitahavya riches spreading far and wide,
give Bharadvaja wide-spread wealth.
4 Him, your refulgent guest, Agni who comes from heaven, the Herald of mankind, well-skilled in sacred rites,
Who, like a holy singer, utters heavenly words, oblation-bearer, envoy, God, I seek with hymns.
5 Who with his purifying, eye-attracting form hath shone upon the earth as with the light of Dawn;
Who speeding on, as in the fight of Etaia, cometh, untouched by age, as one athirst in heat.
6 Worship ye Agni, Agni, with your log of wood; praise your beloved, your beloved guest with songs.
Invite ye the Immortal hither with your hymns. A God among the Gods, he loveth what is choice,
loveth our service, God mid Gods.
7 Agni inflamed with fuel in my song I sing, pure, Cleanser, steadlast, set in tront at sacrifice.
Wise Jatavedas we implore with prayers for bliss the Priest, the holy Singer, bounteous, void of guile.
8 Men, Agni, in each age have made thee, Deathiess One, their envoy, offering-bearer, guard adorable.
With reverence Gods and mortals have established thee, the ever-watchful, omnipresent Household Lord.
9 Thou, Agni, ordering the works and ways of both, as envoy of the Gods traversest both the worlds.
When we lay claim to thy regard and gracious fare, be thou to us a thriceprotecting friendly guard.
10 Him fair of face, rapid, and fair to look on, him very wise may we who know not follow.
Let him who knows all rules invite for worship, Agru announce our offering to the Immortals.
11 Him, Agni, thou deliverest and savest who brings him prayer to thee the Wise, O Hero,
The end of sacrifice or its inception; yea, thou endowest him with power and riches.
12 Guard us from him who would assail us, Agni; preserve us, O thou Victor, from dishonour.
Here let the place of darkening come upon thee: may wealth be ours, desirable in thousands.
13 Agni, the Priest, is King, Lord of the homestead, he, Jatayedas, knows all generations.
Most skilful worshipper mid Gods and mortals, may he begin the sacrifice, the Holy.
14 Whate'er to-day thou, bright-flamed Priest, enjoyest from the man's rite-for thou art sacrificer
Worship, for duly dost thou spread in greatness: bear off thine ofrerings of to-day, Most Youthful.
15 Look thou upon the viands duly laid for thee. Fain would he set thee here to worship Heaven and,Earth.
Help us, O liberal Agni, in the strife for spoil, so that we may o'ercome all things that trouble us,
o'ercome, o'ercome them with thy help.
16 Together with all Gods, O fair-faced Agni, be seated first upon the woollined altar,
Nest-like, bedewed with oil. Bear this our worship to Savitar who sacrifices rightly.
17 Here the arranging priests, as did Atharvan, rub this Agni forth,
Whom, not bewildered, as he moved in winding ways, they brought from gloom.

18 For the Gods' banquet be thou born, for full perfection and for weal.
Bring the Immortal Gods who strengthen holy Law: so let our sacrifice reach the Gods.
19 O Agni, Lord and Master of men's homesteads, with kindled fuel we have made thee mighty.
Let not our household gear be found defective. Sharpen us with thy penetrating splendour.

## [06-016] HYMN XVI. Agni.

1. PRIEST of all sacrifices hast thou been appointed by the Gods, Agni, amid the race of man.
2 So with thy joyous tongues for us sacrifice nobly in this rite.
Bring thou the Gods and worship them.
3 For well, O God, Disposer, thou knowest, straight on, the paths and ways,
Agni, most wise in sacrifice.
4 Thee, too, hath Bharata of old, with mighty men, implored for bliss.
And worshipped thee the worshipful.
5 Thou givest these abundant boons to Divodasa pouring forth,
To Bharadvaja offering gifts.
6 Do thou, Immortal Messenger, bring hither the Celestial Folk;
Hearing the singer's eulogy.
7 Mortals with pious thought implore thee, Agni, God, at holy rites,
To come unto the feast of Gods.
8 I glorify thine aspect and the might of thee the Bountilul.
All those who love shall joy in thee,
9 Invoker placed by Manus, thou, Agni, art near, the wisest Priest:
Pay worship to the Tribes of Heaven.
10 Come, Agni, lauded, to the feast; come to the offering of the gifts.
As Priest be seated on the grass.
11 So, Angiras, we make thee strong with fuel and with holy oil.
Blaze high, thou youngest of the Gods.
12 For us thou winnest, Agni, God, heroic strength exceeding great,
Far-spreading and of high renown.
13 Agni, Atharvan brought thee forth, by rubbing, from the lotus-flower,
The head of Visva, of the Priest.
14 Thee. Vrtra's slayer, breaker down of castles, hath Atharvan's son,
Dadhyac the Rsi, lighted up.
15 The hero Pathya kindled thee the Dasyus'. most destructive foe,
Winner of spoil in every fight.
16 Come, here, O Agni, will I sing verily other songs to thee,
And with these drops shalt thou grow strong.
17 Where'er tby mind applies itself, vigour preeminent bast thou:
There wilt thou gain a dwelling-place.
18 Not for a moment only lasts thy bounty, good to many a one!
Our service therefore shalt thou gain.

19 Agni, the Bharata, hath been sought, the Vrtra-slayer, marked of all,
Yea, Divodasa's Hero Lord.
20 For he gave riches that surpass in greatness all the things of earth,
Fighting untroubled, unsubdued.
21 Thou, Agni, as in days of old, with recent glory, gathered light,
Hast overspread the lofty heaven.
22 Bring to your Agni, O my friends, boldly your laud and sacrifice:
Give the Disposer praise and song.

23 For as sagacious Herald he hath sat through every age of man,
Oblation-bearing messenger.
24 Bring those Two Kings whose ways are pure, Adityas, and the Marut host,
Excellent God! and Heaven and Earth.
25 For strong and active mortal man, excellent, Agni, is the look Of thee Immortal, Son of Strength
26 Rich through his wisdom, noblest be the giver serving thee to-day:
The man hath brought his hymn of praise.
27 These, Agni, these are helped by thee, who strong and active all their lives,
O'ercome the malice of the foe, fight down the malice ofthe foe.
28 May Agni with his pointed blaze cast down each fierce devouring fiend
May Agni win us wealth by war.
29 O active Jatavedas, bring riches with store of hero sons:
Slay thou the demons, O Most Wise.
30 Keep us, O Jatavedas, from the troubling of the man of sin:
Guard us thou Sage who knowest prayer.
31 Whatever sinner, Agni, brings oblations to procure our death,
Save us from woe that he would work.
32 Drive from us with thy tongue, O God, the man who doeth evil deeds,
The mortal who would strike us dead.
33 Give shelter reaching far and wide to Bharadvaja, conquering Lord!
Agni, send wealth most excellent.
34 May Agni slay the Vrtras,-fain for riches, through the lord of song,
Served with oblation, kindled, bright.
35 His Father's Father, shining in his Mother's everlasting side,
Set on the seat of holy Law.
36 O active Jatavedas, bring devotion that wins progeny, Agni,
that it may shine to heaven.
37 O Child of Strength, to thee whose look is lovely we with dainty food,
O Agni, have poured forth our songs.
38 To thee for shelter are we come, as to the shade from fervent heat
Agni, who glitterest like gold.
39 Mighty as one who slays with shafts, or like a bull with sharpened horn,
Agni, thou breakest down the forts.
40 Whom, like an infant newly born, devourer, in their arms they bear,
Men's Agni, skilled in holy rites.
41 Bear to the banquet of the Gods the God best finder-out of wealth,
Let him be seated in his place.
42 In Jatavedas kindle ye the dear guest who hath now appeared
In a soft place, the homestead's Lord.
43 Harness, O Agni, O thou God, thy steeds which are most excellent:
They bear thee as thy spirit wills.
44 Come hither, bring the Gods to us to taste the sacrificial feast,
To drink the draught of Soma juice.

45 O Agni of the Bharatas, blaze high with everlasting might,
Shine forth and gleam, Eternal One.
46 The mortal man who serves the God with banquet, and, bringing gifts at sacrifice, lauds Agni,
May well attract, with prayer and hands uplifted, the Priest of Heaven and Earth, true Sacrificer.
47 Agni, we bring thee, with our hymn, oblation fashioned in the heart.
Let these be oxen unto thee, let these be bulls and kine to thee.

48 The Gods enkindle Agni, best slayer of Vrtra, first in rank,
The Mighty, One who brings us wealth and crushes down the
Raksasas.

## [06-017] HYMN XVII. Indra.

1. DRINK Soma, Mighty One, for which, when lauded, thou
breakest through the cattle-stall, O Indra;
Thou who, O Bold One, armed with thunder smotest Vrtra with
might, and every hostile being.
2 Drink it thou God who art impetuous victor, Lord of our hymns,
with beauteousjaws, the Hero,
Render of kine-stalls, car-borne, thunder-wielding, so pierce thy
way to wondrous strength, O Indra.
3 Drink as of old, and let the draught delight thee. hear thou our
prayer and let our songs exalt thee.
Make the Sun visible, make food abundant, slaughter the foes,
pierce through and free the cattle.
4 These gladdening drops, O Indra, Self-sustainer, quaffed shall
augment thee in thy mighty
splendour.
Yea, let the cheering drops delight thee greatly, great, perfect,
strong, powerful, all-subduing.
5 Gladdened whereby, bursting the firm enclosures, thou gavest
splendour to the Sun and Morning.
The mighty rock that compassed in the cattle, ne'er moved, thou
shookest from its seat, O Indra.
6 Thou with thy wisdom, power, and works of wonder, hast
stored the ripe milk in the raw cows'
udders
Unbarred the firm doors for the kine of Morning, and, with the
Angirases, set free the cattle.
7 Thou hast spread out wide earth, a mighty marvel, and, high
thyself, propped lofty heaven, O Indra.
Both worlds, whose Sons are Gods, thou hast supported, young,
Mothers from old time ofholy Order.
8 Yea, Indra, all the Deities installed thee their one strong
Champion in the van for battle.
What time the godless was the Gods' assailant, Indra they chose
to win the light of heaven.
9 Yea, e'en that heaven itself of old bent backward before thy bolt,
in terror of its anger,
When Indra, life of every living creature, smote down within his
lair the assailing Dragon.
10 Yea, Strong One! Tvastar turned for thee, the Mighty, the bolt
with thousand spikes and hundred
edges,
Eager and prompt at will, wherewith thou crushedst the boasting
Dragon, O impetuous Hero.
11 He dressed a hundred buffaloes, O Indra, for thee whom all
accordant Maruts strengthen.
He, Pusan Visnu, poured forth three great vessels to him, the
juice that cheers, that slaughters Vrtra.
12 Thou settest free the rushing wave of waters, the floods' great
swell encompassed and
obstructed.
Along steep slopes their course thou tumedst, Indra, directed
downward, speeding to the ocean.
13 So may our new prayer bring thee to protect us, thee well-
armed Hero with thy bolt of thunder,
Indra, who made these worlds, the Strong, the ty, who never
groweth old, the victory-giver.
14 So, Indra, form us brilliant holy singers for strength, for glory,
and for food and riches.
Give Bharadvaja hero patrons, Indra Indra, be ours upon the day
of trial.
15 With this may we obtain strength God-appointed, and brave
sons gladden us through a hundred winters.

## [06-018] HYMN XVIII. Indra.

1. GLORIFY him whose might is all-surpassing, Indra the much-
invoked who fights uninjured.
Magnify with these songs the never-vanquished, the Strong, the
Bull of men, the Mighty Victor.
2 He, Champion, Hero, Warrior, Lord of battles, impetuous,
loudly roaring, great destroyer,
Who whirls the dust on high, alone, oerthrower, hath made all
races of mankind his subjects.
3 Thou, thou alone, hast tamed the Dasyus; singly thou hast
subdued the people for the Arya.

In this, or is it not, thine hero exploit, Indra? Declare it at the
proper season.
4 For true, I deem, thy strength is, thine the Mighty, thine, O
Most Potent, thine the Conquering
Victor;
Strong, of the strong, Most Mighty, of the mighty, thine, driver of
the churl to acts of bounty.
5 Be this our ancient bond of friendship with you and with
Angirases here who speak of Vala.
Thou, Wondrous, Shaker of things firm, didst smite him in his
fresh strength, and force his doors and
castles.
6 With holy thoughts must he be called, the Mighty, showing his
power in the great fight with Vrtra.
He must be called to give us seed and offspring, the Thunderer
must be moved and sped to battle.
7 He in his might, with name that lives for ever, hath far
surpassed all human generations.
He, most heroic, hath his home with splendour, with glory and
with riches and with valour.
8 Stranger to guile, who ne'er was false or faithless, bearing a
name that may be well remembered,
Indra crushed Cumuri, Dhuni, Sambara, Pipru, and Susna, that
their castles fell in ruin.
9 With saving might that must be praised and lauded, Indra,
ascend thy car to smite down Vrtra.
In thy right hand hold fast thy bolt of thunder, and weaken,
Bounteous Lord, his art and magic.
10 As Agni, as the dart burns the dry forest, like the dread shaft
burn down the fiends, O Indra;
Thou who with high deep-reaching spear hast broken, hast
covered over mischief and destroyed it.
11 With wealth, by thousand paths come hither, Agni, paths that
bring ample strength, O thou Most
Splendid.
Come, Son of Strength, o'er whom, Invoked of many! the godless
hath no power to keep thee distant.
12 From heaven, from earth is bruited forth the greatness of him
the firm, the fiery, the resplendent.
No foe hath he, no counterpart, no refuge is there from him the
Conqueror full of wisdom
13 This day the deed that thou hast done is famous, when thou,
for him, with many thousand others
Laidest low Kutsa, Ayu, Atithigva, and boldly didst deliver
Turvayana.
14 In thee, O God, the wisest of the Sages, all Gods were joyful
when thou slewest Ahi.
When lauded for thyself, thou gavest freedom to sore-afflicted
Heaven and to the people.
15 This power of thine both heaven and earth acknowledge, the
deathless Gods acknowledge it, O
Indra.
Do what thou ne'er hast done, O Mighty Worker: beget a new
hymn at thy sacrifices.

## [06-019] HYMN XIX. Indra.

1. GREAT, hero-like controlling men is Indra, unwasting in his powers, doubled in vastness.
He, turned to us, hath grown to hero vigour: broad, wide, he hath been decked by those who serve
him.
2 The bowl made Indra swift to gather booty, the High, the Lofty, Youthful, Undecaying,
Him who hath waxed by strength which none may conquer, and even at once grown to complete
perfection.
3 Stretch out those hands of thine, extend to us-ward thy wide capacious arms, and grant us glory.
Like as the household herdsman guards the cattle, so move thou round about us in the combat.
4 Now, fain for strength, let us invite your Indra hither, who lieth hidden with his Heroes,-
Free from all blame, without reproach, uninjured, e'en as were those who sang, of old, his praises.
5 With steadfast laws, wealth-giver, strong through Soma, he hath much fair and precious food to
feed us.
In him unite all paths that lead to riches, like rivers that commingle with the ocean.
6 Bring unto us the mightiest might, O Hero, strong and most potent force, thou great Subduer!
All splendid vigorous powers of men vouchsafe us, Lord of Bay Steeds, that they may make us joyful.
7 Bring us, grown mighty in its strength, O Indra, thy friendly rapturous joy that wins the battle,
Wherewith by thee assisted and triumphant, we may laud thee in gaining seed and offspring.
8 Indra, bestow on us the power heroic skilled and exceeding strong, that wins the booty,
Wherewith, by thine assistance, we may conquer our foes in battle, be they kin or stranger.
9 Let thine heroic strength come from behind us, before us, from above us or below us.
From every side may it approach us, Indra. Give us the glory of the realm of splendour.

10 With most heroic aid from thee, like heroes Indra, may we win wealth by deeds glory.
Thou, King, art Lord of earthly, heavenly treasure: vouchsafe us riches vast, sublime, and lasting.
11 The Bull, whose strength hath waxed, whom Maruts follow, free-giving Indra, the Celestial Ruler,
Mighty, all-conquering, the victory-giver, him let us call to grant us new protection.
12 Give up the people who are high and haughty to these men and to me, O Thunder-wielder!
Therefore upon the earth do we invoke thee, where heroes win, for sons and kine and waters.
13 Through these thy friendships, God invoked of many! may we be victors over every foeman.
Slaying both kinds of foe, may we, O Hero, be happy, helped by thee, with ample riches.

## [06-020] HYMN XX. Indra.

1. GIVE us wealth, Indra, that with might, as heaven o'ertops the earth, o'ercomes our foes in battle
Wealth that brings thousands and that wins the corn-lands, wealth, Son of Strength! that vanquishes
the foeman.
2 Even as the power of Dyaus, to thee, O Indra, all Asura sway was by the Gods entrusted,

When thou, Impetuous! leagued with Visnu, slewest Vrtra the Dragon who enclosed the waters.
3 Indra, Strong, Victor, Mightier than the mighty, addressed with prayer and perfect in his splendour,
Lord of the bolt that breaketh forts in pieces, became the King of the sweet juice of Soma..
4 There, Indra, while the light was won, the Panis fled, 'neath a hundred blows, for wise Dasoni,
And greedy Susna's magical devices nor left he any of their food remaining.
5 What time the thunder fell and Susna perished, all life's support from the great Druh was taken.
Indra made room for his car-driver Kutsa who sate beside him, when he gained the sunlight.
6 As the Hawk rent for him the stalk that gladdens, he wrenched the head from Namuci the Dasa.
He guarded Nam, Sayya's son, in slumber, and sated him with food, success, and riches.
7 Thou, thunder-armed, with thy great might hast shattered Pipru's strong forts who knew the wiles
of serpents.
Thou gavest to thy worshipper Rjisvan imperishable Wealth, O Bounteous Giver.
8 The crafty Vetasu, the swift Dasni, and Tugra speedily with all his servants,
Hath Indra, gladdening with strong assistance, forced near as 'twere to glorify the Mother.
9 Resistless, with the hosts he battles, bearing in both his arms the Vrtra-slaying thunder.
He mounts his Bays, as the car-seat an archer: yoked at a word they bear the lofty Indra.
10 May we, O Indra, gain by thy new favour: so Parus laud thee, with their sacrifices,
That thou hast wrecked seven autumn forts, their shelter, slain Dasa tribes and aided Purukutsa.
11 Favouring Usana the son of Kavi, thou wast his ancient strengthener, O Indra.
Thou gavest Navavastva. as a present, to the great father gavest back his grandson.
12 Thou, roaring Indra, drovest on the waters that made a roaring sound like rushing rivers,
What time, O Hero, o'er the sea thou broughtest, in safety broughtest Turvasa and Yadu.
13 This Indra, was thy work in war: thou sentest Dhuni and Cumuri to sleep and slumber.
Dabhiti lit the flame for thee, and worshipped with fuel, hymns, poured Soma, dressed oblations.

## [06-021] HYMN XXI. Indra. Visvedevas.

1. THESE the most constant singer's invocations call thee who art to be invoked, O Hero;
Hymns call anew the chariot-borne, Eternal: by eloquence men gain abundant riches.
2 I praise that Indra, known to all men, honoured with songs, extolled with hymns at sacrifices,
Whose majesty, rich in wondrous arts, surpasseth the magnitude of earth, and heaven in greatness.
3 He hath made pathways, with the Sun to aid him, throughout the darkness that extended pathless.
Mortals who yearn to worship ne'er dishonour, O Mighty God, thy Law who art Immortal.
4 And he who did these things, where is that Indra? among what tribes? what people doth he visit?
What sacrifice contents thy mind , and wishes? What priest among them all? what hymn, O Indra?
5 Yea, here were they who, born of old, have served thee, thy friends of ancient time, thou active Worker.

Bethink thee now of these, Invoked of many! the midmost and the recent, and the youngest.

6 Inquiring after him, thy later servants, Indra, have gained thy former old traditions.
Hero, to whom the prayer is brought, we praise thee as great for that wherein we know thee mighty.

7 The demon's strength is gathered fast against thee: great as that strength hath grown, go forth to
meet it.
With thine own ancient friend and companion, the thunderbolt, brave Champion! drive it backward.

8 Hear, too, the prayer of this thy present beadsman, O Indra, Hero, cherishing the singer.
For thou wast aye our fathers' Friend aforetime, still swift to listen to their supplication.

9 Bring to our help this day, for our protection, Varuna, Mitra, Indra, and the Maruts,
Pusan and Visnu, Agni and Purandhi, Savitar also, and the Plants and Mountains.

10 The singers here exalt with hymns and praises thee who art very Mighty and Most Holy.
Hear, when invoked, the invoker's invocation. Beside thee there is nonelike thee, Immortal!

11 Now to my words come quickly thou who knowest, O Son of Strength, with all who claim our
worship,
Who visit sacred rites, whose tongue is Agni, Gods who made Manu stronger than the Dasyu.

12 On good and evil ways be thou our Leader, thou who art known to all as Path-preparer.
Bring power to us, O Indra, with thy Horses, Steeds that are best to draw, broad-backed, unwearied.

## [06-022] HYMN XXII. Indra.

1. WITH these my hymns I glorify that Indra who is alone to be invoked by mortals,
The Lord, the Mighty One, of manly vigour, victorious, Hero, true, and full of wisdom.

2 Our sires of old,. Navagvas, sages seven, while urging him to show his might, extolled him,
Dwelling on heights, swift, smiting down opponents, guileless in word, and in his thoughts most
mighty.

3 We seek that Indra to obtain his riches that bring much food, and men, and store of heroes.
Bring us, Lord of Bay Steeds, to make us joyful, celestial wealth, abundant, undecaying.

4 Tell thou us this, if at thy hand aforetime the earlier singers have obtained good fortune,
What is thy share and portion, Strong Subduer, Asura-slayer, rich, invoked of many?

5 He who for car-borne Indra, armed with thunder, hath a hymn, craving, deeply-piercing, fluent,
Who sends a song effectual, firmly-grasping, and strength-bestowing, he comes near the mighty.

6 Strong of thyself, thou by this art hast shattered, with thought-swift Parvata, him who waxed
against thee,
And, Mightiest! roaring! boldly rent in pieces things that were firmly fixed and never shaken.

7 Him will we fit for you with new devotion, the strongest Ancient One, in ancient manner.
So may that Indra, boundless, faithful Leader, conduct us o'er all places hard to traverse.

8 Thou for the people who oppress hast kindled the earthly firmament and that of heaven.

With heat, O Bull, on every side consume them: heat earth and flood for him who hates devotion.

9 Of all the Heavenly Folk, of earthly creatures thou art the King, O God of splendid aspect.
In thy right hand, O Indra, grasp die thunder: Eternal! thou destroyest all enchantments.

10 Give us confirmed prosperity, O Indra, vast and exhaustless for the foe's subduing.
Strengthen therewith the Arya's hate and Dasa's, and let the arms of Nahusas be mighty.

11 Come with thy team which brings all blessings hither, Disposer, much-invoked, exceeding holy.
Thou whom no fiend, no God can stay or hinder, come switly with these Steeds in my direction.

## [06-023] HYMN XXIII. Indra.

1. THOU art attached to pressed-out Soma, Indra, at laud, at prayer, and when the hymn is chanted;
Or when with yoked Bays, Maghavan, thou comest, O Indra, bearing in thine arms the thunder.

2 Or when on that decisive day thou holpest the presser of the juice at Vrtra's slaughter;
Or when thou, while the strong one feared, undaunted, gavest to death, Indra, the daring Dasyus.

3 Let Indra drink the pressed-out Soma, Helper and mighty Guide of him who sings his praises.
He gives the hero room who pours oblations, and treasure even to the lowly singer.

4 E'en humble rites with his Bay steeds he visits: he wields the bolt, drinks Soma, gives us cattle.
He makes the valiant rich in store of heroes, accepts our praise and hears the singer's calling.

5 What he hath longed for we have brought to Indra, who from the days of old hath done us service.
While Soma flows we will sing hymn, and laud him, so that our prayer may streng. then Indra's vigour.

6 Thou hast made prayer the means of thine exalting, therefore we wait on thee with hymns, O Indra.
May we, by the pressed Soma, Somadrinker! bring thee, with sacrifice, blissful sweet refreshment.

7 Mark well our sacrificial cake, delighted Indra, drink Soma and the milk commingled.
Here on the sacrificer's grass be seated: give ample room to thy devoted servant.

8 O Mighty One, be joyful as thou willest. Let these our sacrifices reach and find thee;
And may this hymn and these our invocations turn thee, whom many men invoke, to help us.

9 Friends, when thejuices flow, replenish duly your own, your bounteous Indra with the Soma.
Will it not aid him to support us? Indra. spares him who sheds the juice to win his favour.

10 While Soma flowed, thus Indra hath been lauded, Ruler of nobles, mid the Bharadvajas,
That Indra may become the singer's patron and give him wealth in every kind of treasure.

## [06-024] HYMN XXIV. Indra.

1. STRONG rapturous joy, praise, glory are with Indra: impetuous God, he quaffs the juice of Soma:
That Maghavan whom men must laud with singing, Heaven-dweller, King of songs, whose help is
lasting.

2 He, Friend of man, most wise, victorious Hero, hears, with far-reaching aid, the singer call him.
Excellent, Praise of Men, the bard's Supporter, Strong, he gives strength, extolled in holy synod.

3 The lofty axle of thy wheels, O Hero, is not surpassed by heaven and earth in greatness.
Like branches of a tree, Invoked of many manifold aids spring forth from thee, O Indra.
4 Strong Lord, thine energies, endowed with vigour, are like the paths of kine converging homeward.
Like bonds of cord, Indra, that bind the younglings, no bonds are they, O thou of boundless bounty.
5 One act to-day, another act tomorrow oft Indra makes what is not yet existeni.
Here have we Mitra, Varuna, and Pusan to overcome the foeman's domination.
6 By song and sacrifice men brought the waters from thee, as from a mountain's ridge, O Indra.
Urging thy might, with these fair lauds they seek thee, O theme of song, as horses rush tobattle.
7 That Indra whom nor months nor autumn seasons wither with age, nor fleeting days enfeeble,-
Still may his body Wax, e'en now so mighty, glorified by the lauds and hymns that praise him.
8 Extolled, he bends not to the strong, the steadfast, nor to the bold incited by the Dasyu.
High mountains are as level plains to Indra: even in the deep he finds firm ground to rest on.
9 Impetuous Speeder through all depth and distance, give strengthening food, thou drinker of the juices.
Stand up erect to help us, unreluctant, what time the gloom of night brightens to morning.
10 Hasting to help, come hither and protect him, keep him from harm when he is here, O Indra.
At home, abroad, from injury preserve him. May brave sons gladden us through a hundred winters.

### [06-025] HYMN XXV. Indra.
1. WITH thine assistance, O thou Mighty Indra, be it the least, the midmost, or the highest,-
Great with those aids and by these powers support us, Strong God! in battle that subdues our foemen.
2 With these discomfit hosts that fight against us, and check the opponent's wrath, thyself uninjured.
With these chase all our foes to every quarter: subdue the tribes of Dasas to the Arya.
3 Those who array themselves as foes to smite us, O Indra, be they kin or be they strangers,-
Strike thou their manly strength that it be feeble, and drive in headlong flight our foemen backward.
4 With strength of limb the hero slays the hero, when bright in arms they range them for the combat.
When two opposing hosts contend in battle for seed and offspring, waters, kine, or corn-lands.
5 Yet no strong man hath conquered thee, no hero, no brave, no warrior trusting in his valour.
Not one of these is match for thee, O Indra. Thou far surpassest all these living creatures.
6 He is the Lord of both these armies' valour when the commanders call them to the conflict:
When with their ranks expanded they are fighting with a great foe or for a home with heroes.
7 And when the people stir themselves for battle, be thou their saviour, Indra, and protector,
And theirs, thy manliest of our friends, the pious, the chiefs who have installed us priests, O Indra.
8 To thee for high dominion hath been for evermore, for slaughtering the Vrtras,

All lordly power and might, O Holy Indra, given by Gods for victory in battle.
9 So urge our hosts together in the combats: yield up the godless bands that fight against us.
Singing, at morn may we find thee with favour, yea, Indra, and e'en now, we Bharadvajas.

### [06-026] HYMN XXVI. Indra.
1. O INDRA, hear us. Raining down the Soma, we call on thee to win us mighty valour.
Give us strong succour on the day of trial, when the tribes gather on the field of battle.
2 The warrior, son of warrior sire, invokes thee, to gain great strength that may be won as booty:
To thee, the brave man's Lord, the fiends' subduer, he looks when fighting hand to hand for cattle.
3 Thou didst impel the sage to win the daylight, didst ruin Susna for the pious Kutsa.
The invulnerable demon's head thou clavest when thou wouldst win the praise of Atithigva.
4 The lofty battle-car thou broughtest forward; thou holpest Dasadyu the strong when fighting.
Along with Vetasu thou slewest Tugra, and madest Tuji strong, who praised thee, Indra.
5 Thou madest good the laud, what time thou rentest a hundred thousand fighting foes, O Hero,
Slewest the Dasa Sambara of the mountain, and with strange aids didst succour Divodasa.
6 Made glad with Soma-draughts and faith, thou sentest Cumuri to his sleep, to please Dabhiti.
Thou, kindly giving Raji to Pithinas, slewest with might, at once, the sixty thousand.
7 May I too, with the liberal chiefs, O Indra, acquire thy blin supreme and domination,
When, Mightiest! Hero-girt! Nahusa heroes boast them in thee, the triply-strong Defender.
8 So may we he thy friends, thy best beloved, O Indra, at this holy invocation.
Best be Pratardani, illustrious ruler, in slaying foemen and in gaining riches.

### [06-027] HYMN XXVII. Indra.
1 WHAT deed hath Indra done in the wild transport, in quaffing or in friendship with, the Soma?
What joys have men of ancient times or recent obtained within the chamber of libation?
2 In its wild joy Indra hath proved him faithful, faithful in quaffing, faithful in its friendship.
His truth is the delight that in this chamber the men of old and recent times have tasted.
3 All thy vast power, O Maghavan, we know not, know not the riches of thy full abundance.
No one hath seen that might of thine, productive of bounty every day renewed, O Indra.
4 This one great power of thine our eyes have witnessed, wherewith thou slewest Varasikha's children,
When by the force of thy descending thunder, at the mere solund, their boldest was demolished.
5 In aid of Abhyavartin Cayamana, Indra destroyed the seed of Varasikha.
At Hariyupiya he smote the vanguard of the Vrcivans, and the rear fled frighted.
6 Three thousand, mailed, in quest of fame, together, on the Yavyavati, O much-sought Indra,
Vrcivan's sons, falling before the arrow, like bursting vessels went to their destruction.

7 He, whose two red Steers, seeking goodly pasture, plying their tongues move on 'twixt earth and
heaven,
Gave Turvasa to Srnjaya, and, to aid him, gave the Vrcivans up to Daivavata.
8 Two wagon-teams, with damsels, twenty oxen, O Agni, Abhydvartin Cayamdna,
The liberal Sovran, giveth me. This guerdon of Prthu's seed is hard to win from others.

## [06-028] HYMN XXVIII. Cows.
I. THE Kine have come and brought good fortune: let them rest in the cow-pen and be happy near us.
Here let them stay prolific, many-coloured, and yield through many morns their milk for Indra.
2 Indra aids him who offers sacrifice and gifts: he takes not what is his, and gives him more thereto.
Increasing ever more and ever more his wealth, he makes the pious dwell within unbroken bounds.
3 These are ne'er lost, no robber ever injures them: no evil-minded foe attempts to harass them.
The master of the Kine lives many a year with these, the Cows whereby he pours his gifts and serves
the Gods.
4 The charger with his dusty brow o'ertakes them not, and never to the shambles do they take their
way.
These Cows, the cattle of the pious worshipper, roam over widespread pasture where no danger is.
5 To me the Cows seem Bhaga, they seem Indra, they seem a portion of the first-poured Soma.
These present Cows, they, O ye Indra. I long for Indra with my heart and spirit.
6 O Cows, ye fatten e'en the worn and wasted, and make the unlovely beautiful tolook on.
Prosper my house, ye with auspicious voices. Your power is glorified in our assemblies.
7 Crop goodly pasturage and be prolific drink pure sweet water at good drinking places.
Never be thief or sinful man your matter, and may the dart of Rudra still avoid you.
8 Now let this close admixture be close intermigled with these Cows,
Mixt with the Steer's prolific flow, and, Indra, with thy hero might.

## [06-029] HYMN XXIX Indra.
1. YOUR men have followed Indra for his friendship, and for his loving-kindness glorified him.
For he bestows great wealth, the Thunder-wielder: worship him, Great and Kind, to win his favour.
2 Him to whose hand, men closely cling, and drivers stand on his golden chariot firmly stationed.
With his firm arms he holds the reins; his Horses, the Stallions, are yoked ready for the journey.
3 Thy devotees embrace thy feet for glory. Bold, thunder-armed, rich, through thy strength, in
guerdon,
Robed in a garment fair as heaven to look on, thou hast displayed thee like an active dancer.
4 That Soma when effused hath best consistence, for which the food is dressed and grain is mingled;
By which the men who pray, extolling Indra chief favourites of Gods, recite their praises.
5 No limit of thy might hath been appointed, which by its greatness sundered earth and heaven.

These the Prince filleth full with strong endeavour, driving, as 'twere, with help his flocks to waters.
6 So be the lofty Indra prompt to listen, Helper unaided, golden-visored Hero.
Yea, so may he, shown forth in might unequalled, smite down the many Vrtras and the Dasyus.

## [06-030] HYMN XXX. Indra.
1. INDRA hath waxed yet more for hero prowess, alone, Eternal, he bestoweth treasures.
Indra transcendeth both the worlds in greatness: one half of him equalleth earth and heaven.
2 Yea, mighty I esteem his Godlike nature: none hindereth what he hath once determined.
Near and afar he spread and set the regions, and every day the Sun became apparent.
3 E'en now endures thine exploit of the Rivers, when, Indra, for their floods thou clavest passage.
Like men who sit at meat the mountains settled: by thee, Most Wise! the regions were made
steadfast.
4 This is the truth, none else is like thee, Indra, no God superior to thee, no mortal.
Thou slewest Ahi who besieged the waters, and lettest loose the streams to hurry seaward.
5 Indra, thou breakest up the floods and portals on all sides, and the firmness of the mountain.
Thou art the King of men, of all that liveth, engendering at once Sun, Heaven, and Morning.

## [06-031] HYMN XXXI Indra.
1. SOLE Lord of wealth art thou, O Lord of riches: thou in thine hands hast held the people, Indra!
Men have invoked thee with contending voices for seed and waters, progeny and sunlight.
2 Through fear of thee, O Indra, all the regions of earth, though naught may move them, shake and
tremble.
All that is firm is frightened at thy coming, -the earth, the heaven, the mountain, and the forest.
3 With Kutsa, Indra! thou didst conquer Susna, voracious, bane of crops, in fight for cattle.

In the close fray thou rentest him: thou stolest the Sun's wheel and didst drive away misfortunes.
4 Thou smotest to the ground the hundred castles, impregnable, of Sambara the Dasyu,
When, Strong, with might thou holpest Divodasa who poured libations out, O Soma-buyer, and
madest Bharadvaja rich who praised thee.
5 As such, true Hero, for great joy of battle mount thy terrific car, O Brave and Manly.
Come with thine help to me, thou distant Roamer, and, glorious God, spread among men my glory.

## [06-032] HYMN XXXII Indra.
1. I WITH my lips have fashioned for this Hero words never matched, most plentiful and auspicious,
For him the Ancient, Great, Strong, Energetic, the very mighty Wielder of the Thunder.
2 Amid the sages, with the Sun he brightened the Parents: glorified, he burst the mountain;
And, roaring with the holy-thoughted singers, he loosed the bond that held the beams of Morning.
3 Famed for great deeds, with priests who kneel and laud him, he still hath conquered in the frays for cattle,

And broken down the forts, the Fort-destroyer, a Friend with friends, a Sage among the sages.

4 Come with thy girthed mares, with abundant vigour and plenteous strength to him who sings thy praises.
Come hither, borne by mares with many heroes, Lover of song! Steer! for the people's welfare.

5 Indra with rush and might, sped by his Coursers, hath swiftly won the waters from the southward.
Thus set at liberty the rivers daily flow to their goal, incessant and exhaustless.

## [06-033] HYMN XXXIII. Indra.

1. GIVE us the rapture that is mightiest, Indra, prompt to bestow and swift to aid, O Hero,
That wins with brave steeds where brave steeds encounter, and quells the Vrtras and the foes in battle.

2 For with loud voice the tribes invoke thee, Indra, to aid them in the battlefield of heroes.
Thou, with the singers, hast pierced through the Panis: the charger whom thou aidest wins the booty.

3 Both races, Indra, of opposing foemen, O Hero, both the Arya and the Dasa,
Hast thou struck down like woods with well-shot lightnings: thou rentest them in fight, most manly Chieftain!

4 Indra, befriend us with no scanty succour, prosper and aid us, Loved of all that liveth,
When, fighting for the sunlight, we invoke thee, O Hero, in the fray, in war's division.

5 Be ours, O Indra, now and for the future, be graciously inclined and near to help us.
Thus may we, singing, sheltered by the Mighty, win many cattle on the day of trial.

## [06-034] HYMN XXXIV. Indra.

1. FULL Many songs have met in thee, O Indra, and many a noble thought from thee proceedeth.
Now and of old the eulogies of sages, their holy hymns and lauds, have yearned for Indra.

2 He, praised of many, bold, invoked of many, alone is glorified at sacrifices.
Like a car harnessed for some great achievement, Indra must be the cause of our rejoicing.

3 They make their way to Indra and exalt him, bim whom no prayers and no laudations trouble;
For when a hundred or a thousand singers. laud him who loves the song their praise delights him.

4 As brightness mingles with the Moon in heaven, the offered Soma yearns to mix with Indra.
Like water brought to men in desert places, our gifts at sacrifice have still refreshed him.

5 To him this mighty eulogy, to Indra hath this our laud been uttered by the poets,
That in the great encounter with the foemen, Loved of all life, Indra may guard and help us.

## [06-035] HYMN XXXV. Indra.

1. WHEN shall our prayers rest in thy car beside thee? When dost thou give the singer food for
thousands?
When wilt thou clothe this poet's laud with plenty, and when wilt thou enrich our hymns with booty?

2 When wilt thou gatber men with men, O Indra, heroes with heroes, and prevail in combat?
Thou shalt win triply kine in frays for cattle, so, Indra, give thou us celestial glory.

3 Yea, when wilt thou, O Indra, thou Most Mighty, make the prayer all-sustaining for the singer?

When wilt thou yoke, as we yoke songs, thy Horses, and come to offerings that bring wealth in
cattle?

4 Grant to the Singer food with store of cattle, splendid with horses and the fame of riches.
Send food to swell the milch-cow good at milking: bright be its shine among the Bharadvajas.

5 Lead otherwise this present foeman, Sakra! Hence art thou praised as Hero, foe destroyer
Him who gives pure gifts may I praise unceasing. Sage, quicken the Angirases by devotion.

## [06-036] HYMN XXXVI. Indra.

1. THY raptures ever were for all men's profit: so evermore have been thine earthly riches.
Thou still hast been the dealer-forth of vigour, since among Gods thou hast had power and Godhead.

2 Men have obtained his strength by sacrificing, and ever urged him, on to hero valour.
For the rein-seizing, the impetuous Charger they furnished power even for Vrtra's slaughter.

3 Associate with him, as teams of horses, help, manly might, and vigour follow Indra.
As rivers reach the sea, so, strong with praises, our holy songs reach him the Comprehensive.

4 Lauded by us, let flow the spring, O Indra, of excellent and brightly-shining riches.
For thou art Lord of men, without an equal: of all the world thou art the only Sovran.

5 Hear what thou mayst hear, thou who, fain for worship, as heaven girds earth, guardest thy
servant's treasure;
Tlat thou mayst be our own, joying in power, famed through thy might in every generation.

## [06-037] HYMN XXXVII Indra.

1. LET thy Bay Horses, yoked, O mighty Indra, bring thy car hither fraught with every blessing.
For thee, the Heavenly, e'en the poor invoketh: may we this day, thy feast-companions, prosper.

2 Forth to the vat the brown drops flow for service, and purified proceed directly forward.
May Indra drink of this, our guest aforetime, Celestial King of the strong draught of Soma.

3 Bringing us hitherward all-potent Indra on well-wheeled chariot, may the Steeds who bear him
Convey him on the road direct to glory, and ne'er may Vayu's Amrta cease and fail him.

4 Supreme, he stirs this man to give the guerdon,-Indra, most efficacious of the princes,-
Wherewith, O Thunderer, thou removest sorrow, and, Bold One! partest wealth among the nobles.

5 Indra is hewho gives enduring vigour: may our songs magnify the God Most Mighty.
Best Vrtra-slayer be the Hero Indra these things he gives as Prince, with strong endeavour.

## [06-038] HYMN XXXVIII. Indra.

1. HE hath drunk hence, Most Marvellous, and carried away our great and splendid call on Indra.
The Bounteous, when we serve the Gods, accepteth song yet more famous and the gifts we bring
him.

2 The speaker filleth with a cry to Indra his ears who cometh nigh e'en from a distance.
May this my call bring Indra to my presence, this call to Gods composed in sacred verses.

3 Him have I sung with my best song and praises, Indra of ancient birth and Everlasting.
For prayer and songs in him are concentrated: let laud wax mighty when addressed to Indra:
4 Indra, whom sacrifice shall strengthen, Soma, and song and hymn, and praises and devotion,
Whom Dawns shall strengthen when the night departeth, Indra whom days shall strengthen,
months, and autumns.
5 Him, born for conquering might in full perfection, and waxen strongfor bounty and for glory,
Great, Powerful, will we to-day, O singer, invite to aid. us and to quell our foemen.

## [06-039] HYMN XXXIX Indra.
1. OF this our charming, our celestial Soma, eloquent, wise, Priest, with inspired devotion,

Of this thy close attendant, hast thou drunken. God, send the singer food with milk to grace it.
2 Craving the kine, rushing against the mountain led on by Law, with holyminded comrades,
He broke the never-broken ridge of Vala. With words of might Indra subdued the Panis.
3 This Indu lighted darksome nights, O Indra, throughout the years, at morning and at evening.
Him have they stablished as the days' bright ensign. He made the Mornings to be born in splendour.
4 He shone and caused to shme the worlds that shone not. By Law he lighted up the host of
Mornings.
He moves with Steeds yoked by eternal Order, contenting men with nave that finds the sunlight.
5 Now, praised, O Ancient King! fill thou the singer with plenteous food that he may deal forth
treasures.
Give waters, herbs that have no poison, forests, and kine, and steeds, and men, to him who lauds
thee.

## [06-040] HYMN XL. Indra
1. DRINK, Indra; juice is shed to make thee joyful: loose thy Bay Steeds and give thy friends their
freedom.
Begin the song, seated in our assembly. Give strength for sacrifice to him who singeth.
2 Drink thou of this whereof at birth, O Indra, thou drankest, Mighty One for power and rapture.
The men, the pressing-stones, the cows, the waters have made this Soma ready for thy drinking.
3 The fire is kindled, Soma pressed, O Indra: let thy Bays, best to draw, convey thee hither.
With mind devoted, Indra, I invoke thee. Come, for our great prosperity approach us.
4 Indra, come hither: evermore thou camest through our great strong desire to drink the Soma.
Listen and hear the prayers which now we offer, and let this sacrifice increase thy vigour.
5 Mayst thou, O Indra, on the day of trial, present or absent, wheresoe'er thou dwellest,
Thence, with thy team, accordant with the Maruts, Song-lover! guard our sacrifice, to help us.

## [06-041] HYMN XLL Indra.
1. COME gracious to our sacrifice, O Indra: pressed Soma-drops are purified to please thee.

As cattle seek their home, so Thunderwielder, come, Indra, first of those who claim our worship.
2 With that well-formed most wide-extending palate, wherewith thou ever drinkest streams of
sweetness,
Drink thou; the Adhvaryu standeth up before thee: let thy spoil-winning thunderbolt attend thee.
3 This drop, steer-strong and omniform, the Soma, hath been made ready for the Bull, for India.
Drink this, Lord of the Bays, thou Strong Supporter, this that is thine of old, thy food for ever.
4 Soma when pressed excels the unpressed Soma, better, for one who knows, to give him pleasure.
Come to this sacrifice of ours, O Victor replenish all thy powers with this libation.
5 We call on thee, O Indra: come thou hither: sufficient be the Soma for thy body.
Rejoice thee, Satakratu! in the juices guard us in wars, guard us among our people.

## [06-042] HYMN XLII- Indra.
1. BRING sacrificial gifts to him, Omniscient, for he longs to drink,
The Wanderer who comes with speed, the Hero ever in the van.
2 With Soma go ye nigh to him chief drinker of the Soma's juice:
With beakers to the Impetuous God, to Indra with the drops effused.
3 What time, with Soma, with the juice effused, ye come before the God,
Full wise he knows the hope of each, and, Bold One, strikes this foe and that.
4 To him, Adhvaryu! yea, to him give offerings of the juice expressed.
Will he not keep us safely from the spiteful curse of each presumptuous high-born foe?

## [06-043] HYMN XLIII. Indra
1. IN whose wild joy thou madest once Sambara Divodasa's prey,
This Soma is pressed out for thee, O Indra: drink!
2 Whose gladdening draught, shed from the points, thou guardest in the midst and end,
This Soma is pressed out for thee, O Indra drink!
3 In whose wild joy thou settest free the kine held fast within the rock,
This Soma is pressed out for thee, O Indra: drink!
4 This, in whose juice delighting thou gainest the might of Maghavan,
This Soma is pressed out for thee, O Indra drink!

## [06-044] HYMN XLIV. Indra.
1. THAT which is wealthiest, Wealthy God in splendoursmost illustrious,
Soma is pressed: thy gladdening draught, Indra! libation's Lord! is this.
2 Effectual, Most Effectual One! thine, as bestowing wealth of hymns,
Soma is pressed: thy gladdening draught, Indra! libation's Lord! is this.
3 Wherewith thou art increased in strength, and conquerest with thy proper aids,
Soma is pressed: thy gladdening draught, Indra! libation's Lord! is this.
4 Him for your sake I glorify as Lord of Strength who wrongeth none,
The Hero Indra, conquering all, Most Bounteous, God of all the tribes.

5 Those Goddesses, both Heaven and Earth, revere the power and might of him,
Him whom our songs increase in strength, the Lord of bounty swift to come.
6 To seat your Indra, I will spread abroad with power this song of praise.
The saving succours that abide in him, like songs, extend and grow.
7 A recent Friend, he found the skilful priest: he drank, and showed forth treasure from the Gods.
He conquered, borne by strong all-shaking mares, and was with far-spread power his friends'
Protector.
8 In course of Law the sapient juice was quaffed: the Deities to glory turned their mind.
Winning through hymns a lofty title, he, the Lovely, made his beauteous form apparent.
9 Bestow on us the most illustrious strength ward off men's manifold malignities.
Give with thy might abundant vital force, and aid us graciously in gaining riches.
10 We turn to thee as Giver, liberal Indra. Lord of the Bay Steeds, be not thou ungracious.
No friend among mankind have we to lookto: why have men called thee him who spurs the niggard?
11 Give us not up, Strong Hero! to the hungry: unharmed be we whom thou, so rich, befriendest.
Full many a boon hast thou for men demolish those who present no gifts nor pour oblations.
12 As Indra thundering impels the rain-clouds, so doth he send us store of kine and horses.
Thou art of old the Cherisher of singers let not the rich who bring no gifts deceive thee.
13 Adbyaryu, hero, bring to mighty Indrafor he is King thereof-the pressed-out juices;
To him exalted by the hymns and praises, ancient and modern, of the singing Rsis.
14 In the wild joy of this hath Indra, knowing full many a form, struck down resistless Vrtras.
Proclaim aloud to him the savoury Soma so that the Hero, strong of jaw, may drink it.
15 May Indra drink this Soma poured to please him, and cheered therewith slay Vrtra with his
thunder.
Come to our sacrifice even from a distance, good lover of our songs, the bard's Supporter.
16 The cup whence Indra drinks the draught is present: the Amrta dear to Indra hath been drunken,
That it may cheer the God to gracious favour, and keep far from us hatred and affliction.
17 Therewith enraptured, Hero, slay our foemen, the unfriendly, Maghavan be they kin or strangers,
Those who still aim their hostile darts to smite us, turn them to flight, O Indra, crush and kill them.
18 O Indra Maghavan, in these our battles win easy paths for us and ample freedom.
That we may gain waters and seed and offspring, set thou our princes on thy side, O Indra.
19 Let thy Bay Stallions, harnessed, bring thee hither, Steeds with strong chariot and strong reins to
hold them,
Strong Horses, speeding hither, bearing thunder, well-harnessed, for the strong exciting potion.
20 Beside the vat, Strong God! stand thy strong Horses, shining with holy oil, like waves exulting.
Indra, they bring to thee, the Strong and Mighty, Soma of juices shed by mighty press-stones.

21 Thou art the Bull of earth, the Bull of heaven, Bull of the rivers, Bull of standing waters.
For thee, the Strong, O Bull, hath Indu swollen. juice pleasant, sweet to drink, for thine election.
22 This God, with might, when first he had his being, with Indra for ally, held fast the Pani.
This Indu stole away the warlike weapons, and foiled the arts of his malignant father.
23 The Dawns he wedded to a glorious Consort, and set within the Sun the light that lights him.
He found in heaven, in the third lucid regions, the threefold Amrta in its close concealment.
24 He stayed and held the heaven and earth asunder: the chariot with the sevenfold reins he
harnessed.
This Soma Set with power within the milch-kine a spring whose ripe contents ten fingers empty.

## [06-045] HYMN XLV. Indra.
1. THAT Indra is our youthful Friend, who with his trusty guidance led
Turvasa, Yadu from afar.
2 Even to the dull and uninspired Indra, gives vital power, and wins
Even with slow steed the offered prize.
3 Great are his ways of guiding us, and!nanilbld are Ins eulogies:
His kind protections never fail.
4 Friends, sing your psalm and offer praise to him to whom the prayer is brought:
For our great Providence is he.
5 Thou, Slaughterer of Vrtra, art Guardian and Friend of one and two,
Yea, of a man like one of us.
6 Beyond men's hate thou leadest us, and givest cause to sing thy praise:
Good hero art thou called by men.
7 I call with hymns, as 'twere a cow to milk, the Friend who merits praise,
The Brahman who accepts the prayer.
8 Him in whose hands they say are stored all treasures from the days of old,
The Hero, conquering in the fight.
9 Lord of Strength, Caster of the Stone, destroy the firm forts built by men,
And foil their arts, unbending God!
10 Thee, thee as such, O Lord of Power, O Indra, Soma-drinker, true,
We, fain for glory, have invoked.
11 Such as thou wast of old, and art now to be called on when the prize
lies ready, listen to our call.
12 With hymns and coursers we will gain, Indra, through thee, both steeds and spoil
Most glorious, and the proffered prize.
13 Thou, Indra, Lover of the Song, whom men must stir to help, hast been
Great in the contest for the prize.
14 Slayer of foes, whatever aid of thine imparts the swiftest course,
With that impel our car to speed.
15 As skilfullest of those who drive the chariot, with our art and aim,
O Conqueror, win the proffered prize.
16 Praise him who, Matchless and Alone, was born the Lord of living men,
Most active, with heroic soul.

17 Thou who hast been the singers' Friend, a Friend auspicious with thine aid,
As such, O Indra, favour us.
18 Grasp in thine arms the thunderbolt, O Thunder-armed, to slay the fiends:
Mayst thou subdue the foemen's host.
19 I call the ancient Friend, allied with wealth, who speeds the lowly man,
Him to whom chiefly prayer is brought.
20 For he alone is Lord of all the treasures of the earth: he speeds
Hither, chief Lover of the Song.
21 So with thy yoked teams satisfy our wish with power and wealth in steeds
And cattle, boldly, Lord of kine!
22 Sing this, what time the ' juice is pressed, to him your Hero, Much-invoked,
To please him as a mighty Steer.
23 He, Excellent, withholdeth not his gift of power and wealth in kine,
When he hath listened to our songs.
24 May he with might unclose for us the cow's stall, whosesoe'er it be,
To which the Dasyu-slayer goes.
25 O Indra Satakratu, these our songs have called aloud to thee,
Like mother cows to meet their calves.
26 Hard is thy love to win: thou art a Steer to him who longs for steers:
Be to one craving steeds a Steed.
27 Delight thee with the juice we pour for thine own great munificence:
Yield not thy singer to reproach.
28 These songs with every draught we pour come, Lover of the Song, to thee,
As milch-kine hasten to their young
29 To thee most oft invoked, amid the many singers' rivalry
Who beg with all their might for wealth.
30 Nearest and most attractive may our laud, O Indra come to thee.
Urge thou us on to ample wealth.
31 Brbu hath set himself above the Panis, o'er their highest head,
Like the wide bush on Ganga's bank.
32 He whose good bounty, thousandfold, swift as the rushing of the wind,
Suddenly offers as a gift.
33 So all our singers ever praise the pious Brbu's noble deed,
Chief, best to give his thousands, best to give a thousand liberal gifts.

## [06-046] HYMN XLVI. Indra.

1. THAT we may win us wealth and power we poets, verily, call on thee:
In war men call on thee, Indra, the hero's Lord, in the steed's race-course call on thee.
2 As such, O Wonderful, whose hand holds thunder, praised as mighty, Caster of the Stone!
Pour on us boldly, Indra, kine and chariotsteeds, ever to be the conqueror's strength.
3 We call upon that Indra, who, most active, ever slays the foe:
Lord of the brave, Most Manly, with a thousand powers, help thou and prosper us in fight.
4 Rcisama, thou forcest men as with a bull, with anger, in the furious fray.
Be thou our Helper in the mighty battle fought for sunlight, water, and for life.
5 O Indra, bring us name and fame, enriching, mightiest, excellent,

Wherewith, O Wondrous God, fair-visored, thunder-armed, thou hast filled full this earth and heaven.
6 We call on thee, O King, Mighty amid the Gods, Ruler of men, to succour us.
All that is weak in us, Excellent God, make firm: make our foes easy to subdue.
7 All strength and valour that is found, Indra, in tribes of Nahusas, and all the splendid fame that the
Five Tribes enjoy
Bring, yea, all manly powers at once.
8 Or, Maghavan, what vigorous strength in Trksi lay, in Druhyus or in Paru's folk,
Fully bestow on us, that, in the conquering fray, we may subdue our foes in fight.
9 O Indra, grant a happy home, a triple refuge triply strong.
Bestow a dwelling-place on the rich lords and me, and keep thy dart afar from these.
10 They who with minds intent on spoil subdue the foe, boldly attack and smite him down,-

From these, O Indra Maghavan who lovest song, be closest guardian of our lives.
11 And now, O Indra, strengthen us: come near and aid us in the fight,
What time the feathered shafts are flying in the air, the arrows with their sharpened points.
12 Give us, where heroes strain their bodies in the fight, the shelter that our fathers loved.
To us and to our sons give refuge: keep afar all unobserved hostility.
13 When, Indra, in the mighty fray thou urgest chargers to their speed,
On the uneven road and on a toilsome path, like falcons, eager for renown,
14 Speeding like rivers rushing down a steep descent, responsive to the urging call,
That come like birds attracted to the bait, held in by reins in both the driver's hands.

## [06-047] HYMN XLVII. Indra, Etc.

1. YEA, this is good to taste and full of. sweetness, verily it is strong and rich in flavour.
No one may conquer Indra in the battle when he hath drunken of the draught we offer.
2 This sweet juice here had mightiest power to gladden: it boldened Indra when he siaughtered Vrtra,
When he defeated Sambara's many onslaughts, and battered down his nineand ninety ramparts.
3 This stirreth up my voice when I have drunk it: this hath aroused from sleep my yearning spirit.
This Sage hath measured out the six expanses from which no single creature is excluded.
4 This, even this, is he who hath created the breadth of earth, the lofty height of heaven.
He formed the nectar in three headlong rivers. Soma supports the wide mid-air above us.
5 He found the wavy sea of brilliant colours in forefront of the Dawns who dwell in brightness.
This Mighty One, the Steer begirt by Maruts, hath propped the heavens up with a mighty pillar.
6 Drink Soma boldly from the beaker, Indra, in war for treasures, Hero, Vrtra-slayer!
Fill thyself full at the mid-day libation, and give us wealth, thou Treasury of riches.
7 Look out for us, O Indra, as our Leader, and guide us on to gain yet goodlier treasure.

Excellent Guardian, bear us well through peril, and lead us on to wealth with careful guidance.

8 Lead us to ample room, O thou who knowest, to happiness, security, and sunlight.

High, Indra, are the arms of thee the Mighty: may we betake. us to their lofty shelter.

9 Set us on widest chariot-seat, O Indra, with two steeds best to draw, O Lord of Hundreds!

Bring us the best among all sorts of viands: let not the foe's wealth, Maghavan, subdue us.

10 Be gracious, Indra, let my days be lengthened: sharpen my thought as 'twere a blade of iron

Approve whatever words I speak, dependent on thee, and grant me thy divine protection.

11 Indra the Rescuer, Indra the Helper, Hero who listens at each invocation,

Sakra I call, Indra invoked of many. May Indra Maghavan prosper and bless us.

12 May helpful Indra as our good Protector, Lord of all treasures, favour us with succour,

Baffle our foes, and give us rest and safety, and may we be the lords of hero vigour.

13 May we enjoy the grace of him the Holy, yea, may we dwell in his auspicious favour.

May helpful Indra as our good Preserver drive from us, even from afar, our foemen.

14 Like rivers rushing down a slope, O Indra, to thee haste songs and prayers and linked verses.

Thou gatherest, Thunderer! like widespread bounty, kine, water, drops, and manifold libations.

15 Who lauds him, satisfies him, pays him worship? E'en the rich noble still hath found him mighty.

With power, as when one moves his feet alternate, he makes the last precede, the foremost follow.

16 Famed is the Hero as each strong man's tamer, ever advancing one and then another.

King of both worlds, hating the high and haughty, Indra protects the men who are his people.

17 He loves no more the men he loved aforetime: he turns and moves away allied with others.

Rejecting those who disregard his worship, Indra victorious lives through many autumns.

18 In every figure he hath been the mode: this is his only form for us to look on.

Indra moves multiform by his illusions; for his Bay Steeds are yoked, ten times a hundred.

19 Here Tvastar, yoking to the car the Bay Steeds, hath extended sway.

Who will for ever stand upon the foeman's side, even when our princes sit at ease?

20 Gods, we have reached a country void of pasture the land, though spacious, was too small to hold us.

Brhaspati, provide in war for cattle; find a path, Indra, for this faithful singer.

21 Day after day far from their seat he drove them, alike, from place to place, those darksome creatures.

The Hero slew the meanly-huckstering Dasas, Varcin and Sambara, where the waters gather.

22 Out of thy bounty, Indra, hath Prastoka bestowed ten coffers and ten mettled horses.

We have received in turn from Divodasa Sambara's wealth, the gift of Atithigva.

23 Ten horses and ten treasure-chests, ten garments as an added gift,

These and ten lumps of gold have I received from Divodasa's hand.

24 Ten cars with extra steed to each, for the Atharvans hundred cows,

Hath Asvatha to Payu given.

25 Thus Srnjaya's son honoured the Bharadvajas, recipients of all noble gifts and bounty.

26 Lord of the wood, be firm and strong in body: be, bearing us, a brave victorious hero

Show forth thy strength, compact with straps of leather, and let thy rider win all spoils of battle.

27 Its mighty strength was borrowed from the heaven and earth: its conquering force was brought

from sovrans of the wood.

Honour with holy gifts the Car like Indra's bolt, the Car bound round with straps, the vigour of the floods.

28 Thou Bolt of Indra, Vanguard of the Maruts, close knit to Varuna and Child of Mitra,-

As such, accepting gifts which here we offer, receive, O Godlike Chariot, these oblations.

29 Send forth thy voice aloud through earth and heaven, and let the world in all its breadth regard thee;

O Drum, accordant with the Gods and Indra, drive thou afar, yea, very far, our foemen.

30 Thunder out strength and fill us full of vigour: yea, thunder forth and drive away all dangers.

Drive hence, O War-drum, drive away misfortune: thou art the Fist of Indra: show thy firmness.

31 Drive hither those, and these again bring hither: the War-drum speaks aloud as battle's signal.

Our heroes, winged with horses, come together. Let our car-warriors, Indra, be triumphant.

## [06-048] HYMN XLVIII. Agni and Others.

1. SING to your Agni with each song, at every sacrifice, for strength.

Come, let us praise the Wise and Everlasting God, even as a well-beloved Friend,

2 The Son of Strength; for is he not our gracious Lord? Let us serve him who bears our gifts.

In battle may he be our help and strengthener, yea, be the saviour of our lives.

3 Agni, thou beamest forth with light, great Hero, never changed by time.

Shining, pure Agni! with a light that never fades, beam with thy fair beams brilliantly.

4 Thou worshippest great Gods: bring them without delay by wisdom and thy wondrous power.

O Agni, make them turn hither to succour us. Give strength, and win it for thyself.

5 He whom floods, stones, and trees support, the offspring of eternal Law;

He who when rubbed with force is brought to life by men upon the lofty height of earth;

6 He who hath filled both worlds full with his brilliant shine, who hastens with his smoke to heaven;

He made himself apparent through the gloom by night, the Red Bull in the darksome nights, the Red Bull in the darksome nights.

7 O Agni, with thy lofty beams, with thy pure brilliancy, O God,

Kindled, Most Youthful One! by Bharadvaja's hand, shine on us, O pure God, with wealth, shine,

Purifier! splendidly.

8 Thou art the Lord of house and home of all the tribes, O Agni, of all tribes of men.

Guard with a hundred forts thy kindler from distress, through hundred winters, Youngest God! and
those who make thy singers rich.
9 Wonderful, with thy favouring help, send us thy bounties, gracious Lord.
Thou art the Charioteer, Agni, of earthly wealth: find rest and safety for our seed.
10 With guards unfailing never negligent speed thou our children and our progeny.
Keep far from us, O Agni, all celestial wrath and wickedness of godless men.
11 Hither, O friends, with newest song drive her who freely pours her milk;
Loose her who never turns away;
12 Who, for the host of Maruts bright with native sheen, hath shed immortal fame like milk;
Whom the impetuous Maruts look upon with love, who moves in splendour on their ways.
13 For Bharadvaja she poured down in days of old
The milch-cow yielding milk for all, and food that gives all nourishment.
14 Your friend like Indra passing wise, with magic power like Varuna.
Like Aryaman joy-giving, bringing plenteous food like ViSnxu for my wish, I praise,
15 Bright as the host of Maruts mighty in their roar. May they bring Pusan free from foes;
May they bring hither hundreds, thousands for our men: may they bring hidden stores to light, and
make wealth easy to be found.
16 Haste to me, Pusan, in thine car, bright Deity: I fain would speak:
Most sinful is our foeman's hate.
17 Tear not up by the roots the Kakambira tree: destroy thou all malignity.
Let them not snare by day the neck of that Celestial Bird the Sun.
18 Uninjured let thy friendship be, like the smooth surface of a skin,
A flawless skin, containing curds, full to the mouth, containing curds.
19 For thou art high above mankind, in glory equal to the Gods.
Therefore, O Pusan, look upon us in the fight: now help us as in days of old.
20 May the kind excellence of him the Kind, loud Roarers! be our guide,
Be it the God's, O Maruts, or a mortal man's who worships, ye impetuous Ones!
21 They whose high glory in a moment like the God, the Sun, goes round the space of heaven,
The Maruts have obtained bright strength, a sacred name,
strength that destroys the Vrtras,
strength Vrtra-destroying excellent.
22 Once, only once, the heaven was made, once only once, the earth was formed-
Once, only Prsni's milk was shed: no second, after this, is born.

## [06-049] HYMN XLIX. Visvedevas.

1. I LAUD with newest songs the Righteous People, Mitra and Varuna who make us happy.
Let them approach, here let them listen,Agni, Varuna, Mitra, Lords of fair dominion.
2 Him, to be praised at each tribe's sacrifices, the Two young Matrons' sober-minded Herald,
The Son of Strength, the Child of Heaven, the signal of sacrifice, red Agni will I worship.
3 Unlike in form are the Red God's two Daughters: one is the Sun's, and stars bedeck the other.

Apart, the Sanctifiers, in succession, come to the famed hymn, praised in holy verses.
4 I with a lofty song call hither Vayu, all-bounteous, filler of his car, most wealthy.
Thou, Sage, with bright path, Lord of harnessed horses, impetuous, promptly honourest the prudent.
5 That chariot of the Asvins, fair to look on, pleaseth me well, yoked with a thought, refulgent,
Wherewith, Nasatyas, Chiefs, ye seek our dwelling, to give new strength to us and to our children.
6 Bulls of the Earth, O Vata and Parjanya, stir up for us the regions of the water.
Hearers of truth, ye, Sages, World-Supporters, increase his living wealth whose songs delight you.
7 So may Sarasvati, the Hero's Consort, brisk with rare life, the lightning's Child, inspire us,
And, with the Dames accordant, give the singer a refuge unassailable and flawless.
8 I praise with eloquence him who guards all pathways. He, when his love impelled him, went to Arka.
May he vouchsafe us gear with gold to grace it: may Pusan make each prayer of ours efective.
9 May Herald Agni, fulgent, bring for worship Tvastar adored, in homes and swift to listen,
Glorious, first to share, the life-bestower, the ever active God, fair-armed, fair-handed.
10 Rudra by day, Rudra at night we honour with these our songs, the Universe's Father.
Him great and lofty, blissful, undecaying let us call specially as the Sage impels us.
11 Ye who are youthful, wise, and meet for worship, come, Martits, to the longing of the singer.
Coming, as erst to Angiras, O Heroes, ye animate and quicken e'en the desert.
12 Even as the herdsman driveth home his cattle, I urge my songs to him the strong swift Hero
May he, the glorious, lay upon his body the singer's hymns, as stars bedeck the heaven.
13 He who for man's behoof in his afiliction thrice measured out the earthly regions, Visnu-
When one so great as thou affordeth shelter, may we with wealth and with ourselves be happy.
14 Sweet be this song of mine to Ahibudhnya, Parvata, Savitar, with Floods and Lightnings;
Sweet, with the Plants, to Gods who seek oblations. May liberal Bhaga speed us on to riches.
15 Give riches borne on cars, with many heroes, contenting men, the guard of mighty Order.
Give us a lasting home that we may battle with godless bands of men who fight against us, and meet
with tribes to whom the Gods are gracious.

## [06-050] HYMN L. Visvedevas.

1. I CALL with prayers on Aditi your Goddess, on Agni, Mitra, Varuna for favour,
On Aryaman who gives unasked, the gracious, on Gods who save, on Savitar and Bhaga.
2 Visit, to prove us free from sin, O Surya Lord of great might, the bright Gods sprung from Daksa,
Twice-born and true, observing sacred duties, Holy and full of light, whose tongue is Agni.
3 And, O ye Heaven and Earth, a wide dominion, O ye most blissful Worlds, our lofty shelter,
Give ample room and freedom for our dwelling, a home, ye Hemispheres, which none may rival.
4 This day invited may the Sons of Rudra, resistless, excellent, stoop down to meet us;

For, when beset with slight or sore affliction, we ever call upon the Gods, the Maruts;
5 To whom the Goddess Rodasi clings closely, whom Pusan follows bringing ample bounty.
What time ye hear our call and come, O Maruts, upon your separate path all creatures tremble.
6 With a new hymn extol, O thou who singest, the Lover of the Song, the Hero Indra.
May he, exalted, hear our invocation, and grant us mighty wealth and strength when lauded.
7 Give full protection, Friends of man, ye Waters, in peace and trouble, to our sons and grandsons.
For ye are our most motherly physicians, parents of all that standeth, all that moveth.
8 May Savitar come hither and approach us, the God who rescues, Holy, goldenhanded,
The God who, bounteous as the face of Morning, discloses precious gifts for him who worships.
9 And thou, O Son of Strength, do thou turn hither the Gods to-day to this our holy service.
May I for evermore enjoy thy bounty and, Agni, by thy grace be rich in heroes.
10 Come also to my call, O ye Nasatyas, yea, verily, through my prayers, ye Holy Sages.
As from great darkness ye delivered Atri, protect us, Chiefs, from danger in the conflict.
11 O Gods, bestow upon us riches, splendid with strength and heroes, bringing food in plenty.
Be gracious, helpful Gods of earth, of heaven, born of the Cow, and dwellers in the waters.
12 May Rudra and Sarasvati, accordant, Visnu and Vayu, pour down gifts and bless us;
Rbhuksan, Vaja, and divine Vidhatar, Parjanya, Vata make our food abundant.
13 May this God Savitar, the Lord, the Offspring of Waters, pouring down his dew be gracious,
And, with the Gods and Dames accordant, Tvastar; Dyaus with the Gods and Prthivi with oceans.
14 May Aja-Ekapad and Ahibudhnya, and Earth and Ocean hear our invocation;
All Gods who strengthen Law, invoked and lauded, and holy texts uttered by sages, help us.
15 So with my thoughts and hymns of praise the children of Bharadvaja sing aloud to please you.
The Dames invoked, and the resistless Vasus, and all ye Holy Ones have been exalted.

## [06-051] HYMN LI. Visvedevas.

1. THAT mighty eye of Varuna and Mitra, infallible and dear, is moving upward.
The pure and lovely face of holy Order hath shone like gold of heaven in its arising.
2 The Sage who knows these Gods' three ranks and orders, and all their generations near and distant,
Beholding good and evil acts of mortals, Sura marks well the doing of the pious.
3 I praise you Guards of mighty Law eternal, Aditi, Mitra, Varuna, the noble,
Aryaman, Bhaga, all whose thoughts are faithful: hither I call the Bright who share in common.
4 Lords of the brave, infallible, foe-destroyers, great Kings, bestowers of fair homes to dwell in,
Young, Heroes, ruling heaven with strong dominion, Adityas, Aditi I seek with worship.
5 O Heaven our Father, Earth our guileless Mother, O Brother Agni, and ye Vasus, bless us.

Grant us, O Aditi and ye Adityas, all of one mind, your manifold protection.
6 Give us not up to any evil creature, as spoil to wolf or she-wolf, O ye Holy.
For ye are they who guide aright our bodies, ye are the rulers of our speech and vigour.
7 Let us not suffer for the sin of others, nor do the deed which ye, O Vasus, punish.
Ye, Universal Gods! are all-controllers: may he do harm unto himself who hates Me.
8 Mighty is homage: I adopt and use it. Homage hath held in place the earth and heaven.
Homage to Gods! Homage commands and rules them. I banish even committed sin by homage
9 You Furtherers of Law, pure in your spirit, infallible, dwellers in the home of Order,
To you all Heroes mighty and far-seeing I bow me down, O Holy Ones, with homage.
10 For these are they who shine with noblest splendour; through all our troubles these conduct us
safely-
Varuna, Mitra, Agni, mighty Rulers, trueminded, faithful to the hymn's controllers.
11 May they, Earth, Aditi, Indra, Bhaga, Pusan increase our laud, increase the Fivefold people.
Giving good help, good refuge, goodly guidance, be they our good deliverers, good protectors.
12 Come now, O Gods, to your celestial station: the Bharadvajas' priest entreats your favour.
He, sacrificing, fain for wealth, hath honoured the Gods vath those who sit and share oblations.
13 Agni, drive thou the wicked foe, the evil-hearted thief away,
Far, far, Lord of the brave I and give us easy paths.
14 Soma, these pressing-stones have called aloud to win thee for our Friend.
Destroy the greedy Pani, for a wolf is he.
15 Ye, O most bountiful, are they who, led by Indra, seek the sky.
Give us good paths for travel: guard us ivell at home.
16 Now have we entered on the road that leads to bliss, without a foe,
The road whereon a man escapes all enemies and gathers wealth.

## [06-052] HYMN LIL Visvedevas.

1. THIS I allow not in the earth or heaven, at sacrifice or in these holy duties.
May the huge mountains crush him down: degraded be Atiyaja's sacrificing patron.
2 Or he who holds us in contempt, O Maruts, or seeks to blame the prayer that we are making,
May agonies of burning be his portion. May the sky scorch the man who hates devotion.
3 Why then, O Soma, do they call thee keeper of prayer? Why then our guardian from reproaches?
Why then beholdest thou how men revile us? Cast thy hot dart at him who hates devotion.
4 May Mornings as they spring to life, protect me, and may the Rivers as they swell preserve me.
My guardians be the firmly-seated mountains: the Fathers, when I call on Gods, defend me!
5 Through all our days may we be healthy. minded, and look upon the Sun when he arises.
Grant this the Treasure-Lord of treasures, coming, observant, oftenest of Gods, with succour!
6 Most near, most oft comes Indra with protection, and she Sarasvati, who swells with rivers -
Parjanya, bringing health with herbs, and Agni, well lauded swift to listen, like a father.

7 Hear this mine invocation; come hither, O Universal Gods,
Be seated on this holy grass.
8 To him who comes to meet you, Gods, with offerings bathed in holy oil-
Approach ye, one and all, to him.
9 All Sons of Immortality shall listen to the songs we sing,
And be exceeding good to us.
10 May all the Gods who strengthen Law, with Rtus, listening to our call,
Be pleased with theit appropriate draught.
11 May 1ndra, with the Marut host, with Tvastar, Mitra, Aryaman,
Accept the laud and these our gifts.
12 O Agni, Priest, as rules ordain, offer this sacrifice of ours,
Remembering the Heavenly Folk.
13 Listen, All-Gods, to this mine invocation, Ye who inhabit heaven, and air's midregions,
All ye, O Holy Ones, whose tongue is Agni, seated upon this sacred grass, be joyful.
14 May the All-Gods who claim our worship hear my thought; may the two World-halves hear it, and
the Waters' Child.
Let me not utter words that ye may disregard. Closely allied with you may we rejoice in bliss.
15 And those who, Mighty, with the wiles of serpents, were born on earth, in heaven, where waters
gather-
May they vouchsafe us life of full duration. May the Gods kindly give us nights and mornings.
16 At this my call, O Agni and Parjanya, help, swift to hear, my thought and our laudation.
One generates holy food, the other offspring, so grant us food enough with store of children.
17 When holy grass is strewn and fire enkindled, with hymn and lowly homage I invite you.
All-Gods, to day in this our great assembly rejoice, ye Holy, in the gifts we offer.

### [06-053] HYMN LIII. Pusan.

1. LORD of the path, O Pusan, we have yoked and bound thee to our hymn,
Even as a car, to win the prize.
2 Bring us the wealth that men require, a manly master of a house,
Free-handed with the liberal meed.
3 Even him who would not give, do thou,
O glowing Pusan, urge to give,
And make the niggard's soul grow soft.
4 Clear paths that we may win the prize; scatter our enemies afar.
Strong God, be all our thoughts fulfilled.
5 Penetrate with an awl, O Sage, the hearts of avaricious churls,
And make them subject to our will.
6 Thrust with thine awl, O Pusan: seek that which the niggard's heart holds dear,
And make him subject to our will.
7 Tear up and read in pieces, Sage, the hearts of avaricious churls,
And make them subject to our will.
8 Thou, glowing Pusan, carriest an awl that urges men to prayer;
Therewith do thou tear up and rend to shreds the heart of every one.
9 Thou bearest, glowing Lord! a goad with horny point that guides the cows
Thence do we seek thy gift of bliss.
10 And make this hymn of ours produce kine, horses, and a store of wealth
For our delight and use as men.

### [06-054] HYMN LIV. Pusan.

1. O PUSAN, bring us to the man who knows, who shall direct us straight,
And say unto us, It is here.
2 May we go forth with Pusan who shall point the houses out to us,
And say to us, These same are they.
3 Unharmed is Pusan's chariot wheel; the box ne'er falleth to the ground,
Nor doth the loosened felIy shake.
4 Pusan forgetteth not the man who serveth him with offered gift:
That man is first to gather wealth.
5 May Pusan follow near our kine; may Pusan keep our horses safe:
May Pusan gather gear for us.
6 Follow the kine of him who pours libations out and worships thee;
And ours who sing thee songs of praise.
7 Let none be lost, none injured, none sink in a pit and break a limb.
Return with these all safe and sound.
8 Pusan who listens to our prayers, the Strong whose wealth is never lost,
The Lord of riches, we implore.
9 Secure in thy protecting care, O Pusan, never may we fail.
We here are they who sing thy praise.
10 From out the distance, far and wide, may Pusan stretch his right hand forth,
And drive our lost again to us.

### [06-055] HYMN LV. Pusan.

1. SON of Deliverance, come, bright God!
Let us twain go together: be our charioteer of sacrifice.
2 We pray for wealth to thee most skilled of charioteers, with braided hair,
Lord of great riches, and our Friend.
3 Bright God whose steeds are goats, thou art a stream of wealth, a treasure-heap,
The Friend of every pious man.
4 Pusan, who driveth goats for steeds, the strong and Mighty, who is called
His Sister's lover, will we laud.
5 His Mother's suitor I address. May he who loves his Sister hear,
Brother of Indra, and my Friend.
6 May the sure-footed goats come nigh, conveying Pusan on his car,
The God who visiteth mankind.

### [06-056] HYMN LVI, Pusan.

1. WHOSO remembers Pusan as cater of mingled curd and meal
Need think no more upon the God.
2 And he is best of charioteers. Indra, the hero's Lord, allied
With him as Friend, destroys the foes.
3 And there the best of charioteers hath guided through the speckled cloud
The golden wheel of Sura's car.
4 Whate'er we speak this day to thee, Wise, Wondrous God whom many praise,
Give thou fulfilment of our thought.
5 Lead on this company of ours, that longs for kine, to win the spoil:
Thou, Pusan, art renowned afar.
6 Prosperity we crave from thee, afar from sin and near to wealth,
Tending to perfect happiness both for to. morrow and to-day.

### [06-057] HYMN LVII. Indra and Pusan.

1. INDRA and Pusan will we call for friend ship and prosperity
And for the winning of the spoil.

2 One by the Soma sits to drink juice which the mortar hath expressed:
The other longs for curd and meal.
3 Goats are the team that draws the one: the other hath Bay Steeds at hand;
With both of these he slays the fiends.
4 When Indra, wondrous strong, brought down the streams, the mighty waterfloods,
Pusan was standing by his side.
5 To this, to Pusan's favouring love, and Indra's, may we closely cling,
As to a tree's extended bough.
6 As one who drives a car draws in his reins, may we draw Pusan near,
And Indra, for our great success.

## [06-058] HYMN LVIII. Pusan.

1. LIKE heaven art thou: one form is bright, one holy, like Day and Night dissimilar in colour.
All magic powers thou aidest, self-depen. dent! Auspicious be thy bounty here, O Pusan.
2 Goat-borne, the guard of cattle, he whose home is strength, inspirer of the hymn, set over all the world;
Brandishing here and there his lightly. moving goad, beholding every creature, Pusan, God, goes forth.
3 O Pusan, with thy golden ships that travel across the ocean, in the air's mid-region,
Thou goest on an embassy to Surya, subdued by love, desirous of the glory.
4 Near kinsman of the heaven and earth is Pusan, liberal, Lord of food, of wondrous iustre,
Whom strong and vigorous and swiftlymoving, subdued by love, the Deities gave to Surya.

## [06-059] HYMN LIX. Indra-Agni.

1. I WILL declare, while juices flow, the manly deeds that ye have done:
Your Fathers, enemies of Gods, were smitten down, and, Indra-Agni, ye survive.
2 Thus, Indra-Agnip verily your greatness merits loftiest praise,
Sprung from one common Father, brothers, twins are ye; your Mother is in every place.
3 These who delight in flowing juice, like fellow horses at their food,
Indra and Agni, Gods armed with the thunderbolt, we call this day to come with help.
4 Indra and Agni, Friends of Law, served with rich gifts, your speech is kind
To him who praises you while these libations flow: that man, O Gods, ye ne'er consume.
5 What mortal understands, O Gods, Indra and Agni, this your way?
One of you, yoking Steeds that move to every side, advances in your common car.
6 First, Indra-Agni, hath this Maid come footless unto those with feet.
Stretching her head and speaking loudly with her tongue, she hath gone downward thirty steps.
7 E'en now, O Indra-Agni, men hold in their arms and stretch their bows.
Desert us not in this great fray, in battles for the sake of kine.
8 The foeman's sinful enmities, Indra and Agni, vex me sore.
Drive those who hate me far away, and keep them distant from the Sun.

9 Indra and Agni, yours are all the treasures of the heavens and earth.
Here give ye us the opulence that prospers every living man.
10 O Indra-Agni, who accept the laud, and hear us for our praise,
Come near us, drawn by all our songs, to drink of this our Soma juice.

## [06-060] HYMN LX. Indra-Agni.

1. HE slays the foe and wins the spoil who worships Indra and Agni, strong and mighty Heroes,
Who rule as Sovrans over ample riches, victorious, showing forth their power in conquest.
2 So battle now, O Indra and thou, Agni, for cows and waters, sunlight, stolen Mornings.
Team-borne, thou makest kine thine own, O Agni: thou, Indra, light, Dawns, regions, wondrous waters.
3 With Vrtra-slaying might, Indra and Agni, come, drawn by homage, O ye Vrtra-slayers.
Indra and Agni, show yourselves among us with your supreme and unrestricted bounties.
4 I call the Twain whose deeds of old have all been famed in ancient days
O Indra-Agni, harm us not.
5 The Strong, the scatterers of the foe, Indra and Agni, we invoke;
May they be kind to one like me.
6 They slay our Arya foes, these Lords of heroes, slay our Dasyu foes
And drive our enemies away.
7 Indra and Agni, these our songs of praise have sounded forth to you:
Ye who bring blessings! drink the juice.
8 Come, Indra-Agni, with those teams, desired of many, which ye have,
O Heroes, for the worshipper.
9 With those to this libation poured, ye Heroes, Indra-Agni, come:
Come ye to drink the Soma juice.
10 Glorify him who compasses all forests with his glowing flame,
And leaves them blackened with his tongue.
11 He who gains Indra's bliss with fire enkindled finds an easy way
Over the floods to happiness.
12 Give us fleet coursers to convey Indra and Agni, and bestow
Abundant strengthening food on us.
13 Indra and Agni, I will call you hither and make you joyful with the gifts I offer.
Ye Twain are givers both of food and riches: to win me strength and vigour I invoke you.
14 Come unto us with riches, come with wealth in horses and in kine.
Indra and Agni, we invoke you both, the Gods, as Friends for friendship, bringing bliss.
15 Indra and Agni, hear his call who worships. with libations poured.
Come and enjoy the offerings, drink the sweetly-flavoured Soma juice.

## [06-061] HYMN LXI. Sarasvati.

1. To Vadhryasva when. be worshipped her with gifts she gave fierce Divodasa, canceller of debts.
Consumer of the churlish niggard, one and all, thine, O Sarasvati, are these effectual boons.
2 She with her might, like one who digs for lotus-stems, hath burst with her strong waves the ridges of the hills.
Let us invite with songs and holy hymns for help Sarasvati who slayeth the Paravatas.

3 Thou castest down, Sarasvati, those who scorned the Gods, the brood of every Brsaya skilled in magic arts.
Thou hast discovered rivers for the tribes of men, and, rich in wealth! made poison flow away from them.
4 May the divine Sarasvati, rich in her wealth, protect us well, Furthering all our thoughts with might
5 Whoso, divine Sarasvati, invokes thee where the prize is set, Like Indra when he smites the foe.
6 Aid us, divine Sarasvad, thou who art strong in wealth and power
Like Pusan, give us opulence.
7 Yea, this divine Sarasvati, terrible with her golden path, Foe-slayer, claims our eulogy.
8 Whose limitless unbroken flood, swift-moving with a rapid rush,
Comes onward with tempestuous roar.
9 She hath spread us beyond all foes, beyond her Sisters, Holy One,
As Surya spreadeth out the days.
10 Yea, she most dear amid dear stream, Seven-sistered, graciously inclined,
Sarasvati hath earned our praise.
11 Guard us from hate Sarasvati, she who hath filled the realms of earth,
And that wide tract, the firmament!
12 Seven-sistered, sprung from threefold source, the Five Tribes' prosperer, she must be
Invoked in every deed of might.
13 Marked out by majesty among the Mighty Ones, in glory swifter than the other rapid Streams,
Created vast for victory like a chariot, Sarasvati must be extolled by every sage.
14 Guide us, Sarasvati, to glorious treasure: refuse us not thy milk, nor spurn us from thee.
Gladly accept our friendship and obedience: let us not go from thee to distant countries.

## [06-062] HYMN LXII. Asvins.

1. I LAUD the Heroes Twain, this heaven's Controllers: singing with songs of praise I call the Asvins,
Fain in a moment, when the morns are breaking, to part the earth's ends and the spacious regions.
2 Moving to sacrifice through realms of lustre they light the radiance of the car that bears them.
Traversing many wide unmeasured spaces, over the wastes ye pass, and fields, and waters.
3 Ye to that bounteous path of yours, ye mighty, have ever borne away our thoughts with horses,
Mind-swift and full of vigour, that the trouble of man who offers gifts might cease and slumber.
4 So ye, when ye have yoked your chariothorses, come to the hymn of the most recent singer.
Our true and ancient Herald Priest shall bring you, the Youthful, bearing splendour, food, and vigour.
5 With newest hymn I call those Wonder-Workers, ancient and brilliant, and exceeding mighty,
Bringers of bliss to him who lauds and praises, bestowing varied bounties on the singer.
6 So ye, with birds, out of the sea and waters bore Bhujyu, son of Tugra, through the regions.
Speeding with winged steeds through dustless spaces, out of the bosom of the flood they bore him.
7 Victors, car-borne, ye rent the rock asunder: Bulls, heard the calling of the eunuch's consort.
Bounteous, ye filled the cow with milk for Sayu: thus, swift and zealous Ones, ye showed your favour.

8 Whate'er from olden time, Heaven, Earth! existeth great object of the wrath of Gods and mortals,
Make that, Adityas, Vasus, sons of Rudra, an evil brand to one allied with demons.
9 May he who knows, as Varuna and Mitra, air's realm, appointing both the Kings in season,
Against the secret fiend cast forth his weapon, against the lying words that strangers utter.
10 Come to our home with friendly wheels, for offipring; come on your radiant chariot rich in heroes.
Strike off, ye Twain, the heads of our assailants who with man's treacherous attack approach us.
11 Come hitherward to us with teams of horses, the highest and the midmost and the lowest.
Bountiful Lords, throw open to the singer doors e'en of the firm-closed stall of cattle.

## [06-063] HYMN LXIII. Asvins.

1. WHERE hath the hymn with reverence, like an envoy, found both fair Gods to-day, invoked of many-
Hymn that hath brought the two Nasatyas hither? To this man's thought be ye, both Gods, most friendly.
2 Come readily to this mine invocation, lauded with songs, that ye may drink the juices.
Compass this house to keep it from the foeman, that none may force it, either near or distant.
3 Juice in wide room hath been prepared to feast you: for you the grass is strewn, most soft to tread on.
With lifted hands your servant hath adored you. Yearningfor you the press-stones shed the liquid.
4 Agni uplifts him at your sacrifices: forth goes the oblation dropping oil and glowing.
Up stands the grateful-minded priest, elected, appointed to invoke the two Nasatyas.
5 Lords of great wealth! for glory, Surya's Daughter mounted your car that brings a hundred succours.
Famed for your magic arts were ye, magicians! amid the race of Gods, ye dancing Heroes!
6 Ye Twain, with these your glories fair to look on, brought, to win victory, rich gifts for Surya.
After you flew your birds, marvels of beauty: dear to our hearts! the song, well lauded, reached you.
7 May your winged coursers, best to draw. Nasatyas! convey you to the object of your wishes.
Swift as the thought, your car hath been sent onward to food of many a sort and dainty viands.
8 Lords of great wealth, manifold is your bounty: ye filled our cow with food that never faileth.
Lovers of sweetness! yours are praise and singers, and poured libations which have sought your favour.
9 Mine were two mares of Puraya, brown, swift-footed; a hundred with Sumidha, food with Peruk
Sanda gave ten gold-decked and well-trained horses, tame and obedient and of lofty stature.
10 Nasatyas! Purupanthas offered hundreds, thousands of steeds to him who sang your praises,
Gave, Heroes! to the singer Bharadvaja. Ye-Wonder-Workers, let the fiends be slaughtered.
11 May I with princes share your bliss in freedom.

## [06-064] HYMN LXIV. Dawn.

1. THE radiant Dawns have risen up for glory, in their white splendour like the waves of waters.
She maketh paths all easy, fair to travel, and, rich, hath shown herself benign and friendly.

2 We see that thou art good: far shines thy lustre; thy beams, thy splendours have flown up to heaven.

Decking thyself, thou makest bare thy bosom, shining in majesty, thou Goddess Morning.

3 Red are the kine and luminous that bear her the Blessed One who spreadeth through the distance.

The foes she chaseth like a valiant archer, like a swift warrior she repelleth darkness.

4 Thy ways are easy on the hills: thou passest Invincible! Se1f-luminous! through waters.

So lofty Goddess with thine ample pathway, Daughter of Heaven, bring wealth to give us comfort.

5 Dawn, bring me wealth: untroubled, with thine oxen thou bearest riches at thy will and pleasure;

Thou who, a Goddess, Child of Heaven, hast shown thee lovely through bounty when we called thee early.

6 As the birds fly forth from their restingplaces, so men with store of food rise at thy dawning.

Yea, to the liberal mortal who rernaineth at home, O Goddess Dawn, much good thou bringest.

### [06-065] HYMN LXV. Dawn.

1. SHEDDING her light on human habitations this Child of Heaven hath called us from our slumber;

She who at night-time with her argent lustre hath shown herself e'en through the shades of darkness.

2 All this with red-rayed steeds have they divided: the Dawns on bright cars shine in wondrous fashion.

They, bringing near the stately rite's commencement, drive far away the night's surrounding shadows.

3 Dawns, bringing hither, to the man who worships, glory and power and might and food and vigour,

Opulent, with imperial sway like heroes, favour your servant and this day enrich him.

4 Now is there treasure for the man who serves you, now for the hero, Dawns! who brings oblation;

Now for the singer when he sings the praise-song. Even to one like me ye brought aforetime.

5 O Dawn who standest on the mountain ridges, Angirases now praise thy stalls of cattle.

With prayer and holy hymn they burst them open: the heroes' calling on the Gods was fruitful.

6 Shine on us as of old, thou Child of Heaven,on him, rich Maid! who serves like Bharadvaja.

Give to the singer wealth with noble heroes, and upon us bestow wide-spreading glory.

### [06-066] HYMN LXVI. Maruts.

1. E'EN to the wise let that be still a wonder to which the general name of Cow is given.

The one hath swelled among mankind for milking: Prsni hath drained but once her fair bright udder.

2 They who like kindled flames of fire are glowing,. the Maruts, twice and thrice have waxen mighty.

Golden and dustless were their cars, invested with their great strength and their heroic vigour.

3 They who are Sons of the rain-pouring Rudra, whom the long-lasting One had power to foster:

The Mighty Ones whose germ great Mother Prsni is known to have received for man's advantage.

4 They shrink not from the birth; in this same manner still resting there they purge away reproaches.

When they have streamed forth, brilliant, at their pleasure, with their own splendour they bedew their bodies.

5 Even those who bear the brave bold name of Maruts, whom not the active quickly wins for milking.

Even the liberal wards not off those fierce ones, those who are light and agile in their greatness.

6 When, strong in strength and armed with potent weapons, they had united wellformed earth and heaven,

Rodasl stood among these furious Heroes like splendour shining with her native brightness.

7 No team of goats shall draw your car, O Maruts, no horse no charioteer be he who drives it.

Halting not, reinless, through the air it travels, speeding alone its paths through earth and heaven.

8 None may obstruct, none overtake, O Maruts, him whom ye succour in the strife of battle

For sons and progeny, for kine and waters: he bursts the cow-stall on the day of trial.

9 Bring a bright hymn to praise the band of Maruts, the Singers, rapid, strong in native vigour,

Who conquer mighty strength with strength more mighty: earth shakes in terror at their wars, O
Agni.

10 Bright like the flashing flames of sacrifices, like tongues of fire impetuous in their onset,

Chanting their psalm, singing aloud, like heroes, splendid from birth, invincible, the Maruts.

11 That swelling band I call with invocation, the brood of Rudra, armed with glittering lances.

Pure hymns are meet for that celestial army: like floods and mountains have the Strong Ones battled.

### [06-067] HYMN LXVIL Mitra-Varuna.

1. NOW Mitra-Varuna shall be exalted high by your songs, noblest of all existing;

They who, as 'twere with reins are best Controllers, unequalled with their arms to check the people.

2 To you Two Gods is this my thought extended, turned to the sacred grass with loving homage.

Give us, O Mitra-Varuna, a dwelling safe from attack, which ye shall guard, Boon-Givers!

3 Come hither, Mitra-Varuna, invited with eulogies and loving adoration,

Ye who with your might, as Work-Controllers, urge even men who quickly hear to labour.

4 Whom, of pure origin, like two strong horses, Aditi bore as babes in proper season,

Whom, Mighty at your birth, the Mighty Goddess brought forth as terrors to the mortal foeman.

5 As all the Gods in their great joy and gladness gave you with one accord your high dominion,

As ye surround both worlds, though wide and spacious your spies are ever true and never bewildered.

6 So, through the days maintaining princely power. ye prop the height as 'twere from loftiest heaven.

The Star of all the Gods, established, filleth the heaven and earth with food of man who liveth.

7 Take the strong drink, to quaff till ye are sated, when he and his attendants fill the chamber.

The young Maids brook not that none seeks to win them, when, Quickeners of all! they scatter moisture.

8 So with your tongue come ever, when your envoy, faithful and very wise, attends our worship.

Nourished by holy oil! he this yGur glory: annihilate the sacrificer's trouble.

9 When, Mitra-Varuna, they strive against you and break tlie friendly laws ye have established,

They, neither Gods nor men in estimation, like Api's sons have godless sacrifices.

10 When singers in their song uplift their voices, some chant the Nivid texts with steady purpose.

Then may we sing you lauds that shall be fruitful: dp ye not rival all the Gods in greatness?

11 O Mitra-Varuna, may your large bounty come to us hither, near to this our dwelling,

When the kine haste to us, and when they harness the fleet-foot mettled stallion for the battle.

### [06-068] HYMN LXVIII. Indra-Varuna.

1. HIS honouring rite whose grass is trimmed is offered swiftly to you, in Manu's wise, accordant,

The rite which Indra-Varuna shall carry this day to high success and glorious issue.

2 For at Gods' worship they are best through vigour; they have become the strongest of the Heroes;

With mighty strength, most liberal of the Princes, Chiefs of the host, by Law made Vrtra's slayers.

3 Praise those Twain Gods for powers that merit worship, Indra and Varuna, for bliss, the joyous.

One with his might and thunderbolt slays Vrtra; the other as a Sage stands near in troubles.

4 Though dames and men have waxen strong and mighty, and all the Gods selfpraised among the

Heroes,

Ye, Indra-Varuna, have in might surpassed them, and thus were ye spread wide, O Earth and

Heaven.

5 Righteous is he, and liberal and helpful who, Indra-Varuna, brings you gifts with gladness.

That bounteous man through food shall conquer faemen, and win him opulence and wealthy people.

6 May wealth which ye bestow in food and treasure on him who brings you gifts and sacrifices,

Wealth, Gods! which breaks the curse of those who vex us, be, Indra-Varuna, e'en our own possession.

7 So also, Indra-Varuna, may our princes have riches swift to save, with Gods to guard them-

They whose great might gives victory in battles, and their triumphant glory spreads with swiftness.

8 Indra. and Varuna, Gods whom we are lauding, mingle ye wealth with our heroic glory.

May we, who praise the strength of what is mighty, pass dangers, as with boats we cross the waters.

9 Now will I sing a dear and far-extending hymn to Varuna the God, sublime, imperial Lord,

Who, mighty Governor, Eternal, as with flame, illumines both wide worlds with majesty and power.

10 True to Law, Indra-Varuna, drinkers of the juice, drink this pressed Soma which shall give you rapturous joy.

Your chariot cometh to the banquet of the Gods, to sacrifice, as it were home, that ye may drink.

11 Indra and Varuna, drink your fill, ye Heroes, of this invigorating sweetest Soma.

This juice is shed by us that ye may quaff it: on this trimmed grass be seated, and rejoice you

### [06-069] HYMN LXIX. Indra-Visnu

1. INDRA and Visnu, at my task's completion I urge you on with food and sacred service.

Accept the sacrifice and grant us riches, leading us on by unobstructed pathways.

2 Ye who inspire all hymns, Indra and Visnu, ye vessels who contain the Soma juices,

May hymns of praise that now are sung address you, the lauds that are recited by the singers.

3 Lords of joy-giving draughts, Indra and Visnu, come, giving gifts of treasure, to the Soma.

With brilliant rays of hymns let chanted praises, repeated with the lauds, adorn and deck you.

4 May your foe-conquering horses bring you hither, Indra and Visnu, sharers of the banquet.

Of all our hymns accept the invocations list to my prayers and hear the songs I sing you.

5 This your deed, Indra-Visnu, must be lauded: widely ye strode in the wild joy of Soma.

Ye made the firmament of larger compass, and made the regions broad for our existence.

6 Strengthened with sacred offerings, IndraVisnu, first eaters, served with worship ana oblation,

Fed with the holy oil, vouchsafe us riches ye are the lake, the vat that holds the Soma.

7 Drink of this meath, O Indra, thou, and Visnu; drink ye your fill of Soma, Wonder-Workers.

The sweet exhilarating juice hath reached you. Hear ye my prayers, give ear unto my calling.

8 Ye Twain have conquered, ne'er have yc been conquered: never hath either of the Twain been vanquished.

Ye, Indra-Visnu, when ye fought the battle, produced this infinite with three divisions.

### [06-070] HYMN LXX. Heaven and Earth.

1. FILLED full of fatness, compassing all things that be, wide, spacious, dropping meath, beautiful in their form,

The Heaven and the Earth by Varuna's decree, unwasting, rich in germs, stand parted each from each.

2 The Everlasting Pair, with full streams, rich in milk, in their pure rule pour fatness for the pious man.

Ye who are Regents of this world, O Earth and Heaven, pour into us the genial flow that prospers meit.

3 Whoso, for righteous life, pours offerings to you, O Heaven and Earth, ye Hemispheres, that man succeeds.

He in his seed is born again and spreads by Law: from you flow things diverse in form, but ruled alike.

4 Enclosed in fatness, Heaven and Earth are bright therewith: they mingle with the fatness which they still increase.

Wide, broad, set foremost at election of the priest, to them the singers pray for bliss to further them.

5 May Heaven and Earth pour down the balmy rain for us, balm-dropping, yielding balm, with balm upon your path,

Bestowing by your Godhead sacrifice and wealth, great fame and strength for us and good heroic might.

6 May Heaven and Earth make food swell plenteously for us, all-knowing Father, jother, wondrous in

their works.

Pouring out bounties, may, in union, both the Worlds, all beneficial, send us gain, and power, and

wealth.

### [06-071] HYMN LXXI. Savitar.

1. FULL of effectual wisdom Savitar the God hath stretched out golden arms that he may bring forth life.

Young and most skilful, while he holds the region up, the Warrior sprinkles fatness over both his hands.

2 May we enjoy the noblest vivifying force of Savitar the God, that he may give us wealth:

For thou art mighty to produce and lull to rest the world of life that moves on two feet and on four.

3 Protect our habitation, Savitar, this day, with guardian aids around, auspicious, firm and true.

God of the golden tongue, keep us for newest bliss: let not the evil-wisher have us in his power.

4 This Savitar the God, the golden-handed, Friend of the home, hath risen to meet the twilight.

With cheeks of brass, with pleasant tongue, the Holy, he sends the worshipper rich gifts in plenty.
5 Like a Director, Savitar hath extended his golden arms, exceeding fair to look on.
He hath gone up the heights of earth and heaven, and made each monster fall and cease from
troubling.
6 Fair wealth, O Savitar, to-day, to-morrow, fair wealth produce for us each day that passes.
May we through this our song be happy gainers, God, of a fair and spacious habitation.

## [06-072] HYMN LXXII. Indra-Soma.

1. GREAT is this might of yours, Indra and Soma: the first high exploits were your own achievements.
Ye found the Sun ye found the light of heaven: ye killed all darkness and the Gods' blasphemers.
2 Ye, Indra-Soma, gave her light to Morning, and led the Sun on high with all his splendour.
Ye stayed the heaven with a supporting pillar, and spread abroad apart, the Earth, the Mother.
3 Ye slew the flood -obstructing serpent Vrtra, Indra and Soma: Heaven approved your exploit.
Ye urged to speed the currents of the rivers, and many seas have ye filled full with waters.
4 Ye in the unripe udders of the milch-kine have set the ripe milk, Indra, thou, and Soma.
Ye have held fast the unimpeded whiteness within these many-coloured moving creatures.
5 Verily ye bestow, Indra and Soma, wealth, famed, victorious, passing to our children.
Ye have invested men, ye Mighty Beings, with manly strength that conquers in the battle.

## [06-073] HYMN LXXIII. Brhaspati.

1. SERVED with oblations, first-born, mountain-render, Angiras' son, Brhaspati, the Holy,
With twice-firm path, dwelling in light, our Father, roars loudly, as a bull, to Earth and Heaven.
2 Brhaspati, who made for such a people wide room and verge when Gods were invoked,
Slaying his enemies, breaks down their castles, quelling his foes and conquering those who hate him.
3 Brhaspati in war hath won rich treasures, hath won, this God, the great stalls filled with cattle.
Striving to win waters and light, resistless, Brhaspati with lightning smites the foeman.

## [06-074] HYMN LXXIV. Soma-Rudra.

1. HOLD fast your Godlike sway, O Soma-Rudra: let these our sacrifices quickly reach you.
Placing in every house your seven great treasures, bring blessing to our quadrupeds and bipeds.
2 Soma and Rudra, chase to every quarter the sickness that hath visited our dwelling.
Drive Nirṛti away into the distance, and give us excellent and happy glories.
3 Provide, O Soma-Rudra, for our bodies all needful medicines to heal and cure us.
Set free and draw away the sin committed which we have still inherent in our persons.
4 Armed with keen shafts and weapons, kind and loving, be gracious unto us, Soma and Rudra.
Release us from the noose of Varuna; keep us from sorrow, in your tender loving-kindness.

## [06-075] HYMN LXXV. Weapons of War.

1. THE warrior's look is like a thunderous rain-cloud's, when, armed with mail, he seeks the lap of battle.
Be thou victorious with unwounded body: so let the thickness of thy mail protect thee.
2 With Bow let us win kine, with Bow the battle, with Bow be victors in our hot encounters.
The Bow brings grief and sorrow to the foeman: armed with the Bow may we subdue all regions.
3 Close to his car, as fain to speak, She presses, holding her well-loved Friend in her embraces.
Strained on the Bow, She whispers like a woman-this Bowstring that preserves us in the combat.
4 These, meeting like a woman and her lover, bear, mother-like, their child upon their bosom.
May the two Bow-ends, starting swift asunder, scatter, in unison, the foes who hate us.
5 With many a son, father of many daughters, He clangs and clashes as he goes to battle.
Slung on the back, pouring his brood, the Quiver vanquishes all opposing bands and armies.
6 Upstanding in the Car the skilful Charioteer guides his strong Horses on whithersoe'er he will.
See and admire the strength of those controlling Reins which from behind declare the will of him who
drives.
7 Horses whose hoofs rain dust are neighing loudly, yoked to the Chariots, showing forth their vigour,
With their forefeet descending on the foemen, they, never flinching, trample and destroy them.
8 Car-bearer is the name of his oblation, whercon are laid his Weapons and his Armour.
So let us here, each day that passes, honour the helpful Car with hearts exceeding joyful.
9 In sweet association lived the fathers who gave us life, profound and strong in trouble,
Unwearied, armed with shafts and wondrous weapons, free, real heroes, conquerors of armies.
10 The Brahmans, and the Fathers meet for Soma-draughts, and, graciously inclined, unequalled
Heaven and Earth.
Guard us trom evil, Pusan, guard us strengtheners of Law: let not the evil-wisher master us.
11 Her tooth a deer, dressed in an eagle's feathers, bound with cow-hide, launched forth, She flieth
onward.
There where the heroes speed hither and thither, there may the Arrows shelter and protect us.
12 Avoid us thou whose flight is straight, and let our bodies be as stone.
May Soma kindly speak to us, and Aditi protect us well.
13 He lays his blows upon their backs, he deals his blows upon their thighs.
Thou, Whip, who urgest horses, drive sagacious horses in the fray.
14 It compasses the arm with serpent windings, fending away the friction of the bowstring:
So may the Brace, well-skilled in all its duties, guard manfully the man from every quarter.
15 Now to the Shaft with venom smeared, tipped with deer-horn, with iron mouth,
Celestial, of Parjanya's seed, be this great adoration paid.
16 Loosed from the Bowstring fly away, thou Arrow, sharpened by our prayer.
Go to the foemen, strike them home, and let not one be left alive.
17 There where the flights of Arrows fall like boys whose locks are yet unshorn.

Even there may Brahmanaspati, and Aditi protect us well, protect us well through all our days.

18 Thy vital parts I cover with thine Armour: with immortality King Soma clothe thee.

Varuna give tliee what is more than ample, and in thy triumph may the Gods be joyful.

19 Whoso would kill us, whether he be a strange foe or one of us, May all the Gods discomfit him. My nearest, closest Mail is prayer.

# BOOK SEVEN

### [07-001] HYMN I. Agni.

1. THE men from fire-sticks, with their hands' swift movement, have, in deep thought, engendered

glorious Agni,

Far-seen, with pointed flame, Lord of the homestead.

2 The Vasus set that Agni in the dwelling, fair to behold, for help from every quarter:

Who, in the home for ever, must be honoured.

3 Shine thou before us, Agni, well-enkindled, with flame, Most Youthful God, that never fadeth.

To thee come all our sacrificial viands.

4 Among all fires these fires have shone most brightly, splendid with light, begirt by noble heroes,

Where men of lofty birth sit down together.

5 Victorious Agni, grant us wealth with wisdom, wealth with brave sons, famous and independent,

Which not a foe who deals in magic conquers.

6 To whom, the Strong, at morn and eve comes, maid-like, the ladle dropping oil, with its oblation.

Wealth-seeking comes to him his own devotion.

7 Burn up all malice with those flames, O Agni, wherewith of old thou burntest up Jarutha,

And drive away in silence pain and sickness.

8 With him who lighteth up thy splendour, Agni, excellent, pure, refulgent, Purifier,

Be present, and with us through these our praises.

9 Agni, the patriarchal men, the mortals who have in many places spread thy lustre,-

Be gracious to us here for their sake also.

10 Let these men, heroes in the fight with foemen, prevail against all godless arts of 4magic,-

These who ipprove the noble song I sing thee.

11 Let us not sit in want of men, O Agni, without descendants, heroleu, about thee:

But, O House-Friend, in houses full of children.

12 By sacrifice which the Steeds' Lord ever visits, there make our dwelling rich in seed and offspring,

Increasing still with lineal successors.

13 Guard us, O Agni, from the hated demon, guard us from malice of the churlish sinner:

Allied with thee may I subdue assailants.

14 May this same fire of mine surpass all others, this fire where offspring, vigorous and firm-handed,

Wins, on a thousand paths, what ne'er shall perish.

15 This is that Agni, saviour from the foeman, who guards the kindler of the flame from sorrow:

Heroes of noble lineage serve and tend him.

16 This is that Agni, served in many places, whom the rich lord who brings oblation kindles,

And round him goes the priest at sacrifices.

17 Agni, may we with riches in possession bring thee continual ofierings in abundance,

Using both means to draw thee to our worship.

18 Agni, bear thou, Eternal, these most welcome oblations to the Deities' assembly:

Let them enjoy our very fragrant presents.

19 Give us not up, Agni, to want of heroes, to wretched clothes, to need, to destitution.

Yield us not, Holy One, to fiend or hunger; injure us not at home or in the forest.

20 Give strength and power to these my prayers, O Agni; O God, pour blessings on our chiefs and

nobles.

Grant that both we and they may share thy bounty. Ye Gods, protect us evermore with blessings.

21 Thou Agni, swift to hear, art fair of aspect: beam forth, O Son of Strength, in full effulgence.

Let me not want, with thee, a son for ever: let not a manly hero ever fail us.

22 Condemn us not to indigence, O Agni, beside these flaming fires which Gods have kindled;

Nor, even after fault, let thy displeasure, thine as a God, O Son of Strength, o'ertake us.

23 O Agni, fair of face, the wealthy mortal who to the Immortal offers his oblation.

Hath him who wins him treasure by his Godhead, to whom the prince, in need, goes supplicating.

24 Knowing our chief felicity, O Agni, bring hither ample riches to our nobles,

Wherewith we may enjoy ourselves, O Victor, with undiminished life and hero children.

25 Give strength and power to these my prayers, O Agni; O God, pour blessings on bur chiefs and

nobles.

Grant that both we and they may share thy bounty. Ye Gods, protect us evermore with blessings.

### [07-002] HYMN II. Apris.

1. GLADLY accept, this day, our fuel, Agni: send up thy sacred smoke and shine sublimely.

Touch the celestial summits with thy columns, and overspread thee with the rays of Surya.

2 With sacrifice to these we men will honour the majesty of holy Narasamsa-

To these the pure, most wise, the thought. inspirers, Gods who enjoy both sorts of our oblations.

3 We will extol at sacrifice for ever, as men may do, Agni whom Manu kindled,

Your very skilful Asura, meet for worship, envoy between both worlds, the truthful speaker.

4 Bearing the sacred grass, the men who serve him strew it with reverence, on their knees, by Agni.

Calling him to the spotted grass, oil-sprinkled, adorn him, ye Adhvaryus, with oblation.

5 With holy thoughts the pious have thrown open Doors fain for chariots in the Gods' assembly.

Like two full mother cows who lick their youngling, like maidens for the gathering, they adorn them.

6 And let the two exalted Heavenly Ladies, Morning and Night, like a cow good at milking,

Come, much-invoked, and on our grass be seated ' wealthy, deserving worship, for our welfare.

7 You, Bards and Singers at men's sacrifices, both filled with wisdom, I incline to worship.

Send up our offerings when we call upon you, and so among the Gods obtain us treasures.

8 May Bharati with all her Sisters, Ila accordant with the Gods, with mortals Agni,

Sarasvati with all her kindred Rivers, come to this grass, Three Goddesses, and seat them.

9 Well pleased with us do thou, O God, O Tvastar, give ready issue to our procreant vigour,

Whence springs the hero, powerful, skilled in action, lover of Gods, adjuster of the press-stones.

10 Send to the Gods the oblation, Lord of Forests, and let the Immolator, Agni, dress it.

He as the truer Priest shall offer worship, for the God'sgenerations well he knoweth.

11 Come thou to us, O Agni, duly kindled, together with the potent Gods and Indra.

On this our grass sit Aditi, happy Mother, and let our Hail! delight the Gods Immortal.

## [07-003] HYMN III. Agni.

1. ASSOCIATE with fires, make your God Agni envoy at sacrifice, best skilled in worship,

Established firm among mankind, the Holy, flame-crowned and fed with oil, the Purifier.

2 Like a steed neighing eager for the pasture, when he hath stepped forth from the great enclosure:

Then the wind following blows upon his splendour, and, straight, the path is black which thou hast travelled.

3 From thee a Bull but newly born, O Agni, the kindled everlasting flames rise upward.

Aloft to heaven thy ruddy smoke ascendeth: Agni, thou speedest to the Gods as envoy.

4 Thou whose fresh lustre o'er the earth advanceth when greedily with thy jaws thy food thou eatest.

Like a host hurried onward comes thy lasso: fierce, with thy tongue thou piercest, as 'twere barley.

5 The men have decked him both at eve and morning, Most Youthful Agni, as they tend a courser.

They kindle him, a guest within his dwelling: bright shines the splendour of the worshipped Hero.

6 O fair of face, beautiful is thine aspect when, very near at hand, like gold thou gleamest,

Like Heaven's thundering roar thy might approaches, and like the wondrous Sun thy light thou showest.

7 That we may worship, with your Hail to Agni! with sacrificial cakes and fat oblations,

Guard us, O Agni, with those boundless glories as with a hundred fortresses of iron.

8 Thine are resistless songs for him who offers, and hero-giving hymns wherewith thou savest;

With these, O Son of Strength, O Jatavedas, guard us, preserve these princes and the singers.

9 When forth he cometh, like an axe new-sharpened, pure in his form, resplendent in his body,

Sprung, sought with eager longing, from his Parents, for the Gods' worship, Sage and Purifier:

10 Shine this felicity on us, O Agni: may we attain to perfect understanding.

All happiness be theirs who sing and praise thee. Ye Gods, preserve us evermore with blessings.

## [07-004] HYMN IV. Agni.

1. BRING forth your gifts to his refulgent splendour, your hymn as purest offering to Agni,

To him who goes as messenger with knowledge between all songs of men and Gods in heaven.

2 Wise must this Agni be, though young and tender, since he was born, Most Youthful, of his Mother;

He who with bright teeth seizeth fast the forests, and eats his food, though plenteous, in a moment.

3 Before his presence must we all assemble, this God's whom men have seized in his white splendour.

This Agni who hath brooked that men should seize him hath shone for man with glow insufferable.

4 Far-seeing hath this Agni been established, deathless mid mortals, wise among the foolish.

Here, O victorious God, forbear to harm us: may weforever share thy gracious favour.

5 He who hath occupied his God-made dwelling, Agni, in wisdom hath surpassed Immortals.

A Babe unborn, the plants and trees support him, and the earth beareth him the All-sustainer.

6 Agni is Lord of Amrta. in abundance, Lord of the gift of wealth and hero valour,

Victorious God, let us not sit about thee like men devoid of strength, beauty, and worship.

7 The foeman's treasure may be won with labour: may we be masters of our own possessions.

Agni, no son is he who springs from others: lengthen not out the pathways of the foolish.

8 Unwelcome for adoption is the stranger, one to be thought of as another's offspring,

Though grown familiar by continual presence. May our strong hero come, freshly triumphant.

9 Guard us from him who would assail us, Agni; preserve us O thou Victor, from dishonour.

Here let the place of darkening come upon thee: may wealth be ours, desirable, in thousands.

10 Shine this felicity on us, O Agni: may we attain to perfect understanding.

All happiness be theirs who sing and praise thee. Ye Gods, preserve us evermore with blessings.

## [07-005] HYMN V. Agni.

1. BRING forth your song of praise to mighty Agni, the speedy messenger of earth and heaven,

Vaisvanara, who, with those who wake, hath waxen great in the lap of all the Gods Immortal.

2 Sought in the heavens, on earth is Agni stablished, leader of rivers, Bull of standing waters.

Vaisvanara when he hath grown in glory, shines on the tribes of men with light and treasure.

3 For fear of thee forth fled the dark-hued races, scattered abroad, deserting their possessions,

When, glowing, O Vaisvanara, for Puru, thou Agni didst light up and rend their castles.

4 Agni Vaisvanara, both Earth and Heaven submit them to thy threefold jurisdiction.

Refulgent in thine undecaying lustre thou hast invested both the worlds with splendour.

5 Agni, the tawny horses, loudly neighing our resonant hymns that drop with oil, attend thee;

Lord of the tribes, our Charioteer of riches, Ensign of days, Vaisvanara of mornings.

6 In thee, O bright as Mitra, Vasus seated the might of Aduras, for they loved thy spirit.

Thou dravest Dasyus from their home, O Agni, and broughtest forth broad light to light the Arya.

7 Born in the loftiest heaven thou in a moment reachest, like wind, the place where Gods inhabit.

Thou, favouring thine offspring, roaredst loudly when giving life to creatures, Jatavedas.

8 Send us that strength, Vaisvanara, send it, Agni, that strength, O Jatavedas, full of splendour,

Wherewith, all-bounteous God, thou pourest riches, as fame wide-spreading, on the man who offers.

9 Agni, bestow upon our chiefs and nobles that famous power, that wealth which feedeth many.
Accordant with the Vasus and the Rudras, Agni, Vaisvanara, give us sure protection.

## [07-006] HYMN VI. Agni.

1. PRAISE of the Asura, high imperial Ruler, the Manly One in whom the folk shall triumph
I laud his deeds who is as strong as Indra, and lauding celebrate the Fort-destroyer.
2 Sage, Sing, Food, Light,-they bring him from the mountain, the blessed Sovran of the earth and
heaven.
I decorate with songs the mighty actions which Agni, Fort-destroyer, did aforetime.
3 The foolish, faithless, rudely-speaking niggards, without belief or sacrifice or worship,-
Far far sway hath Agni chased those Dasytis, and, in the east, hath turned the godless westward.
4 Him who brought eastward, manliest with his prowess, the Maids rejoicing in the western
darkness,
That Agni I extol, the Lord of riches, unyielding tamer of assailing foemen.
5 Him who brake down the walls with deadly weapons, and gave the Mornings to anoble Husband,
Young Agni, who with conquering strength subduing the tribes of Nahus made them bring their
tribute.
6 In whose protection all men rest by nature, desiring to enjoy his gracious favour-
Agni Vaisvanara in his Parents. bosom hath found the choicest seat in earth and heaven.
7 Vaisvanara the God, at the sun's setting, hath taken to himself deep-hidden treasures:
Agni hath taken them from earth and heaven, from the sea under and the sea above us.

## [07-007] HYMN VII. Agni.

1. I SEND forth even your God, victorious Agni, like a strong courser, with mine adoration.
Herald of sacrifice be he who knoweth he hath reached Gods, himself, with measured motion.
2 By paths that are thine own come hither, Agni, joyous, delighting in the Gods' alliance,
Making the heights of earth roar with thy fury, burning with eager teeth the woods and forests.
3 The grass is strewn; the sacrifice advances adored as Priest, Agni is made propitious,
Invoking both All-boon-bestowing Mothers of whom, Most Youthful! thou wast born to help us.
4 Forthwith the men, the best of these for wisdom, have made him leader in the solemn worship.
As Lord in homes of men is Agni stablished, the Holy One, the joyous, sweetly speaking.
5 He hath come, chosen bearer, and is seated in man's home, Brahman, Agni, the Supporter,
He whom both Heaven anct Earth exalt and strengthenwhom, Giver of all boons, the Hotar worships.
6 These have passed all in glory, who, the manly, have wrought with skill the hymn of adoration;
Who, listening, have advanced the people's welfare, and set their thoughts on this my holy statute.
7 We, the Vasisthas, now implore thee, Agni, O Son of Strength, the Lord of wealth and treasure.
Thou hast brought food to singers and to nobles. Ye Gods, preserve us evermore with blessings.

## [07-008] HYMN VIII. Agni

1. THE King whose face is decked with oil is kindled with homage offered by his faithful servant.
The men, the priests adore him with oblations. Agni hath shone forth when the dawn is breaking.
2 Yea, he hath been acknowledged as most mighty, the joyous Priest of men, the youthful Agni.
He, spreading o'er the earth, made light around him, and grew among the plants with blackened
fellies..
3 How dost thou decorate our hymn, O Agni? What power dost thou exert when thou art lauded?
When, Bounteous God, may we be lords of riches, winners of precious wealth which none may
conquer?
4 Far famed is this the Bharata's own Agni he shineth like the Sun with lofty splendour.
He who hath vanquished Puru in the battle, the heavenly guest hath glowed in full refulgence.
5 Full many oblations are in thee collected: with all thine aspects thou hast waxen gracious.
Thou art already famed as praised and lauded, yet still, O nobly born, increase thy body.
6 Be this my song, that winneth countless treasure, engendered with redoubled force for Agni,
That, splendid, chasing sickness, slaying demons, it may delight our friend and bless the singers.
7 We, the Vasisthas, now implore thee, Agni, O Son of Strength, the Lord of wealth and riches.
Thou hast brought food to singers and to nobles. Ye Gods, preserve us evermore with blessings.

## [07-009] HYMN IX. Agni.

1. ROUSED from their bosom is the Dawns' beloved, the joyous Priest, most sapient, Purifier.
He gives a signal both to Gods and mortals, to Gods oblations, riches to the pious.
2 Most wise is he who, forcing doors of Panis, brought the bright Sun to us who feedeth many.
The cheerful Priest, men's Friend and home-companion, through still night's darkness he is made
apparent.
3 Wise, ne.'er deceived, uncircumscribed, refulgent, our gracious guest, a Friend with good
attendants,
Shines forth with wondrous light before the Mornings; the young plants hath he entered, Child of
Waters.
4 Seeking our gatherings, he, your Jatavedas, hath shone adorable through human ages,
Who gleams refulgent with his lovely lustre: the kine have waked to meet him when enkindled.
5 Go on thy message to the Gods, and fail not, O Agni, with their band who pray and worship.
Bring all the Gods that they may give us riches, Sarasvati, the Maruts, Asvins, Waters.
6 Vasistha, when enkindling thee, O Agni, hath slain jarutha. Give us wealth in plenty.
Sing praise in choral song, O Jatavedas. Ye Gods, preserve us evermore with blessings.

## [07-010] HYMN X. Agni.

1. HE hath sent forth, bright, radiant, and refulgent, like the Dawn's Lover, his far-spreading lustre.
Pure in his splendour shines the golden Hero: our longing thoughts hath he aroused and wakened.

2 He, like the Sun, hath shone while Morn is breaking, and priests who weave the sacrifice sing
praises,
Agni, the God, who knows their generations and visits Gods, most bounteous, rapid envoy.
3 Our songs and holy hymns go forth to Agni, seeking the God and asking him for riches,
Him fair to see, of goodly aspect, mighty, men's messenger who carries their oblations.
4 joined with the Vasus, Agni, bring thou Indra bring hither mighty Rudra with the Rudras,
Aditi good to all men with Adityas, Brhaspati All-bounteous, with the Singers.
5 Men eagerly implore at sacrifices Agni, Most Youthful God, the joyous Herald.
For he is Lord and Ruler over riches, and for Gods' worship an unwearied envoy.

## [07-011] HYMN XI. Agni.

1. GREAT art thou, Agni, sacrifice's Herald: not without thee are deathless Gods made joyful.
Come hither with all Deities about thee here take thy seat, the first, as Priest, O Agni.
2 Men with oblations evermore entreat thee, the swift, to undertake an envoy's duty.
He on whose sacred grass with Gods thou sittest, to him, O Agni, are the days propitious.
3 Three times a day in thee are shown the treasures sent for the mortal who presents oblation.
Bring the Gods hither like a man, O Agni: be thou our envoy, guarding us from curses.
4 Lord of the lofty sacrifice is Agni, Agni is Lord of every gift presented.
The Vasus were contented with his wisdom, so the Gods made him their oblationbearer.
5 O Agni, bring the Gods to taste our presents: with Indra leading, here let them be joyful.
Convey this sacrifice to Gods in heaven. Ye Gods, preserve us evermore with blessings.

## [07-012] HYMN XII. Agni.

1. WE with great reverence have approached The Youngest who hath shone forth well-kindled in his
dwelling,
With wondrous light between wide earth and heaven, well-worshipped, looking forth in all directions.
2 Through his great might o'ercoming all misfortunes, praised in the house is Agni Jatavedas.
May he protect us from disgrace and trouble, both us who laud him and our noble patrons.
3 O Agni, thou art Varuna and Mitra: Vasisthas with their holy hymns exalt thee.
With thee be most abundant gain of treasure. Ye Gods, preserve us evermore with blessings.

## [07-013] HYMN XIII. Agni.

1. BRING song and hymn to Agni, Asura-slayer, enlightener of all and thought-bestower.
Like an oblation on the grass, to please him, I bring this to Vaisvanara, hymn-inspirer.
2 Thou with thy flame, O Agni, brightly glowing, hast at thy birth filled full the earth and heaven.
TIOU with thy might, Vaisvanara Jatavedas, settest the Gods free frodi the curse that bound them.
3 Agni, when, born thou lookedst on all creatures, like a brisk herdsman moving round his cattle.

The path to prayer, Vaisvanara, thou foundest. Ye Gods, preserve us evermore with blessings.

## [07-014] HYMN XIV Agni.

1. WITH reverence and with offered gifts serve we the God whose flame is bright:
Let us bring Jatavedas fuel, and adore Agni when we invoke the Gods.
2 Agni, may we perform thy rites with fuel, and honour thee, O Holy one, with praises:
Honour thee, Priest of sacrifice! with butter, thee, God of blessed light! with our oblation.
3 Come, Agni, with the Gods to our invoking, come, pleased, to offerings sanctified with Vasat.
May we be his who pays thee, God, due honour. Ye Gods, preserve us evermore with blessings.

## [07-015] HYMN XV. Agni.

1. OFFER oblations in his mouth, the bounteous God's whom we must serve.
His who is nearest kin to us:
2 Who for the Fivefold People's take hath seated him in every home
Wise, Youthful, Master of the house.
3 On all sides may that Agni guard our household folk and property;
May he deliver us from woe.
4 I have begotten this new hymn for Agni, Falcon of the sky:
Will he not give us of his wealth?
5 Whose lories when he glows in front of sacrite are fair to see,
Like wealth of one with hero sons.
6 May he enjoy this hallowed gift, Agni accept our songs, who bears
Oblations, best of worshippers.
7 Lord of the house, whom men must seek, we set thee down, O Worshipped Onel
Bright, rich in heroes, Agni! God
8 Shine forth at night and morn: through thee with fires are we provided well.
Thou, rich in heroes, art our Friend.
9 The men come near thee for their gain, the singers with their songs of praise:
Speech, thousandfold, comes near to thee.
10 Bright, Purifier, meet for praise, Immortal with refulgent glow,
Agni drives Raksasas away.
11 As such, bring us abundant wealth, young Child of Strength, for this thou canst
May Bhaga give us what is choice.
12 Thou, Agni, givest hero fame: Bhaga and Savitar the God,
And Did give us what is good.
13 Agni, preserve us from distress: consume our enemies, O God,
Eternal, with the hottest flames.
14 And, irresistible, be thou a mighty iron fort to us,
With hundred walls for man's defence.
15 Do thou preserve us, eve and morn, from sorrow, from the wicked men,
Infallible! by day and night.

## [07-016] HYMN XVI. Agni.

1. WITH this my reverent hymn I call Agni for you, the Son of Strength,
Dear, wisest envoy, served with noble sacrifice, immortal messenger of all.
2 His two red horses, all-supporting, let him yoke: let him, well-worshipped, urge them fast.
Then hath the sacrifice good prayers and happy end, and heavenly gift of wealth to men.

163

3 The flame of him the Bountiful, the Much-invoked, hath mounted up,
And his red-coloured smoke-clouds reach and touch the sky: the men are kindling Agni well.
4 Thee, thee Most Glorious One we make our messenger. Bring the Gods hither to the feast.
Give us, O Son of Strength, all food that feedeth man: give that for which we pray to thee.
5 Thou, Agni, art the homestead's Lord, our Herald at the sacrifice.
Lord of all boons, thou art the Cleanser and a Sage. Pay worship, and enjoy the good.
6 Give riches to the sacrificer, O Most Wise, for thou art he who granteth wealth.
Inspire with zeal each priest at this our solemn rite; all who are skilled in singing praise.
7 O Agni who art worshipped well, dear let our princes he to thee,
Our wealthy patrons who are governors of men, who part, as gifts, their stalls of kine.
8 They in whose home, her hand bearing the sacred oil, Ila sits down well-satisfied-
Guard them, Victorious God, from slander and from harm. give us a refuge famed afar.
9 Do thou, a Priest with pleasant tongue, most wise, and very near to us,
Agni, bring riches hither to our liberal chiefs, and speed the offering of our gifts.
10 They who bestow as bounty plenteous wealth of steeds, moved by desire of great renown-
Do thou with saving help preserve them from distress, Most Youthful! with a hundred forts.
11 The God who gives your wealth demands a full libation poured to him.
Pour ye it forth, then fill the vessel full again: then doth the God pay heed to you.
12 Him have the Gods appointed Priest of sacrifice, oblation-bearer, passing wise.
Agni gives wealth and valour to the worshipper, to folk who offer up their gifts.

## [07-017] HYMN XVII. Agni.

1. AGNI, be kindled well with proper fuel, and let the grass be scattered wide about thee.
2 Let the impatient Portals be thrown open bring thou the Gods impatient to come hither.
3 Taste, Agni: serve the Gods with our oblation. Offer good sacrifices, Jatavedas!
4 Let Jatavedas pay fair sacrifices, worship andgratify the Gods Immortal.
5 Wise God, win for us things that are all-goodly, and let the prayers, we pray today be fruitful.
6 Thee, even thee, the Son of Strength, O Agni, those Gods have made the bearer of oblations.
7 To thee the God may we perform our worship: do thou, besought, grant us abundant riches.

## [07-018] IIYMN XVIII. Indra.

1. ALL is with thee, O Indra, all the treasures which erst our fathers won who sang thy praises.
With thee are milch-kine good to milk, and horses: best winner thou of riches for the pious.
2 For like a King among his wives thou dwellest: with glories, as a Sage, surround and help us.
Make us, thy servants, strong for wealth, and honour our songs wirth kine and steeds and decoration.
3 Here these our holy hymns with joy and gladness in pious emulation have approached thee.

Hitherward come thy path that leads to riches: may we find shelter in thy favour, Indra.
4 Vasistha hath poured forth his prayers, desiring to milk thee like a cow in goodly pasture.
All these my people call thee Lord of cattle: may Indra. come unto the prayer we offer.
5 What though the floods spread widely, Indra made them shallow and easy for Sudas to traverse.
He, worthy of our praises, caused the Simyu, foe of our hymn, to curse the rivers' fury.
6 Eager for spoil was Turvasa Purodas, fain to win wealth, like fishes urged by hunger.
The Bhrgus and the Druhyus quickly listened: friend rescued friend mid the two distant peoples.
7 Together came the Pakthas, the Bhalanas, the Alinas, the Sivas, the Visanins.
Yet to the Trtsus came the Arya's Comrade, through love of spoil and heroes' war, to lead them.
8 Fools, in their folly fain to waste her waters, they parted inexhaustible Parusni.
Lord of the Earth, he with his might repressed them: still lay the herd and the affrighted herdsman.
9 As to their goal they sped to their destruetion: they sought Parusni; e'en the swift returned not.
Indra abandoned, to Sudas the manly, the swiftly flying foes, unmanly babblers.
10 They went like kine unherded from the pasture, each clinging to a friend as chance directed.
They who drive spotted steeds, sent down by Prsni, gave ear, the Warriors and the harnessed horses.
11 The King who scattered one-and-twenty people of both Vaikarna tribes through lust of glory-
As the skilled priest clips grass within the chamber, so hath the Hero Indra, wrought their downfall.
12 Thou, thunder-armed, o'erwhelmedst in the waters famed ancient Kavasa and then the Druhyu.
Others here claiming friendship to their friendship, devoted unto thee, in thee were joyful.
13 Indra at once with conquering might demolished all their strong places and their seven castles.
The goods of Anu's son he gave to Trtsu. May we in sacrifice conquer scorned Puru.
14 The Anavas and Druhyus, seeking booty, have slept, the sixty hundred, yea, six thousand,
And six-and-sixty heroes. For the pious were all these mighty exploits done by Indra.
15 These Trtsus under Indra's careful guidance came speeding like loosed waters rushing downward.
The foemen, measuring exceeding closely, abandoned to Sudas all their provisions.
16 The hero's side who drank the dressed oblation, Indra's denier, far o'er earth he scattered.
Indra brought down the fierce destroyer's fury. He gave them various roads, the path's Controller.
17 E'en with the weak he wrought this matchless exploit: e'en with a goat he did to death a lion.
He pared the pillar's angles with a needle. Thus to Sudas Indra gave all provisions.
18 To thee have all thine enemies submitted: e'en the fierce Bheda hast thou made thy subject.
Cast down thy sharpened thunderbolt, O Indra, on him who harms the men who sing thy praises.
19 Yamuna and the Trtsus aided Indra. There he stripped Bheda bare of all his treasures.
The Ajas and the Sigrus and the Yaksus brought in to him as tribute heads of horses.

20 Not to be scorned, but like Dawns past and recent, O Indra, are thy favours and thy riches.
Devaka, Manyamana's son, thou slewest, and smotest Sambara from the lofty mountain.
21 They who, from home, have gladdened thee, thy servants Parasara, Vasistha, Satayatu,
Will not forget thy friendship, liberal Giver. So shall the days dawn prosperous for the princes.
22 Priest-like, with praise, I move around the altar, earning Paijavana's reward, O Agni,
Two hundred cows from Devavan's descendant, two chariots from Sudas with mares to draw them.
23 Gift of Paijavana, four horses bear me in foremost place, trained steeds with pearl to deck them.
Sudas's brown steeds, firmly-stepping, carry me and my son for progeny and glory.
24 Him whose fame spreads between wide earth and heaven, who, as dispenser, gives each chief his
portion,
Seven flowing Rivers glorify like Indra. He slew Yudhyamadhi in close encounter.
25 Attend on him O ye heroic Maruts as on Sudas's father Divodasa.
Further Paijavana's desire with favour. Guard faithfully his lasting firm dominion.

## [07-019] HYMN XIX. Indra.

1. HE like a bull with sharpened horns, terrific, singly excites and agitates all the people:
Thou givest him who largely pours libations his goods who pours not, for his own possession.
2 Thou, verily, Indra, gavest help to Kutsa, willingly giving car to him in battle,
When, aiding Arjuneya, thou subduedst to him both Kuyava and the Dasa Susna.
3 O Bold One, thou with all thine aids hast boldly holpen Sudas whose offerings were accepted,
Puru in winning land and slaying foemen, and Trasadasyu son of Purukutsa.
4 At the Gods' banquet, hero-souled! with Heroes, Lord of Bay Steeds, thou slewest many foemen.
Thou sentest in swift death to sleep the Dasyu, both Cumuri and Dhuni, for Dabhiti.
5 These were thy mighty powers that, Thunder-wielder, thou swiftly crushedst nine-and-ninety castles:
Thou capturedst the hundredth in thine onslaught; thou slewest Namuci, thou slewest Vrtra.
6 Old are the blessings, Indra, which thou gavest Sudas the worshipper who brought oblations.
For thee, the Strong, I yoke thy strong Bay Horses: may our prayers reach thee and win strength,
Most Mighty!
7 Give us not up, Lord of Bay Horses, Victor, in this thine own assembly, to the wicked.
Deliver us with true and faithful succours: dear may we be to thee among the princes.
8 May we men, Maghavan, the friends thou lovest, near thee be joyful under thy protection.
Fain to fulfil the wish of Atithigva humble. the pride of Turvasa and Yadva.
9 Swiftly, in truth, O Maghavan, about thee men skilled in hymning sing their songs and praises. '
Elect us also into their assembly who by their calls on thee despoiled the niggards.
10 Thine are these lauds, O manliest of heroes, lauds which revert to us and give us riches.

Favour these, Indra, when they fight with faemen, as Friend and Hero and the heroes' Helper.
11 Now, lauded for thine aid, Heroic Indra, sped by our prayer, wax mighty in thy body.
Apportion to us strength and habitations. Ye Gods, protect us evermore with blessings.

## [07-020] HYMN XX. Indra.

1. STRONG, Godly-natured, born for hero exploit, man's Friend, hedoth whatever deed he willeth.
Saving us e'en from great transgression, Indra, the Youthful, visiteth man's home with favour.
2 Waxing greatness Indra slayeth Vrtra: the Hero with his aid hath helped the singer.
He gave Sudas wide room and space, and often hath granted wealth to him who brought oblations.
3 Soldier unchecked, war-rousing, battling Hero, unconquered from of old, victorious ever,
Indra the very strong hath scattered armies; yea, he hath slain each foe who fought against him.
4 Thou with thy greatness hast filled full, O Indra, even both the worlds with might, O thou Most Mighty.
Lord of Bays, Indra, brandishing his thunder, is gratified with Soma at the banquet.
5 A Bull begat the Bull for joy of battle, and a strong Mother brought forth him the manly.
He who is Chief of men, their armies' Leader, is strong Hero, bold, and fain for booty.
6 The people falter not, nor suffer sorrow, who win themselves this God's terrific spirit.
He who with sacrifices worships Indra is lord of wealth, law-born and law's protector.
7 Whene'er the elder fain would help the younger the greater cometh to the lesser's present.
Shall the Immortal sit aloof' inactive? O Wondrous Indra, bring us wondrous riches.
8 Thy dear folk, Indra, who present oblations, are, in chief place, thy friends, O Thunder-wielder.
May we be best content in this thy favour, sheltered by One who slays not, but preserves us.
9 To thee the mighty hymn hath clamoured loudly, and, Maghavan, the eloquent hath besought thee.
Desire of wealth hath come upon thy singer: help us then, gakra, to our share of riches.
10 Place us by food which thou hast given, O Indra, us and the wealthy patrons who command us.
Let thy great power bring good to him who lauds thee. Ye Gods, preserve us evermore with
blessings.

## [07-021] HYMN XXI. Indra.

1. PRESSED is the juice divine with milk commingled: thereto hath Indra ever been accustomed.
We wake thee, Lord of Bays, with sacrifices: mark this our laud in the wild joy of Soma.
2 On to the rite they move, the grass they scatter, these Soma-drinkers eloquent in synod.
Hither, for men to grasp, are brought the press-stones, far-thundering, famous, strong, that wait on heroes.
3 Indra, thou settest free the many waters that were encompassed, Hero, by the Dragon.
Down rolled, as if on chariots borne, the rivers: through fear of thee all things created tremble.
4 Skilled in all manly deeds the God terrific hath with his weapons mastered these opponents.
Indra in rapturous joy shook down their castles he slew them in his might, the Thunder-wielder.

5 No evil spirits have impelled us, Indra, nor fiends, O Mightiest God, with their devices.
Let our true God subdue the hostile rabble: let not the lewd approach our holy worship.
6 Thou in thy strength surpassest Earth and Heaven: the regions comprehend not all thy greatness.
With thine own power and might thou slewest Vrtra: no foe hath found the end of thee in battle.
7 Even the earlier Deities submitted their powers to thy supreme divine dominion.
Indra wins wealth and deals it out to other's: men in the strife for booty call on Indra.
8 The humble hath invoked thee for protection, thee, Lord of great felicity, O Indra.
Thou with a hundred aids hast been our Helper: one who brings gifts like thee hath his defender.
9 May we, O Indra, be thy friends for ever, eagerly, Conqueror, yielding greater homage.
May, through thy grace, the strength of us who battle quell in the shock the onset of the foeman.
10 Place us by food which thou hast given, O Indra, us and the wealthy patrons who command us.
Let thy great power bring good to him who lauds thee. Ye Gods, preserve us evermore with blessings.

## [07-022] HYMN XXII Indra.

1. DRINK Soma, Lord of Bays, and let it cheer thee: Indra, the stone, like a well guided courser,
Directed by the presser's arms hath pressed it.
2 So let the draught of joy, thy dear companion, by which, O Lord of Bays, thou slayest foemen,
Delight thee, Indra, Lord of princely treasures.
3 Mark closely, Maghavan, the words I utter, this eulogy recited by Vasistha:
Accept the prayers I offer at thy banquet.
4 Hear thou the call of the juice-drinking press-stone: hear thou the Brahman's hymn who sings and lauds thee.
Take to thine inmost self these adorations.
5 I know and ne'er forget the hymns and praises of thee, the Conqueror, and thy strength immortal.
Thy name I ever utter. Self-Refulgent
6 Among mankind many are thy libations, and many a time the pious sage invokes thee.
O Maghavan, be not long distant from us.
7 All these libations are for thee, O Hero: to thee I offer these my prayers. that strengthen.
Ever, in every place, must men invoke thee.
8 Never do men attain, O Wonder-Worker, thy greatness, Mighty One, who must be lauded,
Nor, Indra, thine heroic power and bounty.
9 Among all Rsis, Indra, old and recent, who have engendered hymns as sacred singers,
Even with us be thine auspicious friendships. Ye Gods, preserve us evermore with blessings.

## [07-023] HYMN XXIII. Indra.

1. PRAYERS have been offered up through love of glory: Vasistha, honour Indra in the battle.
He who with might extends through all existence hears words which I, his faithful servant, utter.
2 A cry was raised which reached the Gods, O Indra, a cry to them to send us strength in combat.
None among men knows his own life's duration: bear us in safety over these our troubles.

3 The Bays, the booty-seeking car I harness: my prayers have reached him who accepts them gladly.
Indra, when he had slain resistless foemen, forced with his might the two world-halves asunder.
4 Like barren cows, moreover, swelled the waters: the singen sought thy holy rite, O Indra.
Come unto us as with his team comes Vayu: thou, through our solemn hymns bestowest booty.
5 So may these gladdening draughts rejoice thee, Indra, the Mighty, very bounteous to the singer.
Alone among the Gods thou pitiest mortals: O Hero, make thee glad at this libation.
6 Thus the Vasisthas glorify with praises Indra, the Powerful whose arm wields thunder.
Praised, may he guard our wealth in kine and heroes. Ye Gods, preserve us evermore with blessings.

## [07-024] HYMN XXIV. Indra.

1. A HOME is made for thee to dwell in, Indra: O Much-invoked, go thitherwith the heroes.
That thou, to prosper us, mayst be our Helper, vouchsafe us wealth, rejoice with draughts of Soma.
2 Indra, thy wish, twice-strong, is comprehended: pressed is the Soma, poured are pleasant juices.
This hymn of praise, from loosened tongue, made perfect, draws Indra to itself with loud invoking.
3 Come, thou Impetuous; God, from earth or heaven; come to our holy grass to drink the Soma.
Hither to me let thy Bay Horses bring thee to listen to our hymns and make thee joyful.
4 Come unto us with all thine aids, accordant, Lord of Bay Steeds, accepting our devotions,
Fair-helmeted, o'ercoming with the mighty, and lending us the strength of bulls, O Indra.
5 As to the chariot pole a vigorous courser, this laud is brought to the great strong Upholder.
This hymn solicits wealth of thee: in heaven, as 'twere above the sky, set thou our glory.
6 With precious things. O Indra, thus content us: may we attain to thine exalted favour.
Send our chiefs plenteous food with hero children. Preserve us evermore, ye Gods, with blessings.

## [07-025] HYMN XXV. Indra.

WHEN with thy mighty help, O potent Indra, the armies rush together in their fury.
When from the strong man's arm the lightning flieth, let not the mind go forth to side with others.
2 O Indra, where the ground is hard to traverse, smite down our foes, the mortals who assail us,
Keep far from us the curse of the reviler: bring us accumulated store of treasures.
3 God of the fair helm, give Sudas a hundred succours, a thousand blessings, and thy bounty.
Strike down the weapon of our mortal foeman: bestow upon us splendid fame and riches.
4 I wait the power of one like thee, O Indra, gifts of a Helper such as thou art, Hero.
Strong, Mighty God, dwell with me now and ever: Lord of Bay Horses, do not thou desert us.
5 Here are the Kutsas supplicating Indra for might, the Lord of Bays for God-sent conquest.
Make our foes ever easy to be vanquished: may we, victorious, win the spoil, O Hero.
6 With precious things, O Indra, thus content us: may we attain to thine exalted favour.

Send our chiefs plenteous food with hero children. Preserve us evermore, ye Gods, with blessings.

## [07-026] HYMN XXVI. Indra.

1. SOMA unpressed ne'er gladdened liberal Indra, no juices pressed without a prayer have pleased
him.
I generate a laud that shall delight him, new and heroic, so that he may hear us.
2 At every laud the Soma gladdens Indra: pressed juices please him as each psalm is chanted,
What time the priests with one united effort call him to aid, as sons invoke their father.
3 These deeds he did; let him achieve new exploits, such as the priests declare at their libations.
Indra hath taken and possessed all castles, like as one common husband doth his spouses.
4 Even thus have they declared him. Famed is Indra as Conqueror, sole distributer of treasures;
Whose many succours come in close succession. May dear delightful benefits attend us.
5 Thus, to bring help to men, Vasistha laudeth Indra, the peoples' Hero, at libation.
Bestow upon us strength and wealth in thousands. Preserve us evermore, ye Gods, with blessings.

## [07-027] HYMN XXVII. Indra.

1. MEN call on Indra in the armed encounter that he may make the hymns they sing decisive.
Hero, rejoicing in thy might, in combat give us a portion of the stall of cattle,
2 Grant, Indra Maghavan, invoked of many, to these my friends the strength which thou possessest.
Thou, Maghavan, hast rent strong places open: unclose for us, Wise God, thy hidden bounty.
3 King of the living world, of men, is Indra, of all in varied form that earth containeth.
Thence to the worshipper he giveth riches: may he enrich us also when we laud him.
4 Maghavan Indra, when we all invoke him, bountiful ever sendeth strength to aid us:
Whose perfect guerdon, never failing, bringeth wealth to the men, to friends the thing they covet.
5 Quick, Indra, give us room and way to riches, and let us bring thy mind to grant us treasures,
That we may win us cars and Steeds and cattle. Preserve us evermore, ye Gods, with blessings.

## [07-028] HYMN XXVIII. Indra.

1. COME to our prayers, O Indra, thou who knowest: let thy Bay Steeds be yoked and guided hither.
Though mortal men on every side invoke thee, still give thine ear to us, O All-impeller.
2 Thy greatness reacheth to our invocation, the sages' prayer which, Potent God, thou guardest.
What time thy hand, O Mighty, holds the thunder, awful in strength thou hast become resistless.
3 What time thou drewest both world-halves together, like heroes led by thee who call each other-
For thou wast born for strength and high dominion-then e'en the active overthrew the sluggish.
4 Honour us in these present days, O Indra, for hostile men are making expiation.
Our sin that sinless Varuna discovered, the Wondrous-Wise hath long ago forgiven.
5 We will address this liberal Lord, this Indra, that he may grant us gifts of ample riches,

Best favourer of the singer's prayer and praises. Preserve us evermore, ye Gods, with blessings.

## [07-029] HYMN XXIX Indra.

1. THIS Soma hath been pressed for thee, O Indra: come hither, Lord of Bays, for this thou lovest.
Drink of this fair, this well-effused libation: Maghavan, give us wealth when we implore thee.
2 Come to us quickly with thy Bay Steeds, Hero, come to our prayer, accepting our devotion.
Enjoy thyself aright at this libation, and listen thou unto the prayers we offer.
3 What satisfaction do our hymns afford thee? When, Maghavan? Now let us do thee service.
Hymns, only hymns, with love for thee, I weave thee: then hear, O Indra, these mine invocations.
4 They, verily, were also human beings whom thou wast wont to hear, those earlier sages.
Hence I, O Indra Maghavan, invoke thee: thou art our Providence, even as a Father.
5 We will address this liberal Lord, this Indra, that he may grant us gifts of ample riches,
Best favourer of the singer's prayer and praises. Preserve us evermore, ye Gods, with blessings.

## [07-030] HYMN XXX. Indra.

1. WITH power and strength, O Mighty God, approach us: be the augmenter, Indra, of these riches;
Strong Thunderer, Lord of men, for potent valour, for manly exploit and for high dominion.
2 Thee, worth invoking, in the din of battle, heroes invoke in fray for life and sunlight.
Among all people thou art foremost fighter: give up our enemies to easy slaughter.
3 When fair bright days shall dawn on us, O Indra, and thou shalt bring thy banner near in battle,
Agni the Asura shall sit as Herald, calling Gods hither for our great good fortune.
4 Thine are we, Indra, thine, both these who praise thee, and those who give rich gifts, O God and
Hero.
Grant to our princes excellent protection, may they wax old and still be strong and happy.
5 We will address this liberal Lord, this Indra that he may grant us gifts of ample riches:
Best favourer of the singer's prayer and praises. Preserve us evermore, ye Gods, with blessings.

## [07-031] HYMN XXXI. Indra.

1. SING ye a song, to make him glad, to Indra, Lord of Tawny Steeds,
The Soma-drinker, O my friends.
2 To him the Bounteous say the laud, and let us glorify, as men May do, the Giver of true gifts.
3 O Indra, Lord of boundless might, for us thou winnest strength and kine,
Thou winnest gold for us, Good Lord.
4 Faithful to thee we loudly sing, heroic Indra, songs to thee:
Mark, O Good Lord, this act of ours.
5 Give us not up to man's reproach, to foeman's hateful calumny:
In thee alone is all my strength.
6 Thou art mine ample coat of mail, my Champion, Vrtra-Slayer, thou:
With thee for Friend I brave the foe.
7 Yea, great art thou whose conquering might two independent Powers confess.
The Heaven, O India, and the Earth.

8 So let the voice surround thee, which attends the Maruts on their way,
Reaching thee with the rays of light.
9 Let the ascending drops attain to thee, the Wondrous God, in heaven:
Let all the folk bow down to thee.
10 Bring to the Wise, the Great, who waxeth mighty, your offerings, and make ready your devotion;
To many clans he goeth, man's controller.
11 For Indra, the sublime, the far-pervading, have singers generated prayer and praises:
The sages never violate his statutes.
12 The choirs have stablished Indra King for ever, for victory, him whose anger is resistless:
And, for the Bays' Lord, strengthened those he loveth.

## [07-032] HYMN XXXII. Indra.

1. LET none, no, not thy worshippers, delay thee far away from us.
Even from far away come thou unto our feast, or listen if already here.
2 For here, like flies on honey, these who pray to thee sit by the juice that they have poured.
Wealth-craving singers have on Indra set their hope, as men set foot upon a car.
3 Longing for wealth I call on him, the Thunderer with the strong right hand,
As a son calleth on his sire.
4 These Soma juices, mixed with curd, have been expressed for Indra here.
Come with thy Bay Steeds, Thunder-wielder, to our home, to drink them till they make thee glad.
5 May he whose ear is open hear us. He is asked for wealth: will he despise our prayer?
Him who bestows at once a hundred thousand gifts none shall restrain when he would give.
6 The hero never checked by men hath gained his strength through Indra, he
Who presses out and pours his deep libations forth, O Vrtra-slayer, unto thee.
7 When thou dost drive the fighting men together be, thou Mighty One, the mighty's shield.
May we divide the wealth of him whom thou hast slain: bring us, Unreachable, his goods.
8 For Indra, Soma-drinker, armed with thunder, press the Soma juice.
Make ready your dressed meats: cause him to favour us. The Giver blesses him who gives.
9 Grudge not, ye Soma pourers; stir you, pay the rites, for wealth, to the great Conqueror.
Only the active conquers dwells in peace, and thrives: not for the niggard are the Gods.
10 No one hath overturned or stayed the car of him who freely gives.
The man whom Indra and the Marut host defend comes to a stable full of kine.
11 Indra, that man when fighting shall obtain the spoil, whose strong defender thou wilt be.
Be thou the gracious helper, Hero I of our cars, be thou the helper of our men.
12 His portion is exceeding great like a victorious soldier's spoil.
Him who is Indra, Lord of Bays, no foes subdue. He gives the Soma-pourer strength.
13 Make for the Holy Gods a hymn that is not mean, but well-arranged and fair of form.
Even many snares and bonds subdue not him who dwells with Indra through his sacrifice.

14 Indra, what mortal will attack the man who hath his wealth in thee?
The strong will win the spoil on the decisive day through faith in thee, O Maghavan.
15 In battles with the foe urge on our mighty ones who give the treasures dear to thee,
And may we with our princes, Lord of Tawny Steeds! pass through all peril, led by thee.
16 Thine, Indra, is the lowest wealth, thou cherishest the mid-most wealth,
Thou ever rulest all the highest: in the fray for cattle none resisteth thee.
17 Thou art renowned as giving wealth to every one in all the battles that are fought.
Craving protection, all these people of the earth, O Much-invoked, implore thy name.
18 If I, O Indra, were the Lord of riches ample as thine own,
I should support the singer, God. who givest wealth! and not abandon him to woe.
19 Each day would I enrich the man who sang my praise, in whatsoever place he were.
No kinship is there better, Maghavan, than thine: a father even is no more.
20 With Plenty for his true ally the active man will gain the spoil.
Your Indra, Much-invoked, I bend with song, as bends a wright his wheel of solid wood.
21 A moral wins no riches by unworthy praise: wealth comes not to the niggard churl.
Light is the task to give, O Maghavan, to one like me on the decisive day.
22 Like kine unmilked we call aloud, Hero, to thee, and sing thy praise,
Looker on heavenly light, Lord of this moving world, Lord, Indra, of what moveth not.
23 None other like to thee, of earth or of the heavens, hath been or ever will be born.
Desiring horses, Indra Maghavan! and kine, as men of might we call on thee.
24 Bring, Indra, the Victorious Ones; bring, elder thou, the younger host.
For, Maghavan, thou art rich in treasures from of old, and must be called in every fight.
25 Drive thou away our enemies, O Maghavan: make riches easy to be won.
Be thou our good Protector in the strife for spoil: Cherisher of our friends be thou.
26 O Indra, give us wisdom as a sire gives wisdom to his sons.
Guide us, O Much-invoked, in this our way may we still live and look upon the light.
27 Grant that no mighty foes, unknown, malevolent, unhallowed, tread us to the ground.
With thine assistance, Hero, may we ass through all the waters that are rul`ng down.

## [07-033] HYMN XXXIII Vasistha.

1. THESE who wear hair-knots on the right, the movers of holy thought, white-robed, have won me
over.
I warned the men, when from the grass I raised me, Not from afar can my Vasisthas help you.
2 With soma they brought Indra from a distance, Over Vaisanta, from the strong libation.
Indra preferred Vasisthas to the Soma pressed by the son of Vayata, Pasadyumna.
3 So, verily, with these he crossed the river, in company with these he slaughtered Bheda.

So in the fight with the Ten Kings, Vasisthas! did Indra help Sudas through your devotions.

4 I gladly, men I with prayer prayed by our fathers have fixed your axle: ye shall not be injured:
Since, when ye sang aloud the Sakvari verses, Vasisthas! ye invigorated Indra.

5 Like thirsty men they looked to heaven, in battle with the Ten Kings, surrounded and imploring.
Then Indra heard Vasistha as he praised him, and gave the Trtsus ample room and freedom.

6 Like sticks and staves wherewith they drive the cattle, Stripped bare, the Bharatas were found
defenceless:
Vasistha then became their chief and leader: then widely. were the Trtsus' clans extended.

7 Three fertilize the worlds with genial moisture: three noble Creatures cast a light before them.
Three that give warmth to all attend the morning. All these have they discovered, these Vasisthas.

8 Like the Sun's growing glory is their splendour, and like the sea's is their unfathomed greatness.
Their course is like the wind's. Your laud, Vasisthas, can never be attained by any other.

9 They with perceptions of the heart in secret resort to that which spreads a thousand branches.
The Apsaras brought hither the Vasisthas wearing the vesture spun for them by Yama.

10 A form of lustre springing from the lightning wast thou, when Varuna and Mitra saw thee.
Tliy one and only birth was then, Vasistha, when from thy stock Agastya brought thee hither.

11 Born of their love for Urvasi, Vasistha thou, priest, art son of Varuna and Mitra;
And as a fallen drop, in heavenly fervour, all the Gods laid thee on a lotus-blossorn.

12 He thinker, knower both of earth and heaven, endowed with many a gift, bestowing thousands,
Destined to wear the vesture spun by Yama, sprang from the Apsaras to life, Vasistha.

13 Born at the sacrifice, urged by adorations, both with a common flow bedewed the pitcher.
Then from the midst thereof there rose up Mana, and thence they say was born the sage Vasistha.

14 He brings the bearer of the laud and Saman: first shall he speak bringing the stone for pressing.
With grateful hearts in reverence approach him: to you, O Pratrdas, Vasistha cometh.

## [07-034] HYMN XXXIV Visvedevas.

1. MAY our divine and brilliant hymn go forth, like a swift chariot wrought and fashioned well.

2 The waters listen as they flow along: they know the origin of heaven and earth.

3 Yea, the broad waters swell their flood ior him: of him strong heroes think amid their foes.

4 Set ye for him the coursers to the pole: like Indra Thunderer is the Golden-armed.

5 Arouse you, like the days, to sacrifice speed gladly like a traveller on the way.

6 Go swift to battles, to the sacrifice: set up a flag, a hero for the folk.

7 Up from his strength hath risen as 'twere a light: it bears the load as earth bears living things.

8 Agni, no demon I invoke the Gods: by law completing it, I form a hymn.

9 Closely about you lay your heavenly song, and send your voice to where the Gods abide.

10 Varuna, Mighty, with a thousand eyes, beholds the paths wherein these rivers run.

11 He, King of kings, the glory of the floods, o'er all that liveth hath resistless sway.

12 May he assist us among all the tribes, and make the envier's praise devoid of light.

13 May the foes' threatening arrow pass us by: may he put far from us our bodies' sin.

14 Agni, oblation-eater, through our prayers aid us: to him our dearest laud is brought.

15 Accordant with the Gods choose for our Friend the Waters' Child: may he be good to us.

16 With lauds I sing the Dragon born of floods: he sits beneath the streams in middle air.

17 Ne'er may the Dragon of the Deep harm us: ne'er fail this faithful servant's sacrifice.

18 To these our heroes may they grant renown: may pious men march boldly on to wealth.

19 Leading great hosts, with fierce attacks of these, they burn their foes as the Sun burns the earth.

20 What time our wives draw near to us, may he, left-handed Tvastar, give us hero sons.

21 May Tvastar find our hymn acceptable, and may Aramati, seeking wealth, be ours.

22 May they who lavish gifts bestow those treasures: may Rodasi and Varunani listen.
May he, with the Varutris, be our refuge, may bountiful Tvastar give us store of riches.

23 So may rich Mountains and the liberal Waters, so may all Herbs that grow on ground, and Heaven,
And Earth accordant with the Forest-Sovrans, and both the World-halves round about protect us.

24 To this may both the wide Worlds lend approval, and Varuna in heaven, whose Friend is Indra.
May all the Maruts give consent, the Victors, that we may hold great wealth in firm possession.

25 May Indra, Varuna, Mitra, and Agni, Waters, Herbs, Trees accept the praise we offer.
May we find refuge in the Marut's bosom. Protect us evermore, ye Gods, with blessings.

## [07-035] HYMN XXXV. Visvedevas.

1. BEFRIEND us with their aids Indra and Agni, Indra and Varuna who receive oblations!
Indra and Soma give health, strength and comfort, Indra and Pusan be our help in battle.

2 Auspicious Friends to us be Bhaga, Sathsa, auspicious be Purandhi aid all Riches;
The blessing of the true and well-conducted, and Aryaman in many forms apparent.

3 Kind unto us he Maker and Sustainer, and the far-reaching Pair with God-like natures.
Auspicious unto us be Earth and Heaven, the Mountain, and the Gods' fair invocations.

4 Favour us Agni with his face of splendour, and Varuva and Mitra and the Asvins.
Favour us noble actions of the pious, impetuous vita blow on us with favour.

5 Early invoked, may Heaven and Earth be friendly, and Air's mid-region good for us to look on.
To us may Herbs and Forest-Trees be gracious, gracious the Lord Victorious of the region.

6 Be the God Indra with the Vasus friendly, and, with Adityas, Varuna who blesseth.
Kind, with the Rudras, be the Healer Rudra, and, with the Dames, may Tvastar kindly listen.

7 Blest unto us be Soma, and devotions, blest be the Sacrifice, the Stones for pressing.
Blest be the fixing of the sacred Pillars, blest be the tender Grass and blest the Altar.
8 May the far-seeing Sun rise up to bless us: be the four Quarters of the sky auspicious.
Auspicious be the firmly-seated Mountains, auspicious be the Rivers and the Waters.
9 May Adid through holy works be gracioas, and may the Maruts, loud in song, be friendly.
May Visnu give felicity, and Pusan, the Air that cherisheth our life, and Vayu.
10 Prosper us Savitar, the God who rescues, and let the radiant Mornings be propitious.
Auspicious to all creatures be Parjanya, auspicious be the field's benign Protector.
11 May all the fellowship of Gods befriend us, Sarasvati, with Holy Thoughts, be gracious.
Friendly be they, the Liberal Ones who seek us, yea, those who dwell in heaven, on earth, in waters.
12 May the great Lords of Truth protect and aid us: blest to us be our horses and our cattle.
Kind be the pious skilful-handed Rbhus, kind be the Fathers at our invocations.
13 May Aja-Ekapad, the God, be gracious, gracious the Dragon of the Deep, and Ocean.
Gracious be he the swelling Child of Waters, gracious be Prsni who hath Gods to guard her.
14 So may the Rudras, Vasus, and Adityas accept the new hymn which we now are making.
May all the Holy Ones of earth and heaven, and the Cow's offipring hear our invocation.
15 They who of Holy Gods are very holy, Immortal, knowing Law, whom man must worship,-
May these to-day give us broad paths to travel. Preserve us evermore, ye Gods, with blessings.

### [07-036] HYMN XXXVI. Visvedevas

1. LET the prayer issue from the seat of Order, for Surya with his beams hath loosed the cattle.
With lofty ridges earth is far extended, and Agni's flame hath lit the spacious surface.
2 O Asuras, O Varuna and Mitra, this hymn to you, like food, anew I offer.
One of you is a strong unerring Leader, and Mitra, speaking, stirreth men to labour.
3 The movements of the gliding wind come hither: like cows, the springs are filled to overflowing.
Born in the station e'en of lofty heaven the Bull hath loudly bellowed in this region.
4 May I bring hither with my song, O Indra, wise Aryaman who yokes thy dear Bay Horses,
Voracious, with thy noble car, O Hero, him who defeats the wrath of the malicious.
5 In their own place of sacrifice adorers worship to gain long life and win his friendship.
IIe hath poured food on men whcn thcy havc praiscd him; bc this, the dearest reverence, paid to Rudra.
6 Coming together, glorious, loudly roaring - Sarasvati, Mother of Floods, the seventh-
With copious milk, with fair streams, strongly flowing, full swelling with the volume of their water;
7. And may the mighty Maruts, too, rejoicing, aid our devotion and protect our offspring.
Let not swift-moving Aksara neglect us: they have increased our own appropriate riches,

8 Bring ye the great Aramati before you, and Pusan as the Hero of the synod,
Bhaga who looks upon this hymn with favour, and, as our strength, the bountiful Purandbi.
9 May this our song of praise reach you, O Maruts, and Visnu guardian of the future infant.
May they vouchsafe the singer strength for offspring. Preserve us evermore, ye Gods, with blessings.

### [07-037] HYMN XXXVII. Visvedevas.

1. LET your best-bearing car that must be lauded, ne'er injured, bring you Vajas and Rbhuksans.
Fill you, fair-helmeted! with mighty Soma, thrice-mixed, at our libations to delight you.
2 Ye who behold the light of heaven, Rbhuksans, give our rich patrons unmolested riches.
Drink, heavenly-natured. at our sacrifices, and give us bounties for the hymns we sing you.
3 For thou, O Bounteous One, art used to giving, at parting treasure whether small or ample.
Filled full are both thine arms with great possessions: thy goodness keeps thee not from granting riches.
4 Indra, high-famed, as Vaja and Rbhuksans, thou goest working, singing to the dwelling.
Lord of Bay Steeds, this day may we Vasisthas offer our prayers to thee and bring oblations.
5 Thou winnest swift advancement for thy servant, through hymns, Lord of Bay Steeds, which thou hast favoured.
For thee with friendly succour have we battled, and when, O Indra, wilt thou grant us riches?
6 To us thy priests a home, as 'twere, thou givest: when, Indra wilt thou recognize our praises?
May thy strong Steed, through our ancestral worship, bring food and wealth with heroes to our dwelling.
7 Though Nirrti the Goddess reigneth round him, Autumns with food in plenty come to Indra.
With three close Friends to length of days he cometh, he whom men let not rest at home in quiet.
8 Promise us gifts, O Savitar: may riches come unto us in Parvata's full bounty.
May the Celestial Guardian still attend us. Preserve us evermore, ye Gods, with blessings.

### [07-038] HYMN XXXVIII. Savitar.

1. ON high hath Savitar, this God, extended the golden lustre which he spreads around him.
Now, now must Bhaga be invoked by mortals, Lord of great riches who distributes treasures.
2 Rise up, O Savitar whose hands are golden, and hear this man while sacrifice is offered,
Spreading afar thy broad and wide effulgence, and bringing mortal men the food that feeds them.
3 Let Savitar the God he hymned with praises, to whom the Vasus, cvcn, all sing glory.
Sweet be our lauds to him whose due is worship: may he with all protection guard our princes.
4 Even he whom Aditi the Goddess praises, rejoicing in God Savitar's incitement:
Even he who praise the high imperial Rulers, Varuna, Mitra, Aryaman, sing in concert.
5 They who come emulous to our oblation, dispensing bounty, from the earth and heaven.
May they and Ahibudhnya hear our calling: guard us Varutri with the Ekadhenus.

6 This may the Lord of Life, entreated, grant us,-the wealth which Savitar the God possesses.
The mighty calls on Bhaga for protection, on Bhaga calls the weak to give him riches.
7 Bless us the Vajins when we call, while slowly they move, strong Singers, to the Gods' assembly.
Crushing the wolf, the serpent, and the demons, may they completely banish all affliction.
8 Deep-skilled in Law eternal, deathless, Singers, O Vajins, help us in each fray for booty.
Drink of this meath, be satisfied, be joyful: then go on paths which Gods are wont to travel.

## [07-039] HYMN XXXIX Visvedevas.
1. AGNI, erect, hath shown enriching favour: the flame goes forward to the Gods' assembly.
Like car-borne men the stones their path have chosen: let the priest, quickened, celebrate our
worship.
2 Soft to the tread, their sacred grass is scattered: these go like Kings amid the band around them,
At the folks early call on Night and Morning,-Vayu, and Pusan with his team, to bless us.
3 Here on their path the noble Gods proceeded: in the wide firmament the Beauteous decked them.
Bend your way hither, ye who travel widely: hear this our envoy who hath gone to meet you.
4 For they are holy aids at sacrifices: all Gods approach the place of congregation.
Bring these, desirous, to our worship, Agni, swift the Nisatyas, Bhaga, and Purandhi.
5 Agni, to these men's hymns, from earth, from heaven, bring Mitra, Varuna, Indra, and Agni,
And Aryaman, and Aditi, and Visnu. Sarasvati be joyful, and the Maruts.
6 Even as the holy wish, the gift is offered: may he, unsated, come when men desire him.
Give never-failing ever-conquering riches: with Gods for our allies may we be victors.
7 Now have both worlds been praised by the Vasisthas; and holy Mitra, Varuna, and Agni.
May they, bright Deities, make our song supremest. Preserve us evermore, ye Gods, with blessings.

## [07-040] HYMN XL. Visvedevas.
1. BE gathered all the audience of the synod: let us begin their praise whose course is rapid.
Whate'er God Savitar this day produces, may we be where the Wealthy One distributes.
2 This, dealt from heaven ' may both the Worlds vouchsafe us, and Varuna, Indra, Aryaman, and
Mitra.
May Goddess Aditi assign us riches, Vayu and Bhaga make them ours for ever.
3 Strong be the man and full of power, O Maruts, whom ye, borne on by spotted coursers, favour.
Him, too, Sarasvati and Agni further, and there is none to rob him of his riches.
4 This Varuna is guide of Law, he, Mitra, and Aryaman, the Kings, our work have finished.
Divine and foeless Aditi quickly listens. May these deliver us unharmed from trouble.
5 With offerings I propitiate the branches of this swift-moving God, the bounteous Visnu.
Hence Rudra gained his Rudra-strength: O Asvins, ye sought the house that hath celestial viands.

6 Be not thou angry here, O glowing Pusan, for what Varutri and the Bounteous gave us.
May the swift-moving Gods protect and bless us, and Vata send us rain, wha wanders round us.
7 Now have both worlds been praised by the Vasisthas, and holy Mitra, Varuna, and Agni.
May they, bright Deities, make our song supremest. Preserve us evermore, ye Gods, with blessings.

## [07-041] HYMN XLI. Bhaga.
1. AGNI at dawn, and Indra we invoke at dawn, and Varuna and Mitra, and the Asvins twain.
Bhaga at dawn, Pusan, and Brahmanaspati, Soma at dawn, Rudra we will invoke at dawn.
2 We will invoke strong, early-conquering Bhaga, the Son of Aditi, the great supporter:
Thinking of whom, the poor, yea, even the mighty, even the King himself says, Give me Bhaga.
3 Bhaga our guide, Bhaga whose gifts are faithful, favour this song, and give us wealth, O Bhaga.
Bhaga, augment our store of kine and horses, Bhaga, may we be rich in men and heroes.
4 So may felicity be ours at present, and when the day approaches, and at noontide;
And may we still, O Bounteous One, at sunset be happy in the Deities' loving-kindness.
5 May Bhaga verily be bliss-bestower, and through him, Gods! may happiness attend us.
As such, O Bhaga, all with might invoke thee: as such be thou our Champion here, O Bhaga.
6 To this our worship may all Dawns incline them, and come to the pure place like Dadhikravan.
As strong steeds draw a chariot may they bring us hitherward Bhaga who discovers treasure.
7 May blessed Mornings dawn on us for ever, with wealth of kine, of horses, and of heroes,
Streaming with all abundance, pouring fatness. Preserve us evermore, ye Gods, with blessings.

## [07-042] HYMN XLII Visvedevas.
1. LET Brahmans and Angirases come forward, and let the roar of cloudy heaven surround us.
Loud low the Milch-kine swimming in the waters: set be the stones that grace our holy service.
2 Fair, Agni, is thy long-known path to travel: yoke for the juice tfiy bay, thy ruddy horses,
Or red steeds, Hero-bearing, for the chamber. Seated, I call the Deities' generations.
3 They glorify your sacrifice with worship, yet the glad Priest near them is left unequalled.
Bring the Gods hither, thou of many aspects: turn hitherward Aramati the Holy.
4 What time the Guest hath made himself apparent, at ease reclining in the rich man's dwelling,
Agni, well-pleased, well-placed within the chamber gives to a house like this wealth worth the
choosing.
5 Accept this sacrifice of ours, O Agni; glorify it with Indra and the Maruts.
Here on our grass let Night and Dawn be seated: bring longing Varuna and Mitra hither.
6 Thus hath Vasistha praised victorious Agni, yearning for wealth that giveth all subsistence.
May he bestow on us food, strength, and riches. Preserve us evermore, ye Gods, with blessings.

## [07-043] HYMN XLIII Visvedevas.

1. SING out the pious at your sacrifices to move with adorations Earth and Heaven-

The Holy Singers, whose unmatched devotions, like a tree's branches, part in all directions.

2 Let sacrifice proceed like some fleet courser: with one accord lift ye on high the ladles.

Strew sacred grass meet for the solenm service: bright flames that love the Gods have mounted upward.

3 Like babes in arms reposing on their mother, let the Gods sit upon the grass's summit.

Let general fire make bright the flame of worship: scorn us not, Agni, in the Gods' assembly.

4 Gladly the Gods have let themselves be honoured, milking the copious streams of holy Order.

The highest might to-day is yours, the Vasits': come ye, as many as ye are, one-minded.

5 So, Agni, send us wealth among the people: may we be closely knit to thee, O Victor,

Unharmed, and rich, and taking joy together. Preserve us evermore, ye ods, with blessings.

### [07-044] HYMN XLIV. Dadhikras.

1. I CALL on Dadhikras, the first, to give you aid, the Asvins, Bhaga, Dawn, and Agni kindled well,

Indra, and Visnu, Pusan, Brahmanaspati, Adityas, Heaven and Earth, the Waters, and the Light.

2 When, rising, to the sacrifice we hasten, awaking Dadhikras with adorations.

Seating on sacred grass the Goddess Ila. let us invoke the sage swift-hearing Asvins.

3 While I am thus arousing Dadhikravan I speak to Agni, Earth, and Dawn, and Surya,

The red, the brown of Varuna ever mindful: may they ward off from us all grief and trouble.

4 Foremost is Dadhikravan, vigorous courser; in forefront of the cars, his way he knoweth,

Closely allied with Surya and with Morning, Adityas, and Angirases, and Vasus.

5 May Dadhikras prepare the way we travel that we may pass along the path of Order.

May Agni bear us, and the Heavenly Army: hear us all Mighty Ones whom none deceiveth.

### [07-045] HYMN XLV. Savitar.

1. MAY the God Savitar, rich in goodly treasures, filling the region, borne by steeds, come hither,

In his hand holding much that makes men happy, lulling to slumber and arousing creatures.

2 Golden, sublime, and easy in their motion, his arms extend unto the bounds of heaven.

Now shall that mightiness of his he lauded: even Surya yields to him in active vigour.

3 May this God Savitar, the Strong and Mighty, the Lord of precious wealth, vouchsafe us treasures.

May he, advancing his far-spreading lustre, bestow on us the food that feedeth mortals.

4 These songs praise Savitar whose tongue is pleasant, praise him whose arms are full, whose hands are lovely.

High vital strength, and manifold, may he grant us. Preserve us evermore, ye Gods, with blessings.

### [07-046] HYMN XLVI. Rudra.

1. To Rudra bring these songs, whose bow is firm and strong, the self-dependent God with swiftlyflying shafts,

The Wise, the Conqueror whom none may overcome, armed with sharp-pointed weapons: may he hear our call.

2 He through his lordship thinks on beings of the earth, on heavenly beings through his high imperial sway.

Come willingly to our doors that gladly welcome thee, and heal all sickness, Rudra., in our families.

3 May thy bright arrow which, shot down by thee from heaven, flieth upon the earth, pass us uninjured by.

Thou, very gracious God, bast thousand medicines: inflict no evil on our sons or progeny.

4 Slay us not, nor abandon us, O Rudra let not thy noose, when thou art angry, seize us.

Give us trimmed grass and fame among the living. Preserve us evermore, ye Gods, with blessings.

### [07-047] HYMN XLVII. Waters.

1. MAY we obtain this day from you, O Waters, that wave of pure refreshment, which the pious

Made erst the special beverage of Indra, bright, stainless, rich in sweets and dropping fatness.

2 May the Floods' Offspring, he whose course is rapid, protect that wave most rich in sweets, O Waters,

That shall make Indra and the Vasus joyful. This may we gain from you to-day, we pious.

3 All-purifying, joying in their nature, to paths of Gods the Goddesses move onward.

They never violate the laws of Indra. Present the oil-rich offering to the Rivers.

4 Whom Surya with his bright beams hath attracted, and Indra dug the path for them to travel,

May these Streams give us ample room and freedom. Preserve us evermore, ye Gods, with blessings.

### [07-048] HYMN XLVIII. Rbhus.

1. YE liberal Heroes, Vajas and Rbhuksans, come and delight you with our flowing Soma.

May your strength, Vibhus, as ye come to meet us, turn hitherward your car that brings men profit.

2 May we as Rbhu with your Rbhus conquer strength with our strength, as Vibhus with the Vibhus.

May Vaja aid us in the fight for booty, and helped by Indra may we quell the foeman.

3 For they rule many tribes with high dominion, and conquer all their foes in close encounter.

May Indra, Vibhvan, Vaja, and Rbhuksan destroy by turns the wicked foeman's valour.

4 Now, Deities, give us ample room and freedom: be all of you, one-minded, our protection.

So let the Vasus grant us strength and vigour. Preserve us evermore, ye Gods, with blessings.

### [07-049] HYMN XLIX. Waters.

1. FORTH from the middle of the flood the Waters-their chief the Sea-flow cleansing, never sleeping.

Indra, the Bull, the Thunderer, dug their channels: here let those Waters, Goddesses, protect me.

2 Waters which come from heaven, or those that wander dug from the earth, or flowing free by nature,

Bright, purifying, speeding to the Ocean, here let those Waters. Goddesses, protect me.

3 Those amid whom goes Varuna the Sovran, he who discriminates men's truth and falsehood-

Distilling meath, the bright, the purifying, here let those Waters, Goddesses, protect me.

4 They from whom Varuna the King, and Soma, and all the Deities drink strength and vigour,
They into whom Vaisvanara Agni entered, here let those Waters, Goddesses, protect Me.

## [07-050] HYMN L. Various Deities.

1. O MITRA-VARUNA, guard and protect me here: let not that come to me which nests within and
swells.
I drive afar the scorpion hateful to the sight: let not the winding worm touch me and wound my foot.
2 Eruption that appears upon the twofold joints, and that which overspreads the ankles and the
knees,
May the refulgent Agni banish far away let not the winding worm touch me and wound my foot.
3 The poison that is formed upon the Salmali, that which is found in streams, that which the plants
produce,
All this may all the Gods banish and drive away: let not the winding worm touch me and wound my
foot.
4 The steep declivities, the valleys, and the heights, the channels full of water, and the waterless-
May those who swell with water, gracious Goddesses, never afflict us with the Sipada disease, may
all the rivers keep us free from Simida.

## [07-051] HYMN LI. Adityas.

1 THROUGH the Adityas' most auspicious shelter, through their most recent succour may we
conquer.
May they, the Mighty, giving ear, establish this sacrifice, to make us free and sinless.
2 Let Aditi rejoice and the Adityas, Varuna, Mitra, Aryaman, most righteous.
May they, the Guardians of the world, protect us, and, to show favour, drink this day our Soma.
3 All Universal Deities, the Maruts, all the Adityas, yea, and all the Rbhus,
Indra, and Agni, and the Asvins, lauded. Preserve us evermore, ye Gods, with blessings.

## [07-052] HYMN LII. Adityas.

1. MAY we be free from every bond, Adityas! a castle among Gods and men, ye Vasus.
Winning, may we win Varuna and Mitra, and, being, may we be, O Earth and Heaven.
2 May Varuna and Mitra grant this blessing, our Guardians, shelter to our seed and offspring.
Let us not suffer for another's trespass. nor do the thing that ye, O Vasus, punish.
3 The ever-prompt Angirases, imploring riches from Savitar the God, obtained them.
So may our Father who is great and holy, and all the Gods, accordant, grant this favour.

## [07-053] HYMN LIII. Heaven and Earth.

1. AS priest with solemn rites and adorations I worship Heaven and Earth, the High and Holy.
To them, great Parents of the Gods, have sages of ancient time, singing, assigned precedence.
2 With newest hymns set in the seat of Order, those the Two Parents, born before all others,

Come, Heaven and Earth, with the Celestial People, hither to us, for strong is your protection.
3 Yea, Heaven and Earth, ye hold in your possession full many a treasure for the liberal giver.
Grant us that wealth which comes in free abundance. Preserve us evermore, ye Gods, with blessings.

## [07-054] HYMN LIV. Vastospati.

1. ACKNOWLEDGE us, O Guardian of the Homestead: bring no disease, and give us happy entrance.
Whate'er we ask of thee, be pleased to grant it, and prosper thou quadrupeds and bipeds.
2 Protector of the Home, be our promoter: increase our wealth in kine and steeds, O Indu.

May we be ever-youthful in thy friendship: be pleased in us as in his sons a father.
3 Through thy dear fellowship that bringeth welfare, may we be victors, Guardian of the Dwelling!
Protect our happiness in rest and labour. Preserve us evermore, ye Gods, with blessings.

## [07-055] HYMN LV. Vastospati.

1. VASTOSPATI, who killest all disease and wearest every form,
Be an auspicious Friend to us.
2 When, O bright Son of Sarama, thou showest, tawny-hued! thy teeth,
They gleam like lances' points within thy mouth when thou wouldst bite; go thou to steep.
3 Sarama's Son, retrace thy way: bark at the robber and the thief.
At Indra's singers barkest thou? Why dust thou seek to terrify us? Go to sleep.
4 Be on thy guard against the boar, and let the boar beware of thee.
At Indra's singers barkest thou? Why dost thou seek to terrify us? Go to sleep.
5 Sleep mother, let the father sleep, sleep dog and master of the house.
Let all the kinsmen sleep, sleep all the people who are round about.
6 The man who sits, the man who walks, and whosoever looks on us,
Of these we closely shut the eyes, even as we closely shut this house.
7 The Bull who hath a thousand horns, who rises up from out the sea,-
By him the Strong and Mighty One we lull and make the people sleep.
8 The women sleeping in the court, lying without, or stretched on beds,
The matrons with their odorous sweetsthese, one and all, we lull to sleep.

## [07-056] HYMN LVI. Maruts.

1. Wno are these radiant men in serried rank, Rudra's young heroes borne by noble steeds?
2 Verily no one knoweth whence they sprang: they, and they only, know each other's birth.
3 They strew each other with their blasts, these Hawks: they strove together, roaring like the wind.
4 A sage was he who knew these mysteries, what in her udder mighty Prsni bore.
5 Ever victorious, through the Maruts, be this band of Heroes, nursing manly strength,
6 Most bright in splendour, flectest on their way, close-knit to glory, strong with varied power.

173

7 Yea, mighty is your power and firm your strength: so, potent, with the Maruts, be the band.

8 Bright is your spirit, wrathful are your minds: your bold troop's minstrel is like one inspired.

9 Ever avert your blazing shaft from us, and let not your displeasure reach us here

10 Your dear names, conquering Maruts, we invoke, calling aloud till we are satisfied.

11 Well-armed, impetuous in their haste, they deck themselves, their forms, with oblations: to you,
the pure, ornaments made of gold.

12 Pure, Maruts, pure yourselves, are your oblations: to you, the pure, pure sacrifice I offer.
By Law they came to truth, the Law's observers, bright by their birth, and pure, and sanctifying.

13 Your rings, O Maruts, rest upon your shoulders, and chains of gold are twined upon your bosoms.
Gleaming with drops of rain, like lightning-flashes, after your wont ye whirl about your weapons.

14 Wide in the depth of air spread forth your glories, far, most adorable, ye bear your titles.
Maruts, accept this thousandfold allotment of household sacrifice and household treasure.

15 If, Maruts, ye regard the praise recited here at this mighty singer invocation,
Vouchsafe us quickly wealth with noble heroes, wealth which no man uho hateth us may injure.

16 The Maruts, fleet as coursers, while they deck them like youths spectators of a festal meeting,
Linger, like beauteous colts, about the dwelling, like frisking calves, these who pour down the water.

17 So may the Maruts help us and be gracious, bringing free room to lovely Earth and Heaven.
Far be your bolt that slayeth men and cattle. Ye Vasus, turn yourselves to us with blessings.

18 The priest, when seated, loudly calls you, Maruts, praising in song your universal bounty.
He, Bulls! who hath so much in his possession, free from duplicity, with hymns invokes you.

19 These Maruts bring the swift man to a stand-still, and strength with mightier strength they break
and humble
These guard the singer from the man who hates him and lay their sore displeasure on the wicked.

20 These Maruts rouse even the poor and needy: the Vasus love him as an active champion.
Drive to a distance, O ye Bulls, the darkness: give us full store of children and descendants.

21 Never, O Maruts, may we lose your bounty, nor, car-borne Lords! be hitidmost when ye deal it.
Give us a share in that delightful treasure, the genuine wealth that, Bulls! is your possession.

22 What time the men in fury rush together for running streams, for pastures, and for houses.
Then, O ye Maruts, ye who spring from Rudra, be our protectors in the strife with foemen.

23 Full many a decd ye did for our forcfathcrs worthy of lauds which, even of old, they sang you.
lle strong man, with the Maruts, wins in battle, the charger, with the Maruts, gains the booty.

24 Ours, O ye Maruts, be the vigorous Hero, the Lord Divine of men, the strong Sustainer,
With whom to fair lands we may cross the waters, and dwell in our own home with you beside us.

25 May Indra, Mitra, Varuna and Agni, Waters, and Plants, and Trees accept our praises.

May we find shelter in the Marut's bosom. Preserve us evermore, ye Gods, with blessings.

### [07-057] HYMN LVII. Maruts.

1. YEA, through the power of your sweet juice, ye Holy! the Marut host is glad at sacrifices.
They cause even spacious heaven and earth to tremble, they make the spring flow when they come,
the Mighty.

2 The Maruts watch the man who sings their praises, promoters of the thought of him who worships.
Seat you on sacred grass in our assembly, this day, with friendly minds, to share the banquet.

3 No others gleam so brightly as these Maruts with their own forms, their golden gauds, their
weapons.
With all adornments, decking earth and heaven, they heighten, for bright show, their common
splendour.

4 Far from us be your blazing dart, O Maruts, when we, through human frailty, sin against you.
Let us not he exposed to that, ye Holy! May your most loving favour still attend us.

5 May even what we have done delight the Maruts, the blameless Ones, the bright, the purifying.
Further us, O ye Holy, with your kindness: advance us mightily that we may prosper.

6 And may the Maruts, praised by all their titles, Heroes, enjoy the taste of our oblations.
Give us of Amrta for the sake of offspring: awake the excellent fair stores of riches.

7 Hither, ye Maruts, praised, with all your succours, with all felicity come to our princes,
Who, of themselves, a hundredfold increase us. Preserve us evermore, ye Gods, with blessings.

### [07-058] HYMN LVIII. Maruts.

1. SING to the troop that pours down rain in common, the Mighty Company of celestial nature.
They make the world-halves tremble with their greatness: from depths of earth and sky they reach to
heaven.

2 Yea, your birth, Maruts, was with wild commotion, ye who move swiftly, fierce in wrath, terrific.
Ye all-surpassing in your might and vigour, each looker on the light fears at your coming.

3 Give ample vital power unto our princes let our fair praises gratify the Maruts.
As the way travelled helpeth people onward, so further us with your delightful succours.

4 Your favoured singer counts his wealth by hundreds: the strong steed whom ye favour wins a
thousand.
The Sovran whom ye aid destroys the foeman. May this your gift, ye Shakers, be distinguished.

5 I call, as such, the Sons of bounteous Rudra: will not the Maruts turn again to us-ward?
What secret sin or open stirs their anger, that we implore the Swift Ones to forgive us.

6 This eulogy of the Bounteous hath been spoken: accept, ye Maruts, this our hymn of praises.
Ye Bulls, keep those who hate us at a distance. Preserve us evermore, ye Gods, with blessings.

### [07-059] HYMN LIX. Maruts.

1. WHOMSO ye rescue here and there, whomso ye guide, O Deities,

To him give shelter, Agni, Mitra, Varuna, ye Maruts, and thou Aryaman.
2 Through your kind favour, Gods, on some auspicious day, the worshipper subdues his foes.
That man increases home and strengthening ample food who brings you offerings as ye list.
3 Vasistha will not overlook the lowliest one among you all.
O Maruts, of our Soma juice effused to-day drink all of you with eager haste.
4 Your succour in the battle injures not the man to whom ye, Heroes, grant your gifts.
May your most recent favour turn to us again. Come quickly, ye who fain would drink.
5 Come hitherward to drink the juice, O ye whose bounties give you joy.
These offerings are for you, these, Maruts, I present. Go not to any place but this.
6 Sit on our sacred grass, be graciously inclined to give the wealth for which we long,
To take delight, ye Maruts, Friends of all, with Svaha, in sweet Soma juice.
7 Decking the beauty of their forms in secret the Swans with purple backs have flown down hither.
Around me all the Company hath settled, like joyous Heroes glad in our libation.
8 Maruts, the man whose wrath is hard to master, he who would slay us ere we think, O Vasus,
May he be tangled in the toils of mischief; smite ye him down with your most flaming weapon.
9 O Maruts, ye consuming Gods, enjoy this offering brought for you,
To help us, ye who slay the foe.
10 Sharers of household sacrifice, come, Maruts, stay not far away,
That ye may help us, Bounteous Ones.
11 Here, Self-strong Maruts, yea, even here. ye Sages with your sunbright skins
I dedicate your sacrifice.
12 Tryambaka we worship, sweet augmenter of prosperity.
As from its stem the cucumber, so may I be released from death, not reft of immortality.

## [07-060] HYMN LX. Mitra-Varuna.

1. WHEN thou, O Sun, this day, arising sinless, shalt speak the truth to Varuna and Mitra,
O Aditi, may all the Deities love us, and thou, O Aryaman, while we are singing.
2 Looking on man, O Varuna and Mitra, this Sun ascendeth up by both the pathways,
Guardian of all things fixt, of all that moveth, beholding good and evil acts of mortals.
3 He from their home hath yoked the Seven gold Coursers who, dropping oil and fatness, carry Surya.
Yours, Varuna and Mitra, he surveyeth the worlds and living creatures like a herdsman.
4 Your coursers rich in store of sweets have mounted: to the bright ocean Surya hath ascended,
For whom the Adityas make his pathway ready, Aryaman, Mitra, Varuna, accordant.
5 For these, even Aryaman, Varuna and Mitra, are the chastisers of all guile and falsehood.
These, Aditi's Sons, infallible and mighty, have waxen in the home of law Eternal.
6 These, Mitra, Varuna whom none deceiveth, with great power quicken even the fool to wisdom,
And, wakening, moreover, thoughtful insight, lead it by easy paths o'er grief and trouble.

7 They ever vigilant, with eyes that close not, caring for heaven and earth, lead on the thoughtless.
Even in the river's bed there is a shallow. across this broad expanse may they conduct us.
8 When Aditi and Varuna and Mitra, like guardians, give Sudas their friendly shelter,
Granting him sons and lineal succcession, lct us not, bold ones! move the Gods to anger.
9 May he with ofierings purify the altar from any stains of Varuna's reviler.
Aryaman save us us all those who hate us: give room and freedom to Sudas, ye Mighty.
10 Hid from our eyes is their resplendent meeting: by their mysterious might they hold dominion.
Heroes! we cry trembling in fear before you, even in the greatness of your power have mercy.
11 He who wins favour for his prayer by worship, that he may gain him strength and highest riches,
That good man's mind the Mighty Ones will follow: they have brought comfort to his spacious dwelling.
12 This priestly task, Gods! Varuna and Mitra! hath been performed for you at sacrifices.
Convey us safely over every peril. Preserve us evermore, ye Gods, with blessings.

## [07-061] HYMN LXI. Mitra-Varuna.

1. O VARUNA and Mitra, Surya spreading the beauteous light of you Twain Gods ariseth.
He who beholdetb all existing creatures observetb well the zeal that is in mortals.
2 The holy sage, renowned afar, directeth his hymns to you, O Varuna and Mitra,-
He whose devotions, sapient Gods, ye favour so that ye fill, as 'twere, with power his autumns.
3 From the wide earth, O Varuna and Mitra from the great lofty heaven, ye, Bounteous Givers, -
Have in the fields and houses set your warder-, who visit every spot and watch unceasing.
4 I praise the strength of Varuna and Mitra that strength, by mightiness, keeps both worlds asunder.
Heroless pass the months of the ungodly he who loves sacrifice makes his home enduring.
5 Steers, all infallible are these your people in whom no wondrous thing is seen, no worship.
Guile follows close the men who are untruthful: no secrets may be hidden from your knowledge.
6 I will exalt your sacrifice with homage: as priest, I, Mitra-Varuna, invoke you.
May these new hymns and prayers that I have fashioned delight you to the profit of the singer.
7 This priestly task, Gods! Varuna and Mitra! hath been performed for you at sacrifices.
Convey us safely over every peril. Preserve us evermore, ye Gods, with blessings.

## [07-062] HYMN LXII. Mitra-Varuna.

1. SURYA hath sent aloft his beams of splendour o'er all the tribes of men in countless places.
Together with the heaven he shines apparent, formed by his Makers well with power and wisdom.
2 So hast thou mounted up before us, Surya, through these our praises, with fleet dappled horses.
Declare us free from all offence to Mitra, and Varuna, and Aryaman, and Agni.
3 May holy Agni, Varuna, and Mitra send down their riches upon us in thousands.

May they, the Bright Ones, make our praise-song perfect, and, when we laud them, grant us all our
wishes.
4 O undivided Heaven and Earth, preserve us, us, Lofty Ones! your nobIy-born descendants.
Let us not anger Varuna, nor Vayu, nor him, the dearest Friend of mortals, Mitra.
5 Stretch forth your arms and let our lives be lengthened: with fatness dew the pastures of our cattle.
Ye Youthful, make us famed among the people: hear, Mitra-Varuna, these mine invocations.
6 Now Mitra, Varuna, Aryaman vouchsafe us freedom and room, for us and for our children.
May we find paths all fair and good to travel. Preserve us evermore, ye Gods, with blessings.

### [07-063] HYMN LXIII. Mitra-Varuna.

1. COMMON to all mankind, auspicious Surya, he who beholdeth all, is mounting upward;
The God, the eye of Varuna and Mitra, who rolled up darkness like a piece of leather.
2 Surya's great ensign, restless as the billow, that urgeth men to action, is advancing:
Onward he still would roll the wheel well-rounded, which Etasa, harnessed to the car-pole, moveth.
3 Refulgent from the bosom of the Mornings, he in Whom singers take delight ascendeth.
This Savitar, God, is my chief joy and pleasure, who breaketh not the universal statute.
4 Golden, far-seeing, from the heaven he riseth: far is his goal, he hasteth on resplendent.
Men, verily, inspirited by Surya speed to their aims and do the work assigned them.
5 Where the irrunortals have prepared his pathway he flieth through the region like a falcon.
With homage and oblations will we serve you, O Mitra-Varuna, when the Sun hath risen.
6 Now Mitra, Varuna, Aryaman vouchsafe us freedom and room, for us and for our children.
May we find paths all fair and good to travel. Preserve us evermore, ye Gods, with blessings.

### [07-064] HYMN LXIV. Mitra-Varuna.

1. YE Twain who rule, in heaven and earth, the region, clothed be your clouds in robes of oil and
fatness.
May the imperial Varuna, and Mitra, and high-born Aryaman accept our presents.
2 Kings, guards of rrtighty everlasting Order, come hitherward, ye Princes, Lords of Rivers.
Send us from heaven, O Varuna and Mitra, rain and sweet food, ye who pour down your bounties.
3 May the dear God, and Varuna and Mitra conduct us by the most effective pathways,
That foes may say unto Sudas our chieftain, May, we, too, joy in food with Gods to guard us.
4 IIim who hath wrought for you this car in spirit, who makes the song rise upward and sustains it,
Bedew with fatness, Varuna nd Mitra ye Kings, make glad the pleasant dwelling-places.
5 To you this laud, O Varuna and Mitra is offered like bright Soma juice to Vayu.
Favour our songs of praise, wake thought and spirit. Preserve us evermore, ye Gods, with blessings.

### [07-065] HYMN LXV. Mitra-Varuna.

1. WITH hymns I call you, when the Sun hath risen, Mitra, and Varuna whose thoughts are holy,
Whose Power Divine, supreme and everlasting, comes with good heed at each man's supplication.
2 For they are Asuras of Gods, the friendly make, both of you, our lands exceeding fruitful.
May we obtain you, Varuna and Mitra, wherever Heaven and Earth and days may bless us.
3 Bonds of the sinner, they bear many nooses: the wicked mortal hardly may escape them.
Varuna-Mitra, may your path of Order bear us o'er trouble as a boat o'er waters.
4 Come, taste our offering, Varuna and Mitra: bedew our pasture wil sweet food and fatness.
Pour down in plenty here upon the people the choicest of your fair celestial water.
5 To you this laud, O Varuna and Mitra, is offered, like bright Soma juice to Vayu.
Favour our songs of praise, wake thought and spirit. Preserve us evermore, ye Gods, with blessings.

### [07-066] HYMN LXVI Mitra-Varuna.

1. LET our strong hymn of praise go forth, the laud of Mitra-Varuna,
With homage to that high-born Pair;
2 The Two exceeding wise, the Sons of Daksa, whom the gods ordained
For lordship, excellently great.
3 Such, Guardians of our homes and us, O Mitra-Varuna, fulfil
The thoughts of those who sing your praise.
4 So when the Sun hath risen to-day, may sinless Mitra, Aryaman,
Bhaga, and Savitar sendus forth.
5 May this our home be guarded well forward, ye Bounteous, on the way,
Who bear us safely o'er distress.
6. And those Self-reigning, Aditi, whose statute is inviolate,
The Kings who rule a vast domain.
7 Soon as the Sun hath risen, to you, to Mitra-Varuna, I sing,
And Aryarnan who slays the foe.
8 With wealth of gold may this my song bring unmolested power and might,
And, Brahmans, gain the sacrifice.
9 May we be thine, God Varuna, and with our princes, Mitra, thine.
Food and Heaven's light will we obtain.
10 Many are they who strengthen Law, Sun-eyed, with Agni for their tongue,
They who direct the three great gatherings with their thoughts, yea, all things with surpassing
might.
11 They who have stablished year and month and then the day, night, sacrifice and holy verse,
Varuna, Mitra, Aryarnan, the Kings, have won dominion which none else may gain.
12 So at the rising of the Sun we think of you with hymns to-day,
Even as Varuna, Mitra, Aryaman deserve: ye are the charioteers of Law.
13 True to Law, born in Law the strengtheners of Law, terrible, haters of the false,
In their felicity which gives the best defence may we men and our princes dwell.
14 Uprises, on the slope of heaven, that marvel that attracts die sight
As swift celestial Etasa bears it away, prepared for every eye to see.

15 Lord of each single head, of fixt and moving things, equally through the whole expanse,
The Seven sister Bays bear Surya on his car, to bring us wealth and happiness.
16 A hundred autumns may we see that bright Eye, God-ordained, arise
A hundred autumns may we live.
17 Infallible through your wisdom, come hither, resplendent Varuna,
And Mitra, to the Soma draught.
18 Come as the laws of Heaven ordain, Varuna, Mitra, void of guile:
Press near and drink the Soma juice.
19 Come, Mitra, Varuna, accept, Heroes, our sacrificial gift:
Drink Soma, ye who strengthen Law.

### [07-067] HYMN LXVII. Asvins.

1. I WITH a holy heart that brings oblation will sing forth praise to meet your car, ye Princes,
Which, Much-desired! hath wakened as your envoy. I call you hither as a son his parents.
2 Brightly hath Agni shone by us enkindled: the limits even of darkness were apparent.
Eastward is seen the Banner of the Morning, the Banner born to give Heaven's Daughter glory.
3 With hymns the deft priest is about you, Asvins, the eloquent priest attends you now, Nasatyas.
Come by the paths that ye are wont to travel, on car that finds the light, laden with treasure.
4 When, suppliant for your help, Lovers of Sweetness! I seeking wealth call you to our libation,
Hitherward let your vigorous horses bear you: drink ye with us the well-pressed Soma juices.
5 Bring forward, Asvins, Gods, to its fulfilment my never-wearied prayer that asks for riches,
Vouchsafe us all high spirit in the combat, and with your powers, O Lords of Power, assist us.
6 Favour us in these prayers of ours, O Asvins. May we have genial vigour, ne'er to fail us.
So may we, strong in children and descendants, go, wealthy, to the banquet that awaits you.
7 Lovers of Sweetness, we have brought this treasure to you as 'twere an envoy sent for friendship.
Come unto us with spirits free from anger, in homes of men enjoying our oblation.
8 With one, the same, intention, ye swift movers, o'er the Seven Rivers hath your chariot travelled.
Yoked by the Gods, your strong steeds never weary while speeding forward at the pole they bear you.
9 Exhaustless be your bounty to our princes who with their wealth incite the gift of riches,
Who further friendship with their noble natures, combining wealth in kine with wealth in herses.
10 Now hear, O Youthful Twain, mine invocation: come, Asvins, to the home where food aboundeth.
Vouchsafe us wealth, do honour to our nobles. Preserve us evermore, ye Gods, with blessings.

### [07-068] HYMN LXVIII. Asvins.

1. COME, radiant Asvins, with your noble horses: accept your servant's hymns, ye Wonder-Workers:
Enjoy oblations which we bring to greet you.
2 The gladdening juices stand prepared before you: come quickly and partake of mine oblation.
Pass by the calling of our foe and bear us.
3 Your chariot with a hundred aids, O Asvins, beareth you swift as thought across the regions,
Speeding to us, O ye whose wealth is Surya.
4 What time this stone of yours, the Gods' adorer, upraised, sounds forth for you as Soma-presser,
Let the priest bring you, Fair Ones, through oblations.
5 The nourishment ye have is, truly, wondrous: ye gave thereof a quickening store to Atri,
Who being dear to you, receives your favour.
6 That gift, which all may gain, ye gave Cyavana, when he grew old, who offered you oblations,
When ye bestowed on him enduring beauty.
7 What time his wicked friends abandoned Bhujyu, O Asvins, in the middle of the ocean,
Your horse delivered him, your faithful servant.
8 Ye lent your aid to Vrka when exhausted, and listened when invoked to Sayu's calling.
Ye made the cow pour forth her milk like water, and, Asvins, strengthened with your strength the barren.
9 With his fair hymns this singer, too, extols you, waking with glad thoughts at the break of morning.
May the cow nourish him with milk to feed llim. Preserve us evermore, ye Gods, with blessings.

### [07-069] HYMN LXIX. Asvins.

1. MAY your gold chariot, drawn by vigorous horses, come to us, blocking up the earth
and heaven,
Bright with its fellies while its way drops fatness, food-laden, rich in coursers, man's protector.
2 Let it approach, yoked by thewill, three-seated, extending far and wide o'er fivefold beings,
Whereon ye visit God-adoring races, bending your course whither ye will, O Asvins.
3 Renowned, with noble horses, come ye hither: drink, Wondrous Pair, the cup that holds sweet
juices.
Your car whereon your Spouse is wont to travel marks with its track the farthest ends of heaven.
4 When night was turning to the grey of morning the Maiden, Surya's Daughter, chose your
splendour.
When with your power and might ye aid the pious he comes through heat to life by your assistance.
5 O Chariot-borne, this car of yours invested with rays of light comes harnessed to our dwelling.
Herewith, O Asvins, while the dawn is breaking, to this our sacrifice bring peace and blessing.
6 Like the wild cattle thirsty for the lightning, Heroes, come nigh this day to our libations.
Men call on you with hymns in many places, but let not other worshippers detain you.
7 Bhujyu, abandoned in the midst of ocean, ye raised from out the water with your horses,
Uninjured, winged, flagging not, undaunted, with deeds of wonder saving him, O Asvins.
8 Now hear, O Youthful Twain, mine invocation: come, Asvins, to the home where food aboundeth.
Vouchsafe us wealth, do honour to our nobles. Preserve us evermore, ye Gods, with blessings.

### [07-070] HYMN LXX. Asvins.

1. RICH in all blessings, Asvins come ye hither: this place on earth is called your own possession,
Like a strong horse with a fair back it standeth, whereon, as in a lap, ye seat you firmly.

2 This most delightful eulogy awaits you in the man's house drink-offering hath been heated,
Which bringeth you over the seas and rivers, yoking as'twere two well-matched shining horses.
3 Whatever dwellings ye possess, O Asvins, in fields of men or in the streams of heaven,
Resting upon the summit of the mountain, or bringing food to him who gives oblation,
4 Delight yourselves, ye Gods, in plants and waters when Rsis give them and ye find they suit You.
Enriching us with treasures in abundance ye have looked back to former generations.
5 Asvins, though ye have heard them oft aforetime, regard the many prayers which Rsis offer.
Come to the man even as his heart desireth: may we enjoy your most delightful favour.
6 Come to the sacrifice offered you, Nasatyas, with men, oblations, and prayer duly uttered.
Come to Vasistha as his heart desireth, for unto you these holy hymns are chanted.
7 This is the thought, this is the song, O Asvins: accept this hymn of ours, ye Steers, with favour.
May these our prayers addressed to you come nigh you. Preserve us evermore, ye Gods, with
blessings.

## [07-071] HYMN LXXI. Asvins.

1. THE Night retireth from the Dawn her Sister; the Dark one yieldeth to the Red her pathway.
Let us invoke you rich in steeds and cattle - by day and night keep far from us the arrow.
2 Bearing rich treasure in your car, O Asvins, come to the mortal who presents oblation.
Keep at a distance penury and sickness; Lovers of Sweetness, day and night preserve us.
3 May your strong horses, seeking bliss, bring hither your chariot at the earliest flush of morning.
With coursers yoked by Law drive hither, Asvins, your car whose reins are light, laden with treasure.
4 The chariot, Princes, that conveys you, moving at daylight, triple-seated, fraught with riches,
Even with this come unto us, Nasatyas, that laden with all food it may approach us.
5 Ye freed Cyavana from old age and weakness: ye brought the courser fleet of food to Pedu.
Ye rescued Atri from distress and darkness, and loosed for Jahusa the bonds that bound him.
6 This is the thought, this is the song, O Asvins: accept this hymn of ours, ye Steers, With favour.
May these our prayers addressed to you come nigh you. Preserve us evermore, ye Gods, with
blessings.

## [07-072] HYMN LXXII. Asvins.

1. COME, O Nasatyas, on your car resplendent, rich in abundant wealth of kine and horses.
As harnessed steeds, all our laudations follow you whose forms shine with most delightful beauty.
2 Come with the Gods associate, come ye hither to us, Nasatyas, with your car accordant.
'Twixt you and us there is ancestral friendship and common kin: remember and regard it.
3 Awakened are the songs that praise the Asvins, the kindred prayers and the Celestial Mornings.
Inviting those we long for, Earth and Heaven, the singer calleth these Nasatyas hither.

4 What time the Dawns break forth in light, O Asvins, to you the poets offer their devotions.
God Savitar hath sent aloft his splendour, and fires sing praises with the kindled fuel.
5 Come from the west, come from the cast, Nasatyas, come, Asvins, from below and from above us.
Bring wealth from all sides for the Fivefold People. Preserve us evermore, ye Gods, with blessings.

## [07-073] HYMN LXXIII. Asvins.

1. WE have o'erpassed the limit of this darkness while, worshipping the Gods, we sang their praises.
The song invoketh both Immortal Asvins far-reaching, born of old, great WonderWorkers.
2 And, O Nasatyas, man's dear Priest is seated, who brings to sacrifice and offers worship,
Be near and taste the pleasant juice, O Asvins: with food, I call you to the sacrifices.
3 We choosing you, have let our worship follow its course: ye Steers, accept this hymn with favour.
Obeying you as your appointed servant, Vasistha singing hath with lauds aroused you.
4 And these Two Priests come nigh unto our people, united, demon-slayers, mighty-handed.
The juices that exhilarate are mingled. Injure us not, but come with happy fortune.
5 Come from the west, come from the cast, Nasatyas, come, Asvins, from below and from above us.
Bring wealth from all sides for the Fivefold People. Preserve us evermore, ye Gods, with blessings.

## [07-074] HYMN I.XXIV. Asvins.

1. THESE morning sacrifices call you, Asvins, at the break of day.
For help have I invoked you rich in power and might: for, house by house ye visit all.
2 O Heroes, ye bestow wonderful nourishment. send it to him whose songs are sweet
Accordant, both of you, drive your car down to us, and drink the savoury Soma juice.
3 Approach ye and be near to us. drink, O ye Asvins, of the meath.
Draw forth the milk, ye Mighty, rich in genuine wealth: injure us not, and come to us.
4 The horses that convey you in their rapid flight down to the worshipper's abode,
With these your speedy coursers, Heroes, Asvins, come, ye Gods, come well-inclined to us.
5 Yea, verily, our princes seek the Asvins in pursuit of food.
These shall give lasting glory to our liberal lords, and, both Nasatyas, shelter us.
6 Those who have led the way, like cars, offending none, those who are guardians of the men-
Also through their own might the heroes have grown strong, and dwell in safe and happy homes.

## [07-075] HYMN LXXV. Dawn.

1. BORN in the heavens the Dawn hath flushed, and showing her majesty is come as Law ordaineth.
She hath uncovered fiends and hateful darkness; best of Angirases, hath waked the pathways.
2 Rouse us this day to high and happy fortune: to great felicity, O Dawn, promote us.
Vouchsafe us manifold and splendid riches, famed among mortals, man-befriending Goddess!
3 See, lovely Morning's everlasting splendours, bright with their varied colours, have approached us.
Filling the region of mid-air, producing the rites of holy worship, they have mounted.

4 She yokes her chariot far away, and swiftly visits the lands where the Five Tribes are settled,
Looking upon the works and ways of mortals, Daughter of Heaven, the world's Imperial Lady.
5 She who is rich in spoil, the Spouse of Surya, wondrously opulent, rules all wealth and treasures.
Consumer of our youth, the seers extol her: lauded by priests rich Dawn shines out refulgent.
6 Apparent are the steeds of varied colour, the red steeds carrying resplendent Morning.
On her all-lovely car she comes, the Fair One, and brings rich treasure for her faithful servant.
7 True with the True and Mighty with the Mighty, with Gods a Goddess, Holy with the Holy,
She brake strong fences down and gave the cattle: the kine were lowing as they greeted Morning.
8 O Dawn, now give us wealth in kine and heroes, and horses, fraught with manifold enjoyment.
Protect our sacred grass from man's reproaches. Preserve us evermore, ye Gods, with blessings.

### [07-076] HYMN LXXVI. Dawn.

1. SAVITAR God of all men hath sent upward his light, designed for all mankind, immortal.
Through the Gods' power that Eye was first created. Dawn hath made all the universe apparent.
2 I see the paths which Gods are wont to travel, innocuous paths made ready by the Vasus.
Eastward the flag of Dawn hath been uplifted; she hath come hither o'er the tops of houses.
3 Great is, in truth, the number of the Mornings which were aforetime at the Sun's uprising.
Since thou, O Dawn, hast been beheld repairing as to thy love, as one no more to leave him.
4 They were the Gods' companions at the banquet, the ancient sages true to Law Eternal.
The Fathers found the light that lay in darkness, and with effectual words begat the Morning.
5 Meeting together in the same enclosure, they strive not, ofone mind, one with another.
They never break the Gods' eternal statutes, and injure none, in rivalry with Vasus.
6 Extolling thee, Blest Goddess, the Vasisthas, awake at early morn, with lauds implore thee.
Leader of kine and Queen of all that strengthens, shine, come as first to us, O high-born Morning.
7 She bringeth bounty and sweet charm of voices. The flushing Dawn is sung by the Vasisthas,
Giving us riches famed to distant places. Preserve us evermore, ye Gods, with blessings.

### [07-077] HYMN LXXVIT. Dawn.

1. SHE hath shone brightly like a youthful woman, stirring to motion every living creature.
Agni hath come to feed on mortal? fuel. She hath made light and chased away the darkness.
2 Turned to this All, far-spreading, she hath risen and shone in brightness with white robes about her.
She hath beamed forth lovely with golden colours, Mother of kine, Guide of the days she bringeth.
3 Bearing the Gods' own Eye, auspicious Lady, leading her Courser white and fair to look on,
Distinguished by her bean-is Dawn shines apparent, come forth to all the world with wondrous treasure.

4 Draw nigh with wealth and dawn away the foeman: prepare for us wide pasture free from danger.
Drive away those who hate us, bring us riches: pour bounty, opulent Lady, on the singer.
5 Send thy most excellent beams to shine and light us, giving us lengthened days, O Dawn, O Goddess,
Granting us food, thou who hast all things precious, and bounty rich in chariots, kine, and horses.
6 O Usas, nobly-born, Daughter of Heaven, whom the Vasisthas with their hymns make mighty,
Bestow thou on us vast and glorious riches. Preserve us evermore, ye Gods, with blessings.

### [07-078] HYMN LXXVIII. Dawn.

1. WE have beheld her earliest lights approaching: her many glories part, on high, asunder.
On car sublime, refulgent, wending hither, O Usas, bring the Wealth that makes us happy.
2 The fire well-kindIed sings aloud to greet her, and with their hymns the priests are chaming welcome.
Usas approaches in her splendour, driving all evil darkness far away, the Goddess.
3 Apparent eastward are those lights of Morning, sending out lustre, as they rise, around them.
She hath brought forth Sun, sacrifice, and Agni, and far away hath fled detested darkness.
4 Rich Daughter of the Sky, we all behold her, yea, all men look on Dawn as she is breaking.
fler car that moves self-harnessed hath she mounted, the car drawn onward by her well-yoked horses.
5 Inspired with loving thoughts this day to greet thee, we and our wealthy nobles have awakened.
Show yourselves fruitful, Dawns, as ye are rising. Preserve us evermore, ye Gods, with blessings.

### [07-079] HYMN LXXIX. Dawn.

1. ROUSING the lands where men's Five Tribes are settled, Dawn hath disclosed the pathways of the people.
She hath sent out her sheen with beauteous oxen. The Sun with light hath opened earth and heaven.
2 They paint their bright rays on the sky's far limits. the Dawns come on like tribes arrayed for battle.
Thy cattle, closely shutting up the darkness, as Savitar spreads his arms, give forth their lustre.
3 Wealthy, most like to Indra, Dawn hath risen, and brought forth lauds that shall promote our welfare.
Daughter of Heaven, a Goddess, she distributes, best of Angirases, treasures to the pious.
4 Bestow on us, O Dawn, that ample bounty which thou didst send to those who sang thy praises;
Thou whom with bellowings of a bull they quickened: thou didst unbar the firm-set mountain's portals.
5 Impelling every God to grant his bounty sending to us the charm of pleasant voices,
Vouchsafe us thoughts, for profit, as thou breakest. Preserve us evermore, ye Gods, with blessings.

### [07-080] HYMN LXXX. Dawn.

1 THE priests, Vasisthas, are the first awakened to welcome Usas with their songs and praises,
Who makes surrounding regions part asunder,and shows apparent all existing creatures.

2 Giving fresh life when she hath hid the darkness, this Dawn hath wakened there with new-born
lustre.
Youthful and unrestrained she cometh forward: she hath turned thoughts to Sun and fire and
worship.
3 May blessed Mornings shine on us for ever, with wealth of kine, of horses, and of heroes,
Streaming with all abundance, pouring fatness. Preserve us evermore, ye Gods, with blessings.

## [07-081] HYMN LXXXI. Dawn.

1. ADVANCING, sending forth her rays, the Daughter of the Sky is seen.
Uncovering, that we may see, the mighty gloom, the friendly Lady makes the light.
2 The Sun ascending, the refulgent Star, pours down his beams together with the Dawn.
O Dawn, at thine arising, and the Sun's, may we attain the share allotted us.
3 Promptly we woke to welcome thee, O Usas, Daughter of the Sky,
Thee, Bounteous One, who bringest all we long to have, and to the offerer health and wealth.
4 Thou, dawning, workest fain to light the great world, yea, heaven, Goddess! that it may be seen.
We yearn to be thine own, Dealer of Wealth: may we be to this Mother like her sons.
5 Bring us that wondrous bounty, Dawn, that shall be famed most far away.
What, Child of Heaven, thou hast of nourishment for man, bestow thou on us to enjoy.
6 Give to our princes opulence and immortal fame, and strength in herds of kine to us.
May she who prompts the wealthy, Lady of sweet strains, may Usas dawn our foes away.

## [07-082] HYMN LXXXIT. Indra-Varuna

1. GRANT us your strong protection, IndraVaruna, our people, and our family, for sacrifice.
May we subdue in fight our evil-hearted foes, him who attacks the man steadfast in lengthened rites.
2 O Indra-Varuna, mighty and very rich One of you is called Monarch and One Autocrat.
All Gods in the most lofty region of the air have, O ye Steers, combined all power and might in you.
3 Ye with your strength have pierced the fountains of the floods: the Sun have ye brought forward as
the Lord in heaven.
Cheered by this magic draught ye, Indra-Varuna, made the dry places stream, made songs of praise
flow forth.
4 In battels and in frays we ministering priests, kneeling upon our knees for furtherance of our weal,
Invoke you, only you, the Lords of twofold wealth, you prompt to hear, we bards, O Indra-Varuna.
5 O Indra-Varuna, as ye created all these creatures of the world by your surpassing might,
In peace and quiet Mitra waits on Varuna, the Other, awful, with the Maruis seeks renown.
6 That Varuna's high worth may shine preeminent, these Twain have measured each his proper
power and might.
The One subdueth the destructive enemy; the Other with a few furthereth many a man.
7 No trouble, no misfortune, Indra-Varuna, no woe from any side assails the mortal man

Whose sacrifice, O Gods, ye visit and enjoy: ne'er doth the crafty guile of mortal injure him.
8 With your divine protection, Heroes, come to us: mine invncation hear, if ye be pleased therewith.
Bestow ye upon us, O Indra-Varuna, your friendship and your kinship and your favouring grace.
9 In battle after battle, Indra-Varuna, be ye our Champions, ye who are the peoples' strength,
When both opposing bands invoke you for the fight, and men that they may gain offspring and
progeny.
10 May Indra, Varuna, Mitra, and Aryaman vouchsafe us glory and great shelter spreading far.
We think of the beneficent light of Aditi, and Savitar's song of praise, the God who strengthens Law.

## [07-083] HYMN LXXXIII. Indra-Varuna.

1. LOOKING to you and your alliance, O ye Men, armed with broad axes they went forward, fain for
spoil.
Ye smote and slew his Dasa and his Aryan enemies, and helped Sudas with favour, Indra-Varuna.
2 Where heroes come together with their banners raised, in the encounter where is naught for us to
love,
Where all things that behold the light are terrified, there did ye comfort us, O Indra-Varuna.
3 The boundaries of earth were seen all dark with dust: O Indra-Varuna, the shout went up to
heaven.
The enmities of the people compassed me about. Ye heard my calling and ye came to me with help.
4 With your resistless weapons, Indra-Varuna, ye conquered Bheda and ye gave Sudas your aid.
Ye heard the prayers of these amid the cries of war: effectual was the service of the Trtsus' priest.
5 O Indra-Varuna, the wickedness of foes and mine assailants' hatred sorely trouble me.
Ye Twain are Lords of riches both of earth and heaven: so grant to us your aid on the decisive day.
6 The men of both the hosts invoked you in the fight, Indra and Varuna, that they might win the wealth,
What time ye helped Sudas, with all the Trtsu folk, when the Ten Kings had pressed him down in their attack.
7 Ten Kings who worshipped not, O Indra-Varuna, confederate, in war prevailed not o'er Sudas.
True was the boast of heroes sitting at the feast: so at their invocations Gods were on their side.
8 O Indra-Varuna, ye gave Sudas your aid when the Ten Kings in battle compassed him about,
There where the white-robed Trtsus with their braided hair, skilled in song worshipped you with
homage and with hymn.
9 One of you Twain destroys the Vrtras in the fight, the Other evermore maintains his holy Laws.
We call on you, ye Mighty, with our hymns of praise. Vouchsafe us your protection, Indra-Varuna.
10 May Indra, Varuna, Mitra, and Aryaman vouchsafe us glory and great shelter spreading far.
We think of the beneficent light of Aditi, and Savitar's song of praise, the God who strengthens Law.

## [07-084] HYMN LXXXIV. Indra-Varuna.

1. KINGS, Indra-Varuna, I would turn you hither to this our sacrifice with gifts and homage.
Held in both arms the ladle, dropping fatness, goes of itself to you whose forms are varied.

2 Dyaus quickens and promotes your high dominion who bind with bonds not wrought of rope or
cordage.
Far from us still be Varuna's displeasure may Indra give us spacious room to dwell in.
3 Make ye our sacrifice fair amid the assemblies: make ye our prayers approved among our princes.
May God-sent riches come for our possession: further ye us with your delightful succours.
4 O Indra-Varuna, vouchsafe us riches with store of treasure, food, and every blessing;
For the Aditya, banisher of falsehood, the Hero, dealeth wealth in boundless plenty.
5 May this my song reach Varuna and Indra, and, strongly urging, win me sons and offspring.
To the Gods' banquet may we go with riches. Preserve us evermore, ye Gods, with blessings.

## [07-085] HYMN LXXXV. Indra-Varuna.

1. FOR you I deck a harmless hymn, presenting the Soma juice to Varuna and Indra-
A hymn that shines like heavenly Dawn with fatness. May they be near us on the march and guard
us.
2 Here where the arrows fall amid the banners both hosts invoke the Gods in emulation.
O Indra-Varuna, smite back those-our foemen,yea, smite them withyour shaft to every quarter.
3 Self-lucid in their seats, e'en heavenly Waters endowed with Godhead Varuna and Indra.
One of these holds the folk distinct and sundered, the Other smites and slays resistless foemen.
4 Wise be the priest and skilled in Law Eternal, who with his sacred gifts and oration.
Brings you to aid us with your might, Adityas: let him have viands to promote his welfare.
5 May this my song reach Varuna and Indra, and, strongly urging, win me sons and offspring.
To the Gods' banquet may we go with riches. Preserve us evermore, ye Gods with blessings.

## [07-086] HYMN LXXXVI. Varuna.

1. WISE, verily, are creatures through his greatness who stayed ever, spacious heaven and earth
asunder;
Who urged the high and mighty sky to motion, the Star of old, and spread the earth before him.
2 With mine own heart I commune on the question how Varuna and I may be united.
What gift of mine will he accept unangered? When may I calmly look and find him gracious?
3 Fain to know this in in I question others: I seek the wise, O Varuna, and ask them.
This one same answer even the sages gave me, "Surely this Varuna is angry with thee."
4 What, Varuna, hath been my chief transgression, ihat thou wouldst slay the friend who sings thy
praises?
Tell me, Unconquerable Lord, and quickly sinless will I approach thee with mine homage.
5 Free us from sins committed by our fathers, from those wherein we have ourselves offended.
O King, loose, like a thief who feeds the cattle, as from the cord a calf, set free Vasistha.
6 Not our own will betrayed us, but seduction, thoughtlessness, Varuna wine, dice, or anger.

The old is near to lead astray the younger: even sleep removeth not all evil-doing.
7 Slavelike may I do service to the Bounteous, serve, free from sin, the God inclined to anger.
This gentle Lord gives wisdom to the simple: the wiser God leads on the wise to riches.
8 O Lord, O Varuna, may this laudation come close to thed and lie within thy spirit.
May it be well with us in rest and labour. Preserve us ever-more, ye Gods, with blessings.

## [07-087] HYMN LXXXVII. Varuna.

1. VARUNA cut a pathway out for Surya, and led the watery floods of rivers onward.
The Mares, as in a race, speed on in order. He made great channels for the days to follow.
2 The wind, thy breath, hath sounded through the region like a wild beast that seeks his food in
pastures.
Within these two, exalted Earth and Heaven, O Varuna, are all the forms thou lovest.
3 Varuna's spies, sent forth upon their errand, survey the two world-halves well formed and
fashioned.
Wise are they, holy, skilled in sacrifices, the furtherers of the praise-songs of the prudent.
4 To me who understand hath Varuna spoken, the names borne by the Cow are three times seven.
The sapient God, knowing the place's secret, shall speak as 'twere to teach the race that cometh.
5 On him three heavens rest and are supported, and the three earths are there in sixfold order.
The wise King Varuna hath made in heaven that Golden Swing to cover it with glory.
6 Like Varuna from heaven he sinks in Sindhu, like a white-shining spark, a strong wild creature.
Ruling in depths and meting out the region, great saving power hath he, this world's Controller.
7 Before this Varuna may we be sinless him who shows mercy even to the sinner-
While we are keeping Aditi's ordinances. Preserve us evermore, ye Gods, with blessings.

## [07-088] HYMN LXXXVIII. Varuna.

1. PRESENT to Varuna thine hymn, Vasistha, bright, most delightful to the Bounteous Giver,
Who bringeth on to us the Bull, the lofty, the Holy, laden with a thousand treasures.
2 And now, as I am come before his presence, I take the face of Varuna for Agni's.
So might he bring-Lord also of the darkness-the light in heaven that I may see its beauty!
3 When Varuna and I embark together and urge our boat into the midst of ocean,
We, when we ride o'er ridges of the waters, will swing within that swing and there be happy.
4 Varuna placed Vasistha in the vessel, and deftly with his niight made him a Rsi.
When days shone bright the Sage made him a singer, while the heavens broadened and the Dawns
were lengthened.
5 What hath become of those our ancient friendships, when without enmity we walked together?
I, Varuna, thou glorious Lord, have entered thy lofty home, thine house with thousand portals.
6 If he, thy true ally, hath sinned against thee, still, Varuna, he is the friend thou lovedst.

Let us not, Living One, as sinners I know thee: give shelter, as a Sage, to him who lauds thee.

7 While we abide in these fixed habitations, and from the lap of Aditi win favour,

May Varuna untie the bond that binds us. Preserve us evermore, ye Gods, with blessings.

### [07-089] HYMN LXXXIX Varuna.

1. LET me not yet, King Varuna, enter into the house of clay: Have mercy, spare me, Mighty Lord.

2 When, Thunderer! I move along tremulous like a wind-blown skin,

Have mercy, spare me, Mighty Lord.

3 O Bright and Powerful God, through want of strength I erred and went astray

Have mercy, spare me, Mighty Lord.

4 Thirst found thy worshipper though he stood in the midst of water-fijods:

Have mercy, spare me, Mighty Lord.

5 O Varuna, whatever the offence may be which we as men commit against the heavenly host,

When through our want of thought we violate thy laws, punish us not, O God, for that iniquity.

### [07-090] HYMN XC. Vayu.

1. To you pure juice, rich in meath, are offered by priest: through longing for the Pair of Heroes.

Drive, Vayu, bring thine harnessed horses hither: drink the pressed Soma till it make thee joyful.

2 Whoso to thee, the Mighty, brings oblation, pure Soma unto thee, pure-drinking Vayu,

That man thou makest famous among mortals: to him strong sons are born in quick succession.

3 The God whom both these worlds brought forth for riches, whom heavenly Dhisana for our wealth

appointeth,

His team of harnessed horses waits on Vayu, and, foremost, on the radiant Treasure-bearer.

4 The spotless Dawns with fair bright days have broken; they found the spacious light when they

were shining.

Eagerly they disclosed the stall of cattle: floods streamed for them as in the days aforetime.

5 These with their truthful spirit, shining brightly, move on provided with their natural insight.

Viands attend the car that beareth Heroes, your car, ye Sovran Pair, Indra and Vayu.

6 May these who give us heavenly light, these rulers, with gifts of kine and horses, gold and

treasures.

These princes, through full life, Indra and Vayu! o'ercome in battle with their steeds and heroes.

7 Like coursers seeking fame will we Vasisthas, O Indra-Vayu, with our fair laudations.

Exerting all our power call you to aid us. Preserve us evermore, ye Gods, with blessings.

### [07-091] HYMN XCI. Vayu.

1. WERE not in sooth, the Gods aforetime blameless, whose pleasure was increased by adoration?

For Vayu and for man in his affliction they caused the Morning to arise with Surya.

2 Guardians infallible, eager as envoys' preserve us safe through many months and autumns.

Addressed to you, our fair praise, Indra-Vayu, implores your favour and renewed well-being.

3 Wise, bright, arranger of his teams, he. seeketh men with rich food whose treasures are abundant.

They have arranged them of one mind with Vayu: the men have wrought all noble operations.

4 So far as native power and strength permit you, so far as men behold whose eyes have vision,

O ye pure-drinkers, drink with us pure Soma: sit on this sacred grass, Indra and Vayu.

5 Driving down teams that bear the lovely Heroes, hitherward, Indra-Vayu, come together.

To you this prime of savoury juice is offered: here loose your horses and be friendly-minded.

6 Your hundred and your thousand teams, O Indra and Vayu, all-munificent, which attend you,

With these most gracious-minded come ye hither, and drink, O Heroes of the meath we offer.

7 Like coursers seeking fame will we Vasisthas, O Indra-Vayu, with our fair laudations,

Exerting all our powe-,, call you to aid us. Preserve us evermore, ye Gods, with blessings.

### [07-092] HYMN XCII. Vayu

1. O VAYU, drinker of the pure, be near us: a thousand teams are thine, Allbounteous Giver.

To thee the rapture-bringing juice is offered, whose first draught, God, thou takest as thy portion.

2 Prompt at the holy rites forth came the presser with Soma-draughts for Indra and for Vayu,

When ministering priests with strong devotion bring to you Twain the first taste of the Soma.

3 The teams wherewith thou seekest him who offers, within his home, O Viyu, to direct him,

Therewith send wealth: to us with full enjoyment, a hero son and gifts of kine and horses.

4 Near to the Gods and making Indra joyful, devout and ofFering precious gifts to Vayu,

Allied with princes, smiting down the hostile, may we with heroes conquer foes in battle.

5 With thy yoked teams in hundreds and in thousands come to our sacrifice and solemn worship.

Come, Vayu, make thee glad at this libation. Preserve us evermore, ye Gods, with blessings.

### [07-093] HYMN XCIII. Indra-Agni.

1. SLAYERS of enemies, Indra and Agni, accept this day our new-born pure laudation.

Again, again I call you prompt to listen, best to give quickly strength to him who craves it.

2 For ye were strong to gain, exceeding mighty, growing together, waxing in your vigour.

Lords of the pasture filled with ample riches, bestow upon us strength both fresh and lasting.

3 Yea when the strong have entered our assembly, and singers seeking with their hymns your favour,

They are like steeds who come into the race-course, those men who call aloud on Indra-Agni.

4 The singer, seeking with his hymns your favour, begs splendid riches of their first possessor.

Further us with new bounties, Indra-Agni, armed with strong thunder, slayers of the foeman.

5 When two great hosts, arrayed against each other, meet clothed with brightness, in the fierce encounter

Stand ye beside the godly, smite the godless; and still assist the men who press the Soma.

6 To this our Soma-pressing, Indra-Agni, come ye prepared to show your loving-kindness,

For not at any time have ye despised us. So may I draw you with all strengthenings hither.

7 So Agni, kindled mid this adoration, invite thou Mitra, Varuna, and Indra.

Forgive whatever sin we have committed may Aryaman and Aditi remove it.

8 While we accelerate these our sacrifices, may we win strength from both of you, O Agni:

Ne'er may the Maruts, Indra, Visnu slight us. Preserve us evermore, ye Gods, with blessings.

## [07-094] HYMN XCIV. Indra-Agni.

1. As rain from out the cloud, for you, Indra and Agni, from my soul

This noblest praise hath been produced.

2 Do ye, O Indra-Agni, hear the singer's call: accept his songs.

Ye Rulers, grant his heart's desire.

3 Give us not up to poverty, ye Heroes, Indra-Agni, nor

To slander and reproach of men.

4 To Indra and to Agni we bring reverence, high and holy hymn,

And, craving help, softwords with prayer.

5 For all these holy singers here implore these Twain to succour them,

And priests that they may win them strength.

6 Eager to laudyou, we with songs invoke you, bearing sacred food,

Fain for success in sacrifice.

7 Indra and Agni, come to us with favour, ye who conquer men:

Let not the wicked master us.

8 At no time let the injurious blow of hostile mortal fall on us:

O Indra-Agni, shelter us.

9 Whatever wealth we crave of you, in gold, in cattle, or in steeds,

That, Indra-Agni, let us gain;

10 When heroes prompt in worship call Indra and Agni, Lords of steeds,

Beside the Soma juice effused.

11 Call hither with the song and lauds those who best slay the foemen, those

Who take delight in hymns of praise.

12 Slay ye the wicked man whose thought is evil of the demon kind.

Slay him who stays the waters, slay the Serpent with your deadly dart.

## [07-095] HYMN XCV. Sarasvati.

1. THIS stream Sarasvati with fostering current comes forth, our sure defence, our fort of iron.

As on a car, the flood flows on, surpassing in majesty and might all other waters.

2 Pure in her course from mountains to the ocean, alone of streams Sarasvati hath listened.

Thinking of wealth and the great world of creatures, she poured for Nahusa her milk and fatness.

3 Friendly to man he grew among the women, a strong young Steer amid the Holy Ladies.

He gives the fleet steed to our wealthy princes, and decks their bodies for success in battle.

4 May this Sarasvati be pleased and listen at this our sacrifice, auspicious Lady,

When we with reverence, on our knees, implore her close-knit to wealth, most kind to those she loveth.

5 These offerings have ye made with adoration: say this, Sarasvati, and accept our praises;

And, placing us under thy dear protection, may we approach thee, as a tree, for shelter.

6 For thee, O Blest Sarasvati, Vasistha hath here unbarred the doors d sacred Order.

Wax, Bright One, and give strength to him who lauds thee.

Preserve us evermore, ye Gods, with blessings.

## [07-096] HYMN XCVI. Sarasvati.

1. I SING a lofty song, for she is mightiest, most divine of Streams.

Sarasvati will I exalt with hymns and lauds, and, O Vasistha, Heaven and Earth.

2 When in the fulness of their strength the Purus dwell, Beauteous One, on thy two grassy banks,

Favour us thou who hast the Maruts for thy friends: stir up the bounty of our chiefs.

3 So may Sarasvati auspicious send good luck; she, rich in spoil, is never niggardly in thought,

When praised in jamadagni's way and lauded as Vasistha lauds.

4 We call upon Sarasvan, as unmarried men who long for wives,

As liberal men who yearn for sons.

5 Be thou our kind protector, O Sarasvan, with those waves of thine

Laden with sweets and dropping oil.

6 May we enjoy Sarasvan's breast, all-beautiful, that swells with streams,

May we gain food and progeny.

## [07-097] HYMN XCVIL Brhaspati.

1. WHERE Heaven and Earth combine in men's assembly, and ttose who love the Gods delight in worship,

Where the libations are effused for Indra, may he come first to drink and make him stronger.

2 We crave the heavenly grace of Gods to guard us-so may Brhaspati, O friends, exalt us-

That he, the Bounteous God, may find us sintess, who giveth from a distance like a father.

3 That Brahmanaspati, most High and Gracious, I glorify with offerings and with homage.

May the great song of praise divine, reach Indra who is the King of prayer the Gods' creation.

4 May that Brhaspati who brings all blessings, most dearly loved, be seated by our altar.

Heroes and wealth we crave; may he bestow them, and bear us safe beyond the men who vex us.

5 To us these Deathless Ones, erst born, have granted this laud of ours which gives the Immortal pleasure.

Let us invoke Brhaspati, the foeless, the clear-voiced God, the Holy One of households

6 Him, this Brhaspati, his red-hued horses, drawing together, full of strength, bring hither.

Robed in red colour like the cloud, they carry the Lord of Might whose friendship gives a dwelling.

7 For he is pure, with hundred wings, refulgent, with sword of gold, impetuous, winning sunlight.

Sublime Brhaspati, easy of access granteth his friends most bountiful refreshment.

8 Both Heaven and Earth, divine, the Deity's Parents, have made Brhaspati increase in grandeur.

Glorify him, O friends, who merits glory: may he give prayer fair way and easy passage.

9 This, Brahmanaspati, is your laudation prayer hath been made to thunderwielding Indra.

Favour our songs, wake up our thought and spirit: destroy the godless and our foemen's malice.

10 Ye Twain are Lords of wealth in earth and heaven, thou, O Brhaspati, and thou, O Indra.

Mean though he be, give wealth to him who lauds you. Preserve us evermore, ye Gods, with
blessings.

**[07-098] HYMN XCVIII. Indra.**
1. PRIESTS, offer to the Lord of all the people the milked-out stalk of Soma, radiant-coloured.
No wild-bull knows his drinking-place like Indra who ever seeks him who hath pressed the Soma,
2 Thou dost desire to drink, each day that passes, the pleasant food which thou hast had aforetime,
O Indra, gratified in heart and spirit, drink eagerly the Soma set before thee.
3 Thou, newly-born, for strength didst drink the Soma; the Mother told thee of thy future greatness.
O Indra, thou hast filled mid-air's wide region, and given the Gods by battle room and freedom.
4 When thou hast urged the arrocrant to combat, proud in their strength of arm, we will subdue
them.
Or, Indra, when thou fightest girt by heroes, we in the glorious fray with thee will conquer.
5 I will declare the earliest deeds of Indra, and recent acts which Maghavan hath accomplished.
When he had conquered godless wiles and magic, Soma became his own entire possession.
6 Thine is this world of flocks and herds around thee, which with the eye of Surya thou beholdest.
Thou, Indra, art alone the Lord of cattle; may we enjoy the treasure which thou givest.
7 Ye Twain are Lords of wealth in earth and heaven, thou, O Brhaspati, and thou, O Indra.
Mean though he be, give wealth to him who lauds you. Preserve us evermore, ye Gods, with
blessings.

**[07-099] HYMN XCIX. Visnu.**
1. MEN come not nigh thy majesty who growest beyond all bound and measure with thy body.
Both thy two regions of the earth, O Visnu, we know: thou God, knowest the highest also.
2 None who is born or being born, God Visnu, hath reached the utmost limit of thy grandeur.
The vast high vault of heaven hast thou supported, and fixed earth's eastern pinnacle securely.
3 Rich in sweet food be ye, and rich in milch-kine, with fertile pastures, fain to do men service.
Both these worlds, Visnu, hast thou stayed asunder, and firmly fixed the earth with pegs around it.
4 Ye have made spacious room for sacrificing by generating Surya, Dawn, and Agni.
O Heroes, ye have conquered in your battles even the bull-jawed Dasa's wiles and magic.
5 Ye have destroyed, thou, Indra, and thou Visnu, Sambara's nine-and-ninety fenced castles.
Ye Twain smote down a hundred times a thousand resistless heroes of the royal Varcin.
6 This is the lofty hymn of praise, exalting the Lords of Mighty Stride, the strong and lofty.
I laud you in the solemn synods, Visnu: pour ye food on us in our camps, O Indra.
7 O Visnu, unto thee my lips cry Vasat! Let this mine offering, Sipivista, please thee.
May these my songs of eulogy exalt thee. Preserve us evermore, ye Gods, with blessings.

**[07-100] HYMN C. Visnu.**

1 NE'ER doth the man repent, who, seeking profit, bringeth his gift to the far-striding Visnu.
He who adoreth him with all his spirit winneth himself so great a benefactor.
2 Thou, Visnu, constant in thy courses, gavest good-will to all men, and a hymn that lasteth,
That thou mightst movc us to abundant comfort of very splendid wealth with store of horses.
3 Three times strode forth this God in all his grandeur over this earth bright with a hundred
splendours.
Foremost be Visnu, stronger than the strongest: for glorious is his name who lives for ever.
4 Over this earth with mighty step strode Visnu, ready to give it for a home to Manu.
In him the humble people trust for safety: he, nobly born, hath made them spacious dwellings.
5 To-day I laud this name, O gipivista, I, skilled in rules, the name of thee the Noble.
Yea, I the poor and weak praise thee the Mighty who dwellest in the realm beyond this region.
6 What was there to be blamed in thee, O Visnu, when thou declaredst, I am Sipivista?
Hide not this form from us, nor keep it secret, since thou didst wear another shape in battle.
7 O Visnu, unto thee my lips cry Vasat! Let this mine offering, Sipivista, please thee.
May these my songs of eulogy exalt thee. Preserve us evermore, ye Gods, with blessings.

**[07-101] HYMN CI. Parjanya.**
1 SPEAK forth three words, the words which light precedeth, which milk this udder that produceth
nectar.
Quickly made manifest, the Bull hath bellowed, engendering the germ of plants, the Infant.
2 Giver of growth to plants, the God who ruleth over the waters and all moving creatures,
Vouchsafe us triple shelter for our refuge, and threefold light to succour and befriend us.
3 Now he is sterile, now begetteth offspring, even as he willeth doth he change his figure.
The Father's genial flow bedews the Mother; therewith the Sire, therewith the son is nourished.
4 In him all living creatures have their being, and the three heavens with triplyflowing waters.
Three reservoirs that sprinkle down their treasure shed their sweet streams around him with a
murmur.
5 May this my song to Sovran Lord Parjanya come near unto his heart and give him pleasure.
May we obtain the showers that bring enjoyment, and God-protected plants with goodly fruitage.
6 He is the Bull of all, and their impregner lie holds the life of all things fixed and moving.
May this rite save me till my hundredth autumn. Preserve us evermore, ye Gods, with blessings.

**[07-102] HYMN CII Parjanya.**
1 SING forth and laud Parjanya, son of Heaven, who sends the gift of rain
May he provide our pasturage.
2 Parjanya is the God who forms in kine, in mares, in plants of earth,
And womankind, the germ of life.
3 Offer and pour into his mouth oblation rich in savoury juice:
May he for ever give us food.

## [07-103] HYMN CIII. Frogs.

1. THEY who lay quiet for a year, the Brahmans who fulfil their vows,
The Frogs have lifted up their voice, the voice Parjanya hath inspired.
2 What time on these, as on a dry skin lying in the pool's bed, the floods of heaven descended,
The music of the Frogs comes forth in concert like the cows lowing with their calves beside them.
3 When at the coming of the Rains the water has poured upon them as they yearned and thirsted,
One seeks another as he talks and greets him with cries of pleasure as a son his father.
4 Each of these twain receives the other kindly, while they are revelling in the flow of waters,
When the Frog moistened by the rain springs forward, and Green and Spotty both combine their
voices.
5 When one of these repeats the other's language, as he who learns the lesson of the teacher,
Your every limb seems to be growing larger as ye converse with eloquence on the waters.
6 Onc is Cow-bellow and Goat-bleat the other, one Frog is Green and one of them is Spotty.
They bear one common name, and yet they vary, and, talking, modulate the voice diversely.
7 As Brahmans, sitting round the brimful vessel, talk at the Soma-rite of Atiratra,
So, Frogs, ye gather round the pool to honour this day of all the year, the first of Rain-time.
8 These Brahmans with the Soma juice, performing their year-long rite, have lifted up their voices;
And these Adhvaryus, sweating with their kettles, come forth and show themselves, and none are
hidden.
9 They keep the twelve month's God-appointed order, and never do the men neglect the season.
Soon as the Rain-time in the year returneth, these who were heated kettles gain their freedom.
10 Cow-bellow and Goat-bleat have granted riches, and Green and Spotty have vouchsafed us
treasure.
The Frogs who give us cows in hundreds lengthen our lives in this most fertilizing season.

## [07-104] HYMN CIV. Indra-Soma.

1. INDRA and Soma, burn, destroy the demon foe, send downward, O ye Bulls, those who add gloom
to gloom.
Annihilate the fools, slay them and burn them up: chase them away from us, pierce the voracious
ones.
2 Indra and Soma, let sin round the wicked boil like as a caldron set amid the flames of fire.
Against the foe of prayer, devourer of raw flesh, the vile fiend fierce of eye, keep ye perpetual hate.
3 Indra and Soma, plunge the wicked in the depth, yea, cast them into darkness that hath no support,
So that not one of them may ever thence return: so may your wrathful might prevail and conquer
them.
4 Indra and Soma, hurl your deadly crushing bolt down on the wicked fiend from heaven and from the earth.
Yea, forge out of the mountains your celestial dart wherewith ye burn to death the waxing demon
race.

5 Indra and Soma, cast ye downward out of heaven your deadly darts of stone burning with fiery
flame,
Eternal, scorching darts; plunge the voracious ones within the depth, and let them sink without a
sound.
6 Indra and Soma, let this hymn control you both, even as the girth encompasses two vigorous
steeds-
The song of praise which I with wisdom offer you: do ye, as Lords of men, animate these my prayers.
7 In your impetuous manner think ye both thereon: destroy these evil beings, slay the treacherous
fiends.
Indra and Soma, let the wicked have no bliss who evermore assails us with malignity.
8 Whoso accuses me with words of falsehood when I pursue my way with guileless spirit,
May he, the speaker of untruth, be, Indra, like water which the hollowed hand compresses.
9 Those who destroy, as is their wont, the simple, and with their evil natures harm the righteous,
May Soma give them over to the serpent, or to the lap of Nirrti consign them.
10 The fiend, O Agni, who designs to injure the essence of our food, kine, steeds, or bodies,
May he, the adversary, thief, and robber, sink to destruction, both himself and offspring.
11 May he be swept away, himself and children: may all the three earths press him down beneath
them.
May his fair glory, O ye Gods, be blighted, who in the day or night would fain destroy us.
12 The prudent finds it easy to distinguish the true and false: their words oppose each other.
Of these two that which is the true and honest, Soma protects, and brings the false to nothing.
13 Never doth Soma aid and guide the wicked or him who falsely claims the Warrior's title.
He slays the fiend and him who speaks untruly: both lie entangled in the noose of Indra.
14 As if I worshipped deities of falsehood, or thought vain thoughts about the Gods, O Agni.
Why art thou angry with us, Jatavedas? Destruction fall on those who lie against thee!
15 So may I die this day if I have harassed any man's life or if I be a demon.
Yea, may he lose all his ten sons together who with false tongue hath called me Yatudhana.
16 May Indra slay him with a mi weapon, and let the vilest ofghty all creatures perish,
The fiend who says that he is pure, who calls me a demon though devoid of demon nature.
17 She too who wanders like an owl at night-time, hiding her body in her guile and malice,
May she fall downward into endless caverns. May press-stones with loud ring destroy the demons.
18 Spread out, ye Maruts, search among the people: seize ye and grind the Raksasas to pieces,
Who fly abroad, transformed to birds, at night-time, or sully and pollute our holy worship.
19 Hurl down from heaven thy bolt of stone, O Indra: sharpen it, Maghavan, made keen by Soma.
Forward, behind, and from above and under, smite down the demons with thy rocky weapon.
20 They fly, the demon dogs, and, bent on mischief, fain would they harm indomitable Indra.

Sakra makes sharp his weapon for the wicked: now, let him cast his bolt at fiendish wizards.

21 Indra hath ever been the fiends' destroyer who spoil oblations of the Gods' invokers:
Yea, Sakra, like an axe that spilts the timber, attacks and smashes them like earthen vessels.

22 Destroy the fiend shaped like an owl or owlet, destroy him in the form of dog or cuckoo.
Destroy him shaped as eagle or as vulture as with a stone, O Indra, crush the demon.

23 Let not the fiend of witchcraft-workers reach us: may Dawn drive off the couples of Kimidins.
Earth keep us safe from earthly woe and trouble: from grief that comes from heaven mid-air preserve
us.

24 Slay the male demon, Indra! slay the female, joying and triumphing in arts of magic.
Let the fools' gods with bent necks fall and perish, and see no more the Sun when he arises.

25 Look each one hither, look around Indra and Soma, watch ye well.
Cast forth your weapon at the fiends against the sorcerers hurt your bolt.


# BOOK EIGHT

### [08-001] HYMN I. Indra.

1. GLORIFY naught besides, O friends; so shall no sorrow trouble you.
Praise only mighty Indra when the juice is shed, and say your lauds repeatedly:

2 Even him, eternal, like a bull who rushes down, men's Conqueror, bounteous like a cow;
Him who is cause of both, of enmity and peace, to both sides most munificent.

3 Although these men in sundry ways invoke thee to obtain thine aid,
Be this our prayer, addressed, O Indra, unto thee, thine exaltation every day.

4 Those skilled in song, O Maghavan among these men o'ercome with might the foeman's songs.
Come hither, bring us strength in many a varied form most near that it may succour us.

5 O Caster of the Stone, I would not sell thee for a mighty price,
Not for a thousand, Thunderer! nor ten thousand, nor a hundred, Lord of countless wealth!

6 O Indra, thou art more to me than sire or niggard brother is.
Thou and my mother, O Good Lord, appear alike, to give me wealth abundantly.

7 Where art thou? Whither art thou gone? For many a place attracts thy mind.
Haste, Warrior, Fort-destroyer, Lord of battle's din, haste, holy songs have sounded forth.

8 Sing out the psalm to him who breaks down castles for his faithful friend,
Verses to bring the Thunderer to destroy the forts and sit on Kanva's sacred grass.

9 The Horses which are thine in tens, in hundreds, yea, in thousands thine,
Even those vigorous Steeds, fleet-footed in the course, with those come quickly near to us.

10 This day I call Sabardugiha who animates the holy song,
Indra the richly-yielding Milch-cow who provides unfailing food in ample stream.

11 When Sura wounded Etasa, with Vata's rolling winged car.

Indra bore Kutsa Arjuneya off, and mocked Gandharva. the unconquered One.

12 He without ligature, before making incision in the neck,
Closed up the wound again, most wealthy Maghavan, who maketh whole the injured part.

13 May we be never cast aside, and strangers, as it were, to thee.
We, Thunder-wielding Indra, count ourselves as trees rejected and unfit to bum.

14 O Vrtra-slayer, we were thought slow and unready for the fray.
Yet once in thy great bounty may we have delight, O Hero, after praising thee.

15 If he will listen to my laud, then may out Soma-drops that flow
Rapidly through the strainer gladden Indra, drops due to the Tugryas' Strengthener.

16 Come now unto the common laud of thee and of thy faithful friend.
So may our wealthy nobles' praise give joy to thee. Fain would I sing thine eulogy.

17 Press out the Soma with the stones, and in the waters wash it clean.
The men investing it with raiment made of milk shall milk it forth from out the stems.

18 Whether thou come from earth or from the lustre of the lofty heaven,
Wax stronger in thy body through my song of praise: fill full all creatures, O most Wise.

19 For India press the Soma out, most gladdening and most excellent.
May Sakra make it swell sent forth with every prayer and asking, as it were, for strength.

20 Let me not, still beseeching thee with earnest song at Soma rites,
Anger thee like soma wild beast. Who would not beseech him who hath power to grant his prayer?

21 The draught made swift with rapturous joy, effectual with its mighty strength,
All-conquering, distilling transport, let him drink: for he in ecstasy gives us gifts.

22 Where bliss is not, may he, All-praised, God whom the pious glorify,
Bestow great wealth upon the mortal worshipper who sheds the juice and praises him.

23 Come, Indra, and rejoice thyself, O God, in manifold affluence.
Thou fillest like a lake thy vast capacious bulk with Soma and with draughts besides.

24 A thousand and a hundred Steeds are harnessed to thy golden car.
So may the long-maned Bays, yoked by devotion, bring Indra to drink the Soma juice.

25 Yoked to thy chariot wrought of gold, may thy two Bays with peacock tails,
Convey thee hither, Steeds with their white backs, to quaff sweet juice that makes us eloquent.

26 So drink, thou Lover of the Song, as the first drinker, of this juice.
This the outpouring of the savoury sap prepared is good and meet to gladden thee.

27 He who alone by wondrous deed is Mighty, Strong by holy works,
May he come, fair of cheek; may he not stay afar, but come and turn not from our call.

28 Susna's quick moving castle thou hast crushed to pieces with thy bolts.
Thou, Indra, from of old, hast followed after light, since we have had thee to invoke.

29 My praises when the Sun hath risen, my praises at the time of noon,

My praises at the coming of the gloom of night, O Vasu, have gone forth to thee.

30 Praise yea, praise him. Of princes these are the most liberal of their gifts,
These, Paramajya, Ninditasva, Prapathi, most bounteous, O Medhyatithi.

31 When to the car, by faith, I yoked the horses longing for the way-
For skilled is Yadu's son in dealing precious wealth, he who is rich in herds of kine.

32 May he who gave me two brown steeds together with their cloths of gold,
May he, Asanga's son Svanadratha, obtain all joy and high felicities.

33 Playoga's son Asanga, by ten thousand, O Agni, hath surpassed the rest in giving.
For me ten bright-hued oxen have come forward like lotus-stalks from out a lake upstanding.

34 What time her husband's perfect restoration to his lost strength and manhood was apparent,
His consort Sasvati with joy addressed him, Now art thou well, my lord, and shalt be happy.

## [08-002] HYMN II. Indra.

1. HERE is the Soma juice expressed; O Vasu, drink till thou art full:
Undaunted God, we give it thee.

2 Washed by the men, pressed out with stones, strained through the filter made of wool,
'Tis like a courser bathed in stream.

3 This juice have we made sweet for thee like barley, blending it with milk.
Indra, I call thee to our feast.

4 Beloved of all, Indra alone drinks up the flowing Soma juice
Among the Gods andmortal men.

5 The Friend, whom not the brilliant-hued, the badly-mixt or bitter draught,
Repels, the far-extending God;

6 While other men than we with milk chase him as hunters chase a deer,
And with their kine inveigle him.

7 For him, for Indra, for the God, be pressed three draughts of Soma juice
In the juice-drinker's own abode.

8 Three reservoirs exude their drops, filled are three beakers to the brim,
All for one offering to the God.

9 Pure art thou, set in many a place, and blended in the midst with milk
And curd, to cheer the Hero best.

10 Here, Indra, are thy Soma-draughts pressed out by us, the strong, the pure:
They crave admixture of the milk.

11 O Indra, pour in milk, prepare the cake, and mix the Soma-draught.
I hear them say that thou art rich.

12 Quaffed juices fight within the breast. The drunken praise not by their wine,
The naked praise not when it rains.

13 Rich be the praiser of one rich, munificent and famed like thee:
High rank be his, O Lord of Bays.

14 Foe of the man who adds no milk, he heeds not any chanted hymn
Or holy psalm that may he sung.

15 Give us not, Indra, as a prey unto the scornful or the proud:
Help, Mighty One, with power and might.

16 This, even this, O Indra, we implore. as thy devoted friends,

The Kanvas praise thee with their hymns.

17 Naught else, O Thunderer, have I praised in the skilled singer's eulogy:
On thy land only have I thought.

18 The Gods seek him who presses out the Soma; they desire not sleep
They punish sloth unwcariedly.

19 Come hither swift with gifts of wealth - be not thou angry with us-like
A great man with a youthful bride.

20 Let him not, wrathful with us, spend the evening far from us to-day,
Like some unpleasant son-in-law.

21 For well we know this Hero's love, most liberal of the boons he gives,
His plans whom the three worlds display.

22 Pour forth the gift which Kanvas bring, for none more glorious do we know
Than the Strong Lord with countless aids.

23 O presser, offer Soma first to Indra, Hero, Sakra, him
The Friend of man, that he may drink;

24 Who, in untroubled ways, is best provider, for his worshippers.
Of strength in horses and in kine.

25 Pressers, for him blend Soma juice, each draught most excellent, for him
The Brave, the Hero, for his joy.

26 The Vrtra-slayer drinks the juice. May he who gives a hundred aids
Approach, nor stay afar from us.

27 May the strong Bay Steeds, yoked by prayer, bring hither unto us our Friend,
Lover of Song, renowned by songs.

28 Sweet are the Soma juices, come! Blent are the Soma juices, come!
Rsi-like, mighty, fair of cheek, come hither quickly to the feast.

29 And lauds which strengthen thee for great bounty and valour, and exalt
Indra who doeth glorious deeds,

30 And songs to thee who lovest song, and all those hymns addressed to thee-
These evermore confirm thy might.

31 Thus he, sole doer of great deeds whose hand holds thunder, gives us strength,
He who hath never been subdued.

32 Vrtra he slays with his right hand, even Indra, great with mighty power,
And much-invoked in many a place.

33 He upon whom all men depend, all regions, all achievements, he
Takes pleasure in our wealthy chiefs.

34 All this hath he accomplished, yea, Indra, most gloriously renowned,
Who gives our wealthy princes strength.

35 Who drives his chariot seeking spoil, from afar, to him he loves:
For swift is he to bring men wealth.

36 The Sage who, winning spoil with steeds, slays Vrtra, Hero with the men,
His servant's faithful succourer.

37 O Priyamedhas, worship with collected mind this Indra whom
The Soma hath full well inspired.

38 Ye Kanvas, sing the Mighty One, Lord of the Brave, who loves renown,
All-present, glorified by song.

39 Strong Friend, who, with no trace of feet, restores the cattle to the men,

Who rest their wish and hope on him.
40 Shaped as a Ram, Stone-hurler I once thou camest hither to the son
Of Kanva, wise Medhyatithi.
41 Vibhindu, thou hast helped this man, giving him thousands four times ten,
And afterward eight thousand more.
42 And these twain pouring streams of milk, creative, daughters of delight,
For wedlock sake I glorify.

## [08-003] HYMN III. Indra.

1. DRINK, Indra, of the savoury juice, and cheer thee with our milky draught.
Be, for our weal, our Friend and sharer of the feast, and let thy wisdom guard us well.
2 In thy kind grace and favour may we still be strong: expose us not to foe's attack.
With manifold assistance guard and succour us, and bring us to felicity.
3 May these my songs of praise exalt thee, Lord, who hast abundant wealth.
Men skilled in holy hymns, pure, with the hues of fire, have sung them with their lauds to thee.
4 He, with his might enhanced by Rsis thousandfold, hath like an ocean spread himself.
His majesty is praised as true at solemn rites, his power where holy singers rule.
5 Indra for worship of the Gods, Indra while sacrifice proceeds,
Indra, as worshippers in battle-shock, we call, Indra that we may win the spoil.
6 With might hath Indra spread out heaven and earth, with power hath Indra lighted up the Sun.
In Indra are all creatures closely held; in him meet the distilling Soma-drops.
7 Men with their lauds are urging thee, Indra, to drink the Soma first.
The Rbhus in accord have lifted up their voice, and Rudras sung thee as the first.
8 Indra increased his manly strength at sacrifice, in the wild rapture of this juice.
And living men to-day, even as of old, sing forth their praises to his majesty.
9 I crave of thee that hero strength, that thou mayst first regard this prayer,
Wherewith thou holpest Bhrgu and the Yatis and Praskanva when the prize was staked.
10 Wherewith thou sentest mighty waters to the sea, that, Indra, is thy manly strength.
For ever unattainable is this power of him to whom the worlds have cried aloud.
11 Help us, O Indra, when we pray to thee for wealth and hero might.
First help thou on to strength the man who strives to win, and aid our laud, O Ancient One.
12 Help for us, Indra, as thou holpest Paura once, this man's devotions bent on gain.
Help, as thou gavest Rugama and Syavaka and Svarnara and Krpa aid.
13 What newest of imploring prayers shall, then, the zealous mortal sing?
For have not they who laud his might, and Indra-power won for themselves the light of heaven?
14 When shall they keep the Law and praise thee mid the Gods?
Who counts as Rsi and as sage?
When ever wilt thou, Indra Maghavan, come nigh to presser's or to praiser's call?

15 These songs of ours exceeding sweet, these hymns of praise ascend to thee,
Like ever-conquering chariots that display their strength, gain wealth, and give unfailing aid.
16 The Bhrgus are like Suns, like Kanvas, and have gained all that their thoughts were bent upon.
The living men of Priyamedha's race have sung exalting Indra with their lauds.
17 Best slayer of the Vrtras, yoke thy Bay Steeds, Indra, from afar.
Come with the High Ones hither, Maghavan, to us, Mighty, to drink the Soma juice.
18 For these, the bards and singers, have cried out to thee with prayer, to gain the sacrifice.
As such, O Maghavan, Indra, who lovest song, even as a lover bear my call.
19 Thou from the lofty plains above, O Indra, hurledst Vrtra down.
Thou dravest forth the kine of guileful Mrgaya and Arbuda from the mountain's hold.
20 Bright were the flaming fires, the Sun gave forth his shine, and Soma, Indra's juice, shone clear.
Indra, thou blewest the great Dragon from the air -. men must regard that valorous deed.
21 The fairest courser of them all, who runneth on as 'twere to heaven.
Which Indra and the Maruts gave, and Pakasthaman Kaurayan.
22 To me hath Pakasthaman given, a ruddy horse, good at the pole,
Filling is girth and rousing wealth;
23 Compared with whom no other ten strong coursers, harnessed to the pole,
Bear Tugrya to his dwelling place.
24 Raiment is body, food is life, and healing ointment giveth strength.
As the free-handed giver of the ruddy steed, I have named Pakasthaman fourth.

## [08-004] HYMN IV. Indra.

1. THOUGH, Indra, thou art called by men eastward and westward, north and south,
Thou chiefly art with Anava and Turvasa, brave Champion I urged by men to Come.
2 Or, Indra, when with Ruma, Rusama, Syavaka, and Krpa thou rejoicest thee,
Still do the Kanvas, bringing praises, with their prayers, O Indra, draw thee hither: come.
3 Even as the wild-bull, when he thirsts, goes to the desert's watery pool,
Come hither quickly both at morning and at eve, and with the Kanvas drink thy fill.
4 May the drops gladden thee, rich Indra, and obtain bounty for him who pours the juice.
Soma pressed in the mortar didst thou take and drink, and hence hast won surpassing might.
5 With mightier strength he conquered strength, with energy he crushed their wrath.
O Indra, Strong in youth, all those who sought the fray bent and bowed down to thee like trees.
6 He who wins promise of thine aid goes girt as with a thousand mighty men of war.
He makes his son preeminent in hero might - he serves with reverential prayer.
7 With thee, the Mighty, for our Friend, we will riot fear or feel fatigue.
May we see Turvasa and Yadu: thy great deed, O Hero, must be glorified.

8 On his left hip the Hero hath reclined himself: the proffered feast offends him not.
The milk is blended with the honey of the bee: quickly come hither, haste, and drink.
9 Indra, thy friend is fair of form and rich in horses, cars, and kine.
He evermore hath food accompanied by wealth, and radiant joins the company.
10 Come like a thirsty antelope to the drinking-place: drink Soma to thy heart's desire.
Raining it down, O Maghavan, day after day, thou gainest thy surpassing might.
11 Priest, let the Soma juice flow forth, for Indra longs to drink thereof.
He even now hath yoked his vigorous Bay Steeds: the Vrtra-slayer hath come near.
12 The man with whom thou fillest thee with Soma deems himself a pious worshipper.
This thine appropriate food is here poured out for thee: come, hasten forward. drink of it,
13 Press out the Soma juice, ye priests, for Indra borne upon his car.
The pressing-stones speak loud of Indra, while they shed the juice which, offered, honours him.
14 To the brown juice may his dear vigorous Bay Steeds bring Indra, to our holy task.
Hither let thy Car-steeds who seek the sacrifice bring thee to our drink-offerings.
15 Pusan, the Lord of ample wealth, for firm alliance we elect.
May he with wisdom, Sakra! Looser! Much-invoked! aid us to riches and to seed.
16 Sharpen us like a razor in the barber's hands: send riches thou who settest free.
Easy to find with thee are treasures of the Dawn for mortal man whom thou dost speed.
17 Pusan, I long to win thy love, I long to praise thee, Radiant God.
Excellent Lord, 'tis strange tome, no wish have I to sing the psalm that Pajra sings.
18 My kine, O Radiant God, seek pasture where they will, my during wealth, Immortal One.
Be our protector, Pusan! be, most liberal Lord, propitious to our gathering strength.
19 Rich was the gift Kurunga gave, a hundred steeds at morning rites.
Among the gifts of Turvasas we thought of him, the opulent, the splendid King.
20 What by his morning songs Kanva, the powerful, hath, with the Priyamedhas, gained-
71 The herds of sixty thousand pure and spotless kine, have I, the Rsi, driven away.
21 The very trees were joyful at my coming: kine they obtained in plenty, steeds in plenty.

## [08-005] HYMN V. Asvins.

1. WHEN, even as she were present here, red Dawn hath shone from far away,
She spreadeth light on every side.
2 Like Heroes on your will-yoked car farshining, Wonder-Workers! ye
Attend, O Asvins, on the Dawn.
3 By you, O Lords of ample wealth our songs of praise have been observed:
As envoy have I brought the prayer.
4 Kanvas must praise the Asvins dear to many, making many glad,
Most rich, that they may succour us.

5 Most liberal, best at winning strength, inciters, Lords of splendour who
Visit the worshipper's abode.
6 So for devout Sudeva dew with fatness his unfailing mead,
And make it rich for sacrifice.
7 Hitherward running speedily with horses, as with rapid hawks,
Come, Asvins, to our song of praise
8 Wherewith the three wide distances, and all the lights that are in heaven.
Ye traverse, and three times of night.
9 O Finders of the Day, that we may win us food of kine and wealth,
Open the paths for us to tread.
10 O Asvins, bring us wealth in kine, in noble heroes, and in cars:
Bring us the strength that horses give.
11 Ye Lords of splendour, glorified, ye Wonder-Workers borne on paths
Of gold, drink sweets with Somajuice.
12 To us, ye Lords of ample wealth, and to our wealth chiefs extend
Wide shelter, ne'er to be assailed.
13 Come quickly downward to the prayer of people whom ye favour most:
Approach not unto other folk.
14 Ye Asvins whom our minds perceive, drink of this lovely gladdening draught,
The meath which we present to you.
15 Bring riches hither unto us in hundreds and in thousands, source
Of plenteous food, sustaining all.
16 Verily sages call on you, ye Heroes, in full many a place.
Moved by the priests, O Asvins, conic.
17 Men who have trimmed the sacred grass, bringing oblations and prepared,
O Asvins, are invoking you.
18 May this our hymn of praise to-day, most powerful to bring you, be,
O Asvins, nearest to your hearts.
19 The skin filled full of savoury meath, laid in the pathway of your car-
O Asvins, drink ye both therefrom.
20 For this, ye Lords of ample wealth, bring blessing for our herd, our kine,
Our progeny, and plenteous food.
21 Ye too unclose to us like doors the strengthening waters of the sky,
And rivers, ye who find the day.
22 When did the son of' Tugra serve you, Men? Abandoned in the sea,
That with winged steeds your car might fly.
23 Ye, O Nasatyas, ministered to Kanva with repeated aid,
When cast into the heated pit.
24 Come near with those most recent aids of yours which merit eulogy,
When I invoke you, Wealthy Gods.
25 As ye protected Kanva erst, Priyamedha and Upastuta,
Atri, Sinjara, Asvins Twain
26 And Amsu in decisive fight, Agastya in the fray for kine.
And, in his battles, Sobhari.
27 For so much bliss, or even more, O Asvins, Wealthy Gods, than this,
We pray white singing hymns to you.
28 Ascend your car with golden seat, O Asvins, and with reins of gold,
That reaches even to the sky.
29 Golden is its supporting shaft, the axle also is of gold,
And both the wheels are made of gold.

30 Thereon, ye Lords of ample wealth, come to us even from afar,
Come ye to this mine eulogy.

31 From far away ye come to us, Asvins, enjoying plenteous food
Of Dasas, O Immortal Ones.

32 With splendour, riches, and renown, O Asvins, hither come to us,
Nasatyas, shining brilliantly.

33 May dappled horses, steeds who fly with pinions, bring you hitherward
To people skilled in sacrifice.

34 The whcel delayeth not that car of yours accompanied by song,
That cometh with a store of food.

35 Borne on that chariot wrought of gold, with coursers very fleet of foot,
Come, O Nasatyas, swift as thought.

36 O Wealthy Gods, ye taste and find the brisk and watchful wild beast good.
Associate wealth with food for us.

37 As such, O Asvins, find for me my share of new-presented gifts,
As Kasu, Cedi's son, gave me a hundred head of buffaloes, and ten thousand kine.

38 He who hath given me for mine own ten Kings like gold to look upon.
At Caidya's feet are all the people round about, all those who think upon the shield.

39 No man, not any, goes upon the path on which the Cedis walk.
No other prince, no folk is held more liberal of gifts than they.

## [08-006] HYMN VI Indra

1. INDRA, great in his power and might, and like Parjanya rich in rain,
Is magnified by Vatsa's lauds.

2 When the priests, strengthening the Son of Holy Law, present their gifts,
Singers with Order's hymn of praiser.

3 Since Kanvas with their lauds have made Indra complete the sacrifice.
Words are their own appropriate arms.

4 Before his hot displeasure all the peoples, all the men, bow down,
As rivers bow them to the sea.

5 This power of his shone brightly forth when Indra brought together, like
A skin, the worlds of heaven and earth.

6 The fiercely-moving Vrtra's head he severed with his thunderbolt,
His mighty hundred-knotted bolt.

7 Here are-we sing them loudly forth-our thoughts among-the best of songs.
Even lightnings like the blaze of fire.

8 When bidden thoughts, spontaneously advancing, glow, and with the stream
Of sacrifice the Kanvas shine.

9 Indra, may we obtain that wealth in horses and in herds of cows,
And prayer that may be noticed first.

10 I from my Father have received deep knowledge of the Holy Law
I was born like unto the Sun.

11 After the lore of ancient time I make, like Kanva, beauteous songs,
And Indra's selfgains strength thereby.

12 Whatever Rsis have not praised thee, Indra, or have lauded thee,
By me exalted wax thou strong.

13 When his wrath thundered, when he rent Vrtra to pieces, limb by limb,
He sent the waters to the sea.

14 Against the Dasyu gusna thou, Indra, didst hurl thy during bolt:
Thou, Dread one, hast a hero's fame.

15 Neither the heavens nor firmaments nor regions of the earth contain
Indra, the Thunderer with his might.

16 O Indra him who lay at length staying thy copious waters thou,
In his own footsteps, smotest down

17 Thou hiddest deep in darkness itim, O Indra, who had set his grasp
On spacious heaven and earth conjoined.

18 Indra, whatever Yatis and Bhrgus have offered praise to thee,
Listen, thou Mighty, to my call.

19 Indra, these spotted cows yield thee their butter and the milky draught;
Aiders, thereby, of sacrifice;

20 Which, teeming, have received thee as a life-germ, Indra, with their mouth,
Like Surya who sustaineth all.

21 O Lord of Might, with hymns of praise the Kanvas have increased thy power,
The drops poured forth have strengthened thee.

22 Under thy guidance, Indra, mid thy praises, Lord of Thunder, shall
The sacrifice be soon performed.

23 Indra, disclose much food for us, like a stronghold with store of kine:
Give progeny and heroic strength.

24 And, Indra, grant us all that wealth of fleet steeds which shone bright of old
Among the tribes of Nahusas.

25 Hither thou seemest to attract heaven's fold which shines before our eyes,
When, Indra, thou art kind to us.

26 Yea, when thou puttest forth thy power, Indra, thou governest the folk.
Mighty, unlimited in strength.

27 The tribes who bring oblations call to thee, to thee to give them help,
With drops to thee who spreadest far.

28 There where the mountains downward slope, there by the meeting of the streams
The Sage was manifest with song.

29 Thence, marking, from his lofty place downward he looks upon the sea,
And thence with rapid stir he moves.

30 Then, verify, they see the light refulgent of primeval seed,
Kindled on yonder side of heaven.

31 Indra, the Kanvas all exalt thy wisdom and thy manly power,
And, Mightiest! thine heroic strength.

32 Accept this eulogy of mine, Indra, and guard me carefully:
Strengthen my thought and prosper it.

33 For thee, O Mighty, Thunder-armed, we singers through devotionhave
Fashioned the hymn that we may live.

34 To Indra have the Kanvas sung, like waters speeding down a slope:
The song is fain to go to him.

35 As rivers swell the ocean, so our hymns of praise make Indra strong,
Eternal, of resistless wrath.

36 Come with thy lovely Bay Steeds, come to us from regions far away
O Indra, drink this Soma juice.

37 Best slayer of Vrtras, men whose sacred grass is ready trimmed
Invoke thee for the gain of spoil.
38 The heavens and earth come after thee as the wheel follows Etasa:
To thee flow Sorna-drops effused.
39 Rejoice, O Indra, in the light, rejoice in Saryandyan, be Glad in the sacrificer's hymn.
40 Grown strong in heaven, the Thunder-armed hath bellowed, Vrtra-slayer, Bull,
Chief drinker of the Soma juice.
41 Thou art a Rsi born of old, sole Ruler over all by might:
Thou, Indra, guardest well our wealth.
42 May thy Bay Steeds with beauteous backs, a hundred, bring thee to the feast,
Bring thee to these our Soma-draughts.
43 The Kanvas with their hymns of praise have magnified this ancient thought
That swells with streams of meath and oil.
44 Mid mightiest Gods let mortal man choose Indra at the sacrifice,
Indra, whoe'er would win, for help.
45 Thy steeds, by Priyamedhas praised, shall bring thee, God whom all invoke,
Hither to drink the Somajuice.
46 A hundred thousand have I gained from Parsu, from Tirindira,
And presents of the Yadavas.
47 Ten thousand head of kine, and steeds three times a hundred they bestowed
On Pajra for the Sama-song.
48 Kakuha hath reached up to heaven, bestowing buffaloes yoked in fours,
And matched in fame the Yadavas.

## [08-007] HYMN VII. Maruts.

1. O MARUTS, when the sage hath poured the Trstup forth as food for you,
Ye shine amid the mountain-clouds.
2 When, Bright Ones, fain to show your might ye have determined on your course,
The mountain-clouds have bent them down.
3 Loud roaring with the winds the Sons of Prsni have upraised themselves:
They have poured out the streaming food.
4 The Maruts spread the mist abroad and make mountains rock and reel,
When with the winds they go their way
5 What time the rivers and the hills before your coming bowed them down,
So to sustain your mighty force.
6 We call on you for aid by night, on you for succour in the day,
On you while sacrifice proceeds.
7 These, verily, wondrous, red of hue, speed on their courses with a roar
Over the ridges of the sky.
8 With might they drop the loosened rein so that the Sun may run his course,
And spread themselves with beams of light.
9 Accept, ye Maruts, this my song, accept ye this mine hymn of praise,
Accept, Rbhuksans, this my call.
10 The dappled Cows have poured three lakes, meath for the Thunder-wielding God,
From the great cask, the watery cloud.
11 O Maruts, quickly come to us when, longing for felicity,
We call you hither from the sky.

12 For, Rudras and Rbhuksans, ye, Most Bountiful, are in the house,
Wise when the gladdening draught is drunk.
13 O Maruts, send us down from heaven riches distilling rapturous joy,
With plenteous food, sustaining all.
14 When, Bright Ones, hither from the hills ye have resolved to take your way,
Ye revel in the drops effused.
15 Man should solicit with his lauds happiness which belongs to them,
So great a band invincible.
16 They who like fiery sparks with showers of rain blow through the heaven and earth,
Milking the spring that never fails.
17 With chariots and tumultuous roar, with tempests and with hymns of praise
The Sons of Prsni hurry forth.
18 For wealth, we think of that whereby ye aided Yadu, Turvasa,
And KanVa who obtained the spoil.
19 May these our viands Bounteous Ones I that flow in streams like holy oil,
With Kanva's hymns, increase your might.
20 Where, Bounteous Lords for whom the grass is trimmed, are ye rejoicing now?
What Brahman is adoring you?
21 Is it not there where ye of old, supplied with sacred grass, for lauds
Inspired the strong in sacrifice?
22 They brought together both the worlds, the mighty waters, and the Sun,
And, joint by joint, the thunderbolt.
23 They sundered Vrtra limb from limb and split the gloomy mountain-clouds,
Performing a heroic deed.
24 They reinforced the power and strength of Trita as he fought, and helped
Indra in battle with the foe.
25 They deck themselves for glory, bright, celestial, lightning in their hands,
And helms of gold upon their heads.
26 When eagerly ye from far away came to the cavern of the Bull,
He bellowed in his fear like Heaven.
27 Borne by your golden-footed steeds, O Gods, come hither to receive
The sacrifice we offer you.
28 When the red leader draws along their spotted deer yoked to the car.
The Bright Ones come, and shed the rain.
29 Susoma, Saryakiavan, and Arjika full of homes, have they.
These Heroes, sought with downward car.
30 When, Maruts, ye come to him, the singer who invokes you thus,
With favours to your suppliant?
31 What now? where have ye still a friend since ye left Indra all alone?
Who counteth on your friendship now?
32 The Kanvas sing forth Agni's praise together with our Maruts' who
Wield thunder and wear swords of gold.
33 Hither for new felicity may I attract the Impetuous Ones,
The Heroes with their wondrous strength
34 Before them sink the very hills deerning themseives abysses: yea,
Even the mountains bend them down.
35 Steeds flying on their tortuous path through mid-air carry them, and give

The man who lauds them strength and life.
36 Agni was born the first of all, like Surya lovely with his light:
With lustre these have spread abroad.

## [08-008] HYMN VIII. Asvins.

1. WITH all the succours that are yours, O Asvins, hither come to us:
Wonderful, borne on paths of gold, drink ye the meath with Soma juice.
2 Come now, ye Asvins, on your car decked with a sun-bright canopy,
Bountiful, with your golden forms, Sages with depth of intellect.
3 Come hither from the Nahusas, come, drawn by pure hymns, from mid-air.
O Asvins, drink the savoury juice shed in the Kanvas' sacrifice.
4 Come to us hither from the heavens, come from mid-air, well-loved by us:
Here Kanva's son hath pressed for you the pleasant meath of Soma juice.
5 Come, Asvins, to give car to us, to drink the Soma, Asvins, come.
Hail, Strengtheners of the praise-song speed onward, ye Heroes, with your thoughts.
6 As, Heroes, in the olden time the Rsis called you to their aid,
So now, O Asvins, come to us, come near to this mine eulogy.
7 Even from the luminous sphere of heaven come to us, ye who find the light,
Carers for Vatsa, through our prayers and lauds, O yewho hearour call.
8 Do others more than we adore the Asvins with their hymns of praise?
The Rsi Vatsa, Kanva's son, hath magnified you with his songs.
9 The holy singer with his hymns hath called you, Asvins, hither-ward;
Best Vrtra-slayers, free from stain, as such bring us felicity.
10 What time, ye Lords of ample wealth, the Lady mounted on your car,
Then, O ye Asvins, ye attained all wishes that your hearts desired.
11 Come thence, O Asvins, on your car that hath a thousand ornaments:
Vatsa the sage, the sage's son, hath sung a song of sweets to you.
12 Cheerers of many, rich in goods, discoverers of opulence,
The Asvins, Riders through the sky, have welcomed this my song of praise.
13 O Asvins, grant us all rich gifts wherewith no man mav interfere.
Make us observe the stated times: give us not over to reproach.
14 Whether, Nasatyas, ye be nigh, or whether ye be far away,
Come thence, O Asvins, on your car that hath a thousand ornaments.
15 Vatsa the Rsi with his songs, Nasatyas, hath exalted you:
Grant him rich food distilling oil, graced with a thousand ornaments.
16 Bestow on him, O Asvins, food that strengthens, and that drops with oil,
On him who praises you for bliss, and, Lords of bounty, prays for wealth.
17 Come to us, ye who slay the foe, Lords of rich treasure, to this hymn.
O Heroes, give us high renown and these good things of earth for help.
18 The Priyamedhas have invoked you with all succours that are yours,
You, Asvins, Lords of solemn rites, with calls entreating you to come.
19 Come to us, Asvins, ye Who bring felicity, auspicious Ones,

To Vatsa who with prayer and hymn, lovers of song, hath honoured you.
20 Aid us, O Heroes, for those hymns for which ye helped GoSarya erst,
Gave Vasa, Dasavraja aid, and Kanva and Medhatithi:
21 And favoured Trasadasyu, ye Heroes, in spoil-deciding fray:
For these, O Asvins, graciously assist us in acquiring strength.
22 O Asvins, may pure hymns of ours, and songs and praises, honour you:
Best slayers everywhere of foes, as such we fondly yearn for you.
23 Three places of the Asvins, erst concealed, are made apparent now.
Both Sages, with the flight of Law come hither unto those who live.

## [08-009] HYMN IX. Asvins.

1. To help and favour Vatsa now, O Asvins, come ye hitherward.
Bestow on him a dwelling spacious and secure, and keep malignities away.
2 All manliness that is in heaven, with the Five Tribes, or in mid-air,
Bestow, ye Asvins, upon us.
3 Remember Kanva first of all among the singers, Asvins, who
Have thought upon your wondrous deeds.
4 Asvins, for you with song of praise this hot oblation is effused,
This your sweet Soma juice, ye Lords of ample wealth, through which ye think upon the foe.
5 Whatever ye have done in floods, in the tree, Wonder-Workers, and in growing plants,
Therewith, O Asvins, succour me.
6 What force, Nasatyas, ye exert, whatever, Gods, ye tend and heal,
This your own Vatsa gains not by his hymns alone: ye visit him who offers gifts.
7 Now hath the Rsi splendidly thought out the Asvins' hymn of praise.
Let the Atharvan pour the warm oblation forth, and Soma very rich in sweets.
8 Ye Asvins, now ascend your car that lightly rolls upon its way.
May these my praises make you speed hitherward like a cloud of heaven.
9 When, O Nasatyas, we this day make you speed hither with our hymns,
Or, Asvins, with our songs of praise, remember Kanya specially.
10 As erst Kaksivan and the Rsi Vyasva, as erst Dirghatamas invoked your presence,
Or, in the sacrificial chambers, Vainya Prthi, so be ye mindful of us here, O Asvins.
11 Come as home-guardians, saving us from foemen, guarding our living creatures and our bodies,
Come to the house to give us seed and offspring,
12 Whether with Indra ye be faring, Asvins, or resting in one dwelling-place with Vayu,
In concord with the Rbhus or Adityas, or standing still in Visnu's striding-places.
13 When I, O Asvins, call on you to-day that I may gather strength,
Or as all-conquering might in war, be that the Asvins' noblest grace.
14 Now come, ye Asvins, hitherward: here are oblations set for you;
These Soma-draughts to aid Yadu and
Turvasa, these offered you mid Kaniva's Sons.
15 Whatever healing balm is yours, Nisatyas, near or far away,
Therewith, great Sages, grant a home to Vatsa and to Vimada.
16 Together with the Goddess, with the Asvins' Speech have I awoke.

Thou, Goddess, hast disclosed the hymn, and holy gift from mortal men.

17 Awake the Asvins, Goddess Dawn! Up Mighty Lady of sweet strains!

Rise, straightway, priest of sacrifice! High glory to the gladdening draught!

18 Thou, Dawn, approaching with thy light shinest together with the Sun,

And to this man-protecting home the chariot ofthe Asvins comes.

19 When yellow stalks give forth the juice, as cows from udders pour their milk,

And voices sound the song of praise, the Asvins' worshippers show first.

20 Forward for glory and for strength, protection that shall conquer men,

And power and skill, most sapient Ones!

21 When Asvins, worthy of our lauds, ye seat you in the father's house.

With wisdom or the bliss ye bring.

## [08-010] HYMN X. Asvins.

1. WHETHER ye travel far away or dwell in yonder light of heaven,

Or in a mansion that is built above the sea, come thence, ye Asvins, hitherward.

2 Or if for Manu.ye prepared the sacrifice, remember also Kanva's son.

I call Brhaspati, Indra, Visnu, all the gods, the Asvins borne by rapid steeds.

3 Those Asvins I invoke who work marvels, brought hither to receive,

With whom our friendship is most famed, and kinship passing that of Gods.

4 On whom the solemn rites depend, whose worshippers rise without the Sun:

These who foreknow the holy work of sacrifice, and by their Godhead drink the sweets of Soma juice.

5 Whether ye, Lords of ample wealth, now linger in the cast or west,

With Druhyu, or with Anu, Yadu, Turvaga, I call you hither; come to me.

6 Lords of great riches, whether through the firmament ye fly or speed through heaven and earth,

Or with your Godlike natures stand upon your cars, come thence, O Asvins, hitherward.

## [08-011] HYMN XI. Agni.

1. THOU Agni, God mid mortal men, art guard of sacred rites, thou art

To be adored at sacrifice.

2 O Mighty Agni, thou must be glorified at our festivals,

Bearing our offerings to the Gods.

3 O Jatavedas Agni, fight and drive our foes afar from us,

Themand their godless enmities.

4 Thou, Jatavedas, seekest not the worship of a hostile man,

However nigh itbe to thee.

5 We sages, mortals as we are, adore the mighty name oof thee,

Immortal Jatavedas' name.

6 Sages, we call the Sage to help, mortals, we call the God to aid:

We call on Agni with our songs.

7 May Vatsa draw- thy mind away even from thy loftiest dwelling-place,

Agni, with song that yearns for thee.

8 Thou art the same in many a place: mid all the people thou art Lord.

In fray and fightt we call on thee.

9 When we are seeking strength we call Agni to help us in the strife,

The giver of rich gifts in war.

10 Ancient, adorablie at sacrifices, Priest from of old, meet for our praise, thou sittest.

Fill full and satisfy thy body, Agni, and win us happiness by offering worship.

## [08-012] HYMN XII. Indra.

1. JOY, Mightiest Indra, known and marked, sprung most from Soma-draughts, wherewith

Thou smitest down the greedy fiend, for that we long.

2 Wherewith thou bolpest Adhrigu, the great Dasagva, and the God

Who stirs the sunlight, and the sea, for that we long.

3 Wherewith thou dravest forth like cars Sindhu and all the mighty floods

To go the way ordained by Law, for that we long.

4 Accept this laud for aid, made pure like oil, thou Caster of the Stone,

Whereby even in a moment thou hast waxen great.

5 Be pleased, Song-lover, with this song it flows abundant like the sea.

Indra, with all thy succours thou hast waxen great.

6 The God who from afar hath sent gifts to maintain our friendship's bond,

Thou. spreading them like rain from heaven, hast waxen great.

7 The beams that mark him have grown strong, the thunder rests between his arms,

When, like the Sun, he hath increased both Heaven and Earth.

8 When, Mighty Lord of Heroes, thou didst cat a thousand buffaloes,

Then grew and waxed exceeding great thine Indra-power.

9 Indra consumeth with the rays of Surya the malicious man:

Like Agni conquering the woods, he hath grown strong.

10 This newest thought of ours that suits the time approaches unto thee:

Serving, beloved in many a place it metes and marks.

11 The pious germ of sacrifice directly purifies the soul.

By Indra's lauds it waxes great, it metes and marks.

12 Indra who wins the friend hath spread himself to drink the Soma-draught:

Like worshipper's dilating praise; it metes and marks.

13 He whom the sages, living men, have gladdened, offering up their hymns,

Hath welled like oil of sacrifice in Agni's mouth.

14 Aditi also hath brought forth a hymn for Indra, Sovran Lord:

The work of sacrifice for help is glorified.

15 The ministering priests have sung their songs for aid and eulogy:

God, thy Bays turn not from the rite which Law ordains.

16 If, Indra, thou drink Soma by Visnu's or Trta Aptya's side,

Or with the Maruts take delight in flowing drops;

17 Or, Sakra, if thou gladden thee afar or in the sea of air,

Rejoice thee in this juice of ours, in flowing drops.

18 Or, Lord of Heroes if thou aid the worshipper who shed; the, juice,

Or him whose laud delights thee, and his flowing drops.

19 To magnify the God, the God, Indra, yea, Indra for your help,

And promptly end the sacrifice-this have they gained.

20 With worship, him whom men adore, with Soma, him who drinks it most,

Indra with lauds have they increasedthis have they gained.

21 His leadings are with power and might and his instructions manifold:

He gives the worshipper all wealth: this have they gained.

22 For slaying Vrtra have the Gods set Indra in the foremost place.
Indra the choral bands have sung, for vigorous strength.
23 We to the Mighty with our might, with lauds to him who hears our call,
With holy hymns have sung aloud, for vigorous strength.
24 Not earth, nor heaven, nor firmaments contain the Thunder-wielding God:
They shake before his violent rush and vigorous strength.
25 What time the Gods, O Indra, get thee foremost in the furious fight,
Then thy two beautiful Bay Steeds carried thee on.
26 When Vrtra, stayer of the floods, thou si"est, Thundeicr with might,
Then thy two beautiful Bay Steeds carried thee on.
27 When Visnu, through thine energy, strode wide those three great steps of his,
Then thy two beautiful Bay Steeds carried thee on.
28 When thy two beautiful Bay Steeds grew great and greater day by day,
Even then all creatures that had life bowed down to thee.
29 When, Indra, all the Marut folk humbly submitted them to thee,
Even then all creatures that had life bowed down to thee.
30 When yonder Sun, that brilliant light, thou settest in the heaven above,
Even then all creatures that had life bowed down to thee.
31 To thee, O Indra, with this thought the sage lifts up this eulogy,
Akin and leading as on foot to sacrifice.
32 When in thine own dear dwelling all gathered have lifted up the voice
Milk-streams at worship's central spot, for sacrifice,
33 As Priest, O Indra, give us wealth in brave men and good steeds ana kine
That we may first remember thee for sacrifice.

**[08-013] HYMN XIII. Indra.**
1. INDRA, when Soma juices flow, makes his mind pure and meet for lauds.
He gains the power that brings success, for great is he.
2 In heaven's first region, in the seat of Gods, is he who brings success,
Most glorious, prompt to save, who wins the water-floods.
3 Him, to win strength, have I invoked, even Indra mighty for the fray.
Be thou most near to us for bliss, a Friend to aid.
4 Indra, Song -lover, here for thee the worshipper's libation flows.
Rejoicing in this sacred grass thou shinest forth.
5 Even now, O Indra, give us that which, pressing juice, we crave of thee.
Bring us wealth manifold which finds the light of heaven.
6 What time the zealous worshipper hath boldly sung his songs to thee,
Like branches of a tree up-grows what they desire.
7 Generate songs even as of old, give car unto the singer's call.
Thou for the pious hast grown great at each carouse.
8 Sweet strains that glorify him play like waters speeding down a slope,
Yea, him who in this song is called the Lord of Heaven;
9 Yea, who alone is called the Lord, the single Ruler of the folk,
By worshippers seeking aid: may he joy in the draught.
10 Praise him, the Glorious, skilled in song, Lord of the two victorious Bays:
They seek the worshipper's abode who bows in prayer.
11 Put forth thy strength: with dappled Steeds come, thou of mighty intellect,
With swift Steeds to the sacrifice, for 'tis thy joy.

12 Grant wealth to those who praise thee, Lord of Heroes, Mightiest Indra: give
Our princes everlasting fame and opulence.
13 I call thee when the Sun is risen, I call thee at the noon of day:
With thy car-horses, Indra, come wellpleased to us.
14 Speed forward hither, come to us, rejoice thee in the milky draught:
Spin out the thread of ancient time, as well is known.
15 If, Sakra, Vrtra-slayer, thou be far away or near to us.
Or in the sea, thou art the guard of Soma juice.
16 Let songs we sing and Soma-drops expressed by us make Indra strong:
The tribes who bring oblations find delight in him.
17 Him sages longing for his aid, with offerings brought in eager haste,
Him. even as branches, all mankind have made to grow.
18 At the Trkadrukas the Gods span sacrifice that stirred the mind:
May our songs strengthen him who still hath strengthened us.
19 When, true to duty, at due times the worshipper offers lauds to thee,
They call him Purifier, Pure, and Wonderful.
20 That mind of Rudra, fresh and strong, moves conscious in the ancient ways,
With reference whereto the wise have ordered this.
21 If thou elect to be my Friend drink of this sacrificial juice,
By help whereof we may subdue all enemies.
22 O Indra, Lover of the song, when shall thy praiser be most blest?
When wilt thou grant us wealth in herds of kine and steeds?
23 And thy two highIy-lauded Bays, strong stallions, draw thy car who art
Untouched by age, most gladdening car for which we pray.
24 With ancient offerings we implore the Young and Strong whom many praise.
He from of old hath sat upon dear sacred grass.
25 Wax miglity, thou whom many laud for aids which Rsis have extolled.
Pour down for us abundant food and guard us well.
26 O Indra, Caster of the Stone, thou helpest him who praises thee:
From sacrifice I send to thee a mindyoked hymn.
27 Here, yoking for the Soma-draught these Horses, sharers of thy feast,
Thy Bay Steeds, Indra, fraught with weal tb, consent to come.
28 Attendants on thy glory, let the Rudras roar assent to thee,
And all the Marut companies come tothe feast.
29 These his victorious followers bold in the heavens the place they love,
Leagued in the heart of sacrifice, as well we know.
30 That we may long behold the light, what time the ordered rite proceeds,
He duly measures, as he views, the sacrifice.
31 O Indra, strong is this thy car, and strong are these Bay Steeds of thine:
O Satakratu, thou art strong, strong is our call.
32 Strong is the press-stone, strong thy joy, strong is the flowing Soma juice:
Strong is the rite thou furtherest, strong is our call.
33 As strong I call on thee the Strong, O Thunderer with thy thousand aids:
For thou hast won the hymn of praise. Strong is our call.

**[08-014] HYMN XIV. Indra.**
1. IF I, O Indra, were, like thee, the single Sovran of all wealth,
My worshipper should be rich in kine.

2 I should be fain, O Lord of Power, to strengthen and enrich the sage,
Were I the Lord of herds of kine.
3 To worshippers who press the juice thy goodness, Indra, is a cow
Yielding in plenty kine and steeds.
4 None is there, Indra, God or man, to hinder thy munificence,
The wealth which, lauded, thou wilt give.
5 The sacrifice made Indra strong when he unrolled the earth, and made
Himself a diadem in heaven.
6 Thine aid we claim, O Indra, thine who after thou hast waxen great
Hast won all treasures for thine own.
7 In Soma's ecstasy Indra spread the firmament and realms of light,
When he cleft Vala limb from limb.
8 Showing the hidden he drave forth the cows for the Angirases,
And Vala he cast headlong down.
9 By Indra were the lumirious realms of heaven established and secured,
Firm and immovable from their place.
10 Indra, thy laud moves quickly like a joyous wave of water-floods:
Bright shine the drops that gladden thee.
11 For thou, O Indra, art the God whom hymns and praises magnify:
Thou blessest those who worship thee.
12 Let the two long-maned Bay Steeds bring Indra to drink the Soma juice,
The Bountiful to our sacrifice.
13 With waters' foam thou torest off, Indra, the head of Namuci,
Subduing all contending hosts.
14 The Dasyus, when they fain would climb
by magic arts and mount to heaven,
Thou, Indra, castest down to earth.
15 As Soma-drinker conquering all, thou scatteredst to every side
Their settlement who poured no gifts.

## [08-015] HYMN XV. Indra.

1. SING forth to him whom many men invoke, to him whom many laud.
Invite the powerful Indra with your songs of praise.
2 Whose lofty might-for doubly strong is he-supports the heavens and earth,
And hills and plains and floods and light with manly power.
3 Such, Praised by many! thou art King alone thou smitest Vrtras dead,
To gain, O Indra, spoils of war and high renown.
4 We sing this strong and wild delight of thine which conquers in the fray,
Which, Caster of the Stone! gives room and shines like gold.
5 Wherewith thou also foundest lights for Ayu and for Manu's sake:
Now joying in this sacred grass thou beamest forth.
6 This day too singers of the hymn praise, as of old, this might of thine:
Win thou the waters day by day, thralls of the strong.
7 That lofty Indra-power of thine, thy strength and thine intelligence,
Thy thunderbolt for which we long, the wish makes keen.
8 O Indra, Heaven and Earth augment thy manly power and thy renown;
The waters and thy mountains stir and urge thee on.
9 Visnu the lofty ruling Power, Varuna, Mitra sing thy praise:
In thee the Marut3' company have great delight.

10 O Indra, thou wast born the Lord of men, most liberal of thy gifts:
Excellent deeds for evermore are all thine own.
11 Ever, alone, O highly-praised, thou sendest Vrtras to their rest:
None else than Indra executes the mighty deed.
12 Though here and there, in varied hymns, Indra, men call on thee for aid,
Still with our heroes fight and win the light of heaven.
13 Already have all forms of him entered our spacious dwelling-place:
For victory stir thou Indra, up, the Lord of Might.

## [08-016] HYMN XVI. Indra.

1. PRAISE Indra whom our songs must laud, sole Sovran of mankind, the Chief
Most liberal who controlleth men.
2 In whom the hymns of praise delight, and all the glory-giving songs.
Like the floods' longing for the sea.
3 Him I invite with eulogy, best King, effective in the fight,
Strong for the gain of mighty spoil.
4 Whose perfect ecstasies are wide, profound, victorious, and give joy in the field where heroes win.
5 Him, when the spoils of war are staked, men call to be their advocate:
They who have Indra win the day.
6 Men honour him with stirring songs and magnify with solemn rites:
Indra is he who giveth case.
7 ındra is priest and Rsi, he is much invoked by many men,
And mighty by his mighty powers.
8 Meet to be lauded and invoked, true Hero with his deeds of might,
Victorious even when alone.
9 The men, the people magnify that Indra with their Slina. songs,
With hymns and sacred eulogies
10 Him who advances them to wealth, sends light to lead them in the war,
And quells their foemen in the fray.
11 May he, the saviour much-invoked, may Indra bear us in a ship
Safely beyond all enemies.
12 As such, O Indra, honour us with gifts of booty, further us,
And lead us to felicity.

## [08-017] HYMN XVII Indra.

1. COME, we have pressed the juice for thee; O Indra, drink this Soma here
Sit thou on this my sacred grass.
2 O Indra, let thy long-maned Bays, yoked by prayer, bring thee hitherward
Give car and listen to our prayers.
3 We Soma-bearing Brahmans call thee Soma-drinker with thy friend,
We, Indra, bringing Soma juice.
4 Come unto us who bring the juice, come unto this our eulogy,
Fair-visored! drink thou of the juice.
5 I pour it down within thee, so through all thy members let it spread:
Take with. thy tongue the pleasant drink.
6 Sweet to thy body let it be, delicious be the savoury juice:
Sweet be the Soma to thine heart.
7 Like women, let this Soma-draught, invested with its robe, approach,
O active Indra, close to thee.
8 Indra, transported with the juice, vast in his bulk, strong in his neck
And stout arms, smites the Vrtras down.

9 O Indra, go thou forward, thou who rulest over all by might:
Thou Vrtra-slayer slay the fiends,
10 Long be thy grasping-hook wherewith thou givest ample wealth to him
Who sheds the juice and worships thee.
11 Here, Indra, is thy Soma-draught, made pure upon the sacred grass:
Run hither, come and drink thereof.
12 Famed for thy radiance, worshipped well this juice is shed for thy delight
Thou art invoked, Akhandala!
13 To Kundapayya, grandson's son, grandson of Srngavrs! to thee,
To him have I addressed my thought.
14 Strong pillar thou, Lord of the home armour of Soma-offerers:
The drop of Soma breaketh all the strongholds down, and Indra is the Rsis' Friend.
15 Holy Prdikusanu, winner of the spoil, one eminent o'er many men,
Lead on the wild horse Indra with his vigorous grasp forward to drink the Soma juice.

## [08-018] HYMN XVIII. Adityas.

1. Now let the mortal offer prayer to win the unexampled grace
Of these Adityas and their aid to cherish life.
2 For not an enemy molests the paths which these Adityas tread:
Infallible guards, they strengthen us in happiness.
3 Now soon may Bhaga, Savitar, Varuna, Mitra, Aryaman
Give us the shelter widely spread which we implore.
4 With Gods come thou whose fostering care none checks, O Goddesss Aditi:
Come, dear to many, with the Lords who guard us well.
5 For well these Sons of Aditi know to keep enmities aloof,
Unrivalled, giving ample room, they save from woe.
6 Aditi guard our herd by day, Aditi, free from guile, by night,
Aditi, ever strengthening, save us from grief!
7 And in the day our hymn is this: May Aditi come nigh to help,
With loving-kindness bring us weal and chase our foes.
8 And may the Asvins, the divine Pair of Physicians, send us health:
May they remove iniquity and chase our foes.
9 May Agni bless us with his fires, and Surya warm us pleasantly:
May the pure Wind breathe sweet on us, and chase our foes.
10 Drive ye disease and strife away, drive ye away malignity:
Adityas, keep us ever far from sore distress.
11 Remove from us the arrow, keep famine, Adityas! far away:
Keep enmities afar from us, Lords of all wealth!
12 Now, O Adityas, grant to us the shelter that lets man go free,
Yea, even the sinner from his sin, ye Bounteous Gods 1
13 Whatever mortal with the powe r of demons fain would injure us,
May he, impetuous, suffer harm by his own deeds.
14 May sin o'ertake our human foe, the man who speaketh evil thing,
Him who would cause our misery, whose heart is false.
15 Gods, ye are with the simple ones, ye know each mortal in your hearts;
Ye, Vasus, well discriminate the false and true.
16 Fain would we have the sheltering aid of mountains and of water-floods:
Keep far from us iniquity, O Heaven and Earth.
17 So with auspicious sheltering aid do ye, O Vasus, carry us
Beyond all trouble and distress, borne in your ship.
18 Adityas, ye Most Mighty Ones, grant to our children and their seed
Extended term of life that they may live long days.
19 Sacrifice, O Adityas, is your inward monitor: be kind,
For in the bond of kindred we are bound to you.

20 The Maruts' high protecting aid, the Asvins, and the God who saves,
Mitra and Varuna for weal we supplicate.
21 Grant us a home with triple guard, Aryaman, Mitra, Varuna!
Unthreatened, Maruts! meet for praise, and filled with men.
22 And as we human beings, O Adityas, are akin to death,
Graciously lengthen ye our lives that we may live.

## [08-019] HYMN XIX. Agni.

1. SING praise to hiin, the Lord of Light. The Gods have made the God to be their messenger,
And sent oblation to Gods.
2 Agni, the Bounteous Giver, bright with varied flames, laud thou, O singer Sobhari-
Him who controls this sacred food with Soma blent, who hath first claim to sacrifice.
3 Thee have we chosen skilftillest in sacrifice, Immortal Priest among the Gods,
Wise finisher of this holy rite:
4 The Son of Strength, the blessed, brightly shining One, Agni whose light is excellent.
May he by sacrifice win us in heaven the grace of Mitra, Varuna, and the Floods.
5 The mortal who hath ministered to Agni with oblation, fuel, ritual lore,
And reverence, skilled in sacrifice.
6 Verily swift to run are his fleet-footed steeds, and most resplendent fame is his.
No trouble caused by Gods or wrought by mortal man from any side o'ertaketh him.
7 May we by thine own fires be well supplied with fire, O Son of Strength, O Lord of Might:
Thou as our Friend hast worthy men.
8 Agni, who praises like a guest of friendly mind, is as a car that brings us gear.
Also in thee is found perfect security thou art the Sovran Lord of wealth.
9 That man, moreover, merits praise who brings, auspicious Agni, sacrificial gifts
May he win riches by his thoughts.
10 He for whose sacrifice thou standest up erect is prosperous and rules o'er men.
He wins with coursers and with singers killed in song: with heroes he obtains the prize.
11 He in whose dwelling Agni is chief ornament, and, all-desired, loves his laud well,
And zealously tends his offerings-
12 His, or the lauding sage's word, his, Son of Strength! who Is most prompt with sacred gifts,
Set thou beneath the Gods, Vasu, above mankind, the speech of the intelligent.
13 He who with sacrificial gifts or homage bringeth very skilful Agni nigh,
Or him who flashes fast with song,
14 The mortal who with blazing fuel, as his laws command, adores the Perfect God,
Blest with his thoughts in splendour shall exceed all men, as though he overpassed the floods.
15 Give us the splendour, Agni, which may overcome each greedy fiend in our abode,
The wrath of evil-hearted folk.
16 That, wherewith Mitra, Varuna, and Aryaman, the Asvins, Bhaga give us light,
That may we, by thy power finding best furtherance, worship, O Indra, helped by thee.
17 O Agni, most devout are they, the sages who have set thee Sage exceeding wise,

O God, for men to look upon:

18 Who have arranged thine altar Blessed God, at morn brought thine oblation, pressed the juice.
They by their deeds of strength have won diem, mighty wealth, who have set all their hope in thee.

19 -May Agni worshipped bring us bliss, may the gift, Blessed One, and sacrifice bring bliss;
Yea, may our praises bring us bliss.

20 Show forth the mind that brings success in war with fiends, wherewith thou conquerest in fight.
Bring down the many firm hopes of our enemies, and let us vanquish with thine aid.

21 I praise with song the Friend of man, whom Gods sent down to be herald and messenger,
Best worshipper, bearer of our gifts.

22 Thou unto sharp-toothed Agni, Young and Radiant God, proclaimest with thy song the feast-
Agni, who for our sweet strains moulds heroic strength when sacred oil is offered him,

23 While, served with sacrificial oil, now upward and now downward Agni moves his sword,
As doth the Asura his robe.

24 The God, the Friend of man, who bears our gifts to heaven, the God with his sweet-smelling
mouth,
Distributes, skilled in sacrifice, his precious things, Invoking Priest, Immortal God.

25 Son of Strength, Agni, if thou wert the mortal, bright as Mitra, I worshipped with our gifts!
And I were the Immortal God

26 I would not give thee up, Vasu, to calumny, or misery, O Bounteous One.
My worshipper should feel no hunger or distress, nor, Agni, should he live in sin.

27 Like a son cherished in his father's houi§e, let our oblation rise unto the Gods.

28 With thine immediate aid may I, excellent Agni, ever gain my wish
A mortal with a God to help.

29 O Agni, by thy wisdom, by thy bounties, by thy leading may I gather wealth.
Excellent Agni, thou art called my Providence: delight thou to be liberal.

30 Agni, he conquers by thine aid that brings him store of noble heroes and great strength,
Whose bond of friendship is thy choice.

31 Thy spark is black and crackling, kindled in due time, O Bounteous, it is taken up.
Thou art the dear Friend of the mighty Mornings: thou shinest in glimmerings of the night.

32 We Sobharis have come to him, for succour, who is good to help with thousand powers,
The Sovran, Trasadasyu's Friend.

33 O Agni, thou on whom all other fires depend, as branches on the parent stem,
I make the treasures of the folk, like songs, mine own, while I exalt thy sovran might.

34 The mortal whom, Adityas, ye, Guilelew, lead to the farther bank
Of all the princes, Bounteous Ones

35 Whoe'er he be, Man-ruling Kings! the Regent of the race of men-
May we, O Mitra, Varuna, and Aryaman, like him be furtherers of your law.

36 A gift of fifty female slaves hath Trasadasyu given me, Purukutsa's son,
Most liberal, kind, lord of the brave.

37 And Syava too for me led forth a strong steed at Suvastu's ford:
A herd of three times seventy kine, good lord of gifts, he gave to me.

## [08-020] HYMN XX Maruts.

1. LET none, Swift Travellers! check you: come hither, like-spirited, stay not far away,
Ye benders even of what is firm.

2 Maruts, Rbhuksans, Rudras come ye with your cars strong-fellied and exceeding bright.
Come, ye for whom we long, with food, to sacrifice, come ye with love to Sobbari.

3 For well we know the vigorous might of Rudra's Sons, the Martits, who are passing strong,
Swift Visnu's band, who send the rain.,

4 Islands are bursting forth and misery is stayed: the heaven and earth are joined in one.
Decked with bright rings, ye spread the broad expanses out, when ye, Self. luminous, stirred
yourselves.

5 Even things immovable shake and reel, the mountains and the forest trees at your approach,
And the earth trembles as ye come.

6 To lend free course, O Maruts, to your furious rush, heaven high and higher still gives way,
Where they, the Heroes mighty with their arms, display their gleaming omaments on their forms.

7 After their Godlike nature they, the bull. like Heroes, dazzling and impetuous, wear
Great splendour as they show erect.

8 The pivot of the Sobharis' chariot within the golden box is balmed with milk.
May they the Well-born, Mighty, kindred of the Cow, aid us to food and to delight.

9 Bring, ye who sprinkle balmy drops. oblations to your vigorous Marut company,
To those whose leader is the Bull.

10 Come hither, O ye Mares, on your stronghorsed car, solid in look, with solid naves.
Lightly like winged falcons, O ye Heroes, come, come to enjoy our ofrerings.

11 Their decoration is the same: their omaments of gold are bright upon their arms;
Their lances glitter splendidly.

12 They toil not to defend their bodies from attack, strong Heroes with their mighty arms.
Strong are your bows and strong the weapons in your cars, and glory sits on every face.

13 Whose name extendeth like a sea, alone, resplendent, so that all have joy in it,
And life-power like ancestral might.

14 Pay honour to these Maruts and sing praise to them, for of the wheel-spokes of the car
Of these loud roarers none is last: this is their power, this moves them to give mighty gifts.

15 Blest by your favouring help was he, O Maruts, at the earlier flushings of the morn,
And even now shall he be blest.

16 The strong man to whose sacrifice, O Heroes, ye approach that ye may taste thereof,
With glories and with war that winneth spoil shall gain great bliss, ye Shakers of the world.

17 Even as Rudra's Sons, the brood of the Creator Dyaus, the Asura, desire,
O Youthful Ones, so shall it be:

18 And these the bounteous, worthy of the Maruts who move onward pouring down the rain-

Even for their sake, O Youthful Ones, with kindest heart take us to you to be your own.

19 O Sobhari, with newest song sing out unto the youthful purifying Bulls,
Even as a plougher to his steers.

20 Who, like a celebrated boxer, overcome the challengers in every fight:
They who, like shining bulls, are most illustrious-honour those Maruts with thy song.

21 Allied by common ancestry, ye Maruts, even the Cows, alike in energy,
Lick, all by turns, each other's head.

22 Even mortal man, ye Dancers breast adorned with gold, attains to brotherhood with you.
Mark ye and notice us, O Maruts; evermore your friendship is secured to us.

23 O Maruts, rich in noble gifts, bring us a portion of the Maruts' medicine,
Ye Coursers who are Friends to us.

24 Haters of those who serve you not, bliss-bringers, bring us bliss with those auspicious aids
Wherewith ye are victorious and guard Sindhu well, and succour Krvi in his need.

25 Maruts, who rest on fair trimmed grass, what balm soever Sindhu or Asikni hath,
Or mountains or the seas contain.

26 Ye carry on your bodies, ye who see it all: so bless us graciously therewith.
Cast, Maruts, to the ground our sick man's malady: replace the dislocated limb.

## [08-021] HYMN XXI. Indra.

1. WE call on thee, O Matchless One! We seeking help, possessing nothing firm ourselves,
Call on thee wonderful in fight

2 On thee for aid in sacrifice. This youth of ours, the bold, the mighty, hath gonse forth.
We therefore, we thy friends, Indra, havie chosen thee, free-giver, as our Guardian God.

3 Come hither, for the drops are here, O Lord of corn-lands. Lord of horses, Lord of kine:
Drink thou the Soma, Soma's Lord!

4 For we the kinless singers have drawn hither thee, O Indra, who hast numerous kin.
With all the forms thou hast, comic thou of bull-like strength, come near to drink the Soma juice.

5 Sitting like birds beside thy meath., mingled with milk, that gladdeneth and exalteth thee,
Indra, to thee we sing aloud.

6 We speak to thee with this our reverential prayer. Why art thou pondering yet awhile?
Here are our wishes; thou art liberal, Lord of Bays: we and our hymns are present here.

7 For not in recent times alone, O Indra, Thunder-armed, have we obtained thine aid.
Of old we knew thy plenteous wealth.

8 Hero, we knew thy friendship and thy rich rewards: these, Thunderer, now we crave of thee.
O Vasu, for all wealth that cometh of the kine, sharpen our powers, fair-visored God.

9 Him who of old hath brought to us this and that blessing, him I magnify for you,
Even Indra, O my friends, for help

10 Borne by Bay Steeds, the Lord of heroes, ruling men, for it is he who takes; delight.
May Maghavan bestow on us his worshippers hundreds of cattle and of steeds.

11 Hero, may we, with thee for Friend, withstand the man who pants against us in his wrath,
In fight with people rich in kine.

12 May we be victors in the singer's battlesong, and meet the wicked, Much invoked!
With heroes smite the foeman and show forth our strength. O Indra, further thou our thoughts.

13 O Indra, from all ancient time rivalless ever and companionless art thou:
Thou seekest comradeship in war.

14 Thou findest not the wealthy man to be thy friend: those scorn thee who are flown with wine.
What time thou thunderest and gatherest, then thou, even as a Father, art invoked.

15 O Indra, let us not, like fools who waste their lives at home, with friendship such as thine
Sit idly by the poured-out juice.

16 Giver of kine, may we not miss thy gracious gifts: let us not rob thee of thine own.
Strip even the strong places of the foe, and bring: thy gifts can never be made vain.

17 Indra or blest Sarasvati alone bestows such wealth, treasure so great, or thou,
O Citra, on the worshipper.

18 Citra is King, and only kinglings are the rest who dwell beside Sarasvati.
He, like Parjanya with his rain, hath spread himself with thousand, yea, with myriad gifts.

## [08-022] HYMN XXII. Asvins.

1. HITHERWARD have I called to-day, for succour, that most wondrous car
Which ye ascended, Asvins, ye whose paths are red, swift to give Car, for Surya's sake.

2 Car ever young, much longed-for, easily invoked, soon guided, first in deeds of might,
Which waits and serves, O Sobhari, with benevolence, without a rival or a foe.

3 These Asvins with our homage, these Two Omnipresent Deities Hitherward will we bring for kind help, these who seek the dwelling of the worshipper.

4 One of your chariot wheels is moving swiftly round, one speeds for you its onward course.
Like a milch-cow, O Lords of splendour, and with haste let your benevolence come to us.

5 That chariot of yours which hath a triple seat and reins of gold,
The famous car that traverseth the heaven and earth, thereon Nasatyas, Asvins, come.

6 Ye with your plough, when favouring Manu with your help, ploughed the first harvest in the sky.
As such will we exalt you, Lords of splendour, now, O Asvins, with our prayer and praise.

7 Come to us, Lords of ample wealth, by paths of everlasting Law,
Whereby to high dominion ye with mighty strength raised Trksi, Trasadasyu's son.

8 This Soma pressed with stones is yours, ye Heroes, Lords of plenteous wealth.
Approach to drink the Soma, come, drink in the worshipper's abode.

9 O Asvins, mount the chariot, mount the golden seat, ye who are Lords of plenteous wealth,
And bring to us abundant food.

10 The aids wherewith ye helped Paktha and Adhrigt;, and Babhru severed from his friends,-
With those, O Asvins, come hither with speed and soon, and heal whatever is diseased.

11 When we continually invoke the Asvins, the resistless, at this time of day,
We lovers of the song, with songs.
12 Through these, ye Mighty Ones, come hither to my call which brings all blessings, wears all
forms,-
Tlrough which, All-present Heroes, lavishest of food ye strengthened Krvi, come through these.
13 I speak to both of these as such, these Asvins whom I reverence at this time of day:
With homage we entreat them both.
14 Ye who are Lords of splendour, ye whose paths are red, at eve, at mom, at sacrifice,
Give us not utterly as prey to mortal foe, ye Rudras, Lords of ample wealth.
15 For bliss I call. the blissful car, at morn the inseparable Asvins with their car
I call, like Sobhari our sire.
16 Rapid as thought, and strong, and speeding to thejoy, bringing.your swiftly-coming help,
Be to us a protection even from far away Lords of great wealth, with many aids.'
17 Come, Wonder-Workers, to our home, our home, O Asvins, rich in cattle, steeds, and gold,
Chief drinkers of the Soma's juice
18 Choice-worthy strength, heroic, firm and excellent, uninjured by the Raksas foe,
At this your coming nigh, ye Lords of ample wealth and all good things, may we obtain.

## [08-023] HYMN XXIII. Agni.

1. WORSHIP thou Jatavedas, pray to him who willingly accepts,
Whose smoke wanders at will, and none may grasp his flame.
2 Thou, all men's friend, Visvamanas, exaltest Agni with thy song,
The Giver, and his flames with which no cars contend.
3 Whose resolute assault, to win vigour and food, deserves our praise,-
Through whose discovering power the priest obtaineth wealth.
4 Up springs the imperishable flame, the flame of the Refulgent One
Most bright, with glowing jaws and glory in his train.
5 Skilled in fair sacrifice, extolled, arise in Godlike loveliness,
Shining with lofty splendour, with effulgent light.
6 Called straight to our oblations, come, O Agni, through our eulogies,
As thou hast been our envoy bearing up our gifts.
7 I call your Agni, from of old Invoking Priest of living men:
Him with this song I laud and magnify for you.
8 Whom, wondrous wise, they animate with solemn rites and his fair form,
Kind as a friend to men who keep the holy Law.
9 Him, true to Law, who perfecteth the sacrifice,. Law-loving ones!
Ye with your song have gratified in the place of prayer.
10 May all our sacrifices go to him the truest Angiras,
Who is among mankind the most illustrious Priest.
11 Imperishable Agni, thine are all these high enkindled lights,
Like horses and like stallions showing forth their strength.
12 So give us, Lord of Power and Might, riches combined with hero strength,
And guard us with our sons and grand. sons in our frays.
13 Soon as the eager Lord of men is friendly unto Manti's race,
Agni averteth from us all the demon host.
14 O Hero Agni, Lord of men, on hearing this new laud of mine,
Burn down the Raksasas, enchanters, with thy flame.
15 No mortal foe can e'er prevail by arts of magic over him
Who serveth Agni well with sacrificial gifts.

16 Vyasva the sage, who sought the Bull, hath won thee, finder of good things:
As such may we enkindle thee for ample wealth.
17 Usana Kavya stablished thee, O Agni, as Invoking Priest:
Thee, Jatavedas, Sacrificing Priest for man.
18 All Deities of one accord appointed thee their messenger:
Thou, God, through hearing, hadst first claim to sacrifice.
19 Him may the mortal hero make his own immortal messenger.
Far-spreading, Purifier, him whose path is black.
20 With lifted ladles let us call him splendid with his brilliant flame,
Men's ancient Agni, wasting not, adorable.
21 The man who pays the worship due to him with sacrificial gifts
Obtains both plenteous nourishment and hero fame.
22 To Jatavedas Agni, chief in sacrifices, first of all
With homage goes the ladle rich with sacred gifts.
23 Even as Vyatya did, may we with these most high and liberal hymns
Pay worship unto Agni of the splendid flame.
24 Now sing, as Sthurayupa sang, with lands to him who spreadeth far,
To Agni of the home, O Rsi, Vyasva's son.
25 As welcome guest of human kind, as offspring of the forest kings,
The sages worship ancient Agni for his aid.
26 For men's oblations brought to him who is the mighty Lord of all,
Sit, Agni, mid our homage, on the sacred grass.
27 Grant us abundant. treasures, grant the opulence which many crave,
With store of heroes, progeny, and high renown.
28 Agni, Most Youthful of the Gods, send evermore the gift of wealth
Unto Varosusaman and to all his folk.
29 A mighty Conqueror art thou, O Agni, so disclose to us
Food in our herds of kine and gain of ample wealth.
30 Thou, Agni, art a glorious God: bring hither Mitra, Varuna,
Imperial Sovrans, holy-minded, true to Law.

## [08-024] HYMN XXIV. Indra.

1. COMPANIONS, let us learn a prayer to Indra. whom the thunder arms,
To glorify your bold and most heroic Friend.
2 For thou by slaying Vrtra art the Vrtra-slayer, famed for might.
Thou, Hero, in rich gifts surpassest wealthy chiefs.
3 As such, when glorified, bring us riches of very wondrous fame,
Set in the highest rank, Wealth-giver, Lord of Bays!
4 Yea, Indra, thou disclosest that preeminent dear wealth of men:
Boldly, O Bold One, glorified, bring it to us.
5 The workers of destruction stay neither thy right hand nor thy left:
Nor hosts that press about thee, Lord of Bays, in fight.
6 O Thunder-armed, I come with songs to thee as to a stall with kine:
Fulfil the wish and thought of him who sings thy praise.
7 Chief Vrtra-slayer, through the hymn of Visvamanas think of all,
All that concerneth us, Excellent, Mighty Guide.
8 May we, O Vrtra-slayer, O Hero, find this thy newest boon,
Longed-for, and excellent, thou who art
much invoked!
9 O Indra, Dancer, Much-invoked! as thy great power is unsurpassed,
So be thy bounty to the worshipper unchecked.
10 Most Mighty, most heroic One, for mighty bounty fill thee full.
Though strong, strengthen thyself to win wealth, Maghavan!

11 O Thunderer, never have our prayers gone forth to any God but thee:
So help us, Maghavan, with thine assistance now.
12 For, Dancer, verily I find none else for bounty, saving thee,
For splendid wealth and power, thou Lover of the Song.
13 For Indra pour ye out the drops meath blent with Soma let him drink
With bounty and with majesty will he further us.
14 I spake to the Bay Coursers' Lord, to him who gives ability:
Now hear the son of Asva as he praises thee.
15 Never was any Hero born before thee mightier than thou:
None certairdy like thee in goodness and in wealth.
16 O ministering priest, pour out of the sweet juice what gladdens most:
So is the Hero praised who ever prospers us.
17 Indra, whom Tawny Coursers bear, praise such as thine, preeminent,
None by his power or by his goodness hath attained.
18 We, seeking glory, have invoked this Master of all power and might
Who must be glorified by constant sacri fice.
19 Come, sing we praise to Indra, friends, the Hero who deserves the laud,
Him who with none to aid o'ercomes all tribes of men.
20 To him who wins the kine, who keeps no cattle back, Celestial God,
Speak wondrous speech more sweet than butter and than meath.
21 Whose hero powers are measureless, whose bounty ne'er may be surpassed,
Whose liberality, like light, is over all.
22 As Vyasva did, praise Indra, praise the Strong unfluctuating Guide,
Who gives the foe's possessions to the worshipper.
23 Now, son of Vyasva, praise thou him who to the tenth time still is new,
The very Wise, whom living men must glorify
24 Thou knowest, Indra, Thunder-armed, how to avoid destructive powers,
As one secure from pitfalls each returning day.
25 O Indra, bring that aid wherewith of old, Most Wondrous! thou didst slay
His foes for active Kutsa: send it down to us.
26 So now we seek thee fresh in might, Most Wonderful in act! for gain:
For thou art he who conquers all our foes for us.
27 Who will set free from ruinous woe, or Arya on the Seven Streams:
O valiant Hero, bend the Dasa's weapon down.
28 As to Varosusaman thou broughtest great riches, for their gain,
To Vyasva's sons, Blest Lady, rich in ample wealth!
29 Let Narya's sacrificial meed reach Vyasva's Soma-bearing sons:
In hundreds and in thousands be the great reward.
30 If one should ask thee, Where is he who sacrificed? Whither lookest thou?
Like Vala he hath passed away and dwelleth now on Gomati.

## [08-025] HYMN XXV. Mitra-Varuna.

1. I WORSHIP you who guard this All, Gods, holiest among the Gods,
You, faithful to the Law, whose power is sanctified.
2 So, too, like charioteers are they, Mitra and sapient Varuna,
Sons high-born from of old, whose holy laws stand fast.
3 These Twain, possessors of all wealth, most glorious, for supremest sway
Aditi, Mighty Mother, true to Law, brought forth.

4 Great Varuna and Mitra, Gods, Asuras and imperial Lords,
True to Eternal Law proclaim the high decree.
5 The offspring of a lofty Power, Daksa's Two Sons exceeding strong,
Who, Lords of flowing rain, dwell in the place of food.
6 Ye who have gathered up your gifts, celestial and terrestrial food,
Let your rain come to us fraught with the mist of heaven.
7 The Twain, who from the lofty sky seem to look down on herds below,
Holy, imperial Lords, are set to be revered.
8 They, true to Law, exceeding strong, have sat them down for savran rule:
Princes whose laws stand fast, they have obtained their sway.
9 Pathfinders even better than the eye, with unobstructed sight,
Even when they close their lids, observant, they perceive.
10 So may the Goddess Aditi, may the Nasatyas guard us well,
The Martits guard us well,.endowed with mighty strength.
11 Do ye, O Bounteous Gods, protect our dwelling lace by day and night:
With you for our defenders may we go unharmed.
12 May we, unharmed, serve bountiful Visnu, the God who slayeth none:
Self-moving Sindhu hear and be the first to mark.
13 This sure protection we elect, desirable and reaching far,
Which Mitra, Varuna, and Aryaman afford.
14 And may the Sindhu of the floods, the Maruts, and the ASvin Pair,
Boon Indra, and boon Visnu have one mind with us.
15 Because these warring Heroes stay the enmity of every foe,
As the fierce water-flood repels the furious ones.
16 Here this one God, the Lord of men, looks forth exceeding far and wide:
And we, for your advantage, keep his holy laws.
17 We keep the old accustomed laws, the statutes of supremacy,
The Iong-known laws of Mitra and of Varuna.
18 He who hath measured with his ray the boundaries of heaven and earth,
And with his majesty hath filled the two worlds full,
19 Surya hath spread his light aloft up to the region of the sky,
Like Agni all aflame when gifts are offered him.
20 With him who sits afar the word is lord of food that comes from kine,
Controller of the gift of unempoisoned food.
21 So unto Surya, Heaven, and Earth at morning and at eve I speak.
Bringing enjoyments ever rise thou up for us.
22 From Uksanyayana a bay, from Harayana a white steed,
And from Susaman we obtained a hamessed car.
23 These two shall bring me further gain of troops of tawny-coloured steeds,
The carriers shall they be of active men of war.
24 And the two sages have I gained who hold the reins and bear the whip,
And the two great strong coursers, with my newest song.

## [08-026] HYMN XXVI. Asvins.

1. I CALL your chariot to receive united praise mid princely men,
Strong Gods who pour down wealth, of never vanquished might!
2 Ye to Varosusaman come, Nasatyas, for this glorious rite.
With your protecting aid. Strong Gods, who pour down wealth.
3 So with oblations we invoke you, rich in ample wealth, to-day,
When night hath passed, O ye who send us plenteous food.
O Asvins, Heroes, let your car, famed, best to travel, come to us,
And, for his glory, mark your zealous servant's lauds.
5 Asvins, who send us precious gifts, even when offended, think of him:

For ye, O Rudras, lead us safe beyond our foes.

6 For, Wonder-Workers, with fleet steeds ye fly completely round this All,

Stirring our thoughts, ye Lords of splendour, honey-hued.

7 With all-sustaining opulence, Asvins, come hitherward to us,

Ye rich and noble Heroes, ne'er to be o'erthrown.

8 To welcome this mine offering, O ye Indra-like Nasatyas, come

As Gods of best accord this day with other Gods.

9 For we, like Vyasva, lifting up our voice like oxen, call on you:

With all your loving kindness, Sages, come to us.

10 O Rsi, laud the Asvins well. Will they not listen to thy call?

Will they not bum the Panis who are nearer them?

11 O Heroes, listen to the son of Vyasva, and regard me here,

Varuna, Mitra, Aryaman, of one accord.

12 Gods whom we yearn for, of your gifts, of what ye bring to us, bestow

By princes' hands on me, ye Mighty, day by day.

13 Him whom your sacrifices clothe, even as a woman with her robe,

The Asvins help to glory honouring him well.

14 Whoso regards your care of men as succour widest in its reach,

About his dwelling go, ye Asvins, loving us.

15 Come to us ye who pour down wealth, come to the home which men must guard:

Like shafts, ye are made meet for sacrifice by song.

16 Most fetching of all calls, the laud, as envoy, Heroes, called to you

Be it your own, O Asvin Pair.

17 Be ye in yonder sea of heaven, or joying in the home of food,

Listen to me, Immortal Ones.

18 This river with his lucid flow attracts you, more than all the streams,-

Even Sindhu with his path of gold.

19 O Asvins, with that glorious fame come hither, through our brilliant song,

Come ye whose ways are marked with light.

20 Harness the steeds who draw the car, O Vasu, bring the well-fed pair.

O Vayu, drink thou of our meath: come unto our drink-offerings.

21 Wonderful Vayu, Lord of Right, thou who art Tvastar's son-in-law,

Thy saving succour we elect.

22 To Tvastar's son-in-law we pray for wealth whereof he hath control:

For glory we seek vayu, men with juice effused.

23 From heaven, auspicious Vayu, come drive hither with thy noble steeds:

Come on thy mighty car with wide-extending seat.

24 We call thee to the homes of men, thee wealthiest in noble food,

And liberal as a press-stone with a horse's back.

25 So, glad and joyful in thine heart, do thou, God, Vayu, first of all

Vouchsafe us water, strength, and thought.

## [08-027] HYMN XXVII. Visvedevas.

1. CHEIF Priest is Agni at the laud, as stones and grass at sacrifice:

With song I seek the Maruts, Brahmanaspati, Gods for help much to be desired.

2 I sing to cattle and to Earth, to trees, to Dawns, to Night, to plants.

O all ye Vasus, ye possessors of all wealth, be ye the furtherers of our thoughts.

3 Forth go, with Agni, to the Gods our sacrifice of ancient use,

To the Adityas, Varuna whose Law stands fast, and the all-lightening Marut troop.

4 Lords of all wealth, may they be strengtheners of man, destroyers of his enemies.

Lords of all wealth, do ye, with guards which none may harm, preserve our dwelling free from foes.

5 Come to us with one mind to-day, come to us all with one accord,

Maruts with holy song, and, Goddess Aditi, Mighty One, to our house and home.

6 Send us delightful things, ye Maruts, on your steeds: come ye, O Mitra, to our gifts.

Let Indra, Varuna, and the Adityas sit, swift Heroes, on our sacred grass.

7 We who have trimmed the grass for you, and set the banquet in array,

And pressed the Soma, call you, Varuina, like men, with sacrificial fires aflame.

8 O Maruts, Visinu, Asvins, Pusan, haste away with minds turned hitherward to Me.

Let the Strong Indra, famed as Vrtra's slayer, come first with the winners of the spoil.

9 Ye Guileless Gods, bestow on us a refuge strong on every side,

A sure protection, Vasus, unassailable from near at hand or from afar.

10 Kinship have I with you, and close alliance O ye Gods, destroyers of our foes.

Call us to our prosperity of former days, and soon to new klicity.

11 For now have I sent forth to you, that I may win a fair reward,

Lords of all wealth, with homage, this my song of praise. like a milch-cow that faileth not.

12 Excellent Savitar hath mounted up on high for you, ye sure and careful Guides.

Bipeds and quadrupeds, with several hopes and aims, and birds have settled to their tasks.

13 Singing their praise with God-like thought let us invoke each God for grace,

Each God to bring you help, each God to strengthen you.

14 For of one spirit are the Gods with mortal man, co-sharers all of gracious gifts.

May they increase our strength hereafter and to-day, providing case and ample room.

15 I laud you, O ye Guileless Gods, here where we meet to render praise.

None, Varuna and Mitra, harins the mortal, man who honours and obeys your laws.

16 He makes his house endure, he gathers plenteous food who pays obedience to your will.

Born in his sons anew he spreads as Law commands, and prospers every way unharmed.

17 E'en without war he gathers wealth, and goes hisway on pleasant paths,

Whom Mitra, Varuna and Aryaman protect, sharing the gift,of one accord.

18 E'en on the plain for him ye make a sloping path, an easy way where road is none:

And far away from him the ineffectual shaft must vanish, shot at him in vain.

19 If ye appoint the rite to-day, kind Rulers, when the Sun ascends,

Lords of all wealth, at sunset or at wakingtime, or be it at the noon of day,

20 Or, Asuras, when ye have sheltered the worshipper who goes to sacrifice, at eve

may we, O Vasus, ye possessors of all wealth, come then into the midst of You.

21 If ye to-day at sunrise, or at noon, or in the gloom of eve,

Lords of all riches, give fair treasure to the man, the wise man who hath sacrificed,

22 Then we, imperial Rulers, claim of you this boon, your wide protection, as a son.
May we, Adityas, offering holy gifts, obtain that which shall bring us greater bliss.

## [08-028] HYMN XXVIII. Visvedevas.

1. THE Thirty Gods and Three besides, whose seat hath been the sacred grass,
From time of old have found and gained.
2 Varuna, Mitra, Aryaman, Agnis, with Consorts, sending boons,
To whom our Vasat! is addressed:
3 These are our guardians in the west, and northward here, and in the south,
And on the cast, with all the tribe.
4 Even as the Gods desire so verily shall it be. None minisheth this power of theirs,
No demon, and no mortal
5 The Seven carry seven spears; seven are the splendours they possess,
And seven the glories they assume.

## [08-029] HYMN XXIX Visvedevas.

1. ONE is a youth brown, active, manifold he decks the golden one with ornament.
2 Another, luminous, occupies the place of sacritice, Sage, among the Gods.
3 One brandishes in his hand an iron knife, firm, in his seat amid the Deities.
4 Another holds the thunderbolt, wherewith he slays the Vrtras, resting in his hand.
5 Another bears a pointed weapon: bright is he, and strong, with healing medicines.
6 Another, thief-like, watches well the ways, and knows the places where the treasures lie.
7 Another with his mighty stride hath made his three steps thither where the Gods rejoice.
8 Two with one Dame ride on with winged steeds, and journey forth like travellers on their way.
9 Two, highest, in the heavens have set their seat, worshipped with holy oil, imperial Kings.
10 Some, singing lauds, conceived the Sama-hymn, great hymn whereby they caused the Sun to
shine.

## [08-030] HYMN XXX. Visvedevas.

1. NOT one of you, ye Gods, is small, none of you is a feeble child:
All of you, verily, are great.
2 Thus be ye lauded, ye destroyers of the foe, ye Three-and-Thirty Deities,
The Gods of man, the Holy Ones.
3 As such defend and succour us, with benedictions speak to us:
Lead us not from our fathers' and from Manu's path into the distance far away.
4 Ye Deities who stay with us, and all ye Gods of all mankind,
Give us your wide protection, give shelter for cattle and for steed.

## [08-031] HYMN XXXI. Various Deities.

1. THAT Brahman pleases Indra well, who worships, sacrifices, pours Libation, and prepares the
meal.
2 Sakra protects from woe the man who gives him sacrificial cake.
And offers Soma blent with milk.
3 His chariot shall be glorious, sped by Gods, and mighty shall he be,
Subduing all hostilities.
4 Each day that passes, in his house flows his libation, rich in milk,

Exhaustless, bringing progeny.
5 O Gods, with constant draught of milk, husband and wife with one accord
Press out and wash the Soma juice.
6 They gain sufficient food: they come united to the sacred grass,
And never do they fail in strength.
7 Never do they deny or seek to hide the favour of the Gods:
They win high glory for themselves.
8 With sons and daughters by their side they reach their full extent of life,
Both decked with ornaments of gold.
9 Serving the Immortal One with gifts of sacrificial meal and wealth,
They satisfy the claims of love and pay due honour to the Gods.
10 We claim protection from the Hills, we claim protection of the Floods,
Of him who stands by Visnu's side.
11 May Pusan come, and Bhaga, Lord of wealth, All-bounteous, for our weal
Broad be the path that leads to bliss:
12 Aramati, and, free from foes, Visva with spirit of a God,
And the Adityas' peerless might.
13 Seeing that Mitra, Aryaman, and Varuna are guarding us,
The paths of Law are fair to tread.
14 I glorify with song, for wealth, Agni the God, the first of you.
We honour as a well-loved Friend the God who prospereth our fields.
15 As in all frays the hero, so swift moves his car whom Gods attend.
The man who, sacrificing, strives to win the heart of Deities will conquer those who worship not.
16 Ne'er are ye injured, worshipper, presser of juice, or pious man.
The man who, sacrificing, strives to win the heart of Deities will conquer those who worship not.
17 None in his action equals him, none holds him far or keeps him off.
The man who, sacrificing, strives to win the heart of Deities will conquer those who worship not.
18 Such strength of heroes shall be his, such mastery of fleet-foot steeds.
The man who, sacrificing, strives to win the heart of Deities will conquer those who worship not.

## [08-032] HYMN XXXII. Indra.

1. KANVAS, tell forth with song the deeds of Indra, the Impetuous,
Wrought in the Soma's wild delight.
2 Strong God, he slew Anarsani, Srbinda, Pipru, and the fiend, Ahisuva, and loosed the floods.
3. Thou broughtest down the dwelling-place, the height of lofty Arbuda.
That exploit, Indra, must be famed.
4 Bold, to your famous Soma I call the fair-visored God for aid,
Down like a torrent from the hill.
5 Rejoicing in the Soma-draughts, Hero, burst open, like a fort,
The stall of horses and of kine.
6 If my libation gladdens, if thou takest pleasure in my laud,
Come with thy Godhead from afar.
7 O Indra, Lover of the Song, the singers of thy praise are we:
O Soma-drinker, quicken us.
8 And, taking thy delight with us bring us still undiminished food:
Great is thy wealth, O Maghavan.
9 Make thou us rich in herds of kine, in steeds, in gold: let us exert
Our strength in sacrificial gifts.

10 Let us call him to aid whose hands stretch far, to whom high laud is due.
Who worketh well to succour us.
11 He, Satakratu, even in fight acts as a Vrtra-slayer s,till:
He gives his worshippers much wealth.
12 May he, this A;akra, strengthen us, Boon God who satisfies our needs,
Indra, with all lhis saving helps.
13 To him, the mighty stream of wealth, the Soma-presser's rescuing Friend,
To Indra sing your song of praise;
14 Who bringeth what is great and firm, who winneth glory in his wars,
Lord of vast wealth through power and might.
15 There liveth none to cheek or stay his energies and gracious deeds:
None who can say, He giveth not.
16 No debt is due by Brahmans now, by active men who press the juice:
Well hath each Soma-draught been paid.
17 Sing ye to him who must be praised, say lauds to him who must be praised,
Bring prayer to him who must be praised.
18 May be, unchecked, strong, meet for praise, bring hundreds, thousands forth to light,
Indra who aids the worshipper.
19 Go with thy God-like nature forth, go where the folk are calling thee:
Drink, Indra, of the drops we pour.
20 Drink milky draughts which are thine own, this too which was with Tugrya once,
This is it, Indra, that is thine.
21 Pass him who psours libations out in angry mood or after sin:
Here drink the juice we offer thee.
22 Over the three great distances, past the Five Peoples go thy way,
O Indra, noticing our voice.
23 Send forth thy ray like Surya: let my songs attract thee hitherward,
Like waters gathering to the vale.
24 Now to the Hero fair of cheek, Adhvaryu, pour the Soma forth:
Bring of the juice that he may drink
25 Who cleft the water-cloud in twain, loosed rivers for their downward flow,
And set the ripe milk in the kine.
26 He, meet for praise, slew Vrtra, slew Ahisuva, Urnavabha's son,
And pierced th:rough Arbuda with frost.
27 To him your matchless Mighty One, unconquerable Conqueror,
Sing forth the prayer which Gods have given:
28 Indra, who in the wild delight of Soma juice considers here
All holy Laws among the Gods.
29 Hither let these thy Bays who share thy banquet, Steeds with golden manes,
Convey thee to the feast prepared.
30 Hither, O thou whom many laud, the Bays whom Priyamedha praised,
Shall bring thee to the Soma-draught.

## [08-033] HYMN XXXIII. Indra.

1. WE compass thee like waters, we whose grass is trimmed and Soma pressed.
Here where the filter pours its stream, thy worshippers round thee, O Vrtra-slayer, sit.
2 Men, Vasu! by the Soma, with lauds call thee to the foremost place:

When comest thou athirst unto the juice as home, O Indra, like a bellowing bull?
3 Boldly, Bold Hero, bring us spoil in thousands for the Kanvas' sake.
O active Maghavan, with eager prayer we crave the yellow-hued with store ol kine.
4 Medhyatithi, to Indra sing, drink of the juice to make thee glad.
Close-knit to his Bay Steeds, bolt-armed, beside the juice is he: his chariot is of gold.
5 He Who is praised as strong of hand both right and left, most wise and hold:
Indra who, rich in hundreds, gathers thousands up, honoured as breaker-down of forts.
6 The bold of heart whom none provokes, who stands in bearded confidence;
Much-lauded, very glorious, overthrowing foes, strong Helper, like a bull with might.
7 Who knows what vital ower he wins, drinking beside the flowing juice?
This is the fair-checked God who, joying in the draught, breaks down the castles in his strength.
8 As a wild elephant rushes on this way and that way, mad with heat,'
None may compel thee, yet come hither to the draught: thou movest mighty in thy power.
9 When he, the Mighty, ne'er o'erthrown, steadfast, made ready for the fight,
When Indra Maghavan lists to his praiser's call, he will not stand aloof, but come.
10 Yea, verily, thou art a Bull, with a bull's rush. whom none may stay:
Thou Mighty One, art celebrated as a Bull, famed as a Bull both near and far.
11 Thy reins are very bulls in strength, bulls' strength is in thy golden whip.
Thy car, O Maghavan, thy Bays are strong as bulls: thou, Satakratu, art a Bull.
12 Let the strong presser press for thee. Bring hither, thou straight-rushing Bull.
The mighty makes the mighty run in flowing streams for thee whom thy Bay Horses bear.
13 Come, thou most potent Indra, come to drink the savoury Soma juice.
Maghavan, very wise, will quickly come to hear the songs, the prayer, the hymns of praise.
14 When thou hast mounted on thy car let thy yoked Bay Steeds carry thee,
Past other men's libations, Lord of Hundred Powers, thee, Vrtra-slayer, thee our Friend.
15 O thou Most Lofty One, accept our laud as nearest to thine heart.
May our libations be most sweet to make thee glad, O Soma-drinker, Heavenly Lord.
16 Neither in thy decree nor mine, but in another's he delights,-
The man who brought us unto this.
17 Indra himself hath said, The mind of woman brooks not discipline,
Her intellect hath little weight.
18 His pair of horses, rushing on in their wild transport, draw his car:
High-lifted is the stallion's yoke.
19 Cast down thine eyes and look not up. More closely set thy feet. Let none
See what thy garment veils, for thou, a Brahman, hast become a dame.

## [08-034] HYMN XXXIV. Indra.

1. Come hither, Indra, with thy Bays, come thou to Kanva's eulogy.
Ye by command of yonder Dyaus, God bright by day! have gone to heaven.
2 May the stone draw thee as it speaks, the Soma-stone with ringing voice.
Ye by command of yonder Dyaus, God bright by day! have gone to heaven.
3 The stones' rim shakes the Soma here like a wolf worrying a sheep.
Ye by command of yonder Dyaus, God bright by day! have gone to heaven.
4 The Kanvas call thee hitherward for succour and to win the spoil.
Ye by command of yonder Dyaus, God bright by day! have gone to heaven.
5 I set for thee, as for the Strong, the first draught of the juices shed.
6 Come with abundant blessings, come with perfect care to succour us.
7 Come, Lord of lofty thought, who hast infinite wealth and countless aids.
8 Adorable mid Gods, the Priest good to mankind shall bring thee near.
9 As wings the falcon, so thy Bays rushing in joy shall carry thee.
10 Come from the enemy to us, to svaha and the Soma-draught.
11 Come hither with thine car inclined to hear, take pleasure in our lauds.
12 Lord of well-nourished Horses, come with well-fed Steeds alike in hue.
13 Come hither from the mountains, come from regions of the sea of air.
14 Disclose to us O Hero, wealth in thousands both of kine and steeds.
15 Bring riches hitherward to us in hundreds, thousands, myriads.
Ye by command of yonder Dyaus, God bright by day! have gone to heaven.
16 The thousand steeds, the mightiest troop, which we and Indra have received
From Vasurocis as a gift,
17 The brown that match the wind in speed, and bright bay coursers fleet of foot,
Like Suns, resplendent are they all.
18 Mid the Pargvata's rich gifts, swift steeds whose wheels run rapidly,
I seemed to stand amid a wood.

## [08-035] HYMN XXXV. Asvins.

1. WITH Agni and with Indra, Visnu. Varuna, with the Adityas, Rudras, Vasus, closely leagued;
Accordant, of one mind with Surya and with Dawn, O Asvins, drink the Soma juice.
2 With all the Holy Thoughts, all being Mighty Ones! in close alliance wil the Mountains, Heaven, and Earth;
Accordant. of one mind with Surya and with Dawn, O Asvins, drink the Soma juice.
3 With all the Deities, three times eleven, here, in close alliance with the Maruts, Bhrgus, Floods;
Accordant, of one mind with Surya and with Dawn, O Asvins, drink the Soma juice.
4 Accept the sacrifice, attend to this my call: come nigh, O ye Twain Gods, to all libations here.
Accordant, of one mind with Surya and with Dawn, O Asvins, bring us strengthening food.

5 Accept our praise-song as a youth accepts a maid. Come nigh, O ye Twain Gods, to all libations here.
Accordant, of one mind with Sarya and with Dawn O Asvins, bring us strengthening food.
6 Accept the songs we sing, accept the solemn rite. Conie nigh, O ye Twain Gods, to all libations here.
Accordant, of one mind with Surya and with Dawn, O Asvins, bring us strengthening food.
7 Ye fly as starlings fly unto the forest trees; like buffaloes ye seek the Soma we have shed.
Accordant, of one mind with Surya and with Dawn, come thrice, O Asvins, to our home.
8 Ye fly like swans, like those who travel on their way; like buffaloes ye seek the Soma we have shed.
Accordant, of one mind with Surya and with Dawn, come thrice, O Asvins, to our home.
9 Ye fly to our oblation like a pair of hawks; like buffaloes ye seek the Soma we have shed.
Accordant, of one mind with Surya and with Dawn, come thrice, O Asvins, to our home.
10 Come hitherward and drink and satisfy yourselves, bestow upon us progeny and affluence.
Accordant, of one mind with Surya and with Dawn, O Asvins, grant us vigorous strength.
11 Conquer your foes, protect us, praise your worshippers; bestow upon us progeny and affluence.
Accordant, of one mind with Surya and with Dawn, O Asvins, grant us vigolms strength.
12 Slay enemies, animate men whom ye befriend; bestow upon us progeny and aff luence.
Accordant, of one mind with Surya and with Dawn, O Asvins, grant us vigorous strength.
13 With Mitra, Varuna, Dharma, and the Maruts in your company approach unto your praiser's call.
Accordant, of one mind with Surya and with Dawn, and with the Adityas, Asvins! come.
14 With Visnu and the Angirases attending you, and with the Maruts come unto your praiser's call.
Accordant, of one mind with Surya and with Dawn, and with the Adityas, Asvins! come.
15 With Rbhus and With Vajas. O ye Mighty Ones, leagued with the Maruts come ye to your praiser's call.
Accordant, of one mind with Surya and with Dawn, and with the Adityas, Asvins! come.
16 Give spirit to our prayer and animate our thoughts; slay ye the Raksasas and drive away disease.
Accordant, of One mind with Surya and with Dawn, -the presser's Soma, Asvins drink.
17 Strengthen the Ruling Power, strengthen the men of war; slay ye the Raksasas and drive away disease.
Accordant, of one mind with Surya and with Dawn, the presser's Soma, Asvins drink.
18 Give strength unto the milch-kine, give the people strength, slay ye the Raksasas and drive away disease.
Accordant, of one mind with Surya and with Dawn, the presser's Soma, Asvins drink.
19 As ye heard Atri's earliest eulogy, so hear Syavasva, Soma-presser, ye who reel in joy.
Accordant, of one mind with Surya and with Dawn, drink juice, O Asvins, three days old.
20 Further like running streams Syavasva's eulogies who presses out the Soma, ye who reel in joy.

Accordant, of one mind with Surya and with Dawn, drink juice, O Asvins, three days old.

21 Seize, as ye grasp the reins, Syavasva's solemn rites who presses out the Soma, ye who reel in joy.
Accordant, of one mind with Surya and with Dawn, drink juice, O Asvins, three days old.

22 Drive down your chariot hitherward drink ye the Soma's savoury juice.
Approach, ye Asvins, come to us: I call you, eager for your aid. Grant treasures to the worshipper.

23 When sacrifice which tells our reverence hath begun. Heroes! to drink the gushing juice,
Approach, ye Asvins, come to us: I call you, eager for your aid. Grant treasures to the worshipper.

24 Sate you with consecrated drink, with juice effused, ye Deities.
Approach, ye Asvins, come to us: I call you, eager for your aid. Grant treasures to the worshipper.

## [08-036] HYMN XXXVI. Indra.

1. THOU helpest him whose grass is trimmed, who sheds the juice, O Satakratu, drink Soma to make
thee glad.
The share which they have fixed for thee, thou, Indra, Victor o'er all hosts and space, begirt with
Maruts, Lord of Heroes, winner of the floods.

2 Maghavan, help thy worshipper: let him help thee. O Satakratu, drink Soma to make thee glad.
The share which they have fixed for thee, etc.

3 Thou aidest Gods with food, and that with might aidg thee, O Satakratu, drink Soma to make thee glad.

4 Creator of the heaven, creator of the earth, O Satakratu, drink Soma to make thee glad.

5 Father of cattle, father of all steeds art thou. O Satakratu, drink Soma to make thee glad.

6 Stone-hurler, glorify the Atris' hymn of praise. O Satakratu, drink Soma to make thee glad.

7 Hear thou Syavagva while he pours to thee, as erst thou heardest Atri when he wrought his holy
rites.
Indra, thou only gavest Trasadasyu aid in the fierce fight with heroes, strengthening his prayers.

## [08-037] HYMN XXXVII Indra.

1. THIS prayer, and those who shed the juice, in wars with Vrtra thou holpest, Indra, Lord of
Strength, with all thy succours.
O Vrtra-slayer, from libation poured at noon, drink of the Soma juice, thou blameless Thunderer.

2 Thou mighty Conqueror of hostile armaments, O Indra, Lord of Strength, with all thy saving help.

3 Sole Ruler, thou art Sovran of this world of life, O Indra, Lord of Strength, with all thy saving help.

4 Thou only sunderest these two consistent worlds, O Indra, Lord of Strength, with all thy saving
help.

5 Thou art the Lord supreme o'er rest and energy, O Indra, Lord of Strength, with all thy saving help.

6 Thou helpest one to power, and one thou hast not helped, O Indra, Lord of Strength, with all thy
saving aid.

7 Hear thou Syavasva while he sings to thee, as erst thou heardest Atri when he wrought his holy
rites.
Indra, thou only gavest Trasadasyu aid in the fierce fight with heroes, strengthening his powers.

## [08-038] HYMN XXXVIII. Indra-Angi.

I. YE Twain are Priests of sacrifice, wmners in war and holy works:
Indra and Agni, mark this well.

2 Ye bounteous riders on the car, ye Vrtra-slayers unsubdued:
Indra and Agni, mark this well.

3 The men with pressing-stones have pressed this meath of yours which gives delight:
Indra, and Agni, mark this well.

4 Accept our sacrifice for weal, sharers of praise! the Soma shed:
Indra and Agni, Heroes, come.

5 Be pleased with these libations which attract you to our sacred gifts
Indra and Agni, Heroes, come.

6 Accept this eulogy of mine whose model is the Gayatri:
Indra and Agni, Heroes, Come.

7 Come with the early-faring Gods, ye who are Lords of genuine wealth:
Indra-Agni, to the Soma-draught

8 Hear ye the call of Atris, hear Syavasva as he sheds the juice:
Indra-Agni to the Soma-draught

9 Thus have I called you to our aid as sages called on you of old:
Indra-Agni to the Soma draught!

10 Indra's and Agni's grace I claim, Sarasvati's associates
To whom this psalm of praise is sung.

## [08-039] HYMN XXXIX. Agni.

1. THE glorious Agni have I praised, and worshipped with. the sacred food.
May Agni deck the Gods for us. Between both gathering-places he goes on his embassy, the Sage.
May all the others die away.

2 Agni, burn down the word within their bodies through our newest speech,
All hatreds of the godless, all the wicked man's malignities. Away let the destroyers go. May all the
others die away.

3 Agni, I offer hymns to thee, like holy oil within thy moutlh.
Acknowledge them. among the Gods, for thou art the rmost excellent, the worshipper's blissful
messenger. Let all the others die away.

4 Agni bestows all vital power even as each man supplicates.
He brings the Vasus strengthening gifts, and grants deliglht, in rest and stir, for every calling on the
Gods. Let all the others die away.

5 Agni hath made himself renowned by wonderful victorious act.
He is the Priest of all the tribes, chosen with sacrificial meeds. He urges Deities to receive. Let all the
others die away.

6 Agni knows all that springs from Gods, he knows the mystery of men.
Giver of wealth is Agni, he uncloses both the doors to us when worshipped with our newest gift. Let
all the others die away.

7 Agni inhabiteth with Gods and men who offer sacrifice.
He cherisheth with great delight much wisdom, as all things that be, God among Gods adorable. May
all the others die away.

8 Agni who liveth in all streams, Lord of the Sevenfold Race of men,
Him dweller in three homes we seek, best slayer of the Dasytis for Mandhatar, first in sacrifice. Let all
the others die away.

9 Agni the Wise inhabiteth three gathering-places, triply formed.
Decked as our envoy let the Sage bring hither and conciliate the Thrice Eleven Deities. Let all the
others die away.

10 Our Agni, thou art first among the Gods, and first mid living men.
Thou only rulest over wealth. Round about thee, as natural dams, circumfluous the waters run. Let all the others die away.

## [08-040] HYMN XL. Indra-Agni.

1. INDRA and Agni, surely ye as Conquerors will give us wealth,
Whereby in fight we may o'ercome that which is strong and firmly fixed, as Agni burns the woods
with wind. Let all the others die away.
2 We set no snares to tangle you; Indra we worship and adore,
Hero of heroes mightiest.
Once may he come unto us with his Steed, come unto us to win us strength, and to complete the
sacrifice.
3 For, famous Indra-Agni, ye are dwellers in the midst of frays.
Sages in wisdom, ye are knit to him who seeketh you as friends.
Heroes, bestow on him his wish.
4 Nabhaka-like, with sacred song Indra's and Agni's praise I sing,
Theirs to whom all this world belongs, this heaven and this mighty earth which bear rich treasure in
their lap.
5 To Indra and to Agni send your prayers, as was Nabhaka's wont,-
Who oped with sideway opening the sea with its foundations seven-Indra all powerful in his might.
6 Tear thou asunder, as of old, like tangles of a creeping plant,
Demolish thou the Dasa's might. May we with Indra's help divide the treasure he hath gathered up.
7 What time with this same song these men call Indra-Agni sundry ways,
May we with our own heroes quell those who provoke us to the fight, and conquer those who strive
with us.
8 The Two refulgent with their beams rise and come downward from the sky.
By Indra's and by Agni's hest, flowing away, the rivers, run which they released from their restraint.
9 O Indra, many are thine aids, many thy ways of guiding us,
Lord of the Bay Steeds, Hinva's Son. To a Good Hero come our prayers, which soon shall have
accomplishment.
10 Inspire him with your holy hymns, the Hero bright and glorious,
Him who with might demolisbeth even the brood of Susna, and winneth for us the heavenly streams.
11 Inspire him worshipped with fair rites, the glorious Hero truly brave.
He brake in pieces Susna's brood who still expected not the stroke, and won for us the heavenly
streams. Let all the others die away.
12 Thus have we sung anew to Indra-Agni, as sang our sires,
Angirases, and Mandhatar.
Guard us with triple shelter and preserve us: may we be masters of a store of riches.

## [08-041] HYMN XLI. Varuna.

1. To make this Varuna come forth sing thou a song unto the band of Maruts wiser than thyself,-
This Varuna who guardeth well the thoughts of men like herds of kine.
Let all the others die away.
2 Him altogether praise I with the song and hymns our fathers sang, and with Nabhaka's eulogies,-
Him dwelling at the rivers' source, surrounded by his Sisters Seven.

3 The nights he hath encompassed, and stablished the morns with magic art visible over all is he.
His dear Ones, following his Law, have prospered the Three Dawns for him.
4 He, visible o'er all the earth, stablished the quarters of the sky:
He measured out the eastern place, that is the fold of Varuna: like a strong herdsman is the God.
5 He who supports the worlds of life, he who well knows the hidden names mysterious of the morning beams,
He cherishes much wisdom, Sage, as heaven brings forth each varied form.
6 In whom all wisdom centres, as the nave is set within the wheel.
Haste ye to honour Trita, as kine haste to gather in the fold, even as they muster steeds to yoke.
7 He wraps these regions as a robe; he contemplates the tribes of Gods and all the works of mortal men.
Before the home of Varuna all the Gods follow his decree.
8 He is an Ocean far-removed, yet through the heaven to him ascends the worship which these
realms possess.
With his bright foot he overthrew their magic, and went up to heaven.
9 Ruler, whose bright far-seeing rays, pervading all three earths, have filled the three superior realms
of heaven.
Firm is the seat of Varuna: over the Seven he rules as King.
10 Who, after his decree, o'erspread the Dark Ones with a robe of light;
Who measured out the ancient seat, who pillared both the worlds apart as the Unborn supported
heaven. Let all the others die away.

## [08-042] HYMN XLII Varuna.

1. LORD of all wealth, the Asura propped the heavens, and measured out the broad earth's wide expanses.
He, King supreme, approached all living creatures. All these are Varuna's holy operations.
2 So humbly worship Varuna the Mighty revere the wise Guard of World Immortal.
May he vouchsafe us triply-barred protection. O Earth and Heaven, within your lap preserve us.
3 Sharpen this song of him who strives his utmost, sharpen, God Varuna, his strength and insight;
May we ascend the ship that bears us safely, whereby we may pass over all misfortune.
4 Asvins, with songs the singer stones have made you hasten hitherward,
Nasatyas, to the Soma-draught. Let all the others die away.
5 As the sage Atri with his hymns, O Asvins, called you eagerly,
Nasatyas, to the Soma-draught. Let all the others die away.
6 So have I called you to our aid, even as the wise have called of old,
Nasatyas, to the Soma-draught. Let all the others die away.

## [08-043] HYMN XLIII. Agni.

1. THESE songs of mine go forth as lauds of Agni, the disposing Sage,
Whose worshipper is ne'er o'erthrawn.
2 Wise Agni Jatavedas, I beget a song of praise for thee.
Who willingly receivest it.
3 Thy sharpened flames, O Agni, like the gleams of light that glitter through,
Devour the forests with their teeth.
4 Gold-coloured, bannered with the smoke, urged by the wind, aloft to heaven
Rise, lightly borne, the flames of fire.
5 These lightly kindled fiery flames are all around made visible,

Even as the glearaings of the Dawns.

6 As Jatavedas speeds along, the dust is black beneath his feet,
When Agni spreads upon the earth.

7 Making the plants his nourishment, Agni devours and wearies not,
Seeking the tender shrubs again.

8 Bending him down with all his tongues, he flickers with his fiery glow
Splendid is Agni in the woods.

9 Agni, thine home is in the floods: into the plants thou forcest way,
And as their Child art born anew.

10 Worshipped with offerings shines thy flame, O Agni, from the sacred oil,
With kisses on the ladle's mouth.

11 Let us serve Agni with our hymns, Disposer, fed on ox and cow,
Who bears the Soma on his back.

12 Yea, thee, O Agni, do we seek with homage and with fuel, Priest
Whose wisdom is most excellent.

13 O worshipped with oblations, pure Agni, we call on thee as erst,
Did Bhrgu, Manus, Angiras.

14 For thou, O Agni, by the fire, Sage by the Sage, Good by the Good,
Friend by the Friend, art lighted up.

15 So wealth in thousands, food with store of heroes give thou to the sage,
O Agni, to the worshipper.

16 O Agni, Brother, made by strength, Lord of red steeds and brilliant sway,
Take pleasure in this laud of mine.

17 My praises, Agni, go to thee, as the cows seek the stall to meet,
The lowing calf that longs for milk.

18 Agni, best Angiras, to thee all people who have pleasant homes,
Apart, have turned as to their wish.

19 The sages skilled in holy song and thin. kers with their thoughts have urged
Agni to share the sacred feast.

20 So, Agni, unto thee the Priest, Invoker, strong in forays, pray
'nose who spin out the sacrifice.

21 In many a place, the same in look art thou, a Prince o'er all the tribes
In battles we invoke thine aid.

22 Pray thou to Agni, pray to him who blazes served with sacred oil:
Let him give ear to this our call.

23 We call on thee as such, as one who hears, as Jatavedas, one,
Agni! who beats away our foes.

24 I pray to Agni, King of men, the Wonderful, the President
Of holy Laws: may he give ear.

25 Him like a bridegroom, him who stirs all people, like a noble horse,
Like a fleet steed, we instigate.

26 Slaying things deadly, burning up foes, Riksasas, on every side,
Shine, Agni, with thy sharpened flame.

27 Thou whom the people kindle even as Manus did, best Angiras!
O Agni, mark thou this my speech.

28 O Agni, made by strength! be thou born in the heavens or born in floods,
As such we call on thee with songs.

29 Yea, all the people, all the folk who have good dwellings, each apart,
Send food for thee to eat thereof.

30 O Agni, so may we, devout, gazed at by men, throughout our days,
Pass lightly over all distress.

31 We venerate with cheerful hearts the cheerful Agni, dear to all,
Burning, with purifying flame.

32 So thou, O Agni rich in light, beaming like Surya with thy rays
Boldly demolishest the gloom,

33 We pray to thee for this thy gift, Victor the gift that faileth not,
O Agni, choicest wealth from thee.

## [08-044] HYMN XLIV. Agni.

1. PAY service unto Agni with your fuel, rouse your Guest with oil:
In him present your offerings.

2 Agni, do thou accept my laud, be magnified by this my song:
Welcome my sweedy-spoken words.

3 Agni, envoy, I place in front; the oblation-bearer I address:
Here let him seat the Deities.

4 Agni, the lofty flames of' thee enkindled have gone up on high,
Thy bright flames, thou Refulgent One.

5 Beloved! let my ladles full of sacred oil come near to thee:
Agni, accept our offerings.

6 I worship Agni-may he hear!-the cheerful, the Invoker, Priest,
Of varied splendour, rich in light.

7 Ancient Invoker, meet for praise, beloved Agni, wise and strong,
The visitant of solemn rites.

8 Agni, best Angiras, accept straightway these offerings, and guide
The seasonable sacrifice.

9 Excellent God, with brilliant flames, enkindled bring thou hitherward,
Knowing the way, the Heavenly Host.

10 Him, Sage and Herald, void of guile, ensign of sacrifices, him
Smoke-bannered, rich in light, we seek.

11 O Agni, be our Guardian thou, God, against those who injure us:
Destroy our foes, thou Son of Strength.

12 Making his body beautiful, Agni the Sage hath waxen by
The singer and his ancient hymn.

13 I invocate the Child of Strength, Agni with purifying flame,
At this well-ordered sacrifice.

14 So Agni, rich in many friends, with fiery splendour, seat thyself
With Gods upon our sacred grass.

15 The mortal man who serves the God Agni within his own abode,
For him he causes wealth to shine.

16 Agni is head and height of heaven, the Master of the earth is he:
He quickeneth the watere seed.

17 Upward, O Agni, rise thy flames, pure and resplendent, blazing high,
Thy lustres, fair effulgences.

18 For, Agni, thou as Lord of Light rulest o'er choicest gifts: may I,
Thy singer, find defence in thee.

19 O Agni, they who understand stir thee to action with their thoughts:
So let our songs enhance thy might.

20 We ever claim the friendship of Agni, the singing messenger,
Of God-like nature, void of guile.

21 Agni who bears most holy sway, the holy Singer, holy Sage,
Shines holy when we worship him.

22 Yea, let my meditations, let my songs exalt thee evermore.
Think, Agni, of our friendly bond,

23 If I were thou and thou wert I, O Agni, every prayer of thine
Should have its due fulfilment here.

24 For Excellent and Lord of wealth. art thou O Agni, rich in light:

May we enjoy thy favouring grace.

25 Agni, to thee whose laws stand fast our resonant songs of praise speed forth,
As rivers hasten to the sea.

26 Agni, the Youthful Lord of men, who stirreth much and eateth all,
The Sage, I glorify with hymns.

27 To Agni let us haste with lauds, the Guide of sacrificial rites,
Armed with sharp teeth, the Mighty One.

28 And let this man, good Agni, be with thee the singer of thy praise:
Be gracious, Holy One, to him.

29 For thou art sharer of our feast, wise, ever watchful as a Sage:
Agni, thou shinest in the sky.

30 O Agni, Sage, before our foes, before misfortunes fall on us,
Excellent Lord, prolong our lives.

## [08-045] HYMN XLV. Indra

1. HITHERWARD! they who light flame and straightway trim the sacred grass.
Whose Friend is Indra ever young.

2 High is their fuel, great their laud, wide is their splinter from the stake,
Whose Friend is Indra ever young.

3 Unequelled in fight the hero leads his army with the warrior chiefs.
Whose Friend is Indra ever young.

4 The new-born Vrtra-slayer asked his Mother, as he seized his shaft,
Who are the fierce? Who are renowned?

5 Savasi answered, He who seeks thine enmity will battle like
A stately elephant on a hill.

6 And hear, O Maghavan; to him who craves of thee thou grantest all
Whate'er thou makest firm is firm.

7 What time the Warrior Indra goes to battle, borne by noble steeds,
Best of all charioteers is he.

8 Repel, O Thunder-armed, in all directions all attacks on us:
And be our own most glorious God.

9 May Indra set our car in front, in foremost Place to win the spoil,
He whom the wicked injure not.

10 Thine enmity may we escape, and, gakra, for thy bounty, rich
In kine, may we come near to thee

11 Softly approaching, Thunder-armed wealthy by hundreds, rich in steeds,
Unrivalled, readywith our gifts.

12 For thine exalted excellence gives to thy worshippers each day
Hundreds and thousands of thy boons.

13 Indra, we know thee breaker-down even of trong forts, winner of spoil,
A:one who conquers wealth for us.

14 Though thou art highest, Sage and Bold let the drops cheer thee when we come
To thee as to a trafficker.

15 Bring unto us the treasure of the opulent man who, loth to give,
Hath slighted thee for gain of wealth.

16 Indra, these friends of ours, supplied with Soma, wait and look to thee,
As men with fodder to the herd.

17 And thee who art not deaf, whose cars are quick to listen, for our aid,
We call to us from far away.

18 When thou hast listened, make our call one which thou never wilt forget,

And be our very nearest Friend.

19 When even now, when we have been in trouble, we have thought of thee,
O Indra, give us gifts of kine.

20 O Lord of Strength, we rest on thee, as old men rest upon a staff:
We long to have. thee dwell with us.

21 To Indra sing a song of praise, Hero of mighty valour, him
Whom no one challenges to war.

22 Hero, the Soma being shed, I pour the juice for thee to drink:
Sate thee and finish thy carouse.

23 Let not the fools, or those who mock beguile thee when they seek thine aid
Love not the enemies of prayer.

24 Here let them with rich milky draught cheer thee to great munificence:
Drink as the wild-bull drinks the lake.

25 Proclaim in our assemblies what deeds, new and ancient, far away,
The Vrtra-slayer hath achieved.

26 In battle of a thousand arms Indra drank Kadru's Soma juice:
There he displayed his manly might.

27 True undeniabIc strength he found in Yadu and in Turvasa,
And conquered through the sacrifice.

28 Him have I magnified, our Lord in, common, Guardian of your folk,
Discloser of great wealth in kine;

29 Rbhuksan, not to be restrained, who strengthened Tugra's son in lauds,
Indra beside the flowingjuice;

30 Who for Trisoka clave the hill that formed a wide receptacle,
So that the cows might issue forth.

31 Whate'er thy plan or purpose be, whate'er, in transport, thou wouldst do,
Do it not, Indra, but be kind.

32 But little hath been heard of done upon the earth by one like thee i
Let thine heart, Indra, turn to us.

33 Thine then shall be this high renown, thine shall these lofty praises be,
When, Indra, thou art kind to us.

34 Not for one trespass, not for two, O Hero, slay us, nor for three,
Nor yet for many trespasses.

35 I fear one powerful like thee, the crusherdown of enemies,
Mighty, repelling all attacks.

36 O wealthy God, ne'er may I live to see my friend or son in need*:
Hitherward let thy heart be turned.

37 What friend, O people, unprovoked, hath ever said unto a friend,
He turns and leaves us in distress?

38 Hero, insatiate enjoy this Soma juice so near to thee,
Even as a hunter rushing down.

39 Hither I draw those Bays of thine yoked
by our hymn, with splendid car,
That thou mayst give unto the priests.

40 Drive all our enemies away, smite down the foes who press around,
And bring the wealth for which we long:

41 O Tndra, that which is concealed in strong firm place precipitous:
Bring us the wealth for which we long

42 Great riches which the world of men shall recognize as sent by thbe:
Bring us the wealth for which we long.

**[08-046] HYMN XLVI. Indra.**

1. WE, Indra, Lord of ample wealth, our Guide, depend on one like thee,
Thou driver of the Tawny Steeds.
2 For, Hurler of the Bolt, we know thee true, the giver of our food,
We know the giver of our wealth.
3 O thou whose majesty the bards celebrate with their songs, thou Lord,
Of hundred powers and hundred aids.
4 Fair guidance hath the mortal man whom Aryaman, the Marut host,
And Mitra, void of guile, protect.
5 Kine, steeds, and hero strength he gains, and prospers, by the Adityas sped,
Ever in wealth which all desire.
6 We pray to Indra for his gift, to him the Fearless and the Strong,
We pray to him the Lord of wealth.
7 For verily combined in him are all the fearless powers of aid.
Him, rich in wealth, let swift Steeds bring to us, his Bays, to Soma juice for his carouse:
8 Yea, that most excellent carouse, Indra, which slays most enemies,
With Heroes wins the light of heaven, and is invincible in war:
9 Which merits fame, all-bountiful! and, unsubdued, hath victory in deeds of might.
So come to our libations, Strongest! Excellent! May we obtain a stall of kine.
10 Responding to our wish for cows, for steeds, and chariots, as of old,
Be gracious, Greatest of the Great
11 For, Hero, nowhere can I find the bounds of thy munificence.
Still do thou favour us, O Bolt-armed Maghavan: with strength hast thou rewarded hymns.
12 High, glorifier of his friend, he knows all generations, he whom many praise.
All races of mankind with ladies lifted up invoke that Mighty Indra's aid.
13 Be he our Champion and Protector in great deeds, rich in all wealth, the Vrtra-slayer, Maghavan.
14 In the wild raptures of the juice sing to your Hero with high laud, to him the Wise,
To Indra, glorious in his name, the Mighty One, even as the hymn alloweth it.
15 Thou givest wealth to me myself, thou givest treasure, Excellent! and the strong steed,
O Much-invoked, in deeds of might, yea, even now.
16 Him, Sovran Ruler of all precious things, who even hath power o'er this fair form of his,
As now it taketh shape, and afterward,
17 We praise, so that the Mighty One may speed to you, Pourer of boun ies, Traveller, prepared to go.
Thou favourest the Maruts known to all, by song and sacrifice.
With song and praise I sing to thee.
18 We in the sacrifice perform their will whose voice is lifted high,
The worship of those Thundering Ories who o'er the ridges of these mountains fly in troops.
19 O Indra, Mightiest, bring us that which crushes men of evil minds,
Wealth suited to our needs, O Stirrer of the thought, best wealth,
O thou who stirrest thought.
20 O Winner, noble winner, strong, wondrous, most splendid, excellent,
Sole Lord of victory, bring all-overpowering wealth, joy-giving, chief in deeds of might.
21 Now let the godless man approach who hath received reward so great

As Vasa, Asvya, when this light of morning dawned, received from Prthusravas, from Kanita's son.
22 Steeds sixty thousand and ten thousand kine, and twenty hundred camels I obtained;
Ten hundred brown in hue, and other ten red in three spots: in all, ten thousand kine.
23 Ten browns that make my wealth increase, fleet steeds whose tails are long and fair,
Turn with swift whirl my chariot wheel;
24 The gifts which Prthusravas gave, Kanita's son munificent.
He gave a chariot wrought of gold: the prince was passing bountiful, and won himself most lofty fame.
25 Come thou to this great rite of ours, Vayu! to give us vigorous light.
We have served thee that thou mightest give much to us, yea, mightest quickly give great wealth.
26 Who with thrice seven times seventy horses comes to us, invested with the rays of morn,
Through these our Soma-draughts and those who press, to give, drinker of pure bright Soma Juice.
27 Who hath inclined this glorious one, buunteous himself, to give me gifts.
Borne on firm chariot with the prosperous Nahup, wise, to a man yet more devout.
28 Sole Lord in beauty meet for praise, O Vayu, dropping fatness down,
Hurried along by steeds, by camels, and by hounds, spreads forth thy train: even this it is.
29 So, as a prize dear to the strong, the sixty thousand have I gained,
Bulls that resemble vigorous steeds.
30 To me come oxen like a herd, yea, unto me the oxen come.
31 And in the grazing herd he made a hundred camels bleat for me,
And twenty hundred mid the white.
32 A hundred has the sage received, Dasa Balbutha's and Taruksa's gifts.
These are thy people, Vayu, who rejoice with Indra for their guard, rejoice with Gods for guards.
33 And now to Vasa Asvya here this stately woman is led forth,
Adorned with ornaments of gold.

**[08-047] HYMN XLVII. Adityas.**

1. GREAT help ye give the worshipper, Varuna, Mitra, Mighty Ones! No sorrow ever reaches him
whom ye, Adityas, keep from harm. Yours are incomparable aids, and good the succour they afford.
2 O Gods, Adityas, well ye know the way to keep all woes afar.
As the birds spread their sheltering wings, spread your protection over us.
3 As the birds spread their sheltering wings let your protection cover us.
We mean all shelter and defence, ye who have all things for your own.
4 To whomsoever they, Most Wise, have given a home and means of life,
O'er the whole riches of this man they, the Adityas, have control.
5 As drivers of the car avoid ill roads, let sorrows pass us by.
May we be under Indra's guard, in the Adityas' favouring grace.
6 For verily men sink and faint through loss of wealth which ye have given.
Much hath he gained from you, O Gods, whom ye, Adityas, have approached.
7 On him shall no fierce anger fall, no sore distress shall visit him,
To whom, Adityas, ye have lent your shelter that extendeth far.

8 Resting in you, O Gods, we are like men who fight in coats of mail.
Ye guard us from each great offence, ye guard us from each lighter fault.
9 May Aditi defend us, may Aditi guard and shelter us,
Mother of wealthy Mitra and of Aryaman and Varuna.
10 The shelter, Gods, that is secure, auspicious, free from malady,
A sure protection, triply strong, even that do ye extend to us.
11 Look down on us, Adityas, as a guide exploring from the bank.
Lead us to pleasant ways as men lead horses to an easy ford.
12 Ill be it for the demons' friend to find us or come near to us.
But for the milch-cow be it well, and for the man who strives for fame.
13 Each evil deed made manifest, and that which is concealed, O Gods,
The whole thereof remove from us to Trita Aptya far away.
14 Daughter of Heaven, the dream that bodes evil to us or to our kine,
Remove, O Lady of the Light, to Trita Aptya far away.
15 Even if, O Child of Heaven, it make a garland or a chain of gold,
The whole bad dream, whate'er it be, to Trita Aptya we consign.
16 To him whose food and work is this, who comes to take his share therein,
To Trita, and to Dvita, Dawn! bear thou the evil dream away.
17 As we collect the utmost debt, even the eighth and sixteenth part,
So unto Aptya we transfer together all the evil dream.
18 Now have we conquered and obtained, and from our trespasses are free.
Shine thou away the evil dream, O Dawn, whereof we are afraid.
Yours are incomparable aids, and good the succour they afford.

## [08-048] HYMN XLVIII. Soma.

1. WISELY have I enjoyed the savoury viand, religious-thoughted, best to find out treasure,
The food to which all Deities and mortals, calling it meath, gather themselves together.
2 Tlou shalt be Aditi as thou hast entered within, appeaser of celestial anger.
Indu, enjoying Indra's friendship, bring us - as a swift steed the car - forward to riches.
3 We have drunk Soma and become immortal; we have attained the light, the Gods discovered.
Now what may foeman's malice do to harm us? What, O Immortal, mortal man's deception?
4 Absorbed into the heart, be sweet, O Indu, as a kind father to his son, O Soma,
As a wise Friend to friend: do thou, wide-ruler, O Soma, lengthen out our days for living.
5 These glorious drops that give me freedom have I drunk.
Closely they knit my joints as straps secure a car.
Let them protect my foot from slipping on the way: yea, let the drops I drink preserve me from disease.
6 Make me shine bright like fire produced by friction: give us a clearer sight and make us better.
For in carouse I think of thee, O Soma, Shall I, as a rich man, attain to comfort?
7 May we enjoy with an enlivened spirit the juice thou givest, like ancestral riches.
O Soma, King, prolong thou our existence as Surya makes the shining days grow longer.
8 King Soma, favour us and make us prosper: we are thy devotees; of this be mindful.
Spirit and power are fresh in us, O Indu give us not up unto our foeman's pleasure.

9 For thou hast settled in each joint, O Soma, aim of men's eyes and guardian of our bodies.
When we offend against thine holy statutes, as a kind Friend, God, best of all, be gracious.
10 May I be with the Friend whose heart is tender, who, Lord of Bays! when quaffed will never harm me-
This Soma now deposited within me. For this, I pray for longer life to Indra.
11 Our maladies have lost their strength and vanished: they feared, and passed away into the darkness.
Soma hath risen in us, exceeding mighty, and we are come where men prolong existence.
12, Fathers, that Indu which our hearts have drunken, Immortal in himself, hath entered mortals.
So let us serve this Soma with oblation, and rest securely in his grace and favour.
13 Associate with the Fathers thou, O Soma, hast spread thyself abroad through earth and heaven.
So with oblation let us serve thee, Indu, and so let us become the lords of riches,
14 Give us your blessing, O ye Gods' preservers. Never may sleep or idle talk control us.
But evermore may we, as friends of Soma, speak to the synod with brave sons around us.
15 On all sides,. Soma, thou art our life-giver: aim of all eyes, light-finder, come within us.
Indu, of one accord with thy protections both from behind and from before preserve us.

## [08-049] HYMN XLIX. Agni.

1. AGNI, come hither with thy fires; we choose thee as Invoking Priest.
Let the extended ladle full of oil balm thee, best Priest, to sit on sacred grass.
2 For unto thee, O Angiras, O Son of Strength, move ladles in the sacrifice.
To Agni, Child of Force, whose locks drop oil, we seek, foremost in sacrificial rites.
3 Agni, thou art Disposer, Sage, Herald, bright God! and worshipful,
Best offercr, cheerful, to be praised in holy rites, pure Lord! by singers with their hymns.
4 Most Youthful and Eternal, bring the longing Gods to me, the guileless, for the feast.
Come, Vasu, to the banquet that is well-prepared: rejoice thee, gracious, with our songs.
5 Famed art thou, Agni, far and wide, Preserver, righteous, and a Sage.
The holy singers, O refulgent kindled God! arrangers, call on thee to come -
6 Shine, Most Resplendent! blaze, send bliss unto the folk, and to thy worshipper
Great art thou.
So may my princes, with good fires, subduing foes, rest in the keeping of the Gods.
7 O Agni, as thou burnest down to earth even high-grown underwood,
So, bright as Mitra is, burn him who injures us, him who plots ill against thy friend.
8 Give us not as a prey to mortal enemy, nor to the wicked friend of fiends.
With conquering guards, auspicious, unassailable, protect us, O Most Youthful God.
9 Protect us, Agni, through the first, protect us through the second hymn,

Protect us through three hymns, O Lord of Power and Might, through four hymns, Vasu, guard thou us.

10 Preserve us from each fiend who brings the Gods no gift, preserve thou us in deeds of strength:

For we possess in thee the nearest Friend of all, for service of the Gods and weal.

11 O Holy Agni, give us wealth renowned with men and strengthening life.

Bestow on us, O Helper, that which many crave, more glorious still by righteousness;

12 Wherewith we may o'ercome our rivals in the war, o'erpowering the foe's designs.

So wax thou by our food, O Excellent in strength. Quicken our thoughts that find out wealth.

13 Agni is even as a bull who whets and brandishes his horns. Well-sharpened are his jaws which may not be withstood: the Child of Strength hath powerful teeth.

14 Not to be stayed, O Bull, O Agni, are thy teeth when thou art spreading far and wide.

Make our oblations duly offered up, O Priest, and give us store of precious things.

15 Thou liest in the wood: from both thy Mothers mortals kindle thee.

Unweariedly thou bearest up the offerer's gifts, then shinest bright among the Gods.

16 And so the seven priests, O Agni, worship thee, Free-giver, Everlasting One.

Thou cleavest through the rock with heat and fervent glow. Agni, rise up above the men.

17 For you let us whose grass is trimmed call Agni, Agni, restless God.

Let us whose food is offered call to all the tribes Agni the Invoking Priest of men.

18 Agni, with noble psalm that tells his wish he dwells, thinking on thee who guardest him.

Speedily bring us strength of many varied sorts to be most near to succour us.

19 Agni, Praise-singer! Lord of men, God burner-up of Raksasas, Mighty art thou, the ever-present Household-Lord, Home-friend and Guardian from the sky.

20 Let no fiend come among us, O thou rich in light, no spell of those who deal in spells.

To distant pastures drive faint hunger: far away, O Agni, chase the demons' friends.

## [08-050] HYMN L. Indra.

1. BOTH boons,-may Indra, hitherward turned, listen to this prayer of ours,

And mightiest Maghavan with thought inclined to us come near to drink the Soma juice.

2 For him, strong, independent Ruler, Heaven and Earth have fashioned forth for power and might.

Thou seatest thee as first among thy peers in place, for thy soul longs for Soma juice.

3 Fill thyself full, O Lord of wealth, O Indra, with the juice we shed.

We know thee, Lord of Bay Steeds victor in the fight, vanquishing e'en the invincible.

4 Changeless in truth, O Maghavan Indra, let it be as thou in wisdom willest it.

May we, O fair of check, win booty with thine aid, O Thunderer, swiftly seeking it.

5 Indra, with all thy saving helps give us assistance, Lord of power.

For after thee we follow even as glorious bliss, thee, Hero, finder-out of wealth.

6 Increaser of our steeds and multiplying kine, a golden well, O God, art thou,

For no one may impair the gifts laid up in thee. Bring me whatever thing I ask.

7 For thou,-come to the worshipper!-wilt find great wealth to make us rich.

Fill thyself full, O Maghavan, for gain of kine, full, Indra, for the gain of steeds.

8 Thou as thy gift bestowest many hundred herds, yea, many thousands dost thou give.

With singers' hymns have we brought the Fort-render near, singing to Indra for his grace.

9 Whether the simple or the sage, Indra, have offered praise to thee,

He Satakratu! by his love hath gladdened thee, ambitious! ever pressing on!

10 If he the Strong of arm, the breaker-down of forts, the great Destroyer, hear my call,

We, seeking riches cry to Indra, Lord of wealth, to Satakratu with our lauds.

11 We count not then as sinners, nor as niggardly or foolish men,

When with the Soma juice which we have shed we make Indra, the Mighty One, our Friend.

12 Him have we yoked in fight, the powerful Conqueror, debt-claimer, not to be deceived.

Best charioteer, the Victor marks each fault, he knows the strong to whom he will come near.

13 Indra, give us security from that whereof we are afraid.

Help us, O Maghavan, let thy succour give us this: drive away foes and enemies.

14 For thou, O liberal Lord of bounty, strengthenest his ample home who worships thee.

So Indra, Maghavan, thou Lover of the Song, we with pressed Soma call on thee,

15 Indra is Vrtra-slayer, guard, our best defender from the foe.

May he preserve our last and middlemost, and keep watch from behind us and before.

16 Defend us from behind, below, above, in front, on all sides, Indra, shield us well.

Keep far away from us the terror sent from heaven: keep impious weapons far away.

17 Protect us, Indra, each to-day, each morrow, and each following day.

Our singers, through all days, shalt thou, Lord of the brave, keep safely both by day and night.

18 A crushing Warrior, passing rich is Maghavan, endowed with all heroic might.

Thine arms, O Satakratu, are exceeding strong, arms which have grasped the thunderbolt.

## [08-051] HYMN LI. Indra.

1. OFFER ye up as praise to him that wherein Indra takes delight.

The Soma-bringers magnify Indra's great energy with hymns.

Good are the gifts that Indra gives.

2 Sole among chiefs, companionless, impetuous, and peerless, he Hath waxen great o'er many folk, yea., over all things born, in might.

3 Lord of swift bounty, he will win e'en with a steed of worthless sort.

This, Indra, must be told of thee who wilt perform heroic deeds.

4 Come to us.hither: let us pay devotions that enhance thy might,

For which, Most Potent! thou wouldst fain bless the man here who strives for fame.

5 For thou, O Indra, makest yet more bold the spirit of the bold

Who with strong Soma serveth thee, still ready with his reverent prayers.

6 Worthy of song, he looketh down as a man looketh into wells.

Pleased with the Soma-bringer's skill he maketh him his mate and friend.

7 In strength and wisdom all the Gods, Indra, have yielded unto thee.
Be thou the Guard of all, O thou whom many praise.

8 Praised, Indra, is this might of thine, best for the service of the Gods,
That thou with power dost slay Vrtra, O Lord of Strength.

9 He makes the races of mankind like synods of the Beauteous One.
Indra knows this his manifest deed, and is renowned.

10 Thy might, O Indra, at its birth, thee also, and thy mental power,
In thy care, Maghavan rich in kine! they have increased exceedingly.

11 O Vrtra-slayer, thou and I will both combine for winning spoil.
Even malignity will consent, O Bolt-armed Hero, unto us.

12 Let us extol this Indra as truthful and never as untrue.
Dire is his death who pours no gifts great light hath he who offers them. Good are the gifts that Indra gives.

### [08-052] HYMN LII. Indra.

1. WITH powers of Mighty Ones hath he, Ancient, Beloved, been equipped,
Through whom the Father Manu made prayers cfficacious with the Gods.

2 Him, Maker of the sky, let stones wet with the Soma ne'er forsake,
Nor hymns and prayer that must be said.

3 Indra who knew full well disclosed the kine to the Angirases.
This his great deed must be extolled.

4 Indra, promoter of the song, the sage's Strengthener as of old,
Shall come to bless and succour us at presentation of this laud.

5 Now after their desire's intent the pious singers with the cry
Of Hail! have sung loud hymns to thee, Indra, to gain a stall of kine.

6 With Indra rest all deeds of might, deeds done and yet to be performed,
Whom singers know devoid of guile.

7 When the Five Tribes with all their men to Indra have sent out their voice,
And when the priest hath strewn much grass, this is the Friend's own dwellingpiace.

8 This praise is verily thine own: thou hast performed these manly deeds,
And sped the wheel upon its way.

9 At the o'erflowing of this Steer, boldly he strode for life, and took
Soma as cattle take their corn.

10 Receiving this and craving help, we, who with you are Daksa's sons,
Would fain exalt the Maruts' Lord.

11 Yea, Hero, with the singers we sing.to the duly-coming Band.
Allied with tbee may we prevail.

12 With us are raining Rudras, clouds accordant in call to battle, at the death of Vrtra,
The strong assigned to him who sings and praises. May Gods with Indra at their head protect us.

### [08-053] HYMN LIII. Andra.

1. MAY our hymns give thee great delight. Display thy bounty, Thunderer.
Drive off the enemies of prayer.

2 Crush with thy foot the niggard churls who bring no gifts.
Mighty art thou
There is not one to equal thee.

3 Thou art the Lord of Soma pressed, Soma impressed is also thine.
Thou art the Sovran of the folk.

4 Come, go thou forth, dwelling in heaven and listening to the prayers of men:
Thou fillest both the heavens and earth.

5 Even that hill with rocky heights, with hundreds, thousands, held within.
Thou for thy worshippers brakest through.

6 We call on thee both night and day to taste the flowing Soma juice:
Do thou fulfil our heart's desire.

7 Where is that ever-youthful Steer, strong. necked and never yet bent down?
What Brahman ministers to him?

8 To whose libation doth the Steer, betake him with delight therein?
Who takes delight in Indra now?

9 Whom, Vrtra-slayer, have thy gift and hero powers accompanied?
Who is thy dearest in the laud?

10 For thee among mankind, among the Purus is this Soma shed.
Hasten thou hither: drink thereof.

11 This, growing by Soma and by Saryanavan, dear to thee,
In Arjikiya, cheers thee best.

12 Hasten thou hitherward, and drink this for munificence to-day,
Delightful for thine eager draught.

### [08-054] HYMN LIV. Indra.

1. THOUGH, Indra, thou art called by men from east and west, from north and soutb,
Come hither quickly with fleet steeds

2 If in the effluence of heaven, rich in its light, thou takest joy,
Or in the sea in Soma juice.

3 With songs I call thee, Great and Wide, even as a cow to profit us,
Indra, to drink the Soma-draught.

4 Hither, O Indra, let thy Bays bear up and, bring upon thy car
Thy glory, God! and majesty.

5 Thou, Indra, wouldst be sung and praised as great, strong, lordly in thy deeds
Come hither, drink our Soma juice.

6 We who have shed the Soma and prepared the feast are calling thee.
To sit on this our sacred grass.

7 As, Indra, thou art evermore the common Lord of all alike,
As such we invocate thee now.

8 The men with stones have milked for thee this nectar of the Soma juice:
Indra, be pleased with it, and drink.

9 Neglect all pious men with skill in sacred song: come hitherward,
With speed, and give us high renown.

10 Gods, may the mighty rest unharmed, the King who gives me spotted kine,
Kine decked with golden ornaments.

11 Beside a thousand spotted kine I have received a gift of gold,
Pure, brilliant, and exceeding great.

12 Durgaha's grandsons, giving me a thousand kine, munificent,
Have won renown among the Gods.

### [08-055] HYMN LV. Indra.

1. LOUD singing at the sacred rite where Soma flows we priests invoke

With haste, that he may help, as the bard's Cherisher, Indra who findeth wealth for you.
2. Whom with fair helm, in rapture of the juice, the firm resistless slayers hinder not:
Giver of glorious wealth to him who sing a his praise, honouring him who toils and pours:
3 Sakra, who like a curry-comb for horses or a golden goad,
Indra, the Vrtra-slayer, urges eagerly the opening of the stall of kine:
4 Who for the worshipper scatters forth ample wealth, even though buried, piled in heaps:
May Indra, Lord of Bay Steeds, fair-helmed Thunderer, act at his pleasure, as he lists.
5 Hero whom many praise, what thou hast longed for, oven of old, from men.
All that we offer unto thee, O Indra, now, sacrifice, laud, effectual speech.
6 To Soma, Much-invoked, Bolt-armed! for thy carouse, Celestial, Soma-drinker come.
Thou to the man who- prays and pours the juice hast been best giver of delightful wealth.
7 Here, verily, yesterday we let the Thunder-wielder drink his fill.
So in like manner offer him the jifice today. Now range you by the Glorious One.
8 Even the wolf, the savage beast that rends the sheep, follows the path of his decrees.
So graciously accepting, Indra, this our praise, with wondrous thought come forth to us.
9 What manly deed of vigour now remains that Indra hath not done?
Who hath not heard his glorious title and his fame, the Vrtra-slayer from his birth?
10 'How great his power resistless! how invincible the Vrtra-slayer's matchless might!
Indra excels all usurers who see the day, excels all traffickers in strength.
11 O Indra, Vrtra-slayer, we, thy very constant worshippers,
Bring prayers ne'er heard before to thee, O Much-invoked, O Thunder-armed, to be thy meed.
12 O thou of mighty acts, the aids that are in thee call forward many an eager hope.
Past the drink-offerings, Vasu, even of the good, hear my call, Strongest God, and come.
13 Verily, Indra, we are thine, we worshippers depend on thee.
For there is none but only thou to show us race, O Maghavan, thou much invoked.
14 From this our misery and famine set us free, from this dire curse deliver us.
Succour us with thine help and with tby wondrous thought. Most Mighty, finder of the way.
15 Now let your Soma juice be poured; be not afraid, O Kali's sons.
This darkening sorrow goes away; yea, of itself it vanishes.

## [08-056] HYMN LVI. Adityas.

1. Now pray we to these Ksatriyas, to the Adityas for their aid,
These who are gracious to assist.
2 May Mitra bear us oer distress, and Varuna and Aryaman,
Yea, the Adityas, as they know.
3 For wonderful and meet for praise is these Adityas' saving help
To him who offers and prepares.
4 The mighty aid of you, the Great, Varuna, Mitra, Aryarnan,
We claim to be our sure defence.
5 Guard us, Adityas, still alive, before the deadly weapon strike:
Are yc not they who hear our call?
6 What sheltering defence ye have for him who toils in pouring gifts,

Graciously bless ye us therewith.
7 Adityas, Gods, from sorrow there is freedom; for the sinless, wealth,
O ye in whom no fault is seen.
8 Let not this fetter bind us fast: may he release us for success;
For strong is Indra and renowned.
9 O Gods who fain would lend your aid, destroy not us as ye destroy
Your enemies who go astray.
10 And thee too, O Great Aditi, thee also, Goddess, I address,
Thee very gracious to assist.
11 Save us in depth and shallow from the foe, thbu Mother of Strong Sons
Let no one of our seed be harmed.
12 Far-spread! wide-ruling! grant that we, unharmed by envy, may expand
Grant that our progeny may live.
13 Those who, the Princes of the folk, in native glory, neer deceived,
Maintain their statutes, void of guilt-
14 As such, from mouth of ravening wolves, O ye Adityas, rescue us,
Like a bound thief, O Aditi.
15 Adityas, let this arrow, yea, let this mali. gnity depart
From us or eer it strike us dead.
16 Fori Bountiful Adityas, we have evermore enjoyed your help,
Both now and in die days of old.
17 To every one, O ye Most Wise, who turneth even from sin to you,
Ye Gods vouchsafe that he may live.
18 May this new mercy profit us, which, ye Adityas, frees like one,
Bound from his bonds, O Aditi.
19 O ye Adityas, this your might is not to be despised by us:
So be ye graciously inclined.
20 Let not Vivasvan's weapon nor the shaft, Adityas, wrought with skill,
Destroy us ere old age be nigh.
21 On every side dispel all sin, Adityas, all hostility,
Indigence, and combined attack.

## [08-057] HYMN LVII. Indra.

1. EVEN as a car to give us aid, we draw thee hither for our bliss,
Strong in thy deeds, checking assault, Lord, Mightiest Indra, of the brave!
2 Great in tby power and wisdom, Strong, with thought that comprehendeth all
Thou hast filled full with majesty.
3 Thou very Mighty One, whose hands by virtue of thy greatness grasp,
The golden bolt that breaks its way.
4 Your Lord of might that ne'er hath bent, that ruleth over all mankind,
I call, that he, as he is wont, may aid the chariots and the men.
5 Whom, ever furthering, in frays that win the light, in both the hosts
Men call to succour and to help.
6 Indra, the Strong, the measureless, worthy of praise, Most Bountiful,
Sole Ruler even over wealth.
7 Him, for his ample bounty, him, this Indra do I urge to drink,
Who, as his praise was sung of old, the Dancer, is the Lord of men.
8 Thou Mighty One, whose friendship none of mortals ever hath obtained
None will attain unto thy might.
9 Aided by thee, with thee allied, in frays for water and for sun,
Bolt-armed! may we win ample spoil.

10 So seek we thee with sacrifice and songs, chief Lover of the Song,
As, in our battles Indra, thou to Purumayya gavest help.
11 O Thunderer, thou whose friendship and whose onward guidance both are sweet,
Thy sacrifice must be prepared.
12 To us, ourselves, give ample room, give for our dwelling ample room
Give ample room to us to live.
13 We count the banquet of the Gods a spacious pathway for the men,
And for the cattle, and the car.
14 Six men, yea, two and two, made glad with Soma juice, come near to me
With offerings pleasant to the taste.
15 Two brown-hued steeds, Indrota's gift, two bays from Rksa's son were mine,
From Asvamedha's son two red.
16 From Atithigva good car-steeds; from Arksa rein-obeying steeds,
From Asvamedha beauteous ones.
17 Indrota, Atithigva's son, gave me six horses matched with mares
And Patakratu gave besides.
18 Marked above all, amid the brown, is the red mare Vrsanvati,
Obedient to the rein and whip.
19 O bound to me by deeds of might, not even the man who loves to blame.
Hath found a single fault in you.

## [08-058] HYMN LVIII. Indra.

1. I SEND you forth the song of praise for Indu, hero-gladdener.
With hymn and plenty he invites you to complete the sacrifice.
2 Thou wishest for thy kine a bull, for those who long for his approach,
For those who turn away from him, lord of thy cows whom none may kill.
3 The dappled kine who stream with milk prepare his draught of Soma juice:
Clans in the birth-place of the Gods, in the three luminous realms of heaven.
4 Praise, even as he is known, with song Indra the guardian of the kine,
The Son of Truth, Lord of the brave.
5 Hither his Bay Steeds have been sent, red Steeds are on the sacred grass,,
Where we in concert sing our songs.
6 For Indra Thunder-armed the kine have yielded mingled milk and meath,
What time he found them in the vault.
7 When I and Indra mount on high up to the Bright One's place and home,
We, having drunk of meath, will reach his seat whose Friends are three times seven.
8 Sing, sing ye forth your songs of praise, ye Briyamedhas, sing your songs:
Yea, let young children sing their lauds as a strong castle praise ye him.
9 Now loudly let the viol sound, the lute send out its voice with might,
Shrill be, the music of the string. To Indra. is the hymn up-raised.
10 When bither speed the dappled cows, unflinching, easy to be milked,
Seize quickly, as it bursts away, the Soma juice for Indra's drink.
11 Indra hath drunk, Agni hath drunk. all Deities have drunk their fill.

Here Varuna shall have his home, to whom the floods have sung aloud as motherkine unto their calves.
12 Thou, Varuna, to whom belong Seven Rivers, art a glorious God.
The waters flow into thy throat as 'twere a pipe with ample mouth.
13 He who hath made the fleet steeds spring, well-harnessed, to the worshipper,
He, the swift Guide, is that fair form that loosed the horses near at hand.
14 Indra, the very Mighty, holds his enemies in utter scorn.
He, far away, and yet a child, cleft the cloud smitten by his voice.
15 He, yet a boy exceeding small, mounted his newly-fashioned car.
He for his Mother and his Sire cooked the wild mighty buffalo.
16 Lord of the home, fair-helmeted, ascend thy chariot wrought of gold.
We will attend the Heavenly One, the thousand-footed, red of hue, matchless, who blesses where he goes.
17 With reverence they come hitherward to him as to. a Sovran lord,
That they may bring him near for this man's good success, to prosper and bestow his gifts.
18 The Priyamedhas have observed the offering of the men of old,
Of ancient custom, while they strewed the sacred grass, and spread their sacrificial food.

## [08-059] HYMN LIX. Indra.

1. HE who, as Sovran Lord of men, moves with his chariots unrestrained,
The Vrtra-slayer vanquisher, of fighting hosts, preeminent, is praised with song.
2 Honour that Indra, Puruhanman! for his aid, in whose sustaining hand of old,
The splendid bolt of thunder was deposited, as the great Sun was set in heaven.
3 No one by deed attains to him who works and strengthens evermore:
No, not by sacrifice, to Indra. praised o all, resistless, daring, bold in might.
4 The potent Conqueror, invincible in war, him at whose birth the Mighty Ones,
The Kine who spread aftar, sent their loud voices out, heavens, earths seat their loud voices out,
5 O Indra, if a hundred heavens and if a hundred earths were thine-
No, not a thousand Suns could match thee at thy birth, not both the worlds, O Thunderer.
6 Thou, Hero, hast performed thy hero deeds with might, yea, all with strength, O Strongest One.
Maghavan, help us to a stable full of kine, O Thunderer, with wondrous aids.
7 Let not a godless mortal gain this food, O thou whose life is long!
But one who yokes the bright-hued steeds, the Etasas, even Indra yoker of the Bays.
8 Urge ye the Conqueror to give, your Indra greatly to be praised,
To be invoked in shallow waters and in depths, to be invoked in deeds of might.
9 O Vasu, O thou Hero, raise us up to ample opulence.
Raise us to gain of mighty wealth, O Maghavan, O Indra, to sublime renown.
10 Indra, thou justifiest us, and tramplest down thy slanderers.
Guard thyself, valiant Hero, in thy vital parts: strike down the Dasa with thy blows.

11 The man who brings no sacrifice, inhuman, godless, infidel,
Him let his friend the mountain cast to rapid death, the mountain
cast the Dasyu down.
12 O Mightiest Indra, loving us, gather thou up, as grains of corn,
Within thine hand, of these their kine, to give away, yea, gather
twice as loving us.
13 O my companions, wish for power. How may we perfect Sara's
praise,
The liberal princely patron, never to be harmed?
14 By many a sage whose grass is trimmed thou art continually
praised,
That thou, O Sara, hast bestowed here one and here another'calf.
15 The noble, Suradeva's son, hath brought a calf, led by the car
to three of us.
As a chief brings a goat to milk.

## [08-060] HYMN LX. Agni.

1. O AGNI, with thy mighty wealth guard us from all malignity,
Yea, from all hate of mortal man.
2 For over thee, O Friend from birih, the wrath of man hath no
control:
Nay, Guardian of the earth art thou.
3 As such, with all the Gods, O Son of Strength, auspicious in thy
flame.
Give us wealth bringing all things good.
4 Malignities stay not from wealth the mortal man whom, Agni,
thou
Protectest while he offers gifts.
5 Sage Agni, be whom thou dost urge, in worship of the Gods, to
wealth,
With thine assistance winneth kine.
6 Riches with many heroes thou hast for the man who offers gifts:
Lead thou us on to higher bliss.
7 Save us, O Jatavedas, nor abandon us to him who sins,
Unto the evil-hearted man.
8 O Agni, let no godless man avert thy bounty as a God:
Over all treasures thou art Lord.
9 So, Son of Strength, tbou aidest us to what is great and
excellent.
Those, Vasu! Friend! who sing thy praise.
10 Let our songs come anear to him beauteous and bright with
piercing flame
Our offerings, with our homage, to the
Lord of wealth, to him whom many praise, for help:
11 To Agni Jatavedas, to the Son of Strength, that he may give us
precious gifts,
Immortal, from of old Priest among mortal men, the most
delightful in the house.
12 Agni, made yours by sacrifice, Agni, while holy rites advance;
Agni, the first in songs, first with the warrior steed; Agril to win
the land for us.
13 May Agni who is Lord of wealth vouchsafe us food for
friendship sake.
Agni we ever seek for seed and progeny, the Vasu who protects
our lives.
14 Solicit with your chants, for help, Agni the God with piercing
flame,
For riches famous Agni, Purumilha and ye men! Agni to light our
dwelling well.
15 Agni we laud that he may keep our foes afar, Agni to give us
health and strength.
Let him as Guardian be invoked in all the tribes, the lighter-up of
glowing brands.

## [08-061] HYMN LXI. Agni.

1. PREPARE oblation: let him come; and let the minister serve
again
Who knows the ordering thereof,
2 Rejoicing in his friendship, let the priest be seated over man,
Beside the shoot of active power.
3 Him, glowing bright beyond all thought, they seek among the
race of man;
With him for tougue they seize the food.
4 He hath inflamed the twofold plain: lifegiving, he hath climbed
the wood,
And with his tongue hath struck the rock.
5 Wandering here the radiant Calf finds none to fetter him, and
seeks
The Mother to declare his praise.
6 And now that great and mighty team, the team of horses that
are his,
And traces of his car, are seen.
7 The seven milk a single cow; the two set other five to work,
On the stream's loud-resounding bank.
8 Entreated by Vivasvan's ten, Indra cast down the water-jar
With threefold hammer from the sky.
9 Three times the newIy-kindled flame proceeds around the
sacrifice:
The priests anoint it with the meath.
10 With reverence they drain the fount that circles with its wheel
above,
Exhaustless, with the mouth below.
11 The pressing-stones are set at work: the meath is poured into
the tank,
At the out-shedding of the fount.
12 Ye cows, protect the fount: the two Mighty Ones bless the
sacrifice.
The handles twain are wrought of gold.
13 Pour on the juice the ornament which reaches both the heaven
and earth
Supply the liquid to the Bull.
14 These know their own abiding-place: like calves beside the
mother cows
They meet together with their kin.
15 Devouring in their greedy jaws, they make sustaining food in
heaven,
To Indra, Agni light and prayer.
16 The Pious One milked out rich food, sustenance dealt in
portions seven,
Together with the Sun's seven rays.
17 I took some Soma when the Sun rose up, O Mitra, Varuna.
That is the sick man's medicine.
18 From where oblations must be laid, which is the Well-
beloved's home,
He with his tongue hath compassed heaven.

## [08-062] HYMN LXII. Asvins.

1. ROUSE ye for him who keeps the Law, yoke your steeds,
Aiyins, to your car
Let your protecting help be near.
2 Come, Asvins, with your car more swift than is the twinkling of
an eye
Let your protecting help be near.
3 Asvins, ye overlaid with cold the fiery pit for Atri's sake:
Let your protecting help be near.
4 Where are ye? whither are ye gone? whither, like falcons, have
ye flown?
Let your protecting help be near.
5 If ye at any time this day are listening to this my call,
Let your protecting help be near.
6 The Asvins, fust to hear our prayer, for closest kinship I
approach:

215

Let your protecting help be near.

7 For Atri ye, O Asvins, made a dwellingplace to shield him well,
Let your protecting help be near.

8 Ye warded off the fervent heat for Atri when he sweetly spake:
Let your protecting help be near.

9 Erst Saptavadbri by his prayer obtained the trenchant edge of fire:
Let your protecting help be near.

10 Come hither, O ye Lords of wealth, and listen to this call of mine:
Let your protecting help be near.

11 What is this praise told forth of you as Elders in the ancient way?
Let your protecting help be near.

12 One common brotherhood is yours, Asvins your kindred is the same:
Let your protecting help be near.

13 This is your chariot, Asvins, which speeds through the regions, earth and heaven
Let your protecting aid be near.

14 Approach ye hitherward to us with thousands both of steeds and kine:
Let your protecting help be near.

15 Pass us not by, remember us with thousands both of kine aud steeds:
Let your protecting help be near.

16 The purple-tinted Dawn hath risen, and true to Law hath made the light
Let your protecting help be near.

17 He looked upon the Asvins, as an axearmed man upon a tree:
Let your protecting help be near.

18 By the black band encompassed round, break it down, bold one, like a fort.
Let your protecting help be near.

## [08-063] HYMN LXIII. Agni.

1. EXERTING all our strength with thoughts of power we glorify in speech
Agni your dear familiar Friend, the darling Guest in every home.

2 Whom, served with sacrificial oil like Mitra, men presenting gifts
Eulogize with their songs of praise

3 Much-lauded Jatavedas, him who bears oblations up to heaven
Prepared in service of the Gods.

4 To noblest Agni, Friend of man, best Vrtra-slayer, are we come,
Him in whose presence Rksa's son, mighty Srutarvan, waxes great;

5 To deathless Jatavedas, meet for praise, adored, with sacred oil,
Visible through the gloom o:f night

6 Even Agni whom these priestly men worship with sacrificial gifts,
With lifted ladles offering them.

7 O Agni, this our newest hymn hath been addressed from us to thee,
O cheerful Guest, well-born, most wise, worker of wonders, ne'er deceived.

8 Agni, may it be dear to thee, most grateful, and exceeding sweet:
Grow mightier, eulogized therewith.

9 Splendid with splendours may it be, and in the battle with the foe
Add loftier glory to thy fame.

10 Steed, cow, a lord of heroes, bright like Indra, who shall fill the car.
Whose high renown ye celebrate, and people praise each glorious deed.

11 Thou whom Gopavana made glad with song, O Agni Angiras,

Hear this my call, thou Holy One.

12 Thou whom the priestly folk implore to aid the gathering of the spoil,
Such be thou in the fight with foes.

13 I, called to him who reels with joy, Srutarvan, Rksa's son, shall stroke
The heads of four presented steeds, like the long wool of fleecy rams.

14 Four coursers with a splendid car, Savistha's horses, fleet of foot,
Shall bring me to the sacred feast, as flying steeds brought Tugra's son.

15 The very truth do I declare to thee, Parusni, mighty flood.
Waters! no man is there who gives more horses than Savistha gives.

## [08-064] HYMN LXIV. Agni.

1. YOKE, Agni, as a charioteer, thy steeds who best invite the Gods: As ancient Herald seat thyself.

2 And, God, as skilfullest of all, call for us bitherward the Gods:
Give all our wishes sure effect.

3 For thou, Most Youthful, Son of Strength, thou to whom sacrifice is paid,
Art holy, faithful to the Law.

4 This Agni, Lord of wealth and spoil hundredfold, thousandfold, is head
And chief of riches and a Sage.

5 As craftsmen bend the felly, so bend at our general call: come nigh,
Angiras, to the sacrifice.

6 Now, O Virupa, rouse for him, Strong God who shines at early morn,
Fair praise with voice that ceases not.

7 With missile of this Agni, his who looks afar, will we lay low
The thief in combat for the kine.

8 Let not the Companies of Gods fail us, like Dawns that float away,
Like cows who leave the niggardly.

9 Let not the sinful tyranny of any fiercely hating foe
Smite us, as billows smite a ship.

10 O Agni, God, the people sing reverent praise to thee for strength:
With terrors trouble thou the foe.

11 Wilt thou not, Agni, lend us aid in winning cattle, winning wealth?
Maker of room, make room for us.

12 In this great battle cast us not aside as one who bears a load:
Snatch up the wealih and win it all.

13 O Agni, let this plague pursue and fright another and not us:
Make our impetuous strength more strong.

14 The reverent or unwearied man whose holy labour he accepts,
Him Agni favours with success.

15 Abandoning the foeman's host pass hither to this company:
Assist the men with whom I stand.

16 As we have known thy gracious help, as of a Father, long ago,
So now we pray to thee for bliss.

## [08-065] HYMN LXV. Indra.

I. NOT to forsake me, I invoke this Indra girt by Maruts,
Lord Of magic power who rules with might.

2 This Indra with his Marut Friends clave into pieces Vrtra's bead
With hundred-knotted thunderbolt.

3 Indra, with Marut Friends grown strong, hath rent asunder Vrtra, and
Released the waters of the sea.

4 This is that Indra who, begirt by Maruts, won the light of heaven

That he might drink the Soma juice.
5 Mighty, impetuous, begirt by Maruts, him who loudly roars,
Indra we invocate with songs.
6 Indra begirt by Maruts we invoke after the ancient plan,
That he may drink the Soma juice.
7 O liberal Indra, Marut-girt, much-lauded Satakratu, drink
The Soma at this sacrifice.
8 To thee, O Indra, Marut-girt, these Soma juices, Thunderer!
Are offered from the heart with lauds.
9 Drink, Indra, with thy Marut Friends, pressed Soma at the morning rites,
Whetting thy thunderbolt with strength.
10 Arising in thy might, thy jaws thou shookest, Indra, having quaffed
The Soma which the mortar pressed.
11 Indra, both worlds complained to thee when uttering thy fearful roar,
What time thou smotest Dasyus dead.
12 From Indra have I measured out a song eight-footed with nine parts,
Delicate, faithful. to the Law.

### [08-066] HYMN LXVI. Indra.

1. SCARCELY was Satakratu, born when of his Mother he inquired,
Who are the mighty? Who are famed?
2. Then Savassi declared to him Aurnavabha, Ahisuva:
Son, these be they thou must o'erthrow
3 The Vrtra-slayer smote them all as spokes are hammered into naves:
The Dasyu-killer waxed in might.
4 Then Indra at a single draught drank the contents of thirty pails,
Pails that were filled with Soma juice.
5 Indra in groundless realms of space pierced the Gandharva through, that he
Might make Brahmans' strength increase.
6 Down from the mountains Indra shot hither his well-directed shaft:
He gained the ready brew of rice.
7 One only is that shaft of thine, with thousand feathers, hundred barbs,
Which, Indra, thou hast made thy friend.
8 Strong as the gbhus at thy birth, therewith to those who praise thee, men,
And women, bring thou food to eat.
9 By thee these exploits were achieved, the mightiest deeds, abundantly:
Firm in thy heart thou settest them.
10 All these things Visnu brought, the Lord of ample stride whom thou hadst sent-
A hundred buffaloes, a brew of rice and milk: and Indra, slew the ravening boar
11 Most deadly is thy bow, successful, fashioned well: good is thine arrow, decked with gold.
Warlike and well equipped thine arms are, which increase sweetness for him who drinks the sweet.

### [08-067] HYMN LXVII. Indra.

1. BRING us a thousand, Indra, as our guerdon for the Soma juice:
Hundreds of kine, O Hero, bring.
2 Bring cattle, bring us ornament, bring us embellishment and steeds,
Give us, besides, two rings of gold.
3 And, Bold One, bring in ample store rich jewels to adorn thi; ear,

For thou, Good Lord, art far renowned.
4 None other is there for the priest, Hero! but thou, to give him gifts,
To win much spoil and prosper him.
5 Indra can never be brought low, Sakra can never be subdued:
He heareth and beholdeth all.
6 He spieth out the wrath of man, he who can never be deceived:
Ere blame can come he marketh it.
7 He hath his stomach full of might, the Vrtra-slayer, Conqueror,
The Soma-drinker, ordering all.
8 In thee all treasures are combined, Soma all blessed things in thee,
Uninjured, easy to bestow.
9 To thee speeds forth my hope that craves the gift of corn, and kine and gold,
Yea, craving horses, speeds to thee.
10 Indra, through hope in thee alone even this sickle do I grasp.
Fill my hand, Maghavan, with all that it can hold of barley cut or gathered up.

### [08-068] HYMN LXVIII. Soma.

1. THIS here is Soma, ne'er restrained, active, all-conquering bursting forth,
Rsi and Sage by sapience,
2 All that is bare he covers o'er, all that is sick he medicines;
The blind man sees, the cripple walks.
3 Thou, Soma, givest wide defence against the hate of alien men,
Hatreds that waste and weaken us.
4 Thou by thine insight and thy skill, Impetuous One, from heaven and earth
Drivest the sinner's enmity.
5 When to their task they come with zeal, may they obtain the Giver's grace,
And satisfy his wish who thirsts.
6 So may he find what erst was lost, so may be speed the pious man,
And lengthen his remaining life.
7 Gracious, displaying tender love, unconquered, gentle in thy thoughts,
Be sweet, O Soma, to our heart.
8 O Soma, terrify us not; strike us not with alarm, O King:
Wound not our heart with dazzling flame.
9 When in my dwelling-place I see the wicked enemies of Gods,
King, chase their hatred far away, thou Bounteous One, dispel our foes.

### [08-069] HYMN LXIX. Indra

1. O Sarakratu! truely I have made none else my Comforter.
Indra; be gracious unto us.
2 Thou who hast ever aided us kindly of old to win the spoil,
As such, O Indra, favour us.
3 What now? As prompter of the poor thou helpest him who sheds the juice.
Wilt thou not, Indra, strengthen us?
4 O Indra, help our chariot on, yea, Thunderer, though it lag behind:
Give this my car the foremost place.
5 Ho there! why sittest thou at case? Make thou my chariot to be first
And bring the fame of victory near.
6 Assist our car that seeks the prize. What can be easier for thee?
So make thou us victorious.
7 Indra, be firm: a fort art thou. To thine appointed place proceeds
The auspicious hymn in season due.
8 Let not our portion be disgrace. Broad is the course, the prize is set,

The barriers are opened wide.

9 This thing we wish. that thou mayst take thy fourth, thy sacrificial name.

So art thou held to be our Lord.

10 Ekadyu hath exalted you, Immortals: both Goddesses and Gods hath he delighted.

Bestow upon him bounty meet for praises. May he, enriched with prayer, come soon and early.

### [08-070] HYMN LXX. Indra.

1. INDRA, God of the mighty arm, gather for us with thy right hand

Manifold and nutritious spoil.

2 We know thee mighty in thy deeds, of mighty bounty, mighty wealth,

Mighty in measure, prompt to aid.

3 Hero, when thou art fain to give, neither may Gods nor mortal men

Restrain thee like a fearful Bull.

4 Come, let us glorify Indra, Lord supreme of wealth, Self-ruling King:

In bounty may he harm us not.

5 Let prelude sound and following chant so let him hear the Saman sung,

And with his bounty answer us.

6 O Indra, with thy right hand bring, and with thy left remember us.

Let us not lose our share of wealth.

7 Come nigh, O Bold One, boldly bring hither the riches of the churl

Who giveth least of all the folk.

8 Indra, the booty which thou hast with holy singers to receive,

Even that booty win with us.

9 Indra, thy swiftly-coming spoil, the booty which rejoices all,

Sounds quick in concert with our hopes.

### [08-071] HYMN LXXI. Indra.

1. HASTE forward to us from afar, or, Vrtra-slayer, from anear,

To meet the offering to the meath.

2 Strong are the Soma-draughts; come nigh: the juices fill thee with delight:

Drink boldly even as thou art wont'.

3 Joy, Indra, in the strengthening food et it content thy wish and thought,

And be delightful to thine heart.

4 Come to us thou who hast no foe: we call thee down to hymns of praise,

In heaven's sublimest realm of light.

5 This Soma here expressed with stones and dressed with milk for thy carouse,

Indra, is offered up to thee.

6 Graciously, Indra, hear my call. Come and obtain the draught, and sate

Thyself with juices blent with milk.

7 The Soma, Indra, which is shed in chalices and vats for thee,

Drink thou, for thou art Lord thereof.

8 The Soma seen within themats, as in the flood the Moon is seen,

Drink thou, for thou art Lord thereof.

9 That which the Hawk brought in his claw, inviolate, through the air to thee,

Drink thou, for thou art Lord thereof.

### [08-072] HYMN LXXII. Visvedevas.

1. WE choose unto ourselves that high protection of the Mighty Gods

That it may help and succour us.

2 May they be ever our allies, Varuna, Mitra, Aryaman,

Far-seeing Gods who prosper us.

3 Ye furtherers of holy Law, transport us safe o'er many woes,

As over water-floods in ships.

4 Dear wealth be Aryaman to us, Varuna dear wealth meet for praise:

Dear wealth we choose unto ourselves.

5 For Sovrans of dear wealth are ye, Adityas, not of sinner's wealth,

Ye sapient Gods who slay the foe.

6 We in our homes, ye Bounteous Ones, and while we journey on the road,

Invoke you, Gods, to prosper us.

7 Regard us, Indra, Visnu, here, ye Asvins and the Marut host,

Us who are kith and kin to you.

8 Ye Bounteous Ones, from time of old we here set forth our brotherhood,

Our kinship in. the Mother's womb.

9 Then come with Indra for your chief, as early day, ye Bounteous Gods

Yea, 1 address you now for this.

### [08-073] HYMN LXXIII. Agni.

1. AGNI, your dearest Guest, I laud, him who is loving as a friend,

Who brings us riches like a car.

2 Whom as a far-foreseeing Sage the Gods have, from the olden time,

Established among mortal men.

3 Do thou, Most Youthful God, protect the men who offer, hear their songs,

And of thyself preserve their seed.

4 What is the praise wherewith, O God, Afigiras, Agni, Son of Strength,

We, after thine own wish and thought,

5 May serve thee, O thou Child of Power, and with what sacrifice's plan?

What prayer shall I now speak to thee?

6 Our God, make all of us to dwell in happy habitations, and

Reward our songs with spoil and wealth.

7 Lord of the house, what plenty fills the songs which thou inspirest now,

Thou whose hymn helps to win the kine?

8 Hirn Wise and Strong they glorify, the foremost Champion in the fray,

And mighty in his dwelling-place.

9 Agni, he dwells in rest and peace who smites and no one smites again:

With hero sons he prospers well

### [08-074] HYMN LXXIV. Asvins.

1. To this mine invocation, O ye Asvins, ye Nasatyas, come,

To drink the savoury Soma juice.

2 This laud of mine, ye Asvins Twain, and this mine invitation hear,

To drink the savoury Soma juice.

3 Here Krsna is invoking you, O Asvins, Lords of ample wealth.

To drink the savoury Soma juice.

4 List, Heroes, to the singer's call, the call of Krsna lauding you,

To drink the savoury Soma juice.

5 Chiefs, to the sage who sings your praise grant an inviolable home,

To drink the savoury Soma juice.

6 Come to the worshipper's abode, Asvins, who here is lauding you,

To drink the savoury Soma juice.

7 Yoke to the firmly jointed car the ass which draws you, Lords of wealth.
To drink the savoury Soma juice.
8 Come hither, Asvins, on your car of triple form with triple seat,
To drink the savoury Soma juice.
9 O Asvins, O Nasatyas, now accept with favouring grace my songs,
To drink the savoury Soma juice.

## [08-075] HYMN LXXV. Asvins.

1. YE Twain are wondrous strong, well-skilled in arts that heal, both bringers of delight, ye both won
Daksa's praise.
Visvaka calls on you as such to save his life. Break ye not off our friendship, come and set me free.
2 How shall he praise you now who is distraught in mind? Ye Twain give wisdom for the gainof what
is good.
Visvaka calls on you as such to save his life. Break ye not off our friendship, come and set me free.
3 Already have ye Twain, possessors of great wealth, prospered Visnapu thus for gain of what is
good.
Visvaka calls on you as such to save his life. Break ye not off our friendship, come and set me free.
4 And that Impetuous Hero, winner of the spoil, though he is far away, we call to succour us,
Whose gracious favour, like a father's, is most sweet. Break ye not off our friendship, come and set
me free.
5 About the holy Law toils Savitar the God the horn of holy Law hath he spread far and wide.
The holy Law hath quelled even mighty men of war. Break ye not off our ftiendship, come and act me
free.

## [08-076] HYMN LXXVI. Asvins.

1. SPLENDID, O Asvins, is your praise. Come fountain-like, to pour the stream.
Of the sweet juice effused-dear is it, Chiefs, in heaven-drink like two wild bulls at a pool.
2 Drink the libation rich in sweets, O Asvins Twain: sit. Heroes, on the sacred grass.
Do ye with joyful heart in the abode of man preserve his life by means of wealth.
3 The Priyamedhas bid you come with all the succours that are yours.
Come to his house whose holy grass is trimmed, to dear sacrifice at the morning rites.
4 Drink ye the Soma rich in meath, ye Asvins Twain: sit gladly on the sacred grass.
So, waxen mighty, to our eulogy from heaven come ye as wild-bulls to the pool.
5 Come to us, O ye Asvins, now with steeds of many a varied hue,
Ye Lords of splendour, wondrous, borne on paths of gold, drink Soma, ye who strengthen Law.
6 For we the priestly singers, fain tohymn your praise, invoke you for the gain of strength.
So, wondrous, fair, and famed for great deeds come to us, through our hymn, Asvins, when ye hear.

## [08-077] HYMN LXXVII. Indra.

1. As cows low to their calves in stalls, so with our songs we glorify
This Indra, even your Wondrous God who checks attack, who joys in the delicious juice.

2 Celestial, bounteous Giver, girt about with might, rich, mountain-like, in precious things,
Him swift we seek. for foodful booty rich in kine, brought hundredfold and thousandfold.
3 Indra, the strong and lofty hills are powerless to bar thy way.
None stay that act of thine when thou wouldst fain give wealth to one like me who sings thy praise.
4 A Warrior thou by strength, wisdom, and wondrous deed, in might excellest all that is.
Hither may this our hymn attract thee to our help, the hymn which Gotamas have made.
5 For in thy might thou stretchest out beyond the boundaries of heaven.
The earthly region, Indra, comprehends thee not. After thy Godhead hast thou waxed.
6 When, Maghavan, thou honourest the worshipper, no one is there to stay thy wealth.
Most liberal Giver thou, do thou inspire our song of praise, that we may win the spoil.

## [08-078] HYMN LXXVIII. Indra.

1. To Indra sing the lofty hymn, Maruts that slays the Vrtras best.
Whereby the Holy Ones created for the God the light divine that ever wakes.
2 Indra who quells the curse blew curses far away, and then in splendour came to us.
Indra, refulgent with thy Marut host! the Gods strove eagerly to win thy love.
3 Sing to your lofty Indra, sing, Maruts, a holy hymn of praise.
Let Satakratu, Vrtra-slayer, kill the foe with hundred-knotted thunderbolt.
4 Aim and fetch boldly forth, O thou whose heart is bold: great glory will be thine thereby.
In rapid torrent let the mother waters spread. Slay Vrtra, win the light of heaven.
5 When thou, unequalled Maghavan, wast born to smite the Vrtras dead,
Thou spreadest out the spacious earth and didst support and prop the heavens.
6 Theri was the sacrifice produced for thee, the laud, and song of joy,
Thou in thy might surpassest all, all that now is and yet shall be.
7 Raw kine thou filledst with ripe milk. Thou madest Surya rise to heaven.,
Heat him as milk is heated with pure Sama hymns, great joy to him who loves the song.

## [08-079] HYMN LXXIX. Indra.

1. MAY Indra, who in every fight must be invoked, be near to us.
May the most mighty Vrtra-slayer, meet for praise, come to libations and to hymns.
2 Thou art the best of all in sending bounteous gifts, true art thou, lordly in thine act.
We claim alliance with the very Glorious One, yea, with the Mighty Son of Strength.
3 Prayers unsurpassed are offered up to thee the Lover of the Song.
Indra, Lord of Bay Steeds, accept these fitting hymns, hymns which we have thought out for thee.
4 For thou, O Maghavan, art truthful, ne'er subdued and bringest many a Vrtra low.
As such, O Mightiest Lord, Wielder of Thunder, send wealth hither to the worshipper.
5 O Indra, thou art far-renowned, impetuous, O Lord of Strength.
Alone thou slayest with the guardian of mankind resistless never-conquered foes.

6 As such we seek thee now, O Asura, thee most wise, craving thy bounty as our share.
Thy sheltering defence is like a mighty cloak. So may thy glories reach to us.

## [08-080] HYMN LXXX. Indra.

1. DOWN to the stream a maiden came, and found the Soma by the way.
Bearing it to her home she said, For Indra will I press thee out, for Sakra will I press thee out.
2 Thou roaming yonder, little man, beholding every house in turn,
Drink thou this Soma pressed with teeth, accompanied with grain and curds, with cake of meal and
song of praise.
3 Fain would we learn to know thee well, nor yet can we attain to thee.
Still slowly and in gradual drops, O Indu, unto Indra flow.
4 Will he not help and work for us? Will he not make us wealthier?
Shall we not, hostile to our lord, unite ourselves to Indra now?
5 O Indra, cause to sprout again three places, these which I declare,-
My father's head, his cultured field, and this the part below my waist.
6 Make all of these grow crops of hair, you cultivated field of ours,
My body, and my father's head.
7 Cleansing Apala, Indra! thrice, thou gavest sunlike skin to her,
Drawn, Satakratu! through the hole of car, of wagon, and of yoke.

## [08-081] HYMN LXXXI. Indra

1. INVITE ye Indra with a song to drink your draught of Soma juice,
All-conquering Satakratu, most munificent of all who live.
2 Lauded by many, much-invoked, leader of song, renowned of old:
His name is Indra, tell it forth.
3 Indra the Dancer be to us the giver of abundant strength:
May he, the mighty, bring it near.
4 Indra whose jaws are strong hath drunk of worshipping Sudaksa's draught,
The Soma juice with barley mixt.
5 Call Indra loudly with your songs of praise to drink the Soma juice.
For this is what augments his stiength.
6 When he hath drqnk its gladdening drops, the God with vigour of a God
Hath far surpassed all things that are.
7 Thou speedest down to succour us this ever-conquering God of yours,
Him who is drawn to all our songs
8 The Warrior not to he restrained, the Soma-drinker ne'er o'erthrown,
The Chieftain of resistless might.
9 O Indra, send us riches, thou Omniscient, worthy of our praise:
Help us in the decisive fray.
10 Even thence, O ındra, come to us with food that gives a hundred powers,
With food that gives a thousand powers.
11 We sought the wisdom of the wise. Sakra, Kine-giver, Thunder-armed!
May we with steeds o'ercome in fight.
12 We make thee, Satakratu, find enjoyment in the songs we sing.
Like cattle in the pasture lands.
13 For, Satakratu, Thunder-armed, all that we craved, as men are wont,
All that we hoped, have we attained.

14 Those, Son of Strength, are come to thee who cherish wishes in their hearts
O Indra, none excelleth thee.
15 So, Hero, guard us with thy care, with thy most liberal providence,
Speedy, and terrible to foes.
16 O Satakratu Indra, now rejoice with that carouse of thine
Which is most splendid of them all
17 Even, Indra, that carouse which slays the Vrtras best, most widely famed,
Best giver of thy power and might.
18 For that which is thy gift we know, true Soma-drinker, Thunder-armed,
Mighty One, amid all the folk.
19 For Indra, Lover of Carouse, loud be our songs about the juice:
Let poets sing the song of praise.
20 We summon Indra to the draught, irl whom all glories rest, in whom
The seven communities rejoice.
21 At the Trikadrukas the Gods span sacrifice that stirs the mind:
Let our songs aid and prosper it.
22 Let the drops pass within thee as the rivers flow into the sea:
O fndra, naught excelleth thee.
23 Thou, wakeful Hero, by thy might hast taken food of Soma juice,
Which, Indra, is within thee now.
24 O Indra, Vrtra-slayer, let Soma be ready for thy maw,
The drops be ready for thy forms.
25 Now Srutakaksa sings his song that cattle and the steed may come,
That Indra's very self may come.
26 Here, Indra, thou art ready by our Soma juices shed for thee,
Sakra, at hand that thou mayst give.
27 Even from far away our songs reach thee, O Caster of the Stone:
May we come very close to thee.
28 For so thou art the hero's Friend, a Hero, too, art thou, and strong:
So may thine heart be won to us.
29 So hath the offering, wealthiest Lord, been paid by all the worshippers:
So dwell thou, Indra, even with me.
30 Be not thou like a slothfid priest, O Lord of spoil and wealth: rejoice
In the pressed Soma blent with milk.
31 O Indra, let not ill designs surround us in the sunbeams' light:
This may we gain with thee for Friend.
32 With thee to help us, Indra, let us answer all our enemies:
For thou art ours and we are thine.
33 Indra, the poets and thy friends, faithful to thee, shall loudly sing
Thy praises as they follow thee.

## [08-082] HYMN LXXXII. Indra.

1. SURYA, thou mountest up to meet the Hero famous for his wealth,
Who hurls the bolt and works for man
2 Him who with might of both his arms brake nine-and-ninety castles down,
Slew Vrtra and smote Ahi dead.
3 This Indra is our gracious Friend. He sends us in a full broad stream
Riches in horses, kine, and corn.
4 Whatever, Vrtra-slayer! thou, Surya, hast risen upon to-day,
Tbat, Indra, all is in thy power.
5 When, Mighty One, Lord of the brave, thou thinkest thus, I shall not die,

That thought of thine is true indeed.

6 Thou, Indra, goest unto all Soma libations shed for thee,
Both far away and near at hand.

7 We make this Indra very strong to strike the mighty Vrtra dead:
A vigorous Hero shall he be.

8 Indra was made for giving, set, most mighty, o'er the joyous draught.
Bright, meet for Soma, famed in song.

9 By song as 'twere, the powerful bolt which none may parry was prepared
Lofty, invincible he grew.

10 Indra, Song-lover, lauded, make even in the wilds fair ways for us,
Whenever, Maghavan, thou wilt.

11 Thou whose commandment and behest of sovran sway none disregards,
Neither audacious man nor God.

12 And both these Goddesses, Earth, Heaven, Lord of the beauteous helm! revere
Thy might which no one may resist.

13 Thou in the black cows and the red and in the cows with spotted skin
This white milk hast deposited.

14 When in their terror all the Gods shrank from the Dragon's furious might,
Fear of the monster fell on them.

15 Then he was my Defender, then, Invincible, whose foe is not,
The Vrtra-slayer showed his might.

16 Him your best Vrtra-slayer, him the famous Champion of mankind
I urge to great munificence,

17 To come, Much-lauded! Many-named with this same thought that longs for milk,
Whene'er the Soma juice is shed.

18 Much-honoured by libations, may the Vrtra-slayer wake for us:
May Sakra listen to our prayers.

19 O Hero, with that aid dost thou delight us, with what succour bring
Riches to those who worship thee?

20 With whose libation joys the Strong, the Hero with his team who quells
The foe, to drink the Soma juice?

21 Rejoicing in thy spirit bring thousandfold opulence to us:
Enrich thy votary with gifts.

22 These juices with their wedded wives flow to enjoyment lovingly:
To waters speeds the restless one.

23 Presented strengthening gifts have sent Indra away at sacrifice,
With might, onto the cleansing bath.

24 These two who share his feast, Bay Steeds with golden manes, shall bring him to
The banquet that is laid for him.

25 For thee, O Lord of Light, are shed these Soma-drops, and grass is strewn
Bring Indra to his worshippers.

26 May Indra give thee skill, and lights of heaven, wealth to his votary
And priests who praise him: laud ye him.

27 O Satakratu, wondrous strength and all our lauds I bring to thee:
Be gracious to thy worshippers.

28 Bring to us all things excellent, O Satakratu, food and strength:
For, Indra, thou art kind to us.

2§ O Satakratu, bring to us all blessings, all felicity:

Fbr, Indra, thou art kind to us.

30 Bearing the Soma juice we call, best Vrtra-slayer, unto thee:
For, Indra, thou art kind to us.

31 Come, Lord of rapturous, joys, to our libation with thy Bay Steeds, come
To our libation with thy Steeds.

32 Known as best Vrtra-slaycr crst, as Indra Satakratu, come
With Bay Steeds to the juice we shed.

33 O Vrtra-slayer, thou art he who drinks these drops of Soma: come
With Bay Steeds to the juice we shed.

34 May Indra give, to aid us, wealth handy that rules the Skilful Ones:
Yea, may the Strong give potent wealth.

## [08-083] HYMN LXXXIII. Maruts.

1. THE Cow, the famous Mother of the wealthy Maruts, pours her milk:
Both horses of the cars are yoked,-

2 She in whose bosom all the Gods, and Sun and Moon for men to see,
Maintain their everlasting Laws.

3 This all the pious sing to us, and sacred poets evermore:
The Maruts to the Soma-draught

4 Here is the Soma ready pressed of this the Maruts drink, of this
Self-luminous the Asvins drink.

5 Of this, moreover, purified, set in three places, procreant,
Drink Varuna, Mitra, Aryaman.

6 And Indra, like the Herald Priest, desirous of the milky juice,
At early morn will quaff thereof.

7 When have the Princes gleamed and shone through waters as through troops of foes'?
When hasten they whose might ispure?

8 What favour do I claim this day of you
great Deities, you who are
Wondrously splendid in yourselves?

9 1 call, to drink the Soma, those Maruts who spread all realms of earth
And luminous regions of the sky.

10 You, even such, pure in your might, you, O ye Maruts, I invoke
From heaven to drink this Somajuice.

11 The Maruts, those who have sustained and propped the heavens and earth apart,
I call to drink this Soma juice.

12 That vigorous band of Maruts that abidetb in the mountains, I
Invoke to drink this Soma juice.

## [08-084] HYMN LXXXIV. Indra.

1. SONG-LOVER! like a charioteer come songs to thee when Soma flows.
O Indra, they have called to thee as mother-kine unto their calves.

2 Bright juices bitherward have sped thee, Indra, Lover of the Song.
Drink, Indra, of this flowing sap: in every house 'tis set for thee.

3 Drink Soma to inspirit thee, juice, Indra, which the Falcon brought:
For thou art King and Sovran Lord of all the families of men.

4 O Indra, hear Tirasci's call, the call of him who serveth thee.
Satisfy him with wealth of kine and valiant offspring: Great art thou.

5 For he, O Indra, hath produced for thee the newest gladdening song,
A hymn that springs from careful thought, ancient, and full of sacred truth.

6 That Indra will we laud whom songs and hymns of praise have magnified.
Striving to win, we celebrate his many deeds of hero might.

221

7 Come now and let us glorify pure Indra with pure Sama hymns. Let the pure milky draught delight him strengthened by pure songs of praise.

8 O Indra, come thou pure to us, with pure assistance, pure thyself.
Pure, send thou riches down to us, and, meet for Soma, pure, be glad.

9 O Indra, pure, vouchsafe us wealth, and, pure, enrich the worshipper.
Pure, thou dost strike the Vrtras dead, and strivest, pure, to win the spoil.

## [08-085] HYMN LXXXV. Indra.

1. FOR him the Mornings made their courses longer, and Nights with pleasant voices spake to Indra.
For him the Floods stood still, the Seven Mothers, Streams easy for the heroes to pass over.

2 The Darter penetrated, though in trouble, thrice-seven close-pressed ridges of the mountains.
Neither might God nor mortal man accomplish what the Strong Hero wrought in full-grown vigour.

3 The mightiest force is Indra's bolt of iron when firmly grasped in both the arms of Indra.
His head and mouth have powers that pass all others, and all his people hasten near to listen.

4 1 count thee as the Holiest of the Holy, the caster-down of what hath ne'er been shaken.
I count thee as the Banner of the heroes, I count thee as the Chief of all men living.

5 What time, O Indra, in thine arms thou tookest thy wildly rushing bolt to Slay the Dragon,
The mountains roared, the cattle loudly bellowed, the Brahmans with their hymns drew nigh to Indra.

6 Let us praise him who made these worlds and creatures, all things that after him sprang into being.
May we win Mitra with our songs, and Indra, and. wait upon our Lord with adoration.

7 Flying in terror from the snort of Vrtra, all Deities who were thy friends forsook thee.
So, Indra, be thy friendship with the Maruts: in all these battles thou shalt be the victor.

8 Thrice-sixty Maruts, waxing strong, were with thee, like piles of beaming light, worthy of worship.
We come to thee: grant us a happy portion. Let us adore thy might with this oblation.

9 A sharpened weapon is the host of Maruts. Who, Indra, dares withstand thy bolt of thunder?
Weaponless are the Asuras, the godless: scatter them with thy wheel, Impetuous Hero.

10 To him the Strong and Mighty, most auspicious, send up the beAuteous hymn for sake of cattle.
Lay oa his body many songs for Indra invoked with song, for will not he regard. them?

11 To him, the Mighty, who accepts laudation, send forth thy thought as by a boat o'er rivers,
Stir with thy hymn the body of the Famous and Dearest One, for will not he regard it?

12 Serve him with gifts of thine which Indra welcomes: praise with fair praise, invite him with thine homage.
Draw near, O singer, and refrain from outcry. Make thy voice heard, for will not he regard it?

13 The Black Drop sank in Amsumati's bosom, advancing with ten thousand round about it.
Indra with might longed for it as it panted: the hero-hearted laid aside his weapons.

14 1 saw the Drop in the far distance moving, on the slope bank of Amsumati's river,
Like a black cloud that sank into the water. Heroes, I send you forth. Go, fight in battle.

15 And then the Drop in Amsumati's bosom, splendid with light, assumed its proper body;
And Indra, with Brhaspati to aid him, conquered the godless tribes that came against him.

16 Then, at thy birth, thou wast the foeman, Indra, of those the seven who ne'er had met a rival.
The hidden Pair, the Heaven and Earth, thou foundest, and to the mighty worlds thou gavest pleasure.

17 So, Thunder-armed! thou with thy bolt of thunder didst boldly smite that power which none might equal;
With weapons broughtest low the might of Susna, and, Indra, foundest by thy strength the cattle.

18 Then wast thou, Chieftain of all living mortals, the very mighty slayer of the Vrtras.
Then didst thou set the obstructed rivers flowing, and win the floods that were enthralled by Dasas.

19 Most wise is he, rejoicing in libations, splendid as day, resistless in his anger.
He only doth great deeds, the only Hero, sole Vrtra-slayer he, with none beside him.

20 Indra is Vrtra's slayer, man's sustainer: he must be called; with fair praise let us call him.
Maghavan is our Helper, our Protector, giver of spoil and wealth to make us famous.

21 This Indra, Vrtra-slayer, this Rbhuksan, even at his birth, was meet for invocation.
Doer of many deeds for man's advantage, like Soma quaffed, for friends we must invoke him.

## [08-086] HYMN LXXXVI. Indra.

1. O INDRA, Lord of Light, what joys thou broughtest from the Asuras,
Prosper therewith, O Maghavan, him who lauds that deed, and those whose grass is trimmed for thee.

2 The unwasting share of steeds and kine which, Indra, thou hast fast secured,
Grant to the worshipper who presses Soma and gives guerdon, not unto the churl.

3 The riteless, godless man who sleeps, O Indra, his unbroken steep,-
May he by following his own devices die. Hide from him wealth that nourishes.

4 Whether, O Sakra, thou be far, or, Vrtra-slayer, near at hand,
Thence by heaven-reaching songs he who hath pressed the juice invites thee with thy long-maned Steeds.

5 Whether thou art in heaven's bright sphere, or in the basin of the sea;
Whether, chief Vrtra-slayer, in some place on earth, or in the firmament, approach.

6 Thou Soma-drinker, Lord of Strength, beside our flowing Soma juice
Delight us with thy bounty rich in pleasantness, O Indra, with abundant wealth.

7 O Indra, turn us not away: be the companion of our feast.
For thou art our protection, yea, thou art our kin: O Indra, turn us not away.

8 Sit down with us, O Indra, sit beside the juice to drink the meath.

Show forth great favour to the Singer, Maghavan; Indra, with us, beside the juice.

9 O Caster of the Stone, nor Gods nor mortals have attained to thee.

Thou in thy might surpassest all that hath been made: the Gods have not attained to thee.

10 Of one accord they made and formed for kingship Indra, the Hero who in all encounters

overcometh,

Most eminent for power, destroyer in the conflict, fierce and exceeding strong, stalwart and full of

vigour.

11 Bards joined in song to Indra so that he might drink the Soma juice,

The Lord of Light, that he whose laws stand fast might aid with power and with the help he gives.

12 Tle holy sages form a ring, looking and singing to the Ram.

Inciters, full of vigour, not to he deceived, are with the chanters, nigh to bear.

13 Loudly I call that Indra, Maghavan the Mighty, who evermore possesses power, ever resistless.

Holy, most liberal, may he lead us on to riches, and, Thunder-armed, make all our pathways pleasant

for us.

14 Thou knowest well, O Sakra, thou Most Potent, with thy strength, Indra, to destroy these castles.

Before thee, Thunder-armed! all beings tremble: the heavens and earth before thee shake with terror,

15 May thy truth, Indra, Wondrous Hero be my guard: bear me o'er much woe, Thunderer! as over

floods.

When, Indra, wilt thou honour us with opulence, all-nourishing and much-to-be. desired, O King?

## [08-087] HYMN LXXXVII. Indra.

1. To Indra sing a Sama hymn, a lofty song to Lofty Sage,

To him who guards the Law, inspired, and fain for praise.

2 Thou, Indra, art the Conqueror: thou gavest splendour to the Sun.

Maker of all things, thou art Mighty and All-God.

3 Radiant with light thou wentest to the sky, the luminous realm of heaven.

ne Deities, Indra strove to win thee for their Friend.

4 Come unto us, O Indra, dear, still conquering, unconcealable,

Vast as a mountain spread on all sides, Lord of Heaven.

5 O truthful Soma-drinker, thou art mightier than both the worlds.

Thou strengthenest him who pours libation, Lord of Heaven.

6 For thou art he, O Indra, wiio stormeth all castles of the foe,

Slayer of Dasyus, man's Supporter, Lord of Heaven.

7 Now have we, Indra, Friend of Song, sent our great wishes forth to thee,

Coming like floods that follow floods.

8 As rivers swell the ocean, so, Hero, our prayers increase thy might,

Though of thyself, O Thunderer, waxing day by day.

9 With holy song mey bind to the broad wide-yoked car the Bay Steeds of the rapid God,

Bearers of Indra, yoked by word.

10 O Indra, bring great strength to us, bring valour, Satakratu, thou most active, bring

A hero conquering in war.

11 For, gracious Satakratu, thou hast ever been a Mother and a Sire to us,

So now for bliss we pray to thee.

12 To thee, Strong, Much-invoked, who showest forth thy strength, O Satakratu, do I speak:

So grant thou us heroic strength.

## [08-088] HYMN LXXXVIII. Indra.

1. O THUNDERER, zealous worshippers gave thee drink this time yesterday.

So, Indra, listen here to those who bring the laud: come near unto our dwellingplacc.

2 Lord of Bay Steeds, fair-helmed, rejoice thee: this we crave.

Here the disposers wait on thee.

Thy loftiest glories claim our lauds beside the juice, O Indra, Lover of the Song.

3 Turning, as 'twere, to meet the Sun, enjoy from Indra all good things.

When he who will be born is born with power we look to treasures as our heritage.

4 Praise him who sends us wealth, whose bounties injure none: good are the gifts which Indra.

grants.

He is not worth with one who satisfies his wish: he turns his mind to giving boons.

5 Thou in thy battles, Indra, art subduer of all hostile bands.

Father art thou, aII-conquering, cancelling the curse, thou victor of the vanquisher.

6 The Earth and Heaven clung close to thy victorious might as to their calf two mother-cows.

When thou attackest Vrtra all the hostile bands shrink and faint, Indra, at thy wrath.

7 Bring to your aid the Eternal One, who shoots and none may shoot at him,

Inciter, swift, victorious, best of Charioteers. Tugrya's unvanquished Strengthener;

8 Arranger of things unarranged, e'en Satakratu, source of might, Indra, the Friend of all, for succour we invoke, Guardian of treasure, sendjng wealth.

## [08-089] HYMN LXXXIX Indra. Vak.

1. I MOVE before thee here present in person, and all the Deities follow behind me.

When, Indra, thou securest me my portion, with me thou shalt perform heroic actions.

2 The food of meath in foremost place I give thee, thy Soma shall be pressed, thy share appointed.

Thou on my right shalt be my friend and comrade: then shall we two smite dead full many a foeman.

3 Striving for strength bring forth a laud to Indra, a truthful hymn if he in truth existeth.

One and another say, There is no Indra. Who hath beheld him? Whom then shall we honour?

4 Here am I, look upon me here, O singer. All that existeth 1 surpass in greatness.

The Holy Law's commandments make me mighty. Rending with strength I rend the worlds asunder.

5 When the Law's lovers mounted and ap. proached me as 1 sate lone upon the dear sky's summit.

Then spake my spirit to the heart within me, My friends have cried unto me with their children.

6 All these thy deeds must be declared at Soma-feasts, wrought, Indra, Bounteous Lord, for him who

sheds the juice,

When thou didst open wealth heaped up by many, brought from far away to Sarablia, the Rsi's kin.

7 Now run ye forth your several ways: he is not here who kept you back.

For hath not Indra sunk his bolt deep down in Vrtra's vital part?

8 On-rushing with the speed of thought within the iron fort he pressed:

The Falcon went to heaven and brought the Soma to the Thunderer.

9 Deep in the ocean lies the bolt with waters compassed round about,
And in continuous onward flow the floods their tribute bring to it.

10 When, uttering words which no one comprehended, Vak, Queen of Gods, the Gladdener, was
seated,
The heaven's four regions drew forth drink and vigour: now whither hath her noblest portion
vanished?

11 The Deities generated Vak the Goddess, and animals of every figure speak her.
May she, the Gladdener, yielding food and vigour, the Milch-cow Vak, approach us meetly lauded.

12 Step forth with wider stride, my comrade Visnu; make room, Dyaus, for the leaping of the
lightning.
Let us slay Vrtra, let us free the rivers let them flow loosed at the command of Indra.

## [08-090] HYMN XC. Various.

1. YEA, specially that mortal man hath toiled for service of the Gods,
Who quickly hath brought near Mitra and Varuna. to share his sacrificial gifts.

2 Supreme in sovran power, far-sighted, Chiefs and Kings, most swift to hear from far away,
Both, wondrously, set them in motion as with arms, in company with Surya's beams.

3 The rapid messenger who runs before you, Mitra-Varuna, with iron head, swift to the draught,

4 He whom no man may question, none may summon back, who stands not still for colloquy,-
From hostile clash with him keep ye us safe this day: keep us in safety with your arms.

5 To Aryaman and Mitra sing a reverent song, O pious one,
A pleasant hymn that shall protect to Varuna: sing forth a laud unto the Kings.

6 The true, Red Treasure they have sent, one only Son born of the Three.
They, the Immortal Ones, never deceived, survey the families of mortal men.

7 My songs are lifted up, and acts most splendid are to be performed.
Come hither, ye Nasatyas, with accordant mind, to meet and to enjoy my gifts.

8 Lords of great wealth, when we invoke your bounty which no demon checks,
Both of you, furthering our eastward-offcred praise, come, Chiefs whom Jamadagni lauds!

9 Come, Vayu, drawn by fair hymns, to our sacrifice that reaches heaven.
Poured on the middle of the strainingcloth, and cooked, this bright drink hath been offered ilice.

10 He comes by straightest paths, as ministering Priest, to taste the sacrificial gifts.
Then, Lord of harnessed teams I drink of the twofold draught, bright Soma mingled with the milk.

11 Verily, Surya, thou art great; truly, Aditya, thou art great.
As thou art great indeed, thy greatness is admired: yea, verily, thou, God, art great.

12 Yea, Surya, thou art great in fame thou evermore, O God, art great.
Thou by thy greatness art the Gods' High Priest, divine, far-spread unconquerable light.

13 She yonder, bending lowly down, clothed in red hues and rich in rays,
Is seen, advancing as it were with various tints, amid the ten surrounding arms.

14 Past and gone are three mortal generations: the fourth and last into the Sun hath entered.
He mid the worlds his lofty place hath taken. Into green plants is gone the Purifying.

15 The Rudras' Mother, Daughter of the Vasus, centre of nectar, the Adityas' Sister-
To folk who understand will 1 proclaim it-injure not Aditi, the Cow, the sinless.

16 Weak-minded men have as a cow adopted me who came hither from the Gods, a Goddess,
Who, skilled in eloquence, her voice uplifteth, who standeth near at hand with all devotions.

## [08-091] HYMN XCI. Agni.

1. LORD of the house, Sage, ever young, high power of life, O Agni, God,
Thou givest to thy worshipper.

2 So with our song that prays and serves, attentive, Lord of spreading light,
Agni, bring hitherward the Gods.

3 For, Ever-Youthful One, with thee, best Furtherer, as our ally,
We overcome, to win the spoil.

4 As Aurva Bhrgu used, as Apnavana used, I call the pure
Agni who clothes him with the sea.

5 1 call the Sage who sounds like wind, the Might that like Parjanya roars,
Agni who clothes him with the sea.

6 As Savitar's productive Power, as him who sends down bliss, I call
Agni who clothes him with the sea.

7 Hither, for powerful kirship, I call Agni, him Who prospers you,
Most frequent at our solemn rites

8 That through this famed One's power, he may stand by us even as Tvastar comes
Unto the forms that must he shaped.

9 This Agni is the Lord supreme above all glories mid the Gods:
May he come nigh to us with strength.

10 Here praise ye him the most renowned of all the ministering Priests,
Agni, the Chief at sacrifice;

11 Piercing, with purifying flame, enkindled in our homes, most high,
Swiftest to hear from far away.

12 Sage, laud the Mighty One who wins the spoil of victory like a steed,
And, Mitra like, unites the folk.

13 Still turning to their aim in thee, the oblation-bearer's sister hymns
Have come to thee before the wind.

14 The waters find their place in him, for whom the threefold sacred grass
Is spread unbound, unlimited.

15 The station of the Bounteous God hath, through his aid which none impair,
A pleasant aspect like the Sun.

16 Blazing with splendour, Agni, God, through pious gifts of sacred oil,
Bring thou the Gods and worship them.

17 The Gods as mothers brought thee forth, the Immortal Sage, O Afigiras,
The bearer of our gifts to heaven.

18 Wise Agni, Gods established thee, the Seer, noblest messenger,
As bearer of our sacred gifts.

19 No cow have I to call mine own, no axe at hand wherewith to work,
Yet what is here I bring to thee.
20 O Agni, whatsoever be the fuel that we lay for thee,
Be pleased therewith, Most Youthful God
21 That which the white-ant cats away, that over which the emmet crawls-
May all of this be oil to thee.
22 When he enkindles Agni, man should with his heart attend the song:
I with the priests have kindled him.

## [08-092] HYMN XCII. Agni

1. THAT noblest Furtherer hath appeared, to whom men bring their holy works.
Our songs of praise have risen aloft to Agni who was barn to give the Arya strength.
2 Agni of Divodasa turned, as 'twere in majesty, to the Gods.
Onward he sped along the mother earth, and took his station in the height of heaven.
3 Him before whom the people shrink when he performs his glorious deeds,
Him who wins thousands at the worship of the Gods, himself, that Agni, serve with son s.
4 The mortal man whom thou wouldst lead to opulence, O Vasu, he who brings thee gifts.
He, Agni, wins himself a hero singing lauds, yea, one who feeds a thousand men.
5 He with the steed wins spoil even in the fenced fort, and gains imperishable fame.
In thee, O Lord of wealth, continually we lay all precious offerings to the Gods.
6 To him who dealeth out all wealth, who is the cheerful Priest of men,
To him, like the first vessels filled with savoury juice, to Agni go the songs of praise.
7 Votaries, richly-gifted, deck him with their songs, even as the steed who draws the car.
On both, Strong Lord of men! on child and grandson pour the bounties which our nobles give.
8 Sing forth to him, the Holy, most munificent, sublime with his refulgent glow,
To Agni, ye Upastutas.
9 Worshipped with gifts, enkindled, splendid, Maghavan shall win himself heroic fame.
And will not his most newly shown benevolence come to us with abundant strength?
10 Priest, presser of the juice! praise now the dearest Guest of all our friends,
Agni, the driver of the cars.
11 Who, finder-out of treasures open and concealed, bringeth them hither, Holy One;
Whose waves, as in a cataract, are hard to pass, when he, through song, would win him strength.
12 Let not the noble Guest, Agni, be wroth with us: by many a man his praise is sung,
Good Herald, skilled in sacrifice.
13 O Vasu, Agni, let not them be harmed who come in any way with lauds to thee.
Even the lowly, skilled in rites, with offered gifts, seeketh thee for the envoy's task.
14 Friend of the Maruts, Agni, come with Rudras to the Soma-draught,
To Sobhar's fair song of praise, and be thou joyful in the light.
VALAKHILYA
APPENDIX: (Book VIII. Hymns 49-59. M. Müller.)

## [08-093] HYMN I. Indra.

1. TO you will I sing Indra's praise who gives good gifts as well we know;
The praise of Maghavan who, rich in treasure, aids his singers with wealth thousandfold.
2 As with a hundred hosts, he rushes boldly on, and for the offerer slays his foes.
As from a mountain flow the water-brooks, thus flow his gifts who feedeth many a one.
3 The drops effused, the gladdening draughts, O Indra, Lover of the Son
As waters seek the lake where they are wont to rest, fill thee, for bounty, Thunderer.
4 The matchless draught that strengthens and gives eloquence, the sweetest of the meath drink
thou,
That in thy joy thou maysi scatter thy gifts o'er us, plenteously, even as the dust.
5 Come quickly to our laud, urged on by Soma-pressers like a horse-
Laud, Godlike Indra, which milch-kine make sweet for thee: with Kanva's sons are gifts for thee.
6 With homage have we sought thee as a Hero, strong, preeminent, with unfailing wealth.
O Thunderer, as a plenteous spring pours forth its stream, so, Indra, flow our songs to thee.
7 If now thou art at sacrifice, or if thou art upon the earth,
Come thence, high-thoughted! to our sacrifice with the Swift, come, Mighty with the Mighty Ones.
8 The active, fleet-foot, tawny Coursers that are thine are swift to victory, like the Wind,
Wherewith thou goest round to visit Manus' seed, wherewith all heaven is visible.
9 Indra, from thee so great we crave prosperity in wealth of kine,
As, Maghavan, thou favouredst Medhyatithi, and, in the fight, Nipatithi.
10 As, Maghavan, to Kanva, Trasadasyu, and to Paktha and Dasavraja;
As, Indra, to Gosarya and Rjisvan, thou vouchsafedst wealth in kine and gold.

## [08-094] HYMN II. Indra.

1. SAKRA I praise, to win his aid, far-famed, exceeding bountiful,
Who gives, as 'twere in thousands, precious wealth to him who sheds the juice and worships him.
2 Arrows with hundred points, unconquerable, are this Indra's n-dghty arms in war.
He streams on liberal worshippers like a hill with springs, when juices poured have gladdened him.
3 What time the flowing Soma-drops have gladdened with their taste the Friend,
Like water, gracious Lord! were my libations made, like milch-kine to the worshipper.
4 To him the peerless, who is calling you to give you aid, forth flow the drops of pleasant meath.
The Soloa-drops which call on thee, O gracious Lord, have brought thee to our hymn of praise.
5 He rushes hurrying like a steed to Soma that adorns our rite,
Which hymns make sweet to thee, lover of pleasant food. The call to Paura thou dost love.
6 Praise the strong, grasping Hero, winner of the spoil, ruling supreme oer mighty wealth.
Like a full spring, O Thunderer, from thy store hast thou poured on the worshipper evermore.
7 Now whether thou be far away, or in the heavens, or on the earth,

O Indra, mighty- thoughted, harnessing thy Bays, come Lofty with the Lofty Ones.
8 The Bays who draw thy chariot, Steeds who injure none, surpass the wind's impetuous strength-
With whom thou silencest the enemy of man, with whon; thou goest round the sky.
9 O gracious Hero, may we learn anew to know thee as thou art:
As in decisive fight thou holpest Etasa, or Vasa 'gainst Dasavraja,
10 As, Maghavan, to Kanva at the sacred feast, to Dirghanitha thine home-friend,
As to Gosarya thou, Stone-darter, gavest wealth, give me a gold-bright stall of kine.

## [08-095] HYMN III. Indra.

1. As with Manu Samvarani, Indra, thou drankest Soma juice,
And, Maghavan, with Nipatithi, Medbyatithi, with Pustigu and Srustigu,-
2 T'he son of Prsadvana was Praskaniva's host, who lay decrepit and forlorn.
Aided by thee the Rsi Dasyave-vrka strove to obtain thousands of kine.
3 Call hither with thy newest song Indra who lacks not hymns of praise,
Him who observes and knows, inspirer of the sage, him who seems eager to enjoy.
4 He unto whom they sang the seven-headed hymn, three-parted, in the loftiest place,
He sent his thunder down on all these living things, and so displayed heroic might.
5 We invocate that Indra who bestoweth precious things on us.
Now do we know his newest favour; may we gain a stable that is full of kine.
6 He whom thou aidest, gracious Lord, to give again, obtains great wealth to nourish him.
We with our Soma ready, Lover of the Song! call, Indra Maghavan, on thee.
7 Ne'er art thou fruitless, Indra ne'er dost thou desert the worshipper
But now, O Maghavan, thy bounty as a God is poured forth ever more and more.
8 He who hath. overtaken Krvi with his might, and silenced Susna with deathbolts,-
When he supported yonder heaven and spread it out, then first the son of earth was born.
9 Good Lord of wealth is he to whom all Aryas, Dasas here belong.
Directly unto thee, the pious Rusama Paviru, is that wealth brought nigh.
10 In zealous haste the singers have sung forth a song distilling oil and rich in sweets.
Riches have spread among us and heroic strength, with us are flowing Soma-drops.

## [08-096] HYMN IV. Indra.

1. As, Sakra, thou with Manu called Vivasvan drankest Soma juice,
As, Indra, thou didst love the hymn by Trita's side, so dost thou joy with Ayu now.
2 As thou with Matarisvan, Medhya, Prsadhra, hast cheered thee Indra, with pressed juice,
Drunk Soma with Rjunas, Syumarasmi, by Dasonya's Dasasipra's side.
3 'Tis he who made the lauds his own and boldly drank the Soma juice,
He to whom Visnu came striding his three wide steps, as Mitra's statutes ordered it.

4 In whose laud thou didst joy, Indra, at the great deed, O Satakratu, Mighty One!
Seeking renown we call thee as the milkers call the cow who yields abundant milk.
5 He is our Sire who gives to us, Great, Mighty, ruling as he wills.
Unsought, may he the Strong, Rich, Lord of ample wealth, give us of horses and of kine.
6 He to whom thou, Good Lord, givest that he may give increases wealth that nourishes.
Eager for wealth we call on Indra, Lord of wealth, on Satakratu with our lauds.
7 Never art thou neglectful: thou guardest both races with thy care.
The call on Indra, fourth Aditya! is thine own. Amrta is stablished in the heavens.
8 The offercr whom thou, Indra, Lover of the Song, liberal Maghavan, favourest,-
As at the call of Kanva so, O gracious Lord, hear, thou our songs and eulogy.
9 Sung is the song of ancient time: to Indra have ye said the prayer.
They have sung many a Brhati of sacrifice, poured forth the worshipper's many thoughts.
10 Indra hath tossed together mighty stores of wealth, and both the worlds, yea, and the Sun.
Pure, brightly-shining, mingled with the milk, the draughts of Soma have made Indra glad.

## [08-097] HYMN V. Indra.

1. As highest of the Maghavans, preeminent among the Bulls,
Best breaker-down of forts, kine-winner, Lord of wealth, we seek thee, Indra Maghavan.
2 Thou who subduedst Ayu, Kutsa, Atithigva, waxing daily in thy might,
As such, rousing thy power, we invocate thee now, thee Satakratu, Lord of Bays.
3 The pressing-stones shall pour for us the essence of the meath of all,
Drops that have been pressed out afar among the folk, and those that have been pressed near us.
4 Repel all enmities and keep thern far away: let all win treasure for their own.
Even among Sistas are the stalks that make thee glad, where thou with Soma satest thee.
5 Come, Indra, very near to us with aids of firmly-based resolve;
Come, most auspicious, with thy most auspicious help, good Kinsman, with good kinsmen, come!
6 Bless thou with progeny the chief of men, the lord of heroes, victor in the fray.
Aid with thy powers the men who sing thee lauds and keep their spirits ever pure and bright.
7 May we be such in battle as are surest to obtain thy grace:
With holy offerings and invocations of the Gods, we mean, that we may win the spoil.
8 Thine, Lord of Bays, am I. Prayer longeth for the spoil. Still with thy help I seek the fight.
So, at the raiders' head, I, craving steeds and kine, unite myself with thee alone.

## [08-098] HYMN VI. Indra.

1. INDRA, the poets with. their hymns extol this hero might of thine:
They strengthened, loud in song, thy power that droppeth oil.
With hymns the Pauras came to thee.

2 Through piety they came to Indra for his aid, they whose libations give thee joy.
As thou with, Krsa and Samvarta hast rejoiced, so, Indra, be thou glad with us.
3 Agreeing in your spirit, all ye Deities, come nigh to us.
Vasus and Rudras shall come near to give us aid, and Maruts listen to our call.
4 May Pusan, Visnu, and Sarasvati befriend, and the Seven Streams, this call of mine:
May Waters, Wind, the Mountains, and the Forest-Lord, and Earth give ear unto my cry.
5 Indra, with thine own bounteous gift, most liberal of the Mighty Ones,
Be our boon benefactor, Vrtra-slayer, be our feast-companion for our weal.
6 Leader of heroes, Lord of battle, lead thou us to combat, thou Most Sapient One.
High fame is theirs who win by invocations, feasts and entertainment of the Gods.
7 Our hopes rest on the Faithful One: in Indra is the people's life.
O Maghavan, come nigh that thou mayst give us aid: make plenteous food stream forth for us.
8 Thee would we worship, Indra, with our songs of praise: O Satakratu, be thou ours.
Pour down upon Praskanva bounty vast and firm, exuberant, that shall never fail.

## [08-099] HYMN VII. Praskanva's Gift.

1. GREAT, verily, is Indra's might. I have beheld, and hither comes
Thy bounty, Dasyave-vrka!
2 A hundred oxen white of hue are shining like the stars in heaven,
So tall, they seem to prop the sky.
3 Bamboos a hundred, a hundred dogs, a hundred skins of beasts well-tanned,
A hundred tufts of Balbaja, four hundred red-hued mares are mine.
4 Blest by the Gods, Kinvayanas! be ye who spread through life on life:
Like horses have ye stridden forth.
5 Then men extolled the team of seven not yet full-grown, its fame is great.
The dark mares rushed along the paths, so that no eye could follow them.

## [08-100] HYMN VIII Praskanva's Go.

1. THY bounty, Dasyave-vrka, exhaustless hath displayed itself:
Its fulness is as broad as heaven.
2 Ten thousand Dasyave-vrka, the son of Putakrata, hath
From his own wealth bestowed on me.
3 A hundred asses hath he given, a hundred head of fleecy sheep,
A hundred slaves, and wreaths besides.
4 There also was a mare led forth, picked out for Putakrata's sake,
Not of the horses of the herd.
5 Observant Agni hath appeared, oblation-bearer with his car.
Agni with his resplendent flame hath shone on high as shines the Sun, hath shone like Surya in
theheavens.

## [08-101] HYMN IX. Asvins.

1. ENDOWED, O Gods, with your primeval wisdom, come quickly with your chariot, O ye Holy.
Come with your mighty powers, O ye Nasatyas; come hither, drink ye this the third libation.

2 The truthful Deities, the Three-and-Thirty, saw you approach before the Ever-Truthful.
Accepting this our worship and libation, O Asvins bright with fire, drink ye the Soma.
3 Asvins, that work of yours deserves our wonder,-the Bull of heaven and earth and air's mid region;
Yea, and your thousand promises in battle, -to all of these come near and drink beside us.
4 Here is your portion laid for you, ye Holy: come to these songs of ours, O ye Nasatyas.
Drink among us the Soma full of sweetness, and with your powers assist the man who worships.

## [08-102] HYMN X. Visvedevas.

1. HE whom the priests in sundry ways arranging the sacrifice, of one accord, bring hither,
Who was appointed as a learned Brahman, -what is the sacrificer's knowledge of him?
2 Kindled in many a spot, still One is Agni; Silrya is One though high o'er all he shineth.
Illuminating this All, still One is usas. That which is One hath into All developed.
3 The chariot bright and radiant, treasure-laden, three-wheeled, with easy seat, and lightly rolling,
Which She of Wondrous Wealth was born to harness,-this car of yours I call. Drink what remaineth.

## [08-103] HYMN XI. Indra-Varuna.

1. IN offerings poured to you, O Indra-Varuna, these shares of yours stream forth to glorify your state.
Ye haste to the libations at each sacrifice when ye assist the worshipper who sheds the juice.
2 The waters and the plants, O Indra-Varuna, had efficacious vigour, and attained to might:
Ye who have gone beyond the path of middle air,-no godless man is worthy to be called your foe.
3 True is your Krsa's word, Indra and Varuna: The seven holy voices pour a wave of meath.
For their sake, Lords of splendour! aid the pious man who, unbewildered, keeps you ever in his
thoughts.
4 Dropping oil, sweet with Soma, pouring forth their stream, are the Seven Sisters in the seat of
sacrifice.
These, dropping oil, are yours, O Indra-Varuna: with these enrich with gifts and help the worshipper.
5 To our great happiness have we ascribed to these Two Bright Ones truthfulness, great strength,
and majesty.
O Lords of splendour, aid us through the Three-times-Seven, as we pour holy oil, O Indra-Varuna.
6 What ye in time of old Indra and Varuna, gave Rsis revelation, thought, and power of song,
And places which the wise made, weaving sacrifice,-these through my spirit's fervid glow have I
beheld.,
7 O Indra-Varuna, grant to the worshippers cheerfulness void of pride, and wealth to nourish them.
Vouchsafe us food, prosperity, and progeny, and lengthen out our days that we may see long life.

# BOOK NINE

## [09-001] HYMN I. Soma Pavamana.

1. In sweetest and most gladdening stream flow pure, O Soma, on thy way,

Pressed out for Indra, for his drink.

2 Fiend-queller, Friend of all men, he hath with the wood attained unto
His place, his iron-fashioned home.

3 Be thou best Vrtra-slayer, best granter of bliss, most liberal:
Promote our wealthy princes' gifts.

4 Flow onward with thy juice unto the banquet of the Mighty Gods:
Flow hither for our strength and fame.

5 O Indu, we draw nigh to thee, with this one object day by day:
To thee alone our prayers are said

6 By means of this eternal fleece may Surya's Daughter purify
Thy Soma that is foaming forth.

7 Ten sister maids of slender form seize him within the press and hold
Him firmly on the final day.

8 The virgins send him forth: they blow the the skin musician-like and fuse
The triple foe-repelling meath.

9 Inviolable milch-kine round about him blend for Indra's drink,
The fresh young Soma with their milk.

10 In the wild raptures of this draught, Indra slays all the Vrtras: he,
The Hero, pours his wealth on us.

### [09-002] HYMN II. Soma Pavamana.

1. Soma, flow on, inviting Gods, speed to the purifying cloth:
Pass into Indra, as a Bull.

2 As mighty food speed hitherward, Indu, as a most splendid Steer:
Sit in thy place as one with strength.

3 The well-loved meath was made to flow, the stream of the creative juice
ne Sage drew waters to himself.

4 The mighty waters, yea, the floods accompany thee Mighty One,
When thou wilt clothe thee with the milk.

5 The lake is brightened in the floods. Soma, our Friend, heaven's prop and stay,
Falls on the purifying cloth.

6 The tawny Bull hath bellowed, fair as mighty Mitra to behold:
He shines together with the Sun.

7 Songs, Indu, active in their might are beautified for thee, wherewith
Thou deckest thee for our delight.

8 To thee who givest ample room we pray, to win the joyous draught:
Great are the praise& due to thee.

9 Indu as, Indra's Friend, on us pour with a stream of sweetness, like
Parjanya sender of the rain.

10 Winner of kine, Indu, art thou, winner of heroes, steeds, and strength
Primeval Soul of sacrifice.

### [09-003] HYMN III. Soma Pavamana.

1. HERE present this Immortal God flies, like a bird upon her wings,
To settle in the vats of wood.

2 This God, made ready with the hymn, runs swiftly through the winding ways,
Inviolable as he flows.

3 This God while flowing is adorned, like a bay steed for war, by men
Devout and skilled in holy songs.

4 He, like a warrior going forth with heroes, as he flows along
Is fain to win all precious boons.

5 This God, as he is flowing on, speeds like a car and gives his gifts:
He lets his voice be heard of all

6 Praised by the sacred bards, this God dives into waters, and bestows
Rich gifts upon the worshipper.

7 Away he rushes with his stream, across the regions, into heaven,
And roars as he is flowing on.

8 While flowing, meet for sacrifice, he hath gone up to heaven across
The regions, irresistible.

9 After the 'way of ancient time, this God, pressed out for Deities,
Flows tawny to the straining-cloth.

10 This Lord of many Holy Laws, even at his birth engendering strength,
Effused, flows onward in a stream.

### [09-004] HYMN IV. Soma Pavamana.

1. O Soma flowing on thy way, win thou and conquer high renown;
And make us better than we are.

2 Win thou the light, win heavenly light, and, Soma, all felicities;
And make us better than we are.

3 Win skilful strength and mental power. O Soma, drive away our foes;
And make us better than we are.

4 Ye purifiers, purify Soma for Indra, for his drink:
Make thou us better than we are.

5 Give us our portion in the Sun through thine own mental power and aids;
And make us better than we are.

6 Through thine own mental power and aid long may we look upon the Sun;
Make thou us better than we are.

7 Well-weaponed Soma, pour to usa stream of riches doubly great;
And make us better than we are.

8 As one victorious unsubdued in battle pour forth wealth to us;
And make us better than we are.

9 By worship, Pavamana! men have strengthened thee to prop the Law:
Make thou us better than we are.

10 O Indu, bring us wealth in steeds, manifold. quickening all life;
And mate us better than we are.

### [09-005] HYMN V Apris.

1. ENKINDLED, Pavamana, Lord, sends forth his light on, every side
In friendly show, the bellowing Bull.

2 He, Pavamana, Self-produced, speeds onward sharpening his horns:
He glitters through the firmament.

3 Brilliant like wealth, adorable, with splendour Pavamana shines,
Mightily with the streams of meath.

4 The tawny Pavamana, who strews from of old the grass with might,
Is worshipped, God amid the Gods.

5 The golden, the Celestial Doors are lifted with their frames on high,
By Pavamana glorified.

6 With passion Pavamana longs for the great lofty pair, well-formed
Like beauteous maidens, Night and Dawn

7 Both Gods who look on men I call, Celestial Heralds: Indra's Self
Is Pavamana, yea, the Bull.

8 This, Pavamana's sacrifice, shall the three beauteous Goddesses,
Sarasvati and Bharati and Ila, Mighty One, attend.
9 1 summon Tvastar hither, our protector, champion, earliest-born,
Indu is Indra, tawny Steer; Pavamana is Prajapati.
10 O Pavamana, with the meath in streams anoint Vanaspati,
The ever-green. the golden-hued, refulgent, with a thousand boughs.
11 Come to the consecrating rite of Pavamana, all ye Gods,-
Vayu, Surya, Brhaspati, Indra, and Agni, in accord.

## [09-006] HYMN VI. Soma Pavamana.

1. SOMA, flow on with pleasant stream, a Bull devoted to the Gods,
Our Friend, unto the woollen sieve.
2 Pour hitherward, as Indra's Self, Indu, that gladdening stream of thine,
And send us coursers full of strength.
3 Flow to the filter hitherward, pouring that ancient gladdening juice,
Streaming forth power and high renown.
4 Hither the sparkling drops have flowed, like waters down a steep descent
They have reached Indra purified.
5 Whom, having passed the filter, ten dames cleanse, as 'twere a vigorous steed,
While he disports him in the wood,-
6 The steer-strong juice with milk pour forth, for feast and service of the Gods,
To him who bears away the draught.
7. Effused, the God flows onward with his stream to Indra, to the God,
So that his milk may strengthen him.
8 Soul of the sacrifice, the juice effused flows quickly on: he keeps
His ancient wisdom of a Sage.
9 So pouring forth, as Indra's Friend, strong drink, best Gladdener! for the feast,
Thou, even in secret, storest hymns.

## [09-007] HYMN VII. Soma Pavamana.

1. FORTH on their way the glorious drops have flowed for maintenance of Law,
Knowing this sacrifice's course.
2 Down in the mighty waters sinks the stream of meath, most excellent,
Oblation best of all in worth.
3 About the holy place, the Steer true, guileless, noblest, hath sent forth
Continuous voices in the wood.
4 When, clothed in manly strength, the Sage flows in celestial wisdom round,
The Strong would win the light of heaven.
5 When purified, he sits as King above the hosts, among his folk,
What time the sages bring him nigh.
6 Dear, golden-coloured, in the fleece he sinks and settles in the wood:
The Singer shows his zeal in hymns.
7 He goes to Indra, Vayu, to the Asvins, as his custom is,
With gladdening juice which gives them joy.
8 Tle streams of pleasant Soma flow to Bhaga, Mitra-Varuna,-
Well-knowing through his mighty powers.
Heaven and Earth, riches of meath to win us wealth:
Gain for us treasures and renown.

## [09-008] HYMN VIII. Soma Pavamana.

1. OBEYING Indra's dear desire these Soma juices have flowed forth,
Increasing his heroic might.
2 Laid in the bowl, pure-flowing on to Vayu and the Asvins, may
These give us great heroic strength.
3 Soma, as thou art purified, incite to bounty Indra's heart,
To sit in place of sacrifice.
4 The ten swift fingers deck thee forth, seven ministers impel thee on:
The sages have rejoiced in thee.
5 When through the filter thou art poured, we clothe thee with a robe of milk
To be a gladdening draught for Gods.
6 When purified within the jars, Soma, brightred and golden-hued,
Hath clothed him with a robe of milk.
7 Flow on to us and make us rich. Drive all our enemies away.
O Indu, flow into thy Friend.
Send down the rain from heaven, a stream of opulence from earth. Give us,
O Soma, victory in war.
9 May we obtain thee, Indra's drink, who viewest men and findest light,
Gain thee, and progeny and food.

## [09-009] HYMN IX. Soma Pavamana.

I. THE Sage of Heaven whose heart is wise, when laid between both hands and pressed,
Sends us delightful powers of life.
2 On, onward to a glorious home; dear to the people void of guile,
With excellent enjoyment, flow.
3 He, the bright Son, when born illumed his Parents who had sprung to life,
Great Son great Strengtheners of Law.
4 Urged by the seven devotions he hath stirred the guileless rivers which
Have magnified the Single Eye.
5 These helped to might theYouthful One, high over all, invincible,
Even Indu, Indra! in thy law.
6 The immortal Courser, good to draw, looks down upon the Seven: the fount
Hath satisfied the Goddesses
7 Aid us in holy rites, O Man: O Pavamana, drive away
Dark shades that must be met in fight.
8 Make the paths ready for a hymn newer and newer evermore:
Make the lights shine as erst they shone.
9 Give, Pavamana, high renown, give kine and steeds and hero sons:
Win for us wisdom, win the light.

## [09-010] HYMN X. Soma Pavamana.

1. LIKE cars that thunder on their way, like coursers eager for renown,
Have Soma-drops flowed forth for wealth.
2 Forth have they rushed from holding hands, like chariots that are urged to speed,
Like joyful songs of singing-men.
3 The Somas deck themselves with milk, as Kings are graced with eulogies,
And, with seven priests, the sacrifice.
4 Pressed for the gladdening draught, the drops flow forth abundantly with song,
The Soma juices in a stream.
5 Winning Vivasvan's glory and producing Morning's light, the Suns
Pass through the openings of the cloth.

6 The singing-men of ancient time open the doors of sacred songs,-
Men, for the mighty to accept.
7 Combined in close society sit the seven priests, the brotherhood,
Filling the station of the One.
8 He gives us kinship with the Gods, and with the Sun unites our eye:
The Sage's ofrspring hath appeared.
9 The Sun with his dear eye beholds that quarter of the heavens which priests
Have placed within the sacred cell.

## [09-011] HYMN XL Soma Pavamana.

1. SING forth to Indu, O ye men, to him who is purified,
Fain to pay worship to the Gods.
2 Together with thy pleasant juice the Atharvans have commingled milk,
Divine, devoted to the God.
3 Bring, by thy flowing, weal to kine, weal to the people, weal to steeds.
Weal, O thou King, to growing plants
4 Sing a praise-song to Soma brown of hue, of independent might.
The Red, who reaches up to heaven.
5 Purify Soma when effused with stones which bands move rapidly,
And pour the sweet milk in the meath.
6 With humble homage draw ye nigh; blend the libation with the curds:
To Indra offer Indu up.
7 Soma, foe-que chief o'er men, doing the will of pour forth
Prosperity upon our kine.
8 Heart-knower, Sovran of the heart, thou art effused, O Soma, that Indra may drink thee and rejoice.
9 O Soma Pavamana, give us riches and heroic strength,-
Indu! with. Indra for ally.

## [09-012] HYMN XII. Soma Pavamana.

1. To Indra have the Soma drops, exceeding rich in sweets, been poured,
Shed in the seat of sacrifice.
2 As mother kine low to their calves, to Indra have the sages called,
Called him to drink the Soma juice.
3 In the stream's wave wise Soma dwells, distilling rapture, in his seat,
Resting upon a wiId-cow's hide.
4 Far-sighted Soma, Sage and Seer, is worshipped in the central point
Of heaven, the straining-cloth of wool.
5 In close embraces Indu holds Soma when poured within the jars.
And on the. purifying sieve.
6 Indu sends forth a voice on high to regions of the sea of air,
Shaking the vase that drops with meath.
7 The Tree whose praises never fail yields heavenly milk among our hymns,
Urging men's generations on.
8 The Wise One, with the Sage's stream, the Soma urged to speed, flows on
To the dear places of the sky.
9 O Pavamana, bring us wealth bright with a thousand splendours. Yea.
O Indu, give us ready help.

## [09-013] HYMN XIII. Soma Pavamana.

1. PASSED through, the fleece in thousand streams the Soma, purified, flows on
To Indra's, Viyu's special place.
2 Sing forth, ye men who long for help, to Pavamana, to the Sage,
Effused to entertain the Gods.
3 The Soma-drops with thousand powers are purified for victory,
Hymned to become the feast of Gods.
4 Yea, as thou flowest bring great store of food that we may win the spoil
Indu, bring splendid manly might.
5 May they in flowing give us wealth in thousands, and heroic power,-
These Godlike Soma-drops effused.
6 Like coursers by their drivers urged, they were poured forth, for victory,
Swift through the woollen straining-cloth.
7 Noisily flow the Soma-drops, like milch-kine lowing to their calves:
They have run forth from both the hands.
8 As Gladdener whom Indra loves, O Pavamana, with a roar
Drive all our enemies away.
9 O Pavamamas, driving off the godless, looking on the light,
Sit in the place of sacrifice.

## [09-014] HYMN XIV. Soma Pavamana.

1. REPOSING on the river's wave the Sage hath widely flowed around,
Bearing the hymn which many love.
2 When the Five kindred Companies, active in duty, with the song
Establish him, the Powerful,
3 Then in his juice whose strength is great, have all the Gods rejoiced themselves,
When he hath clothed him in the milk.
4 Freeing himself he flows away, leaving his body's severed limbs,
And meets his own Companion here.
5 He by the daughters of the priest, like a fair youth, hath been adorned,
Making the milk, as 'twere, his robe.
6 O'er the fine fingers, through desire of milk, in winding course he goes,
And utters voice which he hath found.
7 The nimble fingers have approached, adorning him the Lord of Strength:
They grasp the vigorous Courser's back.
8 Comprising all the treasures that are in the heavens and on the earth,
Come, Soma, as our faithful Friend.

## [09-015] HYMN XV. Soma Pavamana.

1. THROUGH the fine fingers, with the song, this Hero comes with rapid ears,
Going to Indra's special place.
2 In holy thought he ponders much for the great worship of the Gods.
Where the Immortals have their seat.
3 Like a good horse is he led out, when on the path that shines with light
The mettled steeds exert their strength.
4 He brandishes his horns on high, and whets them Bull who leads the herd,
Doing with might heroic deeds.
5 He moves, a vigorous Steed, adorned with beauteous rays of shining gold,
Becoming Sovran of the streams.
6 He, over places rough to pass, bringing rich treasures closely packed.
Descends into the reservoirs.

7 Men beautify him in the vats, him worthy to be beautified,
Him who brings forth abundant food.
8 Him, even him, the fingers ten and the seven songs make beautiful,
Well-weaponed, best of gladdeners.

## [09-016] HYMN XVI. Soma Pavamana.

1. THE pressers from the Soma-press send forth thy juice for rapturous joy
The speckled sap runs like a flood.
2 With strength we follow through the sieve him who brings might and wins the kine,
Enrobed in water with his juice.
3 Pour on the sieve the Soma, ne'er subdued in waters, waterless,
And make it pure for Indra's drink.
4 Moved by the purifier's thought, the Soma flows into the sieve:
By wisdom it hath gained its home.
5 With humble homage, Indra, have the Soma-drops flowed forth to thee,
Contending for the glorious prize.
6 Purified in his fleecy garb, attaining every beauty, he
Stands, hero-like, amid the kine.
7 Swelling, as 'twere, to heights of heaven, the stream of the creative juice
Falls lightly on the cleansing sieve.
8 Thus, Soma, purifying him who knoweth song mid living men,
Thou wanderest through the cloth of wool.

## [09-017] HYMN XVII. Soma Pavamana.

1. LIKE rivers down a steep descent, slaying the Vrtras, full of zeal,
The rapid Soma-streams have flowed.
2 The drops of Soma juice effused fall like the rain upon the earth:
To Indra flow the Soma-streams.
3 With swelling wave the gladdening drink, the Soma, flows into.the sieve,
Loving the Gods and slaying fiends.
4 It hastens to the pitchers, poured upon the sieve it waxes strong
At sacrifices through the lauds.
5 Soma, thou shinest mounting heaven as 'twere above light's triple realm,
And moving secm'st to speed the Sun.
6 To him, the head of sacnfice, singers and bards have sung their songs,
Offering what he loves to see.
7 The men, the sages with their hymns, eager for help, deck thee strong &teed,
Deck thee for service of the Gods.
8 Flow onward to the stream of meath rest efficacious in thy home,
Fair, to be drunk at sacrifice.

## [09-018] HYMN XVIII. Soma Pavamana.

1. THOU, Soma, dweller on the hills, effused, hast flowed into the sieve,:
All-bounteous art thou in carouse.
2 Thou art a sacred Bard, a Sage; the meath is offipring of thy sap:
All-bountcous art thou in carouse.
3 All Deities of one accord have come that they may drink of thee:
All-bounteous art thou in carouse.
4 He who containeth in his hands all treasures much to be desired:
All-bounteous art thou in carouse.
5 Who milketh out this mighty Pair, the Earth and Heaven, like mother kine

All-bounteous art thou in carouse.
6 Who in a moment mightily floweth around these two world-halvcs:
All-bounteous art thou in carouse.
7 The Strong One, being purified, hath in the pitchers cried aloud:
All-bounteous art thou in carouse.

## [09-019] HYMN XIX. Soma Pavamana.

1. O SOMA, being purified bring us the wondrous treasure, meet
For lauds, that is in earth and heaven.
2 For ye Twain, Indra, Soma, are Lords of the light, Lords of the kine:
Great Rulers, prosper ye our songs.
3 The tawny Steer, while cleansed among the living, bellowing on the grass,
Hath sunk and settled in his home.
4 Over the Steer's productive flow the sacred songs were resonant,
The mothers of the darling Son.
5 Hath he not, purified, impregned the kine whb long to meet their Lord,
The kine who yield the shining milk?
6 Bring near us those who stand aloof strike fear into our enemies:
O Pavamana, find us wealth.
7 Soma, bring down the foeman's might, his vigorous strength and vital powe'r,
Whether he be afar or near.

## [09-020] HYMN XX Soma Pavamana.

1. FORTH through the straining-cloth the Sage flows to the banquet of the Gods,
Subduing all our enemies.
2 For he, as Pavamana, sends thousandfold treasure in the shape
Of cattle to the singing-men.
3 Thou graspest all things with thy mind, and purifiest thee with thoughts
As such, O Soma, find us fame.
4 Pour lofty glory on us, send sure riches to our liberal lords,
Bring food to those who sing thy praise.
5 As thou art cleansed, O Wondrous Steed, O Soma, thou hast entered, like
A pious King, into the songs.
6 He, Soma, like a courser in the floods invincible, made clean
With hands, is resting in the jars.
7 Disporting, like a liberal chief, thou goest, Soma, to the sieve,
Lending the laud a Hero's strength.

## [09-021] HYMN XXI. Soma Pavamana.

1. To Indra flow these running drops, these Somas frolicsome in mood.
Exhilarating, finding light;
2 Driving off foes, bestowing room upon the presser, willingly
Bringing their praiser vitalforce.
3 Lightly disporting them, the drops flow to one common reservoir,
And fall into the river's wave.
4 These Pavamanas have obtained all blessings much to be desired,
Like coursers harnessed to a car.
5 With view to us, O Soma-drops, bestow his manifold desire
On him who yet hath given us naught.
6 Bring us our wish with this design, as a wright brings his new-wrought wheel:
Flow pure and shining with the stream.
7 These drops have cried with resonant voice: like swift steeds they have run the course,

And roused the good man's hymn to life.

## [09-022] HYMN XXII. Soma Pavamana.

1. THESE rapid Soma-streams have stirred themselves to motion like strong steeds,
Like cars, like armies hurried forth.
2 Swift as wide winds they lightly move, like rain-storms of Parjanya, like
The flickering flames of burning fire.
3 These Soma juices, blent with curds, purified, skilled in sacred hymns,
Have gained by song their hearts'desire.
4 Immortal, cleansed, these drops, since first they flowed, have never wearied, fain
To reach the regions and their paths.
5 Advancing they have travelled o'er the ridges of the earth and heaven,
And this the highest realm of all.
6 Over the heights have they attained the highest thread that is spun out,
And this which must be deemed most high.
7 Thou, Soma, boldest wealth in kine which thou hast seized from niggard churls:
Thou calledst forth the outspun thread.

## [09-023] HYMN XXIII. Soma Pavamana.

1. SWIFT Soma drops have been effused in streams of meath, the gladdening drink,
For sacred lore of every kind.
2 Hither to newer. resting-place the ancient Living Ones are come.
They made the Sun that he might shine.
3 O Pavamana, bring to us the unsacrificing foeman's wealth,
And give us food with progeny.
4 The living Somas being cleansed diffuse exhilarating drink,
Turned to the vat which drips with meath.
5 Soma gows on intelligent, possessing sap and mighty strength,
Brave Hero who repels the curse.
6 For Indra, Soma! thou art cleansed, a feast-companion for the Gods:
1ndu, thou fain wilt win us strength
7 When he had drunken draughts of this, Indra smote down resistless foes:
Yea, smote them, and shall smite them still.

## [09-024] HYMN XXIV.Soma Pavamana.

1. HITHERWARD have the Soma streamed,
the drops while they are purified:
When bIent, in waters they are rinsed.
2 The milk hath run to meet them like floods rushing down a precipice:
They come to Indra, being cleansed.
3 O Soma Pavamana, thou art flowing to be Indra's drink:
The men have seized and lead thee forth.
4 Victorious, to be hailed with joy, O Soma, flow, delighting men,
To him who ruleth o'er mankind.
5 Thou, Indu, when, effused by stones, thou runnest to the filter, art,
Ready for Indra's high decree.
6 Flow on, best Vrtra-slayer; flow meet to be hailed with joyful lauds.
Pure, purifying, wonderful.
7 Pure, purifying is he called the Soma of the meath eflused,
Slayer of sinners, dear to Gods.

## [09-025] HYMN XXV. Soma Pavamana.

1. GREEN-HUED! as one who giveth strength flow on for Gods to drink, a draught
For Vayu and the Marut host.
2 O Pavamana, sent by song, roaring about thy dwelling-place,
Pass into Vayu as Law bids.
3 The Steer shines with the Deities, dear Sage in his appointed home,
Foe-Slayer, most beloved by Gods.
4 Taking each beauteous form, he goes, desirable, while purified,
Thither where- the Immortals sit.
5 To Indra Soma flows, the Red, engendering song, exceeding wise,
The visitor of living men.
6 Flow, best exhilarator, Sage, flow to the filter in a stream
To seat thee in the place of song.

## [09-026] HYMN XXVI. Soma Pavamana.

1. THE sages with the fingers' art have dressed and decked that vigorous Steed
Upon the lap of Aditi,
2 The kine have called aloud to him exhaustless with a thousand streams,
To Indu who supporteth heaven.
3 Him, nourisher of many, Sage, creative Pavamana, they
Have sent, by wisdom, to the sky.
4 Him, dweller with Vivasvan, they with use of both arms have sent forth,
The Lord of Speech infallible.
5 Him, green, beloved, many eyed, the Sisters with prosing stones
Send down to ridges of the sieve.
6 O Pavamana, Indu, priests hurry thee on to Indra, thee
Who aidest song and cheerest him.

## [09-027] HYMN XXVII. Soma Pavamana.

1. THIS Sage, exalted by our lauds, flows to the purifying cloth,
Scattering foes as he is cleansed.
2 As giving power and winning light, for Indra and for Vayu he
Is poured upon the filtering-cloth.
3 The men conduct him, Soma, Steer, Omniscient, and the Head of Heaven,
Effused into the vats of wood.
4 Longing for kine, longing for gold hath Indu Pavamana lowed,
Still Conqueror, never overcome.
5 This Pavamana, gladdening draught, drops on the filtering cloth, and then
Mounts up with Surya to the sky.
6 To Indra in the firmament this mighty tawny Steer hath flowed,
This Indu, being purified.

## [09-028] HYMN XXVIII. Soma Pavamana.

1. URGED by the men, this vigorous Steed, Lord of the mind, Omniscient,
Runs to the woollen straining-cloth.
2 Within the filter hath he flowed, this Soma for the Gods effused,
Entering all their essences.
3 He shines in beauty there, this God Immortal in his dwelling-place,
Foe-slayer, dearest to the Gods.
4 Directed by the Sisters ten, bellowing on his way this Steer
Runs onward to the wooden vats.
5 This Pavamana, swiftand strong, Omniscient, gave spleudour to
The Sun and all his forms of light.
6 This Soma being purified, flows mighty and infallible,
Slayer of sinners, dear toGods.

## [09-029] HYMN XXIX. Soma Pavamana.

1. FORWARD with mighty force have flowed the currents of this Steer effused,
Of him who sets him by the Gods.
2 The singers praise him with their song, and learned priests adorn the Steed,
Brought forth as light that merits laud.
3 These things thou winnest lightly while purified, Soma, Lord of wealth:
Fill full the sea that claims our praise.
4 Winning all precious things at once, flow on, O Soma, with thy stream
Drive to one place our enemies.
5 Preserve us from the godless, from ill-omened voice of one and all,
That so we may be freed from blame.
6 O Indu, as thou flowest on bring us the wealth of earth and heaven,
And splendid vigour, in thy stream.

## [09-030] HYMN XXX. Soma Pavamana.
1. STREAMS of this Potent One have flowed easily to the straining-cloth:
While he is cleansed he lifts his voice.
2 Indu, by pressers urged to speed, bellowing out while beautified.
Sends forth a very mighty sound.
3 Pour on us, Soma, with thy stream manconquering might which many crave,
Accompanied with hero sons.
4 Hither hath Pavamana flowed, Soma flowed hither in a stream,
To settle in the vats of wood.
5 To waters with the stones they drive thee tawny-hued, most rich in sweets,
O Indu, to be Indra's drink.
6 For Indra, for the Thunderer press the Soma very rich in sweets,
Lovely, inspiriting, for strength.

## [09-031] HYMN XXXI. Soma Pavamana.
1. THE, Soma-drops, benevolent, come forth as they are purified,
Bestowing wealth which all may see.
2 O Indu, high o'er heaven and earth be thou, increaser of our might:
The Master of all strength be thou.
3 The winds are gracious in their love to thee, the rivers flow to thee
Soma, they multiply thy power.
4 Soma, wax great. From every side may vigorous powers unite in thee:
Be in the gathering-Place of strength.
5 For thee, brown-hued! the kine have poured imperishable oil and milk.
Aloft on the sublimest height.
6 Friendship, O Indu, we desire with thee who bearest noble arms,
With thee, O Lord of all that is.

## [09-032] HYMN XXXII. Soma Pavamana.
1. THE rapture-shedding Soma-drops, effused in our assembly, have
Flowed forth to glorify our prince.
2 Then Trita's Maidens onward urge the Tawny-coloured with the stones,
Indu for Indra, for his drink.
3 Now like a swan he maketh all the company sing each his hymn:
He, like a steed, is bathed in milk.

4 O Soma, viewing heaven and earth, thou runnest like a darting deer
Set in the place of sacrifice.
5 The cows have sung with joy to him, even as a woman to her love
He came as to a settled race.
6 Bestow illustrious fame on us, both on our liberal lords and me,
Glory, intelligence, and wealth.

## [09-033] HYMN XXXIII. Soma Pavamana.
1. LIKE waves of waters, skilled in song the juices of the Soma speed
Onward, as buffaloes to woods.
2 With stream of sacrifice the brown bright drops have flowed with strength in store
Of kine into the wooden vats.
3 To Indra, Vayu, Varuna, to Visnu, and the Maruts, flow
The drops of Soma juice effused.
4 Three several words are uttered: kine are lowing, cows who give their milk:
The Tawny-hued goes bellowing on.
5 The young and sacred mothers of the holy rite have uttered praise:
They decorate the Child of Heaven.
6 From every side, O Soma, for our profit, pour thou forth four seas
Filled full of riches thousandfold.

## [09-034] HYMN XXXIV. Some Pavamana.
1. THE drop of Soma juice effused flows onward with this stream impelled.
Rending strong places with its might.
2 Poured forth to Indra, Varuna, to Vayu and the Marut hosts,
To Visnu, flows the Soma juice.
3 With stones they press the Soma forth, the Strong conducted by the strong:
They milk the liquor out with skill.
4 'Tis he whom Trita must refine, 'tis he who shall make Indra glad:
The Tawny One is decked with tints.
5 Him do the Sons of Prsni milk, the dwelling-place of sacrifice,
Oblation lovely and most dear.
6 To him in one united stream th-,se songs flow on straight forward. he,
Loud voiced, hath made the milch-kine low.

## [09-035] HYMN XXXV. Soma Pavamana.
1. Pour forth on us abundant wealth, O Pavamana, with thy stream.
Wherewith thou mayest find us light
2 O Indu, swayer of the sea, shaker of all things, flow thou on,
Bearer of wealth to us with might.
3 With thee for Hero, Valiant One! may we subdue our enemies:
Let what is precious flow to us.
4 Indu arouses strength the Sage who strives for victory, winning power,
Discovering holy works and means.
5 Mover of speech, we robe him with our songs as he is purified
Soma, the Guardian of the folk;
6 On whose way, Lord of Holy Law, most richi as he is purified.
The people all have set their hearts.

## [09-036] HYMN XXXVI. Soma Pavamana.
1. FORTH from the mortar is the juice sent, like a car-horse, to the sieve:
The Steed steps forward to the goal.

2 Thus, Soma, watchful, bearing well, cheering the Gods, flow past the sieve,
Turned to the vat that drops with meath.
3 Excellent Pavamana, make the lights shine brightly out for us.
Speed us to mental power and skill.
4 He, beautified by pious men, and coming from their hands adorned,
Flows through the fleecy straining-cloth.
5 May Soma pour all treasures of the heavens, the earth, the firmament
Upon the liberal worshipper.
6 Thou mountest to the height of heaven, O Soma, seeking steeds and kine,
And seeking heroes, Lord of Strength!

### [09-037] HYMN XXXVII. Soma Pavamana.

1. SOMA, the Steer, effused for draught, flows to the purifying sieve,
Slaying the fiends, loving the Gods.
2 Far-sighted, tawny-coloured, he flows to the sieve, intelligent,
Bellowing, to his place of rest.
3 This vigorous Pavamana runs forth to the luminous realm of heaven,
Fiend-slayer, through the fleecy sieve.
4 This Payamana up above Trita's high ridge hath made the Sun,
Together with the Sisters, shine.
5 This Vrtra-slaying Steer, effused, Soma room-giver, ne'er deceived,
Hath gone, as 'twere, to win the spoil.
6 Urged onward by the sage, the God speeds forward to the casks of wood,
Indu to Indra willingly.

### [09-038] HYMN XXXVIII. Soma Pavamana.

1. THIS Steer, this Chariot, rushes through the woollen filter, as he goes
To war that wins a thousand spoils.
2 The Dames of Trita with the stones onward impel this Tawny One
Indu to Indra for his drink.
3 Ten active fingers carefully adorn him here; they make him bright
And beauteous for the gladdening draught.
4 He like a falcon settles down amid the families of men.
Speeding like lover to his love.
5 This young exhilarating juice looks downward from its place in heaven,
This Soma-drop that pierced the sieve.
6 Poured for the draught, this tawny juice
flows forth, intelligent, crying out,
Unto the well-beloved place.

### [09-039] HYMN XXXIX Soma Pavamana.

1. FLOW On, O thou of lofty thought, flow swift in thy beloved form,
Saying, I go where dwell the Gods.
2 Preparing what is unprepared, and bringing store of food to man,
Make thou the rain descend from heaven.
3 With might, bestowing power, thejuice enters the purifying sieve,
Far-seeing, sending forth its light.
4 This is it which in rapid course hath with the river's wave flowed down
From heaven upon the straining cloth.
5 Inviting him frorh far away, and even from near at hand, the juice

For Indra is poured forth as meath.
6 In union they have sung the hymn: with stones they urge the Tawny One.
Sit in the place of sacrifice.

### [09-040] HYMN XL. Soma Pavamana.

1. THE Very Active hath assailed, while purified, all enemies:
They deck the Sage with holy songs.
2 The Red hath mounted to his place; to India, goes the mighty juice:
He settles in his firm abode.
3 O Indu, Soma, send us now great opulence from every side,
Pour on us treasures thousandfold.
4 O Soma Pavamana, bring, Indu, all splcndours hitherward:
Find for us food in boundless store.
5 As thou art cleansed, bring hero strength and riches to thy worshipper,
And prosper thou the singer's hymns.
6 O Indu, Soma, being cleansed, bring hither riches doublypiled,
Wealth, mighty Indu, meet for lauds.

### [09-041] HYMN XLI. Soma Pavamana.

1. ACTIVE and bright have they come forth, impetuous in speed like bulls,
Driving the black skin far away.
2 Quelling the riteless Dasyu, may we think upon the bridge of bliss,
Leaving the bridge of woe behind.
3 The mighty Pavamana's roar is heard as 'twere the rush of rain
Lightnings are flashing to the sky.
4 Pour out on us abundant food, when thou art pressed, O Indu wealth
In kine and gold and steeds and spoil.
5 Flow on thy way, Most Active, thou. fill full the mighty heavens and earth,
As Dawn, as Surya with his beams.
6 On every side, O Soma, flow round us with thy protecting stream,
As Rasa flows around the world.

### [09-042] HYMN XLII. Soma Pavamana.

1. ENGENDERING the Sun in floods, engendering heaven's lights, green-hued,
Robed in the waters and the milk,
2 According to primeval plan this Soma, with his stream, effused
Flows purely on, a God for Gods.
3 For him victorious, waxen great, the juices with a thousand powers
Are purified for winning spoil.
4 Shedding the ancient fluid he is poured into the cleansing sieve:
He, thundering, hath produced the Gods.
5 Soma, while purifying, sends hither all things to be desired,
He sends the Gods who strengthen Law.
6 Soma, effused, pour on us wealth in kine, in heroes, steeds, and spoil,
Send us abundant store of food.

### [09-043] HYMN XLIII. Soma Pavamana.

1. WE will enrobe with sacred song the Lovely One who, as a Steed,
Is decked with milk for rapturous joy.
2 All songs of ours desiring grace adorn him in the ancient way,
Indu for Indra, for his drink.
3 Soma flows on when purified, beloved and adorned with songs,
Songs of the sage Medhyatithi.
4 O Soma Pavamana, find exceeding glorious wealth for us,
Wealth, Indu, fraught with boundless might.

5 Like courser racing to the prize Indu, the lover of the Gods,
Roars, as he passes, in the sieve.
6 Flow on thy way to win us strength, to speed the sage who
praises thee:
Soma, bestow heroic power.

### [09-044] HYMN XLIV. Soma Pavamana.

1. INDU, to us for this great rite, bearing as 'twere thy wave to
Gods,
Unwearied, thou art flowing forQh.
2 Pleased with the hymn, impelled by prayer, Soma is hurried far
away,
The Wise One in the Singer's stream.,
3 Watchful among the. gods, this juice advances to the cleansing
sieve
Soma, most active, travels on.
4 Flow onward, seeking strength for us, embellishing the
sacrifice:
The priest with trimmed grass calleth thee.
5 May Soma, ever bringing power to Bhaga and to Vayu, Sage
And Hero, lead us to the Gods.
6 So, to increase our wealth to-day, Inspirer, best of Furtherers,
Win for us strength and high renown.

### [09-045] HYMN XLV. Soma Pavamana.

1. FLOW, thou who viewest men, to give delight, to entertain the
Gods,
Indu, to Indra for his drink.
2 Stream to thine embassy for us: thou hastenest, for Indra, to
The Gods, O better than our friends.
3 We balm thee, red of hue, with milk to fit thee for the rapturous
joy:
Unbar for us the doors of wealth.
4 He through the sieve hath passed, as comes a courser to the
pole, to run
Indu belongs unto the Gods.
5 All friends have lauded him as he sports in the wood, beyond
the fleece:
Singers have chanted Indu's praise.
6 Flow, Indu, with that stream wherein steeped thou announcest
to the man
Who worships thee heroic strength.

### [09-046] HYMN XLVI. Soma Pavamana.

1. LIKE able coursers they have been sent forth to be the feast of
Gods,
joying in mountains, flowing on.
2 To Vayu flow the Soma-streams, the drops of juice made
beautiful
Like a bride dowered by her sire.
3 Pressed in the mortar, these, the drops of
juice, the Somas rich in food,
Give strength to Indra with their work.
4 Deft-handed men, run hither, seize the brilliant juices blent
with meal,
And cook with milk the gladdening draught.
5 Thus, Soma, Conqueror of wealth! flow, finding furtherance for
us,
Giver oF ample opulence.
6 This Pavamana, meet to be adorned, the fingers ten adorn,
The draught that shall make Indra glad.

### [09-047] HYMN XLVII. Soma Pavamana.

1. GREAT as he was, Soma hath gained strength by this high
solemnity:
joyous he riseth like a bull.

2 His task is done: his crushings of the Dasyus are made
manifest:
He sternly reckoneth their debts.
3 Soon as his song of praise is born, the Soma, Indra's juice,
becomes
A thousand-winning thunderbolt.
4 Seer and Sustainer, hc himself dcsireth riches for the sage
When he embellisheth his songs.
5 Fain would they both win riches as in races of the steeds. In war
Thou art upon the conquerors' side.

### [09-048] HYMN XLVIII. Soma Pavamana.

1. WITH sacrifice we seek to thee kind Cherisher of manly might
In mansions of the lofty heavens;
2 Gladdening crusher of the bold, ruling with very mighty sway,
Destroyer of a hundred forts.
3 Hence, Sapient One! the Falcon, strong of wing, unwearied,
brought thee down,
Lord over riches, from the sky.
4 That each may see the light, the Bird brought us the guard of
Law, the Friend
Of all, the speeder through the air.
5 And now, sent forth, it hath attained to mighty power and
majesty,
Most active, ready to assist.

### [09-049] HYMN XLIX. Soma Pavamana.

1. Poust down the rain upon us, pour a wave of waters from the
sky,
And plenteous store of wholesome fbod.
2 Flow onward with that stream of thine, whereby the cows have
come to us,
The kine of strangers to our home.
3 Chief Friend of Gods in sacred rites, pour on us fatness with thy
stream,
Ppur down on us a flood of rain.
4 To give us vigour, with thy stream run through the fleecy
straining-cloth
For verily the Gods will bear.
5 Onward hath Pavamana flowed and beaten off the Raksasas,
Flashing out splendour as of old.

### [09-050] HYMN L. Soma Pavamana.

1. LOUD as a river's roaring wave thy powers have lifted up
themselves:
Urge on thine arrow's sharpened point.
2 At thine effusion upward rise three voices full of joy, when thou
Flowest upon the fleecy ridge.
3 On to the fleece they urge with stone the tawny well-beloved
One,
Even Pavamana, dropping meath.
4 Flow with thy current to the sieve, O Sage most powerful to
cheer,
To seat thee in the place of song.
5 Flow, Most Exhilarating! flow anointed with the milk for balm,
Indu, for Indra, for his drink.

### [09-051] HYMN LI. Soma Pavamana.

1. ADHVARYU, on the filter pour the Soma juice expressed with
stones,
And make it pure for Indra's drink.
2 Pour out for Indra, Thunder-armed, the milk of heaven,, the
Soma's juice,
Most excellent, most rich in sweets.
3 These Gods and all the Marut host, Indu enjoy this juice of
thine,
This Pavamana's flowing meath.

4 For, Soma, thou hast been effused, strengthening for the wild carouse,
O Steer, the singer, for our help.
5 Flow with thy stream, Far-sighted One, effused, into the cleansing sieve:
Flow on to give us strength and fame.

## [09-052] HYMN LII. Soma Pavamana.

1. WEALTH-WINNER, dwelling in the sky, bringing us vigour with the juice,
Flow to the filter when effused.
2 So, in thine ancient ways, may he, beloved, with a thousand streams
Run o'er the fleecy straining-cloth.
3 Him who is like a caldron shake: O Indu, shake thy gift to us
Shake it, armed Warrior! with thine arms.
4 Indu, invoked with many a prayer, bring down the vigour of these men,
Of him who threatens us with war.
5 Indu, Wealth-giver, with thine help pour out for us a hundred, yea,
A thousand of thy pure bright streams.

## [09-053] HYMN LIII. Soma Pavamana.

1. O THOU with stones for arms, thy powers, crushing the fiends, have raised themselves:
Chase thou the foes who compass us.
2 Thou conquerest thus with might when car meets car, and when the prize is staked:
With fearless heart will I sing praise.
3 No one with evil thought assails this Pavamana's holy laws:
Crush him who fain would fight with thee.
4 For Indra to the streams they drive the tawny rapture-dropping Steed,
Indu the bringer of delight.

## [09-054] HYMN LIV. Soma Pavamana.

1. AFTER his ancient splendour, they, the bold, have drawn the bright milk from
The Sage who wins a thousand gifts.
2 In aspect he is like the Sun; he runneth forward to the lakes,
Seven currents flowing through the sky.
3 He, shining in his splendour, stands high over all things that exist-
Soma, a God as Surya is.
4 Thou, Indu, in thy brilliancy, pourest on us, as Indra's Friend,
Wealth from the kine to feast the Gods.

## [09-055] HYMN LV. Soma Pavamana.

1. POUR on us with thy juice all kinds of corn, each sort of nourishment,
And, Soma, all felicities.
2 As thine, O Indu, is the praise, and thine what springeth from the juice,
Seat thee on the dear sacred grass.
3 And, finding for us kine and steeds, O Soma, with thy juice flow on
Through days that fly most rapidly.
4 As one who conquers, ne'er subdued, attacks and stays the enemy,
Thus, Vanquisher of thousands! flow.

## [09-056] HYMN LVI. Soma Pavamana.

1. SWIFT to the purifying sieve flows Soma as exalted Law,
Slaying the fiends, loving the Gods.

2 When Soma pours the strengthening food a hundred ever-active streams
To Indra's friendship win theirway.
3 Ten Dames have sung to welcome thee, even as a maiden greets her love:
O Soma, thou art decked to win.
4 Flow hitherward, O Indu, sweet to Indra and to Visnu: guard
The men, the singers, from distress.

## [09-057] HYMN LVII. Soma Pavamana.

1. THY streams that never fail or waste flow forth like showers of rain from heaven,
To bring a thousand stores of strength.
2 He flows beholding on his way all wellbeloved sacred lore,
Green-tinted, brandishing his, arms.
3 He, when the people deck him like a docile king of elephants.
Sits as a falcon in the, wood.
4 So bring thou hitherward to us, Indu, while thou art purified,
All treasures both of heaven and earth.

## [09-058] HYMN LVIII. Soma Pavamana.

1. SWIFT runs this giver of delight, even the stream of flowing juice:
Swift runs this giver of delight.
2 The Morning knows all precious things, the Goddess knows her grace to man:
Swift runs this giver of delight.
3 We have accepted thousands from Dhvasra's and Purusanti's hands:
Swift runs this giver of delight.
4 From whom we have accepted thus thousands and three times ten beside:
Swift runs this giver of delight.

## [09-059] HYMN LIX. Soma Pavamana.

1. FLOW onward, Soma, winning kine, and steeds, and all that gives delight:
Bring hither wealth with progeny.
2 Flow onward from the waters, flow, inviolable, from the plants:
Flow onward from the pressing-boards.
3 Soma, as Pavamana, pass over all trouble and distress:
Sit on the sacred grass, a Sage.
4 Thou, Pavamana, foundest light; thou at thy birth becamest great:
O Indu, thou art over all.

## [09-060] HYMN LX. Soma Pavamana.

1. SING forth and laud with sacred song most active Pavamana, laud
Indu who sees with thousand eyes.
2 Thee who hast thousand eyes to see, bearer of thousand burthens, they
Have filtered through the fleecy cloth.
3 He, Pavamana, hath streamed through the fleece then: he runs into the jars,
Finding his way to Indra's heart.
4 That Indra may be bounteous, flow, most active Soma, for our weal:
Bring genial seed with progeny.

## [09-061] HYMN LXI. Soma Pavamana.

1. FLOW onward, Indu, with this food for him who in thy wild delight

Battered the nine-and-ninety down,

2 Smote swiftly forts, and gambara, then Yadu and that Turvaga,
For pious Divodasa's sake.

3 Finder of horses, pour on us horses and
wealth in kine and gold,
And, Indu, food in boundless store.

4 We seek to win thy friendly love, even Pavamana's flowing o'er
The limit of the cleansing sieve.

5 With those same waves which in their stream oyerflow the
purifying sieve,
Soma; be gracious unto us.

6 O Soma, being purified, bring us from all sides,-for thou canst,-
Riches and food with hero sons.

7 Him here, the Child whom streams have borne, the ten swift
fingers beautify
With the Adityas is he seen.

8 With Indra and with Vayu he, effused, flows onward with,the
beams
Of Surya to the cleansing sieve.

9 Flow rich in sweets and lovely for our Bhaga, Vayu, Pusan flow
For Mitra and for Varuna.

10 High is thy juice's birth: though set in heaven, on earth it hath
obtained
Strong sheltering power and great renown.

11 Striving to win, with him we gain all wealth from the ungodly
man,
Yea, all the glories of mankind.

12 Finder of room and freedom, flow for Indra whom we must
adore,
For Varuna and the Marut host.

13 The Gods have come to Indu well-descended, beautified with
milk,
The active crusher of the foe.

14 Even as mother cows their calf, so let our praise-songs
strengthen him,
Yea, him who winneth Indra's heart.

15 Soma, pour blessings on our kine, pour forth the food that
streams with milk
Increase the sea that merits laud.

16 From heaven hath Pavamana made, as 'twere, the marvellous
thunder, and
The lofty light of all mankind.

17 The gladdening and auspicious juice of thee, of Pavamana,
King!
Flows o'er the woollen straining-cloth.

18 Thy juice, O Pavamana, sends its rays abroad like splendid
skill,
Like lustre, all heaven's light, to see.

19 Flow onward with that juice of thine most excellent, that
brings delight,
Slaying the wicked, dear to Gods.

20 Killing the foeman and his hate, and winning booty every day,
Gainer art thou of steeds and kine.

21 Red-hued, be blended with the milk that seems to yield its
lovely breast,
Falcon-like resting in thine home.

22 Flow onward thou who strengthenedst Indra to slaughter
Vrtra who
Compassed and stayed the mighty floods.

23 Soma who rainest gifts, may we win riches with our hero sons:
Strengthen, as thou art cleansed, our hymns.

24 Aided by thee, and through thy grace, may we be slayers when
we war:
Watch, Soma, at our solemn rites.

25 Chasing our foemen, driving off the godless, Soma flowcth on,
Going to Indra's special place.

26 O Pavamana, hither bring great riches, and destroy our foes:

O Indu, grant heroic fame.

27 A hundred obstacles have ne'er checked
thee when fain to give thy boons,
When, being cleansed, thou combatest.

28 Indu, flow on, a mighty juice; glorify us among the folk:
Drive all our enemies away.

29 Indu, in this thy friendship most lofty and glorious may we
Subdue all those who war with us.

30 Those awful weapons that thou hast, sharpened at point to
strike men down-
Guard us therewith from every foe.

## [09-062] HYMN LXII. Soma Pavamana.

1. THESE rapid Soma-drops have been poured through the
purifying sieve
To bring us all felicities.

2 Dispelling manifold mishap, giving the courser's progeny,
Yea, and the warrior steed, success.

3 Bringing prosperity to kine, they make perpetual Ila flow
To us for noble eulogy.

4 Strong, mountain-born, the stalk hath been
pressed in the streams for rapturous joy:
Hawk-like he settles in his home.

5 Fair is the God-loved juice; the plant is washed in waters,
pressed by men
The milch-kine sweeten it with milk.

6 As drivers deck a courser, so have they adorned the meath's
juice for
Ambrosia, for the festival.

7 Thou, Indu, with thy streams that drop sweet juices, which were
poured for
help,
Hast settled in the cleansing sieve.

8 So flow thou onward through the fleece, for Indra flow, to be his
drink,
Finding thine home in vats of wood.

9 As giving room and freedom, as most sweet, pour butter forth
and milk,
O Indu, for the Angirases.

10 Most active and benevolent, this Pavamana, sent to us
For lofty friendship, meditates.

11 Queller of curses, mighty, with strong sway, this Pavamana
shall
Bring treasures to the worshipper.

12 Pour thou upon us thousandfold possessions, both of kine and
steeds,
Exceeding glorious, much-desired.

13 Wandering far, with wise designs, the juice here present is
effused,
Made beautiful by living men.

14 For Indra flows the gladdening drink, the measurer of the
region, Sage,
With countless wealth and endless help.

15 Born on the inountain, lauded here, Indu for Indra is set down,
As in her sheltering nest a bird.

16 Pressed by the men, as 'twere to war hath Soma Pavamana
sped,
To test with might within the vats.

17 That he may move, they yoke him to the three-backed triple-
seated car
By the Seven Rsis' holy songs.

18 Drive ye that Tawny Courser, O ye pressers, on his way to war,
Swift Steed who carries off the spoil.

19 Pouring all glories hither, he, effused and entering the jar,
Stands like a hero mid the kine.

20 Indu, the living men milk out the juice to make the rapturous
draught:

Gods for the Gods milk out the meath.

21 Pour for the Gods into the sieve our Soma very rich in sweets,
Him whom the Gods most gladly hear.

22 Into his stream who gladdens best these Soma juices have been poured,
Lauded with songs for lofty fame.

23 Thou flowest to enjoy the milk, and bringest valour, being cleansed:
Winning the spoil flow hitherward.

24 And, hymned by Jamadagnis, let all nourishment that kine supply,
And general praises, flow to us.

25 Soma, as leader of the song flow onward with thy wondrous aids,
For holy lore of every kind.

26 Do thou as leader of the song, stirring the waters of the sea,
Flow onward, thou who movest all.

27 O Soma, O thou Sage, these worlds stand ready to attest thy might:
For thy behoof the rivers flow.

28 Like showers of rain that fall from heaven thy streams perpetually flow
To the bright fleece spread under them.

29 For potent Indra purify Indu effectual and strong,
Enjoyment-giver, Mighty Lord.

30 Soma, true, Pavamana, Sage, is seated in the cleansing sieve,
Giving his praiser hero strength.

## [09-063] HYMN LXIII. Soma Pavanana.

1. POUR hitherward, O Soma, wealth in thousands and heroic strength,
And keep renown secure for us.

2 Thou makest food and vigour swell for Indra, best of gladdeners!
Within the cups thou seatest thee.

3 For Indra and for Visnu poured, Soma hath flowed into the jar:
May Vayu find it rich in sweets.

4 These Somas swift and brown of hue, in stream of solemn sacrifice
Have flowed through twisted obstacles,

5 Performing every noble work, active, augmenting Indra's strength,
Driving away the godless ones.

6 Brown Soma-drops, effused that seek Indra, to their appropriate place
Flow through the region hitherward.

7 Flow onward with that stream of thine wherewith thou gavest Surya light,
Urging on waters good to men.

8 He, Pavamana, high o'er man yoked the Sun's courser Etasa
To travel through the realm of air.

9 And those ten Coursers, tawny-hued, he harnessed that the Sun might come
Indu, he said, is Indra's self.

10 Hence, singers, pour the gladdeningjuice to Vayu and to Indra, pour
The drops upon the fleecy cloth.

11 O Soma Pavamana, find wealth for us not to be assailed,
Wealth which the foeman may not win.

12 Send riches hither with thy stream in thousands, both of steeds and kine,
Send spoil of war and high renown.

13 Soma the God, expressed with stones, like Surya, floweth on his way,
Pouring the juice within the jar.

14 These brilliant drops have poured for us, in stream of solemn sacrifice,

Worshipful laws and strength in kine.

15 Over the cleansing sieve have flowed the Somas, blent with curdled milk,
Effused for Indra Thunder-armed.

16 Soma, do thou most rich in sweets, a gladdening drink most dear to Gods,
Flow to the sieve to bring us wealth.

17 For Indra, living men adorn the Tawny Courser in the streams,
Indu, the giver of delight.

18 Pour for us, Soma, wealth in gold, in horses and heroic sons,
Bring hither strength in herds of kine.

19 For Indra pour ye on the fleece him very sweet to taste, who longs.
For battle as it were in war.

20 The singers, seeking help, adorn the Sage who must be decked with songs:
Loud bellowing the Steer comes on,

21 The singers with their thoughts and hymns have, in the stream of sacrifice,
Caused Soma, active Steer, to roar.

22 God, working with mankind, flow on; to Indra go thy gladdening juice:
To Vayu mount as Law commands

23 O Soma, Pavamana, thou pourest out wealth that brings renown:
Enter the lake, as one we love.

24 Soma thou flowest chasing foes and bringing wisdom and delight:
Drive off the folk who love not Gods.

25 The Pavamanas have been poured, the brilliant drops of Soma juice,
For holy lore of every kind.

26 The Pavamanas have been shed, the beautiful swift Soma-drops,
Driving all enemies afar.

27 From, heaven, from out the firmament, hath Pavamana been effused
Upon the summit of the earth.

28 O Soma, Indu, very wise, drive, being purified, with thy stream
All foes, all Raksasas away.

29 Driving the Raksasas afar, O Soma, bellowing, pour for us
Most excellent and splendid strength.

30 Soma, do thou secure for us the treasures of the earih and heaven,
Indu, all boons to be desired.

## [09-064] HYMN LXIV. Soma Pavamana.

1. Soma, thou art a splendid Steer, a Steer, O God, with steerlike sway:
Thou as a Steer ordainest laws.

2 Steer-strong thy might is as a steer's, steerstrong thywood, steer-like thy drink
A Steer indeed, O Steer, art thou.

3 Thou, Indu, as a vigorous horse, hast neighed together steeds and kine:
Unbar for us the doors to wealth.

4 Out of desire of cows and steeds and horses. potent Soma-drops,
Brilliant and swift, have been effused.

5 They purified in both the hands, made beautiful by holy men,
Flow onward to the fleecy cloth.

6 These Soma juices shall pour forth all treasures for the worshipper
From heaven and earth and firmament.

7 The streams of Pavamana, thine, Finder of all, have been effused,
Even as Surya's rays of light.

8 Making the light that shines from heaven thou flowest on to every form
Soma, thou swellest like a sea.

9 Urged on thou sendest out thy voice, O Pavamana; thou hast moved,
Like the God Surya, to the sieve.

10 Indu, Enlightener, Friend, hath been purified by the sages' hymns:
So starts the charioteer his steed-

11 Thy God-delighting wave which hath flowed to purifying seive,
Alighting in the home of Law.

12 Flow to our sieve, a gladdening draught that hath most intercourse with Gods,
Indu, to Indra for his drink.

13 Flow onward with a stream for food, made beautiful by sapient men:
Indu with sheen approach the milk.

14 While thou art cleansed, Song-Lover, bring comfort and vigour to the folk,
Poured, Tawny One! on milk and curds.

15 Purified for the feast of Gods, go thou to Indra's special place,
Resplendent, guided by the strong.

16 Accelerated by the hymn, the rapid drops of Soma juice
Have flowed, urged onward, to the lake.

17 Easily have the living drops, made beautiful, approached the lake,
Yea, to the place of sacrifice.

18 Compass about, our faithful Friend, all our possessions with thy might:
Guard, hero like, our sheltering home.

19 Loud neighs the Courser Etasa, with singers, harnessed for the place,
Guided for travel to the lake.

20 What time the Swift One resteth in the golden place of sacrifice,
He leaves the foolish far away.

21 The friends have sung in unison, the prudent wish to sacrifice:
Down sink the unintelligent.

22 For Indra girt by Maruts, flow, thou Indu, very rich in sweets,
To sit in place of sacrifice.

23 Controlling priests and sages skilled in holy song adorn thee well:
The living make thee beautiful.

24 Aryaman, Mitra, Varuna drink Pavamana's juice, yea, thine:
O Sage, the Maruts drink thereof.

25 O Soma, Indu, thou while thou art purified urgest onward speech.
Thousandfold, with the lore of hymns.

26 Yea, Soma, Indu, while thou art purified do thou bring to us
Speech thousandfold that longs for war.

27 O Indu, Much-invoked, while thou art purifying, as the Friend.
Of these men enter thou the lake.

28 Bright are these Somas blent with milk, with light that flashes brilliantly. And form that utters
loud acclaim.

29 Led by his drivers, and sent forth, the Strong Steed hath come nigh for spoil,
Like warriors when they stand arrayed.

30 Specially, Soma, coming as a Sage from heaven to prosper us,
Flow like the Sun for us to see.

**[09-065] HYMN LXV. Soma Pavamana.**

1. THE, glittering maids send Sura forth, the glorious sisters, close-allied,
Send Indu forth, their mighty Lord.

2 Pervade, O Pavamana, all our treasures with repeated light,
God, coming hither from the Gods.

3 Pour on us, Pavamana, rain, as service and rain praise for Gods:
Pour all to be our nourishment.

4 Thou art a Steer by lustre: we, O Pavamana, faithfully
Call upon thee the Splendid One.

5 Do thou, rejoicing, nobly-armed! pour upon us heroic strength:
O Indu, come thou bitherward.

6 When thou art cleansed with both the hands and dipped in waters, with the wood.
Thou comest to the gathering-place.

7 Sing forth your songs, as Vyasva sang, to Soma Pavamana, to,
The Mighty One with thousand eyes;

8 Whose coloured sap they drive with stones, the yellow meath-distilling juice,
Indu for Indra, for his drink.

9 We seek to gain the friendly love of thee that Strong and Mighty One,
Of thee the winner of all wealth.

10 Flow onward with thy stream, a Steer, inspiriting the Maruts' Lord,
Winning all riches by thy might.

11 I send thee forth to battle from the press, O Pavamana, Strong,
Sustainer, looker on the light.

12 Acknowledged by this song of mine, flow, tawny-coloured, with thy stream
Incite to battle thine ally.

13 O Indu, visible to all pour out for us abundant food:
Soma, be thou our prosperer.

14 The pitchers, Indu, with thy streams have sung aloud in vigorous might
Enter them, and let Indra drink.

15 O thou whose potent gladdening juice they milk out with the stones, flow on,
Destroyer of our enemies.

16 King Pavamana is implored with holy songs, on man's behalf,
To travel through the firmament.

17 Bring us, O Indu, hundredfold increase of kine, and noble steeds,
The gift of fortune for our help.

18 Pressed for the banquet of the Gods, O Soma, bring us might, and speed,
Like beauty for a brilliant show.

19 Soma, flow on exceeding bright with loud roar to the wooden vats,
Falcon-like resting in thine home.

20 Soma, the Water-winner flows to Indra, Vayu, Varuna,
To Visnu and the Marut host.

21 Soma , bestowing food upon our progeny, from every sides,
Pour on us riches thousandfold

22 The Soma juices which have been expressed afar or near at hand,
Or there on Saryanavan's bank,

23 Those pressed among Arjikas, pressed among the active, in men's homes,
Or pressed among the Races Five-

24 May these celestial drops, expressed, pour forth upon us, as they flow,
Rain from the heavens apd hero strength.

25 Urged forward o'er the ox-hide flows the Lovely One of tawny hue,
Lauded by Jamadagni's song.

26 Like horses urged to speed, the drops, bright, stirring vital power, when blent
With milk, are beautified in streams.

27 So they who toil with juices send thee forward for the Gods' repast:
So with this splendour flow thou on.

28 We choose to-day that chariot-steed of thine, the Strong, that brings us bliss,
The Guardian, the desire of all,
29 The Excellent, the Gladdener, the Sage with heart that understands,
The Guardian, the desire of all;
30 Who for ourselves, O thou Most Wise, is wealth and fair intelligence,
The Guardian, the desire of all.

### [09-066] HYMN LXVI. Soma Pavamana.

1. FOR holy lore of every sort, flow onward thou whom all men love.
A Friend to be besought by friends.
2 O'er all thou rulest with these Two which, Soma Pavamana, stand,
Turned, as thy stations, hitherward.
3 Wise Soma Pavamana, thou encompassest on every side
Thy stations as the seasons come.
4 Flow onward, generating food, for precious boons of every kind,
A Friend for friends, to be our help.
5 Upon the lofty ridge of heaven thy bright rays with their essences,
Soma, spread purifying power.
6 O Soma, these Seven Rivers flow, as being thine, to give command:
The Streams of milk run forth to thee.
7 Flow onward, Soma in a stream, effused to gladden Indra's heart,
Bringing imperishable fame.
8 Driving thee in Vivasvan's course, the Seven Sisters with their hymns
Made melody round thee the Sage.
9 The virgins deck thee o'er fresh streams to drive thee to the sieve when thou,
A singer, bathest in the wood.
10 The streams of Pavamana, thine, Sage, Mighty One, have pouredthem forth.
Like coursers eager for renown.
11 They have been poured upon the fleece towards the meath-distilling vat:
The holy songs have sounded forth.
12 Like milch-kine coming home, the drops of Soma juice have reached the lake,
Have reached the place of sacrifice.
13 O Indu, to our great delight the running waters flow to us,
When thou wilt robe thyself in milk.
14 In this thy friendship, and with thee to help us, fain to sacrifice,
Indu, we crave thy friendly love.
15 Flow on, O Soma, for the great Viewer of men, for gain of Idne
Enter thou into Indra's throat.
16 Best art thou, Soma, of the great, Strongest of strong ones, Indu: thou
As Warrior ever hast prevailed.
17 Mightier even than the strong, more valiant even than the brave,
More libpral than the bountiful,
18 Soma, as Sura, bring us food, win offspring of our bodies: we
Elect thee for our friendship, we elect thee for companionship.
19 Agni, thou pourest life; send down upon us food and vigorous strength;
Drive thou misfortune far away,
20 Agni is Pavamana, Sage, Chief Priest of all the Races Five:
To him whose wealth is great we pray.
21 Skilled in thy task, O Agni, pour splendour with hero strength on us,

Granting me wealth that nourishes.
22 Beyond his enemies away to sweet praise Pavamana flows,
Like Surya visible to all.
23 Adorned by living men, set forth for entertainment, rich in food,
Far-sighted Indu is a Steed.
24 He, Pavamana, hath produced the lofty Law, the brilliant light,
Destroying darkness black of hue.
25 From tawny Pavamana, the Destroyer, radiant streams have sprung,
Quick streams from him whose gleams are swift.
26 Best rider of the chariot, praised with fairest praise mid beauteous ones,
Gold-gleaming with the Marut host,
27 May Pavamana, best to win the booty, penetrate with rays,
Giving the singer hero strength.
28 Over the fleecy sieve hath flowcd thc drop cffuscd: to Indra comes
Indu while he is purified
29 This Soma, through the pressing-stones, is sporting on the oxhide, and
Summoning Indra to the draught.
30 O Pavamana, bless us, so that we may live, with that bright milk
Of thine which hath been brought from heaven.

### [09-067] HYMN LXVII. Soma and Others.

1. THOU, Soma, hast a running stream, joyous, most strong at sacrifice:
Flow bounteously bestowing wealth.
2 Effused as cheerer of the men, flowing best gladdener, thou art
A Prince to Indra with thy juice.
3 Poured forth by pressing-stones, do thou with loud roar send us in a stream
Most excellent illustrious might.
4 Indu, urged forward, floweth through the fleecy cloth: the Tawny One
With his loud roar hath brought as strength.
5 Indu, thou flowest through the fleece, bringing felicities and fame,
And, Soma, spoil and wealth in kine.
6 Hither, O Indu, bring us wealth in steeds and cattle hundredfold:
Bring wealth, O Soma, thousandfold.
7 In purifying, through the sieve the rapid drops of Soma juice
Come nigh to Indra in their course.
8 For Indra floweth excellent Indu, the noblest Soma juice
The Living for the Living One.
9 The glittering maids send Sura forth they with their song have sung aloud
To Pavamana dropping meath.
10 May Pusan, drawn by goats, be our protector, and on all his paths
Bestow on us our share of maids.
11 This Soma flows like gladdening oil for him who wears the braided locks:
He shall give us our share of maids.
12 This Soma juice, O glowing God, flows like pure oil, effused for thee:
He shall give us our share of maids.
13 Flow onward, Soma, in thy stream, begetter of the sages' speech:
Wealth-giver among Gods art thou.
14 The Falcon dips within the jars: he wrap.him in his robe and goes
Loud roaring to the vats of wood.

15 Soma, thy juice hath been effused and poured into the pitcher: like
A rapid hawk it rushes on.
16 For Indra flow most rich in sweets, O Soma, bringing him delight.
17 They were sent forth to feast the Gods, like chariots that display their strength.
18 Brilliant, best givers of delight, these juices have sent Vayu forth.
19 Bruised by the press-stones and extolled, Soma, thou goest to the sieve,
Giving the worshipper hero strength.
20 This juice bruised by the pressing-stones and lauded passes through the sieve,
Slayer of demons, through the fleece.
21 O Pavamana, drive away the danger, whether near at hand
Or far remote, that finds me here.
22 This day may Pavamana cleanse us with his purifying power,
Most active purifying Priest.
23 O Agni, with the cleansing light diffused through all thy fiery glow,
Purify thou this prayer of ours.
24 Cleanse us with thine own cleansing power, O Agni, that is bright with flame,
And by libations poured to thee.
25 Savitar, God, by both of these, libation, purifying power,
Purify me on every side.
26 Cleanse us, God Savitar, with Three, O Soma, with sublimest forms,
Agni, with forms of power and might.
27 May the Gods' company make me clean, and Vasus make rue pure by song.
Purify me, ye General Gods; O Jatavedas, make me pure.
28 Fill thyself full of juice, flow forth, O Soma, thou with all thy stalks,
The best oblation to the Gods.
29 We with our homage have approached the Friend who seeks our wondering praise,
Young, strengthener of the solemn rite.
30 Lost is Alayya's axe. O Soma, God do thou send it back hither in thy flow
Even, Soma, God, if 'twere a mole.
31 The man who reads the essence stored by saints, the Pavamani hymns,
Tastes food completely purified, made sweet by Matarisvan's touch.
32 Whoever reads the essence stored by saints, the Pavamani hymns,
Sarasvati draws forth for him water and butter, milk and meath.

## [09-068] HYMN LXVIII. Soma Pavamana.

1. THE drops of Soma juice like cows who yield their milk have flowed forth, rich in meath, unto the
Shining One,
And, seated on the grass, raising their voice, assumed the milk, the covering robe wherewith the
udders stream.
2 He bellows with a roar arourd the highest twigs: the Tawny One is sweetened as he breaks them
up.
Then passing through the sieve into the ample room, the God throws off the dregs according to his
wish.
3 The gladdening drink that measured out the meeting Twins fills full with milk the Eternal Everwaxing
Pair.

Bringing to light the Two great Regions limitless, moving above them he gained sheen that never
fades.
4 Wandering through, the Parents, strengthening the floods, the Sage makes his place swell with his
own native might.
The stalk is mixed with grain: he comes led by the men together with the sisters, and preserves the
Head.
5 With energetic intellect the Sage is born, deposited as germ of Law, far from the Twins.
They being young at first showed visibly distinct the Creature that is half-concealed and halfexposed.
6 The sages knew the form of him the Gladdener, what time the Falcon brought the plant from far
away.
Him who assures success they beautified in streams, the stalk who yearned therefor, mighty and
meet for praise.
7 Together with the Rsis, with their prayers and hymns ten women deck thee, Soma, friendly when
effused.
Led by the men, with invocations of the Gods, through the fleece, thou hast given us strength to win
the spoil.
8 Songs resonant with praise have celebrated him. Soma, Friend, springing forth with his fair
company.
Even him who rich in meath, with undulating stream, Winnner of Wealth, Immortal, sends his voice
from heaven,
9 He sends it into all the region forth from heaven. Soma, while he is filtcred, settles in the jars.
With milk and waters is he decked when pressed with stones: Indu, when purified, shall find sweet
rest and room.
10 Even thus poured forth How on thy way, O Soma, vouchsafing us most manifold lively vigour.
We will invoke benevolent Earth and Heaven. Give us, ye Gods, riches with noble heroes.

## [09-069] HYMN LXIX. Soma Pavamana.

1. LAID like an arrow on the bow the hymn hath been loosed like a young calf to the udder of its dam.
As one who cometh first with full stream she is milked the Soma is impelled to this man's holy rites.
2 The thought is deeply fixed; the savoury juice is shed; the tongue with joyous sound is stirring in
the mouth;
And Pavamana, like the shout of combatants, the drop rising in sweet juice, is flowing through the
fleece.
3 He flows about the sheep-skin, longing for a bride: he looses Aditi's Daughters for the worshipper.
The sacred drink hath come, gold-tinted, well-restrained: like a strong Bull he shines, whetting his
manly might.
4 The Bull is bellowing; the Cows are coming nigh: the Goddesses approach the God's own restingplace.
Onward hath Soma passed through the sheep's fair bright fleece, and hath, as 'twere, endued a
garment newly washed.
5 The golden-hued, Immortal, newly bathed, puts on a brightly shining vesture that is never harmed.
He made the ridge of heaven to be his radiant robe, by sprinkling of the bowls from moisture of the
sky.

241

6 Even as the beams of Surya, urging men to speed, that cheer and send to sleep, together rush they
forth,
These swift outpourings in long course of holy rites: no form save only Indra shows itself so pure.
7 As down the steep slope of a river to the vale, drawn from the Steer the swift strong draughts have
found a way.
Well be it with the men and cattle in our home. May powers, O Soma, may the people stay with us.
8 Pour out upon us wealth in goods, in gold, in steeds, in cattle and in corn, and great heroic strength.
Ye, Soma, are my Fathers, lifted up on high as heads of heaven and makers of the strength of life.
9 These Pavamanas here, these drops of Soma, to Indra have sped forth like cars to booty.
Effused, they pass the cleansing fleece, while, gold-hued, they cast their covering off to pour the rain
down.
10 O Indu, flow thou on for lofty Indra, flow blameless, very gracious, foe-destroyer.
Bring splendid treasures to the man who lauds thee. O Heaven and Earth, with all the Gods protect.
us.

## [09-070] HYMN LXX. Soma Pavamana.

1. THE three times seven Milch-kine in the eastern heaven have for this Soma poured the genuine
milky draught.
Four other beauteous Creatures hath he made for his adornment, when he waxed in strength
through holy rites.
2 Longing for lovely Amrta, by his wisdom he divided, each apart from other, earth and heaven.
He gladly wrapped himself in the most lucid floods, when through their glory they found the God's
resting-place.
3 May those his brilliant rays be ever free from death, inviolate, for both classes of created things,-
Rays wherewith powers of men and Gods are purified. Yea, even for this have sages welcomed him as
King.
4 He, while he is adorned by the ten skilful ones, that he too in the Midmost Mothers may create,
While he is watching o'er the lovely Amrta's ways, looks on both races as Beholder of mankind.
5 He, while he is adorned to stream forth mighty strength, rejoices in his place between the earth and
heaven.
The Steer dispels the evil-hearted with his might, aiming at offerings as an archer at the game.
6 Beholding, as it were, Two Mother Cows, the Steer goes roaring on his way even as the Maruts
roar.
Knowing Eternal Law, the earliest light of heaven, he, passing wise, was chosen out to tell it forth.
7 The fearful Bull is bellowing with violent might, far-sighted, sharpening his yellowcoloured horns.
Soma assumes his seat in the well-fashioned place: the cowhide and the sheepskin are his ornament.
8 Bright, making pure his body free from spot and stain, on the sheep's back the Golden-coloured
hath flowed down.
Acceptable to Mitra, Vayu, Varuna, he is prepared as threefold meal by skilful men.
9 Flow on for the God's banquet, Soma, as a Steer, and enter Indra's heart, the Soma's reservoir.

Bear us beyond misfortune ere we be oppres. sed. the man who knows the land directs the man who
asks.
10 Urged like a car-steed flow to strength, O Soma: Indu, flow onward to the throat of Indra.
Skilled, bear us past, as in a boat o'er water: as battling Hero save us from the foeman.

## [09-071] HYMN LXXI. Soma Pavamana,

1. THE guerdon is bestowed: the Mighty takes his Seat, and, ever-Watchful, guards from fiend and
evil sprite.
Gold-hued, he makes the cloud his diadem, the milk his carpet in both worlds, and prayer his robe of
state.
2 Strong, bellowing, he goes, like one who slays the folk; he lets this hue of Asuras flow off from him,
Throws off his covering, seeks his father's meeting-place, and thus makes for himself the bright robe
he assumes.
3 Onward he flows, from both the hands, pressed out with stones: excited by the prayer, the water
makes him wild.
He frolics and draws near, completes his work with song, and bathes in streams to satisfy the
worshipper.
4 They pour out meath around the Master of the house, Celestial Strengthener of the mountain that
gives might;
In whom, through his great powers, oblation-eating cows in their uplifted udder mix their choicest
milk.
5 They, the ten sisters, on the lap of Aditi, have sent him forward like a car from both the arms.
He wanders and comes near the Cow's mysterious place, even the place which his inventions have
produced.
6 Like as a falcon to his home, so speeds the God to his own golden wisely-tashioned place to rest.
With song they urge the darling to the sacred grass: the Holy One goes like a courser to the Gods.
7 From far away, from heaven, the redhued noted Sage, Steer of the triple height, hath sung unto the
kine.
With thousand guidings he, leading this way and that, shines, as a singer, splendidly through many a
morn.
8 His covering assumes a radiant hue; where'er he comes into the fight he drives the foe afar.
The Winner of the Floods, with food he seeks the host of heaven, he comes to praises glorified with
milk.
9 Like a bull roaming round the herds he bellows: he hath assumed the brilliancy of Surya.
Down to the earth hath looked the heavenly Falcon: Soma with wisdom views all living creatures.

## [09-072] HYMN LXXII. Soma Pavamana.

1. THEY cleanse the Gold-hued: like a red Steed is he yoked, and Soma in the jar is mingled with the
milk.
He sendeth out his voice, and many loving friends of him the highly lauded hasten with their songs.
2 The many sages utter words in unison, while into Indra's throat they pour the Soma juice,
When, with the ten that dwell together closely joined, the men whose hands are skilful cleanse the

lovely meath.

3 He goes upon his way, unresting, to the cows, over the roaring sound which Sarya's Daughter
loves.
The Falcon brought it to him for his own delight: now with the twofold kindred sisters is his home.

4 Washed by the men, stone-pressed, dear on the holy grass, faithful to seasons, Lord of cattle from
of old,
Most liberal, completing sacrifice for men, O Indra, pure bright Soma, Indu, flows for thee.

5 O Indra, urged by arms of men and poured in streams, Soma flows on for thee after.his Godlike kind.
Plans thou fulfillest, gatherest thoughts for sacrifice: in the bowls sits the Gold-hued like a roosting
bird.

6 Sages well-skilled in work, intelligent, drain out the stalk that roars, the Sage, the Everlasting One.
The milk, the hymns unite them with him in the place of sacrifice, his seat who is produced anew.

7 Earth's central point, sustainer of the mighty heavens, distilled into the streams, into the waters'
wave,
As Indra's thunderbolt, Steer with farspreading wealth, Soma is flowing on to make the heart rejoice.

8 Over the earthly region flow thou on thy way, helping the praiser and the pourer, thou Most Wise.
Let us not lack rich treasure reaching to our home, and may we clothe ourselves in manifold bright
wealth.

9 Hither, O Indu, unto us a hundred gifts of steeds, a thousand gifts of cattle and of gold,
Measure thou forth, yea, splendid ample strengthening food do thou, O Pavamana, heed this laud of
ours.

### [09-073] HYMN LXXIII. Soma Pavamana.

1. THEY from the spouting drop have sounded at the rim: naves speed together to the place of
sacrifice.
That Asura hath formed, to seize, three lofty heights. The ships of truth have borne the pious man
across.

2 The strong Steers, gathering, have duly stirred themselves,and over the stream's wave the friends
sent forth the song.
Engendering the hymn, with flowing streams of meath, Indra's dear body have they caused to wax in
strength.

3 With sanctifying gear they sit around the song: their ancient Father guards their holy work from
harm.
Varuna hath o'erspread the mighty sea of air. Sages had power to hold him in sustaining floods.

4 Sweet-tongued, exhaustless, they have sent their voices down togetlier, in heaven's vault that
pours a thousand streams.
His wildly-restless warders never close an eye: in every place are found the bonds that bind man last.

5 O'er Sire and Mother they have roared in unison bright with the verse of praise, burning up riteless
men,
Blowing away with supernatural might from earth and from the heavens the swarthy skin which
Indra hates.

6 Those which, as guides of song and counsellors of speed, were manifested from their ancient

dwelling place,-
From these the eyeless and the deaf have turned aside: the wicked travel not the pathway of the
Law.

7 What time the filter with a thousand streams is stretched, the thoughtful sages purify their song
therein.
Bright-coloured are their spies, vigorous, void of guile, excellent, fair to see, beholders of mankind.

8 Guardian of Law, most wise, he may not be deceived: three Purifiers hath he set within his heart.
With wisdom he beholds all creatures that exist: he drives into the pit the hated riteless ones.

9 The thread of sacrifice spun in the cleansing sieve, on Varuna's tongue-tip, by supernatural might,-
This, by their striving, have the prudent ones attained: he who hath not this power shall sink into the
pit.

### [09-074] HYMN LXXIV. Soma Pavamana

1. BORN like a youngling he hath clamoured in the wood, when he, the Red, the Strong, would win
the light of heaven.
He comes with heavenly seed that makes the water swell: him for wide-spreading shelter we implore
with prayer.

2 A far-extended pillar that supports the sky the Soma-stalk, filled full, moves itself every way.
He shall bring both these great worlds while the rite proceeds: the Sage holds these who move!
together and all food.

3 Wide space hath he who follows Aditi's right path, and mighty, well-made food, meath blent with
Soma juice;
He who from hence commands the rain, Steer of the kine, Leader of floods, who helps us hence, who
claims our laud.

4 Butter and milk are drawn from animated cloud; thence Amrta is produced, centre of sacrifice.
Hini the Most Bounteous Ones, ever united, love; him as ouir Friend the Men who make all swell rain
down.

5 The Soma-stalk hath roared, following with the wave: he swells with sap for man the skin which
Gods enjoy.
Upon the lap of Aditi he lays the germ, by means whereof we gain children and progeny.

6 In the third region which distils a thousand streams, may the Exhaustless Ones descend with
procreant power.
The kindred Four have been sent downward from the heavens: dropping with oil they bring Amrta
and sacred gifts.

7 Soma assumes white colour when he strives to gain: the bounteous Asura knows full many a
precious boon.
Down the steep slope, through song, he comes to sacrifice, and he will burst the water-holding cask
of heaven,

8 Yea, to the shining milk-anointed beaker, as to his goal, hath stepped the conquering Courser.
Pious-souled men have sent their giffi of cattle unto Kaksivan of the hundred winters.

9 Soma, thy juice when thou art blended with the streams, flows, Pavamana, through the long wool
of the sheep.

243

So, cleansed by sages. O best giver of delight, grow sweet for Indra, Pavamana! for his drink.

## [09-075] HYMN LXXV. Soma Pavamana.

1. GRACIOUSLY-MINDED he is flowing on his way to win dear names o'er which the Youthful One
grows great.
The Mighty and Far-seeing One hath mounted now the mighty Surya's car which moves to every
side.
2 The Speaker, unassailable Master of this hymn, the Tongue of sacrifice pours forth the pleasant
meath.
Within the lustrous region of the heavens the Son makes the third secret name of Mother and of Sire.
3 Sending forth flashes he hath bellowed to the jars, led by the men into the golden reservoir.
The milky streams of sacrifice have sung to him: he of the triple height shines brightly through the
morns.
4 Pressed by the stones, with hymns, and graciously inclined, illuminating both the Parents, Heaven
and Earth,
He flows in ordered season onward through the flee, a current of sweet juice still swelling day by
day.
5 Flow onward, Soma, flow to bring prosperity: cleansed by the men, invest thee with the milky
draught.
What gladdening drinks thou hast, foaming, exceeding strong, even with these incite Indra to give us
wealth.

## [09-076] HYMN LXXVI. Soma Pavamana.

1. ON flows the potent juice, sustainer of the heavens, the strength of Gods, whom men must hail
with shouts of joy.
The Gold-hued, started like a courser by brave men, impetuously winneth splendour in the streams.
2 He takes his weapons, like a hero, in his hands, fain to win light, car-borne, in forays for the kine.
Indu, while stimulating India's might, is urged forward and balmed by sages skilful in their task.
3 Soma, as thou art purified with flowing wave, exhibiting thy strength enter thou Indra's throat.
Make both worlds stream for us, as lightning doth the clouds: mete out exhaustless powers for us, as
'twere through song.
4 Onward he flows, the King of all that sees the light: the Rsis' Lord hath raised the song of sacrifice;
Even he who is adorned with Surya's arrowy beam, Father of hymns, whose wisdom is beyond our
reach.
5 Like as a bull to herds, thou flowest to the pail, bellowing as a steer upon the water's lap.
So, best of Cheerers, thou for Indra flowest on that we, with thy protection, may o'ercome in fight.

## [09-077] HYMN LXXVII. Soma Pavamana.

1. MORE beauteous than the beautiful, as Indra's bolt, this Soma, rich in sweets, hath clamoured in
the vat.
Dropping with oil, abundant, streams of sacrifice flow unto him like milch-kine, lowing, with their
milk.
2 On flows that Ancient One whom, hitherward, from heaven, sped through the region of the air, the

Falcon snatched.
He, quivering with alarm and terrified in heart before bow-armed Krsanu, holdeth fast the sweet.
3 May those first freshest drops of Soma juice effused flow on, their way to bring us mighty strength
in kine.
Beauteous as serpents, worthy to be looked upon, they whom each sacred gift and all our prayers
have pleased.
4 May that much-lauded Indu, with a heart inclined to us, well-knowing, fight against our enemies.
He who hath brought the germ beside the Strong One's seat moves onward to the widely-opened stall of kine.
5 The active potent juice of heaven is flowing on, great Varuna whom the forward man can ne'er
deceive.
Mitra, the Holy, hath been pressed for troubled times, neighing like an impatient horse amid the herd,

## [09-078] HYMN LXXVIII. Soma Pavamana.

1. RAISING his voice the King hath flowed upon his way: invested with the waters he would win the
kine.
The fleece retains his solid parts as though impure, and bright and cleansed he seeks the special
place of Gods.
2 Thou, Soma, art effused for Indra by the men, balmed in the wood as wave, Sage, Viewer of mankind.
Full many are the paths whereon thou mayest go: a thousand bay steeds hast thou resting in the
bowls.
3 Apsarases who dwell in waters of the sea, sitting within, have flowed to Soma wise of heart.
They urge the Master of the house upon his way, and to the Eternal Pavamana pray for bliss.
4 Soma flows on for u's as winner of the kine, winner of thousands, cars, water, and light, and gold;
He whom the Gods have made a gladdening draught to drink, the drop most sweet to taste, wealbringing,
red of hue.
5 Soma, as Pavamana thou, our faithful Friend, making for us these real treasures, flowest on.
Slay thou the enemy both near and, far away: grant us security and ample pasturage.

## [09-079] HYMN LXXIX. Soma Pavamana.

1. SPONTANEOUS let our drops of Soma juice flow on, pressed, golden-hued, among the Gods of lofty
heaven.
Perish among us they who give no gifts of food! perish the godless! May our prayers obtain success.
2 Forward to us the drops, distilling meath, shall flow, like riches for whose sake we urge the horses on.
Beyond the crafty hindering of all mortal men may we continually bear precious wealth away.
3 Yea, yerily, foe of hate shown to himself is he, yea, verity, destroyer too of other hate.
As thirst subdueth in the desert, conquer thou, O Soma Pavarnana, men of evil thoughts.
4 Near kin to thee is he, raised loftiest in the heavens: upon the earth's high ridge thy scions have grown forth.
The press-stones chew and crunch thee on the ox's hide: sages have milked thee with their hands into the streams.
5 So do they hurry on thy strong and beauteous juice, O Indu, as the first ingredient of the draught.
Bring low, thou Pavamana, every single foe, and be thy might shown forth as sweet and gladdening

drink.

**[09-080] HYMN LXXX. Soma Pavamana.**

1. ON flows the stream of Soma who beholds mankind: by everlasting Law he calls the Gods from
heaven.
He lightens with the roaring of Br aspati: h the lakes have not contained the pourings of juice.

2 Thou, powerful Soma, thou to whom the cows have -lowed, ascendest bright with sheen, thine ironfashioned home.
Thou, lengthening our princes' life and high renown, flowest for Indra as his might to gladdening drink.

3 Best giver of delight, he flows to Indra's throat, robing himself in might, Auspicious One, for fame.
He spreads himself abroad to meet all things that be: the vigorous Tawny Steed flows sporting on his way.

4 The men, the ten swift fingers, milk thee out for Gods, even thee most rich in meath, with thousand
flowing streams.
Soma who winnest thousands, driven by the men, expressed with stones, bring, as thou flowest, all
the Gods.

5 Deft-handed men with stones, the ten swift fingers, drain thee into waters, thee, the Steer enriched
with sweets.
Thou, Soma, gladdening Indra, and the Heavenly Host, flowest as Pavamana like a river's wave.

**[09-081] HYMN LXXXI. Soma Pavamana.**

1. ONWARD to Indra's throat move, beauteously adorned, the waves of Soma as he purifies himself,
When they, brought forward with the lovely curd of kine, effused, have cheered the Hero to bestow his gifts.

2 Hither hath Soma flowed unto the beakers, like a chariot-horse, a stallion swift upon his way.
Thus, knowing both the generations, he obtains the rights and dues of Gods from yonder and from hence.

3 While thou art cleansed, O Soma, scatter wealth on us; Indu, bestow great bounty as a liberal Prince.
Giver of life, with wisdom help to opulence; strew not our home possessions far away from us.

4 Hither let Pusan Pavamana come to us, Varuna, Mitra, bountiful, of one accord,
The Maruts, Asvins, Vayu, and Brhaspati, Savitar, Tvastar, tractable Sarasvati.

5 Both Heaven and Earth, the all-invigorating Pair, Vidhatar, Aditi, and Aryaman the God,
Bhaga who blesses men, the spacious Firmament,-let all the Gods in Pavamana take delight.

**[09-082] HYMN LXXXII. Soma Pavamana.**

1. EVEN as a King hath Soma, red and tawny Bull, been pressed: the Wondrous One hath bellowed to
the kine.
While purified he passes through the filtering fleece to seat him hawk-like on the place that drops with oil.

2. To glory goest thou, Sage with disposing skill, like a groomed steed thou rushest forward to the prize.
O Soma, be thou gracious, driving off distress: thou goest, clothed in butter, to a robe of state.

3 Parjanya is the Father of the Mighty Bird: on mountains, in earth's centre hath he made his home.
The waters too have flowed, the Sisters, to the kine: he meets the pressing-stones at the beloved rite.

4 Thou givest pleasure as a wife delights her lord. Listen, O Child of Pajri, for to thee I speak.

Amid the holy songs go on that we may live: in time of trouble, Soma, watch thou free from blame.

5 As to the men of old thou camest, Indu unharmed, to strengthen, winning hundreds, thousands,
So now for new felicity flow onward: the waters follow as thy law ordaineth.

**[09-083] HYMN LXXXIII. Soma Pavamana.**

1. SPREAD is thy cleansing filter, Brahmanaspati: as Prince, thou enterest its limbs from every side.
The raw, whose mass hath not been heated gains not this: they only which are dressed, which bear,
attain to it.

2 High in the seat of heaven is spread the Scorcher's sieve: its threads are standing separate,
glittering with light.
The Swift Ones favour him who purifieth this: with consciousness they stand upon the height of heaven.

3 The foremost spotted Steer hath made the Mornings shine, and yearning after strength sustains all
things that be.
By his high wisdom have the mighty Sages wrought: the Fathers who behold mankind laid down the
germ,

4 Gandharva verily protects his dwellingplace; Wondrous, he guards the generations of the Gods.
Lord of the snare, he takes the foeman with the snare: those who are most devout have gained a share of meath.

5 Rich in oblations! robed in cloud, thou corapassest oblation, sacrifice, the mighty seat of Gods.
King, on thy chariot-sieve thou goest up to war, and with a thousand weapons winnest lofty fame.

**[09-084] HYMN LXXXIV. Soma Pavamana.**

1. FLOW, cheering Gods, most active, winner of the flood, for Indra, and for Vayu, and for Varuna.
Bestow on us to-day wide room with happiness, and in tbine ample dwelling laud the Host of
Heaven.

2 He who hath come anear to creatures that have life, Immortal Soma flows onward to all of them.
Effecting, for our aid, both union and release, Indu, like Surya, follows closely after Dawn.

3 He who is poured with milk, he who within the plants hastes bringing treasure for the happiness of Gods,
He, poured forth in a stream flows with the lightning's flash, Soma who gladdens Indra and the Host
of Heaven.

4 Winner of thousands, he, this Soma, flows along, raising a vigorous voice that wakens with the dawn.
Indu with winds that drives on the ocean of the air, he sinks within the jars, he rests in Indra's heart.

5 The kine with milk dress him who makes the milk increase, Soma, amid the songs, who finds the light of heaven.
Winner of wealth, the effectual juice is flowing on, Singer and Sage by wisdom, dear as heaven itself.

**[09-085] HYMN LXXXV. Soma Pavamana.**

I. FLOW on to Indra, Soma, carefully effused: let sickness stay afar together with the fiends.
Let not the double-tongued delight them with thy juice. here be thy flowing drops laden with
opulence.

2 O Pavamana, urge us forward in the fight thou art the vigour of the Gods, the well-loved drink.
Smite thou our enemies who raise the shout of joy: Indra, drink Soma juice, and drive away our foes.

3 Unharmed, best Cheerer, thou, O Indu, flowest on: thou, even thou thyself, art Indra's noblest food.
Full many a wise man lifts to thee the song of praise, and hails thee with a kiss as Sovran of this
world.
4 Wondrous, with hundred streams, hymned in a thousand songs, Indu pours out for Indra his
delightrul meath.
Winning us land and waters, flow thou hitherward: Rainer of bounties, Soma, make broad way for us.
5 Roaring within the beaker thou art balmed with milk: thou passest through the fleecy filter all at
once.
Carefully cleansed and decked like a prizewinning steed, O Soma, thou hast flowed down within
Indra's throat.
6 Flow onward sweet of flavour for the Heavenly Race, for Indra sweet, whose name is easily
invoked:
Flow sweet for Mitra, Varuna, and Vayu, rich in meath, inviolable for Brhaspati.
7 Ten rapid fingers deck the Courser in the jar: with hymns the holy singers send their voices forth.
The filtering juices hasten to their eulogy, the drops that gladden find their way to Indra's heart.
8 While thou art purified pour on us hero strength, great, far-extended shelter, spacious pasturage.
Let no oppression master this our holy work: may we, O Indu, gain all opulence through thee.
9 The Steer who sees afar hath risen above the sky: the Sage hath caused the lights of heaven to give
their shine.
The. King is passing through the filter with a roar: they drain the milk of heaven from him who looks
on men.
10 High in the vault of heaven, unceasing, honey-tongued, the Loving Ones drain out the mountainhaunting
Steer,-
The drop that hath grown great in waters, in the lake meath-rich, in the stream's wave and in the
cleansing sieve.
11 The Loving Ones besought with many voices the Eagle who had flown away to heaven.
Hymns kiss the Youngling worthy of laudation, resting on earth, the Bird of golden colour.
12 High to heaven's vault hath the Gandharva risen, beholding all his varied forms and figures.
His ray hath shone abroad with gleaming splendour: pure, he hath lighted both the worlds, the
Parents.

## [09-086] HYMN LXXXVI. Soma Pavamana.

1. THY gladdening draughts, O Pavamana, urged by song flow swiftly of themselves like sons of fleetfoot
mares.
The drops of Soma juice, those eagles of the heavens, most cheering, rich in meath, rest in the
reservoir.
2 As rapid chariot-steeds, so turned in several ways have thine exhilarating juices darted forth,
Soma-drops rich in meath, waves, to the Thunder-armed, to Indra, like milch-kine who seek their calf
with milk.
3 Like a steed urged to battle, finder of the light; speed onward to the cloud-born reservoir of heaven,
A Steer that o'er the woolly surface seeks the sieve, Soma while purified for Indra's nourishment.

4 Fleet as swift steeds, thy drops, divine, thought-swift, have been, O Pavamana, poured with milk
into the vat.
The Rsis have poured in continuous Soma drops, ordainers who adorn thee, Friend whom Rsis love.
5 O thou who seest all things, Sovran as thou art and passing strong, thy rays encompass all abodes.
Pervading with thy natural powers thou flowest on, and as the whole world's Lord, O Soma, thou art
King.
6 The beams of Pavamana, sent from earth and heaven, his ensigns who is ever steadfast, travel
round.
When on the sieve the Golden-hued is cleansed, he rests within the vats as one who seats him in his
place.
7 Served with fair rites he flows, ensign of sacrifice: Soma advances to the special place of Gods.
He speeds with thousand currents to the reservoir, and passes through the filter bellowing as a bull.
8 The Sovran dips him in the seain and the streams, and set in rivers with the waters' wave moves
on.
High heaven's Sustainer at the central point of earth, raised on the fleecy surface Pavamana stands.
9 He on whose high decree the heavens and earth depend nath roared and thundered like the
summit of the sky.
Soma flows on obtaining Indra's friendly love, and, as they purify him, settles in the jars.
10 He, light of sacrifice distils delicious meath, most wealthy, Father and begetter of the Gods.
He, gladdening, best of Cheerers, juice!hat Indra loves, enriches with mysterious treasure earth and
heaven.
11 The vigorous and far-seeing one, the Lord of heaven, flows, shouting to the beaker, with his
thousand streams.
Coloured like gold he rests in seats where Mitra dwells, the Steer made beautiful by rivers and by
sheep.
12 In forefront of the rivers Pavamana speeds, in forefront of the hymn, foremost among the kine.
He shares the mighty booty in the van of war: the well-armed Steer is purified by worshippers.
13 This heedful Pavamana, like a bird sent forth, hath with his wave flowed onward to the fleecy
sieve.
O Indra, through thy wisdom, b thy thought, O Sage, Soma flows bright and pure between the earth
and heaven.
14 He, clad in mail that reaches heaven, the Holy One, filling the firmament stationed amid the
worlds,
Knowing. the realm of light, hath come to us in rain: he summons to himself his own primeval Sire.
15 He who was first of all to penetrate his form bestowed upon his race wide shelter and defence.
From that high station which he hath in loftiest heaven he comes victorious to all encounters here.
16 Indu hath started for Indra's special place and slights not as a Friend the promise of his Friend.
Soma speeds onward like a youth to youtlitial maids, and gains the beaker by a course of bundred
paths.
17 Your songs, exhilarating, tuneful, uttering praise, are come into the placns where the people meet.

Worshippers have exalted Soma with their hymns, and milch kine have come near to meet him with
their milk.
18 O Soma, Indu, while they cleanse thee, pour on us accumulateds Plentiful, nutritious food,
Which, ceaseless, thrice a day shall yield us hero power enriched with store of nourishment, and
strength, and Meath.
19 Far-seeing Soma flows, the Steer, the Lord of hymns, the Furtherer of day, of morning, and of
heaven.
Mixt with the streams he caused the beakers to resound, and with the singers' aid they entered
Indra's heart.
20 On, with the prudent singers, flows the ancient Sage and guided by the men hath roared about
the vats.
Producing Trita's name, may he pour forth the meath, that Vayu and that Indra may become his
Friends.
21 He, being purified, hath made the Mornings shine: this, even this is he who gave the rivers room.
He made the Three Times Seven pour out the milky flow: Soma, the Cheerer, yields whate'er the
heart finds sweet.
22 Flow, onward, Soma, in thine own celestial forms, flow, Indu, poured within the beaker and the
sieve.
Sinking into the throat of Indra with a roar, led by the men thou madest Surya mount to heaven.
23 Pressed out with stones thou flowest onward to the sieve, O Indu, entering the depths of Indra's
throat.
Far-sighted Soma, now thou lookest on mankind: thou didst unbar the cowstall for the Angirases.
24 In thee, O Soma, while thou purifitedst thee, high-thoughted sages, seeking favour, have rejoiced.
Down from the heavens the Falcon brought thee hitherward, even thee, O Indu, thee whom all our
hymns adorn.
25 Seven Milch-kine glorify the Tawny-coloured One while with his wave in wool he purifies himself.
The living men, the mighty, have impelled the Sage into the waters' lap, the place of sacrifice.
26 Indu, attaining purity, plunges through the foe, making Ilis ways all easy for the pious man.
Making the kine his mantle, he, the lovely Sage, runs like a sporting courser onward through the
fleece.
27 The ceaseless watery fountains with their hundred streams sing, as they hasten near, to him the
Golden-hued
Him, clad in robes of milk, swift fingers beautify on the third height and in the luminous realm of
heaven.
28 These are thy generations of celestial seed thou art the Sovran Lord of all the world of life.
This universe, O Pavamana, owns thy sway; thou, Indu, art the first establisher of Law.
29 Thou art the sea, O Sage who bringest alf to light: under thy Law are these five regions of the
world.
Tlou reachest out beyond the earth, beyond the heavens: thine are the lights, O Pavamana, thine the
Sun.
30 Thou in the filter, Soma Pavamana, art purified to support the region for the Gods.

The chief, the longing ones have sought to hold thee fast, and all these living creatures have been
turned to thee.
31 Onward the Singer travels o'er the fleecy sieve. the Tawny Steer hath bellowed in the wooden
vats.
Hymns have been sung aloud in resonant harmony, and holy songs kiss him, the Child who claims
our praise.
32 He hath assumed the rays of Surya for his robe, spinning, as he knows bow, the triply-twisted
thread.
He, guiding to the newest rules of Holy Law, comes as the Women's Consort to the special place.
33 On flows the King of rivers and the Lord of heaven: he follows with a shout the paths of Holy Law.
The Golden-hued is poured forth, with his hundred streams, Wealth-bringer, lifting up his voice while
purified.
34 Fain to be cleansed, thou, Pavamana, pourest out, like wondrous Surya, through the fleece, an
ample sea.
Purified with the hands, pressed by the men with stones, thou speedest on to mighty booty-bringing
war.
35 Thou, Pavamana, sendest food and power in streams. thou sittest in the beakers as a hawk on
trees,
For Indra poured as cheering juice to make him glad, as nearest and farseeing bearer-up of heaven.
36 The Sisters Seven, the Mothers, stand around the Babe, the noble, new-born Infant, skilled in holy
song,
Gandharva of the floods, divine, beholding men, Soma, that he may reign as King of all the world.
37 As Sovran Lord thereof thou Passest through these worlds, O Indu, harnessing thy tawny wellwinged
Mares.
May they pour forth for thee milk and oil rich in sweets: O Soma, let the folk abide in thy decree.
38 O Soma, thou beholdest men from every side: O Pavamana, Steer, thou wanderest through these.
Pour out upon us wealth in treasure and in gold: may we have strength to live among the things that
be.
39 Winner of gold and goods and cattle flow thou on, set as impregner, Indu, mid the worlds of life.
Rich in brave men art thou, Soma, who winnest all: these holy singers wait upon thee with the song.
40 The wave of flowing meath hath wakened up desires: the Steer enrobed in milk plunges into the
streams.
Borne on his chariot-sieve the King hath risen to war, and with a thousand rays hath won him high
renown.
41 Dear to all life, he sends triumphant praises forth, abundant, bringing offspring, each succeeding
day.
From Indra crave for us, Indu, when thou art quaffed, the blessing that gives children, wealth that
harbours steeds.
42 When days begin, the strong juice, lovely, golden-hued, is recognized by wisdom more and more
each day,
He, stirring both the Races, goes between the two, the bearer of the word of men and word of Gods.

43 They balm him, balm him over balm him thoroughly, caress the mighty strength and balm it with
the meath.
They seize the flying Steer at the stream's breathing-place: cleansing with gold they grasp the
Animal herein.
44 Sing forth to Pavamana skilled in holy song: the juice is flowing onward like a mighty stream.
He.glideth like a serpent from his ancient skin, and like a playful horse the Tawny Steer hath run.
45 Dweller in floods, King, foremost, he displays his might, set among living things as measurer of
days.
Distilling oil he flows, fair, billowy, golden-hued, borne on a car of light, sharing one hom-e with
wealth.
46 Loosed is the heavens! support, the uplifted cheering juice: the triply-mingled draught flows round
into the worlds.
The holy hymns caress the stalk that claims our praise, when singers have approached his beauteous
robe with song.
47 Thy strearns that flow forth rapidly collected run over the fine fleece of the sheep as thou art
cleansed.
When, Indu, thou art. balmed with milk within the bowl, thou sinkest in the jars, O Soma, when
expressed.
48 Winner of' power, flow, Soma, worthy of our laud: run onward to the fleece as well-beloved meath.
Destroy, O Indu, all voracious Raksasas. With brave sons in the assembly let our speech be bold.

## [09-087] HYMN LXXXVII. Soma Pavamana.

1. RUN onward to the reservoir and seat thee: cleansed by the men speed forward to the battle.
Making thee beauteous like an able courser, forth to the sacred grass with reins they lead thee.
2 Indu, the well-armed God, is flowing onward, who quells the curse and guards from treacherous
onslaught,
Father, begetter of the Gods, most skilful, the buttress of the heavens and earth's supporter.
3. Rsi and Sage, the Champion of the people, cleft and sagacious, Usana in wisdom,
He hath discovered even their hidden nature, the Cows' concealed and most mysterious title.
4 This thine own Soma rich in meath, O Indra, Steer for the Steer, hath flowed into the filter.
The strong Free-giver, winning hundreds, thousands, hath reached the holy grass that never fails
him.
5 These Somas are for wealth of countless cattle, renown therefor, and mighty strength immortal.
These have been sent forth, urified by strainers, like steeds who rusg to battle fain for glory.
6 He, while he cleanses him, invoked of many, hath flowed to give the people all enjoyment.
Thou whom the Falcon brought, bring, dainty viands, bestir thyself and send us wealth and booty.
7 This Soma, pressed into the cleansing filter, hath run as 'twere a host let loose, the Courser;
Like a strong bull who whets his horns kpen-pointed, like a brave warrior in the fray for cattle.
8 He issued forth from out the loftiest mountain, and found kine hidden somewhere in a stable.

Soma's stream clears itself for thee, O Indra, like lightning thundering through the clouds of heaven,
9 Cleansing thyselr, and borne along with Indra, Soma, thou goest round the herd of cattle.
May thy praise help us, Mighty One, prompt Giver, to the full ample food which thou bestowest.

## [09-088] HYMN LXXXVIII. Soma Pavamana.

1. FOR thee this Soma is effused, O Indra: drink of this juice; for thee the stream is flowing-
Soma, which thou thyself hast made and chosen, even Indu, for thy special drink to cheer thee.
2 Like a capacious car hath it been harnessed, the Mighty; to acquire abundant treasures.
Then in the sacrifice they celebrated all triumphs won by Nahus - n the battle.
3 Like Vayu with his team, moving at pleasure, most gracious when invoked like both Nasatyas,
Thou art thyself like the Wealth-Giver, Soma! who grants all boons, like song-inspiring Pusan.
4 Like Indra who hath done great deeds, thou, Soma, art slayer of the Vrtras, Fort-destroyer.
Like Pedu's horse who killed the brood of serpents, thus thou, O Soma, slayest every Dasyu.
5 Like Agni loosed amid the forest, fiercely he winneth splendour in the running waters.
Like one who fights, the roaring of the mighty, thus Soma Pavamana sends his current.
6 These Somas passing through the fleecy filter, like rain descending from the clouds of heaven,
Have been effused and poured into the beakers, swiftly like rivers running lowly seaward.
7 Flow onward like the potent band of Maruts, like that Celestial Host whom none revileth.
Quickly be gracious unto us like waters, like sacrifice victorious, thousand-fashioned.
8 Thine are King Varuna's eternal statutes, lofty and deep, O Soma, is thy glory.
All-pure art thou like Mitra the beloved, adorable, like Aryaman, O Soma.

## [09-089] HYMN LXXXIX. Soma Pavamana.

1. THIS Chariot-horse hath moved along the pathways, and Pavamana flowed like rain from heaven.
With us hath Soma with a thousand currents sunk in the wood, upon his Mother's bosom.
2. King, he hath clothed him in the robe of rivers, mounted the straightest-going ship of Order.
Sped by the Hawk the drop hath waxed in waters: the father drains it, drains the Father's offspring.
3 They come to him, red, tawny, Lord of Heaven, the watchful Guardian of the meath, the Lion.
First, Hero in the fight, he seeks the cattle, and with his eye the Steer is our protector.
4 They harness to the broad-wheeled car the mighty Courser whose back bears meath, unwearied,
awful.
The twins, the sisters brighten him, and strengthen-these children of one damethe vigorous Racer.
5 Four pouring out the holy oil attend him, sitting together in the same container.
To him they flow, when purified, with homage, and still, from every side, are first about him.
6 He is the buttress of the heavens, supporter of earth, and in his hand are all the people.
Be the team's Lord a well to thee the singer: cleansed is the sweet plant's stalk for deed of glory.

7 Fighting, uninjured come where Gods are feasted; Soma, as Vitra-slayer flow for Indra.
Vouchsafe us ample riches very splendid may we be masters of heroic vigour.

### [09-090] HYMN XC. Soma Pavamana,

1. URGED On, the Father of the Earth and Heaven hath gone forth like a car to gather booty,
Going to Indra, sharpening his weapons, and in his hand containing every treasure.
2 To him the tones of sacred song have sounded, Steer of the triple height, the Life-bestower.
Dwelling in wood as Varuna in rivers, lavishing treasure he distributes blessings
3 Great Conqueror, warnor-girt, Lord of all heroes, flow on thy way as he who winneth riches;
With sharpened. arms, with swift bow, never vanquished in battle, vanquishing in fight the foemen.
4 Giving security, Lord of wide dominion, send us both earth and heaven with all their fulness.
Striving to win the Dawns, the light, the waters, and cattle, call to us abundant vigour.
5 O Soma, gladden Varuna and Mitra; cheer, Indu Pavamana! Indra, Visnu.
Cheer thou the Gods, the Company of Maruts: Indu, cheer mighty Indra to rejoicing.
6 Thus like a wise and potent King flow onward, destroying with thy vigour all misfortunes.
For our well-spoken hymn give life, O Indu. Do ye preserve us evermore with blessings.

### [09-091] HYMN XCI. Soma Pavamana.

1. As for a chariot-race, the skilful Speaker, Chief, Sage, Inventor, hath, with song, been started.
The sisters ten upon the fleecy summit drive on the Car-horse to the resting places.
2 The drop of Soma, pressed by wise Nahusyas, becomes the banquet of the Heavenly People-
Indu, by hands of mortal men made beauteous, immortal, with the sheep and cows and waters.
3 Steer roaring unto Steer, this Pavamana, this juice runs to the white milk of the milch-cow.
Through thousand fine hairs goes the tuneful Singer, like Sura by his fair and open pathways.
4 Break down the, strong seats even of the demons: cleansing thee, Indu, robd thyself in vigour.
Rend with thy swift bolt, coming from above them, those who are near and those who yet are distant.
5 Prepare the forward paths in ancient manner for the new bymn, thou Giver of all bounties.
Those which are high and hard for foes to conquer may we gain from thee, Active! Food-bestower!
6 So purifying thee vouchsafe us waters, heaven's light, and cows, offlpring and many children.
Give us health, ample land, and lights, O Soma, and grant us long to look upon the sunshine.

### [09-092] HYMN XCII. Soma Pavamana.

1. THE gold-hued juice, poured out upon the filter, is started like a car sent forth to conquer.
He hath gained song and vigour while they cleansed him, and hath rejoiced the Gods with entertainments.
2 He who beholdeth man hath reached the filter: bearing his name, the Sage hath sought his dwelling.
The Rsis came to him, seven holy singers, when in the bowls he settled as Invoker.
3 Shared by all Gods, mobt wise, propitious, Soma goes, while they cleanse him, to his constant station.
Let him rejoice in all his lofty wisdom to thc Five Tribes the Sage attains with labour.
4 In thy mysterious place, O Pavamana Soma, are all the Gods, the Thrice-Eleven.
Ten on the fleecy height, themselves, self-prompted, and seven fresh rivers, brighten and adorn thee.
5 Now let this be the truth of Pavamana, there where all singers gather them together,
That he hath given us room and made the daylight, hath holpen Manu and repelled the Dasyu.
6 As the priest seeks the station rich in cattle, like a true King who goes to great assemblies,
Soma hath sought the beakers while they cleansed him, and like a wild bull, in the wood hath settled.

### [09-093] HYMN XCIII. Soma Pavamana.

1. TEN sisters, pouring out the rain together, swift-moving thinkers of the sage, adorn him.
Hither hath run the gold-hued Child of Surya and reached the vat like a fleet vigorous courser.
2 Even as a youngling crying to his mothers, the bounteous Steer hath flowed along to waters.
As youth to damsel, so with milk he hastens on to the. chose meeting-place, the beaker.
3 Yea, swollen is the udder of the milch-cow: thither in streams goes very sapient Indu.
The kine make ready, as with new-washed treasures, the Head and Chief with milk within the vessels.
4 With all the Gods, O Indu Pavamana, while thou art roaring send us wealth in horses.
Hither upon her car come willing Plenty, inclined to us, to give us of her treasures.
5 Now unto us mete riches, while they cleansethee, all-glorious, swelling wealth, with store of heroes.
Long be his life who worships, thee, O Indu. May he, enriched with prayer, come soon and early.

### [09-094] HYMN XCIV. Soma Pavamana.

1. WHEN beauties strive for him as for a charger, then strive the songs like soldiers for the sunlight.
Acting the Sage, he flows enrobed in waters and song as 'twere a stall that kine may prosper.
2 The worlds expand to hirn who from aforetime found light to spread the law of life eternal.
The swelling songs, like kine within the stable, in deep devotion call aloud on Indu.
3 When the sage bears his holy wisdom round him, like a car visiting all worlds, the Hero,
Becoming fame, mid Gods, unto the mortal, wealth to the skilled, worth praise mid the Ever-present,
4 For glory born be hath come forth to glory: he giveth life and glory to the singers.
They, clothed in glory, have become immortal. He, measured in his course, makes frays successful.
5 Stream to us food and vigour, kine and horses: give us broad lights and fill thGods with rapture.
All ther are easy things for thee to master thou, Pavamana Soma, quellest foemen.

**[09-095] HYMN XCV Soma Pavamana.**

1. Loud neighs the Tawny Steed when started, settling deep in the wooden vessel while they cleanse him.
Led by the men he takes the milk for raiment: then shall he, through his powers, engender praisesongs.

2 As one who rows drives on his boat, he, Gold-hued, sends forth his voice, loosed on the path of Order.
As God, the secret names of Gods he utters, to be declared on sacred grass more widely.

3 Hastening onward like the waves of waters, our holy hymns are pressing nigh to Soma.
To him they come with lowly adoration, and, longing, enter him who longs to meet them.

4 They drain the stalk, the Steer who dwells on mountains, even as a Bull who decks him on the upland.
Hymns follow and attend him as he bellows: Trita bears Varuna aloft in ocean.

5 Sending thy voice out as Director, loosen the Invoker's thought, O Indu, as they cleanse thee.
While thou and Indra rule for our advantage, may we be masters of heroic vigour.

**[09-096] HYMN XCVI. Soma Pavamana**

1. IN forefront of the cars forth goes the Hero, the Leader, winning spoil: his host rejoices.
Soma endues his robes of lasting colours, and blesses, for his friends, their calls on Indra.

2 Men decked with gold adorn his golden tendril, incessantly with steed-impelling homage.
The Friend of Indra mounts his car well-knowing, he comes thereon to meet the prayer we offer.

3 O God, for service of the Gods flow onward, for food sublime, as Indra's drink, O Soma.
Making the floods, bedewing earth and heaven, come from the vast, comfort us while we cleanse thee

4 Flow for prosperity and constant Vigour, flow on for happiness and high perfection.
This is the wish of these friends assembled: this is my wish, O Soma Pavamana.

5 Father of holy hymns, Soma flows onward the Father of the earth, Father of heaven:
Father of Agni, Surya's generator, the Father who begat Indra and Visnu.

6 Brahman of Gods, the Leader of the poets, Rsi of sages, Bull of savage creatures,
Falcon amid the vultures, Axe of forests, over the cleansing sieve goes Soma singing.

7 He, Soma Pavamana, like a river, hath stirred the wave of voice, our songs and praises.
Beholding these inferior powers in cattle, he rests among them as a Steer well-knowing.

8 As Gladdener, Warrior never harmed in battle, with thousand genial streams, pour strength and vigour.
As thoughtful Pavamana, urge O Indu, speeding the kine, the plant's wave on to Indra.

9 Dear, grateful to the Gods, on to the beaker moves Soma, sweet to Indra, to delight him.
With hundred powers, with thousand currents, Indu, like a strong car-horse, goes to the assembly.

10 Born in old time as finder-out of treasures, drained with the stone, decking himself in waters,
Warding off curses, King of all existence, he shall find way for prayer the while they cleanse him.

11 For our sage fathers, Soma Pavamana, of old performed, by thee, their sacred duties.
Fighting unvanquished, open the enclosures: enrich us with large gifts of steeds and heroes.

12 As thou didst flow for Manu Life-bestowing, Foe-queller, Comforter, rich in oblations,
Even thus flow onward now conferring riches: combine with Indra, and bring forth thy weapons.

13 Flow onward, Soma, rich in sweets and holy,. enrobed in waters on the fleecy summit.
Settle in vessels that are full of fatness, as cheering and most gladdening drink for Indra.

14 Pour, hundred-streamed, winner of thousands, mighty at the Gods' banquet, Pour the rain of heaven,
While thou with rivers roarest in the beaker, and blent with milk prolongest our existence.

15 Purified with our holy hymns, this Soma o'ertakes malignities like some strong charger,
Like fresh milk poured by Aditi, like passage in ample room, or like a docile car-horse.

16 Cleansed by the pressers, armed with noble weapons, stream to us the fair secret name thou bearest.
Pour booty, like a horse, for love of glory God, Soma, send us kine, and send us Vayu.

17 They deck him at his birth, the lovely Infant, the Maruts with their troop adorn the Car-horse.
By songs a Poet and a Sage by wisdom, Soma joes singing through the cleansing filter.

18 Light-winner, Rsi-mindcd, Rsi-maker, hymned in a thousand hymns, Leader of sages,
A Steer who strives to gain his third form, Soma is, like Viraj, resplendent as a Singer.

19 Hawk seated in the bowls, Bird wide-extended, the Banner seeking kine and wielding weapons,
Following close the sea, the wave of waters, the great Bull tells his fourth form and declares it.

20 Like a fair youth who decorates his body, a courser rushing to the gain of riches,
A steer to herds, so, flowing to the pitcher, he with a roar hath passed into the beakers.

21 Flow on with might as Pavamana, Indu flow loudly roaring through the fleecy filter.
Enter the beakers sporting, as they cleanse thee, and let thy gladdening juice make Indra joyful.

22 His streams have been effused in all their fulness, and he hath entered, balmed with milk, the goblets.
Singing his psalm, well-skilled in song, a Chanter, be comes as 'twere to his friend's sister roaring.

23 Chasing our foes thou comest, Pavamana Indu, besting, as lover to his darling.
As a bird flies and settles in the forest, thus Soma settles, purified, in goblets.

24 With full stream and abundant milk, O Soma, thy beams come, like a woman, as they cleanse thee.
He, gold-hued, rich in boons, brought to the waters, hath roared within the goblet of the pious.

**[09-097] HYMN XCVII. Soma Pavamana**

1. MADE pure by this man's urgent zeal and impulse the God hath to the Gods his juice imparted.
He goes, effused and singing, to the filter, like priest to measured seats supplied with cattle.

2 Robed in fair raiment meet to wear in battle, a mighty Sage pronouncing invocations.
Roll onward to the beakers as they cleanse thee, far-seeing at the feast of Gods, and watchful.

3 Dear, he is brightened on the fleecy summit, a Prince among us, nobler than the noble.
Roar out as thou art purified, run forward. Do ye preserve us evermore with blessings.

4 Let us sing praises to the Gods: sing loudly, send ye the Soma forth for mighty riches.

Let him flow, sweetly-flavoured, through the filter, and let our pious one rest in the pitcher.

5 Winning the friendship of the Deities, Indu flows in a thousand streams to make them joyful.

Praised by the men after the ancient statute, he hath come nigh, for our great bliss, to Indra.

6 Flow, Gold-hued, cleansing thee, to enrich the singer: let thy juice go to Indra to support him.

Come nigh, together with the Gods, for bounty. Do ye preserve us evermore with blessings.

7 The God declares the Deities' generations, like Usana, proclaiming lofty wisdom.

With brilliant kin, far-ruling, sanctifying, the Boar advances, singing, to the places.

8 The Swans, the Vrsaganas from anear us have brought their restless spirit to our dwelling.

Friends come to Pavamana meet for praises, and sound in concert their resistless music.

9 He follows the Wide-strider's rapid movement: cows low, as 'twere, to him who sports at pleasure.

He with the sharpened horns brings forth abundance: the Silvery shines by night, by day the Golden.

10 Strong Indu, bathed in milk, flows on for Indra, Soma exciting strength, to make him joyful.

He quells malignities and slays the demons, the King of mighty power who brings us comfort.

11 Then in a stream he flows, milked out with press-stones, mingled with sweetness, through the fleecy filter-

Indu rejoicing in the love of Indra, the God who gladdens, for the God's enjoyment.

12 As he is purified he pours out treasures, a God bedewing Gods with his own juices.

Indu hath, wearing qualities by seasons, on the raised fleece engaged, the ten swift fingers.

13 The Red Bull bellowing to the kine advances, causing the heavens and earth to roar and tbunder.

Well is he beard like Indra's shout in battle: letting this voice be known he hastens hither.

14 Swelling with milk, abounding in sweet flavours, urging the meath-rich plant thou goest onward.

Raising a shout thou flowest as they cleanse thee, when thou, O Soma, art effused for Indra.

15 So flow thou on inspiriting, for rapture, aiming deatb-shafts at him who stays the waters,

Flow to us wearing thy resplendent colour, effused and eager for the kine, O Soma.

16 Pleased with us, Indu, send us as thou flowest good easy paths in ample space and comforts.

Dispelling, as 'twere with a club, misfortunes, run o'er the height, run o'er the fleecy summit.

17 Pour on us rain celestial, quickly streaming, refreshing, fraught with health and ready bounty.

Flow, Indu, send these Winds thy lower kinsmen, setting them free like locks of hair unbraided.

18 Part, like a knotted tangle, while they cleanse thee, O Soma, righteous and unrighteous conduct.

Neigh like a tawny courser who is loosened, come like a youth, O God, a house-possessor.

19 For the God's service, for delight, O Indu, run o'er the height, run o'ver the fleecy summit.

With thousand streams, inviolate, sweet-scented, flow on for gain of strength that conquers heroes.

20 Without a car, without a rein to guide them, unyoked, like coursers started in the contest,

These brilliant drops of Soma juice run forward. Do ye, O Deities, come nigh to drink them.

21 So for our banquet of the Gods, O Indu, pour down the rain of heaven into the vessels.

May Soma grant us riches sought with longing, mighty, exceeding strong, with store of heroes.

22 What time the loving spirit's word had formed him Chief of all food, by statute of the Highest,

Then loudly lowing came the cows to Indu, the chosen, well-loved Master in the beaker.

23 The Sage, Celestial, liberal, raining bounties, pours as he flows the Genuine for the Truthful.

The King shall be effectual strength's upholder: he by the ten bright reins is mostly guided.

24 He who beholds mankind, made pure with filters, the King supreme of Deities and mortals,

From days of old is Treasure-Lord of riches: he, Indu, cherishes fair well-kept Order.

25 Haste, like a steed, to vittory for glory, to Indra's and to Vayu's entertainment.

Give us food ample, thousandfold: be, Soma, the finder-out of riches when they cleanse thee.

26 Effused by us let God-delighting Somas bring as they flow a home with noble heroes.

Rich in all boons like priests acquiring favour, the worshippers of heaven, the best of Cheerers.

27 So, God, for service of the Gods flow onward, flow, drink of Gods, for ample food, O Soma.

For we go forth to war against the mighty make heaven and earth well stablished by thy cleansing.

28 Thou, yoked by strong men, neighest like a courser, swifter than thought is, like an awful lion.

By paths directed hitherward, the straightest, send thou us happiness, Indu, while they cleanse thee.

29 Sprung from the Gods, a hundred streams, a thousand, have been effused: sages prepare and purge them.

Bring us from heaven the means of winnning, Indu; thou art-forerunnner of abundant riches.

30 The streams of days, were poured as 'twere from heaven: the wise King doth not treat his friend unkindly.

Like a son following his father's wishes, grant to this family success and safety.

31 Now are thy streams poured forth with all their sweetness, when, purified. thou goest through the filter.

The race of kine is thy gift, Pavarridna: when born thou madest Surya rich with brightness.

32 Bright, bellowing aiong the path of Order, thou shinest as the form of life eternal.

Thou flowest on as gladdening drink for Indra, sending thy voice out with the hymns of sages.

33 Pouring out streams at the Gods' feast with service, thou, Soma, lookest down, a heavenly Eagle.

Enter the Soma-holding beaker, Indu, and with a roar approach the ray of Sarya.

34 Three are the voices that the Courser utters: he speaks the thought of prayer, the law of Order.

To the Cow's Master come the Cows inquiring: the hymns with eager longing come to Soma.

35 To Soma come the Cows, the Milch-kine longing, to Soma sages with their hvmns inquiring.

Soma, effused, is purified and blended our hymns and Trstup songs unite in Soma.

36 Thus, Soma, as we pour thee into vessels, while thou art purified flow for our welfare.

Pass into Indra with a mighty roaring make the voice swell, and generate abundance.

37 Singer of true songs, ever-watchful, Soma hath settled in the ladles when they cleanse him.

Him the Adhvaryus, paired and eager, follow, leaders of sacrifice and skilful-handed.

38 Cleansed near the Sun as 'twere he as Creator hath filled full heaven and earth, and hath disclosed
them.

He by whose dear help men gain all their wishes shall yield the precious meed as to a victor.

39 He, being cleansed, the Strengthener and Increaser, Soma the Bounteous, helped us with his
lustre,

Wherewith our sires of old who knew the footsteps found light and stole the cattle from the
mountain.

40 In the first vault of heaven loud roared the Ocean, King of all being, generating creatures.

Steer, in the filter, on the fleecy summit, Soma, the Drop effused, hath waxen mighty.

41 Soma the Steer, in that as Child of Waters he chose the Gods, performed that great achievement.

He, Pavamana, granted strength to Indra; he, Indu, generated light in Surya.

42 Make Vayu glad,, for furtherance and bounty: cheer Varuna and Mitra, as they cleanse thee.

Gladden the Gods, gladden the host of Maruts: make Heaven and Earth rejoice, O God, O Soma.

43 Flow onward righteous slayer of the wicked, driving away our enemies and sickness,

Blending thy milk with milk which cows afford us. We are thy friends, thou art the Friend of Indra.

44 Pour us a fount of meath, a spring of treasure; send us a hero son and happy fortune.

Be sweet to India when they cleanse thee, Indu, and pour down riches on us from the ocean.

45 Strong Soma, pressed, like an impetuous courser, hath flowed in stream as a flood speeding
downward.

Cleansed, he hath settled in his wooden dwelling: Indu hath flowed with milk and with the waters.

46 Strong, wise, for thee who longest for his coming this Soma here flows to the bowls, O Indra.

He, chariot-borne, sun-bright, and truly potent, was poured forth like the longing of the pious.

47 He, purified with ancient vital vigour, pervading all his Daughter's forms and figures,

Finding his threefold refuge in the waters, goes singing, as a priest, to the assemblies.

48 Now, chariot-borne, flow unto us, God Soma, as thou art purified flow to the saucers,

Sweetest in waters, rich in meath, and holy, as Savitar the God is, truthfulminded.

49 To feast him, flow mid song and hymn, to Vayu, flow purified to Varuna and Mitra.

Flow to the song-inspiring car-borne Hero, to mighty Indra, him who wields the thunder.

50 Pour on us garments that shall clothe us meetly, send, purified, miIch-kine, abundant yielders.

God Soma, send us chariot-drawing horses that they may bring us treasures bright and golden.

51 Send to us in a stream celestial riches, send us, when thou art cleansed, what earth containeth,

So that thereby we may acquire possessions and Rsihood in Jamadagni's manner.

52 Pour forth this wealth with this purification: flow onward to the yellow lake, O Indu.

Here, too, the Ruddy, wind-swift, full of wisdom, Shall give a son to him who cometh quickly.

53 Flow on for us with this purification to the famed ford of thee whose due is glory.

May the Foe-queller shake us down, for triumph, like a tree's ripe fruit, sixty thousand treasures.

54 Eagerly do we pray for those two exploits, at the blue lake and Prsana, wrought in battle.

He sent our enemies to sleep and slew thern, and turned away the foolish and unfriendly.

55 Thou comest unto three extended filters, and hasteriest through each one as they cleanse thee.

Thou art the giver of the gift, a Bhaga, a Maghavan for liberal lords, O Indu.

56 This Soma here, the Wise, the All-obtainer, flows on his way as King of all existence.

Driving the drops at our assemblies, Indu completely traverses the fleecy filter.

57 The Great Inviolate are kissing Indu, and singing in his place like eager sages.

The wise men send him forth with ten swift fingers, and balm his form with essence of the waters.

58 Soma, may we, with thee as Pavamana, pile up together all our spoil in battle.

This boon vouchsafe us Varuna and Mitra, and Aditi and Sindhu, Earth and Heaven.

## [09-098] HYMN XCVIII. Soma Pavamana

1. STREAM on us riches that are sought by many, best at winning strength

Riches, O Indu, thousandfold, glorious, conquering the great.

2 Effused, he hath, as on a car, invested him in fleecy mail:

Onward hath Indu flowed in streams, impelled, surrounded by the wood.

3 Effused, this Indu hath flowed on, distilling rapture, to the fleece:

He goes erect, as seeking kine in stream, with light, to sacrifice.

4 For thou thyself, O Indu, God, to every mortal worshipper

Attractest riches thousandfold, made manifest in hundred forms.

5 Good Vrtra-slayer, may we be still nearest to this wealth of thine

Which many crave, nearest to food and happiness, Resistless One!

6 Whom, bright with native splendour, crushed between the pair of pressingstones-

The wavy Friend whom Indra loves-the twice-five sisters dip and bathe,

7 Him with the fleece they purify, brown, golden-hued, beloved of all,

Who with exhilarating juice goes forth to all the Deities.

8 Through longing for this sap of yours ye drink what brings ability,

Even him who, dear as heaven's own light, gives to our princes high renown.

9 Indu at holy rites produced you, Heaven and Earth, the Friends of men,

Hill-haunting God the Goddesses. They bruised him where the roar was loud.

10 For Vrtra-slaying Indra, thou, Soma, art poured that he may drink,

Poured for the guerdon-giving man, poured for the God who sitteth there.

11 These ancient Somas, at the break of day, have flowed into the sieve,

Snorting away at early morn these foolish evil-hearted ones.

12 Friends, may the princes, ye and we, obtain this Most Resplendent One.
Gain him who hath the smell of strength, win him whose home is very strength.

## [09-099] HYMN XCIX. Soma Pavamana.

1. THEY for the Bold and Lovely One ply manly vigour like a bow: joyous, in front of songs they weave bright raiment for the Lord Divine.
2 And he, made beautiful by night, dips forward into strengthening food',
What time the sacrificer's thoughts speed on his way the Golden-hued.
3 We cleanse this gladdening drink of his the juice which Indra chiefly drinks---
That which kine took into their mouths, of old, and princes take it now.
4 To him, while purifying, they have raised the ancient psalm of praise:
And sacred songs which bear the names of Gods have supplicated him.
5 They purify him as he drops, courageous, in the fleecy sieve.
Him they instruct as messenger to bear the sage's morning prayer.
6 Soma, best Cheerer, takes his seat, the while they cleanse him in the bowls.
He as it were impregns the cow, and babbles on, the Lord of Song.
7 He is effused and beautified, a God for Gods, by skilful men.
He penetrates the mighty floods collecting all he knows therein.
8 Pressed, Indu, guided by the men, thou art led to the cleaning sieve.
Thou, yielding Indra highest joy, takest thy seat within the bowls.

## [09-100] HYMN C. Soma Pavamana.

I. THE Guileless Ones are singing praise to Indra's well beloved Friend,
As, in the morning of its life, the mothers lick the new-born calf.
2 O Indu, while they cleanse thee bring, O Soma, doubly-waxing wealth
Thou in the worshipper's abode causest all treasures to increase.
3 Set free the. song which mind hath yoked, even as thunder frees the rain:
All treasures of the earth and heaven, O Soma, thou dost multiply.
4 Thy stream when thou art pressed runs on like some victorious warrior's steed
Hastening onward through the fleece like a fierce horse who wins the prize.
5 Flow on, Sage Soma, with thy stream to give us mental power and strength,
Effused for Indra, for his drink, for Mitra and for Varuna.
6 Flow to the filter with thy stream, effused, best winner, thou, of spoil,
O Soma, as most rich in sweets for Indra, Visnu, and the Gods.
7 The mothers, void of guiles, caress thee Golden-coloured, in the sieve,
As cows, O Pavamana, lick the new-born calf, as Law commands.
8 Thou, Pavamana, movest on with wondrous rays to great renown.
Striving within the votary's house thou drivest all the glooms away.
9 Lord of great sway, thou liftest thee above the heavens, above the earth.
Thou, Pavamana hast assumed thy coat of mail in majesty.

## [09-101] HYMN CI. Soma Pavamana

1. FOR first possession of your juice, for the exhilarating drink,
Drive ye away the dog, my friends, drive ye the long-tongued dog away.
2 He who with purifying stream, effused, comes flowing hitherward,
Indu, is like an able steed.
3 The men with all-pervading song send unassailable Soma forth,
By pressing-stones, to sacrifice.
4 The Somas, very rich in sweets, for which the sieve is destined, flow,
Effused, the source of Indra's joy: may your strong juices reach the Gods.
5 Indu flows on for Indra's sake: thus have the Deities declared.
The Lord of Speech exerts himself, Ruler of all, because of might.
6 Inciter of the voice of song, with thousand streams the ocean flows,
Even Soma, Lord of opulence, the Friend of Indra, day by day.
7 As Pusan, Fortune, Bhaga, comes this Soma while they make him pure.
He, Lord of the multitude, hath looked upon the earth and heaven.
8 The dear cows lowed in joyful mood together to the gladdening drink.
The drops as they were purified, the Soma juices, made then paths.
9 O Pavamana, bring the juice, the mightiest, worthy to be famed,
Which the Five Tribes have over them, whereby we may win opulence.
10 For us the Soma juices flow, the drops best furtherers of our weal,
Effused as friends without a spot, benevolent, finders of the light.
11 Effused by means of pressing-stones, upon the ox-hide visible,
They, treasure-finders, have announced food unto us from every side.
12 Tlese Soma juices, skilled in song, purified, blent with milk and curd,
When moving and when firmly laid in oil, resemble lovely Suns.
13 Let not the power of men restrain the voice of the outpouring juice:
As Bhrgu's sons chased Makha, so drive ye the greedy hound away.
14 The Friend hath wrapped him in his robe, as in his parents arms, a son.
He went, as lover to a dame, to take his station suitor-like.
15 That Hero who produces strength, he who hath propped both worlds apart,
Gold-hued, hath wrapped him in the sieve, to settle, priest-like, in his place.
16 Soma upon the ox's skin through the sheep's wool flows purified.
Bellowing out, the Tawny Steer goes on to Indra's special place.

## [09-102] HYMN CIL Soma Pavamana.

1. THE Child, when blended with the streams, speeding the plan of sacrifice,
Surpasses all things that are dear, yea, from of old.
2 The place, near the two pressing-stones of Trita, hath he occupied,
Secret and dear through seven lights of sacrifice.
3 Urge to three courses, on the heights of Trita, riches in a stream.
He who is passing wise measures his courses out.
4 Even at his birth the Mothers Seven taught him, for glory, like a sage,
So that he, firm and sure, hath set his mind on wealth.
5 Under his sway, of one accord, are all the guileless Deities:
Warriors to be envied, they, when they are pleased.

6 The Babe whom they who strengthen Law have generated fair to see,
Much longed for at the sacrifice, most liberal Sage,-
7 To him, united, of themselves, come the young Parents of the rite,
When they adorn him, duly weaving sacrifice.
8 With wisdom and with radiant eyes unbar to us the stall of heaven,
Speeding at solemn rite the plan of Holy Law.

## [09-103] HYMN CIII. Soma Pavamana.

1. To Soma who is purified as ordering Priest the song is raised:
Bring meed, as 'twere, to one who makes thee glad with hymns.
2 Blended with milk and curds he flows on through the long wool of the sheep.
The Gold-hued, purified, makes him three seats for rest.
3 On through the long wool of the sheep to the meath-dropping vat he flows:
The Rsis' sevenfold quire hath sung aloud to him.
4 Shared by all Gods, Infallible, the Leader of our holy hymns,
Golden-hued Soma, being cleansed, hath reached the bowls.
5 After thy Godlike qualities, associate with Indra, go,
As a Priest purified by priests, Immortal One.
6 Like a car-horse who shows his strength, a God effused for Deities.
The penetrating Pavamana flows along.

## [09-104] HYMN CIV. Soma Pavamana.

1. SIT down, O friends, and sing aloud to him who purifies himself:
Deck him for glory, like a child, with holy rites.
2 Unite him bringing household wealth, even as a calf, with mother kine,
Him who hath double strength, the God, delighting juice.
3 Purify him who gives us power, that he, most Blessed One, may be
A banquet for the Troop, Mitra, and Varuna.
4 Voices have sung aloud to thee as finderout of wealth for us:
We clothe the hue thou wearest with a robe of milk.
5 Thou, Indu, art the food of Gods, O Sovran of all gladdening drinks:
As Friend for friend, be thou best finder of success.
6 Drive utterly away from us each demon, each voracious fiend,
The godless and the false: keep sorrow far away.

## [09-105] HYMN CV. Soma Pavamana

1. SING; ye aloud, O friends, to him who makes him pure for gladdening drink:
They shall make sweet the Child with sacrifice and laud.
2 Like as a calf with mother cows, so Indu is urged forth and sent,
Glorified by our hymns, the God-delighting juice.
3 Effectual means of power is he, he is a banquet for the Troop,
He who hath been effused, most rich in meath, for Gods.
4 Flow to us, Indu, passing, strong, effused, with wealth of kine and steeds:
I will spread forth above the milk thy radiant hue.
5 Lord of the tawny, Indu thou who art the God's most special food,
As Friend to friend, for splendour be thou good to men.
6 Drive utterly, far away from us each godless, each voracious foe.
O Indu, overcome and drive the false afar.

## [09-106] HYMN CVI. Soma Pavamana.

1. To Indra, to the Mighty Steer, may these gold-coloured juices go,
Drops rapidly produced, that find the light of heaven.

2 Effused, this juice victorious flows for Indra, for his maintenance.
Soma bethinks him of the Conqueror, as he knows.
3 May Indra in his raptures gain from him the grasp that gathers spoil,
And, winning waters, wield the steerstrong thunderbolt.
4 Flow vigilant for Indra, thou Soma, yea, Indu, run thou on:
Bring hither splendid strength that finds the light of heaven.
5 Do thou, all-beautiful, purify for Indra's sake the mighty juice,
Path-maker thou, far seeing, with a thousand ways.
6 Best finder of prosperity for us, most rich in sweets for Gods,
Proceed thou loudly roaring on a thousand paths.
7 O Indu, with thy streams, in might, flow for the banquet of the Gods:
Rich in meath, Soma, in our beaker take thy place.
8 Thy drops that swim in water have exalted Indra to delight:
The Gods have drunk thee up for immortality.
9 Stream opulence to us, ye drops of Soma, pressed and purified,
Pouring down rain from heaven in hoods, and finding light.
10 Soma, while filtered, with his wave flows through the long wool of the sheep,
Shouting while purified before the voice of song.
11 With songs they send the Mighty forth, sporting in wood, above the fleece:
Our psalms have glorified him of the triple height.
12 Into the jars hath he been loosed, like an impetuous steed for war,
And lifting up his voice, while filtered, glided on.
13 Gold-hued and lovely in his course, through tangles of the wool he flows,
And pours heroic fame upon the worshippers.
14 Flow thus, a faithful votary: the streams of meath have been effused.
Thou comest to the filter, singing, from each side.

## [09-107] HYMN CVII. Soma Pavamana.

I., HENCE sprinkle forth the juice effused,. Soma, the best of sacred gifts,
Who, friend of man, hath run amid the water-streams. He hath pressed Soma out with stones.
2 Now, being purified, flow hither through the fleece inviolate and most odorous.
We ladden thee in waters when thou art effused, blending thee still with juice and milk.
3 Pressed out for all to see, delighting Gods, Indu, Far-sighted One, is mental power.
4 Cleansing thee, Soma, in thy stream, thou flowest in a watery robe:
Giver of wealth, thou sittest in the place of Law, O God, a fountain made of gold.
5 Milking the heavenly udder for dear meath, he hath sat in the ancient gatheringplace.
Washed by the men, the Strong Farseeing One streams forth nutriti us food that all desire.
6 O Soma, while they cleanse thee, dear and watchful in the sheep's long wool,
Thou hast become a Singer most like Angiras: thou madest Surya mount to heaven.
7 Bountiful, best of furtherers, Soma floweth on, Rsi and Singer, keen of sight.
Thou hast become a Sage most welcome to the Gods: thou madest Surya mount to heaven.
8 Pressed out by pressers, Soma goes over the fleecy backs of sheep,
Goes, even as with a mare, in tawnycoloured stream, goes in exhilarating stream.

9 Down to the water-Soma, rich in kine hath flowed with cows, with cows that have been milked.

They have approached the mixing-vessel as a sea: the cheerer streams for the carouse.

10 Effused by stones, O Soma, and urged through the long wool of the sheep,

Thou, entering the saucers as a man the fort, gold-hued hast settled in the wood.

11 He beautifies himself through the sheep's long fine wool, like an impetuous steed in war,

Even Soma Pavamana who shall be the joy of sages and of holy bards.

12 O Soma,-for the feast of Gods, river-like he hath swelled with surge,

With the stalk's juice, exhilarating, resting not, into the vat that drops with meath.

13 Like a dear son who must be decked, the Lovely One hath clad him in a shining robe.

Men skilful at their work drive him forth, like a car, into the rivers from their bands.

14 The living drops of Soma juice pour, as they flow, the gladdening drink,

Intelligent drops above the basin of the sea, exhilarating, finding light.

15 May Pavamana, King and God, speed with his wave over the sea the lofty rite:

May he by Mitra's and by Varuna's decree flow furthering the lofty rite.

16 Far-seeing, lovely, guided by the men, the God whose home is in the sea-

17 Soma, the gladdening juice, flows pressed for Indra with his Marut host:

He hastens o'er the fleece with all his thousand streams: men make him bright and beautiful.

18 Purified in the bowl and gendering the hymn, wise Soma joys among the Gods.

Robed in the flood, the Mighty One hath clad himself with milk and settled in the vats.

19 O Soma, Indu, every day thy friendship hath been my delight. Many fiends follow me; help me, thou Tawny-hued; pass on beyond these barriers.

20 Close to thy bosom am I, Soma, day and night. O Tawny-hued, for friendship sake.

Surya himself refulgent with his glow have we o'ertaken in his course like birds.

21 Deft-handed! thou when purified liftest thy voice amid the sea.

Thou, Pavamana, makest riches flow to us, yellow, abundant, much-desifed.

22 Making thee pure and bright in the sheep's long wool, tbou hast bellowed, steerlike, in the wood.

Thou flowest, Soma Pavamana, balmed with milk unto the special place of Gods.

23 Flow on to win us strength, flow on to lofty lore of every kind.

Thou, Soma, as Exhilarator wast the first to spread the sea abroad for Gods.

24 Flow to the realm of earth, flow to the realm of heaven, O Soma, in thy righteous ways.

Fair art thou whom the sages, O Far-seeing One, urge onward with their songs and hymns.

25 Over the cleansing sieve have flowed the Pavamanas in a stream,

Girt by the Maruts, gladdening, Steeds with Indra's stiength, for wisdom and for dainty food.

26 Urged onward by the pressers, clad in watery robes, Indu is speeding to the vat.

He gendering light, hath made the glad Cows low, while he takes them as his garb of state.

## [09-108] HYMN CVIII. Soma Pavamana.

1. FOR Indra, flow thou Soma on, as gladdening juice most sweet, intelligent,

Great, cheering, dwelling most in heaven.

2 Thou, of whom having drunk the Steer acts like a steer. drinking of this that finds the light,

He, Excellently Wise, is come to strengthening food, to spoil and wealth like Etasa.

3 For, verily, Pavamana, thou bast, splendidest, called all the generations of

The Gods to immortality.

4 By whom Dadhyac Navagva opens fastened doors, by whom the sages gained their wish,

By whom they won the fame of lovely Amrta in the felicity of Gods.

5 Effused, he floweth in a stream, best rapture-giver, in the long wool of the sheep,

Sporting, as 'twere the waters' wave.

6 He who from out the rocky cavern took with might the redmrefulgent watery Cows,

Thou masterest the stable full of kine and steeds: burst it, brave Lord, like one in mail.

7 Press ye and pour him, like a steed, laudworthy, speeding through the region and the flood,

Who swims in water, roan in wood;

8 Increaser of the water, Steer with thousand streams, dear to the race of Deities;

Who born in Law hath waxen mighty by the Law, King, God, and lofty Ordinance.

9 Make splendid glory shine on us, thou Lord of strengthening food, God, as the Friend of Gods:

Unclose the fount of middle air.

10 Roll onward to the bowls, O Mighty One, effused, as Prince supporter of the tribes.

Pour us rain from heaven, send us the waters' flow: incite our thoughts to win the spoil.

11 They have drained him the Steer of heaven, him with a thousand streams, distilling rapturous joy,

Him who brings all things excellent.

12 The Mighty One was born Immortal, giving life, lightening darkness with his shine.

Wcll-praised by. sages he hath. by his wondrous power assumed the Threefold as his robe.

13 Effused is he who brings good things, who brings us bounteous gifts and sweet refreshing food,

Soma who brings us quiet homes:

14 He whom our Indra and the Marut host shall drink, Bhaga shall drink with Aryarnan,

By whom we bring to us Mitra and Varuna and Indra for our great defence.

15 Soma, for Indra's drink do thou, led by the men, well-wcaponcd and most gladdening,

Flow on with greatest store of sweets.

16 Enter the Soma-holder, even Indra's heart, as rivers pass into the sea,

Acceptable to Mitra, Vayu, Varuna, the noblest Pillar of the heavens.

## [09-109] HYMN CIX. Soma Pavamana.

1. PLEASANT to Indra's Mitra's, Pusan's Bhaga's taste, sped onward, Soma, with thy flowing stream.

2 Let Indra drink, O Soma, of thy juice for wisdom, and all Deities for strength.

3 So flow thou on as bright celestial juice, flow to the vast, immortal dwelling-place.

4 Flow onward, Soma, as a mighty sea, as Father of the Gods to every form.

5 Flow on, O Soma, radiant for the Gods and Heaven and Earth and bless our progeny.

6 Thou, bright Juice, art Sustainer of the sky: flow, mighty, in accordance with true Law.

7 Soma, flow splendid with thy copious stream through the great fleece as in the olden time.

8 Bom, led by men, joyous, and purified, let the Light-finder make all blessings flow:

9 Indu, while cleansed, keeping the people safe, shall give us all possessions for our own.

10 Flow on for wisdom, Soma, and for power, as a strong courser bathed, to win the prize.

11 The pressers purify this juice of thine, the Soma, for delight, and lofty fame

12 They deck the Gold-hued Infant, newlyborn, even Soma, Indu, in the sieve for Gods.

13 Fair Indu hath flowed on for rapturous joy, Sage for good fortune in the waters' lap.

14 He bears the beauteous name of Indra, that wherewith he overcame all demon foes.

15 All Deities are wont to drink of him, pressed by the men and blent with milk and curds.

16 He hath flowed forth with thousand streams effused, flowed ihsough the filter and the sheep's long wool.

17 With endless genial flow the Strong hath run, purified by the waters, blent with milk.

18 Pressed out with stones, directed by the men, go fortli, O Soma, into Indra's throat.

19 The mighty Soma with a thousand streams is poured to Indra through the cleansing sieve.

20 Indu they balm with pleasant milky juice for Indra, for the Steer, for his delight.

21 Lightly, for sheen, they cleanse thee for the Gods, gold-coloured, wearing water as thy robe.

22 Indu to Indra streams, yea, downward streams, Strong, flowing to the floods, and mingling -there.

## [09-110] HYMN CX. Soma Pavamana.

1. O'ERPOWERING Vrtras, forward run to win great strength: Thou speedest to subdue like one exacting debts.

2 In thee, effused, O Soma, we rejoice ourselves for great supremacy in fight.
Thou, Pavamana, enterest into mighty deeds,

3 O Pavamana, thou didst generate the Sun, and spread the moisture out with power,
Hasting to us with plenty vivified with milk.

4 Thou didst produce him, Deathless God mid mortal men for maintenance of Law and lovely Amrta:
Thou evermore hast moved making strength flow to us.

5 All round about hast thou with glory pierced for us as 'twere a never-failing well for men to drink,
Borne on thy way in fragments from the presser's arms.

6 Then, beautifully radiant, certain Heavenly Ones, have sung to him their kinship as they looked thereon,
And Savitar the God opens as 'twere a stall.

7 Soma, the men of old whose grass was trimmed addressed the hymn to thee for mighty strength
and for renown:
So, Hero, urge us onward to heroic power.

8 They have drained forth from out the great depth of the sky the old primeval milk of heaven that
claims the laud:
They lifted up their voice to Indra athis birth.

9 As long as thou, O Pavamana, art above this earth and heaven and all existence in thy might,
Thou standest like a Bull the chief amid the herd.

10 In the sheep's wool hath Soma Pavamana flowed, while they cleanse him, like a playful infant,
Indu with hundred powers and hundred currents.

11 Holy and sweet, while purified, this Indu flows on, a wave of pleasant taste, to Indra,-
Strength-winner, Treasure-finder, Life. bestower.

12 So flow thou on, subduing our assailants, chasing the demons hard to beencountered,
Well-armed and conquering our foes, O Soma.

## [09-111] HYMN CXI. Soma Pavamana.

1. WITH this his golden splendour purifying him, he with his own allies subdues all enemies, as Sara
with his own allies.
Cleansing himself with stream of juice he shines forth yellow-hued and red, when with the praisers
he encompasses all forms, with praisers having seven mouths.

2 That treasure of the Panis thou discoveredst; thou with thy mothers deckest thee in thine abode,
with songs of worship in thine home.
As 'twere from far, the hymn is heard, where holy songs resound in joy. He with the ruddy-hued,
threefold hath won life-power, he, glittering, hath won life-power.

3 He moves intelligent, directed to the East. The very beauteous car rivals the beams of light, the beautiful celestial car.
Hymns, lauding manly valour, came, inciting Indra to success, that ye may be unconquered, both thy
bolt and thou, both be unconquered in the war.

## [09-112] HYMN CXII. Soma Pavamana.

1. WE all have various thoughts and plans, and diverse are the ways of men.
The Brahman seeks the worshipper, wright seeks the cracked, and leech the maimed. Flow, Indu,
flow for Indra's sake.

2 The smith with ripe and seasoned plants, with feathers of the birds of air,
With stones, and with enkindled flames, seeks him who hath a store of gold. Flow, Indu, flow for
Indra's sake.

3 A bard am I, my dad's a leech, mammy lays corn upon the stones.
Striving for wealth, with varied plans, we follow our desires like kine. Flow, Indu, flow for Indra's sake.

4 The horse would draw an easy car, gay hosts attract the laugh and jest.
The male desires his mate's approach, the frog is eager for the flood, Flow, Indu, flow for Indra's sake.

## [09-113] HYMN CXIII. Soma Pavamana.

1. LET Vrtra-slaying Indra drink Soma by Saryanavan's side,
Storing up vigour in his heart, prepared to do heroic deeds. Flow, Indu, flow for Indra's sake.

2 Lord of the Quarters, flow thou on, boon Soma, from Arjika land,
Effused with ardour and with faith, and the true hymn of sacrifice. Flow, Indu, flow for Indra's sake.

3 Hither hath Surya's Daughter brought the wild Steer whom Parjanya nursed.
Gandharvas have seized bold of him, and in the Soma laid the juice. Flow, Indu, flow for Indra's sake.

4 Splendid by Law! declaring Law, truthspeaking, truthful in thy works,

Enouncing faith, King Soma! thou, O Soma, whom thy maker decks. Flow, Indu, flow for Indra's sake.

5 Together flow the meeting streams of him the Great and truly Strong.
The juices of the juicy meet. Made pure by prayer, O Golden-hued, flow, Indu, flow for Indra's sake.

6 O Pavamana, where the priest, as he recites the rhythmic prayer,
Lords it o'er Soma with the stone, with Soma bringing forth delight, flow, Indu, flow for Indra's sake.

7 O Pavarnana, place me in that deathless, undecaying world
Wherein the light of heaven is set, and everlasting lustre shines. Flow, Indu, flow for Indra's sake.

8 Make me immortal in that realm where dwells the King, Vivasvan's Son,
Where is the secret shrine of heaven, where are those waters young and fresh. Flow, Indu, flow for
Indra's sake.

9 Make me immortal in that realm where they move even as they list,
In the third sphere of inmost heaven where lucid worlds are full of light. Flow, Indu, flow for Indra's
sake.

10 Make me immortal in that realm of eager wish and strong desire,
The region of the radiant Moon, where food and full delight are found. Flow, Indu, flow for Indra's sake:

11 Make me immortal in that realm where happiness and transports, where
Joys and felicities combine, and longing wishes are fulfilled. Flow, Indu, flow for Indra's sake.

## [09-114] HYMN CXIV. Soma Pavamana.

1. THE man who waIketh as the Laws of Indu Pavamana bid,-
Men call him rich in children, him, O Soma, who hath met thy thought. Flow, Indu, flow for Indra's
sake.

2 Kasyapa, Rsi, lifting up thy voice with hymn-composers' lauds,
Pav reverence to King Soma born the Sovran Ruler of the plants. Flow, Indu, flow for Indra's sake.

3 Seven regions have their several Suns; the ministering priests are seven;
Seven are the Aditya Deities,-with these, O Soma, guard thou us. Flow, Indu, flow for Indra's sake.

4 Guard us with this oblation which, King Soma, hath been dressed for thee.
Let not malignity conquer us, let nothing evil do us harm. Flow, Indu, flow for Indra's sake.

# BOOK TEN

## [10-001] HYMN I. Agni.

1. HIGH hath the Mighty risen before the dawning, and come to us with light from out the darkness.
Fair-shapen Agni with white-shining splendour hath filled at birth all human habitations.

2 Thou, being born, art Child of Earth and Heaven, parted among the plants in beauty, Agni!
The glooms of night thou, Brilliant Babe, subduest, and art come forth, loud roaring, from thy Mothers.

3 Here, being manifested, lofty Visnu, full wise, protects his own supremest station.
When they have offered in his mouth their sweet milk, to him with one accord they sing forth praises.

4 Thence bearing food the Mothers come to meet thee, with food for thee who givest food its increase.

These in their altered form again thou meetest. Thou art Invoking Priest in homes of mortals.

5 Priest of the holy rite, with car that glitters, refulgent Banner of each act of worship,
Sharinging every God through might and glory, even Agni Guest of men I summon hither.

6 So Agni stands on earth's most central station, invested in well-decorated garments.
Born, red of hue, where men pour out libations, O King, as great High Priest bring the Gods hither.

7 Over the earth and over heaven, O Agni, thou, Son, hast ever spread above thy Parents.
Come, Youthfullest! to those who long to meet thee, and hither bring the Gods, O Mighty Victor.

## [10-002] HYMN II. Agni.

1. GLADDEN the yearning Gods, O thou Most Youthful: bring them, O Lord of Seasons, knowingseasons,
With all the Priests Celestial, O Agni. Best worshipper art thou of all Invokers.

2 Thine is the Herald's, thine the Cleanser's office, thinker art thou, wealth-giver, true to Order.
Let us with Svaha offer up oblations, and Agni, worthy God, pay the Gods worship.

3 To the Gods' pathway have we travelled, ready to execute what work we may accomplish.
Let Agni, for he knows, complete the worship. He is the Priest: let him fix rites and seasons.

4 When we most ignorant neglect the statutes of you, O Deities with whom is knowledge,
Wise Agni shall correct our faults and failings, skilled to assign each God his fitting season.

5 When, weak in mind, of feeble understanding, mortals bethink them not of sacrificing,
Then shall the prudent and discerning Agni worship the Gods, best worshipper, in season.

6 Because the Father hath produced thee, Leader of all our solemn rites, their brilliant Banner:
So win by worship pleasant homes abounding in heroes, and rich food to nourish all men.

7 Thou whom the Heaven and Earth, thou whom the Waters, and Tvastar, maker of fair things, created,
Well knowing, all along the Fathers' pathway, shine with resplendent light, enkindled, Agni.

## [10-003] HYMN III. Agni.

1. O KING, the potent and terrific envoy, kindled for strength, is manifest in beauty.
He shines, all-knowing, with his lotty splendour: chasing black Night he comes with white-rayed
Morning.

2 Having o'ercome the glimmering Black with beauty, and bringing forth the dame the Great Sire's
Daughter,
Holding aloft the radiant light of Surya, as messenger of heaven he shines with treasures.

3 Attendant on the Blessed Dame the Blessed hath come: the Lover followeth his Sister.
Agni, far-spreading with conspicuous lustre, hath compassed Night with whitelyshining garments.

4 His goings-forth kindle as 'twere high voices the goings of the auspicious Friend of Agni.
The rays, the bright beams of the strong-jawed, mighty, adorable Steer are visible as he cometh.

5 Whose radiant splendours flow, like sounds, about us, his who is lofty, brilliant, and effulgent,

Who reaches heaven with best and brightest lustres, sportive and piercing even to the summit.
6 His powers, whose chariot fellies gleam and glitter have loudly roared while, as with teams, he
hasted.
He, the most Godlike, far-extending envoy, shines with flames ancient, resonant, whitely-shining.
7 So bring us ample wealth: seat thee as envoy of the two youthful Matrons, Earth and Heaven.
Let Agni rapid with his rapid, horses, impetuous with impetuous Steeds, come hither.

### [10-004] HYMN IV. Agni.

1. To thee will send praise and bring oblation, as thou hast merited lauds when we invoked thee.
A fountain in the desert art thou, Agni, O Ancient King, to man who fain would worship,
2 Thou unto whom resort the gathered people, as the kine seek the warm stall, O Most Youthful.
Thou art the messenger of Gods and mortals, and goest glorious with thy light between them.
3 Making thee grow as 'twere some noble infant, thy Mother nurtures thee with sweet affection.
Over the desert slopes thou passest longing, and seekest, like some beast set free, thy fodder.
4 Foolish are we, O Wise and free from error: verily, Agni, thou dost know thy grandeur.
There lies the form: he moves and licks, and swallows, and, as House-Lord, kisses the Youthful
Maiden.
5 He rises ever fresh in ancient fuel: smoke-bannered, gray, he makes the wood his dwelling.
No swimmer, Steer, he presses through the waters, and to his place accordant mortals bear him.
6 Like thieves who risk their lives and haunt the forest, the twain with their ten girdles have secured
him.
This is a new hymn meant for thee, O Agni: yoke as it were thy car with parts that glitter.
7 Homage and prayer are thine, O Jatavedas, and this my song shall evermore exalt thee.
Agni, protect our children and descendants, and guard with ever-watclful care our bodies.

### [10-005] HYMN V. Agni.

1. HE only is the Sea, holder of treasures: born many a time he views the hearts within us.
He hides him in the secret couple's bosom. The Bird dwells in the middle of the fountain.
2 Inhabiting one dwelling-place in common, strong Stallions and the Mares have come together.
The sages guard the seat of Holy Order, and keep the highest names concealed within them.
3 The Holy Pair, of wondrous power, have coupled: they formed the Infant, they who bred produced
him.
The central point of all that moves and moves not, the while they wove the Sage's thread with insight
4 For tracks of Order and refreshing viands attend from ancient times the goodly Infant.
Wearing him as a mantle, Earth and Heaven grow strong by food of pleasant drink and fatness.
5 He, calling loudly to the Seven red Sisters, hath, skilled in sweet drink, brought them to be looked
on.
He, born of old, in middle air hath halted, and sought and found the covering robe of Pusan.

6 Seven are the pathways which the wise have fashioned; to one of these may come the troubled
mortal.
He standeth in the dwelling of the Highest, a Pillar, on sure ground where paths are parted.
7 Not Being, Being in the highest heaven, in Aditi's bosom and in Daksa's birthplace,
Is Agni, our first-born of Holy Order, the Milch-cow and the Bull in life's beginning.

### [10-006] HYMN VI Agni

1. THIS is that Agni, he by whose protection, favour, and help. the singer is successful;
Who with the noblest flames of glowing fuel comes forth encompassed with far-spreading lustre.
2 Agni, the Holy One, the everlasting, who shines far beaming with celestial splendours;
He who hath come unto his friends with friendship, like a fleet steed who never trips or stumbles.
3 He who is Lord of all divine oblation, shared by all living men at break of morning,
Agni to whom our offerings are devoted, in whom rests he whose car, through might, is scatheless.
4 Increasing by his strength. while lauds content him, with easy flight unto the Gods he travels.
Agni the cheerful Priest, best Sacrificer, balms with his tongue the Gods with whom he mingles.
5 With songs and adorations bring ye hither Agni who stirs himself at dawn like Indra,
Whom sages laud with hymns as Jatavedas of those who wield the sacrificial ladle.
6 In whom all goodly treasures meet together, even as steeds and riders for the booty.
Inclining hither bring us help, O Agni, even assistance most desired by Indra.
7 Yea, at thy birth, when thou hadst sat in glory, thou, Agni, wast the aim of invocations.
The Gods came near, obedient to thy sunimons, and thus attained their rank as chief Protectors.

### [10-007] HYMN VII. Agni.

1. O AGNI, shared by all men living bring us good luck for sacrifice from earth and heaven.
With us be thine intelligence, WonderWorker! Protect us, God, with thy far-reaching blessings.
2 These hymns brought forth for thee, O Agni, laud thee for bounteous gifts, with cattle and with
horses.
Good Lord, when man from thee hath gained enjoyment, by hymns, O noblyborn, hath he obtained it.
3 Agni I deem my Kinsman and my Father, count him my Brother and my Friend for ever.
I honour as the face of lofty Agni in heaven the bright and holy light of Surya.
4 Effectual, Agni, are our prayers for profit. He whom, at home thou, Priest for ever, guardest
Is rich in food, drawn by red steeds, and holy: by day and night to him shall all be pleasant.
5 Men with their arms have generated Agni, helpful as some kind friend, adorned with splendours,
And stablished as Invoker mid the people the ancient Priest the sacrifice's lover.
6 Worship, thyself, O God, the Gods in heaven: what, void of knowledge, shall the fool avail thee?
As thou, O God, hast worshipped Gods by seasons, so, noblyborn! to thine own self pay worship.

7 Agni, be thou our Guardian and Protector bestow upon us life and vital vigour.

Accept, O Mighty One, the gifts we offer, and with unceasing care protect our bodies.

## [10-008] HYMN VIII. Agni.

1. AGNI advances with his lofty banner: the Bull is bellowing to the earth and heavens.

He hath attained the sky's supremest limits. the Steer hath waxen in the lap of waters.

2 The Bull, the youngling with the hump, hath frolicked, the strong and never-ceasing Calf hath
bellowed.

Bringing our offerings to the God's assembly, he moves as Chief in his own dwelling-places.

3 Him who hath grasped his Parents' head, they stablished at sacrifice a wave of heavenly lustre.

In his swift flight the red Dawns borne by horses refresh their bodies in the home of Order.

4 For, Vasu thou precedest every Morning, and still hast been the Twins' illuminator.

For sacrifice, seven places thou retainest while for thine own self thou engenderest Mitra.

5 Thou art the Eye and Guard of mighty Order, and Varuna when to sacrifice thou comest.

Thou art the Waters' Child O Jatavedas, envoy of him whose offering thou acceptest.

6 Thou art the Leader of the rite and region, to which with thine auspicious teams thou teadest,

Thy light-bestowing head to heaven thou liftest, making thy tongue the oblationbearer, Agni.

7 Through his wise insight Trita in the cavern, seeking as ever the Chief Sire's intention,

Carefully tended in his Parents' bosom, calling the weapons kin, goes forth to combat.

8 Well-skilled to use the weapons of his Father, Aptya, urged on by Indra, fought the battle.

Then Trita slew the foe seven-rayed, three-headed, and freed the cattle of the Son of Tvastar.

9 Lord of the brave, Indra cleft him in pieces who sought to gain much strength and deemed him
mighty.

He smote his three heads from his body, seizing the cattle of the oniniform Son of Tvastar.

## [10-009] HYMN IX. Waters.

1. YE, Waters, are beneficent: so help ye us to energy

That we may look on great delight.

2 Give us a portion of the sap, the most auspicious that ye have,

Like mothers in their longing love.

3 To you we gladly come for him to whose abode ye send us on;

And, Waters, give us procreant strength.

4 The Waters. be to us for drink, Goddesses for our aid and bliss:

Let them stream to us health and strength.

5 1 beg the Floods to give us balm, these Queens who rule o'er precious things,

And have supreme control of men.

6 Within the Waters-Soma thus hath told me-dwell all balms that heal,

And Agni, he who blesseth all.

7 O Waters, teem with medicine to keep my body safe from harm,

So that I long may see the Sun.

8 Whatever sin is found in me, whatever evil I have wrought,

If I have lied or falsely sworn, Waters, remove it far from me.

9 The Waters I this day have sought, and to their moisture have we come:

O Agni, rich in milk, come thou, and with thy splendour cover me.

## [10-010] HYMN X.Yama Yami.

1. FAIN would I win my friend to kindly friendship. So may the Sage, come through the air's wide
ocean,

Remembering the earth and days to follow, obtain a son, the issue of his father.

2 Thy friend loves not the friendship which considers her who is near in kindred as stranger.

Sons of the mighty Asura, the Heroes, supporters of the heavens, see far around them.

3 Yea, this the Immortals seek of thee with longing, progeny of the sole existing mortal.

Then let thy soul and mine be knit together, and as a loving husband take thy consort.

4 Shall we do now what we ne'er did aforetime? we who spake righteously now talk impurely?

Gandharva in the floods, the Dame of Waters-such is our bond, such our most lofty kinship.

5 Even in the womb God Tvastar, Vivifier, shaping all forms, Creator, made us consorts.

None violates his holy ordinances: that we are his the heavens and earth acknowledge.

6 Who knows that earliest day whereof thou speakest? Who hatb beheld it? Who can here declare it?

Great is the Law of Varuna and Mitra. What, wanton! wilt thou say to men to tempt them?

7 I, Yami, am possessed by love of Yama, that I may rest on the same couch beside him.

I as a wife would yield me to my husband. Like car-wheels let us speed to meet each other.

8 They stand not still, they never close their eyelids, those sentinels of Gods who wander round us.

Not me-go quickly, wanton, with another, and hasten like a chariot wheel to meet him.

9 May Surya's eye with days and nights endow him, and ever may his light spread out before him.

In heaven and earth the kindred Pair commingle. On Yam! be the unbrotherly act of Yama.

10 Sure there will come succeeding times when brothers and sisters will do acts unmeet for kinsfolk.

Not me, O fair one,-seek another husband, and make thine arm a pillow for thy consort.

11 Is he a brother when no lord is left her? Is she a sister when Destruction cometh?

Forced by my love these many words I utter. Come near, and hold me in thy close embraces.

12 I will not fold mine arms about thy body: they call it sin when one comes near his sister.

Not me,-prepare thy pleasures with another: thy brother seeks not this from thee, O fair one.

13 Alas! thou art indeed a weakling, Yama we find in thee no trace of heart or spirit.

As round the tree the woodbine clings, another will cling albout thee girt as with a girdle.

14 Embrace another, Yami; let another, even as the woodbine rings the tree, enfold thee.

Win thou his heart and let him win thy fancy, and he shall form with thee a blest alliance.

## [10-011] HYMN XI. Agni

1. THE Bull hath yielded for the Bull the milk of heaven: the Son of Aditi can never be deceived.

According to his wisdom Varuna knoweth all: may he, the Holy, hallow times for sacrifice.

2 Gandharvi spake: may she, the Lady of the flood, amid the river's roaring leave my heart untouched.
May Aditi accomplish all that we desire, and may our eldest Brother tell us this as Chief.
3 Yea, even this blessed Morning, rich in store of food, splendid, with heavenly lustre, hath shone out
for man,
Since they, as was the wish of yearning Gods, brought forth that yearning Agni for the assembly as
the Priest.
4 And the fleet Falcon brought for sacrifice from afar this flowing Drop most excellent and keen of
sight,
Then when the Aryan tribes chose as Invoking Priest Agni the Wonder-Worker, and the hymn rose
up.
5 Still art thou kind to him who feeds thee as with grass, and, skilled in sacrifice, offers thee holy
gifts.
When thou, having received the sage's strengthening food with lauds, after long toil, cornest with
many more.
6 Urge thou thy Parents, as a lover ' to delight: the Lovely One desires and craves it from his heart.
The priest calls out, the sacrificer shows his skill, the Asura tries his strength, and with the hymn is
stirred.
7 Far-famed is he, the mortal man, O Agni, thou Son of Strength, who hath obtained thy favour.
He, gathering power, borne onward by his horses, makes his days lovely in his might and splendour.
8 When, Holy Agni, the divine assembly, the sacred synod mid the Gods, is gathered,
And when thou, Godlike One, dealest forth treasures, vouchsafe us, too, our portion of the riches.
9 Hear us, O Agni, in your common dwelling: harness thy rapid car of Amrta.
Bring Heaven and Earth, the Deities' Parents, hither: stay with us here, nor from the Gods be distant.

## [10-012] HYMN XII. Agni

1. HEAVEN and Earth, first by everlasting Order, speakers of truth, are near enough to hear us,
When the God, urging men to worship. sitteth as Priest, assuming all his vital vigour.
2 As God comprising Gods by Law Eternal, bear, as the Chief who knoweth, our oblation,
Smoke-bannered with the fuel, radiant, joyous, better to praise and worship, Priest for ever.
3 When the cow's nectar wins the God completely, men here below are heaven's sustainers.
All the Gods came to this thy heavenly Yajus which from the motley Pair milked oil and water.
4 1 praise your work that ye may make me prosper: hear, Heaven and Earth, Twain Worlds that drop
with fatness.
While days and nights go to the world of spirits, here let the Parents with sweet meath refresh us
5 Hath the King siezed us? How have we offended against his holy ordinance? Who knoweth?
For even Mitra mid the Gods is angry there are both song and strength for those who come not.
6 'Tis hard to understand the Immortal's nature, where she who is akin becomes astranger.
Guard ceaselessly, great Agni, him who ponders Yama's name, easy to be comprehended.

7 They in the synod where the Gods rejoice them, where they are seated in Vivasvan's dwelling,
Have given the Moon his beams, the Sun his splendour-the Two unweariedly maintain their
brightness.
8 The counsel which the Gods meet to consider, their secret plan,-of that we have no knowledge.
There let God Savitar, Aditi, and Mitra proclaim to Varuna that we are sinless.
9 Hear us, O Agni, in your comninn dwell ing: harness thy rapid car, the car of Amrta.
Bring Heaven and Earth, the Deities' Parents, hither: stay with us here, nor from the Gods be distant.

## [10-013] HYMN XIII Havirdhanas.

1. I YOKE with prayer your ancient inspiration: may the laud rise as on the prince's pathway.
All Sons of Immortality shall hear it, all the possessors of celestial natures.
2 When speeding ye came nigh us like twin sisters, religious-hearted votaries brought you forward.
Take your place, ye who know your proper station: be near, be very near unto our Soma.
3 Five paces have I risen from Earth. I follow her who hath four feet with devout observance.
This by the Sacred Syllable have I measured: I purify in the central place of Order,
4 He, for God's sake, chose death to be his portion. He chose not, for men's good, a life eternal
They sacrificed Brhaspati the Rsi. Yama delivered up his own dear body.
5 The Seven flow to the Youth on whom the Maruts wait: the Sons unto the Father brought the
sacrifice.
Both these are his, as his they are the Lords of both: both toil; belonging unto both they prosper well.

## [10-014] HYMN XIV. Yama.

1. HONOUR the King with thine oblations, Yama, Vivasvan's Son, who gathers men together,
Who travelled to the lofty heights above us, who searcbes out and shows the path to many.
2 Yama first found for us a place to dwell in: this pasture never can be taken from
Us.
Men born on earth tread their own paths that lead them whither our ancient Fathers have departed.
3 Mitali prospers there with Kavyas, Yama with Angiras' sons, Brhaspati with Rkvans:
Exalters of the Gods, by Gods exalted, some joy in praise and some in our oblation.
4 Come, seat thee on this bed of grass, O Yama, in company with Angirases and Fathers.
Let texts recited by the sages bring thee O King, let this oblation make thee joyful.
5 Come, Yama, with the Angirases the Holy, rejoice thee here with children of Virupa.
To sit on sacred grass at this our worship, I call Vivasvan, too, thy Father hither.
6 Our Fathers are Angirases, Navagvas, Atharvans, Bhrgus who deserve the Soma.
May these, the Holy, look on us with favour, may we enjoy their gracious loving-kindness.
7 Go forth, go forth upon the ancient pathways whereon our sires of old have gone before us.
'Mere shalt thou look on both the Kings enjoying their sacred food, God Varuna and Yama.

8 Meet Yama, meet the Fathers, meet the merit of free or ordered acts, in highest heaven.
Leave sin and evil, seek anew thy dwelling, and bright with glory wear another body.
9 Go hence, depart ye, fly in all directions: this place for him the Fathers have provided.
Yama bestows on him a place to rest in adorned with days and beams of light and waters.
10 Run and outspeed the two dogs, Sarama's offspring, brindled, four-eyed, upon thy happy pathway.
Draw nigh then to the gracious-minded Fathers where they rejoice in company with Yama.
11 And those two dogs of thine, Yama, the watchers, four-eyed, who look on men and guard the pathway,-
Entrust this man, O King, to their protection, and with prosperity and health endow him.
12 Dark-hued, insatiate, with distended nostrils, Yama's two envoys roam among the People;
May they restore to us a fair existence here and to-day, that we may see the sunlight.
13 To Yama pour the Soma, bring to Yama consecrated gifts:
To Yama sacrifice prepared and heralded by Agni goes.
14 Offer to Yama holy gifts enriched with butter, and draw near:
So may he grant that we may live long days of life among the Gods.
15 Offer to Yama, to the King, oblation very rich in meath:
Bow down before the Rsis of the ancient times, who made this path in days of old.
16 Into the six Expanses flies the Great One in Trkadrukas.
The Gayatri, the Trstup, all metres in Yama are contained.

## [10-015] HYMN XV. Fathers.

1. MAY they ascend, the lowest, highest, midmost, the Fathers who deserve a share of Soma-
May they who have attained the life of spirits, gentle and righteous, aid us when we call them.
2 Now let us pay this homage to the Fathers, to those who passed of old and those who followed,
Those who have rested in the earthly region, and those who dwell among the Mighty Races.
3 1 have attained the gracious-minded Fathers, I have gained son and progeny from Visnu.
They who enjoy pressed juices with oblation seated on sacred grass, come oftenest hither.
4 Fathers who sit on sacred grass, come, help us: these offerings have we made for you; accept them.
So come to us with most auspicious favour, and give us health and strength without a trouble.
5 May they, the Fathers, worthy of the Soma, invited to their favourite oblations.
Laid on the sacred grass, come nigh and listen: may they be gracious unto us and bless us.
6 Bowing your bended knees and seated southward, accept this sacrifice of ours with favour.
Punish us not for any sin, O Fathers, which we through human frailty have committed.
7 Lapped in the bosom of the purple Mornings, give riches to the man who brings oblations.
Grant to your sons a portion of that treasure, and, present, give them energy, ye Fathers.
8 Our ancient Fathers who deserve the Soma, who came, most noble, to our Soma banquet,-
With these let Yama, yearning with the yearning, rejoicing eat our offerings at his pleasure.
9 Come to us, Agni, with the gracioug Fathers who dwell in glowing light, the very Kavyas,

Who thirsted mid the Gods, who hasten hither, oblation winners, theme of singers' praises.
10 Come, Agni, come with countless ancient Fathers, dwellers in light, primeval, God-adorers,
Eaters and drinkers of oblations, truthful, who travel with the Deities and Indra.
11 Fathers whom Agni's flames have tasted, come ye nigh: ye kindly leaders, take ye each your proper place.
Eat sacrificial food presented on the grass: grant riches with a multitude of hero sons.
12 Thou, Agni Jatavedas, when entreated, didst bear the offerings which thou madest fragrant,
And give them to the Fathers who did cat them with Svadha. Eat, thou God, the gifts we bring thee.
13 Thou, Jatavedas, knowest well the number of Fathers who are here and who are absent,
Of Fathers whom we know and whom we know not: accept the sacrifice wellprepared with portions.
14 They who, consumed by fire or not cremated, joy in their offering in the midst of heaven,-
Grant them, O Sovran Lord, the world of spirits and their own body, as thy pleasure wills it.

## [10-016] HYMN XVI. Agni.

1. Burn him not up, nor quite consume him, Agni: let not his body or his skin be scattered.
O Jatavedas, when thou hast matured him, then send him on his way unto the Fathers.
2 When thou hast made him ready, Jatavedas, then do thou give him over to the Fathers.
When he attains unto the life that waits him, he shall become the Deities' controller.
3 The Sun receive thine eye, tne Wind thy spirit; go, as thy merit is, to earth or heaven.
Go, if it be thy lot, unto the waters; go, make thine home in plants with all thy members.
4 Thy portion is the goat: with heat consume him: let thy fierce flame, thy glowing splendour, burn him
With thine auspicious forms, o Jatavedas, bear this man to the region of the pious.
5 Again, O Agni, to the Fathers send him who, offered in thee, goes with our oblations.
Wearing new life let him increase his offspring: let him rejoin a body, Jatavedas.
6 What wound soe'er the dark bird hath inflicted, the emmet, or the serpent, or the jackal,
May Agni who devoureth all things heal it and Soma who hath passed into the Brahmans.
7 Shield thee with flesh against the flames of Agni, encompass thee about with fat and marrow,
So will the Bold One, eager to attack thee with fierce glow fail to girdle and consume thee.
8 Forbear, O Agni, to upset this ladle: the Gods and they who merit Soma love it.
This ladle, this which serves the Gods to drink from, in this the Immortal Deities rejoice them.
9 1 send afar flesh eating Agni, bearing off stains may he depart to Yama's subjects.
But let this other Jatavedas carry oblation to the Gods, for he is skilful.
10 I choose as God for Father-worship Agni, flesh-eater, who hath past within your dwelling,
While looking on this other Jatavedas. Let him light flames in the supreme assembly.
11 With offerings meet let Agni bring the Fathers who support the Law.
Let him announce oblations paid to Fathers and to Deities.

12 Right gladly would we set thee down, right gladly make thee burn and glow.
Gladly bring yearning Fathers nigh to cat the food of sacrifice.
13 Cool, Agni, and again refresh the spot which thou hast scorched and burnt.
Here let the water-lily grow, and tender grass and leafy herb.
14 O full of coolness, thou cool Plant, full of fresh moisture, freshening Herb,
Come hither with the female frog: fill with delight this Agni here.

## [10-017] HYMN XVII. Various Deities.
1. TVASTAR prepares the bridal of his Daughter: all the world hears the tidings and assembles.
But Yama's Mother, Spouse of great Vivasvan, vanished as she was carried to her dwelling.
2 From mortal men they hid the Immortal Lady, made one like her and gave her to Vivasvan.
Saranyu brought to him the Asvin brothers, and then deserted both twinned pairs of children.
3 Guard of the world, whose cattle ne'er are injured, may Pusan bear thee hence, for he hath knowledge.
May he consign thee to these Fathers' keeping, and to the gracious Gods let Agni give thee.
4 May Ayu, giver of all life, protect thee, and bear thee forward on the distant pathway.
Thither let Savitar the God transport thee, where dwell the pious who have passed-before thee.
5 Pusan knows all these realms: may he conduct us by ways that are most free from fear and danger.
Giver of blessings, glowing, all-heroic, may he, thewise and watchful, go before us.
6 Pusan was born to move on distant pathways, on the road far from earth and far from heaven.
To both most wonted places of assembly he travels and returns with perfect knowledge.
7 The pious call Sarasvati, they worship Sarasvati while sacrifice proceedeth.
The pious called Sarasvati aforetime. Sarasvati send bliss to him who giveth.
8 Sarasvati, who camest with the Fathers, with them rejoicing thee in our oblations,
Seated upon this sacred grass be joyful, and give us strengthening food that brings no sickness.
9 Thou, called on as Sarasvati by Fathers who come right forward to our solemn service,
Give food and wealth to present sacrificers, a portion, worth a thousand, of refreshment.
10 The Mother Floods shall make us bright and shining, cleansers of holy oil, with oil shall cleanse us:
For, Goddesses, they bear off all defilement: I, rise up from them purified and brightened.
11 Through days of earliest date the Drop descended on this place and on that which was before it.
I offer up, throughout the seven oblations, the Drop which still to one same place is moving.
12 The Drop that falls, thy stalk which arms have shaken, which from the bosom of the press hath fallen,
Or from the Adhvaryu's purifying filter, I offer thee with heart and cry of Vasat!
13 That fallen Drop of thine, the stalk which from the ladle fell away,
This present God Brhaspati shall pour it forth to make us rich.
14 The plants of earth are rich in milk, and rich in milk is this my speech;
And rich in milk the essence of the Waters: make me pure therewith.

## [10-018] HYMN XVIII. Various Deities.
1. Go hence, O Death, pursue thy special pathway apart from that which Gods are wont to travel.
To thee I say it who hast eyes and hearest: Touch not our offspring, injure not our heroes.
2 As ye have come effacing Mrtyu's footstep, to further times prolonging your existence,
May ye be rich in children and possessions. cleansed, purified, and meet for sacrificing.
3 Divided from the dead are these, the living: now be our calling on the Gods successful.
We have gone forth for dancing and for laughter, tofurther times prolonging our existence.
4 Here I erect this rampart for the living; let none of these, none other, reach this limit.
May they survive a hundred lengthened autumns, and may they bury Death beneath this mountain.
5 As the days follow days in close succession, as with the seasons duly come the seasons,
As each successor fails not his foregoer, so form the lives of these, O great Ordainer.
6 Live your full lives ap! find old age delightful, all of you striving one behind the other.
May Tvastar, maker of fair things, be gracious and lengthen out the days of your existence.
7 Let these unwidowed dames with noble husbands adorn themselves with fragrant balm and unguent.
Decked with fair jewels, tearless, free from sorrow, first let the dames go up to where he lieth.
8 Rise, come unto the world of life, O woman: come, he is lifeless by whose side thou liest.
Wifehood with this thy husband was thy portion, who took thy hand and wooed thee as a lover.
9 From his dead hand I take the bow be carried, that it may be our power and might and glory.
There art thou, there; and here with noble heroes may we o'ercome all hosts that fight against us.
10 Betake thee to the Iap of Earth the Mother, of Earth far-spreading, very kind and gracious.
Young Dame, wool-soft unto the guerdongiver, may she preserve tbee from Destruction's bosom.
11 Heave thyself, Earth, nor press thee downward heavily: afford him easy access, gently tending him.
Cover him, as a mother wraps her skirt about her child, O Earth.
12 Now let the heaving earth be free from motion: yea,- let a thousand clods remain above him.
Be they to him a home distilling fatness, here let them ever be his place of refuge.
13 I stay the earth from thee, while over thee I place this piece of earth. May I be free from injury.
Here let the Fathers keep this pillar firm for thee, and there let Yama make thee an abiding-place.
14 Even as an arrow's feathers, they have set me on a fitting day.
The fit word have I caught and held as 'twere a courser with the rein.

## [10-019] HYMN XIX. Waters or Cows.
1. TURN, go not farther on your way: visit us, O ye Wealthy Ones.
Agni and Soma, ye who bring riches again, secure us wealth.
2 Make these return to us again, bring them beside us once again.
May. Indra give them back to us, and Agni drive them hither-ward.
3 Let them return to us again: under this herdsman let them feed.
Do thou, O Agni, keep them here, and let the wealth we have remain.

4 1 call upon their herdsman, him who knoweth well their coming nigh,

Their parting and their home-return, and watcheth their approach and rest.

5 Yea, let the herdsman, too, return, who marketh well their driving-forth;

Marketh their wandering away, their turning back and coming home.

6 Home-leader, lead them home to us; Indra, restore to us our kine:

We will rejoice in them alive.

7 1 offer you on every side butter and milk and strengthening food.

May all the Holy Deities pour down on us a flood of wealth.

8 O thou Home-leader, lead them home, restore them thou who bringest home.

Four are the quarters of the earth; from these bring back to us our kine,

## [10-020] HYMN XX. Agni.

1. SEND unto us a good and happy mind.

2 1 worship Agni, Youthfullest of Gods, resistless, Friend of laws;
Under whose guard and heavenly light the Spotted seek the Mother's breast:

3 Whom with their mouth they magnify, bannered with flame and homed in light.
He glitters with his row of teeth.

4 Kind, Furtherer of men, he comes, when he hath reached the ends of heaven,
Sage, giving splendour to the clouds.

5 To taste man's offerings, he, the Strong, hath risen erect at sacrifice:
Fixing his dwelling he proceeds.

6 Here are oblation, worship, rest: rapidly comes his furtherance.
To sword-armed Agni come the Gods.

7 With service for chief bliss I seek the Lord of Sacrifice, Agni, whom
They call the Living, Son of Cloud.

8 Blest evermore be all the men who come from us, who magnify Agni with sacrificial gifts.

9 The path he treads is black and white and red, and striped, and brown, crimson, and glorious.
His sire begat him bright with hues of gold.

10 Thus with his thoughts, O Son of Strength, O Agni, hath Vimada, accordant with the Immortals,
Offered thee hymns, soliciting thy favour. Thou hast brought all food, strength, a prosperous
dwelling.

## [10-021] HYMN XXI. Agni.

1. WITH offerings of our own we choose thee, Agni, as Invoking Priest,
For sacrifice with trimmed grass,-at your glad carouse-piercing and brightly shining. Thou art waxing
great.

2 The wealthy ones adorn thee, they who bring us horses as their gift:
The sprinkling ladle, Agni,-at your glad carouse -and glowing offering taste thee. Thou art waxing great.

3 The holy statutes rest by thee, as 'twere with ladles that o'erflow.
Black and white-gleaming colours,-at your glad carouse-all glories thou assurnest. Thou art waxing great.

4 O Agni, what thou deemest wealth, Victorious and Immortal One!
Bring thou to give us vigour,-at your glad carouse -splendid at sacrifices. Thou art waxing great.

5 Skilled in all lore is Agni, he whom erst Atharvan brought to life.
He was Vivasvan's envoy, at your glad carouse-the weIl-loved friend of Yama, Thou art waxing great.

6 At sacrifices they adore thee, Agni, when the rite proceeds.
All fair and lovely treasures-at your glad carouse-thou givest him who offers. Thou art waxing great.

7 Men, Agni, have established thee as welcome Priest at holy rites,
Thee whose face shines with butter,-at your glad carouse-bright, with eyes most observant. Thou art waxing great.

8 Wide and aloft thou spreadest thee, O Agni, with tby brilliant flame.
A Bull art thou when bellowing,-at your glad carouse-thou dost impregn the Sisters. Thou art waxinggreat.

## [10-022] HYMN XXII. Indra.

1. WHERE is famed Indra heard of? With what folk is he renowned to-day as Mitra is,-
Who in the home of Rsis and in secret is extolled with song?

2 Even here is Indra famed, and among us this day the glorious Thunderer is praised,
He who like Mitra mid the folk hath won complete and full renown.

3 He who is Sovran Lord of great and perfect strength, exerter of heroic might,
Who bears the fearless thunder as a father bears his darling son.

4 Harnessing to thy car, as God, two blustering Steeds Of the Wind-God, O Thunderer,
That speed along the shining path, thou making ways art glorified.

5 Even to these dark Steeds of Wind thou of thyself hast come to ride,
Of which no driver may be found, none, be he God or mortal man.

6 When ye approach, men ask you, thee and Usana: Why come ye to our dwelling-place?
Why are ye come to mortal man from distant realms of eapth and heaven?

7 O Indra, thou shalt speak us fair: our holy prayer is offered up.
We pray to thee for help as thou didst strike the monster Susna dead.

8 Around us is the Dasyu, riteless, void of sense, inhuman, keeping alien laws.
Baffle, thou Slayer of the foe, the weapon which this Dasa wields.

9 Hero with Heroes, thou art ours: yea, strong are they whom thou dost help.
In many a place are thy full gifts, and men, like vassals, sing thy praise.

10 Urge thou these heroes on to slay the enemy, brave Thunderer! in the fight with swords.
Even when hid among the tribes of Sages numerous as stars.

11 Swift come those gifts of thine whose hand is prompt to rend and burn, O Hero Thunder-armed:
As thou with thy Companions didst destroy the whole of SuSnia's brood.

12 Let not thine excellent assistance come to us, O Hero Indra, profitless.
May we, may we enjoy the bliss of these thy favours, Thunderer!

13 May those soft impulses of thine, O Indra, be fruitful and innocent to us.
May we know these whose treasures are like those of milch-kine, Thunderer!

14 That Earth, through power of knowing things that may be known, handless and footless yet might
thrive,
Thou slewest, turning to the right, gu;na for every living man.

15 Drink, drink the Soma, Hero Indra; be not withheld as thou art good, O Treasure-giver.
Preserve the singers and our liberal princes, and make us wealthy with abundant riches.

## [10-023] HYMN XXIII. Indra.

1. INDRA, whose right hand wields the bolt, we worship, driver of Bay Steeds seeking sundered
courses.
Shaking his beard with might he hath arisen, casting his weapons forth and dealing bounties.
2 The treasure which his Bay Steeds found at sacrifice,-this wealth made opulent Indra slayer of the
foe.
Rbhu, Rbhuksan, Vaja-he is Lord of Might. The Dasa's very name I utterly destroy.
3 When, with the Princes, Maghavari, famed of old, comes nigh the thunderbolt of gold, and the
Controller's car
Which his two Tawny Coursers draw, then Indra is the Sovran Lord of power whose glory spreads
afar.
4 With him too is this rain of his that comes like herds: Indra throws drops of moisture on his yellow
beard.
When the sweet juice is shed he seeks the pleasant place, and stirs the worshipper as wind disturbs
the wood.
5 We laud and praise his several deeds of valour who, fatherlike, with power hath made us stronger;
Who with his voice slew many thousand wicked ones who spake in varied manners with
contemptuous cries.
6 Indra, the Vimadas have formed for thee a laud, copious, unparalleled, for thee Most Bountiful.
We know the good we gain from him the Mighty One when we attract him as a herdsman calls the
kine.
7 Ne'er may this bond of friendship be dissevered, the Rsi Vimada's and thine, O Indra.
We know thou carest for us as a brother with us, O God, be thine auspicious friendship.

## [10-024] HYMN XXIV. Indra. Asvins.

1. O INDRA, drink this Soma, pressed out in the mortar, full of sweets.
Send down to us great riches,-at your glad carouse-in thousands, O Most healthy. Thou art waxing
great.
2 To thee with sacrifices, with oblations, and with lauds we come.
Lord of all strength and power, grant-at your glad carouse-the best choiceworthy treasure. Thou art
waxing great.
3 Thou who art Lord of precious boons, inciter even of the churl.
Guardian of singers, Indra,-at your glad carouse-save us from woe and hatred. Thou art waxing great.
4 Strong, Lords of Magic power, ye Twain churned the united worlds apart,
When ye, implored by Vimada, Nasatyas, forced apart the pair.
5 When the united pair were rent asunder all the Gods complained.
The Gods to the Nasatyas cried, Bring these together once again.
6 Sweet be my going forth, and rich in sweets be my approach to home.
So, through your Deity, both Gods, enrich us with all pleasantness.

## [10-025] HYMN XXV. Soma.

1. SEND us a good and happy mind, send energy and mental power.
Then-at your glad carouse-let men joy in thy love, Sweet juice! as kine in pasture. Thou. art waxing
great.
2 rn all thy forms, O Soma, rest thy powers that influence the heart.
So also these my longings-at your glad carouse-spread themselves seeking riches. Thou art waxing
great.
3 Even if, O Soma, I neglect thy laws through my simplicity,
Be gracious-at your glad carouse-as sire to son. Preserve us even from slaughter. T'hou. art waxing
great.
4 Our songs in concert go to thee as streams of water to the wells.
Soma, that we may live, grant-at your glad carouse-full powers of mind, like beakers. Thou art waxing
great.
5 O Soma, through thy might who art skilful and strong, these longing men,
These sages, have thrown open-at your glad carouse-the stall of kine and horses. Thou art waxing
great
6 Our herds thou guardest, Soma, and the moving world spread far and wide.
Thou fittest them for living,-at your glad carouse-looking upon all beings. Thou art waxing great.
7 On all sides, Soma, be to us a Guardian ne'er to be deceived.
King, drive away our foemen-at your glad carouse:-let not the wicked rule us. Thou art waxing great.
8 Be watchful, Soma, passing wise, to give us store of vital strength.
More skilled than man to guide us,-at your glad carouse-save us from harm and sorrow. Thou art
waxing great.
9 Chief slayer of our foemen, thou, Indu, art Indra's gracious Friend,
When warriors invoke him-at your glad carouse -in fight, to win them offspring. Thou art waxing
great.
10 Victorious is this gladdening drink: to Indra dear it grows in strength.
This-at your glad carouse -enhanced the mighty hymn of the great sage Kaksivan. Thou art waxing
great.
11 This to the sage who offers gifts brings power that comes from wealth in kine.
This, better than the seven, hath-at your glad carouse-furthered the blind, the cripple. Thou art
waxing great.

## [10-026] HYMN XXVI. Pusan.

1. FORWARD upon their way proceed the ready teams, the lovely songs.
Further them glorious Pusan with yoked chariot, and the Mighty Twain!
2 With sacred hymns let this man here, this singer, win the God to whom
Belong this majesty and might. He hath observed our eulogies.
3 Pusan the Strong hath knowledge of sweet praises even as Indu hath.
He dews our corn with moisture, he bedews the pasture of our kine.
4 We will bethink ourselves of thee, O Pusan, O thou God, as One.
Who brings fulfilment of our hymns, and stirs the singer and the sage.

5 joint-sharer of each sacrifice, the driver of the chariot steeds;
The Rsi who is good to man, the singer's Friend and faithful Guard.
6 One who is Lord of Suca, Lord of Suca caring for herself:
Weaving the raiment of the sheep and making raiment beautiful.
7 The mighty Lord of spoil and wealth, Strong Friend of all prosperity;
He with light movement shakes his beard, lovely and ne'er to be deceived.
8 O Pusan, may those goats of thine turn hitherward thy chariot-pole.
Friend of all suppliants; art thou, born in old time, and arm and sure.
9 May the majestic Pusan speed our chariot with his power and might.
May he increase our store of wealth and listen to this call of ours.

## [10-027] HYMN XXVII. Indra.

1. THIS, singer, is my firm determination, to aid the worshipper who pours the Soma.
I slay the man who brings no milkoblation, unrighteous, powerful, the truth's perverter.
2 Then Will I, when I lead my friends to battle against the radiant persons of the godless,
Prepare for thee at home a vigorous bullock, and pour for thee the fifteen-fold strong juices.
3 I know not him who sayeth and declareth that he hath slain the godless in the battle.
Soon as they see the furious combat raging, men speak forth praises of my vigorous horses.
4 While yet my deeds of might were unrecorded, all passed for Maghavans though I existed.
The potent one who dwelt in peace I conquered, grasped by the foot and slew him on the mountain.
5 None hinder me in mine heroic exploits, no, not the mountains when I will and purpose.
Even the deaf will tremble at my roaring, and every day will dust be agitated.
6 To see the Indraless oblation-drinkers, mean offerers, o'ertaken by destruction!
Then shall the fellies of my car pass over those who have blamed my joyous Friend and scorned him.
7 Thou wast, thou grewest to full vital vigour: an earlier saw, a later one shall see thee.
Two canopies, as 'twere, are round about him who reacheth to the limit of this region.
8 The freed kine eat the barley of the pious. 1 saw them as they wandered with the herdsman.
The calling of the pious rang around them. What portion will these kine afford their owner?
9 When we who cat the grass of men are gathered I am with barley-eaters in the corn-land.
There shall the captor yoke the yokeless bullock, and he who hath been yoked seek one to loose him.
10 There wilt thou hold as true my spoken purpose, to bring together quadrupeds. and bipeds.
I will divide, without a fight, his riches who warreth here, against the Bull, with women.
11 When a man's daughter hath been ever eyeless, who, knowing, will be wroth with her for blindness?
Which of the two will loose on him his anger-the man who leads her home or he who woos her?
12 How many a maid is pleasing to the suitor who fain would marry for her splendid riches?
If the girl be both good and fair of feature, she finds, herself, a friend among the people.

13 His feet have grasped: he eats the man who meets him. Around his head he sets the head for shelter.
Sitting anear and right above he smites us, and follows earth that lies spread out beneath him.
14 High, leafless, shadowless, and swift is Heaven: the Mother stands, the Youngling, loosed, is feeding.
Loud hath she lowed, licking Another's offspring. In what world hath the Cow laid down her udder?
15 Seven heroes from the nether part ascended, and from the upper part came eight together.
Nine from behind came armed with winnowing-baskets: ten from the front pressed o'er the rock's high ridges.
16 One of the ten, the tawny, shared in common, they send to execute their final purpose.
The Mother carries on her breast the Infant of noble form and soothes it while it knows not.
17 The Heroes dressed with fire the fatted wether: the dice were thrown by way of sport and gaming.
Two reach the plain amid the heavenly waters, hallowing and with means of purifying.
18 Crying aloud they ran in all directions: One half of them will cook, and not the other.
To me hath Savitar, this God, declared it: He will perform, whose food is wood and butter.
19 I saw a troop advancing from the distance moved, not by wheels but their own God-like nature.
The Friendly One seeks human generations, destroying, still new bands of evil beings.
20 These my two Bulls, even Pramara's, are harnessed: drive them not far; here let them often linger.
The waters even shall aid him to his object, and the all-cleansing Sun who is above us.
21 This is the thunderbolt which often whirleth down from the lofty misty realm of Surya.
Beyond this realm there is another glory so through old age they pass and feel no sorrow.
22 Bound fast to,every tree the cow is lowing, and thence the man-consuming birds are flying,
Then all this world, though pressing juice for Indra and strengthening the Rsi, is affrighted.
23 In the Gods' mansion stood the first-created, and from their separation came the later.
Three warm the Earth while holding stores of water, and Two of these convey the murmuring moisture.
24 This is thy life: and do thou mark and know it. As such, hide not thyself in time of battle.
He manifests the light and hides the vapour: his foot is never free from robes that veil it.

## [10-028] HYMN XXVIII. Indra. Vasukra.

1. Now all my other friends are here assembled: my Sire-in-law alone hath not come hither.
So might he eat the grain and drink the Soma, and, satisfied, return unto; his dwelling.
2 Loud belloweth the Bull whose horns are sharpened: upon the height above earth's breadth he standeth.
That man I guard and save in all his troubles who fills my flanks when he hath shed the Soma.
3 Men with the stone press out for thee, O Indra, strong, gladdening Soma, and thereof thou drinkest.
Bulls they dress for thee, and of these thou eatest when, Maghavan, with food thou art invited.

4 Resolve for me, O singer, this my riddle: The rivers send their swelling water backward:

The fox steals up to the approaching lion: the jackal drives the wild-boar from the brushwood.

5 How shall I solve this riddle, I, the simple, declare the thought of thee the Wise and Mighty?

Tell us, well knowing, as befits the season: Whitherward is thy prosperous car advancing?

6 Thus do they magnify me, me the mighty higher than even high heaven is my car-pole.

I all at once demolish many thousands: my Sire begot me with no foe to match me.

7 Yea, and the Gods have known me also, Indra, as mighty, fierce and strong in every exploit.

Exulting with the bolt I slaughtered Vrtra, and for the offerer oped with might the cow-stall.

8 The Deities approached, they carried axes; splitting the wood they came with their attendants.

They laid good timber in the fire-receivers, and burnt the grass up where they found it growing.

9 The hare hath swallowed up the opposing razor: I sundered with a clod the distant mountain.

The great will I make subject to the little: the calf shall wax in strength and eat the bullock.

10 There hath the strong-winged eagle left his talon, as a snared lion leaves the trap that caught him.

Even the wild steer in his thirst is captured: the leather strap still holds his foot entangled.

11 So may the leather strap their foot entangle who fatten on the viands of the Brahman.

They all devour the bulls set free to wander, while they themselves destroy their bodies' vigour.

12 They were well occupied with holy duties who sped in person with their lauds to Soma.

Speaking like man, mete to us wealth and booty: in heaven thou hast the name and fame of Hero.

## [10-029] HYMN XXIX. Indra.

1. As sits the young bird on the tree rejoicing, ye, swift Pair, have been roused by clear laudation,

Whose Herald-Priest through many days is Indra, earth's Guardian, Friend of men, the best of Heroes.

2 May we, when this Dawn and the next dance hither, be thy best servants, most heroic Hero!

Let the victorious car with triple splendour bring hitherward the hundred chiefs with Kutsa.

3 What was the gladdening draught that pleased thee, Indra? Speed through our doors to songs, for

thou art mighty.

Why comest thou to me, what gift attracts thee? Fain would I bring thee food most meet to offer.

4 Indra, what fame hath one like thee mid heroes? With what plan wilt thou act? Why hast thou

sought us?

As a true Friend, Wide-Strider! to sustain us, since food absorbs the thought of each among us.

5 Speed happily those, as Surya ends his journey, who meet his wish as bridegrooms meet their

spouses;

Men who present, O Indra strong by nature, with food the many songs that tell thy praises.

6 Thine are two measures, Indra, wide-wellmeted, heaven for thy majesty, earth for thy wisdom.

Here for thy choice are Somas mixed with butter: may the sweet meath be pleasant for thy drinking.

7 They have poured out a bowl to him, to Indra, full of sweet juice, for faithful is his bounty.

O'er earth's expanse hath he grown great by wisdom, the Friend of man, and by heroic exploits.

8 Indra hath conquered in his wars, the Mighty: men strive in multitudes to win his friendship.

Ascend thy chariot as it were in battle, which thou shalt drive to us with gracious favour.

## [10-030] HYMN XXX. Waters.

1. As 'twere with swift exertion of the spirit, let the priest speed to the celestial Waters,

The glorious food of Varuna and Mitra. To him who spreadeth far this laud I offer.

2 Adhvaryus, he ye ready with oblations,, and come with longing to the longing Waters,

Down on which looks the. purple-tinted Eagle. Pour ye that flowing wave this day, deft-handed.

3 Go to the reservoir, O ye Adhvaryus worship the Waters' Child with your oblations.

A consecrated wave he now will give you, so press for him the Soma rich in sweetness.

4 He who shines bright in floods, unfed with fuel, whom sages worship at their sacrifices:

Give waters rich in sweets, Child of the Waters, even those which gave heroic might to Indra:

5 Those in which Soma joys and is delighted, as a young man with fair and pleasant damsels.

Go thou unto those Waters, O Adhvaryu, and purify with herbs what thou infusest.

6 So maidens bow before the youthful gallant who comes with love to them who yearn to meet him.

In heart accordant and in wish one-minded are the Adhvaryus and the heavenly Waters.

7 He who made room for you when fast imprisoned, who freed you from the mighty imprecation,-

Even to that Indra send the meath-rich current, the wave that gratifies the Gods, O Waters.

8 Send forth to him the meath-rich wave, O Rivers, which is your offspring and a well of sweetness,

Oil-balmed, to be implored at sacrifices. Ye wealthy Waters, hear mine invocation.

9 Send forth the rapture-giving wave, O Rivers, which Indra drinks, which sets the Twain in motion;

The well that springeth from the clouds, desirous, that wandereth triple-formed, distilling transport.

10 These winding Streams which with their double current, like cattle-raiders, seek the lower pastures,-

Waters which dwell together, thrive together, Queens, Mothers of the world, these, Rsi, honour.

11 Send forth our sacrifice with holy worship send forth the hymn and prayer for gain of riches.

For need of sacrifice disclose the udder. Give gracious hearing to our call, O Waters.

12 For, wealthy Waters, ye control all treasures: ye bring auspicious intellect and Amrta.

Ye are the Queens of independent riches Sarasvati give full life to the singer!

13 When I behold the Waters coming hither, carrying with them milk and meath and butter,

Bearing the well-pressed Soma juice to Indra, they harmonize in spirit with Adhvaryus.

14 Rich, they are come with wealth for living beings, O friends, Adhvaryus, seat them in their places.

Seat them on holy grass, ye Soma-bringers in harmony with the Offspring of the Waters.

15 Now to this grass are come the longing Waters: the Pious Ones are seated at our worship.

Adbvaryus, press the Soma juice for Indra so will the service of the Gods be easy.

## [10-031] HYMN XXXI. Visvedevas.

1. MAY benediction of the Gods approach us, holy, to aid us with all rapid succours.
Therewith may we be happily befriended, and pass triumphant over all our troubles.
2 A man should think on wealth and strive to win it by adoration on the path of Order,
Counsel himself with his own mental insight, and grasp still nobler vigour with his spirit.
3 The hymn is formed, poured are the allotted portions: as to a ford friends come unto the Wondrous.
We have obtained the power of case and comfort, we haVe become acquainted, with Immortals.
4 Pleased be the Eternal Lord who loves the household with this man whom God Savitar created.
May Bhaga Aryaman grace him with cattle: may he appear to him, and be, delightful.
5 Like the Dawns' dwelling-place be this assembly, where in their might men rich in food have
gathered.
Striving to share the praises of this singer. To us come strengthening and effectual riches!
6 This Bull's most gracious far-extended favour existed first of all in full abundance.
By his support they are maintained in common who in the Asura's mansion dwell together.
7 What was the tree, what wood, in sooth, produced it, from which they fashioned forth the Earth
and Heaven?
These Twain stand fast and wax not old for ever: these have sung praise to many a day and morning.
8 Not only here is this: more is beyond us. He is the Bull, the Heaven's and Earth's supporter.
With power divine he makes his skin a filter, when the Bay Coursers bear him on as Surya.
9 He passes o'er the broad earth like a Stega: he penetrates the world as Wind the mist-cloud.
He, balmed with oil, near Varuna and Mitra, like Agni in the wood, hath shot forth splendour.
10 When suddenly called the cow that erst was barren, she, self-protected, ended all her troubles.
Earth, when the first son sprang from sire and mother, cast up the gami, that which men were
seeking.
11 To Nrsad's son they gave the name of Kainva, and he the brown-hued courser won the treasure.
For him dark-coloured streamed the shining udder: none made it swell for him. Thus Order willed it.

## [10-032] HYMN XXXII. Indra.

1. FORTH speed the Pair to bring the meditating God, benevolent with boons sent in return for
boons.
May Indra graciously accept both gifts from us, when he hath knowledge of the flowing Soma juice.
2 Thou wanderest far, O Indra, through the spheres of light and realms of earth, the region, thou
whom many praise!
Let those who often bring their solemn rites conquer the noisy babblers who present no gifts.
3 More beautiful than beauty must this seem to me, when the son duly careth for his parents' line.
The wife attracts the husband: with a shout of joy the man's auspicious marriage is performed aright.

4 This beauteous place of meeting have I looked upon, where, like milch-cows, the kine order the
marriage train;
Where the Herd's Mother counts as first and best of all, and round her are the seven-toned people of
the choir.
5 The Pious One hath reached your place before the rest: One only moves victorious with the Rudras'
band.
To these your helpers pour our meath, Immortal Gods, with whom your song of praise hath power to
win their gifts.
6 He who maintains the Laws of God informed me that thou wast lying hidden in the waters.
Indra, who knoweth well, beheld and showed thee. By him instructed am I come, O Agni.
7 The stranger asks the way of him who knows it: taught by the skilful guide he travels onward.
This is, in truth, the blessing of instruction: he finds the path that leads directly forward.
8 Even now he breathed: these days hath he remembered. Concealed, he sucked the bosom of his
Mother.
Yet in his youth old age hath come upon him: he hath grown gracious, good, and free from anger.
9 O Kalasa, all these blessings will we bring them, O Kurusravana, who give rich presents.
May he, O wealthy princes, and this Soma which I am bearing in my heart, reward you.

## [10-033] HYMN XXXIII. Various Deities.

1. THE urgings of the people have impelled me, and by,the nearest way I bring you Pusan.
The Universal Gods have brought me safely. The cry was heard, Behold, Dubsasu cometh!
2 The ribs that compass me give pain and trouble me like rival wives.
Indigence, nakedness, exhaustion press me sore: my mind is fluttering like a bird's.
3 As rats eat weavers' threads, cares are consuming me, thy singer, gatakratu, me.
Have mercy on us once, O Indra, Bounteous Lord: be thou a Father unto us.
4 I the priests' Rsi chose as prince most liberal Kurusravana, The son of Trasadasyu's son,
5 Whose three bays harnessed to the car bear me straight onward: I will laud
The giver of a thousand meeds,
6 The sire of Upamasravas, even him whose words were passing sweet,
As a fair field is to its lord.
7 Mark, Upamasravas, his son, mark, grandson of Mitratithi: I am thy father's eulogist.
8 If I controlled Immortal Gods, yea, even were I Lord of men, My liberal prince were living still.
9 None lives, even had he hundred lives, beyond the statute of the Gods
So am I parted from my friend.

## [10-034] HYMN XXXIV. Dice, Etc.

1. SPRUNG from tall trees on windy heights, these rollers transport me as they turn upon the table.
Dearer to me the die that never slumbers than the deep draught of Mujavan's own Soma.
2 She never vexed me nor was angry with me, but to my friends and me was ever gracious.

For the die's sake, whose single point is final, mine own devoted wife I alienated.
3 My wife holds me aloof, her mother hates me: the wretched man finds none to give him comfort.
As of a costly horse grown old and feeble, I find not any profit of the gamester.
4 Others caress the wife of him whose riches the die hath coveted, that rapid courser:
Of him speak father, mother, brothers saying, We know him not: bind him and take him with you.
5 When I resolve to play with these no longer, my friends depart from me and leave me lonely.
When the brown dice, thrown on the board, have rattled, like a fond girl I seek the place of meeting.
6 The gamester seeks the gambling-house, and wonders, his body all afire, Shall I be lucky?
Still do the dice extend his eager longing, staking his gains against his adversary.
7 Dice, verily, are armed with goads and driving-hooks, deceiving and tormenting, causing grievous woe.
They give frail gifts and then destroy the man who wins, thickly anointed with the player's fairest good.
8 Merrily sports their troop, the three-and-fifty, like Savitar the God whose ways are faithful.
They bend not even to the mighty's anger: the King himself pays homage and reveres them.
9 Downward they roll, and then spring quickly upward, and, handless, force the man with hands to serve them.
Cast on the board, like lumps of magic charcoal, though cold themselves they bum the heart to ashes.
10 The gambler's wife is left forlorn and wretched: the mother mourns the son who wanders homeless.
In constant fear, in debt, and seeking riches, he goes by night unto the home of others.
11 Sad is the gambler when he sees a matron, another's wife, and his well-ordered dwelling.
He yokes the brown steeds in the early morning, and when the fire is cold sinks down an outcast.
12 To the great captain of your mighty army, who hath become the host's imperial leader,
To him I show my ten extended fingers: I speak the truth. No wealth am I withholding.
13 Play not with dice: no, cultivate thy corn-land. Enjoy the gain, and deem that wealth sufficient.
There are thy cattle there thy wife, O gambler. So this good Savitar himself hath told me.
14 Make me your friend: show us some little mercy. Assail us not with your terrific fierceness.
Appeased be your malignity and anger, and let the brown dice snare some other captive.

### [10-035] HYMN XXXV. Visvedevas.
1. THESE fires associate with Indra are awake, bringing their light when first the Dawn begins to shine.
May Heaven and Earth, great Pair, observe our holy work. We claim for us this day the favour of the Gods.
2 Yea, for ourselves we claim the grace of Heaven and Earth, of Saryanavan, of the Hills and Mother Streams.
For innocence we pray to Surya and to Dawn. So may the flowing Soma bring us bliss to-day.
3 May the great Twain, the Mothers, Heaven and Earth, this day preserve us free from sin for peace and happiness.
May Morning sending forth her light drive sin afar. We pray to kindled Agni for felicity.

4 May this first Dawn bring us the host of gracious Gods: rich, may it richly shine for us who strive for wealth.
The wrath of the malignant may we keep afar. We pray to kindled Agni for feilicity.
5 Dawns, who come forward with the bright beams of the Sun, and at your earliest flushing bring to us the light,
Shine ye on us to-day auspicious, for renown. We pray to kindled Agni for felicity.
6 Free from all sickness may the Mornings come to us, and let our fires mount upward with a lofty blaze.
The Asvin Pair have harnessed their swift-moving car. We pray to kindled Agni for felicity.
7 Send us to-day a portion choice and excellent, O Savitar, for thou art he who dealeth wealth.
I cry to Dhisana, Mother of opulence. We pray to kindled Agni for felicity.
8 Further me this declaring of Eternal Law, the Law of Gods, as we mortals acknowledge it!
The Sun goes up beholding all the rays of morn. We pray to kindled Agni for felicity.
9 This day we pray with innocence in strewing grass, adjusting pressing-stones, and perfecting the hymn.
Thou in the Adityas' keeping movest restlessly. We pray to kindled Agni for felicity.
10 To our great holy grass I bid the Gods at morn to banquet, and will seat them as the seven priests,-
Varuna, Indra, Mitra, Bhaga for our gain. We pray to kindled Agni for felicity.
11 Come hither, O Adityas, for our perfect weal: accordant help our sacrifice that we may thrive.
Pusan, Brhaspati, Bhaga, both Asvins, and enkindled Agni we implore for happiness.
12 Adityas, Gods, vouchsafe that this our home may be praise-worthy, prosperous, our heroes' sure defence,
For cattle, for our sons, for progeny, for life. We pray to kindled Agni for felicity.
13 This day may all the Maruts, all he near us with aid: may all our fires be well enkindled.
May all Gods come to us with gracious favour. May spoil and wealth he ours, and all possessions.
14 He whom ye aid, O Deities, in battle, whom ye protect and rescue from affliction,
Who fears no danger at your milk-libation, -such may we be to feast the Gods, ye Mighty.

### [10-036] HYMN XXXVI. Visvedevas.
1. THERE are the Dawn and Night, the grand and beauteous Pair, Earth, Heaven, and Varuna, Mitra, and Aryaman.
Indra I call, the Maruts, Mountains, and the Floods, Adityas, Heaven and Earth, the Waters, and the Sky.
2 May Dyaus and Prthivi, wise, true to Holy Law, keep us in safety from distress and injury.
Let not malignant Nirrti rule over us. We crave to-day this gracious favour of the Gods.
3 Mother of Mitra and of opulent Varuna, may Aditi preserve us safe from all distress.
May we obtain the light of heaven without a foe. We crave this gracious favour of the Gods to-day.
4 May ringing press-stones keep the Raksasas afar, ill dream, and Nirrti, and each voracious fiend.
May the Adityas and the Maruts shelter us. We crave this gracious favour of the Gods to-day.
5 Full flow libations; on our grass let Indra sit; Brhaspati the singer laud with Sama hymns!
Wise be our hearts' imaginings that we may live. We crave this gracious favour of the Gods to-day.

6 Ye Asvins, make our sacrifice ascend to heaven, and animate the rite that it may send us bliss,
Offered with holy oil, with forward-speeding rein. We crave the gracious favour of the Gods to-day.
7 Hither I call the band of Maruts, swift to hear, great, purifying, bringing bliss, to he our Friends.
May we increase our wealth to glorify our name. We crave this graciousfavour of the Gods to-day.
8 We bring the Stay of Life, who makes the waters swell, swift-hearing, Friend of Gods, who waits on sacrifice.
May we control that Power, Soma whose rays are bright. We crave this gracious favour of the Gods to-day.
9 Alive ourselves, with living sons, devoid of guilt, may we win this with winners by fair means to win.
Let the prayer-haters bear our sin to every side. We crave this gracious favour of the Gods to-day.
10 Hear us, O ye who claim the worship of mankind, and give us, O ye Gods, the gift for which we pray,
Victorious wisdom, fame with heroes and with wealth. We crave to-day this gracious favour of the Gods.
11 We crave the gracious favour of the Gods to-day, great favour of great Gods, sublime and free from foes,
That we may gain rich treasure sprung from hero sons. We crave this gracious favour of the Gods today.
12 In great enkindled Agni's keeping, and, for bliss, free from all sin before Mitra and Varuna.
May we share Savitar's best animating help. We crave this gracious favour of the Gods to-day.
13 All ye, the Gods whom Savitar the Father of truth, and Varuna and Mitra govern,
Give us prosperity with hero children, and opulence in kine and various treasure.
14 Savitar, Savitar from cast and westward, Savitar, Savitar from north and southward,
Savitar send us perfect health and comfort, Savitar let our days of life be lengthened!

## [10-037] HYMN XXXVII. Surya.

1. Do homage unto Varuna's and Mitra's Eye: offer this solemn worship to the Mighty God,
Who seeth far away, the Ensign, born of Gods. Sing praises unto Surya, to the Son of Dyaus.
2 May this my truthful speech guard me on every side wherever heaven and earth and days are spread abroad.
All else that is in motion finds a place of rest: the waters ever flow and ever mounts the Sun.
3 No godless man from time remotest draws thee down when thou art driving forth with winged dappled Steeds.
One lustre waits upon thee moving to the cast, and, Surya, thou arisest with a different light.
4 O Surya, with the light whereby thou scatterest gloom, and with thy ray impellest every moving thing,
Keep far from us all feeble, worthless sacrifice, and drive away disease and every evil dream.
5 Sent forth thou guardest well the Universe's law, and in thy wonted way arisest free from wrath.
When Surya, we address our prayers to thee to-day, may the Gods favour this our purpose and desire.
6 This invocation, these our words may Heaven and Earth, and Indra and the Waters and the Maruts hear.
Ne'er may we suffer want in presence of the Sun, and, living happy lives, may we attain old age.
7 Cheerful in spirit, evermore, and keen of sight, with store of children, free from sickness and from sin,
Long-living, may we look, O Surya, upon thee uprising day by day, thou great as Mitra is!

8 Surya, may we live long and look upon thee still, thee, O Far-seeing One, bringing the glorious light,
The radiant God, the spring of joy to every eye, as thou art mounting up o'er the high shining flood.
9 Thou by whose lustre all the world of life comes forth, and by thy beams again returns unto its rest,
O Surya with the golden hair, ascend for us day after day, still bringing purer innocence.
10 Bless us with shine, bless us with perfect daylight, bless us with cold, with fervent heat and lustre.
Bestow on us, O Surya, varied riches, to bless us in our home and when we travel.
11 Gods, to our living creatures of both kinds vouchsafe protection, both to bipeds and to quadrupeds,
That they may drink and eat invigorating food. So grant us health and strength and perfect innocence.
12 If by some grievous sin we have provoked the Gods, O Deities, with the tongue or thoughtlessness of heart,
That guilt, O Vasus, lay upon the Evil One, on him who ever leads us into deep distress.

## [10-038] HYMN XXXVIII. Indra.

1. O INDRA, in this battle great and glorious, in this loud din of war help us to victory,
Where in the strife for kine among bold ring-decked men arrows fly all around and heroes are subdued.
2 At home disclose to us opulence rich in food, streaming with milk, O Indra, meet to be renowned.
Sakra, may we be thine, the friendly Conqueror's: even as we desire, O Vasu, so do thou.
3 The godless man, much-lauded Indra, whether he be Dasa or be Arya, who would war with us,-
Easy to conquer he for thee, with us, these foes: with thee may we subdue them in the clash of fight.
4 Him who must be invoked by many and by few, who standeth nigh with comfort in the war of men,
Indra, famed Hero, winner in the deadly strife, let us bring hitherward to-day to favour us.
5 For, Indra, I have heard thee called Self. capturer, One, Steer! who never yields, who urges even the churl.
Release thyself from Kutsa and come hither. How shall one like thee sit still bound that he may not move?

## [10-039] HYMN XXXIX. Asvins.

1. As 'twere the name of father, easy to invoke, we all assembled here invoke this Car of yours,
Asvins, your swiftly-rolling circumambient Car which he who worships must invoke at eve and dawn.
2 Awake all pleasant strains and let the hymns flow forth: raise up abundant fulness: this is our desire.
Asvins, bestow on us a glorious heritage, and give our princes treasure fair as Soma is.
3 Ye are the bliss of her who groweth old at home, and helpers of the slow although he linger last.
Men call you too, Nasatyas, healers of the blind, the thin and feeble, and the man with broken bones.
4 Ye made Cyavana, weak and worn with length of days, young again, like a car, that he had power to move.
Ye lifted up the son of Tugra from the floods. At our libations must all these your acts be praised.
5 We will declare among the folk your ancient deeds heroic; yea, ye were Physicians bringing health.
You, you who must be lauded, will we bring for aid, so that this foe of ours, O Asvins, may believe.

6 Listen to me, O Asvins; I have cried to you. Give me-your aid as sire and mother aid their son.

Poor, without kin or friend or ties of blood am I. Save me before it be too late, from this my curse.

7 Ye, mounted on your chariot brought to Vimada the comely maid of Purumitra as a bride.

Ye, came unto the calling of the weakling's dame, and granted noble offspring to the happy wife.

8 Ye gave a ain the vigour of his youthful life to tge sage Kali when old age was coming nigh.

Ye rescued Vandana and raised him from the pit, and in a moment gave Vispala power to move.

9 Ye Asvins Twain, endowed with manly strength, brought forth Reblia when hidden in the cave and well-nigh dead,

Freed Saptavadliri, and for Atri caused the pit heated with fire to be a pleasant resting-place.

10 On Pedu ye bestowed, Asvins, a courser white, mighty with nine-and-ninety varied gifts of strength,

A horse to be renowned, who bore his friend at speed, joy-giving, Bhaga-like to be invoked of men.

11 From no side, ye Two Kings whom none may check or stay, doth grief, distress, or danger come u on the man

Whom, Asvins swift to hear, borne on your glowing path, ye with your Consort make the foremost in the race.

12 Come on that Chariot which the Rbhus wrought for you, the Chariot, Asvins, that is speedier than thought,

At harnessing whereof Heaven's Daughter springs to birth, and from Vivasvan come auspicious Night and Day.

13 Come, Conquerors of the sundered mountain, to our home, Asvins who made the cow stream milk for Sayu's sake,

Ye who delivered even from the wolf's deep throat and set again at liberty the swallowed quail.

14 We have prepared this laud for you, O Asvins, and, like the Bhrgus, as a car have framed it,

Have decked it as a maid to meet the bridegroom, and brought it as a son, our stay for ever.

## [10-040] HYMN XL. Asvins.

1. YOUR radiant Chariot-whither goes it on its way?-who decks it for you, Heroes, for its happy course,

Starting at daybreak, visiting each morning every house, borne hitherward through prayer unto the sacrifice?

2 Where are ye, Asvins, in the evening, where at morn? Where is your haltingplace, where rest ye for the night?

Who brings you homeward, as the widow bedward draws her husband's brother, as the bride attracts the groom?

3 Early ye sing forth praise as with a herald's voice, and, meet for worship, go each morning to the house.

Whom do ye ever bring to ruin? Unto whose libations come ye, Heroes, like two Sons of Kings?

4 Even as hunters follow two wild elephants, we with oblations call you down at morn and eve.

To folk who pay you offierings at appointed times, Chiefs, Lords of splendour, ye bring food to strengthen them.

5 To you, O Asvins, came the daughter of a King, Ghosa, and said, O Heroes, this I beg of you:

Be near me in the day, he near me in the night: help me to gain a car-borne chieftain rich in steeds.

6 O Asvins, ye are wise: as Kutsa comes to men, bring your car nigh the folk of him who sings your praise.

The bee, O Asvins, bears your honey in her mouth, as the maid carries it purified in her hand.

7 To Bhujyu and to Vasa ye come near with help, O Asvins, to Sinjara and to Usana.

Your worshipper secures your friendship for himself. Through your protection I desire felicity.

8 Krsa and Sayu ye protect, ye Asvins Twain: ye Two assist the widow and the worshipper;

And ye throw open, Asvins, unto those who win the cattle-stall that thunders with its serenfold mouth.

9 The Woman hath brought forth, the Infant hath appeared, the plants of wondrous beauty

straightway have sprung up.

To him the rivers run as down a deep descent, and he this day becomes their master and their lord.

10 They mourn the living, cry aloud, at sacrifice: the men have set their thoughts upon a distant cast.

A lovely thing for fathers who have gathered here,-a joy to husbands,-are the wives their arms shall clasp

11 Of this we have no knowledge. Tall it forth to us, now the youth rests within the chambers of the bride.

Fain would we reach the dwelling of the vigorous Steer who loves the kine, O Asvins: this is our dcsirc.

12 Your favouring grace hath come, ye Lords of ample wealth: Asvins, our longings are stored up within your hearts.

Ye, Lords of splendour, have become our twofold guard: may we as welcome friends reach Aryaman's abode.

13 Even so, rejoicing in the dwelling-place of man, give hero sons and riches to the eloquent.

Make a ford, Lords of splendour, where men well may drink: remove the spiteful tree-stump standing in the path.

14 O Asvins, Wonder-Workers, Lords of lustre, where and with what folk do ye delight yourselves today?

Who hath detained them with him? Whither are they gone? Unto what sage's or what worshipper's abode?

## [10-041] HYMN XLI. Asvins.

1. THAT general Car of yours, invoked by many a man, that comes to our libations, three-wheeled,

meet for lauds,

That circumambient Car, worthy of sacrifice, we call with our pure hymns at earliest flush of dawn.

2 Ye, O Nasatyas, mount that early-harnessed Car, that travels early, laden with its freight of balm,

Wherewith ye, Heroes, visit clans who sacrifice, even the poor man's worship where the priest attends.

3 If to the deft Adhvaryu with the meath in hand, or to the Kindler firm in strength, the household friend,

Or to the sage's poured libations ye approach, come thence, O Asvins, now to drink the offered meath.

## [10-042] HYMN XLII. Indra.

1. EVEN as an archer shoots afar his arrow, offer the laud to him with meet adornment.

Quell with your voice the wicked's voice, O sages. Singer, make Indra rest beside the Soma.

2 Draw thy Friend to thee like a cow at milking: O Singer, wake up Indra as a lover.

Make thou the Hero haste to give us riches even as a vessel filled brimful with treasure.

3 Why, Maghavan, do they call thee Bounteous; Giver? Quicken me: thou, I hear, art he who quickens.

Sakra, let my intelligence be active, and bring us luck that finds great wealth, O Indra.

4 Standing, in battle for their rights, together, the people, Indra, in the fray invoke thee.

Him who brings gifts the Hero makes his comrade: with him who pours no juice he seeks not friendship.

5 Whoso with plenteous food for him expresses strong Somas as much quickly-coming treasure,

For him he overthrows in early morning his swift well-weaponed foes, and slays the tyrant.

6 He unto whom we offer praises, Indra, Maghavan, who hath joined to ours his wishes,-
Before him even afar the foe must tremble: low before him must bow all human glories.
7 With thy fierce bolt, O God invoked of many, drive to a distance from afar the foeman.
O Indra, give us wealth in corn and cattle, and make thy singer's prayer gain strength and riches.
8 Indra, the swallower of strong libations rich in the boons they bring, the potent Somas,
He, Maghavan, will not restrict his bounty he brings much wealth unto the Soma-presser.
9 Yea, by superior play he wins advantage, when he, a gambler, piles his gains in season.
Celestial-natured, he o'erwhelms with riches the devotee who keeps not back his treasure.
10 O Much-invoked, may we subdue all famine and evil want with store of grain and cattle.
May we allied, as first in rank, with princes obtain possessions by our own exertion.
11 Brhaspati protect us from the rearward, and from above, and from below, from sinners!
May Indra from the front, and from the centre, as Friend to friends, vouchsafe us room and freedom.

## [10-043] HYMN XLIII. Indra.

1. IN perfect unison all yearning hymns of mine that find the light of heaven have sung forth Indra's praise.
As wives embrace their lord, the comely bridegroom, so they compass Maghavan about that he may help.
2 Directed unto thee my spirit never strays, for I have set my hopes on thee, O Much-invoked!
Sit, Wonderful! as King upon the sacred grass, and let thy drinking-place be by the Soma juice.
3 From indigence and hunger Indra turns away: Maghavan hath dominion over precious wealth.
These the Seven Rivers flowing on their downward path increase the vital vigour of the potent Steer.
4 As on the fair-leafed tree rest birds, to Indra flow the gladdening Soma juices that the bowls contain.
Their face that glows with splendour through their mighty power hath found the shine of heaven for man, the Aryas' light.
5 As in the game a gambler piles his winnings, so Maghavan, sweeping all together, gained the Sun
This mighty deed of thine none other could achieve, none, Maghavan, before thee, none in recent time.
6 Maghavan came by turns to all the tribes of men: the Steer took notice of the people's songs of praise.
The man in whose libations Sakra hath delight by means of potent Somas vanquisheth his foes.
7 When Soma streams together unto Indra flow like waters to the river, rivulets to the lake,
In place of sacrifice sages exalt his might, as the rain swells the corn by moisture sent from heaven.
8 He rushes through the region like a furious Bull, he who hath made these floods the dames of worthy lords.
This Maghavan hath found light for the man who brings oblation, sheds the juice, and promptly pours his gifts.
9 Let the keen axe come forth together with the light: here be,.as erst, the teeming cow of sacrifice.
Let the Red God shine bright with his refulgent ray, and let the Lord of heroes glow like heaven's clear sheen.
10 O Much-invoked, may we subdue all famine and evil want with store of grain and cattle.
May we allied, as first in rank, with princes obtain possessions by our own exertion.

11 Brhaspati protect us from the rearward, and from above, and from below, from sinners.
May Indra from the front, and from the centre, as Friend to friends, vouchsafe us room and freedom.

## [10-044] HYMN XLIV. Indra.

1. MAY Sovran Indra come to the carousal, he who by Holy Law is strong and active,
The overcomer of all conquering forces with his great steer-like power that hath no limit.
2 Firm-seated is thy car, thy Steeds are docile; thy hand, O King, holds, firmly grasped, the thunder.
On thy fair path, O Lord of men, come quickly: we will increase thy powers when thou hast drunken.
3 Let strong and mighty Steeds who bear this Mighty Indra, the Lord of men, whose arm wields thunder,
Bring unto us, as sharers of our banquet, the Steer of conquering might, of real vigour.
4 So like a Bull thou rushest to the Lord who loves the trough, the Sage, the prop of vigour, in the vat,
Prepare thine energies, collect them in thyself: be for our profit as the Master of the wise.
5 May precious treasures come to us-so will I pray. Come to the votary's gift offered with beauteous laud.
Thou art the Lord, as such sit on this holy grass: thy vessels are inviolate as Law commands.
6 Far went our earlist invocation of the Gods, and won us glories that can never be surpassed.
They who could not ascend the ship of sacrifice, sink down in desolation, trembling with alarm.
7 So be the others, evil-hearted, far away, whose horses, difficult to harness, have been yoked.
Here in advance men stand anear to offer gifts, by whom full many a work that brings reward is done.
8 He firmly fixed the plains and mountains as they shook. Dyaus thundered forth and made the air's mid-region quake.
He stays apart the two confronting worlds; he sings lauds in the potent Soma's joy when he hath drunk.
9 I bear this deftly-fashioned goad of thine, wherewith thou, Maghavan, shalt break the strikers with the hoof.
At this libation mayst thou be well satisfied. Partake the juice, partake the worship, Maghavan.
10 O Much-invoked, may we subdue all famine and evil want with store of grain and cattle.
May we allied, as first in rank, with princes obtain possessions by our own exertion.
11 Brhaspati protect us from the rearward, and from above, and from below, from sinners.
May Indra from the front and from the centre, as Friend to friends, vouchsafe us room and freedom.

## [10-045] HYMN XLV. Agni.

1. FIRST Agni sprang to life from out of Heaven: the second time from us came Jatavedas.
Thirdly the Manly-souled was in the waters. The pious lauds and kindles him the Eternal.
2 Agni, we know thy three powers in three stations, we know thy forms in many a place divided.
We know what name supreme thou hast in secret: we know the source from which thou hast proceeded.
3 The Manly-souled lit thee in sea and waters, man's Viewer lit thee in the breast of heaven,
There as thou stoodest in the third high region the Steers increased thee in the water's bosom.

4 Agni roared out, like Dyaus what time he thunders: he licked the ground about the plants he flickered.
At once, when born, he looked around enkindled, and lightened heaven and earth within with splendour.
5 The spring of glories and support of riches, rouser of thoughts and guardian of the Soma,
Good Son of Strength, a King amid the waters, in forefront of the Dawns he shines enkindled.
6 Germ of the world, ensign of all creation, be sprang to life and filled the earth and heavens.
Even the firm rock he cleft when passing over, when the Five Tribes brought sacrifice to Agni.
7 So among mortals was Immortal Agni stablished as holy wise and willing envoy.
He waves the red smoke that he lifts above him, striving to reach the heavens with radiant lustre.
8 Like gold to look on, far he shone refulgent, beaming imperishable life for glory,
Agni by vital powers became immortal when his prolific Father Dyaus begat him.
9 Whoso this day, O God whose flames are lovely, prepares a cake, O Agni, mixt with butter,
Lead thou and further him to higher fortune, to bliss bestowed by Gods, O thou Most Youthful.
10 Endow him, Agni, with a share of glory, at every song of praise sung forth enrich him.
Dear let him be to Surya, dear to Agni, preeminent with son and children's children.
11 While, Agni, day by day men pay thee worship they win themselves all treasures worth the wishing.
Allied with thee, eager and craving riches, they have disclosed the stable filled with cattle.
12 Agni, the Friend of men, the Soma's keeper, Vaisvanara, hath been lauded by the Rsis.
We will invoke benignant Earth and Heaven: ye Deities, give us wealth with hero children.

## [10-046] HYMN XLVI. Agni.

1. STABLISHED for thee, to lend thee vital forces, Giver of wealth, Guard of his servant's body.
The Great Priest, born, who knows the clouds, Abider with men, is seated in the lap of waters.
2 Worshipping, seeking him with adoration like some lost creature followed by its footprints,
Wise Bhrgus, yearning in their hearts, pursued him, and found him lurking where the floods are gathered.
3 On the Cow's forehead, with laborious searching, Trita, the offspring of Vibhiavas, found him.
Born in our houses, Youthful, joy-bestower, he now becomes the central point of brightness.
4 Yearning, with homage, they have set and made him blithe Priest among mankind, oblation-bearer,
Leader of rites and Purifier, envoy of men, as sacrifice that still advances.
5 The foolish brought the ne'er-bewildered forward, great, Victor, Song-inspirer, Fort-destroyer.
Leading the Youth gold-bearded, like a courser gleaming with wealth, they turned their hymn to profit.
6 Holding his station firmly in the houses, Trita sat down within his home surrounded
Thence, as Law bids, departs the Tribes' Companion having collected men with no compulsion.
7 His are the fires, eternal, purifying, that make the houses move, whose smoke is shining,
White, waxing in their strength, for ever stirring, and sitting in the wood; like winds are Somas.

8 The tongue of Agni bears away the praisesong, and, through his care for Earth, her operations.
Him, bright and radiant, living men have stablished as their blithe Priest, the Chief of Sacrificers.
9 That Agni, him whom Heaven and Earth engendered, the Waters. Tvastar, and with might, the Bhrgus,
Him Matarisvan and the Gods have fashioned holy for man and first to be entreated.
10 Agni, whom Gods have made oblationbearer, and much-desiring men regard as holy,
Give life to him who lauds thee when he worships, and then shall glorious men in troops adore thee.

## [10-047] HYMN XLVII. Indra Vaikuntha.

1. THY right hand have we grasped in ours, O Indra, longing for treasure, Treasure-Lord of treasures!
Because we know thee, Hero, Lord of cattle: vouchsafe us mighty and resplendent riches.
2 Wealth, fully armed, good guard and kind protector, sprung from four seas, the prop and stay of treasures,
Fraught with great bounties, meet for praise and glory; vouchsafe us mighty and resplendent riches.
3 Wealth, with good Brahmans, Indra! God-attended, high, wide, and deep, arid based on broad foundations,
Strong, with famed Rsis, conquering our foemen: vouchsafe us mighty and resplendent riches.
4 Victorious, winning strength, with hero sages, confirmed in power, most useful, wealth-attracting,
True, Indra! crushing forts and slaying Dasyus: vouchsafe us mighty and resplendent riches.
5 Wealthy in heroes and in cars and horses, strength hundredfold and thousandfold, O Indra,
With manly sages, happy troops, Iight-winning: vouchsafe us mighty and resplentdent riches.
6 To Saptagu the sage, the holy-minded, to him, Brhaspati, the song approaches,
Angiras' Son who must be met with homage: vouchsafe us mighty and reslendent riches.
7 My lauds, like envoys, craving loving-kindness, go forth to Indra with their strong entreaty,
Moving his heart and uttered by my spirit: vouchsafe us mighty and resplendent riches.
8 Grant us the boon for which I pray, O Indra, a spacious home unmatched among the people.
To this may Heaven and Earth accord approval: vouchsafe us mighty and resplendent riches.

## [10-048] HYMN XLVIII. Indra Vaikuntha.

1. I WAS the first possessor of all precious gear: the wealth of every man I win and gather up.
On me as on a Father living creatures call; I deal enjoyment to tho. man who offers gifts.
2 I, Indra, am Atharvan's stay and firm support: I brought forth kine to Trita from the Dragon's grasp.
I stripped the Dasyus of their manly might, and gave the cattle-stalls to Matarigvan and Dadhyac.
3 For me hath Tvastar forged the iron thunderbolt: in me the Gods have centred intellectual power.
My sheen is like the Sun's insufferably bright: men honour me as Lord for past and future deeds.
4 I won myself these herdi of cattle, steeds and kine, and gold in ample store, with my destructive bolt.
I give full many a thousand to the worshipper, what time the Somas and the lauds have made me glad.
5 Indra am I none ever wins my wealth from me never at any time am I a thrall to death.

Pressing the Soma, ask riches from me alone: ye, Purus, in my friendship shall not suffer harm.

6 These, breathing loud in fury, two and two, who caused Indra to bring his bolt of thunder to the fray,
The challengers, I struck with deadly weapon down: firm stand what words the God speaks to his worshippers.

This One by stronger might I conquered singly; yea, also two: shall three prevail against me?
Like many sheaves upon the floor I thrash them. How can my foes, the Indraless, revile me?

8 Against the Gungus I made Atithigva strong, and kept him mid the folk like Vrtra-conqueringstrength,
When I won glory in the great foe-slaying fight, in battle where Karanja fell, and Parnaya.

9 With food for mine enjoyment Sapya Nami came: he joined me as a friend of old in search of kine.
As I bestowed on him an arrow for the fight I made him worthy of the song apd hymn of praise.

10 One of the two hath Soma, seen within it; the Herdsman with the bone shows forth the other.
He, fain to fight the Bull whose horns were sharpened, stood fettered in the demon's ample region.

11 I, as a God, ne'er violate the statutes of Gods, of Vasus, Rudriyas, Adityas.
These Gods have formed me for auspicious vigour, unconquered and invincible for ever.

### [10-049] HYMN XLIX. Indra Vaikuntha.

1. I HAVE enriched the singer with surpassing wealth; I have allowed the holy hymn to strengthen me.
I, furtherer of him who offers sacrifice, have conquered in each fight the men who worship not.

2 The People of the heavens, the waters, and the earth have stablished me among the Gods with Indra's name.
I took unto myself the two swift vigorous Bays that speed on divers paths, and the fierce bolt for strength.

3 With deadly blows I smote Atka for Kavi's sake; I guarded Kutsa well with these saving helps.
As Susna's slayer I brandished the dart of death: I gave not up the Aryan name to Dasyu foes.

4 Smadibha, Tugra, and the Vetasus I gave as prey to Kutsa, father-like, to succour him.
I was a worthy King to rule the worshipper, when I gave Tuji dear inviolable gifts.

5 I gave up Mrgaya to Srutarvan as his prey because he ever followed me and kept my laws.
For Ayu's sake I caused Veta to bend and bow, and into Savya's hand delivered Padgrbhi.

6 1, I crushed Navavastva of the lofty car, the Dasa, as the Vrtra-slayer kills the fiends;
When straightway on the region's farthest edge I brought the God who makes the lights to broaden and increase.

7 I travel round about borne onward in my might by the fleet-footed dappled Horses of the Sun.
When man's libation calls me to the robe of state I soon repel the powerful Dasyu with my blows.

8 Stronger am I than Nabus, I who slew the seven: I glorified with might Yadu and Turvaga.
I brought another low, with strength I bent his strength: I let the mighty nine-and-ninety wax in power.

9 Bull over all the streams that flow along the earth, I took the Seven Rivers as mine own domain.
I, gifted with great wisdom, spread the floods abroad: by war I found for man the way to high success.

10 I set within these cows the white milk which no God, not even Tvastar's self, had there deposited,-

Much-longed-for, in the breasts, the udders of the kine, the savoury sweets of meath, the milk and Soma juice.

11 Even thus hath Indra Maghavan, truly bounteous, sped Gods and men with mighty operation.
The pious glorify all these thine exploits, Lord of Bay Coursers, Strong, and Selfresplendent.

### [10-050] HYMN L. Indra Vaikuntha.

1. I LAUD your Mighty One who joyeth in the juice, him who is shared by all men, who created all;
Indra, whose conquering strength is powerful in war, whose fame and manly vigour Heaven and Earth revere.

2 He with his friend is active, lauded, good to man, Indra who must be glorified by one like me.
Hero, Lord of the brave, all cars are thy delight, warring with Vrtra, or for waters, or for spoil.

3 Who are the men whom thou wilt further, Indra, who strive to win thy bliss allied with riches?
Who urged thee forward to exert thy power divine, to valour, in the war for waters on their fields?

4 Thou, Indra, through the holy prayer art mighty, worthy of sacrifice at all libations.
In every fight thou castest heroes on the ground: thou art the noblest song, O Lord of all the folk.

5 Help now, as Highest, those who toil at sacrifice: well do the people know thy great protecting might.
Thou shalt be Everlasing, Giver of success yea, on all these libations thou bestowest strength.

6 All these libations thou makest effectual, of which thou art thyself supporter, Son of Power.
Therefore thy vessel is to be esteemed the best, sacrifice, holy text, prayer, and exalted speech.

7 They who with flowing Soma pray to thee, O Sage, to pour on them thy gifts of opulence and wealth,
May they come forward, through their spirit, on the path of bliss, in the wild joy of Soma juice effused.

### [10-051] HYMN LI. Agni. Gods.

1. LARGE was that covering, and firm of texture, folded wherein thou enteredst the waters.
One Deity alone, O Jatavedas Agni, saw all thy forms in sundry places.

2 What God hath seen me? Who of all their number clearly beheld my forms in many places?
Where lie, then, all the sacred logs of Agni that lead him God-ward, Varuna and Mitra?

3 In many places, Agni Jatavedas, we sought thee hidden in the plants and waters.
Then Yama marked thee, God of wondrous splendour! effulgent from thy tenfold secret dwelling,

4 I fled in fear from sacrificial worship, Varuna, lest the Gods should thus engage me.
Thus were my forms laid down in many places. This, as my goal, I Agni saw before me.

5 Come; man is pious and would fain do worship, he waits prepared: in gloom thou, Agni, dwellest.
Make pathways leading God-ward clear and easy, and bear oblations with a kindly spirit.

6 This goal mine elder brothers erst selected, as he who drives a car the way to travel.
So, Varuna, I fled afar through terror, as flies the wild-bull from an archer's bowstring.

7 We give thee life unwasting, Jatavedas, so that, employed, thou never shalt be injured.
So, nobly born! shalt thou with kindly spirit bear to the Gods their share of men's oblations.

8 Grant me the first oblations and the latter, entire, my forceful shares of holy presents,
The soul of plants, the fatness of the waters, and let there be long life, ye Gods, to Agni.
9 Thine be the first oblations and the latter, entire, thy forceful shares of holy presents.
Let all this sacrifice be thine, O Agni, and let the world's four regions bow before thee.

### [10-052] HYMN LII. Gods.

1. INSTRUCT me, all ye Gods, how I, elected your Priest, must seat me here, and how address you.
Instruct me how to deal to each his portion, and by what ' path to bring you man's oblation.
2 I sit as Priest most skilled in sacrificing: the Maruts and all Deities impel me.
Asvins, each day yours is the Adhvaryu's duty: Brahman and wood are here: 'tis yours to offer.
3 Who is the Priest? Is he the Priest of Yama? On whom is thrust this God-appointed honour?
He springs to life each month, each day that passes; so Gods have made him their oblation-bearer.
4 The Gods have made me bearer of oblations, who slipped away and passed through many troubles.
Wise Agni shall ordain for us the worship, whether five-wayed, threefold, or seven-threaded.
5 So will I win you strength and life for ever. O Gods, that I may give you room and freedom.
To Indra's arms would I consign the thunder; in all these battles shall he then be victor.
6 The Deities three hundred and thirty-nine, have served and honoured Agni,
Strewn sacred grass, anointed him with butter, and seated him as Priest, the Gods' Invoker.

### [10-053] HYMN LIII. Agni Saucika Gods.

1. HE hath arrived, he whom we sought with longing, who skilled in sacrifice well knows its courses.
Let him discharge his sacrificial duties: let him sit down as Friend who was before Us.
2 Best Priest, he hath been won by being seated, for he hath looked on the well-ordered viands.
Come, let us worship Gods who must be worshipped, and pouring oil, laud those who should be lauded.
3 Now hath he made the feast of Gods effective: now have we found the secret tongue of worship.
Now hath he come, sweet, robed in vital vigour, and made our calling on the Gods effective.
4 This prelude of my speech I now will utter, whereby we Gods may quell our Asura foemen.
Eaters of strengthening food who merit worship, O ye Five Tribes, be pleased with mine oblation.
5 May the Five Tribes be pleased with mine oblation, and the Cow's Sons and all who merit worship.
From earthly trouble may the earth protect us, and air's mid realm from woe that comes from heaven.
6 Spinning the thread, follow the region's splendid light: guard thou the path ways well which wisdom hath prepared.
Weave ye the knotless labour of the bards who sing: be Manu thou, and bring the Heavenly People forth.
7 Lovers of Soma, bind the chariot traces fast: set ye the reins in order and embellish them.
Bring hitherward the car with seats where eight may sit, whereon the Gods have brought the treasure that we love.

8 Here flows Asmanvati: hold fast each other, keep yourselves up, and pass, my friends, the river.
There let us leave the Powers that brought no profit, and cross the flood to Powers that are auspicious.
9 Tvastar, most deft of workmen, knew each magic art, bringing most blessed bowls that hold the drink of Gods.
His axe, wrought of good metal, he is sharpening now, wherewith the radiant Brahmanaspati will cut.
10 Now, O ye Sapient Ones, make ye the axes sharp wherewith ye fashion bowls to hold the Amrta.
Knowing the secret places make ye ready that whereby the Gods have gotten immortality.
11 Ye with a secret tongue and dark intention laid the maiden deep within, the calf within the mouth.
They evermore are near us with their gracious help: successful is the song that strives for victory.

### [10-054] HYMN LIV. Indra.

1. I SING thy fame that, Maghavan, through thy Greatness the heavens and earth invoked thee in their terror,
Thou, aiding Gods, didst quell the power of Dasas, what time thou holpest many a race, O Indra.
2 When thou wast roaming, waxen strong in body, telling thy might, Indra, among the people,
All that men called thy battles was illusion: no foe hast thou to-day, nor erst hast found one.
3 Who are the Rsis, then, who comprehended before our time the bounds of all thy greatness?
For from thy body thou hast generated at the same time the Mother and the Father.
4 Thou, Mighty Steer, hast four supremest natures, Asura natures that may ne'er be injured.
All these, O Maghavan, thou surely knowest, wherewith thou hast performed thy great achievements.
5 Thou hast all treasures in thy sole possession, treasures made manifest and treasures hidden.
Defer not thou, O Maghavan, my longing: thou, art Director, Indra, thou art Giver.
6 To him who set the light in things of splendour, and with all sweetness blent essential sweetness,
To Indra hath this welcome hymn that strengthens been uttered by the votary Brhaduktha.

### [10-055] HYMN LV. Indra.

1. FAR is that secret name by which, in terror, the worlds invoked thee and thou gavest vigour
The earth and heaven thou settest near each other, and Maghavan, madest bright thy Brother's Children.
2 Great is that secret name and far-extending, whereby thou madest all that is and shall be.
The Five Tribes whom he loveth well have entered the light he loveth that was made aforetime.
3 He filled the heaven and earth and all between them, Gods five times sevenfold in their proper seasons.
With four-and-thirty lights he looks around him, lights of one colour though their ways are divers.
4 As first among the lights, O Dawn, thou shonest, whereby thou broughtest forth the Stay of Increase,
Great art thou, matchless is thine Asura nature, who, high above, art kin to those beneath thee.
5 The old hath waked the young Moon from his slumber who runs his circling course with many round him.

Behold the Gods' high wisdom in its greatness: he who died yesterday to-day is living.

6 Strong is the Red Bird in his strength, great Hero, who from of old hath had no nest to dwell in.

That which he knows is truth and never idle: he wins and gives the wealth desired of many.

7 Through these the Thunderer gained strong manly vigour, through whom he waxed in power to

smite down Vrtra,-

Who through the might of Indra's operation came forth as Gods in course of Law and Order.

8 All-strong, performing works with his companion, All-marking, rapid Victor, Curse-averter,

The Hero, waxing, after draughts of Soma, blew far from heaven the Dasyus with his weapon.

## [10-056] HYMN LVI. Visvedevas.

1. HERE is one light for thee, another yonder: enter the third and he therewith united.

Uniting with a body be thou welcome, dear to the Gods in their sublimest birthplace.

2 Bearing thy body, Vajin, may thy body afford us blessing and thyself protection.

Unswerving, stablish as it were in heaven thine own light as the mighty God's supporter.

3 Strong Steed art thou: go to the yearning Maidens with vigour, happily go to heaven and praises:

Fly happily to the Gods with easy passage, according to the first and faithful statutes.

4 Part of their grandeur have the Fathers also gained: the Gods have seated mental power in them as

Gods.

They have embraced within themselves all energies, which, issuing forth, again into their bodies pass.

5 They strode through all the region with victorious might, establishing the old immeasurable laws.

They compassed in their bodies all existing things, and streamed forth offspring in many successive forms.

6 In two ways have the sons established in his place the Asura who finds the light, by the third act,

As fathers, they have set their heritage on earth, their offspring, as a thread continuously spun out.

7 As in a ship through billows, so through regions of air, with blessings, through toils and troubles

Hath Brhaduktha brought his seed with glory, and placed it here and in the realms beyond us.

## [10-057] HYMN LVII. Visvedevas.

1. LET us not, Indra, leave the path, the Soma-presser's sacrifice: Let no malignity dwell with us.

2 May we obtain, completely wrought, the thread spun out to reach the Gods,

That perfecteth the sacrifice.

3 We call the spirit hither with the Soma of our parted sires, Yea, with the Fathers' holy hymns.

4 Thy spirit come to thee again for wisdom, energy, and lire, That thou mayst long behold the sun!

5 O Fathers, may the Heavenly Folk give us our spirit once again, That we may be with those who live.

6 O Soma with the spirit still within us, blest with progeny, May we be busied in the law.

## [10-058] HYMN LVIII. Manas or Spirit.

1. THY spirit, that went far away to Yama to Vivasvan's Son, We cause to come to thee again that thou mayst live and sojourn here.

2 Thy spirit, that went far away, that passed away to earth and heaven,

We cause to come to thee again that thou mayst live and sojourn here.

3 Thy spirit, that went far away, away to the four-cornered earth, We cause to come to thee again that thou mayst live and sojourn here.

4 Thy spirit, that went far away to the four quarters of the world, We cause to come to thee again that thou mayst live and sojourn here.

5 Thy spirit, that went far away, away unto the billowy sea, We cause to come to thee again that thou mayst live and sojourn here.

6 Thy spirit, that went far away to beams of light that flash and flow,

We cause to come to thee again that thou mayst live and sojourn here.

7 Thy spirit, that went far away, went to the waters and the plants,

We cause to come to thee again that thou mayst live and sojourn here.

8 Thy spirit, that went far away, that visited the Sun and Dawn. We cause to come to thee again that thou mayst live and sojourn here.

9 Thy spirit, that went far away, away to lofty mountain heights, We cause to come to thee again that thou mayst live and sojourn here.

10 Thy spirit, that went far away into this All, that lives and moves,

We cause to come to thee again that thou mayst live and sojourn here.

11 Thy spirit, that went far away to distant realms beyond our ken,

We cause to come to thee again that thou mayst live and sojourn here.

12 Thy spirit, that went far away to all that is and is to be, We cause to come to thee again that thou mayst live and sojourn heie.

## [10-059] HYMN LIX. Nirrti and Others.

1. His life hath been renewed and carried forward as two men, car-borne, by the skilful driver.

One falls, then seeks the goal with quickened vigour. Let Nirrti depart to distant places.

2 Here is the psalm for wealth, and food, in plenty: let us do many deeds to bring us glory.

All these our doings shall delight the singer. Let Nirrti depart to distant places.

3 May we o'ercome our foes with acts of valour, as heaven is over earth, hills over lowlands.

All these our deeds the singer hath considered. Let Nirrti depart to distant places.

4 Give us not up as prey to death, O Sorna still let us look upon the Sun arising.

Let our old age with passing days be kindly. Let Nirrti depart to distant places.

5 O Asuniti, keep the soul within us, and make the days we have to live yet longer.

Grant that we still may look upon the sunlight: strengthen thy body with the oil we bring thee.

6 Give us our sight again, O Asuniti, give us again our breath and our enjoyment.

Long may we look upon the Sun uprising; O Anumati, favour thou and bless us.

7 May Earth restore to us our vital spirit, may Heaven the Goddess and mid-air restore it.

May Soma give us once again our body, and Pusan show the Path of peace and comfort.
8 May both Worlds bless Subandhu, young Mothers of everlasting Law.
May Heaven and Earth uproot and sweep iniquity and shame away: nor sin nor sorrow trouble thee.
9 Health-giving medicines descend sent down from heaven in twos and threes,
Or wandering singly on the earth. May Heaven and Earth uproot and sweep iniquity and shame
away: nor sin nor sorrow trouble thee.
10 Drive forward thou the wagon-ox, O Indra, which brought Usinarani's wagon hither.
May Heaven and Earth uproot and sweep iniquity and shame away: nor sin nor sorrow trouble thee.

## [10-060] HYMN LX. Asamati and Others.-

1. BRINGING our homage we have come to one magnificent in look.
Glorified of the mighty Gods
2 To Asamati, spring of gifts, lord of the brave, a radiant car,
The conqueror of Bhajeratha
3 Who, when the spear hath armed his hand, or even weaponless o'erthrows
Men strong as buffaloes in fight;
4 Him in whose service flourishes Iksvaku, rich and dazzling-bright.
As the Five Tribes that are in heaven.
5 Indra, support the princely power of Rathaprosthas matched by none,
Even as the Sun for all to see.
6 Thou for Agastya's sister's sons yokest thy pair of ruddy steeds.
Thou troddest niggards under foot, all those, O King, who brought no gifts.
7 This is the mother, this the sire, this one hath come to be thy life.
What brings thee forth is even this. Now come, Subandhu, get thee forth.
8 As with the leather thong they bind the chariot yoke to hold it fast,
So have I held thy spirit fast, held it for life and not for death, held it for thy security.
9 Even as this earth, the mighty earth, holds fast the monarchs of the wood.
So have I held thy spirit fast, held it for life and not for death, held it for thy security.
10 Subandlin's spirit I have brought from Yarna, from Vivasvan's Son,
Brought it for life and not for death, yea, brought it for security.
11 The wind blows downward from on high, downward the Sun-God sends his heat,
Downward the milch-cow pours her milk: so downward go thy pain and grief.
12 Felicitous is this mine hand, yet more felicitous is this.
This hand contains all healing balms, and this makes whole with gentle touch.

## [10-061] HYMN LXI. Visvedevas.

1. THE welcome speaker in the storm of battle uttered with might this prayer to win the Asvins,
When the most liberal God, for Paktha, rescued his parents, and assailed the seven Hotras.
2 Cyavana, purposing deceptive presents, with all ingredients, made the altar ready.
Most sweet-voiced Turvayana poured oblations like floods of widely fertilizing water.

3 To his oblations, swift as thought, ye hurried, and welcomed eagerly the prayers he offered.
With arrows in his hand the Very Mighty forced from him all obedience of a servant.
4 I call on you the Sons of Dyaus, the Asvins, that a dark cow to my red kine be added.
Enjoy my sacrifice, come to my viands contented, not deceiving expectation. '
10 Uttering praise to suit the rite Navagvas came speedily to win the damsel's friendship.
They who approached the twice-strong stable's keeper, meedless would milk the rocks that naught
had shaken.
11 Swift was new friendship with the maid they quickly accepted it as genuine seed and bounty.
Milk which the cow Sabardugha had yielded was the bright heritage which to thee they offered.
12 When afterwards they woke- and missed the cattle, the speaker thus in joyful mood addressed
them:
Matchless are singers through the Vasu's nature; he bringeth them all food and all possessions.
13 His followers then who dwelt in sundry places came and desired too slay the son of Nrsad.
Resistless foe, be found the hidden treasure of Susna multiplied in numerous offipring.
14 Thou, called Effulgence, in whose threefold dwelling, as in the light of heaven, the Gods are
sitting,
Thou who art called Agni or Jatavedas, Priest, hear us, guileless Priest of holy worship.
15 And, Indra, bring, that I may laud and serve them, those Two resplendent glorious Nasatyas,
Blithe, bounteous, man-like, to the sacrificer, honoured among our men with offered viands.
16 This King is praised and honoured as Ordainer: himself the bridge, the Sage speeds o'er the
waters.
He hath stirred up Kaksivan, stirred up Agni, as the steed's swift wheel drives the felly onward.
17 Vaitarana, doubly kinsman, sacrificer, shall milk the cow who ne'er hath calved, Sabardhu,
When I encompass Varuna and Mitra with lauds, and Aryaman in safest shelter.
18 Their kin, the Prince in heaven, thy nearest kinsman, turning his thought to thee thus speaks in
kindness:
This is our highest bond: I am his offspring. How many others came ere I succeeded?
19 Here is my kinship, here the place I dwell in: these are my Gods; I in full strength am present.
Twice-born am I, the first-born Son of Order: the Cow milked this when first she had her being.
20 So mid these tribes he rests, the friendly envoy, borne on two paths, refulgent Lord of fuel.
When, like a line, the Babe springs up erectly, his Mother straight hath borne him strong to bless us.
21 Then went the milch-kine forth to please the damsel, and for the good of every man that liveth.
Hear us, O wealthy Lord; begin our worship. Thou hast grown mighty through Asvaghna's virtues.
22 And take thou notice of us also, Indra, for ample riches, King whose arm wields thunder!
Protect our wealthy nobles, guard our princes unmenaced near thee, Lord of Tawny Coursers.
23 When he goes forth, ye Pair of Kings, for booty, speeding to war and praise to please the singer,-

I was the dearest sage of those about him,-let him lead these away and bring them safely.

24 Now for this noble man's support and comfort, singing with easy voice we thus implore thee:
Impetuous be his son and fleet his courser: and may I be his priest to win him glory.

25 If, for our strength, the priest with adoration to win your friendship made the laud accepted,
That laud shall be a branching road to virtue for every one to whom the songs are suited.

26 Glorified thus, with holy hymns and homage:-Of noble race, with Waters, God-attended
May he enrich us for our prayers and praises: now can the cow be milked; the path is open.

27 Be to us, then, ye Gods who merit worship, be ye of one accord our strong protection,
Who went on various ways and brought us vigour, ye who are undeceivable explorers.

## [10-062] HYMN LXII. Visvedevas, Etc.

1. YE, who, adorned with guerdon through the sacrifice, have won you Indra's friendship and eternal
life,
Even to you be happiness, Angirases. Welcome the son of Manu, ye who are most wise.

2 The Fathers, who drave forth the wealth in cattle, have in the year's courses cleft Vala by Eternal
Law:
A lengthened life be yours, O ye Angirases. Welcome the son of Manu, ye who are most wise.

3 Ye raised the Sun to heaven by everlasting Law, and spread broad earth, the Mother, out on every
side.
Fair wealth of progeny be yours, Angirases. Welcome the son of Manu, ye who are most wise.

4 This kinsman in your dwellingplace speaks pleasant words: give ear to this, ye Rsis, children of the
Gods.
High Brahman dignity be yours, Angirases. Welcome the son of Manu, ye who are most wise.

5 Distinguished by their varied form, these Rsis have been deeply moved.
These are the sons of Angirases: from Agni have they sprung to life.

6 Distinguished by their varied form, they sprang from Agni, from the sky.
Navagva and Dasagva, noblest Angiras, he giveth bounty with the Gods.

7 With Indra for associate the priests have cleared the stable full of steeds and kine,
Giving to me a thousand with their eightmarked cars, they gained renown among the Gods.

8 May this man's sons be multiplied; like springing corn may Manu grow,
Who gives at once in bounteous gift a thousand kine, a hundred steeds.

9 No one attains to him, as though a man would grasp the heights of heaven.
Savarnya's sacrificial meed hath broadened like an ample flood.

10 Yadu and Turva, too, have given two Dasas, well-disposed, to serve,
Together with great store of kine.

11 Blest be the hamlet's chief, most liberal Manu, and may his bounty rival that of Surya.
May the God let Ssvarni's life be leng
thened, with whom, unwearied, we have lived and prospered.

## [10-063] HYMN LXIII. Visvedevas.

1. MAY they who would assume kinship from far away, Vivasvan's generations, dearly loved of men,
Even the Gods who sit upon the sacred grass of Nahusa's son Yayati, bless and comfort us.

2 For worthy of obeisance, Gods, are all your names, worthy of adoration and of sacrifice.
Ye who were born from waters, and from Aditi, and from the earth, do ye here listen to my call.

3 I will rejoice in these Adityas for my weal, for whom the Mother pours forth water rich in balm,
And Dyaus the Infinite, firm as a rock, sweet milk,-Gods active, strong through lauds, whose might
the Bull upholds.

4 Looking on men, ne'er slumbering, they by their deserts attained as Gods to lofty immortality.
Borne on refulgent cars, sinless, with serpents' powers, they robe them, for our welfare, in the height
of heaven.

5 Great Kings who bless us, who have come to sacrifice, who, ne'er assailed, have set their mansion
in the sky,-
These I invite with adoration and with hymns, mighty Adityas, Aditi, for happiness.

6 Who offereth to you the laud that ye accept, O ye All-Gods of Manu, many as ye are?
Who, Mighty Ones, will prepare for you the sacrifice to bear us over trouble to felicity?

7 Ye to whom Manu, by seven priests, with kindled fire, offered the first oblation with his heart and
soul,
Vouchsafe us, ye Adityas, shelter free from fear, and make us good and easy paths to happiness.

8 Wise Deities, who have dominion o'er the world, ye thinkers over all that moves not and that
moves,
Save us from uncommitted and committed sin, preserve us from all sin to-day for happiness.

9 In battles we invoke Indra still swift to hear, and all the holy Host of Heaven who banish grief,
Agni, Mitra, and Varuna that we may gain, Dyays, Bhaga, Maruts, Prthivi for happiness:

10 Mightily-saving Earth, incomparable Heaven the good guide Aditi who gives secure defence
The well-oared heavenly Ship that lets no waters in, free from defect, will we ascend for happiness.

11 Bless us, all Holy Ones, that we may have your help, guard and protect us from malignant injury.
With fruitful invocation may we call on you, Gods, who give ear to us for grace, for happiness.

12 Keep all disease afar and sordid sacrifice, keep off the wicked man's malicious enmity.
Keep far away from us all hatred, O ye Gods, and give us ample shelter for our happiness.

13 Untouched by any evil, every mortal thrives, and, following the Law, spreads in his progeny.
Whom ye with your good guidance, O Adityas, lead safely through all his pain and grief to happiness.

14 That which ye guard and grace in battle, O ye Gods, ye Maruts, where the prize is wealth, where
heroes win,
That conquering Car, O Indra, that sets forth at dawn, that never breaks, may we ascend for
happiness.

15 Vouchsafe us blessing in our paths and desert tracts, blessing in waters and in battle, for the light;

Blessing upon the wombs that bring male children forth, and blessing, O ye Maruts, for the gain of
wealth.
16 The noblest Svasti with abundant riches, who comes to what is good by distant pathway,-
May she at home and far away preserve us, and dwell with us under the Gods' protection
17 Thus hatb the thoughtful sage, the son of Plati, praised you, O Aditi and all Adityas,
Men are made rich by those who are Immortal: the Heavenly Folk have been extolled by Gaya.

## [10-064] HYMN LXIV. Visvedevas.

1. WHAT God, of those who hear, is he whose well-praised name we may record in this our sacrifice;
and how?
Who will be gracious? Who of many give us bliss? Who out of all the Host will come to lend us aid?
2 The will and thoughts within my breast exert their power: they yearn with love, and fly to all the
regions round.
None other comforter is found save only these: my longings and my hopes are fixt upon the Gods.
3 To Narasamsa and to Pusan I sing forth, unconcealable Agni kindied by the Gods.
To Sun and Moon, two Moons, to Yama in the heaven, to Trita, Vata, Dawn, Night, and the Atvins
Twain.
4 How is the Sage extolled whom the loud singers praise? What voice, what hymn is used to laud
Brhaspati?
May Aja-Ekapad with Rkvans swift to hear, and Ahi of the Deep listen unto our call.
5 Aditi, to the birth of Daksa and the vow thou summonest the Kings Mitra and Varuna.
With course unchecked, with many chariots Aryaman comes with the seven priests to tribes of varied
sort.
6 May all those vigorous Coursers listen to our cry, hearers of invocation, speeding on their way;
Winners of thousands where the priestly meed is won, who gather of themselves great wealth in
every race.
7 Bring ye Purandbi, bring Vayu who yokes his steeds, for friendship bring ye Pusan with your songs
of praise:
They with one mind, one thought attend the sacrifice, urged by the favouring aid of Savitar the God.
8 The thrice-seven wandering Rivers, yea, the mighty floods, the forest trees, the mountains, Agni to
our aid,
Krsanu, Tisya, archers to our gathering-place, and Rudra strong amid the Rudras we invoke.
9 Let the great Streams come hither with their mighty help, Sindhu, Sarasvati, and Sarayu with
waves.
Ye Goddess Floods, ye Mothers, animating all, promise us water rich in fatness and in balm.
10 And let Brhaddiva, the Mother, hear our call, and Tvastar, Father, with the Goddesses and Dames.
Rbhuksan, Vaja, Bhaga, and Rathaspati, and the sweet speech of him who labours guard us well!
11 Pleasant to look on as a dwelling rich in food is the blest favour of the Maruts, Rudra's Sons.
May we be famed among the folk for wealth in kine. and ever come to you, ye Gods, with sacred food.

12 The thought which ye, O Maruts, Indra and ye Gods have given to me, and ye, Mitra and Varuna,-
Cause this to grow and swell like a milchcow with milk. Will ye not bear away my songs upon your
car?
13 O Maruts, do ye never, never recollect and call again to mind this our relationship?
When next we meet together at the central point, even there shall Aditi confirm our brotherhood.
14 The Mothers, Heaven and Earth, those mighty Goddesses, worthy of sacrifice, ecune with the race
of Gods.
These Two with their support uphold both Gods and men, and with the Fathers pour the copious
genial stream.
15 This invocation wins all good that we desire Brhaspati, highly-praised Aramati, are here,
Even where the stone that presses meath rings loudly out, and where the sages make their voices
heard with hymns.
16 Thus hath the sage, skilled in loud singers' duties, desiring riches, yearning after treasure,
Gaya, the priestly singer, with his praises and hymns contented the Celestial people.
17 Thus hath the thoughtful sage the son of Plati, praised you, O Aaiti and all Adityas.
Men are made rich by those who are Immortal: the Heavenly Folk have been extolled by Gaya.

## [10-065] HYMN LXV. Visvedevas.

I. MAY Agni, Indra, Mitra, Varuna consent, Aryaman, Vayu, Pusan, and Sarasvati,
Adityas, Maruts, Visnu, Soma, lofty Sky, Rudra and Aditi, and Brahmanaspati.
2 Indra and Agni, Hero-lords when Vrtra fell, dwelling together, speeding emulously on,
And Soma blent with oil, putting his greatness forth, have with their power filled full the mighty
firmament.
3 Skilled in the Law I lift the hymn of praise to these, Law-strengtheners, unassailed, and great in
majesty.
These in their wondrous bounty send the watery sea: may they as kindly Friends send gifts to make
us great.
4 They with their might have stayed Heaven, Earth, and Prthivi, the Lord of Light, the firmament, -
the lustrous spheres.
Even as fleet-foot steeds who make their masters glad, the princely Gods are praised, most bountiful
to man.
5 Bring gifts to Mitra and to Varuna who, Lords of all, in spirit never fail the worshipper,
Whose statute shines on high through everlasting Law, whose places of sure refuge are the heavens
and earth.
6 The cow who yielding milk goes her appointed way hither to us as leader of holy rites,
Speaking aloud to Varuna and the worshipper, shall with oblation serve Vivasvan and the Gods.
7 The Gods whose tongue is Agni dwell in heaven, and sit, aiders of Law, reflecting, in the seat of
Law.
They propped up heaven and then brought waters with their might, got sacrifice and in a body made
it fair.

8 Born in the oldest time, the Parents dwelling round are sharers of one mansion in the home of Law.
Bound by their common vow Dyaus, Prthivi stream forth the moisture rich in oil to Varuna the Steer.
9 Parjanya, Vata, mighty, senders of the rain, Indra and Vayu, Varuna, Mitra, Aryaman:
We call on Aditi, Adityas, and the Gods, those who are on the earth, in waters, and in heaven.
10 Tvastar and Vayu, those who count as Rbhus, both celestial Hotar-priests, and Dawn for happiness,
Winners of wealth, we call, and wise Brhaspati, destroyer of our foes, and Soma Indra's Friend.
11 They generated prayer, the cow, the horse, the plants, the forest trees, the earth, the waters, and the hills.
These very bounteous Gods made the Sun mount to heaven, and spread the righteous laws of Aryas o'er the land.
12 O Asvins, ye delivered Bhujyu from distress, ye animated Syava, Vadhrmati's son.
To Vimada ye brought his consort Kamadyu, and gave his lost Visnapu back to Visvaka.
13 Thunder, the lightning's daughter, Aja-Ekapad, heaven's bearer, Sindhu, and the waters of the sea:
Hear all the Gods my words, Sarasvati give ear together with Purandhi and with Holy Thoughts.
14 With Holy Thoughts and with Purandhi may all Gods, knowing the Law immortal, Manu's Holy Ones,
Boon-givers, favourers, finders of light, and Heaven, with gracious love accept my songs, my prayer, my hymn.
15 Immortal Gods have I, Vasistha, lauded, Gods set on high above all other beings.
May they this day grant us wide space and freedom: ye Gods, preserve us evermore with blessings.

## [10-066] HYMN LXVI. Visvedevas.

1. I CALL the Gods of lofty glory for our weal, the makers of the light, well-skilled in sacrifice;
Those who have waxen mightily, Masters of all wealth, Immortal, strengthening Law, the Gods whom Indra leads.
2 For the strong band of Maruts will we frame a hymn: the chiefs shall bring forth sacrifice for Indra's troop,
Who, sent by Indra and advised by Varuna, have gotten for themselves a share of Surya's light
3 May Indra with the Vasus keep our dwelling safe, and Aditi with Adityas lend us sure defence.
May the God Rudra with the Rudras favour us, and Tvastar with the Dames further us to success.
4 Aditi, Heaven and Earth, the great eternal Law, Indra, Visnu, the Maruts, and the lofty Sky.
We call upon Adityas, on the Gods, for help, on Vasus, Rudras, Savitar of wondrous deeds.
5 With Holy Thoughts Sarasvan, firm-lawed Varuna, great Vayu, Pusan, Visnu, and the Asvins Twain,
Lords of all wealth, Immortal, furtherers of prayer, grant us a triply-guarding refuge from distress.
6 Strong be the sacrifice, strong be the Holy Ones, strong the preparers of oblation, strong the Gods.
Mighty be Heaven and Earth, true to eternal Law, strong be Parjanya, strong be they who laud the Strong.

7 To win us strength I glorify the Mighty Twain, Agni and Soma, Mighty Ones whom many laud.
May these vouchsafe us shelter with a triple guard, these whom the strong have served in worship of the Gods.
8 Potent, with firm-fixt laws, arranging sacrifice, visiting solemn rites in splendour of the day,
Obeying Order, these whose priest is Agni, free from falsehood, poured the waters out when Vrtra died.
9 The Holy Ones engendered, for their several laws, the heavens and earth, the waters, and the plants and trees.
They filled the firmament with heavenly light for help: the Gods embodied Wish and made it beautiful.
10 May they who bear up heaven, the Rbhus deft of hand, and Vata and Parjanya of the thundering Bull,
The waters and the plants, promote the songs we sing: come Bhaga, Rati, and the Vaijns to my call.
11 Sindhu, the sea, the region, and the firmament, the thunder, and the ocean, Aja-Ekapad,
The Dragon of the Deep, shall listen to my words, and all the Deities and Princes shall give ear.
12 May we, be yours, we men, to entertain the Gods: further our sacrifice and give it full success.
Adityas, Rudras, Vasus, givers of good gifts, quicken the holy hymns which we are singing now
13 I follow with success upon the path of Law the two celestial Hotars, Priests of oldest time.
We pray to him who dwelleth near, Guard of the Field, to all Immortal Gods who never are remiss.
14 Vasistha's sons have raised their voices, like their sire. Rsi-like praying to the Gods for happiness.
Like friendly-minded kinsmen, come at our desire, O Gods, and shake down treasures on us from above.
15 Immortal Gods have I, Vasistha, lauded, Gods set on high above all other beings.
May they this day grant us wide space and freedom: ye Gods, preserve us evermore with blessings.

## [10-067] HYMN LXVII. Brhaspati.

1. THIS holy hymn, sublime and sevenheaded, sprung from eternal Law, our sire discovered.
Ayasya, friend of all men, hath engendered the fourth hymn as he sang his laud to Indra.
2 Thinking aright, praising eternal Order, the sons of Dyaus the Asura, those heroes,
Angirases, holding the rank of sages, first honoured sacrifice's holy statute.
3 Girt by his friends who cried with swanlike voices, bursting the stony barriers of the prison,
Brhaspati spake in thunder to the cattle, and uttered praise and song when he had found them.
4 Apart from one, away from two above him, he drave the kine that stood in bonds of falsehood.
Brhaspati, seeking light amid the darkness, drave forth the bright cows: three he made apparent.
5 When he had cleft the lairs and western castle, he cut off three from him who held the waters.
Brhaspati discovered, while he thundered like Dyaus, the dawn, the Sun, the cow, the lightning.
6 As with a hand, so with his roaring Indra cleft Vala through, the guardian of the cattle.

279

Seeking the milk-draught with sweatshining comrades he stole the Pani's kine and left him weeping.
7 He with bright faithful Friends, winners of booty, hath rent the milker of the cows asunder.
Brhaspati with wild boars strong and mighty, sweating with heat, hath gained a rich possession.
8 They, longing for the kine, with faithful spirit incited with their hymns the Lord of cattle.
Brhaspati freed the radiant cows with comrades self-yoked, averting shame from one another.
9 In our assembly with auspicious praises exalting him who roareth like a lion,
Maywe, in every fight where heroes conquer, rejoice in strong Brhaspati the Victor.
10 When he had won him every sort of booty and gone to heaven and its most lofty mansions,
Men praised Brhaspati the Mighty, bringing the light within their mouths from sundry places.
11 Fulfil the prayer that begs for vital vigour: aid in your wonted manner even the humble.
Let all our foes be turned and driven backward. Hear this, O Heaven and Earth, ye All-producers.
12 Indra with mighty strength cleft asunder the head of Arbuda the watery monster,
Slain Ahi, and set free the Seven Rivers. O Heaven and Earth, with all the Gods protect us.

## [10-068] HYMN LXVIII. Brhaspati.

1. LIKE birds who keep their watch, plashing in water, like the loud voices of the thundering raincloud,
Like merry streamlets bursting from the mountain, thus to Brhaspati our hymns have sounded.
2 The Son of Angirases, meeting the cattle, as Bhaga, brought in Aryaman among us.
As Friend of men he decks the wife and husband: as for the race, Brhaspati, nerve our coursers.
3 Brhaspati, having won them from the mountains, strewed down, like barley out of winnowingbaskets,
The vigorous, wandering cows who aid the pious, desired of all, of blameless form, well-coloured.
4 As the Sun dews with meath the seat of Order, and casts a flaming meteor down from heaven.
So from the rock Brhaspati forced the cattle, and cleft the earth's skin as it were with water.
5 Forth from mid air with light he drave the darkness, as the gale blows a lily from the fiver.
Like the wind grasping at the cloud of Vala, Brhaspati gathered to himself the cattle,
6 Brhaspati, when he with fiery lightnings cleft through the weapon of reviling Vala,
Consumed.him as tongues cat what teeth have compassed: he threw the prisons of the red cows open.
7 That secret name borne by the lowing cattle within the cave Brhaspati discovered,
And drave, himself, the bright kine from the mountain, like a bird's young after the egg's disclosure.
8 He looked around on rock-imprisoned sweetness as one who eyes a fish in scanty water.
Brhaspati, cleaving through with varied clamour, brought it forth like a bowl from out the timber.
9 He found the light of heaven, and fire, and Morning: with lucid rays he forced apart the darkness.
As from a joint, Brhaspati took the marrow of Vala as he gloried in his cattle.
10 As trees for foliage robbed by winter, Vala mourned for the cows Brhaspati had taken.

He did a deed ne'er done, ne'er to be equalled, whereby the Sun and Moon ascend alternate.
11 Like a dark steed adorned with pearl, the Fathers have decorated heaven With constellations.
They set the light in day, in night the darkness. Brhaspati cleft the rock and found the cattle.
12 This homage have we.offered to the Cloud God who thunders out to many in succession.
May this Brhaspati vouchsafe us fulness of life with kine and horses, men, and heroes.

## [10-069] HYMN LXIX. Agni.

1. Auspicious is the aspect of Vadhryasva's fire good is its guidance, pleasant are its visitings.
When first the people Of Sumitra kindle it, with butter poured thercon it crackles and shines bright.
2 Butter is that which makes Vadhryaiva's fire growstrong: the butter is its food, the butter makes it fat.
It spreads abroad when butter hath been offered it, and balmed with streams of butter shines forth like the Sun.
3 Still newest is this face of thine, O Agni, which Manu and Sumitra have enkindled.
So richly shine, accept our songs with favour, so give us strengthening food, so send us glory.
4 Accept this offering, Agni, whom aforetime Vadhryasva, hath entreated and enkindled.
Guard well our homes and ople, guard our bodies, protect thy girt to us which thou hast granted.
5 Be splendid, guard us Kinsman of Vadhryasva: let not the enmity of men o'ercome thee,
Like the bold hero Cyavana, I Sumitra tell forth the title of Vadhryaiva's Kinsman.
6 All treasures hast thou won, of plains and mountains, and quelled the Dasas' and Aryas' hatred.
Like the bold hero Cyavana, O Agni, mayst thou subdue the men who long for battle.
7 Deft Agni hath a lengthened thread, tall oxen, a thousand heifers, numberless devices.
Decked by the men, splendid among the splendid, shine brightly forth amid devout Sumitras.
8 This is Thine the teeming cow, O Jatavedas, who pours at once her ceaseless flow, Sabardhuk,
Thou. art lit up by men enriched with guerdon, O Agni, by the pious-souled Sumitras.
9 Even Immortal Gods, O Jatavedas, Vadhryasva's Kinsman, have declared thy grandeur.
When human tribes drew near with supplication thou conqueredst with men whom thou hadst strengthened.
10 Like as a father bears his son, O Agni, Vadhryasva bare thee in his lap and served thee.
Thou, Youngest God, having enjoyed his fuel, didst vanquish those of old though they were mighty.
11 Vadhryasva's Agni evermore hath vanquished his foes with heroes who had pressed the Soma.
Lord of bright rays, thou burntest up the battle, subduing, as our help, e'en mighty foemen.
12 This Agni of Vadhryasva, Vrtra-slayer, lit from of old, must be invoked with homage.
As such assail our enemies, Vadhryasva, whether the foes be strangers or be kinsmen.

## [10-070] HYMN LXX. Apris.

1. ENJOY, O Agni, this my Fuel, welcome the oil-filled ladle where we pour libation.

Rise up for worship of the Gods, wise Agni, on the earth's height, while days are bright with beauty.

2 May he who goes before the Gods come hither with steeds whose shapes are varied, Narasarhsa.
May he, most Godlike, speed our offered viands with homage God-ward on the path of Order.

3 Men with oblations laud most constant Agni, and pray him to perform an envoy's duty.
With lightly-rolling car and best draught-horses, bring the Gods hither and sit down as Hotar.

4 May the delight of Gods spread out transversely: may it be with us long in length and fragrant.
O Holy Grass divine, with friendly spirit bring thou the willing Gods whose Chief is Indra.

5 Touch ye the far-extending height of heaven or spring apart to suit the wide earth's measure.
Yearning, ye Doors, with those sublime in greatness, seize eagerly the heavenly Car that cometh.

6 Here in this shrine may Dawn and Night, the Daughters of Heaven, the skilful Goddesses, be
seated.
In your wide lap, auspicious, willing Ladies may the Gods seat them with a willing spirit.

7 Up stands the stone, high burns the fire enkindled: Aditi's lap contains the Friendly Natures
Ye Two Chief Priests who serve at this our worship, may ye, more skilled, win for us rich possessions.

8 On our wide grass, Three Goddesses be seated: for you have we prepared and made it pleasant.
May Ila, she whose foot drops oil, the Goddess, taste, man-like, sacrifice and well-set presents.

9 Since thou, God Tvastar, hast made beauty perfect, since hou hast been the Angirases' Companion,
Willing, most wealthy, Giver of possessions, grant us the Gods' assembly, thou who knowest.

10 Well-knowing, binding with thy cord, bring hither, Lord of the Wood, the Deities' assembly.
The God prepare and season our oblations may Heaven and Earth be gracious to my calling.

11 Agni, bring hither Varuna to help us, Indra from heaven, from air's mid-realm the Maruts.
On sacred grass all Holy ones be seated and let the Immortal Gods rejoice in Svaha.

### [10-071] HYMN LXXI. Jnanam

1. WHEN-men, Brhaspati, giving names to objects, sent out Vak's first and earliest utterances,
All that was excellent and spotless, treasured within them, was disclosed through their affection.

2 Where, like men cleansing corn-flour in a cribble, the wise in spirit have created language,
Friends see and recognize the marks of friendship: their speech retains the blessed sign imprinted.

3 With sacrifice the trace of Vak they foIlowed, and found her harbouring within the Rsis.
They brought her, dealt her forth in many places: seven singers make her tones resound in concert.

4 One man hath ne'er seen Vak, and yet he seeth: one man hath hearing but hath never heard her.
But to another hath she shown her beauty as a fond well-dressed woman to her husband.

5 One man they call a laggard, dull in friendship: they never urge him on to deeds of valour.
He wanders on in profitless illusion: the Voice he heard yields neither fruit,nor blossom.

6 No part in Vak hath he who hath abandoned his own dear friend who knows the truth of friendship.

Even if he hears her still in vain he listens: naught knows he of the path of righteous action.

7 Unequal in the quickness of their spirit are friends endowed alike with eyes and hearing.
Some look like tanks that reach the mouth or shoulder, others like pools of water fit to bathe in.

8 When friendly Brahmans sacrifice together with mental impulse which the heart hath fashioned,
They leave one far behind through their attainments, and some who count as Brahmans wander
elsewhere.

9 Those men who step not back and move not forward, nor Brahmans nor preparers of libations,
Having attained to Vak in sinful fashion spin out their thread in ignorance like spinsters.

10 All friends are joyful in the friend who cometh in triumph, having conquered in assembly.
He is their blame-averter, food-provider prepared is he and fit for deed of vigour.

11 One plies his constant task reciting verses. one sings the holy psalm in Sakvari measures.
One more, the Brahman, tells the lore of being, and one lays down the rules of sacrificing.

### [10-072] HYMN LXXII. The Gods.

1. LET US with tuneful skill proclaim these generations of the Gods,
That one may see them when these hymns are chanted in a future age.

2 These Brahmanaspati produced with blast and smelting, like a Smith,
Existence, in an earlier age of Gods, from Non-existence sprang.

3 Existence, in the earliest age of Gods, from Non-existence sprang.
Thereafter were the regions born. This sprang from the Productive Power.

4 Earth sprang from the Productive Power the regions from the earth were born.
Daksa was born of Aditi, and Aditi was Daksa's Child.

5 For Aditi, O Daksa, she who is thy Daughter, was brought forth.
After her were the blessed Gods born sharers of immortal life.

6 When ye, O Gods, in yonder deep closeclasping one another stood,
Thence, as of dancers, from your feet a thickening cloud of dust arose.

7 When, O ye Gods, like Yatis, ye caused all existing things to grow,
Then ye brought Surya forward who was lying hidden in the sea.

8 Eight are the Sons of Adid who from her body sprang to life.
With seven she went to meet the Gods she cast Martanda far away.

9 So with her Seven Sons Aditi went forth to meet the earlier age.
She brought Martanda thitherward to spring to life and die again.

### [10-073] HYMN LXXIII. Indra.

1. THOU wast born mighty for victorious valour, exulting, strongest, full of pride and courage.
There, even there, the Maruts strengthened Indra when. his most rapid Mother stirred the Hero.

2 There with fiend's ways e'en Prsni was seated: with much laudation they exalted Indra.
As if encompassed by the Mighty-footed, from darkness, near at hand, forth came the Children.

3 High are thy feet when on thy way thou goest: the strength thou foundest here hath lent thee
vigour.

Thousand hyenas in thy mouth thou holdest. O Indra, mayst thou turn the Asvins hither.

4 Speeding at once to sacrifice thou comest for friendship thou art bringing both Nasatyas.
Thou hadst a thousand treasures in possession. The Asvins, O thou Hero, gave thee riches.

5 Glad, for the race that rests on holy Order, with friends who hasten to their goal, hath Indra
With these his magic powers assailed the Dasyu: he cast away the gloomy mists, the darkness.

6 Two of like name for him didst thou demolish, as Indra striking down the car of Usas.
With thy beloved lofty Friends thou camest, and with the assurance of thine heart thou slewest.

7 War-loving Namuci thou smotest, robbing the Dasa of his magic for the Rsi.
For man thou madest ready pleasant pathways, paths leading as it were directly God-ward.

8 These names of thine thou hast fulfilled completely: as Lord, thou boldest in thine arm, O Indra.
In thee, through thy great might, the Gods are joyful: the roots of trees hast thou directed upward.

9 May the sweet Soma juices make him happy to cast his quoit that lies in depth of waters.
Thou from the udder which o'er earth is fastened hast poured the milk into the kine and herbage.

10 When others call him offspring of the Courser, my meaning is that Mighty Power produced him.
He came from Manyu and remained in houses: whence he hath sprung is known to Indra only.

11 Like birds of beauteous wing the Priyamedhas, Rsis, imploring, have come nigh to Indra:
Dispel the darkness and fill full our vision deliver us as men whom snares entangle.

### [10-074] HYMN LXXIV. Indra.

1. I AM prepared to laud with song or worship the Noble Ones who are in earth and heaven,
Or Coursers who have triumphed in, the contest, or those who famed, have won the prize with glory.

2 Their call, the call of Gods, went up to heaven: they kissed the ground with glory-seeking spirit,
There where the Gods look on for happy fortune, and like the kindly heavens bestow their bounties.

3 This is the song of those Immortal Beings who long for treasures in their full perfection.
May these, completing prayers and sacrifices, bestow upon us wealth where naught is wanting.

4 Those living men extolled thy deed, O Indra, those who would fain burst through the stall of cattle,
Fain to milk her who bare but once, great, lofty, whose Sons are many and her streams past number.

5 Sacivan, win to your assistance Indra who never bends, who overcomes his foemen.
Rbhuksan, Maghavan, the hymn's upholder, who, rich in food, bears man's kind friend, the thunder.

6 Since he who won of old anew hath triumphed, Indra hath earned his name of Vrtra-slaycr.
He hath appeared, the mighty Lord of Conquest. What we would have him do let him accomplish.

### [10-075] HYMN LXXV. The Rivers.

1. THE singer, O ye Waters in Vivasvan's place, shall tell your grandeur forth that is beyond compare.
The Rivers have come forward triply, seven and seven. Sindhu in might surpasses all the streams that

flow.

2 Varuna cut the channels for thy forward course, O Sindhu, when thou rannest on to win the race.
Thou speedest o'er precipitous ridges of the earth, when thou art Lord and Leader of these moving floods.

3 His roar is lifted up to heaven above the earth: he puts forth endless vigour with a flash of light.
Like floods of rain that fall- in thunder from the cloud, so Sindhu rushes on bellowing like a bull.

4 Like mothers to their calves, like milch kine with their milk, so, Sindhu, unto thee the roaring rivers run.
Thou leadest as a warrior king thine army's wings what time thou comest in the van of these swift streams.

5 Favour ye this my laud, O Ganga, Yamuna, O Sutudri, Parusni and Sarasvati:
With Asikni, Vitasta, O Marudvrdha, O Arjikiya with Susoma hear my call.

6 First with Trstama thou art eager to flow forth, with Rasa, and Susartu, and with Svetya here,
With Kubha; and with these, Sindhu and Mehatnu, thou seekest in thy course Krumu and Gomati.

7 Flashing and whitely-gleaming in her mightiness, she moves along her ample volumes through the realms,
Most active of the active, Sindhu unrestrained, like to a dappled mare, beautiful, fair to see.

8 Rich in good steeds is Sindhu, rich in cars and robes, rich in gold, nobly-fashioned, rich in ample wealth.
Blest Silamavati and young Urnavati invest themselves with raiment rich in store of sweets.

9 Sindhu hath yoked her car, light-rolling, drawn by steeds, and with that car shall she win booty in this fight.
So have I praised its power, mighty and unrestrained, of independent glory, roaring as it runs.

### [10-076] HYMN LXXVI. Press-stones.

1. I GRASP at you when power and strength begin to dawn: bedew ye, Indra and the Maruts, Heaven and Earth,
That Day and Night, in every hall of sacrifice, may wait on us and bless us when they first spring forth.

2 Press the libation out, most excellent of all: the Pressing-stone is grasped like a hand-guided steed.
So let it win the valour that subdues the foe, and the fleet courser's might that speeds to ample wealth.

3 Juice that this Stone pours out removes defect of ours, as in old time it brought prosperity to man.
At sacrifices they established holy rites on Tvastar's milk-blent juice bright with the hue of steeds.

4 Drive ye the treacherous demons far away from us: keep Nirrti afar and banish Penury.
Pour riches forth for us with troops of hero sons, and bear ye up, O Stones, the song that visits Gods.

5 To you who are more mighty than the heavens themselves, who, finishing your task with more than Vibhvan's speed,
More rapidly than Vayu seize the Soma juice, better than Agni give us food, to you I sing.

6 Stirred be the glorious Stones: let it press out the juice, the Stone with heavenly song that reaches

up to heaven,
There where the men draw forth the meath for which they long, sending their voice around in rivalry
of speed.
7 The Stones press out the Soma, swift as car-borne men, and, eager for the spoil, drain forth the sap
thereof
To fill the beaker, they exhaust the udder's store, as the men purify oblations with their lips.
8 Ye, present men, have been most skilful in your work, even ye, O Stones who pressed Soma for
Indra's drink.
May all ye have of fair go to the Heavenly Race, and all your treasure to the earthly worshipper.

## [10-077] HYMN LXXVII. Maruts.

1. As with their voice from cloud they sprinkle treasure so are the wise man's liberal sacrifices.
I praise their Company that merits worship as the good Martits' priest to pay them honour.
2 The youths have wrought their ornaments for glory through many nights,-this noble band of
Maruts.
Like stags the Sons of Dyatis have striven onward, the Sons of Aditi grown strong like pillars.
3 They who extend beyond the earth and heaven, by their own mass, as from the cloud spreads
Surya;
Like mighty Heroes covetous of glory, like heavenly gallants who destroy the wicked.
4 When ye come nigh, as in the depth of waters, the earth is loosened, as it were, and shaken.
This your all-feedin sacrifice approaches: come all united, fraught, as 'twere with viands.
5 Ye are like horses fastened to the chariot poles, luminous with your beams, with splendour as at
dawn;
Like self-bright falcons, punishers of wicked men, like hovering birds urged forward, scattering rain
around.
6 When ye come forth, O Maruts, from the distance, from the great treasury of rich possessions,
Knowing, O Vasus, boons that should be granted, even from afar drive back the men who hate us.
7 He who, engaged in the rite's final duty brings, as a man, oblation to the Maruts,
Wins him life's wealthy fulness, blest with heroes: he shall be present, too, where Gods drink Soma.
8 For these are helps adored at sacrifices, bringing good fortune by their name Adityas.
Speeding on cars let them protect our praises, delighting in our sacrifice and worship.

## [10-078] HYMN LXXVIII. Maruts.

1. Ye by your hymns are like high-thoughted singers, skilful, inviting Gods with sacrifices;
Fair to behold, like Kings, with bright adornment, like spotless gallants, leaders of the people:
2 Like fire with flashing flame, breast-bound with chains of gold, like tempest-blasts, self-moving,
swift to lend your aid;
As best of all foreknowers, excellent to guide, like Somas, good to guard the man who follows Law.
3 Shakers of all, like gales of wind they travel, like tongues of burning fires in their effulgence.
Mighty are they as warriors clad in armour, and, like the Fathers' prayers, Most Bounteous Givers.

4 Like spokes of car-wheels in one nave united, ever victorious like heavenly Heroes,
Shedding their precious balm like youthful suitors, they raise their voice and chant their psalm as
singers.
5 They who are fleet to travel like the noblest steeds, long to obtain the prize like bounteous
charioteers,
Like waters speeding on with their precipitous floods, like omniform Angirases with Sama-hymns.
6 Born from the stream, like press-stones are the Princes, for ever like the stones that crush in pieces;
Sons of a beauteous Dame, like playful children, like a great host upon the march with splendour.
7 Like rays of Dawn, the visitors of sacrifice, they shine with ornaments as eager to be bright.
Like rivers hasting on, glittering with their spears, from far away they measure out the distances.
8 Gods, send us happiness and make us wealthy, letting us singers prosper, O ye Maruts.
Bethink you of our praise and of our friendship: ye from of old have riches to vouchsafe us.

## [10-079] HYMN LXXIX. Agni.

1. I HAVE beheld the might of this Great Being. Immortal in the midst of tribes of mortals.
His jaws now open and now shut together: much they devour, insatiately chewing.
2 His eyes are turned away, his head is hidden: unsated with his tongue he eats the fuel.
With hands upraised, with reverence in the houses, for him they quickly bring his food together.
3 Seeking, as 'twere, his Mother's secret bosom, he, like a child, creeps on through wide-spread
bushes.
One he finds glowing like hot food made ready, and kissing deep within the earth's recmes.
4 This holy Law I tell you, Earth and Heaven: the Infant at his birth dovours his Parents.
No knowledge of the God have I, a mortal. Yea, Agni knoweth best, for he hath wisdom.
5 This man who quickly gives him food, who offers his gifts of oil and butter and supports him, -
Him with his thousand eyes he closely looks on: thou showest him thy face from all sides, Agni.
6 Agni, hast thou committed sin or treason among the Gods? In ignorance I ask thee.
Playing, not playing, he gold-hued and toothless, hath cut his food up as the knife a victim.
7 He born in wood hath yoked his horses rushing in all directions, held with reins that glitter.
The well-born friend hath carved his food with Vasus: in all his limbs he hath increased and
prospered.

## [10-080] HYMN LXXX. Agni.

1. AGNI bestows the fleet prize-winning courser: Agni, the hero famed and firm in duty.
Agni pervades and decks the earth and heaven, and fills the fruitful dame who teems with heroes.
2 Blest be the wood that feeds the active Agni: within the two great worlds hath Agni entered.
Agni impels a single man to battle, and with him rends in pieces many a foeman.
3 Agni rejoiced the car of him who praised lim, and from the waters burnt away jarutha.

Agni saved Atri in the fiery cavern, and made Nrmedha rich with troops of children.
4 Agni hath granted wealth that decks the hero, and sent the sage who wins a thousand cattle.
Agni hath made oblations rise to heaven: to every place are Agni's laws extended.
5 With songs of praise the Rsis call on Agni; on Agni, heroes worsted in the foray.
Birds flying in the region call on Agni around a thousand cattle Agni wanders.
6 Races of human birth pay Agni worship, men who have sprung from Nahus' line adore him.
Stablished in holy oil is Agni's pasture, on the Gandharva path of Law and Order.
7 The Rbhus fabricated prayer for Agni, and we with mighty hymns have called on Agni.
Agni, Most Youthful God, protect the singer: win us by worship, Agni, great possessions.

## [10-081] HYMN LXXXI. Visvakarman.

1. HE who sate down as Hotar-priest, the Rsi, our Father, offering up all things existing,-
He, seeking through his wish a great possession, came among men on earth as archetypal.
2 What was the place whereon he took his station? What was it that supported him? How was it?
Whence Visvakarman, seeing all, producing the earth, with mighty power disclosed the heavens.
3 He who hath eyes on all sides round about him, a mouth on all sides, arms and feet on all sides,
He, the Sole God, producing earth and heaven, weldeth them, with his arms as wings, together.
4 What was the tree, what wood in sooth produced it, from which they fashioned out the earth and heaven?
Ye thoughtful men inquire within your spirit whereon he stood when he established all things.
5 Nine highest, lowest, sacrificial natures, and these thy mid-most here, O Visvakarman,
Teach thou thy friends at sacrifice, O Blessed, and come thyself, exalted, to our worship.
6 Bring thou thyself, exalted with oblation, O Visvakarman, Earth and Heaven to worship.
Let other men around us live in folly here let us have a rich and liberal patron.
7 Let us invoke to-day, to aid our labour, the Lord of Speech, the thought-swift Visvakarman.
May he hear kindly all our invocations who gives all bliss for aid, whose works are righteous.

## [10-082] HYMN LXXXII. Visvakarman.

1. THE Father of the eye, the Wise in spirit, created both these worlds submerged in fatness.
Then when the eastern ends were firmly fastened, the heavens and the earth were far extended.
2 Mighty in mind and power is Visvakarman, Maker, Disposer, and most lofty Presence.
Their offerings joy in rich juice where they value One, only One, beyond the Seven Rsis.
3 Father who made us, he who, as Disposer, knoweth all races and all things existing,
Even he alone, the Deities' narne-giver,him other beings seek for information.
4 To him in sacrifice they offered treasures,-Rsis of old, in numerous troops, as singers,
Who, in the distant, near, and lower region, made ready all these things that have existence.

5 That which is earlier than this earth and heaven, before the Asuras and Gods had being,-
What was the germ primeval which the waters received where all the Gods were seen together?
6 The waters, they received that germ primeval wherein the Gods were gathefed all together.
It rested set upon the Unborn's navel, that One wherein abide all things existing.
7 Ye will not find him who produced these creatures: another thing hath risen up among you.
Enwrapt in misty cloud, with lips that stammer, hymn-chanters wander and are discontented.

## [10-083] HYMN LXXXII. Manyu.

1. HE who hath reverenced thee, Manyu, destructive bolt, breeds for himself forthwith all conquering
energy.
Arya and Dasa will we conquer with thine aid, with thee the Conqueror, with conquest conquestsped.
2 Manyu was Indra, yea, the God, was Manyu, Manyu was Hotar, Varuna, Jatavedas.
The tribes of human lineage worship Manyu. Accordant with thy fervour, Manyu, guard us.
3 Come hither, Manyu, mightier tham the mighty; chase, with thy fervour for ally, our foemen.
Slayer of foes, of Vrtra, and of Dasyu, bring thou to us all kinds of wealth and treasure.
4 For thou art, Manyu, of surpassing vigour, fierce, queller of the foe, and self-existent,
Shared by all men, victorious, subduer: vouchsafe to us superior strength in battles.
5 I have departed, still without a portion, wise God! according to thy will, the Mighty.
I, feeble man, was wroth thee, O Manyu I am myself; come thou to give me vigour.
6 Come hither. I am all thine own; advancing turn thou to me, Victorious, All-supporter!
Come to me, Manyu, Wielder of the Thunder: bethink thee of thy friend, and slay the Dasyus.
7 Approach, and on my right hand hold thy station: so shall we slay a multitude of foemen.
The best of meath I offer to support thee: may we be first to drink thereof in quiet.

## [10-084] HYMN LXXXIV. Manyu.

1. BORNE on with thee, O Manyu girt by Maruts, let our brave men, impetuous, bursting forward,
March on, like flames of fire in form, exulting, with pointed arrows, sharpening their weapons.
2 Flashing like fire, be thou, O conquering Manyu, invoked, O Victor, as our army's leader.
Slay thou our foes, distribute their possessions: show forth thy vigour, scatter those who hate us.
3 O Manyu, overcome thou our assailant on! breaking, slaying, crushing down the foemen.
They have not hindered thine impetuous vigour: Mighty, Sole born! thou makest them thy subjects.
4 Alone or many thou art worshipped, Manyu: sharpen the spirit of each clan for battle.
With thee to aid, O thou of perfect splendour, we will uplift the glorious shout for conquest.
5 Unyielding bringing victory like Indra, O Manyu, be thou here our Sovran Ruler.
To thy dear name, O Victor, we sing praises: we know the spring from which thou art come hither.
6 Twin-born with power, destructive bolt of thunder, the highest conquering might is thine, Subduer!

Be friendly to its in thy spirit, Manyu, O Much-invoked, in shock of mighty battle.

7 For spoil let Varuna and Manyu give us the wealth of both sides gathered and collected;

And let our enemies with stricken spirits, o'erwhelmed with terror, slink away defeated.

## [10-085] HYMN LXXXV. Surya's Bridal.

1. TRUTH is the base that bears the earth; by Surya are the heavens sustained.

By Law the Adityas stand secure, and Soma holds his place in heaven.

2 By Soma are the Adityas strong, by Soma mighty is the earth.

Thus Soma in the midst of all these constellations hath his place.

3 One thinks, when they have brayed the plant, that he hath drunk the Soma's juice;

Of him whom Brahmans truly know as Soma no one ever tastes.

4 Soma, secured by sheltering rules, guarded by hymns in Brhati,

Thou standest listening to the stones none tastes of thee who dwells on earth.

5 When they begin to drink thee then, O God, thou swellest out again.

Vayu is Soma's guardian God. The Moon is that which shapes the years.

6 Raibhi was her dear bridal friend, and Narasamsi led her home.

Lovely was Surya's robe: she came to that which Gatha had adorned.

7 Thought was the pillow of her couch, sight was the unguent for her eyes:

Her treasury was earth and heaven..when Surya went unto her Lord.

8 Hymns were the cross-bars of the pole, Kurira-metre decked the car:

The bridesmen were the Asvin Pair Agni was leader of the train.

9 Soma was he who wooed the maid: the groomsmen were both Asvins, when

The Sun-God Savitar bestowed his willing Surya on her Lord.

10 Her spirit was the bridal car; the covering thereof was heaven:

Bright were both Steers that drew it when Surya approached her husband's, home.

11 Thy Steers were steady, kept in place by holy verse and Sama-hymn:

All car were thy two chariot wheels: thy path was tremulous in the sky,

12 Clean, as thou wentest, were thy wheels wind, was the axle fastened there.

Surya, proceeding to her Lord, mounted a spirit-fashioried car.

13 The bridal pomp of Surya, which Savitar started, moved along.

In Magha days are oxen slain, in Arjuris they wed the bride.

14 When on your three-wheeled chariot, O Asvins, ye came as wooers unto Surya's bridal,

Then all the Gods agreed to your proposal Pusan as Son elected you as Fathers.

15 O ye Two Lords of lustre, then when ye to Surya's wooing came,

Where was one chariot wheel of yours? Where stood ye for die Sire's command?

16 The Brahmans, by their seasons, know, O Surya, those two wheels of thine:

One kept concealed, those only who are skilled in highest truths have learned.

17 To Surya and the Deities, to Mitra and to Varuna.

Who know aright the thing that is, this adoration have I paid.

18 By their own power these Twain in close succession move;

They go as playing children round the sacrifice.

One of the Pair beholdeth all existing things; the other ordereth seasons and is born again.

19 He, born afresh, is new and new for ever ensign of days he goes before the Mornings

Coming, he orders f6r the Gods their portion. The Moon prolongs the days of our existence.

20 Mount this, all-shaped, gold-hued, with strong wheels, fashioned of Kimsuka and Salmali, lightrolling,

Bound for the world of life immortal, Surya: make for thy lord a happy bridal journey.

21 Rise up from hence: this maiden hath a husband. I laud Visvavasu with hymns and homage.

Seek in her father's home another fair one, and find the portion from of old assigned thee.

22 Rise up from hence, Visvavasu: with reverence we worship thee.

Seek thou another willing maid, and with her husband leave the bride.

23 Straight in direction be the path:s, and thornless, whereon our fellows travel to the wooing.

Let Aryaman and Bhaga lead us: perfect, O Gods, the union of the wife and husband.

24 Now from the noose of Varuna I free thee, wherewith Most Blessed Savitar hath bound thee.

In Law's seat, to the world of virtuous action, I give thee up uninjured with thy consort.

25 Hence, and not thence, I send these free. I make thee softly fettered there.

That, Bounteous Indra, she may live blest in her fortune and her sons.

26 Let Pusan take thy hand and hence conduct thee; may the two Asvins on their car transport thee.

Go to the house to be the household's mistress and speak as lady ito thy gathered people.

27 Happy be thou and prosper witlh thy children here: be vigilant to rule thy household in this home.

Closely unite thy body with this; man, thy lord. So shall ye, full of years, address your company.

28 Her hue is blue and red: the fienod who clingeth close is driven off.

Well thrive the kinsmen of this bride the husband is bourid fast in bonds.

29 Give thou the woollen robe away: deal treasure to the Brahman priests.

This female fiend hath got her feet, and as a wife attends her lord.

30 Unlovely is his body when it glistens with this wicked fiend,

What time the husband wraps about his limbs the garment of his wife.

31 Consumptions, from her people, which follow the bride's resplendent train,-

These let the Holy Gods again bear to the place from which they came.

32 Let not the highway thieves who lie in ambush find the wedded pair.

By pleasant ways let them escape the danger, and let foes depart.

33 Signs of good fortune mark the bride come all of you and look at her.

Wish her prosperity, and then return unto your homes again.

34 Pungent is this, and bitter this, filled, as it were, with arrow-barbs, Empoisoned and.not fit for use.

The Brahman who knows Surya well deserves the garment of the bride.

35 The fringe, the cloth that decks her head, and then the triply parted robe,-

Behold the hues which Surya wears these doth the Brahman purify.

36 I take thy hand in mine for happy fortune that thou mayst reach old age with me thy husband.

Gods, Aryaman, Bhaga, Savitar, Purandhi, have given thee to be my household's mistress.

37 O Pusan, send her on as most auspicious, her who shall be the sharer of my pleasures;
Her who shall twine her loving arms about me, and welcome all my love and mine embraces.

38 For thee, with bridal train, they, first, escorted Surya to her home.
Give to the husband in return, Agni, the wife with progeny.

39 Agni hath given the bride again with splendour and with ample life.
Long lived be he who is her lord; a hundred autumns let him live.

40 Soma obtained her first of all; next the Gandharva was her lord.
Agai was thy third husband: now one bornof woman is thy fourth.

41 Soma to the Gandharva, and to Agni the Gandharva gave:
And Agni hath bestowed on me riches and sons and this my spouse.

42 Be ye not parted; dwell ye here reach the full time of human life.
With sons and grandsons sport and play, rejoicing in your own abode.

43 So may Prajapati bring children forth to us; may Aryaman adorn us till old age come nigh.
Not inauspicious enter thou thy husband's house: bring blessing to our bipeds and our quadrupeds.

44 Not evil-eyed, no slayer of thy husband, bring weal to cattle, radiant, gentlehearted;
Loving the Gods, delightful, bearing heroes, bring blessing to our quadrupeds and bipeds.

45 O Bounteous Indra, make this bride blest in her sons and fortunate.
Vouchsafe to her ten sons, and make her husband the eleventh man.

46 Over thy husband's father and thy husband's mother bear full sway.
Over the sister of tby lord, over his brothers rule supreme.

47 So may the Universal Gods, so may the Waters join our hearts.
May Matarisvan, Dhatar, and Destri together bind us close.

## [10-086] HYMN LXXXVI. Indra.

1. MEN have abstained from pouring juice they count not Indra as a God.
Where at the votary's store my friend Vrsakapi hath drunk his fill. Supreme is Indra over all.

2 Thou, Indra, heedless passest by the ill Vrsakapi hath wrought;
Yet nowhere else thou findest place wherein to drink the Soma juice. Supreme is Indra over all.

3 What hath he done to injure thee, this tawny beast Vrsakapi,
With whom thou art so angry now? What is the votary's foodful store? Supreme is Indra over all.

4 Soon may the hound who hunts the boar seize him and bite him in the car,
O Indra, that Vrsakapi whom thou protectest as a friend, Supreme is Indra over all.

5 Kapi hath marred the beauteous things, all deftly wrought, that were my joy.
In pieces will I rend his head; the sinner's portion sball be woo. Supreme is Indra over all.

6 No Dame hath ampler charms than 1, or greater wealth of love's delights.
None with more ardour offers all her beauty to her lord's embrace. Supreme is Indra over all.

7 Mother whose love is quickly wibn, I say what verily will be.
My,breast, O Mother, and my head and both my hips seem quivering. Supreme is Indra over all.

8 Dame with the lovely hands and arms, with broad hair-plaits add ample hips,
Why, O thou Hero's wife, art thou angry with our Vrsakapi? Supreme is Indra over all.

9 This noxious creature looks on me as one bereft of hero's love,
Yet Heroes for my sons have I, the Maruts' Friend and Indra's Queen. Supreme is Indra over all.

10 From olden time the matron goes to feast and general sacrifice.
Mother of Heroes, Indra's Queen, the rite's ordainer is extolled. Supreme is Indra over all.

11 So have I heard Indrani called most fortunate among these Dames,
For never shall her Consort die in future time through length of days. Supreme is Indra overall.

12 Never, Indralni, have I joyed without my friend Vrsakapi,
Whose welcome offering here, made pure with water, goeth to the Gods. Supreme is Indra over all.

13 Wealthy Vrsakapayi, blest with sons and consorts of thy sons,
Indra will eat thy bulls, thy dear oblation that effecteth much. Supreme is Indra over all.

14 Fifteen in number, then, for me a score of bullocks they prepare,
And I devour the fat thereof: they fill my belly full with food. Supreme is Indra over all.

15 Like as a bull with pointed horn, loud bellowing amid the herds,
Sweet to thine heart, O Indra, is the brew which she who tends thee pours. Supreme is Indra over all.

18 O Indra this Vrsakapi hath found a slain wild animal,
Dresser, and new-made pan, and knife, and wagon with a load of wood. Supreme is Indra over all.

19 Distinguishing the Dasa and the Arya, viewing all, I go.
I look upon the wise, and drink the simple votary's Soma juice. Supreme is Indra over all.

20 The desert plains and steep descents, how many leagues in length they spread!
Go to the nearest houses, go unto thine home, Vrsakapi. Supreme is Indra over all.

21 Turn thee again Vrsakapi: we twain will bring thee happiness.
Thou goest homeward on thy way along this path which leads to sleep. Supreme is Indra over all.

22 When, Indra and Vrsakapi, ye travelled upward to your home,
Where was that noisome beast, to whom went it, the beast that troubles man? Supreme is Indra over all.

23 Daughter of Manu, Parsu bare a score of children at a birth.
Her portion verily was bliss although her burthen caused her grief.

## [10-087] HYMN LXXXVII. Agni.

1. I BALM with oil the mighty Raksas-slayer; to the most famous Friend I come for shelter
Enkindled, sharpened by our rites, may Agni protect us in the day and night from evil.

2 O Jatavedas with the teeth of iron, enkindled with thy flame attack the demons.
Seize with thy longue the foolish gods' adorers: rend, put within thy mouth the raw-flesh caters.

3 Apply thy teeth, the upper and the lower, thou who hast both, enkindled and destroying.
Roam also in the air, O King, around us, and with thy jaws assail the wicked spirits.

4 Bending thy shafts through sacrifices, Agni, whetting their points with song as if with whetstones,
Pierce to the heart therewith the Yatudhanas, and break their arms uplifed to attack thee.

5 Pierce through the Yatudhana's skin, O Agni; let the destroying dart with fire consume him.
Rend his joints, Jatavedas, let the cater of flesh, flesh-seeking, track his mangled body.
6 Where now thou seest Agni Jatavedas, one of these demons standing still or roaming,
Or flying on those paths in air's midregion, sharpen the shaft and as an archer pierce him.
7 Tear from the evil spirit, Jatavedas, what he hath seized and with his spears hath captured.
Blazing before him strike him down, O Agni; let spotted carrion-eating kites devour him.
8 Here tell this forth, O Agni: whosoever is, he himself, or acteth as, a demon,
Him grasp, O thou Most Youthful, with thy fuel. to the Mati-seer's eye give him as booty.
9 With keen glance guard the sacrifice, O Agni: thou Sage, conduct it onward to the Vasus.
Let not the fiends, O Man-beholder, harm thee burning against the Raksasas to slay them.
10 Look on the fiend mid men, as Man-beholder: rend thou three extremities in pieces.
Demolish with thy flame his ribs, O Agni, the Yatudhana's root destroy thou triply.
11 Thrice, Agni, let thy noose surround the demon who with his falsehood injures Holy Order.
Loud roaring with thy flame, O Jatavedas, crush him and cast him down before the singer.
12 Lead thou the worshipper that eye, O Agni, wherewith thou lookest on the hoof-armed demon.
With light celestial in Atharvan's manner burn up the foot who ruins truth with falsehood.
13 Agni, what curse the pair this day have uttered, what heated word the worshippers have spoken,
Each arrowy taunt sped from the angry spirit,-pierce to the heart therewith the Yatudhanas.
14 With fervent heat exterminate the demons; destroy the fiends with burning flame, O Agni.
Destroy with fire the foolish gods' adorers; blaze and destrepy the insatiable monsters.
15 May Gods destroy this day the evil-doer may each hot curse of his return and blast him.
Let arrows pierce the liar in his vitals, and Visva's net enclose the Yatudhana.
16 The fiend who smears himself with flesh of cattle, with flesh of horses and of human bodies,
Who steals the milch-cow's milk away, O Agni,-tear off the heads of such with fiery fury.
17 The cow gives milk each year, O Man-regarder: let not the Yatudhana ever taste it.
If one would glut him with the biesting, Agni, pierce with thy flame his vitals as he meets thee.
18 Let the fiends drink the poison of the cattle; may Aditi cast off the evildoers.
May the God Savitar give them up to ruin, and be their share of plants and herbs denied them.
19 Agni, from days of old thou slayest demons: never shall Raksasas in fight o'ercome thee.
Burn up the foolish ones, the flesh-devourers: let none of them escape thine heavenly arrow.
20 Guard us, O Agni, from above and under, protect us fl-om behind us and before us;
And may thy flames, most fierce and never wasting, glowing with fervent heat, consume the sinner.
21 From rear, from front, from under, from above us, O King, protect us as a Sage with wisdom.

Guard to old age thy friend, O Friend, Eternal: O Agni, as Immortal, guard us mortals.
22 We set thee round us as a fort, victorious Agni, thee a Sage, Of hero lineage, day by day, destroyer of our treacherous foes.
23 Burn with thy poison turned against the treacherous brood of Raksasas,
O Agni, with thy sharpened glow, with lances armed with points of flame.
24 Burn thou the paired Kimidins, brun, Agni, the Yatudhana pairs.
I sharpen thee, Infallible, with hymns. O Sage, be vigilant.
25 Shoot forth, O Agni, with thy flame demolish them on every side.
Break thou the Yatudhana's strength, the vigour of the Raksasa.

## [10-088] HYMN LXXXVIII. Agni.

1. DEAR, ageless sacrificial drink is offered in light-discovering, heaven-pervading Agni.
The Gods spread forth through his Celestial Nature, that he might bear the world up and sustain it.
2 The world was swallowed and concealed in darkness: Agni was born, and light became apparent.
The Deities, the broad earth, and the heavens, and plants, and waters gloried in his friendship.
3 Inspired by Gods who claim our adoration, I now will laud Eternal Lofty Agni,
Him who hath spread abroad the earth with lustre, this heaven, and both the worlds, and air's midregion.
4 Earliest Priest whom all the Gods accepted, and chose him, and anointed him with butter,
He swiftly made all things that fly, stand, travel, all that hath motion, Agni Jatavedas.
5 Because thou, Agni, Jatavedas, stoodest at the world's head with thy refulgent splendour,
We sent thee forth with hymns and songs and praises: thou filledst heaven and earth, God meet for worship.
6 Head of the world is Agni in the night-time; then, as the Sun, at morn springs up and rises.
Then to his task goes the prompt Priest foreknowing the wondrous power of Gods who must be
honoured.
7 Lovely is he who, kindled in his greatness, hath shone forth, seated in the heavens, refulgent.
With resonant hymns all Gods who guard our bodies have offered up oblation in this Agni.
8 First the Gods brought the hymnal into being; then they engendered Agni, then oblation.
He was their satrifice that guards our bodies: him the heavens know, the earth, the waters know him.
9 He, Agni, whom the Gods have generated, in whom they offered up all worlds and creatures,
He with his bright glow heated earth and heaven, urging himself right onward in his grandeur.
10 Then by the laud the Gods engendered Agni in heaven, who fills both worlds through strength and vigour.
They made him to appear in threefold essence: he ripens plants of every form and nature.
11 What time the Gods, whose due is worship, set him as Surya, Son of Aditi, in heaven,
When the Pair, ever wandering, sprang to being, all creatures that existed looked upon them.
12 For all the world of life the Gods made Agni Vaisvanara to be the days' bright Banner,-
Him who hath spread abroad the radiant Mornings, and, coming with his light, unveils the darkness.
13 The wise and holy Deities engendered Agni Vaisvanara whom age ne'er touches.

The Ancient Star that wanders on for ever, lofty and. strong, Lord of the Living Being.
14 We call upon the Sage with holy verses, Agni Vaisvanara the ever-beaming,
Who hath surpassed both heaven and earth in greatness: lie is a God below, a God above us.
15 I have heard mention of two several pathways, ways of the Fathers and of Gods and mortals.
On these two paths each moving creature travels, each thing between the Father and the Mother.
16 These two united paths bear him who journeys born from the head and pondered with the spirit
He stands directed to all things existing, hasting, unresting in his fiery splendour.
17 Which of us twain knows where they speak together, upper and lower of the two rite-leaders?
Our friends have helped to gather our assembly. They came to sacrifice; who will announce it?
18 How many are the Fires and Suns in number? What is the number of the Dawns and Waters?
Not jestingly I speak to you, O Fathers. Sages, I ask you this for information.
19 As great as is the fair-winged Morning's presence to him who dwells beside us, matarisvan!
Is what the Brahman does when he approaches to sacrifice and sits below the Hotar.

## [10-089] HYMN LXXXIX. Indra.

1. I WILL extol the most heroic Indra who with his might forced earth and sky asunder;
Who hath filled all with width as man's Upholder, surpassing floods and rivers in his greatness.
2 Surya is he: throughout the wide expanses shall Indra turn him, swift as car-wheels, hither,
Like a stream resting not but ever active he hath destroyed, with light, the blackhued darkness.
3 To him I sing a holy prayer, incessant new, matchless, common to the earth and heaven,
Who marks, as they were backs, all living creatures: ne'er doth he fail a friend, the noble Indra.
4 I will send forth my songs in flow unceasing, like water from the ocean's depth, to Indra.
Who to his car on both its sides securely hath fixed the earth and heaven as with an axle.
5 Rousing with draughts, the Shaker, rushing onward, impetuous, very strong, armed as with arrows
Is Soma; forest trees and all the bushes deceive not Indra with their offered likeness.
6 Soma hath flowed to him whom naught can equal, the earth, the heavens, the firmament, the mountains,-
When heightened in his ire his indignation shatters the firm and breaks the strong in pieces.
7 As an axe fells the tree so be slew Vrtra, brake down the strongholds and dug out the rivers.
He cleft the mountain like a new-made pitcher. Indra brought forth the kine with his Companions.
8 Wise art thou, Punisher of guilt, O Indra. The sword lops limbs, thou smitest down the sinner,
The men who injure, as it were a comrade, the lofty Law of Varuna and Mitra.
9 Men who lead evil lives, who break agreements, and injure Varuna, Aryaman and Mitra,-
Against these foes, O Mighty Indra, sharpen, as furious death, thy Bull of fiery colour.
10 Indra is Sovran Lord of Earth and Heaven, Indra is Lord of waters and of mountains.

Indra is Lord of prosperers and sages Indra must be invoked in rest and effort.
11 Vaster than days and nights, Giver of increase, vaster than firmament and flood of ocean,
Vaster than bounds of earth and wind's extension, vaster than rivers and our lands is Indra.
12 Forward, as herald of refulgent Morning, let thine insatiate arrow fly, O Indra.
And pierce, as 'twere a stone launched forth from heaven, with hottest blaze the men who love deception.
13 Him, verily, the moons, the mountains followed, the tall trees followed and the plants and herbage.
Yearning with love both Worlds approached, the Waters waited on Indra when he first had being.
14 Where was the vengeful dart when thou, O Indra, clavest the demon ever beat on outrage?
When fiends lay there upon the ground extended like cattle in the place of immolation?
15 Those who are set in enmity against us, the Oganas, O Indra, waxen mighty,-
Let blinding darkness follow those our fbemen, while these shall have bright shining nights to light them.
16 May plentiful libations of the people, and singing Rsis' holy prayers rejoice thee.
Hearing with love this common invocation, come unto us, pass by all those who praise thee.
17 O Indra, thus may we be made partakers of thy new favours that shall bring us profit.
Singing with love, may we the Visvamitras win daylight even now through thee, O Indra.
18 Call we on Maghavan, auspicious Indra, best hero in the fight where spoil is gathered,
The Strong who listens, who gives aid in battles, who slays the Vrtras, wins and gathers riches.

## [10-090] HYMN XC. Purusa.

1. A THOUSAND heads hath Purusa, a thousand eyes, a thousand feet.
On every side pervading earth he fills a space ten fingers wide.
2 This Purusa is all that yet hath been and all that is to be;
The Lord of Immortality which waxes greater still by food.
3 So mighty is his greatness; yea, greater than this is Purusa.
All creatures are one-fourth of him, three-fourths eternal life in heaven.
4 With three-fourths Purusa went up: onefourth of him again was here.
Thence he strode out to every side over what cats not and what cats.
5 From him Viraj was born; again Purusa from Viraj was born.
As soon as he was born he spread eastward and westward o'er the earth.
6 When Gods prepared the sacrifice with Purusa as their offering,
Its oil was spring, the holy gift was autumn; summer was the wood.
7 They balmed as victim on the grass Purusa born in earliest time. With him the Deities and all Sadhyas and Rsis sacrificed.
8 From that great general sacrifice the dripping fat was gathered up.
He formed the creatures of-the air, and animals both wild and tame.
9 From that great general sacrifice Rcas and Sama-hymns were born:
Therefrom were spells and charms produced; the Yajus had its birth from it.

10 From it were horses born, from it all cattle with two rows of teeth:
From it were generated kine, from it the goats and sheep were born.
11 When they divided Purusa how many portions did they make? What do they call his mouth, his arms? What do they call his thighs and feet?
12 The Brahman was his mouth, of both his arms was the Rajanya made.
His thighs became the Vaisya, from his feet the Sudra was produced.
13 The Moon was gendered from his mind, and from his eye the Sun had birth;
Indra and Agni from his mouth were born, and Vayu from his breath.
14 Forth from his navel came mid-air the sky was fashioned from his head
Earth from his feet, and from his car the regions. Thus they formed the worlds.
15 Seven fencing-sticks had he, thrice seven layers of fuel were prepared,
When the Gods, offering sacrifice, bound, as their victim, Purusa.
16 Gods, sacrificing, sacrificed the victim these were the earliest holy ordinances.
The Mighty Ones attained the height of heaven, there where the Sidhyas, Gods of old, are dwelling.

## [10-091] HYMN XCI. Agni.

1. BRISK, at the place of Ila, hymned by men who wake, our own familiar Friend is kindled in the house;
Hotar of all oblation, worthy of our choice, Lord, beaming, trusty friend to one who loveth him.
2 He, excellent in glory, guest in every house, finds like a swift-winged bird a home in every tree.
Benevolent to men, he scorns no living man: Friend to the tribes of men he dwells with every tribe.
3 Most sage with insight, passing skilful with thy powers art thou, O Agni, wise with wisdom,
knowing all.
As Vasu, thou alone art Lord of all good things, of all the treasures that the heavens and earth
produce.
4 Foreknowing well, O Agni, thou in Ila's place hast occupied thy regular station balmed with oil.
Marked are thy comings like the comings of the Dawns, the rays of him who shineth spotless as the Sun.
5 Thy glories are, as lightnings from the rainy cloud, marked, many-hued, like heralds of the Dawns'approach,
When, loosed to wander over plants and forest trees, thou crammest by thyself thy food into thy
mouth.
6 Him, duly coming as their germ, have plants received: this Agni have maternal Waters brought to
life.
So in like manner do the forest trees and plants bear him within them and produce him evermore.
7 When, sped and urged by wind, thou spreadest thee abroad, swift piercing through thy food according to thy will,
Thy never-ceasing blazes, longing to consume, like men on chariots, Agni, strive on every side.
8 Agni, the Hotar-priest who fills the assembly full, Waker of knowledge, chief Controller of the thought,-
Him, yea, none other than thyself, doth man elect at sacrificial offerings great and small alike.
9 Here, Api, the arrangers, those attached to thee, elect thee as their Priest in sacred gatherings,

When men with strewn clipt grass and sacrificial gifts offer thee entertainment, piously inclined.
10 Thine is the Herald's task and Cleanser's duly timed; Leader art thou, and Kindler for the pious man.
Thou art Director, thou the ministering Priest: thou art the Brahman, Lord and Master in our home.
11 When mortal man presents to thee Immortal God, Agni, his fuel or his sacrificial gift,
Then thou art his Adhvaryu, Hotar, messenger, callest the Gods and orderest the sacrifice.
12 From us these hymns in concert have gone forth to him, these. holy words, these Rcas, songs and
eulogies,
Eager for wealth, to Jatavedas fain for wealth: when they have waxen strong they please their
Strengthener.
13 This newest eulogy will I speak forth to him, the Ancient One who loves it. May he hear our voice.
May it come near his heart and make it stir with love, as a fond well-dressed matron clings about her
lord.
14 He in whom horses, bulls, oxen, and barren cows, and rams, when duly set apart, are offered up,-
To Agni, Soma-sprinkled, drinker of sweet juice, Disposer, with my heart I bring a fair hymn forth.
15 Into thy mouth is poured the offering, Agni, as Soma into cup, oil into ladle.
Vouchsafe us wealth. strength-winning, blest with heroes, wealth lofty, praised by men, and full of
splendour.

## [10-092] HYMN XCII. Visvedevas.

1. I PRAISE your Charioteer of sacrifice, the Lord of men, Priest of the tribes, refulgent, Guest of night.
Blazing amid dry plants, snatching amid the green, the Strong, the Holy Herald hath attained to heaven.
2 Him, Agni, Gods and men have made their chief support, who drinks the fatness and completes the sacrifice.
With kisses they caress the Grandson of the Red, like the swift ray of light, the Household Priest of Dawn.
3 Yea, we discriminate his and the niggard's ways: his branches evermore are sent forth to consume.
When his terrific flames have reached the Immortal's world, then men remember and extol the Heavenly Folk.
4 For then the net of Law, Dyaus, and the wide expanse, Earth, Worship, and Devotion meet for
highest praise,
Varuna, Indra, Mitra were of one accord, and Savitar and Bhaga, Lords of holy might.
5 Onward, with ever-roaming Rudra, speed the floods: over Aramati the Mighty have they run.
With them Parijman, moving round his vast domain, loud bellowing, bedews all things that are within.
6 Straightway the Rudras, Maruts visiting all men, Falcons of Dyaus, home-dwellers with the Asura,-
Varuna, Mitra, Aryaman look on with these, and the swift-moving Indra with swift-moving Gods.
7 With Indra have they found enjoyment, they who toil, in the light's beauty, in the very Strong One's
strength;
The singers who in men's assemblies forged for him, according to his due, his friend the thunderbolt.
8 Even the Sun's Bay Coursers hath lie held in check: each one fears Indra as the mightiest of all.
Unhindered, from the air's vault thunders day by day the loud triumphant breathing of the fearful Bull.

9 With humble adoration show this day your song of praise to mighty Rudra, Ruler of the brave:
With whom, the Eager Ones, going their ordered course, he comes from heaven Self-bright,
auspicious, strong to guard.
10 For these have spread abroad the fame of human kind, the Bull Brhaspati and Soma's brotherhood.
Atharvan first by sacrifices made men sure: through skill the Bhrgus were esteemed of all as Gods.
11 For these, the Earth and Heaven with their abundant seed, four-bodied Narasmsa, Yama, Aditi,
God Tvastar Wealth-bestower, the Rbhuksanas, Rodasi, Maruts, Visnu, claim and merit praise.
12 And may he too give car, the Sage, from far away, the Dragon of the Deep, to this our yearning
call.
Ye Sun and Moon who dwell in heaven and move in turn, and with your thought, O Earth and Sky,
observe this well.
13 Dear to all Gods, may Pasan guard the ways we go, the Waters' child and Vayu help us to success.
Sing lauds for your great bliss to Wind, the breath of all: ye Asvins prompt to hear, hear this upon
your way.
14 With hymns of praise we sing him who is throned as Lord over these fearless tribes, the Selfresplendent
One.
We praise Night's youthful Lord benevolent to men, the foeless One, the free, with all celestial
Dames.
15 By reason of his birth here Angiras first sang: the pressing-stones upraised bebeld the sacrifice-
The stones through which the Sage became exceeding vast, and the sharp axe obtains in fight the
beauteous place.

## [10-093] HYMN XCIII. Visvedevas.

1. MIGHTY are ye, and far-extended, Heaven and Earth: both Worlds are evermore to us like two
young Dames.
Guard us thereby from stronger foe; guard us hereby to give us strength.
2 In each succeeding sacrifice that mortal honoureth the Gods,
He who, most widely known and famed for happiness, invitetb them.
3 Ye who are Rulers over all, great is your sovran power as Gods.
Ye all possess all majesty: all must be served in sacrifice.
4 These are the joyous Kings of Immortality, Parijman, Mitra, Aryaman, and Varuna.
What else is Rudra, praised of men? the Maruts, Bhaga, Pusana?
5 Come also to our dwelling, Lords of ample wealth, common partakers of our waters, Sun and Moon,
When the great Dragon of the Deep hath settled down upon their floors.
6 And let the Asvins, Lords of splendour, set us free,- both Gods, and, with their Laws, Mitra and Varuna.
Through woes, as over desert lands, he speeds to ample opulence.
7 Yea, let the Asvins Twain be gracious unto us, even Rudras, and all Gods, Bhaga, Rathaspati;
Parijman, Rbhu, Vaja, O Lords of all wealth Rbhuksanas.
8 Prompt is Rbhuksan, prompt the worshipper's strong drink: may thy fleet Bay Steeds, thine who
sperdest on, approach.
Not mans but God's is sacrifice whose psalm is unassailable.
9 O God Savitar, harmed by none, lauded, give us a place among wealthy princes.

With his Car-steeds at once 'hath our Indra guided the reins and the car of these men.
10 To these men present here, O Heaven and Earth, to us grant lofty fame extending over all
mankind.
Give us a steed to win us strength, a steed with wealth for victory.
11 This speaker, Indra-for thou art our Friend-wherever he may be, guard thou, Victor! for help, ever
for help
Thy wisdom, Vasu! prosper him.
12 So have they strengthened this mine hymn which seems to take its bright path to the Sun, and
reconciles the men:
Thus forms a carpenter the yoke of horses, not to be displaced.
13 Whose chariot-seat hath come again laden with wealth and bright with gold,
Lightly, with piercing ends, as 'twere two ranks of heroes ranged for fight.
14 This to Duhsima Prthavana have I sung, to Vena, Rama, to the nobles, and the King.
They yoked five hundred, and their love of us was famed upon their way.
15 Besides, they showed us seven -and-seventy horses here.
Tanva at once displayed his gift, Parthya at once displayed his gift; and straightway Mayava showed his.

## [10-094] HYMN XCIV. Press-stones.

1. LET these speak loudly forth; let us speak out aloud: to the loud speaking Pressing-stones address
the speech;
When, rich with Soma juice, Stones of the mountain, ye, united, swift to Indra bring the sound of
praise.
2 They speak out like a hundred, like a thousand men: they cry aloud to us with their green-tinted mouths,
While, pious Stones, they ply their task with piety, and, even before the Hotar, taste the offered food.
3 Loudly they speak, for they have found the savoury meath: they make a humming sound over the meat prepared.
As they devour the branch of the Red-coloured Tree, these, the well-pastured Bulls, have uttered bellowings.
4 They cry aloud, with strong exhilarating drink, calling on Indra now, for they have found the meath.
Bold, with the sisters they have danced, embraced by them, making the earth reecho with their
ringing sound.
5 The Eagles have sent forth their cry aloft in heaven; in the sky's vault the dark impetuous ones
have danced.
Then downward to the nether stone's fixt place they sink, and, splendid as the Sun, effuse their
copious stream.
6 Like strong ones drawing, they have put forth all their strength: the Bulls, harnessed together, bear
the chariot-poles.
When they have bellowed, panting, swallowing their food, the sound of their loud snorting is like that
of steeds.
7 To these who have ten workers and a tenfold girth, to these who have ten yoke-straps and ten binding thongs,
To these who bear ten reins, the eternal, sing ye praise, to these who bear ten car-poles, ten when they are yoked.
8 These Stones with ten conductors, rapid in their course, with lovely revolution travel round and round.
They have been first to drink the flowing Soma juice, first to enjoy the milky fluid of the stalk.

9 These Soma-eaters kiss Indra's Bay-coloured Steeds: draining. the stalk they sit upon the ox's hide.

Indra, when he hath drunk Soma-nicath drawn by them, waxes in strength, is famed, is mighty as a Bull.

10. Strong is your stalk; ye, verily, never shall be harmed; ye have refreshment, ye are ever satisfied.

Fair are ye, as it were, through splendour of his wealth, his in whose sacrifice, O Stones, ye find delight.

11 Bored deep, but not pierced through with holes, are ye, O Stones, not loosened, never weary, and
exempt from death,

Eternal, undiseased, moving in sundry ways, unthirsting, full of fatness, void of all desire.

12 Your fathers, verily, stand firm from age to age: they, loving rest, are not dissevered from their seat.

Untouched by time, ne'er lacking green plants and green trees, they with their voice have caused the
heavens and earth to hear.

13 This, this the Stones proclaim, what time they are disjoined, and when with ringing sounds they move and drink the balm.
Like tillers of the ground when they are sowing seed, they mix the Soma, nor, devouring, minish it.

14 They have raised high their voice for juice, for sacrifice, striking the Mother earth as though they danced thereon.
So loose thou too his thought who hath effused the sap, and let the Stones which we are honouring be disjoined.

## [10-095] HYMN XCV. Urvasi. Pururavas.

1. Ho there, my consort! Stay, thou fierce-souled lady, and let us reason for a while together.
Such thoughts as these of ours, while yet unspoken in days gone by have never brought us comfort.

2 What am I now to do with this thy saying? I have gone from thee like the first of Mornings.
Pururavas, return thou to thy dwelling: I, like the wind, am difficult to capture.

3 Like a shaft sent for glory from the quiver, or swift-steed winning cattle winning hundreds.
The lightning seemed to flash, as cowards planned it. The minstrels bleated like a lamb in trouble.

4 Giving her husband's father life and riches, from the near dwelling, when her lover craved her,
She sought the home wherein she found her pleasure, accepting day and night her lord's embraces.

5 Thrice in the day didst thou embrace thy consort, though coldly she received thy fond caresses.
To thy desires, Pururavas, I yielded: so wast thou king, O hero, of my body.

6 The maids Sujirni, Sreni, Sumne-api, Charanyu, Granthini, and Hradecaksus,-
These like red kine have hastened forth, the bright ones, and like milch-cows have lowed in emulation.

7 While he was born the Dames sate down together, the Rivers with free kindness gave him nurture;
And then, Pururavas, the Gods increased thee for mighty battle, to destroy the Dasyus.

8 When I, a mortal, wooed to mine embraces these heavenly nymphs who laid aside their raiment,
Like a scared snake they fled from me in terror, like chariot horses when the car has touched them.

9 When, loving these Immortal Ones, the mortal hath converse with the nymphs as they allow him.
Like swans they show the beauty of their bodies, like horses in their play they bite and nibble.

10 She who flashed brilliant as the falling lightning brought me delicious presents from the waters.

Now from the flood be born a strong young hero May Uruvasi prolong her life for ever

11 Thy birth hath made me drink from earthly milch-kine: this power, Pururavas, hast thou
vouchsafed me.
I knew, and, warned thee, on that day. Thou wouldst not hear me. What sayest thou, when naught avails thee?

12 When will the son be born and seek his father? Mourner-like, will he weep when first he knows him?
Who shall divide the accordant wife and husband, while fire is shining with thy consort's parents?

13 I will console him when his tears are falling: he shall not weep and cry for care that blesses.
That which is thine, between us, will I send thee. Go home again, thou fool;.thou hast not won me.

14 Thy lover shall flee forth this day for ever, to seek, without return, the farthest distance.
Then let his bed be in Destruction's bosom, and there let fierce rapacious wolves devour him.

15 Nay, do not die, Pururavas, nor vanish: let not the evil-omened wolves devour thee.
With women there can be no lasting friendship: hearts of hyenas are the hearts of women.

16 When amid men in altered shape I sojourned, and through four autumns spent the nights among them,
I tasted once a day a drop of butter; and even now with that am I am contented.

17 I, her best love, call Urvasi to meet me, her who fills air and measures out the region.
Let the gift brought by piety approach thee. Turn thou to me again: my heart is troubled.

18 Thus speak these Gods to thee, O son of Ila: As death hath verily got thee for his subject,
Thy sons shall serve the Gods with their oblation, and thou, moreover, shalt rejoice in Svarga.

## [10-096] HYMN XCVI. Indra.

1 In the great synod will I laud thy two Bay Steeds: I prize the sweet strong drink of thee the Warrior- God,
His who pours lovely oil as 'twere with yellow drops. Let my songs enter thee whose form hath golden tints.

2 Ye who in concert sing unto the goldhued place, like Bay Steeds driving onward to the heavenly seat,
For Indra laud ye strength allied with Tawny Steeds, laud him whom cows content as 'twere with yellow drops.

3 His is that thunderbolt, of iron, goldenhued, gold-coloured, very dear, and yellow in his arms;
Bright with strong teeth, destroying with its tawny rage. In Indra are set fast all forms of golden hue.

4 As if a lovely ray were laid upon the sky, the golden thunderbolt spread out as in a race.
That iron bolt with yellow jaw smote Ahi down. A thousand flames had he who bore the tawny-hued.

5 Thou, thou, when praised by men who sacrificed of old. hadst pleasure in their lauds, O Indra golden-haired.
All that befits thy song of praise thou welcornest, the perfect pleasant gift, O Golden-hued from birth.

6 These two dear Bays bring hither Indra on his car, Thunder-armed, joyous, meet for laud, to drink his fill.
Many libations flow for him who loveth them: to Indra have the gold-hued Soma juices run.

7 Tle gold-hued drops have flowed to gratify his wish: the yellow dro s have urged the swift Bays to the Strong.
He who speeds on with Bay Steeds even as he lists hath satisfied his longing for the golden drops.

8 At the swift draught the Soma-drinker waxed in might, the Iron One with yellow beard and yellow hair.

291

He, Lord of Tawny Coursers, Lord of fleet-foot Mares, will bear his Bay Steeds safely over all distress.

9 His yellow-coloured jaws, like ladles move apart, what time, for strength, he makes the yellowtinted stir,

When, while the bowl stands there, he grooms his Tawny Steeds, when he hath drunk strong drink, the sweet juice that he loves.

10 Yea, to the Dear One's seat in homes of heaven and earth the Bay Steeds' Lord hath whinnied like a horse for food.

Then the great wish hath seized upon him mightily, and the Beloved One hath gained high power of life,

11 Thou, comprehending with thy might the earth and heaven, acceptest the dear hymn for ever new and new.

O Asura, disclose thou and make visible the Cow's beloved home to the bright golden Sun.

12 O Indra, let the eager wishes of the folk bring thee, delightful, golden-visored, on thy car,

That, pleased with sacrifice wherein ten fingers toil, thou mayest, at the feast, drink of our offered meath.

13 Juices aforetime, Lord of Bays, thou drankest; and thine especially is this libation.

Gladden thee, Indra, with the meath-rich Soma: pour it down ever, Mighty One! within thee.

## [10-097] HYMN XCVII. Praise of Herbs.

1. HERBS that sprang up in time of old, three ages earlier than the Gods,-

Of these, whose hue is brown, will I declare the hundred powers and seven.

2 Ye, Mothers, have a hundred homes, yea, and a thousand are your growths.

Do ye who have a thousand powers free this my patient from disease.

3 Be glad and joyful in the Plants, both blossoming and bearing fruit,

Plants that will lead us to success like mares who conquer in the race.

4 Plants, by this name I speak to you, Mothers, to you the Goddesses:

Steed, cow, and garment may I win, win back thy very self, O man.

5 The Holy Fig tree is your home, your mansion is the Parna tree:

Winners of cattle shall ye be if ye regain for me this man.

6 He who hath store of Herbs at hand like Kings amid a crowd of men,-

Physician is that sage's name, fiend-slayer, chaser of disease.

7 Herbs rich in Soma, rich in steeds, in nourishments, in strengthening power,-

All these have I provided here, that this man may be whole again.

8 The healing virtues of the Plants stream forth like cattle from the stall,-

Plants that shall win me store of wealth, and save thy vital breath, O man.

9 Reliever is your mother's name, and hence Restorers are ye called.

Rivers are ye with wings that fly: keep far whatever brings disease.

10 Over all fences have they passed, as steals a thief into the fold.

The Plants have driven from the frame whatever malady was there.

11 When, bringing back the vanished strength, I hold these herbs within my hand,

The spirit of disease departs ere he can seize upon the life.

12 He through whose frame, O Plants, ye creep member by member, joint by joint,-

From him ye drive away disease like some strong arbiter of strife.

13 Fly, Spirit of Disease, begone, with the blue jay and kingfisher.

Fly with the wind's impetuousspeed, vanish together with the storm.

14 Help every one the other, lend assistance each of you to each,

All of you be accordant, give furtherance to this speech of mine.

15 Let fruitful Plants, and fruitless, those that blossom, and the blossomless,

Urged onward by Brhaspati, release us from our pain and grief;

16 Release me from the curse's plague and woe that comes from Varuna;

Free me from Yama's fetter, from sin and offence against the Gods.

17 What time, descending from the sky, the Plants flew earthward, thus they spake:

No evil shall befall the man whom while he liveth we pervade,

18 Of all the many Plants whose King is, Soma, Plants of hundred forms,

Thou art the Plant most excellent, prompt to the wish, sweet to the heart.

19 O all ye various Herbs whose King is Soma, that o'erspread the earth,

Urged onward by Brhaspati, combine your virtue in this Plant.

20 Unharmed be he who digs you up, unharmed the man for whom I dig:

And let no malady attack biped or quadruped of ours.

21 All Plants that hear this speech, and those that have departed far away,

Come all assembled and confer your healing power upon this Herb.

22 With Soma as their Sovran Lord the Plants hold colloquy and say:

O King, we save from death the man whose cure a Brahman undertakes.

23 Most excellent of all art thou, O Plant thy vassals are the trees.

Let him be subject to our power, the man who seeks to injure us.

## [10-098] HYMN XCVIII. The Gods.

1. COME, be thou Mitra, Varuna, or Pusan, come, O Brhaspati, to mine oblation:

With Maruts, Vasus, or Adityas, make thou Parjanya pour for Santanu his rain-drops.

2 The God, intelligent, the speedy envoy whom thou hast sent hath come to me, Devapi:

Address thyself to me and turn thee hither within thy lips will I put brilliant language.

3 Within my mouth, Brhaspati, deposit speech lucid, vigorous, and free from weakness,

Thereby to win for Santanu the rain-fall. The meath-rich drop from heaven hath passed within it.

4 Let the sweet drops descend on us, O Indra: give us enough to lade a thousand wagons.

Sit to thy Hotar task; pay worship duly, and serve the Gods, Devapi, with oblation.

5 Knowing the God's good-will, Devapi, Rsi, the son of Rstisena, sate as Hotar.

He hath brought down from heaven's most lofty summit the ocean of the rain, celestial waters.

6 Gathered together in that highest ocean, the waters stood by deities obstructed.

They buried down set free by Arstisena, in gaping clefts, urged onward by Devapi.

7 When as chief priest for Santanu, Devapi, chosen for Hotar's duty, prayed beseeching,

Graciously pleased Brhaspati vouchsafed him a voice that reached the Gods and won the waters.

8 O Agni whom Devapi Arstisena, the mortal man, hath kindled in his glory,

Joying in him with all the Gods together, urge on the sender of the rain, Parjanya.

9 All ancient Rsis with their songs approached thee, even thee, O Much-invoked, at sacrifices.
We have provided wagon-loads in thousands: come to the solemn rite, Lord of Red Horses.

10 The wagon-loads, the nine-and-ninety thousand, these have been offered up to thee, O Agni.
Hero, with these increase thy many bodies, and, stimulated, send us rain from heaven.

11 Give thou these ninety thousand loads, O Agni, to Indra, to the Bull, to be his portion.
Knowing the paths which Deities duly travel, set mid the Gods in heaven Aulana also.

12 O Agni, drive afar our foes, our troubles chase malady away and wicked demons.
From this air-ocean, from the lofty heavens, send down on us a mighty flood of waters.

## [10-099] HYMN XCIX. Indra.

I. WHAT Splendid One, Loud-voiced, Farstriding, dost thou, well knowing, urge us to exalt with praises?
What give we him? When his might dawned, he fashioned the Vrtra-slaying bolt, and sent us waters.

2 He goes to end his work with lightning flashes: wide is the seat his Asura glory gives him.
With his Companions, not without his Brother, he quells Saptatha's magic devices.

3 On most auspicious path he goes to battle he toiled to win heaven's light, full fain to gain it;
He seized the hundred-gated castle's treasure by craft, unchecked, and slew the lustful demons.

4 Fighting for kine, the prize of war, and I roaming among the berd be brings the young streams hither,
Where, footless, joined, without a car to bear them, with jars for steeds, they pour their flood like butter.

5 Bold, unsolicited for wealth, with Rudras he came, the Blameless, having left his dwelling,
Came, seized the food of Vamra and his consort, and left the couple weeping and unsheltered.

6 Lord of the dwelling, he subdued the demon who roared aloud, six-eyed and triple-headed.
Trta, made stronger by the might he lent him, struck down the boar with shaft whose point was iron.

7 He raised himself on high and shot his arrow against the guileful and oppressive foeman.
Strong, glorious, manliest, for us he shattered the forts of Nabus when he slew the Dasyus.

8 He, like a cloud that rains upon the pasture, hath found for us the way to dwell in safety.
When the Hawk comes in body to the Soma, armed with his iron claws he slays the Dasyus.

9 He with his potent Friends gave up the mighty, gave gusnia up to Kutsa for affliction.
He led the lauded Kavi, he delivered Atka as prey to him and to his heroes.

10 He, with his Gods who love mankind, the Wondrous, giving like Varuna who works with magic,
Was known, yet young as guardian of the seasons; and he quelled Araru, four-footed dernon.

11 Through lauds of him hath Ausija Rjisvan burst, with the Mighty's aid, the stall of Pipru.
When the saint pressed the juice and shone as singer, he seized the forts and with his craft subdued them.

12 So, swiftly Asura, for exaltation, hath the great Vamraka come nigh to Indra.

He will, when supplicated, bring him blessing: he hath brought all, food, strength, a happy dwelling.

## [10-100] HYMN C. Visvedevas.

1. Be, like thyself, O Indra, strong for our delight: here lauded, aid us, Maghavan, drinker of the juice.
Savitar with the Gods protect us: hear ye Twain. We ask for freedom and complete felicity.

2 Bring swift, for offering, the snare that suits the time, to the pure-drinker Vayu, roaring as he goes,
To him who hath approached the draught of shining milk. We ask for freedom and complete felicity.

3 May Savitar the God send us full life, to each who sacrifices, lives aright and pours the juice
That we with simple hearts may wait upon the Gods. We ask for freedom and complete felicity.

4 May Indra evermore be gracious unto us, and may King Soma meditate our happiness,
Even as men secure the comfort of a friend. We ask for freedom and complete felicity.

5 Indra hath given the body with its song and strength: Brhaspati, thou art the lengthener of life.
The sacrifice is Manu, Providence, our Sire. We ask for freedom and complete felicity.

6 Indra possesseth might celestial nobly formed: the singer in the hotise is Agni, prudent Sage.
lie is the sacrifice in synod, fair, most near. We ask for freedom and complete felicity,

7 Not often have we sinned against you secretly, nor, Vasus, have we openly provoked the Gods.
Not one of its, ye Gods, hath worn an alien shape. We ask for freedom and complete felicity.

8 May Savitar remove from us our malady, and may the Mountains keep it far away from where
The press-stone as it sheds the meath rings loudly forth. We ask for freedom and complete felicity.

9 Ye Vasus, let the stone, the presser stand erect: avert all enmities and keep them far remote.
Our guard to be adored is Savitar this God. We ask for freedom and complete felicity.

10 Eat strength and fatness in the pasture, kine, who are balmed at the reservoir and at the seat of Law.
So let your body be our body's medicine. We ask for freedom and complete felicity.

11 The singer fills the spirit: all mens, love hath he. Indra takes kindly care of those who pour the juice.
For his libation is the heavenly udder full. We ask for freedom and complete felicity.

12 Wondrous thy spirit-filling light, triumpliant; thy hosts save from decay and are resistless.
The pious votary by straightest pathway speeds to possess the best of all the cattle.

## [10-101] HYMN CI. Visvedevas.

1. WAKE with one mind, my friends, and kindle Agni, ye who are many and who dwell together.
Agni and Dadhikras and Dawn the Goddess, you, Gods with Indra, I call down to help us.

2 Make pleasant hymns, spin out your songs and praises: build ye a ship equipped with oars for transport.
Prepare the implements, make all things ready, and let the sacrifice, my friends, go forward.

3 Lay on the yokes, and fasten well the traces: formed is the furrow, sow the seed within it.
Through song may we find bearing fraught with plenty: near to the ripened grain approach the sickle.

4 Wise, through desire of bliss from Gods, the skilful bind the traces fast, And lay the yokes on either side.

5 Arrange the buckets in their place securely fasten on the straps. We will pour forth the well that hath a copious stream, fair-flowing well that never fails.

6 I pour the water from the well with pails prepared and goodly straps,
Unfailing, full, with plenteous stream.

7 Refresh the horses, win the prize before you: equip a chariot fraught with happy fortune.
Pour forth the well with stone wheel, wooden buckets, the drink of heroes, with the trough for armour.

8 Prepare the cow-stall, for there drink your heroes: stitch ye the coats of armour, wide and many.
Make iron forts, secure from all assailants let not your pitcher leak: stay it securely.

9 Hither, for help, I turn the holy heavenly mind of you the Holy Gods, that longs for sacrifice.
May it pour milk for us, even as a stately cow who, having sought the pasture, yields a thousand streams.

10 Pour golden juice within the wooden vessel: with stone-made axes fashion ye and form it.
Embrace and compass it with tenfold girdle, and to both chariot-poles attach the car-horse.

11 Between both poles the car-horse goes pressed closely, as in his dwelling moves the doublywedded.
Lay in the wood the Soviran of the Forest, and sink the well although ye do not dig it.

12 Indra is he, O men, who gives us happiness: sport, urge the giver of delight to win us strength
Bring quickly down, O priests, hither to give us aid, to drink the Soma, Indra Son of Nistigri.

## [10-102] HYMN CII. Indra.

1. FOR thee may Indra boldly speed the car that works on either side.
Favour us, Much-invoked! in this most glorious fight against the raiders of our wealth.

2 Loose in the wind the woman's robe was streaming what time she won a car-load worth a thousand.
The charioteer in fight was Mudgalani: she Indra's dart, heaped up the prize of battle.

3 O Indra, cast thy bolt among assailants who would slaughter us:
The weapon both of Dasa and of Arya foe keep far away, O Maghavan.

4 The bull in joy had drunk a lake of water. His shattering horn encountered an opponent.
Swiftly, in vigorous strength, eager for glory, he stretched his forefeet, fain to win and triumph.

5 They came anear the bull; they made him thunder, made him pour rain down ere the fight was ended.
And Mudgala thereby won in the contest well-pastured kine in hundreds and in thousands.

6 In hope of victory that bull was harnessed: Kesi the driver urged him on with shouting.
As he ran swiftly with the car behind him his lifted heels pressed close on Mudgalani.

7 Deftly for him he stretched the car-pole forward, guided the bull thereto and firmly yoked him.
Indra vouchsafed the lord of cows his favour: with mighty steps the buffalo ran onward.

8 Touched by the goad the shaggy beast went nobly, bound to the pole by the yoke's thong of leather.
Performing deeds of might for many people, he, looking on the cows, gained strength and vigour.

9 Here look upon this mace, this bull's companion, now lying midway on the field of battle.

Therewith hath Mudgala in ordered contest won for cattle for himself, a hundred thousand.

10 Far is the evil: who hath here beheld it? Hither they bring the bull whom they are yoking..
To this they give not either food or water. Reaching beyond the pole it gives directions.

11 Like one forsaken, she hath found a husband, and teemed as if her breast were full and flowing.
With swiftly-racing chariot may we conquer, and rich and blessed be our gains in battle.

12 Thou, Indra, art the mark whereon the eyes of all life rest, when thou,
A Bull who drivest with thy bull, wilt win the race together with thy weakling friend.

## [10-103] HYMN CIII. Indra.

1. SWIFT, rapidly striking, like a bull who sharpens his horns, terrific, stirring up the people,
With eyes that close not, bellowing, Sole Hero, Indra. subdued at once a hundred armies.

2 With him loud-roaring, ever watchful, Victor, bold, hard to overthrow, Rouser of battle,
Indra. the Strong, whose hand bears arrows, conquer, ye warriors, now, now vanquish in the combat.

3 He rules with those who carry shafts and quivers, Indra who with his band rings hosts together,
Foe-conquering, strong of arm, the Soma-drinker, with mighty bow, shooting with well-laid arrows.

4 Brhaspati, fly with thy chariot hither, slayer of demons, driving off our foemen.
Be thou protector of our cars, destroyer, victor in battle, breaker-up of armies.

5 Conspicuous by thy strength, firm, foremost fighter, mighty and fierce, victorious, all-subduing,
The Son of Conquest, passing men and heroes, kine-winner, mount thy conquering car, O Indra.

6 Cleaver of stalls, kine-winner, armed with thunder, who quells an army and with might destroys it.-
Follow him, brothers! quit yourselves like heroes, and like this Indra show your zeal and courage.

7 Piercing the cow-stalls with surpassing vigour, Indra, the pitiless Hero, wild with anger,
Victor in fight, unshaken and resistless,may he protect our armies in our battles.

8 Indra guide these: Brhaspati precede them, the guerdon, and the sacrifice, and Soma;
And let the banded Maruts march in forefront of heavenly hosts that conquer and demolish.

9 Ours be the potent host of mighty Indra, King Varuna, and Maruts, and Adityas.
Uplifted is the shout of Gods who conquer high-minded Gods who cause the worlds to tremble.

10 Bristle thou up, O Maghavan, our weapons: excite the spirits of my warring heroes.
Urge on the strong steeds' might, O Vrtra-slayer, and let the din of conquering cars go upward.

11 May Indra aid us when our flags are gathered: victorious be the arrows of our army.
May our brave men of war prevail in battle. Ye Gods, protect us in the shout of onset.

12 Bewildering the senses of our foemen, seize thou their bodies and depart, O Apva.
Attack them, set their hearts on fire and burn them: so let our foes abide in utter darkness.

13 Advance, O heroes, win the day. May Indra be your sure defence.

Exceeding mighty be your arms, that none may wound or injure you.

## [10-104] HYMN CIV. Indra.

1. Soma hath flowed for thee, Invoked of mat Speed to our sacrifice with both thy Coursers.
To thee have streameld the songs or mighty singers, imploring, Indra, drink of our libation.
2 Drink of the juice which men have washed in waters, and fill thee full, O Lord of Tawny Horses.
O Indra, hearer of the laud, with Soma which stones have mixed for thee enhance thy rapture.
3 To make thee start, a strong true draught I offer to thee, the Bull, O thou whom Bay Steeds carry.
Here take delight, O Indra, in our voices while thou art hymned with power and all our spirit.
4 O Mighty Indra, through thine aid, thy prowess, obtaining life, zealous, and skilled in Order,
Men in the house who share the sacred banquet stand singing praise that brings them store of children.
5 Through thy directions, Lord of Tawny Coursers, thine who art firm, splendid, and blest, the people
Obtain most liberal aid for their salvation, and praise thee, Indra, through thine excellencies.
6 Lord of the Bays, come with thy two Bay Horses, come to our prayers, to drink the juice of Soma.
To thee comes sacrifice which thou acceptest: thou, skilled in holy rites, art he who giveth.
7 Him of a thousand powers, subduing foemen, Maghavan praised with hymns and pleased with Soma,-
Even him our songs approach, resistless Indra: the adorations of the singer laud him.
8 The way to bliss for Gods and man thou foundest, Indra, seven lovely floods, divine, untroubled,
Wherewith thou, rending forts, didst move the ocean, and nine-and-ninety flowing streams of water.
9 Thou from the curse didst free the mighty Waters, and as their only God didst watch and guard them.
O Indra, cherish evermore thy body with those which thou hast won in quelling Vrtra.
10 Heroic power and noble praise is Indra yea, the song worships him invoked of many.
Vrtra he quelled, and gave men room and freedom: gakra, victorious, hath conquered armies.
11 Call we on Maghayan, auspicious Indra. best Hero in this fight where spoil is gathered,
The Strong, who listens, who gives aid in battles, who slays the Vrtras, wins and gathers riches.

## [10-105] HYMN CV. Indra.

1. WHEN, Vasu, wilt thou love the laud? Now let the channel bring the stream.
The juice is ready to ferment.
2 He whose two Bay Steeds harnessed well, swerving, pursue the Bird's tail-plumes,
With Rowing manes, like heaven and earth, he is the Lord with power to give.
3 Bereft of skill is Indra, if, like some outwearied man he fears
The sinner, when the Mighty hath prepared himself for victory.
4 Indra with these drives round, until he meets with one to worship him:
Indra is Master of the pair who snort and swerve upon their way.
5 Borne onward by the long-maned Steeds who stretch themselves as 'twere for food,
The God who wears the helm defends them with his jaws.
6 The Mighty sang with Lofty Ones: the Hero fashioned with his strength,

Like skilful Matarisvan with his power and might,
7 The bolt, which pierced at once the vitals of the Dasyu easy to be slain,
With jaw uninjured like the wondrous firmament.
8 Grind off our sins: with song will we conquer the men who sing no hymns:
Not easily art thou pleased with prayerless sacrifice.
9 When threefold flame burns high for thee, to rest on poles of sacrifice,
Thou with the living joyest in the self-bright Ship.
10 Thy glory was the speckled cup, thy glory was the flawless scoop.
Wherewith thou pourest into thy receptacle.
11 As hundreds, O Immortal God, have sung to thee, so hath Sumitra, yea, Durmitra praised thee here,
What time thou holpest Kutsa's son, when Dasyus fell, yea, holpest Kutsa's darling when the Dasyus died.

## [10-106] HYMN CVI. Asvins.

1. THIS very thing ye Twain hold as your object: ye weave your songs as skilful men weave garments.
That ye may come united have I waked you: ye spread out food like days of lovely weather.
2 Like two plough-bulls ye move along in traces, and seek like eager guests your bidder's banquet.
Ye are like glorious envoys mid the people: like bulls, approach the place where ye are watered.
3 Like the two pinions of a bird, connected, like two choice animals, ye have sought our worship.
Bright as the fire the votary hath kindled, ye sacrifice in many a spot as roamers.
4 Ye are our kinsmen, like two sons, two fathers, strong in your splendour and like kings for conquest;
Like rays for our enjoyment, Lords to feed us, ye, like quick bearers, have obeyed our calling.
5 You are like two pleasantly moving well-fed (hills) like Mitra and Varuna, the two bestowers of
felicity, veracious, possessors of infinite wealth, happy, like two horses plump with fodder, abiding in
the firmament, like two rams (are you) to be nourished with sacrificial food, to be cherished (with oblations).
6 You are like two mad elephants bending their forequarters and smiting the foe, like the two sons of
Nitosa destroying (foes), and cherishing (friends); you are bright as two water-born (jewels), do you,
who are victorious, (render) my decaying mortal body free from decay.
7 Fierce (Asvins), like two powerful (heroes), you enable this moving, perishable mortal (frame) to
cross over to the objects (of its destination) as over water; extremely strong, like the Rbhus, your
chariot, attained its destination swift as the wind, it pervaded (everywhere), it dispensed riches.
8 With your bellies full of the Soma, like two saucepans, preservers of wealth, destroyers of enemies.
(you are) armed with hatchets, moving like two flying (birds) with forms like the moon, attaining
success through the mind, like two laudable beings, (you are) approaching (the sacrifice).
9 Like giants, ye will find firm ground to stand on in depths, like feet for one who fords a shallow.
Like cars ye will attend to him who orders: ye Two enjoy our wondrous work as sharers.
10 Like toiling bees ye bring to us your honey, as bees into the hide that opens downward.
11 May we increase the laud and gain us vigour: come to our song, ye whom one chariot carries.

Filled be our kine with ripened meath like glory: Bhutamsa hath fulfilled the Asvins' longing.

## [10-107] HYMN CVII. Daksina.

1. THESE men's great bounty hath been manifested, and the whole world of life set free from darkness.
Great light hath come, vouchsafed us by the Fathers: apparent is the spacious path of Guerdon.

2 High up in heaven abide the Guerdon-givers: they who give steeds dwell with the Sun for ever.
They who give gold are blest with life eternal. they who give robes prolong their lives, O Soma.

3 Not from the niggards-for they give not fireely-comes Meed at sacrifice, Gods' satisfaction:
Yea, many men with hands stretched out with Guerdon present their gifts because they dread dishonour.

4 These who observe mankind regard oblation as streamy Vayu and light-finding Arka.
They satisfy and give their gifts in synod, and pour in streams the seven-mothered Guerdon.

5 He who brings Guerdon comes as first invited: chief of the hamlet comes the Guerdon-bearer.
Him I account the ruler of the people who was the first to introduce the Guerdon.

6 They call him Rsi, Brahman, Sama-chanter, reciter of the laud, leader of worship.
The brightly-shining God's three forms he knoweth who first bestowed the sacrificial Guerdon.

7 Guerdon bestows the horse, bestows the bullock, Guerdon bestows, moreover, gold that Rsisters.
Guerdon gives food which is our life and spirit. He who is wise takes Guerdon for his armour.

8 The liberal die not, never are they ruined: the liberal suffer neither harm nor trouble.
The light of heaven, the universe about us,-all this doth sacrificial Guerdon give them.

9 First have the liberal gained a fragrant dwelling, and got themselves a bride in fair apparel.
The liberal have obtained their draught of liquor, and conquered those who, unprovoked, assailed them.

10 They deck the fleet steed for the bounteous giver: the maid adorns herself and waits to meet him.
His home is like a lake with lotus blossoms, like the Gods' palaces adorned and splendid.

11 Steeds good at draught convey the liberal giver, and lightly rolling moves the car of Guerdon.
Assist, ye Gods, the liberal man in battles: the liberal giver conquers foes in combat.

## [10-108] HYMN CVIII. Sarama. Panis.

1. WHAT wish of Sarama hath brought her hither? The path leads far away to distant places.
What charge hast thou for us? Where turns thy journey? How hast thou made thy way o'er Rasa's waters.

2 I come appointed messenger of Indra, seeking your ample stores of wealth, O Panis.
This hath preserved me from the fear of crossing: thus have I made my way o'er Rasa's waters.

3 What is that Indra like, what is his aspect whose envoy, Sarama, from afar thou comest?
Let him approach, and we will show him friendship: he shall be made the herdsman of our cattle.

4 I know him safe from harm: but he can punish who sent me hither from afar as envoy.
Him rivers flowing with deep waters bide not. Low will ye be, O Panis, slain by Indra.

5 These are the kine which, Sarama, thou seekest, flying, O Blest One, to the ends of heaven.
Who will loose these for thee without a battle? Yea, and sharp-pointed are our warlike weapons.

6 Even if your wicked bodies, O ye Panis, were arrow-proof, your words are weak for wounding;
And were the path to you as yet unmastered, Brhaspati in neither case will spare you.

7 Paved with the rock is this our treasure-chamber; filled full of precious things, of kine, and horses.
These Panis who are watchful keepers guard it. In vain hast thou approached this lonely station.

8 Rsis will come inspirited with Soma, Angirases unwearied, and Navagvas.
This stall of cattle will they part among them: then will the Panis wish these words unspoken.

9 Even thus, O Sarama, hast thou come hither, forced by celestial might to make the journey.
Turn thee not back, for thou shalt be our sister: O Blest One, we will give thee of the cattle.

10 Brotherhood, sisterhood, I know not either: the dread Angirases and Indra know them.
They seemed to long for kine when I departed. Hence, into distance, be ye gone, O Panis.

11 Hence, far away, ye Panis! Let the cattle lowing come forth as holy Law commandeth,
Kine which Brhaspati, and Soma, Rsis, sages, and pressing-stones have found when hidden.

## [10-109] HYMN CIX. Visvedevas.

1. THESE first, the boundless Sea, and Matarisvan, fierce-glowing Fire, the Strong, the Blissbestower.
And heavenly Floods, first-born by holy Order, exclaimed against the outrage on a Brahman.

2 King Soma first of all, without reluctance, made restitution of the Brahman's consort.
Mitra and Varuna were the inviters: Agni as Hota; took her hand and led her.

3 The man, her pledge, must by her hand be taken when they have cried, She is a Brahman's consort.
She stayed not for a herald to conduct her: thus is the kingdom of a ruler guarded.

4 Thus spake of her those Gods of old, Seven Rsis who sate them down to their austere devotion:
Dire is a Brahman's wife led home by others: in the supremest heaven she plants confusion.

5 The Brahmacari goes engaged in duty: he is a member of the Gods' own body.
Through him Brhaspati obtained his consort, as the Gods gained the ladle brought by Soma.

6 So then the Gods restored her, so men gave the woman back again.
The Kings who kept their promises restored the Brahman's wedded wife,

7 Having restored the Brahman's wife, and freed them, with Gods' aid, from sin,
They shared the fulness of the earth, and won themselves extended sway.

## [10-110] HYMN CX. Apris.

1. THOU in the house of man this day enkindled worshippest Gods as God, O Jatavedas.
Observant, bright as Mitra, bring them hither: thou art a sapient and foreknowing envoy.

2 Tanunapat, fair-tongued, with sweet meath balming the paths and waysof Order, make them pleasant.
Convey our sacrifice to heaven, exalting with holy thoughts ourhymns of praise and worship.
3 Invoked, deserving prayer and adoration, O Agni, come accordant with the Vasus.
Thou art, O Youthful Lord, the Gods' Invoker, so, best of Sacrificers, bring them quickly.
4 By rule the Sacred Grass is scattered eastward, a robe to clothe this earth when dawns are breaking.
Widely it spreads around and far-extended, fair for the Gods and bringing peace and freedom.
5 Let the expansive Doors be widely opened, like wives who deck their beauty for their husbands.
Lofty, celestial, all-impelling Portals, admit the Gods and give them easy entrance.
6 Pouring sweet dews let holy Night and Morning, each close to each, be seated at their station,
Lofty, celestial Dames with gold to deck them. assuming all their fair and radiant beauty.
7 Come the two first celestial sweet-voiced Hotars, arranging sacrifice for man to worship
As singers who inspire us in assemblies, showing the eastward light with their direction.
8 Let Bharati come quickly to our worship, and Ila showing like a human being.
So let Sarasvati and both her fellows, deft Goddesses, on this fair grass be seated.
9 Hotar more skilled in sacrifice, bring hither with speed to-day God Tvastar, thou who knowest.
Even him who formed these two, the Earth and Heaven the Parents, with their forms, and every creature.
10 Send to our offerings which thyself thou balmest the Companies of Gods in ordered season.
Agni, Vanaspati the Immolator sweeten our offered gift with meath and butter.
11 Agni, as soon as he was born, made ready the sacrifice, and was the Gods' preceder.
May the Gods cat our offering consecrated according to this true Priest's voice and guidance.

## [10-111] HYMN CXI. Indra.

1. BRING forth your sacred song ye prudent singers, even as are the thoughts of human beings.
Let us draw Indra with true deeds anear us: he loves our songs, the Hero, and is potent.
2 The hymn shone brightly from the seat of worship: to the kine came the Bull, the Heifer's Offpring
With mighty bellowing hath he arisen, and hath pervaded even the spacious regions.
3 Indra knows, verily, how to hear our singing, for he, victorious, made a path for Surya.
He made the Cow, and be became the Sovran of Heaven, primeval, matchless, and unshaken.
4 Praised by Angirases, Indra demolished with might the works of the great watery monster
Full many regions, too, hath he pervaded, and by his truth supported earth's foundation.
5 The counterpart of heaven and earth is Indra: he knoweth all libations, slayeth Susna.
The vast sky with the Sun hath he extended, and, best otpillars, stayed it with a pillar.
6 The Vrtra-slaver with his bolt felled Vrtra: the magic of the godless, waxen mighty,
Here hast thou, Bold Assailant, boldly conquered. Yea, then thine arms, O Maghavan, were potent.

7 When the Dawns come attendant upon Surya their rays discover wealth of divers colours.
The Star of heaven is seen as 'twere approaching: none knoweth aught of it as it departeth.
8 Far have they gone, the first of all these waters, the waters that flowed forth when Indra sent them.
Where is their spring, and where is their foundation? Where now, ye Waters, is your inmost centre?
9 Thou didst free rivers swallowed by the Dragon; and rapidly they set themselves in motion,
Those that were loosed and those that longed for freedom. Excited now to speed they run unresting.
10 Yearning together they have sped to Sindhu: the Fort-destroyer, praised, of old, hath loved them.
Indra, may thy terrestrial treasures reach us, and our full songs of joy approach thy dwelling.

## [10-112] HYMN CXII. Indra.

1. DRINK of the juice, O Indra, at thy plea. sure, for thy first draught is early morn's libation.
Rejoice, that thou mayst slay our foes, O Hero, and we with lauds will tell thy mighty exploits.
2 Thou hast a car more swift than thought, O Indra; thercon come hither, come to drink the Soma.
Let thy Bay Steeds, thy Stallions, hasten hither, with whom thou cornest nigh and art delighted.
3 Deck out thy body with the fairest colours, with golden splendour of the Sun adorn it.
O Indra, turn thee hitherward invited by us thy friends; be seated and be joyful.
4 O thou whose grandeur in thy festive transports not even these two great worlds have comprehended.
Come, Indra, with thy dear Bay Horses harnessed, come to our dwelling and the food thou lovest.
5 Pressed for thy joyous banquet is the Soma, Soma whereof thou, Indra, ever drinking,
Hast waged unequalled battles with thy foemen, which prompts the mighty flow of thine abundance.
6 Found from of old is this thy cup, O Indra: Satakratu, drink therefrom the Soma.
Filled is the beaker with the meath that gladdens, the beaker which all Deities delight in.
7 From many a side with proffered entertainment the folk are calling thee, O Mighty Indra.
These our libations shall for thee be richest in sweet meath: dvink thereof and find them pleasant.
8 I will declare thy deeds of old, O Indra, the mighty acts which thou hast first accomplished.
In genuine wrath thou loosenedst the mountain so that the Brahman easily found the cattle.
9 Lord of the hosts, amid our bands be seated: they call thee greatest Sage among the sages.
Nothing is done, even far away, without thee: great, wondrous, Maghavan, is the hymn I sing thee.
10 Aim of our eyes be thou, for we implore thee, O Maghavan, Friend of friends and Lord of treasures.
Fight, Warrior strong in truth, fight thou the battle: give us our share of undivided riches.

## [10-113] HYMN CXTII. Indra.

1. THE Heavens and the Earth accordant with all Gods encouraged graciously that vigorous might of his.
When he came showing forth his majesty and power, he drank of Soma juice and waxed exceeding strong.
2 This majesty of his Visnu extols and lauds, making the stalCthat gives the meath flow forth with inight.

When Indra Maghavan with those who followed him had smitten Vrtra he deserved the choice of
Gods.

3 When, bearing warlike weapons, fain to win thee praise, thou mettest Vrtra, yea, the Dragon, for the fight,
Then all the Maruts who were gathered with dice there extolled, O Mighty One, thy powerful majesty.

4 Soon as he sprang to life he forced asun. der hosts: forward the Hero looked to manly deed and war.
He cleft the rock, he let concurrent streams flow forth, and with his skilful art stablished the heavens'
wide vault.

5 Indra hath evermore possessed surpassing power: he forced, far from each other, heaven and earth apart.
He hurled impetuous down his iron thunderbolt, a joy to Varuna's and Mitra's worshipper.

6 Then to the mighty powers of Indra, to his wrath, his the fierce Stormer, loud of voice, they came
with speed;
What time the Potent One rent Vrtra with his strength, who held the waters back, whom darkness compassed round.

7 Even in the first of those heroic acts which they who strove together came with might to execute,
Deep darkness fell upon the slain, and Indra won by victory the right of being first invoked.

8 Then all the Gods extolled, with eloquence inspired by draughts of Soma juice, thy deeds of manly might.
As Agni eats the dry food with his tcetlv, he ate Vrtra, the Dragon, maimed by Indra's deadly dart.

9 Proclaim his many friendships, met with friendship, made with singers, with the skilful and the eloquent.
Indra, when he subdues Dhuni and Cumuri, lists to Dabhiti for his faithful spirit's sake.

10 Give riches manifold with noble horses, to be remembered while my songs address thee.
May we by easy paths pass all our troubles: find us this day a ford wide and extensive.

## [10-114] HYMN CXIV. Visvedevas.

1. Two perfect springs of heat pervade the Threefold, and come for their delight is Matarisvan.
Craving the milk of heaven the Gods are present: well do they know the praisesong and the Saman.

2 The priests beard far away, as they are ordered, serve the three Nirrtis, for well they know them.
Sages have traced the cause that first produced them, dwelling in distant and mysterious chambers.

3 The Youthful One, well-shaped, with four locks braided, brightened with oil, puts on the ordinances.
Two Birds of mighty power are seated near her, there where the Deities receive their portion.

4 One of these Birds hath passed into the sea of air: thence he looks round and views this universal world.
With simple heart I have beheld him from anear: his Mother kisses him and he returns her kiss.

5 Him with fair wings though only One in nature, wise singers shape, with songs, in many figures.
While they at sacrifices fix the metres, they measure out twelve chalices of Soma.

6 While they arrange the four and six-and-thirty, and duly order, up to twelve, the measures,
Having disposed the sacrifice thoughtful sages send the Car forward with the Rc and Saman.

7 The Chariot's majesties are fourteen others: seven sages lead it onward with their Voices.
Who will declare to us the ford Apnana, the path whereby they drink first draughts of Soma?

8 The fifteen lauds are in a thousand places that is as vast as heaven and earth in measure.
A thousand spots contain the mighty thousand. Vak spreadeth forth as far as Prayer extendeth.

9 What sage hath learned the metres' application? Who hath gained Vak, the spirit's aim and object?
Which ministering priest is called eighth Hero? Who then hath tracked the two Bay Steeds of Indra?

10 Yoked to his chariot-pole there stood the Coursers: they only travel round earth's farthest limits.
These, when their driver in his home is settled, receive the allotted meed of their exertion.

## [10-115] HYMN CXV. Agni.

1. VERILY wondrous is the tender Youngling's growth who never draweth nigh to drink his Mothers'
milk.
As soon as she who hath no udder bore him, he, faring on his great errand, suddenly grew strong.

2 Then Agni was his name, most active to bestow, gathering up the trees with his consuming tooth;
Skilled in fair sacrifice, armed with destroying tongue, impetuous as a bull that snorteth in the mead.

3 Praise him, yourGod who, bird-like, rests upon a tree, scattering drops of juice and pouring forth his flood,
Speaking aloud with flame as with his lips a priest, and broadening his paths like one of high command.

4 Thou Everlasting, whom, far-striding fain to burn, the winds, uninterrupted, never overcome,
They have approached, as warriors eager for the fight, heroic Trita, guiding him to gain his wish.

5 This Agni is the best of Kanvas, Kanvas' Friend, Conqueror of the foe whether afar or near.
May Agni guard the singers, guard the princes well: may Agni grant to us our princes' gracious help.

6 Do thou, Supitrya, swiftly following, make thyself the lord of Jatavedas, mightiest of all,
Who surely gives a boon even in thirsty land most powerful, prepared to aid us in the wilds.

7 Thus noble Agni with princes and mortal men is lauded, excellent for conquering strength with chiefs,
Men who are well-disposed as friends and true to Law, even as the heavens in majesty surpass mankind.

8 O Son of Strength, Victorious, with this title Upastuta's most potent voice reveres thee.
Blest with brave sons by thee we will extol thee, and lengthen out the days of our existence.

9 Thus, Agni, have the sons of Vrstihavya, the Rsis, the Upastutas invoked thee.
Protect them, guard the singers and the princes. With Vasat! have they come, with hands uplifted,
with their uplifted hands and cries of Glory!

## [10-116] HYMN CXV1. Indra.

1. DRINK Soma juice for mighty power and vigour, drink, Strongest One, that thou mayst smite down Vrtra.
Drink thou, invoked, for strength, and riches: drink thou thy fill of meath and pour it down, O Indra.

2 Drink of the foodful juice stirred into motion, drink what thou choosest of the flowing Soma.
Giver of weal, be joyful in thy spirit, and turn thee hitherward to bless and prosper.

3 Let heavenly Soma gladden thee, O Indra, let that effused among mankind delight thee.
Rejoice in that whereby thou gavest freedom, and that whereby thou conquerest thy foemen.

4 Let Indra come, impetuous, doubly mighty, to the poured juice, the Bull, with two Bay Coursers.
With juices pressed in milk, with meath presented, glut evermore thy bolt, O Foe-destroyer.
5 Dash down, outffaming their sharp flaming weapons, the strong-holds of the men urged on by demons.
I give thee, Mighty One, great strength and conquest: go, meet thy foes and rend them in the battle.
6 Extend afar the votary's fame and glory, as the firm archer's strength drives off the foeman.
Ranged on our side, grown strong in might that conquers, never defeated, still increase thy body.
7 To thee have we presented this oblation: accept it, Sovran Ruler, free from anger.
Juice, Maghavan, for thee is pressed and ripened: eat, Indra, drink of that which stirs to meet thee.
8 Eat, Indra, these oblations which approach thee: be pleased with food made ready and with Soma.
With entertainment we receive thee friendly: effectual be the sacrificer's wishes.
9 I send sweet speech to Indra and to Agni: with hymns I speed it like a boat through waters.
Even thus, the Gods seem moving round about me, the fountains and bestowers of our riches.

## [10-117] HYMN CXVII. Liberality.

1. THE Gods have not ordained hunger to be our death: even to the well-fed man comes death in varied shape.
The riches of the liberal never waste away, while he who will not give finds none to comfort him.
2 The man with food in store who, when the needy comes in miserable case begging for bread to eat,
Hardens his heart against him-even when of old he did him service-finds not one to comfort him.
3 Bounteous is he who gives unto the beggar who comes to him in want of food and feeble.
Success attends him in the shout of battle. He makes a friend of him in future troubles.
4 No friend is he who to his friend and comrade who comes imploring food, will offer nothing.
Let him depart-no home is that to rest in-, and rather seek a stranger to support him.
5 Let the rich satisfy the poor implorer, and bend his eye upon a longer pathway.
Riches come now to one, now to another, and like the wheels of cars are ever rolling.
6 The foolish man wins food with fruitless labour: that food -I speak the truth- shall be his ruin.
He feeds no trusty friend, no man to love him. All guilt is he who eats with no partaker.
7 The ploughshare ploughing makes the food that feeds us, and with its feet cuts through the path it follows.
Better the speaking than the silent Brahman: the liberal friend outyalues him who gives not.
8 He with one foot hath far outrun the biped, and the two-footed catches the three-footed.
Four-footed creatures come when bipeds call them, and stand and look where five are met together.
9 The hands are both alike: their labour differs. The yield of sister milch-kine is unequal.
Twins even differ in their strength and vigour: two, even kinsmen, differ in their bounty.

## [10-118] HYMN CXVIII. Agni.

1. AGNI, refulgent among men thou slayest the devouring fiend, Bright Ruler in thine own abode.

2 Thou springest up when worshipped well the drops of butter are thy joy
When ladies are brought near to thee.
3 Honoured with gifts he shines afar, Agni adorable with song: The dripping ladle balms his face.
4 Agni with honey in his mouth, honoured with gifts, is balmed with oil,
Refulgent in his wealth of light.
5 Praised by our hymns thou kindlest thee, Oblation-bearer, for the Gods
As such do mortals call on thee.
6 To that Immortal Agni pay worship with oil, ye mortal men,- Lord of the house, whom none deceives.
7 O Agni, burn the Raksasas with thine unconquerable flame Shine guardian of Eternal Law.
8 So, Agni, with thy glowing face burn fierce against the female fiends,
Shining among Uruksayas.
9 Uruksayas have kindled thee, Oblation-bearer, thee, with hymns.
Best Worshipper among mankind.

## [10-119] HYMN CXIX. Indra.

1. THIS, even this was my resolve, to win a cow, to win a steed: Have I not drunk of Soma juice?
2 Like violent gusts of wind the draughts that I have drunk have lifted me
Have I not drunk of Soma juice?
3 The draughts I drank have borne me up, as fleet-foot horses draw a car:
Have I not drunk of Soma juice?
4 The hymn hath reached me, like a cow who lows to meet her darling calf:
Have I not drunk of Soma juice?
5 As a wright bends a chariot-seat so round my heart I bend the hymn:
Have I not drunk of Soma juice?
6 Not as a mote within the eye count the Five Tribes of men with me:
Have I not drunk of Soma juice?
7 The heavens and earth themselves have not grown equal to one half of me
Have I not drunk of Soma juice?
8 I in my grandeur have surpassed the heavens and all this spacious earth
Have I not drunk of Soma juice?
9 Aha! this spacious earth will I deposit either here or there Have I not drunk of Soma juice?
10 In one short moment will I smite the earth in fury here or there:
Have I not drunk of Soma juice?
11 One of my flanks is in the sky; I let the other trail below: Have I not drunk of Soma juice?
12 1, greatest of the Mighty Ones, am lifted to the firmament: Have I not drunk of Soma juice?
13 I seek the worshipper's abode; oblation-bearer to the Gods: Have I not drunk of Soma juice?

## [10-120] HYMN CXX. Indra.

1. IN all the worlds That was the Best and Highest whence sprang the Mighty Gods, of splendid
valour.
As soon as born he overcomes his foemen, be in whom all who lend him aid are joyful.
2 Grown mighty in his strength, with ample vigour, he as a foe strikes fear into the Dasa,

Eager to win the breathing and the breathless. All sang thy praise at banquet and oblation.

3 All concentrate on thee their mental vigour, what time these, twice or thrice, are thine assistants.

Blend what is sweeter than the sweet with sweetness: win. quickly with our meath that meath in battle.

4 Therefore in thee too, thou who winnest riches, at every banquet are the sages joyful.

With mightier power, Bold God, extend thy firmness: let not malignant Yatudhanas harm thee.

5 Proudly we put our trust in thee in battles, when we behold great wealth the prize of combat.

I with my words impel thy weapons onward, and sharpen with my prayer thy vital vigour.

6 Worthy of praises, many-shaped, most skilful, most energetic, Aptya of the Aptyas:

He with his might destroys the seven Danus, subduing many who were deemed his equals.

7 Thou in that house which thy protection guardeth bestowest wealth, the higher and the lower.

Thou stablishest the two much-wandering Mothers, and bringest many deeds to their completion.

8 Brhaddiva, the foremost of light-winners, repeats these holy prayers, this strength of Indra.

He rules the great self-luminous fold of cattle, and all the doors of light hath he thrown open.

9 Thus hath Brhaddiva, the great Atharvan, spoken to Indra as himself in person.

The spotless Sisters, they who are his Mothers, with power exalt him and impel him onward.

### [10-121] HYMN CXXI. Ka.

1. IN the beginning rose Hiranyagarbha, born Only Lord of all created beings.

He fixed and holdeth up this earth and heaven. What God shall we adore with our oblation?

2 Giver of vital breath, of power and vigour, he whose commandments all the Gods acknowledge -.

The Lord of death, whose shade is life immortal. What God shall we adore with our oblation?

3 Who by his grandeur hath become Sole Ruler of all the moving world that breathes and slumbers;

He who is Loord of men and Lord of cattle. What God shall we adore with our oblation?

4 His, through his might, are these snow-covered mountains, and men call sea and Rasa his possession:

His arms are these, his are these heavenly regions. What God shall we adore with our oblation?

5 By him the heavens are strong and earth is stedfast, by him light's realm and sky-vault are supported:

By him the regions in mid-air were measured. What God shall we adore with our oblation?

6 To him, supported by his help, two armies embattled look while trembling in their spirit,

When over them the risen Sun is shining. What God shall we adore with our oblation?

7 What time the mighty waters came, containing the universal germ, producing Agni,

Thence sprang the Gods' one spirit into being. What God shall we adore with our oblation?

8 He in his might surveyed the floods containing productive force and generating Worship.

He is the God of gods, and none beside him. What God shall we adore with our oblation?

9 Neer may he harm us who is earth's Begetter, nor he whose laws are sure, the heavens' Creator,

He who brought forth the great and lucid waters. What God shall we adore with our oblation?

10 Prajapati! thou only comprehendest all these created things, and none beside thee.

Grant us our hearts' desire when we invoke thee: may we have store of riches in possession.

### [10-122] HYMN CXXII. Agni.

1. I PRAISE the God of wondrous might like Indra, the lovely pleasant Guest whom all must welcome.

May Agni, Priest and Master of the household, give hero strength and all-sustaining riches.

2 O Agni, graciously accept this song of mine, thou passing-wise who knowest every ordinance.

Enwrapped in holy oil further the course of prayer: the Gods bestow according to thy holy law.

3 Immortal, wandering round the seven stations, give, a liberal Giver, to the pious worshipper,

Wealth, Agni, with brave sons and ready for his use: welcome the man who comes with fuel unto thee.

4 The seven who bring oblations worship thee, the Strong, the first, the Great Chief Priest, Ensign of sacrifice,

The oil-anointed Bull, Agni who hears, who sends as God full hero strength to him who freely gives.

5 First messenger art thou, meet for election: drink thou thy fill invited to the Anirta,

The Maruts in the votary's house adorned thee; with lauds the Bhrgus gave thee light and glory.

6 Milking the teeming Cow for all-sustaining food. O Wise One, for the worship-loving worshipper,

Thou, Agni, dropping oil, thrice lighting works of Law, showest thy wisdom circling home and sacrifice.

7 They who at flushing of this dawn appointed thee their messenger, these men have paid thee reverence.

Gods strengthened thee for work that must be glorified, Agni, while they made butter pure for sacrifice.

8 Arrangers in our synods, Agni, while they sang Vasisistha s sons have called thee down, the Potent One.

Maintain the growth of wealth with men who sacrifice. Ye Gods, preserve us with your blessings evermore.

### [10-123] HYMN CXXIII. Vena.

1. SEE, Vena, born in light, hath driven hither, on chariot of the air, the Calves of Prsni.

Singers with hymns caress him as an infant there where the waters and the sunlight mingle.

2 Vena draws up his wave from out the ocean. mist-born, the fair one's back is made apparent,

Brightly he shone aloft on Order's summit: the hosts sang glory to their common birthplace.

3 Full many, lowing to their joint-possession, dwelling together stood the Darling's Mothers.

Ascending to the lofty height of Order, the bands of singers 'sip the sweets of Amrta.

4 Knowing his form, the sages yearned to meet him: they have come nigh to hear the wild Bull's bellow.

Performing sacrifice they reached the river: for the Gandharva found the immortal waters.

5 The Apsaras, the Lady, sweetly smiling, supports her Lover in sublimest heaven.

In his Friend's dwelling as a Friend he wanders: he, Vena, rests him on his golden pinion.

6 They gaze on thee with longing in their spirit, as on a strong-winged bird that mounteth sky-ward;

On thee with wings of gold, Varuna's envoy, the Bird that hasteneth to the home of Yama.

7 Erect, to heaven hath the Gandharva mounted, pointing at us his many-coloured weapons;
Clad in sweet raiment beautiful to look on, for he, as light, produceth forms that please us.
8 When as a spark he cometh near the ocean, still looking with a vulture's eye to heaven,
His lustre, joying in its own bright splendour, maketh dear glories in the lowest region.

## [10-124] HYMN CXXIV. Agni, Etc.

1. COME to this sacrifice of ours, O Agni, threefold, with seven threads and five divisions.
Be our oblation-bearer and preceder: thou hast lain long enough in during darkness.
2 I come a God foreseeing from the godless to immortality by secret pathways,
While I, ungracious one, desert the gracious, leave mine own friends and seek the kin of strangers.
3 1, looking to the guest of other lineage, have founded many a rule of Law and Order.
I bid farewell to the Great God, the Father, and, for neglect, obtain my share of worship.
4 I tarried many a year within this altar: I leave the Father, for my choice is Indra.
Away pass Agni, Varuna and Soma. Rule ever changes: this I come to favour.
5 These Asuras have lost their powers of magic. But thou, O Varuna, if thou dost love me,
O King, discerning truth and right from falsehood, come and be Lord and Ruler of my kingdom.
6 Here is the light of heaven, here allis lovely; here there is radiance, here is air's wide region.
Let us two slaughter Vrtra. Forth, O Soma! Thou art oblation: we therewith will serve thee.
7 The Sage hath fixed his form by wisdom in the heavens: Varuna with no violence let the waters flow.
Like women-folk, the floods that bring prosperity have eau lit his hue and colour as they gleamed and shone.
8 These wait upon his loftiest power and vigour: he dwells in these who triumph in their Godhead;
And they, like people who elect their ruler, have in abhorrence turned away from Vrtra.
9 They call him Swan, the abhorrent floods' Companion, moving in friendship with celestial Waters.
The poets in their thought have looked on Indra swiftly approaching when Anustup calls him.

## [10-125] HYMN CXXV. Vak.

1. I TRAVEL with the Rudras and the Vasus, with the Adityas and All-Gods I wander.
I hold aloft both Varuna and Mitra, Indra and Agni, and the Pair of Asvins.
2 I cherish and sustain high-swelling Soma, and Tvastar I support, Pusan, and Bhaga.
I load with wealth the zealous sdcrificer who pours the juice and offers his oblation
3 I am the Queen, the gatherer-up of treasures, most thoughtful, first of those who merit worship.
Thus Gods have stablished me in many places with many homes to enter and abide in.
4 Through me alone all eat the food that feeds them,-each man who sees, brewhes, hears the word outspoken
They know it not, but yet they dwell beside me. Hear, one and all, the truth as I declare it.
5 1, verily, myself announce and utter the word that Gods and men alike shall welcome.

I make the man I love exceeding mighty, make him a sage, a Rsi, and a Brahman.
6 I bend the bow for Rudra that his arrow may strike and slay the hater of devotion.
I rouse and order battle for the people, and I have penetrated Earth and Heaven.
7 On the world's summit I bring forth the Father: my home is in the waters, in the ocean.
Thence I extend o'er all existing creatures, and touch even yonder heaven with my forehead.
8 I breathe a strong breath like the wind and tempest, the while I hold together all existence.
Beyond this wide earth and beyond the heavens I have become so mighty in my grandeur.

## [10-126] HYMN CXXVI. Visvedevas.

1. No peril, no severe distress, ye Gods, affects the mortal man,
Whom Aryaman and Mitra lead, and Varima, of one accord, beyond his foes.
2 This very thing do we desire, Varuna, Mitra, Aryaman,
Whereby ye guhrd the mortal man from sore distress, and lead him safe beyond his foes.
3 These are, each one, our present helps, Varuna, Mitra, Aryaman.
Best leaders, best deliverers to lead us on and bear as safe beyond our foes.
4 Ye compass round and guard each man, Varuna, Mitra, Aryaman:
In your dear keeping may we be, ye who are excellent as guides beyond our foes.
5 Adityas are beyond all foes,-Varuna, Mitra, Aryaman:
Strong Rudra with the Marut host, Indra, Agni let us call for weal beyond our foes.
6 These lead us safely over all, Varuna, Mitra, Aryaman,
These who are Kings of living men, over all troubles far away beyond our foes.
7 May they give bliss to aid us well, Varuna, Mitra, Aryaman:
May the Adityas, when we pray, grant us wide shelter and defence beyond our foes.
8 As in this place, O Holy Ones, ye Vasus freed even the Gaud when her feet were fettered.
So free us now from trouble and affliction: and let our life be lengthened still, O Api.

## [10-127] HYMN CXXVII. Night.

1. WITH all her eyes the Goddess Night looks forth approaching many a spot:
She hath put all her glories on.
2 Immortal. she hath filled the waste, the Goddess hath filled height and depth:
She conquers darkness with her light.
3 The Goddess as she comes hath set the Dawn her Sister in her place:
And then the darkness vanishes.
4 So favour us this night, O thou whose pathways we have visited As birds their nest upon the tree.
5 The villagers have sought their homes, and all that walks and all that flies,
Even the falcons fain for prey.
6 Keep off the she-wolf and the wolf, O Urmya, keep the thief away;
Easy be thou for us to pass.
7 Clearly hath she come nigh to me who decks the dark with richest hues:
O Morning, cancel it like debts.
8 These have I brought to thee like kine. O Night, thou Child of Heaven, accept

This laud as for a conqueror.

## [10-128] HYMN CXXVIII. Visvedevas.

1. LET me win glory, Agni, in our battles: enkindling thee, may we support our bodies.
May the four regions bend and bow before me: with thee for guardian may we win in combat.
2 May all the Gods be on my side in battle, the Maruts led by Indra, Visnu, Agni.
Mine be the middle air's extended region, ani may the wind blow favouring these my wishes.
3 May the Gods grant me riches; may the blessing and invocation of the Gods assist me.
Foremost in fight be the divine Invokers: may we, unwounded, have brave heroes round us.
4 For me let them present all mine oblations, and let my mind's intention be accomplished.
May I he guiltless of the least transgression: and, all ye Go-is, do ye combine to bless us.
5 Ye six divine Expanses, grant us freedom: here, all ye Gods, acquit yourselves like heroes.
Let us not lose our children or our bodies: let us not benefit the foe, King Soma!
6 Baffling the wrath of our opponents, Agni, guard us as our infallible Protector.
Let these thy foes turn back and seek their houses, and let their thought who watch at home be ruined.
7 Lord of the world, Creator of creators the saviour God who overcomes the foeman.
May Gods, Brhaspati, both Asvins shelter from ill thii sacrifice and sacrificer.
8 Foodful, and much-invoked, at this our calling mty the great Bull vouchsafe us wide protection.
Lord of Bay Coursers, Indra, blew our children: harm us not, give us riot as prey to others.
9 Let those who are our foemen stay. afar from us: with Indra and with Agni we will drive them off.
Vasus, Adityas, Rudras have exalted me, made me far-reaching, inighty, thinker, sovran lord.

## [10-129] HYMN CXXIX. Creation.

1. THEN was not non-existent nor existent: there was no realm of air, no sky beyond it.
What covered in, and where? and what gave shelter? Was water there, unfathomed depth of water?
2 Death was not then, nor was there aught immortal: no sign was there, the day's and night's divider.
That One Thing, breathless, breathed by its own nature: apart from it was nothing whatsoever.
3 Darkness there was: at first concealed in darknew this All was indiscriminated chaos.
All that existed then was void and form less: by the great power of Warmth was born that Unit.
4 Thereafter rose Desire in the beginning, Desire, the primal seed and germ of Spirit.
Sages who searched with their heart's thought discovered the existent's kinship in the non-existent.
5 Transversely was their severing line extended: what was above it then, and what below it?
There were begetters, there were mighty forces, free action here and energy up yonder
6 Who verily knows and who can here declare it, whence it was born and whence comes this creation?
TheGods are later than this world's production. Who knows then whence it first came into being?

7 He, the first origin of this creation, whether he formed it all or did not form it,
Whose eye controls this world in highest heaven, he verily knows it, or perhaps he knows not.

## [10-130] HYMN CXXX. Creation.

1. THE sacrifice drawn out with threads on every side, stretched by a hundred sacred ministers and one,-
This do these Fathers weave who hitherward are come: they sit beside the warp and cry, Weave forth, weave back.
2 The Man extends it and the Man unbinds it: even to this vault of heaven hath he outspun, it.
These pegs are fastened to the seat of worship: they made the Sama-hymns their weaving shuttles.
3 What were the rule, the order and the model? What were the wooden fender and the butter?
What were the hymn, the chant, the recitation, when to the God all Deities paid worship?
4 Closely was Gayatri conjoined with Agni, and closely Savitar combined with Usnih.
Brilliant with Ukthas, Soma joined Anustup: Brhaspati's voice by Brhati was aided.
5 Viraj adhered to Varuna and Mitra: here Tristup day by day was Indra's portion.
Jagati entered all the Gods together: so by this knowledge men were raised to Rsis.
6 So by this knowledge men were raised to Rsis, when ancient sacrifice sprang up, our Fathers.
With the mind's eye I think that I behold them who first performed this sacrificial worship.
7 They who were versed in ritual and metre, in hymns and rules, were the Seven Godlike Rsis.
Viewing the path of those of old, the sages have taken up the reins like chariot-drivers.

## [10-131] HYMN CXXXI. Indra.

1. DRIVE all our enemies away, O Indra, the western, mighty Conqueror, and the eastern.
Hero, drive off our northern foes and southern, that we in thy wide shelter may be joyful.
2 What then? As men whose fields are full of barley reap the ripe corn removing it in order,
So bring the food of those men, bring it hither, who went not to prepare the grass for worship.
3 Men come not with one horse at sacred seasons; thus they obtain no honour in assemblies.
Sages desiring herds of kine and horses strengthen the mighty Indra for his friendship.
4 Ye, Asvins, Lords of Splendour, drank full draughts of grateful Soma juice,
And aided Indra in his work with Namuci of Asura birth.
5 As parents aid a son, both Asvins, Indra, aided thee with their wondrous Powers and wisdom.
When thou, with might. hadst drunk the draught that gladdens, Sarasvati, O Maghavan, refreshed thee.-
6 Indra is strong to save, rich in assistance may he, possessing all, be kind and gracious.
May he disperse our foes and give us safety, and may we be the lords of hero vigou r.
7 May we enjoy his favour, his the Holy may we enjoy his blessed loving kindness.
May this rich Indra, as our good Protector, drive off and keep afar all those who hate us.

## [10-132] HYMN CXXXII. Mitra. Varuna.

1. MAY Dyaus the Lord of lauded wealth, and Earth stand by the man who offers sacrifice,
And may the Asvins, both the Gods, strengthen the worshipper with bliss.
2 As such we honour you, Mitra and Varuna, with hasty zeal, most blest, you who sustain the folk.
So may we, through your friendship for the worshipper, subdue the fiends.
3 And when we seek to win your love and friendship, we.who have precious wealth in our possession,
Or when the worshipper augments his riches let not his treasures be shut up
4 That other, Asura! too was born of Heaven. thou art, O Varuna, the King of all men.
The chariot's Lord was well content, forbearing to anger Death by sin so great.
This sin hath Sakaputa here committed. Heroes who fled to their dear friend he slayeth,
When the Steed bringeth down your grace and favour in bodies dear and worshipful.
6 Your Mother Aditi, ye wise, was purified with water even as earth is purified from heaven.
Show love and kindness here below: wash her in rays of heavenly light.
7 Ye Twain have seated you as Lords of Wealth, as one who mounts a car to him who sits upon the pole, upon the wood.
These our disheartened tribes Nrmedhas saved from woe, Sumedhas saved from Woe.

## [10-133] HYMN CXXXIII. Indra.

1. SING strength to Indra that shall set his chariot in the foremost place.
Giver of room in closest fight, slayer of foes in shock of war, be thou our great encourager. Let the
weak bowstrings break upon the bows of feeble enemies.
2 Thou didst destroy the Dragon: thou sentest the rivers down to earth.
Foeless, O Indra, wast thou born. Thou tendest well each choicest thing. Therefore we draw us close to thee. Let the weak bowstrings break upon the bows of feeble enemies.
3 Destroyed be all malignities and all our enemy's designs.
Thy bolt thou castest, at the foe, O Indra, who would srnite us dead: thy liberal bounty gives us wealth.
4 The robber people round about, Indra, who watch and aim at us,-
Trample them down beneath thy foot; a conquering scatterer art thou.
5 Whoso assails us, Indra, be the man a stranger or akin,
Bring down, thyself, his strength although it be as vast as are the heavens.
6 Close to thy friendship do we cling, O Indra, and depend, or, thee.
Lead us beyond all pain and grief along the path of holy Law.
7 Do thou bestow upon us her, O Indra, who yields according to the singer's longing,
That the great Cow may, with exhaustless udder, pouring a thousand streams, give milk to feed us.

## [10-134] HYMN CXXXIV. Indra.

1. As, like the Morning, thou hast filled, O Indra, both the earth and heaven.
So as the Mighty One, great King of all the mighty world of men, the Goddess Mother brought thee
forth, the Blessed Mother gave thee life.
2 Relax that mortal's stubborn strength whose heart is bent on wickedness.

Trample him down beneath thy feet who watches for and aims at us. The Goddess Mother brought
thee forth, the Blessed Mother gave thee life.
3 Shake down, O Slayer of the foe, those great all splendid enemies.
With all thy powers, O Sakra, all thine helps, O Indra, shake them down:
4 As thou, O Satakratu, thou, O Indrv, shakest all things down
As wealth for him who sheds the juice, with thine assistance thousandfold.
5 Around, on every side like drops of sweat let lightning-flashes fall.
Let all malevolence pass away from us like threads of Darva grass.
6 Thou bearest in thine hand a lance like a long hook, great Counsellor!
As with his foremost foot a goat, draw down the branch, O Maghavan.
7 Never, O Gods, do we offend, nor are we ever obstinate: we walk as holy texts command.
Closely we clasp and cling to you, cling to your sides, beneath your arms.

## [10-135] HYMN CXXXV. Yama.

1. IN the Tree clothed with goodly leaves where Yama drinketh with the Gods,
The Father, Master of the house, tendeth with love our ancient Sires.
2 I looked reluctantly on him who cherishes those men of old,
On him who treads that evil path, and then I yearned for this again.
3 Thou mountest, though thou dost not see, O Child, the new and wheel-less car
Which thou hast fashioned mentally, onepoled but turning every way.
4 The car which thou hast made to roll hitherward from the Sages, Child!
This hath the Saman followed close, hence, laid together on a ship.
5 Who was the father of the child? Who made the chariot roll away?
Who will this day declare to us how the funeral gift was made?
6 When the funeral gift was placed, straightway the point of flame appeared.
A depth extended in the front: a passage out was made behind.
7 Here is the seat where Yama dwells, that which is called the Home of Gods:
Here minstrels blow the flute for him here he is glorified with songs.

## [10-136] HYMN CXXXVI. Kesins.

1. HE with the long loose locks supports Agni, and moisture, heaven, and earth:
He is all sky to look upon: he with long hair is called this light.
2 The Munis, girdled with the wind, wear garments soiled of yellow hue.
They, following the wind's swift course go where the Gods have gone before.
3 Transported with our Munihood we have pressed on into the winds:
You therefore, mortal men. behold our natural bodies and no more.
4 The Muni, made associate in the holy work of every God,
Looking upon all varied forms flies through the region of the air.
5 The Steed of Vata, Vayu's friend, the Muni, by the Gods impelled,
In both the oceans hath his home, in eastern and in western sea.
6 Treading the path of sylvan beasts, Gandharvas, and Apsarases,

He with long locks, who knows the wish, is a sweet most delightful friend

7 Vayu hath churned for him: for him he poundeth things most hard to bend,

When he with long loose locks hath drunk, with Rudra, water from the cup.

## [10-137] HYMN CXXXVII Visvedevas.

1. YE Gods, raise up once more the man whom ye have humbled and brought low.

O Gods, restore to life again the man who hatb committed sin.

2 Two several winds are blowing here, from Sindhu, from a distant land.

May one breathe energy to thee, the other blow disease away.

3 Hither, O Wind, blow healing balm, blow all disease away, thou Wind;

For thou who hast all medicine comest as envoy of the Gods.

4 I am come nigh to thee with balms to give thee rest and keep thee safe.

I bring thee blessed strength, I drive thy weakening malady away.

5 Here let the Gods deliver him, the Maruts' band deliver him:

All things that be deliver him that he be freed from his disease.

6 The Waters have their healing power, the Waters drive disease away.

The Waters have a balm for all: let them make medicine for thee.

7 The tongue that leads the voice precedes. Then with our ten-fold branching hands,

With these two chasers of disease we stroke thee with a gentle touch.

## [10-138] HYMN CXXXVIII. Indra.

1. ALLIED with thee in friendship, Indra, these, thy priests, remembering Holy Law, rent Vrtra limb
from limb,

When they bestowed the Dawns and let the waters flow, and when thou didst chastise dragons at Kutsa's call.

2 Thou sentest forth productive powers, clavest the hills, thou dravest forth the kine, thou drankest pleasant meath.

Thou gavest increase through this Tree's surpassing might. The Sun shone by the hymn that sprang from Holy Law.

3 In the mid-way of heaven the Sun unyoked his car: the Arya found a match to meet his Dam foe.

Associate with Rjisvan Indra overthrew the solid forts of Pipru, conjuring Asura.

4 He boldly cast down forts which none had e'er assailed: unwearied he destroycd the godless
treasure-stores.

Like Sun and Moon he took the stronghold's wealth away, and, praised in song, demolished foes with
flashing dart.

5 Armed with resistless weapons, with vast power to cleave, the Vrtra-slayer whets his darts and deals fordi wounds.

Bright Usas was afraid of Indra's slaughtering bolt: she went upon her way and left her chariot there.

6 These are thy famous exploits, only thine, when thou alone hast left the other reft of sacrifice.

Thou in the heavens hast set the ordering of the Moons: the Father bears the felly portioned out by thee.

## [10-139] HYMN CXXXIX. Savitar.

1. SAVITAR, golden-haired, hath lifted eastward, bright With the sunbeams, his eternal lustre;

He in whose energy wise Pusan marches, surveying all existence like a herdsman.

2 Beholding men he sits amid the heaven filling the two world-halves and air's wide region.

He looks upon the rich far-spreading pastures between the eastern and the western limit.

3 He, root of wealth, the gatherer-up of treasures, looks with his might on every form and figure.

Savitar, like a God.whose Law is constant, stands in the battle for the spoil like Indra.

4 Waters from sacrifice came to the Gandharva Visvavasu, O Soma, when they saw him.

Indra, approaching quickly, marked their going, and looked around upon the Sun's enclosures.

5 This song Visvavasu shall sing us, meter of air's mid-realm celestial Gandharva,

That we may know aright both truth and falsehood: may he inspire our thoughts and help our praises.

6 In the floods' track he found the bootyseeker: the rocky cow-pen's doors he threw wide open.

These, the Gandharva told him, flowed with Amrta. Indra knew well the puissancc of the dragons.

## [10-140] HYMN CXL. Agni.

1. AGNI, life-power and fame are thine: thy fires blaze mightily, thou rich in wealth of beams!

Sage, passing bright, thou givest to the worshipper, with strength, the food that merits laud.

2 With brilliant, purifying sheen, with perfect sheen thou liftest up thyself in light.

Thou, visiting both thy Mothers, aidest them as Son: thou joinest close the earth and heaven.

3 O Jatavedas, Son of Strength, rejoice ihyself, gracious, in our fair hymns and songs.

In thee are treasured various forms of strengthening food, born nobly and of wondrous help.

4 Agni, spread forth, as Ruler, over living things: give wealth to us, Immortal God.

Thou shinest out from beauty fair to look upon: thou leadest us to conquering power.

5 To him, the wise, who orders sacrifice, who hath great riches un der his control,

Thou givest blest award of good, and plenteous food, givest him wealth that conquers all.

6 The men have set before them them for their welfare Agni, strong, visible to all, the Holy.

Thee, Godlike One, with ears to hear, most famous, men's generations magnify with praise-songs.

## [10-141] HYMN CXLI. Visvedevas.

1. TURN hither, Agni, speak to us: come to us with a gracious mind.

Enrich us, Master of the house: thou art the Giver of our wealth.

2 Let Aryarnan vouchsafe us wealth, and Bhaga, and Brhaspati.

Let the Gods give their gifts, and let Sunrta, Goddess, grant us wealth.

3 We call King Soma to our aid, and Agni with our songs and hymns,

Adityas, Visnu, Surya, and the Brahman Priest Brhaspati.

4 Indra, Vayu, Brhaspati, Gods swift to listen, we invoke,

That in the synod all the folk may be benevolent to us.

5 Urge Aryaman to send us gifts, and Indra, and Brhaspati,

Vata, Visnu, Sarasvati and the Strong Courser Savitar.

6 Do thou, O Agni, with thy fires strengthen our prayer and sacrifice:

Urge givers to bestow their wealth to aid our service of the Gods.

## [10-142] HYMN CXLII. Agni.

1. WITH thee, O Agni, was this singer of the laud: he hath no other kinship, O thou Son of Strength.

Thou givest blessed shelter with a triple guard. Keep the destructive lightning far away from us.
2 Thy birth who seekest food is in the falling flood, Agni: as Comrade thou winnest all living things.
Our coursers and our songs shall be victorious: they of themselves advance like one who guards the herd.
3 And thou, O Agni, thou of Godlike nature, sparest the stones, while caring up the brushwood.
Then are thy tracks like deserts in the corn-lands. Let us not stir to wrath thy mighty arrow.
4 O'er hills through vales devouring as thou goest, thou partest like an army fain for booty
As when a barber shaves a beard, thou shavest earth when the wind blows on thy flame and fans it.
5 Apparent are his lines as he approaches the course is single, but the cars are many,
When, Agni, thou, making thine arms resplendent, advancest o'er the land spread out beneath thee.
6 Now let thy strength, thy burning flames fly upward, thine energies, O Agni, as thou toilest.
Gape widely, bend thee, waxing in thy vigour: let all the Vasus sit this day beside thee.
7 This is the waters' reservoir, the great abode of gathered streams.
Take thou another path than this, and as thou listest walk thereon.
8 On thy way hitherward and hence let flowery Durva grass spring up
Let there be lakes with lotus blooms. These are the mansions of the flood.

## [10-143] HYMN CXLIII. Asvins.

1. YE made that Atri, worn with eld, free as a horse to win the goal.
When ye restored to youth and strength Kaksivan like a car renewed,
2 Ye freed that Atri like a horse, and brought him newly-born to earth.
Ye loosed him like a firm-tied knot which Gods unsoiled by dust had bound.
3 Heroes who showed most wondrous power to Atri, strive to win fair songs;
For then, O Heroes of the sky, your hymn of praise shall cease no more.
4 This claims your notice, Bounteous Gods! - oblation, Asvins! and our love,
That ye, O Heroes, in the fight may bring us safe to ample room.
5 Ye Twain to Bhujyu tossed about in ocean at the region's end,
Nasatyas, with your winged sterds came nigh, and gave him strength to win.
6 Come with your joys, most liberal Gods, Lords of all treasures, bringing weal.
Like fresh full waters to a well, so, Heroes come and be with us.

## [10-144] HYMN CXLIV. Indra.

1. THIS deathless Indu, like a steed, strong and of full vitality,
Belongs to thee, the Orderer.
2 Here, by us, for the worshipper, is the wise bolt that works with skill.
It brings the bubbling beverage as a dexterous man brings the effectual strong drink.
3 Impetuous Ahisuva, a bull among cows of his,
looked down upon the restless Hawk.
4 That the strong-pinioned Bird hath brought, Child of the Falcon, from afar,
What moves upon a hundred wheels along the female Dragon's path.

5 Which, fair, unrobbed, the Falcon brought thee in his foot, the red-hued dwelling of the juice;
Through this came vital power which lengthens out our days, and kinship through its help awoke.
6 So Indra is by lndu's power; e'en among Gods will it repel great treachery.
Wisdom, Most Sapient One, brings force that lengthens life. May wisdom bring the juice to us.

## [10-145] HYMN CXLV. Sapatnibadhanam.

1. FROM out the earth I dig this plant, a herb of most effectual power,
Wherewith one quells the rival wife and gains the husband for oneself.
2 Auspicious, with expanded leaves, sent by the Gods, victorious plant,
Blow thou the rival wife away, and make my husband only mine.
3 Stronger am 1, O Stronger One, yea, mightier than the mightier;
And she who is my rival wife is lower than the lowest dames.
4 Her very name I utter not: she takes no pleasure in this man.
Far into distance most remote drive we the rival wife away.
5 I am the conqueror, and thou, thou also act victorious:
As victory attends us both we will subdue my fellow-wife.
6 I have gained thee for vanquisher, have grasped thee with a stronger spell.
As a cow hastens to her calf, so let thy spirit speed te me, hasten like water on its way.

## [10-146] HYMN CXLVI. Aranyani.

1. GODDESS of wild and forest who seemest to vanish from the sight.
How is it that thou seekest not the village? Art thou not afraid?
2 What time the grasshopper replies and swells the shrill cicala's voice,
Seeming to sound with tinkling bells, the Lady of the Wood exults.
3 And, yonder, cattle seem to graze, what seems a dwelling-place appears:
Or else at eve the Lady of the Forest seems to free the wains.
4 Here one is calling to his cow, another there hath felled a tree:
At eve the dweller in the wood fancies that somebody hath screamed.
5 The Goddess never slays, unless some murderous enemy approach.
Man eats of savoury fruit and then takes, even as he wills, his rest.
6 Now have I praised the Forest Queen, sweet-scented, redolent of balm,
The Mother of all sylvan things, who tills not but hath stores of food.

## [10-147] HYMN CXLVII Indra.

1. I TRUST in thy first wrathful deed, O Indra, when thou slewest Vrtra and didst work to profit man;
What time the two world-halves fell short of thee in might, and the earth trembled at thy force, O Thunder-anned.
2 Thou with thy magic powers didst rend the conjurer Vrtra, O Blameless One, with heart that longed for fame.
Heroes elect thee when they battle for the prey, thee in all sacrifices worthy of renown.
3 God Much-invoked, take pleasure in these princes here, who, thine exalters, Maghavan, have come to wealth.
In synods, when the rite succeeds, they hymn the Strong for sons and progeny and riches undisturbed.
4 That man shall find delight in well-protected wealth whose care provides for him the quick-sought
joyous draught.

Bringing oblations, strengthened Maghavan, by thee, he swiftly wins the spoil with heroes in the
fight.
5 Now for our band, O Maghavan, when lauded, make ample room with might, and grant us riches.
Magician thou, our Varuna and Mitra, deal food to us, O Wondrous, as Dispenser.

## [10-148] HYMN CXLVIII. Indra.

1. WHEN we have pressed the juice we laud thee, Indra, and when, Most Valorous we have won the
booty.
Bring us prosperity, as each desires it under thine own protection may we conquer.
2 Sublime from birth, mayst thou O Indra, Hero, with Surya overcome the Dasa races.
As by a fountain's side, we bring the Soma that lay concealed, close-hidden in the waters.
3 Answer the votary's hymns, for these thou knowest, craving the Rsis' prayer, thyself a Singer
May we be they who take delight in Somas: these with sweet food for thee, O Chariot-rider.
4 These holy prayers, O Indra, have I sung thee: grant to the men the strength of men, thou Hero.
Be of one mind with those in whom thou joyest: keep thou the singers safe and their companions.
5 Listen to Prthi's call, heroic Indra, and be thou lauded by the hymns of Venya,
Him who hath sung thee to thine oil-rich dwelling, whose rolling songs have sped thee like a torrent.

## [10-149] HYMN CXLIX. Savitar.

1. SAVITAR fixed the earth with bands to bind it, and made heaven stedfast where no prop
supported.
Savitar milked, as 'twere a restless courser, air, sea bound fast to what no foot had trodden.
2 Well knoweth Savitar, O Child of Waters, where ocean, firmly fixt, o'erflowed its limit.
Thence sprang the world, from that uprose the region: thence heaven spread out and the wide earth
expanded.
3 Then, with a full crowd of Immortal Beings, this other realm came later, high and holy.
First, verily, Savitar's strong-pinioned Eagle was born: and he obeys his law for ever.
4 As warriors to their steeds, kine to their village, as fond milk giving cows approach their youngling,
As man to wife, let Savitar come downward to us, heaven's bearer, Lord of every blessing.
5 Like the Angirasa Hiranvastupa, I call thee, Savitar, to this achievement:
So worshipping and lauding thee for favour I watch for thee as for the stalk of Soma.

## [10-150] HYMN CL. Agni.

1. THOU, bearer of oblations, though kindled, art kindled for the Gods.
With the Adityas, Rudras, Vasus, come to us: to show us favour come to us.
2 Come hither and accept with joy this sacrifice and hymn of ours.
O kindled God, we mortals are invoking thee, calling on thee to show us grace.
3 I laud thee Jatavedas, thee Lord of all blessings, with my song.
Agni, bring hitherward the Gods whose Laws we love, whose laws we love, to show us grace.

4 Agni the God was made the great High-Priest of Gods, Rsis have kindled Agni, men of mortal
mould.
Agni I invocate for winning ample wealth. kindly disposed for winning wealth.
5 Atri and Bharadvaja and Gavisthira, Kanva and Trasadasyu, in our fight he helped.
On Agni calls Vasistha, even the household priest, the household priest to win his grace.

## [10-151] HYMN CLI. Faith.

1. By Faith is Agni kindled, through Faith is oblation offered up.
We celebrate with praises Faith upon the height of happiness.
2 Bless thou the man who gives, O Faith; Faith, bless the man who fain would give.
Bless thou the liberal worshippers: bless thou the word that I have said.
3 Even as the Deities maintained Faith in the mighty Asuras,
So make this uttered wish of mine true for the liberal worshippers.
4 Guarded by Vayu, Gods and men who sacrifice draw near to Faith.
Man winneth Faith by yearnings of the heart, and opulence by Faith.
5 Faith in the early morning, Faith at noonday will we invocate,
Faith at the setting of the Sun. O Faith, endow us with belief.

## [10-152] HYMN CLII. Indra.

1. A MIGHTY Governor art thou, Wondrous, Destroyer of the foe,
Whose friend is never done to death, and never, never overcome.
2 Lord of the clan, who brings us bliss, Strong, Warrior, Slayer of the fiend,
May India, Soma-drinker, go before us, Bull who gives us peace.
3 Drive Raksasas and foes away, break thou in pieces Vrtra'sjaws:
O Vrtra-slaying Indra, quell the foeman's wrath who threatens us.
4 O Indra, beat our foes away, humble the men who challenge us:
Send down to nether darkness him who seeks to do us injury.
5 Baffle the foeman's plan, ward off his weapon who would conquer us.
Give shelter from his furious wrath, and keep his murdering dart afar.

## [10-153] HYMN CLIII. Indra.

1. SWAYING about, the Active Ones came nigh to Indra at his birth,
And shared his great heroic might.
2 Based upon strength and victory and power, O Indra is thy birth:
Thou, Mighty One, art strong indeed.
3 Thou art the Vrtra-slayer, thou, Indra, hast spread the firmament:
Thou hast with might upheld the heavens.
4 Thou, Indra, bearest in thine arms the lightning that accords with thee,
Whetting thy thunderbolt with might.
5 Thou, Indra, art preeminent over all creatures in thy might:
Thou hast pervaded every place.

## [10-154] HYMN CLIV. New Life.

1. FOR some is Soma purified, some sit by sacrificial oil:
To those for whom the meath flows forth, even to those let him depart.
2 Invincible through Fervour, those whom Fervour hath advanced to heaven,
Who showed great Fervour in their lives, -even to those let him depart.
3 The heroes who contend in war and boldly cast their lives away,

Or who give guerdon thousandfold, -even to those let him depart.
4 Yea, the first followers of Law, Law's pure and holy strengtheners,
The Fathers, Yama! Fervour-moved,even to those let him depart.
5 Skilled in a thousand ways and means, the sages who protect the Sun,
The Rsis, Yama! Fervour-moved,-even to those let him depart.

## [10-155] HYMN CLV. Various.

1. ARAYI, one-eyed limping hag, fly, ever-screeching, to the hill.
We frighten thee away with these, the heroes of Sirimbitha.
2 Scared from this place and that is she, destroyer of each germ unborn.
Go, sharp-horned Brahmanaspti and drive Arayi far away.
3 Yon log that floats without a man to guide it on the river's edge,-
Seize it, thou thing with hideous jaws, and go thou far away thereon.
4 When, foul with secret stain and spot, ye hastened onward to the breast,
All Indra's enemies were slain and passed away like froth and foam.
5 These men have led about the cow, have duly carried Agni round,
And raised their glory tg the Gods. Who will attack them with success?

## [10-156] HYMN CLVI. Agni.

1. LET songs of ours speed Agni forth like a fleet courser in the race,
And we will win each prize through him.
2 Agni the dart whereby we gain kine for ourselves with help from thee,-
That send us for the gain of wealth.
3 O Agni, bring us wealth secure, vast wealth in horses and in kine:
Oil thou the socket, turn the wheel.
4 O Agni, thou hast made the Sun, Eternal Star, to mount the sky,
Bestowing light on living men.
5 Thou, Agni, art the people's light, best, dearest, seated in thy shrine:
Watch for the singer, give him life.

## [10-157] HYMN CLVII. Visvedevas.

1. WE will, with Indra and all Gods to aid us, bring these existing worlds into subjection.
2 Our sacrifice, our bodies, and our offspr. let Indra form together with Adityas.
3 With the Adityas, with the band of Maruts, may Indra be Protector of our bodies.
4 As when the Gods came, after they had slaughtered the Asuras, keeping safe their Godlike nature,
5 Brought the Sun hitherward with mighty powers, and looked about them on their vigorous Godhead.

## [10-158] HYMN CLVIII. Surya.

1. MAY Surya guard us out of heaven, and Vata from the firmament,
And Agni from terrestrial spots.
2 Thou Savitar whose flame deserves hundred libations, be thou pleased:
From failing lightning keep us safe.
3 May Savitar the God, and may Parvata also give us sight;
May the Creator give us sight.
4 Give sight unto our eye, give thou our bodies sight that they may see:
May we survey, discern this world.

5 Thus, Surya, may we look on thee, on thee most lovely to behold,
See clearly with the eyes of men.

## [10-159] HYMN CLIX. Saci Paulomi.

1. YON Sun hath mounted up, and this my happy fate hate mounted high.
I knowing this, as conqueror have won my husband for mine own.
2 I am the banner and the head, a mighty arbitress am I:
I am victorious, and my Lord shall be submissive to my will.
3 My Sons are slayers of the foe, my Daughter is a ruling Queen:
I am victorious: o'er my Lord my song of triumph is supreme.
4 Oblation, that which Indra gave and thus grew glorious and most high,-
This have I offered, O ye Gods, and rid me of each rival wife.
5 Destroyer of the rival wife, Sole Spouse, victorious, conqueror,
The others' glory have I seized as 'twere the wealth of weaker Dames.
6 I have subdued as conqueror these rivals, these my fellow-wives,
That I may hold imperial sway over this Hero and the folk.

## [10-160] HYMN CLX. Indra.

1. TASTE this strong draught enriched with offered viands: with all thy chariot here unyoke thy
Coursers.
Let not those other sacrificers stay thee, Indra: these juices shed for thee are ready.
2 Thine is the juice effused, thine are the juices yet to be pressed: our resonant songs invite thee.
O Indra, pleased to-day with this libation, come, thou who knowest all and drink the Soma.
3 Whoso, devoted to the God, effuses Soma for him with yearning heart and spirit,-
Never doth Indra give away his cattle: for him he makes the lovely Soma famous.
4 He looks with loving favour on the mortal who, like a rich man, pours for him the Soma.
Maghavan in his bended arm supports him: he slays, unasked, the men who hate devotion.
5 We call on thee to come to us, desirous of goods and spoil, of cattle, and of horses.
For thy new love and favour are we present: let us invoke thee, Indra, as our welfare.

## [10-161] HYMN CLXI. Indra.

1. FOR life I set thee free by this oblation from the unknown decline and from Consumption;
Or, if the grasping demon have possessed him, free him from her, O Indra, thou and Agni.
2 Be his days ended, be he now departed, be he brought very near to death already,
Out of Destruction's lap again I bring him, save him for life to last a hundred autumns.
3 With hundred-eyed oblation, hundred-autumned, bringing a hundred lives, have I restored him,
That Indra for a hundred years may lead him safe to the farther shore of all misfortune.
4 Live, waxing in thy strength, a hundred autumns, live through a hundred springs, a hundred winters.
Through hundred-lived oblation Indra, Agni, Brhaspati, Savitar yield him for a hundred!
5 So have I found and rescued thee thou hast returned with youth renewed.

Whole in thy members! I have found thy sight and all thy life for thee.

## [10-162] HYMN CLXII. Agni

1. MAY Agni, yielding to our prayer, the Raksas-slayer, drive away
The malady of evil name that hath beset thy labouring womb.
2 Agni, concurring in the prayer, drive off the eater of the flesh,
The malady of evil name that hath attacked thy babe and womb.
3 That which destroys the sinking germ, the settled, moving embryo,
That which will kill the babe at birth,even this will we drive far away.
4 That which divides thy legs that it may lie between the married pair,
That penetrates and licks thy side,-even this will we exterminate.
5 What rests by thee in borrowed form of brother, lover, or of lord,
And would destroy thy Progeny,-even this will we exterminate.
6 That which through sleep or darkness hath deceived thee and lies down by thee,
And will destroy thy progeny,--even this will we exterminate.

## [10-163] HYMN CLXIII

1. FROM both thy nostrils, from thine eyes, from both thine ears and from thy chin,
Forth from thy head and brain and tongue I drive thy malady away.
2 From the neck-tendons and the neck, from the breast-bones and from the spine,
From shoulders, upper, lower arms, I drive thy malady away.
3 From viscera and all within, forth from the rectum, from the heart,
From kidneys, liver, and from spleen, I drive thy malady away.
4 From thighs, from knee-caps, and from heels, and from the forepart of the feet,
From hips from stomach, and from groin I drive thy malady away.
5 From what is voided from within, and from thy hair, and from they nails,
From all thyself from top to toe, I drive thy malady away.
6 From every member, every hair, disease that comes in every joint,
From all thyself, from top to toe, I drive thy malady away.

## [10-164] HYMN CLXIV. Dream-charm.

1. AVAUNT, thou Master of the mind Depart, and vanish far away.
Look on Destruction far from hence. The live man's mind is manifold.
2 A happy boon do men elect, a mighty blessing they obtain.
Bliss with Vaivasvata they see. The live man's mind seeks many a place.
3 If by address, by blame, by imprecation we have committed sin, awake or sleeping,
All hateful acts of ours, all evil doings may Agni bear away to distant places.
4 When, Indra, Brahmanaspati, our deeds are wrongful and unjust,
May provident Angirasa prevent our foes from troubling, us.
5 We have prevailed this day and won: we are made free from sin and guilt.
Ill thoughts, that visit us awake or sleeping, seize the man we hate, yea, seize the man who hateth us.

## [10-165] HYMN CLXV. Visvedevas.

1. GODS, whatsoe'er the Dove came hither seeking, sent to us as the envoy of Destruction,

For that let us sing hymns and make atonement. Well be it with our quadrupeds and bipeds.
2 Auspicious be the Dove that hath been sent us, a harmless bird, ye Gods, within our dwelling.
May Agni, Sage, be pleased with our oblation, and may the Missile borne on wings avoid us.
3 Let not the Arrow that hath wings distract us: beside the fire-place, on the hearth it settles.
May, it bring welfare to our men and cattle: here let the Dove, ye Gods, forbear to harm us.
4 The screeching of the owl is ineffective and when beside the fire the Dove hath settled,
To him who sent it hither as an envoy, to him be reverence paid, to Death, to Yama.
5 Drive forth the Dove, chase it with holy verses: rejoicing, bring ye hither food and cattle,
Barring the way against all grief and trouble. Let the swift bird fly forth and leave us vigour.

## [10-166] HYMN CLXVI. Sapatnanasanam.

1. MAKE me a bull among my peers, make me my rivals, conqueror:
Make me the slayer of my foes, a sovran ruler, lord of kine
2 I am my rivals' slayer, like Indra unwounded and unhurt,
And all these enemies of mine are vanquished and beneath my feet.
3 Here, verily, I bind you fast, as the two bow-ends with the string.
Press down these men, O Lord of Speech, that they may humbly speak to me.
4 Hither I came as conqueror with mighty all-effecting power,
And I have mastered all your thought, your synod, and your holy work.
5 May I be highest, having gained your strength in war, your skill in peace
my feet have trodden on your heads.
Speak to me from beneath my feet, as frogs from out the water croak, as frogs from out the water croak.

## [10-167] HYMN CLXVII. Indra.

1. THIS pleasant meath, O Indra, is effused for thee: thou art the ruling Lord of beaker and of juice.
Bestow upon us wealth with many hero sons: thou, having glowed with Fervour, wortnest heavenly light.
2 Let us call Sakra to libations here effused, winner of light who joyeth in the potent juice.
Mark well this sacrifice of ours and come to us: we pray to Maghavan the Vanquisher of hosts.
3 By royal Soma's and by Varuna's decree, under Brhaspati's and Anumati's guard,
This day by thine authority, O Maghavan, Maker, Disposer thou! have I enjoyed the jars.
4 1, too, urged on, have had my portion, in the bowl, and as first Prince I drew forth this my hymn of praise,
When with the prize I came unto the flowing juice, O Visvamitra, Jamadagni, to your home.

## [10-168] HYMN CLXVIII. Vayu.

1. O THE Wind's chariot, O its power and glory! Crashing it goes and hath a voice of thunder.
It makes the regions red and touches heaven, and as it moves the dust of earth is scattered.
2 Along the traces of the Wind they hurry, they come to him as dames to an assembly.

Borne on his car with these for his attendants, the God speeds forth, the universe's Monarch.

3 Travelling on the paths of air's midregion, no single day doth he take rest or slumber.

Holy and earliest-born, Friend of fhe waters, where did he spring and from what region came he?

4 Germ of the world, the Deities' vital spirit, this God moves ever as his will inclines him.

His voice is heard, his shape is ever viewless. Let us adore this Wind with our oblation.

## [10-169] HYMN CLXIX. COWS.

1. MAY the wind blow upon our Cows with healing: may they eat herbage full of vigorous juices.

May they drink waters rich in life and fatness: to food that moves on feet be gracious, Rudra.

2 Like-coloured, various-hued, or single-coloured, whose names through sacrifice are known to Agni,

Whom the Angirases produced by Fervour,vouchsafe to these, Parjanya, great protection.

3 Those who have offered to the Gods their bodies, whose varied forms are all well known to Soma,-

Those grant us in our cattle-pen, O Indra, with their full streams of milk and plenteous offspring.

4 Prajapati, bestowing these upon me, one-minded with all Gods and with the Fathers,

Hath to our cow-pen brought auspicious cattle: so may we own the offspring they will bear us.

## [10-170] HYMN CLXX. Surya.

1. MAY the Bright God drink glorious Soma-mingled meath, giving the sacrifice's lord uninjured life;

He who, wind-urged, in person guards our offspring well, hath nourished them with food and shines o'er many a land.

2 Radiant, as high Truth, cherished, best at winning strength, Truth based upon the statute that supports the heavens,

He rose, a light, that kills Vrtras and enemies, best slayer of the Dasyus, Asuras, and foes.

3 This light, the best of lights, supreme, all-conquering, winner of riches, is exalted with high laud.

All-lighting, radiant, mighty as the Sun to see, he spreadeth wide unfailing victory and strength.

4 Beaming forth splendour with thy light, thou hast attained heaven's lustrous realm.

By thee were brought together all existing things, possessor of all Godhead, All-effecting God.

## [10-171] HYMN CLXXI. Indra.

1. FOR Ita's sake who pressed the juice, thou, Indra, didst protect his car,

And hear the Soma-giver's call.

2 Thou from his skin hast borne the head of the swift-moving combatant,

And sought the Soma-pourer's home.

3 Venya, that mortal man, hast thou, for Astrabudhna the devout, O Indra, many a time set free.

4 Bring, Indra, to the east again that Sun who now is in the west, Even against the will of Gods.

## [10-172] HYMN CLXXII. Dawn.

1. WITH all thy beauty come: the kine approaching with full udders follow on thy path.

2 Come with kind thoughts, most liberal, rousing the warrior's hymn of praise, with bounteous ones,

3 As nourishers we tie the thread, and, liberal with our bounty, offer sacrifice.

4 Dawn drives away her Sister's gloom, and, through her excellence, makes her retrace her path.

## [10-173] HYMN CLXXIII. The King.

1. BE with us; I have chosen thee: stand stedfast and immovable.

Let all the people wish for thee let not thy kingship fall away.

2 Be even here; fall not away be like a mountain unremoved.

Stand stedfast here like Indra's self, and hold the kingship in the grasp.

3 This man hath Indra stablished, made secure by strong oblation's power.

May Soma speak a benison, and Brahmanaspati, on him.

4 Firm is the sky and firm the earth, and stedfast also are these hills.

Stedfast is all this living world, and stedfast is this King of men.

5 Stedfast, may Varuna the King, stedfast, the God Brhaspati, Stedfast, may Indra, stedfast too, may Agni keep thy stedfast reign.

6 On constant Soma let us think with constant sacrificial gift And then may Indra make the clans bring tribute unto thee alone.

## [10-174] HYMN CLXXIV. The King.

1. WITH offering for success in fight whence Indra was victorious.

With this, O Brahmanaspati, let us attain to royal sway.

2 Subduing those who rival us, subduing all malignities,

Withstand the man who menaces, withstand the man who angers us.

3 Soma and Savitar the God have made thee a victorious King

All elements have aided thee, to make thee general conqueror.

4 Oblation, that which Indra. gave and thus grew glorious and most high,-

This have I offered, Gods! and hence now, verily, am rivalless.

5 Slayer of rivals, rivalless, victorious, with royal sway,

Over these beings may I rule, may I be Sovran of the folk.

## [10-175] HYMN CLXXV. Press-stones.

I. MAY Savitar the God, O Stones, stir you according to the Law:

Be harnessed to the shafts, and press.

2 Stones, drive calamity away, drive ye away malevolence:

Make ye the Cows our medicine.

3 Of one accord the upper Stones, giving the Bull his bull-like strength,

Look down with pride on those below.

4 May Savitar the God, O Stones, stir you as Law commands for him

Who sacrifices, pouring juice.

## [10-176] HYMN CLXXVI. Agni.

1. WITH hymns of praise their sons have told aloud the Rbhus' mighty deeds.

Who, all-supporting, have enjoyed the earth as, twere a mother cow.

2 Bring forth the God with song divine, being Jatavedas hitherward,

To bear our gifts at once to heaven.

3 He here, a God-devoted Priest, led forward comes to sacrifice.

Like a car covered for the road, he, glowing, knows, himself, the way.

4 This Agni rescues from distress, as 'twere from the Immortal Race,

A God yet mightier than strength, a God who hath been made for life.

## [10-177] HYMN CLXXVII. Mayabheda.

1. THE sapient with their spirit and their mind behold the Bird adorned with all an Asura's magic
might.
Sages observe him in the ocean's inmost depth: the wise disposers seek the station of his rays.
2 The flying Bird bears Speech within his spirit: erst the Gandharva in the womb pronounced it:
And at the seat of sacrifice the sages cherish this radiant, heavenly-bright invention.
3 I saw the Herdsman, him who never resteth, approaching and departing on his pathways.
He, clothed in gathered and diffusive splendour, within the worlds continually travels.

## [10-178] HYMN CLXXVIII. Tarksya.

1. THIS very mighty one whom Gods commission, the Conqueror of cars, ever triumphant,
Swift, fleet to battle, with uninjured fellies, even Tarksya for our weal will we call hither.
2 As though we offered up our gifts to Indra, may we ascend. him as a ship. for safety.
Like the two wide worlds, broad, deep far-extended, may we be safe both when he comes and leaves
you.
3 He who with might the Five Lands hath pervaded, like Surya with his lustre, and the waters-
His strength wins hundreds, thousands none avert it, as- the young maid repelleth not her lover.

## [10-179] HYMN CLXXIX. Indra.

1. Now lift ye up yourselves and look on Indra's seasonable share.
If it be ready, offer it; unready, ye have been remise.
2 Oblation is prepared: come to us, Indra; the Sun hath travelled over half his journey.
Friends with their stores are sitting round thee waiting like lords of clans for the tribe's wandering
chieftain.
3 Dressed in the udder and on fire, I fancy; well-dressed, I fancy, is this recent present.
Drink, Indra, of the curd of noon's libation with favour, Thunderer, thou whose deeds are mighty.

## [10-180] HYMN CLXXX. Indra.

1. O MUCH-INVOKED, thou hast subdued thy foemen: thy might is loftiest; here display thy bounty.
In thy right hand, O Indra, bring us treasures: thou art the Lord of rivers filled with riches.
2 Like a dread wild beast roaming on the mountain thou hast approached us from the farthest
distance.
Whetting thy bold and thy sharp blade, O Indra, crush thou the foe and scatter those who hate us.
3 Thou, mighty Indra, sprangest into being as strength for lovely lordship o'er the people.
Thou drovest off the folk who were unfriendly, and to the Gods thou gavest room and freedom.

## [10-181] HYMN CLXXXl. Visvedevas.

1. VASISTHA mastered the Rathantara, took it from radiant Dhatar, Savitar, and Visnu,
Oblation, portion of fourfold oblation, known by the names of Saprathas and Prathas.
2. These sages found what lay remote and hidden, the sacrifice's loftiest secret essence.
From radiant Dhatar, Savitar, and Visnu, from Agni, Bharadvaja brought the Brhat.

3 They found with mental eyes the earliest Yajus, a pathway to the Gods, that had descended.
From radiant Dhitar, Savitar, and Visnu, from Surya did these sages bring the Gharma.

## [10-182] HYMN CLXXXII. Brhaspati.

1. BRHASPATI lead us safely over troubless and turn his evil thought against the sinner;
Repel the curse, and drive away ill-feeling, and give the sacrificer peace and cornfort!
2 May Naratarhsa aid us at Prayaja: blest be our Anuyaja at invokings.
May he repel the curse, and chase ill-feeling, and give the sacrificer peace and comfort.
3 May he whose head is flaming burn the demons, haters of prayer, so that the arrow slay them.
May he repel the curse and chase ill-feeling, and give the sacrificer peace and comfort.

## [10-183] HYMN CLXXXIII. The Sacrificer, Etc.

1. I SAW thee meditating in thy spirit what sprang from Fervour and hath thence developed.
Bestowing offspring here, bestowing riches, spread in thine offspring, thou who cravest children.
2 I saw thee pondering in thine heart, and praying that in due time thy body might be fruitful.
Come as a youthful woman, rise to meet me: spread in thine offspring, thou who cravest children.
3 In plants and herbs, in all existent beings I have deposited the germ of increase.
All progeny on earth have I engendered, and sons in women who will be hereafter.

## [10-184] HYMN CLXXXIV.

1. MAY Visnu form and mould the womb, may Tvastar duly shape the forms,
Prajapati infuse the stream, and Dhatar lay the germ for thee.
2 O Sinivali, set the germ, set thou the germ, Sarasvati:
May the Twain Gods bestow the germ, the Asvins crowned with lotuses.
3 That which the Asvins Twain rub forth with the attrition-sticks of gold,-
That germ of thine we invoke, that in the tenth month thou mayst bear.

## [10-185] HYMN CLXXXV. Aditi.

1. GREAT, unassailable must he the heavenly favour of' Three Gods,
Varuna, Mitra, Aryaman.
2 O'er these, neither at home nor yet abroad or pathways that are Strange,
The evil-minded foe hath power
3 Nor over him,. the man on whom the Sons of Aditi bestow Eternal light that he may live.

## [10-186] HYMN CLXXXVI. Vayu.

1. FILLING our hearts with health and joy, may Vata breathe his balm on us
May he prolong our days of life.
2 Thou art our Father, Vata, yea, thou art a Brother and a friend,
So give us strength that we may live.
3 The store of Amrta laid away yonder, O Vata, in thine home,-
Give us thereof that we may live.

## [10-187] HYMN CLXXXVII. Agni.

1. To Agni send I forth my song, to him the Bull of all the folk:
So may he bear us past our foes.

2 Who from the distance far away shines brilliantly across the wastes:
So may he bear us past our foes.
3 The Bull with brightly-gleaming flame who utterly consumes the fiends
So may he bear us past our foes.
4 Who looks on all existing things and comprehends them with his view:
So may he bear us past our foes.
5 Resplendent Agni, who was born in farthest region of the air:
So may he bear us past our foes.

### [10-188] HYMN CLXXXVIII. Agni.
1. Now send ye Jatavedas forth, send hitherward the vigorous Steed
To seat him on our sacred grass.
2. I raise the lofty eulogy of Jatavedas, raining boons,
With sages for his hero band.
3 With flames of Jatavedas which carry oblation to the Gods,
May he promote our sacrifice.

### [10-189] HYMN CLXXXIX. Surya.
1. THIS spotted Bull hath come, and sat before the Mother in the east,
Advancing to his Father heaven.
2 Expiring when he draws his breath, she moves along the lucid spheres:
The Bull shines out through all the sky.
3 Song is bestowed upon the Bird: it rules supreme through thirty realms
Throughout the days at break of morn.

### [10-190] HYMN CXC. Creation.
1. FROM Fervour kindled to its height Eternal Law and Truth were born:
Thence was the Night produced, and thence the billowy flood of sea arose.
2 From that same billowy flood of sea the Year was afterwards produced,
Ordainer of the days nights, Lord over all who close the eye.
3 Dhatar, the great Creator, then formed in due order Sun and Moon.
He formed in order Heaven and Earth, the regions of the air, and light.

### [10-191] HYMN CXCI. Agni.
1. THOU, mighty Agni, gatherest up all that is precious for thy friend.
Bring us all treasures as thou art enkindled in libation's place
2 Assemble, speak together: let your minds be all of one accord,
As ancient Gods unanimous sit down to their appointed share.
3 The place is common, common the assembly, common the mind, so be their thought united.
A common purpose do I lay before you, and worship with your general oblation.
4 One and the same bt your resolve, and be your minds of one accord.
United be the thoughts of all that all may happily agree.

Made in the USA
San Bernardino, CA
16 March 2019